SECOND EDITION

Sociology Now

THE ESSENTIALS

Michael Kimmel
Stony Brook University

Amy Aronson
Fordham University

With the assistance of Jeffery Dennis,
Wright State University

Allyn & Bacon

Boston • Columbus • Indianapolis • New York • San Francisco • Upper Saddle River
Amsterdam • Cape Town • Dubai • London • Madrid • Munich • Paris • Montreal • Toronto
Delhi • Mexico City • Sao Paulo • Sydney • Hong Kong • Seoul • Singapore • Taipei • Tokyo

Executive Editor: *Jeff Lasser*
Senior Development Editor: *Leah R. Strauss*
Senior Development Editor: *Jessica Carlisle*
Associate Editor: *Lauren Macey*
Editorial Assistant: *Elaine Almquist*
Executive Marketing Manager: *Kelly May*
Marketing Assistant: *Gina Lavagna*
Senior Production Project Manager: *Roberta Sherman*
Manufacturing Buyer: *Debbie Rossi*
Editorial Production and Composition Service: *Nesbitt Graphics, Inc.*
Interior Designer: *Ellen Pettengell*
Photo Researcher: *Debbie Needleman*
Cover Designer: *Joel Gendron*

Credits appear on page 543, which constitutes an extension of the copyright page.

Library of Congress Cataloging-in-Publication Data

Kimmel, Michael S.
  Sociology now : the essentials / Michael Kimmel, Amy Aronson ; with the assistance of Jeffery Dennis. -- 2nd ed.
      p. cm.
  Includes bibliographical references and index.
  ISBN-13: 978-0-205-73199-2 (alk. paper)
  ISBN-10: 0-205-73199-6 (alk. paper)
 1. Sociology. 2. Sociology--Study and teaching. I. Aronson, Amy.
II. Dennis, Jeffery P. III. Title.
  HM585.K57 2011
  301--dc22
                              2009050884

10 9 8 7 6 5 4 3 2 1   Q-TAU   14 13 12 11 10

Allyn & Bacon
is an imprint of

www.pearsonhighered.com

ISBN 10: 0-205-73199-6
ISBN 13: 978-0-205-73199-2

Brief Contents

Contents

PART I Foundations of the Field

PART II Identities and Inequalities

PART III Social Institutions

11 The Family 320

12 Economy and Work 354

15 Sociology of Environments: The Natural, Physical, and Human Worlds   462

Features

What Do You Think? What Does America Think?

U.S. / Them

Preface

I am a sociologist—both by profession and by temperament. It's what I do for a living and how I see the world. I consider myself enormously lucky to have the kind of job I have, teaching and writing about the world in which we live.

I love sociology. I love that it gives us a way to see the world that is different from any other way of seeing the world. It's a lens, and when I hold that lens up to the world, I see shapes and patterns that help me understand it, colors and movement that enable me to perceive depth and shading. I love sociology because when I see those shapes, those patterns, and those shades of gray, I feel hopeful that we can, as citizens and sociologists, contribute to making that world a better place for all of us.

Teachers in general are a pretty optimistic bunch. When we work with you to develop your own critical engagement with the world—developing ideas, using evidence to back up assertions, deepening and broadening your command of information—we believe that your life will be better for it. You will get a better job, be a more engaged and active citizen, maybe even be a better parent, friend, or partner than you might otherwise have been. We believe that education is a way to improve your life on so many different levels. Pretty optimistic, no?

In this book, we have tried to communicate that way of seeing and that optimism about how you can use a sociological lens.

Why Study Sociology? A Message to Students

So, what did people say when you told them you were taking sociology? They probably looked at you blankly, "Like, what is sociology?" They might say, "And what can you do with it?" Sociology is often misunderstood. Some think it's nothing more than what my roommate told me when I said I was going to go to graduate school in sociology. (He was pre-med.) "Sociology makes a science out of common sense," he said dismissively.

It turns out he was wrong: What we think of as common sense turns out to be wrong a lot of the time. The good news is that sociologists are often the ones who point out that what "everybody knows" isn't necessarily true. In a culture saturated by self-help books, pop psychology, and TV talk shows promising instant and complete physical makeovers and utter psychological transformation, sociology says, "Wait a minute, not so fast."

Our culture tells us that all social problems are really individual problems. Poor people are poor because they don't work hard enough, and racial discrimination is simply the result of prejudiced individuals.

And the "solutions" offered by TV talk shows and self-help books also center around individual changes. If you work hard, you can make it. If you want to change, you can change. Social problems, they counsel, are really a set of individual problems all added together. Racism, sexism, or homophobia is really the result of unenlightened people holding bad attitudes. If they changed their attitudes, those enormous problems would dissolve like sugar in your coffee.

Sociology has a different take. Sociologists see society as a dynamic interaction between individuals and institutions, like education, economy, and government. Changing yourself might be necessary for you to live a happier life, but it has little impact on the effects of those institutions. And changing attitudes would make social life far more pleasant, but problems like racial or gender inequality are embedded in the ways those institutions are organized. It will take more than attitudinal shifts to fix that.

One of sociology's greatest strengths is also what makes it so elusive or discomfiting. We often are in a position in which we contrast American mythologies with sociological realities.

I remember a song as I was growing up called "Only in America" by Jay and the Americans, which held that only in this country could "a guy from anywhere," "without a cent" maybe grow up to be a millionaire or president. Pretty optimistic, right? And it takes a sociologist, often, to burst that bubble, to explain that it's really not true—that the likelihood of a poor boy or girl making it in the United States is minuscule and that virtually everyone ends up in the same class position as his or her parents. It sounds almost unpatriotic to say that the best predictors of *your* eventual position in society are the education and occupation of your parents.

Sociology offers some answers to questions that may therefore be unpopular—because they emphasize the social and the structural over the individual and psychological, because they reveal the relationship between individual experience and social reality, and because structural barriers impede our ability to realize our dreams.

This often leads introductory students to feel initially depressed. Because these problems are so deeply embedded in our society, and because all the educational enlightenment in the world might not budge these powerful institutional forces—well, what's the use? Might as well just try and get yours, and the heck with everyone else.

But then, as we understand the real mission of sociology, students often feel invigorated, inspired. Sociology's posture is exactly the opposite—and that's what makes it so compelling. Understanding those larger forces means, as the Who put it, "we won't get fooled again!"

What also makes sociology compelling is that it connects those two dimensions. It is *because* we believe that all social problems are really the result of individual weaknesses and laziness that those social problems remain in place. It is *because* we believe that poverty can be eliminated by hard work that poverty doesn't get eliminated. If social problems are social, then reducing poverty, or eliminating racial or gender discrimination, will require more than individual enlightenment; it will require large-scale political mobilization to change social institutions. And the good news is that sociologists have also documented the ways that those institutions themselves are always changing, always being changed.

Why Study Sociology Right Now?
A Message to Students and Instructors

Understanding our society has never been more important. Sociology offers perhaps the best perspective on what are arguably the two dominant trends of our time, globalization and multiculturalism.

Globalization refers to the increasingly interlocked processes and institutions that span the entire world rather than in one country. Goods and services are produced and distributed globally. Information moves instantly. You want to know how much things have changed? More than 2,000 soldiers in both the Union and Confederate armies were killed in the summer of 1865—that is, *after* the Civil War had ended. Why? Because no one had told them the war was over.

Globalization makes the world feel smaller, leaves us all far more intimately connected. And because people all over the world are wearing the same sneakers, eating the same fast food, and connecting by the Internet and texting each other, we are becoming more and more similar.

On the other hand, multiculturalism makes us keenly aware of how we are different. Globalization may make the world smaller, but we remain divided by religious-inspired wars, racial and ethnic identities, blood feuds, tribal rivalries, and what is generally called "sectarian violence."

Multiculturalism describes the ways in which we create identities that at once make us "global citizens" and also, at the same time, local and familial, based on our membership in racial, ethnic, or gender categories. Here in the United States, we have not become one big happy family, as some predicted a century ago. Instead of the "melting pot" in which each group would become part of the same "stew," we are, at our best, a "beautiful mosaic" of small groups that, when seen from afar, creates a beautiful pattern while each tile retains its distinct shape and beauty.

> *Globalization and multiculturalism make the world feel closer and also more divided; and they make the distances between us as people seem both tiny and unbridgeably large.*

Globalization and multiculturalism are not only about the world—they are about us, individually. We draw our sense of who we are, our **identities**, from our membership in those diverse groups into which we are born or that we choose. Our identities—who we think we are—come from our gender, race, ethnicity, class, sexuality, age, religion, region, nation, and tribe. From these diverse locations, we piece together an identity, a sense of self. Sometimes one or another feels more important than others, but at other times other elements emerge as equally important.

And these elements of our identities also turn out to be the bases on which social hierarchies are built. Social inequality is organized from the same elements as identity—resources and opportunities are distributed in our society on the basis of race, class, ethnicity, age, sexuality, gender, and so forth.

A sociological perspective has never been more important to enabling us to understand these problems because sociology has become the field that has most fully embraced globalization and multiculturalism as the central analytic lenses through which we view social life.

Why Use *Sociology Now*? A Message to Instructors

The field of sociology has changed enormously since I first went to graduate school in the mid-1970s. At the time, two paradigms, functionalism and conflict theory, battled for dominance in the field, each one claiming to explain social processes better than the other. At the time, symbolic interactionism seemed a reasonable way to understand microlevel processes.

That was an era of great conflict in our society: the civil rights, women's, and gay and lesbian movements; protests against the Vietnam War; hippies. On campuses these groups vied with far more traditional, conservative, and career-oriented students whose collegiate identity came more from the orderly 1950s than the tumultuous 1960s.

Just as the world has changed since then, so, too, has sociology—both substantively and demographically. New perspectives have emerged from older models, and terms like *rational choice, poststructuralism, collective mobilization, cultural tool kit*—not to mention *multiculturalism* and *globalization*—have become part of our daily lexicon.

Demographically, sociology is the field that has been most transformed by the social movements of the last decades of the twentieth century. Because sociology interrogates the connections between identities and inequalities, it has become a home to those groups who were historically marginalized in American society: women, people of color, and gays and lesbians. The newest sections in the American Sociological Association are those on the Body, Sexualities, and Race, Class, and Gender; the largest sections are no longer Medical Sociology and Organizational Sociology, but now Sex and Gender, Culture, and Race.

It turned out that symbolic interactionism was resilient enough to remain a theoretical lens through which social interaction and processes can still be understood. That's largely because the old textbook model of "three paradigms" placed the three in a somewhat stilted competition: Conflict and functionalism were the macro theories; interactionism stood alone as a micro theory.

Themes: Exploring the Questions of Today

One of the biggest differences you'll see immediately in *Sociology Now* is that we have built on older functionalism–conflict theory–interactionism models with a contemporary approach. We no longer believe these paradigms are battling for dominance; students needn't choose between competing models. Sociology is a synthetic discipline—*for us the question is almost never "either/or," and thus the answer is almost always "both/and."*

Sociology is also, often, a debunking discipline, rendering old truisms into complex, contextualized processes and interactions. What "everybody knows" to be true often turns out not to be. We didn't learn everything we needed to know in kindergarten. It's more complicated than that!

And using globalization and multiculturalism as the organizing themes of the book helps to illustrate exactly how "both/and" actually works. The world isn't smaller or bigger—it's both. We're not more united or more diverse—we're both. We're not more orderly or more in conflict—we're both. And sociology is the field that explains the way that "both" sides exist in a dynamic tension with each other. What's more, sociology explains why, and how, and in what ways they exist in that tension.

This way of expressing where sociology is now turned out to be quite amenable to the traditional architecture of a sociology textbook. The general sections of the book, and the individual chapter topics, are not especially different from the chapter organization of other textbooks.

There are, however, some important differences.

First, **globalization** is not the same as cross-national comparisons. Globalization is often imagined as being about "them"—other cultures and other societies. And while examples drawn from other cultures are often extremely valuable to a sociologist, especially in challenging ethnocentrism, globalization is about processes that link "us" and "them." Thus, many of our examples, especially our cultural references, are about the United States—in relation to the rest of the world. This enables students both to relate to the topic and also to see how it connects with the larger global forces at work.

> *Globalization is woven into every chapter—and, perhaps more important, every American example is connected to a global process or issue.*

Second, **multiculturalism** is not the same as social stratification. Every sociology textbook has separate chapters on class, race, age, and gender. (We have added a few, which I will discuss below.) But in some books, that's about as far as it goes—chapters on "other topics" do not give adequate sociological treatment to the ways in which our different positions affect our experience of other sociological institutions and processes.

> *Multiculturalism is used as a framing device in every chapter. Every chapter describes the different ways in which race, class, age, ethnicity, sexuality, and gender organize people's experiences within institutions.*

Within Part Two, on "Identities and Inequalities," we deal with each of these facets of identity—age, class, race, ethnicity, gender, sexuality—separately, of course. But we are vitally concerned, also, with the ways in which they intersect with each other. When, after all, do you start being middle class and stop being Black? Contemporary sociological inquiry requires that we examine the intersections among these various elements of identity and inequality, understanding how they interact, amplify, and contradict each other.

These aspects of identity both unite us (as elements of identity) and divide us—into groups that compete for scarce resources. These are the dimensions of social life that organize inequality. Thus we explore both—identity and inequality.

Multiculturalism requires not just that we "add women (or any other group) and stir"—the ways that some courses and textbooks tried to revamp themselves in the last few decades of the twentieth century to embrace diversity. Multiculturalism requires that we begin from questions of diversity and identity, not end there. This book attempts to do that.

Organization

In this second edition of *Essentials*, we've reorganized several chapters and departed somewhat from standard introductory textbook formats (as well as from the complete edition of this text).

Chapter 10: The "Sociological Body": Age, Health, and Sexuality. We've included a chapter on age, health, and sexuality, not because it's trendy but because it's sociologically accurate. We've reorganized the chapter to stress the centrality of the body in society. As in other chapters, we see the body as a place where we express our identity as individuals and as a social site of inequality and conflict.

While most other textbooks might have a chapter on age, they are often really relabeled gerontology chapters and deal exclusively with aging—that is, with old people. We've added new material on youth. A large part of the chapter focuses on youth as an identity and as a source of inequality. After all, when we discuss age stratification, it is *both* old and young who experience discrimination. Our students know this; we should acknowledge it in our textbooks. And, again, it has been sociologists who have been at the forefront of exploring and understanding youth—as identity and as a basis for inequality.

We've brought a discussion of health and medicine into this chapter because health issues—from illness and pandemics to the social organization of health care—are urgent social issues that cry out for sustained sociological analysis. Again, students and instructors ask for these topics to be covered.

Over the past several decades, sexuality has emerged as one of the primary foundations of identity, while, at the same time, inequalities based on sexuality have emerged as among the nation's (and the world's) most charged arenas of inequality. And sociologists were in the forefront of the effort to identify sexuality as a primary foundation of identity. Chapter 10 acknowledges that.

Students today are eager to discuss these issues. Textbooks developed in the late twentieth century have not fully taken account of the massive changes that our current interest in sexuality has wrought—changes augured by movements both to liberalize and to restrict sexual expression and to multiply the variations of sexual identities, the importance of HIV in reconstituting sexual behaviors, and current campus sexual behaviors.

Chapter 13: Politics and Media. Paired with the discussion of politics, we have included a detailed treatment of media because the world has changed so enormously in the past few decades, and the media have been among the most important causes, and consequences, of those changes. Few institutions are more centrally involved in both globalization and multiculturalism. And, again, it has been sociologists who have come to see the increased centrality of the media in both the creation of identity and the global distribution of information. Sociologists have insisted that media (and peer groups) must take their place as equally important agents of childhood socialization as the former "big three"—family, religion, and education. And while some of us are zooming down the information superhighway, others are stuck on barely passable dirt tracks.

Chapter 14: Education, Religion, and Science. For the second edition of *Essentials,* we have added a section on religion and science, partly in response to requests from students and professors who had adopted the book. Sociological understandings of both religion and science—how they are organizationally similar even if they are theoretically different—are increasingly vital for an engaged citizenry, to be able to sift through seemingly contradictory claims and use of evidence. Simply put, we are often asked to believe the choice is either religion or science: We believe that a sociological perspective on both religion and science can enable us to better understand our social world.

What's more, many of the debates about religion and science are played out in educational arenas. What sorts of theories about the origins of human life should—and should not—be taught in schools? What standards of evidence are acceptable for scientific theories? Are prayers permitted at the beginning of the school day? We have therefore paired the discussion of science and religion with the discussion of education.

Finally, we add a sociological reason for this pairing. After family, the greatest social and institutional influences on the development of our identities are schools and religious institutions. Family, church, and school are the traditional sociological trinity of the institutions of socialization. We thought that covering them together here, as social institutions, parallels the discussion of education and religion (and family) in the chapter on socialization and therefore helped the chapter cohere better.

Chapter 15: Sociology of Environments: The Natural, Physical, and Human Worlds. Students are eager to discuss the environment. Few issues are more pressing to the current generation of college students than the environment. Indeed, few issues seem to be more pressing to our society as a whole. Yet while many textbooks discuss aspects of the environment, they typically focus on the "human" environment (chapters on demography and population) or the "built" environment (a chapter on urbanization). While fundamental and necessary, these books often leave out the third element of the environmental equation: the natural environment.

We have reconceptualized the chapter on the environment to focus on all three elements: human, built, and natural. It is, after all, the interaction among these three elements that structures the sorts of issues we face and constructs and constrains the sorts of policy options available to meet environmental needs. We believe that this framing will better equip a new generation of sociology students to understand and engage with the vital environmental issues of our time.

Chapter 4: How Do We Know What We Know? The Methods of the Sociologist. We believe that methods don't exist in a conceptual vacuum. Strategies of researching sociological problems come only after one has a problem to investigate. We have placed the discussion of classical and contemporary theory (Chapter 1) and of the conceptual foundations of sociology—culture, society, organization, interaction (Chapters 2 and 3)—before the discussion of methods because, we believe, it's more sociological to do so. When sociologists do research, they don't begin with a method and then go looking for a problem. They begin with a problem, drawn from the conceptual foundations of the field, and then determine the sorts of methodological strategies that they might use to comprehend it.

What's more, we believe that sociological methods are so important that we should not end our discussion of methodology with the individual methods chapter. One of the distinctive elements of *Sociology Now: The Essentials* is the "How Do We Know What We Know?" feature box. In each chapter, we stop and ask exactly *how* sociologists have come to know what we know about a certain topic. That is, we discuss different methods used in sociological research. Thus the discussion of methods is woven into each chapter, and it is woven in *in context* with substantive sociological questions.

Distinctive Features

The "How Do We Know What We Know?" box is only one of several features of *Sociology Now* that are fresh and exciting for students, enhancing their enjoyment of the text without sacrificing any of the substance.

rituals not only bind people to the specific group of which they are a member but also bind them across generations to past and future members. While many rituals are secular— pledging allegiance to the flag, college graduation ceremonies— rituals are most often associated with religion, where participation in the ritual cements one's sense of belonging to the community and its shared cultural history. Most cultures have specific rituals to mark the specific transitions in a person's life: birth, coming of age, marriage,

Eskimo Words for Snow

You've probably heard that the Eskimo have many different words for snow. It's a myth. Actually, the language of the Inuit (native peoples of the Arctic regions) creates words out of many different ideas, so it seems that they have many words for the same thing. In English, we use separate words in the phrase "the snow under the tree"; an Inuit might express this in one word. In fact, English has more words for different types of snow than most Inuit languages (Pullum, 1991).

Did You Know?

Elements of Culture   43

◄ **Did You Know?** Each chapter is punctuated by several "Did You Know?" boxes. These are generally short sociological factoids, tidbits of information that are funny, strange, a little offbeat, but illustrate the sociological ideas being discussed.

For example, did you know that the notion that the Eskimos have 24 different words for snow is a myth? Did you know that at the turn of the last century, baby boys were supposed to be dressed in red or pink and little girls in blue?

You won't draw their attention to all of these factoids, but the students are going to enjoy reading them. And we guarantee that there are at least a few that you didn't know!

► **Sociology and Our World.** Among the most exciting and rewarding parts of teaching introductory sociology is revealing to students how what we study is so immediately applicable to the world in which we all live. Thus, each chapter has at least two boxes that make this connection explicit. They're there to help the student see the connections between their lives, which they usually think are pretty interesting, and sociology, which they might, at first, fear as dry and irrelevant. And these boxes also are there to facilitate classroom discussions, providing only a couple of examples of what could be numerous possibilities to apply sociology to contemporary social questions.

Sociology and Our World

Six Degrees of Kevin Bacon

Did you know that the versatile actor Kevin Bacon is the center of the film universe? In 1994, three students at Albright College in Pennsylvania were hanging around a dorm room during a snowstorm and watching Bacon's film *Footloose*. When that film was followed by another Bacon film, *Quicksilver*, they began to speculate about how many different actors he had worked with. "It became one of our stupid party tricks," said one of the students. "People would throw names at us, and we'd connect them to Kevin Bacon." The three wrote to talk show host Jon Stewart, and a fad was quickly born.

To play, pick any actor in history and see how many connections it takes to connect that actor to a Kevin Bacon movie. For example neither John Wayne nor Marilyn Monroe ever appeared in a movie with Bacon. But Wayne was in *El Dorado* with James Caan, who was in *New York I Love You* with Kevin Bacon. Monroe was in *The Misfits* with Eli Wallach, who was also in *New York I Love You*. (Students at the University of Virginia have computed the "Bacon number" for any actor in history: see http://oracleofbacon.org.) Wayne and Monroe have Bacon numbers of 2. (So does 10-year-old Khail Bryant, who is our classm...

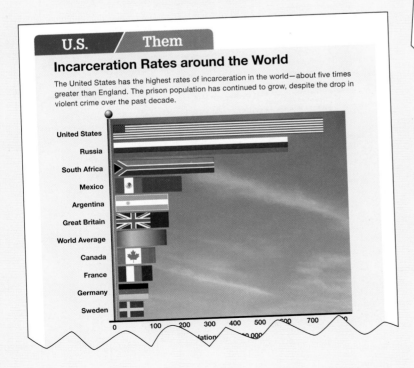

U.S. / Them
Incarceration Rates around the World

The United States has the highest rates of incarceration in the world—about five times greater than England. The prison population has continued to grow, despite the drop in violent crime over the past decade.

United States
Russia
South Africa
Mexico
Argentina
Great Britain
World Average
Canada
France
Germany
Sweden

0   100   200   300   400   500   600   700

◄ **U.S./Them** To better grasp globalization, we've added a new graphic feature in each chapter in which a sociological issue is framed comparatively, comparing U.S. data with data from the rest of the world. We try to set the United States in a global context, comparing it both to countries similar to the United States (other G7 countries, for example) as well as to countries very different from ours in the developing world. To see a list of the U.S./Them features, turn to p. xiv.

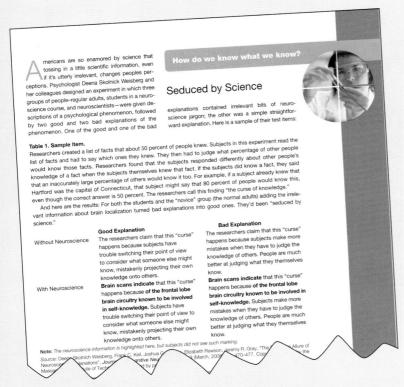

◄ How Do We Know What We Know? As mentioned above, this feature enables us to show students how methods actually work in the exploration of sociological problems. Instead of confining methods to its own chapter and then ignoring it for the remainder of the book, we ask, for example, how sociologists measure social mobility (Chapter 7), or how we use statistics to examine the relationship between race and intelligence (Chapter 8).

Sometimes, we show how *bad* methods have been used to support various arguments, such as nineteenth-century arguments against women entering higher education (Chapter 9), or even the recent claim by economist Steven Levitt that the legalization of abortion in 1973 led to the decline in violent crime two decades later (Chapter 6).

In this way, students can see method-in-action as a tool that sociologists use to discover the patterns of the social world.

► What Do You Think? What Does America Think? Part of an introductory course requires students to marshal evidence to engage with and often reevaluate their opinions. Often our job is to unsettle their fallback position of "this is just my own personal opinion"—which floats unhinged from any social contexts. We ask that they contextualize, that they refer to how they formed their opinions and to what sorts of evidence they might use to demonstrate the empirical veracity of their position. How they came to think what they think is often as important as what they think.

But students often benefit enormously from knowing what *other people* think as well. What percentage of Americans agrees with you? In each chapter, we've included a boxed feature that asks students questions taken directly from the General Social Survey. We include information about what a representative sample of Americans thinks about the same topic, to give a student a sense of where his or her opinion fits with the rest of the country. Critical-thinking questions based on the data encourage students to think about how factors like race, gender, and class influence our perceptions and attitudes.

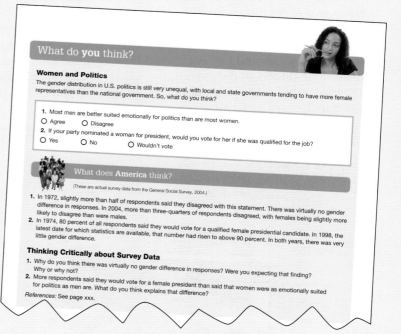

▶ **Chapter Review.** To help students master the material in each chapter, we've expanded the review section at the end of each chapter. It now includes:

- A summary of the chapter that includes key terms and definitions, organized by section
- A multiple-choice self-test
- Open-ended critical-thinking questions
- Links to related multimedia assets on mysoclab.com

Chapter Review

1. The Social Body

Our bodies are subject to natural processes, but our understandings of our bodies are social constructs, varying by time and place, and we transform them accordingly. Beauty, for example, is a social construct, and ideals of beauty vary by culture, and even economic climate. The beauty standard in the United States is unnaturally thin or muscular but highly valued. **Anorexia nervosa** and **bulimia** rates among young women here are the highest worldwide, and men suffer from **muscle dysmorphia** and the **Adonis complex,** while our population is increasingly obese. Globally more people are overweight, although there are still nations combating malnutrition. As nations gain wealth, they gain weight, but the richest people are the healthiest as a result of diet and exercise, while the poor suffer ill health. Tattooing today exemplifies the body as a projection of our identity and a work in progress, subject to transformation. Plastic surgery is also increasingly common, and even **transgenderism** is more common than previously.

anorexia nervosa A potentially fatal syndrome characterized by chronic and dangerous starvation dieting and exercise. (p. 286)

[...] potentially fatal syndrome characterized by food [...] purging [...] the qua[...]

worse than those in other developed nations. As we've seen in the United States, the rich do very well, but everyone else does poorly.

chronological age A person's age as determined by the actual date of his or her birth. (p. 290)

functional age A set of observable characteristics and attributes that are used to categorize people into different age cohorts. (p. 290)

age cohort A group of people who are born within a specific time period and therefore assumed to share both chronological and functional characteristics, as well as life experiences. (p. 290)

gerontology Scientific study of the biological, psychological, and sociological phenomena associated with old age and aging. (p. 290)

life span The average or the maximum amount of time an organism or object can be expected to live or last. (p. 290)

age norms Distinctive cultural values, pursuits, and pastimes that are culturally prescribed for each age cohort. (p. 290)

life expectancy The average number of years a person can expect to live; varies greatly by country and region. (p. 290)

adolescence Term coined by psychologist G. Stanley Hall (1904) to name [...] coinciding with [...] erty as a dis[...]

Self-Test: Check Your Understanding

1. Which of the following is not one of the causes for the increase in the percentage of elderly in the American population identified in the text?
   a. Decline in birth rate
   b. Increased life expectancy
   c. The large cohort of baby boomers reaching retirement age
   d. All of the above are factors identified in the text, resulting in an increase in the percentage of elderly in America.

2. Who lives longer, men or women?
   a. Men
   b. Women
   c. Men live longer in developing countries, but women live longer in industrialized countries.
   d. Women live longer in developing countries, but men live longer in industrialized countries.

3. Where does the United States rank in life expectancy compared with other nations worldwide?
   a. Number 1, with the longest life expectancy
   b. In the top ten
   c. In the top 20
   d. 4[...] and dropping

5. Cross-cultural studies reveal that the rates of preference for exclusively same-sex partners
   a. are similar across cultures.
   b. vary widely across cultures.
   c. are similar for men across cultures but [...] women.
   d. are impossible to assess, because of ho[...] this practice is believed to be.

6. Which of the following is the most effect[...] negative consequences of sexual behavio[...] of abortion, unwanted pregnancy, and s[...] ted diseases, according to the text?
   a. Abstinence-based education
   b. Comprehensive sex education
   c. Government-subsidized free birth c[...]
   d. All of the above have been shown t[...] effective, according to the text.

7. The majority of slaves in captivity toda[...]
   a. sub-Saharan Africa.
   b. Asian countries.
   c. South American countries.
   d. Thailand.
   [...]e trend in [...]

Integrate and Explore: Points to Consider

1. Why are some sexual behaviors considered deviant in some cultures and normal in others? What challenges with regard to sexual behavior might be expected with increased globalization, since sexual scripts vary by cultures? Do you expect multiculturalism to result in greater or decreased tolerance for diverse sexual behaviors and identities?

2. What does it mean to say that age is a social construct? Do all nations experience each age the same, or are there differences? How much do life expectancies differ? How has the social experience of age changed as a result of ind[...]alization and d[...]lopment?

succeed with mysoclab

Self-scoring practice tests, flashcards for learning key terms, streaming audio of the entire text, and multimedia, including:

Watch—*Sexual Violence Billboards*
Watch—Mindy Stombler, *What is "Social" About Sex?*
Explore—*Gen X-ers and Boomers*
MySocLibrary—Greg Critser, *Let Them Eat Fat*

An Engaging Writing Style. All textbook writers strive for clarity; a few even reach for elegance. This book is no exception. We've tried to write the book in a way that conveys a lot of information but also in a way that engages the students where *they* live. Not only are concepts always followed by examples, but we frequently use examples drawn from pop culture—from TV, movies, and music—and even from videos and video games.

This will not only make the students' reading experience seem more immediate but should also enable the instructor to illustrate the relevance of sociological concepts to the students' lives.

New to This Edition

Every book is a conversation—between authors and readers. And many books, like this, one, also hope to start conversations—between faculty and students, among students themselves, and between the authors and readers. A new edition of a book provides an opportunity to continue that conversation, to try and listen to those who read the book, assign the book, and even those whose job it is to sell the book. We have tried to listen to the concerns and questions from students, faculty, reviewers, and sales people (who are often a marvelous conduit of informal reviews and concerns). Many of the revisions in this edition of the book—adding the "U.S./Them" box feature, adding health to Chapter 10, and completely reorganizing the chapter around "the sociological body"—are responses to concerns raised by you.

One thing you'll notice is that the book *looks* different. Not only does the book include a vibrant new layout and design, but also more and more-sophisticated graphics, as well as new photos and cartoons. The end-of-chapter review section has been redesigned to provide a summary of each section of the chapter that includes the key terms and their definitions. A multiple-choice self-test has been added, as well as open-ended critical-thinking questions. Links to online assets from the Multimedia Library on mysoclab.com are also provided.

Of course, we've updated the data in each chapter, and we've tried to present the most current and relevant information to you. But more than that, we have tried to bring forward a distinctly sociological understanding of the statistics and studies that we cite. With a journalistic commitment to currency and a sociological commitment to context, we've brought in discussions of the 2008 presidential vote (in Chapter 13, Politics and Media, and also to some extent in Chapter 7, Stratification and Social Class) and of the economic crisis and its consequences, both domestically and globally; and we've also introduced a new section on health as an institution and health care reform (Chapter 10, The "Sociological Body": Age, Health, and Sexuality), just to name a few.

Specifically, here's what you'll find:

Chapter 1 What Is Sociology? New section "Sociology Comes to the United States" integrates women (such as Margaret Fuller and Charlotte Perkins Gilman) and minorities (such as W.E.B. DuBois) into the discussion of the sociological canon (they are not presented as a separate group). ▪ Updated chapter-opening vignette includes reference to President Obama's inaugural address. ▪ New map shows world regions according to GNP (Figure 1.1: An Alternative View of the World).

Chapter 2 Culture and Society New chapter-opening vignette launches discussion of culture by discussing "branding" (wearing an article of clothing that indicates membership in a group). ▪ Streamlined discussion of American values, with a new table that includes: Core Values (according to Williams), Opposite Values, and Our Contradictory Values (Table 2.2). ▪ New *What Do You Think/What Does America Think* box poses questions about America's ethnocentrism. ▪ New *Sociology and Our World* box, "Changing Language" talks about new words in the American lexicon, such as, "hockey mom." ▪ Section on popular culture and globalization includes example of the global hip hop scene. ▪ Updated Figure 2.1: American Attitudes about Nonmarital, Heterosexual Sex.

Chapter 3 Society: Interactions, Groups, and Organizations New chapter-opening vignette references Putnam's "bowling alone" while also discussing contemporary society's new communities. ▪ New *Sociology and Our World* box, "Six Degrees of Kevin Bacon." ▪ New Figure 3.1: Ascribed, Achieved, and Master Statuses. ▪ New Figure 3.2: Characteristics of Bureaucracy.

Chapter 4 How Do We Know What We Know? The Methods of the Sociologist Clarified information in "Types of Sociological Research Methods" section. ▪ Added more detailed discussion of all methods and variables. ▪ New figures and tables added to illustrate and clarify categories and issues, including: Figure 4.1: Inductive and Deductive Research Models; Figure 4.2: Types of Variables; Table 4.2: The General Social Survey; and Revised Table 4.3: Research Methodologies.

Chapter 5 Socialization Streamlined discussion of "Psychological Stage Theories of Development." ▪ Added "Genie" to discussion of isolated children. ▪ New *Sociology and Our World* box, "Different Access Means Different Adolescences" discusses the role of SNS (social networking sites) as a primary 'institution' of peer culture for U.S. teens. ▪ Revised Figure 5.2: Piaget's Cognitive Stages of Development.

Chapter 6 Deviance and Crime Deviance is discussed with a contemporary viewpoint. ▪ Updated section on white collar and business crime (using examples from the current economic crisis). ▪ New section on organized crime. ▪ Section "The Social Organization of Crime" includes updates with regard to gender, race, age, and class. ▪ Expanded section on incarceration and prisons, including coverage of privatization, costs, and global perspectives. ▪ New discussion of drugs (i.e., global networks of production and distribution) added to globalization and crime section. ▪ New figures on the reporting of gang activity by law enforcement, and the race/ethnicity and gender of gang members (Figures 6.1, 6.2, and 6.3). ▪ New data on computer security incidents (Figure 6.4). ▪ New data on regional crime rates (Figure 6.5), the U.S. incarceration rate (Figure 6.6), and the race of defendants executed in the U.S. since 1976 (Figure 6.8).

Chapter 7 Stratification and Social Class Greatly expanded sections on poverty (U.S. and global), inequality, and global inequalities. ▪ New section on class and culture. ▪ Enhanced section on social mobility, with updated discussion of intersections with race, class, gender, and also global comparisons. ▪ Discussion of the rhetoric used in the 2008 Presidential election with regard to class. ▪ New figure about American class structure (Figure 7.1). ▪ Updated Figure 7.2: Share of U.S. Median Income Received by Low- and High-Income OECD Households. ▪ New figures on Population Living on Less than $1 per Day, global comparison (Figure 7.3), Poverty Rates by Sex and Age (Figure 7.4), Women in Poverty (Figure 7.5), Causes of Moving Down the Economic Ladder (Figure 7.6), new map that shows the world by income (Figure 7.8), and Wallerstein's World System Theory Model (Figure 7.9). ▪ New tables include: Table 7.1: Occupational Prestige: 31-year Trend and Table 7.2: The Material Hardship of Poverty.

Chapter 8 Race and Ethnicity Streamlined chapter organization by grouping "Prejudice, Discrimination, and Racism" in one cohesive section. ▪ Updated discussion of biraciality. ▪ Enhanced discussion of persistence of racism and discrimination. ▪ New figures include: Figure 8.1: Extreme States (the states with the highest share of population that is either white or black); Figure 8.2: Race Relations (survey about biraciality); Figure 8.3: Multiracial Coupling (data and survey); Figure 8.4: U.S. Population Profile by Race: 2000, 2005, 2050; Figure 8.6: Subtle Discrimination; Figure 8.8: Percentage of Legal Immigrants Reporting European Origins, 1820–2006; Figure 8.9: U.S. Hispanic Population by County; and Figure 8.10: Major Asian American Groups.

Chapter 9 Sex and Gender Increased emphasis on youth and intersectionality. ▪ Increased emphasis on both femininity and masculinity. ▪ Updated coverage of the wage gap and the "glass ceiling," including the Lilly Ledbetter Fair Pay Act. ▪ New coverage on the gender of friendship and cross-race friendships. ▪ Discussion of "third wave" feminism includes example of a Guerrilla Girls poster. ▪ Updated Table 9.1: The Most Male- and Female-Dominated Occupations. ▪ New Figure 9.1: Overall Wage Gap: Median Weekly Earnings for Men and Women. ▪ New Figure 9.2: The Wage Gap: Median Annual Earnings by Race and Sex.

Chapter 10 The "Sociological Body": Age, Health, and Sexuality New sections on health as an institution and healthcare reform. ▪ New section on race, class, and health. ▪ Increased emphasis on youth—both in terms of identity and in terms of inequality. ▪ Enhanced section on global distribution of health and illness. ▪ New section on HIV/AIDS, both domestic and, especially, global. ▪ New data updates on sex education. ▪ New figures include: Figure 10.1: The Global Obesity Forecast; Figure 10.2: Percent of Population Age 65 or Older by Region: 2000, 2015, 2030; Figure 10.3: Poverty Among the Elderly (Age 65 and Older); Figure 10.4: Young Children in Low-Income Families in the U.S., by Race; Figure 10.5: Percentage of AIDS Cases by Race/Ethnicity in the U.S.; Figure 10.6: OECD Health Spending as a percentage of GDP; Figure 10.7: LGBTI Rights in the World; and Figure 10.9: Acceptance of Homosexuality by Society: Survey Results.

Chapter 11 The Family Enhanced section on cohabitation according to race, class, and also sexuality. ▪ New discussion of divorce rates in the U.S. by region. ▪ New *Sociology and Our World* box, "Instant Divorce." ▪ Updated section on "Not Parenting." ▪ New coverage of Intimate Partner Violence (IPV). ▪ Updated section "Family Violence between Generations" includes new section on corporal punishment of children and new section on elder abuse. ▪ New figures include: Figure 11.1: Trends in Coupling; Figure 11.2: Living Together (global comparison);

Figure 11.5: Changing Household Composition, 1995 and 2010; and Figure 11.7: Intimate Partner Violence among Females by Race/Ethnicity and Age.

Chapter 12 Economy and Work Updates on the financial crisis and its consequences, broken out by race, class, gender, and global dimensions. ▪ Coverage of the American economy in global perspective. ▪ New section on "Green-Collar Jobs." ▪ Enhanced coverage of illegal immigration and working "off the books." ▪ New *Sociology and Our World* box, "The Sociology of the Current Recession." ▪ Updated data on unemployment rates, U.S. and global. ▪ Expanded section on work-family dynamics including new data on percentage of mothers in the workforce. ▪ New figures include: Figure 12.1: Global Changes in Employment, by Sector of the Economy, 1997–2007; Figure 12.3: What Americans Think about Global Regulation and the Economy; Figure 12.4: Top Ten Fastest-Growing Occupations, 2006–2016; Figure 12.6: Unemployment Rates Total and Youth, World and Regions; Figure 12.7: Unemployment Rates by Race/Ethnicity and Education; and Figure 12.8: U.S. Women in Business. ▪ New tables include: Table 12.1: Top Ten Occupations Most Vulnerable to Offshoring; and Table 12.2: Who Earns Minimum Wage?

Chapter 13 Politics and Media New chapter-opening vignette discusses the 2008 U.S. Presidential campaign and Barack Obama's election. ▪ Streamlined coverage of political systems. ▪ Expanded section "Class, Race, Gender, and Power" includes more on the inter-connections between the wealthy and the powerful. ▪ Analysis of the 2008 Presidential vote with regard to class, education, race, gender and age. ▪ Updated discussion of the state of print media (especially the challenges faced by newspapers). ▪ New material on youth and political activism (including, "slacktivism"). ▪ Updated material on Internet use (by race, class, and gender) and its uses (pornography, blogs, Twitter). ▪ Updated discussion of global media. ▪ New figures include: Figure 13.1: Number of Democracies Worldwide, 1989-2008; Figure 13.2 Popular Vote in 2008: Presidential Election by Race/Ethnicity; Figure 13.3: Deaths Due to Terrorism, 1998–2007; Figure 13.4: Global Bloggers; Figure 13.5: BET Viewership; and Figure 13.6: Top Ten Grossing Films at International Box Office.

Chapter 14 Education, Religion, and Science Enhanced section on inequality and attainment. ▪ Updated discussion of U.S. high school and college graduation rates by race and class. ▪ Updated section on education reform and policy (including bilingual education, privatization, charter schools, homeschooling). ▪ New section on the transformation of higher education and community colleges. ▪ New section comparing religion and science. ▪ New sections on world religions and religious experience and identity. ▪ New section on science in the sociological perspective. ▪ New figures include: Figure 14.1: U.S. High School Graduation Rate; Figure 14.3: Undergraduate Enrollment; Figure 14.4: Soaring College Tuitions; and Figure 14.7: How Americans Describe Their Religious Identity.

Chapter 15 Sociology of Environments: The Natural, Physical, and Human Worlds Updated discussion of emigration and refugees. ▪ Updated coverage of U.S. internal migration. ▪ Updated section on waste and recycling—U.S. and global. ▪ Updates to sections on energy and climate change. ▪ New figures include: Figure 15.1: The Birth Dearth in Sociological Context; Figure 15.2: Major Refugee-Hosting Countries; Figure 15.3: Interstate Migration in the U.S.; Figure 15.5: World Population, 1950–2050; Figure 15.6: U.S. Cities and Prosperity; and Figure 15.8: Fossil Fuel Usage per Capita (global comparison).

We hope as you use the book—as a reader or as an instructor—that you will continue to tell us what works and what doesn't, how you respond to different features, and what we might do in the future to improve the book. The conversation continues!

Acknowledgments

To say that every book is a conversation is true, but insufficient. Every book is many conversations at once. To be sure, it's a conversation between authors and readers, and it's designed to stimulate conversations among readers themselves. But writing a book is itself saturated with other conversations, and though I cannot possibly do justice to them all, it is important to acknowledge their presence in this process.

First, there is my conversation, as an author, with my chosen field, my profession. How have I understood what others have written, their research, their way of seeing the world? How can I best communicate that to a new generation of students encountering sociology for the very first time?

I've had conversations with dozens of other sociologists who have read these chapters and provided enormously helpful feedback. Their candor has helped us revise, rethink, and reimagine entire sections of the book, and we are enormously grateful.

Manuscript Reviewers
Sociology Now: The Essentials, Second Edition:

Andre Arceneaux, *St. Louis University*
Sheli Bernstein-Goff, *West Liberty University*
Shannon Carter, *University of Central Florida*
Ruth A. Chananie-Hill, *University of Northern Iowa*
Erica Chito Childs, *Hunter College*
Susan Ciriello, *Naugatuck Valley Community College*
Theodore Cohen, *Ohio Wesleyan University*
Laura Colmenero-Chilberg, *Black Hills State University*
Jason Cummings, *Indiana University*
Louwanda Evans, *Texas A&M University / Blinn College*
Siddig Fageir, *Tougaloo College*
Paul Farcus, *Mt. Aloysius College*
Carol Fealey, *Farmingdale State College*
Kathleen Fitzgerald, *Columbia College*
Pamela J. Forman, *University of Wisconsin—Eau Claire*
Anita Gardner, *Cleveland Community College*
Heather Griffiths, *Fayetteville State University*
Kellie Hagewen, *University of Nebraska—Lincoln*
Lisa Handler, *Community College of Philadelphia*
Laura Hansen, *University of Massachusetts—Boston*
Jennifer Hartsfield, *University of Oklahoma*
Theresa Hibbert, *University of Texas at El Paso*
Xuemei Hu, *Union County College*
A. J. Jacobs, *East Carolina University*
Tiffany Jenson, *University of Oklahoma*
Kimberly M. Johanek, *Boise State University*
Irwin Kantor, *Middlesex County College*
Mara Kent-Skruch, *Anne Arundel Community College*

Brian Klocke, *SUNY Plattsburgh*
Caroline Kozojed, *Bismarck State College*
Jamee Kristen, *University of Nebraska*
Todd Krohn, *The University of Georgia*
Amy Lane, *University of Missouri*
Jynette Larshus, *Georgia Southern University*
Dwayne Lee, *Midlands Technical College*
Shelby Longard, *Belmont University*
Cheryl Maes, *University of Nevada, Rio*
Fortunata Songora Makene, *Worcester State College*
Harry Mersmann, *San Joaquin Delta College*
Melinda Miceli, *University of Hartford*
Amanda Miller, *Ohio State University*
Jane Morgan, *Cuesta College*
David Nicholson, *University of Oklahoma*
Amy Palder, *Georgia State University*
Harriet H. Perry, *University of Texas at El Paso*
Joleen L. Pietrzak, *University of South Dakota*
Pam Rosenberg, *Shippensburg University*
Michael Ryan, *Dodge City Community College*
Teresa Sobieszczyk, *University of Montana*
Richard Steinhaus, *New Mexico Junior College*
LaRoyce Sublett, *Georgia Perimeter College*
Laura Toussaint, *Green River Community College*
Rollin Watson, *Somerset Community College*
Joann Watts Sietas, *Palomar College*
Michael Wehrman, *Ohio University*
Michael Weissbuch, *Xavier University*
Shonda Whetstone, *Blinn College*
Elena Windsong, *University of New Mexico*
Susan Wortmann, *University of Nebraska—Lincoln*

Manuscript Reviewers
for the first edition of *Sociology Now:*

Boyd Bergeson, *Oregon Health and Sciences University*
Susan Blackwell, *Delgado Community College*
Ralph Brown, *Brigham Young University*
Philip J. Crawford, *San Jose Community College*
Kris de Welde, *University of Colorado at Boulder*
Brenda Donelan, *Northern State University*
Catherine Felton, *Central Piedmont Community College*
Dian Fitzpatrick, *East Stroudsburg University*
Risa L. Garelick, *Coconino Community College*
Ann Marie Hickey, *University of Kansas*
Candace L. Hinson, *Tallahassee City College*
Michael L. Hirsch, *Huston-Tillotson University*
Amitra Hodge, *Buffalo State College*
Lynette F. Hoelter, *University of Michigan*
Amy Holzgang, *Cerritos College*
William Housel, *Northwestern Louisiana State University*

H. David Hunt, *University of Southern Mississippi*
Judi Kessler, *Monmouth College*
Amy Manning Kirk, *Sam Houston State University*
Jennifer Lerner, *Northern Virginia Community College*
Ami Lynch, *George Washington University*
Karen E. B. McCue, *University of New Mexico*
Shelley A. McGrath, *Southern Illinois University*
Abigail McNeely, *Austin Community College*
Stephanie R. Medley-Rath, *University of West Georgia*
Sharon Methvin, *Clark College*
Barbara J. Miller, *Pasadena City College*
Beth Mintz, *University of Vermont*
Monique Moleon-Mathews, *Indian River Community College*
Adam Moskowitz, *Columbus State Community College*
Elizabeth Pare, *Wayne State University*
Joseph Keith Price, *West Texas A&M University*
Cynthia K. S. Reed, *Tarrant Community College*
Susan Smith-Cunnien, *University of St. Thomas*
Ryan Spohn, *Kansas State University*
Marybeth C. Stalp, *University of Northern Iowa*
Kell J. A. Stone, *El Camino College*
Richard Valencia, *Fresno City College*
Dean Wagstaffe, *Indian River Community College*
Georgie Ann Weatherby, *Gonzaga University*
Pamela Williams-Paez, *Canyons College*
S. Rowan Wolf, *Portland Community College*

We would also like to thank the following instructors whom we consulted to create the table of contents for the first edition of the *Essentials* edition of the text:

Roger C. Barnes, *University of the Incarnate Word*
Roberta Campbell, *Miami University—Hamilton*
Karyn Daniels, *Long Beach Community College*
Amitra A. Hodge, *Buffalo State University*
Lynette Hoelter, *University of Michigan*
Barry D. Kass, *SUNY—Orange*
Karen McCue, *University of New Mexico*
Richard B. Miller, *Missouri Southern State University*
John Mitrano, *Central Connecticut State University*
Timothy E. Nissen, *University of Wisconsin—River Falls*
Scott Potter, *Marion Technical College*
J. Keith Price, *West Texas A&M University*
Lesley Williams Reid, *Georgia State University*
George Wilson, *University of Miami*

Each chapter includes a box called "What Do You Think? What Does America Think?"—all of which were contributed by Kathleen Dolan of North Georgia College and State University. These help the students gauge their own opinions next to the results of GSS and other surveys of Americans' opinions. Such a gauge is pedagogically vital. Often my students begin a response to a question with a minimizing feint: "This is just my own personal opinion . . . " What a relief and revelation to see their opinions as socially shared (or not) with others. I'm grateful to Kathleen for her efforts to contextualize those "personal opinions."

At the end of each chapter, the "Chapter Review" section provides students with a quick, effective review of the chapter's material—all of which were contributed by Lisa Jane Thomassen of Indiana University. I'm grateful to Lisa for her efforts to create precise summaries and interesting review questions for each chapter.

I've also carried on a conversation with my colleagues at SUNY, Stony Brook, where I have been so fortunate to work for two decades in a department that strongly values high-quality teaching. In particular, I'm grateful to my chair, Diane Barthel-Bouchier, for managing such a diverse and collegial department where I have felt so comfortable. Every single one of my colleagues—both past and present—has assisted me in some way in the work on this book, guiding my encounter with areas of his or her expertise, providing an example he or she has used in class, or commenting on specific text. I am grateful to them all.

There has also been an ongoing conversation with my students, both graduate and undergraduate, throughout my career. They've kept me attentive to the shifts in the field and committed to working constantly on my own pedagogical strategies to communicate them. My teaching assistants over the years have been especially perceptive—and unafraid to communicate their thoughts and opinions!

I have spent my entire career teaching in large public universities—UC Berkeley, UC Santa Cruz, Rutgers, and now Stony Brook—teaching undergraduate students who are, overwhelmingly, first-generation college students, and most often immigrants and members of minority groups. They represent the next generation of Americans, born not to privilege but to hope and ambition. More than any other single group, they have changed how I see the world.

Many other sociologists have influenced my thinking over the years. I suspect I may be a rather impressionable guy, because were I to list them all, I think the list would go on for pages! So I will only thank some recent friends and colleagues who have contributed their advice, comments, or criticisms on specific items in this book, and those old friends who have shared their passion for sociology with me for decades: Elizabeth Armstrong, Troy Duster, Paula England, Cynthia and Howard Epstein, Abby Ferber, John Gagnon, Josh Gamson, Barry Glassner, Erich Goode, Cathy Greenblat, Michael Kaufman, Mike Messner, Rebecca Plante, Lillian Rubin, Don Sabo, Wendy Simonds, Arlene and Jerry Skolnick, Jean-Anne Sutherland, and Suzanna Walters.

For the rest of my far-flung friends and colleagues, I hope that you will find the fruits of those conversations somewhere in these pages.

One person stands out as deserving of special thanks. Jeffery Dennis began his career as my graduate student—an enormously gifted one at that. We engaged Jeff as a colleague to work with us to develop this book—to help us develop chapters, explore arguments, clarify examples, track down obscure factoids, organize thematic presentations—and with everything we asked of him, he delivered far more than we hoped. He's been a most valued contributor to this project and a major participant in its conversations.

A textbook of this size and scale is also the result of a conversation between author and publisher—and there we have been enormously lucky to work with such a talented and dedicated team as we have at Allyn and Bacon. As the editor, Jeff Lasser does more than acquire a book, he inhabits it—or, more accurately, it inhabits him. He thinks about it constantly and engages with the authors with just the right balance of criticism and support. He knows when to push—and when not to.

Jessica Carlisle has been simply the ideal development editor. Her instincts were almost always flawless—she held aloft a concern for both the form and the content of this book in equal measure, helping us revise, trim, cut, and add in a way that made the book better, stronger, and tighter. And Leah Strauss has been far more than a maternity leave pinch hitter, but a vital member of the starting team.

The rest of the production team, including Patty Bergin, Roberta Sherman, and Susan McNally, were as professional and dedicated to the project as we were.

At the beginning of this preface, I said I was really lucky because my job is so amazingly rewarding and because I get to do something that is in harmony with my values, with how I see the world.

But I'm also really lucky because I get to do virtually everything—including the writing of this book—with my wife, Amy Aronson. Amy is a professor of journalism and media studies at Fordham University; she comes to her sociological imagination through her background in the humanities and her experiences as a magazine editor (*Working Woman*). In the writing of this book, we have been completely equal partners—this is the only part I have written myself. (Don't worry: She edited it!)

Amy thanks her colleagues at Fordham University, Lincoln Center, for their support and various helpful comments. She's grateful always to Robert Ferguson for his unwavering encouragement over the years.

And we both thank our respective families—Winnie Aronson, Nancy Aronson, Barbara and Herb Diamond, Sandi Kimmel and Patrick Murphy, Ed Kimmel, Bill Diamond, Jeff Diamond, Leslie and Bruce Hodes, and Lauren Kaplan—for believing in us and cheering us on.

And we thank Zachary, our son. At age 11, he's been a lively critic of some of our ideas, a curious listener, and a patient family member. (He helped pick some of the pictures!) Every single day, when he recounts the day's events at school, or is at soccer or ice hockey practice, or observes something in the neighborhood, or asks a question about the news—he reminds us of the importance of a sociological perspective in making sense of the world.

And finally I thank Amy. As partners in our lives, as parents to our son, and in our collaboration on this and other books, we work toward a marriage of equals, in which the idea of gender equality is a lived reality, not some utopian dream.

Michael Kimmel

To learn more about this text and the authors, watch video of Michael Kimmel and Amy Aronson discussing *Sociology Now* at www.pearsonhighered.com/showcase/kimmel2e.

About the Authors

Michael Kimmel, Professor of Sociology at Stony Brook University, is one of the pioneers in the sociology of gender and one of the world's leading experts on men and masculinities. He was the first man to deliver the International Women's Day lecture at the European Parliament; was the first man to be named the annual lecturer by the Sociologists for Women in Society; and has been called as an expert witness in several high-profile gender discrimination cases. Among his many books are *Men's Lives, The Gendered Society, Manhood in America,* and *Revolution: A Sociological Perspective.* He is also known for his ability to explain sociological ideas to a general audience. His articles have appeared in dozens of magazines and newspapers, including the *New York Times, The Nation,* the *Village Voice,* the *Washington Post,* and *Psychology Today.*

Amy Aronson is Assistant Professor of Journalism and Media Studies at Fordham University. She is the author of *Taking Liberties: Early American Women's Magazines and Their Readers* and an editor of the international quarterly, *Media History.* She has coedited several books, including a centennial edition of Charlotte Perkins Gilman's *Women and Economics* and the two-volume *Encyclopedia of Men and Masculinities,* which was honored by the New York Public Library with a Best of Reference Award in 2004. A former editor at *Working Woman* and *Ms.,* she has also written for publications including *BusinessWeek, Global Journalist,* and the Sunday supplement of *The Boston Globe*.

About the Supplements

Instructor Supplements

Unless otherwise noted, instructor's supplements are available at no charge to adopters and available in printed or duplicated formats, as well as electronically through the Pearson Higher Education Instructor Resource Center (www.pearsonhighered.com/irc).

Instructor's Manual (*Shelly McGrath, Southern Illinois University*) For each chapter in the text, the Instructor's Manual provides chapter summaries and outlines, learning objectives, key terms and people, teaching suggestions (which include film suggestions, projects, and homework exercises), and references for further research and reading. 0-205-75710-3

Test Bank (*Pam Rosenberg, Shippensburg University*) The Test Bank contains approximately 100 questions per chapter in multiple-choice, fill-in-the-blank, true-false, short answer, essay, and open-book formats. The open-book questions challenge students to look beyond words and answer questions based on the text's figures, tables, and maps. All questions are labeled and scaled according to Bloom's Taxonomy. 0-205-75711-1

MyTest Computerized Test Bank The printed Test Bank is also available online through Pearson's computerized testing system, MyTest. This fully networkable test-generating program is available online. The user-friendly interface allows you to view, edit, and add questions; transfer questions to tests; and print tests in a variety of fonts. Search and sort features allow you to locate questions quickly and to arrange them in whatever order you prefer. The Test Bank can be accessed anywhere with a free MyTest user account. There is no need to download a program or a file to your computer. 0-205-75716-2

Interactive PowerPoint™ Presentation Completely new PowerPoint™ slides bring the powerful Kimmel design right into the classroom, drawing students into the lecture and providing wonderful interactive activities, visuals, and animation. 0-205-81822-6

Secondary PowerPoint™ Presentation (*Akello "Kell" Stone, El Camino College*) These PowerPoint slides on a CD, created especially for *Sociology Now: The Essentials*, feature lecture outlines for every chapter and many of the tables, charts, and maps from the text. PowerPoint software is not required, as a PowerPoint viewer is included. 0-205-71183-9

Sociology Active Learning Library (*General Editor Kathy Rowell, Sinclair Community College*) Sociology Active Learning Library (SALLY) is a website where we are collecting class-tested, hands-on learning activities from instructors across the country. Learning activities have been evaluated and developed to make sure they are pedagogically complete and ready to use in the classroom (www.sally.pearsoncmg.com).

Student Supplements

Study Guide (*Shelly McGrath, Southern Illinois University*) The Study Guide is designed to help students prepare for quizzes and exams. For every chapter in the text, it contains a chapter summary, lists of key terms and people, and a practice test with 25 multiple-choice, 10 true-false, 10 fill-in-the blank, 3–5 essay questions and an answer key. It can be packaged on request with the text at no additional cost. 0-205-75712-X

Study Card for Introduction to Sociology Compact, efficient, and laminated for durability, the Allyn and Bacon Study Card for Introductory Sociology condenses course information down to the basics, helping students quickly master fundamental facts and concepts or prepare for an exam. It can be packaged on request with this text at no additional charge. 0-205-44608-6

Online Course Management

MySocLab MySocLab is a dynamic website that provides a wealth of resources geared to meet the diverse teaching and learning needs of today's instructors and students. MySocLab is built around a complete e-Text version of the book and is designed to be used either as a supplement to a traditional lecture course or to completely administer an online course. MySocLab offers superior tools to enhance learning and teaching, including many assignable exercises and activities:

- **A complete eText** of the book enables students to save time by having access to their book online. Students can highlight and add their own notes.
- **Self-scoring Pre & Post Tests with Individualized Study Plans** allow students to review their knowledge of course material and concepts. Pre and Post Test results generate a customized study plan that enables students to identify and focus on what they don't know.
- **MySocLibrary** offers electronic access to over 100 classic and contemporary readings, accompanied by

introductions, essay/discussion questions, and automatically graded multiple-choice questions.

- **Social Explorer** provides access to Census data from 1790 to 2007, with visually engaging interactive maps that enable exploration of data from the country level all the way down to the Census tract level.

MySocLab is available at no additional cost to the student when a text is packaged with a *MySocLab Student Access Code Card*, (0-205-66917-4).

WebCT and Blackboard Test Banks For colleges and universities with WebCT™ and Blackboard™ licenses, we have converted the complete Test Bank into these popular course management platforms. Adopters can download the electronic file by logging in to our Instructor Resource Center. (www.pearsonhighered.com/irc) 0-205-83207-5 and 0-205-83205-9

Additional Supplements

The Allyn and Bacon Social Atlas of the United States (*William H. Frey, University of Michigan, with Amy Beth Anspach and John Paul DeWitt*) This brief and accessible atlas uses colorful maps, graphs, and some of the best social science data available to survey the leading social, economic, and political indicators of American society. It is available for purchase separately or packaged with this text at a significant discount, 0-205-43917-9.

Careers in Sociology, **Third Edition** (*W. Richard Stephens, Jr., Eastern Nazarene College*) This supplement explains how sociology can help students prepare for careers in such fields as law, gerontology, social work, business, and computers. It also examines how sociologists entered the field. The supplement is packaged on request with this text at no additional charge, 0-205-37922-2.

1

What Is Sociology?

It was the best of times, it was the worst of times, it was the age of wisdom, it was the age of foolishness, it was the epoch of belief, it was the epoch of incredulity, it was the season of Light, it was the season of Darkness, it was the spring of hope, it was the winter of despair, we had everything before us, we had nothing before us, we were all going direct to Heaven, we were all going direct the other way—in short, the period was so far like the present period.

Charles Dickens (1859)

These are the first lines of one of Western literature's greatest novels, *A Tale of Two Cities* by Charles Dickens. In it, Dickens recounts the saga of the French Revolution, a period of unparalleled optimism about the possibilities of human freedom and some of the most barbaric and repressive measures ever taken in the name of that freedom.

One hundred and fifty years later, Barack Obama echoed some of Dickens's sentiments when he was inaugurated as the nation's 44th president. Although the United States is "the most prosperous, powerful nation on earth," we are "in the midst of a crisis." Our workers are productive, our minds inventive, our values timeless and enduring; yet "gathering clouds and raging storms" threaten everything we have built, everything we stand for.

Well, which is it: best or worst, most prosperous or in the throes of economic crisis? Dickens and President Obama insisted that it was both—and there lies the essence of sociological thinking. It's difficult to hold both ideas in our heads at the same time. More often, we take a position—usually at one extreme or the other—and then try to hold it in the face of evidence that suggests otherwise. Logic and common sense insist that it can't possibly be both.

That's what makes sociology so fascinating. Sociology is constantly wrestling with two immense and seemingly contradictory questions, social order and social disorder—how it often feels that everything fits together perfectly, like a smoothly functioning machine, and how it often feels as if society is coming apart at the seams. If every single individual is simply doing what is best for him- or herself, why is there any social order at all? Why are we not constantly at war with each other? And how is order maintained? How is society possible in the first place?

On the other hand, why does it often seem that society is falling apart? Why do so many people in society disobey its laws, disagree about its values, and differ about the political and social goals of the society? Why is there so much crime and delinquency? Why is there so much inequality? Why does society keep changing?

These sorts of giant questions are what sociology sets out to answer. Sociologists analyze the ways that institutions like family, marketplace, military, and government serve to sustain social order and how problems like inequality, poverty, and racial or gender discrimination make it feel as if it is falling apart. And it turns out that most of the answers aren't so obvious or commonsensical after all.

> "Sociology is a way of seeing the world. It takes us beyond the "either/or" framing of common sense and looks at how most social issues are really "both/and."

Sociology as a Way of Seeing

If you're like most people, you know that sociology is "the study of society." But we don't typically know much more than that. What is society? And how do we study it?

Unlike other social sciences, the field of sociology is not immediately evident from just its name, like economics or political science. Nor are there many TV or movie characters who are sociologists, as there are psychologists (like Dr. Phil) or anthropologists (Indiana Jones). In the classic movie *Animal House* (1979), the protagonist encounters two sorority girls at a party. The writers wanted to portray these girls as gum-chomping, airheaded idiots. So what are they majoring in? Right—sociology.

Sociology sets for itself the task of trying to answer certain basic questions about our lives: the nature of identity, the relationship of the individual to society, our relationships with others. Sociologists try to explain the paradoxes that we daily observe in the world around us: for example, how economic changes bring us closer and closer, and, at the same time, we fragment into smaller religious, tribal, or ethnic enclaves. Or we observe that society is divided into different unequal groups based on class, race, ethnicity, and gender, and yet, at the same time, everyone's values are remarkably similar.

Sociology is both a field of study and a way of seeing. As a field, perhaps the pithiest definition was written 50 years ago, by C. Wright Mills (1959), a professor at Columbia University. Sociology, he wrote, is an "imagination," a way of seeing, a way of "connecting biography to history." What Mills means is that the **sociological imagination** sees our lives as *contextual* lives—our individual identities are understandable only in the social contexts—such as family, or our jobs, or our set of friends—in which we find ourselves. A sociological perspective is a perspective that sees connections and contexts. Sociology connects individuals to the worlds in which we live. Stated most simply, **sociology** *is the study of human behavior in society.*

Beyond Either/Or: Seeing Sociologically

To help orient you to the field of sociology, read again the quote that begins this chapter. Now, take a look at your local daily newspaper or watch your local TV news. Notice how often they're telling you how things are getting worse, much worse than they've ever been. Crime threatens our safety, teenage drinking and drug use are epidemic, fundamentalist fanatics make the entire world unsafe. The media fret about the spiraling divorce rate, teen pregnancies, and the collapse of marriage; or we worry about new strains of diseases, like "swine flu," or about "old" diseases like smallpox being unleashed as weapons, and about the microbial dangers lurking in our food. We fret about the collapse of morality and the decline in religion. Is the country falling apart?

Perhaps the opposite is true. We're also bombarded with stories about the enormous social changes that have made the world a smaller and smaller place, where millions of people can communicate with one another in an instant. Dramatic technological breakthroughs expand the possibilities for trade, cultural exchange, and economic development. Scientific advances make it possible to live longer, healthier lives than any people who have ever lived. The mapping of the human genome may enable scientists to elim-

Sociology and Our World

The Sociological Imagination

In his famous essay, C. Wright Mills argued that the sociological imagination "enables us to grasp history and biography and the relations between the two within society. That is its task and its promise." This means connecting our individual lives to the large-scale events in the world, seeing the impact of such things as climate change, economic shifts, or immigration on our sense of ourselves and on our day-to-day interactions with others. This sometimes comes as a great relief, to know that we don't create our lives in some vacuum but rather in relationship to others, in a specific time and place. We're not alone. On the other hand, it does mean that we are less "special" than we might like to think: that the unique people we feel ourselves to be are in constant relationship to the world around us. We may choose our own direction, but we choose from a rather limited set of options. And it's sociology's task to explore what those options are by examining the forces that limit our choices. Thus, sociology is about how we create our identity, but also about what sorts of resources we use to construct it.

inate many of the diseases that have plagued human beings for millennia while the rise of the Internet will enable us to communicate that knowledge in a heartbeat. Americans are going to college in greater numbers, and today we have women, African American, Asian American, Hispanic, and gay CEOs, corporate board members, and business owners. Freedom and democracy have spread throughout the world. Is society getting better and better?

To the sociologist, neither of these polar positions is completely true. The sociologist is as concerned about the collapse of traditional social institutions and values as he or she is about the extraordinary ways society is improving. Sociologists see *both* sides at once. They don't think in "either/or"; they usually think in "both/and." And what's more, sociologists don't see the glass half full or half empty, as the classic formulation of optimist or pessimist goes. Sociologists see the glass half full—and want to know about the quality of the air in the glass. They see the glass half empty and want to know about the quality of the water as well.

For example, as you'll see in this book, most sociologists believe our identities come from *both* nature and nurture; that people are getting *both* richer and poorer (it depends on which people in what places); that our racial and ethnic identities *both* draw us closer together and further fragment us.

Making Connections: Sociological Dynamics

The sociologist is interested in the connections between things getting better and things getting worse. In our globalizing world, where daily the farthest reaches of the world are ever more tightly connected to every other part,

where changes in one remote corner of Earth ripple through the rest of society, affecting every other institution—in such a world, the sociologist attempts to see both integration and disintegration and the ways in which the one is related to the other.

Take one example. In New York City, we are occasionally aghast that some innocent person, calmly waiting on a subway platform, is pushed in front of an oncoming train and killed—all for apparently no reason at all. On the freeway, we daily hear of cases of "road rage" that got a little out of control. Instead of being content with giving each other the finger and cursing at the tops of our lungs, occasionally someone gets really carried away and pulls a gun out of the glove compartment and opens fire on a stranger, whose only "crime" might have been to have cut that person off. Immediately, the headlines blare that society is falling apart, that violence is on the rise. Psychologists offer therapeutic salve and warn of the increasing dangers of urban or suburban life. "It's a jungle out there," we'll say to ourselves. "These people are nuts."

But sociologists also ask another sort of question: How can so many people drive on clogged freeways, on too-little sleep, inching along for hours, surrounded by maniacs who are gabbing on their cell phones, ignoring speed limits and basic traffic safety—many also going either toward or away from stressful jobs or unbalanced home lives? How can we stuff nearly 2 million human beings, who neither know one another nor care very much for any of them, into large metal containers, packed like sardines, hurtling through dark tunnels at more than 60 miles an hour? How is it possible that these same people don't get so murderously angry at their conditions that people aren't pushed

Half full or half empty? We often think we have to choose, but sociologists see the glass as both half full and half empty—and explore the relationship between the two halves. Context also matters: when are we seeing the picture? if the water's just been poured, the glass is half full. if you've just been drinking from it, it's half empty. Besides, how big is the glass? A champagne glass or takeout coffee cup?

in front of subway trains at every single subway stop every single day of the year? How come more people aren't driving armed and dangerous, ready to shoot anyone who worsens an already difficult morning commute?

To a sociologist, social *order* is as intriguing as social breakdown. Sociologists want to know what keeps us from fragmenting into 280 million different parts, and, at the same time, we want to know what drives us in so many millions of directions. We want to know what holds us together and what drives us apart. How is social order possible—especially in a nation in which we believe that each individual is completely free to do as he or she sees fit, where we're all supposed to be "looking out for number 1"? How come, despite all our protests, we also tend to "look out for number 2"?

Is it simply the threat of coercion—that we'd all be wreaking murder and mayhem if we weren't afraid of getting caught? We think it's something more, and that's what sociology—and this book—is about.

Sociological Understanding

Our interest is not entirely in social order, nor is it entirely social disintegration and disorder. Let's return for a moment to that person who pushed someone in front of a subway train. Sure, that person probably needs to have his or her head examined. But a sociologist might also ask about governmental policies that deinstitutionalized millions of mentally ill people, forcing them onto ever-shrinking welfare rolls and often into dramatically overcrowded prisons. And perhaps we need also to examine the income disparities that collide in our major cities—disparities that make the United States perhaps the most unequal industrial country and the modern city as the most heterogeneous collection of people from different countries, of different races, speaking different languages, in the entire world.

And what about that person who opened fire on a passing motorist? Can we discuss this frightening event without also discussing the availability of guns in America and the paucity of effective gun control laws? Shouldn't we also discuss suburban and urban sprawl, overwork, the number and size of cars traveling on decaying roads built for one-tenth that many? Or maybe it's just those shock jocks that everyone is listening to in their cars—the guys who keep telling us not to just get mad but to get even?

A comparison with other countries is usually helpful. No other industrial country has this sort of road rage deaths; they are far more common in countries ruled by warlords, in which a motorist might unknowingly drive on "their" piece of the highway. And though many other industrial nations have intricate and elaborate subway systems, people being pushed in front of trains is exceedingly rare. And are those same countries far more homogeneous than the United States with well-financed institutions for the mentally ill or with a more balanced income structure? Or maybe it's that people who live in those countries are just more content with their lives than we are.

These are just two examples of how a sociologist looks at both social order and social breakdown. There are many others that we will discuss in this book. For example, the much-lamented decline in marriage and increase in divorce are accompanied by a dramatic increase in people who want to marry and start families (like lesbians, gay men, and transgendered people) and the dramatically high percentage of people who remarry within three years of divorce—which indicates that most people still believe in the institution. The oft-criticized decline in literacy and numeracy among American teenagers is accompanied by equally astonishing increases in competition at America's most elite schools—so much so that many who attended elite schools in the past would not be admitted now.

Chaos or order? Cars, buses, rickshaws, bicycles and pedestrians crowd the street in Dhaka, Bangladesh in what appears to be a jumble. Yet everyone manages to get where they are going, without much violence or many accidents.

U.S. / Them

How Globalized Are We?

The forces of globalization are evident in our daily lives, from the 4.7 billion people worldwide who watched the Beijing Olympics in 2008, to the financial crisis that began with mortgage lenders in the United States and quickly sapped markets around the world. Four components have been used to measure the level of globalization: trade and investment flows, the migration of people across borders, use of communication technologies, and participation in international organizations. Which countries are the most globalized in the world—and which are the least?

TOP 10 MOST
Globalized Countries

Singapore   (#1 Globalization score: 1000)
Hong Kong
Netherlands
Switzerland
Ireland
Denmark
United States
Canada
Jordan
Estonia

TOP 10 LEAST
Globalized Countries

Pakistan
Bangladesh
Turkey
China
Brazil
Venezuela
Indonesia
Algeria
India
Iran   (#72 Globalization score: 120)

Source: A.T. Kearney, *Foreign Policy* Globalization Index.

1. What factors do you think might explain the discrepancies between the most and the least globalized countries?

2. What social effects do you think the size of the globalization gap might have?

Doing Sociology

Sure, sociology is an academic field, with a clear object of study and theories that inform that inquiry and various methods that we use to understand it. But just as important, sociology is a kind of posture, a perspective, a way of seeing the world.

Take a look at the course offerings in your school's catalog. Most courses in most fields seem to present part of the field's object of study—except sociology. While about half of our course offerings are about what sociology *is* and *does*—that is, about sociological theory, methods, and specific areas of study—the other half are often listed as what we might call the "sociology ofs"—they offer a sociological perspective on other fields. So we have sociology of alcohol, art, crime, culture, delinquency, drugs, gender, literature, mass communications, media, music, science, sexuality, technology, and work.

Sociology is, of course, also a defined subject—and as such it uses theoretical models of how the world works and various methods to understand that world. But sociology is equally a "way of seeing"—a way of organizing all these seemingly contradictory trends—indeed a way of looking at the objects of study of all the other disciplines.

The sociological perspective itself is dynamic. It is a difficult position to maintain in the wake of moral certainties asserted from both sides. But it is precisely the fact that such moral certainties are asserted from both sides that makes the mapping of relationships—seeing vices as well as virtues, stability as well as change, order as well as disintegration—that much more imperative. Sociologists see both trends simultaneously, as well as seeing how they are interrelated.

The sociological perspective is not avoidance, nor is it an unwillingness to take a position. In fact, sociologists are involved in designing policies to ameliorate many of the world's most pressing problems. Nor is it the same thing as moral relativism, which is a form of apolitical resignation. Most sociologists have strong political commitments to using their research to make other people's lives better, though they inevitably disagree about what "better" might mean and how best to accomplish it. Finally, the sociological perspective is not to be confused with indifference. Seeing problems as analytically complex doesn't mean that one is uninterested in solving them.

To be a sociologist is to recognize the social complexity of problems—the events we seek to understand have many parts, each connected to the others. It requires that we step back from the immediate pulls of political positions and take into account larger contexts in which problems take shape. And it requires a certain intellectual humility, to acknowledge that none of us can completely grasp the fullness of any problem because the parts are so connected. None of us can see the complete picture.

You probably recall the famous story of the blind men asked to describe an elephant. (The story originated in India, but there are also versions of this folktale in ancient China, twelfth-century Islam, and nineteenth-century England, which gives you the idea that it's a parable that strikes a cross-cultural nerve.) In the story, each man touches a different part of the elephant, and then each, in his arrogance, describes the entire animal. One declares the elephant to be a tree (he felt the leg), another a wall (the side), and others declare it a spear (the tusk), a snake (the trunk), and so forth. The sociologist realizes that his or her view is partial, and we rely on the perceptions and observations (research) of other social scientists to complete our understanding of the whole picture.

More polluted and less: Industrial countries may produce more pollution, but they also have higher standards for cleaning it up. Globally, countries must achieve a balance.

Sociology and Science

Sociology is a social science. To some, this phrase is an oxymoron—a phrase where the terms are opposites, sort of like "jumbo shrimp." It's true that the social sciences cannot match the predictive power of natural science because people don't behave as predictably as rocks or bacteria or planets. But that doesn't mean that we cannot test hypotheses to discern patterns of behaviors, clusters of attitudes, and structures and institutions that make social life possible.

Some sociologists would not look out of place in a science department: They create hypotheses based on empirical observations of social phenomena, then test them. In other words, they are looking for scientific facts. Other sociologists would not look out of place in a humanities department: They ask open-ended questions to find out what it feels like to belong to a certain social group. In other words, they are looking for the human spirit.

One sort of sociologist believes that social phenomena like race, class, deviance, and injustice are as real as natural phenomena and should be studied just as objectively. The other sort believes that social phenomena exist only through human interaction, so they can't be studied objectively at all. One uses numbers (quantitative methods), and the other uses words (qualitative methods). Sometimes departments are split into two camps, each accusing the other of not doing "real sociology."

However, a sociologist who sits down to compare research methods with a chemist or even biologist will find substantial differences. Other scientists work with objects (carbon isotopes, microorganisms) that have no volition, no motivation, no emotion. When the object of study is intelligent and aware, you need different techniques and different propositions. For this reason, sociology is a *social* science.

On the other end of the conference table, the sociologist talking to the humanities scholar will also find substantial differences. Humanities scholars look at texts (books, movies, art, music, philosophical treatises) for their own sake. The artists may have described the society they lived in, but the description is always an artistic vision, not real life. Sociologists try to get at real life. They engage in systematic observation and hypothesis testing and draw samples to test for relationships. And they claim that their

"I'm a social scientist, Michael. That means I can't explai electricity or anything like that, but if you ever want to kn about people I'm your man."

research has revealed something about what it was really like to live in a society. For this reason, sociology is a social *science*.

Some of the questions that sociology poses for itself also distinguish it from the other social sciences. For example, economists follow the processes of individuals who act rationally in markets, such as the labor market. Sociologists are interested in such rational economic calculation but also study behavior that is not rational and that is collective—that is, sociologists typically understand that behavior cannot be reduced to the simple addition of all the rational individuals acting in concert. Psychologists may focus on those group processes—there are branches of psychology and sociology that are both called "social psychology"—but our everyday understandings of psychology are that the problems we observe in our lives can be remedied by adequate therapeutic intervention. Sociologists think these "private troubles" actually more often require social solutions. For example, your individual income may be enhanced by working harder, changing your job, or winning the lottery, but the social problem of poverty will never be solved like that—even if every person worked harder, switched jobs, or won the lottery.

What do **you** think?

Some people see a very strong line between what they call the "hard" and "soft" sciences. So, what do you think? How scientific is sociology?

1. Very scientific   **3.** Not too scientific   **5.** Haven't heard of it
2. Pretty scientific   **4.** Not scientific at all

What does **America** think?

(Actual Survey Data from General Social Survey, 2006.)

Less than 10 percent of respondents thought sociology was very scientific. Another 44 percent thought it was pretty scientific. Eight percent had not heard of it, with most of those folks being from the lower or working class.

Think about It Some More

1. How might you explain the social class difference in responses? What does social class correlate with that might have an effect here?

References: See Davis et al., page 511.

Getting beyond "Common Sense"

However, sociology is not just "common sense" —the other rhetorical retreat from engagement with complex social issues. In fact, very often what we observe to be true turns out, after sociological examination, not to be true. Commonsense explanations trade in stereotypes—"women are more nurturing"; "men are more aggressive"—that are never true for everyone. What's more, common sense assumes that such patterns are universal and timeless—that, for example, men and women are from different planets (Mars and Venus) and that we're programmed somehow to be completely alien creatures. But what if you actually decide you want to be different—that you want to be an aggressive woman or a nurturing man? Can you? Commonsense explanations have no room for variation, and they have no history. And they leave no room for freedom of choice.

You know that old, tired, argument between "nature" and "nurture"? It describes a debate about whether we behave the ways we do because our biology, our "nature," determines our actions—as they say, because we are "hard-

wired" to do so—or because our ancestors millions of years ago found it to their evolutionary advantage to behave in such a way to ensure their survival? Or, in contrast, do we do the things we do because we have been taught to do them, socialized virtually from the moment we are born by institutions that are bigger and more powerful than we are?

To the sociologist, the answer is clear but complex. Our behavior does not result from *either* nature *or* nurture; our behavior results from *both* nature *and* nature. Looking through a sociological lens reveals that it's not a question of either/or. It's all about seeing the both/and and investigating how that relationship is playing out. Of course the things we do are the result of millennia of evolutionary adaptation to our environments, and of course we are biologically organized to do some things and not others. But that environment also includes the social environment. We adapt to the demands and needs of the social contexts in which we find ourselves, too. And we frequently override our biological drives to do things that we are *also* biologically programmed to do. Just as we are hardwired to preserve ourselves at all costs, we are also biologically programmed to sacrifice our own lives for the survival of the group or for our offspring.

But to the sociologist, the two sides of the nature–nurture debate share one thing in common: They make the individual person a passive object of larger forces, with no real ability to act for him- or herself and therefore no role in history. According to nature lovers and nurturers, we can't help doing what we do: We're either biologically destined or socially programmed to act as we do. "Sorry, it's in my genes!" is pretty much the same thing as "Sorry, I was socialized to do it!"

Neither of these positions sees the *interaction* of those forces as decisive. That is the domain of sociology.

What makes a more thorough analysis of social life possible and makes the sociological perspective possible is the way we have crafted the lens through which we view social problems and processes. It is a lens that requires that we see events in their contexts and yet remain aware of how we, as individuals, shape both the contexts and the events in which we participate.

A sociological perspective helps you to see how the events and problems that preoccupy us today are timeless; they do not come from nowhere. They have a history. They are the result of the actions of large-scale forces— forces that are familial, communal, regional, national, or global. And they enable you to see the connections between those larger-scale forces and your own experience, your own participation in them. Sociologists understand that this history is not written beforehand; it is changeable, so that you can exert some influence on how it turns out.

That's why Mills's definition of the sociological imagination, the connection between biography and history, is as compelling today as when it was written half a century ago. Sociology connects you, as an individual, to the larger processes of both stability and change that compose history.

*Nature **and** nurture: Tiger Woods may have been born with prodigious talent, but if he didn't have lots of help along the way, and practice extraordinarily hard, he would never have become the world's greatest golfer.*

Where Did Sociology Come From?

The questions that animate sociology today— individuals, progress, freedom, inequality, power—were the founding ideas of the field. Sociology emerged in Europe in the early nineteenth century. At that time, European society had just passed through a calamitous period in which the Enlightenment, the French Revolution, and the beginnings of the Industrial Revolution had dramatically transformed European society.

Before Sociology

Even in the seventeenth and eighteenth centuries, philosophers were attempting to understand the relationship of the individual and society. Political revolutions and intellectual breakthroughs led to this period being called the "Age of Reason" or the "Enlightenment." Theorists challenged the established social order, like the rule of the monarchy and hereditary aristocracy, and the ideas that justified it, like the "divine right of kings." It was during the Enlightenment of the seventeenth and eighteenth centuries that the idea of the "individual" took shape.

John Locke (1632–1704), for example, believed that society was formed through the rational decisions of free individuals, who join together through a "social contract" to form society. Society permits and even facilitates the free movement of goods, making life easier and more predictable. The purpose of government, Locke argued ([1689] 1988), was to resolve disagreements between individuals and ensure people's rights—but that's all. If the government goes too far, Locke believed, and becomes a sort of omnipotent state, the people have a right to revolution and to institute a new government.

In France, meanwhile, Jean-Jacques Rousseau (1712–1788) had a rather different perspective. Rousseau ([1754] 2007) believed that people were basically good and innocent but that private property creates inequality and with it unhappiness and immorality. Rousseau believed that a collective spirit, what he called the "general will," would replace individual greed and that through social life people could be free—but only if they were equal.

These two themes—Locke's emphasis on individual liberty and Rousseau's idea that society enhanced freedom—came together in the work of Thomas Jefferson, when he penned the Declaration of Independence in 1776, the founding document of the United States. That document asserted that all men are equal in rights and that government is the servant, not the master, of human beings. Jefferson fused Rousseau's vision of a community with Locke's ideal of limited government into a document that continues to inspire people the world over.

Mary Wollstonecraft (1759–1797), a passionate advocate of the equality of the sexes, has been called the first major feminist. She argued that society couldn't progress if half its members are kept backward, and she proposed broad educational changes for both boys and girls. But she also suggested the problems are cultural. Women accept their powerlessness in society because they can use their informal interpersonal power to seduce men. Men who value women only as objects of pleasure and amusement allow themselves to be manipulated, and so the prison of self-indulgence corrupts both sexes. Wollstonecraft was the first classical theorist to apply the ideas of the Enlightenment to the position of women—and find the Enlightenment, not women, to be the problem!

These ideas—"discovery" of the individual, the relationship of the individual to society, the position of women (and minorities), and the regulation of individual freedom by governments—were the critical ideas circulating in Europe on the eve of the nineteenth century.

And these were among the fundamental questions addressed by the new field of sociology.

The Invention of Sociology

The economic and political changes heralded by the American Revolution of 1776 and the French Revolution of 1789 were in part inspired by the work of those Enlightenment thinkers. Between 1776 and 1838, European society underwent a dramatic change—politically, economically, and intellectually. The American and French revolutions replaced absolutist monarchs with republics, where power rested not on the divine right of kings and queens but on the consent of the people. The Industrial Revolution reorganized the production and distribution of goods from the quaint system of craft production, in which apprentices learned trades and entered craft guilds, to large-scale factory production in which only the very few owned the factories and many workers had only their ability to work to sell to the highest bidder.

The foundation of society, one's identity, the nature of politics, and economics changed fundamentally between the collapse of the "old regime" in the late eighteenth century, and the rise of the new "modern" system in the middle of the nineteenth century (Table 1.1).

These changes also changed the way we saw the world. Even the language that we used to describe that world was transformed. It was during this era that the following words were first used with the meaning they have today: *industry, factory, middle class, democracy, class, intellectual, masses, commercialism, bureaucracy, capitalism, socialism, liberal, conservative, nationality, engineer, scientist, journalism, ideology*—and, of course, *sociology* (Hobsbawm, 1962). Politically, some revolutionists thought we should continue those great movements; conservatives thought we'd gone too far, and it was time to retreat to more familiar social landscapes. Sociologists both praised and criticized these new developments.

Table 1.1
Contrasting the "Old Regime" and the New Social Order

	Old Regime	New Order
Basis of economy	Land	Property
Location of economic activity	Rural manors	Urban factories
Source of identity	Kinship	Work
	Status/caste	Class
Ideology	Religion	Science
Type of government	Monarchy	Republic
Basis of government	Divine right	Popular consent

Classical Sociological Thinkers

The word *sociology* itself was introduced in 1838 by a French theorist, Auguste Comte. To him, it meant "the scientific study of society." Most of the earliest sociologists embraced a notion of progress—that society passed through various stages from less developed to more developed and that this progress was positive, both materially and morally. This notion of progress is central to the larger intellectual project of "modernism" of which sociology was a part. *Modernism*—the belief in evolutionary progress, through the application of science—challenged tradition, religion, and aristocracies as remnants of the past and saw industry, democracy, and science as the wave of the future.

Auguste Comte. Comte (1798–1857) believed that each society passed through three stages of development based on the form of knowledge that provided its foundation: religious, metaphysical, and scientific. In the religious or theological stage, supernatural forces are understood to control the world. In the metaphysical stage, abstract forces and what Comte called "destiny" or "fate" are perceived to be the prime movers of history. Religious and metaphysical knowledge thus rely on superstition and speculation, not science. In the scientific, or "positive," stage (the origin of the word *positivism*) events are explained through the scientific method of observation, experimentation, and analytic comparison.

Comte believed that, like the physical sciences, which explain physical facts, sociology must rely on science to explain social facts. Comte saw two basic facts to be explained: "statics," the study of order, persistence, and organization; and "dynamics," the study of the processes of social change. Comte believed that sociology would become "the queen of the sciences," shedding light on earlier sciences and synthesizing all previous knowledge about the natural world with a science of the social world. Sociology, he believed, would reveal the principles and laws that affected the functioning of all societies. Comte hoped that the scientific study of society would enable sociologists to guide society toward peace, order, and reform.

Comte's preoccupation with sociology as a science did not lead him to shy away from moral concerns; indeed, Comte believed that a concern for moral progress should be the cen-

Auguste Comte coined the term sociology as the scientific study of society.

tral focus of all human sciences. Sociology's task was to help society become better. In fact, sociology was a sort of "secular religion," a religion of humanity, Comte argued. And he, himself, was its highest minister. Toward the end of his life, he fancied himself a secular prophet and signed his letters "the Founder of Universal Religion, Great Priest of Humanity." (Some sociologists today also suffer from a similar lack of humility!)

After Comte, the classical era of sociological thought began. Sociologists have never abandoned his questions: The questions of order and disorder, persistence and change, remain foundations of contemporary and classical sociological thought.

Alexis de Tocqueville. Alexis de Tocqueville (1805–1859), a French social theorist and historian, is known for studies of American democracy and the French Revolution. Tocqueville saw the United States as the embodiment of democracy. Without a feudal past that tied us to outdated ideas of monarchy or aristocracy and with nearly limitless land on which the country could grow prosperous, democracy flourished. But democracy contains tensions and creates anxieties that European societies did not face.

Tocqueville's greatest insight is that democracy can either enhance or erode individual liberty. On the one hand, democracy promises increasing equality of conditions and increasingly uniform standards of living. On the other hand, it also concentrates power at the top and weakens traditional

Tocqueville and America

Tocqueville's most famous book, *Democracy in America* ([1835] 2004), is perhaps the most famous analysis of American society ever written. But it actually happened by accident. Tocqueville came to the United States to study a major innovation in the American penal system that he regarded as especially enlightened. The reform? Solitary confinement, which was initially a reform that would give the otherwise "good" person a chance to reflect on his actions and begin to reform himself.

sources of liberty, like religion or the aristocracy (which he believed were strong enough to protect individuals from encroachments by the state). Democracies can lead to mass society, in which individuals feel powerless and are easily manipulated by the media. As a result, democratic societies are faced with two possible outcomes, free institutions or despotism. When he tried to predict the direction America was heading, he thought it depended on Americans' ability to prevent the concentration of wealth and power and on the free spirit of individuals. And the solution, he believed, lay in "intermediate institutions"—the way that Americans, as a nation of "joiners," developed small civic groups for every conceivable issue or project.

Karl Marx. Karl Marx (1818–1883) was the most important of all socialist thinkers. Marx's greatest sociological insight was that class was the organizing principle of social life; all other divisions would eventually become class divisions.

Marx's great intellectual and political breakthrough came in 1848 (Marx and Engels, [1848] 1998). Before that, he had urged philosophers to get their heads out of the clouds and return to the real world—that is, he urged them toward "materialism," a focus on the way people organize their society to solve basic "material" needs such as food, shelter, and clothing as the basis for philosophy, not "idealism," with its focus on society as the manifestation of either sacred or secular ideas. As revolutions were erupting all across Europe, he saw his chance to make that philosophy into a political movement. With Engels, he wrote *The Communist Manifesto*. Asserting that all history had "hitherto been the history of class struggles," the *Manifesto* linked the victory of the proletariat (the working class) to the development of capitalism itself, which dissolved traditional bonds, like fam-

Marx the Journalist

To earn enough money to write his books, Marx also served as a journalist. His coverage of the American Civil War, which he saw as a clash between the feudal South and the capitalist North, was published all over Europe.

Did You Know?

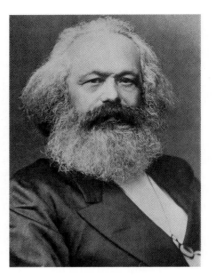

Karl Marx argued that, as capitalism progressed, the rich would get richer and the poor would get poorer—until it exploded in revolution.

ily and community, and replaced them with the naked ties of self-interest.

Initially, Marx believed, capitalism was a revolutionary system itself, destroying all the older, more traditional forms of social life and replacing them with what he called "the cash nexus"—one's position depended only on wealth, property, and class. But eventually, capitalism suppresses all humanity, drowning it in "the icy waters of egotistical calculation." We are not born greedy or materialistic; we become so under capitalism.

His central work was *Capital* (Marx, [1867] 1998), a three-volume work that laid out a theory of how capitalism worked as a system. His central insight was that the exchange of money and services between capitalists (those who own the means of production) and labor (those who sell their "labor power" to capitalists for wages) is unequal. Workers must work longer than necessary to pay for the costs of their upkeep, producing what Marx called "surplus value." And because of competition, capitalists must try to increase the rate of surplus value. They do this by replacing human labor with machines, lowering wages (and cutting any benefits) until workers can't afford even to consume the very products they are producing, and by centralizing their production until the system reaches a crisis. Thus capitalists are not only fighting against labor, but they are also competing against each other. Eventually, Marx believed, it would all come tumbling down.

This work inspired socialists all over the world who saw the growing gap between rich and poor as both a cause for despair about the conditions of the poor and an occasion for political organizing. Marx believed that the "laws of motion" of capitalism would bring about its own destruction as the rich got so rich and the poor got so poor that they would revolt against the obvious inequity of the system. Then workers would rise up and overthrow the unequal capitalist system and institute communism—the collective ownership of all property.

Marx believed this would take place first in the industrial countries like Britain and Germany, but the socialist revolutions of the twentieth century that used Marx as inspiration were in largely peasant societies, like Russia and China, for example. Nowhere in the world has Marx's political vision been implemented. His economic theory that the development of capitalism tends to concentrate wealth and power, however, has never been more true than today, when the gap between rich and poor is greater than ever in U.S. history. Currently, the richest 1 percent of people in the world receives as much income as the bottom 5 percent. Globally, the United States has the most unequal distribution of income of all high-income nations (UC Atlas of Global Inequality, 2007).

Emile Durkheim. Emile Durkheim (1858 –1917) was a master of sociological inquiry. He searched for distinctly social origins of even the most individual and personal of issues. His greatest work, *Suicide* ([1897] 2007), is a classic example of his sociological imagination. On the surface, suicide appears to be the ultimate individual act. Yet Durkheim argued that suicide is profoundly social, an illustration of how connected an individual feels to others. Durkheim tried to measure the amount of integration (how connected we feel to social life) and regulation (the amount that our individual freedoms are constrained) by empirically examining what happens when those processes fail.

In a sense, Durkheim turned the tables on economists who made a simple linear case that freedom was an unmitigated good and that the more you have the happier you will be. Durkheim argued that too much freedom might reduce the ties that one feels to society and therefore make one *more* likely to commit suicide, not less!

Durkheim's study of suicide illustrated his central insight: that society is held together by "solidarity," moral bonds that connect us to the social collectivity. "Every society is a moral society," he wrote. Social order, he claimed, cannot be accounted for by the pursuit of individual self-interest; solidarity is emotional, moral, and nonrational. Rousseau had called this "the general will," Comte called it "consensus," but neither had attempted to actually study it (see also Durkheim, [1893] 1997).

In traditional society, solidarity is relatively obvious: Life is uniform and people are similar; they share a common culture and sense of morality that Durkheim characterizes as **mechanical solidarity.** In modern society, with its division of labor and diverse and conflicting interests, common values are present but less obvious. People are interdependent, and Durkheim calls this **organic solidarity.**

Durkheim's influence has been immense, not only in sociology, where he ranks with Marx and Weber as one of the founders of the discipline, but also in anthropology, social psychology, and history. Durkheim's use of statistics was pioneering for his time, and his concept of the "social fact," his rigorous comparative method, and his functional style of analysis have been widely adopted (Durkheim, [1895] 1997). His emphasis on society as a moral entity has served as a powerful critique of abstract individualism and rationality and of a definition of freedom that places human liberty in opposition to society.

Max Weber. Max Weber (1864–1920) was an encyclopedic scholar whose expertise left hardly a field untouched. But his chief interest in all his studies was the extraordinary importance of "rationality" in the modern world. His major

Max Weber introduced purely social processes, like charisma and status, as sources of identity and inequality.

Suicide Is *Not* an Individual Act

On the surface, there is no act more personal or individual than suicide. Taking your own life is almost always explained by individual psychopathology because a person must be crazy to kill him- or herself. If that's true, Durkheim reasoned, suicide would be distributed randomly among the population; there would be no variation by age, religion, region, or marital status, for example.

Yet that is exactly what he found; suicide varies by:

1. *Religion.* Protestants commit suicide far more often than Catholics, and both commit suicide more often than Jews (he did not measure Muslims).
2. *Age.* Young people and old people commit suicide more often than middle-aged people.
3. *Marital status.* Single people commit suicide more often than married people.
4. *Gender.* Men commit suicide more often than women.
5. *Employment.* Unemployed people commit suicide more often than the employed.

Because we can assume that unemployed, unmarried young male Protestants are probably no more likely to be mentally ill than any other group, Durkheim asked what each of these statuses might contribute to keeping a person from suicide. And he determined that the "function" of each status is to embed a person in a community, to provide a sense of belonging, of "integrating" the person into society.

What's more, these statuses also provided rules to live by, solid norms that constrain us from spinning wildly out of control, that "regulate" us. The higher the level of integration and regulation, Durkheim reasoned, the lower the level of suicide. Too little integration leads to what Durkheim called "egoistic" suicide, in which the individual kills him- or herself because he or she doesn't feel the connection to the group. Too little regulation led to what Durkheim called "anomic" suicide, in which the person floats in a sense of normlessness and doesn't know the rules that govern social life or when those rules change dramatically.

But sometimes there can be too much integration, where the individual completely loses him- or herself in the group and therefore would be willing to kill him- or herself to benefit the group. A suicide that resulted from too much integration is one Durkheim called "altruistic"—think of suicide bombers, for example. And sometimes people feel overregulated, trapped by rules that are not of their own making, that lead to what Durkheim called "fatalistic" suicide. Durkheim saw this type of suicide among slaves, for example, or, as he also hypothesized, "very young husbands." Why do you think he thought that?

Types of Suicide and Integration and Regulation

	Too little	Too much
Level of integration	Egoistic	Altruistic
Level of regulation	Anomic	Fatalistic

Durkheim's methodological innovation was to find a way to measure something as elusive as integration or regulation—the glue that holds society together and connects us to each other. Ironically, he found the way to "see" integration and regulation at those moments it wasn't there!

Weber Inspired by Franklin

Weber began the work on *The Protestant Ethic and the Spirit of Capitalism* when he was invited to give a lecture at the World's Fair in St. Louis in 1900. He stopped off in Philadelphia to read some of Benjamin Franklin's papers and believed he had discovered the kernel of the spirit of capitalism. All his major works appeared after he returned from that trip.

Did You Know?

insights were that rationality was the foundation of modern society and that while rationality organized society in more formal, legal, and predictable ways, it also trapped us in an "iron cage" of bureaucracy and meaninglessness.

To understand society, Weber developed a sociology that was both "interpretive" and "value free." Weber's interpretive sociology understands social relationships by showing the sense they make to those who are involved in them. Weber also insisted that experts separate their personal evaluations from their scientific pronouncements because such value judgments cannot be logically deduced from facts. By protecting science from the taint of ideology, Weber hoped also to protect political debate from unwarranted claims by experts. "Value freedom" does not mean sociologists should not take political positions but that we must use value judgments to select subjects deemed worthy of research and must engage with the minds and feelings of the people being studied.

Weber's most famous work, *The Protestant Ethic and the Spirit of Capitalism* ([1904, 1905] 2004), was a study of the relationship of religious ideas to economic activity. What made European capitalism unique, he argued, was its connection to the ideas embodied in the Protestant Reformation, ideas that enabled individuals to act in this world. Essentially, Weber argued that the Puritan ethic of predestination led to a deep-seated need for clues about whether one is saved or not. Seeking some indication, Protestants, particularly Calvinists, began to value material success and worldly profit as signs of God's favor.

At the end, however, Weber was pessimistic. Rationality can free us from the theocratic past but also imprison us in an "iron cage"—an utterly dehumanized and mechanized world. Like Marx, Weber believed that the modern capitalist order brought out the worst in us: "In the field of its highest development, in the United States, the pursuit of wealth, stripped of its religious and ethical meaning, tends to become associated with purely mundane passions, which often actually give it the character of sport."

And, like Marx, Weber believed that, in the long run, class was the most significant division among people. But Weber had a more complicated understanding. At any one moment, he wrote, there are other less economic factors that divide people from each other, as well as unite them into groups. To class, Weber added the idea of "status" and "party." "Party" referred to voluntary organizations that people would enter together to make their voices heard collectively because individually we would be unable to affect real change.

While one's class position was objective, based on the position in the labor market, status groups were based, Weber believed, on social factors—what other people thought about one's lifestyle. Class is based on one's relationship to production; status is based on one's relationship to consumption. While people really couldn't do much about class, they can definitely try to transform their status because it depends on how others see them. The desire to have others see one as belonging to a higher status group than one actually belongs to leads to extraordinary patterns of consumption—buying very expensive cars and homes to "show off" or "keep up with the Joneses," for example.

In later writings, Weber argued that the characteristic form of modern organization—whether in the state, the corporation, the military, university, or church—is bureaucratic. Whereas Marx predicted a revolution that would shatter capitalism, and Durkheim foresaw new social movements that would reunify people, Weber saw a bleak future in which individual freedom is increasingly compressed by corporations and the state.

Weber's often dense and difficult prose was matched by the enormous range of his writings and the extraordinary depth of his analysis. He remains the most deft thinker of the first generation of classical theorists, both appreciating the distinctiveness of Western society's promotion of individual freedom and deploring its excesses, celebrating rational society, and fearing the "iron cage" of an overly rational world.

Georg Simmel. Georg Simmel (1858–1918) is among the most original and far-ranging members of the founding generation of modern sociology. Never happy within the academic division of labor, he contributed to all of the social sciences but remained primarily a philosopher.

Simmel was on a quest for a subject matter for sociology that would distinguish it from the other social sciences and the humanistic disciplines. He found this not in a new set of topics but in a method, or rather, in a special point of view. The special task of sociology is to study the *forms* of social interaction apart from their content. Simmel assumes that the same social forms—competition, exchange, secrecy, domination—could contain quite different content and that the same social content could be embodied in different forms. It mattered less to Simmel what a person was competing about, or whether domination was based on sheer force, monetary power, or some other basis: What mattered to him was the ways that these forms of domination or competition had specific, distinctive properties.

Forms arise as people interact with one another for the sake of certain purposes or to satisfy certain needs. They are the processes by which individuals combine into groups, institutions, nations, or societies. Forms may gain autonomy from the demands of the moment, becoming larger, more solid structures that stand detached from, even opposed to, the continuity of life. Some forms may be historical, like "forms of development"—stages that societies might pass through. Unlike Marx, Durkheim, or Weber, then, Simmel never integrated his work into an overarching scheme. Instead he gathered a rich variety of contents under each abstract form, allowing for new and startling comparisons among social phenomena.

While this all sounds somewhat "formal" and abstract, Simmel's major concern was really about individualism. His work is always animated by the question of what the social conditions are that make it easier for persons to discover and express their individuality. In modern society, with its many cultural and social groups, individuals are caught in crosscutting interests and expectations. We belong to so many groups, and each demands different things of us. Always aware of the double-edged sword that characterizes sociology, Simmel saw both sides of the issue. For example, in his major philosophical work on money, he argued that money tends to trivialize human relationships, making them more instrumental and calculable, but it also enlarges the possibilities of freedom of expression and expands the possibilities for action. Like a good sociologist, Simmel argued that money is neither the root of all evil nor the means to our emancipation: It's both.

Sociology Comes to the United States

Sociology arrived in the United States at the end of the nineteenth century. These American sociologists took the pivotal ideas of European sociology and translated them for the American experience. They have each, since, joined the classical **canon** or officially recognized set of foundational sociologists.

Margaret Fuller. Margaret Fuller (1810–1850) was America's first female foreign correspondent. Her book *Woman in the Nineteenth Century* ([1845] 1994) became the intellectual foundation of the American women's movement. The book is a bracing call for complete freedom and equality, a call that "every path be open to woman as freely as to man." Fuller calls on women to become self-reliant and not expect help from men and introduces the concept of sisterhood—women must help one another, no matter whether they are scholars, servants, or prostitutes. Her research documents women's capabilities from an immense catalogue of mythology, folklore, the Bible, classical antiquity, fiction, and history. She explores the image of woman, in all its ambiguity, within literature and myth, and

Margaret Fuller had been editor of the important Transcendentalist journal, The Dial, *for two years and was literary critic for Horace Greeley's famous paper*, The New York Tribune, *when she published* Women in the Nineteenth Century *(1845), a variegated argument for women's independence and critique of gender inequality in nineteenth-century American society.*

asserts "no age was left entirely without a witness of the equality of the sexes in function, duty, and hope." She also calls for an end to sexual stereotyping and the sexual double standard.

Frederick Douglass. Frederick Douglass (1817–1895) was the most important African American intellectual of the nineteenth century. He lived 20 years as a slave and nearly nine as a fugitive slave and then achieved international fame as an abolitionist, editor, orator, and the author of three autobiographies. These gave a look into the world of oppression, resistance, and subterfuge within which the slaves lived.

Sociologically, Douglass's work stands as an impassioned testament to the cruelty and illogic of slavery, claiming that *all* human beings were equally capable of being full individuals. His work also reveals much about the psychological world of slaves: its sheer terror but also its complexities. Its portraits of slave owners range from parody to denunciation and, in one case, even respect, and all serve Douglass's principal theme: that slaveholding, no less than the slave's own condition, is learned behavior and presumably can be unlearned.

Lester Ward. Lester Ward (1841–1913) was one of the founders of American sociology and the first to free it from the biological fetters of the Darwinian model of social change. Ward rebelled against **social Darwinism,** which saw each succeeding society as improving on the one before it. Instead, Ward stressed the need for social planning and reform, for a "sociocratic" society that later generations were to call a welfare state.

Ward argued that, unlike Darwinist predictions, natural evolution proceeded in an aimless manner, based on adaptive reactions to accidents of nature. In nature, evolution was more random, chaotic, and haphazard than social Darwinists imagined. But in society, evolution was informed by purposeful action, which he called "social telesis."

Ward welcomed the many popular reform movements because he saw enlightened government as the key to social evolution. Education would enable the common man and woman to participate as democratic citizens. The bottom layers of society, the proletariat, women, even the underclass of the slums, are by nature the equals of the "aristocracy of brains," he wrote. They lack only proper instruction.

Charlotte Perkins Gilman. Most readers who know Charlotte Perkins Gilman (1860–1935) at all know her for her short story "The Yellow Wallpaper" (1899) or for her novel *Herland* ([1915] 1998). But sociologists know her for her groundbreaking *Women and Economics* ([1898] 1998), a book in which she explores the origin of women's subordination and its function in evolution. Woman makes a living by marriage, not by the work she does, and so man becomes her economic environment. As a consequence her female qualities dominate her human ones because it is the female traits through which she earns her living. Women are raised to market their feebleness, their docility, and so on, and these qualities are then called "feminine."

Gilman was one of the first to see the need for innovations in child rearing and home maintenance that would ease the burdens of working women. She envisaged housework as being like any other kind of work—as a public, social activity no different from shoemaking or shipbuilding. In her fiction she imagines a range of institutions that overcome the isolation of women and children, such as communal kitchens, day-care centers, and city plans that foster camaraderie rather than withdrawal. For women, as well as for men, she wrote in her autobiography, "The one predominant duty is to find one's work and do it."

Charlotte Perkins Gilman argued that defining women solely by their reproductive role is harmful to women—as well as to men, children, and society.

Thorstein Veblen. Thorstein Veblen (1857–1929) is best known for his bitingly satirical work, *The Theory of the Leisure Class* ([1899] 1994). Here, he argued that America was split in two, between the "productive class"—those who work—and the "pecuniary class"—those who have the money. That is, he divided Americans into workers and owners, respectively. The wealthy, he argued, weren't productive; they lived off the labor of others, like parasites. They spent their time engaged in competitive displays of wealth and prestige, which he called "conspicuous consumption"—consumption that is done because it is visible and because it invites a certain social evaluation of "worth." One comes to advertise wealth through wasteful consumption.

He also saw a tension between the benevolent forces of technology and the profit system that distorts them. He contrasted the rationality of work, of the machine process and its personnel, to the irrational caprices of speculators, financiers, and the wealthy who squander valuable goods so as to win prestige. Modern society was neither a simple Marxian class struggle between the malevolent wealthy owners and their naïve and innocent workers, nor was technology inevitably leading to either social uplift or social decay. It was not a matter of the technology but of its ownership and control and the uses to which it was put.

W. E. B. DuBois. W. E. B. DuBois (1868–1963) was the most original, and widely read advocate for the civil rights of Black people for a period of over 30 years. A social scientist, political militant, essayist, and poet, he wrote 19 books and hundreds of articles, edited four periodicals, and was a founder of the NAACP

W. E. B. DuBois identified racism as the most pressing social problem in America—and the world.

First African American to Receive a Ph.D.

W. E. B. DuBois was the first African American to receive a Ph.D. from Harvard University (1895). It was only the fifth Ph.D. ever awarded to an African American in the United States.

Did You Know?

and the Pan-African movement. His work forms a bridge between the nineteenth century and the Civil Rights movement of the 1960s. Today he is recognized as one of the greatest sociologists in our history, and the American Sociological Association recently voted to name the annual award for the most influential book after him.

DuBois believed that race was the defining feature of American society, that, as he put it, "the problem of the twentieth century was the problem of the color line," and that, therefore, the most significant contribution he could make toward achieving racial justice would be a series of scientific studies of the Negro. In 1899, he published *The Philadelphia Negro,* the first study ever of Black people in the United States; he planned an ambitious set of volumes that would together finally understand the experiences of the American Negro (DuBois, [1899] 1996).

In his most famous work, *The Souls of Black Folk,* DuBois explored the psychological effects of racism, a lingering inner conflict. "One feels ever his two-ness —an American, a Negro, two souls, two thoughts, two unreconciled strivings; two warring ideals in one dark body, whose dogged strength alone keeps it from being torn asunder." His work defines a "moment in history when the American Negro began to reject the idea of the world belonging to white people" (DuBois, [1903] 1999). Gradually disillusioned with White people's resistance to integration, DuBois eventually called for an increase in power and especially economic autonomy, the building of separate Black businesses and institutions.

George Herbert Mead. George Herbert Mead (1863–1931) studied the development of individual identity through social processes. He argued that identity is the product of our interactions with ourselves and with others, which is based on the distinctly human capacity for self-reflection. He distinguished between the "I," the part of us that is inherent and biological, from the "me," the part of us that is self-conscious and created by observing ourselves in interaction. The "me" is created, he said, by managing the **generalized other,** by which he meant a person's notion of the common values, norms, and expectations of other people in a society. Thus Mead developed a distinctly *social* theory of the self (the "me")—one that doesn't bubble up from one's biology alone but a self that takes shape only through interaction with society (Mead, 1967).

This "pragmatic" approach—in which one examines social phenomena as they occur— actually made Mead optimistic. Mead believed that each of us develops through play, first by making up the rules as we go along, then later by being able to follow formal rules, and still later by learning to "take the role of the other"—to put ourselves in others' shoes. The ability to step outside of ourselves turns out to be the crucial step in developing a "self" that is fully able to interact with others. Mead's work is the foundation for much of the sociological research in interactionism.

Because several of these founders of sociological thought were minorities or women, they were constantly defiled and denounced because of their views. Indeed, sociology's historical difficulty to establish itself as a credible social science may have been because so many of its pioneers were women or minorities. DuBois and Gilman were denounced because each gave such weight to economic independence for Blacks and for women; they were accused of reducing social issues to simple economic autonomy. And Frederick Douglass was consistently denounced because he extended his cry for Black freedom to women as well. It was Douglass who provided the oratorical support for the suffrage plank at the first convention for women's rights in Seneca Falls, New York, in 1848—for which he was denounced the next day as an "Aunt Nancy man," the nineteenth-century equivalent of a wimp.

Doing sociology is not always comfortable, nor is sociology done only by those whose material lives are already comfortable. Sometimes sociology challenges common sense and the status quo.

Contemporary Sociology

Contemporary sociologists return constantly to the ideas of its founders for inspiration and guidance as they develop their own questions about how society works—and doesn't work. Classical theories provide orientation for the development of sociological thinking.

In the United States, sociology developed as an academic field in the period between 1930 and 1960. It promised to be a social science that could explain the historical origins and dynamics of modern society. Two questions dominated the field: What could sociology contribute to the study of the self? And what processes ensure social order? Stated differently, the first question was about the distinction of sociology from psychology: What is the self, and how is it different from what psychologists call "personality"? And the second question was really about why there had been such dramatic political upheavals in Europe (Nazism, Fascism, Communism) and why, despite the terrible ravages of the Great Depression and the instability of World War II, the United States remained relatively stable and orderly.

Symbolic Interactionism and the Sociology of the Self

The creation of a stable social "self" rested on interest in microlevel interactions, interactions among individuals, and sociologists who called themselves "symbolic interactionists." **Symbolic interactionism** examines how an individual's interactions with his or her environment—other people, institutions, ideas—help people develop a sense of "self." The "symbolic" part was the way we use symbol systems—like language, religion, art, or body language and decoration—to navigate the social world. Symbolic interactionists follow in the sociological tradition of George Herbert Mead.

Herbert Blumer, who studied with Mead at the University of Chicago, actually coined the term *symbolic interactionism* in 1937. According to Blumer, people were active agents in the construction of their identities and the meanings they give to their experiences. According to Blumer, the way people view the objects in

their environment depends on the meanings that these things have for them. These meanings are the result of social interaction, and, Blumer argued, they change over time. Here Blumer echoes one of the most famous sociological axioms, written by W. I. Thomas, another Chicago School sociologist: "Those things which men believe to be true, are true in their consequences." That is, if we perceive something to be true, we ordinarily will act on those perceptions, and that therefore, the "consequences"—namely, our actions—confirm that perception.

Erving Goffman, an influential symbolic interactionist, used what he called a *dramaturgical* model to understand social interaction. Like an actor preparing to perform a part in a play, a *social* actor practices a part "backstage," accumulating props and testing out different ways to deliver his or her lines. The actual "front-stage" performance, in front of the intended audience, helps us refine our presentation of self: If the people we want to like us do, in fact, like us, we realize that our performance is successful, and we will continue it. But if they reject us or don't like us, we might try a different strategy, rehearse that "backstage," and then try again. If that fails, our identity might get "spoiled," and we would have to either change the venue of our performance, alter our part significantly, or accept society's critical reviews.

In one of Goffman's most important works, he looked at what happens to individuals' identities when all their props are removed and they are forced to conform to an absolutely rigid regime. In *total institutions* such as prisons, mental hospitals, and concentration camps, Goffman discerned that individuals are routinely stripped of anything that identifies them as individuals. And yet, still, they try to assert something that is theirs alone, something that enables them to hold on to their individual senses of themselves.

In his conclusion to his book *Asylums* (1961), Goffman describes this dynamic. He writes that

> without something to belong to, we have no
> stable self, and yet total commitment and
> attachment to any social unit implies a kind of
> selflessness. Our sense of being a person can

come from being drawn into a wider social unit; our sense of selfhood can arise through the little ways in which we resist the pull. Our status is backed by the solid buildings of the world, while our sense of personal identity often resides in the cracks. (Goffman, 1961, p. 320)

Structural Functionalism and Social Order

At the larger, structural, or "macro" level, sociologists were preoccupied with political and social stability and order. Talcott Parsons (1902–1979), the leading exponent of what he called **structural functionalism,** looked to Durkheim's idea of organic solidarity—the idea that society is held together as an organic whole through shared values and norms and the division of labor—as the inspiration for his theory. According to Parsons, social life consisted of several distinct integrated levels that enable the world—and individuals who are within it—to find stability, order, and meaning. Functionalism offers a **paradigm,** a coherent model of how society works and how individuals are socialized into their roles within it (Parsons, 1937, 1951).

Parsons believed that like most natural phenomena, societies tend toward balance—balance within all their component parts and balance within each individual member of society. The functionalist model stresses balance and equilibrium among the values of the society, its norms, and the various institutions

that develop to express and sustain those values over time.

According to this perspective, every institution, every interaction has a "function"—the reproduction of social life. Thus, for example, educational institutions function to ensure the steady transmission of social values to the young and to filter their entry into the labor force until the labor force can accommodate them. (If every 18-year-old simply went off to work, more than half wouldn't find jobs!) Families "function" to regulate sexual relationships and to ensure the socialization of the young into society.

It was left to Robert K. Merton (1910–2003), Parsons's former student and colleague, to clarify functionalism and also extend its analysis. Like Parsons, he argued that society tends toward equilibrium and balance. Those processes, events, and institutions that facilitate equilibrium he called "functional," and those that undermine it he called "dysfunctional." In this way, Merton understood both the forces that maintain social order and those that do not (Merton, [1949] 1976).

Merton argued that the functions of any institution or interaction can be either "manifest" or "latent." **Manifest functions** are overt and obvious, the intended functions, while **latent functions** are hidden and unintended but nonetheless important. For example, the manifest function of going to college used to be that a person educated in the liberal arts would be a better, more productive citizen. The latent function was that going to college would also enable the graduate to get a better job. However, that's changed significantly, and the manifest function for most college students today is that a college education is a prerequisite for getting a good job. Latent functions today might include escape from parental control or access to a new set of potential dating partners, because many people meet their future spouses in college.

Functionalists believed that every social institution helped to integrate individuals into social life. What *was,* they argued, "was" for a reason—it worked. When there was a problem, such as, for example, juvenile delinquency, it was not because delinquents were bad people but because the system was not socializing young boys adequately. Poverty was not the result of the moral failings of the poor but a systemic incapacity to adequately provide jobs and welfare to all. Although functionalism was criticized for its implicit

The British say the king (or queen) "reigns but does not rule." To the sociologist, the monarchy symbolically represents the nation, providing a sense of unity and shared purpose.

Rich or poor? No, rich and poor. Conflict theorists argue that society is held together by the tensions of inequality and conflict. Globally, relations between countries often mirror relations within a country. In Sao Paulo, Brazil, the favela (shanty town) shares a border with a luxury high-rise apartment.

conservatism—if it exists it serves a purpose and shouldn't be changed—the theory also expressed a liberal faith in the ability of American institutions to eventually respond to social problems.

Functionalism was, itself, "functional" in explaining society during a period of stability and conformity like the 1950s. But by the end of the decade there were rumblings of change—from individuals and groups who came to believe that what functioned for some groups wasn't so functional for other groups. They pushed sociologists to see the world differently.

Conflict Theories: An Alternative Paradigm

In the 1960s, many sociologists, inspired more by Marx and Weber than by Durkheim and Parsons, argued that this celebrated ability of American institutions to respond to social problems was itself the problem. American institutions did not solve problems; they caused them by allocating resources unequally. The United States was a society based on structural inequality, on the unequal distribution of rewards. The rich got richer, and the poor got poorer—and the institutions of the economy, the political process, and social reforms often perpetuated that inequality.

Generally, these sociologists adopted a theoretical paradigm that was called **conflict theory**—a theory that suggested that the dynamics of society, both of social order and social resistance, were the result of the conflict among different groups. Like Marx and Weber before them, conflict theorists believed that those who had power sought to maintain it; those who did not have power sought to change the system to get it. The constant struggles between the haves and the have-nots were the organizing principle of society, and the dynamic tension between these groups gave society its motion and its coherence. Conflict theories included those that stressed gender inequality (feminist theory), racial inequality (critical race theory), or class-based inequality (Marxist theory or socialist theory).

For two decades, the 1970s and 1980s, these two theories, functionalism and conflict theory, were themselves in conflict as the dominant theoretical perspectives in sociology. Were you to pick up an introductory sociology textbook originally written in the last two decades of the twentieth century, between 1980 and 2000, it would likely describe these two theoretical perspectives (as well as symbolic interactionism to describe microlevel social interactions) as the dominant and competing perspectives of the field (Table 1.2).

Today the dramatic global economic and political shifts of the past decades, the rise of new transnational institutions like the EU (European Union) and trade agreements like

Table 1.2
Major Sociological
Schools of
Thought,
1950–2000

Theory	Level of Analysis	Order: What Holds Society Together?	Individual to Society	Change	Direction of Change
Structural-functionalism	Macro	Society is a stable system of interrelated elements—shared values, institutions—and there is general agreement (consensus) about how society should work.	Individuals are integrated into society by socialization.	Incomplete integration leads to deviance. Change is progressive.	Positive: Society is evolving to more and more equality.
Conflict theory	Macro	Society is a dynamic tension among unequal groups marked by an unequal distribution of rewards and goods.	Individuals belong to different groups that compete for resources.	Groups mobilize to get greater goods.	Short term: conflict. Longer term: greater equality.
Symbolic interactionism	Micro	Society is a set of processes among individuals and groups, using symbolic forms (language, gestures, performance) to create identity and meaning.	Individuals connect to others symbolically.	Tension between institutions and individual identity.	No direction specified.

NAFTA (the North American Free Trade Act), and the rise of new social movements based on ethnicity or religion to challenge them require that sociologists shift the lenses through which they view the social world.

Globalization and Multiculturalism: New Issues, New Lenses

The events of the past few decades have seen these older divisions among sociologists subsiding and the incorporation of new lenses through which to view sociological issues. Probably the best terms to describe these new lenses are *globalization* and *multiculturalism*. By **globalization,** we mean that the interconnections—economic, political, cultural, social—among different groups of people all over the world, the dynamic webs that connect us to one another, and the ways these connections also create cleavages among different groups of people. By **multiculturalism,** literally the understanding of many different cultures, we come to understand the very different ways that different groups of people approach issues,

construct identities, and create institutions that express their needs.

Globalization focuses on larger, **macro-level analysis,** which examines large-scale institutional processes such as the global marketplace, corporations, and transnational institutions such as the United Nations or World Bank. Multiculturalism stresses both the macrolevel unequal distribution of rewards based on class, race, region, gender, and the like and also the **microlevel analysis,** which focuses on the ways in which different groups of people and even individuals construct their identities based on their membership in those groups. For example, the globalization of the media industries allows books, magazines, movies, television programs, and music from almost every country to be consumed all over the world. A macrolevel analysis of globalization might point to ways global information exchange promotes interconnection and mutual understanding. A microlevel, multiculturalist analysis might point out, however, that the flow of information is mostly one way, from the West and particularly the United States into other countries, dominating other cultures, reinforcing global economic inequalities, and promoting a homogeneous, Westernized global society. Or a multiculturalist might argue that global media, particularly the Internet, are playing a role in reinvigorating local cultures and identities by promoting mixing and fusion and by allowing a diversity of voices—including "alternative" and "radical" ones—to be heard (Williams, 2003).

Globalization and Multiculturalism: Interrelated Forces. Today the world often seems to alternate between feeling like a centrifuge, in which everything at the center is scattered into millions of individual, local particles, and a great gravitational vacuum that collects all these local, individual particles into a congealing center.

There are numerous, formerly unimaginable changes that go under the heading of "globalization"—scientific advances, technological breakthroughs that connect people all over the globe, the speed and integration of commercial and economic decisions, the coherence of multinational political organizations and institutions—like the recently "invented" European Union and G8 organizations, not to mention the older and venerable organizations like the United Nations (founded in 1945) and NATO (the North Atlantic Treaty Organization, founded in 1950). The increased globalization of production of the world's goods—companies doing business in every other country—is coupled with increasingly similar patterns of consumption as teenagers all over the world are listening to Cold Play or Rihanna on portable stereo equipment made in Japan, talking on cell phones made in Finland, wearing clothing from the Gap that is manufactured in Thailand, walking in Nikes or Reeboks, shopping at malls that feature the same boutiques, which they drive to in cars made in Germany or Japan, using gasoline refined by American or British companies from oil extracted from the Arabian peninsula.

Just as our societies are changing dramatically, bringing the world closer and closer together, so too are those societies changing, becoming multiracial and multicultural. Increasingly, in industrial societies, the old divisions between women and men and among various races and ethnicities are breaking down. Women and men are increasingly similar: Both work, and both care for children, and the traits that were formerly associated with one sex or the other are increasingly blurred. Most of us know that we possess both the capacities for aggression, ambition, and technical competence as well as the abilities to be compassionate and caring. Industrial countries like the United States or the nations of Europe are increasingly multicultural: Gone are the days when to be American meant being able to trace your lineage to the Mayflower or when to be Swedish meant uniformly blond hair and blue eyes. Today, even the U.S. Census cannot keep up with how much we're changing: The fastest growing racial category in the United States in the year 2005 was "biracial." Just who are "we" anyway?

At the same time that we've never been closer or more similar to each other, the boundaries between us have never been more sharply drawn. The collapse of the Soviet Union led to the establishment of dozens of new nations, based entirely on ethnic identity. The terrifying explosion of a murderous strain of Islamic fundamentalism vows to purify the world of all nonbelievers. Virtually all the wars of the past two decades have been interethnic conflicts, in which one ethnic group has attempted to eradicate another from within the nation's borders—not necessarily because of some primitive bloodlust on the part of those neighboring cultures but because the political entities in which they were forced to live, nation-states, were themselves the artificial creations of powerful nations at the end of the past century. The Serbian aggression against Bosnia, Croatia, and Kosovo; the Hutu and Tutsi in Rwanda; the past or current tribal civil wars in Somalia or Congo; plus dozens of smaller-scale interethnic wars have given the world a new term for the types of wars we witness now—*ethnic cleansing*.

The drive for uniformity as the sole basis for unity, for sameness as the sole basis for security, leads to internal efforts at perpetual self-purification—as if by completely excluding "them," we get to know what "us" means. Such efforts are accompanied by a dramatic (and often violent) restoration of traditional roles for women and men. Women are "refeminized" by being forced back into the home, under lock and key as well as under layers of physical concealment;

Sociology and Our World

Defining Globalization

There are many definitions of globalization. The one here is from the Carnegie Endowment for International Peace, a major research and policy institution.

What Is Globalization?

Globalization is a process of interaction and integration among the people, companies, and governments of different nations. The process is driven by international trade and investment and is aided by information technology. Its effects extend from the environment, to culture, to political systems, to economic development and prosperity, to human physical well-being in societies around the world.

Globalization is not new. For thousands of years, people—and, later, corporations—have been buying from and selling to each other in lands at great distances, such as through the famed Silk Road across Central Asia that connected China and Europe during the Middle Ages. Likewise, for centuries, people and corporations have invested in enterprises in other countries. In fact, many of the features of the current wave of globalization are similar to those prevailing before the outbreak of World War I in 1914.

But policy and technological developments of the past few decades have spurred increases in cross-border trade, investment, and migration so large that many observers believe the world has entered a qualitatively new phase in its economic development. Since 1950, for example, the volume of world trade has increased twentyfold, and from just 1997 to 1999 flows of foreign investment nearly doubled, from $468 billion to $827 billion. Distinguishing this current wave of globalization from earlier ones, author Thomas Friedman has said that today globalization is "farther, faster, cheaper, and deeper" (Friedman, 2005, p. 12).

Globalization is deeply controversial. Proponents of globalization claim that it allows poor countries and their citizens to develop economically and raise their standards of living. Opponents of globalization argue that the creation of an unfettered international free market has benefited multinational corporations in the Western world at the expense of local enterprises, local cultures, and common people. Resistance to globalization has therefore taken shape both at a popular and at a governmental level as people and governments try to manage the flow of capital, labor, goods, and ideas that constitute the current wave of globalization.

men are "remasculinized" by being required to adopt certain physical traits and return to traditional clothing and the imposition of complete control over women.

Religion, blood, folk, nation—these are the terms we use to specify who we are and who they are not. The boundaries between us have never been more sharply drawn—nor have they ever been so blurred.

These trends play themselves out not only on the global stage but also within each society. In the economic North, there are calls for returns to some idealized visions of pristine purity of racial bloodlines, to religious fundamentals, to basics like the '50s vision of the family—the 1850s, that is. And in many societies in Africa or Latin America, there are signs of increased multiculturalism, tolerance for difference, the embracing of technological

innovation and secular humanist science. Neither side is as monochromatic as stereotypes might imagine it to be.

We often imagine the past and the present as a set of opposites. The past was bucolic, stable, unchanging; society today is a mad rush of dizzying social changes that we can barely grasp. But neither vision is completely true. "Just as there was more change among past peoples than often meets the eye," writes sociologist Harvey Molotch, "so there is more stability in the modern world than might be thought" (Molotch, 2003, p. 94).

And most of us adopt an idiosyncratic combination of these trends. The terrorists of al-Qaeda, who seek a return to a premodern Islamic theocracy, keep in touch with wireless Web access and a sophisticated technological system while Americans, their sworn

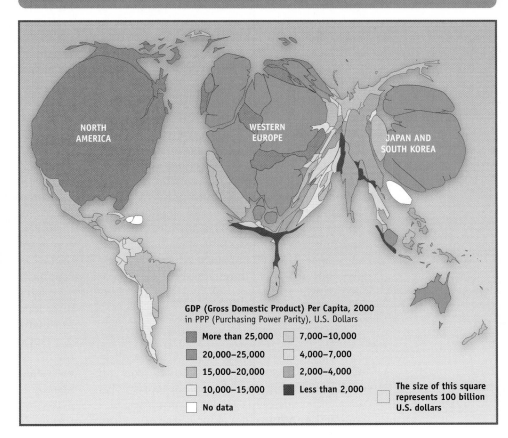

Religion can bring us together in joy and song . . .

. . . or drive us apart in anger and hatred.

archenemy, the embodiment of secularism, stream to church every Sunday in numbers that dwarf those of European nations. We speak with patriotic fervor of closing our borders to non-Americans, while we merrily consume products from all over the world. (I recently saw a bumper sticker that said "Buy American"—on a Honda Civic.)

Global Tensions. These two master trends—globalization and particularism; secular, scientific, and technological advances; and religious fundamentalism, ethnic purification, and local tribalisms—are not simply the final conflict between two competing worldviews, a "clash of civilizations" as one eminent political scientist calls it. Such a view imagines these as two completely separate entities, now on a collision course for global conflagration, and ignores the ways in which each of these trends is a reaction to the other, is organized in response to the other, is, in the end, *produced* by the other. And such a view also misses the ways in which these master trends are contained within any society—indeed, within all of us.

Globalization is often viewed as increasing homogeneity around the world. The sociologist George Ritzer calls it **McDonaldization** —the homogenizing spread of consumerism around the globe (1996). *New York Times* columnist Thomas Friedman (2000) once predicted that "no two countries

which both have a McDonald's will go to war with each other."

Friedman's prediction turned out to be wrong—in part because he saw only that part of globalization that flattens the world and minimizes cultural and national differences. But globalization is also accompanied by multiculturalism, an increased awareness

Figure 1.1 An Alternative View of the World

GDP (Gross Domestic Product) Per Capita, 2000 in PPP (Purchasing Power Parity), U.S. Dollars

More than 25,000	7,000–10,000
20,000–25,000	4,000–7,000
15,000–20,000	2,000–4,000
10,000–15,000	Less than 2,000
No data	

The size of this square represents 100 billion U.S. dollars

(*Source:* From United Nations Environment Programme/GRID-Arendal website, maps.grids.no. Cartogram reproduced by permission of the authors, Vladimir Tikunov [Department of Geography, University of Moscow] and Philippe Rekacewicz [Le Monde diplomatique, Paris].)

of the particular aspects of our specific identities, and a resistance to losing them to some global identity, which most people find both grander and blander. In the words of political scientist Benjamin Barber (1996), our world is characterized by *both* "McWorld" and "Jihad"—the integration into "one commercially homogeneous network" and also increased tribalization and separation.

Globalization and multiculturalism express *both* the forces that hold us together—whether the repression of armies, police forces, and governments or the shared values of nationalism or ethnic pride—*and* the forces that drive us apart. These are, actually, the same forces.

For example, religion both maintains cohesiveness among members and serves as one of the principal axes of division among people in the world today. Ethnicity provides a sense of stable identity and a way of distinguishing ourselves from others, as well as a way that society unequally allocates resources. Gender, race, youth/age, and social class also contribute to stable identity and can help us feel connected to groups, but they similarly serve as major contributors to social inequality, thus pulling society apart.

One impetus for the recognition of globalization and multiculturalism as among the central organizing principles of society is the continued importance of *race, class,* and *gender* in social life. In the past half century, we've become increasingly aware of the centrality of these three categories of experience. Race, class, and gender are among the most important axes around which social life revolves, the organizing mechanisms of institutions, the foundations of our identities. Along with other forms of identity and mechanisms of inequality—ethnicity, sexuality, age, and religion—they form a matrix through which we understand ourselves and our world.

Sociology and Modernism

One of the central themes of virtually all of the classical sociological theories was an abiding faith in the idea of progress. This idea—that society is moving from a less developed to a more developed (and therefore better) stage—is a hallmark of the idea of **modernism.** In classical sociological theory, modernism was expressed as the passage from religious to scientific forms of knowledge (Comte), from mechanical to organic forms of solidarity (Durkheim), from feudal to capitalist to communist modes of production (Marx), from traditional to legal forms of authority (Weber). In the twentieth century, structural functionalists hailed the movement from extended to nuclear family forms and from arbitrary rule by aristocrats to universal legal principles as emblems of social progress.

Yet many of the founders of sociology were also deeply ambivalent about progress. Tocqueville saw democracy as inevitable but potentially dangerous to individual freedom. Durkheim saw that organic solidarity required constant effort to maintain the levels of integration that individuals would feel, so they would not drift away from social life. Marx bemoaned the fact that members of the working class would have to experience great deprivation before they would rise up against capitalism. And Weber saw the very mechanism of individual freedom, rationality, coming back to trap us in an iron cage of meaninglessness.

Today, we live in an age in which the very idea of progress from one stage to the next has been called into question. For one thing, it's clear that no society ever passes from one stage fully into the next. We can see pieces of both mechanical and organic solidarity all around us. In the most advanced societies, kinship, "blood," and primordial ethnic identity continue to serve as a foundation for identity; in some of the least developed countries, young people are using the Internet and hanging out on Facebook. Societies maintain both feudal relations and capitalist ones—including those countries that call themselves communist! We are governed by authorities that rely on traditional, charismatic, and legal rationales.

What's more, the world has become so interdependent that one society cannot exist in isolation from others. The development of one society toward different ways of organizing social life (replacing tribal elders with elected representatives, for example) is heavily influenced by the global marketplace, by transnational organizations like the United Nations, and by ideas that circulate over the globe via transportation, telecommunications, and the media faster than any classical theorist could ever have imagined.

We no longer see less-developed societies as the image of our past, any more than they see Europe or the United States as an image of their future.

Sociology remains a deeply "modern" enterprise: Most sociologists believe that science and reason can solve human problems and that people's lives can be improved by the application of these scientifically derived principles. Yet sociologists are also reexamining the fixed idea of progress and seeing a jumble of conflicting possibilities that exist at any historical moment rather than the inevitable unfolding of a single linear path. As a concept, postmodernism originated in architecture, as a critique of the uniformity of modern buildings. Using elements from classical and modern, postmodernists prefer buildings that are not fixed and uniform but rather a collage, a collision of styles in a new form.

In sociology, **postmodernism** suggests that the meaning of social life may not be found in conforming to rigid patterns of development but rather in the creative assembling of interactions and interpretations that enable us to negotiate our way in the world. In the postmodern conception of the world, the fundamentals of society—structure, culture, agency—are all challenged and in flux. Thus we are simultaneously freer and more creative and also potentially more frightened, more lost, and more alone.

In the face of these postmodernist ideas, the modern world has also witnessed a rebirth of "premodern" ideas. Premodern ideas—kinship, blood, religion, tribe—were the ideas first challenged by the Enlightenment view of the world, from which sociology emerged in the nineteenth century. The increased freedom of postmodern society—the ability to make up the rules as you go along—is accompanied by increased fatalism, a belief that all is entirely preordained.

There has been a dramatic increase in religious beliefs, New Age consciousness, and other nonscientific ways of explaining our lives and our place in the universe. The forces that were supposed to disappear as the bases for social life have remained and even strengthened as some of the world's most powerful mechanisms for uniting people into connected clans and dividing us into warring factions. The global economy, potentially an unprecedented force for economic growth and development worldwide, brings us together into a web of interconnected interests and also widens the ancient divide between rich and poor, haves and have-nots, chosen and dispossessed.

Contemporary society consists of all these elements; just as modern society is the collision of premodern and postmodern. Understanding this collision—creative and chaotic, compassionate and cruel—is the task of sociology in the twenty-first century.

Sociology in the Twenty-First Century: Sociology and You

Sociologists are part of a larger network of social scientists. Sociologists work in colleges and universities, teaching and doing research, but they also work in government organizations, doing research and policy analysis; in social movements, developing strategies; and in large and small organizations, public and private.

Sociologists reflect and embody the processes we study, and the changes in the field of sociology are, in a way, a microcosm of the changes we observe in the society in which we live. And, over the past few decades, the field has undergone more dramatic changes than many of the other academic fields of study. Sociology's mission is the understanding—without value judgments—of different groups, and, as you will see, to understand the dynamics of both *identity* and *inequality* that belonging to these groups brings, as well as the different institutions—the family, education, workplace, media, religious institution, and the like—in which we experience social life. It makes a certain logical sense, therefore, that many members of marginalized groups, such as racial, sexual, and ethnic minorities and women, would find a home in sociology.

Did You Know?

Once, of course, all academic fields of study were the dominion of White men. Today, however, women and racial, ethnic, and sexual minorities have transformed collegiate life. Not that long ago, women were excluded from many of the most prestigious colleges and universities; now women outnumber men on virtually every college campus. Not that long ago, racial minorities were excluded from many of America's universities and colleges; today universities have special recruiting task forces to ensure a substantial minority applicant pool. Not that long ago, gays and lesbians, bisexuals, and transgendered people were expelled from colleges and universities for violating ethics or morals codes; today there are LGBT (lesbian, gay, bisexual, transgender) organizations on most college campuses.

Sociology has been one of the fields that has pioneered this inclusion. It is a source of pride to most sociologists that today sociology is among the most diverse fields on any campus.

In the past 50 years (since 1966), the percentage of BA degrees in sociology awarded to women has increased 98.7 percent, while the percentage of MA degrees rose 336.9 percent, and the percentage of PhD degrees rose a whopping 802.5 percent (Figure 1.2). At the same time, the percentage of African American PhDs in sociology has more than doubled, while the percentage of Hispanic PhDs nearly tripled in the same period, and Asian American degrees more than doubled—all of these are the highest percentages of any social science (American Sociological Association, 2007).

We live in a society composed of many different groups and many different cultures, subcultures, and countercultures, speaking different languages, with different kinship networks and different values and norms. It's noisy, and we rarely agree on anything. And yet we also live in a society where the overwhelming majority of people obey the same laws and are civil to one another and in which we respect the differences among those different groups. We live in a society characterized by a fixed hierarchy and in a society in which people believe firmly in the idea of mobility, a society in which one's fixed, ascribed characteristics (race, class, and sex) are the single best determinants of where one will end up, and a society in which we also believe anyone can make it if he or she works hard enough.

This is the world sociologists find so endlessly fascinating. This is the world about which sociologists develop their theories, test their hypotheses, and conduct their research. Sociology is the lens through which we look at this dizzying array of social life—and begin to try and make sense of it. Welcome to it—and welcome to sociology as a new way of seeing that world.

Figure 1.2 Sociology Degrees Awarded to Women

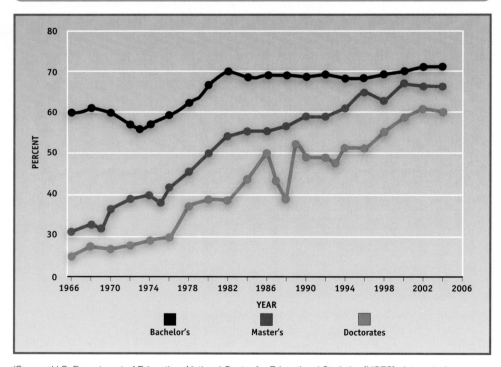

(*Source:* U.S. Department of Education, National Center for Educational Statistics [NCES], Integrated Postsecondary Education Data System (IPEDS) Completions, 1966–2004 [Washington, DC: NCES, 2006]. Retrieved on November 8, 2006, from: http://caspar.nsf.gov.)

Chapter Review

1. Sociology as a Way of Seeing

Sociologists use their **"sociological imagination"** as a lens to see beyond individual behavior to the larger social forces and regularities that affect society and the people who comprise it. This allows us to consider social behavior from numerous perspectives, across a wide variety of social phenomena, at many levels of analysis. We can focus on regularities, or on divergences from the usual; on social order or on disorder. As sociologists recognize, what appear to be contradictions are part of the whole fabric of society. The discipline of **sociology** considers the context for human behavior and looks beyond the individual experience. When seen through the lens of the sociological imagination, the invisible and dynamic connections at play in the social order are revealed. Sociological understanding goes beyond either/or.

sociological imagination The ability to see the connection between our individual identities and the social contexts (family, friends, and institutions) in which we find ourselves. (p. 4)

sociology The study of human behavior in society. (p. 4)

2. Doing Sociology

Social behavior is complex. It can be studied at many levels; for example, we can consider small groups, countries, cultures, or even a global economy. For a sociologist, seemingly private or personal problems are seen as public, or societal, issues. Because they study a broad array of topics and complex issues, sociologists use many methods to get beyond commonsense understandings. The methods depend on the topic. Some methods are very quantitative; others are more qualitative. But no matter what a sociologist studies, or the methods used, sociologists are doing science—making systematic observations, generating hypotheses that are tested with reliable and valid data, and constructing theories that help us understand behavior and make predictions for future testing. Through these techniques we can see what would otherwise be invisible and go beyond overly simplistic or false commonsense understandings, and either/or approaches, to social behavior.

3. Where Did Sociology Come From?

Historical changes in governments, economies, and beliefs raised questions about the nature of society. During the Enlightenment, as science gained credence, secularism advanced, religion receded from civic life, and monarchy subjects became citizens, philosophers explored the relationship of the individual to society. Ideas formative for new republics, including France and America, were important in the emergence of *sociology*, the name Comte gave the science that studied the changes and challenges facing society in order to help it progress. Durkheim, one of sociology's founders, explored changes in the individual's relationship to others as societies moved toward modernization in his discussion of **mechanical solidarity** and **organic solidarity,** fundamental to the **canon.** Ward, an American sociologist, like Comte

believed that sociology could improve society through planning and reform, instead of allowing **social Darwinism** to prevail, to the detriment of society. Mead's work in identity developed the idea of the self as social, internalizing the **generalized other.** White males dominated sociology, but recently Black and female theorists who explored inequality, long ignored, are now recognized for their contributions.

canon The officially recognized set of foundational sociologists. (p. 18)

mechanical solidarity Durkheim's term for a traditional society where life is uniform and people are similar. They share a common culture and sense of morality that bonds them. (p. 15)

organic solidarity Emile Durkheim's term for a modern society where people are interdependent because of the division of labor; they disagree on what is right and wrong but share solidarity because the division of labor makes them dependent on each other. (p. 15)

social Darwinism A model of social change that saw each succeeding society as developing through evolution and the "survival of the fittest." (p. 19)

generalized other The organized rules, judgments, and attitudes of an entire group. If you try to imagine what is expected of you, you are taking on the perspective of the generalized other. (p. 20)

4. Contemporary Sociology

Twentieth-century sociology emphasized the self in society and social stability amidst change, with three main paradigms emerging. **Symbolic interactionism** emphasizes the role of microlevel interaction in the construction of self and society, while **structural functionalism** developed a **paradigm** of societal equilibrium and order through institutions, which serve both **manifest functions** and **latent functions.** In the turbulent 1960s, as society grappled with issues of inequality, **conflict theory** held great relevance. Based on the writings of Marx and Weber, it emphasizes social conflict, identifying structural inequities in power and resources as the source of social inequality. Today, the twin lenses of **globalization,** emphasizing cross-cultural interaction and integration, and **multiculturalism,** awareness of cross-cultural differences, are used to view social issues, applicable for **macrolevel analysis** and **microlevel analysis. McDonaldization** is one charge against globalization. The orderly progression of development **modernism** envisioned gave way to divergent worldviews and juxtapositions in **postmodernism.**

symbolic interactionism Sociological perspective that examines how individuals and groups interact, focusing on the creation of personal identity through interaction with others. Of particular interest is the relationship between individual action and group pressures. (p. 21)

functionalism (or structural functionalism) Sociological theory that stressed the interconnectedness of social institutions forming stable and orderly social systems. (p. 22)

paradigm An example, pattern, or model, especially an outstandingly clear or typical example or archetype. (p. 22)

manifest functions The intended consequences of an action or event. (p. 22)

latent function Any function of an institution or process that is unintended, such as education keeps the streets safer, since young people are inside. (p. 22)

conflict theory Theoretical approach that stresses the competition for scarce resources and unequal distribution of those resources based on social status (such as class, race, gender). (p. 23)

globalization A set of processes leading to the development of patterns of economic, cultural, and social relationships that transcend geographical boundaries; a widening, deepening, and speeding up of worldwide interconnectedness in all aspects of contemporary life. (p. 24)

multiculturalism The doctrine that several different cultures (rather than one national culture) can coexist peacefully and equitably in a single country. (p. 24)

macrolevel analysis Analysis of the large-scale patterns or social structures of society, such as economies or political systems. (p. 24)

microlevel analysis Analysis of small-scale social patterns, such as individual interactions or small group dynamics. (p. 24)

McDonaldization The homogenizing spread of consumerism around the globe. (p. 27)

modernism In sociology, a belief in progress that challenged tradition, religion, and aristocracies as remnants of the past and saw industry, democracy, and science as the wave of the future. (p. 28)

postmodernism A late-twentieth-century worldview that emphasizes the existence of different worldviews and concepts of reality, rather than one "correct" or "true" one. Postmodernism emphasizes that a particular reality is a social construction by a particular group, community, or class. (p. 29)

5. Sociology in the Twenty-First Century: Sociology and You

Race, sex, and class are good predictors of where we will end up in life, but we believe in opportunity and mobility. We live in a world that is connected globally, yet even within a single nation there are numerous distinct cultural identities. Today, in a world of contradictions, sociology helps us make sense of complex phenomenon and gain insight into confusing situations. It is time for *Sociology Now*.

Self-Test: Check Your Understanding

1. The term *sociological imagination* refers to
   a. a personality trait shared by all sociologists.
   b. an analytic perspective that considers the context for individual behavior.
   c. the ability to come up with creative explanations for unusual human behavior.
   d. the fact that sociologists find people fascinating, which fuels their curiosity.

2. Which of the following best typifies the approach a sociologist might take toward understanding the situation faced by a father who is depressed because he lost his job?
   a. Figuring out which sort of psychiatric treatment would be most appropriate as an intervention to restore individual functioning
   b. Prescribing a medication that alleviates the symptoms of depression
   c. Exploring factors of the global economy that result in job loss or studying gender identities related to wage-earning.
   d. Developing an essay that compares representations of despair in postmodern societies found in paintings and literature

3. According to the text, the discipline of sociology is an example of
   a. an art.
   b. a political science.
   c. a philosophy.
   d. a social science.

4. Sociologists approach social issues by
   a. focusing solely on stability and the social order.
   b. focusing primarily on disorder and chaos.
   c. concentrating on what is unique in an individual's experience.
   d. recognizing both stability and disorder.

5. Which of the following was not identified in the text examples of societal changes influenced by ideas important in the development of sociology?
   a. The American Revolution
   b. The Industrial Revolution
   c. The Cognitive Revolution
   d. The French Revolution

6. Durkheim found that suicides varied by age, religion, marital status, and employment status because of differences in
   a. integration and regulation.
   b. intelligence and mental illness.
   c. spirituality and morals.
   d. locus of control and education.
7. Goffman's dramaturgical model emphasizing people as social actors in roles is based on which paradigm?
   a. Symbolic interactionism
   b. Structural functionalism
   c. Conflict theory
   d. Globalization

8. Which of the following is based on the assumption that societies would progress toward increasingly higher levels of development?
   a. McDonaldization
   b. Multiculturalism
   c. Modernism
   d. Postmodernism

Self-Test Answers: 1. b, 2. c, 3. d, 4. d, 5. c, 6. a, 7. a, 8. c

Integrate and Explore: Points to Consider

1. How can a discipline that studies human behavior be scientific? What are the principles of a scientific investigation, and how can these principles be applied to the study of human behavior in society?
2. Which historical events occurred during the period in which sociology emerged as a science? Identify the common themes or ideas that were driving these changes. What changes were taking place in society during this time? Which aspects of life were affected, and how?
3. Discuss the roots and development of sociology that make it conducive to the inclusion of diverse perspectives. What were the goals of the new discipline? How did women and minorities contribute to historical sociological thought? Are women and minorities well represented in sociology today?

succeed with PEARSON mysoclab

Self-scoring practice tests, flashcards for learning key terms, streaming audio of the entire text, and multimedia, including:

Watch—Michael Kimmel, *The Big Questions Sociologists Ask Today*
Watch—Michael Kimmel, *What is Multiculturalism?*
Watch—Michael Kimmel, *What is Globalization?*
MySocLibrary—Peter Berger, *Invitation to Sociology*
MySocLibrary—C. Wright Mills, *The Promise*

Culture and Society

Look around your class. Odds are that some students are wearing a team logo on a T-shirt or jersey. Someone will be wearing something that proclaims the name of the school or perhaps a team or club at your school. Someone may even be wearing something with the name of another school on it. Some will wear easily identifiable athletic logos, like swooshes or stripes, and others will have large or discrete insignias that denote the designer of the clothing.

An enormous number of people are "branded"—wearing an article of clothing that indicates membership in a group. We often signal our membership by what we wear, what sorts of things we buy, or the kind of music we listen to. Branding is a way of connecting, a way of being a part of something greater than ourselves.

We may be branded, but at the same time, we don't really like to be "labeled." We resist the stereotypes that might be associated with someone who is a loyal adherent to a particular brand. We're more than that, different from that. We're unique individuals and are not reducible to what we wear and what bands we like.

We are constantly constructing our identities—that sense of who we are that feels both internally authentic and that we present to others. And the way we construct that identity is through culture. Culture provides both the arena in which we interact, the various symbols we use to signal our identity to others, and the means by which we do it. That Green Day T-shirt and those Nike shoes, that butterfly tattoo and that earring all signal to others who we think we are.

As we saw in the last chapter, one of the most concise yet profound definitions of sociology is C. Wright Mills's idea that sociology "connects biography and history"— that is, it connects you, as an individual, to the larger social *contexts* in which you find yourself. This connection raises important questions for us: How much "free will" do I actually have? Can I control my own destiny or am I simply the product of those larger contexts? Both—and neither. We have an enormous amount of freedom to choose our paths—probably more than any entire population in history. And yet, as we will see, those choices are constrained by circumstances that we neither chose nor created. Another way of saying this is found in the first paragraphs of a book by Karl Marx (1965):

Men make their own history, but they do not make it as they please; they do not make it under self-selected circumstances, but under circumstances existing already, given and transmitted from the past.

It is this connection—between the personal and the structural—that defines the sociological perspective. The sociological perspective enables us to see how nature and nurture combine, how things are changing and how they are eternal and timeless, how we are shaped by our societies and how we in turn shape them—to see, in essence, how it can be both the best of times and the worst of times.

> "What makes human life different from other species is that we alone have a conscious 'history,' a continuity of generations and a purposive direction of change. Humans have culture."

Culture
Cultural Diversity
Subcultures and
  Countercultures

Elements of Culture
Material Culture
Symbols
Language
Ritual
Norms
Values

Cultural Expressions
Universality and
  Localism
High Culture and
  Popular Culture
Forms of Popular
  Culture
The Politics of
  Popular Culture
The Globalization of
  Popular Culture
Culture as a Tool Kit

Cultural Change

Culture in the Twenty-First Century

Culture

Sociology uses specific terms and concepts that enable us to see those linkages discussed above and to make sense of both ourselves and the world we live in. Every academic field uses certain concepts as the lenses through which it sees and therefore understands the world, much like the lenses of eyeglasses help us see what we need to see much more clearly. For example, psychologists might use terms like *cognition, unconscious,* or *ego;* economists would use terms like *supply and demand, production cycle,* or *profit margins.*

The lenses through which sociologists see the world are broad terms like *society* and *culture;* structural terms like *institutions;* and cultural terms like *values* and *norms.* (We will discuss all these terms in the coming chapters.) Larger structures—institutions and/or organizations like the economy, government, family, or corporation—offer the larger, general patterns of things. And *agency* stresses the individual decisions that we make, ourselves, to create and shape our own destiny.

What makes us human? What differentiates human life from other animals' lives? One answer is culture. **Culture** refers to the sets of values and ideals that we understand to define morality, good and evil, appropriate and inappropriate. Culture defines larger structural forces and also how we perceive them. While dogs or horses or chimpanzees live in social groupings, they do not transmit their culture from one generation to the next. Although they learn and adapt to changing environmental conditions, they do not consciously build on the experiences of previous generations, transmitting to their children the wisdom of their ancestors. What makes human life different is that we alone have a conscious "history," a continuity of generations and a purposive direction of change. Humans have culture.

Culture is the foundation of society—both the material basis for social life and the ideas, beliefs, and values that people have. **Material culture** consists of the things people make and the things they use to make them—the tools they use, the physical environment they inhabit (forests, beaches, mountains, fertile farmlands, or harsh desert). **Nonmaterial culture** consists of the ideas and beliefs that people develop about their lives and their world. Anthropologists have explained how people who live near dense forests, where animals are plentiful and food abundant, will develop very different cultural values from a culture that evolves in the desert, in which people must constantly move to follow an ever-receding water supply.

Our culture shapes more than what we know, more than our beliefs and our attitudes; culture shapes our human nature. Some societies, like the Yanomamo in Brazil, "know" that people are, by nature, violent and aggressive, and so they raise everyone to be violent and aggressive. But others, like the Tasaday tribe in the Philippines, "know" that people are kind and generous, and so everyone is raised to be kind and generous. In the United States, our culture is diverse enough that we can believe both sides. On the one hand, "everybody knows" that everyone is only out for him- or herself, and so it shouldn't surprise us that people cheat on exams or their taxes or drive over the speed limit. On the other hand, "everybody knows" that people are neighborly and kind, and so it doesn't surprise us that most people *don't* cheat on exams or their taxes and they drive under the speed limit.

Cultural Diversity

Cultural diversity means that the world's cultures are vastly different from each other. Their rich diversity sometimes appears exotic, sometimes tantalizing, and sometimes even disgusting. Even within American culture, there are subcultures that exhibit beliefs or behaviors that are vastly different from those of other groups. And, of course, culture is hardly static: Our culture is constantly changing, as beliefs and habits change. For example, in the early nineteenth century, it was a common prescribed cultural practice among middle-class New Englanders for a dating couple to be expected to share a bed together with a board placed down the middle, so that they could become accustomed to each other's sleeping behavior but without having sex. Parents would welcome their teenage children's "bundling" in a way they might not feel particularly comfortable doing today.

What do **you** think?

America is famously egocentric, and the stereotype of the insensitive, ignorant American tourist is pervasive and persistent. When any group is in power, it is easy to grow unaware of the cultures of others and to judge and dismiss them. So, what do you think? How much do you agree or disagree with the following statement?

> The world would be a better place if people from other countries were more like Americans.
>
> **1.** Strongly agree **3.** Neither agree nor disagree **5.** Strongly disagree
>
> **2.** Agree **4.** Disagree

What does **America** think?

(Actual Survey Data from the General Social Survey.)

Thirty-four percent of the respondents said they had no opinion. Forty-two percent said they thought the world would be a better place if people from other countries were more like Americans, and 24 percent disagree. There was a big difference in opinion by social class.

More Like Americans by Class %

	Lower	Working	Middle	Upper	Row Total
Strongly Agree	27.5	17.4	14.2	5.4	15.9
Agree	28.6	24.5	27.3	20.2	26.1
Neither Agree nor Disagree	33.9	37.4	31.7	34.0	34.2
Disagree	6.9	16.6	19.9	26.9	18.1
Strongly Disagree	3.2	4.0	6.9	13.5	5.8

Think about It Some More

1. How do you explain the social class differences in response?

2. Do you think this kind of ethnocentrism is unique to the United States?

References: See Davis et al., page 511.

Often, when we encounter a different culture, we experience **culture shock,** a feeling of disorientation, because the cultural markers that we rely on to help us know where we are and how to act have suddenly changed. Sometimes, the sense of disorientation leads us to retreat to something more comfortable and reassert the values of our own cultures. We find other cultures weird, or funny, or sometimes we think they're immoral. In the 2003 movie *Lost in Translation*, Bill Murray and Scarlett Johansson experience the strange limbo of living in a foreign culture during an extended stay at a Tokyo hotel. They develop an unlikely bond of friendship, finding each other as a source of familiarity and comfort.

The condemnation of other cultures because they are different is called **ethnocentrism,** a belief that one's culture is superior to others. We often use our own culture as the reference point by which we evaluate others. William Graham Sumner, the sociologist who first coined the term, described ethnocentrism

Oppression or freedom? To many Westerners, the hijab is a symbol of woman's subordinate status. But this Muslim woman thinks otherwise.

as seeing "one's own group is the center of everything, and all others are scaled and rated with reference to it" (Sumner, [1906] 2002, p. 12). Ethnocentrism can be relatively benign, as a quiet sense of superiority or even cultural disapproval of the other culture, or it can be aggressive, as when people try to impose their values on others by force.

Sociologists must constantly guard against ethnocentrism because it can bias our understandings of other cultures. It's helpful to remember that each culture justifies its beliefs by reference to the same guiding principles, so when Yanomamo people act aggressively, they say, "Well, that's just human nature," which is exactly what the Tasaday say when they act kindly toward each other. Because each culture justifies its activities and organization by reference to these universals—God's will, human nature, and the like—it is difficult for any one of us to stand in judgment of another's way of doing things. Therefore, to a large extent, sociologists take a position of **cultural relativism,** a position that all cultures are equally valid in the experience of their own members.

At the same time, many sociologists also believe that we should not shy away from claiming that some values are, or should be, universal values to which all cultures should subscribe. For example, the ideals of human rights that all people share—these are values that might be seen as condemning slavery, female genital mutilation, the killing of civilians during wartime, the physical or sexual abuse of children, the exclusion of married men from prosecution for rape of their wives. Some have suggested that these universal human rights are themselves the ethnocentric imposition of Western values on other cultures, and they may be. But they also express values that virtually every culture claims to hold, and so they may be close to universal. Cultural relativism makes us sensitive to the ways other people organize their lives, but it does not absolve us from taking moral positions ourselves.

Cultures vary dramatically in the ways they go about the most basic activities of life: eating, sleeping, producing goods, raising children, educating them, making friends, making love, forming families. This diversity is sometimes startling; and yet, every culture shares some central elements. Every culture has history, a myth of origin, a set of guiding principles that dictates right and wrong, with justifications for those principles.

Subcultures and Countercultures

Even within a particular culture there are often different subgroups. Subcultures and countercultures often develop within a culture.

Subcultures. A **subculture** is a group of people within a culture who share some distinguishing characteristics, beliefs, values, or attributes that set them apart from the dominant culture. Some groups within a society create their own subcultures, with norms and values distinct from the mainstream, and usually their own separate social institutions. Roman Catholics were once prohibited from joining fraternal organizations such as the Masons, so they founded their own, the Knights of Columbus. Because ethnic and sexual minorities are often subjected to negative stereotyping, they often produce their own organizations, media, and even travel agencies.

Subcultures are communities that constitute themselves through a relationship of *difference* to the dominant culture. They can be a subset of the dominant culture, simply exaggerating their set of interests as the glue that holds them together as a community. So, for example, generation Y is a youth subculture, a group for which membership is limited to those of a certain age who believe they have characteristics that are different from the dominant culture. Members of a subculture are part of the larger culture, but they may draw more on their subcultural position for their identity. Membership in a subculture enables you to feel "one" with others and "different" from others at the same time.

Countercultures. Subcultures that identify themselves through their *difference and opposition* to the dominant culture are called countercultures. Like subcultures, **countercultures** offer an important grounding for identity, but they do so in opposition to the dominant culture. As a result, countercultures demand a lot of conformity from members because they define themselves in opposition, and they may be more totalistic than a subculture. One can imagine, for example, belonging to several different subcultures, and these may exist in tandem with membership in the official culture. But countercultural membership often requires a sign of separation from the official culture. And it would be hard to belong to more than one.

As a result, countercultures are more often perceived as a threat to the official culture than a subculture might be. Countercultures may exist parallel to the official culture, or they may be outlawed and strictly policed. For example, the early Christians thought they were a subculture, a group with a somewhat separate identity from the Jews (another subculture) and the Romans. But the Romans were too threatened, and the Christians were seen as a counterculture that had to be destroyed.

Like subcultures, countercultures create their own cultural forms—music, literature, news media, art. Sometimes these may be incorporated into the official culture as signs of rebellion. For example, blue jeans, tattoos, rock and rap music, leather jackets, and wearing black pants and shirts together all have their origins as signs of countercultural rebellion from the hippie, ghetto, or fringe sexual cultures. But they were incorporated into consumerism and have now achieved mainstream respectability.

Sometimes a countercultural movement can change a society. In 1989, writer Vaclav Havel led the "Velvet Revolution" in Czechoslovakia and became the country's president.

The term *counterculture* came into widespread use during the 1960s to describe an emerging subculture based on age (youth), behaviors (marijuana and psychedelic drug use, "free" sexual practices), and political sensibilities (liberal to radical). Gradually, this subculture became well defined in opposition to the official culture, and membership required wearing certain androgynous fashions (tie-dyed shirts, sandals, bell-bottom blue jeans, "peasant" blouses), bodily practices (everyone wearing their hair long), musical preferences, drug use, and anti-Vietnam War politics. Other countercultures sprang up in many other countries, and some, like those in the Czech Republic and Poland, even became the dominant political parties during periods of radical reform.

Countercultures are not necessarily on the left or the right politically—what they are is oppositional. In the contemporary United States, there are groups such as White supremacist survivalists as well as back-to-the-land hippies on communes: Both represent countercultures (and, given that they tend to be rural and isolated, they may also be neighbors!).

Elements of Culture

All cultures share six basic elements: material culture, symbols, language, rituals, norms, and values.

Material Culture

As we mentioned earlier, material culture consists of both what people make and what they make it with. Every society must solve basic needs of subsistence: provision of food and shelter from the elements for both the person and the family (shelter and clothing). Material culture includes the environment we inhabit and the tools we develop to survive in it. Those tools are the level of technology. We organize our societies to enable us to collectively meet these basic subsistence needs for food, clothing, and shelter. We develop different cultures based on the climate, the available food supply, and the geography of our environment.

Symbols

As humans wrestle with the meanings of their material environment, we attempt to represent our ideas to others. We translate what we see and think into symbols. A **symbol** is anything—an idea, a marking, a thing—that carries additional meanings beyond itself to others who share in the culture. Symbols come to mean what they do only in a culture; they would have no meaning to someone outside. Take, for example, one of the most familiar symbols of all, the cross. If one is Christian, the cross carries with it certain meanings. But to someone else, it might be simply a decoration or a reference to the means of execution in the Roman era. And to some who have seen crosses burning on their lawns, they may be a symbol of terror. That's what we mean when we say that symbols take on their meaning only inside culture.

Symbols are representations of ideas or feelings. In a single image, a symbol suggests and stands in for something more complex and involved. The donkey and elephant stand for America's Democratic and Republican parties; a smiley face stands for happiness (even if it also stands for shallowness); red parentheses stand for Bono's Red Campaign to fight AIDS; the bald eagle represents the American nation.

Symbols can be created at any time. Witness the recent various ribbons—red for AIDS awareness, pink for breast cancer awareness. But many symbols developed over centuries and in relative isolation from one another. In the case of older symbols, the same ones may mean completely different things in different cultures. For example, the color red means passion, aggression, or danger in the United States, while it signifies purity in India and is a symbol of celebration and luck in China. White symbolizes purity in the West, but in Eastern cultures is the color of mourning and death.

Symbols are not always universally shared, and many cultural conflicts in society are over the meaning and appropriateness of certain symbols. Consider flags, for example. Many people around the world feel deeply patriotic at the sight of their nation's flag. My grandfather would actually often weep when he saw the American flag because it reminded him of his family's arduous journey to this country as an immigrant and the men who fought and died alongside him in World War I. Flags are important symbols and are displayed at solemn ceremonial moments and at festivals and sports events. Is burning the American flag a protected form of speech, a way for Americans to express their dissent from certain policies, or is it the deliberate destruction of the symbol of the nation, tantamount to an act of treason? And what about waving the flag of a different nation, like the one where your ancestors may have come from? To some, it's harmless, an expression of ethnic pride, like waving Irish flags on St. Patrick's Day; but others think it borders on treason, like waving the flag of the former Soviet Union or the Iraqi flag at a demonstration. To some, waving the Confederate flag is a symbol of civic pride, or of Southern heritage, while to others the Confederate flag is a symbol of racism.

These examples illustrate how symbols can often become politicized, endowed with meaning by different groups, and used as forms of political speech. Symbols elicit powerful emotions because they express the emotional foundations of our culture.

Language

Language is an organized set of symbols by which we are able to think and communicate with others. Language is also the chief vehicle by which human beings create a sense of self. It is through language that we pose questions of identity—"Who am I?"—and through our linguistic interactions with others that we constitute a sense of ourselves. We need language to know what we think as well as who we are.

In the thirteenth century, Frederick II, Holy Roman emperor, decided to perform an experiment to see if he could discover the "natural language of man." What language would we speak if no one taught us language? He selected some newborn babies and decreed that no one speak to them. The babies were suckled and nursed and bathed as usual, but speech and songs and lullabies were strictly prohibited. All the babies died. We need to interact with other people to survive, let alone thrive. And language enables us to accomplish this interaction.

Language is not solely a human trait. There is ample evidence that other animals use sounds, gestures, facial expressions, and touch to communicate with each other. But these expressions seem to always relate to events in the present—nearby food sources, the presence of

danger—or immediate expressions of different feelings or moods. What makes the human use of language different from that of animals is that we use language to transmit culture, to connect us to both the past and the future, to build on the experiences of previous generations. Even the most linguistically capable chimps cannot pass that kind of language on to their offspring.

Language does not merely reflect the world as we know it; language actually shapes our perceptions of things. In 1929, two anthropologists, Edward Sapir and Benjamin Whorf, noticed that the Hopi Indians of the Southwest seemed to have no verb tenses, no ways for them to state a word in the past, present, or future tense. Imagine speaking to your friends without being able to put your ideas in their proper tense. Although common sense held that the function of language was to express the world we already perceived, Sapir and Whorf concluded that language, itself, provides a cultural lens through which people

Did You Know?

(Flags can be powerful cultural symbols, eliciting strong emotions. To some, the Stars and Bars (a battle flag of the Confederate states during the Civil War) is a symbol of Southern heritage; to the majority of Americans (and people around the world), it is a symbol of racism and a reminder of slavery.

Michelle Obama (at left) and Cindy McCain (at right), the wives of the 2008 presidential contenders, may have dressed similarly, but cultural meanings of that similarity may have been different. A Georgia Congressman called Obama "uppity" evoking a long-discredited term from the Jim Crow south, "applied to African-Americans who tried to rise above servile positions," according to the Atlanta Constitution.

No Country Code Required

Even language in cyberspace shapes how we see the world. If you've written e-mail messages to people in other countries, you've probably noticed that those countries have "country codes" at the end: .za for South Africa, .jp for Japan, and so on. American addresses end with .gov, .edu, .net, or .com. Why doesn't the United States have a country code? Perhaps because when you are the dominant power in the world, everyone else needs to be named. In the world of the Internet, as Michael Jackson sang, "We are the world."

Did You Know?

perceive the world. What became known as the **Sapir-Whorf hypothesis** states that language shapes our perception (Sapir, 1921; Whorf, 1956).

Sociologist Eviatar Zerubavel (1989) noted that, in English, there are different words for "jelly" and "jam," while Hebrew, his native language, did not distinguish between the two and had only one word. Only when he learned English, he writes, did he actually "see" that they were different. Having the language for the two things made it possible for him to see them. In France, there is a spe-

cific ailment called a pain in the liver, a *crise de foie*. Americans find the idea strange because that sort of pain is given a generic "stomach ache." (In fact, when I lived in France, I found it somewhat amusing to think that they knew exactly which internal organ was in pain!) And there is no word for "gentrification" in Spanish. An Argentine colleague of mine first heard the word when he moved to New York City, and when he returned to Buenos Aires, he couldn't believe how different the city looked to him, now that he had the language to describe the changes he saw. Ask yourself or anyone you know who speaks more than one language about how different things actually *are* different when you speak Chinese, or Russian, or French, or Spanish.

We often say that we'll "believe it when we see it"—that empirical proof is required for us to believe something. But it's equally true that we "see it when we believe it"—we cannot "see" what we don't have the conceptual framework to understand.

Because language not only reflects the world in which we live but also shapes our perception of it, language is also political. Consider, for example, the battles over the implicit gender bias of using the word *man* to include both women and men, and the use of the masculine pronoun *he* as the "inclusive" generic term. Some words, such as *chairman* or *policeman,* make it clear that the position carries a gender—whether the occupant of the position is male or female.

Even the appellation for women and men was made the object of political struggle. While referring to a man as "Mr." indicates nothing about his marital status, appellations for women referred only to their status as married (Mrs.) or unmarried (Miss). To create a neutral, parallel term for women, Ms., took several years before it became commonplace.

Similarly, language conveys cultural attitudes about race and ethnicity. This happens not simply through the use of derogatory slang terms but also in the construction of language itself. Adjectives or colloquial phrases may convey ideas about the relative values of different groups, simply through the association of one with the other: "a black mark against you," "good guys wear white hats," "a Chinaman's chance," or "to Jew someone down" all encode stereotypes in language. During the 2008 presidential campaign, Georgia Congressman Lynn Westmorland called Barack Obama "uppity," a term with racist associations to the pre–Civil Rights era, used to describe Black people who "didn't know their place" (Weisman, 2008).

The idea of a single unifying language has also become a hot-button issue in the United States. If language is central to the smooth functioning of society, what does it imply about that unity when "only" 82 percent of Americans speak only English at home and more than 17 percent speak a different language (10 percent of them speaking Spanish)?

Ritual

Shared symbols and language are two of the most important processes that enable cultures to cohere and persist over time. Another process is **rituals,** by which members of a culture engage in a routine behav-

Changing Language

Language unites a people through a shared symbol system; and, like those people, language is constantly changing. Here are some of the new words that were added to the American lexicon in 2008:

age-doping: the falsification of records, usually a birth certificate, to enable an athlete to compete in sports (an issue that arose with the Chinese women's gymnastic team at the 2008 Olympic games)

hockey mom: a mother who is involved in her children's youth hockey participation; generally considered more aggressive and competitive than a "soccer mom" (coined by Alaska Governor Sarah Palin during the 2008 presidential campaign)

fish pedicure: a cosmetic procedure in which fish eat the dead skin from the bottom of the foot

D.W.T.: driving while texting

hypermiling: an attempt to maximize your car's gas mileage by adjusting the car and your driving techniques to beat the EPA estimates (*The Oxford English Dictionary* rated this the "Word of the Year, 2008.")

tweet: the verb for posting your momentary experience on Twitter,

See Leibovich, 2008, p. 3.

ior to express their sense of belonging to the culture. Rituals both symbolize the culture's coherence by expressing our unity and also create that coherence by enabling each member to feel connected to the culture.

Rituals are typically ceremonial; they are performed at significant times and often in exactly the same way each time. In this way, rituals not only bind people to the specific group of which they are a member but also bind them across generations to past and future members. While many rituals are secular—pledging allegiance to the flag, college graduation ceremonies—rituals are most often associated with religion, where participation in the ritual cements one's sense of belonging to the community and its shared cultural history. Most cultures have specific rituals to mark the specific transitions in a person's life: birth, coming of age, marriage,

Eskimo Words for Snow

You've probably heard that the Eskimo have many different words for snow. It's a myth. Actually, the language of the Inuit (native peoples of the Arctic regions) creates words out of many different ideas, so it seems that they have many words for the same thing. In English, we use separate words in the phrase "the snow under the tree"; an Inuit might express this in one word. In fact, English has more words for different types of snow than most Inuit languages (Pullum, 1991).

Did You Know?

children, and death. It's often through our participation in these rituals that we know how to feel about our stage of life and our place in the community.

Norms

Norms are the rules a culture develops that define how people should act and the consequences of failure to act in the specified ways. Cultural "norms" and cultural "values" are often discussed together; values are the ideas that justify those standards, or norms. Norms prescribe behavior within the culture, and values explain to us what the culture has determined is right and wrong. Norms tell us *how* to behave; values tell us *why*. Norms and values not only guide our own goals and actions but also inform our judgments of others.

The basic set of norms in Western societies was set down in the Ten Commandments and other ancient texts and includes prescriptions to remain humble and religiously obedient to both God and one's parents, as well as normative prohibitions on theft, adultery, murder, and desiring what you don't have. The

Beware of cross–cultural PDAs. In April 2007, a judge in Jaipur, India, issued an arrest warrant for the actor Richard Gere. Why? Because Gere had hugged and kissed Bollywood actress Shilpa Shetty at a televised AIDS benefit. The crowd cheered, and Shetty, herself, thought it was harmless, but effigies of Gere were burned all over the country, and the judge declared that the kiss was "highly sexually erotic" and "transgressed all limits of vulgarity." In India, public displays of affection not only violate customs, but they are against the law.

New Testament is filled with values as well, such as reciprocity ("do unto others as you would have them do unto you") and "let he who is without sin cast the first stone," which implies self-knowledge, restraint, and refusal to judge others.

Like the other components of culture, norms and values vary from place to place. What might be appropriate behavior in one culture, based on its values, might be inappropriate or even illegal in another. While eating together in a restaurant, for example, Americans might feel insulted if they didn't get to order their own meals. Individual choice is very important, and often others (the waiter, our dining companions) will compliment us on our choice. In China, the person at the top of the hierarchy typically orders for everyone, and it is assumed the food will be shared. Individual choice matters little; self-esteem is gained through group participation.

Similarly, in China, when opening a new restaurant, the owner typically will invite local leaders, including police, the tax collector, and political officials, for free meals. It is understood that, in exchange for these free meals, the officials will treat the new business kindly. This is because the culture stresses social reciprocity and mutual obligations to each other. In the United States, however, such behavior would be seen as corruption, attempted bribery; and both the restaurant owner and the officials who accepted such "gifts" would be breaking the law.

Norms and values also vary within cultures. For example, while images of wealth and success may be inspiring to some Americans, Hispanics tend not to approve of overt materialistic displays of success. While Americans over the age of 40 might find it inappropriate for you to text message in a social situation, younger people often feel virtual relationships are just as important and "present" as interpersonal ones right in the same room (Twenge, 2006). Enforcement varies, too. Teenagers, for example, may care deeply about norms and standards of their peers but not about the judgment of others.

Norms also change over time. Not that long ago, norms surrounding the use of telephones included not calling someone or talking on the phone during the dinner hour unless it was an emergency. Now telemarketers target that time slot to call people because they are likely to be home from work, and people routinely talk on cell phones right at the dinner table, even in restaurants. People check voice mail and Facebook and text message each other during college classes (!) and during business meetings, when it used to be considered highly inappropriate to initiate or allow interruptions in these settings, again, except in an emergency. People walk around plugged into iPods and MP3 players even on the job, at museums or other cultural events, and in social groups.

Technology has been a major driver of new norms and new mores over the past several decades. After all, technological inventions have created some entirely new social situations, new kinds of encounters and relationships, which have spawned new social norms and mores to organize them. Think about it—there are sets of informal rules about appropriate behavior on elevators, in airplanes, or at urinals, to name just a few examples. The Internet has spawned a particularly wide range of new norms, mores, and language. "Netiquette" is now so elaborate that book-length manuals are written about it, and magazines frequently offer service features to help their readers avoid a Web faux pas (Table 2.1).

Norms consist of folkways, mores, and laws, depending on their degree of formality in society. **Folkways** are relatively weak and informal norms that are the result of patterns of action. Many of the behaviors we call "manners" or etiquette are folkways. Other people may notice when we break them, but infractions are seldom punished. For example, there are no formal laws that prohibit women guests from wearing white to a wedding, which is informally reserved for the bride alone. But people might think you have bad taste or bad manners, and their informal evaluation is often enough to enforce those unwritten rules.

Mores (pronounced more-ayz) are informal norms about moral behavior that members of a society feel are especially important. These are perceived as more than simple violations of etiquette; they are moral attitudes that are seen as serious even if there are no actual laws that prohibit them. Today, some would argue that showing up for a college interview wearing flip-flops or with hair still wet from a shower violates mores; it doesn't break any laws, but it would probably sink your application.

Each culture develops norms surrounding basic life experiences. For example, table manners—how we dress, the utensils we use, and dining etiquette—vary considerably from one culture to the other.

Laws are norms that have been organized and written down. Breaking these norms involves the disapproval not only of immediate community members but also the agents of the state, who are charged with publishing such norm-breaking behavior. Laws both restrict our activities, prohibiting certain behaviors (like theft, for example), and enhance our experiences by requiring other activities. For example, the Social Security law requires that both employers and employees contribute to their retirement funds, whether they want to or not, so that we will have some income when we retire.

Values

Values are the ethical foundations of a culture, its ideas about right and wrong, good and bad. They are among the most basic lessons a culture can transmit to its young because values constitute what a society thinks about itself. (The process of value transmission is called *socialization,* discussed in Chapter 5.)

As such, values are the foundation for norms, and norms express those values at different levels of complexity and formality. When members of a culture decide that something is right or wrong, they often enact

The Pledge of Allegiance

The flag is a national symbol everywhere, but only the United States has a Pledge of Allegiance. Why? The answer is economic, not patriotic. Originally, the pledge was part of an advertising campaign for a magazine that was selling flags to subscribers. In 1892, President Benjamin Harrison decreed it should be recited daily in schools (to help immigrants adjust to new symbols). It was officially recognized in 1945 and the words "under God" were added in 1954 during the Cold War.

Did You Know?

Table 2.1
Internet Slang

Many of the English speakers on the Web (366 million of them!) use and invent Internet slang—shortcuts and stylized renderings of common expressions. Popular terms include:

L8r	Later			
IRL	In real life			
TY	Thanks			
YW	You're welcome			
TMI	Too much information			
NP	No problem			
O Rly	Oh, really			
OMG	Oh my God		JOOC	Just out of curiosity
zOMG	A variation on OMG (Oh my God)		BTDT	Been there, done that
AFK	Away from keyboard		SCNR	Sorry, could not resist
IMHO	In my humble opinion		W/E	Whatever!
HAND	Have a nice day		GAL	Get a Life
LOL	Laugh out loud		:-)	smile or happy
ROFL	Roll on the floor laughing		:-(	frown or sad
LMAO	Laugh my ass off		:-O	surprised
WURSC	Wow, you are so cool		:-D	open-mouthed smile, "rly" happy

a law to prescribe or proscribe it. Less than 100 years ago, women were not permitted to vote, because they were not considered rational enough to make an informed decision or because, as married women, they were the property of their husbands. Less than 40 years ago, women were prohibited from service alongside men in the nation's military, police forces, and fire departments. Today, our values have changed about women's abilities, and discriminatory laws have been defeated.

Values respond to norms, and changes in our laws are often expected to produce a change in values over time. When our values about racial equality began to change, laws were enacted to prohibit discrimination. These laws were not completely popular when they were first enacted, but over time our values have shifted to better conform to the laws. Seat belt and helmet laws were incredibly unpopular when they were first passed, over significant resistance from both individuals and the automobile manufacturers. But now most Americans conform to these laws, even when there are no police around to watch them.

Even the values we hold are more fluid than we often think. Values are both consistent abstract ethical precepts *and* convenient, fluid, and internally contradictory rationalizations of our actions. Sometimes we consider them before we act; other times we apply them after the fact. In that sense they're more like contradictory childhood aphorisms—"he who hesitates is lost" versus "look before you leap"—than they are the Ten Commandments.

What Are American Values? In the United States, many of our values are contained in the Pledge of Allegiance: political unity in the face of a crisis ("one nation," "indivisible"), religious belief ("under God"), freedom and equality ("with liberty and justice for all"). In his inaugural address in January, 2009, President Barack Obama listed these as the values that define America: "honesty and hard work, courage and fair play, tolerance and curiosity, loyalty and patriotism." And like all such statements, there are inconsistencies, even within the "one nation." For example, to be free implies the absence of restraints on individual behavior, as in doing

We often think of our values as a consistent set of ethical principles that guide all our actions, but the reality is more complex. Anyone who has ever made, but not kept, a New Year's resolution knows that there are often big gaps between our values and our actions. As a result, sociologists point to a difference between "ideal" cultures, the values, norms, and ideals to which we aspire, and "real" cultures, which represent those ideals as we enact them on a daily basis. It turns out we are quite forgiving of our own failures to live up those ideal values, although we are often less forgiving of others' failures. We hold others to higher standards than we hold ourselves. And we also believe that we live closer to our values than others do.

For example, the Pew Research Center, a research and charitable foundation, completed a survey in which Americans were asked about their own values and the values they perceive that others hold. An overwhelming majority of Americans said responsibility (92 percent), family life (91 percent), and friendship

Our Values—and Others' Values

(85 percent) were their primary guiding principles. But they also felt that less than half of other Americans felt that way. Over two-thirds listed generosity (72 percent) and religious faith (68 percent) as guiding principles for themselves, but only about one-fifth (20 percent) for their fellow citizens. By contrast, only 37 percent of these same Americans thought prosperity and wealth were important values for them but for 58 percent of others (Pew, 2007). Perhaps we consider ourselves more moral than other people; perhaps we just let ourselves off the hook more readily. Or perhaps it's a little bit of each.

whatever you please to the environment or underpaying workers in the name of making money. But "justice for all" may require just those constraints so that each person would have an equal chance. "Fair play" implies applying the rules evenly, but "loyalty" may ask us to bend those rules just a little bit to help those to whom we are loyal.

In his famous studies of American values, sociologist Robin Williams Jr. (1970) enumerated a dozen "core" American values. (These are listed in Table 2.2 as "Core Values.") You'll notice that these values are internally inconsistent: The beliefs in equality and group superiority, for example, or humanitarianism and achievement, can be contradictory. In fact, we might even say that Americans hold the opposite of these 12 values at the same time (these are listed as "Opposite Values").

How can we hold contradictory values at the same time? For one thing, we don't apply them all to every situation: We apply values situationally. And we often hold those values more fervently with others than we do with ourselves—"it's true for thee but not for me"—that is, we employ those values strategically, depending on the person and the situation. One of the wonderful things about human beings is that we are able to hold contradictory views: We can believe that "he who hesitates is lost" and caution others to "look before you leap."

Emerging Values. Values aren't timeless; they all have histories. They change. As a result, there may be some values that are emerging now as new values. Some of these may become core values; others may be absorbed or discarded. Those recently observed by sociologists include physical fitness, environmentalism, and diversity/multiculturalism. And yet each of these emerging values may actually contradict others: We want to

Americans both love and distrust the rich and famous. We both emulate them and often take a secret pleasure in their downfall. Here, celebrity Paris Hilton greets fans as she leaves prison, June 2007.

Table 2.2 Core American Values

Core Value (according to Williams, 1970)	Opposite Values	Our Contradictory Values
Achievement and success	Luck and pluck	We value success, but we may not care how one achieves it.
Individualism	Community	Americans may believe in individualism, but we are also a nation of civic-minded volunteers who help their neighbors in times of crisis.
Activity and work	Leisure and cheating	While we value affluence, we often don't really want to work hard to achieve it.
Efficiency and practicality	Luxury	We value being practical, but we also believe that indulging in luxury is a virtue as well as a vice. We like bling.
Science and technology	Religion	We believe that science can save us, but we also believe that salvation can be realized only through religion. Three times as many Americans believe in the virgin birth of Jesus as believe in evolution.
Progress	"Karma"	We believe that everything should be constantly new and improving, that "every day in every way I am getting better and better," and at the same time that everything happens for a reason and that "what goes around comes around."
Material comfort	Distrust the rich	We want to live large but also believe that the rich are immoral and probably unhappy. "Living well is the best revenge," and "money is the root of all evil."
Humanitarianism	Entitlement	We believe in helping our neighbors and value personal kindness and also believe in "looking out for number one." (This is the flip side of Individualism vs. Community.)
Freedom	Tolerance has its limits	Americans believe that everyone should be free, but we also believe they should not be so different from us, and they should express that freedom only where we feel it's appropriate to do so.
Democracy	Security	We believe that the government should represent the people and protect their individual rights but that sometimes those rights need to be curtailed in the name of national security.
Equality	Inequality	We believe that everyone is created equal and entitled to the same rights and also believe that inequality is justified based on different abilities and motivations.
Racism and group superiority	We're all just people	Americans believe that some people are superior to others by birth; at the same time, we do not like to be seen as members of a group (although we don't mind seeing others that way).

stay in shape but do not want to work hard at exercise or diets; we want to protect the environment but not at the expense of developing roads, housing, and extracting natural resources or driving the cars we want to drive; we believe in multiculturalism but oppose political efforts that would force different groups of people to go to school together or live closer to each other. Though we believe that everyone is equal, we increasingly marry people with similar education levels and befriend people whose backgrounds are similar to our own (Brooks, 2004). With more and more women in the workforce, Americans are also pairing up with those people who share the same jobs (Arnold, 2007).

Changing and Contradictory Values. One good example of this difference is Americans' attitudes about homosexuality. Most Americans agree with the statement that homosexuality is "wrong" and have felt that way for the past 40 years. In 1991, the General Social Survey (GSS), perhaps the most definitive ongoing study of Americans' attitudes, found that 71 percent said gay sex was always wrong. By 2006, the percentage of Americans who felt that homosexuality was always wrong had fallen to just under 53 percent—barely a majority.

Yet few would disagree that Americans' attitudes about homosexuality have changed dramatically in those 40 years. The difference is that most Americans are unlikely to apply that "ideal" value to their own interactions. So most Americans may hold an opinion that homosexuality is wrong, but they also believe that their gay or lesbian friend, colleague, or relative should be free to pursue his or her life without discrimination.

On the other hand, the recent visibility of homosexuality—the Supreme Court's decision striking down antisodomy laws, the popularity of gay-themed television shows, the ordination of an openly gay Episcopal bishop, and the debate about states legalizing gay marriage—has led to a slight downturn in support for equality. Support for equality for gays and lesbians seems to stop at the marriage altar.

American attitudes about heterosexual sex often show a similar pattern. In 1972, the GSS found that 49 percent of Americans felt sex before marriage is always wrong. By 2006, that figure had dropped to only 29 percent (Figure 2.1). Yet nonmarital sex has become an accepted feature of American life during the past 25 years. The number of cohabitating couples has grown 1,000 percent in the United States since 1960, with more

Values are often deeply felt, and inspire passionate and symbolic expression. Both supporters and opponents of gay marriage claim that their position is "American" and use the American flag in their protests. Matthew Arnold-Loyd confronted an opponent of gay marriage at an Empire State Pride Agenda rally in April outside the state capitol in Albany.

Figure 2.1 American Attitudes about Nonmarital, Heterosexual Sex, 1972–2006

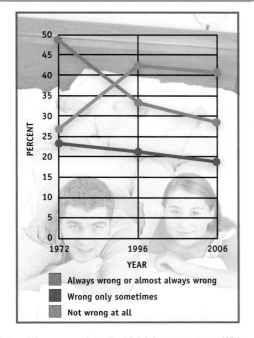

- Always wrong or almost always wrong
- Wrong only sometimes
- Not wrong at all

Notes: Women consistently think it is more wrong; White people are more likely than Black people to say it is wrong; and the upper class is least likely to think it is wrong. (*Source:* General Social Survey Data, 1972–2006.)

than 4.7 million couples currently living together. Between 1965 and 1974, only 10 percent of marriages were preceded by a period of cohabitation. But between 1990 and 1994, that number increased to 57 percent, and it remains there today. Nonmarital sex is a standard plot element routinely portrayed in American TV programs, movies, books, even commercials, with little public outcry.

There are two consequences of holding such contradictory and inconsistent values. For one thing, it means that values are less the guiding principles of all our actions and more a sort of collection of attitudes we can hold situationally to justify and rationalize our beliefs and actions. And it also means that we become a deeply divided nation, in which clusters of attitudes seem to cohere around two separate poles. In the 2004 presidential election, these were the "red" states (those that voted for George W. Bush) and the "blue states" (those that voted for John Kerry).

Sometimes expressed as a "culture war" between the left and the right, liberals and conservatives, these clusters suggest that the United States is a deeply and fundamentally divergent society, in which attitudes and behaviors tend to revolve around two opposing positions. Many different groups may also hold different sets of values.

Cultural Expressions

Cultures are the sets of symbols and rituals that unite groups of people, enable them to feel part of something bigger and more enduring than just their own individual existence. Despite the remarkable diversity in the world's cultures, they also share certain features in common.

Universality and Localism

Culture is both universal and local. Every culture has families, legal systems, and religion. All cultures engage in sports and music, dancing and jokes. All cultures prescribe some forms of bodily rituals—from adorning the body to styling the hair to transforming the body. The specific forms of these universals may vary from one culture to another, but all cultures exhibit these forms.

The anthropologist George Murdock (1945) identified 67 **cultural universals**— that is, rituals, customs, and symbols—that are evident in all societies (Table 2.3). What purpose do these rituals serve that they would appear everywhere? Another anthropologist, A. R. Radcliffe-Brown (1952), argued that these cultural universals permit the society to function smoothly and continuously. Other sociologists have disputed the inevitability of some universals, arguing that some may have been imposed from outside through conquest or even cross-cultural contact.

Cultural universals are broad and basic categories, allowing for significant variation as well. Although all cultures manifest religious beliefs, some may lead to behaviors that are tolerant and peace loving, while others may lead to violence and war. Cultural universals are expressed locally, experienced at the level of families, communities, and regions in ways that connect us not only to large and anonymous groups like our country but also to smaller, more immediate groups. Culture is not *either* universal or local; rather, to the sociologist, culture is *both* universal *and* local. Sometimes we feel our connection more locally and resent efforts to connect us to larger organizations. And then, often at times of crisis like September 11, 2001, Americans put aside their cultural differences and feel passionately connected.

High Culture and Popular Culture

Typically, when we hear the word *culture,* we think of an adjective describing someone (a "cultured" person) or a possession, as in a line in a song by Paul Simon, "The man ain't got no culture." In the common usage, *culture* refers to having refined aesthetic sensibilities, knowing fine wines, classical music, opera, and great works of literature. That is, the word *culture* is often synonymous with what we call *high culture*. High culture attracts audiences drawn from more affluent and largely White groups, as any visit to a major art museum will attest.

High culture is often contrasted with "popular culture," the culture of the masses, the middle and working class. **Popular culture** includes a wide variety of popular music, nonhighbrow forms of literature (from dime novels to comic books), any forms of spectator sports, and other popular forms of entertainment, like television, movies, and video games. Again, sociologists are interested less in what sorts of cultural activities are classified as high or low and more interested in the relationships between those levels, who gets to decide what activities are classified as high or low, and how individuals negotiate their way through both dimensions. And sociologists are interested in the way that certain cultural forms shift their position, from low to high or high to low. Notice, for example, how comic books have been the subject of major museum shows in recent years, and they are now being seen as high culture *and* popular culture. "I get so tired of people saying 'this is classical' and 'this is jazz,' " said noted pianist Jean-Yves Thibaudet. "At the time of Chopin, everything was pop."

This contrast is often value laden, as if it is somehow morally superior to attend an opera sung in a language you do not understand than it is to go see a performance by the Dixie Chicks, or somehow better to view modern art in a museum than to watch NASCAR on television. (Or better to do anything than to watch television!) The split between high culture and popular culture is

Table 2.3
Cultural Universals

Contemporary anthropologists have identified these categories of cultural universals:

1. *Material Culture*—food, clothing (and adornment of the body), tools and weapons, housing and shelter, transportation, personal possessions, household articles

2. *The Arts, Play, and Recreation*—folk art, fine arts, standards of beauty and taste

3. *Language and Nonverbal Communication*—nonverbal communication, language

4. *Social Organization*—societies, families, kinship systems

5. *Social Control*—governmental institutions, rewards, and punishments

6. *Conflict and Warfare*

7. *Economic Organization*—trade and exchange, production and manufacturing, property, division of labor, standard of living

8. *Education*—formal and informal education

9. *World View*—belief systems, religion

(*Source:* George P. Murdock, "On the Universals of Culture," in Linton, *The Science of Man in the World Crisis* (1945); *Universals of Culture*, Alice Ann Cleveland, Jean Craven, and Maryanne Danfelser: Intercom, 92/93.)

often coded in our language—some people "see films" and others "watch movies." Other linguistic codes are also used; for example, only the upper class uses the word "summer" as a verb, as in, "We summer in Maine." One rarely claims to "summer" in Toledo.

Sociologists approach this divide between high culture and popular culture as, itself, a sociological issue. French sociologist Pierre Bourdieu (1984) argued that different groups possess what he called "cultural capital," a resource that those in the dominant class can use to justify their dominance. **Cultural capital** is any "piece" of culture—

an idea, an artistic expression, a form of music or literature—that a group can use as a symbolic resource to exchange with others. If I have access to this form of culture, and you want to have access to it, then I can "exchange" my access to access to those forms of capital that you have.

If there is a divide between high culture and popular culture, Bourdieu argues, then the dominant class can set the terms of training so that high culture can be properly appreciated. That is, the proper appreciation of high culture requires the acceptance of certain rules, certain sets of criteria for evaluation. And this establishes certain cultural

The actress Lily Tomlin used to delight her audiences with a clever critique of this distinction. Portraying a homeless "bag lady," she professed confusion about modern culture. She held up a picture of a big Campbell's soup can (on right). "Soup," she said. Then she held up a poster of the Andy Warhol painting of that same soup can—a poster from the Museum of Modern Art. "Art," she said. Back and forth she went. "Soup." "Art." "Soup." "Art." Confusing, huh? The soup can sells for $.89 at the supermarket; the painting of the soup can (at left) sold for $11.7 million at auction.

elites with privileged knowledge: the proper ways to like something. These elites are cultural "gatekeepers" who permit entry into high culture circles only to those whom the elites have deemed worthy of entry. Such gatekeeping is far less about aesthetic taste and far more about social status.

Actually, both high and popular culture consumption have such rules for appreciation. For example, imagine someone who doesn't know these rules attending the opera in the way he or she might attend a U2 concert: singing along loudly with each aria, holding up a cell phone to take pictures, standing on his or her chair, and swaying to the music. Now, imagine an opera buff attending a U2 concert, sitting politely, applauding only at the end of the concert, and calling out "Bravo!" to the band. Both concertgoers will have gotten it wrong—both of them will have failed to express the appropriate ways to show they like something.

Sociology and Our World

The High Culture– Low Culture Divide

The divide between popular culture and high culture is not nearly as clear as we like to think. In fact, the strict separation is bad history, because many of those cultural products that are now enshrined in "high culture" were originally popular forms of entertainment. Take Shakespeare, for example. Did you know that originally, Shakespeare's plays were performed for mass audiences, who would shout out for the performers to do encores of their favorite scenes? In fact, Shakespeare himself added a little blood and gore to his tragedies to appeal to the mass audience. Opera also was originally a mass entertainment, which was appropriated by music critics in the nineteenth century, when they developed rules for appreciating it that excluded all but the richest and most refined (see Levine, 1988).

Some popular culture can become high culture. Recall Andy Warhol's painting of a soup can or "designer" jeans. Similarly, jazz was initially denounced as racially based, sexually charged popular culture. Now some people believe you need a PhD in music theory just to "appreciate" John Coltrane or Miles Davis.

Equally, some elements of high culture can become part of popular culture. For example, various fashion styles of upper-class life—collared "polo" shirts, even those decorated with little polo players—are worn by large numbers of people who would never set foot in the upper-class arena of the polo field.

The sociologist tries to make no value judgment about which form of culture one appreciates—actually, virtually all of us combine an appreciation of both popular and high culture at various times and places. And both carry specific norms about value and criteria for evaluating whether something is good or not. To the sociologist, what is interesting is how certain cultural forms become established as high or popular and how they change, which groups promote which forms of culture, and the debates we have about whether something is really art—or a can of soup.

Forms of Popular Culture

Popular culture refers not only to the forms of high culture (like art, music, or literature) that are enjoyed by the middle and working classes. Popular culture also refers to those objects, ideas, and values that people may hold at a specific moment. While we have seen that high culture changes, one of popular culture's defining qualities is its fluidity: It is constantly changing, constantly establishing new trends and discarding old ones. We can differentiate between two types of popular culture trends, fads and fashions.

Fads. **Fads** are defined by being short-lived, highly popular, and widespread behaviors, styles, or modes of thought. Often they are associated with other cultural forms. They are often created and marketed to generate "buzz" because if they catch on they can be enormously profitable. Sociologist John Lofland (1993) identified four types of fads:

1. *Objects.* These are objects people buy because they are suddenly popular, whether or not they have any use or intrinsic value. Hula hoops, yo-yos, poodle skirts, Pet Rocks, Beanie Babies, Cabbage Patch Kids, Furbies, Pokemon or Yu-Gi-Oh! trading cards, and various children's confections are often good examples of object fads. As are Crocs, the colored plastic clog-style shoes.
2. *Activities.* These are behaviors that suddenly everybody seems to be doing, and you decide to do it also, or else you'll feel left out. These can include various risk-taking behaviors—car surfing—or sports like rock climbing, or leisure activities like Sudoku. Dances like the moonwalk or the twist and the watusi are activity fads. Diets are top examples of activity fads today.

3. *Ideas*. Sometimes an idea will spread like wildfire, and then, just as suddenly, slip out of view. The Celestine prophesy, beliefs in UFOs, various New Age ideas, and "everything you needed to know you learned in kindergarten" are examples of idea fads.

4. *Personalities*. Some celebrities burst on the scene for their accomplishments, for example, athletes (Tiger Woods, Lebron James) or rock stars (Lil' Wayne, Bono, Eminem). Yet others are simply "famous for being famous"—everyone knows about them and seems to care about them, but few actually know what they've done to merit the attention. "Celebutantes" like Paris Hilton, Kim Kardashian, and Jessica Simpson are examples of the latter.

5. *Internet Memes*. Today there are also Internet fads, which suddenly circulate wildly and/or draw millions of hits through the World Wide Web. Internet memes, defined as "self-propagating units of culture," include people (like Mr. T, the A-Team actor who is considered one of the earliest Internet fads), audio clips, animation segments, or video clips such as "Ken Lee," a short clip from the auditions of the Bulgarian version of *American Idol*, which drew over 10 million in its first six months in 2008, or "Rick Roll," a homemade karaoke music video that drew more than 15 million hits that year. More generally, various websites and blogs can be Internet fads, when they quite suddenly become "in" places to read and post.

Fashion. A **fashion** is a behavior, style, or idea that is more permanent than a fad. It may originate as a fad and become more widespread and more acceptable over time. For example, the practice of tattooing, once associated with lower-class and even dangerous groups, became a fad in the 1990s but is today an accepted part of fashion, with over one-fourth of Americans under 25 years old having at least one tattoo.

Fashions involve widespread acceptance of the activity, whether it is music, art, literature, clothing, or sports. Because fashions are less fleeting than fads, they involve the cultural institutions that mediate our relationships with culture. Fashions may become institutionalized and aggressively marketed to ensure that people know that unless you subscribe to a particular fashion, you will be seen as an outsider. While fads may appear to bubble up from below, fashions are often deliberately created. (In reality, fads are also likely to have been created.)

The Politics of Popular Culture

Most cultural elites are culturally conservative (regardless of how they vote or what sorts of policies they favor). That is, they wish to conserve the cultural forms that are currently in place and the hierarchies of value that are currently given to them. The status quo, as Bourdieu argued, reproduces their cultural dominance. As a result, changes in popular culture typically come from the margins, not the center—from those groups who have been excluded from the cultural elites and thus develop cultural expressions that are, at least in part, forms of cultural resistance.

Take clothing, for example. Blue jeans were once a workingman's attire. In fact, Levi Strauss invented blue jeans to assist gold miners in California in their muddy work. Appropriated by the youth culture in the 1960s as a form of clothing rebellion against the bland conformity of 1950s campus fashion, blue jeans were considered a fad—until kids' parents started to wear them. Then fashion designers got into the act, and the fad became a fashion. Today these symbols of a youthful rejection of materialism can cost up to $500 a pair.

Trends in clothing, music, and other tastes in popular culture often originate today among three marginalized groups: African Americans, young people, and gay men and lesbians. As we've seen, blue jeans were once a youthful fashion

Fads are often short-lived and wildly popular. Over 5 million pet rocks were sold in six months in 1975—and celebrities attended shows to learn how to "train" and "care for" their pets.

Global hip hop scene: A group of rappers and their audience at the Shelter, a nightclub in Shanghai. What is seen as "rebellious" in one culture can transform into another culture's "style." (A note on symbols: Note the New York Yankees hat, which has become a universal symbol of urban style.)

television industries and the Internet, it is taking hold among youths seeking expressions of resistance and authenticity around the world (Chang, 2007; Pennycock, 2007). The music, dance, and clothing styles have been adopted and adapted by young people in countries across Northern and Western Europe; in Asia, including South Korea and Japan; as well as in African countries such as Senegal, Middle Eastern countries like Lebanon, and in Latin American countries including Brazil, Chile, and Argentina.

Sometimes culture is exported deliberately. Popular culture—movies, music, books, television programs—is the second largest category of American export to the rest of the world (the first is aircraft). Large corporations like Nike, Disney, Coca-Cola, and Warner Brothers work very hard to ensure that people in other countries associate American products with hip and trendy fashions in the States.

Some see this trend as a form of **cultural imperialism,** which is the deliberate imposition of one's country's culture on another country. The global spread of American fashion, media, and language (English as the world's lingua franca in culture, arts, business, and technology) is often seen as an imposition of American values and ideas as well as products. Cultural imperialism is not usually imposed by governments that require citizens to consume some products and not others. It is cultural in that these products become associated with a lifestyle to which citizens of many countries aspire. But it is criticized as imperialist in that the profits from those sales are returned to the American corporation, not the home country.

On the other hand, cultural transfer is not nearly as one directional as many critics contend. There are many cultural trends among Americans that originated in other countries. Imported luxury cars, soccer, reggae, wine, beer, and food fads all originate in other countries and become associated with exotic lifestyles elsewhere.

And sometimes, global cultural trends emerge from below, without deliberate marketing efforts. In the 1970s, when I was doing my dissertation research in Paris, I kept seeing young men wearing navy blue V-neck sweaters with UCLA imprinted on the chest. Since I was a student at Berkeley, UCLA was familiar (even though a rival), and so one day I approached one guy and asked, in French, if he had gone to UCLA. He looked blankly at me. I asked again,

statement of rebellion. Many men's fashions in clothing or accessories often have their origins among gay men (clothing styles, pierced ears) or Black inner-city youth (hoodie sweatshirts, skater shoes and pants). White suburban embrace of hip-hop and rap echoes the same embrace of soul and R&B in the 1960s (see the movie *Animal House*), or even the same embrace of jazz and bebop in successive generations. Clever marketers are constantly on the lookout for trends among the marginalized groups that can be transformed into luxury items. If you want to know what White suburban boys will be wearing and what music they'll be listening to in five years, take a look at what Black teenagers or gay men are wearing and listening to today.

The Globalization of Popular Culture

It's not just American teenagers who are dressing in the latest fashions. Tourists visiting in other countries are often surprised at how closely the fashion styles resemble those in the United States. Interestingly, this occurs both through the deliberate export of specific cultural items and also through the ways in which cultural forms of resistance are expressed by young people and minorities. For example, hip-hop culture, which originated among Blacks in American inner cities, has gone global. Spread by the global music and

pointing to his sweater. He shrugged his shoulders and said what sounded like "oooo-klah?" a reasonable French phonetic pronunciation. He had no idea it was a university, but it was simply the fashion among French students to wear "American-style" sweaters. Even today, you can see sweatshirts on Europeans that advertise incorrectly "University of Yale" or "California University."

Culture as a Tool Kit

The social movement of popular culture from margin to center reveals a final element in the sociological approach to culture. Culture is not a thing one does or does not have, nor is it a level of refinement of taste and sensibility. It is not a constant throughout our lives, and it doesn't simply evolve and grow as we mature and develop.

Culture is a complex set of behaviors, attitudes, and symbols that individuals *use* in their daily relationships with others. It is, as sociologist Ann Swidler (1986) calls it, a "tool kit," a sort of repertoire of habits, skills, and styles from which people construct their identities. Culture is not passively inherited, transmitted

Cultural heroes and artifacts are often exported to other societies, which can incorporate them into their own frameworks. Soccer fans in the U.S. or Great Britain may "worship" David Beckham as a star athlete, but in Thailand, they can literally worship at his religious shrine.

from one generation to the next through various institutions, so that each generation eventually obtains all the requisite symbols, linguistic skills, and values of the society. Culture is diverse, and one uses different parts of it in different circumstances with different groups for different reasons.

Cultural Change

Cultures are dynamic, constantly changing. Sometimes that rate of change may seem faster or slower than at other times. And sometimes change feels sudden and dramatic, producing conflict between those who support change and those who resist it. Culture wars often are symbolic clashes—of ideas, symbols, values—between groups who support certain changes and those who want to resist change. And while some change is inevitable, not every change is necessarily beneficial.

Although cultures are constantly changing, all the elements of culture do not change at the same time or in the same ways. In some cases, as we saw, changes among some marginalized groups become fashions for the mainstream after a period of time. It is often the case that changes in material culture—the level of technology, material resources—change more rapidly than changes in cultural institutions like the family or religion. At those moments, societies experience what sociologist William Ogburn called **culture lag**—the gap between

technology and material culture and its social beliefs and institutions.

At those times, the beliefs and values of a society have to catch up to the changes in technology or material life (Ogburn, [1922] 1966). For example, changes in communication technology have dramatically transformed social life, but our values have failed to keep pace. Cell phones, text messaging, and instant messaging, combined with e-mail and other Internet-based modes of communication, have dramatically altered the ways in which people interact. Yet the cultural mores that govern such interaction—etiquette, manners, norms governing appropriate behavior—have not yet caught up to the technology. Occasionally, this results in confusion, discomfort, or conflict. We're constantly creating new norms to respond to these changes—like laws regarding cell phone use while driving or policies on text messaging in class.

Culture lag is a relatively gradual process by which nonmaterial elements of culture catch up with material culture. In this instance, we can also speak of **cultural diffusion,** which means the spreading of new ideas through a society, independent of population movement. As the impact of the technological innovation ripples through the rest of society, eventually a new equilibrium will be reached. Then all goes smoothly until the next technological breakthrough. If you can, ask your own grandparents what they think of twitter, Facebook, and iPhone apps, and you'll get the idea.

But sometimes, technological breakthroughs also enable groups within a society, or an entire society, to impose its values on others. Cultures can change dramatically and suddenly by conquest as well as by diffusion. The impact is often stark, sudden, and potentially lethal. Sometimes conquest can deliberately transform the culture of the colonized, as when missionaries force conquered groups to convert to the religion of the conqueror or be put to death. In those instances, the entire belief system of the culture, its foundation, is dismantled and replaced by a foreign one.

In other cases, it is less immediate or direct but no less profound. The first European colonists who came to the New World in the sixteenth century were able to subdue the indigenous peoples of North America by superior technology (like muskets and artillery), by the manipulation of religious beliefs about the potential benevolent foreigners, and by the coincidental importation of diseases, like syphilis, which killed millions more Native Americans than the colonists' bullets. It is possible that other food-borne diseases, like avian flu and mad cow disease, could have an almost equally devastating impact on local cultures today.

Intercultural contact need not be accomplished through force. Today, global cultural

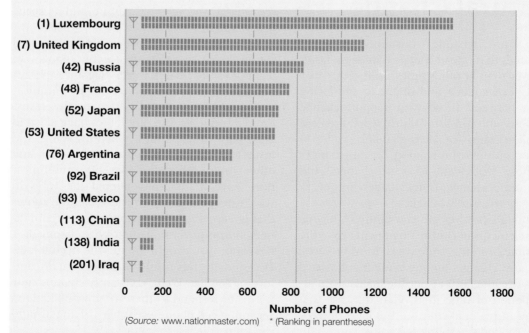

U.S. / Them

Material Culture: Inclusion and Inequality

Culture is not just about attitudes and values but also about access to the tool kit that enables cultural communication. Some cultural forms that are indispensable means of communication in one place may be virtually unheard of in other places.

Number of Cell Phones per Thousand People
(The number of phones is often higher than the number of people)*

- (1) Luxembourg
- (7) United Kingdom
- (42) Russia
- (48) France
- (52) Japan
- (53) United States
- (76) Argentina
- (92) Brazil
- (93) Mexico
- (113) China
- (138) India
- (201) Iraq

0   200   400   600   800   1000   1200   1400   1600   1800

Number of Phones

(*Source:* www.nationmaster.com)   * (Ranking in parentheses)

1. What does the incidence of cell phone ownership mean to a sociologist?

2. In what ways does cell phone use tell us something about the culture we are studying? What other measures might we use?

forms are emerging that diffuse across national boundaries and are incorporated, unevenly and incompletely, into different national and local cultures. These often result in odd juxtapositions—a consultant in rural Africa talking on a cell phone or downloading information from a laptop standing next to a woman carrying a pail of water on her head. But these are no odder than a scene you might well have witnessed in many parts of the United States just 70 years ago—cars speeding past homes with outhouses and outdoor water pumps. Culture spreads unevenly and unequally and often is accompanied by significant opposition and conflict.

Culture in the Twenty-First Century

Concepts such as culture, values, and norms help orient the sociologist, providing a way to understand the world he or she is trying to study. They provide the context, the "field" in which myriad individual experiences, motivations, and behaviors take place. They are necessary to situate our individual experiences; they are the concepts by which sociologists connect individual biography and history. They are the concepts that we'll use to understand the forces that hold society together and those that drive it apart.

Cultures are constantly changing—from within and through their contact with other cultures. A global culture is emerging of shared values and norms, shared technologies enabling common behaviors and attitudes. Increasingly, we share habits, fashions, language, and technology with a wider range of people than ever in human history. We are in that sense all becoming "one." And, at the same time, in our daily lives, we often resist the pull of these global forces and remain steadfastly loyal to those ties that bind us to local cultural forms—kinship and family, our ethnic group, religion, or community.

The cultural diversity that defines most industrialized societies also defines American society, and that diversity will continue to provide moments of *both* combination *and* collision, of separation and synthesis. Most people are rarely "all-American" or feel completely like members of one ethnic or racial subculture. We're both. To be a hyphenated American—an Asian-American or Italian-American, for example—is a way of expressing the fact that we don't have to choose. Sometimes you may feel more "Italian" than American, and other times you may feel more "American" than Italian. And then, finally, there are times when you feel specifically Italian-American, poised somewhere between, distinct and unique, and yet not completely fitting into either. As Bono sings in the U2 song "One": "We're one but we're not the same."

Chapter Review

1. Culture

Culture is a uniquely human phenomenon. Both **material culture** and **nonmaterial culture** are common to a group and shared by its members, and both shape society. Cultures differ from one another and even change over time, which may be unsettling. When confronted with **cultural diversity** we may experience **culture shock. Ethnocentrism** is a common response to different cultures, but sociologists strive for **cultural relativism.** There are subgroups within cultures, and these subcultures often provide an important source of identity for members. Developing in instances when members are different from the mainstream culture and consequently experience prejudice, yet also possess social power, a **subculture** is embedded within, yet distinct from, the larger, dominant culture. A **counterculture** is a subculture that is in opposition to the larger culture and hence often threatening to the dominant culture.

culture Both the material basis for social life and the sets of values and ideals that we understand to define morality, good and evil, appropriate and inappropriate. (p. 36)

material culture The things people make and the things they use to make them—the tools they use, the physical environment they inhabit (forests, beaches, mountains, fertile farmlands, or harsh desert). (p. 36)

nonmaterial culture Often just called "culture," the ideas and beliefs that people develop about their lives and their world. (p. 36)

cultural diversity Describes the vast differences between the cultures of the world as well as the differences in belief and behavior that exist within cultures. (p. 36)

culture shock A feeling of disorientation when the cultural markers that we rely on to help us know where we are and how to act have suddenly changed. (p. 36)

ethnocentrism The use of one's own culture as the reference point by which to evaluate other cultures; it often depends on or leads to the belief that one's own culture is superior to others. (p. 37)

cultural relativism A position that all cultures are equally valid in the experience of their own members. (p. 38)

subculture Group within a society that creates its own norms and values distinct from the mainstream and usually its own separate social institutions as well. (p. 39)

counterculture Subculture that identifies itself through its difference and opposition to the dominant culture. (p. 39)

2. Elements of Culture

All cultures share six basic elements: material culture, symbols, language, rituals, norms, and values. The content and nature of each of these vary widely, change over time, and are often unique to the culture, providing great diversity across cultures. Material culture (see above) arises as a result of solving the basic problem of survival and includes everything created and used for meeting needs, including the environment itself. Nonmaterial culture also varies widely. A **symbol** conveys meaning within a culture, while **language** transmits culture, and, according to the **Sapir-Whorf hypothesis,** shapes perception. **Ritual** binds members of a culture together, often transcending time. A **norm** sets the standards or expectations for situation-specific behavior. Norms are of varying types, depending on the formality, and sanctions for violating them. A **folkway** is informal, **mores** are stronger and informally enforced, and **laws** are codified and formally enforced. A **value** captures what a culture finds desirable and may be in contradiction with other aspects of the culture, including other values.

symbol Anything—an idea, a marking, a thing—that carries additional meanings beyond itself to others who share in the culture. Symbols come to mean what they do only in a culture; they would have no meaning to someone outside. (p. 40)

language An organized set of symbols by which we are able to think and communicate with others; the chief vehicle by which human beings create a sense of self. (p. 41)

Sapir-Whorf hypothesis A theory that language shapes our reality because it gives us a way to talk about the categories of life that we experience. (p. 42)

ritual Enactment by which members of a culture engage in a routine behavior to express their sense of belonging to the culture. (p. 43)

norm One of the rules a culture develops that defines how people should act and the consequences of failure to act in the specified ways. (p. 44)

folkway One of the relatively weak and informal norms that is the result of patterns of action. Many of the behaviors we call "manners" are folkways. (p. 45)

mores Informally enforced norms based on strong moral values, which are viewed as essential to the proper functioning of a group. (p. 45)

law One of the norms that has been organized and written down. Breaking these norms involves the disapproval not only of immediate community members but also of the agents of the state, who are charged with punishing such norm-breaking behavior. (p. 45)

value If norms tell us how to behave, values tell us why. Values constitute what a society thinks about itself and so are among the most basic lessons that a culture can transmit to its young. (p. 45)

3. Cultural Expressions

All societies have **cultural universals,** although whether they always develop without outside influence is unclear. There is great local variety in the way in which these broad categories are realized. Sociologists go beyond the content of culture to explore the construction of meaning surrounding it; for example, how **popular culture** has less **cultural capital** than high culture, with elites investing high culture with status and controlling access and consumption. Popular culture is more dynamic than high culture, with passing **fads** and **fashions.** The global distribution of popular culture has been seen as **cultural imperialism,** in which money flows out of a country to add to the wealth of a foreign corporation. Cultural transfer flows both ways, with people using culture as a "tool kit" to construct their selves.

cultural universal One of the rituals, customs, and symbols that are evident in all societies. (p. 50)

popular culture The culture of the masses, the middle and working classes, that includes a wide variety of popular music, nonhighbrow forms of literature, any forms of spectator sports, and other popular forms of entertainment, like television, movies, and video games. (p. 50)

cultural capital French sociologist Pierre Bourdieu's term for the cultural articles—ideas, artistic expressions, forms of music or literature—that function as resources that people in the dominant class can use to justify their dominance. (p. 51)

fad Short-lived, highly popular, and widespread behavior, style, or mode of thought. (p. 52)

fashion A behavior, style, or idea that is more permanent and often begins as a fad. (p. 53)

cultural imperialism The deliberate imposition of one country's culture on another country. (p. 54)

4. Cultural Change

Culture is dynamic, always changing, but different aspects change at different rates, so that conflict, discontent, or dissatisfaction with cultural changes is not unusual. With **cultural diffusion,** there is often **culture lag.** Technological advancements in particular result in fast cultural changes, as do contacts with outside cultures, which have historically often been the result of technological advances leading to subsequent conquest or colonization.

cultural diffusion The spreading of new ideas through a society, independent of population movement. (p. 55)

culture lag The relatively gradual process by which non-material elements of culture catch up with changes in material culture and technology. (p. 55)

5. Culture in the Twenty-First Century

Even as technology pulls us into a global culture, our identities remain bound up with local forms of culture in multicultural societies. This dichotomy of cultural membership is not either/or; we are both locally diverse and globally unified.

Self-Test: Check Your Understanding

1. Identify which of the following is true, according to the text:
   a. Members of a subculture have no power.
   b. Members of a counterculture are in opposition to the dominant culture.
   c. Members of a subculture appear indistinguishable from the larger culture.
   d. Members of a counterculture wish to be members of the dominant culture.
2. Which of the following is the most dynamic, fluid, quickest to change, and of shortest duration?
   a. Fad
   b. Fashion
   c. High culture
   d. All of these are equally dynamic and of equal duration.
3. Of the following, which did the text identify as an agent of great change and cultural diffusion?
   a. Religion   c. Language
   b. Art   d. Technology
4. The relatively gradual process by which nonmaterial elements of culture catch up with changes in material culture is known as
   a. cultural diffusion.   c. cultural relativism.
   b. cultural lag.   d. culture shock.

5. A nation's flag is an example of a
   a. value.   c. folkway.
   b. norm.   d. symbol.
6. Coca-Cola is available worldwide, although the company's home is in Atlanta, Georgia. Critics of this brand's popularity overseas, which results in the transfer of revenue from local economies to America, accuse Coca-Cola of
   a. multiculturalism.   c. cultural imperialism.
   b. cultural diffusion.   d. ethnocentrism.
7. The unsettled or disoriented feeling experienced by a traveler to another land, where all the habits are unfamiliar, is known as:
   a. ethnocentrism.   c. cultural imperialism.
   b. culture shock.   d. cultural diffusion.
8. Many cultures have a traditional ceremony in the days or months following the birth of a baby, recognizing and welcoming the child into the group. These events are examples of
   a. norms.   c. rituals.
   b. folkways.   d. laws.

Self-Test Answers: 1. b, 2. a, 3. d, 4. b, 5. d, 6. c, 7. b, 8. c

Integrate and Explore: Points to Consider

1. Identify a technology that has resulted in cultural diffusion and discuss the changes that have occurred in your culture as a result. Which aspects have changed the most as a result? Which have changed the least? Where do you see the greatest cultural lag?
2. Discuss how multiculturalism within a society relates to the values held by the culture. Will the values of a subculture necessarily be in accord with the mainstream culture, or might they be in contradiction? Give an example of each.
3. Choose a fad or a fashion that was initially used to express diversity or a unique cultural identity and discuss the subculture where it developed. In what ways did members of that subculture differ from the mainstream

culture? How did it spread to the mainstream culture? Has it become a part of global culture? How has the meaning changed?

succeed with PEARSON mysoclab

Self-scoring practice tests, flashcards for learning key terms, streaming audio of the entire text, and multimedia, including:

Watch—*Pledge of Allegiance Controversy*
MySocLibrary—Horace Miner, *Body Ritual Among the Nacirema*
MySocLibrary—Joel Charon, *What Does It Mean to be Human?*

3

Society:
Interactions, Groups,
and Organizations

In 2001, Harvard political scientist Robert Putnam proclaimed the end of American community. We were estranged from our neighbors, geographically separate from our families, and maintained little civic sense of connectedness. Where once America was a nation of joiners—clubs, fraternal lodges, community organizations—we were now, as he put it in the title of his book, "bowling alone."

And yet nearly every day, we receive a request from someone we barely know to be our friend on Facebook or MySpace or LinkedIn—

or any of the dozens of new networking sites. It's become so common that the word "friend" has become a verb, as in "Do you want to friend me?" A stroll across most campuses, even Professor Putnam's beloved Harvard, reveals a majority of students wearing some clothing item that indicates their community membership—mostly school logos but also allegiances to particular rock bands, sports teams, fashion designers, or skateboard makers.

So which is it? Are we a nation of disconnected atoms, drifting aimlessly without the traditional anchors of community and family, or are we completely connected into new communities via our educational communities, athletic allegiances, or fashion tastes?

Sociologists think it's both. It's true that the traditional ties of civic engagement have waned, but our sense of allegiances and identification with groups outside of ourselves has not diminished. It's been transferred from those traditional anchors of community and family to our consumer tastes and leisure activities.

In the 1960s, sociologist David Riesman called our society a "lonely crowd." Perhaps the flip side is also true and we are also "intimate strangers" (see Rubin, 1983). Sociology's chief concern is to understand the constituent elements of society—the immediate interactions, the groups we

"So which is it? Are we a nation of disconnected atoms, drifting aimlessly without the traditional anchors of community and family, or are we completely connected into new communities via our educational communities, athletic allegiances, or fashion tastes? Sociologists think it's both."

belong to, the networks that connect us, and the organizations in which we work and live. These are the core units of society.

Society: Putting Things in Context

Sociology is a way of seeing that can be described as "contextualizing"—that is, sociologists try to understand the social *contexts* in which our individual activity takes place, the other people with whom we interact, the dynamics of interaction, and the institutions in which that activity takes place. Sociologists are less concerned with the psychological motivations for your actions and more concerned with the forces that shape your motivation, the forces that push you in one direction and pull you in another, other people with whom you interact, and meanings you derive from the action. Understanding social behavior is a constant process of "contextualizing" that behavior—placing it in different frameworks to better understand its complexity. (The importance of the term *context* cannot be overstated. The American Sociological Association's magazine, designed to present sociology's message to the wider public outside the field, is called *Contexts*. When this title was announced, the universal praise among sociologists indicated a collective nod of understanding.)

The chief context in which we try to place individuals, locate their identity, and chart their experiences is generally called *society*. But what is this thing called "society" that we study?

Some people don't even believe it exists. In 1987, British Prime Minister Margaret Thatcher caused an uproar when she told an interviewer, "There's no such thing as society. There are individual men and women, and there are families" (Keay, 1987). Is society simply a collection of individuals, or is it something more than that?

Society can be defined as *an organized collection of individuals and institutions, bounded by space in a coherent territory, subject to the same political authority, and organized through a shared set of cultural expectations and values.* But what does that mean? Let's look at each element:

- *Organized collection of individuals.* Society isn't a random collection but purposive and organized.

- *And institutions.* Society is composed not only of individuals but also all the institu-

tions in which we find ourselves. What sociologists call a **social institution** is an organized and established set of social relationships and networks, bounded by relatively fixed boundaries, that meet specific social needs. Family, economy, and school are all examples of institutions. (We will discuss this further below.)

- *Bounded by space in a coherent territory.* This adds a spatial dimension to society. Society exists someplace, not only in our imaginations.

- *Subject to the same political authority.* Everyone in the same place is also subject to the same rules.

- *Organized through a shared set of cultural expectations and values.* Our behaviors are not only governed by what people expect of us but also motivated by common values.

The definition of society here is somewhat top heavy—that is, it rests on large-scale structures and institutions, territorial arrangements, and uniform political authority. But society doesn't arrive fully formed from out of the blue: Societies are made, constructed, built from the bottom up as well. In this chapter, we will look at the basic building blocks of society from the smallest elements (interactions) to coherent sets of interactions with particular members (groups) and within particular contexts (organizations). From the ground up, societies are composed of *structured social interactions*. Again, let's look at each of these terms individually:

- *Structured* means that our actions, our interactions with others, do not occur in a vacuum. *Structured* refers to the contexts in which we find ourselves—everything from our families and communities, to religious groups, to states and countries, and even to groups of countries. We act in the world in ways that are structured, which makes them (for the most part) predictable and orderly; our actions are, in large part, bound by norms and motivated by values.

- *Social* refers to the fact that we don't live alone; we live in groups, families, networks. Sociologists are interested in the social dynamics of our interaction, how we interact with others.

- *Interaction* refers to the ways we behave in relation to others. Even when we are just sitting around in our homes or dorm rooms with a bunch of friends, "doing nothing," we are interacting in structured, patterned ways.

These two definitions are complementary; they are the micro- and the macrolevels of society. Sociologists believe that society is greater than the sum of its parts. Sociologists examine those parts, from the individual to the largest institutions and organizations. Sociologists have discovered that even a small group of friends makes different decisions than the individual members would alone. And it doesn't end there. Groups are embedded in other groups, in social institutions, in identities, in cultures, in nation-states, until we come to that enormous edifice, society. It turns out to be not a mass of individuals at all but an intricate pattern of groups within groups. What's more, it's not the mere *fact* of different types of groups but how we interact with others in society that structures our behavior, our experiences, and even ourselves.

Since the early twentieth century, sociologists have attempted to understand exactly how we "construct" a sense of self, an identity through our interaction with the world around us. Instead of being "blank slates" on which society imprints its dictates, sociologists see individuals as actively engaged in the process. We create identities through our interactions with the world around us, using the materials (biological inheritance, cultural context, social position) that we have at hand. Our identities, sociologists believe, are socially constructed.

Sociologists use certain conceptual tools to understand the ways in which we construct these identities. Some, like *socialization,* refer to processes by which the culture incorporates individuals, makes them part of the collectivity. Other terms, like *roles, statuses, groups,* and *networks,* help us understand the ways in which individuals negotiate with others to create identities that feel stable, consistent, and permanent. Finally, other terms, like *organizations* and *institutions,* describe more formal and stable patterns of interactions among many individuals that enable us to predict and control behavior. *Society* refers to the sum of all these other elements.

Societies cohere through social structure. **Social structure** is a complex framework, composed of both patterned social interactions and institutions that together both organize social life and provide the context for individual action. It consists of different positions, resources, groups, and relationships. Social structure is both formal and informal, fluid and fixed. It is both a web of affiliations that supports and sustains us and a solid walled concrete building from which we cannot escape.

The Social Construction of Reality

Social life is essentially patterns of **social interaction**—behaviors that are oriented toward other people. Other people are also interacting as well, and these near-infinite interactions cohere into patterns. While we are performing in the gigantic drama of social life, everyone around is also performing, trying to present the best role possible and trying to avoid losing face. Because everyone has different ideas, goals, beliefs, and expectations, how does it all fit together into a social world with some semblance of order? Commonsense knowledge—things that we take for granted as "obvious"—differs among people from different cultures and even among different people within the same culture. Even empirical data—what we see, hear, smell, and taste—differ. One person may watch a movie and be thrilled, another bored, and a third outraged.

There is no objective social reality, no one "true" way of interpreting the things that happen to us. The job of the physical scientist is to find out what is "true" about the physical world, but with no "true" social world, the job of the social scientist is to find out how people come to perceive something as true.

According to Peter Berger and Thomas Luckmann (1966), we "construct" social reality through social interaction. We follow conventions that everyone (or almost everyone) in the group learns to accept: that grandmothers and buddies are to be treated differently, for instance, or that teachers like students who express their own opinions. These conventions become social reality, "the way things are." We do not challenge them or even think about them very much.

Cooley and the Looking-Glass Self

One of the first sociologists to argue that the identity is formed through social interaction was Charles Horton Cooley (1864–1929), who coined the term **looking-glass self** to describe the process by which our identity develops (Cooley, [1902] 1983). He argued that we develop our looking-glass self or mirror self in three stages:

1. *We imagine how we appear to others around us.* We think other people see us as smart or stupid, good or bad. Our conclusions do not need to be accurate. Misinterpretations, mistakes, and misunderstandings can be just as powerful as truthful evaluations.

Remaking the Self: Angelina Jolie is now a U.N. Goodwill Ambassador, an icon of international cooperation and human rights advocate. Not that long ago, she wore black leather to her wedding with the name of her spouse (Jonny Lee Miller) etched in blood on her clothing.

2. *We draw general conclusions based on the reactions of others.* If I imagine that many people think I am stupid, or just one important person (like a teacher or a parent), then I will conclude that I am indeed stupid.

3. *Based on our evaluations of others' reactions, we develop our sense of personal identity.* That is, I imagine that many people think I am stupid, so I "become" stupid or at least hide my intelligence. A favorable reaction in the "social mirror" leads to a positive self-concept; a negative reaction leads to a negative self-concept.

This is never a finished process. We are constantly meeting new people and getting new reactions, so we are revising our looking-glass self throughout our lives.

George Herbert Mead (1863–1931), a sociologist, believed that our self arises through taking on the role of others. Mead used interaction as the foundation for this theory of the construction of identity: We create a "self" through our interactions with others. (We will discuss Mead further in Chapter 5.) Mead said that there were two parts of the self, the "I" and the "me." The "I" is the self as subject, needs, desires, and impulses that are not channeled into any social activity, an agent, the self that thinks and acts. The "me" is self as object—the attitudes we internalize from interactions with others, the social self. We achieve our sense of self-awareness when we learn to distinguish the two.

Goffman and the "Dramaturgical" Self

Erving Goffman (1922–1982) went beyond the concept of the looking-glass self. He believed that our selves change not only because of other people's reactions but also because of the way we actively try to present ourselves to other people. Early in life, we learn to modify our behavior in accordance with what particular people expect of us. Perhaps when I am with my buddies, I tell vulgar jokes and playfully insult them because they approve of this sort of behavior as a form of male bonding. However, I would never consider such behavior when I am visiting my grandmother: Then I am quiet and respectful. Goffman calls this **impression management** (1959). I am not merely responding to the reactions of others. I am actively trying to control how others perceive me by changing my behavior to correspond to an ideal of what they will find most appealing.

We change our behavior so easily and so often, without even thinking about it, that Goffman called his theory **dramaturgy.** Social life is like a stage play, with our performances changing according to the characters on stage at the moment. Everyone tries to give the best performance possible, to convince other "characters" that he or she is corresponding to an ideal of the best grandchild, buddy, or whatever role is being played.

Our attempt to give the best possible performance is called **face work,** because when we make a mistake or do something wrong, we feel embarrassed, or "lose face." We are always in danger of losing face because no performance is perfect. We may not fully understand the role, we may be distracted by another role, or others may have a different idea of what the role should be like.

For example, students who come to the United States from some Asian countries often "lose face" in class because they believe that the "ideal student" should sit quietly and agree with everything the professor says, whereas in American colleges the "ideal student" is expected to ask questions, share personal opinions, and perhaps disagree with the professor. Potential pitfalls are endless, and we learn to avoid them only through years of observation and experimentation.

If we have little to lose during the scene, if the other "characters" are not very important to us or we don't have a lot of emotional investment in the role, we often "front," simply pretend to have a role that we do not. We may pretend to be an expert on gourmet cuisine to impress a date or a high school sports hero to impress our children. But the more important the role, the more adept we must become in playing the role.

How do we interact? What tools do we use?

Nonverbal Communication

One of the most important ways of constructing a social reality is through nonverbal communication: our body movements, gestures, and facial expressions; our placement in relation to others. There is evidence that some basic nonverbal gestures are universal, so they may be based in biological inheritance rather than socialization. Ekman and Friesen (1978) studied New Guinea natives who had almost no contact with Westerners and found that they identified facial expressions of six emotions (happiness, sadness, anger, disgust, fear, and surprise) in the same way that Westerners did. Later, they discovered that the facial expression associated with another emotion, contempt, was not culture specific either; it was recognized by people from Germany, Hong Kong, and Italy to West Sumatra, as well as the United States (Ekman and Friesen, 1986).

However, most facial expressions must be interpreted depending on social situations that vary from culture to culture and era to era and must be learned through socialization: A New Guinean and a Westerner would certainly disagree over what sort of smile people use when they are pretending to be unhappy over an incident but are really thrilled or when they have hurt feelings but are trying not to show it. And while a visitor to Russia might think that people are especially serious and glum, it's because Russians smile only when they feel they have a good reason to do so—and only if the reason is obvious to those around them (Krakovsky, 2009, p. 20). Through socialization, observing, and experimenting in a wide variety of social situations, we learn the conventions of nonverbal communication. What is a comfortable distance for standing near another person? It differs depending on whether the person is a friend, relative, or stranger; male or female; in private or in pubic. People raised in the Middle East are socialized to want a very close speaking distance, so close that you can feel the breath of your partner, and they often find people raised in the United States, accustomed to a farther distance, cool and unfriendly.

Here's another good example of how nonverbal communication is a form of social "glue" that holds us together as a group and maintains social cohesion even in groups that are based on inequality: laughing. Theorists have often misunderstood laughter, assuming that it was a cognitive reaction: You hear a joke, you get the joke, you laugh at it—because the joke is funny. Laughter is not about getting the joke.

Face Work: While our facial expression registers emotions, we also use our faces and gestures to communicate those emotions to others in culturally-specific ways.

Successful social interactions are governed by cultural conventions that are often unstated. If this theater were nearly full, it would be perfectly acceptable to sit next to any of these people. But with the theater nearly empty, it would be seen as a violation of personal space.

It's about getting along. Researchers have found that about 80 to 90 percent of the time, laughter is social, not intellectual. Laughter is a powerful bonding tool that is used to signal readiness for friendship and reinforce group solidarity by mocking deviants or insulting outsiders. It also expresses who belongs where in the status hierarchy. Women tend to laugh more than men, and everyone laughs at jokes by the boss—even if the jokes he or she tells aren't funny. Maybe *especially* if they aren't funny (Tierney, 2007)!

Verbal Communication

Nonverbal communication is so subtle that it requires a great deal of socialization, but talking is not straightforward either. Consider how many times someone has said the right words but his or her tone of voice or posture hinted at something else entirely. Even the most inconsequential statements, a "Hello" or "How are you?," can be full of subtle meanings. Sociologists often study these verbal and nonverbal interactions, trying to understand how we communicate information and validate our sense of belonging at the same time.

Ethnomethodology and the Study of Communicative Acts. Sociologist Harold Garfinkel (1967) asked his students to engage in conversations with family and friends that violated social norms. People frequently ask us "How are you?" as a polite greeting, and they expect to hear "Fine!" as a response, even if we are not fine at all (those who are really interested in our condition might ask "How are you feeling?" instead). But Garfinkel's students took the question at face value and asked for clarification: "How am I in regard to what? My health, my finances, my peace of mind? . . ." Their "victims" usually became annoyed or angry, without really knowing why: The students had violated a convention of social interaction that we depend on to maintain a coherent society. Garfinkel called this form of research **ethnomethodology,** in which the researcher tried to expose the common unstated assumptions that enable such conversational shortcuts to work.

Ethnomethodologists don't break social norms frivolously—although, truth be told, participating in a norm-breaking experiment can be fun—but rather to expose the unstated, nonverbal agreements that have to be in place in order for those norms to work in the first place. For example, try getting on an elevator and singing, staring at other people instead of the elevator floors, or striking up a conversation with a stranger. Nowhere has anyone written "the norms of elevator riding," but you know you've broken the norm when you do it! A recent commercial portrayed an out-of-towner (nicely dressed, with a thick Southern accent) who walks into a working-class urban bar. "How you doin'?" one guy asks, clearly with no expectation of a reply except a nod and a "how you doin'?" back. "Why, I'm doin' fine," the out-of-towner replies, and he then proceeds to give a long litany of the day's events. All the men roll their eyes; he's clearly breaking a norm—acknowledge others but don't actually engage with them. The punchline is when another guy, a bar regular, walks into the bar and says, "How you doin'?" to the others, and the others try to warn him with their eyes. The out-of-towner could have been a student of Garfinkel's: We would never have known what the rules were until someone deliberately broke them to find out. (Check it out at: http://www.youtube.com/watch?v=igh6A0qFS14.)

Patterns of Social Interaction

There are five basic patterns of social interaction, what sociologist Robert Nisbet (1970) calls the "molecular cement" that links individuals in groups from the smallest to the largest:

1. *Exchange*. According to sociologist Peter Blau (1964), exchange is the most basic form of social interaction: We give things to people after they give things to us or in expectation of receiving things in the future. In traditional societies, the exchange can take the form of extravagant gifts or violent retribution; but, most often in modern societies, the exchange is symbolic: Smiles or polite words symbolize welcome or friendship, and vulgar gestures or harsh words are exchanged to symbolize hostility. Individuals, groups, organizations, and nations keep an informal running count of the kindnesses and slights they have received and act according to the "norm of reciprocity."

2. *Cooperation*. The running counts of good and bad exchanges are forgotten when we must work together toward a common goal: growing food, raising children, and protecting our group from enemies. And building civilizations: Without cooperation, social organization more complex than a small group of family and friends would be impossible. In modern societies, our jobs are usually a tiny part of an enterprise requiring the cooperation of hundreds or thousands of people. Sometimes we can even be persuaded to abandon our own goals and interests in favor of group goals. Soldiers, police officers, and others may even be asked to sacrifice their lives.

3. *Competition*. Sometimes the goal is not one of common good: Several advertising agencies may be interested in a prized account, but only one will get the contract. When resources are limited, claimants must compete for them. In modern societies, competition is especially important in economies built around capitalism, but it affects every aspect of social life. Colleges compete for the best students; religious groups compete for members.

4. *Conflict*. In a situation of conflict, the competition becomes more intense and hostile, with the competitors actively hating each other and perhaps breaking social norms to acquire the prized goal. In its basic form, conflict can lead to violence, in the form of schoolyard fights, terrorist attacks, or the armed conflicts of nations. However, sociologist Lewis Coser argued that conflict can also be a source of solidarity. In cases of conflict, the members of each group will often develop closer bonds with each other in the face of the common enemy. Conflict can also lead to positive social change, as groups struggle to overcome oppression (Coser, 1956).

5. *Coercion*. The final form of social interaction is coercion, in which individuals or groups with social power, called the **superordinate,** use the threat of violence, deprivation, or some other punishment to control the actions of those with less power, called the **subordinate** (Simmel, [1908] 1956). Coercion is often combined with other forms of social interaction. For instance, we may obey the speed limit on the highway through coercion, the threat of getting a traffic ticket, as well as through cooperation, the belief that the speed limit has been set for the public good. A great deal of our interactions are coercive, though very often the threat is not violence but being laughed at, stared at, or otherwise embarrassed. Think of how hard you might find it to be friends with uncool people—not because you don't want to but because peer pressure is a powerful form of coercion.

In December, 2008, Iraqi journalist Muntadar Al Zaidi hurled one, then a second shoe at then President George W. Bush as a protest against the Iraqi war. According to the British Broadcasting Company (BBC), in Arab cultures, it's considered rude to display the sole of one's shoe to a fellow human being, because shoes are considered ritually unclean in the Muslim faith.

Elements of Social Structure

Social life requires us to adopt many roles. We must behave according to the role of "parent" around our children, "student" while in class, and "employee" at work. We know the basic rules of each role: that "students" sit in chairs facing a central podium or desk, keep quiet unless we raise our hands, and so on—but we also have a great deal of freedom and, as we become more experienced in playing the role, we can become quite creative. The particular emphasis or interpretation we give a role, our "style," is called **role performance.**

Sociologists use two terms, *status* and *role,* to describe the elementary forms of interaction in society.

Status

In everyday life we use the term *status* to refer to people who have a lot of money, power, and influence. But sociologists use **status** to refer to any social identity recognized as meaningful by the group or society. A status is a position that carries with it certain expectations, rights, and responsibilities. Being a Presbyterian, an English major, or a teenager is a status in contemporary American society, but having red hair or liking pizza is not. Many statuses are identities that are fixed at birth, like race, sex, or ethnicity; others we enter and exit, like different age statuses or, perhaps, class.

Statuses change from culture to culture and over time. Having red hair was once a negative status, associated with being quick tempered, cruel, and possibly demonic. When pizza was first introduced into the United States in the early 1900s, only a few people knew what it was, and "liking pizza" was a status. Many statuses are identical to roles—son or daughter, student, teacher—but others, like resident of Missouri or cyberathlete, are more complex, based on a vast set of interlocking and perhaps contradictory roles (Merton, 1968). There are two kinds of statuses.

Ascribed Status. An **ascribed status** is a status that we receive involuntarily, without regard to our unique talents, skills, or accomplishments: for instance, our place of birth, parents, first language, ethnic background, gender, sexual identity, and age (Figure 3.1). Many ascribed statuses are based on genetics or physiology, so we can do little or nothing to change them. We have the ascribed status as "male" or "female," whether we want it or not. Some people do expend a great deal of time and effort to change their appearance and physiological functioning, but they end up with a new ascribed status of "transsexual."

Sociologists find ascribed statuses interesting because they are often used to confer privilege and power. Some statuses (White, native born, male, heterosexual) are presented as "naturally" superior and others (non-White, immigrant, elderly, female, gay, or lesbian) as "naturally" inferior so often and so effectively that sometimes even people who have the "inferior" statuses agree with the resulting economic, political, and social inequality. Just what statuses are presented as superior and inferior differ from culture to culture and across eras.

Though we usually cannot change our ascribed statuses, we can work to change the characteristics associated with them. If being female or African American, both ascribed statuses, are negatively valued, then people can mobilize to change the perception of those statuses. Many of the "new social movements" of the twentieth century, such as the Civil Rights movement, the women's movement, and the gay/lesbian movement, were dedicated to changing a negative ascribed social status.

Achieved Status. An **achieved status** is a status that we attain through talent, ability, effort, or other unique personal characteristics. Some of the more common achieved statuses are being a high school or college graduate; being rich or poor; having a certain occupation; being married or in a romantic relationship; belonging to a church or club; being good at a sport, hobby, or leisure pursuit; or having a specific point of view on a social issue. If you like big band or heavy metal music, for instance, you have an achieved status.

Achieved statuses are often dependent on ascribed statuses. Fans of big band music tend to be considerably older than fans of rap. Some ascribed statuses make it more difficult to achieve other statuses. Race, gender, and ethnicity all affect our abilities to achieve certain statuses. The status of "male" vastly increases your likelihood of being hired as an airline pilot or dentist, and the status of "female" increases your potential of being hired for a job involving child care. In the United States, while we profess a belief that achieved statuses should be the outcome of individual abilities, ascribed statuses continue

to exert a profound influence on them. Social movements for equality often organize around a sense of injustice and seek to reduce the importance of ascribed statuses.

We are able to change achieved statuses. We can change jobs, religions, or political affiliations. We can learn new skills, develop new interests, meet new people, and change our minds about issues. In fact, we usually do. I have most of the same ascribed statuses now that I did when I was 16 years old (all except for age), but my achieved statuses are dramatically different: I have changed jobs, political views, taste in music, and favorite television programs.

In traditional societies, most statuses are ascribed. People are born rich or poor and expect to die rich or poor. They have the same jobs that their parents had and cannot even think of changing their religion because only one religion is practiced throughout the society. They dress the same and listen to the same songs and stories, so they can't even change their status based on artistic taste.

> **"Old" as a Positive Term**
> In the United States, the status of "elderly" is often negative, associated with being weak, feeble minded, decrepit, and useless; but in China, the status is associated with wisdom and strength, so you might call a 25-year-old teacher "old teacher" to indicate respect.

Did You Know?

Figure 3.1 Ascribed, Achieved, and Master Statuses: Kris Allen

ASCRIBED STATUS

24 years old
Male
Able-bodied
White
Straight

MASTER STATUS

Singer

Married
American Idol winner
Attended college

ACHIEVED STATUS

However, in modern societies, we have many more choices, and more and more statuses are attained.

Master Status. When ascribed or achieved status is presumed so important that it overshadows all of the others, dominating our lives and controlling our position in society, it becomes a **master status** (Hughes, 1945). Being poor or rich tends to be a master status because it dramatically influences other areas of life, such as education, health, and family stability. People who have cancer or AIDS often find that all of the other statuses in their lives become subsidiary. They are not "college student" or "Presbyterian" but "college student with cancer," "Presbyterian with cancer," or just "cancer patient." People who suddenly become disabled find that co-workers, acquaintances, and even their close friends ignore all their other statuses, seeing only "disabled." Other common master statuses are race, ethnicity, religion, and sexual identity (Figure 3.1). Members of ethnic, religious, and sexual minorities often complain that their associates treat them as representatives of their status rather than as individuals, asking "What do gay people think about this?" or "Why do Muslims do that?" but never about last night's ball game. Occupation may also be a master status; the first question you are likely to be asked at a gathering is, "What do you do for a living?"

Roles

Social **roles** are sets of behaviors that are expected of a person who occupies a certain status. In the dramaturgical analogy, a social role is like the role an actor plays in a drama: It includes the physical presentation, props, and costume; the actor's motivation and perspective; and all the actor's lines, as well as the physical gestures, accent, and timing.

As in the theatrical world, our experience of roles is a negotiation between role *expectations* and role *performances*. We learn what sorts of behaviors are expected from specific roles, and then we perform those roles in conformity with those expectations. Our roles are constantly being evaluated: When we do them right, we may receive praise; when we do them wrong, we may be admonished or even punished. And if we begin to dislike the expectations that accompany a role, we may try to modify it to suit our needs, convince others that our performance is better than the expectations, or even reject the role altogether. Role expectations may be independent of the individuals who play them, but each individual does it slightly differently.

Because roles contain many different behaviors for use with different people in different situations, sometimes the behaviors contradict each other. We experience **role strain** when the same role has demands and expectations that contradict each other, so we cannot possibly meet them all at once. For instance, the role of "student" might ask us to submit to the professor's authority *and* exercise independent thought. How can a single behavior fill both demands?

Role strain makes us feel worried, doubtful, and insecure, and it may force us to abandon the role altogether. Goode (1960) found that we often solve the problem of role strain by *compartmentalizing*, depending on subtle cues to decide if we should submit or exercise independent thought *right now* and often never even noticing the contradiction.

A related problem, **role conflict,** happens when we try to play different roles with extremely different or contradictory rules at the same time. If I am out with my buddies, playing the cool, irreverent role of "friend," and I see my teacher, who expects the quiet, obedient student, I may have a problem. If I suddenly become polite, I will lose face with my friends. If I remain irreverent, I will lose face with my teacher. Because everyone is playing multiple roles all the time, role conflict is a common problem.

What happens when we must leave a role that is central to our identity? **Role exit** describes the process of adjustment that takes place when we move out of such a role. Sometimes we leave roles voluntarily: We change jobs or religions, get divorced and leave the "married" role, and so on. Sometimes we leave roles involuntarily: We change age groups (suddenly our parents say, "You're not a kid anymore"), get arrested, get fired. Whether we leave voluntarily or involuntarily, we are likely to feel lost, confused, and sad. Helen Rose Fuchs Ebaugh (1988) notes four stages in voluntarily exiting from significant social roles:

1. *Doubt.* We are frustrated, burned out, or just unhappy with our role.
2. *Search for alternatives.* We observe people in other roles or perhaps try them out

ourselves temporarily. This may be a life-long process.

3. *Departure.* Most people can identify a turning point, a specific moment or incident that marked their departure from the role, even though they might continue to play it for some time.

4. *New role.* It is very important to find a new role to take the place of the old. People who leave a role involuntarily must start the search for alternatives after departure, and it is quite likely that they will try out several new roles before finding one that they like.

Roles and statuses give us, as individuals, the tools we need to enter the social world. We feel grounded in our statuses; they give us roots. And our roles provide us with a playbook, a script, for any situation. We are ready to join others.

Ballplayer or babe? Women who enter traditionally male domains—from the operating room to the boardroom to the sports stadium—must constantly negotiate between different sets of role expectations. Jennie Finch may be an Olympic softball gold medalist and the holder of the NCAA record for most consecutive wins, but she still has to look like a cover girl to reaffirm traditional gender expectations.

Groups

"The world is too much with us," the great British poet William Wordsworth once complained. He believed that immersion in the world kept us from the divine realm of nature. But sociologists are more likely to side with John Donne: "No man is an island, entire of itself . . ."

Even by yourself, sociologists believe, you are "in society." Brought up within culture, the very ideas you carry around about who you are and what you think and feel—these are already conditioned and shaped by society. It is our experience in society that makes us human.

Apart from individuals, then, the smallest unit of society is a group. To sociologists, a **group** is any assortment of people who share (or believe that they share) the same norms, values, and expectations. And the smallest group is a **dyad,** a group of two. Anytime you meet with another person, you are in a group. And every time the configuration of people meeting changes, the group changes. Two different classes may have the same professor, the same subject matter, and most of the same students, but they comprise different groups, and they are often completely different environments. Groups can be for-

mal organizations, with well-defined rules and procedures, or they may be informal, like friends, co-workers, or whoever happens to be hanging around at that moment.

A group can be very small, such as your immediate family and friends, or very large, such as your religion or nation, but the most significant groups in our lives are the ones so large that we don't personally know everyone but small enough so we can feel that we play an important role in them: not your occupation but your specific place of business; not all skateboarders in the world but your specific skateboarding club.

Passengers on the airplane or the customers in a restaurant are not a group. Strictly speaking, they are a **crowd,** an aggregate of individuals who happen to be together but experience themselves as essentially independent. But the moment something goes wrong—the flight is cancelled or the service is inexplicably slow—they will start looking to each other for validation and emotional support, and chances are they will become a group. On the TV series *Lost,* an airplane crashes on a mysterious island in the South Pacific, and the survivors band together to fight a series of weird supernatural threats. On the airplane, they had been reading, napping, or staring into space, basically

Passengers on an airplane are a crowd—there remain individuals who happen to be in the same place, but do not experience group cohesion. That is, unless there is a crisis, when they may become a group. The passengers on USAir 1549 shared an experience that drew them together into a group—on the wings of the plane in the icy Hudson River!

ignoring each other, but now they are becoming a group.

Groups differ from crowds in their **group cohesion,** the degree to which the individual members identify with each other and with the group. In a group with high cohesion, individual members will be more likely to follow the rules and less likely to drop out or defect to another group. Because every group, from business offices to religious cults to online newsgroups, wants to decrease deviance and keep the members from leaving, studies about how to increase cohesion have proliferated. It's not hard to do: You need to shift the group importance from second place to first place, transforming the office or cult into "a family," by forcing members to spend time together and make emotional connections. Wilderness retreats and "trust exercises" are meant to jump-start this connection. And you need to find a common enemy, a rival group or a scapegoat, someone for the group members to draw together to fight.

Groups and Identity

Everyone belongs to many different groups: families, friends, co-workers, classmates, churches, clubs, organizations, plus less tangible groups. Are you a fan of blues music? David Beckham? Even if you never seek out an organized club, you belong to the group of blues fans or soccer fans. Do you favor gun control? Even if you don't feel strongly about the issue, you belong to the group of people who favor gun control. Your gender, sexual orientation, race, ethnicity, age, class, nationality, and even your hair color place you in groups and form part of your identity. Often our membership in a group is a core element of our identities. And other times, other people assume that just because we are members of a particular group, that this membership forms that core of identity—when it may, in fact, do nothing of the sort. Imagine an Asian American gay man who is an avid mountain biker. So avid, in fact, that he joins every mountain biking club in his community and is a central person in all its activities. It is the core of his identity, he believes. But without his bicycle, other people assume that the core of his identity is his membership in a racial and sexual group. "I'm a mountain biker who happens to be Asian American and gay," he insists, "not a gay Asian American who happens to be a mountain biker." The various elements of our identity may fit together neatly, or we may struggle to integrate them. And the rest of society must see our priorities the way we do, or we will experience conflict. Your gender, sexual orientation, race, ethnicity, age, class, nationality, and even your hair color place you in groups and form part of your identity.

What's visible and invisible to us as a facet of our identity is often related to the organization of society. I recently asked my stu-

Even though this man may identify himself as a tennis player, co-workers, acquaintances, and even his close friends may ignore all of his other statuses, seeing only "disabled," and thus force him to root his identity more firmly in that group.

dents in an introductory sociology class to list the five most important elements of their identities on a piece of paper. Every African American student listed their race as the first or second item, but not one White student listed being "White" anywhere on their answers. Every woman listed being a woman, but only 10 percent of men thought to put "male." And while many students listed a "gay" or "lesbian" sexual orientation, not one student wrote "heterosexual." Virtually every student put his or her ethnicity, especially those who were Latino or Asian; among European Americans, only the Italian, Irish, and Russian put their ethnicity (no Germans, Swedes, French, or Swiss). The majority of Jews and Muslims listed religion; half of all Protestants put "Christian," but only 2 percent listed a denomination. And only a quarter of the Catholics listed "Catholic."

Why would that be? Sociologists understand that identities based on group membership are not neutral, but hierarchically valued. Those identities that are most readily noticeable are those where we do not fit in with others, not those in which we are most like everyone else. We're more aware of where we stand out as different, not where we fit in.

Types of Groups

There are many different types of groups, depending on their composition, permanence, fluidity of boundaries, and membership criteria. You are born into some groups (family, race). In other groups, you may be born into the group, but membership also depends on your own activities and commitments, like ethnic or religious groups. Some are based entirely on expression of interest (clubs, fans), and others are based on formal application for membership.

Primary and Secondary Groups. Small groups (small enough so that you know almost everybody) are divided into two types, primary and secondary. According to the sociologist Charles Horton Cooley ([1909] 1990), **primary groups,** such as friends and family, come together for *expressive reasons:*

What do **you** think?

Group Membership

Research shows that those with stronger social ties and networks lead happier, healthier lives. So, what do you think?

- Are there any activities that you do with the same group of people on a regular basis, even if the group doesn't have a name, such as a bridge group, exercise group, or a group that meets to discuss individual or community problems?

What does **America** think?

(These are actual survey data from the General Social Survey, 2004.)

Almost three-quarters of respondents reported not being part of a regular informal group. White respondents (29.3 percent) were more likely than Black respondents (19.1 percent) to be part of such a group. Those who were of another racial classification were least likely to report being part of a group (14.1 percent). There was no difference in group membership by gender.

Thinking Critically about Survey Data

1. Were you surprised that so few respondents report being members of informal groups? Do you think these numbers reflect reality? Why do you think so few people belong to groups? Why do you think Black respondents were less likely to report belonging to an informal group than were White respondents?

References: see Davis et al., page 511.

Sleeping with the enemy? Democratic Party strategist James Carville is married to Republican strategist Mary Matlin. Her marital philosophy: Pick your battles. His? Surrender. He claims to be 0 for 5,211 in marital fights.

They provide emotional support, love, companionship, and security. **Secondary groups,** such as co-workers or club members, come together for *instrumental reasons:* They want to work together to meet common goals. Secondary groups are generally larger and make less of an emotional claim on your identity. In real life, most groups have elements of both: You may join the local chapter of the Green Party because you want to support its political agenda, but you are unlikely to stay involved unless you form some emotional connections with the other members.

In-Groups and Out-Groups. William Graham Sumner ([1906] 2002) identified two different types of groups that depend on membership and affinity. An **in-group** is a group I feel positively toward and to which I actually belong. An **out-group** is one to which I don't belong and do not feel very positively toward. We may feel competitive or hostile toward members of an out-group. Often we think of members of out-groups as bad, wrong, inferior, or just weird, but the specific reactions vary greatly. An avid tennis player may enjoy a wonderful friendship or romance with someone who hates tennis, with only some occasional teasing to remind that friend that he or she belongs to an out-group.

Sometimes, groups attempt to create a sense of superiority for members of the in-group—or to constitute themselves as an in-group in the first place. For example, mem-

bers of a club want to create an aura of importance to their weekly meetings. They may charge a massive "initiation" fee that only other rich people could afford to pay or insist that membership is open only to graduates of an Ivy League college. Creating an in-group can be conscious and deliberate. But for the in-group to be successful, members of the out-group (those not in the in-group) must actually want to join. Otherwise all those secret codes and handshakes just look silly.

Sometimes, however, especially when in-groups and out-groups are divided on the basis of race, nationality, gender, sexuality, or other ascribed status, reactions become more severe and violent. The Holocaust of World War II, the ethnic cleansings of Armenia and Serbia, and the lynchings of the American South were all based on an in-group trying to control or eliminate out-groups.

In-groups and out-groups do not have to be built around any sort of socially meaningful characteristic. Gerald Suttles (1972), studying juvenile groups in Chicago housing projects, found that boys formed in-groups and out-groups based on whether the brick walls of their buildings were lighter or darker in color.

In the 1960s, an Iowa grade school teacher named Jane Elliot (Elliot, 1970; Verhaag, 1996) tried an experiment: She created an out-group from the students with blue eyes, telling the class that the lack of melanin in blue eyes made you inferior. Though she did not instruct the brown-eyed students to treat the blue-eyed students differently, she was horrified by how quickly the out-group was ostracized and became the butt of jokes, angry outbursts, and even physical attacks. What's more, she found that she could not call off the experiment: Blue-eyed children remained a detested out-group for the rest of the year!

Membership in a group changes your perception entirely. You become keenly aware of the subtle differences among the individual members of your group, which we call **in-group heterogeneity,** but tend to believe that all members of the out-group are exactly the same, which we call **out-group homogeneity** (Meissner, Brigham, and Butz, 2005; Mullen and Hu, 1989; Quattrone, 1986; Voci, 2000). Researchers at my university asked some members of fraternities and sororities, as well as some dormitory residents, about the people in their own living group and the people in others. What were they like? Consistently, people said of their in-group that they were "too different," each member being "unique" and everyone "too diverse" to categorize (in-group heterogeneity). When asked about the other groups, though, they were quick to respond, "Oh, they're all jocks," or "That's the egghead nerd house" (out-group homogeneity).

The finding that we tend to perceive individual differences in our in-group and not perceive them in out-groups holds mainly in Western societies. It doesn't hold, or it holds only weakly, for China, Korea, and Japan. The Chinese, in particular, tend to believe too much that everyone is alike to perceive subtle differences (Quattrone, 1986).

Reference Groups. Our membership in groups not only provides us with a source of identity, but it also orients us in the world, like a compass. We *refer* to our group memberships as a way of navigating everyday life. We orient our behavior toward group norms and consider what group members would say before (or after) we act. A **reference group** is a group toward which we are so strongly committed or one that commands so much prestige that we orient our actions around what we perceive that group's perceptions would be. In some cases the reference group is the in-group, and the rest are "wannabes."

Ironically, one need not be a member of the reference group to have it so strongly influence your actions. In some cases, a reference group can be *negative*—as in when you think to yourself that you will do everything that the members of that other group do not like or when your identity becomes dependent on doing the opposite of what members of a group do. Some of these may be political (Nazis or the Ku Klux Klan are familiar negative reference groups) or simply competitive, like a neighboring clan, a fraternity, or students at another school.

In other cases, your reference group can be one to which you aspire. For example, assume that you have decided that despite your poor upbringing in rural Kentucky, you know you will eventually be one of the richest people in the world and will eventually be asked to go yachting with European aristocracy. You may feel this so strongly that you begin, while in college, to act as you imagine those in your reference group act: You wear silk ascots and speak in a fake British accent. Despite the fact that your classmates might think you're a little bit strange, you are developing a reference group. It just happens to be one that no one else around you shares. In these cases, reference groups do not just guide your actions as a member of a group but guide your actions as a *future* member of a different group.

Your reference group and your membership groups are thus not always the same. Both reference groups and membership groups will change over the course of your life, as your circumstances change as well.

Cliques. One of the best illustrations of group dynamics is the high school clique. All across the United States, middle and high school students seem to form the same groups: jocks, nerds, preps, skaters, posers, gang-bangers, wannabes, wiggers, princesses, stoners, brainiacs (Milner, 2006). Cliques are organized around inclusion and exclusion. Ranked hierarchically, those at the bottom are supposed to aspire to be in the cliques at the top. Cliques provide protection, elevate one's status, and teach outsiders a lesson. Many high schools are large enough to accommodate several cliques, and not belonging to the social pinnacle is not so painful because there are so many other cliques to which you can belong (and you can more easily say you don't care what those people think). In smaller schools, though, exclusion

One of the best illustrations of group dynamics is the high school clique. Cliques are organized around inclusion and exclusion—and who has the power to enforce it. In the hit movie Mean Girls (2004), Lindsay Lohan is reminded that only the most popular girls can eat their lunch at this table.

Group Conformity

How can we observe these processes of conformity to group norms? In a classic experiment in social psychology (Asch, 1955), a group of strangers was gathered together under the pretense of testing their visual acuity. They were shown two cards, one with one line and one with three lines of different lengths. (In the group, however, only one person was really the subject of the experiment; all the rest were research assistants!) The group was then asked which of the lines on the second card matched the line on the first. When the subject was asked first, he or she answered correctly. (It didn't matter what others said.) But when the first group members to respond were the research assistants, they gave wrong answers, picking an obviously incorrect line and insisting it was the match.

Surprisingly, the test subjects would then most often give the wrong answers as well, preferring to follow the group norm rather than trust their own perceptions. When asked about it, some claimed that they felt uncomfortable but that they actually came to see the line they chose as the correct one. Psychologist Solomon Asch concluded that our desire to "fit in" is very powerful, even in a group that we don't belong to.

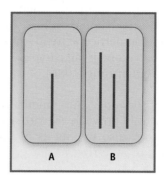

from the most popular group may be a source of significant pain. In the late 1940s, sociologist James Coleman studied high school cliques and found, much to his distress, that popularity was not at all related to intelligence, that student norms, and clique composition, were the result of social factors alone. The "hidden curriculum" of social rankings continues today. Being smart may make you popular, but it is just as likely to have nothing to do with it. In fact, being smart can make you extremely unpopular.

Group Dynamics

Groups exhibit certain predictable dynamics and have certain characteristics. Often these dynamics are simply a function of formal characteristics—size or composition—and other times they are due more to their purpose.

Size. When it comes to groups, size matters. Small groups, in which all members know each other and are able to interact simultaneously, exhibit different features than larger groups, in which your behaviors are not always observed by other members of your group. Large groups may be able to tolerate more diversity than small groups, although the bonds among small groups may be more intense than those in larger groups. Small groups may engage us the most, but larger groups are better able to influence others.

Structure. Every group, even the smallest, has a structure that sociologists can analyze and study. There is always a **leader,** someone in charge, whether that person was elected, appointed, or just informally took control, and a small number of **hardcore members,** those with a great deal of power to make policy decisions. Leaders and hardcore members spend an enormous amount of time and energy on the group; it forms an important part of their identity. As a consequence, they have a vested interest in promoting the norms and values of the group. They are most likely to punish deviance among group members and to think negatively about other groups. Ordinary members split their time and energies among several groups, so they are not as likely to be strongly emotionally invested. They are more likely to commit minor acts of deviance, sometimes because they confuse the norms of the various groups they belong to and sometimes because they are not invested enough to obey every rule.

Conformity. The groups we belong to hold a powerful influence over our norms, values, and expectations. Group members yield to others the right to make decisions about their behavior, their ideas, and their beliefs. When we belong to a group, we prize conformity over "rocking the boat," even in minor decisions and even if the group is not very important to us.

Conformity may be required by the norms of the group. Some groups have formal requirements. For example, cadets at military schools often have their heads shaved on their enrollment, and members of some groups wear specific clothing or get identical tattoos. If you do not conform, you cannot be a member. Other times, however, we volunteer our conformity. We will often imitate the members of our reference group and use it as a "frame of reference" for self-evaluation and attitude formation (Deux and Wrightsman, 1988; Merton, 1968), even if we don't belong to it. For instance, you may have paid special attention to the popular clique in high school and modeled your dress, talk, and other behaviors on them. Other common reference groups are attractive people, movie stars, or sports heroes. Marketing makes use of this dynamic, aiming to get the "opinion leaders" in selected reference groups to use, wear, or tout a product, in the hopes that others will imitate them (Gladwell, 1997; PBS, 2001). The most familiar example of group conformity is peer pressure.

Psychologist Irving Janis called the process by which group members try to preserve harmony and unity in spite of their individual judgments **groupthink** (Janis, 1972). Sometimes groupthink can have negative or tragic consequences. For example, on January 28, 1986, the Space Shuttle *Challenger* exploded shortly after takeoff, killing the seven astronauts aboard. A study afterward revealed that many of the NASA scientists in charge of the project believed that the O-ring seal on the booster rocket was unstable and that the shuttle was not ready to be launched, but they invariably deferred their judgments to the group. The project went on according to schedule.

Diffusion of Responsibility. One of the characteristics of large groups is that responsibility is diffused. The chain of command can be long enough or authority can seem dispersed enough that any one individual, even the one who actually executes an order, may avoid taking responsibility for his or her actions. If

Group conformity and large bureaucratic organizations can often lead to a diffusion of responsibility. Which bankers and financial investors were "responsible" for the financial meltdown of 2008? Everyone was just "doing their job."

you are alone somewhere and see a person in distress, you are far more likely to help that person than if you are in a big city with many other people streaming past.

This dynamic leads to the problem of bystanders: those who witness something wrong, harmful, dangerous, or illegal, yet do nothing to intervene. In cases where there is one bystander, he or she is more likely to intervene than when there are more bystanders. In some cases, bystanders simply assume that as long as others are observing the problem, they are no more responsible than anyone else to intervene. Sometimes, bystanders are afraid that if they do get involved the perpetrators will turn on them; that is, they will become targets themselves. Bystanders often feel guilty or sheepish about their behavior.

In one of the most famous cases, a woman named Kitty Genovese in a quiet residential neighborhood in New York City was murdered outside her apartment building in 1964. Though she screamed as her attacker beat and stabbed her, more than 30 people looked out of their apartment windows and heard her screaming, and yet none called the police. When asked later, they said that they "didn't want to get involved" and that they "thought someone else would call the police, so it would be OK."

Groups in Cyberspace

Bloggers often rail against "old media" as elitists and insiders who rely on status and social networks to get and do their jobs, keeping out the voices of "regular people." But are online groups such liberated spaces, where members are free of stifling norms and conformity to group behavior?

Sociologists find that group behavior in cyberspace can be just as patterned and policed as it is in the "real" social world. In the 1990s, McLaughlin, Osborne, and Smith (1995) found that online groups consciously develop specific types of acceptable group behaviors, and anyone who persists in "reproachable" acts will be threatened with expulsion and may ultimately be kicked out of the group. Today, many larger online communities, such as Slashdot or Kuro5hin, use more collaborative filtering systems to develop and enforce rules of behavior (Bruns, 2005; Rettberg, 2008).

Many popular news communities use what are called reputation systems to promote valued material and deter those who are unskilled, undesirable, or dishonest. Slashdot.com, for example, is organized so all posts are filtered by moderators, who are members in good standing with the group. These participants are overseen by metamoderators, who make sure these members don't wield too much control. Finally, they offer "karma," a means for new or less-valued members to gain recognition for their contributions and good behavior. Reputation systems aim to broaden access while preventing "capture" of the site by outsiders.

Despite this more "democratic" approach to participation and rules of governance, online groups tend to develop such clear values and norms of behavior that the vast majority of subscribers never venture beyond being "lurkers" who read postings but do not post messages of their own (Croteau and Hoynes, 2003).

Stereotyping. Stereotyping is another dynamic of group life. **Stereotypes** are assumptions about what people are like or how they will behave based on their membership in a group. Often our stereotypes revolve around ascribed or attained statuses, but any group can be stereotyped. Think of the stereotypes we have of cheerleaders, jocks, and nerds. In the hit movie series *High School Musical* (2006, 2007, 2008), members of each group try to downplay the stereotypes and be seen as full human beings: The jock/basketball star wants to be lead in the school play; his Black teammate is a wonderful chef who can make a fabulous crème brûlée.

Sometimes you don't even need a single case to have a stereotype; you can get your associations from the media, from things people around you say, or from the simple tendency to think of out-groups as somehow bad or wrong. In Jane Elliott's experiment, the blue-eyed students were not associated with any negative characteristics at all until they became an out-group. Then they were stereotyped as stupid, lazy, shiftless, untrustworthy, and evil.

Stereotypes are so strong that we tend to ignore behaviors that don't fit. If we have a stereotype of teenagers as lazy and irresponsible, we will ignore hardworking, responsible teenagers, maybe thinking of them as exceptions to the rule. Stereotypes are a foundation of *prejudice,* where we "prejudge" people based on their membership in a specific group. (We will discuss this more fully in Chapter 8.)

Social Networks

A **network** is a type of group that is both looser and denser than a formal group. Sociologist Georg Simmel used the term *web* to describe the way our collective membership in different groups constitutes our sense of identity.

Sociologists often use this metaphor to describe a network as a web of social relationships that connect people to each other, and, through those connections, with other people. A network is both denser than a group, with many more connecting nodes, and looser, in that (people are at some remove from) you and exert very little influence on your behavior.

The interconnectedness of these webs—how they connect, overlap, intermingle—has become a major way we understand our world.

Networks and Social Experience

The social connectedness of certain groups in the society can produce interaction patterns that have a lasting influence on the lives of people both within and without the network. For example, prep schools not only offer excellent educations but also afford social networks among wealthy children who acquire "cultural capital" (those mannerisms, behaviors, affectations that mark one as a member of the elite, as we discussed in Chapter 2) that prepares them for life among the elite (Cookson and Persell, 1985). Sociologist G. William Domhoff found that many of the boards of directors of the largest corporations in the world are composed of people who went to prep school together or at least who went to the same Ivy League college (Domhoff, 2002).

Social networks provide support in times of stress or illness; however, some research finds that social networks are dependent on people's ability to offer something in exchange, such as fun, excitement, or a sparkling personality. Therefore, they tend to shrink precisely during the periods of stress and illness when they are needed the most. If you are sick for a few days, you may be mobbed by friends armed with soup and get-well cards. But if your sickness lingers, you will gradually find yourself more alone.

Networks exert an important influence on the most crucial aspects of our lives; our membership in certain networks is often the vehicle by which we get established in a new country or city, meet the person with whom we fall in love, or get a job. Examine your own networks. There are your friends and relatives, your primary ties. Then there are those people whom you actually know, but who are a little less close—classmates and co-workers. These are your secondary ties. Together they form what sociologist Mark Granovetter (1973, 1974) calls your "strong ties"—people who actually know you. But your networks also include "weak ties"—people whom you may not know personally, but perhaps you know *of* them, or they know *of* you. They may have strong ties to one of your strong ties. By the time you would calculate your strong and weak ties, the numbers might reach into the thousands.

Interestingly, it is not only your strong ties that most influence your life, but possibly, centrally, your weak ties. Granovetter (1995) calls this "the strength of weak ties." While one might think strong interpersonal ties are more significant than weak ones because close friends are more interested than acquaintances in helping us, this may not be so, especially when what people need is information. Because our close friends tend to move in the same circles that we do, the information they receive overlaps considerably with what we already know. Acquaintances, by contrast, know people whom we do not and thus receive more novel information. This is in part because acquaintances are typically less similar to one another than close friends and in part because they spend less time together. Moving in different circles from ours, they connect us to a wider world.

Some new Internet companies, such as LinkedIn or SocialSplash, seek to expand the range of our networks. Friendster, Facebook, MySpace, and others use the ever-expanding web of the Internet to create new network configurations with people whom you will never meet but rather get to know because they are a friend of a friend of a friend of a friend of—your friend.

Networks and Globalization

New technology, such as text messaging, satellite television, and especially the Internet, has allowed us to break the bounds of geography

Sociology and Our World

Six Degrees of Kevin Bacon

Did you know that the versatile actor Kevin Bacon is the center of the film universe? In 1994, three students at Albright College in Pennsylvania were hanging around a dorm room during a snowstorm and watching Bacon's film *Footloose*. When that film was followed by another Bacon film, *Quicksilver*, they began to speculate about how many different actors he had worked with. "It became one of our stupid party tricks," said one of the students. "People would throw names at us, and we'd connect them to Kevin Bacon." The three wrote to talk show host Jon Stewart, and a fad was quickly born.

To play, pick any actor in history and see how many connections it takes to connect that actor to a Kevin Bacon movie. For example neither John Wayne nor Marilyn Monroe ever appeared in a movie with Bacon. But Wayne was in *El Dorado* with James Caan, who was in *New York I Love You* with Kevin Bacon. Monroe was in *The Misfits* with Eli Wallach, who was also in *New York I Love You*. (Students at the University of Virginia have computed the "Bacon number" for any actor in history: see http://oracleofbacon.org.) Wayne and Monroe have Bacon numbers of 2. (So does 10-year-old Khail Bryant, who is our son's classmate and friend. Khail was in *Perfect Holiday* with Queen Latifah, who was also in *Beauty Shop* with . . . Kevin Bacon.) About 12 percent of all actors have no "Bacon number"—that is, they cannot be connected to him. Bacon, a good sport about it all, started a charitable organization in 2007 called SixDegrees.org.

and form groups made up of people from all over the world. The Internet is especially important for people with very specialized interests or very uncommon beliefs: You are unlikely to find many people in your hometown who collect antique soda bottles or who believe that Earth is flat, but you can go online and meet hundreds. People who are afraid or embarrassed to discuss their interests at home, such as practitioners of witchcraft or S&M, also find that they can feel safe in Internet message boards and chat rooms. However, there are also thousands of Internet groups formed around more conventional interests, such as sports or movie thrillers.

Blogs and message boards allow us more creativity in playing roles than we have in live interaction. Even in everyday social interactions, we often engage in impression management (Goffman, 1959), emphasizing some aspects of our lives and minimizing or ignoring others. We may pretend to have beliefs, interests,

and skills that we do not, to fit better into a role. Yet online we can adopt completely new roles and statuses, changing not only our skills and interests, but our age, ethnicity, gender, and sexuality at will. Researchers are still studying the impact of this fluidity on the sense of self, exploring issues from avatars, to identity tourism, to racial passing.

Social networks sustain us; they are what communities are made of. At the same time our networks are expanding across the globe at the speed of light, there is also some evidence that these networks are shrinking. A recent study by sociologists found that Americans are far more socially isolated than we were even in the 1980s. Between 1985 and 2004 the size of the average network of confidants (someone with whom you discuss important issues) fell from just under three other people (2.94) to just over two people (2.08). And the number of people who said that there is no one with

U.S / Them

Social Networking: How the Word *Friend* Became Both a Noun and a Verb

More and more people are using social networking sites like Facebook.com, but you may be surprised at just where in the world this growth is occurring. While the number of new users of social networking sites is starting to level off in North America (only 9 percent growth in 2008) the world audience of social networks has grown by 25 percent!

Source: Comscore.com. Reproduced by permission of Comscore, Inc.

1. What have been the benefits of the increased density of our social networks? What are the problems with it?

2. How can a sociologist study networks sites as a research site? What might they be interested in finding out?

whom they discuss important issues nearly tripled. In 1985, the modal respondent (the most frequent response) was three; in 2004, the modal respondent had no confidants. Both kin (family) and nonkin (friendship) confidants were lost (McPherson, Smith-Lovin, and Brashears, 2006).

On the other hand, in some ways, young people today are far *less* isolated than their parents might be. The Internet has provided users with a dizzying array of possible communities of potential confidants, friends, and acquaintances. People who have never met find love, romance, sex, and friendship in cyberspace. Some specific forums like eharmony.com and match.com have been created to assist us—from finding potential cybersex partners to marriage-minded others. People report revealing things about themselves that they might not even tell their spouse. And some participants in these forums actually meet in person—and a few actually marry!

Organizations

Organizations are large secondary groups designed to accomplish specific tasks in an efficient manner. They are thus defined by their (1) size—they are larger, more formal secondary groups; (2) purpose—they are purposive, intent to accomplish something; and (3) efficiency—they determine their strategies by how best to accomplish their goals. We typically belong to several organizations—corporations, schools and universities, churches and religious organizations, political parties. Organizations tend to last over time, and they are independent of the individuals who compose them. They develop their own formal and informal organizational "culture"—consisting of norms and values, routines and rituals, symbols and practices. They tend to maintain their basic structure over a long time to achieve their goals.

Types of Organizations

Sociologists categorize organizations in different ways. One of the most common is by the nature of membership. Sociologist Amitai Etzioni (1975) identified three types of organizations: normative, coercive, and utilitarian.

Normative Organizations. People join a normative organization to pursue some interest or to obtain some form of satisfaction that they consider worthwhile. **Normative organizations** are typically voluntary organizations; members receive no monetary rewards and often have to pay to join. Members therefore serve as unpaid workers; they participate because they believe in the goals of the organization. They can be service organizations (like Kiwanis), charitable organizations (like the Red Cross), or political parties or lobbying groups. Many political organizations, such as the Sierra Club, AARP, or the National Rifle Association are normative organizations: They seek to influence policies and people's lives.

Race, ethnicity, gender, and class all play a part in membership in voluntary organizations. In fact, many such organizations come into being to combat some groups' exclusion from other organizations! For example, the National Women's Suffrage Association came into being in 1869 to oppose the exclusion of women from the voting booth, just as the Congress for Racial Equality (CORE) was formed in 1942 to press for removal of racial discrimination in voting in the segregated South. Other organizations, such as the Ku Klux Klan in the late nineteenth century, were founded for the opposite reason, to keep newly freed Blacks from exercising their right to vote.

Because these organizations make no formal claims on one's time or energy, people tend to remain active members only as long as they feel the organization is serving their interests. With no formal controls, they may lose members as quickly as they gain them. Sometimes the groups dissolve when their immediate objectives have been secured, and individual members drift off to find other groups to join and other causes to embrace. The National Women's Suffrage Association had little reason to exist after women's suffrage was won in 1920; members became involved in other campaigns and other organizations.

Coercive Organizations. There are some organizations that you do not volunteer to join; you are forced to. **Coercive organizations** are organizations in which membership is not voluntary. Prisons, reform schools, and mental institutions are examples of coercive institutions. Coercive organizations tend to have very elaborate formal rules and severe sanctions for those seeking to exit voluntarily. They also tend to have elaborate informal cultures, as individuals try to create something that makes their experience a little bit more palatable.

Coercive institutions are sometimes what sociologist Erving Goffman (1961) called **total institutions.** A total institution is one that completely formally circumscribes your everyday life. Total institutions cut you off from life before you enter and seek to regulate every part of your behavior. They use what social theorist Michel Foucault called a "regime of surveillance"—constant scrutiny of everything you do (Foucault, [1975] 1995, p. 26). Total institutions are fairly dichotomous: One is either an inmate or a "guard." Goffman argued that total institutions tend to follow certain methods to incorporate a new inmate. First, there is a ceremonial stripping of the "old self" to separate you from your former life: Your head may be shaved, your personal clothes may be replaced with a uniform, you may be given a number instead of your name. Once the "old" self is destroyed, the total institution tries to rebuild an identity through conformity with the institutional definition of what you should be like.

Goffman suggested, however, that even total institutions are not "total." Individuals confined to mental hospitals, prisoners, and other inmates often find some clandestine way to hold onto a small part of their prior existence, to remind them that they are not only inmates but also individuals. Small reminders of your former life enable inmates to retain a sense of individuality and dignity. A tattoo, a cross, a family photo—any of these can help the individual resist the total institution.

Utilitarian Organizations. **Utilitarian organizations** are those to which we belong for a specific, instrumental purpose, a tangible material reward. To earn a living or to get an advanced degree, we enter a corporation or university. We may exercise some choice about which university or which corporation, but the material rewards (a paycheck, a degree) are the primary motivation. A large business organization is designed to generate revenues for the companies, profits for shareholders, and wages and salaries for employees. That's what they're there for. We remain in the organization as long as the material rewards we seek are available. If, suddenly, businesses ceased requiring college degrees for employment, and the only reason to stay in school was the sheer joy of learning, would you continue reading this book?

This typology distinguishes between three different types of organizations. But there is considerable overlap. For example, some coercive organizations also have elements of being utilitarian organizations. The recent trend to privatize mental hospitals and prisons, turning them into for-profit enterprises, has meant that the organizational goals are changed to earning a profit, and guards' motivations may become more pecuniary.

Are We a Nation of Joiners?

In his nineteenth-century study of America, *Democracy in America,* the French sociologist Alexis de Tocqueville called America "a nation of joiners." It was the breadth and scale of our organizations—everything from local civic organizations to large formal institutions—that gave American democracy its vitality. A century later, the celebrated historian Arthur Schlesinger (1944, p. 1) pointed out that it seems paradoxical "that a country famed for being individualistic should provide the world's greatest example of joiners." That is another sociological paradox: How can we be so individualistic *and* so collective minded—at the same time?

But recently it appears this has been changing. As we saw at the beginning of the chapter, Robert Putnam argued that the organizations that once composed daily life—clubs, churches, fraternal organizations, civic organizations—had been evaporating in American life. In the

Total institutions use regimentation and uniformity to minimize individuality and replace it with a social, organizational self.

1950s, two-thirds of Americans belonged to some civic organization, but today that percentage is less than one-third. It is especially among normative organizations that membership has decreased most dramatically.

For example, if your parents were born and raised in the United States, it is very likely that *their* parents (your grandparents) were members of the PTA and regularly went to functions at school. It is very likely that your grandparents were members of local civic organizations, like Kiwanis, or a fraternal organization (like Elks or Masons). But it is far less likely that your parents are members. And very *unlikely* that you will join them.

On the other hand, as we also have seen, we join more forums, Internet groups, chat groups, and the like than any people in history—and it is pretty unlikely that our parents or grandparents are going to join them. It isn't so much that we are, or are not, a nation of joiners. Rather, it is what organizations and networks we choose to join and the impact they have on the rest of our lives. Here, Putnam may have a point: We still may join groups, but they may also exert far less influence over our daily lives than they once did.

Organizations: Race and Gender and Inequality?

We often think that organizations and bureaucracies are formal structures that are neutral. They have formal criteria for membership, promotion, and various rewards, and to the extent that any member meets these criteria, the rules are followed without prejudice. Everyone, we believe, plays by the same rules.

What that ignores, however, is that the rules themselves may favor some groups over other groups. They may have been developed by some groups to make sure that they remain in power. What appear to be neutral criteria are also socially weighted in favor of some and against others.

To give one example, membership in a political party was once restricted to those who could read and write, who paid a tax, and whose fathers were members of the party. This effectively excluded poor people, women, and Black people in the pre–Civil Rights South.

Sociologists of gender have identified many of the ways in which organizations reproduce gender inequality. In her now-classic work, *Men and Women of the Corporation,* Rosabeth Moss Kanter (1977) demonstrated that the dif-

Bureaucratic organizations are both rational systems and engines of inequality. Through formal rules, clear lines of authority, and structured roles, the "old boys' network" appears to be based strictly on merit.

ferences in men's and women's behaviors in organizations had far less to do with their characteristics as individuals than they had to do with the structure of the organization. Organizational positions "carry characteristic images of the kinds of people that should occupy them," she argued, and those who do occupy them, whether women or men, exhibited those necessary behaviors. Though the criteria for evaluation of job performance, promotion, and effectiveness seem to be gender neutral, they are, in fact, deeply gendered. "While organizations were being defined as sex-neutral machines," she writes, "masculine principles were dominating their authority structures." The "gender" of the organization turns out to be male.

Here's an example. Many doctors complete college by age 21 or 22 and medical school by age 25 to 27 and then face three more years of internship and residency, during which time they are occasionally on call for long stretches of time, sometimes even two or three days straight. They thus complete their residencies by their late 20s or early 30s. Such a program is designed not for a doctor, but for a *male* doctor—one who is not pressured by the ticking of a biological clock, for whom the birth of children will not disrupt these time demands, and who may even have someone at home taking care of the children while he sleeps at the hospital. No wonder women in medical school—who number nearly one-half of all medical students today—often complain that they were not able to balance pregnancy and motherhood with their medical training.

Bureaucracy: Organization and Power

When we hear the word *bureaucracy*, we often think it means "red tape"—a series of increasingly complex hoops through which you have to jump to realize your goals. In our encounters with bureaucracies, we often experience them as either tedious or formidable obstacles that impede the purpose of the organization.

In a sense we're right. When we encounter a bureaucracy as an applicant, as one who seeks to do something, it can feel like the bureaucracy exists only to thwart our objectives. But if you were at the top of the bureaucracy, you might experience it as a smoothly functioning machine in which every part fits effortlessly and fluidly into every other part, a complex machine of rules and roles.

The sociologist is interested in both aspects of bureaucracies. A **bureaucracy** is a formal organization, characterized by a division of labor, a hierarchy of authority, formal rules governing behavior, a logic of rationality, and an impersonality of criteria (Figure 3.2). It is also a form of domination, by which those at the top stay at the top and those at the bottom believe in the legitimacy of the hierarchy. Part of the reason those at the bottom accept the legitimacy of the power of those at the top is that bureaucracy appears to be simply a form of organization. But, as the great sociologist Max Weber understood, it is by embedding power in formal rules and procedures that it is most efficiently exercised. Bureaucracies are thus the most efficient organizations in getting things done *and* for maintaining the power of those at the top.

Characteristics of Bureaucracies. Max Weber is credited with first describing the essential characteristics of bureaucracies (Weber, 1978). While these characteristics are not necessarily found in every single bureaucratic organization, they represent the *ideal type* of bureaucracy, an abstract mental concept of what a pure version of the phenomenon (in this case a bureaucracy) would look like:

1. *Division of labor.* Each person in a bureaucratic organization has a specific role to play, a specific task to perform. People often become specialists, able to perform a few functions exceptionally well, but they might be unable to do what their colleagues or co-workers do.
2. *Hierarchy of authority.* Positions in a bureaucracy are arranged vertically, with a clear reporting structure, so that each person is under the supervision of another person. Those at the top have power over those below them, all along what is often called the "chain of command." The chain of command is impersonal; the slots held by individuals are independent of the individual occupying the position. If your supervisor leaves a position to move to another part of the company, you no longer report to that person. You report to the new holder of the position of supervisor. The hierarchy of a bureaucratic organization often resembles a pyramid.
3. *Rules and regulations.* Those in the hierarchy do not exert power on a whim: They follow clearly defined rules and regulations that govern the conduct of each specific position in the organization and define the appropriate procedures for the function of each unit and the organization as a whole. These rules and regulations are formalized, "codified" (organized into a coherent structure), and written down, which further reduces the individual discretion supervisors may have and increases the formal procedures of the organization.

Figure 3.2 Characteristics of Bureaucracy

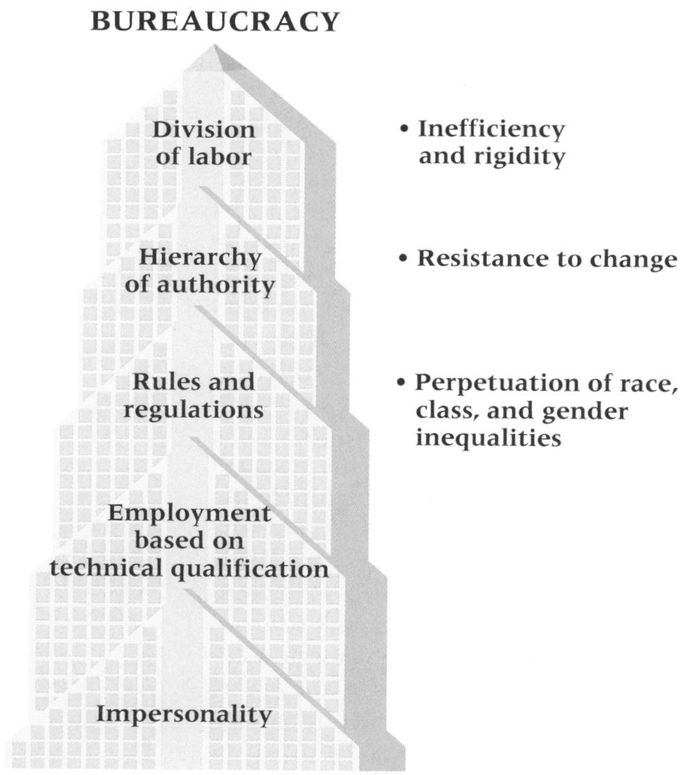

BUREAUCRACY

- Division of labor
- Hierarchy of authority
- Rules and regulations
- Employment based on technical qualification
- Impersonality

- Inefficiency and rigidity
- Resistance to change
- Perpetuation of race, class, and gender inequalities

4. *Impersonality*. Formal and codified rules and regulations and a hierarchy of positions (instead of people) lead to a very impersonal system. Members of bureaucratic organizations are detached and impersonal, and interactions are to be guided by instrumental criteria—what is the right and appropriate decision for the organization, according to its rules, not how a particular decision might make you feel. There is a strict separation of personal and official business and income.

5. *Career ladders*. Bureaucratic organizations have clearly marked paths for advancement, so that members who occupy lower positions on the hierarchy are aware of the formal requirements to advance. They thus are more likely to see their participation as "careers" rather than as "jobs" and further commit themselves to the smooth functioning of the organization. Formal criteria govern promotion and hiring; incumbents cannot leave their positions to their offspring.

6. *Efficiency*. The formality of the rules, the overarching logic of rationality, the clear chain of command, and the impersonal networks enable bureaucracies to be extremely efficient, coordinating the activities of a large number of people.

Why do our experiences with bureaucracies often feel so unsatisfying? Why do we commonly criticize bureaucracies as too large, too unwieldy, and too impenetrable to be efficient forms of organization?

Problems with Bureaucracy

Bureaucracies exhibit many of the other problems of groups—groupthink, stereotypes, and pressure to conform. But as much as they make life more predictable and efficient, bureaucracies also exaggerate certain problems of all groups:

1. *Overspecialization*. Individuals may become so specialized in their tasks that they lose sight of the larger picture and the broader consequences of their actions.

2. *Rigidity and inertia*. Rigid adherence to rules makes the organization cumbersome and resistant to change and leads to a sense of alienation of personnel. This can make bureaucracies inefficient.

3. *Ritualism*. Formality, impersonality, and alienation can lead individuals to simply "go through the motions" instead of maintaining their commitment to the organization and its goals.

4. *Suppression of dissent*. With clear and formal rules and regulations, there is little room for individual initiative, alternate strategies, and even disagreement. Often bureaucracies are characterized by a hierarchy of "yes-men"; each incumbent simply says "yes" to his or her supervisor.

5. *The bureaucratic "catch-22."* This phenomenon, named after a famous novel by Joseph Heller, refers to a process by which the bureaucracy creates more and more rules and regulations, which result in greater complexity and overspecialization, which actually reduce coordination, which results in the creation of contradictory rules.

As a result of these problems, individual members of the bureaucratic organization may feel alienated and confused. Sociologist Robert Merton (1968) identified a specific personality type that he called the **bureaucratic personality** to describe those people who become more committed to following the correct procedures than they are in getting the job done. In the classic comedy movie *Ferris Bueller's Day Off* (1986), school Vice Principal Rooney is so focused on catching Ferris Bueller skipping class that he abandons his work for the day, embarrasses himself in front of his secretary, breaks into the family's home, and is mauled by their dog—and still fails to catch Ferris breaking the rules. At times, these problems may drag the bureaucracy toward the very dynamics that the organization was supposed to combat. Instead of a smoothly functioning, formal, and efficient organizational machine, the bureaucracy can become large, chaotic, inefficient, and homogeneous.

Bureaucracy and Accountability. The mechanisms that enable bureaucracies to be efficient and formal enterprises also have the effect of reducing an individual's sense of accountability. In a chilling example, psychiatrist Robert Jay Lifton (1986) studied doctors who worked at the Nazi death camps. His work shows how bureaucratic organizations can create a sense of alienation that shields people from the consequences of their own actions. In the massive bureaucratic death camps, where processing inmates for extermination was the "business" of the organization, doctors focused on (1) the internal formal administrative tasks that were germane only to their position in the hierarchy

Do Formal or Informal Procedures Result in Greater Productivity?

Does the informal culture of bureaucracy enhance or detract from worker productivity? In a classic study of a Western Electric factory in Hawthorne, Illinois, in the 1930s, Elton Mayo and W. Lloyd Warner found that the informal worker culture ran parallel to the official factory norms. In the experiment, a group of 14 men who put together telephone-switching equipment were paid according to individual productivity. But their productivity did not increase because the men feared that the company would simply raise the expectations for everyone (Mayo, 1933; Roethlisgerberger & Dickson, 1939).

In another classic study, though, Peter Blau (1964) found informal culture increased both productivity and effectiveness. Blau studied a government office charged with investigating possible tax violations. When agents had questions about how to handle a particular case, the formal rules stated they should consult their supervisors. However, the agents feared this would make them look incompetent in the eyes of higher-ups. So, they asked their co-workers, violating the official rules. The result? Not only did they get concrete advice about ways to solve the problem, but the group then began to evolve a range of informal procedures that permitted more initiative and responsibility than the formal rules did, probably enhancing the quantity and quality of work the agents produced.

Formal procedures, according to Meyer and Rowan (1977), are often quite distant from the actual ways people work in bureaucratic organizations. People will often make a show of conforming to them and then proceed with their work using more informal methods. They may use "the rules" to justify the ways a task was carried out, then depart considerably from how things are supposed to be done in actually performing the tasks at hand.

(making sure everything went smoothly), and (2) the informal culture of personal relationships among staff. Lifton describes how these doctors would often come home to their families after a "hard day at the office" and complain only about how a nurse wasn't feeling well or that another doctor was boasting about his car. In this way, Lifton says, the bureaucratic organization led the doctors to experience a form of "psychic numbing"—a psychological distancing from the human consequences of their actions—especially because their "day at the office" consisted of participation in mass murder.

Recall the last few times you've dealt with a bureaucracy. You may have pleaded your case and had a really, really good reason why you were asking them to bend a rule a little bit. And remember how frustrated you were when they waved you away, saying, "There is nothing I can do," "My hands are tied," "I'm only following orders."

If you have ever been on the other side of the desk, though, and faced someone who is trying to plead an excuse, recall how comforting it might have felt that you could refer to specific rules in turning them down and how it supported you in doing your job. It may also have absolved you from feeling bad about it: "I would if I could, honest."

Bureaucracy and Democracy. Weber also identified another potential problem with bureaucracies: a formal structure of accountability that is, ironically, undemocratic. Elected officials are accountable to the public because they have fixed terms of office. They must stand for reelection after a specified term. But officeholders in a bureaucracy tend to stay on for many years, even for their entire careers. (Of course, you can be fired or dismissed by those above you, but your clients or subordinates have no power to remove you.)

There is another reason that bureaucracies do not tend to be democratic organizations. While the formal rules and regulations govern the conduct of each officeholder at every rank, these rules are rarely applied at the top, where more informal and personal rules might apply. For example, those at the top of a bureaucratic hierarchy are likely to forgive minor transgressions when they are performed by their immediate colleagues and friends but are likely to punish underlings quite severely for the same infractions.

In addition, "old boys' networks" can circumvent the formal procedures of the bureaucracy, making sure that personal connections—the children of the bosses' friends or those who went to prep school with them—

are favored candidates for jobs, promotions, or plum assignments. Some positions, whether they are in politics or organized crime, are filled only through such networks of friends, relatives, or friends of friends. In this way, informal networks and cultures within bureaucracies, which can sometimes work to humanize conditions or enhance productivity, can in other situations perpetuate race, class, and gender inequalities. When questioned, the personnel department can point to the formal requirements for the job and declare that the person who got hired was simply the "best qualified" for it.

Bureaucracies appear rational and impersonal, and the criteria they employ are thought to be applied equally and uniformly. But that turns out to be more true at the bottom than at the top (Weber, 1978).

The "Iron Cage" of Bureaucracy. As a result of this difference between appearance and reality, Weber was deeply ambivalent about bureaucracy. On the one hand, bureaucracies are the most efficient, predictable organizations, and officials within them all approach their work rationally and according to formal rules and regulations. But on the other hand, the very mechanisms that make bureaucracies predictable, meaningful, efficient, and coherent and enable those of us who participate in them to see clearly all the different lines of power and control, efficiency and accountability, often lead those organizations to become their opposites. Sometimes, for example, students feel trapped in an avalanche of requirements and large classes, and the purpose of their educa-

tion slips away. At such times, they may go through the motions—sitting in class, taking exams—but they don't feel meaningful. When that happens on a large scale, the organization becomes unwieldy and unequal; officials become alienated, going through the motions with no personal stake in the outcome. Even the professors may "phone it in." The very things we thought would give meaning to our lives end up trapping us in what Weber called the "iron cage." The iron cage describes the increasing rationalization of social life that traps people in the rules, regulations, and hierarchies that they developed to make life sensible, predictable, and efficient. Ironically, mechanisms such as bureaucracies, which promised to illuminate all the elements of an organization, make life more transparent, and enable us to see with greater clarity, could end up ushering in the "polar night of icy darkness." They could crush imagination and destroy the human spirit (Weber, 1958, p. 128).

The Peter Principle

The "Peter Principle" is wrong. The principle holds that "people rise in an organization to their level of incompetence" (Peter and Hull, 1969), but if it were true, most bureaucratic organizations would fail. In one sociological study, central bureaucracies promoted development and prosperity, as they hired on the basis of merit and offered workers rewarding work (Evans and Rauch, 1999).

Did You Know?

Globalization and Organizations

In large complex societies, bureaucracies are the dominant form of organization. We deal with bureaucracies every day—when we pay our phone bill, register for classes on our campus, go to work in an office or factory, see a doctor, or have some interaction with a local, state, or federal government. And when we do, we act as *social actors*—we adopt roles, interact in groups, and collectively organize into organizations.

Groups and organizations are increasingly globalized. Global institutions like the World Bank, or International Monetary Fund, or even private commercial banks like UBS or Bank of America are increasingly the institutional form in which people all over the world do their business. It is likely that if you have a checking account, it is at a major bank with branches in dozens of countries; 50 years ago, if you had a checking account at all, it would have been at the "Community Savings and Loan," and your banker would have known you by name. Most of your bank transactions will be done online, and if you call your bank, you'll

SHAME REALLY, HER ENTHUSIASM AND QUALIFICATIONS WERE EXCELLENT BUT SHE WAS LET DOWN BY HER ATTITUDE TOWARDS VERY IMPORTANT BITS OF PAPER

Source: Fran. Reproduced by permission of www.cartoonstock.com

Bureaucracies depend on the impersonal application of rules. In the 2002 film John Q, *a young father (played by Denzel Washington) is nearly driven to violence when his son needs a heart transplant and is denied treatment by a hospital administrator because the family has surpassed its annual limit aon health insurance coverage. The father points to her heartlessness; the administrator points to the rules and believes her hands are clean*

probably be speaking to someone in another city—probably in another country. Political institutions like the United Nations, or regional organizations like the European Union, attempt to bring different countries together under one bureaucratic organization and even a single monetary system (the euro).

And, of course, even the reactions *against* globalization use the forms and institutions of globalization to resist it. Religious fundamentalists or political extremists who want to return to a more traditional society all use the Internet to recruit members. Global media organizations like Al Jazeera (a global Arabic Muslim media source, with TV and online outlets) spread a specific form of Islam as if it were the only form of Islam—and Muslims in Indonesia begin to act more like Muslims in Saudi Arabia. Every antiglobalization political group—from patriot groups on the far right to radical environmentalists on the far left—uses websites, bloggers, and Internet chat rooms to recruit and spread its message. Globalization may change some of the dynamics of groups and organizations—some new ones emerge, and others fade—but the importance of groups and organizations in our daily lives cannot be overstated.

Groups 'R' Us: Groups and Interactions in the Twenty-First Century

Although we belong to fewer groups than our parents might have, these groups may also be increasingly important in our lives, composing more and more the people with whom we interact and the issues with which we concern ourselves. We're lonelier than ever, and yet we continue to be a nation of joiners, and we locate ourselves still within the comfortable boundaries of our primary groups.

We live in a society composed of many different groups and many different cultures, subcultures, and countercultures, speaking different languages, with different kinship

networks and different values and norms. It's noisy, and we rarely agree on anything. And yet we also live in a society where the overwhelming majority of people obey the same laws and are civil to one another and in which we respect the differences among those different groups. We live in a society characterized by a fixed, seemingly intransigent hierarchy and a society in which people believe firmly in the idea of mobility; a society in which your fixed, ascribed characteristics (race, class, sex) are the single best determinants of where you will end up and a society in which we also believe anyone can make it if he or she works hard enough.

It is a noisy and seemingly chaotic world and also one that is predictable and relatively calm. The terms we have introduced in these two chapters—*culture, society, roles, status, groups, interaction,* and *organizations*—are the conceptual tools that sociologists use to make sense of this teeming tumult of disparate parts and this orderly coherence of interlocking pieces.

Chapter Review

1. Society: Putting Things in Context

Sociologists view **society** from a macrolevel perspective, in terms of institutions and other large, more stable social structures, while also recognizing that **social structure** is created in the face-to-face microlevel emergent interactions between people. After all, institutions are made up of the people in them. These are the contexts in which we exist in society, and which sociologists explore.

society An organized collection of individuals and institutions, bounded by space in a coherent territory, subject to the same political authority, and organized through a shared set of cultural expectations and values. (p. 62)

social institution A formal organized system of roles, norms, and values that are the major foundations of social life (i.e. the family, education) (p. 62)

social structure A complex framework composed of both patterned social interactions and institutions that together organize social life and provide the context for individual action. (p. 63)

2. The Social Construction of Reality

For a sociologist, there is no objective reality, as people's locations in the social structure, group memberships, particular interests, and so forth lend us each a unique perspective; and yet, through **social interaction,** we are creating the social structure together and creating the social reality that exists outside of any one person's perceptions. How can this happen? In part, because we are social creatures who consider the perspectives of others even in our construction of our own identities, as in the **looking-glass self** and in the organization of our behavior, for example, in **impression management** and the **dramaturgy** of social life, which includes **face work.** Social interaction includes both verbal and nonverbal behavior. **Ethnomethodology** focuses on the unspoken assumptions we share in our interactions. Social interactions have a number of basic patterns, including exchange, cooperation, competition, conflict, and coercion, in which the **superordinate** controls the **subordinate.**

social interaction The dynamic process by which two (dyad), three (triad) or more individuals relate to one another. (p. 63)

looking-glass self Cooley's term for the process of how identity is formed through social interaction. We imagine how we appear to others and thus develop our sense of self based on the others' reactions, imagined or otherwise. (p. 64)

impression management Erving Goffman's term for our attempts to control how others perceive us by changing our behavior to correspond to an ideal of what they will find most appealing. (p. 64)

dramaturgy Erving Goffman's conception of social life as being like a stage play wherein we all work hard to convincingly play ourselves as "characters," such as grandchild, buddy, student, employee, or other roles. (p. 65)

face work In dramaturgical theory, the possible performance of ourselves, because when we make a mistake or do something wrong, we feel embarrassed, or "lose face." (p. 65)

ethnomethodology The study of the social knowledge, codes, and conventions that underlie everyday interactions and allow people to make sense of what others say and do. (p. 66)

superordinate Individual or group that possesses social power. (p. 67)

subordinate Individual or group that possesses little or comparatively less social power. (p. 67)

3. Elements of Social Structure

As we encounter social situations, we engage in **role performance,** which is our own interpretation of the behavior appropriate to the situation. Each **status** we have, whether an **ascribed status,** an **achieved status,** or a **master status,** carries with it social expectations, as well as particular rights and responsibilities, which make up the social **role** we enact in our performance. Because we have multiple statuses, and hence multiple roles, it is inevitable that sometimes we experience **role strain** and **role conflict,** and we lose roles. The term **role exit** refers to the process of leaving a role that is important to our identity.

role performance The particular emphasis or interpretation each of us gives a social role. (p. 68)

status One's socially defined position in a group; it is often characterized by certain expectations and rights. (p. 68)

ascribed status Status that is assigned to a person and over which he or she has no control. (p. 68)

achieved status Status or social position based on one's accomplishments or activities. (p. 69)

master status An ascribed or achieved status presumed so important that it overshadows all of the others, dominating our lives and controlling our position in society. (p. 70)

role Behavior expected of people who have a particular status. (p. 70)

role strain The experience of difficulty in performing a role. (p. 70)

role conflict What happens when we try to play different roles with extremely different or contradictory rules at the same time. (p. 70)

role exit The process we go through to adjust when leaving a role that is central to our identity. (p. 70)

4. Groups

The smallest unit sociologists study is the **group.** Groups may be any size, from a **dyad** up, but **crowds** are not groups, as they lack **group cohesion. Primary group** members are bound by expressive ties, while **secondary group** members are together for instrumental reasons. We identify with an **in-group** and are in opposition to an **out-group.** Even our perceptions are influenced by our small group memberships, such that we perceive **in-group heterogeneity** but **out-group homogeneity.** A **reference group** can influence us even if we aren't members. Groups have predictable dynamics. In large groups, responsibility is diffused. In small groups, the **leader** and **hardcore members** have greater investment in the group, conformity is an aspect of group membership, and members work to preserve group cohesion and harmony at the expense of autonomy, even at times exhibiting **groupthink.** We often **stereotype** group members, rather than perceiving distinctions between them.

group Collection of individuals who are aware that they share something in common and who interact with one another on the basis of their interrelated roles and statuses. (p. 71)

dyad A group of two people, the smallest configuration defined by sociologists as a group. (p. 71)

crowd An aggregate of individuals who happen to be together but experience themselves as essentially independent. (p. 71)

group cohesion The degree to which individual members of a group identify with each other and with the group as a whole. (p. 72)

primary group One such as friends and family, which comes together for expressive reasons, providing emotional support, love, companionship, and security. (p. 73)

secondary group Co-workers, club members, or another group that comes together for instrumental reasons, such as wanting to work together to meet common goals. Secondary groups make less of an emotional claim on one's identity than do primary groups. (p. 74)

in-group A group with which you identify and that you feel positively toward, producing a "we" feeling. (p. 74)

out-group One to which you do not belong and toward which you feel either neutral or hostile; the "they" who are perceived as different from and of lower stature than ourselves. (p. 74)

in-group heterogeneity The social tendency to be keenly aware of the subtle differences among the individual members of your group (while believing that all members of out-groups are exactly the same). (p. 74)

out-group homogeneity The social tendency to believe that all members of an out-group are exactly the same (while being keenly aware of the subtle differences among the individual members of one's own group). (p. 74)

reference group A group toward which one is so strongly committed, or one that commands so much prestige, that we orient our actions around what we perceive that group's perceptions would be. (p. 75)

leader All groups have leaders, people in charge, whether they were elected, appointed, or just informally took control. (p. 76)

hardcore members The small number of group members, the "inner circle," who wield a great deal of power to make policy decisions. (p. 76)

groupthink Irving Janis's term for social process in which members of a group attempt to conform their opinions to what they believe to be the consensus of the group, even if, as individuals, they may consider that opinion wrong or unwise. (p. 77)

stereotype Generalization about a group that is oversimplified, selective, exaggerated and usually pejorative, which fails to acknowledge the individual differences in a group. (p. 78)

5. Social Networks

We are connected to others through social **networks.** Members of our primary and secondary groups are obvious members of our networks, but we are also connected less directly to others, including acquaintances, and people we know of, or who know of us. These weaker ties can be an important resource. Social networking websites are an example of how people can connect globally today.

network Often conceived as a web of social relationships, a type of group that is both looser and denser than a formal group but connects people to each other, and, through those connections, with other people. (p. 78)

6. Organizations

An **organization** is a large, stable, secondary group, independent of its members. A **normative organization** is composed of volunteers who come together for personal satisfaction, while membership in a **coercive organization,** which Goffman identified as a **total institution,** is mandatory and exerts total control. A **utilitarian organization** fulfills specific instrumental purposes for its members. Americans used to be a nation of joiners, belonging to numerous civic organizations, but this has changed. While the formal structures of organizations make them appear neutral, they may actually institutionalize inequality. A **bureaucracy** is an efficient hierarchical formal organization with clear rules and regulations and division of labor, which tends to concentrate power at the top, where the rules often don't seem to apply, and often rigidity and ritualism at the lower levels, which gives rise to the **bureaucratic personality.** Today, compared with the past, organizations we encounter are often global bureaucracies.

organization A formal group of people with one or more shared goals. (p. 81)

normative organization Voluntary organization wherein members serve because they believe in the goals of the organization. (p. 81)

coercive organization One in which membership is not voluntary, with elaborate formal rules and sanctions. (p. 81)

total institution An institution that completely circumscribes your everyday life, cutting you off from life before you entered and seeking to regulate every part of your behavior. (p. 82)

utilitarian organization Organization, like the college we attend or the company we work for, whose members belong for a specific, instrumental purpose or tangible material reward. (p. 82)

bureaucracy Originally derived from the French word *bureau,* or office, a formal organization characterized by a division of labor, a hierarchy of authority, formal rules governing behavior, a logic of rationality, and an impersonality of criteria. (p. 84)

bureaucratic personality Robert Merton's term to describe those people who become more committed to following the correct procedures than they are to getting the job done. (p. 85)

7. Groups 'R' Us: Groups and Interactions in the Twenty-First Century

Society today is vastly different than bygone centuries, with great diversity, and global networking, yet we still locate ourselves within primary group memberships. Our values are often in contradiction with our social realities. In the midst of seeming chaos and contradiction, there are regular and predictable patterns of human behavior, and sociology provides the conceptual tools for identifying them. Our group memberships are an important aspect of ourselves and our society.

Self-Test: Check Your Understanding

1. Cooley used the term _____ for the process by which we construct our identities from the imagined response of others.
   a. looking-glass self
   b. impression management
   c. ethnomethodology
   d. dramaturgy

2. As the text points out, race and ethnicity are both examples of a(n)
   a. role performance.
   b. achieved status.
   c. master status.
   d. group.

3. Goffman's view of social interaction as the performance of roles is known as
   a. ethnomethodology.
   b. dramaturgy.
   c. groupthink.
   d. looking-glass self.

4. The Los Angeles Lakers basketball team is an example of a
   a. primary group.
   b. secondary group.
   c. dyad.
   d. crowd.

5. A workgroup maintained cohesion and consensus to the extent that members kept their concerns about the project to themselves, instead of voicing them. This is an example of
   a. impression management.
   b. diffusion of responsibility.
   c. in-group heterogeneity.
   d. groupthink.

6. Identify which of the following is not a characteristic of bureaucracies identified by Max Weber:
   a. Efficiency
   b. Division of labor
   c. Hierarchy of authority
   d. Bureaucratic personality

7. Compared with the last century, for Americans in the twenty-first century participation in organizations overall has
   a. increased.
   b. declined.
   c. remained constant.
   d. failed to follow a consistent pattern.

8. According to the text, the dominant form of organizations we encounter in large complex societies like America are
   a. normative organizations.
   b. total institutions.
   c. bureaucracies.
   d. primary groups.

Self-Test Answers: 1. a, 2. c, 3. b, 4. b, 5. d, 6. d, 7. b, 8. c

Integrate and Explore: Points to Consider

1. How have the organizations and groups we belong to changed in the twenty-first century? Which group memberships have remained largely the same? Which have changed dramatically? In what ways have our lives, as social actors, changed as a result?

2. Identify a number of group memberships you hold and a number of organization memberships. Discuss the type of group and organization each is, and the characteristics of members of the group that are shared, contrasting this with the ways in which members are diverse. Are there any patterns to be found? Do you find greater diversity among members of your own groups or among members of groups other than your own?

succeed with mysoclab PEARSON

Self-scoring practice tests, flashcards for learning key terms, streaming audio of the entire text, and multimedia, including:

Watch—*Facebook Etiquette*
Watch—Michael Kimmel, *Multiculturalism and Identity*
MySocLibrary—Philip Meyer, *If Hitler Asked You to Electrocute a Stranger…*
MySocLibrary—George Ritzer, *The McDonaldization of Society*

How Do We Know
What We Know?
The Methods of the Sociologist

Everybody knows that divorce is bad for children. It's a daily staple on TV talk shows that children of divorced parents are less emotionally well adjusted and have lower rates of achievement in school, poorer grades, lower self-esteem, and higher rates of depression than kids from intact families.

What everybody knows is based on two sorts of studies. First, child psychologists indicate that the majority of the kids they see are children from families of divorce. And there are studies comparing the experiences and achievements of children from divorced families with those of children from intact families. Therefore, we are constantly advised, parents should stay together "for the good of the children."

To a sociologist, though, both sources of data are riddled with problems. How does the population of children in therapy compare with the population of children who are not in therapy? Could it be that children whose parents are divorcing are sent to therapists by courts or mediators? Could it be that whatever problems children might have, they are attributed to the divorce by well-meaning therapists—even if the problems have nothing to do with the divorce?

And comparing children from families of divorce with children in intact families compares two incomparable groups. After all, divorce is not an alternative to marriage, it's an alternative to an *unhappy* marriage. And if you were to compare children from families of divorce with children from intact families in which there was a lot of conflict between the parents, the children from divorced families actually are doing *better!*

"It turns out that much of what passes for common sense turns out to be wrong. Sociology enables us to use scientific thinking to see the complexity of various issues."

It turns out, in a sense, that what "everybody knows" is wrong. Sociologists Paul Amato and Paul Booth found that children from intact high-conflict families fare worse than children in intact, low-conflict families and children from divorced families. And while we would never prescribe divorce "for the sake of the children," it's clear that the impact of divorce is far more complicated, and

children far more resilient, than many popular pundits might imagine (Amato, 2000; Booth and Amato, 2001).

How could these conclusions have been so wrong? It turns out that the populations they chose for their sample, the way they constructed comparisons, and the manner in which they analyzed data led the researchers down an errant path. Most researchers are honest and well intentioned. But the methods they choose can often lead them astray.

This example shows how false it is to dismiss sociology as simply "making a science out of common sense." It turns out that much of what passes for common sense turns out to be wrong. Sociology enables us to use scientific thinking to see the complexity of various issues.

Why Sociological Methods Matter

Sociology is a "social science," a phrase that requires some consideration. As a social *science,* sociology, like economics or political science, uses methods derived from the natural sciences to study social phenomena. Sociologists study group dynamics as an economist might study price fluctuations: When some new element is introduced to the situation, we can measure its direct impact on its surroundings.

But sociology is also a *social* science, like anthropology or history, attempting to study human behavior as it is lived by conscious human beings. As a result of that consciousness, human beings don't behave in exactly the same ways all the time, the ways that natural phenomena like gravity, or planetary orbits, might. People possess **subjectivity**—a complex of individual perceptions, motivations, ideas, and really messy things like emotions. "Imagine how hard physics would be if particles could think" is how the Nobel Prize–winning physicist Murray Gell-Mann once put it (cited by Angle, 1997).

Thus, sociology uses a wide variety of methodologies—perhaps a greater variety than any other academic field. The range of different methods sociologists use extends from complex statistical models, carefully controlled experiments, and enormous surveys to such methods as the literary analysis of texts, linguistic analysis of conversations, ethnographic and field research, "participant observation," and historical research in archives. That is because the range of questions that sociologists pose for research is also enormous. Students of sociology should be exposed to a wide variety of methodologies. The method we use should depend less on some preexisting prejudice and more on what we want to study.

You might think that the choice of method and the type of data that you use are of little importance. After all, if you are trying to find out the truth, won't every method basically get you to the same results? In fact, though, the methods we use and the kinds of questions we ask are often so important that they actually lead to some answers and away from others. And such answers have enormous implications for public policy.

Here's a recent example. For centuries people have argued about "nature" versus "nurture." Which is more important in determining your life course, heredity or environment? In recent years, the argument has been tilting increasingly toward nature. These days, "everybody knows" intelligence is largely innate, genetically transmitted. The most famous—or, to schoolchildren, infamous—

Is intelligence the result of nature or nurture? Both. Class matters also. Poor twins show greater differences in IQ than do middle class twins, whose IQs are very similar.

Chapter 4 How Do We Know What We Know? The Methods of the Sociologist

test of all is the IQ test, a test designed to measure your "innate" intelligence, or aptitude, the natural genetically based ability you have to understand things. Sure, good schools and good environments can help, but most studies have found that about 75 percent of intelligence is hereditary. Typically, these sorts of studies are used by opponents of affirmative action to argue that no amount of intervention is going to help those at the bottom—they're at the bottom for a reason.

It turns out, though, that this "fact" was the result of the methods being used to find it out. Most of the data for the genetic basis for intelligence are based on studies of twins. Identical twins share exactly the same DNA; fraternal twins, or other siblings, share only half. Researchers have thus taken the finding that the IQs of identical twins were more similar than for nonidentical twins and other siblings as a demonstration that heredity determines intelligence.

But recently, Eric Turkheimer (Turkheimer et al., 2003, 2005) and his colleagues reexamined those studies and found a curious thing. Almost all the studies of twins were of *middle-class* twins (poor people tend not to volunteer for research studies). When he examined the results from a massive study of more than 50,000 children and factored in the class background of the families, a startling picture emerged. For the children from wealthy families, virtually all the differences in IQ could be attributed to heredity. But among poor children, the IQs of identical twins varied a lot—as much as the IQs of fraternal twins.

The impact of growing up in poverty (an environmental effect) completely offset the effects of heredity. For the poor, home life and environment are absolutely critical. "If you have a chaotic environment, kids' genetic potential doesn't have a chance to be expressed," Turkheimer told a journalist. "Well-off families can provide the mental stimulation needed for genes to build the brain circuitry for intelligence" (Turkheimer, cited in Kirp, 2006).

It turns out that a certain environmental threshold has to be reached before heredity can kick in and "determine" anything. Only under some environmental conditions can the genetic ability emerge. It is a clear indication that it's rarely either/or—either nature *or* nurture. It's almost always both. But it took careful research to see the shortcomings in those previous studies and help to correct the misunderstanding that resulted. And think, then,

"*Are you just pissing and moaning, or can you verify what you're saying with data?*"

of the potential geniuses whose environments have never enabled their ability to emerge!

Sociology and the Scientific Method

As social scientists, sociologists follow the rules of the scientific method. As in any argument or debate, science requires the use of evidence, or data, to demonstrate a position. The word **data** (the plural of datum) refers to formal and systematic information, organized and coherent. Data are not simply a collection of anecdotes; they are systematically collected and systematically organized.

To gather data, sociologists use a variety of methods. Sociologists share many of these methods with other social scientists. To the sociologist, the choice of method is often determined by the sorts of questions you want to answer. Some sociologists perform experiments just as natural scientists do. Other times they rely on large-scale surveys to provide a general pattern of behaviors or attitudes. They may use historical materials found in archives or other historical sources, much as any historian would. Sociologists will reexamine data from other sources. They might analyze systematically the content of a cultural product, such as a novel, a magazine, a film, or a conversation. Some sociologists rely on interviews or focus groups with particular kinds of people to understand how they see things. Another sociologist might go into the field and live in another culture, participating in its customs and rituals much as an anthropologist might do.

Some of these research methods use **deductive reasoning**—they logically proceed from one demonstrable fact to the next and deduce their results. These are more like the methods of the natural sciences, and the results we obtain are independent of any feelings that the researchers or their subjects may have. It's often impossible to then reason from the general to the specific: If you were to find out that a majority of American teachers supported the use of corporal punishment in the schools, you wouldn't be able to predict what your own teacher will do if you misbehave. (Don't worry, it's not true: Most teachers oppose it.)

In other situations, the feelings of our research subjects are exactly what we are trying to study, and we will need to rely on **inductive reasoning,** which will help us to understand a problem using our own human capacity to put ourselves in the other person's position. In this case, the research leads the researcher to a conclusion about all or many members of a class based on examination of only a few members of that class. For example, if you want to understand *why* teachers support corporal punishment, you might interview a few of them in depth, go observe their classrooms for a period of time, or analyze a set of texts that attempt to explain it from the inside (Figure 4.1).

Inductive reasoning is also what Max Weber called **verstehen,** a method that uses "intersubjective understanding." By this he meant that you use your own abilities to see the world from others' point of view. Sometimes sociologists want to check all emotions at the door of their research lab, lest they contaminate their findings with human error. At other times, it is our uniquely human capacity for empathic connection that is the source of our understanding.

Sociologists study an enormous range of issues. Virtually every area of human behavior is studied, from the large-scale activities of governments, corporations, and international organizations like the European Union or the United Nations, to the most minute and intimate decision making about sexual practices or conversations or self-presentation. As a result, the methods that we use to study sociological problems depend more on the kind of problem we want to study than whether one method is better than any other. Each method provides different types of data, and each type can be enormously useful and illuminate a different part of the problem.

Research methods are like the different ways we use glass to see objects. Some of us will want a magnifying glass, to bring the object so close that we can see every single little feature of the particular object. Others will prefer a prism, by which the object is fragmented into hundreds of tiny parts. A telescope is useful if the object is really far away but pretty useless if you need to see what's happening next door. Bifocals are best if you want to view both close and distant objects through the same lens.

Each of these ways of seeing is valuable. A specific method may be inappropriate to adequately study a specific problem, but no research method should be dismissed as inadequate or inappropriate in all situations. It depends on what you want to know.

The Qualitative/ Quantitative Divide

Most often we think that the real divide among social science methods is between quantitative and qualitative methods. Using **quantitative methods,** one uses powerful statistical tools to help understand patterns in which the behaviors, attitudes, or traits under study can be translated into numerical values. Typically, quantitative methods rely on deductive reason-

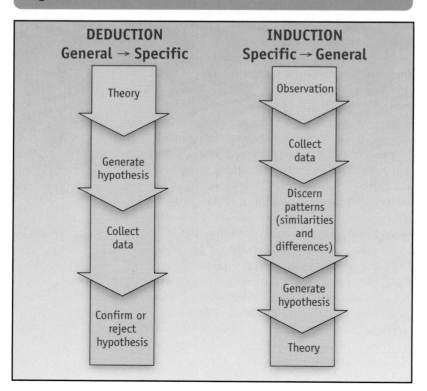

Figure 4.1 Inductive and Deductive Research Models

DEDUCTION
General → Specific

Theory
↓
Generate hypothesis
↓
Collect data
↓
Confirm or reject hypothesis

INDUCTION
Specific → General

Observation
↓
Collect data
↓
Discern patterns (similarities and differences)
↓
Generate hypothesis
↓
Theory

ing. So, for example, checking a box on a survey that gives your sex as "male" or "female" might enable the researcher to examine the relative percentages of men and women who subscribe to certain ideas, vote for a particular political party, or avoid certain behaviors.

Qualitative methods often rely on more inductive and inferential reasoning to understand the texture of social life, the actual felt experience of social interaction. Qualitative methods are often derided as less scientific, as quantitative researchers often assume that their own methods eliminate bias and that therefore only quantitative methods are scientific.

These are convenient myths, but they are incorrect; they are, themselves, the result of bias. Both quantitative and qualitative methods are capable of understanding social reality—although each type of method illuminates a different part of that reality. Both types of methodologies have biases, but qualitative methodologists struggle to make their biases explicit (and thus better control them), while quantitative researchers, assuming they have no biases, sometimes don't see them. Personal values always influence the sorts of questions we ask, the hypotheses we develop and test, and the interpretation of the results.

After all, most great scientific discoveries initially relied on simple and close observation of some phenomenon—like the apple falling on the head of Sir Isaac Newton leading to his "discovery" of gravity. Gradually, from such observations, other scientists are able to expand the reach of explanation to include a wider variety of phenomena, and these are then subject to more statistical analysis.

Social surveys generate large bodies of data for quantitative analysis.

What do **you** think?

Large-scale representative surveys can tell us a lot about our population, about social trends, and about attitudes, behaviors, and beliefs. National survey data tell us that, in general, Americans say they are happy. So where do you fit in that survey?

> Would you say that you are very happy, pretty happy, or not too happy?
>
> O Very happy
>
> O Pretty happy
>
> O Not too happy

What does **America** think?

(These are actual survey data from the General Social Survey, 2004.)

In 1971, 17 percent of respondents said they were not too happy; in 2004 it was much lower, at 12 percent. Differences between Whites and Blacks were significant in 1972, with 32 percent of White respondents and 19 percent of Black respondents saying they were very happy. Black respondents were almost twice as likely to say they were not too happy than were Whites. By 2004, those differences had evened out; 34.8 percent of White respondents and 34.0 percent of Black respondents said they were very happy. In 2004, 10.5 percent of White respondents and 16.4 percent of Black respondents reported being not too happy.

Think about It Some More

1. What do you think the researchers were actually measuring with their survey question? If you were going to measure happiness in a survey, how would you operationalize the term *happiness*?

   References: see Davis et al., page 511.

Table 4.1
Quantitative
and Qualitative
Research
Methods

Method	Reasoning	Examples	Tools
Quantitative	Deductive-	-Large-scale survey -Public opinion polls -Secondary analysis of large-scale data set	-Statistical analysis -Sampling
Qualitative	Inductive	-Ethnography -Interviews -Focus groups -Field studies -Historical research	-Observation -Document and archival research -Small group experiments -Textual analysis

Here's an example. Recently, a study found that nationally, 72 percent of the girls and 65 percent of the boys in the high school class of 2003 actually earned their diplomas and graduated from high school (Lewin, 2006). One can interpret this in several different ways: (1) Things are going well, and the overwhelming majority of boys and girls do earn their diplomas; (2) things are going terribly for everyone because nearly one in every three high school students did not earn his or her diploma; (3) things are going significantly worse for boys than for girls, as there is a significant "gender gap" in high school graduation. (Each of these interpretations was made by a different political group.)

Debates among sociologists and other social scientists often focus on which method leads to the "truth." But the correct answer is *both* methods lead us to the "truth"—that is, each method is adept at revealing a different part of the entire social experience.

Types of Sociological Research Methods

Sociologists typically use one of two basic types of research methods. One type of method relies on the observation of behavior, either in a controlled setting, like a lab, or, more often in sociology, in its natural setting, where people usually do the behavior you're studying (what we call the "field"). Another type relies on analysis of accumulated data, either from surveys or from data already collected by others. Each of these basic types is composed of several subtypes.

What social scientists call *variables* help us measure whether, how, and in what ways something changes (varies) as a result of the research. There are different kinds of variables. An **independent variable** is the event or item in your experiment that is considered to be the cause or influence of the other, dependent, variables. You will manipulate the independent variable to see if that difference has an impact. If it does, it will affect what's called the dependent variable.

The **dependent variable** gets its name because it depends on, or is caused or influenced by, the independent variable. The dependent variable is the variable that the researcher thinks might *depend on* the independent variable. It is what gets measured in an experiment; it's the change to the dependent variable that constitutes your results. Overall, your research results are the relationships between the independent and dependent variables.

These are the key types of variables (see Figure 4.2). But there are others. Let's say you want to test whether heating coffee causes it to boil. Get two pots of coffee, put one on the burner and the other in the freezer, and check it out. In this simple example, there are **extraneous variables** that may influence the outcome of the research but are not actually of interest to the researcher. Extraneous variables might include the material the coffeepot is made of and whether your stove uses gas or electricity. (These might influence the speed of the boiling, or how high the temperature is, but they're not what you are interested in.) And there are **confounding variables** that may be affecting the results of the study but for which you haven't adequately accounted.

Again, in the example above, if the researcher forgot to pay the electric bill and therefore the stove doesn't work, or if the researcher isn't smart enough to correctly sort the pots, it might confound, or complicate, the result. Finally, an **intervening variable** is a variable that intervenes—that is, gets in between—the two variables and thus makes accurate measurement difficult.

Here's another example of the different types of variables, offered by one of my colleagues, Arnout van de Rijt. Let's say that a friend of yours challenges the value of taking sociology courses. She says that if the course was any good, smart students should do better than dumb students. She shows you her evidence. She correlated the IQ scores for all the students in the class with the grades the students received on their sociology exam. IQ had no noticeable effect on the students' grades. She concludes, therefore, that dumb students can be just as successful as smart students. That is, she concludes that because the independent variable (IQ) did *not* change the dependent variable (students' grades), intelligence doesn't matter in sociology!

However, being a sociology student, you know better! You say that you just learned in your sociology course that such evidence is far from conclusive. There are many other variables that can affect your grade. For example, a barking dog could have kept you awake all night before the exam (an extraneous variable). Or you may have had a lot of exposure in your youth to the kinds of tricky puzzles typically found on IQ tests (a confounding variable). And what about the number of hours that you studied for the test (an intervening variable)? Doesn't that affect your grade? In this case, a variety of variables that have nothing whatever to do with IQ will all have dramatically affected the dependent variable.

Sociologists are likely to engage in the following types of research:

- *Observation*. Observing people in their natural habitat, joining their clubs, going to their churches, getting jobs in their offices. This is usually called *participant observation*.
- *Interviews*. Asking a small group of people open-ended questions, such as "Can you describe your last road rage experience?"
- *Surveys*. Asking a lot of people closed-ended questions, such as "How many times have you gotten angry in traffic in the last month?"

Figure 4.2 Types of Variables

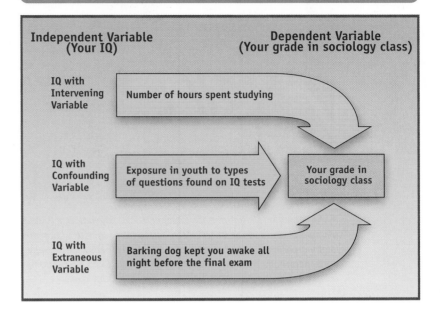

- *Content analysis*. Analyzing artifacts (books, movies, TV programs, magazine articles, and so on) instead of people.

What about going to the library and looking things up in books? Isn't that doing research? Sociologists would call that an incomplete literature review. A real **literature review** needn't perform any original or new research, but it must carefully examine all available research already done on a topic or at least a systematic sample of that research, through a specific critical and theoretical lens.

Let's look at each of these methods in a bit more detail.

Observational Methods

In all observational studies, we directly observe the behavior we are studying. We can do this in a laboratory, conducting an experiment, or we can do it in the place where it more "naturally" occurs. The latter is more common today. For one thing, in lab experiments it is too difficult to change the independent variable. Say you want to know if children of divorced parents are more likely to become juvenile delinquents. You can hardly divide children into two groups and force the parents of the first to divorce and the second to stay together. But in either case, when we observe phenomena, we do more than just watch—we watch scientifically, testing hypotheses against evidence.

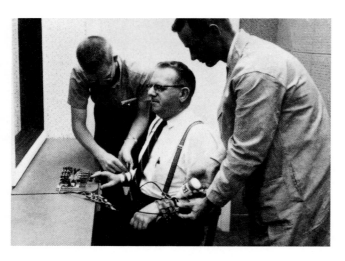

In the "Obedience to Authority" studies, social psychologist Stanley Milgram pretended to attach electrodes to his associate to administer increasingly painful electric shocks when he answered questions incorrectly. Two out of every three test subjects (65 percent) administered shocks all the way up to the maximum level.

Experiments. An **experiment** is a controlled form of observation in which one manipulates independent variables to observe their effects on a dependent variable. To make an experiment valid, one typically uses two groups of people. One is the **experimental group,** and they are the group that will have the change introduced to see what happens. The other is the **control group,** and they will not experience the manipulation of the variable.

A control group enables us to compare the outcomes of the experiment to determine if the changes in the independent variable had any effects on the dependent variable. It is therefore very important that the experimental group and the control group be as similar as possible (by factors such as age, race, religion, class, gender, and so on) so that we can reduce any possibility that one of these other factors may have caused the effects we are examining.

In one of the most famous, or infamous, experiments in social psychology, Stanley Milgram (1963, 1974) wanted to test the limits of people's obedience to authority. During the trials that followed the end of World War II, many Nazis defended themselves by claiming that they were "only following orders." Americans were quick to assume that this blind obedience to some of the most horrifying orders was a character trait of Germans and that such obedience could never happen in the United States. Milgram decided to test this assumption.

He designed an experiment in which a subject was asked to participate in an experiment ostensibly about the effects of negative reinforcement on learning. The "learner" (a colleague of the experimenter) was seated at a table and hooked up to a machine that would supposedly administer an electric shock of increasing voltage every time the learner answered the question wrong. The "teacher" (the actual subject of the experiment) sat in another room, asked the questions to the learner, and had to administer the electric shock when the learner gave the wrong answer.

The machine that administered the shocks had a dial that ranged from "Minor" at one end of the dial to a section marked in red that said "Danger—Severe Shock." And when the teacher reached that section, the "learner" would scream in apparent agony. (Remember, no shocks were actually administered; the experiment was done to see how far the teacher would go simply by being told to do so by the experimenter. The researcher would only say, "Please continue," or "The experiment requires that you continue.")

Milgrim's experiment did not use the two groups—experimental and control—but it did include the essential element of experiments: an intervention or manipulation by the researcher. The independent variables included the orders given by the researcher and the distance between the "teacher" and the "learner"; the dependent variable was the amount of "shock."

What would you have done? What percentage of Americans do you think administered a shock to another human being simply because a psychologist told them to? And what percentage would have administered a potentially lethal electric shock? What would you do if your sociology professor told you to give an electric shock to the person sitting next to you in class?

The results were startling. Most people, when asked, say they would be very unlikely to do such a thing. But, in the experiment, over two-thirds of the "teachers" administered shocks that would have been lethal to the learners. They simply did what they were told to do, despite the facts that they could hear the learners screaming in pain and the shocks were clearly labeled as potentially fatal. (After the experiment was over, the teacher and learner met, and the teachers were relieved to realize that they did not actually kill the learners.) And virtually no one refused to administer any shocks to another person. From this, Milgram concluded that

Nazism was not the result of a character flaw in Germans but that even Americans, with their celebrated rebelliousness and distaste for authority, would obey without much protest.

Let's look at an equally startling but far less controversial experiment. In the late 1960s and early 1970s, sociologists Robert Rosenthal and Lenore Jacobson decided to test the *self-fulfilling prophesy*—the idea that you get what you expect or that you see what you believe (Rosenthal and Jacobson, 1968). They hypothesized that teachers had expectations of student performance and that students performed to those expectations. That is, the sociologists wanted to test their hypothesis that teachers' expectations were actually the cause of student performance, not the other way around. If the teacher thinks a student is smart, the student will do well in the class. If the teacher expects the student to do poorly, the student will do poorly.

Rosenthal and Jacobson administered an IQ test to all the children in an elementary school. Then, without looking at the results, they randomly chose a small group of students and told their teachers that the students had extremely high IQs. This, Rosenthal and Jacobson hypothesized, would raise the teachers' expectations for these randomly chosen students (the experimental group), and these expectations would be reflected in better performance by these students compared with other students (the control group).

At the end of the school year, Rosenthal and Jacobson returned to the school and administered another IQ test to all the students. The "chosen few" performed better on the test than their classmates, yet the only difference between the two groups was the teachers' expectations. It turned out that teacher expectations were the independent variable, and student performance was the dependent variable—not the other way around.

(Before you blame your teachers' expectations for your own grades, remember that professors have been made aware of these potential biases and have, in the past 40 years, developed a series of checks on our expectations. Your grades probably have at least as much to do with your own effort as they do your professors' expectations!)

Neither of these experiments could be conducted in this way today because of changes in the laws surrounding experiments with human subjects. This is another reason sociologists are doing fewer experiments now than they once did.

Field Studies. Many of the issues sociologists are concerned with are not readily accessible in controlled laboratory experiments. Instead, sociologists go "into the field" to conduct research among the people they want to study. (The field is any site where the interactions or processes you want to study are taking place, such as an institution like a school or a specific community.) In observational studies, we rely on ourselves to interpret what is happening, and so we test our sociological ways of seeing.

Some observational studies require **detached observation,** a perspective that constrains the researcher from becoming in any way involved in the event he or she is observing. This posture of detachment is less about some notion of objectivity—after all, we are relying on our subjective abilities as an observer—and more because being detached and away from the action reduces the amount that our observation will change the dynamic we're watching. (Being in the field, even as an observer, can change the very things we are trying to study.)

For example, let's say you want to see if there is a gender difference in children's play. If you observe boys and girls unobtrusively from behind a one-way mirror or screen, they'll play as if no one was watching them. But if they know there are grownups watching, they might behave differently. Detached observation is useful, but it doesn't enable you as a researcher to get inside the experience. For that you'll have to participate in the activities of the people you are studying. **Participant observation** requires that the researcher do both, participate and observe. Many participant observers conceal their identity to blend in better with the group they're studying.

Juggling these two activities is often difficult. In one famous case, Leon Festinger (1957) studied a cult that predicted the end of the world on a certain date. All cult members were required to gather at the leader's house and wait for the end of the world. Festinger participated in the group's activities and every hour or so rushed to the bathroom to record what he was observing. Other cult members assumed he had some digestive distress!

In another famous study, Laud Humphreys (1970) was interested in the negotiation of anonymous homosexual sex in public restrooms. He volunteered to act as a lookout for the men who waited at a rest stop along the

Ethnographers travel to "exotic" locales or study neighborhoods closer to home: urban street vendors, street gangs, or the close-knit community of Italian Americans in Little Italy to name a few.

New Jersey Turnpike because it was against the law to have sex in public restrooms. As the lookout, he was able to observe the men who stopped there to have sex and jotted down their license plate numbers. Later, he was able to trace the men's addresses through their license plate numbers and went to their homes posing as a researcher doing a general sociological study. (This allowed him to ask many questions about their backgrounds.) His findings were as astonishing as they were controversial. Most of the men who stopped at public restrooms to have sex with other men were married and considered themselves heterosexual. Most were working class and politically conservative and saw their behavior simply as sexual release, not as an expression of "who they really were."

Humphreys's research has been severely criticized because he deceived the men he was studying, and he disguised his identity. As a result, universities developed institutional review boards (IRBs) to insure that researchers comply with standards and ethics

in conducting their research. But Humphreys was also able to identify a population of men who had sex with other men who did not identify as gay, and this was later thought to be one of the possible avenues of transmission for HIV from the urban gay population into heterosexual suburban homes.

Increasingly, field researchers use the ethnographic methods of cultural anthropology to undertake sociological research. **Ethnography** is a field method used most often by anthropologists when they study other cultures. While you don't pretend to be a participant (and you identify yourself as a researcher), you try to understand the world from the point of view of the people whose lives you are interested in and attempt, as much as possible, to put your own values and assumptions about their activities "on hold." This avoids two extreme outcomes: (1) If you try to forget your own cultural assumptions and immerse yourself, you risk "going native"—which means you uncritically embrace the group's way of seeing things. (2) If you see the other group only through the filter of your own values, you impose your way of seeing things and can't really understand how they see the world. At its most extreme, this is a form of cultural imperialism—imposing your values on others. Ethnographers attempt to steer a middle path between these extremes.

Ethnographers live and work with the group they're studying to try to see the world from the others' point of view. Two of the most famous of such studies are William F. Whyte's *Street Corner Society* ([1943] 1993) and Elliot Liebow's *Tally's Corner* (1968). Both studies examined the world of working-class and poor men; Whyte's subjects were White and Italian in Boston; Liebow's were Black men in Washington, D.C. In both cases, readers learned more about the complexity in these men's lives than anyone had ever imagined.

Recent field work among urban minorities has echoed these themes. Martin Sanchez-Jankowski (1991) lived with Latino gangs in Los Angeles. Contrary to popular assumptions that might hold that gangs are composed of children from broken homes, adrift and delinquent because they are psychologically maladjusted, Sanchez-Jankowski found that most came from intact families, were psychologically better adjusted than non–gang members, and saw gang membership as a reasonable economic alternative to unemployment and poverty. Gangs provided good steady jobs, high wages (with high risks), and the rich social relationships that come from community. Similarly, Elijah Anderson's research on young Black men in the inner city (1992, 2000) gave a far deeper understanding of the complex of meanings and motives for behavior that had often been reduced to rather one-dimensional stereotypes.

Ethnography taxes our powers of observation and stretches our sociological muscles to try to see the world from the point of view of other people. Philippe Bourgois (1995) lived for three years in New York City's Spanish Harlem, studying the culture of crack dealers. Loic Wacquant (2003) trained for over three years right alongside local boxers in a training gym in Chicago's South Side. Mitch Duneier (1999) hung out with unlicensed and often homeless street vendors in New York. And Sudhir Venkatesh (2008) was "gang leader for a day" in a gang on Chicago's South Side. Ethnographic methods enable us to see people's worlds up close, in intimate detail, bringing out both subtle patterns and structural forces that shape social realities.

Interview Studies. The most typical type of qualitative study uses **interviews** with a small sample. These studies use a **purposive sample,** which means that respondents are not selected randomly and not representative of the larger population but selected purposively—that is, each subject is selected precisely because he or she possesses certain characteristics that are of interest to the researcher.

One problem with interview studies is not the size of the sample but the fact that the sample is not a probability sample—that is, it is not a random sample, but rather the sample is selectively drawn to make sure that specific characteristics are included or excluded. Purposive samples do not allow sociologists to generalize about their results as reliably as they can with random samples. However, they do enable researchers to identify common themes in the data and can sensitize us to trends in attitudes or behaviors among specifically targeted groups of people.

For example, let's say you wanted to study feelings of guilt among new mothers, to see how much these feelings were influenced by television shows and magazine articles that instruct women on how to be good mothers.

It wouldn't make much sense to conduct a random sample, because you wouldn't get enough new mothers in the sample. You could use a "snowball" technique—asking one new mother to refer you to others. Or you could draw a random sample from a nonrandom population—if, for example, the manufacturers of baby foods could be persuaded to give you their mailing lists of new mothers and you selected every hundredth name on the list. (We discuss sampling further below.)

All the methods above involve actually interacting with real people—either in a controlled environment or in their natural habitat. These methods give us a kind of up-close and personal feel to the research, an intimate knowledge with fine nuance and detail.

You know the old expression of being unable to see the forest for the trees. Field methods such as ethnographies are often so focused on the minute patterns of leaves and bark on an individual tree that they lose a sense of the shape and size of the forest. Because the researcher wants to understand broad patterns of behaviors and attitudes, sociologists also use more quantitative methods involving our interaction not with people but with data. Of course, these methods might reveal the larger patterns, but it's hard to make out the nuances and subtleties of the individual trees.

Ethnography enables researchers to see people's worlds up close, in intimate detail, bringing out both subtle patterns and structural forces that shape social realities. Here you can see an ethnographer talking with villagers in Bundu Tuhan, Malaysia.

Analysis of Quantitative Data

Quantitative data analysis involves the use of surveys and other instruments to understand those larger patterns mentioned previously.

Surveys. **Surveys** are the most common method that sociologists use to collect information about attitudes and behaviors. For example, you might be interested in how religion influences sexual behavior. A survey might be able to tell you whether an adolescent's religious beliefs influence whether he or she has had sex (it does) or whether a married person has committed adultery (it doesn't). Or a survey might address whether being a registered Republican or Democrat has any relationship to the types of sports one likes to watch on television (it does).

To construct a survey, we first decide the sorts of questions we want to ask and how best to ask them. While the simplest question would be a dichotomous question, in which "yes" and "no" were the only choices, this form

Sociology and Our World

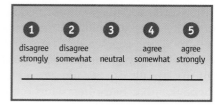

How to "Read" a Survey

- Four out of five doctors recommend Zytrolvan.
- Forty-three percent of Americans support the president's policy.

We hear statements like these all the time. But what do they mean?

According to the American Association for Public Opinion Research, an intelligent analysis of survey results requires that you know some minimal information:

- Who sponsored the survey, and who conducted it?
- What is the population being studied?
- What is the sample selection procedure?
- What are the size of the sample and the completion rates?
- What is the wording of the questions?
- What are the method, location, and dates of data collection?
- How precise are the findings, including weighting or estimating procedures and sampling error?
- Are some results based on parts of the sample rather than the whole sample?

Unfortunately, very few of the survey results you hear about in the mass media (or, for that matter, in many textbooks) include all of the necessary information. Therefore you cannot be sure of their accuracy. If the accuracy of the numbers is important to you, look up the references. If there are no references, start to worry.

Figure 4.3 A Likert Scale

1	2	3	4	5
disagree strongly	disagree somewhat	neutral	agree somewhat	agree strongly

of question can provide only limited information. For example, if you asked, "Do you believe that sex before marriage is always wrong?," you might find out some distribution of moral beliefs, but such answers would tell you little about how people *use* that moral position, whether they apply it to themselves or to others, and how they might deal with those who transgress.

Usually, we ask questions that can be graded on a scale. The most common form is a **Likert scale** that arranges possible responses from lowest to highest. Instead of a simple "yes" or "no" answer, survey respondents are asked to place themselves on a continuum at one of five points or one of seven points. When respondents answer a question on a survey by saying whether we "strongly agree," "agree," "neither agree nor disagree," "disagree," or "disagree strongly," the researchers are using a Likert scale (Figure 4.3).

Once we've decided what questions to ask, we have to decide to whom to ask them. But you can't ask everyone: It would cost too much, take too long, and be impossible to analyze. Sociologists take a **sample** (or a subset) of the population they want to study. (We've already discussed the purposive sampling of interview studies; sampling is part of almost all research; sociologists always have to decide who to study.) Surveys are often done by telephone or by mail. If you want to know what Americans think about an issue, you can't ask all of them. A **random sample** asks a number of people, chosen by an abstract and arbitrary method, like tossing a piece of paper with each person's name on it into a hat. In this way, each person has an equal chance of being selected. Another good type of sample, the **systematic sample,** is done by choosing every tenth name in a telephone book or every thousandth name on the voter registration list. Technically, this sample is not random, because the researcher

Calculating the number of deaths as a consequence of war is a gruesome but difficult task. We might know how many troops armies have, but what about civilian casualties? In Iraq, for example, different sources of data—hospital records, media reports, police reports, or mortuary data—all provide conflicting numbers. (These numbers are low because many people don't go to hospitals, are buried by their families, and are not reported to the media or police. What's more, Iraq has never had a national census, so random sampling would be uncertain because the lists of residents from which such a sample might be drawn would be incomplete.)

Demographer Gilbert Burnham and his colleagues at the Johns Hopkins School of Public Health conducted cluster samples in which they picked out neighborhoods at random and surveyed all the people living in them. They examined data from 47 neighborhoods, each of which had about 40

Finding Hard-to-Get Answers through Sampling

residents living in it. They asked residents whether anyone had died since the U.S. invasion and what the cause of death was and certified over 90 percent of the deaths. They compared this to data from before the invasion, and they calculated that about 650,000 more people had died than would have died had the war never begun, a number significantly higher than earlier estimates (*The Economist*, October 12, 2006).

The statistical methods we use often have significant impact on how we perceive an event.

is following a system, but it is still a good method because it is not biased.

When you take a random sample, you assume that those not in the population from which you are choosing your sample are themselves random. For example, choosing from the phone book would exclude those people who don't have telephones (who tend to be rural and conservative) as well as those who use only their cell phones and are not listed (who tend to be urban and liberal). Using voter registration rolls would exclude those who are not registered, but researchers assume an equal number of liberals and conservatives are not registered.

Often the differences between different groups of people are what you actually want to study. In that case, you'd take a **stratified sample,** in which you divide people into different groups before you construct your sample and make sure that you get an adequate number of members of each of the groups. A stratified sample divides the sample into proportions equal to the proportions found in the population at large.

Let's say you wanted to do a study of racial attitudes in Chicago Heights, Illinois. (Chicago Heights is 38 percent African American, 37 percent White, 24 percent Hispanic, 13.5 percent other, 2.7 percent multiracial, 0.8 percent Native American.) A random sample might actually give you an inaccurate portrait because you might, inadvertently,

have an unrepresentative sample, with too few or too many of a particular group. What if your random sample was gathered through voter records, a common method? You'd lose all those residents who were not registered to vote, who tend to be concentrated among minorities and the poor, as well as the young (and the median age in Chicago Heights is 30.6 years old). What if you called every one-hundredth number in the phone book—you'd lose all those who were unlisted or who don't have landline phones and overrepresent statistically those who have several numbers (and would therefore stand a higher chance of being called). So your random sample could turn out to be not very representative. A stratified sample would enable you to match, in the sample, the percentages in the actual population, making the data much more reliable.

Another type of sample is a **cluster sample.** In these, the researcher might choose a systematic sample of neighborhoods—say every tenth block in a town—and then survey every person in that "cluster." This sort of sample often provides a richer "local" feel to a more representative sample.

Surveys are extremely common in the contemporary United States. There are dozens of organizations devoted to polling Americans on every possible attitude or behavior on a daily basis. Politicians rely on survey data to tailor their policies and shape their message.

Table 4.2
The General
Social Survey
(GSS)

The General Social Survey (GSS; www.norc.org/GSS+Website/) has been surveying American attitudes and behaviors since 1972. Here is a sample of some of the categories that the GSS asks about. Let's look at Americans' attitudes on the government's spending priorities over a 20-year period, 1986 to 2006. More Americans think we spend "too much" on the following:

	1986	1996	2006
Aid to Foreign Countries	75.0%	75.1	64.6
Defense	38.7%	32.9	39.4

More Americans think we spend "too little" on the following:

	1986	1996	2006
Education	65.0%	73.0	74.1
Health Care	60.6%	65.6	73.5
Crime	66.4%	69.3	61.2
The Environment	62.4%	62.0	68.9

(*Source:* Tom W. Smith, "Trends in National Spending Priorities, 1973–2006." General Social Survey National Opinion Research Center, University of Chicago, 2007.)

These are often so targeted and biased that they may make the politicians feel more comfortable, but they may tell us little about what the actual citizenry thinks about a particular issue. Some surveys are created by websites or popular magazines, and these sometimes get attention for their results even though most fail to use valid methods of sampling and questioning. Still, numerous surveys that we see, hear, or read about are developed and privately administered by bona fide research organizations like Roper or Gallup; other sound surveys are publicly financed and available to all researchers for low or no cost, such as the General Social Survey at the National Opinion Research Center in Chicago. The General Social Survey has been surveying American attitudes since 1972, and so one can easily track changes in those attitudes over time. (See Table 4.2.)

Survey Questions. Surveys are the mainstay of sociological research, but coming up with good survey questions is hard. The wording of the question, the possible answers, even the location of the question in the survey questionnaire can change the responses.

Take a classic example (Rugg, 1941). In a national survey, respondents were asked two slightly different questions about freedom of speech:

- Do you think the United States should forbid public speeches against democracy?
- Do you think the United States should allow public speeches against democracy?

When the results came in, 75 percent of respondents would *not allow* the speeches, but only 54 percent would *forbid* them. Surely *forbid* and *not allow* mean the same thing in practice, but the wording changed the way people thought about the issue. In many cases asking both questions helps us test the validity of our methods—whether the question is measuring what we think it is measuring. But researchers are still trying to figure how to avoid this problem.

Have you ever shoplifted? No? Well, then, have you ever taken an object from a store without paying for it? Respondents are much more likely to answer "yes" to the second version because it somehow doesn't seem as bad, even though it's really the same thing.

Do you think women should have the right to have an *abortion?* How about the right to *end their pregnancy?* You guessed it—far more respondents favor the right to end a pregnancy than to have an abortion.

How about the placement of the question in the survey? Respondents are much more likely to respond honestly to the shoplifting question if it's near the end of the survey. When sensitive or embarrassing questions come early, respondents are put off, wondering how intimate the questions are going to get. After they get a little practice by answering questions about their gender, race, age, and occupation, then they are able to handle the tough questions more readily.

Secondary Analysis of Existing Data. Given the enormous amount of time and money it takes to conduct a survey from scratch, many sociologists rely on the survey data previously collected from others. **Secondary analysis** involves reanalyzing data that have already been collected. Often this new analysis looks at the data in a different way or compares different variables.

Others may need to use existing historical data. After all, if you're interested in political debates in seventeenth-century France, you can't very well conduct a survey or interview the participants. Still others use content analysis to explore what people actually mean when they give the sorts of responses they do.

For example, let's say you were interested in the effect of political persuasions on moral attitudes and behavior. Perhaps your hypothesis was that the more conservative one is politically, the more conservative one might be morally. You've operationalized your variables on political persuasion by assuming conservatives are registered Republican and liberals are registered Democratic and that morally conservative people will disapprove of divorce and be less likely to get a divorce. You decide to test the hypothesis that because Republicans are less likely to approve of divorce than Democrats are, then Republicans are less likely to get divorced (attitudes lead to behavior).

You find that a reputable social scientific researcher had done a survey of a sample of Americans, but this researcher was interested only in gender and racial differences in moral attitudes and behavior. It's possible that the research contains other background variables, such as age, political persuasion, educational background, or occupation. Secondary analysis of the existing data will enable you to answer your questions. In addition, you might be able to find data on statewide divorce rates and statewide political attitudes; while these will not answer the question at the more indivi-dual level, they can point to broad patterns about whether conservatives are true to their beliefs and so less likely to divorce. (The answer is apparently no; states that voted Republican in the last three presidential elections have higher divorce rates than states that voted Democratic; 11 "red states" recorded higher divorce rates than any "blue state" in 2000 and 2004, and in 2008 "red states" were eight of the top 10) (Crary, 1999; Dossier: Red State Values, 2006; U.S. Census Bureau, 2009).

Also, there may be different forms of data you can use. Sometimes, for example, researchers will conduct an *interview* and use only a numeric scale to register responses. But then certain answers to certain questions might prompt the interviewer to ask for more information. These responses may be written down as notes or sentences on the initial interview forms. Going back to these forms might require you to do content analysis of the narrative responses people gave to the questions.

While field studies do not permit exact replication—the cultural group you study is indelibly changed by the fact that you have studied it—one can reasonably "replicate" (reproduce) a field study by careful research. For example, if you are in the field, doing an ethnography, and you keep a running record of both your observations and the research strategies and decisions you made while in the field, other researchers can follow your decision making and attempt to understand a similar phenomenon.

One of my graduate students had gone to college at the University of New Mexico. As an undergraduate, one of her professors told me,

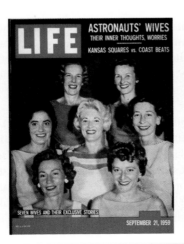

Content analysis of media (such as movies and magazines) can be used to chart the differences in gender ideals. Women today are less likely to be defined only as mothers, or in relation to their husbands' occupations, and more likely to be seen as independent and complex individuals.

she had done a marvelous ethnographic study of local "taggers"—kids who develop elaborate signatures in writing graffiti on walls and public buildings. For several months she hung out with these taggers and interviewed many of them. Just after she wrote her honors thesis, she discovered that someone had just published an ethnographic study of taggers in Denver (Ferrell and Stewart-Huidobro, 1996). She was heartbroken to discover that their conclusions were similar to her own; as she saw it, they had "scooped" her, beaten her to the punch. But her professor explained that actually each researcher had replicated the study of the other researcher, and thus their conclusions were supported, not weakened. This student's work had been validated, not undermined. Although they were not identical, the fact that two teams researching two different examples of a phenomenon in two different cities came to similar conclusions actually strengthens the **generalizability** of the findings of each. We can learn a great deal by such replication because it suggests the extent to which the results of a study can be generalized to other circumstances.

Content Analysis

Content analysis is usually not a quantitative method but instead involves an intensive reading of certain "texts"—perhaps books, or pieces of conversation, or a set of articles from a newspaper or magazine, or even snippets from television shows. Some content analysis involves taking a random, systematic, or other type of sample of such pieces of conversation or media representations and then develops intricate coding procedures for analyzing them. These answers can then be analyzed quantitatively, and one can generate observable variations in the presentations of those texts.

If you want to know if the media images of girls or boys have changed much over the past ten years, then content analysis might enable you to do this. You might choose ten magazines, the five most popular among boys and girls of a certain age. Then you might look at all the issues of those magazines in the month of August of every year for the past ten years and look at the sections called "Back-to-School Fashions." You could devise a coding scheme for these fashions, to judge whether they are more or less gender conforming in terms of style, color, and the like. Then you could see if and how the race or class of the models who are wearing those clothes change. Each of the factors you are measuring is a variable: The independent variable is type of magazine (whether it is intended for boys or intended for girls); and the dependent variables are the details of the way fashions are shown: the models' race, the color and style of the clothes.

Making the Right Comparisons

No matter what research method we choose, it is always important to make sure we are comparing things that are, in fact, comparable (Table 4.3). Otherwise, one risks making claims that turn out not to be true. For example, as we saw at the beginning of the chapter, it is often assumed that divorce has negative consequences for children, both in terms of their school achievement and in terms of their psychological health. But such studies were based on comparisons of children from divorced and married parents and never examined the quality of the marriage. Then, as we saw, children from intact *but unhappy* marriages actually do worse (have lower grades and more psychological problems) than children from divorced families!

Such an example reminds us that researchers in this case needed to distinguish between two types of married parents, happy and unhappy. They needed to include another independent variable: happiness of parents. Policies derived from the original study would have disastrous results for the children who lived in families in which there was a lot of conflict and the parents were really unhappy—even worse consequences than had the parents divorced (Booth and Amato, 2001).

Take another example of how researchers compared the wrong groups. You've probably heard the idea that homosexuality is often the result of a certain family dynamic. Specifically, psychiatrists found that the gay men they saw in therapy often had overdominant mothers and absent fathers (which, the theory goes, caused their homosexuality by preventing the men from making the healthy gender transition away from mother and identifying with

Political Parties and Sex

Republicans have better sex than Democrats. Surveys indicate that Republicans are happier with their sex lives than Democrats. Why? Because Republicans are sexier? Or because they're richer, and thus able to afford more elaborate sex toys? Not at all. It turns out that more men than women are registered Republicans, and more women than men are registered Democrats, and men say that they are more satisfied with their sex lives than women say they are. Party affiliation is irrelevant.

Did You Know?

Table 4.3
Research
Methodologies

Method	Key Points	Problems
Experiments	Some variables can be tightly controlled and monitored. Replication is easy and convenient.	It is difficult to control the independent variable. Ethical considerations prevent many experiments with human subjects.
Field Studies	Sociologists can conduct research directly with the people they want to study.	Research findings may be hard to generalize to other populations.
Interview Studies	A carefully selected sample makes it easy to identify common themes and highlights trends and behaviors within a very specific group.	Generalizing about results is not reliable because the sample group is so targeted.
Surveys	It is easy and convenient to collect large amounts of data about equally large numbers of people.	Data may be corrupt due to poor methodology, including poorly worded questions and answer ordering.
Secondary Analysis of Existing Data	It is often easier and cheaper to rely on information collected by others; sometimes it's the only way to replicate a field study.	You are completely dependent on the original sources and can't use common follow-up methods.
Content Analysis	A researcher can quantitatively analyze an existing text and make generalizable observations based on it.	You may have unacknowledged biases in the sample of texts. You may have unconscious biases in the coding of texts. (It helps to have more than one coder and to compare notes).

father [Bieber et al., 1962]). Such a dynamic would, the researchers believed, keep them "identified" with their mothers and therefore "feminine" in their psychological predisposition. For decades, this family dynamic was the foundation of the psychological treatment of homosexual men. The problem was in the comparative group. The gay men in therapy were compared with the family arrangements of heterosexual men who were not in therapy.

It turned out, though, that the gay men who were not in therapy did not have overdominant mothers and absent fathers. And it also turned out that heterosexual men in therapy *did* have overdominant mothers and absent fathers. In other words, having an overdominant mother and an absent father didn't seem to be the cause of homosexuality but was probably a good predictor of whether a man, straight or gay, decided to go into therapy.

Social Science and the Problem of "Truth"

One thing that is certain about social life is that nothing is certain about social life. Sociology is both a social *science*, sharing basic strategies and perspectives with the natural sciences, and a *social* science, attempting to study living creatures who often behave unpredictably and irrationally, for complex rational, emotional, or psychological reasons. Because a single "truth" is neither knowable nor even possible, social scientists approach their research with the humility of the curious but armed with a vast array of techniques that can help them approach "truths."

Even if truth is impossible, we can approach it. Like all other sciences, we approach it through addressing two central concerns, predictability and causality. **Predictability** refers to the ability to generate testable hypotheses from data and to "predict" the outcomes of some phenomenon or event. **Causality** refers to the relationship of some variable to the effects it produces. According to scientific requirements, a cause is termed "necessary" when it always precedes an effect and "sufficient" when it initiates or produces the effect.

Predictability and Probability

Auguste Comte (1798–1857), often considered the founder of sociology, actually founded something that he called "social physics." He believed that human society follows permanent, unchangeable laws, just as the natural world does. If they know just two variables, temperature and air pressure, chemists can predict with 100 percent certainty whether a vial of H_2O will be solid, liquid, or gas. In the same way, social physicists would be able to predict with 100 percent certainty the behavior of any human population at any time. Will the crowd outside the football game get violent? What political party will win the election? The answer should be merely a matter of analyzing variables.

For 50 years, sociologists analyzed variables. They made a lot of predictions. Some were accurate, many not particularly accurate at all. It turns out that human populations have many more variables than the natural world. Yet predictability is of central concern to sociologists because we hope that if we can understand the variations of enough variables—like race, ethnicity, age, religion, region, and the like—we can reasonably guess what you would be more likely to do in a particular situation. And that—being able to use these variables to predict future behavior—is the essence of predictability.

The number of predictive variables increases dramatically as the group gets bigger and the behavior more complex, until the sociologist has no chance of ever finding them all. But even if we could, predicting human behavior would still be inaccurate because of the observer effect: People *know* that they are being studied. People change their behavior, and even their beliefs and attitudes, based on the situation that they are in, so the variables that are predictive today may not be tomorrow or even five minutes from now.

Causality

Students who take a foreign language in high school tend to be less xenophobic (fearful or suspicious of people from foreign countries). Does taking a foreign language decrease their level of xenophobia, or are xenophobic people less likely to sign up for foreign language classes?

Causality attempts to answer the question we have asked each other since primary school: Which came first, the chicken or the egg? Which "caused" which to happen? Which is the independent variable

---

The Chicken or the Egg

Which came first, the chicken or the egg? Actually, we know. Because living things evolve through changes in their DNA, and because in each animal the DNA is the same in every single cell (beginning with the first cell in reproduction, the zygote), then chickens evolved from nonchickens through a series of tiny changes caused by mutations in the male and female DNA in the process of reproduction. Such changes would only have an effect when a new zygote was created. So, what happened was that two nonchickens mated, but the zygote contained the mutations that produced the first "chicken." When it broke through its shell—presto, the first chicken. So the egg came first.

Did You Know?

(the cause), and which is the dependent variable (the effect)?

In quantitative research, variable *A* is supposed to have a causal impact on variable *B,* but it is not always easy to decide which is the cause and which is the effect. Scientists use a number of clues. Let's look at the old saw that watching violence on television and in the movies (variable *A*) makes children violent (variable *B*).

Imagine I place 50 children at random into two groups. One group of 25 children watches a video about bears learning to share, and the other watches a video about ninjas chopping each others' heads off. I then monitor the children at play. Sure enough, most of the children who watched the sharing video are playing nicely, and the ones who watched the ninjas are pretending to chop each others' heads off. Can I establish a causal link?

The answer is "maybe." There are several other questions that you have to answer:

1. Does variable *B* come after variable *A* in time? Were the children calm and docile until after they watched the ninja video?
2. Is there a high correlation between variable *A* and variable *B?* That is, are all or almost all of the children who watched the ninja video behaving aggressively and all those who watched the bear video behaving calmly?
3. Are there any extraneous variables that might have contaminated the data? Maybe the sharing bears were so boring that the children who watched them are falling asleep.
4. Is there an observer effect that might be contaminating the data? Maybe I'm more likely to classify the behaviors of the ninja video kids as aggressive.

Any or all of these questions might render your assertion that watching ninja videos "causes" violent behavior unreliable. Sociologists must constantly be aware of possible traps and biases in their research—even in a controlled experimental setting like this one (see Table 4.4).

One must also always be on guard against logical fallacies that can lead you in the wrong direction. One problem is what is called the "compositional fallacy" in logic: comparing two groups that are different, assuming they are the same, and drawing an inference between them. Even if all members of category *A* are also members of category *B* doesn't necessarily mean that all members of category *B* are members of category *A*. In its classic formulation: Just because all members of the Mafia (*A*) are Italian (*B*) doesn't mean that all Italians (*B*) are members of the Mafia (*A*).

Storks Really Bring Babies

Where there are more storks, there are more babies. That's true! The higher the number of storks in an area, the higher the birthrate. Could it be that storks actually do bring babies? Well, no. It turns out that storks tend to inhabit rural areas, and rural areas have higher birthrates than urban areas. That is, an extraneous variable (urban versus rural) is the variable that connects those two causally unrelated variables.

Did You Know?

Issue	Question to Ask	Applied?
Sequence	Does *A* come before *B* in time?	Were the children calm and docile when they watched the ninja video?
Correlation	Is there a high correlation between *A* and *B?*	Are all or almost all the children who watched the ninja video behaving aggressively?
Variables	Are there other variables that might have contaminated the data?	Is it possible that the sharing bears video is so boring that everyone just fell asleep?
You (the Researcher)	Is there an observer effect?	Are you more likely to classify the behaviors of ninja video kids as aggressive?

Table 4.4 Potential Traps in Experimental Research

Doing Sociological Research

The research method you use usually depends on the question you want to address in your research. Once you have formulated your research question, you'll begin to think about the best method you can use to generate the sort of information you will need to address it. And once you've chosen the method that would be best to use, you are ready to undertake the sociological research project. Research in the social sciences follows eight basic steps (Figure 4.4):

1. *Choosing an issue.* What sort of issue interests you? Sometimes sociologists follow their curiosity, and sometimes they are invited to study an issue by an agency that will give them a grant for the research. Sometimes sociologists select a problem for research in the hopes that better understanding of the problem can lead to the formulation of policies that can improve people's lives.

   Let's take the example that we used at the beginning of this chapter. Let's say you've read an article in the newspaper in which a politician said that we should make divorce more difficult to obtain because divorce always harms children. This is interesting, you might think. What is the impact of divorce on children?

2. *Defining the problem.* Once you've chosen the issue you want to understand, you'll need to refine your questions and shape them into a manageable research topic. Here, you'll have to decide what sorts of impacts divorce may have on children you might want to explore. How do these children do in school? What is the likelihood that such children would, themselves, have their marriages end in divorce? How do they adjust to divorce socially and psychologically?

3. *Reviewing the literature.* Chances are that other social scientists have already done research on the issue you're interested in. You'll need to critically read and evaluate the previous research on the problem to help you refine your own thinking and to identify gaps in the research. Sometimes a review of the literature will find that previous research has actually yielded contradictory findings. Perhaps you can shed a clearer light on the issue. Or perhaps you'll find the research has already been done conclusively, in which case you'll probably want to find another research question.

4. *Developing a hypothesis.* Having now reviewed the literature, you can state what you anticipate will be the result of your research. A **hypothesis** predicts a relationship between two variables, independent and dependent.

5. *Operationalize your variables.* In our example, you might develop a hypothesis that "children from divorced families are likely to have more psychological problems and lower school achievement than children in intact families." Now you have to figure out what sorts of variables will enable you to address this hypothesis. In this case, you might use the marital status of the parents—whether or not they are divorced—as the independent variable. That's the aspect you would manipulate to see if it causes change in the dependent variable(s). The psychological and educational consequences are those dependent variables; changes in those areas are the things you would measure to get your results.

6. *Designing a project.* Now that you've developed a hypothesis, you are ready to design a research project to find out the answer. Choose the method best suited to the question or questions you want to ask. Would quantitative or qualitative methods be more appropriate to address this question? What sorts of data might enable you

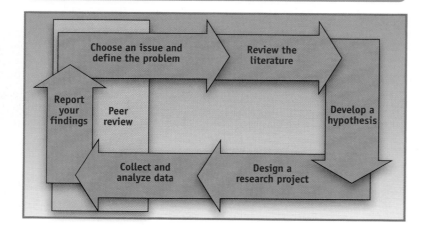

Figure 4.4 Research in the Social Sciences

Choose an issue and define the problem → Review the literature → Develop a hypothesis → Design a research project → Collect and analyze data → Peer review → Report your findings

to test your hypotheses? For example, let's say the question you're interested in is the effect of divorce on children's educational achievement. You might consider a large survey project in which you compare students' test scores and their parents' marital status. But if you wanted to know how divorce makes children feel, you might consider interviewing children from divorced and intact families to understand their emotional experiences.

7. *Collecting data.* The next step of the research is to collect data that will help you answer your research question. The types of data that you collect will depend a lot on the research method you will use. But whatever research method you use, you must ensure that the data are valid and reliable. Validity means that your data must actually enable you to measure what you want to measure. And reliability means that another researcher can use the same data you used and would find similar results. (We discuss validity and reliability later in this chapter.)

Researching the impact of divorce on children, you might design a survey that would assess whether divorce has any impact on school achievement or psychological problems. (You would have to ensure that the participants represent all different groups, so that you don't inadvertently measure the effect of race or class on children.) You might choose several different schools (to make sure they were representative of the nation as a whole) and would code all the children as to whether their parents were divorced or not. Then you could see if there were any differences in their grades or if there were any differences in how often they were reported to the school principal for disciplinary problems. You might find that there already was a survey that had questions that could address your research question. Then you would use the existing data and look for those variables that would describe the impact of divorce. (This "secondary" analysis of existing data might sound like duplication, but it also ensures that the data you use will be valid and reliable.)

You might decide to use more qualitative methods and do in-depth interviews with children of divorced parents and children from intact couples to see if there were any differences between them.

8. *Analyzing the data.* There are several different ways to analyze the data you have collected, and the technique you choose will depend on the type of method you have adopted. Large surveys need to be coded and analyzed statistically, to discern whether there are relationships among the variables that you predicted in your hypotheses and, if there are such relationships, how strong they are or whether they might have been produced by chance. If you've used qualitative techniques, interviews would need to be coded for their narrative content, and observational field notes would need to be organized and systematically examined. Requiring care, precision, and patience, data analysis is often the most cumbersome and tedious element in the research process, whether you are "crunching the numbers" or transcribing interviews.

9. *Reporting the findings.* No research project is of much use unless you share it with others. Typically, one seeks to publish the results of research as an article in a peer-reviewed journal or in an academic book, which also passes peer review. Peer review is a process by which others in the field are asked to anonymously evaluate the article or book, to make sure the research meets the standards of adequate research. Peer review is essential because it ensures the acceptance of the research by one's colleagues. More than simple gatekeeping, peer review provides a valuable service to the author, enabling him or her to see how others read the work and providing suggestions for revision.

Even a student research project needs to experience peer review (as well as review by professors). You should plan to distribute your research projects to other students in the class to see how they react to it and to hear their advice for revision.

Sociological research is a statement in a conversation between the researcher and the public. One needs to report one's findings to a larger community to get their feedback as part of a dialogue. Sometimes, that community is your fellow students or other sociologists. But sometimes one also shares the findings with the larger public because the public at large might be interested in the results. Many sociologists also make sure to share their findings with the people they studied because the researcher might feel that his or her research might actually be useful to the subjects of the study.

How Important Is Sociology?

Countries differ on the level of funding for social science research.

Share of Academic Research and Development Funding in Social Science in Selected Countries

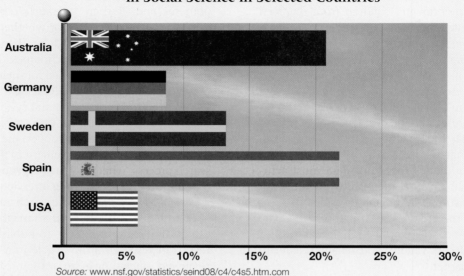

Source: www.nsf.gov/statistics/seind08/c4/c4s5.htm.com

1. What is the significance of government support for social science research? Why should the government fund it?

2. Why do different governments fund social sciences at such different levels?

Issues in Conducting Research

No research project involving human beings is without controversy. Debates have always raged about the validity of studies, and we often come to believe that we can explain anything by statistics. That may be true—that you can prove even the most outrageously false things by the use of statistical manipulations—but not all "proofs" will be equally valid or hold up in the court of review by other social scientists. Most sociological research is published in academic or scholarly journals—such as the *American Sociological Review, Social Problems, Social Forces,* or the *American Journal of Sociology.* The American Sociological Association sponsors several "flagship" journals and controls the selection of editors to ensure that the entire

range of topics and perspectives is covered. Each subfield of sociology has its own journals, devoted to those specific areas of research. In the sociology of gender alone, for example, there are dozens of journals, including *Gender & Society* or *Men and Masculinities,* a scholarly journal that I edit.

In all such reputable journals, articles are subject to "peer review"—that is, each article is evaluated by a set of reviewers who are, themselves, competent researchers in that field. Peer review accomplishes two tasks: (1) It ensures that the research is evaluated by those who are competent to evaluate it and assess the adequacy of the research; and (2) it ensures that the editor's own particular biases do not prejudice her or him in the decision to accept or reject the article. Peer review is the standard model for all serious academic and scholarly journals.

In completing the research, there are three issues that you always need to keep in mind.

Remain Objective and Avoid Bias

You must strive for objectivity, to make sure that your prejudices and assumptions do not contaminate the results you find. That is not to say that your political persuasion or your preconceived assumptions cannot guide your research: They can. Indeed, they will even if you don't want them to. You'll invariably want to do research on something that interests you, and things usually interest us because we have a personal stake in understanding or changing them.

Despite these assumptions, though, you must be careful to construct the research project so that you find out what is really there and not merely develop an elaborate way to confirm your stereotypes. The research methods you use and the questions you ask have to allow for the possibility that you're wrong. And you, as a researcher, have to be prepared to be surprised, because we often find things we didn't expect to find.

Sociologists use the term *value neutrality* to describe the posture of the researcher. We strive to keep our own values and biases from distorting the results of our research. Objectivity doesn't mean not having any values; it means being aware of them so that we are not blinded by them.

There are two kinds of biases that we must be aware of:

1. There are your own sets of assumptions and values, your political positions on specific issues. Everyone has these, as they are based on widely held cultural values (although, as we saw in the first chapter, they are often contradictory). These may determine what you might be interested in studying, but this kind of bias should not make it impossible for the results to surprise you.
2. A second kind of bias is not the values that inform your choice of subject but biases *in the research design itself* that corrupt your results and make them unreliable and invalid. One must be sure to be as conscientious as possible in the integrity of the research design to avoid excluding specific groups from your sample.

For example, if you are vehemently anti-choice, you might decide to research the moral and religious status of women who have abortions. You might hypothesize that abortion is morally wrong and those women who had an

"That's the gist of what I want to say. Now get me some statistics to base it on."

abortion were not informed by morality or committed to any religion. That research question is informed by your biases, which is fine. But if you do a survey of women who have had abortions and find out that about a quarter of them did so even though they claimed that it was morally wrong or that nearly one-fifth of them were born-again or evangelical Christians, you are obligated by your commitment to science to report those findings honestly. (Incidentally, that is what you would find were you to study the question [Alan Guttmacher Institute, 1996; Henshaw and Kost, 1996; Henshaw and Martire, 1982; Medical World News, 1987].)

If you find that most women don't regret their decision and then readminister the survey this time only to women who identify as evangelicals and exclude any women who voted Democratic in the last election, you might find the results you were hoping for. But now your survey would be biased because you systematically excluded some particular group, which skews the results.

Avoid Overstating Results

Overstating one's findings is one of the biggest temptations to any sociological researcher. Findings are often not "newsworthy" unless you find something really significant; and funding sources, such as governmental research institutes and private foundations, often link continuing funding to such glamorous and newsworthy findings. Even when you do your first research project, you'll likely be tempted to overstate your results, if for no other reason than to impress your professor with some "big" finding and get a better grade.

But there are temptations to overstate within the research methodologies themselves. In ethnographic research, for example, one can say a lot about a little—that is, one's insights are very deep, but one has only examined a very small phenomenon or group of people. One cannot pretend that such insights can be generalized to larger populations without adequate comparisons. In survey research one can say a little about a whole lot: By writing a lot of questions and choosing a large sample, one can find out the attitudes or behaviors of Americans, but one cannot explain why they hold such beliefs or take such actions, nor can one explain how they "use" their beliefs.

Researchers must be cautious about inferring why something happens from the fact that it does happen. A **correlation,** or some relationship between two phenomena, doesn't necessarily mean that one is the *cause* of the other. A correlation between a dependent variable and an independent variable tells you that they are related to each other, that one varies when the other varies. Finding a relationship between two variables tells you nothing about the *direction* of that relationship. And it doesn't tell you *why* they both vary together.

For example, there is a strong correlation between the amount of ice cream sold in the United States and the number of deaths by drowning. The more ice cream sold, the higher the number of drowning deaths. Does eating ice cream lead to drowning? Of course not. Both ice cream sales and deaths by drowning happen during the summer, when the temperature gets hot and people eat more ice cream and go swimming more often. The temperature causes both, and so it appears that there is a relationship between them.

Another potential problem is that events in society are not isolated from other events. To measure the impact of one variable on another might be possible in a social vacuum, but in real life, there are so many other things that might get in the way of accurate measurement. Confounding variables need

Sociology and Our World

Major League Baseball Prevents Divorce?

I recently read in the "relationships" section of my Internet server's webpage that cities with major league baseball teams have lower divorce rates than those that do not. Cities that introduced teams in the past decade have seen their divorce rates decline up to 28 percent. This led a University of Denver psychologist to claim that having a major league baseball team leads to greater compatibility among couples. "One way to get going is to head for your nearest ballpark," he said (Mattox, 1999).

A simple correlation between two variables—in this case rates of divorce and proximity to major league baseball teams—is often offered as "proof" that going to major league baseball games helps to sustain marriages. (This might prompt some government agency to give away a lot of tickets to struggling marriages!) But for what other reasons might there be a correlation between baseball teams and low divorce rates?

Could it be that baseball teams are located in major cities, which have lower divorce rates than the suburbs or rural areas? Could those cities also be places where there are a lot of *other* things going on (theater, movies, concerts, and the like) that enrich one's life? Don't those cities also have basketball teams and football teams? Or major symphonies and large libraries? Could it be that cities with major league teams are also those with the lowest rates of *marriage?* Could it be that those cities that introduced teams in the past decade are those in the Sun Belt where many retirees live—that is, people who are unlikely to get divorced?

It's also true that cities with major league baseball teams are in the North, where there are far more Catholics and Jews, who have lower divorce rates than Protestants, who are the overwhelming majority in the South, where there are fewer teams.

And besides, the divorce rate in the United States has been declining *overall* since 1992, so it's no surprise that those cities with new teams would also have a decline in the divorce rate.

Americans are so enamored by science that tossing in a little scientific information, even if it's utterly irrelevant, changes peoples perceptions. Psychologist Deena Skolnick Weisberg and her colleagues designed an experiment in which three groups of people–regular adults, students in a neuroscience course, and neuroscientists—were given descriptions of a psychological phenomenon, followed by two good and two bad explanations of the phenomenon. One of the good and one of the bad

Seduced by Science

explanations contained irrelevant bits of neuroscience jargon; the other was a simple straightforward explanation. Here is a sample of their test items:

Table 1. Sample Item.

Researchers created a list of facts that about 50 percent of people knew. Subjects in this experiment read the list of facts and had to say which ones they knew. They then had to judge what percentage of other people would know those facts. Researchers found that the subjects responded differently about other people's knowledge of a fact when the subjects themselves knew that fact. If the subjects did know a fact, they said that an inaccurately large percentage of others would know it too. For example, if a subject already knew that Hartford was the capital of Connecticut, that subject might say that 80 percent of people would know this, even though the correct answer is 50 percent. The researchers call this finding "the curse of knowledge."

And here are the results: For both the students and the "novice" group (the normal adults) adding the irrelevant information about brain localization turned bad explanations into good ones. They'd been "seduced by science."

	Good Explanation	**Bad Explanation**
Without Neuroscience	The researchers claim that this "curse" happens because subjects have trouble switching their point of view to consider what someone else might know, mistakenly projecting their own knowledge onto others.	The researchers claim that this "curse" happens because subjects make more mistakes when they have to judge the knowledge of others. People are much better at judging what they themselves know.
With Neuroscience	**Brain scans indicate** that this "curse" happens because **of the frontal lobe brain circuitry known to be involved in self-knowledge.** Subjects have trouble switching their point of view to consider what someone else might know, mistakenly projecting their own knowledge onto others.	**Brain scans indicate** that this "curse" happens because **of the frontal lobe brain circuitry known to be involved in self-knowledge.** Subjects make more mistakes when they have to judge the knowledge of others. People are much better at judging what they themselves know.

Note: *The neuroscience information is highlighted here, but subjects did not see such marking*

Source: Deena Skolnich Weisberg, Frank C. Keil, Joshua Goodstein, Elizabeth Rawson, Jeremy R. Gray, "The Seductive Allure of Neuroscience Explanations", *Journals of Cognitive Neuroscience,* 20:3 (March, 2008), pp. 470–477. Copyright © 2008 by the Massachusetts Institute of Technology. Reprinted by permission.

to be assessed in some fashion—by trying to measure them, by minimizing their impact, or by assuming that they confound everything equally and therefore can be safely ignored.

As a result of all these potential problems, researchers must be careful not to overstate their information and aware of a variety of possible explanations for the results they find. And when we read the results of others' research, we must also maintain a critical posture, and not be seduced by science.

Maintain Professional Ethics

The researcher must also be ethical. As scientists, sociologists are constantly confronted with ethical issues. For example, what if you were interested in studying the social impact of oil drilling in the Alaska wilderness on indigenous people who live near the oil wells? And suppose that the research would be funded by a generous grant from the oil companies who would profit significantly if you were to find that the impact would be either minimal or beneficial. Even if your research

Did You Know?

were completely free of corporate influence, people would still be suspicious of your results. Research must be free of influence by outside agencies, even those that might provide research grants to fund the research. And it must be free of the perception of outside influence as well. Much research is funded by foundations or by government agencies, more disinterested funding sources than, for example, a private company that might try to design its research to produce results favorable to its products.

The most important ethical issue is that your research should not actually hurt the people you are researching. Recall the example of psychologist Stanley Milgram's experiment on obedience to authority in which one subject administered "shocks" to another.

The psychological consequences of deceptive research led to significant changes in research ethics. An act of Congress in 1970 made "informed consent" a requirement of research. Only after all adult subjects of research (or the parents of minors) are clearly informed about its object and assured of confidentiality can they consent to participate. And only then can the experiment proceed. Today, all major research universities have a committee on research involving human subjects (CORIHS) or an institutional review board (IRB) that oversees all research undertaken at the university.

The Institutional Review Board

Every research project that goes through a university must pass the inspection of an institutional review board that has strict guidelines to protect test subjects. The researcher cannot even begin the data collection unless he or she can guarantee:

- *Informed consent.* Generally, research subjects must be informed, in advance, of the nature of the project, what it's about, what

they will have to do in it, and any potential risks and benefits they will face. It's possible to waive informed consent but only under certain circumstances. If the subjects are not being harmed, and if full information would affect the results, then it's OK not to have informed consent. For example, you might not tell subjects that you were focusing specifically on racial or gender attitudes because then they might tend to answer "the right way." Instead, you might say you were asking "general" questions. Or, in a more extreme example, say you want to study hired killers; you would not need to get consent waived—because your subjects might kill you if they discovered that they were being studied!

- *Continuous consent.* Research subjects must be informed that they can back out of the project at any time for any reason, no questions asked.

- *Confidentiality.* Any information that would allow the subject to be identified must be stored separately from the other research data, and it must never be published.

- *Anonymity.* Research subjects must be anonymous. Pseudonyms must be used instead of real names; and, if there is any question, even the respondents' biographical data must be modified.

- *Freedom from deception.* Research subjects must not be deceived unless it is absolutely necessary, the deception is unlikely to cause major psychological trauma, and they are debriefed immediately afterwards.

- *Freedom from harm.* Research subjects must not be subjected to any risk of physical or psychological injury greater than they would experience in real life, unless it is absolutely necessary—and then they must be warned in advance. "Psychological injury" extends to embarrassing questions like "Have you ever been pregnant?"

- *Protected groups.* Children and adolescents, college students, prisoners, and other groups have a protected status because they cannot really give consent (children are too young, and college students may believe that they must participate or their grade will suffer). The IRB requires special procedures for studies involving these groups.

In recent years, IRBs have expanded the scope of their review to include any research that involves human subjects in any way whatever. Sometimes, this has resulted in oversight leading to "overreach." For example, one review board asked a linguist studying a preliterate culture to "have the subjects read and sign a consent form." Another IRB forbade a White student studying ethnicity from interviewing African American PhD students "because it might be traumatic for them" (Cohen, 2007, p. 1).

But what if the questions you want to answer are answerable only by deception? Sociologist Erich Goode undertook several research projects that used deceptive research practices (Goode, 1996a, 1996b, 2002). Refusing to submit his research proposals to his university's CORIHS guidelines, he took personal ads in a local magazine to see the sorts of responses he would receive. (Though the ads were fictitious, the people responding to them were real and honestly thought they were replying to real ads. They thus revealed personal information about themselves.)

He took out four ads to determine the relative importance of physical attractiveness and financial success in the dating game. One was from a beautiful waitress (high attractiveness, low financial success); one was from an average-looking female lawyer (low attractiveness, high success). One was from a handsome male taxicab driver (high attractiveness, low success), and the final one was from an average-looking male lawyer (low attractiveness, high success). While about ten times more men than women replied to the ads at all, the two ads that received the most replies from their intended audience were for the beautiful waitress and the average-looking male lawyer. Goode concluded that in the dating marketplace, women and men often rank potential mates differently, with men seeking beauty and women seeking financial security.

One of the most infamous research studies in U.S. history was the Tuskegee experiment, in which nearly 400 African American men with late-stage syphilis were deliberately left untreated to test what the disease would do to them.

While these were interesting findings, many sociologists question Goode's research methods (Saguy, 2002). Goode defended his behavior by saying that the potential daters didn't know that they were responding to fake ads and that therefore no harm was done because people often receive no reply when they respond to ads. But ask yourself: Did he have to deceive people to find this out? How else might he have obtained this information? Do you think he crossed a line?

In every research project, you must constantly balance the demands of the research (and your own curiosity) against the rights of the research subjects. This is a delicate balance, and different people may draw their lines in different places. But to cause possible harm to a research subject is not only unethical, it is also illegal.

Social Science in the Twenty-First Century: Emergent Methodologies

New technologies provide opportunities for new research methods. For example, a new methodology called "field experiments" combines some of the benefits of both field methods and experimental research. On the one hand, they are experiments, using matched pairs and random assignment, so that one can infer causality. On the other hand, they take place "in the field"; that is, in real-life situations. You've probably seen field experiments reported on television because they often reveal hidden biases in employment, housing markets, or consumer behavior.

Recently, field experiments have revealed what minorities had long suspected but could never prove: They are discriminated against by taxi drivers who do not stop for them.

Here are some examples of how field methods reveal biases and discrimination in employment, housing, and consumerism. Matched pairs of prospective "car buyers" go to an auto showroom, or prospective "tenants" walk into a real estate office, or "job seekers" answer a help wanted ad. In each case, the prospects consist of a White couple and a minority couple, or a man and a woman. They go to the same showroom, and look at the same cars, and get very different price quotes. Or the White couple is shown several houses that are listed with the real estate broker, but the Black couple is told they've been rented or sold. And while a male and female applicant answered the same job ad, the male job applicant is told about a managerial opening and the female applicant is given a typing test. Because the experiment was conducted in real time in real life, the discrimination is readily evident because the only variable that was different was race or gender. (When shown on TV, the news reporter will often go back to the car showroom or real estate office with videotape made by the participants and confront the dealer or agent with the evidence of the discrimination [Ayres and Siegelman, 1995; Cross et al., 1990; Yinger, 1998].)

Just as social scientists are finding new methods, they are always trying to refine older survey techniques to obtain the most accurate data. For example, surveys of sexual behavior always find that people are somewhat self-conscious about revealing their sexual behav-iors to strangers talking to them on the phone—let alone someone sitting across from them in a face-to-face survey interview. Researchers have developed a new survey tech-nology—telephone audio computer-assisted self-interviewing—that greatly reduces the requirement of revealing your sexual behavior to a stranger. And some of the results indicate that a significantly higher percentage of Americans report same-sex sexual behavior than previously estimated (Villarroel et al., 2006).

Perhaps the most significant new technology is the proliferation of Internet chat rooms and listservs that has created virtual online communities of people who are drawn to particular issues and interests. If you want to study, for example, collectors of Ming dynasty pottery or buffalo head nickels, you would find several chat groups of such people online. Imagine how much time and energy you would save trying to track them down! They're all in one place, and they all are guaranteed to be exactly what you are looking for. Or are they?

Here's a good example. For the past few years, I have been doing research on White supremacist and Aryan youth in the United States and several European countries. There are many Internet chat rooms and portals through which one can enter the virtual world of the extreme right wing. Online, I can enter a place where eight White suprema-cists, neo-Nazis, and White power young peo-ple are discussing current events. I can listen in, perhaps even participate and ask them some questions. (Professional ethics require that whenever you are doing research you must disclose to them that you are doing re-search.) I could get some amazing "data" that way. But how can I be sure it's reliable?

After all, what if several of them aren't really White supremacists at all, but a couple of high school kids goofing around, a couple of graduate students in anthropology or soci-ology doing their "field work," or even a stu-dent in an introductory sociology course doing research for a term paper for my class? Have you ever gone online and pretended to be someone you weren't? How many peo-ple do you know have done that?

Obviously, one cannot rely solely on the information gathered in such chat rooms. (In my case, I decided I had to interview them in person.) But any new method can be embraced only with caution and only when accompanied by research using more tradi-tional methodologies.

In fact, it is often the combination of different methods—secondary analysis of already existing large-scale survey data coupled with in-depth interviews of a subsample—that are today providing the most exciting research findings in the social sciences. You needn't choose one method over another; all methods allow you to approach social life in different ways. Combined in creative combinations, research methods can shed enough light on a topic that many of its characteristics and dynamics can become clear.

Chapter Review

1. Why Sociological Methods Matter

Sociologists measure social phenomenon scientifically. We study a wide range of topics, from emergent social interaction and groups to large organizations, and it is all the more challenging because of **subjectivity**—people don't just react, they also plan, think, and act. Fortunately, sociologists have many different methods to draw upon in collecting **data,** each of which may yield different insights. Some methods aid in **deductive reasoning;** for others, **inductive reasoning** is used to gain **verstehen. Quantitative methods** use statistical analysis of numerical data to deduce results, while **qualitative methods** gather rich detail to find regular patterns of behavior. Both methods have strengths and weaknesses, and good sociology can be done with both. They reveal different aspects of social phenomenon. The methods used depend on the research question.

subjectivity The complex of individual perceptions, motivations, ideas, and emotions that give each of us a point of view. (p. 94)

data The plural of datum. Data are systematically collected and systematically organized bits of information. (p. 95)

deductive reasoning Reasoning that logically proceeds from one demonstrable fact to the next. It often moves from the general to the more specific. (p. 96)

inductive reasoning Research in which one reasons to a conclusion about all or many members of a class based on examination of only a few members of that class. Loosely, it is reasoning from the specific to the general. (p. 96)

verstehen Max Weber's term for "intersubjective understanding," or the ability to understand social behavior from the point of view of those the sociologist is observing. (p. 96)

quantitative methods Numerical means to drawing sociological conclusions using powerful statistical tools to help understand patterns in which the behaviors, attitudes, or traits under study can be translated into numerical values. (p. 96)

qualitative methods Inductive and inferential means to drawing sociological understanding, usually about less tangible aspects of social life, such as the actual felt experience of social interaction. (p. 97)

2. Types of Sociological Research Methods

Researchers explore how an **independent variable** affects the **dependent variable,** ensuring the results are not due to **extraneous variables, confounding variables,** or an **intervening variable.** Research goes beyond the **literature review** of a research paper for new insights. An **experiment** is a controlled observational method where something is manipulated for the **experimental group,** but not the **control group,** to see the manipulation's effect. Milgram's study of obedience is a famous experiment. Field studies are observational, gathering data where they occur naturally, using **detached observation** or **participant observation.** In an **ethnography,** the researcher gains deeper understanding from the participants' perspective, through immersion. **Interview** of a **purposive sample** is a typical qualitative method. It is useful, although less generalizable. **Survey** is a common quantitative method, gathering data on attitudes and behavior, often using a **Likert scale. Sample** types include **random sample, systematic sample, stratified sample,** or **cluster sample. Secondary analysis** uses existing data sets. Whichever method is used, **generalizability** is desirable. **Content analysis** is another method used sometimes. Whichever method is used, making the right comparisons matters.

independent variable In an experimental study, the agent of change, the ingredient that is added to set things in motion. (p. 98)

dependent variable The variable whose change depends on the introduction of the independent variable. (p. 98)

extraneous variables Variables that influence the outcome of an experiment but are not the variables that are actually of interest. (p. 98)

confounding variables The things that might get in the way of an accurate measurement of the impact of one variable on another. (p. 98)

intervening variable A variable that helps explain a perceived relationship between an independent variable and a dependent variable. For example, in Pavlov's experiment on bell-ringing (independent) and dogs salivating (dependent), an intervening variable might have been the relative intelligence of the dogs themselves. (p. 99)

literature review Reading and summary of other research on or closely related to the topic of a study. (p. 99)

experiment A testing process that is performed under controlled conditions to examine the validity of a hypothesis. (p. 100)

experimental group In an experiment, the group that will have the change introduced to see what happens. *See control group.* (p. 100)

control group In an experiment, the comparison group that will not experience the manipulation of the independent variable (the experimental group). Having a control group enables sociologists to compare the outcomes of the experiment to determine if the changes in the independent variable had any effects on the dependent variable. (p. 100)

detached observation A perspective that constrains the researcher from becoming in any way involved in the event he or she is observing. This reduces the amount that the researchers' observations will change the dynamic that they are watching. (p. 101)

participant observation Sociological research method in which one observes people in their natural habitat. (p. 101)

ethnography A type of field method in which the researcher inserts him- or herself into the daily world of the people he or she is trying to study to understand the events from the point of view of the actors themselves. (p. 102)

interview Research method in which a researcher asks a small group of people open-ended questions. (p. 103)

purposive sample Sample in which respondents are not selected randomly and are not representative of the larger population but are selected precisely because they possess certain characteristics that are of interest to the researcher. (p. 103)

survey Research method in which one asks a sample of people closed-ended questions and tabulates the results. (p. 104)

Likert scale The most common form of survey coding; arranges possible responses from lowest to highest. (p. 104)

sample A limited group of research subjects whose responses are statistically developed into a general theme or trend that can be applied to the larger whole. (p. 104)

random sample A sample chosen by an abstract and arbitrary method, that gives each person an equal chance of being selected, such as tossing a piece of paper with each person's name on it into a hat. (p. 104)

systematic sample A type of sample that starts at a random position on a list and selects every *n*th unit (skip interval) of a population until the desired sample size is reached. Choosing every 100th name in a phone book or on a voter registration is a systematic sample. (p. 104)

stratified sample Sample in which research subjects are divided into proportions equal to the proportions found in the population at large. (p. 105)

cluster sample A sampling technique used when "natural" groupings are evident in the population. The total population is divided into these groups (or clusters), and a sample of the groups is selected. Then the required information is collected from the elements within each selected group. (p. 105)

secondary analysis Analysis conducted on data previously collected by others for other reasons. (p. 107)

generalizability Also called external validity or applicability; the extent to which the results of a study can be generalized to the general population. (p. 108)

content analysis Research method in which one analyzes artifacts (books, movies, TV programs, magazine articles, and so on) instead of people. (p. 108)

3. Social Science and the Problem of "Truth"

Because human society is dynamic and changing, with so many variables, and values, there is no single unchanging truth sociologists can hope to find, but Comte understood that, as scientists, sociologists can conduct research scientifically. This allows us to gain **predictability** and find relationships and **causality** in social behavior.

predictability The degree to which a correct prediction of a research outcome can be made. (p. 110)

causality The term used when one variable causes another to change. (p. 110)

4. Doing Sociological Research

There are eight steps in sociological research. After choosing an issue, defining the problem, and reviewing the literature, a **hypothesis** is developed, variables are operationalized, the project is designed, data are collected and analyzed, and findings are reported.

hypothesis A testable prediction for an event or phenomenon that assumes a relationship between two or more variables. (p. 112)

5. Issues in Conducting Research

Sociologists must be careful to avoid bias and not infer causality where a **correlation** has been observed. Peer review by other scientists prior to journal publication is a check on bias, and methodology—data, analysis, and conclusions. Researchers have ethical obligations, not only to conduct their work as free of bias or values as possible, honestly reporting only what is found, but to be beyond influence and avoid doing harm, too. Informed consent is required by law, and all institutional research is approved by a review board (IRB), ensuring compliance with research ethics, including obtaining informed consent, protecting participant confidentiality and anonymity, protecting special populations, limiting deception, and ensuring that participants are not harmed.

correlation The term for the fact of some relationship between two phenomena. (p. 116)

6. Social Science in the Twenty-First Century: Emergent Methodologies

Researchers are innovative and find new ways of collecting data. Field experiments are one example. Like society itself, sociology is dynamic, and responsive to changes, and new methods of research take advantage of technological advances and changes in how people connect. The Internet is a place where people of similar interests come together and can be a rich source of data. Surveys are yielding more accurate data today, through the use of computer-assisted techniques that allow participants to avoid disclosing sensitive information to another person.

Self-Test: Check Your Understanding

1. According to the text, which type of research primarily uses statistics to deduce findings?
   a. Qualitative methods
   b. Quantitative methods
   c. Both qualitative and quantitative methods
   d. Neither qualitative nor quantitative methods

2. Which method gathers data on attitudes and behaviors using numerically coded measurement instruments such as a Likert scale?
   a. Surveys
   b. Experiments
   c. Participant observation
   d. Interviews

3. Identify the correct order for the basic steps of sociological research, according to the text:
   a. Define problem, design project, review literature, choose issue, develop hypothesis, analyze data, operationalize variables, report findings
   b. Design project, review literature, choose issue, operationalize variables, develop hypothesis, analyze data, define problem, report findings
   c. Review literature, define problem, operationalize variables, design project, choose issue, develop hypothesis, analyze data, report findings
   d. Choose issue, define problem, review literature, develop hypothesis, operationalize variables, design project, analyze data, report findings

4. Which of the following methods is used for the GSS?
   a. Content analysis
   b. Survey
   c. Field experiment
   d. Ethnography

5. A sociologist interested in studying the impact of coal mining on Appalachian people cannot receive funding from a coal producer because of problems with
   a. research ethics.
   b. causality.
   c. predictability.
   d. generalizability.

6. A researcher studying alcoholism attends a meeting of Alcoholics Anonymous (AA) and interviews people there. This is an example of which type of sample?
   a. Random sample
   b. Cluster sample
   c. Purposive sample
   d. Stratified sample

7. Verstehen can best be accomplished through
   a. content analysis.
   b. surveys.
   c. experimentation.
   d. ethnography.

8. An act of Congress mandated that all researchers must
   a. avoid deception.
   b. protect the anonymity of participants.
   c. obtain informed consent.
   d. All of the above

Self-Test Answers: 1. b, 2. a, 3. d, 4. b, 5. a, 6. c, 7. d, 8. c

Integrate and Explore: Points to Consider

1. Is verstehen easier or more difficult to accomplish today than it was in Weber's time? Why might it be more difficult? Why might it be easier? Which research tools or techniques might be most effective to accomplish this understanding?

2. If you were conducting sociological research, what would you like to study? Pick a qualitative method and a quantitative method and discuss the strengths and weaknesses of each, the different kinds of questions each might answer, and types of insights each might reveal, for your topic of interest.

succeed with PEARSON mysoclab

Self-scoring practice tests, flashcards for learning key terms, streaming audio of the entire text, and multimedia, including:

Explore—*Measures of Central Tendency: Mean, Median and Mode*
Explore—*Corrections Do Not Show Causation*
Watch—Jeff Lucas, *Zimbardo's Prison Experiment*
Watch—Judith Stacey, *Qualitative Research*

Socialization

In my high school yearbook, probably the single most common inscription from friends and classmates was a variation of, "Stay the same great guy you are now. Don't ever change." Yet countless conversations from college on have charted exactly such a trajectory of change. "Well, when I was younger I felt this way. But *now* I see it differently!" And how many relationships pivot on whether or not someone will "change"— either to stop doing something hurtful or bad or to start doing something better? How many self-help books are written to help us change? Or maybe the fact that there are so many self-

help books to help us change actually indicates that we really want to change but actually can't!

On the one hand, we are constantly growing and changing. On the other hand, we believe we have a core self, something constant and unchanging, a place deep down that is who we "really are."

Sociologists are interested in "both" of you—the part that feels eternal and constant and the part that is constantly changing. In fact, sociologists may believe that you don't have multiple personality disorder but that these two parts are actually the same person.

Most of the time, we think of our "self," our identity, as a thing that we possess, like a car. I might decide to hide my "true self," "who I really am," in some situations and reveal it in others. But is there really a single, permanent true self, buried deep inside our minds or our souls? Is there really a "who I really am"?

The sociological perspective sees identity not as a possession but as a process, not a thing that you have but a collection of ideas, desires, beliefs, and behaviors that is constantly changing as we grow, experience new situations, and interact with other people. We are different today than we were ten years ago, or even last month, and we will be different tomorrow. We are different at home and at school, when talking to our boss and when talking to our grandmother: not just a different front on a "true self" but a

"The sociological perspective sees identity not as a possession but as a process, not a thing that you have but a collection of ideas, desires, beliefs, and behaviors that is constantly changing"

different self, a different person. Our identity is a process, in constant motion.

The sociological perspective may make us feel more creative because we are constantly revising our identity to meet new challenges, but it may also make us feel more insecure and unstable because it argues that there is nothing permanent or inevitable about the self. Change means creative potential, but it also means instability and the potential for chaos.

Socialization and Biology

Our identity is based on the interplay of nature and nurture. *Nature* means our physical makeup: our anatomy and physiology, our genes and chromosomes. *Nurture* means how we grow up: what we learn from our physical environment and our encounters with other people. Nature and nurture both play a role in who we are, but scientists and philosophers have debated for centuries over how much each contributes and how they interrelate.

Before the Enlightenment of the seventeenth and eighteenth centuries, nature was supreme: Our identity was created by God along with the natural world and could not be changed by mere circumstances. Nurture played virtually no part at all: As many fairy tales assure us, a princess raised in poverty was still a princess. Theologian John Calvin taught that we were predestined to be good or evil, and there was nothing we could do about it. But in the seventeenth century, British philosophers like John Locke rejected the idea that nature is solely responsible for our identity, that biology or God places strict limits on what we can become. They went in the other direction, arguing that each of us is born as *tabula rasa*—a blank slate—and our environment in early childhood determines what we become.

The French philosopher Jean-Jacques Rousseau proposed a compromise. He argued that human beings do inherit identities: All children, and adults in their natural state, are "noble savages," naturally warm, sociable, and peace loving. However, their environment can also change them. Industrial civilization teaches children to become competitive, belligerent, and warlike. Thomas Jefferson based his ideas for the American experiment on Locke and Rousseau: "All men are created equal," that is, they derive some basic qualities from nature.

In the nineteenth century, the nature side of the debate got a boost when Charles Darwin observed that animal species evolve, or change over time. He was not aware of genetic evolution, so he theorized that they develop new traits to adapt to changing food supplies, climates, or the presence of predators. Because human beings, too, are the result of millions of years of adaptation to the physical changes in their world, identity is a product of biological inheritance, unchangeable (at least during any one individual's lifetime).

But growing up in different environments changes our ideas about who we are and where we belong without having to wait millions of years. For example, a person who grows up on an Arctic tundra, with rough weather and scarce food, will think and act differently from a person who grows up in a tropical paradise, where the weather is mild and food is abundant. The former might consider the world harsh, a struggle for survival, and human nature communal and cooperative. The latter might think life is easy, and it is human nature to compete with everyone else to see who can gather the most coconuts. Or it could go the opposite direction: The tundra dweller might think life is so harsh that you need to compete with everyone else to even have a chance at survival, and the tropical paradise resident might think life is so easy that one can lie back on a hammock, with a pina colada in hand, and wait for the coconuts to drop. Or consider how different would be the worldview of the daughter of a European aristocrat compared to a mother in an impoverished family in sub-Saharan Africa.

The type of environment doesn't determine what sort of "human nature" you will think you have, but the environment definitely plays a part in calculating it. Even

Socialization varies significantly by race, class, or gender. When White middle-class people see a police officer, they are likely to feel safer; when Black people see a police officer, they often feel more vulnerable—as these California high school boys express (even when confronted by a Hispanic police officer and a Black probation officer).

identical twins, separated at birth and raised in these two different areas, would think and act differently (Farber, 1982; Loehlin and Nichols, 1976).

The choice is not *either* nature *or* nurture, but both: Our biological inheritance, physical surroundings, history, civilization, culture, and personal life experiences all interact to create our identity. Sociologists tend to stress nurture, not because we think nature unimportant but because the ongoing interaction with people and objects in the real world throughout our life course has a profound impact on the creation of individual identity. Biology and the physical world give us the raw materials from which to create an identity, but it is only through human interactions that identity coheres and makes sense to us.

Socialization is the process by which we become aware of ourselves as part of a group, learn how to communicate with others in the group, and learn the behavior expected of us: spoken and unspoken rules of social interaction, how to think, how to feel. Socialization imbues us with a set of norms, values, beliefs, desires, interests, and tastes to be used in specific social situations.

Socialization can take place through formal instruction, but usually we are socialized informally by observing other people's behaviors and reactions. If you are rewarded for a behavior (or see someone else rewarded for it), you will tend to imitate it. If you are punished for a behavior (or see someone else being punished for it), you will tend to avoid it.

Socialization is at its busiest during childhood, but it also happens throughout our lives. Every time we join a new group, make new friends, change residences or jobs, we are being socialized, learning new expectations of the group and modifying our behavior, thoughts, and beliefs accordingly. And others are being socialized by watching us.

Socialization in Action

Most animals are born with all of the information they need to survive already imprinted in their brains. But some, especially the mammals, must spend some time "growing up," learning how to find food and shelter, elude predators, and get along with others. The period of learning and growth usually lasts for just a few months or, in the case of the higher primates, a few years. But human beings need an extraordinary amount of time, over a third of our lives.

Compare a horse and a human. If you have ever watched a foal being born, in real life or on film, you will recall that it will try to stand up on its wobbly legs shortly after birth. It can walk and run on its own by the next day. After a few weeks, the foal can forage for its own food without depending on its mother's milk. It still has some growing to do, but it is basically as capable as an adult horse.

Human babies do not begin to crawl until about eight months after birth, and they do not take their first hesitant steps for about a year. They can walk and run on their own by the time they are 2 or 3 years old, but

they are still virtually helpless and dependent on their parents for food, shelter, and protection from predators (or other dangers) for at least another ten years. If suddenly abandoned in a big city without any adult supervision, they would be unable to survive. Even after puberty, when they have reached physical adulthood, they are often unprepared to buy their own groceries or live by themselves until they have graduated from high school, college, or even graduate school! By that time, about a quarter of their life is over.

Socialization extends long after early childhood. Even in one's workplace, you learn new roles and norms. Here, new employees of Wal-Mart rehearse before the opening ceremony of the first supercenter of Wal-Mart in Beijing China.

Why do human beings require so many years of dependency? What are they learning during all those years? Of course they are developing physically, from childhood to full-grown adulthood, but they are also learning the skills necessary to survive in their community. Some of the instruction is formal, but most of it is informal, through daily interactions with the people and objects around them and learning an ever-changing array of roles and expectations. Socialization works with the basic foundation of our biology to unleash (or stifle) our individual identity.

Feral Children

In Edgar Rice Burroughs's novel *Tarzan of the Apes* (1914), the infant Lord Greystoke is orphaned on the coast of Africa and raised by apes. A childhood without human contact does not affect him at all; the adult Tarzan is fluent in English, French, and many African languages and fully comfortable in human society. But real "feral children," who spend their toddler years in the wilderness, are not so lucky.

The most famous feral child was the "Wild Boy of Aveyron," probably 12 years old when he was discovered in the woods of southern France in 1800. No one knew where he came from or how long he had been alone. He was unable to speak or communicate, except by growling like an animal. He refused to wear clothes. A long, systematic attempt at "civilizing" him was only partially successful. He was toilet trained, and he learned to wear clothes. He exhibited some reasoning ability. But he never learned to speak more than a few words (Lane, 1979; Shattuck, 1980).

Isolated Children

Though feral children may be largely a myth, some children have been isolated from almost all human contact by abusive caregivers. They can also be studied to determine the impact of little or no early childhood socialization.

One of the best-documented cases of an isolated child was "Isabelle," who was born to an unmarried, deaf-mute teenager. The girl's parents were so afraid of scandal that they kept both mother and daughter locked away in a darkened room, where they had no contact with the outside world. In 1938, when she was 6 years old, Isabelle escaped from her confinement. She was unable to speak except to make croaking sounds, she was extremely fearful of strangers, and she reacted to stimuli with the instinct of a wild animal. Gradually she became used to being around people, but she expressed no curiosity about them; it was as if she did not see herself as one of them. But doctors and social scientists began a long period of systematic training. Within a year she was able to speak in complete sentences, and soon she was able to attend school with other children. By the age of 14, she was in the sixth grade, happy and well adjusted. She managed to overcome her lack of early childhood socialization, but only through exceptional effort.

"Genie" was found in 1970, at the age of 13. Since she was 20 months old, she had been locked in a bedroom, either strapped to a potty-chair or into a sleeping bag. She was fed baby food, beaten if she ever cried. And she had never heard a human voice because she was deprived of radio and television and no one had ever spoken to her. When she was found,

The Wild Boy of Aveyron

When a mother sees her newborn baby for the first time, we expect her to feel a special bond of love and devotion: The maternal "instinct" has kicked in. If she had planned to give the baby up for adoption, she might suddenly change her mind. Even after the child grows up and moves away, she may feel a pang whenever the child is lonely or upset. Suddenly her career, her other relationships, and her other interests dim into insignificance against a life fully and completely devoted to caring for the child. The Romantic poet William Wordsworth said that "maternal sympathy" is a "joyless tie of naked instinct, wound about the heart." But how instinctive is it?

In *Mother Nature: A History of Mothers, Infants, and Natural Selection* (1999), Sarah Hrdy points out that little actual research has been done on mothers and children. Scientists assume that they have an instinct bond based on millions of years of evolution and leave it at that. But even in the animal kingdom, many mothers neglect or abandon their offspring. Rhesus monkeys who have been raised in isolation, without seeing other monkeys mothering their offspring, refuse to nurse or interact with their own. Among humans, women raised by abusive parents tend to be abusive to their own children, and women raised by indifferent parents tend to be indifferent.

Social expectations also play a role in how mothers respond to their children. In some human cultures, mothers are supposed to be cool and unfriendly

Maternal "Instinct"

to their children. In others, they are not supposed to know them at all. Children are raised by uncles and aunts, or by strangers, and the biological mother ignores them. In *Death Without Weeping: The Violence of Everyday Life in Brazil* (1992) Nancy Scheper-Hughes examines a culture of such grinding poverty that children often die at an early age, and she wonders why their mothers seem indifferent. She concludes that maternal devotion is a luxury that only the affluent can afford. Every now and then the newspapers in India report of parents who deliberately disfigure their children to make them more hideous looking and thus more pitifully "attractive" beggars.

Mothers are certainly capable of profound love and devotion to their children, but so are fathers, grandparents, uncles, aunts, brothers, sisters, and adults who have no biological connection at all. And not every mother is capable of such devotion. Biological instinct may play a part in the bond between mother and child, but early training at home and social expectations later in life make all the difference.

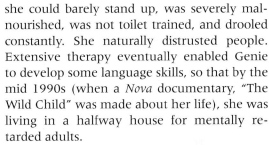

she could barely stand up, was severely malnourished, was not toilet trained, and drooled constantly. She naturally distrusted people. Extensive therapy eventually enabled Genie to develop some language skills, so that by the mid 1990s (when a *Nova* documentary, "The Wild Child" was made about her life), she was living in a halfway house for mentally retarded adults.

Studies of other isolated children reveal that some can recover, with effort and specialized care, but others suffer permanent damage. It is unclear exactly why, but no doubt some contributing factors are the duration of the isolation, the child's age when the isolation began, the presence of some human contacts (like Isabelle's mother), other abuse accompanying the isolation, and the child's intelligence (Birdsong, 1999; Candland, 1993; Newton, 2003). But lack of socialization has serious consequences; it is socialization that makes human beings human.

Primates

Obviously children can't be deliberately raised in isolation for the sake of scientific research, but we can study primates, who require the longest period of socialization other than humans. Psychologists Harry Harlow and Margaret Harlow studied rhesus monkeys raised apart from others of their species and found severe physical and emotional problems. The monkeys' growth was stunted, even when they received adequate nutrition. They were fearful of others in their group and refused to mate or associate with them socially. Those returned after three months managed to reintegrate with the group, but after six months the damage was irreparable. The females who gave birth (through artificial insemination) neglected their offspring, suggesting that "maternal instincts" must be learned through the experience of being nurtured as a child (Griffin and Harlow, 1966; Harlow, Dodsworth, and Harlow, 1965; Harlow et al., 1966; Harlow and Suomi, 1971).

In an experiment, Harry Harlow offered baby monkeys a "choice" between two surrogate mothers. One was made entirely of cold wire, but offered a bottle with milk. The other had soft terrycloth, but no milk. The monkeys consistently chose the terrycloth mother, even though it did not provide food. Harlow hypothesized that monkeys—and all primates—crave emotional attachment, sometimes even more than they crave food.

Models of Socialization

Socialization doesn't happen all at once but proceeds in stages. Both psychologists and sociologists have proposed different stages, based on the accomplishment of specific tasks.

Mead and Taking the Role of Others

George Herbert Mead, whose notions of the difference between the "I" and the "me" we discussed in Chapter 3, developed a stage theory of socialization, stages through which children pass as they become better integrated into society.

Mead argued that there are three stages in the development of the perspective of the other:

1. *Imitation*. Children under the age of 3 can imitate others, but they cannot usually put themselves into the role of others.

2. *Play*. Children aged 3 to 6 pretend to be specific people or kinds of people that they think are important (their parents, doctors, firefighters, Batman). They say and pretend to do things that these people might say and do. But they are learning more than a repertoire of behaviors. Mead saw children's play as crucial to the development of their ability to take the perspective of others. They must anticipate how the people they are pretending to be would think, feel, and behave in various situations, often playing multiple roles: As "parents," for instance, they may play at disciplining their "children," first playing a parent who believes that a misdeed was deliberate and then a child who insists that it was an accident.

3. *Games*. In early school years, children learn to play games and team sports. Now they must interpret and anticipate how other players will act, who will do what when the ball is hit, kicked, passed, or thrown. Complex games like chess and

checkers require strategy, the ability to anticipate the thoughts of others. And, perhaps most important, the children are learning to place value on actions, to locate behavior within a sense of generalized morality (Mead, 1935).

Only in this last phase do children "internalize" the expectations of more and more people, until eventually they can take on the role of their group as a whole. This is what Mead called the **generalized other**—the collection of roles and attitudes that people use as a reference point as they figure out how to behave in any given situation. It is the generalized other that surrounds you in most contexts and provides a constant internalized reference point to guide your actions.

Psychological Stage Theories of Development

Understanding the process of development has been an important part of other social sciences, such as psychology and anthropology. Psychologists have studied different aspects of socialization to explain the different stages through which we pass to become healthy, functioning adults.

Freud's Theory of Sexual Development. Psychiatrist Sigmund Freud (1856–1939), the founder of psychoanalysis, believed that the self consisted of three elements. Of course, they are always interrelated:

1. *The id*. The inborn drive for self-gratification, the **id** is pure impulse, without worrying about social rules, consequences, morality, or other people's reactions; so, if unbridled, it could get you into trouble.

2. *The superego*. The **superego** is internalized norms and values, the "rules" of our social group, learned from family, friends, and social institutions. It provokes feelings of shame or guilt when we break the "rules," pride and self-satisfaction when we follow them.

3. *The ego*. The balancing force between the id and the superego, or impulses and social rules, the **ego** channels impulses into socially acceptable forms. Sometimes it can go wrong, creating neuroses or psychoses (Figure 5.1).

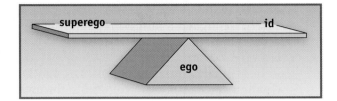

Figure 5.1 The Human Psyche According to Freud

Because the id can never have everything it wants, the task of socialization is twofold. First the ego must be strong enough to handle being rebuffed by reality and able to find acceptable substitutes for what the id originally wanted. (Psychoanalysis is supposed to strengthen the ego to handle this task.) And second, the superego must be strong enough to prevent the id from going after what it wants in the first place. Thus, the superego is the home of guilt, shame, and morality.

Freud believed that each child passes through three stages of development to become a healthy adult man or woman. These stages are based on the strategies that the ego devises to obtain gratification for its bodily urges. The stages are gendered—that is, there are different developmental tasks for girls and boys—but once we pass through them, Freud believed, our gender identity as men and women is fixed and permanent.

Imitation is not only "the sincerest form of flattery," it is also a crucial element of socialization, according to George Herbert Mead. Children imitate the behaviors, and adopt the prejudices, of their parents.

Piaget and Cognitive Development. Swiss psychologist Jean Piaget (1896–1980) studied children of different ages to see how they solve problems, how they make sense of the world (Piaget, 1928, 1932, 1953, 1955). He argued that their reasoning ability develops in four stages, each building on the last (Figure 5.2).

In the *sensorimotor stage* (birth to age 2), children experience the world only through their senses. In the *preoperational stage* (about ages 2 through 7), children can draw a square to symbolize a house or a stick with a blob at the end to symbolize a tree. But they are not yet able to understand common concepts like size, speed, or weight. In one of his most famous experiments, Piaget poured water from a short, fat glass into a tall, skinny glass. Children at the ages of 5 and 6 were unable to determine that the glasses contained the same amount of water; when they saw higher, they thought "more."

In the *concrete operational stage* (about ages 7 through 12), children's reasoning is more developed; they can understand size, speed, and weight; they can use numbers. They can perceive causal connections. But their reasoning is still concrete; they are not able to reach conclusions based on general principles.

In the *formal operational stage* (after about age 12), children are capable of abstract and critical thinking. They can talk about general concepts like "truth." They can reach con-

Figure 5.2 Piaget's Cognitive Stages of Development

Stage	Age Range	Characteristics
Sensorimotor stage 	Birth–2 years	Still in the sensory phase; can understand only what they see, hear, or touch
Preoperational stage 	2–7 years	Capable of understanding and articulating speech and symbols, but can't understand common concepts like weight
Concrete operational stage 	7–12 years	Causal relationships are understood, and they understand common concepts, but they can't reach conclusions through general principles
Formal operational stage 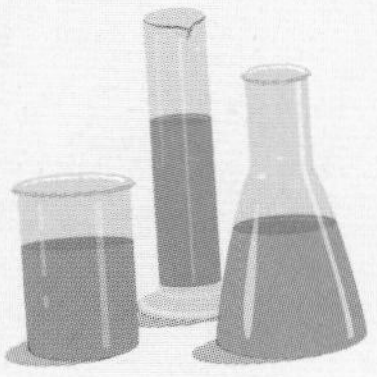	12 years and up	Capable of abstract thought and reasoning

clusions based on general principles, and they can solve abstract problems.

Piaget believed, along with other social scientists, that social interaction is the key to cognitive development. Children learn critical and abstract thinking by paying careful attention to other people behaving in certain ways in specific situations. Therefore, they need many opportunities to interact with others.

Kohlberg, Gilligan, and Moral Development.

According to Piaget, morality is an essential part of the development of cognitive reasoning. Children under 8 years old have a black-and-white view of morality: Something is either good or bad, right or wrong. They can't see "extenuating circumstances," acts that could be partially right, partially wrong, or right under some circumstances, wrong under others. As they mature, they begin to experience moral dilemmas of their own, and they develop more complex reasoning.

Psychologist Lawrence Kohlberg argued that our sense of morality developed from the concrete to the abstract, that is, from real-life situations to the ability to apply abstract principles. (The notion that "justice is blind" is the apex of this sort of thinking.)

Kohlberg's famous question set up the ethical dilemma: Your wife is sick, and you cannot afford the necessary medication. Should you break into the pharmacy and steal it? Stealing is wrong, but does the situation merit it anyway (Kohlberg, 1971)?

Kohlberg's graduate student Carol Gilligan wondered why women usually scored much lower than men on Kohlberg's morality scale. Were they really less moral? Instead, she hypothesized that Kohlberg assumed a male subject. (Notice the dilemma posed that "your wife" is sick.) He interviewed only men, made up a story about a man breaking into the pharmacy, and assumed that moral reasoning was dictated by masculine-coded justice asking "What are the rules?" instead of a more feminine-coded emotion asking "Who will be hurt?" She argued that there is a different guide to moral reasoning, one more often exhibited by women, called "an ethic of care," which is based on people sacrificing their own needs and goals for the good of people around them (Gilligan, 1982). While all of us exhibit characteristics of both justice and care as ethical systems, women tend to gravitate toward care and men toward ethics. Gilligan's argument is that, by focusing only on justice, we will miss an equally important ethical system.

Most social scientists do not believe that women and men have completely different forms of moral reasoning. Both women and men develop ethics of care and ethics of justice. These systems are not gender specific. They are simply different ways of solving moral dilemmas.

Problems with Stage Theories

Stage theories are extremely popular. Many best-sellers describe the "seasons of a man's life," "passages," or "the fountain of age." And we often use stage theory to describe a problem, preferring to believe that someone will "grow out of" a problematic behavior than to believe that such a behavior is part of who they "really are." It is interesting, and often amusing, to try to fit our own experiences into the various theorists' stages of human development, but the whole idea of stages has some problems in the real world:

In his studies of the development of moral reasoning, psychologist Lawrence Kohlberg argued that an abstract "ethic of justice," as in this symbol of American jurisprudence, was the highest form of ethical thought. His student, Carol Gilligan, disagreed, arguing that just as important, though not as recognized, was an "ethic of care," in which people's moral decision making is based on how it will actually affect people.

We socialize ourselves in anticipation of the positions we hope to occupy. These teenagers act so "grown up" as they head to their high school prom in 1953.

- The stages are rigidly defined, but many of the challenges are lifelong. Erikson (1959) puts the conflict between being part of a group and having a unique identity in adolescence, but every time we join a new club, get a new job, move to a new town, or make new friends, we face the same conflict, even in old age.

- It is not clear that failure to meet the challenges of one stage means permanent failure. Maybe we can fix it during the next stage.

- The theorists usually maintain that the stages are universal, but do people in all cultures and all time periods really develop in the same way? In cultures where there are no schools, is there a preadolescence? In many parts of the world, the life expectancy is about 40; are middle adulthood and old age the same there as in the United States, where we can expect to live to about 80? Even within the same culture, people do not develop in the same way. Piaget argued that the formal operational stage of abstract reasoning begins during adolescence, but Kohlberg and Gilligan (1971) found that 30 percent of the U.S. population never develop it at all.

Two other problems with stage theories result from the fact that we assume that one passes through a stage fully and never returns to that stage. But we are also constantly cross-cutting stages, moving back and forth. Socialization turns out to be a lifelong and fluid process.

There are two other socialization processes that are important to consider.

Anticipatory Socialization. Even while you occupy one status, you may begin to anticipate moving to the next stage and begin a future-oriented project of acting *as if* you were already there. **Anticipatory socialization** is when you begin to enact the behaviors and traits of the status that you expect to occupy. For example, young adolescents might decide to begin drinking coffee, in anticipation of the onset of adulthood, when they will drink coffee the same as grownups do. Often people

At Virginia Military Institute, upper-class cadets are in charge of the resocialization of first-year students (called "rats").

begin to imitate those who occupy the statuses *to which we believe we will eventually belong.* This can result in some confusion and even some anger from your friends, especially if you start acting like a "snob" because you are anticipating becoming rich when you graduate from college and join the Fortune 500.

Resocialization. Moving from one stage to another doesn't happen easily, but we often have to relearn elementary components of the role when we enter a new status. **Resocialization** involves learning new sets of values, behaviors, and attitudes that are different from those you previously held. Resocialization is also something that happens all through your life, and failure to adequately resocialize into a new status can have dire consequences. Some resocialization is coerced: Let's say you are a happy-go-lucky sort of person, loud and rambunctious, and you are arrested for disturbing the peace and sent to jail. Failure to resocialize to a docile, obedient, and silent prisoner can result in serious injury. For some psychiatric patients, failure to become a docile patient can lead to an even more serious diagnosis! Some resocialization is voluntary, as when someone joins the military or enters a monastery or convent.

One of the more shocking moments in resocialization happens to college students during their first year in school. Expectations in college are often quite different from high school, and one must "resocialize" to these new institutional norms. When resocialization is successful, one moves easily into a new status. When it is unsuccessful, or only partially realized, you will continue to stick out uneasily.

Agents of Socialization

Agents of socialization are people, groups, or social institutions that socialize new members, either formally (as in lessons about traffic safety in school) or informally (as in cartoon characters on television behaving according to social expectations). **Primary socialization,** which occurs during childhood, gives us basic behavioral patterns but allows for adaptation and change later on. **Secondary socialization** occurs throughout life, every time we start a new class or a new job, move to a new neighborhood, make new friends, or change social roles, allowing us to abandon old, outdated, or unnecessary behavior patterns, giving us new behavioral patterns necessary for the new situation.

Socialization is not necessarily a positive ideal, helping the child adjust to life in the best of all possible worlds. Some of the norms we are socialized into are oppressive, short-sighted, and wrong. We can be socialized into believing stereotypes, into hating out-groups, into violence and abuse. Children of different cultures might be curious about differences they see, even somewhat uneasy, but they aren't biologically programmed to commit genocide as adults. That is learned.

For a long time psychologists and sociologists argued that the major agent of primary socialization was the family, with school and religion becoming increasingly important as childhood proceeded. These three institutions—family, school, religion—and the three primary actors within those institutions—parents, teachers, clergy—were celebrated as the central institutions and agents of socialization.

Of course, they are central; no institutions are more important. But from the point of view of the child, these three institutional agents—parents, teachers, clergy—are experienced as "grownups, grownups, and grownups." Asking children today about their socialization reveals that two other institutions—mass media and peer groups—are also vital in the socialization process. These two institutions become increasingly important later in childhood and especially in adolescence. Later, as adults, government, the workplace, and other social institutions become important. Agents of socialization tend to work together, promoting the same norms and values, and they socialize each other as well as the developing individual. It is often impossible to tell where the influence of one ends and the influence of another begins, and even a list seems arbitrary. (Each of these institutions is so important that we return to each one in a separate chapter.)

"Be Like Me/Don't Be Like Me"

For decades, sociologists believed that parents socialized their children to grow up like them; that is, parents saw themselves as positive role models for their children. And that was true for middle-class parents. Middle-class fathers see themselves as role models for their children, saying, in effect, "You can grow up to be like me if you study and work hard."

But this isn't true for the working class. In a landmark study, *The Hidden Injuries of Class* (1973), sociologists Richard Sennett and Jonathan Cobb interviewed hundreds of working-class women and men, many of whom were immigrants or children of immigrants. They found that these people felt inade-

quate, sometimes like frauds or imposters, ambivalent about their success. They had worked hard but hadn't succeeded, and because they were fervent believers in the American Dream—where even a poor boy can grow up to be the president—they blamed themselves for their failure. Sennett and Cobb attributed this to "status incongruity"—living in two worlds at the same time.

And how did they manage to ward off despair when they were at fault for their own failures? They deferred success from their own lives to the lives of their children. They worked at difficult, dirty, and dangerous jobs not because they were failures but because they were sacrificing to give their children a better life. They were noble and honorable.

But they saw themselves not as role models to be emulated but as cautionary tales to be avoided. "You could grow up to be like me if you don't study and work hard," they were saying. It turns out that whether you see yourself as a positive or a negative role model depends on what class you belong to (Sennett and Cobb, 1993).

Socialization is not always positive. One can be socialized to hate and fear; indeed, you can be socialized to be a ruthless killer as were many child soldiers in the ethnic conflict in Sierra Leone.

Family

There are many different child-rearing systems in cultures around the world. In the United States, we are most familiar with nuclear families (father, mother, children) and extended families (parents, children, uncles, aunts, grandparents), but in some cultures everyone in the tribe lives together in a longhouse; or men, women, and children occupy separate dormitories. Sometimes the biological parents have little responsibility for raising their children or are even forbidden from seeing them. But there is always a core of people—parents, brothers, sisters, and others—who interact with the children constantly as they are growing, giving them their first sense of self and setting down their first motivations, social norms, values, and beliefs. From our family we receive our first and most enduring ideas about who we are and where we are going in life.

Our family also gives us our first statuses, our definitions of ourselves as belonging to a certain class, nationality, race, ethnicity, religion, and gender. In traditional societies, these remain as permanent parts of our self-concept. We would live in the same village as our parents, work at their occupation, and never aspire to an economic success greater than they enjoyed. In modern societies, we are more likely to be mobile, choosing occupations and

is appropriate to have fun and how to have it. Today, there is more anxiety and tension surrounding middle age than in the past. When so much mass media glorify youth, it is easy for people in middle age to think of themselves as deficient or diminished.

Above age 60 has generally been referred to as "old age." In earlier cultures, few people lived to see their old age, and those who did were revered because they had the job of passing on the wisdom of earlier generations to the later. To call someone "Grandfather" or "Grandmother" was to put them at the pinnacle of social status. Nowadays, we may say, "Get out of the way, Grandpa!" as an insult to an older person who is moving too slowly for us. On *The Simpsons*, Homer's father Abraham is constantly ridiculed for his physical disabilities and for being forgetful, longwinded, narrow minded, and fantasy prone.

Because older people often move to retirement communities and nursing homes far from their children, grandchildren, and friends, they must make social connections all over again, and many find old age to be the loneliest time of their lives. It is also the poorest, because they are not working, and their only source of income may be a small pension or Social Security check. The longevity revolution in industrialized countries means that most people can expect to live 20 or more years in old age.

Old age was historically a stage of life characterized by boredom, loneliness, and poverty. As people are living longer, they are also re-creating communities, and, in those countries with adequate Social Security, living happier and healthier— as well as longer—lives.

Sixty-five no longer seems doddering and decrepit, and the mandatory retirement age has been raised to 70 in some states or eliminated altogether. Will such a long life span transform old age, restoring to it some of its lost prestige? The longevity revolution has ushered in new terms for the aged, as we will see later in this book, from the "young old" to the "old old." If 30 is the new 20, then today 90 is the new 70.

Gender Socialization

Each of these age categories provides new arenas and new institutions for socialization. From the nursery to the nursing home, we are surrounded by people from whom we learn appropriate behaviors and emotions and inhabit institutions that have their own norms for behaviors and values that underlie them. We actively engage in socialization throughout our lives. When we get a new job, we are socialized into the spoken and unspoken rules of the job: Do you eat your lunch at your desk, in the employee lounge, or out at a restaurant? Are you supposed to discuss your personal life with your co-workers or limit your interaction to polite greetings? Should you profess an interest in opera or the Superbowl? The socialization is usually what "should" be done, not

what "must" be done. You will not be thrown out onto the street for mentioning the Superbowl when the social norm is to like opera, but you will find your prestige lessened. You will be less likely to belong to the most coveted peer groups and less likely to rise to positions of leadership in the group.

Socialization into gender is one of the most important elements of socialization, occupying a great deal of the time and energy of a great many agents of socialization throughout the life course. From the moment babies return from the hospital in pink or blue blankets, or wear their first outfits marked with "Daddy's Little Princess" or "Daddy's Little Slugger," they undergo **gender socialization:** the active learning of the socially acceptable attitudes, traits, and behaviors that are seen by one's society as appropriate for males or females. In the United States, boys and girls are expected to learn two entirely different sets of social norms.

Gender and the Boy Code

In their best-selling books about boys, psychologists such as William Pollack (1999), James Garbarino (1999), Michael Thompson and Dan Kindlon (2000), and others argue that, from an early age, boys are taught to refrain from crying, to suppress their emotions, never to display vulnerability. As a result, they argue, boys feel effeminate not only if they express their emotions but if they even feel emotions.

Young boys begin to embrace what Pollack calls "the boy code" by age 4 or 5, when they enter kindergarten, and they get a second jolt when they hit adolescence. Think of the messages boys get: "Stand on your own two feet! Don't cry! Don't be a sissy! Don't be a mama's boy!" As one boy in Pollack's book summarizes it: "Shut up and take it, or you'll be sorry."

Consider the parallel for girls. Carol Gilligan (1982) describes how assertive, confident, and proud young girls "lose their voices" when they hit adolescence. At the same moment, Pollack notes, boys become more confident, even beyond their abilities. You might even say that boys find their voices, but they are inauthentic voices of bravado,

risk taking, and foolish violence. The boy code teaches them that they are supposed to be in power, and they begin to act like it. What is the cause of all this posturing and posing? It's not testosterone, but privilege. In adolescence both boys and girls get their first real dose of gender inequality. Therefore, girls suppress ambition, boys inflate it.

The boy code leaves boys disconnected from many of their emotions and keeps them from sharing their feelings with their peers. As they grow older, they feel disconnected from adults, as well, unable to experience the guidance toward maturity that adults can bring. When they turn to anger and violence it is because they believe that these are the only acceptable forms of emotional expression.

Where do they learn the boy code (or, as teenagers and adults, the guy code)? From teachers and parents certainly, but mostly from their peers. The guy code offers a specific blueprint for being accepted as a guy. But just as "the first rule of *Fight Club*" (1996)—perhaps the touchstone text for thousands of guys—says, "You can tell no one about Fight Club," the guy code is never written down or verbalized. Rather, it is passed from guy to guy in locker rooms and gyms, bars and frat houses, workplaces and churches, all across the nation. The guy code teaches exaggerated versions of the ideology of masculinity, with certain modifications: "Be tough! Be strong! Laugh at weakness! Do not feel!"

Boys are expected to be tough, aggressive, loud, and athletic and girls to be sensitive, passive, quiet, and nonathletic. (In recent years, girls have found it far easier to reject or resist this polarized view of things; boys tend to remain committed to the strong silent jock model.)

Throughout childhood, both groups are punished for transgressions by every agent of

socialization: parents, teachers, peers. Perhaps the boys get more punishment. Girls who are tough, aggressive, loud, and athletic are labeled "tomboys," while boys who are sensitive, passive, quiet, and not good at sports are labeled with the much worse term "sissies." The difference is one of gender privilege. Because "masculine" things are powerful, girls who do

Boys may be called "sissies" when they defy gender expectations (as in this image from the movie Billy Elliot) *and girls called "tomboys." But sanctions for gender nonconformity are more severe for boys than for girls.*

"masculine" things may be praised as just trying to increase their prestige, but boys who do "feminine" things are "acting like a girl"; that is, they get less prestige.

Growing up does not lessen the intensity of gender socialization. We are bombarded with media images every day about appropriate masculinity and femininity. On television, commercials instruct men to order a "Manwich" rather than, say, a salad. Our romances are expected to be gender polarized, with heterosexual men from Mars, heterosexual women from Venus, and gay men and lesbians the reverse, even in such trivialities as handling the television remote (men flip quickly from channel to channel, women stick with one channel). Our churches and temples are sites of performing gender, our jobs dependent on demonstrating gender-appropriate skills and attitudes. Even at home, among our friends, we cannot relax: Our peer groups are constantly enforcing the rules, policing everyone and punishing any transgression with snubs, stares, jokes, or ostracism.

Socialization in the Twenty-First Century

The socialization process is dynamic and continuous. Across the life span, more and different agents of socialization can come into play. One never achieves or reaches a "true" identity but is always interacting and reacting to create what can only be a temporary or partial "self." While this complex process potentially offers us constant opportunities for self-creation and growth, it is also rife with tensions between autonomy and belonging, individuality and group identification.

Next time someone gives you his or her yearbook to inscribe, consider writing, "Change! And keep changing! For the rest of your life!"

Chapter Review

1. Socialization and Biology

Humans have long pondered what makes us who we are—nature or nurture? Prior to the Enlightenment, the prevailing European view was that we are creatures of nature, as made by God. This began to change as environment was recognized as a force shaping human nature; in Locke's view, we are born as blank slates, wholly shaped by environment. Rousseau tempered this view, recognizing nature and nurture, and Darwin's work supported the primacy of biology. We are products of both, but biology focuses on the nature and the basic physiological aspect of our being, and sociology focuses on **socialization;** how we develop, becoming who we are, and continually changing, through social interaction.

socialization The process by which we become aware of ourselves as part of a group, learn to communicate with others, and learn how to behave as expected. (p. 127)

2. Socialization in Action

Compared with other species, even other primates, humans are helpless and dependent the longest—up to a quarter of the normal life span. As we develop physically, we develop socially, not just through formal instruction but more often informally through social interaction. The popular Tarzan story portrayed a feral child who became socialized in adulthood, but real-world examples show that childhood socialization is critical. Experimental work with monkeys confirms the importance of early social interaction. Even things thought biologically innate, like the maternal instinct, are socialization dependent.

3. Models of Socialization

Stage theories dominate developmental models, in sociology and psychology, too. Mead discussed three stages in childhood—first imitation, then role play in the play stage, and finally, in the game stage, taking the role of the other, ultimately internalizing the **generalized other.** In Freud's theory of sexual development we go through three stages of developing gender identity, each oriented around how the **ego** meets the **id's** urges. Successfully socialized adults have egos that channel the id's impulses in socially acceptable ways and **superegos** that internalize society's rules. Piaget studied cognitive development, identifying four stages: sensorimotor, preoperational, concrete operational, and finally, formal operational, which is adultlike in reasoning ability. Kohlberg's view of moral development, from concrete to abstract principles, was challenged by Gilligan for neglecting other equally moral ethical systems. Stage theories are criticized because development may not be as invariant, discrete, or progressive as these theories present, nor are they necessarily universal. For example, socialization continues throughout life, with **anticipatory socialization** and **resocialization.**

generalized other The organized rules, judgments, and attitudes of an entire group. If you try to imagine what is expected of you, you are taking on the perspective of the generalized other. (p. 131)

id Sigmund Freud's label for that part of the human personality that is pure impulse, without worrying about social rules, consequences, morality, or other people's reactions. (p. 131)

superego Freud's term for the internalized norms, values, and "rules" of our social group that are learned from family, friends, and social institutions. (p. 131)

ego Freud's term for the balancing force between the id and the superego; it channels impulses into socially acceptable forms. (p. 131)

anticipatory socialization The process of learning and adopting the beliefs, values, and behaviors of groups that one anticipates joining in the future. (p. 134)

resocialization Learning a new set of beliefs, behaviors, and values that depart from those held in the past. (p. 135)

4. Agents of Socialization

We encounter **agents of socialization** throughout our lives. Much of the socialization is unintentional. **Primary socialization** occurs during childhood, through family, school, and religion, with mass media and our **peer group** gaining considerable influence in middle and late childhood. **Secondary socialization** occurs during adulthood, through the workplace and other structural institutions, like the government. Aspects of self developed during primary socialization may always influence us, in one form or another, particularly social statuses, such as religion, even though values, beliefs, and behaviors are not always explicitly taught. Education teaches but also sorts and socializes by gender and class; this is the "hidden curriculum." Religion is a source of community and culture but divides societies, too, sometimes demonizing out-groups. Peer groups informally reinforce the socialization of other institutions in interaction, through encouragement, bullying, and coercion. Mass media (television, movies, magazines, video games, social networking, and the like), are extraordinarily influential and create global connections. For adults, the workplace is so important that we identify ourselves by our job.

agents of socialization The people, groups, or institutions that teach people how to be functioning members of their society. (p. 135)

primary socialization A culture's most basic values, which are passed on to children beginning in earliest infancy. (p. 135)

secondary socialization Occurring throughout the life span, it is the adjustments we make to adapt to new situations. (p. 135)

peer group Our group of friends and wider group of acquaintances who have an enormous socializing influence, especially during middle and late childhood. (p. 139)

5. Socialization and the Life Course

Stages of life may be marked by distinct physiological changes, but meanings associated with life stages are socially constructed, varying by culture and even by status within a culture; for example, by gender, race, or social class. Childhood is a relatively recent construct. In some parts of the world, children still work like adults. Adolescence has developed as separate from adulthood. During this time of extended education, we are shielded from all of the responsibilities and rights of adulthood. Cultures often mark passage into adulthood by ritual. The sociological markers of adulthood—finishing school, getting a job, moving out, marrying, having a child—now occur later. Young adulthood refers to the period before adulthood. Middle age and old age happen later than at any time in the past, due to delay reaching adulthood, and longer life spans.

6. Gender Socialization

There are different expectations for behavior for boys and girls, and behaving appropriately masculine or feminine is a result of the process of **gender socialization,** which begins the moment the sex of the baby is identified, and continues throughout life from all of the agents of socialization. Failing to follow the expectations for gender behavior meets with negative consequences, more so for boys than girls because power and privilege are associated with the male role. A girl who is a "tomboy" is not ridiculed as much as boys who do "feminine" things, which are perceived as weaker and less prestigious. Boys subsequently shun emotional vulnerability, masking it with shows of bravado, fulfilling expectations for masculinity, while girls, in recognition of their lower social status, follow gender expectations, becoming less confident and powerful.

gender socialization Process by which males and females are taught the appropriate behaviors, attitudes, and traits for their biological sex. It begins at birth and continues throughout their lives. (p. 145)

7. Socialization in the Twenty-First Century

We have selves, supported by the social structure, and our primary socialization, but we are also continually changing, responsive to our current social environments, in interaction with increasing numbers of agents of socialization. This is the dynamic tension of self in society, which Goffman understood so well.

Self-Test: Check Your Understanding

1. Which of the following is an example of secondary socialization?
   a. A child develops the understandings that pink is for girls, blue is for boys, and she is supposed to be afraid of spiders instead of interested in them, from things other children say at preschool.
   b. Pointed remarks from co-workers help a college graduate realize that casual Friday means khaki pants and a sport shirt with a collar, instead of cut-off shorts and a T-shirt.
   c. Factory workers on the line are obedient and deferential to all authorities in their workplace, just as they were to their teachers in grade school.
   d. A young adult continues to give up candy and sweets for Lent.

2. According to the text, which of the following agents of socialization are especially influential during adolescence?
   a. The family and education
   b. Mass media and peers
   c. Education and the workplace
   d. The government

3. During which stage of Mead's theory are the expectations of society internalized as the generalized other?
   a. Imitation stage
   b. Play stage
   c. Games stage
   d. In Mead's theory, during all of the above stages, children have internalized the generalized other.

4. Kohn's research found that working-class families instill in their children the importance of _____, while middle-class and affluent families encourage the development of _____.
   a. discretion; industriousness
   b. friendliness; courage
   c. good judgment; self-control
   d. conformity; creativity

5. Sociologists find that the transition to adulthood is marked by the completion of which of the following?
   a. Finishing school and getting a job
   b. Getting married and having a child
   c. Leaving their parents' home for one of their own
   d. All of the above are markers of the transition to adulthood.

6. How do peer groups enforce gender-appropriate behavior?
   a. Teasing and jokes
   b. Hostility and threats
   c. Hazing and beatings
   d. None of the above, as peer groups do not enforce gender norms.

7. Gilligan's description of how young girls "lose their voices" when they reach adolescence refers to:
   a. how their voices crack and change as they physically mature.
   b. their development of an inauthentic voice of bravado.
   c. an unwritten code that is shared tacitly.
   d. losing their confidence and becoming less assertive.

8. The first year of college is often difficult as expectations are very different from high school. Successful adjustment to college the first year is an example of:
   a. primary socialization.
   b. secondary socialization.
   c. resocialization.
   d. anticipatory socialization.

Self-Test Answers: 1. b, 2. b, 3. c, 4. d, 5. d, 6. a, 7. d, 8. c

Integrate and Explore: Points to Consider

1. Which agents of socialization seem to have become more influential as a result of globalization? Which have become less so? How have societies changed, as a result of the growth, and decline, of these influences? Do these changes affect people at different stages of the life course similarly or differently?

2. Thinking about multiculturalism and the life course, consider how the experiences of a 75-year-old member of an ethnic group that reveres the wisdom of the elderly might vary as he or she goes about the day in a society that does not? What challenges might face an adolescent from a culture where children work and adulthood begins relatively early in a society that delays adulthood until the 20s and 30s?

succeed with PEARSON mysoclab

Self-scoring practice tests, flashcards for learning key terms, streaming audio of the entire text, and multimedia, including:

Watch—Michael Kimmel, *Agents of Socialization Today*
Watch—Amy Aronson, *The Power of Media*
MySocLibrary—Gwynn Dyer, *Anybody's Son Will Do*

Deviance and Crime

There's a good chance that every person reading this book is a law-abiding citizen. We don't steal each other's cars; we don't open fire at the quarterback or point guard of opposing teams; we don't burn down dormitories or plunder the provost's office. We pay our taxes and drive under the speed limit, at least most of the time.

Yet there is an equally good chance that each person reading this book is a "criminal"—that is, has done something illegal. We may have run a red light, had a drink while underage, or gambled on a sporting event in an unauthorized setting or while underage. We may have stolen a library book or plagiarized a paper. (These last few might not land you in jail, but they could get you kicked out of school.)

Most of us probably shave the rules a little bit. But we're also likely to get outraged, even to the point of violence, if someone cuts into a line for tickets at the movie theater. Is it just because it's OK for us and not OK for others? Or is it because we carry inside us a common moral standard, and we are willing to cheat a little to make things come out the way we think they are supposed to but resent it when others violate that same moral contract?

So, is the question whether you are a law-abiding citizen or a criminal? To the sociologist, you're both. The more interesting questions are when and where you are one or the other, under what circumstances you obey or disobey the law, and what the social and legal consequences of your behavior are. Do you get away with it or get sent to jail?

And how do we think about crime? What crimes should be punished, and how severe should those punishments be? In some respects, one might say that America is soft on crime: Most arrests are not prosecuted, most prosecutions do not result in jail time, and most prisoners are paroled before they serve their full terms. In other respects, America is hard on crime: It is the number one jailer in the world and the only industrialized nation that still has the death penalty.

> "So, is the question whether you are a law-abiding citizen or a criminal? To the sociologist, you're both. The more interesting questions are when and where you are one or the other. . . ."

It seems to be a matter of working very hard to achieve very limited results. In fact, we are both soft *and* hard on crime; to the sociologist what is most interesting is the how and why of that "softness" and "hardness" and measuring the effectiveness of the institutions that are designed to handle deviance and crime.

What Is Deviance?

Breaking a social rule, or refusing to follow one, is called **deviance.** Deviant acts may or may not be illegal; they can also violate a moral or a social rule that may or may not have legal consequences. This week, many of you will do something that could be considered deviant—from the illegal behaviors like shoplifting, underage drinking, or speeding, to arriving at a party too soon or leaving too late.

We can also be considered deviant without doing, saying, or believing anything bad or wrong but just by belonging to the "wrong" group in some circumstances (Hispanic, gay, Jewish, for example) or by having some status that goes against what's considered "normal" (mentally ill, disabled, atheist, being overweight at a fitness club). There is even deviance by association: If you have a friend who belongs to the minority group, or a family member with a deviant status, you may be labeled as deviant just for being seen with him or her.

Most deviance is not illegal, and many illegal acts are only mildly deviant or not deviant at all. But when lawmakers consider a deviant act bad enough to warrant formal sanctions, it becomes a *crime,* and the government goes into regulating it. Some common sexual practices—like oral sex or masturbation—are illegal in a number of states because lawmakers at one time found them sufficiently deviant to be criminal.

Some sociologists study minor forms of deviance, but most are interested in the major forms of deviance. These are acts that can get you shunned or labeled an "outsider" (Becker, 1966); or they are the sorts of crimes that get you thrown in prison. These are not matters of mere carelessness: The rules come from many important agents of socialization, and the penalties for breaking them are high. With some, like burglary or fraud, you have to consciously plan to commit the act, and the law distinguishes between those crimes that are the result of intention and those that could be the result of negligence or even an accident (and we adjust our penalties accordingly).

So why do people break them? And why don't most of us break them all the time? What makes a deviant or a criminal? Who decides? How does what is considered deviance vary from society to society? How does it change over time? What can we do about

Did You Know?

We can also be considered deviant without doing, saying, or believing anything bad or wrong but just by having some status that goes against what's considered "normal," like this overweight woman at a fitness club or "Lizardman" (at left) who breaks social norms about appearance.

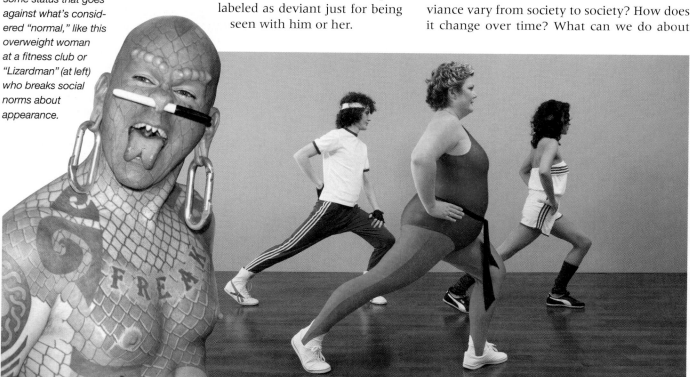

it? These are the central questions to a sociologist because they illustrate our concern for social order and control—both when they are present and people obey the rules and when they are absent and people feel unconstrained by those same rules.

Why do most of us conform to social norms most of the time, and why do most of us decide to break some of them at other times? Sociologists want to know: What accounts for conformity? What accounts for deviance? And who decides which is which?

Conformity and Social Control

Each culture develops different types of rules that prescribe what is considered appropriate behavior in that culture. They vary by how formalized they are, how central to social life, and the types of sanctions that are threatened should you break them:

1. **Folkways** are routine, usually unspoken conventions of behavior; our culture prescribes that we do some things in a certain way, although other ways might work just as well. For example, we face forward instead of backward in an elevator, and answer the question "How are you?" with "Fine." Breaking a folkway may make others in the group uncomfortable (although they sometimes don't understand why they're uncomfortable), and violators may be laughed at, frowned on, or scolded. Folkways are rarely made into laws.

2. **Mores** are norms with a strong moral significance, viewed as essential to the proper functioning of the group: We absolutely should or should not behave this way. You might break a *mos* (the singular form of mores) by assaulting someone or speaking abusively to someone, or even flaming someone in a chat room or in an email. Breaking mores makes others in the group upset, angry, or afraid, and they are likely to consider violators bad or immoral. Mores are often made into laws.

3. **Taboos** are prohibitions viewed as essential to the well-being of humanity. To break a taboo is unthinkable, beyond comprehension. For example, Sigmund Freud considered the incest taboo—one should not have sex with one's own children—to be a foundation of all societies. If parents and children had sex, then lines of inheritance, family name, and orderly property transfer would be completely impossible. Taboos are so important that most cultures

have only a few. In the United States, for instance, murder and assault break mores, not taboos. Breaking taboos causes others to feel disgusted. The violators are considered sick, evil, and monstrous. Taboos are always made into laws, unless they are so unthinkable that lawmakers cannot believe that anyone would break them.

Stigma

If some part of you—your race or sexuality, for example—is considered deviant, without your actually having to do anything, you would be considered "stigmatized." The sociologist Erving Goffman (1963) used the term **stigma** to mean an attribute that changes you "from a whole and usual person to a tainted and discounted one." Deviant behavior or a deviant master status creates stigma, although not in every case. Other people might ignore our deviance or "forgive" it as an anomaly. Goffman believed that people with stigmatized attributes are constantly practicing various strategies to ensure minimal damage. Because being stigmatized will "spoil" your identity, you are likely to adopt one of three strategies to alleviate it.

Goffman identified three strategies to neutralize stigma and save yourself from having a spoiled identity. He listed them in order of increased social power—the more power you have, the more you can try and redefine the situation. (These terms reflect the era in which he was writing; he obviously uses the Civil Rights movement as the reference.)

1. *Minstrelization:* If you're virtually alone and have very little power, you can overconform to the stereotypes that others have about you. To act like a minstrel, Goffman

A Crush on Alice?

For a hundred years, scholars believed that Lewis Carroll had a romantic and probably a sexual interest in 7-year-old Alice Liddell and that he wrote *Alice in Wonderland* and *Through the Looking-Glass* as a means of courting her. But in her 1999 book Karoline Leach concludes he was really having an affair with Alice's mother. After his death, his sister was so worried about a scandal that she manipulated his papers to make it appear that he was interested in Alice instead. In 1898, pedophilia was much less taboo than an extramarital fling!

Did You Know?

Deviants or folk heroes? Jesse James and the Black Panthers were considered criminals by law enforcement agencies, but they were folk heroes in their communities, celebrated in folk songs and tributes.

says, is to exaggerate the differences between the stigmatized and the dominant group. Thus, for example, did African Americans overact as happy-go-lucky entertainers when they had no other recourse? A contemporary example might be women who act ultrafeminine—helpless and dependent—in potentially harassing situations. Note that minstrels exaggerate difference in the face of those with more power; when they are with other stigmatized people, they may laugh about the fact that the powerful "actually think we're like this!" That's often the only sort of power that they feel they have.

2. *Normification:* If you have even a small amount of power, you might try to *minimize* the differences between the stigmatized groups. "Look," you'll say, "we're the same as you are, so there is no reason to discriminate against us." Normification is the process that gays and lesbians refer to when they argue for same-sex marriage or that women use when they say they want to be engineers or physicists. Normification involves exaggerating similarities and downplaying differences.

3. *Militant chauvinism:* When your group's level of power and organization is highest, you may decide to again *maximize* differences with the dominant group. But militant chauvinists don't just say "we're different," they say "we're also better." For example, there are groups of African Americans ("Afrocentrists" or even some of the Nation of Islam) who proclaim Black superiority. Some feminist women proclaim that women's ways are better than the dominant "male" way. These trends try to turn the tables on the dominant group. (*Warning:* Do not attempt this if you are the only member of your group in a confrontation with members of the dominant group.)

These three responses to stigma depend on the size and strength of the stigmatized group. If you're all alone, minstrelizing may be a lifesaving technique. If there are many of you and you are strong, you might try to militantly turn the tables.

Deviant Subcultures

A **subculture** is a group that evolves within a dominant culture, always more or less hidden and closed to outsiders. It may be a loose association of friends who share the same interests, or it may be well organized, with its own alternative language, costumes, and media. While most subcultures are not deviant, the separation from the dominant culture allows deviant subcultures to develop their own norms and values. For a deviant subculture to develop, the activity, condition, identity, and so on must meet three characteristics:

1. It must be punished but not punished too much. If it is not punished enough, potential recruits have no motivation to seek out the subculture. If it is punished too much, the risks of membership are too great.

2. It must have enough participants but not too many. If it has too few participants,

it will be hard to seek them out locally. If it has too many, it would be pointless.

3. It must be complex but not too complex. If it is not complex enough, you could engage in it by yourself. If it is too complex, it could exist only within a counterculture or dominant culture: You would need a college degree.

Notice that each of these criteria is not a simple either/or proposition but rather the achievement of a balance or middle way between heavy punishment and leniency and between size and complexity.

There are many different kinds of deviant subcultures. Many are based on lifestyle differences—sex, or drugs, or rock and roll. Deviant sexual subcultures, for example, might include people whose sexualities are organized around practices outside prescribed patterns, like S&M (sadomasochism) or B&D (bondage and discipline). Drug subcultures range from small groups of potheads to crack cocaine dens run by drug cartels. (Participants in drug cartels are typically not, themselves, users of the drugs; they are simply traffickers whose motives are money and power.) And anyone who has ever been to a Grateful Dead or a Phish concert knows what a musical deviant subculture looks like. One thing is certain: Wherever there are deviant subcultures, there are sociologists studying them.

Youth Gangs as Deviant Subculture. Youth gangs are a good example of a deviant subculture. Before the 1950s, we often considered youth gangs as relatively innocent. Their deviance consisted of swiping apples from fruit stands and swimming in the East River in spite of the "no trespassing" signs. Meanwhile they helped out mothers and friends in distress and sometimes even cooperated with the police. They were juvenile delinquents with hearts of gold, mischievous but not bad. It was the adult gangsters who posed a threat, trying to seduce them into lives of adult, hard-core crime.

Today, though, our image of youth gangs is quite different, closer to the film *Boyz in the Hood* (1991). And they no longer swipe the occasional apple. There are some nearly 31,000 youth gangs in the United States, with about 785,000 active members aged 12 to 24, according to the National Youth Gang Center—a figure that doesn't even include informal ganglike cliques, crews, and posses

who may dress alike and share common customs and rituals but do not engage in organized criminal activity (National Gang Intelligence Center, 2009). Nearly eight in ten cities with populations of 50,000 or more now have a "gang problem." (See Figure 6.1.)

Most gangs are composed of poor or working-class adolescents, typically male (Sanchez-Jankowski, 1991). Members are startlingly young, often preteen when they start, and they generally retire (or go to prison or die) by their mid-twenties. Ethnic minorities are overrepresented, in part because, as numerical minorities, they often feel a stronger need to belong to a group that can provide identity and protection. The National Youth Gang Survey found that 49 percent of gang members are Hispanic, 37 percent Black, 8 percent White, 5 percent Asian, and 1 percent all others (Snyder and Sickmund, 2006). The racial composition of gangs, however, reflects the characteristics of the larger community and so varies considerably with location (Howell, Egley, and Gleason, 2002; see Egley and O'Donnell, 2009) (see Figure 6.2).

Youth gangs are seen as deviant subcultures, with their own norms, values, and rules of conduct. The number of female gang members has been increasing, but most gang members are male.

Figure 6.1 Percentage of State and Local Law Enforcement Agencies Reporting Gang Activity by Region

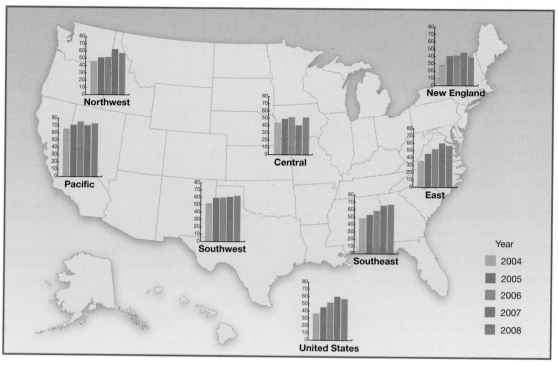

(*Source:* "Gang Proliferation," National Gang Information Center, January 2009.)

While females represent a small proportion of youth gang members, their numbers have been increasing in recent years (Moore

Figure 6.2 Race and Ethnicity of Gang Members

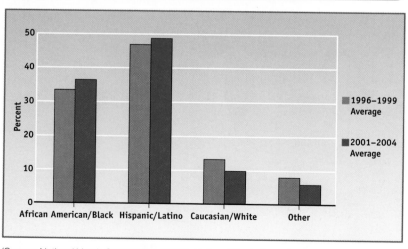

(*Source:* National Youth Gang Center [2007]. National Youth Gang Survey Analysis, www.iir.com/nygc/nygsa/Reprinted by permission of Institute for Intergovernmental Research.)

and Hagedorn, 2001; National youth Gang Center, 2007) (see Figure 6.3). As young teenagers, roughly one-third of all youth gang members are female (Esbensen and Winfree, 1998; Gottfredson and Gottfredson, 2001; U.S. Department of Justice, 2008a); however, females tend to leave gangs at an earlier age than males (Gottfredson and Gottfredson, 2001; Hunt, Joe-Laidler, and MacKenzie, 2005; Thornberry et al., 2003). Emerging research has begun to suggest that the gender composition of a gang affects its delinquency rates. In one study, females in all- or majority-female gangs had the lowest delinquency rates, while both males and females in majority-male gangs had the highest—including higher rates than males in all-male gangs (Fleisher and Krienert, 2004; Peterson, Miller, and Esbensen, 2001; U.S. Department of Justice, 2008a).

Sociologist Sudhir Venkatesh (2008) lived with a gang in Chicago. He found that those at the top do well financially, but regular members averaged only about $3.30 an hour. (Some even supplemented their gang income by working at McDonald's.) But he also found that gangs are active in the local community, creating stability and providing resources that the city did not: paying the women who look after children and the elderly in the housing projects, for example.

Venkatesh found that the gang he worked with prohibited members from using hard drugs (it would spoil the gang's image) and insisted that young members stay in school—that is, gangs may give young people a coherent structure to their lives. But most of all, they have good parties, provide easy access to alcohol and drugs, and "know how to have fun," as one gang member told me.

Figure 6.3 Gender of Gang Members

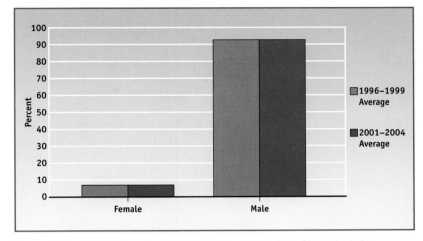

(*Source:* National Youth Gang Center [2007]. National Youth Gang Survey Analysis, www.iir.com/nygc/nygsa/.)

What do **you** think?

Following the Law

Some people feel the law is the bedrock of a civil society and without law anarchy would result. Others are socialized to conform and obey. Would you say that people should obey the law without exception, or are there exceptional occasions on which people should follow their consciences even if it means breaking the law?

1. Always obey law
2. Follow conscience

What does **America** think?

(These are actual Survey Data from the General Social Survey 2006).

Slightly more than half of all respondents (54.6 percent) said they thought people should always obey the law, whereas slightly less than half (45.4 percent) thought people should follow their conscience.

Think about It Some More

1. Can you think of situations where you might follow your conscience even if it conflicts with the law?
2. What are some historical examples of law breaking that were good (functional) for society?

References: See Davis et al., page 511.

Deviance and Social Coherence

Because there is always deviance in society, some sociologists ask what purpose it might serve. One of the founders of modern sociology, Émile Durkheim, wrote that having some members of a society castigated as deviant actually helps the society maintain itself as a coherent entity (Durkheim [1893] 1997a). Durkheim argued that deviance is useful to society in four ways:

1. *It affirms cultural norms and values.* Without defining what is wrong, we do not know what is right: There can be no good without evil, no justice without crime. Deviance is needed to define and sustain morality.
2. *It clarifies moral boundaries.* We don't really know what the rule is until we see someone breaking it. Deviance lets societies draw a clear distinction between good and bad, right and wrong. If there are no clear distinctions, the society falls victim to **anomie** (normlessness).
3. *It heightens group solidarity.* When someone commits an act of major deviance, other people in the society react with collective anger: They are outraged. In responding to the deviant, they reaffirm the moral ties that bind them together.
4. *It encourages social change.* Someone who breaks a social rule makes us wonder if the rule is all that important after all. Deviant people push moral boundaries, suggesting alternatives to the status quo. Today's deviance can be tomorrow's morality (Durkheim, 1997a,b).

Deviance is socially useful because it reminds "us" that we are "normal"—it's *they* who are different and deviant.

Explaining Deviance

Durkheim's explanation explains what deviance *does* for the larger society, but it doesn't explain why deviance happens, especially major acts of deviance that will result in major punishment.

Differential Association. Edwin H. Sutherland's theory of **differential association** (1940) suggests that it is a matter of rewards and punishment: Deviance occurs when an individual receives more prestige and less punishment by violating norms rather than by following them. What is deviant to one group might be something that enhances our status in another group. For example, students who behave in an irreverent, disrespectful fashion in class may be seen as deviant by the teachers and even punished for it, but they might also receive a great deal of prestige from their peers. They may calculate that the benefit (increased prestige) is better than the minor punishment they might receive. Thus, Sutherland argued, individuals become deviant by associating with people or joining groups that are already deviant and therefore are in the position to reward

Differential association means choosing which direction you're going to go, and which group you want to associate with.

deviant behavior (Sutherland, 1940). Deviance is learned.

Sutherland's theory helps to explain the way we sometimes have multiple moral voices in our heads—like the little devil and angel versions of ourselves often depicted on TV—and why sometimes we choose to be deviant. But the theory does not explain how the "carriers of criminality" became deviant in the first place. It also does not explain acts that occur without a community, when everyone around disapproves, or when no one is even aware of the deviance.

Control Theory. Travis Hirschi (1969; Gottfredson and Hirschi, 1995) argued that people do not obey lots of hidden forces: They are *rational,* so they decide whether to engage in an act by weighing the potential outcome. If you knew that there would be absolutely no punishment, no negative consequences of any sort, you would probably do a great many things that you would never dream of otherwise, like propositioning an attractive co-worker or driving like a maniac. Why don't people commit crime? Because we are constrained by the fear of punishment.

Hirschi imagined that people do a "cost-benefit analysis" during their decision making process to determine how much punishment is worth a degree of satisfaction or prestige. In a cost-benefit analysis, you weigh the respective costs of doing something (the likelihood or severity of punishment, for example) against the benefits of doing it (the money you might get, the increased prestige, the thrill of doing it in the first place). People who have very little to lose are therefore most likely to become rule-breakers because for them the costs will almost always be less than the potential benefits.

Hirschi assumes that most people have the same motivation to commit crime, so the differences are that people vary more in the way they control themselves and the way they weigh the costs of doing something against the benefits of doing it.

Walter Reckless (1973), on the other hand, suggests that such cost-benefit analysis really concerns our connections to others. **Social control theory** suggests that people are constrained from deviance by the social ties within their immediate communities. These can be formal and coercive, like the police and prison system, or informal, like familial disapproval. (Sometimes you might do the

We often fail to break rules even when the benefits would be great and the punishment minimal. I often arrive on campus at 6:00 a.m., and just inside, I usually have to stop at a stoplight that feels as if it takes five minutes to change from red to green. I could easily run it. There would be a substantial benefit, in arriving at the office five minutes early and not wasting the gas and oil it takes to just sit there. There would be no punishment: No one is around, and I am certain that no police officers are monitoring a deserted intersection from a hidden camera. Stoplights are a good idea in general, but forcing a driver to wait five minutes to cross a deserted street is idiotic. Nevertheless, in spite of my objections, in spite of the benefits and lack of punishment, I always wait for the light to change.

right thing because you just can't bear to disappoint your elderly grandparent or face the disapproving sneer and rolling eyes of your parent. If you really think that you'll get caught, you are subject to *outer controls:* family, social institutions, and authority figures (like the police) who influence us into obeying social rules (Costello and Vowell, 1999). But even when you know there is no one looking, you are subject to *inner controls:* internalized socialization, religious principles, your self-conception as a "good person" (Hirschi, 1969; Rogers and Buffalo, 1974). Self-control theory places the emphasis on inadequate socialization and thus a weakened internal monitor system.

Inner and outer controls do their job in four ways (Hirschi, 1969):

1. *Attachment.* Strong attachments encourage conformity; weak attachments encourage deviance.
2. *Commitment.* The greater our commitment to the norms and values of the group, the more advantages we derive from conforming and the more we have to lose through deviance.

3. *Involvement.* Extensive involvement in group activities—job, school, sports—inhibits deviance.
4. *Belief.* A strong belief in conventional morality and respect for authority figures inhibit deviance.

Labeling Theory. We used to think that the wrongdoing in deviance resided somewhere in the wrongdoer: You break a social rule because you are "that kind of person," with faulty genes, a criminal personality, or a defective soul. But now we know that wrongdoing is not inherent in an act or an actor but in the social context that determines whether an act is considered deviant or not and how much punishment it warrants.

Howard Becker (1966) used the term *labeling theory* to stress the relativity of deviance. Labeling describes a relationship between a dominant group and the actor. For something to be deviant, it has to be labeled as deviant by a powerful group—a group powerful enough to make that label stick. (If you do something wrong and your little sister declares it deviant, it doesn't have the same sort of weight as if all your friends label it deviant, or, even more, if the police and the juvenile courts call it deviant.) **Labeling theory** understands deviance to be a *process*, not

Deviant or not? A sociology student did a project on gender and video games. She found that being good at video games was "normative" for boys, but girls who were really good gamers might be labeled deviant. "I cannot say how many times boys have been astonished at some of my game playing abilities. Thus, it may seem that a girl playing video games is a type of deviant behavior."

a categorical difference between the deviant and the nondeviant. The label depends on the group's relative amount of power.

The same act might be deviant in some groups and not in others. It might be deviant when one person commits it but not when another person commits it. In fact, an action, belief, or condition is neutral in itself. It only becomes "deviant" when someone decides that it is wrong, bad, or immoral and labels it as deviant. For example, think of women who are sexually aggressive or enjoy pornography. Society might call them "sluts" and shun them. But if a man did any of those things, other men might call him a "stud" and perhaps hang out with him.

But deviance does not only reside in whether other people apply the label "deviant" to your acts. To become a deviant actor, you also have to believe the deviant label; you have to agree with the labels other people ascribe to you. When I was in graduate school, there was a male student who went everywhere, including classes, with no clothes on. Andrew Martinez, known as "The Naked Guy," believed that society's power to label him was the problem, not his nudity. In a 1992 op-ed in *The Oakland Tribune,* he wrote that "When I walk around nude, I am acting how I think it is reasonable to act, not how middle-class values tell me I should act."

Edwin Lemert (1972) theorized that most deviant acts, which he called **primary deviance,** provoke very little reaction and therefore have little effect on your self-concept. If I decide one day to run that red light on campus at 6:00 a.m., a passing police officer may label me as reckless and irresponsible, but I am unlikely to believe it. Only when I repeatedly break a norm, and people start making a big deal of it, does **secondary deviance** kick in. My rule breaking is no longer a momentary lapse in judgment, or justifiable under the circumstances, but an indication of a permanent personality trait: I have acquired a deviant identity. Finally, sociologists also have identified **tertiary deviance,** in which a group formerly labeled deviant attempts to redefine their acts, attributes, or identities as normal—even virtuous. John Kitsuse (1980) and others point to the ways some formerly deviant groups have begun to stand up for their rights, demanding equality with those considered "normals." Similar to "militant chauvinism" defined by Goffman when discussing stigma,

examples might include the disability rights movement, which has attempted to redefine disabilities from deviant to "differently abled."

Deviance and Inequality

Some sociologists argue that deviance is not solely a product of "bad" people or "wrong" behaviors but also of the bad, wrong, and/or unfair social conditions of people's lives. What is labeled as deviant is applied differently to different people. The powerful and the privileged escape the label and the punishment. Therefore, deviance in itself is the product of social inequality.

In a groundbreaking article entitled "Nuts, Sluts, and Perverts: The Poverty of the Sociology of Deviance" (1972), Alexander Liazos noted that the people commonly labeled deviant are always powerless. Why? The answer is not simply that the rich and powerful make the rules to begin with or that they have the resources to avoid being labeled deviant. The answer lies in the fact that those who have the power can make us believe that the rules are "natural" and "good" to mask their political agenda. They can then label actors and acts deviant to justify inequalities in gender, sexual orientation, race, ethnicity, and social class (Daly, 1989; Daly and Chesney-Lind, 1988; Hagan and Peterson, 1995).

In a classic study of a suburban high school, there were two "gangs" of boys, what the researcher called the "Saints" and the "Roughnecks." The Roughnecks were working-class boys, who were in the vocational track and not college bound. Teachers thought of them as deviant, and they wore clothing styles like those in the movie *Grease*— black leather jackets, jeans, and white T-shirts. They were known to commit petty crimes and were called "hooligans" by the school administrators. The "Saints," by contrast, were middle-class boys, and they dressed the part—crew cuts, button-down "preppy" shirts, and penny loafers. They played sports, were popular, and were headed for college. They also spent their weekends breaking into people's homes and committing serious burglaries. But they were not considered deviant because they were "wholesome" and middle class (Chambliss, 2000).

Ironically, the relationship of inequality and deviance often leads us to see and punish the behaviors of the less fortunate and forgive the behavior of the more fortunate. From this perspective, it is more likely that a poor person who stole a few dollars from a company would end up in jail than a CEO who steals millions of dollars from millions of shareholders.

Sociological Theories of Deviance and Crime

Most theories of deviance also apply to crime, which is simply a legally regulated form of extreme deviance. **Crime** can be defined as any act that violates a formal normative code that has been enacted by a legally constituted body. Simple violation of a more or folkway may not be a crime, unless you violate a formal code. Likewise, you can commit a crime (actually break a law) and not be seen as deviant if other people see your act as acceptable. Sometimes, people commit crimes and are seen as heroes, like Robin Hood.

Some crimes are defined by being bad in and of themselves—bad because they violate formal group norms—like homicide, rape, or assault. Other crimes are not as obvious violations of group norms and are considered bad mostly because they have been prohibited. In some cultures or contexts they might not be crimes at all; but because they are illegal, they are crimes.

For example, smoking marijuana is illegal in the United States, yet public opinion polls show many Americans don't see it as "bad" at all times and favor its legal use for medical purposes. Internationally, some countries, including Japan, Thailand, and Honduras, maintain strict laws against pot use for any reason, while others have more relaxed attitudes about pot use, especially for medical purposes. In the Netherlands, pharmacies have been legally obliged to stock and dispense medical marijuana since 2003.

The efforts to control and punish crime have become so extensive and the institutions that have developed—prisons, courts, police, to name a few—so large, that the study of crime, criminology, has developed into a subdiscipline separate from the sociology of deviance, with its own special theories about the causes and consequences of different kinds of crimes.

What causes crime? Sociologists have many theories.

Strain Theory

Robert K. Merton (1938) argued that while some deviance benefits society, some deviance also puts an enormous *strain* on social life. He argued that excessive deviance is a by-product of inequality. When a society promotes certain goals but provides unequal means of acquiring them, the result is anomie, a sense of normlessness, or a feeling that accepted norms conflict with social reality. This is called **strain theory.**

For instance, in the United States, and to some degree in all industrialized societies, we promote the *goal* of financial success and claim that it can be achieved through the *means* of self-discipline and hard work. But these qualities will lead to financial success only when channeled through a prestigious education or network of prestigious social contacts, advantages that many people do not have. They will therefore feel pressured to use alternative *means,* legitimate or illegitimate, to reach the goal (Merton, 1967).

According to Merton, there are five potential reactions to the tension between widely endorsed values and limited means of achieving them:

1. *Conformism* accepts both the means and the values, whether they achieve the goal or not. Conformists may not achieve financial success, but they will still believe that it is important and that self-discipline and hard work are appropriate means of achieving it. Most people are conformists.
2. *Innovation* accepts the values but rejects the means. Innovators believe that financial success is an important goal but not that self-discipline and hard work are effective means of achieving it. Instead, they seek out new means to financial success. They may try to win the lottery, or they may become con artists or thieves.
3. *Ritualism* accepts the means but rejects the values. Ritualists follow rules for their own sake, conforming to standards even though they have lost sight of the values behind them. They will work hard but have no aspirations to financial success.
4. *Rebellion* rejects both the means and the values and substitutes new ones. Instead of financial success, for instance, rebels may value the goal of spiritual fulfillment,

to be achieved not through hard work but through quiet contemplation.

5. *Retreatism* rejects both the means and the values and replaces them with nothing. Retreatists do not accept the value of working hard, and they have not devised any alternative means. They have no aspirations to financial success or any alternative goal, such as spiritual or artistic fulfillment.

Critics of strain theory point out that not everyone shares the same goals, even in the most homogeneous society. There are always many potential goals, conflicting and sometimes contradictory. And while strain theory may adequately explain some white-collar crime, such as juggling the books at work, and some property crimes, such as stealing a television set, it is less effective when explaining those crimes that lack an immediate financial motive.

Broken Windows Theory

Sociologists James Q. Wilson and George Kelling proposed the **broken windows theory** to explain how social controls can systematically weaken and minor acts of deviance can spiral into severe crime and social decay (Wilson and Kelling, 1982). Their theory was based on an experiment by social psychologist Philip Zimbardo who placed cars without license plates and with their hoods up, but otherwise in good condition, in two different social settings, one in wealthy, mostly White Palo Alto, California (the home of Stanford University, where he worked), and the other in a poor, mostly Black neighborhood in the Bronx, in New York City (Zimbardo, 1969). The social class and race of passersby made no difference: In both sites, cars were quickly gutted. One person would conclude that the car was abandoned and "no one cared" and break a side window. The next person would see the side window broken and feel it was acceptable to smash the windshield.

The pattern would continue and escalate from there. Zimbardo concluded that breaking more windows, committing more serious crimes and acts of deviance, is a rational response to situations of social disorder. Wilson and Kelling expanded this thesis to conclude that community characteristics, such as de-

cayed housing, preexisting crime, and the like, contributed to increased crime. Crime rates go up, they argued, in blighted areas where people think no one cares and no one is watching. The societal response has been proactive: policing directed at maintaining public order. However, this has often been misused by conservative politicians to police poor and minority neighborhoods more strictly. A recent National Research Council report on a five-city experiment found no empirical evidence to support this theory, and the most current sociological perspective is that scarce police resources would be better used in other ways (Harcourt and Ludwig, 2006).

Studying Criminal "Subcultures"

In 1955, juvenile delinquency was getting a lot of publicity in the United States. Albert Cohen wondered why young people, mostly working-class and poor boys, were spurning the values of the dominant society and committing so many crimes. After studying working-class and poor youth gangs, he concluded that strain theory wouldn't work: As lower-class youths, they had the least opportunity to achieve economic success, but their crimes were usually not economically motivated. They were not trying to get rich (1955).

Cohen drew upon Edward Sutherland's theory of differential association (which we discussed earlier in the chapter) to propose that the gang members were not being socialized with the same norms and values as lower-class non–gang members or the middle class. They were being subjected to differential association, socialized into a new set of norms and values that allowed them to succeed on their own terms.

Walter B. Miller ([1958] 1970) agreed, but he argued that it is not just lower-class boys in gangs whose norms and values differ from those of the dominant society; it's the entire lower class. In other words, behavior that the main society might consider deviant actually reflects the social norms of the lower-class *subculture*.

Miller implied that lower-class culture was conducive to crime, despite the overwhelming number of lower-class people who are law-abiding, decent citizens and the many upper-class people who reverse Robin Hood's ethic and rob from the poor to give to themselves.

Opportunity Theory

Richard Cloward and Lloyd Ohlin (1960) also built on Sutherland and argued that crime actually arises from opportunity to commit crime. **Opportunity theory** holds that those who have many opportunities—and good ones at that—will be more likely to commit crimes than those with few good opportunities. They agreed, with Merton, that those who don't have equal access to acceptable means to achieve material success may experience strain, but that doesn't explain why most poor people are not criminals. In fact, studies show that most are "conformists," with the same values and goals as the dominant society.

Like Sutherland, Cloward and Ohlin emphasized *learning*—people have to learn how to carry out particular forms of deviance, and they must have the opportunity to actually deviate. They revised differential association theory to propose several different types of deviant subcultures based on the opportunities to deviate:

1. In stable neighborhoods where most people know each other throughout their lives, *criminal subcultures* develop, devoted to such activities as burglary and theft. Young men can rely on social contacts with experienced older men to learn the roles of being a criminal, and the older men in turn can depend on the availability of younger protégés as they go to prison or retire.

2. In unstable neighborhoods where people are constantly moving in and out, there are few opportunities to learn about burglary and theft, and boys who are mostly strangers to each other must find some way to establish dominance. They develop *violence subcultures,* gaining tough reputations through fighting and assaults.

3. In neighborhoods too disorganized for either crime or violence to succeed, people withdraw from society altogether through the use of alcohol and drugs. They develop *retreatist* subcultures.

These are not necessarily exclusive groups. A gang that may start out as part of a violent subculture in an unstable neighborhood may become a criminal subculture as the members become involved in more stable criminal activities like protection rackets and drug trafficking and begin recruiting younger members.

Some aspects of opportunity theory have been confirmed by subsequent research (Allan and Steffensmeier, 1989; Uggen, 1999). But as with many typologies, the theory ignores the interrelation of types of crimes: Drug dealers and users often depend on property crime to finance their drug use and violence for territorial defense; violence often occurs in tandem with property crime. Also, the theory defines deviance in a way that targets poor people—if we include white-collar crimes like stock fraud, neighborhood dynamics become much less significant.

Conflict and Inequality Theories

We may condemn the unequal application of the law, but we give little thought to whether the laws themselves are inherently unfair. **Conflict theories** of crime resemble inequality theories of deviance—they rest on a larger structural analysis of inequalities based on class, or race, or gender for their explanation of crime. Richard Quinney (1977) argued that the dominant class produces deviance by making and enforcing laws that protect its own interest and oppress the subordinate class. Law becomes an instrument of oppression, designed to maintain the powerful in their privileged position (Chambliss and Zatz, 1993). It's not simply that basically neutral and equal laws are applied unequally, meaning that poor people get longer and harsher sentences when they commit the same crimes as upper-class people. That's true. But it's also that the laws themselves are designed to make sure that the rich stay rich and the poor stay poor. When I was in college, a student who lived in my dorm was arrested very early one morning for stealing some fresh-baked bread that had been delivered to a local grocery store. When he was arraigned, the local magistrate looked at him sternly. "I assume this is a fraternity prank," the magistrate said, "and so I'm going to let you go with a warning. If this had been a real crime, if you had really needed the bread, you'd be going to jail for 10 years for theft."

Types of Crimes

There are many different types of crimes. Some are crimes against other people; others are crimes against property. They are handled differently by the police, courts, and penal system, depending on how serious the society believes the crime to be. In the United States, crimes against people are almost always heard in criminal court, while crimes against property may be heard in criminal or civil courts.

Sociologists study all types of crimes, from crimes against other people, like homicide, assault, and rape, to crimes against property, like burglary, motor vehicle theft, and arson. **Violent crime** consists of four offenses, according to the FBI's definitions: murder and nonnegligent manslaughter, forcible rape, robbery, and aggravated assault. **Property crime** includes offenses like burglary and motor vehicle theft, where the object is the taking of money or property, but there is no force or threat of force against the victims (some have historically been called "victimless" crimes, because they involve a willing exchange of illegal goods or services between adults). Earlier, social scientists discussed prostitution or pornography, for example, as victimless, but the realities of sex trafficking, and physical and economic coercion have led most sociologists to realize that the phrase "victimless crime" is an oxymoron.

Crime at Work

Theft at work, whether simply pocketing office supplies or exercising the "100 percent employee discount" at the department store, costs U.S. employers nearly $20 billion a year (National Retail Federation, 2007). But there are many other crimes that you can commit at work, using the authority of your position, with the direct or indirect consent of the boss. In 1940, Edwin Sutherland introduced the term **white-collar crime** for the illegal actions of a corporation or people acting on its behalf (Sutherland, 1940). Today, white-collar crime is a problem across the globe, with more than 43 percent of companies worldwide falling victim to employee fraud between 2005 and 2007 alone (PriceWaterhouseCoopers, 2007). Some white-collar crimes are **consumer crimes** such as credit card fraud, in which the criminal uses a fake or stolen credit card to buy things for him- or herself or for resale. Such purchases cost both retailers and, increasingly, "e-tailers" over $1 billion per year, or nearly 5 cents for every dollar spent online (Berner and Carter, 2005).

White-collar criminals might commit **occupational crime,** using their professional position to illegally secure something of value for themselves or the corporation. Some of the more common occupational crimes include income tax evasion, stock manipulation, bribery, and embezzlement. Media entrepreneur Martha Stewart went to prison for lying about her insider trading when she used her fame to find out that a company whose stock she owned was about to suffer a significant setback; she sold her stock the day before its price collapsed. (She claimed it was a coincidence.) Periodically, a famous Wall Street tycoon will be arrested for manipulating stocks or fraudulently reporting distorted earnings.

Or they might commit **organizational crime,** illegal actions committed in accordance with the operative goals of an organization. Some of the more common organizational crimes are stock manipulation, anti-trust violations, false advertising, and price fixing. Periodically, some corporate whistle-blower notices the remarkable coincidence that all the gasoline companies charge about the same amount for their gas, despite the fact that they are supposed to be competing with each other. Financier Bernard Madoff was arrested in 2009 for defrauding thousands of investors out of more than $50 billion in the largest fraud ever undertaken in the country. Madoff undertook a massive "Ponzi scheme" in which new investors are constantly brought in and their new money is used to pay off the old investors in a large pyramid. They inevitably collapse because the number of new investors required to sustain the older ones increases exponentially, and eventually no new investors can be found.

Such high-profile arrests for white-collar crime may provide the rest of us with the

The Ponzi Scheme

The original Ponzi scheme was perpetrated in 1920 by Charles Ponzi, an Italian immigrant living in Boston. He offered investors a 50 percent return in 45 days if they invested in his international postal coupon scam and 100 percent in 90 days. About 40,000 people gave him a total of about $15 million, and Ponzi became an instant millionaire, living in a lavish mansion—until he got caught.

Did You Know?

illusion that the system works, that criminals always get caught, and that the "little guy" can beat the big wheels. In fact, these high-profile cases are rare. And it is exceptionally rare for corporate violators to ever spend a day in jail (Hagan and Parker, 1985; Sasseen, 2006). Madoff's 150-year jail sentence is notable because it broke precedent rather than sustained it—but he pleaded guilty to the 11 counts of securities fraud, international money laundering, and perjury against him.

The cost of white-collar crime is substantial—between $300 and $600 billion a year in the United States alone, which is far more than the "paltry" $15 billion for "regular" street crime (National White Collar Crime Center, 2009). And of course, corporate officers or their agents are breaking the law, and they can be subject to criminal prosecution. Yet most cases of white-collar crime go unpunished. Many white-collar crimes are not prosecuted or are settled out of court, so they never become part of the public record.

In rare cases when white-collar criminals are charged and convicted, odds are that they will not go to jail. White-collar offenders are more likely to receive fines than prison sentences. Even if they do go to jail, white-collar criminals are typically sentenced to terms averaging less than three years (Pizzo and Muolo, 1994). In other countries, or in white-collar crime in nonprofit organizations, the penalties may be more severe. In one study, 70 percent of Canadian executives who defrauded nonprofits saw jail time, with sentences ranging from three months to seven and a half years (Salterio and Chen, 2008).

Cybercrime

Cybercrime—the use of the Internet and World Wide Web to commit crime—is a relatively new form of crime. Some of these crimes involve fraudulent maneuvers to get victims to reveal personal information that can then be used to

Charles Ponzi.

commit crimes; others involve theft of cyberidentities. Some cybercrime is simply the adaptation of old crimes to new technology—the fraudulent messages, called *phishes,* designed to get you to part with credit card information or to make bogus purchases, are simply the latest version of an old telephone scam that preyed especially on retirees.

The rise of personal computers and the Internet have made some criminal activities, such as money laundering and fraud, easier, and this situation has spawned a whole new field of crime. Internet-based crime is the fastest growing category of crime in the United States. The year 2008 marked the ninth year in a row that identity theft topped the list of consumer complaints with the U.S. Federal Trade Commission, accounting for 36 percent of the total (Federal Trade Commission, 2009). The FBI estimates that nearly 10 million Americans have been victimized by identity theft and have experienced losses totaling $52.6 billion. Elderly people are most vulnerable, in part because they are less technically savvy; the states that have the highest number of identity thefts (Arizona, Nevada, Florida) are also places with large numbers of retirees.

But hackers are often responsible. Hackers have tapped into customer information as well as proprietary company information stored online by credit bureaus, marketing agencies, banks, credit card companies, and other financial services firms. Of the top global financial services organizations, 83 percent had some kind of hacker attack on their computer information systems in 2004, but the numbers have steadily declined for five straight years (see Figure 6.4). In 2008, the average loss per respondent was $288,618 down from $345,005 last year, but up from the low of $167,713 two years ago. Why? Both governments and private companies have developed increasingly sophisticated firewalls and anti-virus protections. But it may also be the case that a significant number of these intrusions go unreported because private companies fear undermining the confidence of their customers and shareholders (Computer Security Institute, 2008).

Organized Crime

Like corporate or white-collar crime, organized crime is a business operation, whose purpose is to supply illegal goods and services to others. Often these goods and services are widely desired but still illegal. During Prohibition, for example, organized crime syndicates provided alcohol to a thirsty public and gambling venues to circumvent prohibitions on gambling. Contemporary organized criminal activities include loan-sharking, prostitution, money laundering, drug trafficking, and warehouse or truck theft.

Although glamorized by television shows such as *The Sopranos,* by movies such as *The Godfather* and *Scarface,* and by celebrity criminals such as "The Teflon Don," organized crime is often routine and boring work, making rounds to small businesses who pay "protection money" (bribes to prevent being the victims of even more serious crimes), keeping track of the finances of a large-scale enterprise, and managing subordinates in a large-scale hierarchical organization. Organized crime has also found legitimate businesses to be quite lucrative. Criminal enterprises have infiltrated such legitimate organizations as unions, the construction industry, international banking, and transportation (trucking and shipping).

Hate Crime

A **hate crime** is a criminal act committed by an offender motivated by bias against race, ethnicity, religion, sexual orientation, or disability status. Anyone can commit a hate crime, but perpetrators usually belong to dominant groups (White, Christian, straight) and victims to disenfranchised groups (Black, Jewish, Muslim, or gay). The FBI records over 7,000 hate crimes per year, but because state and local law enforcement agencies differ in their reporting procedures, and some do not report at all, this

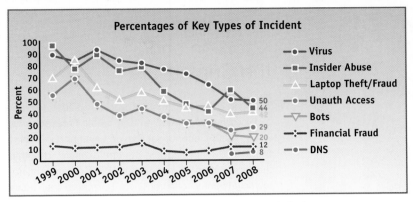

Figure 6.4 Computer Security Incidents

(*Source:* Computer Security Institute, 2008. Reprinted by permission.)

number is no doubt extremely low. Bias based on race seems to be the largest motivating factor in hate crimes (51 percent of cases), followed by religion (18 percent), sexual orientation (16.5 percent), ethnicity (14 percent), and disability (less than 1 percent).

Legislators approve of hate crime legislation sometimes and disapprove at other times. Advocates of these laws argue that hate crimes affect not only the individual but the entire community, so they should be punished more harshly than ordinary crime. The lynchings in the American South were used not only to victimize an individual but to terrorize the entire Black population, and contemporary antigay hate crimes are not meant to express hatred of a single gay person but to demonstrate to all gay people that they are unwelcome and unsafe in the community.

But opponents of these laws argue that they punish attitudes, not actions. Why does the motivation of a crime matter? If I am planning to commit a robbery, I may select a gay man, believing the stereotype that he is fragile and weak and therefore unlikely to resist. My prejudice didn't motivate the crime, merely my choice of an appropriate victim.

Crime in the United States

In 2007, there were more than 1.4 million violent crimes in the United States, a rate of 466.9 per 100,000 inhabitants. There were nearly 10 million property crimes committed, at a rate of 3,263.5 per 100,000 inhabitants (U.S. Department of Justice, 2008b). While these statistics are considerably lower than they were 30 years ago, the United States still has higher crime rates than many other countries in the world: It ranks third in drug offenses per capita, fifth in assaults, eighth in murders with firearms, ninth in rape, eleventh in robberies, and sixteenth in burglaries.

Abortion and the Crime Rate

Did the legalization of abortion cause the decline of crime? In the book *Freakonomics* (2005), economist Steven Levitt and journalist Stephen Dubner suggest the controversial idea that the legalization of abortion in 1973 meant that far fewer unwanted children were born, and that these children would have had fewer economic opportunities and lower levels of education and employment. They would have become adults in the mid-1990s—which is exactly when the crime rate began to decline. Thus, many would-be criminals—those with the demographic "profile" of criminals—were simply never born. Some disagree with their calculations (Foote and Goetz, 2005).

This is a marvelous example of what sociologists call a specious correlation. Sure, the two variables may be correlated, but there are so many intervening variables, not to mention 20 years of other factors that might have influenced things, that one cannot possibly say with any certainty that this one variable caused another. For one thing, how do we know that the fetuses that were aborted were more likely to be criminals? Or that the legalization of abortion was not also connected to a larger set of social and economic reforms that reduced the crime rate? Do you think, perhaps, that all the recent efforts to make abortions more difficult will result in a dramatic increase in crime 20 years from now? We doubt it.

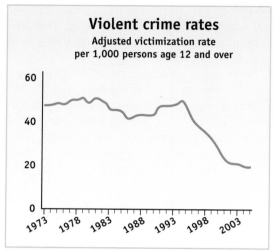

Source: United States Department of Justice Bureau of Justice Statistics, National Crime VictimizationSurvey; available at: http://www.ojp.usdof.gov/bjs/glance/viort_htm

---

When compared with most other advanced countries, the United States stands out for its very high homicide rates (Kurki, 1997; Van Kesteren, Mayhew, and Nieuwbeerta, 2000). With six murders for every 100,000 people, the rate of lethal violence in America is nearly five times higher than that of France, Germany, or England (van Kesteren, Mayhew, and Nieuwbeerta, 2000; Wacquant, 2006; Zimring and Hawkins, 1997).

What social factors explain our rates of crime? Sociologists have considered three explanations:

1. American culture emphasizes individual economic success as *the* measure of self-worth, at the expense of family, neighborhood, artistic accomplishment, and spiritual well-being (Currie, 1985).
2. Not everyone has a high standard of living. The United States has one of the largest income differentials in the world. When the gap begins to shrink, as it did during Clinton-era prosperity, the crime rate declines (Martens, 2005).
3. Guns—that is, the easy availability of guns and the lax enforcement of loose gun control measures, coupled with an American value system that places gun ownership as a sacred right—are a contributor to the crime rate.

Despite the fact that our overall crime rates are higher than some other advanced countries, such as Ireland and Austria, and our outsize homicide rate distinguishes the United States from all of Western Europe (Wacquant, 2006), it is also true that crime rates in the United States have been falling. The National Crime Victimization Survey (2008), which addresses victims of crime (and therefore leaves out murder), reports that the violent crime rate has dropped by nearly 60 percent and the property crime rate has dropped by more than 50 percent since 1973. Violent crime dropped 14 percent in just *two years,* between 2001 and 2003, and has dropped slightly every year since (U.S. Department of Justice, 2008). (See Figure 6.5.)

Crime and Guns

The United States has the weakest laws on handgun ownership in the industrialized world. As a result, there are as many guns as there are people, and it shows in crime statistics. Four million Americans carry a gun on a daily basis. Half of all U.S. households have a gun at home (Wacquant, 2006). Over 70 percent of murders, 48 percent of robberies, and 22 percent of aggravated assaults are committed with guns (U.S. Department of Justice, 2008b).

Globally, the United States ranks in the middle of all countries' rates of deaths by guns. But no other industrialized country comes close to the United States; indeed our rate is nearly double that of our nearest "rival." The United States has had difficulty passing minimal regulations to monitor the distribution of guns. Federal efforts to institute simple safeguards such as criminal background checks on prospective gun owners have met with fierce opposition from gun lobbyists. Many efforts—such as attempts to block convicted criminals from obtaining guns or to revoke the licenses of gun dealers who break the law—remain under attack by gun advocates. In fact, since approximately 2000, some of the scattered state laws that had been in effect for a decade or more have been weakened or repealed, particularly in

the South (Hemenway, 2005). For example, although criminologists have shown that limiting volume purchases of handguns is effective at stemming illegal gun trafficking, South Carolina abolished a one-per-month purchase rule in 2004 that had been in place for nearly 30 years. That same year, the state of Virginia weakened a similar law that had been on the books since 1993 (Wirzbicki, 2005). In June, 2008, the U.S. Supreme Court rejected an argument that the Second Amendment protects only the right of gun ownership by militias. The ruling prohibits the kind of outright ban on handguns that had existed in Washington, D.C.

The Social Organization of Crime

Gender. When looking at crime statistics, we are often astonished by the gender gap. In the United States in 2007, only 24 percent of people arrested for all crimes were women. Women committed only 18 percent of violent crimes. The gender gap narrowed only in two white-collar crimes—forgery and fraud—and women outranked men in embezzlement,

Figure 6.5 Regional Crime Rates

Violent and Property Crimes per 100,000 Inhabitants

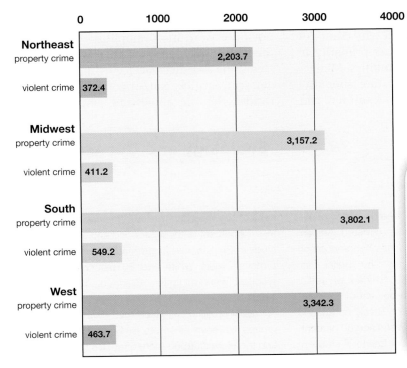

- Northeast property crime: 2,203.7
- Northeast violent crime: 372.4
- Midwest property crime: 3,157.2
- Midwest violent crime: 411.2
- South property crime: 3,802.1
- South violent crime: 549.2
- West property crime: 3,342.3
- West violent crime: 463.7

Overall:

- Arrests for violent crimes decreased 1.1% (from previous year)
- Arrests for property crime increased 5.4% (from previous year)

- The estimated number of violent crimes deceased in three of the four regions, with the only increase, 1.6%, occurring in the South

- The estimated number of property crimes nationwide decreased 1.4 % in 2007 (when compared to previous year)

- The estimated number of motor vehicle thefts and forcible rape offenses decreased in all four regions, with the biggest drop in the Northeast

- The Nation's Capital, Washington D.C., has the highest robbery rate; murder rate, and violent crime rate

(*Source:* Crime in the United States, 2007.)

prostitution, and runaways. Otherwise, women were significantly less likely to be arrested, less likely to be convicted, and less likely to serve sentences. And yet the United States has the largest female arrest and conviction rate in the world: 8.54 per 1,000, nearly double the United Kingdom and four times higher than Canada (Schaffner, 2006). Nonetheless, when we say *crime,* we might as well say *male.*

The gender gap may be influenced by the "chivalry effect": Police, judges, and juries are likely to perceive women as less dangerous and their criminal activities less consequential, so they are more often let go with a warning (Pollak, [1950] 1978). Women who belong to stigmatized groups—who are Black, Hispanic, or lesbian—are more likely to be arrested and convicted, perhaps because they are not granted the same status as women in the mainstream. Feminists note that women receive harsher treatment when their behavior deviates from feminine stereotypes, that is, when they "act like a man" (Edwards, 1986).

But even when we take the chivalry effect into account, men still commit more violent crimes and property crimes than women. Some criminologists argue that, biologically, males are a lot more aggressive and violent, and that explains the high levels of assaults and other violent crimes. However, this biological theory does not explain why crime (or at least criminal arrests) occurs primarily in working-class and poor communities. Middle-class men have testosterone, too; shouldn't they be committing assault and murder? Nor

can "male aggression" explain the gender gap in property crime.

A more sociological explanation is the model of working-class masculinity: In the working-class and poor subcultures where most crimes (or at least most criminal arrests) occur, men are socialized to believe that "defending" themselves, violently if necessary, is appropriate masculine behavior (see, for example, Willis, 1977). On television, *Judge Joe Brown* is quite lenient on men and boys who have assaulted each other: "Part of being a man is learning how to fight," he intones.

Men are further socialized to believe that they must provide the sole financial support in a heterosexual household. Judge Joe Brown is constantly berating his litigants (mostly working class or poor) when a man allows his mother, wife, or girlfriend to pay some of the household bills: "Be a man!" he yells. "Take care of your woman!" And when no legitimate opportunity is available, "taking care of your women" may involve property crime.

Nonviolent crimes can also be gender coded. Stick-up burglars, who rob people face-to-face, usually by threatening them with a gun, are almost always male. Shoplifters, by contrast, are predominantly female. Sociologist Jack Katz (1988) studied what he called "sneaky thrills," crimes like shoplifting, burglary, joyriding, and vandalism committed by amateurs, mostly adolescents, for the fun of it, not necessarily to acquire money or property. He found that not only were most shoplifters female, but they also steal artifacts that were notably "feminine"—a necklace, earrings, sexy underwear, lipstick. Katz theorized that sneaky thrills offer the adolescent perpetrators an

Sociology and Our World

"DWB"

The perceived connection between race and crime is often painful to those who are targeted. African Americans sometimes refer to the phenomenon of being constantly stopped by the police as "DWB"—"driving while Black." Studies of traffic stops have found that while 5 percent of the drivers on Florida highways were Black or Latino, nearly 70 percent of those stopped and 80 percent of those searched were Black or Latino. A study in Maryland found that although Blacks were 17 per-

cent of the motorists on one freeway, they were also 73 percent of those stopped and searched. A study in Philadelphia found that 75 percent of the motorists were White and 80 percent of those stopped were minorities (Cannon, 1999; Cole, 1999). Stopping and searching minorities is a form of "racial profiling" in which members of minority groups are seen as "more likely" to be criminals and therefore stopped more often. It's more a self-fulfilling prophecy: Believing is seeing.

experience similar to sexual experimentation. The stick-up artist enters the victim's world, demonstrates that he is in control, and forcibly leads the action to his desired conclusion. The shoplifters often tell tales of seduction, using metaphors of flirting and enticement, "a rush of excitement as contact is made with the item and inserted into a private place" (p. 71).

Race. If we were to judge solely by arrest and conviction rates, we might conclude that if the gender of crime is male, the race of crime is Black (Pettit and Western, 2004; U.S. Department of Justice, 2009). African Americans are arrested at a rate two, three, or even five times greater than statistical probability: They comprise 12.5 percent of the population but almost 57 percent of arrests for robbery, 50.4 percent for murder, more than 35 percent for drug use. And they are considerably more likely to become the victims of crime (U.S. Department of Justice, 2009). Blacks are also overrepresented among arrestees for offenses that involve considerable discretion at the scene, such as loitering (34.3 percent), disorderly conduct (34.2 percent), or suspicion (41.3 percent) (U.S. Department of Justice, 2009).

Black overrepresentation does not happen only in America. In the United Kingdom, Blacks are three times more likely than Whites or Asians to be arrested. In Britain,

however, Blacks and Whites are equally likely to be crime victims, and it is Asians who face a significantly higher risk (Home Office, 2006).

But it isn't just African Americans; Latinos are overrepresented in the U.S. criminal justice system as well. While Latinos make up about 13 percent of the U.S. population, they are 31 percent of those incarcerated in the federal system. Latino defendants are imprisoned three times as often as Whites and are detained before trial for first-time offenses almost twice as often as Whites, despite the fact that they are the least likely of all ethnic groups to have a criminal history (Walker et al., 2004). They are also disproportionately charged with nonviolent drug offenses and represent the vast majority of those arrested for immigration violations (Human Rights Watch [HRW], 2002; National Council of La Raza, 2004; Weich and Angulo, 2000).

What is the link between crime and race? Each of the theories we have discussed in this chapter offers a perspective on this issue:

Strain theory. It's really a matter of social class, not race. Blacks are more likely to be poor, and poor people living amid affluence are more likely to perceive society as unjust and turn to crime (Anderson, 1994; Blau and Blau, 1982). This theory fails to take into account the fact that, even within the lower classes,

Blacks are significantly more likely to be arrested and sentenced than Whites.

Differential opportunity. Black children are much more likely to be raised by single mothers than are White children. They receive less supervision, so they turn to crime. But the vast majority of children raised by single parents (mostly mothers) do not turn to crime. No significant correlation has been found between growing up in single-parent households and juvenile or adult crime.

Labeling. Being Black is a master status, automatically labeled deviant, equated with violence and criminality. So people (Black or White) tend to view Black behavior as more threatening and report on it more often, police officers (Black or White) tend to arrest Blacks more often, and juries (Black or White) tend to give them stiffer sentences.

Conflict. The crime records omit fraud, income tax evasion, embezzlement, and other crimes that are more often committed by Whites, thus producing misleading statistics.

Age. When we say *crime,* we might just as well say *young.* Since the rise of the first adolescent subcultures in the 1940s, minors have been committing far more than their share of crimes. In 2007, 15- to 24-year-olds constituted about 14 percent of the U.S. population but nearly 55 percent of arrests for property crime and more than 43 percent of arrests for violent crime. Young people under 25 were arrested for over half of all murders, 65 percent of all robberies, and 67 percent of all vandalism (U.S. Department of Justice, 2009).

In search of explanations, many sociologists point to gang activity, which has infiltrated every aspect of community life. Also, because most of the youthful offenders are male, the culture of masculinity may also be at fault: A 15-year-old boy can hardly demonstrate his "masculine" toughness, aggression, and control through academic or artistic accomplishments. He can go out for sports; but, in the inner city, school sports have substandard facilities and underpaid staff, and there are few private after-school programs. He proves his masculinity by violence and crime.

Certainly, there are female gangs, and crimes by young females have increased in recent decades. But even the phrase "prove your femininity" is hard to translate into a provocation to crime. And the data make it clear that crime is largely an activity of young males—and it has been for some time.

Just because other males are the most frequent victims of violent crimes doesn't mean that girls are not also vulnerable. They are. In 2005, according to the FBI, 2,053 boys under the age of 18 were arrested on charges of rape and sexual assault (9.5 percent of the total). Over 30 percent (632) were under the age of 15. There are over 1,000 treatment programs in the United States devoted solely to treating youthful sex offenders. Psychologists believe that these boys are still developing their notions of appropriate sexual behavior, so their preference for coercive and violent sexual activity is capable of change.

But college students are old enough to have already developed their sexual "scripts"—their cognitive map about how to have sex and with whom—and they sometimes exhibit a similar interest in sexual coercion. According to a 2003 Bureau of Justice Statistics study, rape is the most common violent crime at colleges and universities in the United States; 2.8 percent of college women experience either a completed rape or an attempted rape every year, most often by a male peer, boyfriend, or classmate (90 percent of college women know their assailants) (Cole, 2006; U.S. Department of Justice, 2003). Another 13 percent of college women have been stalked, as compared with 8 percent of women of all ages. Aggression and control seem still integral to hegemonic masculinity in young adulthood.

Class. Historically, those with less power in society—women, minorities, young people—have been more likely to be arrested. So, too, with class. The poorer you are, the more likely that you will be arrested for a crime. While the crime rate goes up as the person's socioeconomic status goes down, this may be caused less by economic deprivation—people stealing because they are hungry or don't have enough money to pay their rent—and more because their crimes are more visible and their "profile" is more likely to fit a criminal profile. When the poor rob the rich, it makes the papers; when the rich rob the poor, it's often called "business."

Equally, the poorer you are, the more likely you are to be the victim of crime, both property crime and violent crime. The wealthy are more insulated in their neighborhoods, better served by the police, and more likely to press charges against offenders. Men are far more likely to be victims of a violent crime than women, and Blacks are more likely to be victims than Whites. Teens and young adults aged 12 through 24 experience the highest rates of violent crime as compared with those in older age groups.

The Criminal Justice System

"In the criminal justice system, there are two separate but equally important groups: the police who investigate crimes and the district attorneys who prosecute the offenders. These are their stories." So says the narrator at the beginning of each episode of *Law and Order,* the most successful crime series in television history.

It's mostly right. The criminal justice system is a complex of institutions that includes the police and the courts, a wide range of prosecuting and defense lawyers, and also the prison system.

Police

The number of police officers in the United States has roughly doubled over the past 30 years. In 2005, there were nearly 582,000 full-time law enforcement employees in the United States, or about three for every 1,000 people (U.S. Department of Justice, 2005a). This is more than most countries: France has 2.06, Japan 1.81, and Canada 1.73.

But police officers actually spend only about 20 percent of their time in crime-fighting activity. A surprising amount of their daily routine involves completing departmental paperwork: arrest and accident reports, patrol activity reports, and judicial statements. Their "on" time mostly involves routine public order activity and communicating information about risk control to other institutions in society (insurance companies, public health workers, social welfare agencies, and schools). Today the police have become "knowledge workers" as much as they are "crime fighters" (Ericson and Haggerty, 1997): They offer tips and techniques, such as "stay in well-lighted areas," but in the end you are responsible for your own safety.

The police have a split image. To some people, seeing a police officer on the street makes them feel safe and secure, as if no harm will come to them. To others, seeing that same police officer is a terrible threat, and they might feel that they are in danger of being arrested or killed simply for being there. Some people see the police as protection; others see them as an occupying army.

The police understand this dichotomy. In many cities, like Los Angeles, their motto is "to protect and to serve"—they want people to feel safe, and they want to be of service to those who feel threatened. The most important trends in police forces across the country have been to embed the police within the communities they serve; to encourage more minority police, especially in minority areas; and also to train new groups of female officers, especially to respond to complaints about domestic violence. Since the 1990s, the number of female and minority police officers has increased. Minority representation among local police officers increased from 14.6 percent in 1987 to about 24 percent today. Women's representation increased from 9 percent in 1990 to 11.7 percent in 2007 (U.S. Department of Justice, 2007).

Courts

The court system is an important arena of the criminal justice system. In criminal court, the district attorney's office prosecutes those arrested by the police for criminal offenses; the

"You look like this sketch of someone who's thinking about committing a crime."

Source: © David Sipress/Condé Nast Publications/www.cartoonbank.com
Reprinted by Permission.

accused are defended in adversarial proceedings by a defense attorney. Thus, criminal proceedings pit the government (its agents, the police, lawyers, and the like) against a defendant, unlike civil courts in which the court is an arbiter of arguments between two individuals or groups. While the criminal courtroom drama is a staple of American movies and television, over 90 percent of criminal cases never go to trial. Instead, most are resolved by plea bargaining or pleading guilty to a lesser crime.

In the early 1990s, mandatory sentencing rules were enacted across the United States. These laws applied to about 64,000 defendants a year and required certain sentences for certain crimes, allowing no room for discretion. The laws were supposed to be tough on crime and eliminate bias in prosecutions and sentencing. However, the main result has been an explosion in the prison population. Bias remains in both arrests and prosecutions. Only under mandatory sentencing judges couldn't take circumstances—which could help the poor, minorities, mentally unstable, the sick, or addicted—into account. In early 2005, the Supreme Court ruled that federal judges no longer must abide by the guidelines, saying they violated a defendant's right to a fair trial.

Punishment and Corrections

Today the United States has 2.3 million people in jail or prison, 7.1 per 1,000 people, many more than any country in the world (see the nearby "U.S./Them" feature). Russia is in second place, with 5.8. The United States has more total inmates than the 26 European countries with the largest inmate populations put together—even though we have 500 million fewer people than the total population of those countries (Pew Center on the States, 2008). (See Figure 6.6.) We also imprison at least three times more women than any other nation in the world (Hartney, 2006). And it's not because the United States has higher crime rates; with the single exception of incarceration rates in Russia for robbery, we lock up more people per incident than any other country in the world (National Council on Crime and Delinquency, 2006). (Prisons are different from jails: Jails are detention facilities for suspects and defendants before they make bail, or places for incarcerating people who have committed a misdemeanor. Prisons are facilities for the incarceration of felons—persons who are convicted of committing a crime that draws a penalty of a year and a day, or more.)

Figure 6.6 The United States Has the Most Inmates

The U.S. inmate population dwarfs those of Europe. In fact, the United States has nearly 1.5 million more people in prison than the total of the 26 European countries with the largest inmate populations.

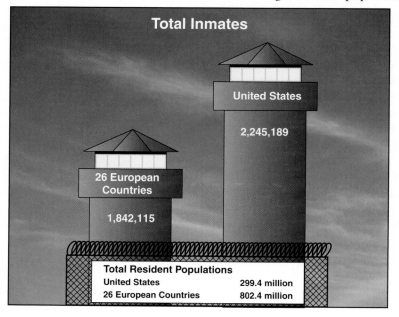

(*Source:* "One in 100: Behind Bars in America 2008" a report by Pew Center on the States and the Public Safety Performance Project, The Pew Charitable Trusts, www.pewcenteronthestates.org, February, 2008. Reproduced by permission.)

When we add the 4.8 million people on probation or parole, we come up with an amazing statistic: 3.2 percent of the adult American population is currently immersed somewhere in the criminal justice system. And the numbers are increasing dramatically (Figure 6.7). Between 1987–2007, the national prison population has nearly tripled (Pew Center on the States, 2008). Over the same time period, state spending on corrections has increased 127 percent. Today, five states—Vermont, Michigan, Oregon, Connecticut, and Delaware—now spend as much or more on corrections as on higher education (Pew Center on the States, 2008).

Prisons. People convicted of crimes may be asked to pay fines and restitution to victims or to engage in community service; but, for most offenses, the main penalty is incarceration: jail or prison terms of up to 84 months for violent crimes, 48 months for drug crimes, and 41 months for property crimes (not including those rare instances when life in prison or the death penalty is imposed). But criminologists, lawgivers, and private individuals have often wondered *why:* What are the goals of incarceration, and are they being achieved? Four goals have been proposed (Goode, 2004; Siegel, 2000):

1. *Retribution.* People who break rules must be punished; they "owe a debt to society." Children who break their parents' rules are often grounded, temporarily losing their liberty and some of their privileges (the freedom to watch television or play video games, for instance). In the same way, adults who break laws can be effectively punished through the loss of their liberty and some of their citizenship privileges (the freedom to vote, sign contracts, take gainful employment, and so on).

   A problem with the retribution goal is that we believe that the punishment should fit the crime: The greater the degree of social harm, the worse the punishment. However, incarceration can only be extended, not worsened. Also, justice is not blind: Prison terms are longer for minorities than Whites, and for men than for women, even when both have been convicted of the same offense (Mustard, 2001).

2. *Deterrence.* Children may not understand or agree with the reasoning behind their

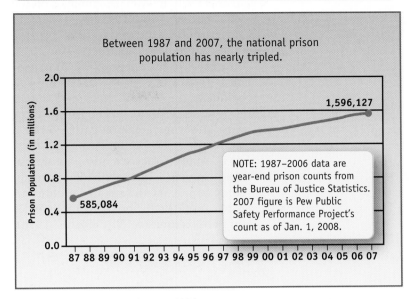

Figure 6.7 Prison Count Pushes Up

Between 1987 and 2007, the national prison population has nearly tripled.

1,596,127

585,084

NOTE: 1987–2006 data are year-end prison counts from the Bureau of Justice Statistics. 2007 figure is Pew Public Safety Performance Project's count as of Jan. 1, 2008.

(*Source:* Pew Center on the States, 2008.)

parents' rules, but threat of grounding deters them from most rule breaking in the first place, and the memory of punishment is sufficient to hinder future rule breaking. In the same way, the threat of prison decreases the likelihood of a first offense, and the memory of prison is assumed to deter people from future crimes.

But does it? Between 30 and 50 percent of people released from prison commit new crimes, often of the same sort that got them the prison sentence in the first place. Criminologists have found that fear of prison itself plays virtually no role in the decision-making process of either first-time or repeat offenders, although quality of life in prison can affect criminal behavior (Katz, Levitt, and Shustorovich, 2003). To people who belong to criminal subcultures, prison is seen as an occupational hazard. Inside or out makes little difference in their social network, their norms and values, their goals, their problem-solving techniques, their social world. In some ways, inside is

The Largest Ethnic Group in Prisons

Did you know that Hispanics are the largest ethnic group in federal prisons? This is due, in part, to the tightening of immigration laws. In 2007, 29,281 Hispanics were sentenced to federal prisons (14,074 for immigration issues), compared to 19,583 Whites and 16,415 Blacks (*New York Times*, 2009).

Did You Know?

even preferable, offering regular meals and free medical care.

3. *Protection*. When we "take criminals off the streets," they will not be able to commit further crimes (at least, not on the streets), and society is protected.

However, only a few of the most violent criminals stay off the streets forever. Nationally, more than half of criminals released are back in prison within three years, either for breaking parole or for a new crime (Pew Center on the States, 2008). Many social scientists argue that while serving time, offenders are in "crime school," with seasoned professionals teaching them how to commit more and better crimes (e.g., Califano, 1998).

4. *Rehabilitation*. Criminals lack the skills necessary to succeed (or even survive) in mainstream society. The National Literacy Survey of 16,000 inmates found that 63 percent were at the lowest levels of functional illiteracy. Less than half have high school diplomas or GEDs. So prison time can be used for rehabilitation. They can get drug and alcohol therapy, learn a trade, get their GED, and even take college classes. A four-year study conducted by the Department of Education found that inmates who participate in any education program are 23 percent less likely to be reincarcerated. A CUNY study at Bedford Hills Correctional Facility, New York's only maximum-security women's prison, found

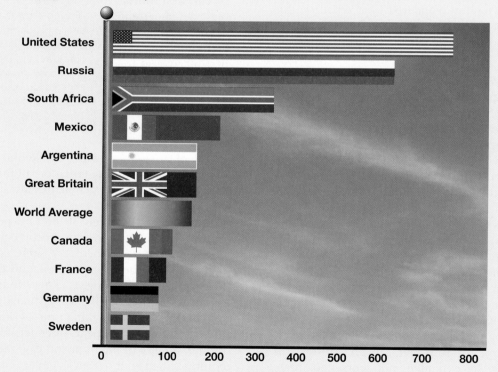

U.S. / Them

Incarceration Rates around the World

The United States has the highest rates of incarceration in the world—about five times greater than England. The prison population has continued to grow, despite the drop in violent crime over the past decade.

Prison Populations (per 100,000 population)

(Source: Roy Walmsley, *World Prison Population List*, 8th Edition. London: International Center for Prison Studies, King's College, 2009. Available at: www.kcl.ac.uk/depsta/law/research/icps/downloads/wppl-8th_41.pdf.)

1. How can sociologists explain our high rates?

2. Or, conversely, how would sociologists explain that rates in other advanced industrial countries, like France, Canada, and Germany, are so much lower?

that prisoners who took college courses were over 60 percent less likely to return than those who did not (Clark, 1991). An extensive study of rearrests, reconvictions, and reincarcerations found that prison education reduces overall relapses into crime by nearly 30 percent (Coley and Barton, 2006; Steurer and Smith, 2003).

But prisons actually offer few rehabilitation programs, and those available are seriously understaffed and underfunded. Most prisoners do not receive counseling or drug and alcohol therapy, and budget cuts terminated almost all of the prison education programs in 1994. Those prisoners who do take classes often find that they have not acquired the skills for real-world jobs, nor have they received any training on how to find work.

The Death Penalty. Fewer than half of the countries in the world (69) currently have death penalties—countries like Algeria, Benin, China, Mongolia, Thailand, and Uganda. There is only one in the industrialized West. The European Union will not accept as a new member any country that has the death penalty.

This means the United States could not become a member of the EU. As of this writing, the death penalty exists in all but 14 of the states. In 2007, the United States ranked sixth in the number of executions, after China, Iran, Pakistan, Iraq, and Sudan (Amnesty International, 2009). The use of the death penalty has steadily dropped in the United States; in 2008, 37 inmates were executed, a 14-year low (Moore, 2008). (See Figure 6.8.)

What crimes are heinous enough to deserve death? Most countries that have capital punishment invoke it only for extraordinary crimes (murder or war-related crimes), while others, like China, Malaysia, Saudi Arabia, and Singapore, use it for some business and drug-related offenses. In the United States, it is usually invoked only in cases of murder and treason.

Who can be executed? In 1989, the Supreme Court decided that it was constitutional to execute John Paul Penry, a 44-year-old man who had the reasoning ability of a 6-year-old. However, in 2002, the Supreme Court reversed its earlier ruling and held that the death penalty constituted "cruel and unusual punishment" for mentally retarded persons.

What about kids? It was once commonplace to execute children as young as 12 or 13 for everyday sorts of crimes. In 2005, the Supreme Court outlawed the death penalty for crimes committed by persons under the age of 18, leaving only two countries in the world where juvenile executions are still legal (Iran and Congo).

The American public generally favors the death penalty for adult offenders—by about two to one, with more support among men than women and more among Whites than among minorities. They typically cite the death penalty's value in deterring crime.

Prisoners and Profit

The American prison system has become partially privatized. That means that prisons are run like a business, with an eye toward profits. The more prisoners, the more profit. And the cheaper it is to house them—including food, computers and television, libraries—the higher the profit. A large number of people now have a vested interest in making the prison system even bigger and perhaps also less "hospitable."

Did You Know?

Figure 6.8 Race of Defendants Executed in the United States since 1976

Black	397	34%
Hispanic	82	7%
White	646	57%
Other	24	2%

NOTE: The federal government counts some categories, such as Hispanics, as an ethnic group rather than a race. DPIC refers to all groups as races because the sources for much of our information use these categories.

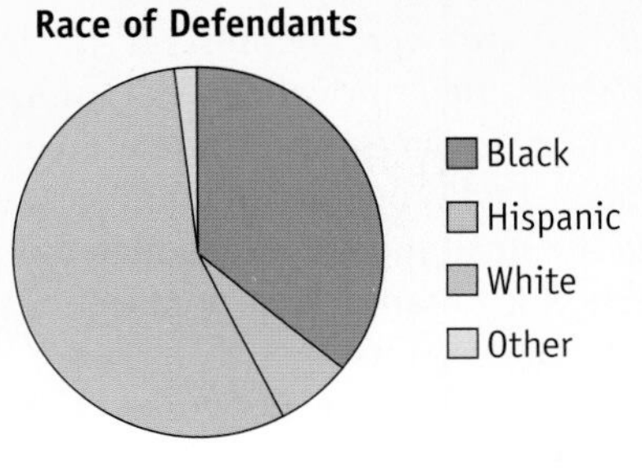

Race of Defendants

- Black
- Hispanic
- White
- Other

(*Source:* Death Penalty Information Center, February 13, 2009; http://deathpenaltyinfo.org. Copyright © 2009 Death Penalty Information Center. Reproduced with permission.)

However, few, if any, offenders actually stop to consider the prospect of being executed before committing the crime. Many violent crimes are committed in the heat of passion, when rational calculation is largely or entirely blocked by emotion (Bouffard, 2002). Besides, for deterrence to work, the punishment must be swift and certain. Neither is the case in the U.S. criminal justice system.

Many scholars have noted that the death penalty is unjustly applied. Race plays a major factor: Blacks convicted of murdering Whites are most likely to get the death penalty, and Whites convicted of murdering Blacks are the least likely (Phillips, 2008; Paternoster, Brame, and Bacon, 2007; Baldus, Woodworth, 1990; General Accounting Office, 1990).

Location also plays a factor. Some states, such as Illinois and New York, have strong public defender offices with sufficient financial resources to attract the top lawyers. Cases can then be assured of vigorous defense through several appeals. Other states, such as Texas and Alabama, do not coordinate public defense or fund it at the state level—the judge appoints a lawyer, who is paid on a fixed scale that does not cover federal appeals. Cases there are represented by inexperienced lawyers who often lack the resources to mount a vigorous defense and the incentive to stick through the appeals process. As a result, a crime committed in Texas is much more likely to get a conviction than the same type of crime committed in Illinois, where two-thirds of capital cases are overturned (Liebman, Fagan, and West, 2000).

Finally, the death penalty, once applied, is irreversible, leading to worries that innocent people might be wrongly executed. In the twentieth century, at least 18 executed offenders were later found innocent (Radelet and Bedau, 1992), and today new techniques of DNA analysis are thinning the ranks of death row.

Globalization and Crime

Every day I receive an email message informing me that I've won a national lottery in England, giving me a hot stock tip, or saying that the wife of a dearly departed African dictator would like my help in spiriting away several million dollars (for which I will be handsomely compensated). These are phishes, and they originate in many different crime cells all over the world.

While the Internet may have expanded the global networks of crime, crime as a global enterprise has a long history, from ancient slave traders (who kidnapped their "cargo") to criminal networks operating in many different countries. There were pirates on the seven seas, hoisting their proverbial black flags beyond territorial waters; and there are contemporary pirates who operate in countries where it is legal to steal and duplicate material from the Internet or to ransack corporate funds into offshore bank accounts.

Today, global criminal networks operate in every arena, from the fake Gucci handbags for sale on street corners to the young girls who are daily kidnapped in Thailand and other countries to serve as sex slaves in brothels around the world; from street gangs and various ethnic and national organized crime networks (the "Russian Mafia," the Italian Mafia) to the equally well-organized and equally illegal offshore bankers and shady corporate entities that incorporate in countries that have no regulations on toxic dumping, environmental devastation, or fleecing stockholders.

In the early twenty-first century, piracy has experienced a revival. Not the Disney-fied Johnny Depp flying the Jolly Roger, but young Somali men, with small arms, trolling the shores off eastern Africa looking for luxury cruise ships, cargo vessels, ships carrying food from the World Food Program, or oil tankers carrying oil through the Gulf of Aden. These are held for ransom, from governments and corporations, totaling $150 million by November 2008. In October, 2008, the United Nations adopted a resolution calling on all governments to apply military force to halt the spread of piracy.

And yet much crime also remains decidedly "local"—an individual is assaulted or robbed, raped, or murdered in his or her own neighborhood. Despite the massive networks of organized global crime, it is still true that the place where you are most likely to be the victim of a violent crime is your own home (U.S. Department of Justice, 2005b, 2009).

When we ask that question, we are really concerned with causality: Does knowing about the possibility of going to the gas chamber or electric chair *cause* people to reconsider their murder plans?

The best way to determine causality is through experiment: Introduce variable *A* into a situation and determine if variable *B* results. If *B* only happens after *A* is introduced, and never before *A* or without *A*, then we can state with some certainty that *A* caused *B*.

But sociologists obviously can't turn the death penalty on and off to look at the results. Instead, we turn to the somewhat riskier business of correlation. We look at places where the death penalty has ended, or where it has been instated, to see what happens to the serious crime rate.

Imagine a country that has no death penalty and a murder rate of 0.10 per 1,000 people, significantly higher than that of the United States (0.04). The country decides to institute the death penalty, and within five years the death penalty drops 10 percent, to 0.09. Sociologists all over the world would stare at the statistics in amazement: The death penalty (variable *A*) is correlated with a decrease in the murder rate (variable *B*)! Is it possible that someone stops to consider the consequences before he sets out to shoot his nuisance of a brother-in-law?

Maybe. Correlation cannot prove causality. Maybe the country is enjoying a period of remarkable economic prosperity, so there is less crime in general. Maybe it has instituted strict gun control laws, so there is no way for anyone to shoot his brother-in-law. Maybe the population is aging, and murder is mostly a young person's activity. We can never know for sure that the death penalty, and not

Does the Death Penalty Act as a Deterrent to Crime?

other intervening variables, caused the drop in the murder rate.

Even though a positive correlation is not always a good indication of a causal relationship, the *lack* of correlation is a pretty good indicator of *a lack* of causality. If *B* happens sometimes before *A*, sometimes after *A*, and sometimes without *A*, we can be reasonably sure that the two variables are not causally linked. When real-life countries and states put in a death penalty, or revoke one, the rate of murder and other serious crime does not go up or down in any systematic fashion. There is no significant correlation.

In fact, it might actually seem to go the other way. Florida and Texas, the two states with the highest numbers of executions, actually have higher murder rates than states with no death penalty or that have death penalties on the books but few or no executions. Is there another variable behind both the executions and the murder rate?

Of course, no one would seriously make the argument that the death penalty *causes* murders! But neither can anyone make a convincing argument that the death penalty deters murder either.

Therefore, despite what "everybody knows" sociologists conclude that the death penalty has no significant effect on serious crime. What "everybody knows" in this case turns out to be wrong.

A good example of this connection between the local and the global is the subject of drugs.

Examining the sociology of drug use provides a window into the various aspects of deviance and crime that sociologists study. Among the issues sociologists have addressed are:

Drug Use: About 8,000 Americans try drugs for the first time every single day. (More than half of them are female and under 18.) Over 3.5 million Americans are dependent on drugs. And nearly a million Americans are in treatment for their addiction. It's become common for celebrities to disappear for a few months and emerge from rehab clinics confessing their former dependency on a talk show. The most commonly used drugs are marijuana, cocaine,

and pain killers. Using some drugs is illegal, and abusing others (such as prescription medications) is illegal, but is it "deviant"? While some sociologists have examined the different rates of use of different drugs by different groups—and the consequences of those differences in arrests and prison sentences—other sociologists examine the social processes by which someone "becomes" a marijuana user—a process that resembles the socialization into any other social group, deviant or not.

Globalization: Networks of Production, Distribution, and Protection: Because drug use is illegal, different types of criminals produce and distribute them. Sociologists of organizations can examine how different networks may connect your local campus

The image of pirates hoisting the Jolly Roger pirate flag and perhaps looking like Johnny Depp as Jack Sparrow has been replaced by a new revived form of piracy. Somali pirates, armed with assault weapons, routinely capture oil tankers and merchant vessels sailing through their coastal waters, leading to new international efforts to curb piracy.

pot dealer with murderous organized drug cartels in other countries—from the local peasants who grow various drugs to large bureaucratic organizations that handle production, transportation, distribution, and protection. In some countries, illegal drugs are among that country's leading exports. Sociologists can use various methods to study the global organizations that compose the drug pipelines—pipelines of production and distribution that resemble pipelines for other natural resources, such as oil—and the dense networks of distribution in local areas.

Drugs and the Criminal Justice System: According to the U.S. Department of Justice, nearly one out of every five adults in state prison is serving time for a drug offense. More than one-fourth are incarcerated for simple possession, and nearly 70 percent are there for trafficking (Mumola and Karberg, 2006; Sabol et al., 2007). The War on Drugs propelled the incarceration rate to a nearly tenfold rate of convictions. But that war's casualties have been distributed unequally toward poor and minority males, who compose the large majority of all drug-related convictions. Incarceration for drug offenses accounts for 17 percent of the increase among Whites but 36 percent among Blacks and 32 percent among Hispanics (Blumstein and Beck, 1999).

Drugs and Public Policy: In 2009, New York State abolished the punitive "Rockefeller Drug Laws," which severely punished possession and use of drugs like marijuana with significant prison sentences. (Defendants convicted of selling two ounces, or possessing four ounces, faced a mandatory sentence of 15 years to life in prison.) Sociologists study drug policies ranging from legalization of drugs, drug law reform, funding for rehabilitation and treatment, to medical use of marijuana.

Deviance and Crime in the Twenty-First Century

The main question in deviance and crime is not only why so many people break the rules. It's also why so many people don't. The question of order is the flip side of the question of deviance—and both are of significant interest. We may all be deviants, but we're also, most of the time, law-abiding citizens. And we obey the law not only because we are afraid to get caught but because, deep down, we believe that the system of laws is legitimate and that we all will benefit somehow from everyone obeying them.

In the future, we'll continue to obey most of the rules and also decide which ones we can break and legitimate their breaking to ourselves. Our society will likely continue its anticrime spending spree, and the number of prisoners will continue to spiral upward. The crime rate will shift unevenly; some crimes will increase and some decrease. And we'll continue to debate the age-old questions of guns and the death penalty.

The sociological questions will remain the same: How do people make the sorts of decisions about what laws to obey and which ones to break? Who decides what laws are, how they are to be enforced, and how equally the law is to be applied? How does our understanding of deviance and crime reflect and reinforce the inequalities of our society even as the institutions that administer them—the police, courts, and prisons—also reflect and reinforce those inequalities? What are the possibilities of more equitable understandings and policies?

Chapter Review

1. What Is Deviance?

Deviance may be minor or major, from talking too loudly at a movie or engaging in a common but illegal sexual practice to burglary or murder. Even the most moral or law-abiding among us sometime speed, litter, fail to recycle when others do, skateboard where we shouldn't, break a social rule or law, or even find aspects of ourselves make us deviant—sometimes being the wrong sort of person. Mostly we conform, but sometimes we don't. Sociologists are interested in what accounts for deviance and for conformity and who decides or defines what is, or is not, deviant.

deviance Breaking or refusing to follow a social rule. The rule can be societywide or specific to a particular group or situation. (p. 152)

2. Conformity and Social Control

Rules about acceptable behavior vary by culture. They are of varying degree of formality, enforced to varying degrees, depending on how important they are, ranging from a **folkway** and **mores** to rules and laws. The most serious violations of culturally acceptable behavior are **taboo** and usually illegal, although they may be so unthinkable or repellent that there may not be laws prohibiting them. We may have a particular characteristic of ourself that is a **stigma,** resulting in a spoiled identity, unless we use one of the strategies Goffman identified for neutralizing stigma. A **subculture** may be deviant, as well. Youth gangs are typical of deviant subcultures—although members are at odds with society, they conform within the group.

folkway One of the relatively weak and informal norms that are the result of patterns of action. Many of the behaviors we call "manners" are folkways. (p. 153)

mores These are informally enforced norms based on strong moral values, which are viewed as essential to the proper functioning of a group. (p. 153)

taboo The strongest form of norms, a taboo is a prohibition viewed as essential to the well-being of humanity. (p. 153)

stigma An attribute that changes you "from a whole and usual person to a tainted and discounted one," as sociologist Erving Goffman (1963) defined it. A stigma discredits a person's claim to be normal. (p. 153)

subculture Group within a society that creates its own norms and values distinct from the mainstream and usually its own separate social institutions as well. (p. 154)

3. Deviance and Social Coherence

Durkheim observed that deviance serves society—providing cohesion, drawing people together through shared morality, defining boundaries for behavior. Without this social coherence, there is **anomie.** But why individuals are deviant is another question for sociologists. Why people engage in deviant activities may be explained by **differential association,** in which conformity is relatively less attractive than is deviance, if there are more influences in our lives supporting deviance. **Control theory** posits crime results from rational analysis. **Social con-**

trol theory sees social ties exerting control on our behavior, while **labeling theory** emphasizes the process in which deviance is constructed, focusing on the power to define who, and what, is or isn't deviant. **Primary deviance** passes unnoticed, but deviant identities develop with **secondary deviance,** which **tertiary deviance** normalizes. Some sociologists see deviance as social inequality because punished deviants are typically powerless, with their fate justified by the powerful and privileged, who themselves evade similar treatment.

anomie A term developed by Emile Durkheim to describe a state of disorientation and confusion that results from too little social regulation, in which institutional constraints fail to provide a coherent foundation for action. (p. 158)

differential association Edwin H. Sutherland's theory suggesting that deviance occurs when an individual receives more prestige and less punishment by violating norms than by following them (p. 158)

control theory Travis Hirschi's theory that people perform a cost-benefit analysis about becoming deviant, determining how much punishment is worth the degree of satisfaction or prestige the deviance will confer. (p. 159)

social control theory As Walter Reckless theorized, people don't commit crimes even if they could probably get away with them due to social controls. There are outer controls—family, friends, teachers, social institutions, and authority figures (like the police)—who influence (cajole, threaten, browbeat) us into obeying social rules; and inner controls—internalized socialization, consciousness, religious principles, ideas of right and wrong, and one's self-conception as a "good person." (p. 159)

labeling theory Howard Becker's term stresses the relativity of deviance, naming the mechanism by which the same act is considered deviant in some groups but not in others. Labels are used to categorize and contain people. (p. 160)

primary deviance Any minor, usually unnoticed, act of deviance committed irregularly that does not have an impact on one's self-identity or on how one is labeled by others. (p. 160)

secondary deviance The moment when someone acquires a deviant identity, occurring when he or she repeatedly breaks a norm and people start making a big deal of it, so the rule breaking can no longer be attributed to a momentary lapse in judgment or justifiable under the circumstances but is an indication of a permanent personality trait. (p. 160)

tertiary deviance Occurs when members of a group formerly labeled deviant attempt to redefine their acts, attributes, or identities as normal—even virtuous. (p. 160)

4. Sociological Theories of Deviance and Crime

Crime is a form of deviance that has large institutions devoted to prevention and control and a whole field of study, with many theories addressing the causes. Theories of crime include **strain theory,** which views crime as a response to inequality and the gap between society's goals and individual means to meet them. Although not supported by research, the **broken windows**

theory is often used to justify enforced policing. Some views emphasize socialization into criminal subcultures, or different norms of the underclass subculture as causes, although the lower classes are mostly law-abiding citizens. **Opportunity theory** looks at subcultures that structure opportunity for crime. Some theories focus on whether criminal laws are fair. **Conflict theories** consider the role of structural inequality in crime, like the perspective on which it is based.

crime A deviant act that lawmakers consider bad enough to warrant formal laws and sanctions. (p. 162)

strain theory Robert K. Merton's concept that excessive deviance is a by-product of inequality within societies that promote certain norms and versions of social reality yet provide unequal means of meeting or attaining them. Individuals respond to this strain either by conforming or by changing the goals or means of obtaining goals accepted by society. (p. 162)

broken windows theory Philip Zimbardo's proposition that minor acts of deviance can spiral into severe crime and social decay. Atmosphere and context are keys to whether deviance occurs or spirals. (p. 163)

opportunity theory Cloward and Ohlin's 1960 theory of crime, which holds that those who have many opportunities—and good ones at that—will be more likely to commit crimes than those with few good opportunities. (p. 164)

conflict theory Theoretical approach that stresses the competition for scarce resources and unequal distribution of those resources based on social status (such as class, race, gender). (p. 164)

5. Types of Crimes

Crimes are categorized as being against people, which includes **violent crime,** or as **property crime.** We usually conceptualize workplace crime as office theft, or shoplifting, but **white-collar crime** is actually far more costly to society. **Consumer crime** is a comparatively recent phenomenon. **Occupational crime** and **organizational crime** are forms of white-collar crime that cost society tremendously more than "regular" crime, although the perpetrators are rarely caught, and, when caught, they don't serve long prison terms; fines and light sentences are more common, in contrast with other property crime. Lower social status often means greater victimization and greater punishment. Crime using the Internet is the fastest-growing category. Pervasive computer use has led to **cybercrime,** from new versions of old crimes, like phishing, to identity theft. **Hate crime** is dramatically underreported, so true rates are hidden, but race is the most common category of bias.

violent crime A crime of violence or one in which violence is a defining feature. According to the FBI, violent crime consists of four offenses: murder and nonnegligent manslaughter, forcible rape, robbery, and aggravated assault. (p. 165)

property crime A crime committed involving property, such as burglary, car theft, or arson, where there is no force or threat of force against a person. (p. 165)

white-collar crime Edward Sutherland's term for the illegal actions of a corporation or people acting on its behalf, by using the authority of their position to commit crime. (p. 165)

consumer crime Crime in which the perpetrator uses a fake or stolen credit card to buy things for him- or herself or for

resale. Such purchases cost both retailers and, increasingly, "e-tailers" over $1 billion per year, or nearly five cents for every dollar spent online. (p. 165)

occupational crime The use of one's professional position to illegally secure something of value for oneself or for the corporation. (p. 165)

organizational crime Illegal actions committed in accordance with the operative goals of an organization, such as antitrust violations, false advertising, or price fixing. (p. 165)

cybercrime The growing array of crimes committed via the Internet and World Wide Web, such as Internet fraud and identity theft. (p. 166)

hate crime A criminal act committed by an offender motivated by bias against race, ethnicity, religion, sexual orientation, or disability status. (p. 167)

6. Crime in the United States

America has very high crime rates and stands out from other advanced countries in homicides, due to our emphasis on individual economic success to the exclusion of other indicators of success like accomplishment or social relationships, the ever-widening gap between haves and have-nots, and the availability of guns. Crime is differentially distributed by social category. Men commit far more crimes than women, except for gender-coded crimes like shoplifting. Racial minorities are overrepresented in the criminal justice system; a number of theories address this inequity, including labeling and conflict theories. Young people and the poor are overrepresented as both perpetrators and victims of crime, following the pattern that lower status relates to both more arrests and greater victimization for crimes against both persons and property, compared with those of high status.

7. The Criminal Justice System

America has more police per capita than most countries, but more time is spent doing paperwork than making arrests in the criminal justice system bureaucracy. Police today are often embedded in the community for improved effectiveness. Most criminal cases never make it to trial, through guilty pleas or pleading lesser charges. Mandatory sentencing laws led to exploding prison populations before their repeal, but although violent crime has dropped here, prison populations still rise. Incarceration is the primary sentence for offenders, in contrast with other countries. Retribution, deterrence, protection, and rehabilitation are justifications given for incarceration. Rehabilitation may work, but recidivism rates are high, as prisons typically serve as "crime schools" with few rehabilitation opportunities. Capital punishment is used by fewer than half the countries worldwide; crimes receiving this sentence vary. Capital punishment varies by state in the United States, and whether it is used varies by locality, victim and offender race, and resources.

8. Globalization and Crime

Global crime has existed as long as there has been travel and trade. We still have pirates, kidnapping, and slavery, and global crime has expanded to include international crime organizations, counterfeit products, and Internet crime. We are still more likely to be victims of violent crime in our own homes. Drugs provide a good example for observing how sociologists view the construction of deviance, and the intersection of local and global factors, at various levels of organization and analysis, from production and distribution to legislation, policy and use, and the criminal justice system.

9. Deviance and Crime in the Twenty-First Century

Although deviance occurs, most of the time we conform. Most of the time we obey laws, too, with the belief that justice prevails in an impartial system. Sociologists are interested in why and when we conform and why and when deviance occurs. Often the answer lies in the definition of what is criminal or what is deviant, and who holds the power to define. Although we strive to correct inequities and create fairer policies, our tacit belief in the system perpetuates inequalities in society through the institutions that administer and apply the laws. It is likely that we will continue to see the same debates and policies and increasing prison populations in the years ahead.

Self-Test: Check Your Understanding

1. Belching loudly during meals and picking your nose publicly are violations of:
   a. folkways.
   b. mores.
   c. taboos.
   d. laws.
2. Goffman identified an attribute that is discrediting, changing us from a normal person to a tainted one, as:
   a. a taboo.
   b. a stigma.
   c. deviance.
   d. anomie.
3. Pat and Chris are both overweight. Pat acts like a jolly, happy-go-lucky clown. Chris is an activist against negative portrayals of big people, in a group that believes they are superior for rebelling against the unrealistic, damaging body images portrayed in the media. Which of Goffman's strategies for neutralizing stigma are Pat and Chris using?
   a. Pat is using normification; Chris is using minstrelization.
   b. Pat is using minstrelization; Chris is using militant chauvinism.
   c. Pat is using militant chauvinism; Chris is using minstrelization.
   d. Pat is using minstrelization; Chris is using normification.
4. Durkheim's view of deviance is that:
   a. it is harmful to society because it corrupts the social order, which is why people work to stamp it out.
   b. it is helpful to society, as it gives people who don't fit in a way to join others like themselves in society, where they can conform.
   c. it is harmful to society for violating group norms, and it undermines social unity.
   d. it is helpful to society by bringing people together uniting against it, and it defines the boundaries of what is acceptable.
5. Which theory of deviance emphasizes the process by which deviance is constructed, focusing on the power needed to define deviance?
   a. Control theory
   b. Differential association theory
   c. Labeling theory
   d. Social control theory
6. To be a crime, an act of deviance must:
   a. be bad in and of itself.
   b. violate a folkway or more.
   c. violate a formal code enacted by a legally constituted body.
   d. All of the above are necessary for an act of deviance to be a crime.
7. Which theory of crime argued that crime results from inequality and the gap between the goals of society and the means to reach the goals?
   a. Strain theory
   b. Broken window theory
   c. Opportunity theory
   d. Conflict theory
8. Which of the following is far and away the most costly, at $600 billion per year for the United States alone?
   a. Consumer crimes
   b. Cybercrime, including identity theft
   c. Workplace theft, including retail shoplifting
   d. White-collar crime

Self-Test Answers: 1. a, 2. b, 3. b, 4. d, 5. c, 6. c, 7. a, 8. d

Integrate and Explore: Points to Consider

1. Which groups or social categories are seen as deviant? Which are overrepresented as victims of crime? Which are overrepresented as perpetrators of crime? Which groups are underrepresented as victims and perpetrators of crime and for identification as deviant? Identify the characteristics of each group that might be important in their relationship to definitions of deviance or crime.
2. Identify the factors that distinguish America from other countries with regard to crime rates, policing, and incarceration. Find a crime, and punishment, in which America differs dramatically from other countries, and one in which America is similar to other countries. What reasons might there be for these similarities and differences?

succeed with mysoclab PEARSON

Self-scoring practice tests, flashcards for learning key terms, streaming audio of the entire text, and multimedia, including:

Watch—*Corrupt Politicians*
Map—Social Explorer, *Increases in Prison Populations*
MySocLibrary—Elijah Anderson, *The Code of the Streets*
MySocLibrary—William Chambliss, *The Saints and the Rednecks*

7

Stratification and Social Class

There's an old British joke that goes something like this:

Two Oxford professors, a physicist and a sociologist, were walking across a leafy college green. "I say, old chap," said the physicist, "What exactly do you teach in that sociology course of yours?"

"Well," replied the sociologist, "This week we're discussing the persistence of the class structure in America."

"I didn't even know they had a class structure in America," said the physicist.

The sociologist smiled. "How do you think it persists?"

Most countries are aware of their own class structure—the physics professor didn't need a sociology course to know that England has social classes—but in the United States, class seems to be invisible. Many people don't even believe it exists. Surely, they say, we're an equal-opportunity country. Class is a relic of old European monarchies, where princes scandalize the media by consorting with commoners.

But the United States does have a class structure. Every country does; social class is present in some form in every human society. Even the Old Order Amish, perhaps the most egalitarian society that has ever existed, have three social classes ranked by occupational prestige: traditional farmers, business owners, and day laborers (Kraybill, 2001). The details may shift and change somewhat over time, but class structure is omnipresent, always operating in our lives, and, paradoxically, especially powerful in countries where people don't believe it exists. Their inability to "see," as the joke suggests, helps class persist from generation to generation.

And the entire world has a global class system, in which some countries get far more of their share of the pie than others, and in which different national groups can connect across national boundaries because of their shared culture. Although both global and local class systems seem invisible, sociologists believe that social class remains the single best indicator of your "life chances"—of the sort of life you are likely to have—where you

"Although it seems invisible, social class remains the single best indicator of . . . the sort of life you are likely to have—where you will go to school, what you think, and even whom you will marry (or if you will) and even how you like to have sex!"

will go to school, what you think, and even whom you will marry (or if you will) and even how you like to have sex! Even focusing so much on your individual choices and individual talents is a reflection of your class position. (Middle-class people believe in the meritocracy more than upper-class people.)

This chapter will explore the importance of class in our society—as a source of identity and as a structure of inequality, in both the national and the global arenas.

What Is Social Stratification?

The system of structured social inequality and the structure of mobility in a society is called **social stratification.** Stratification is concerned with the ranking of people. Social stratification takes its name from geology: Imagine a society looking very much like the side of a mountain made of sedimentary rock: each layer—or "stratum"—carefully demarcated and sitting on the top of another well-defined layer.

All societies rank people. The criteria for the ranking vary: In the contemporary United States, perhaps it's the size of your bank account; in traditional societies, perhaps it's the size of your yam crop. But once you are ranked, you enjoy benefits and rewards "appropriate" to your social location. You get more or less money, fame, prestige, and power throughout your life, regardless of your individual talent, intelligence, and drive to succeed.

In almost every society, an entrepreneurial genius born in a hovel dies in a hovel, and a person of, shall we say, limited ability born in a palace dies in a palace. Almost nobody moves from hovel to palace, except in fairy tales. Your social position is a matter of birth, passed on from parents to children, from generation to generation. Some societies, mostly extremely wealthy ones, like our own, allow for some social mobility, so entrepreneurial geniuses born in hovels can found megasuccessful corporations, or the children of solidly middle-class shop owners can find themselves punching time clocks. But even where social mobility is possible, most people remain at the same social location throughout their lives. If your father was a janitor, it is very unlikely that you will one day be the president—even if you get the right education.

Social stratification involves inequalities not only in wealth and power but also in belief systems. It gives some people more benefits and rewards than others and also defines the arrangement as fair, just, and reasonable. The explanation offered for *why* it is fair, just, and reasonable differs from society to society. Often no explanation is offered at all: Both the "haves" and the "have-nots" accept the system without question (Crompton, 1993; Kerbo, 1996; Saunders, 1990).

Why Do We Have Social Stratification?

What purpose does stratification serve? Classical sociologists disagreed on this question. Some, like Durkheim, believed that stratification was a necessary organizing principle of a complex society and that it served to create interdependence among society's members, so that everyone "needed" the activities of everyone else (Filoux, 1993). Marx, on the other hand, stressed the ways the stratification system benefited those at the top—at the expense of those at the bottom. He spoke of oppression and exploitation, not integration and interdependence (Resnick and Wolff, 1987).

In the middle of the twentieth century, many sociologists followed Durkheim, saw stratification as integrative, and claimed that it allowed for significant mobility. For example, Kingsley Davis and Wilber Moore (1945) argued that as long as some degree of social mobility was possible, stratification is essential to the proper functioning of a society. Some jobs (say, brain surgeon) are extremely important, and other jobs (say, serving hamburgers at the student union) are relatively unimportant. Social stratification creates a **meritocracy,** a system in which those who are the most "meritorious" will rise to the top and those who are less so will sink to the bottom. Meritocracy is the rule by those who deserve to rule. The greater the functional importance of the job, the more rewards it brings, in salary, perks, power, and prestige. Therefore people will work better, longer, and harder in hopes of getting a high-prestige job. Of course, some will not succeed; *most* will not succeed. But the society benefits from everyone working very hard. If a brain surgeon and a burger flipper suddenly started getting the same salary, perks, and prestige, no one would be motivated to work hard. Severing rewards from performance leads to low quality and low productivity.

However, those arguments came at a far more optimistic time in American society; today, the persistence—and even the intensification—of class-based inequalities has rendered that vision obsolete. Sociologists now understand that social mobility occurs in only a few societies, and it is not common anywhere.

This woman is an untouchable, one of the 160 million people who occupy India's lowest caste. No matter how hard or diligently she works, she won't escape the poverty and discrimination into which she was born.

Social stratification divides us far more than it unites us. Stratification is a form of inequality. Elites maintain inequality for their own advantage, prohibiting many of the most talented and intelligent people from making favorable contributions to the society and giving less talented, less intelligent people tremendous amounts of power. Even where some people do get to move up in the rankings, this situation is so infrequent that elites still manage to retain control, and the possibility of mobility ensures that the disenfranchised remain docile: They assume that if they don't succeed, it's their own fault (McAll, 1990).

Systems of Stratification

Societies reproduce social stratification in different ways. Sometimes boundaries are relatively fluid, and sometimes they are etched in stone. The most common forms of stratification are the caste system, feudalism, and class.

Castes. Castes, found in many traditional agricultural societies, divide people by occupation: farmers, merchants, priests, and so on. A **caste system** is fixed and permanent; you are assigned to your position at birth, without any chance of getting out. Perhaps the most famous example of a caste system has been India. India had four castes, or *varnas: Brahmin* (priests), *Kshatriyas* (warriors and other political elites), *Vaishyas* (farmers and merchants), and *Shudras* (servants), plus the untouchables, a "casteless" group at the bottom of the society. Your *varna* determined not only your occupation but where you could live, whom you could talk to on the street (and the terms

you would use to address them), your gods, and even your chances of a favorable afterlife: Only a Brahmin could hope to escape samsara, the cycle of endless deaths and rebirths. Modern India prohibits discrimination on the basis of caste and reserves a percentage of government jobs and university admissions to untouchables. However, the traditional system is still strong, especially in rural areas (Gupta, 2000).

Feudalism. In medieval Europe, between the eleventh and sixteenth centuries; in nineteenth-century Japan; and in a few other regions, there were a few merchants and "free men," but most of the population consisted of peasants and serfs who worked the estates belonging to a small group of feudal lords. **Feudalism** was a fixed and permanent system: If you were born a lord or a serf, you stayed there your whole life.

The classic feudal relationship was one of mutual obligation. The feudal lords housed and fed serfs, offered protection inside the castle walls, and decided on their religion and whether they would be educated. Peasants had no right to seek out other employment or other masters. In effect, they were property. Their only avenue to social advancement was to enter a convent or monastery (Backman, 2002).

Feudalism endured in Germany through the nineteenth century and in Russia until the Bolshevik Revolution of 1917. A person's wealth—and the taxes owed to the Tsar—was gauged not by how much land that person owned but by how many serfs (or "souls") he owned.

Feudalism began to disappear as the class of free men in the cities—artisans, shopkeepers, and merchants—grew larger and more prosperous, and the center of society began to shift from the rural manor to the urban factory. International trade shifted the social world to the city from the countryside, and global networks of commerce—trade, credit, banking, and the like—linked urban centers in new ways that further isolated rural feudal manors. Industrial society dispensed with feudal rankings and ushered in the modern class system.

Class System. Class is the most modern form of stratification. **Class** is based on economic position—a person's occupation, income, or possessions. Of the major forms of stratification, class systems are the most open—that is, they permit the greatest amount of **social mobility,** which is the ability to move up—or down—in the rankings. **Class systems** are systems of stratification based on economic position, and people are ranked according to achieved status (as opposed to ascribed status). Each system of stratification creates a belief system that declares it legitimate, that those at the top "deserve" to be there through divine plan, the natural order of things. Class systems "feel" the most equitable to us today because they appear to justify one's ranking solely on his or her own initiative, hard work, and talent.

Social Class

Many Americans believe that a class system is a relic from our European past and that it exerts far less influence—if any—in the modern world. After all, the very idea of American democracy is that an individual should be able to rise as far as his or her talents, aspirations, and hard work can take that person.

Yet, we also have seen ample evidence that the importance of class is increasing. The frequent appeals to "Joe Lunchbucket," "people who shower after work, not before," and "working families" in the rhetoric of the 2008 presidential election suggests important class distinctions within American society and culture. The continued commentary on the rescue and cleanup efforts in New Orleans in the aftermath of Hurricane Katrina exposes America's persistent class and racial inequalities.

Yet if we openly acknowledge class at all, it is usually the class to which we are aspiring, not the class into which we were born. But it turns out your class of origin is a very reliable measure of where you will end up. Your class background is just about the best predictor of many things, from the seemingly important—what college you go to (or if you go to college at all), what job you have—to the seemingly trivial—what your favorite sexual position is, what music you like, and even what you probably had for dinner last night.

Class also operates on the global level. Just as there are upper-, middle-, and lower-class people, there are upper-, middle-, and lower-class countries. These, too, shift and change over time—a tycoon country today might be a pauper country tomorrow, and vice versa—but the hierarchy of rich and poor, weak and strong, high status and low status doesn't seem to go away. (We will return to the global dimension of class later in the chapter.)

Theories of Social Class

The analysis of social stratification in general, and class in particular, is one of the defining interests of the founders of sociology—as well as a central concern among sociologists today.

Marx and Class. Karl Marx (1818–1883) was the first social scientist to make class the foundation of his entire theory. Marx argued that human survival depends on producing things. How we, as a society, organize ourselves to do this, and how we distribute the rewards, is what Marx called the *mode of production*—the organization of society to produce what people need to survive.

There are many ways to do this. We could imagine a system in which one person owns everything, and everyone else works for him or her. Or we could imagine a system in which everyone owns everything, and you simply take what you need—and leave the rest for others. Or we could imagine a system in which a very few people had far more than they could possibly ever need, and the

Class inequality often combines other forms of inequality to create a complex hierarchical order. The government's response to Hurricane Katrina in 2005 exposed persistent class and racial inequalities in the United States.

Marx argued that the poor are poor because *the rich are rich. Here, a poor woman poses in the doorway of her one room shack with three of her seven children. The despair and depression that often accompany poverty make it difficult to understand how the poor will organize to rise up and take over the system, as Marx predicted.*

large majority had very little; but, instead of giving the rest away to others who need it, the wealthy would simply throw it away. All of these are systems that organize production, the creation of the goods we need for survival, and the relations of production—the relationships people enter into to facilitate production and allocate its rewards.

Marx argued that, historically, it has always been the case that some people own means of production—the cornfields, the cows, and the factories—and everyone else works for them. With ownership comes control: If you own the only cornfield in town, everyone else has to listen to you or go without corn. Therefore there are two types of people, the owners and workers.

In Marx's day, capitalists or what he called the **bourgeoisie** owned the means of production, only now they owned factories instead of farms, and the working classes or the **proletariat** were forced to become wage laborers or go hungry. They received no share of the profits and lived in perpetual poverty. Ironically, they used their wages to buy the very products that they were helping to manufacture.

Marx believed that this system was inherently unfair. He also believed that classes were in intractable and inevitable conflict. He predicted that eventually the proletariat would organize, rebel, and overthrow capitalism altogether in favor of a socialist economy where the workers owned the means of production (Smelser, 1975).

Weber and Class. Max Weber (1864–1920) doubted that overthrowing capitalism would significantly diminish social stratification. It might address economic inequality, but what about other forms of inequality? In one of his most celebrated essays, "Class, Status and Party" (1946), Weber argued that there were three components to social class: economic (class position), social (status), and political (power). Often they were interrelated, but sometimes they operated independently: You could be at the top of the economic ladder, but at the bottom of the social ladder, and somewhere in the middle of the political ladder. So are you a member of the upper, middle, or lower class? Or all three? Social class, it turns out, is a complex, multidimensional hierarchy.

Table 7.1
Occupational
Prestige: 31-Year
Trend

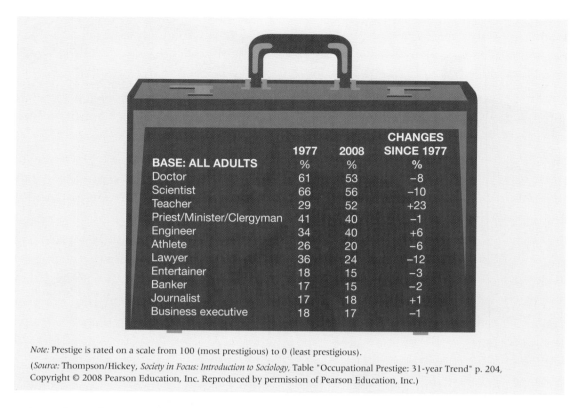

BASE: ALL ADULTS	1977 %	2008 %	CHANGES SINCE 1977 %
Doctor	61	53	−8
Scientist	66	56	−10
Teacher	29	52	+23
Priest/Minister/Clergyman	41	40	−1
Engineer	34	40	+6
Athlete	26	20	−6
Lawyer	36	24	−12
Entertainer	18	15	−3
Banker	17	15	−2
Journalist	17	18	+1
Business executive	18	17	−1

Note: Prestige is rated on a scale from 100 (most prestigious) to 0 (least prestigious).

(*Source:* Thompson/Hickey, *Society in Focus: Introduction to Sociology,* Table "Occupational Prestige: 31-year Trend" p. 204, Copyright © 2008 Pearson Education, Inc. Reproduced by permission of Pearson Education, Inc.)

In Weber's theory, stratification is based on three dimensions:

1. *Class position.* It can determine whether you are an owner or a worker; how much money you make (your income); your property, stocks, bonds, and money in the bank (your wealth). Wealth is more important than income because the legal system, with its laws concerning private property and inheritance, ensures that wealth will pass on to your heirs and endow them with a class position similar to yours—or higher. Class is based simply on your relationship to production—what you do for a living and what you earn.

2. *Status.* Social **prestige** is what other people think of you. If class is based on your relationship to the marketplace, **status** is based on your lifestyle. Status refers to other people's social evaluation of your lifestyle. People see what you have and how you live and make judgments about how much wealth and power you have. This results in people often buying higher-priced luxury goods—"status symbols"—even if they have a hard time paying for them.

   People with higher class positions tend to enjoy higher status, but not necessarily: The status of your job or occupation is often measured as **"occupational prestige"**—the degree of status accorded to an occupation. For example, in the United States, college professors enjoy high status, but (unfortunately) they don't make much money, compared to other high-status professions. Accountants, bankers, and real estate brokers have some of the lowest status ratings in America, but they tend to command high salaries (Harris Interactive, 2008). High and low status differs from society to society and changes over time (Table 7.1). Status does not pass from generation to generation automatically, like wealth, but it can still be transmitted. Upper-class parents teach their children the social skills expected of people with high status, perhaps an appreciation for classical music or modern art, and send them to exclusive schools and colleges where they can prepare for high-status lives. Meanwhile lower-middle-class and working-class parents teach their children the skills necessary for lives of somewhat lower expectations.

3. *Power.* **Power** is the ability to do what you want to do. This may mean a certain amount of control over your own working situation. People in higher class or status positions can set their own hours, disregard punching time clocks, and work to their own rhythm.

Power also resides in your ability to influence the actions of others. People with high power dictate, order, command, or make "requests" that are really commands issued in a nice way, as when a police officer "asks" to see your driver's license. People such as the police officer can have a great deal of power but comparatively low class position or social status (Weber, 1958). But people with higher class positions and social status tend to have more power. As the tyrannical king tells us in the *Wizard of Id* comic strip, "Remember the Golden Rule: He who has the gold makes the rules."

Class position, status, and power remain the major components of social class, but sociologists after Max Weber have continued to postulate new ones: your social connections, your taste in art, your ascribed and attained statuses, and so on. Because there are so many components, sociologists today tend to prefer the term **socioeconomic status** (abbreviated as **SES**) over *social class* to emphasize that people are ranked through the intermingling of many factors, economic, social, political, cultural, and community. Socioeconomic status refers to a position in the social stratification system based on the combined weights of class position, status evaluation, and power.

Class in the United States

Karl Marx divided the world into two simple classes, the rich and the poor. But the sweeping economic and social changes of the past century and the recognition of multiple components to socioeconomic status have pushed sociologists to redefine these class categories and to further delineate others (Grusky, 2000; Lenski, 1984).

Today most sociologists argue for six or more socioeconomic classes in the United States. (See Figure 7.1.) They are usually divided on the basis of household income because that information is easily obtained in census reports, but bear in mind that there are many other factors, and income is not always the best indicator. Our class position is both an ascribed status (the class we are born into) and an achieved status (the class we end up in). Unfortunately for the myth of American mobility, these are far more likely to be the same than they are to be different. In fact, class is the single best predictor of a person's **life chances**—a person's abilities to have access to material goods (food and shelter) and social resources (health care, education) that together control the quality of life.

Figure 7.1 American Class Structure

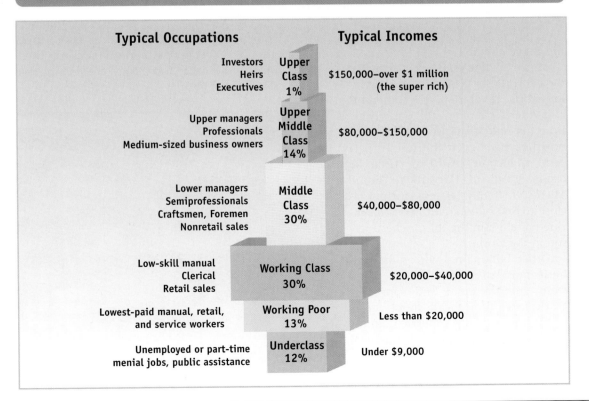

Typical Occupations	Class	Typical Incomes
Investors, Heirs, Executives	Upper Class 1%	$150,000–over $1 million (the super rich)
Upper managers, Professionals, Medium-sized business owners	Upper Middle Class 14%	$80,000–$150,000
Lower managers, Semiprofessionals, Craftsmen, Foremen, Nonretail sales	Middle Class 30%	$40,000–$80,000
Low-skill manual, Clerical, Retail sales	Working Class 30%	$20,000–$40,000
Lowest-paid manual, retail, and service workers	Working Poor 13%	Less than $20,000
Unemployed or part-time menial jobs, public assistance	Underclass 12%	Under $9,000

(*Source:* Based on Gilbert, Dennis L. *The American Class Structure in an Age of Growing Inequality,* 7th ed. © 2008 Pine Forge Press, an imprint of Sage Publications, Inc.)

The upper classes are the prime consumers of high-end luxury brands. Their tastes, however, often trickle down to the middle classes, who consume these same brands as a way to exhibit their mobility and status.

The superrich are usually invisible to the rest of the world. They have people to do their shopping and other chores. They have private jets, so they rarely stand in line at airports.

Lower Upper Class. With annual household incomes of more than $150,000 but less than $1 million, the lower upper class are the "everyday" rich. They tend to have advanced degrees from high-ranking colleges. Though they have substantial investment incomes, they still have to work: They are upper-level CEOs, managers, doctors, and engineers. Much more visible than the superrich, they still protect their privacy. They do not participate extensively in civic and community organizations. They live in gated communities, vacation at exclusive resorts, and send their children to prestigious private schools.

Upper Middle Class. With household incomes above $80,000 but less than $150,000, these are the high-end professionals and corporate workers. Most have college degrees. Only a small percentage of their income comes from investments. They tend to be community leaders, very active in civic organizations and the arts. The audience in performances of the local philharmonic is likely to be mostly upper middle class (the upper class is in Vienna, and the lower middle and working classes are at home watching television).

The Upper Upper Class. These are the superrich, with annual incomes of over $1 million. They include the older established wealthy families, born into massive fortunes that their ancestors amassed during the industrial boom of the nineteenth-century Gilded Age. While the original fortunes were amassed through steel, railroads, or other industries, recent generations depend on extensive worldwide investments. They are neither the "haves" nor the "have nots"—they are the "have mores."

Many of the superrich amassed their fortunes recently, during the information revolution, in computers and other technology. Bill Gates came from an elite background but was nowhere near even the top 10 percent in income in 1975, when he dropped out of Harvard to found Microsoft. Today, Gates's fortune is close to $60 billion, and *Forbes* magazine named him the third richest person in the world.

Other billionaires who didn't inherit most of their fortunes come from entertainment and sports. A blockbuster movie can shoot actors to the ranks of the superrich almost overnight, after years of financial hardship. (Of course, it usually doesn't; the mean salary for entry-level actors in 2009 was $37,000.)

Middle Middle Class. With household incomes between $40,000 and $80,000, these are the "average" American citizens. Most hold white-collar jobs: They are technicians, salespeople, business owners, educators. How-

In the United States and other high-income countries, college is a necessary prerequisite for a middle-class life but no longer guarantees it.

ever, many blue-collar workers and high-demand service personnel, such as police, firefighters, and military, have acquired incomes large enough to place them in the middle class. Most have attended college, and many have college degrees. They have very little investment income but generally enough savings to weather brief periods of unemployment and provide some degree of retirement security. They are also in a precarious position: Shrewd career decisions could propel them into the upper middle class, while a few faulty career decisions could send them plummeting down to the working class. However, they are usually able to buy houses, drive new cars, and send their children to college. They tend to have small families and are very active in community civic life.

Working Class. Also called "lower middle class" to avoid the stigma of *not* being middle class in America, this group has a household income of between $20,000 and $40,000. They tend to be blue-collar workers, involved in manufacturing, production, and skilled trades, but there are also some low-level white-collar workers and professionals (such as elementary school teachers) and some high-level clerical and service industry workers, especially those in two-income households.

They make things and build things. They usually have high school diplomas, and many have been to college. Their savings accounts are usually minimal, so a few missed paychecks can be devastating, and for retirement they will have to depend on government programs such as Social Security or union pensions. Nevertheless, they can often buy houses, drive inexpensive cars, take occasional vacations, and send their children to public college.

They are not heavily involved in local civic and community organizations; instead, their social lives revolve around home, church, and may-be some hobby or sports groups. Extended family appears to be extremely important, more significant in the daily lives of the working class than of the middle class or upper class, who usually live hundreds or thousands of miles away from aunts, uncles, and cousins.

Lower Class. Also called the "working poor" to avoid the stigma of being called lower class, this group has a household income of less than $20,000 per year. They have unskilled and semiskilled jobs: They are service workers, maintenance workers, clerical

Did You Know?

Sociology and Our World

The Hidden Injuries of Class

In a now-classic study, sociologists Richard Sennett and Jonathan Cobb interviewed working-class and poor men and women whose jobs were difficult, demeaning, low paying, and dead end. Sennett and Cobb expected to hear about hardship and deprivation, but they also heard working-class men judging themselves by middle-class standards. They believed in the American dream, where a poor boy can grow up to be president, where all it takes to get rich is perseverance and hard work. Yet they weren't rich—and they blamed themselves. They thought their "failure" was a matter of laziness, lack of ambition, or stupidity.

How did they ward off despair, when they believed themselves fully to blame for their lives of deprivation? They deferred success from their own lives onto the lives of their children. They were working at difficult, dirty, and dangerous jobs not because they were failures but because they were sacrificing to give their children a better life. They were noble and honorable. Middle-class fathers tried to be role models to their children, saying, in effect, "You can grow up to be like me if you study and work hard." But working-class fathers tried to be cautionary tales: "You could grow up to be like me if you *don't* study and work hard."

Living through one's children proved to be enormously damaging. Fathers were resentful if their children were successful and perhaps even more resentful if they weren't, and all of the deprivation was for nothing. Successful children felt ashamed of their parents, and unsuccessful children felt guilt and despair of their own. Following the American dream can also produce painful feelings.

What do **you** think?

Conflict between Poor and Rich in the United States

Because capitalist countries are built on a profit-based economy, they can be especially prone to inequality based on economic status, and this inequality often leads to conflict between the rich and the poor. So, what do you think?

In your opinion, in America, how much conflict is there between poor people and rich people?

○ Very strong conflict   ○ Not strong conflict

○ Strong conflict   ○ No conflict

What does **America** think?

(Actual survey data from the General Social Survey, 1972–2004.)

In the 2000 General Social Survey, more than half of all respondents said they thought there was either strong or very strong conflict between the rich and the poor. Those who identified as lower class were far more likely than others to say there was strong (47.1 percent) or very strong (39.2 percent) conflict. With regard to race, Blacks were far more likely than Whites to report they thought there was strong (42.9 percent) or very strong (27.3 percent) conflict.

Thinking Critically about Survey Data

1. The social class difference in responses was significant. What explains the social class differences?
2. In sociology, we study the intersections between race, class, and gender. How does the intersection of race and class help explain these survey results?

References: See Davis et al., page 511.

---

workers. They deliver pizzas, wait on customers at retail stores, and clean homes and offices. Most do not have high school diplomas: They have an average of 10.4 years of education, as compared with 11.9 for the working class, 13.4 for the middle class, and 14.3 for the upper class.

It's hard to accumulate any money on $20,000 per year, so they usually live from paycheck to paycheck, and even a brief period of unemployment can be catastrophic. And because service jobs rarely include health benefits, illnesses and accidents also have a devastating effect. They often cannot afford houses or cars or college educations for their children. They are not heavily involved in any activity besides making ends meet.

The Underclass. The **underclass** has no income and no connection to the job market. Their major support comes from welfare and food stamps. Most live in substandard housing, and some are homeless. They have inad-

equate education, inadequate nutrition, and no health care. They have no possibility of social mobility and little chance of achieving the quality of life that most people would consider minimally acceptable. Most members of the underclass are not born there: They grow up working poor, or working class, or middle class, and gradually move down through a series of firings, layoffs, divorces, and illnesses.

America and the Myth of the Middle Class

Generally, Americans believe that class is even less important than ever and that most Americans are middle class. On the other hand, class inequality has never been greater, and it is growing wider, not narrower. How can it be both?

Since the beginning of the twentieth century, the middle class has expanded dramatically, and the classes of the very rich and the very poor have declined. (This is true despite the dramatic increase in the gap between the richest and the poorest Americans.) Home ownership has risen, incomes have risen, and many more people own stock through mutual funds, pensions, and retirement accounts than ever before. (This is also true despite the recent economic recession.) They thus own at least a fraction of the means of production—and identify not with workers but with owners.

At the same time that boundaries of the middle class are expanding to the breaking point, with almost everyone thinking that they are middle class (or upper middle class or lower middle class), fully invested in the system, the lifestyle associated with middle class is in obvious decline: less money, a smaller house or no house, a worse job or no job, and less financial security.

Economist Michael Lind (2004) argues that the middle class has always been a product of social engineering by the government. Today's middle class emerged during the "New Deal" of the 1930s when technological innovation, a home front relatively unscathed by war, and a large population of young, well-educated people led to a climate just right for an unprecedented expansion of the middle class. In the early 1970s, a college graduate earned about 45 percent more than a high school graduate. By 2008, that number had jumped to 84 percent more, the result of increased demand for higher skills (Glenn, 2008).

But the current economic downturn has reversed some of these trends: Two of the most important factors, a superior education and a favorable investment climate, have begun to decline in significance. The increases in the percentage of the labor force with college degrees has slowed to less than 5 percent, and America's massive trade deficit and the supercharged economies of Asia make America less attractive for investment. And white-collar jobs are in steady decline. Knowing about computers is no longer key to instant success. The jobs with the biggest numerical gains in the next 10 years are expected to be in food service, customer service, retail sales, clerical work, and private security. We may be seeing the rise of a new feudalism, with a few elites sitting in their skyscraper condos while the rest of the population—the new serfs—cook, clean, park the cars, and patrol the grounds.

Income Inequality

At the same time that most people believe that they are middle class and believe that the system works for them, the United States is increasingly a nation of richer and poorer. Sociologists measure the income inequality in a society by comparing the top incomes with the bottom incomes. In the United States, the top 5 percent earn an average of 11 times more than the bottom 20 percent—this is the most extreme example of income inequality in the developed world. In contrast, the top 20 percent in Sweden earn less than four times the bottom 20 percent, and in Japan, it's three to one (Economic Policy Institute, 2007). In fact, the income gap in the United States is the widest of any industrialized country among all countries included in the Organization for Economic Cooperation and Development (OECD), an international organization that measures and assists in economic development (Figure 7.2).

The income gap in the United States actually seems to be widening: The gap between rich and poor has grown to its widest level since the 1920s (CNNMoney.com, 2007). The richest 1 percent has more money to spend after taxes than the entire bottom 40 percent put together. According to the Congressional Budget Office, income for the bottom half of American households rose six percent since 1979 but, through 2005, the income of the top one percent skyrocketed—by 228 percent (CBS News, May 3, 2008). The richest 10 percent of Americans control 34 percent of the nation's wealth (up a few percentage points since 1990), and the bottom 10 percent virtually none (Economic Policy Institute, 2007).

Even at the top, the gaps are growing enormously. Over the past 30 years or so, the wages and salaries of the top 10 percent of earners have grown nearly 35 percent—about 1 percent a year. That means that being in the top 10 percent did not pay off handsomely. But income at the 99th percentile, the top 1 percent of earners, rose more than 180 percent during that same period. And income at the 99.99th percentile (the top one-hundredth of 1 percent) rose nearly 500 percent. That's for those earning over $6 million a year (Krugman, 2006). An old expression tells us, "A rising tide lifts all boats." But it seems that nowadays the rising tide lifts only the yachts.

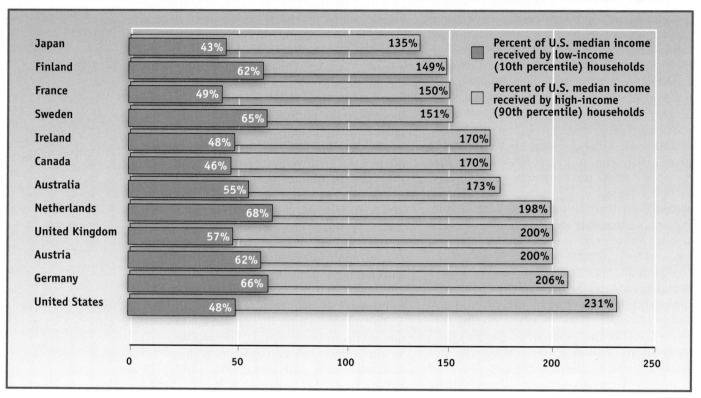

Note: These relative income measures compare the gap between the top 10 percent and the bottom 10 percent of household income in each country to the U.S. median income in purchasing-power-parity terms.
(*Source:* Coder, Rainwater, and Smeeding [2001]; and Smeeding [2006]. Figure 8E, taken from the Economic Policy Institute's *State of Working America 2008/2009*, available at www.epi.org.)

Globally, the United States looks more unequal—both in terms of the gap between the haves and the have-nots and also the relationship of those at the top of the corporate ladder to those below them. In 1970, the average CEO made 28 times more than what the average worker earned; today, it is 275 times more. The average CEO earns $14.2 million in total compensation, more in one workday than the typical worker earns all year (Mischel, Bernstein, and Shierholz, 2009). The U.S. ratio of CEO to average worker compensation is more than double the ratio in Australia, Spain, and Sweden, and nearly three times that of Japan (International Labor Organization [ILO], 2008).

These averages mask even greater disparities between Whites and people of color. The median wealth (net worth less home equity) of White households is $88,000, 11 times more than Hispanic households ($7,932) and 14 times more than that of African American

households ($5,988) (Pew Hispanic Center, 2005).

Class and Race

Class position is based on your position in the economic world. And while it is more flexible than your race or gender statuses that are fixed, or ascribed, at birth it is also less an achieved status than our ideology would often imagine. There is less than a 2 percent chance that someone whose parents are in the bottom 60 percent of all incomes will ever end up in the top 5 percent. And if you are born in the bottom 20 percent, you have a 40 percent chance of staying there (Hertz, 2007).

This means that the historical legacy of racism has enormous consequences for class position. Given how little mobility there actually is, the descendants of poor slaves were unlikely to rise very much in the class hierarchy—even over several generations. Race and class tend to covary—being African American is a better predictor of a lower-class position than being White.

Yet a few do make it, and at the same time as African Americans are overrepresented among the poor, there is also a growing Black middle class, a class of professionals, corporate entrepreneurs, and other white-collar workers. While the existence of this Black middle class reveals that there is some mobility in American society, its small size also illustrates the tremendous obstacles facing any minority member who is attempting to become upwardly mobile.

And, on the other side, there are significant numbers of poor Whites in America. Largely in rural areas, former farmers, migrants, and downsized and laid-off White workers have also tumbled below the poverty line. In cities like Flint, Michigan, where a large GM auto manufacturing plant closed, former workers, both White and Black, were suddenly and dramatically downwardly mobile. Race may be a predictor of poverty, but poverty surely knows no race.

Globally, poverty is also unequally distributed by race. The economic south, largely composed of Africans, South Asians, and Latin Americans, is the home to more than four-fifths of all the world's poor—and a similar percentage of the world's people of color. On the other side of the global divide, the predominantly White nations of Europe are among those with the highest standards of living and the lowest levels of poverty. From 1995 to today, wage inequality between the top and bottom earners worldwide has increased by two-thirds. Among developed countries, Germany, Poland, and the United States are the countries where the gap between top and bottom wages has increased most rapidly, although wage inequality has also increased sharply in some countries, including Thailand, Argentina, and China (ILO, 2009).

Class and Culture

Class is not only about income and poverty. It's more than standard of living. It's about lifestyle as well. Sociologists have found that your class position is a pretty reliable indicator not only of how much you have but of *what* you have, what you want to have, and what you think it's important to have. Class helps sociologists predict what sorts of things you do in your spare time, how you raise your children, the kinds of books you read, the TV shows you watch—or whether you watch TV at all. Class even helps sociologists predict how thin or fat you are. Class, it turns out, is culture: Classes develop different cultural standards—values, norms, and lifestyles.

Some elements of class culture are evident in what we consume: Consumption is one of the chief ways in which we both reveal our class position and also try to hide it. For many Americans, consumption indicates the class to which we aspire, and so because we want to be of a higher class, we consume as if we were, buying those products we associate with "lifestyles of the rich and famous." Many of us who buy shirts with little polo players on them, for example, will never play the actual game of polo. But we wouldn't be caught dead wearing a shirt with a little bowler on it—even though we do go bowling! As Max Weber understood: Class is also often associated with status, with lifestyle.

Class is about more than what we buy and where and what we eat. It's also evident in how we raise our children.

More recently, sociologist Annette Lareau (2003) studied a group of third graders, Black and White, wealthy and poor. The wealthier parents were extremely involved in the children's lives and talked constantly with their children; the kids' lives were a blur of sports practice, musical instrument lessons, and family cultural outings. The poorer kids experienced no such parental involvement or structured activities. They spent their time outside school hanging out at home making up games with the neighbors and friends.

While both of these styles have their advantages—middle-class kids are comfortable in a world of adult culture and are far more assertive, while working-class kids can be more creative figuring out what to do with themselves without formal structure—Lareau stresses that these differences are *cultural* differences, and that in a world where those middle-class skills are more heavily valued, classes tend to socialize their children to remain in the class into which they are born. Class culture, then, is a way that class structure is reproduced.

> ### Does Money Buy Happiness?
> We all know the expression: Money can't buy happiness. And it was long assumed that economic growth did not necessarily lead to greater happiness. But maybe it does. Two young economists found that the richer the country, the happier people are. Given a 10-point scale, the richest countries had the largest numbers who rated their happiness as 8, 9, or 10. In the United States, 90 percent of people making more than $250,000 called themselves "very happy," while only 42 percent of those in families making less than $30,000 said they were happy (Leonhardt, 2008).

Did You Know?

Poverty: Local, National, and Global

When sociologists think about poverty, they usually use one of two terms. **Absolute poverty** is when people do not have the ability to sustain their lives and lack the most basic necessities like food and shelter. **Relative poverty** describes those who may be able to afford the basic necessities of life but still are unable to maintain an adequate standard of living.

Half the world's population—three billion people—live in absolute poverty, on less than $1 a day (Figure 7.3). In fact, the gross domestic product of the poorest 48 nations in the world—that is, 25 percent of the world's nations—is less than the wealth of the world's three richest *people* combined (*The Economist*, 2009; Shah, 2007).

And yet the actual number of the world's poor has been declining. In 2001, there were 390 million *fewer* people living in poverty than 20 years earlier. What happened?

For one thing, China happened. There are 400 million fewer poor people in China today than in 1981. China's growth, coupled with the growth of the economies of East and South Asia, has shifted the global distribution of poverty, so that today the region with the greatest depth of poverty is sub-Saharan

Africa. By 2015, that region will be the epicenter of world poverty in both absolute and relative term (Chen and Ravallon, 2006).

In the United States, we gauge poverty with a calculation devised in 1964 by President Lyndon Johnson. When Johnson declared "war on poverty" in America as part of his dream of a Great Society, he asked economist Mollie Oshansky to devise a poverty threshold, a minimum income necessary to not be poor. She decided that poverty meant "insufficient income to provide the food, shelter, and clothing needed to preserve health." That is, she defined absolute poverty. Minimal requirement of shelter and clothing was hard to gauge, but not food: The Department of Agriculture prescribed several diets that provided minimal nutritional requirements. So she took the least expensive of the diets, multiplied it by three (one-third food, one-third shelter, one-third clothes), and voilà! She estimated the poverty threshold—or the **poverty line.** It was the line below which you would be considered "poor" (Andrew, 1999).

This system is not without its problems. First, its calculations are amazingly low because shelter and clothing cost far more than food. In 2005, the poverty line was $10,400 for an individual (about $5.00 per hour), and $21,200 for a family of four (about $5.25 per hour if two adults work).

The calculations also don't take into account significant differences in cost of living in various regions of the United States: In Omaha, groceries cost 24 percent less than they do in Chicago, 22 percent less than in Boston, and 30 percent less than in Queens, New York. Housing in Omaha runs half of the average price in Chicago and 53 percent less than in Boston or Queens. But the same poverty threshold is used to determine who is poor and who isn't in all four cities (CNN has a city and state calculator for cost of living at http://cgi.money.cnn.com/tools/costofliving/costofliving.html).

The poverty line doesn't take into account things besides food, shelter, and clothes that are equally necessary to preserve health—things like child care, medical care, and transportation. The Economic Policy Institute offers a basic family budget calculator, including all of these necessities. For Omaha, it comes to $31,000 for a four-person household (two adults, two chil-

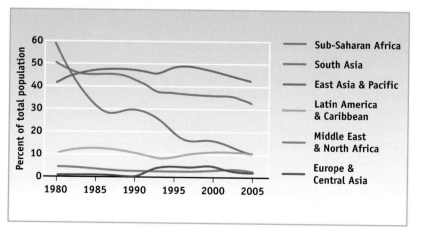

Figure 7.3 Population Living on Less Than $1 per Day

(*Source:* World Development Indicators, 2007. Copyright © 2007 World Bank. Reproduced with permission of World Bank via Copyright Clearance Center.)

dren). For Nassau-Suffolk County (part of New York City), it comes to $52,114. And the percentage of the population that can't meet the budget increases to 23.4 percent and 37.5 percent, respectively.

Yet these statistics are still sobering. The United States has the highest GDP (Gross Domestic Product) in the world and is in the top ten worldwide in GDP per capita (Central Intelligence Agency [CIA], 2008; International Monetary Fund, 2008; World Bank, 2008), yet 12.6 percent of its people fall below the poverty threshold—more than Croatia (11 percent) or Syria (11.9 percent), only a little less than Thailand (13.1 percent) (CIA, 2008; World Bank, 2008). ("GDP per capita" is the gross domestic product, the total value of all goods produced in the country, divided by the number of inhabitants—a standard measure of the total wealth and economic development of a country. GDP per capita tells us little about the *distribution* of that wealth—whether one family owns everything or whether it's distributed exactly equally to everyone.)

Recently, sociologist Fred Block (2005) began to calculate somewhat different measures to illustrate poverty and standards of living. Instead of the "poverty line," Block calculated the "dream line"—estimates of the cost of a no-frills version of the American dream for an urban or suburban family of four. This includes the "four Hs"—housing (owning a single-family home), high-quality child care (for one child), full health coverage, and higher education (enough savings to make sure that both children can attend a public, four-year college or university). The "dream line" comes out to $46,509—and that estimate is low, because it's a national average and cannot even approach what people pay for these services in major metropolitan areas. Currently, if both parents work at minimum wage jobs, they earn $20,600—less than half of the American dream. It appears that the American dream is out of reach for many Americans. What's worse, the American dream is harder to achieve than it was a generation ago. Between the

Percent of households reporting problems with components of well-being:	
Food Insecurity	**Percent**
Food did not last	11.5
Did not eat balanced meals	9.7
Skipped meals	4.4
Housing Conditions	
Insect, pest problems	12.7
Roof leaks	6.9
Broken windows	4.1
Neighborhood Conditions	
Noise problems	21.4
Street repair problems	16.4
Trash, litter	8.2
Abandoned buildings	8.0
Difficulty Meeting Basic Needs	
Could not meet expenses	14.0
Did not pay utility bill	9.2
Did not visit doctor	6.1
Threat of Crime	
Nearby place afraid to walk	28.8
Stay at home out of fear	12.9
Home is unsafe	4.1

Table 7.2
The Material Hardship of Poverty

(*Source:* Reprinted from *Journal of Socio-Economics*, Volume 36, Issue 3, June 2007, John Iceland and Kurt J. Bauman, "Income poverty and material hardship: How strong is the association?" pp. 376-396, Copyright 2007, with permission from Elsevier.)

1970s and today, housing costs increased by more than 500 percent, child care by more than 700 percent, higher education by more than 675 percent, and health insurance by more than 1,775 percent. During this same period, the average income for a family of four increased by 21.9 percent. It is hardly surprising that more American children live in poverty than in any other industrial nation except Russia (Luxembourg Income Study, 2007).

Who Is Poor in America?

The poor are probably not who you think they are. Contrary to stereotypes and media images:

- *Not all poor people are ethnic minorities.* The poverty rate for Whites is a low 8.2 percent, compared to that of Blacks (24.5 percent), Native Americans (23 percent), Hispanics (21.5 percent), and Asians (10.2 percent). However, 116.8 million Whites were living in poverty in the United States in 2007, nearly one-third of the total 373 million (DeNavas-Walt, Proctor, and Smith, 2008).

- *Not all poor people live in the inner city.* In fact, the highest percentages of poor people live in the rural South. In 2007, only Louisiana, Mississippi, Texas, and New Mexico had poverty rates above 16 percent, compared to 9.7 percent in the urban north (U.S. Census Bureau, September 2008). The rural poor are less skilled and less educated than their urban counterparts, and the jobs available to them pay less than similar jobs in urban areas (Dudenhefer, 1993). And their numbers are increasing: Of the 100 counties with the highest child poverty rates in 2005, 95 are rural counties (nearly three-fourths of them—74 percent—are in the rural South) (Weber, 2007). But poverty is becoming more suburban as well; the number of poor Americans living in suburbs is now greater than those living in the 100 largest metropolitan areas by about one million (Children's Defense Fund, 2008).

- *Not all poor people are unemployed.* A 2008 study found that more than 28 percent of American families with one or both parents employed are living below the poverty line (Working Poor Families Project, 2008). And *more*, not less, than full time: Working families work an average of 2,552 hours a year (or 1.25 full-time jobs) (Working Poor Families, 2008). Seventy percent of poor children are in working families (Children's Defense Fund, 2008).

- *Children are more likely than others to be poor.* Right now, 18 percent of children (13.3 million) in America live in poverty—10 percent of white children, 29 percent of Hispanic children, and 35 percent of Black children (*America's Children*, 2009). The child poverty rate in America is often two to three times higher than that of other major industrial nations. Children suffer more than adults from limited health care, poor nutrition, and unsanitary living conditions. Plus, low income tends to increase stress and conflict within families, hamper early cognitive development, hamper educational achievement, and increase the likelihood of participation in serious criminal activity (Children's Defense Fund, 2008).

- *Mothers are more likely than others to be poor.* The poverty rate among female-headed households is more than six times that of married couple families. About half of all poor families are depending on a mother alone to support them (U.S. Census Bureau, 2008).

- *The elderly are less likely than others to be poor.* A generation ago, in 1967, 30 percent of Americans over the age of 65 were living in poverty. By 2007, government intervention through such programs as Social Security, subsidized housing and food, and Medicare lowered the poverty rate to 9.8 percent, a little less than the elderly population in general (12.4 percent) (U.S. Census Bureau, 2008). However, poverty places more of a burden on elderly people than others. They are more likely to suffer from chronic illnesses that require expensive treatment (my mother takes a dozen pills a day, and if she had no health insurance, her monthly pharmacy bill would run about $1,000). They are more likely to live alone and lack the social support networks that other poor people use to get by. And, as the population ages and people live longer, the government subsidy safety nets will be strained to the breaking point.

Figure 7.4 Poverty Rates by Sex and Age

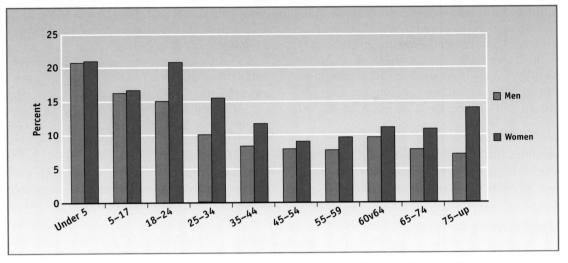

(*Source:* U.S. Census Bureau, *Current Population Survey, 2008 Annual Social and Economic Supplement.*)

The Feminization of Poverty

Social scientists often argue that poverty is also being increasingly "feminized"—that is, women compose an increasing number of poor people. The image of the itinerant (male) pauper has largely faded, replaced today by a single mother. This **feminization of poverty** has never been more obvious: today, nearly 14 percent of all U.S. women are poor, as compared with 11 percent of men (U.S. Census Bureau, 2008). While African American and Hispanic women face proportionally higher poverty rates, the disparity between women and men holds true for all racial and ethnic groups: 26.5 percent of African American women are poor compared with 22 percent of African American men; for Hispanics, it's 23.6 percent of women versus 19.6 percent of men; for Asian Americans, it's 10.7 percent women versus 9 percent men; for Whites, it's 11.6 percent for women as compared to 9.6 percent for men. Poverty rates are highest for families headed by single women (28.3 percent in 2007 versus 13.6 percent of single-parent households headed by men), yet the majority of all poor adult women—54 percent—are single women without kids (Cawthorne, 2008; National Poverty Center, 2008; U.S. Census Bureau, 2008). Still, the widest gender gap in poverty rates occurs during the childbearing years (U.S. Census Bureau, 2008). Supporting a family is difficult for single mothers because women's salaries are often lower anyway, and many single mothers have left the labor force, paused their education, or worked part time to provide unpaid caregiving to children or elderly or disabled family members (see Figure 7.5 on page 202). The lack of adequate child support in the United States—from parental leave to affordable day care to adequate health care—exacerbates the problem (Cawthorne, 2008; McLanahan and Kelly, 2006). For women of color and their children, these problems can be even more acute (National Poverty Center, 2008; U.S. Census Bureau, 2008).

While the gender gap in U.S. poverty rates is wider in America than anywhere else in the Western world (Cawthorne, 2008), this disparity is often magnified in the global arena. In poor countries, women suffer double deprivation, the deprivation of living in a poor country and the deprivation imposed because they are women. In high-income countries, women

It Costs More to Be Poor

- Housing. Renting rooms by the week or apartments by the month costs more than signing a lease, but signing a lease usually requires you to put down first and last months' rent and a security deposit.

- Food. Cheap housing has no kitchen, so you must subsist on more costly takeout. If you have a kitchen, supermarkets are often miles away, so you have to buy your food at expensive convenience stores.

- Furniture. Without a credit card, you can't buy furniture or appliances, so you rent them, for two or three times the price.

- Money. You probably can't get a checking account, and so you cash your checks at a check-cashing service and pay your bills with money orders (for hefty fees).

Did You Know?

live much longer than men: 8.26 years in France, 7.35 years in Switzerland, 6.55 years in the United States. But in low-income countries, the gap in life expectancy is much narrower: 3.20 years in Zaire, 2.40 years in Sudan, 1.10 years in India. In Nepal and Guinea, the gap is even reversed: Men live slightly longer than women. Some commentators believe that the reason for the narrowed gap in life expectancy is a high death rate among the *men,* due to high levels of crime, occupational accidents, and chronic warfare. But certainly women suffer in societies where their life chances are composed entirely of bearing and raising children.

Explaining Poverty

Why are poor people poor? Is it because they are born into poverty, or because they don't work hard enough to get themselves out of it, or because they have some physical, intellectual, or emotional problem that prevents them from getting out?

Personal Initiative. One common explanation is that people are poor because they lack something—initiative, drive, ambition, discipline. An item in the General Social Survey stated, "Differences in social standing between people are acceptable because they basically reflect what people made out of the opportunities they had," and 74 percent of respondents agreed. They were expressing a long-standing belief that people are poor because they are unmotivated and lazy. They do not try hard

enough. They don't want to work. While we often excuse widows, orphans, children, and the handicapped—the "deserving poor"—who can't help it (Katz, 1990), most Americans believe that the vast majority of poor people are "undeserving" poor.

Sociologists, however, understand poverty differently—as a structural problem, not a personal failing. In fact, it's often the other way around: People are unmotivated and lack ambition *because they are poor,* not poor because they lack ambition. No matter how hard they try and how motivated they are, the cards are so heavily stacked against them that they eventually give up—as would any sensible person. In *Nickel and Dimed* (2001), renowned journalist Barbara Ehrenreich tried an experiment: to live on minimum wage for a year. "Disguised" as a poor person, she applied for and received jobs as a waitress in Florida, a maid in Maine, and a Wal-Mart employee in Minnesota. At first she worried that she would not be able to maintain the ruse: Surely coworkers would notice her superior intelligence and competence and realize that she wasn't "one of them," or else the boss would notice and fast-track her into a managerial position. But neither happened. She was no smarter and *less* competent than anyone else in minimum wage jobs. Back home as a renowned journalist, she had to conclude that her privileged lifestyle had a little to do with her drive, ambition, intelligence, and talent, and a lot to do with her social location. Anthropologist Katherine Newman found that poor people actually work harder than wealthy people— often in two demeaning, difficult, and exhausting dead-end jobs (Newman, 1999).

The Culture of Poverty. In 1965, sociologist Oscar Lewis introduced the influential **culture of poverty** thesis (Lewis, 1965) that argued that poverty is not a result of individual inadequacies but of larger social and cultural factors. Poor children are socialized into believing that they have nothing to strive for, that there is no point in working to improve their conditions. As adults, they are resigned to a life of poverty, and they socialize their children the same way. Therefore, poverty is transmitted from one generation to another.

This notion of resignation has often been challenged. For example, the General Social Survey states: "America has an open society. What one achieves in life no longer depends on one's family background, but on the abilities

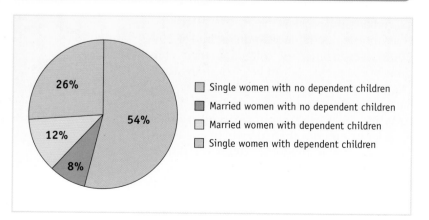

Figure 7.5 Women in Poverty: Family Composition of Household

26%
54%
12%
8%

☐ Single women with no dependent children
■ Married women with no dependent children
☐ Married women with dependent children
☐ Single women with dependent children

(*Source:* U.S. Census Bureau, *Current Population Survey, 2008 Annual Social and Economic Supplement.*)

one has and the education one acquires," and 76 percent of lower-class respondents agree, only a little less than the working class (84 percent), middle class (87 percent), or upper class (80 percent). Certainly these percentages don't indicate any culture of complacency.

Structures of Inequality. Today sociologists know that poverty results from nationwide and worldwide factors that no one individual has any control over, such as economic changes, globalization, racism, and government policies (the minimum wage, Social Security, publicly funded or subsidized health care and day care, and other antipoverty initiatives). Today we also understand that though people living in poverty are not necessarily resigned to their situation, they face structural disadvantages that are nearly impossible to overcome. They would like to lift themselves out of poverty and lead better lives, but they suffer from:

- Poor nutrition
- Poor education
- Higher rates of chronic diseases
- Poor or nonexistent health care
- Inferior housing
- A greater likelihood of being victimized by crime and a greater likelihood of being labeled criminals

We may believe that wealth or poverty is an attribute of individuals—those who work hard enough and sacrifice enough get ahead, and those who don't, well, don't—but, in reality, wealth and poverty are structural features of society. Your relative wealth or poverty depends on who you are more than on how hard you work.

What's more, wealth and poverty are related to each other. Sociologists have argued that the poor are poor *because* the rich are rich. Maintaining a wealthy (or middle-class) lifestyle requires that some people be poor.

Poverty leads to reduced life chances, limited opportunities for securing everything from health care to education, from job autonomy to leisure, from safety at home to the potential for a long life. People at the top of the social hierarchy have resources that enable them to respond to opportunities when they arise, like choosing a prestigious internship or job even if it doesn't pay or relocating to an expensive city or area in order to garner better education or experience. What's more, their superior resources allow people at the

The poor often work harder than the rich. The working poor often work very hard, but their wages are still inadequate to live on.

top to weather problems, from illnesses to accidents to lawsuits to unemployment, that ruin the already precarious lives of the poor. Advantages start early and persist throughout life. And they are virtually invisible—unless you don't have them.

Reducing Poverty

When President Johnson declared a "war on poverty" in 1964, he assumed, optimistically, that it was a war that could be won. The ensuing half century has shown that poverty is a more difficult enemy than anyone originally believed—not because poor people have it so good that they don't want to work to get themselves out of poverty but because the structural foundations of poverty seem to be so solidly entrenched.

A greater proportion of families and children in America today live in poverty (12.6 percent) than in 1973—when the 11.1 percent poverty figure was the lowest ever on record (U.S. Census Bureau, 2008). Dramatic structural, demographic, and policy shifts keep the number of poor high but also obscure just how many poor people have struggled to get themselves out of poverty.

Different societies have tried different sorts of strategies to alleviate poverty. Virtually all industrial nations have a welfare system that guarantees all citizens the basic structural opportunities to work their way out of poverty: free education, national health care, welfare subsistence, housing allowances. Only the United States does not provide those basic structural requirements, and so poor people spend most of their money on housing, health care, and food. As a result, the United States has the highest percentage of poor people of all industrialized countries. While many Americans believe, as the Bible says, "blessed are the poor," the country, as a whole, does little more than bless them and send them on their way.

Global efforts to reduce poverty on a global scale have historically relied on "outside" help: the direct aid of wealthier countries, global organizations devoted to the issue, or large-scale philanthropic foundations. The United States spends billions in direct aid to poor nations. And the World Health Organization, the Red Cross and Red Crescent, and other global organizations channel hundreds of billions of dollars to poorer nations. Finally, foundations such as the Ford and Gates Foundations and the Open Society Institute funnel massive amounts of aid to poor nations to improve health care and education and to reduce poverty, disease, and violence. In 2001, the United Nations announced the "Millennium Project"—a global effort to identify the causes of poverty and to eradicate extreme poverty and hunger by 2015.

This strategy is vital in creating the infrastructure (roads, hospitals, schools) and sustaining agricultural food production (irrigation, seed technologies) that will enable nations to combat poverty. Yet this strategy of direct payments to governments has also received criticism because some of these funds have been terribly misspent by corrupt political regimes, and often little of the money collected actually reaches the poor themselves.

Several newer strategies target local people more directly. In the poorer rural areas of Latin America, the governments of Mexico and Brazil, for example, have embraced "conditional cash transfer schemes" (CCTS) by which the government gives direct payments to poor families of about $50 a month. This may mark the difference between too little food to feed the family and just barely enough. CCTS are "conditional": In return, the beneficiaries must have their children vaccinated and their health monitored and must keep them in school (*The Economist*, 2005c).

In Pakistan, economist Muhammad Yunus has developed a system of "microcredit" by which his bank lends tiny amounts to local poor people. Initially, as a young professor, he loaned a group of women $27 to buy straw to make stools. Over the past 30 years, Grameen Bank has lent $5.72 billion to 6.61 million borrowers—some loans as low as $9—including beggars who wanted to start small businesses or a group of women who needed start-up funds to start a cell phone business or to buy basket-weaving supplies. The bank claims a 98 percent repayment rate (Moore, 2006). In 2006, Yunus received the Nobel Peace Prize in recognition of his work to end poverty one person at a time.

Microcredit helps individuals pull themselves out of poverty by providing tiny loans—some as little as $9—that enable borrowers to start businesses. Most microcredit participants worldwide are women.

Social Mobility

Social mobility means the movement from one class to another. It can occur in two forms: (1) *intergenerational*—that is, your parents are working class, but you became lower, or your parents are middle class, but you became upper class; and (2) *intragenerational*—that is, you move from working to lower, or from middle to upper, all within your lifetime. Social mobility remains one of America's most enduring beliefs, but it is far less common in reality than we imagine. One of the most important studies of mobility was undertaken in the 1960s by Peter Blau and Otis Dudley Duncan (Blau and Duncan, 1967). In their studies of the American occupational structure, they found actually very little mobility between classes, although they found a lot of mobility within any particular class. People moved up or down a little bit from the position of their parents, but movement from one class to another was extremely rare.

Intergenerational mobility seems to have increased since Blau and Duncan. Hout (1984) found that 65 percent of sons were not in the occupational category of their fathers. And Solon (1992) found that while intergenerational mobility was less than he originally expected, it was still significant. Generations do seem to be mobile, but almost as many went from riches to rags as went from rags to riches.

Whatever the American dream may promise about equal opportunity and pulling yourself up by your bootstraps, it is actually far more likely that either you are born with opportunity or you aren't. Most of the sons stayed squarely in the social class of their fathers. Although America doesn't have the same rigid standards as some other societies, it still makes the primary determinant of your social class your parents.

Dynamics of Mobility

Much of the upward mobility that Blau and Duncan found was **structural**—a general upward trend of the entire society, not the result of either intergenerational or intragenerational mobility. Structural mobility means that the entire society got wealthier. Because of the post–World War II economic boom, many working-class families found themselves enjoying middle-class incomes. Similar structural mobility occurred during the Industrial Revolution, when the labor force shifted from farming/agriculture to manufacturing.

More recently, the pattern has been downward mobility, caused by the decline in manufacturing jobs (40 percent disappeared between 1970 and 2000), coupled with the growth of service jobs. Service jobs tend to pay low wages (averaging about half the wages of manufacturing jobs) and offer few or no benefits (averaging 60 percent less than manufacturing jobs). As a result, many people who grew up or spent most of their lives in the middle class find themselves working class or even working poor (Uchitelle, 2006).

Many Americans are underemployed—highly educated and qualified for positions higher than the ones they occupy. On *The Simpsons*, the proprietor of the comic book store defends his bitter outlook on life by saying, "I have a master's degree in folklore and mythology." Millions of Americans have had similar experiences. They acquire college degrees, with dreams of a white-collar job and a middle-class lifestyle, only to find that the jobs simply aren't there. So they take jobs for which they are vastly overqualified in the service industry or as clerical workers, with low salaries, no benefits, and no possibility of career advancement, and join the ranks of the working poor.

Another way to move down from the middle class is to become a permanent temp or part-time worker. Employers prefer temporary employees, even for contracts that will last years, because "temps" command lower salaries and receive neither benefits nor severance pay. Sometimes, employers demote full-time employees to a "part-time" status of 38 hours per week, because employment laws require benefits to be offered only to full-time employees. The result is that employees suffer from the reduced salary and benefits but corporate profits increase (Cummings, 2004).

Intergenerational mobility, the kind Blau and Duncan studied, takes place largely within groups, not between them. Your chances of getting ahead or falling behind are largely influenced by family income—that is, by where you started. Only 6 percent of

> ### The Big Middle Class
>
> In 2006, one-half the world's population was middle class. A century ago, it was only 12 percent (*The Economist*, 2009).

Did You Know?

Mobility Studies

In their effort to understand the *American Occupational Structure* (the title of their 1967 book, which summarized two decades of research), Blau and Duncan created a "path diagram" of American intergenerational mobility using four key variables: father's level of education, father's occupation, son's level of education, and son's occupation. (These questions were asked only of White men.) One version is shown in the diagram.

Here, the son's education and occupation depend on both ascriptive characteristics (the father's occupation and education are fixed, and the son is born with them) and achieved characteristics (the "e" refers to external factors). The son's education is seen as an intervening variable because it affects occupation all by itself, as well as being influenced by his father's education and occupation.

Blau and Duncan were interested in the relative weight of these ascribed or achieved characteristics to measure the "openness" of the American class system and the amount of mobility in it. One of their key findings was that the effects of father's occupa-

tion and education were both direct and indirect. They directly confer some advantages and also indirectly enhance their sons' education, which furthers the sons' success as well.

Among their key findings were that 40 percent of the sons of blue-collar workers *moved up* to white-collar jobs. Perhaps even more intriguing, almost 30 percent of the sons of white-collar workers *moved down* to blue-collar jobs. Today, though, we would also question the idea that we can chart "American" mobility patterns by using data drawn only from White men.

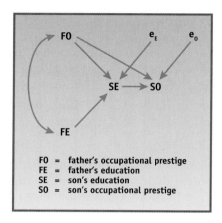

(*Source:* Pew Charitable Trusts, *Economic Mobility Project*, 2009.)

children born to low-income parents make it to the top of the income ladder. Forty-two percent of children in the bottom of the income distribution remain there as adults (Pew Economic Mobility Project, 2009). What's more, the children of high-income groups also experience greater income growth: Families with a median income in the top quintile ($100,100) see their children's income grow by 52 percent in a single generation; families with incomes in the bottom quintile ($23,100) see their children's income grow only 18 percent across their working lives (Isaacs, 2007). But a significant portion of Americans at both the top and the bottom of the income distribution experience little or no economic mobility at all. Thirty-six percent of children born to parents in the bottom wealth quintile remain in the bottom as adults, and 36 percent of children born to parents in the top quintile remain in the top as adults (Isaacs, 2007; Pew Economic Mobility Project, 2009).

Mobility is also affected by race and ethnicity. White people have higher upward

mobility. For example, in every income group Blacks are less likely than Whites to surpass their parents' family income and more likely to fall down the economic ladder (Isaacs, 2008). Only 31 percent of Black children born to middle-income parents end up making more than their parents' family income, compared with 68 percent of White children. And African Americans experience significantly more downward mobility than White people do: Almost half of Black children born to middle-income parents fall to the bottom of the income ladder as adults (Pew Economic Mobility Project, 2009).

Men and women have similar rates of **intragenerational mobility;** that is, the family income of both sons and daughters resembles their parents' to a similar degree. The one big exception is children born to parents on the bottom rung of the economic ladder: 47 percent of daughters born there, stay there, as compared to 35 percent of sons (Pew Economic Mobility Project, 2009). But when it comes to mobility within

Social Mobility in Comparative Context

The United States has less relative mobility than many other industrialized countries. Large social welfare bureaucracies, as in social democratic countries in Scandinavia (Norway, Sweden, and Denmark), are often criticized for stifling social mobility because mobility is thought to be based on individual initiative and hard work. But mobility in the Nordic countries is often more than double that of the United States.

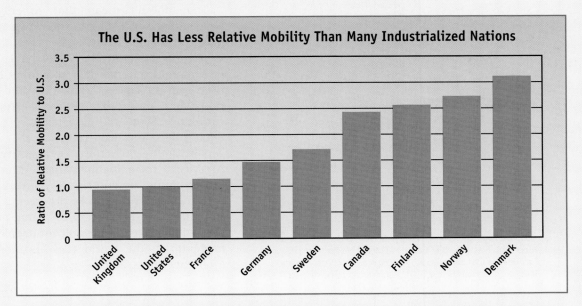

The U.S. Has Less Relative Mobility Than Many Industrialized Nations

(*Source:* Sawhill, Isabel V. and John E. Morton. 2007. "Economic Mobility: Is the American Dream Alive and Well?" Economic Mobility Project, an Initiative of The Pew Charitable Trusts. Washington. http://www.economicmobility.org/assets/pdfs/EMP%20American%20Dream%20Report.pdf. Reproduced by permission.)

1. Why would social democracies, with large-scale health care, state-supported education, and state-supported child care and family policies actually *increase* mobility?

2. What other factors might explain the differences in mobility?

a single generation—what sociologists call intergenerational mobility—men experience greater upward mobility than women (Pew Economic Mobility Project, 2009).

Historically, women have had less opportunity for upward mobility than men because of the types of jobs they were permitted: mostly clerical and service positions that do not offer many opportunities for promotion or increased responsibility. And when they married, they were expected to quit even those jobs or else decrease their hours to part time.

Today, many middle-class women still do not pursue careers that afford middle-class lifestyles because they curtail career ambitions for household and child care responsibilities. As a result, if they divorce, they experience downward mobility. Not only do

they lose the second (and often higher) income from their husband, they also lose benefits like health care and insurance (Weitzman, 1996).

Despite these structural causes of downward mobility, most Americans believe that mobility is largely their own fault. In a Pew Foundation study, most Americans believed that downward mobility was attributed to the way we live and the choices we make. (See Figure 7.6.)

Social Mobility Today

Since the beginning of the twenty-first century, the United States has become less mobile than it has ever been in its history. According to a recent survey, Americans are more likely than they were 30 years ago to

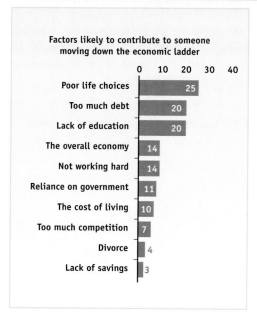

Figure 7.6 Causes of Moving Down the Economic Ladder

Factors likely to contribute to someone moving down the economic ladder

Poor life choices	25
Too much debt	20
Lack of education	20
The overall economy	14
Not working hard	14
Reliance on government	11
The cost of living	10
Too much competition	7
Divorce	4
Lack of savings	3

(*Source:* Findings from the National Survey & Focus Groups on Economic Mobility. 2009. Economic Mobility Project, an Initiative of The Pew Charitable Trusts. Washington. http://economicmobility.org/tools/assets/files/0001. Reproduced by permission.)

end up in the class into which they were born. Rates of mobility are about the same as France or England—countries with hereditary aristocracies and, in the case of Britain, a hereditary monarch. American levels of mobility are significantly lower than Canada and most Scandinavian countries (Pew Economic Mobility Project, 2009).

That doesn't mean that Americans have stopped believing in their own mobility, though. Today, 40 percent of Americans believed that the chance of moving up from one class to another had risen over the last 30 years—the same period when those chances were actually shrinking (Scott and Leonhardt, 2005). Even amidst the deep recession that began in 2008–2009, the vast majority of Americans, including many hardest hit by the economic downturn—83 percent of African Americans, 86 percent of Hispanics, and 88 percent of young people—still believe it is possible for people to move up in the world (Pew Economic Mobility Project, 2009).

Global Inequality

Global inequality is the systematic differences in wealth and power among countries. These differences among countries coexist alongside differences within countries. Increasingly, the upper classes in different countries are more similar to each other—especially in their patterns of consumption—than they are to the middle classes in their own countries. The world seems to be developing a global class structure.

The same processes we observed in the United States are happening on a world scale. For example, over the past 30 years, the overall standard of living in the world has risen. Illiteracy is down, the infant mortality rate is down, the average income is up, and life expectancy is up. But many of these gains are in countries that were high or middle income to begin with, such as the advanced industrial economies of Europe. The standard of living in many of the poorest countries has actually declined. Rich countries are getting richer; poor countries are getting poorer.

The income gap between rich and poor that we see in the United States is becoming the

pattern worldwide. The richest 20 percent of the world's population receives about 80 percent of the global income and accounts for 86 percent of total private consumption, while the poorest 20 percent survives on just 1 percent of the global income and accounts for 1.3 percent of private consumption (Figure 7.7). Actually, the three richest U.S. individuals together—Warren Buffett, Carlos Slim Helu, and Bill Gates—earn as much as the annual economic output of the world's 48 poorest countries combined.

Globalization has increased the economic, political, and social interconnectedness of the world. It has also resulted in staggering disparities in the basics that provide quality of life. The difference between the "haves" and the "have-nots" in our world has never been greater. The $13 billion Americans spend on pet food each year is the same amount it would take to ensure basic health care and nutrition for every person on Earth. Europeans spend more every year on ice cream ($11 billion) than it would take to install water and sanitation for all ($9 billion). Americans spend $12 billion a year on cosmetics, much more than the $8 billion it would take to provide basic education for every person in the world (Aziz, 2008).

Classifying Global Economies

Social scientists used to divide the world into three socioeconomic categories: high-, middle-, and low-income countries (see Figure 7.8).

High-Income Countries. There are about 40 high-income countries, including the United States ($46,000 per capita GDP), Switzerland ($39,800), Japan ($33,800), and Spain ($33,700). These 40 countries cover 25 percent of the world's land surface and are home to 17 percent of its population. Together they enjoy more than half of the world's total income and control the world's financial markets. Most of these nations' populations live in or near cities. Industry is dominated by large-scale factories, big machinery, and advanced technology; however, these countries are also at the forefront of the Information Revolution, with the most companies that make and sell computers and the most computer users; 72.5 percent of the U.S. population and 76 percent of Switzerland's are on the Internet. Because they have access to better nutrition and expert medical care, residents of these countries tend to have high life expectancies (82 in Japan) and low infant mortality rates (4.23 per 100,000 in Switzerland). Because the population is mostly urban and well educated, the birth rate tends to be low (9.87 per thousand in Spain) and the literacy rate high (99 percent in Switzerland).

Middle-Income Countries. There are about 90 middle-income countries, divided into high middle-income countries like Portugal ($21,800 per capita GDP), Uruguay ($10,700), and South Africa ($10,600) and low middle-income countries like Brazil ($9,700), Ukraine ($6,900), and China ($5,300). These countries cover 47

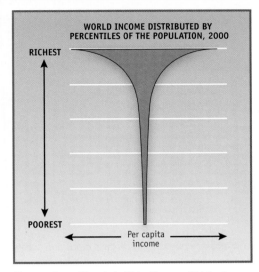

Figure 7.7 Where the Money Is

(*Source:* From "Trends in Global Income Distribution 1970–2015," by Yuri Dikhanov, Human Development Report 2005, p. 37. Reprinted by permission of Yuri Dikhanov, www.hdr.undp.org.)

Figure 7.8 The World by Income

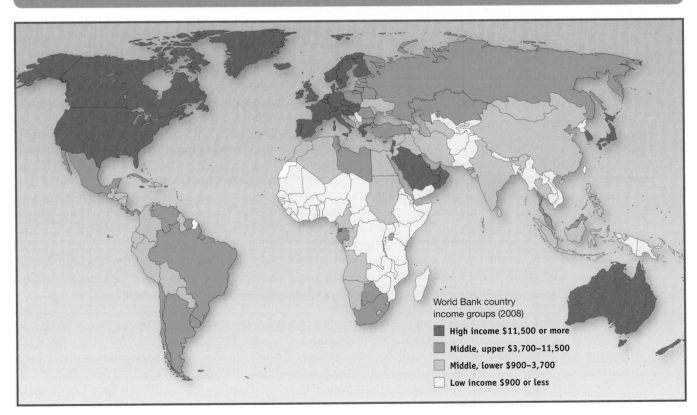

(*Source:* World Bank, 2008, http://maps.grida.no/go/graphic/world-bank-country-income-groups.)

Low income countries rely on cash crops and subsistence agriculture. Rice farming, pictured here in Vietnam, is especially labor intensive, requiring great care and attention to detail.

percent of Earth's land area and are home to more than half of its population. Only two-thirds of the people live in or near cities. There are many industrial jobs, but the Information Revolution has had only a minor impact: Less than 40 percent of Portugal's residents and 9.4 percent of South Africa's are on the Internet. Demographic indicators vary from country to country: In South Africa, the life expectancy is very low (49.5), but in China it is quite high (71). The infant mortality rate is 4.85 deaths per 1,000 births in Portugal and 23.33 in Brazil. Middle countries are not staying in the middle: They are getting either richer or poorer. (And in those countries, the rich are also getting richer and the poor are getting poorer.)

Low-Income Countries. There are about 60 low-income countries, including Jamaica ($4,800 per capita GDP), India ($2,700), Kenya ($1,600), and Somalia ($600). These countries cover 28 percent of the world's land area and are home to 28 percent of its population. Most people live in villages and on farms, as their ancestors have for centuries; only about a third live in cities. They are primarily agricultural, with only a few sustenance industries and virtually no access to the Information Revolution: There are 3 million Internet users among Kenya's 38 million people (7.9 percent) and 98,000 among Somalia's 9.6 million (1 percent). They tend to have low life expectancies (49 in Somalia, 51 in Kenya), high infant mortality rates (56.1 deaths per 1,000 births in Kenya), high

birth rates (37.89 per thousand in Kenya), and low literacy rates (65 percent in India, 38 percent in Somalia). Hunger, disease, and unsafe housing frame their lives (CIA, 2008).

Explaining Global Inequality

For many years, sociologists weren't worried about the causes of global inequality as much as its cure, how to help the underprivileged countries "get ahead." Today, social scientists are less optimistic and are at least equally concerned with what keeps poor countries poor.

Market Theories. These theories stress the wisdom of the capitalist marketplace. They assume that the best possible economic consequences will result if individuals are free to make their own economic decisions, uninhibited by any form of governmental constraint; government direction or intervention, the theorists say, will only block economic development. However, they shouldn't make just any economic decisions: The only avenue to economic growth is unrestricted capitalism (Berger, 1986; Ranis and Mahmood, 1991; Rostow, 1962).

By far the most influential market theory was devised by W. W. Rostow, an economic advisor to President Kennedy. His **modernization theory** focuses on the conditions necessary for a low-income country to develop economically. He argued that a nation's poverty is largely due to the cultural failings of its people. They lack a "work ethic" that stresses thrift and hard work. They would rather consume today than invest in the future. Such failings are reinforced by government policies that set wages, control prices, and generally interfere with the operation of the economy. They can develop economically only if they give up their "backward" way of life and adopt modern Western economic institutions, technologies, and cultural values that emphasize savings and productive investment.

It is somewhat difficult to believe that the people of Somalia, with per capita income of about $500, or Mali, at $900, fail to stash their money in savings accounts and IRAs because they are so eager to consume or that their path to economic solvency lies in abandoning their traditional laziness for good old Yankee elbow grease. Sociologists have been quick to criticize this theory for its ethnocentrism (using the United States as the "model" for what development should look like), its suggestion that people are responsible for their own poverty, and for its curious assurance that wealthy countries act as benevolent Big Brothers to the rest of the world, when in fact they often take advantage of poor countries and block their economic development. Besides, it is not simply a matter of "us" versus "them," rich and poor countries occupying separate social worlds: In a global economy, every nation is affected by the others.

Nevertheless, Rostow's theory is still influential today (Firebaugh, 1996, 1999; Firebaugh and Beck, 1994; Firebaugh and Sandu, 1998). It is sometimes argued that global free trade, achieved by minimizing government restrictions on business, will provide the only route to economic growth. Calls for an end to all restrictions on trade, an end to minimum wage and other labor laws, and an end to environmental restrictions on business are part of this set of policies.

State-Centered Theories. Perhaps the solution is not the market, operating on its own, but active intervention by the government (or by international organizations). State-centered theories argue that appropriate government policies do not interfere with economic development but that governments play a key role in bringing it about. For proof, they point to the newly developed economies of East Asia, which grew in conjunction with, and possibly because of, government intervention (Appelbaum and Henderson, 1992; Cumings, 1998). The governments have acted aggressively, sometimes violently, to ensure economic stability: They outlaw labor unions, jail labor leaders, ban strikes, repress civil rights. They have been heavily involved in social programs such as low-cost housing and universal education. The costs have been enormous: horrible factory conditions, widespread environmental degradation, exploitation of female workers and "guest workers" from impoverished neighboring countries. But the results have been spectacular: Japan enjoyed an economic growth of 10 percent per year through the 1960s, 5 percent through the 1970s, and 4 percent through the 1980s (followed by a slowdown to 1.8 percent). It has a national reserve of $664 billion and has donated $7.9 billion in economic aid to other countries.

Dependency Theory. **Dependency theory** focuses on the unequal relationship between wealthy countries and poor countries, arguing that poverty is the result of exploitation. Wealthy countries (and the multinational corporations based in them) try to acquire an ever-increasing share of the world's wealth by pursuing policies and practices that block the economic growth of the poor countries. Capitalist countries exploit worker countries, just as Karl Marx predicted, thereby ensuring that the rich get richer and the poor get poorer.

The exploitation began with **colonialism,** a political-economic system under which powerful countries established, for their own profit, rule over weaker peoples or countries (Cooper, 2005). The most extensive colonialism occurred between 1500 and 1900, when England, Spain, France, and some other European countries exercised control over the entire world—only Ethiopia, Japan, and Thailand were free of European domination throughout the 400 years. Europeans immigrated in large numbers only to regions with low native populations—the Americas, southern Africa, Australia, and New Zealand—which soon became colonial powers in their own right. Other nations were merely occupied and mined for the raw materials necessary to maintain European wealth—petroleum, copper, iron, sugar, tobacco, and even people (the African slave trade was not finally outlawed until 1830).

After World War II, colonialism gradually ended, today only a few colonial possessions are left, mostly small islands (Bermuda, Guam, Martinique). However, the exploitation did not end. **Multinational corporations,** often with the support of powerful banks and governments of rich countries, established factories in poor countries, using cheap labor and raw materials to minimize their production costs without governmental interference. Today corporations engage in "offshoring," setting up factories in poor countries where the cost of materials and wages is low.

The exercise of power is crucial to maintaining these dependent relationships on the global level. Local businesses cannot compete with the strength of multinational corporations, and former self-subsisting peasants have no other economic options but to work at near-starvation wages at foreign-controlled mines and factories. In 2001, the average Mexican maquiladora worker (employee of a foreign corporation) earned the equivalent of $5.31 per day (with benefits) or $3.56 (without).

Sometimes individual economic pressure is backed up by force. When local leaders question the unequal arrangements, they are suppressed. When people elect an opposition government, it is likely to be overthrown by the country's military—backed by armed forces of the industrialized countries themselves. For example, the CIA played a major role in overthrowing the Marxist governments of Guatemala in 1954 and Chile in 1973 and in undermining the leftist government of Nicaragua in the 1980s.

Dependency theory has been criticized for being simplistic and for putting all blame for global poverty on high-income countries and multinational corporations. Some social scientists, such as Enrique Fernando Cardoso (also a past president of Brazil) argue that, under certain circumstances, poor countries can still develop economically, although only in ways shaped by their reliance on wealthier countries (Cardoso and Faletto, 1978).

World System Theory. **World system theory** draws on dependency theory but focuses on the global economy as an international network dominated by capitalism. It argues that the global economy cannot be understood merely as a collection of countries, some rich and some poor, operating independently of each other except for a dynamic of exploitation and oppression: It must be understood as a single unit. Rich and poor countries are intimately linked.

Immanuel Wallerstein, who founded world system theory and coined the term *world economy* (1974, 1979, 1984, 2004), argued that interconnectedness of the world system began in the 1500s, when Europeans began their economic and political domination of the rest of the world (see Figure 7.9). Because capitalism depends on generating the maximum profits for the minimum of expenditures, the world system continues to benefit rich countries (which acquire the profits) and harm the rest of the world (by minimizing local expenditures and therefore perpetuating poverty).

According to Wallerstein, the world system is composed of four interrelated elements: (1) a global market of goods and labor; (2) the division of the population into different economic classes, based loosely on the Marxian division of owners and workers; (3) an international system of formal and informal political relations among the most powerful countries, who compete or cooperate with each other to shape the world economy; and (4) the division of countries into three broad economic zones—core, periphery, and semiperiphery.

The *core countries* include Western Europe and places where Western Europeans immigrated in large numbers: the United States, Canada, Australia, New Zealand, and South Africa, plus Japan, the only non-European country to become a colonial power in its own right. These are the most advanced industrial countries, and they take the lion's share of profits in the world economic system. Goods, services, and people tend to flow *into* the core.

The *periphery* is the opposite zone, corresponding roughly with the Third World, and includes countries that were under Western European domination but did not receive many permanent settlers: sub-Saharan Africa (other than South Africa), India and Pakistan, parts of Latin America, most of East and Southeast Asia, and Oceania. These countries are low income, largely agricultural, and often manipulated by core countries for their economic advantage. Goods, services, and people tend to flow *away from* the periphery.

Did You Know?

Figure 7.9 Wallerstein's World System Theory Model

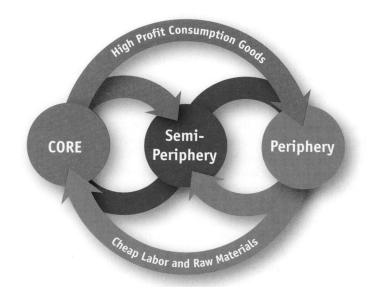

High Profit Consumption Goods

CORE   Semi-Periphery   Periphery

Cheap Labor and Raw Materials

(*Source:* From *The Modern World System: Capitalist Agriculture and the Origins of the European World Economy in the Sixteenth Century* by Immanuel Maurice Wallerstein. Copyright © 1974 Academic Press in 1974. Reproduced by permission.

Globalization has increased the economic, political, and social interconnectedness of the world. It has also increased some staggering inequalities between the world's rich and its poor.

Finally, the *semiperiphery* is an intermediate zone between the core and the periphery. This includes the former Soviet Union, Eastern Europe, countries that were under Western European domination only briefly (the Middle East, parts of East Asia), or countries that received a substantial number of immigrants but not as many as the core (parts of Latin America). These are semi-industrialized, middle-income countries that often form their own local core–periphery systems. For example, goods and services flow *into* Russia from its own periphery states in Eastern Europe, the Baltic, and Central Asia, but they also flow *from* Russia into Western Europe and the United States. The semiperiphery functions much as the middle class does in any country: It both is a buffer zone between rich and poor and exhibits elements of both rich and poor, depending on the position of the other country it is dealing with.

World system theory emphasizes **global commodity chains**—worldwide networks of labor and production processes, consisting of all pivotal production activities, that form a tightly interlocked "chain" from raw materials to finished product to retail outlet to consumer (Gereffi and Korzeniewicz, 1993; Hopkins and Wallerstein, 1996). The most profitable activities in the commodity chain (engineering, design, advertising) are likely to be done in core countries, while the least profitable activities (mining or growing the raw materials, factory production) are likely to be done in peripheral countries. Some low-profit factories (or "sweat-shops") are appearing in core countries, often underground to avoid minimum wage laws; but, paradoxically, they tend to employ mostly immigrants from peripheral countries, who are willing to settle for the poor pay (still better than they would get at home), minimal or nonexistent benefits, and terrible working conditions.

The world system theory has been criticized for depicting the process as only one way, with goods and services flowing from periphery to

Sociology and Our World

Prostitution and the World System

In the world system, it is not only goods and services that flow from periphery to core. People do, too, in the form of slaves, foreign workers, and prostitutes (or sex workers). Interviews with sex workers in dozens of countries around the world reveal that in Japan (core), they tend to come from Korea (semiperiphery) or the Philippines (periphery). In Thailand (semiperiphery), they tend to come from Vietnam or Burma (periphery). In France (core), they tend to come from Turkey or North Africa (semiperiphery). In Germany, they tend to come from Bosnia, Slovenia, or the Czech Republic (semiperiphery). However, in the Czech Republic, they tend to come from Poland, Slovakia, and Hungary (semiperiphery).

Why does a country in the semiperiphery draw sex workers from the semiperiphery? Perhaps the answer lies in relative wealth: The average GDP per capita in the Czech Republic is $23,194, compared to $18,679 in Hungary and $15,800 in Poland. Or perhaps it lies in the mechanics of global sex tourism, in which people (mostly men) from the core take vacations in periphery or semiperiphery states with the intention of having sex, either with prostitutes or with impoverished local "friends" willing to spend the night in exchange for dinner or gifts. Prostitution in the Czech Republic really means Prague, about two hours by train from Dresden and four hours from Munich, a perfect distance for German businessmen to get away for a weekend sex holiday (Kempadoo, Saghera, and Pattanaik, 2005).

core. However, some goods and services flow from core to periphery, and of course states within a zone trade with each other. There are innumerable currents, eddies, undertows, and whirlpools in the economic sea.

Global Mobility

Just as people can move up and down the socioeconomic ladder from generation to generation, and even within a single generation, rich countries can become poor, and poor countries can become rich. Great Britain, the richest country in the world a century ago, today ranks number 30 in per capita GDP (not exactly poor, but moving toward middle income). The United Arab Emirates, impoverished peripheral sheikdoms before the discovery of oil, now rank higher than Canada, Australia, Denmark, Belgium, Germany, and Spain (all core). A generation ago, the Soviet Union was an economic and political superpower. But the collapse of communism and the move to a capitalist economy had a devastating impact. In 2008, 25 percent of the population of Russia lived below the poverty level, and its per capita GDP ranked below its former satellite states, Poland, Slovakia, Slovenia, and the Czech Republic, and is tied with Botswana. Times change, economies change, the world system changes.

Recently there has been a trend of newly industrializing economies (NIEs), countries that move from poor to rich in a matter of a few years. Japan was the first, beginning in the 1950s, and now most of East Asia and Southeast Asia have moved up to middle income and Hong Kong, Japan, South Korea, Singapore, and Taiwan have moved up to high income (Brohman, 1996). Several of these have risen not because of valuable raw materials but because these former colonial trading centers easily adapted to become large-scale manufacturing and global financial centers.

But Japan was never a European colony and in fact had its own colonial empire before World War II. None of these countries received significant European economic assistance until the Cold War, when the world was taking up sides in the apocalyptic conflict between the United States and the Soviet Union. Japan, South Korea, and Taiwan, just a few miles from the Communists, could function as political (and symbolic) bulkheads of democracy, so the United States and its allies poured money and military aid into them. Later, when increasingly efficient global transportation and communication systems made importing manufactured items from long distances economically viable, they began aggressively exporting locally produced merchandise, until "made in Japan" and "made in Korea" became clichés for cheap, mass-produced articles. Once, when I was in Paris, I picked up a cheap ceramic gargoyle in one of the tourist kiosks that line the Left Bank. It wasn't until I got back to my hotel that I checked the bottom and saw the words—in English: "Made in Japan."

Class Identity and Inequality in the Twenty-First Century

Today, class continues to have a remarkable impact on our lives—from the type of education or health care you receive to the type of job you'll have, whom you'll marry, and even how long you'll live and how many children you'll have. The decline in social mobility in the United States makes America increasingly a nation of rich and poor, as in every country there are rich people and poor people, as well as rich countries and poor countries. The gap grows daily. As a result, "being born in the elite in the U.S. gives you a constellation of privileges that very few people in the world have ever experienced," notes David Levine, an economist who researches social mobility and class in America. But, comparatively, "being poor in the U.S. gives you disadvantages unlike anything in Western Europe and Japan and Canada" (cited in Scott and Leonhardt, 2005).

Just as class increases in importance and class inequality increases in its impact on our everyday lives and our society, so too do Americans continue to disavow its importance. We may be becoming a nation of rich and poor, but we continue to assert that we're all middle class, and that class has little bearing on our lives. Perhaps that Oxford professor was onto something.

Chapter Review

1. What Is Social Stratification?

Some societies have more obvious class structures, while in others **social stratification** is less apparent, or, as in the United States, hidden by ideology or beliefs. Nations are globally stratified. Social class is the single best predictor of the life you will have, as resources, opportunities, and prestige are differentially distributed in ways that are unquestioned or justified. **Social mobility** is rare. Because social stratification pervades society, sociologists have questioned why it exists and found different answers. Durkheim found that social stratification creates interdependence in complex societies, while Marx's analysis highlighted how social stratification serves the powerful and wealthy at the expense of those at the bottom of the hierarchy. Stratification does provide incentive for achievement in a **meritocracy;** but, because advancement is rare, stratification mainly justifies the status quo. Historically there have been different social stratification arrangements, including **caste systems, feudalism,** and, more recently, in industrialized societies, **class.** There is some social mobility within a **class system.**

social stratification Taken from the geological term for layers of rock, or "strata," the ranking of people into defined layers. Social stratification exists in all societies and is based on things like wealth, race, and gender. (p. 186)

meritocracy Social system in which the greater the functional importance of the job, the more rewards it brings in salary, perks, power, and prestige. (p. 186)

caste system A fixed and permanent stratification system to which one is assigned at birth. (p. 187)

feudalism A fixed and permanent social structure based on mutual obligation, in which peasants worked the estates belonging to a small group of feudal lords, who fed and protected them. A peasant's only avenue to social advancement was to enter a convent or monastery. (p. 187)

class A group of people sharing the same social position in society. Class is based on income, power, and prestige. (p. 187)

social mobility The movement from one class to another, it can occur in two forms: intergenerational—that is, your parents are working class, but you became lower, or your parents are middle class, but you became upper-class; and intragenerational—that is, you move from working to lower, or from middle to upper, all within your lifetime. (p. 188)

class system System of stratification in which people are ranked according to their economic position. (p. 188)

2. Social Class

Social stratification and class are classic sociological concerns. The kind of life you will have, your **life chances,** is determined by social class, which is pervasive. Marx analyzed society in terms of production, identifying the inequity and conflict between the **bourgeoisie** and **proletariat.** For Weber, stratification was not just economic but composed of dimensions that even today we can observe tend to covary but don't always go together; for example, **prestige, status, occupational prestige,** and **power.** Sociologists today use **socioeconomic status (SES)** when studying social stratification, which is multidimensional. In the United States, there

are at least six socioeconomic statuses, from the upper upper class to the **underclass,** yet we all believe we are middle class, even though the United States has the widest gap between the haves and have-nots of all industrialized nations. Race is a predictor of class here, and globally, as well. Within any society, members of different classes share different cultural experiences, including lifestyles, values, and norms.

bourgeoisie Popularized by Karl Marx, term for the upper-class capitalists who owned the means of production. In Marx's time, they owned factories instead of farms. Today the term is also used to refer to upper-class managers who wield a lot of power. (p. 189)

proletariat Popularized by Karl Marx, the term for the lower classes who were forced to become wage laborers or go hungry. Today, the term is often used to refer to the working class. (p. 189)

prestige The amount of honor, respect or deference accorded to social roles or statuses. (p. 190)

status One's socially defined position in a group; it is often characterized by certain expectations and rights. (p. 190)

occupational prestige The degree of status accorded to an occupation. (p. 190)

power The ability to extract compliance despite resistance or the ability to get others to do what you want them to do, regardless of their own desires. (p. 190)

socioeconomic status (SES) Your social connections, your taste in art, your ascribed and attained statuses, and more. Because there are so many components, sociologists today tend to prefer the concept of socioeconomic status to that of social class, to emphasize that people are ranked through the intermingling of many factors, economic, social, political, cultural, and community. (p. 191)

life chances A person's abilities to have access to material goods (food and shelter) and social resources (health care, education) that together control the quality of life. (p. 191)

underclass About 4 percent of the U.S. population, this group has no income, no connection to the job market, little education, inadequate nutrition, and substandard housing or none at all. They have no possibility of social mobility and little chance of achieving the quality of life that most people would consider minimally acceptable. (p. 194)

3. Poverty: Local, National, and Global

Poverty, an aspect of stratification, can be defined as **absolute poverty** or **relative poverty.** The **poverty line** is another measure, although a conservative measure and uncorrected for local cost of living and other expenses. Poverty is not equally distributed. There is **feminization of poverty;** children are more likely to be poor; and minorities are also overrepresented. The **culture of poverty** view is popular, but it is not lack of initiative, hard work, or despondency that leads to poverty; rather, the poor face insurmountable challenges in overcoming the structural forces that constrain opportunity. Modern methods of combating poverty globally focus on local assistance and developing economic independence. Of all industrialized countries, the United States offers far less in the way of basic assistance and so has the highest level of poverty.

absolute poverty A global problem that afflicts half the world's population, the term for people who are so poor they do not have the ability to sustain their lives and lack the most basic necessities like food and shelter. (p. 198)

relative poverty A measure of the extent to which a household's financial resources fall below an average income threshold for that economy. (p. 198)

poverty line Estimated minimum income required to pay for food, shelter, and clothing. Anyone falling below this income is categorized as poor. (p. 198)

feminization of poverty A worldwide phenomenon that also afflicts U.S. women, this term describes women's over-representation among the world's poor and tendency to be in worse economic straits than men in any given nation or population. (p. 201)

culture of poverty Oscar Lewis's theory that poverty is not a result of individual inadequacies but larger social and cultural factors. Poor children are socialized into believing that they have nothing to strive for, that there is no point in working to improve their conditions. As adults, they are resigned to a life of poverty, and they socialize their children the same way. Therefore poverty is transmitted from one generation to another. (p. 202)

4. Social Mobility

America believes in social mobility, but very little change in social class actually occurs here, although there have been periods of **structural mobility. Intergenerational mobility** is rare; parent income is a good predictor of their children's income. Mobility typically takes place within, not across, classes, and varies by group, with upward mobility more likely to occur for White males, while minorities and middle-class women are more likely to experience downward mobility.

structural mobility a general upward trend of the entire society. Structural mobility means that the entire society got wealthier, as occurred in post-World War II America. (p. 205)

intergenerational mobility Change in social class position, upward or downward, that takes place between generations. Your chances of getting head or falling behind the social class position of your parents is largely influenced by family income; those at the top tend to stay at the top or move even higher; those at the bottom tend to stay at the bottom or move even lower. (p. 205)

intragenerational mobility Change in social class position between members of the same generation, such as between sons and daughters or between Blacks and Whites of the same age group. (p. 206)

5. Global Inequality

The widening gap between rich and poor is happening globally, as well. Studies of **global inequality** show three socioeconomic categories into which countries fall, by income per capita. Typically countries within each category share characteristics, including literacy, infant mortality, birthrate, and whether they are industrialized or primarily agricultural. Poor countries typically stay poor, and a number of theories have sought to explain this phenomenon, including the influential but antiquated **modernization theory. Dependency theory** considers historical exploitation through **colonialism** as a cause of inequal-

ity among nations, which continued into the modern day with **multinational corporations** exploiting poorer countries for gain in wealthier nations. **World system theory** looks at a nation's relations to production in the **global commodity chain** for understanding a country's relative wealth. Today, economies change, and so does global mobility, with some countries gaining while others suffer downward mobility.

global inequality Systematic differences in wealth and power among countries, often involving exploitation of the less powerful by the more powerful countries. (p. 208)

modernization theory W. W. Rostow's theory focusing on the conditions necessary for a low-income country to develop economically. Arguing that a nation's poverty is largely due to the cultural failings of its people, Rostrow believed poor countries could develop economically only if they give up their "backward" way of life and adopt modern Western economic institutions, technologies, and cultural values that emphasize savings and productive investment. (p. 210)

dependency theory Theory of poverty that focuses on the unequal relationship between wealthy countries and poor countries, arguing that poverty is caused by policies and practices by the rich that block economic growth of poor countries and exploit workers. (p. 211)

colonialism A political-economic system under which powerful countries establish, for their own profit, rule over weaker peoples or countries and exploit them for natural resources and cheap labor. (p. 211)

multinational corporations Large, international companies that manage production and/or deliver services in more than one country at once. Multinational corporations have a powerful influence in the local economies of the countries in which they operate, and in the global economy. (p. 211)

world system theory Immanuel Wallerstein's theory that the interconnectedness of the world system began in the 1500s, when Europeans began their economic and political domination of the rest of the world. Because capitalism depends on generating the maximum profits for the minimum of expenditures, the world system continues to benefit rich countries (which acquire the profits) and harm the rest of the world (by minimizing local expenditures and therefore perpetuating poverty). (p. 212)

global commodity chain Worldwide network of labor and production processes, consisting of all pivotal production activities that form a tightly interlocked "chain" from raw materials to finished product to retail outlet to consumer. The most profitable activities in the commodity chain (engineering, design, advertising) are likely to be done in core countries, while the least profitable activities (mining or growing the raw materials, factory production) are likely to be done in peripheral countries. (p. 213)

6. Class Identity and Inequality in the Twenty-First Century

Although social mobility has declined in the United States as the gap between the rich and poor continues to widen, we continue to believe that we are all middle class, free from the impact of a class system. Class has a pervasive impact on our lives, whether we are at the top, benefiting more than almost everyone in the world, or at the bottom, where our poorest citizens suffer more than those of any other industrial nation.

Self-Test: Check Your Understanding

1. According to the text, which of the following is true of the United States?
   a. There is no social mobility, as no one changes from the social class into which he or she was born.
   b. There is very little social mobility; relatively few people change social class.
   c. There is a great deal of social mobility.
   d. The United States does not have social classes—everyone is equal.

2. Which of the following systems of stratification is found in the United States?
   a. Caste system
   b. Feudalism
   c. Class system
   d. There is no social stratification in the United States, as everyone is a member of the middle class.

3. Identify Durkheim's view of social stratification and class.
   a. It results from ownership of means of production, which benefits the owners, while those who work for the owners are exploited.
   b. There are many dimensions to social stratification, including power and status, and you can be high on some and low on others.
   c. Stratification integrates society, creating interdependence.
   d. Stratification serves society by rewarding those who make the greatest contribution.

4. Identify Marx's view of social stratification and class.
   a. It results from ownership of means of production, which benefits the owners, while those who work for the owners are exploited.
   b. There are many dimensions to social stratification, including power and status, and you can be high on some and low on others.

   c. Stratification integrates society, creating interdependence.
   d. Stratification serves society by rewarding those who make the greatest contribution.

5. How many social classes have been identified in the United States today, according to the text?
   a. There is only one class—the middle class.
   b. There are no social classes in the United States, as everyone is equal in this country.
   c. Three
   d. Six or more

6. Of the following, which was identified as being a problem with using the poverty line as an indicator of poverty?
   a. It does not take into account expenses other than food, housing, and shelter, such as medical expenses, child care, and transportation.
   b. It is not corrected for location, and some places have a significantly higher cost of living.
   c. The amount is much too low because the formula counts each of the categories as the same, when some cost much more than others.
   d. All of these are problems with the use of the poverty line as an indicator of poverty identified in the text.

7. Which of the following is not included in the poverty line calculation?
   a. Medical costs
   b. Food
   c. Housing
   d. Clothing

8. Members of which of the following groups are most likely to be poor?
   a. Racial minorities
   b. Ethnic minorities
   c. People living in rural areas
   d. Children

Self-Test Answers: 1. b, 2. c, 3. c, 4. a, 5. d, 6. d, 7. a, 8. d

Integrate and Explore: Points to Consider

1. What characteristics are shared by wealthy nations? What characteristics are shared by poor nations? Is global stratification stable or undergoing changes? What characteristics do the poor typically share globally? What characteristics do the wealthy typically share?

2. How wealthy are Americans, compared with citizens of other nations? Are people in the United States more or less well off than citizens of similar industrialized nations? Are poor Americans better off than the poor in other industrialized nations? Are poor Americans better off than the poor in agricultural nations?

succeed with PEARSON mysoclab

Self-scoring practice tests, flashcards for learning key terms, streaming audio of the entire text, and multimedia, including:

Watch—*United Nations World Inequality Report*
Map—Social Explorer, *Education Extremes and Income Levels*
MySocLibrary—Herbert Gans, *Positive Functions of Underserving Poor*
MySocLibrary—Jeffrey Reiman, *. . . and the Poor Get Prison*

Deutscher. Araber. Chinese. Eskimo.

Indianer (Patagonier) Australier. Malaye. Neger.

8

Race and Ethnicity

In his inaugural address, Barack Obama, the nation's 44th president, observed the symbolic milestone his election represented, that "a man whose father less than 60 years ago might not have been served at a local restaurant can now stand before you . . ." From segregated South to the Oval Office in the course of a generation is a dramatic shift. But has the issue of race disappeared? Or does race remain one of the organizing poles around which social life revolves?

Obama's election made me recall my grade school social studies textbook. Race, I learned there, was fixed, permanent, and primordial. There were only three races: "Negroid, Mongoloid, and Caucasoid." Nobody could

be a member of any other race, and nobody could belong to more than one race.

To me, the most interesting part of the book chapter was the illustrations. There were three: a black guy in a loincloth, holding a spear, standing in front of a grass hut; an Asian guy in a silk kimono, holding some sort of scroll, standing in front of a pagoda; and a White guy in a business suit, holding a briefcase, standing in front of a skyscraper. All were men. We were supposed to classify the three races, from the least to the most civilized, technologically sophisticated, inventive, and intelligent. It doesn't take a genius to figure out which of the three "races" the illustrator belonged to.

How do sociologists think about race? Sociologists tend not to see fixed, immutable biologically based characteristics but the ways in which we have come to see those characteristics as timeless and universal. Race is less fixed than fluid, less eternal and more historical. In fact, the concept of race is relatively recent, an invention of Europeans in the eighteenth century. Rather than immutable, it is among the part of our identity that is in greatest flux at the present, as individuals are increasingly biracial or even multiracial. With race, as with other features of social life, believing is seeing: When we believe that there are only a certain number of races, then we will "see" those, and only those, races.

To a sociologist, race is more than a system of classification, a system that categorizes people. Race is also one of the bases on which

"Race is more than a system . . . that categorizes people [according to physical characteristics]. . . . [It] is a foundation of identity and a basis for social inequality."

our society perceives, rewards, and punishes people. Being from different races is often a primary marker of structured social inequality and a justification for discrimination. Race is among the foremost predictors of your experience in society. Along with class, gender, age, and ethnicity, race is a foundation of identity and a basis for social inequality—at the individual level, in our society, and across the globe.

The Sociology of Race and Ethnicity

Sociologists see race and ethnicity as two of the ways that many societies organize the allocation of goods and resources. Some people are set apart for unequal treatment, receiving more or less political power, economic resources, and social prestige. Assumed physical or cultural characteristics called "race" or "ethnicity" are arbitrary markers that serve to legitimate social inequality.

Just what are race and ethnicity? Although the terms are sometimes used interchangeably, they are based on two different assumptions. **Race** depends on the assumption of biological distinctions. You can be Black or White and live in any country in the world, have any religion, and speak any language. All that matters is your skin color and whatever other physical trait counts. However, **ethnicity** defines a cultural group, distinct not by biology but by cultural practices. You can belong to any race and have a Swedish ethnicity—if you speak Swedish at home, attend the Swedish Lutheran Church, eat lutefisk (cod soaked in lye and served with bacon fat), and celebrate St. Lucia's Day on December 13 by walking with lit candles on your head, as many young girls still do in Sweden.

Or if you do none of those things at all. Few Swedish American students at undergraduate colleges today eat lutefisk or wear crowns of candles! There are likely few, if any, cultural differences between Swedish students and everyone else on campus. In fact, you'd probably never know they are Swedish, except for last names like "Swenson" and a few Swedish flags on dorm room walls. Their Swedish ethnicity resided entirely in how their ancestors might have lived.

Neither race nor ethnicity has any basis in biological or genetic fact. In 2000, Craig Venter, one of the lead scientists of the Human Genome Project, which has mapped the human genetic code, concluded that "the concept of race has no genetic or scientific basis." Race is a social concept, not a scientific one.

Yet race and ethnicity are the single most predictive factors in determining a person's eventual social position. Race and ethnicity can be used to predict how you vote, whom you will marry, and what sort of job you will have when you graduate from college. Race and ethnicity can predict your attitudes on birth control, your musical tastes, and whether or not you go to church. They can even be used to predict what church you go to! In spite of repeated, extensive attempts at racial integration, Americans tend to live in segregated neighborhoods, go to segregated churches, make friends almost entirely within their own race or ethnic group, and date almost entirely within their own race or ethnic

Sociology and Our World

Why Do All the Black Kids Sit Together in the Cafeteria?

Psychologist Beverly Daniel Tatum (1997) noticed Black and White kids separating in classes, in clubs, and in tables in the cafeteria, even when there seemed to be little bad feeling between the groups, even when the teachers encouraged them to "not notice" race at all. In *Why Are All the Black Kids Sitting Together in the Cafeteria?* she argues that the reason that the Black kids are all sitting together is because . . . the White kids are all sitting together in the cafeteria! We tend to notice when the minority does something that expresses community or solidarity, but we do not tend to notice that it is often a response to what the majority is doing. Tatum suggests that this separation is not always a bad thing. White privilege so pervades our society that the Black kids tend to grow up with internalized oppression, a negatively stereotyped "ethnic self." Even if few of the White people around are actively trying to be racist, being the "only one" invariably leads to feelings of isolation and lower self-worth. Minorities must find ways to be in the majority, to be the "norm" some of the time, to establish and affirm a positive identity. So they seek each other out in the classroom and the cafeteria, in response to their exclusion from the "White kids' tables."

group. (There's an old joke among Protestant clergy that the most segregated time in American history is 10 a.m. every Sunday.)

Students often say they are amazed at how race and ethnicity are experienced in class. Students may sit anywhere they wish, but by the third day of the semester the African American, White, and Hispanic groups are as strictly segregated as if they had been assigned that way. If forced to integrate, they will separate again as soon as they are divided into small discussion groups. Why?

How can a category be nothing and so obviously something, at the same time?

Defining Race

To this day, we still do not have a good definition of race. Some textbooks say, "a set of obvious physical traits singled out by members of a community or society as socially significant." Others say "a set of social relationships that allows attributes or competencies to be assigned on the basis of biologically grounded features." But what's "obvious," and what features are "biologically grounded"? Head shape? Eye color? Earwax? There are only two major types of earwax; and, according to the experts who study such things, about 90 percent of Asians and Native Americans but less than 20 percent of other racial groups have the type known as *gray-grainy*. No other "biologically grounded feature" appears nearly as often, although no one has ever suggested that earwax is an indicator of cultural superiority!

What about skin color? In the United States we assign people to "White," "Black," and "yellow" categories, but in Central and South America, there are a dozen or more shades (in Brazil, over 40), and we can perceive thousands of color gradients. Even within a single individual, skin color can change daily, darkening or lightening due to such factors as diet, exposure to the sun, or age. Trying to pinpoint a race based on skin color is absurd.

This is why sociologists have come to understand that race as a biological distinction has no basis in any empirical fact. To sociologists, race is more of a social construction.

Most cultures divide people into good and bad types on the basis of their cultural traits, usually "us," the real people, against "them," the cannibals (who eat the wrong food), barbarians (who speak the wrong language), or infidels (who worship the wrong god). But physical appearance rarely enters the equation. Historically, the word *race* meant the same thing as *culture:* The French "race" lived in France and spoke French, and the Russian "race" lived in Russia and spoke Russian.

Not until the eighteenth century did physical attributes become determining factors in "race." In the United States, debates about the morality of "Negro slavery" indicated a concern for skin color that was more important than the very different cultures from which those Negro slaves came. By the nineteenth century, "race science" tried to give the real people/barbarian division a scientific-sounding gloss arguing that some "races" of people were more highly evolved than others, just as mammals are more highly evolved than reptiles and fish. And, just as mammals are physiologically different from reptiles and fish, the more highly evolved races differed from the less highly evolved, not only culturally, but physiologically.

It turns out that the race scientists got it wrong. People are actually far more physiologically similar than different to suggest we are from different races. Genetic makeup, blood type, facial type, skin color, and every other physical attribute vary more within the groups we call races than between them. You can get distinct races only if a group is isolated for many generations, which prevents any forms of crossbreeding. No human group has ever been isolated long enough (the Australian aboriginals

Differences within racial categories are often greater than differences between them—even among beauty queens.

come closest, cut off from the mainland of Asia for 40,000 years, but they're still 100,000 or more years short). Sociologically, then, race isn't "real"—that is, there are no distinct races that are pure and clearly demarcated from others. And there haven't been such things in millennia. However, it is a sociological maxim (first offered by sociologists W. I. Thomas and D. S. Thomas in 1928) that "things that are perceived as real are real in their consequences." Most people believe there are distinct races, with distinct characteristics, and therefore social life is often arranged as if there were (see Figure 8.1). It's less that we believe it when we see it and more that we see it when we believe it.

Sociologists see race and ethnicity as two of the ways that many societies organize the allocation of goods and resources. Some people are set apart for unequal treatment, receiving more or less political power, economic resources, and social prestige. Assumed physical or cultural characteristics called "race" or "ethnicity" are arbitrary markers that serve to legitimate social inequality.

Race and ethnicity are not all about inequality. They also give us a profound sense of identity. If you are African American, you have access to an enormous infrastructure of political, social, and economic organizations, churches, colleges, fine arts, and mass media that you might not want to give up even if your race became irrelevant. People lacking recognizable ethnic heritages often envy those whose grandparents told stories about the old country, or who can plan a visit overseas to connect with their roots, or who can point to a famous novel and say "it's about us." The story of being a racial or ethnic minority in America is as often a story of pride as it is of prejudice.

Biraciality and Multiraciality

There is no such thing as a "pure" race. Every human group has mixed ancestry, even President Obama, who is literally "African American" (his father was a Black African, from Kenya, and his mother was a White American, from Kansas). An estimated 30 to 70 percent of North American Blacks have some White European ancestors (Herskovits, 1930; Roberts, 1975), and 30 to 50 percent of North American Whites have some Native American ancestors (see Figure 8.2). Even so, interracial romantic relationships have often been considered deviant and forbidden. Such relationships were labeled *miscegenation* and punishable by prison sentences in all but nine states until 1967 (Sollors, 2000). Lawmakers argued that they were against nature and against God's law, that they were an insult to the institution of marriage and a threat to the social fabric. Children of mixed-race unions were called half-breeds or, to be more precise, mulattos (Black–White) or mestizos (White–Indian) and considered morally and intellectually inferior to members of both races.

The legal restrictions against intermarriage have been gone for nearly 40 years, and popular support has shifted considerably: In 1958, 96 percent of Whites disapproved of Black–White intermarriage, but today, upwards of 80 percent *approve* (*Newsweek,* 2009). (Although they have increased in recent years, intermarriage and interracial romantic relationships are still stigmatized, and certainly multiracial couples and families are much more common in some places than in others (see Figure 8.3). It is interesting that just as magazine articles and dire warnings were given to White Americans at the turn of the last century about "race suicide," now some popular magazine articles and films suggest that a Black person who dates or marries a White person is betraying his or her race. On MTV's *The Real World: Philadelphia,* Karamo, who is Black, is outraged when a White guy and a Black girl start dating; he even threatens, "jokingly," to cut the White guy's throat. But then he dates

Figure 8.1 Extreme States: The Whitest and the Blackest

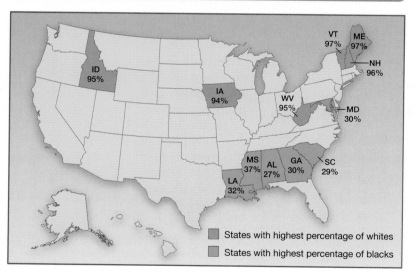

(*Source:* U.S. Census Bureau, *Statistical Abstract 2009,* Table 18. Available at www.census.gov/compendia/statab/tables/09s0018.xls.)

a Latino with impunity, perhaps thinking that it is acceptable because they are gay and will not produce children.

In the 2006 census, there were at least 7 million of those children: Of the population, 2.1 percent were identified as biracial and multiracial (U.S. Census Bureau, 2006a). Half were under the age of 18, so it is evident that the population will grow. Perhaps *biracial* will become a new ethnicity. In the past, people of mixed races usually just "picked one."

Minority Groups and "Majority" Groups

A racial or ethnic minority group is not defined strictly by being a numerical minority. In fact, there are more "minorities" in the United States than the "majority" population. Blacks constitute 71 percent of the population of Allendale County, South Carolina, and 0.3 percent of the population of Blaine County, Montana, but no one would say they are a minority group in only one of those places. And not all groups that are few in numbers are necessarily minorities. There are only 2.8 million people of Swedish ethnicity in the United States, a relatively small number, but according to the most recent Census, 27 percent have graduated from college, 33 percent are in managerial/professional jobs, and their median household income is $42,500, all higher than the national average. Clearly, they are not subjected to significant amounts of discrimination.

Figure 8.2 Race Relations: Do Any of the Following Apply to You?

THOSE RESPONDING 'YES'	1995	TODAY	PERCENTAGE INCREASE
You are of mixed race	16%	16%	0%
Have a child of mixed race	8	11	3
Know a person of mixed race	74	82	8
Know an interracial couple	58	79	21
Speak a foreign language	25	27	1

*2001

(*Source:* The People Speak: "Yes, He Can," *Newsweek*, [January 26, 2009].)

For a race or ethnic group to be classified as a **minority group,** it needs to have four characteristics:

1. *Differential power.* There must be significant differences in access to economic, social, and political resources. Group members may hold fewer professional jobs and have a higher poverty rate, a lower household income, greater incidence of disease, or a lower life expectancy, all factors that point to lifelong patterns of discrimination and social inequality.

2. *Identifiability.* Minority group members share (or are assumed to share) physical or cultural traits that distinguish them from the dominant group.

3. *Ascribed status.* Membership is something you are born with. Membership is not voluntary. You are born into it, and you

Figure 8.3 Multiracial Coupling

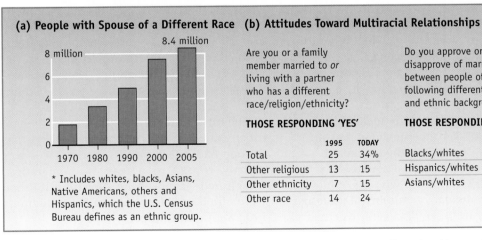

(a) People with Spouse of a Different Race

8.4 million

* Includes whites, blacks, Asians, Native Americans, others and Hispanics, which the U.S. Census Bureau defines as an ethnic group.

(b) Attitudes Toward Multiracial Relationships

Are you or a family member married to *or* living with a partner who has a different race/religion/ethnicity?

THOSE RESPONDING 'YES'

	1995	TODAY
Total	25	34%
Other religious	13	15
Other ethnicity	7	15
Other race	14	24

Do you approve or disapprove of marriages between people of the following different racial and ethnic backgrounds?

THOSE RESPONDING 'APPROVE'

	1997	TODAY
Blacks/whites	63	80%
Hispanics/whites	72	83
Asians/whites	70	84

(*Sources:* [a] Todd Lewan, Multiracial Nation," Associated Press, Sunday, June 15, 2008. Reproduced by permission of the YGS Group; [b] The People Speak: "Yes, He Can" *Newsweek*, [January 26, 2009]. Reproduced by permission.)

cannot change it. Affiliation in many ethnic groups is a matter of choice—you can decide how much of your French heritage, if any, you want to embrace—but you can't wake up one morning and decide to be Japanese.

4. *Solidarity and group awareness.* There must be awareness of membership in a definable category of people, so that there are clearly defined "us" and "them." The minority becomes an **in-group** (Sumner, [1906] 2002), and its members tend to distrust or dislike members of the dominant **out-group.** When a group is the object of long-term prejudice and discrimination, feelings of "us versus them" can become intense.

Minority groups and **majority groups** are often constructed in the United States not so much through race as through skin color: dark people versus light people, people "of color" versus people who are "White." In an interesting linguistic experiment called the Implicit Association Test, students were given word association tests, and all of them, regardless of their own race, tended to associate "White" with purity, goodness, and happiness, and "Black" with corruption, evil, and sadness (Greenwald, McGhee, and Schwartz, 1998; Hofmann et al., 2005).

Within racial groups, people who are lighter are privileged over people who are darker (Greenwald and Farnham, 2000; Greenwald, McGhee, and Schwartz, 1998). When the African American sports legend O. J. Simpson was arrested on suspicion of murdering his estranged wife and her companion, he appeared on the cover of *Time* magazine. The photograph was manipulated to make him look considerably darker than he did in real life.

Whiteness becomes the standard, the "norm," like being male and heterosexual. It is invisible, at least to those who are White (or male or heterosexual). A number of years ago, in a seminar, we were discussing whether all women were, by definition, "sisters," in spite of race and ethnicity, because they all had essentially the same life experiences and because

all women faced a common oppression by men. A White woman asserted that simply being women created bonds that transcended racial differences. A Black woman disagreed.

"When you wake up in the morning and look in a mirror, what do you see?" she asked the White woman.

"I see a woman," replied the White woman.

"That's precisely the problem," responded the Black woman. "I see a *Black* woman."

The White woman saw only *woman,* not *White,* because she enjoyed privilege—such as never having to think about the implications of being White or the impact race had on her everyday interactions. "Whiteness" was invisible to her, just as "maleness" is invisible to men, and "heterosexuality" invisible to heterosexuals. The Black woman saw race because race was how she was *not* privileged; it was there in every interaction every day, in every glimpse in the mirror (Kimmel, 1996). Being the "majority" group is not simply numerical: It is social. In the United States, the majority group is the dominant group.

How We Got White People. The privilege of Whiteness does not depend on your skin color. It has a history and is the result of social positioning. During the nineteenth century, ethnologists, anthropologists, and sociologists traveled around the world, dividing people into races, ordering them from the most to least intelligent, moral, interesting, and evolved. They found hundreds of races and divided them into ten broad categories.

Teutonic people (from England, Germany, and Scandinavia) were defined as White, but people from other parts of Europe were not. The U.S. Census separated them on forms. Magazine illustrations, popular songs, and sociology textbooks characterized these "others" as savage, lazy, sexually promiscuous, born criminals, and responsible for the "social disintegration" of the slums. They were denied jobs and places to live. In the South, many were lynched along with Blacks.

The furor of racial classification in the late nineteenth century and the "discovery" that Europe had inferior and superior races was directly related to a fear of immigration. Established groups from Northern Europe were afraid of being overrun by immigrants from Southern Europe.

Before 1880, most European immigrants were German, French, English, or Scots-Irish. They were mostly middle class and Protestant,

Multiracial Stars

Bob Marley, one of the greatest voices for pan-African liberation, was biracial. (His father was a White Englishman and his mother was a Black Jamaican.) So is Sade (Black Nigerian father and White English mother), Lisa Bonet (Black father and Jewish mother), Alicia Keys (Black father and White mother), Vin Diesel (Italian American and African American), Lenny Kravitz (Black mother and White father), Derek Jeter (Black father and White mother), and Mariah Carey (White mother and Black Venezuelan father), the best-selling female vocalist ever.

Did You Know?

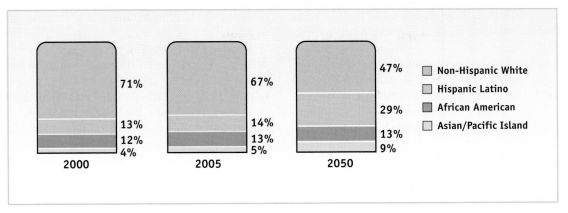

Figure 8.4 U.S. Population Profile, 2000, 2005, 2050

Non-Hispanic White
Hispanic Latino
African American
Asian/Pacific Island

(*Source:* Pew Hispanic Center Report "U.S. Population Projections: 2005–2050" by Jeffrey S. Passel and D'Vera Cohn, http://pewhispanic.org/reports/report.php?ReportID=85. Copyright © 2008 Pew Hispanic Center, a project of the Pew Research Center. Reproduced by permission.)

and they settled in small towns, where they assimilated quickly into the middle-class, Protestant population. But between 1880 and 1920, 23 million immigrants came to the United States, too fast to disperse and blend. Instead they piled up in cities; in 1900, immigrants and their children made up more than 70 percent of populations of New York, Boston, Philadelphia, and Chicago. They were primarily working class and poor; they spoke Italian, Polish, or Yiddish; and they were more often Catholic or Jewish (Van Vugt, 1999; Walch, 1994).

The U.S.–born English-German, Protestant, small-town elite feared these new "primitive" groups (Roediger, 1991). By 1924 the door to immigration from most of Europe (not England) slammed shut (Saxton, 1971, 1990). Because the immigrants tended to have larger families than the native elites, President Theodore Roosevelt raised the alarm of "race suicide" and urged Anglo-Saxon women to have more children, just as poor and immigrant families were advised to limit the number of children they had. By the 1920s and 1930s, scientists developed theories of *eugenics,* the science of "breeding," and encouraged laws that would help the country breed a superior race (Mowry, 1958; Selden, 1999).

By the 1920s, racialist "science" was being taught as fact in American universities. Some early sociologists and anthropologists attempted to demonstrate that these immigrants from "primitive" societies were inferior to native-born Americans (Schwendinger and Schwendinger, 1974).

But gradually the Irish, the Italians, the European Jews, and other European ethnic

groups became categorized as "White." The 1930 census distinguishes ten races (White, Negro, American Indian, Chinese, Japanese, Korean, Filipino, Hindu, Mexican, and Other) and further classifies White people into only three types: native White with native White parents; native White with immigrant parents; and immigrant White. The 1940 census distinguishes only native White and immigrant White. How did that happen? Was it because many had become middle class? Or did expanded versions of Whiteness mean that employers and apartment owners took the "No Irish Need Apply" or "No Bohunks Allowed" placards from their windows, allowing the middle class to enter? (A "Bohunk" is an immigrant from central Europe, a combination of "Bohemian" and "Hungarian.")

Both, and neither. Historian Noel Ignatiev maintains that the Irish deliberately positioned themselves in opposition to Blacks, visibly participating in the massive anti-Black violence in the northeastern United States in the 1840s, to posture for a place at the table of "Whiteness." Anthropologist Karen Brodkin (1998) similarly maintains that Jews began to "speak of a mythic whiteness" that both they and the Anglo-Saxons participated in, transcending the separate categories that scientific racism put them in. The Irish and the Jews "chose" to be White and then set about trying to convince native-born Protestant Whites that they were White.

We also can't discount the 1930s rise of Nazi Germany, where race science was taken to its logical conclusion: The Aryan "master race" protecting its "stock" with military aggression and death camps. By the time Ashley Montagu published *Man's Most Dangerous Myth: The Fallacy of Race* in 1942, a book that declared "race science" to threaten the foundations of modern society itself, race science had the taint of Nazi tyranny, and using ethnography to analyze culture was gaining ground over measuring skull capacity to prove biological distinction. Instead of dirty and dangerous "races" that must be kept separate, immigrants became "ethnic groups" who could easily assimilate into the mainstream. Instead of a nation of Northern European Protestants worried about race mixing or "mongrelization," the United States became a *melting pot,* where each different group blended into a unique whole and with immigrant economic and social success praised as a triumph of democracy over the superstition of race science.

However, the melting pot seemed to work only with Europeans and with some drawbacks: Assimilation meant abandoning cultural traditions. Immigrant parents punished their children for speaking the language from back home, and in a generation or two an entire cultural heritage was nearly forgotten. That was the price they paid for becoming White.

Prejudice, Discrimination, and Racism

The perception of racial and ethnic difference is a foundation of how we see and interact with other people. These perceptions also inform the way we organize society and distribute rewards.

Prejudice is a set of beliefs and attitudes that cause us to negatively "prejudge" people based on their social location. In the classic work on the subject, psychologist Gordon Allport defined prejudice as "a pattern of hostility in interpersonal relations which is directed against an entire group, or against its individual members; it fulfills a specific irrational function for its bearer" (Allport, 1954, p. 12). For example, you may decide not to sell your car to an Asian American because you believe they are bad drivers, or you may decline to rent an apartment from a Hispanic owner because you believe the building would be sloppily maintained. **Racism** is a set of attitudes, an ideology that holds that inequality based on race is justified because of the assumed natural differences between the races. **Discrimination** is a pattern of interactions, a set of behaviors, by which one denies some rewards to some groups based on prejudice.

Prejudice and Stereotypes

Often prejudices are based on **stereotypes,** generalizations about a group that are oversimplified and exaggerated and fail to acknowledge individual differences in the group. For instance, if you believe the stereotype that Asians are gifted in science, you will believe that it is true of all Asians, without exception.

You will believe that any Asian selected at random will be able to answer scientific questions and will score better on science exams than any person randomly selected from another race. Most likely, however, you will not reason it out in any systematic way: You will just ask an Asian when you have a scientific question or be surprised when you meet an Asian who is an art history major.

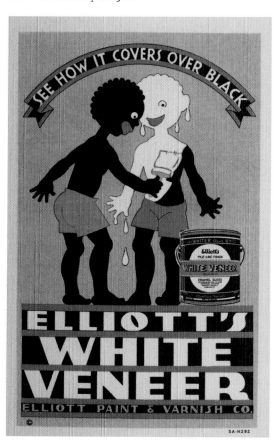

For a very long time, racism was taken for granted in American society—so that racist images were casually used in all sorts of places. This ad singing the praises of white paint was made in 1935.

Most stereotypes, like the association of "Asian" and "science," refer to traits that only a small percentage of group members actually possess or that are no more common to group members than to anyone else, so they are simply inaccurate and unfair. However, some stereotypes are downright wrong: No one (or almost no one) in the group possesses the trait.

In the early 1960s, Bull Connor, a sheriff in Alabama, commented that "Blacks are intellectually inferior" and that therefore integration would fail. In the 1980s, Al Campanis, an official with the Los Angeles Dodgers, commented that "Blacks are better athletes." One occasionally hears that Blacks are more "naturally" gifted basketball players but that White players are "smarter" or "have a better work ethic." And for years football quarterbacks were White, on the assumption that you had to be a brilliant tactician, not a powerful athlete, to play the position. There have also been several celebrated cases in which public speakers spoke about these stereotypes, indicating that they believe them to be true, that races and ethnic groups *are* significantly different in their strength, physical power, intelligence, musical ability, or other characteristics. sometimes these public pronouncements cost them their jobs.

Today, such arguments have become more subtle and sophisticated, but no less stereotypic, with "culture" merely substituted for "biology" as an explanation of the differences. For instance, they argue that, because of social discrimination, Blacks have less stimulating intellectual environments than Whites during their formative years, so they end up with lower intelligence. Or their parents reward playing basketball instead of cracking books, while the parents of White children reward academic skills, so the Black children

Sociology and Our World

What's in a Name? The Sociology of Racial Terminology

Names have power. They define us and show others how we define them. There are often conflicts between what we want to call ourselves and what other people want to call us. They can be good in some situations, bad in others. *Queer* is fine when you're giving an academic lecture on queer theory, but not when you are yelling it out of a passing car. Who gets to make the decisions?

When Richard Wright wrote a book entitled *Black Boy* in 1945, he was trying to shock people with derogatory slang. No one would have dreamed of calling him- or herself "Black" in 1945. The proper term was "colored person" or "Negro."

During the Civil Rights movement of the 1960s, social activists tried to rehabilitate the once-derogatory term *Black*, capitalizing it and insisting that "Black is beautiful." And it worked: In 1965 the word *Negro* appeared in dozens of titles of books and magazine articles, but by 1967 those titles almost always referred to "Black."

Today, many people disapprove of the name "Black," pointing out that it is inaccurate: Skin comes in many shades of brown. But equally inaccurate is "Negro" (which means "black" in Latin), "colored person," and "person of color" (because everyone has color). Afro-American, later African American, appeared about the same time as "Black" to denote ethnicity, someone whose ancestors came from sub-Saharan Africa. But not everyone. If your parents were White South Africans who immigrated to the United States in 1960, you do not get to call yourself African American (well, you can try). When White people use the term *European American* they often do so in defensive reaction against "African Americans."

But surely some names are undeniably offensive, right? Harvard law professor Randall Kennedy isn't sure. He wrote a book called *Nigger* (2002), pointing out that it is sometimes used to identify and fight racism rather than to promote racism; and, within some Black subcultures, it is used commonly "with undertones of warmth and good will." (Often when the subordinate appropriates a term used by the dominant group to demean them, it can take much of the sting away from the word.) Should it really be eradicated from our language, or should it remain, Kennedy asks, as a "reminder of the ironies and dilemmas, the tragedies and glories, of the American experience" (Kennedy, 2002, p. 2)?

Race and Intelligence

In 1994, Harvard psychologist Richard Herrnstein and public policy analyst Charles Murray stirred up a cloud of controversy with their book *The Bell Curve: Intelligence and Class Structure in American Life.* They argued that intelligence—measured by the speed with which you learn new skills and adapt to new situations—is the key to social success and that low intelligence is an important root cause of crime, poverty, unemployment, bad parenting, and many other social problems. In other words, intelligent people succeed more often than stupid people.

But the controversy came when Herrnstein and Murray presented the results of their research to demonstrate that this essential intelligence is correlated with race: African Americans on the average scored significantly lower than White Americans on standard intelligence tests. Scientists have known about racial differences on intelligence tests for many years and explain that they are due to cultural bias in the testing instrument or social inequality during the crucial period of primary socialization, rather than to differences in the way brains actually process information. But Herrnstein and Murray argue that intelligence is 40 to 80 percent inherited, based on genetics.

Now people got angry. Murray was labeled "America's most dangerous conservative" by the *New York Times Magazine* (Herrnstein died in 1994) (Kirp, 2006). When conservative columnist Andrew Sullivan published an excerpt in the magazine *The New Republic,* the entire editorial board vehemently protested. When *The Bell Curve* was assigned to a class, some students refused to read it, and some complained of racism to the dean.

But the most important objection to *The Bell Curve* is that it is just bad science. In *Inequality by Design: Cracking the Bell Curve Myth,* sociologists Claude Fischer and Mike Hout and their colleagues show the methodological flaws in the bell curve research: Neither "intelligence" nor "race" is a purely biological phenomenon, so their correlation cannot be purely biological either (Fischer et al., 1996). Plus, as we saw in the methodology chapter, demonstrating correlation between two variables cannot tell you the direction or cause of the relationship.

And how can we account for the impact of institutional racism, the structures of discrimination that have nothing to do with individual abilities? Social structures set "the rule of the game" whereby individual differences matter. If you have high intelligence but no access to the elite education necessary for social prestige, you might learn the skills of drug dealing or adapt to the new situation of a federal penitentiary rather than going for a Berkeley PhD. On the other hand, if you have low intelligence but the right social connections, you just might inherit the family fortune.

grow up to be better athletes. This is still stereotyping. No study has demonstrated that Black parents regularly discourage their children from getting good grades or that White parents are never obsessed with their children's sports accomplishments.

Racism

Racism describes a set of attitudes; racism is prejudice that is systematically applied to members of a group. It can be **overt racism,** in speech, manifest in behaviors such as discrimination or a refusal to associate with members of that group; it can also be **subtle racism** and even unconscious racism, simply a set of mental categories that we possess about the "other" based on stereotypes.

Racism is a particularly powerful form of prejudice, not only a belief in general stereotypes but a belief that one race (usually White) is inherently superior to the others. It

is not necessary to belong to the "superior" race to buy into racism. Race science, with its "evidence" of the superiority of White people, was quite common 50 or 60 years ago and still pops up from time to time in academic or popular discussions (along with its opposite, "evidence" of the superiority of Black people).

We still hear racist sentiments from time to time. A few years ago in an introductory sociology class, I mentioned that by 2050, White people will be a numerical minority in the United States. A student gasped. "That's terrible! Doesn't that scare you?" It didn't scare me at all, so I said, "What's the problem? America will still be here." She responded, "Yeah, but it won't be our America!" I doubt that she had ever heard of race science, but she was expressing the same fear of losing "our" country to the incursion of minorities that prompted the immigration quotas 70 years ago, or that politician Pat Buchanan expresses in *The Death of the West*

(2002), about the decline of "our America" due to immigration and low birth rates among White people.

Discrimination

Discrimination is a set of actions based on prejudice and stereotypes. They often, but need not, negatively affect the group in question. For instance, if I believe that Asians are academically gifted, I may ask Asian students more questions in class, assign them more difficult projects, or grade their papers more leniently, giving them the "benefit of the doubt." But I may also be especially aware of an Asian student who is disruptive in class.

Some acts of discrimination are responses to specific stereotypes, but more often discrimination occurs as general negative treatment. A waiter or waitress may exercise discrimination against minority customers by waiting on non-minority customers first, rushing them out when they have finished eating, or behaving in an unfriendly or hostile manner. Of course, the victims never know for sure if they are facing discrimination or just bad service. Minority students who get low grades on tests might suspect that the professor is discriminating, but they will never know for sure unless they do some detective work and uncover a pattern of low grades for minority students.

Prejudice and discrimination are not always causally connected. I can be prejudiced but not discriminate, if none of my friends is discriminating and I don't want to appear different or do something socially unacceptable. Or I can discriminate without being prejudiced, if all of my friends are discriminating, if I believe that it is "the thing to do." Studies show that many of the perpetrators of hate crimes are no more prejudiced than those who do not commit hate crimes: They are just "going along for the ride" (Boyd, Berk, and Hamner, 1996; Craig and Waldo, 1996; Morsch, 1991).

Sociologist Robert Merton divided prejudice and discrimination into four categories:

1. *All-weather bigots* are prejudiced against some minority groups, and they discriminate against group members. If they do not discriminate in certain social situations, it is because they do not care to, not because they are worried about losing face. They may even take pride in their prejudice. They might tell a racist joke, for instance, even if they know that the people around them will disapprove, to demonstrate their "heroic" refusal to be swayed by politically correct tolerance.

2. *Fair-weather bigots* are prejudiced against some minority groups, but they do not discriminate when there may be negative consequences. This category includes most prejudiced people: They may dislike minorities, but they will not show it when they have something to lose. They will tell a racist joke only when they are sure they will receive a positive reaction.

3. *Fair-weather liberals* are not prejudiced, but they do discriminate when it is profitable for them to do so. They will not tell a racist joke, but they may laugh at one to avoid being embarrassed or starting an argument.

4. *All-weather liberals* are not prejudiced and do not discriminate. They adhere to the American ideal of equal opportunity for all, regardless of the situation. They will not tell a racist joke or respond favorably to one (Merton, [1949] 1976).

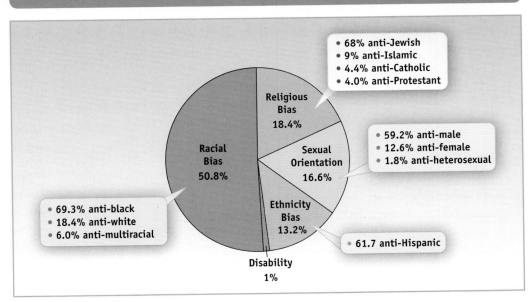

Figure 8.5 Offenses by Bias Motivation

Religious Bias 18.4%
- 68% anti-Jewish
- 9% anti-Islamic
- 4.4% anti-Catholic
- 4.0% anti-Protestant

Racial Bias 50.8%
- 69.3% anti-black
- 18.4% anti-white
- 6.0% anti-multiracial

Sexual Orientation 16.6%
- 59.2% anti-male
- 12.6% anti-female
- 1.8% anti-heterosexual

Ethnicity Bias 13.2%
- 61.7 anti-Hispanic

Disability 1%

(*Source:* Based on data from *Crime in the United States*, U.S. Department of Justice, 2007.)

This typology assumes that prejudice is a quality that you have—you are either prejudiced or not—and that discrimination consists of specific, deliberate acts. However, there is a great degree of variation in prejudice and discrimination. Many people who would never dream of telling or laughing at a racist joke, and who fully support equal rights for minorities, still harbor prejudices—they believe, perhaps subconsciously, that being White is just better than being something else. Similarly, many acts of discrimination are so subtle, almost unconscious, that we are barely aware of them. Even in a social climate where open acts of discrimination are frowned on, members of minority groups suffer many acts of personal discrimination every day, ranging from hostile or frightened stares to unconscious stereotyping to insults and jokes and sometimes to violence. When discrimination comes from someone with power, the power to give you a job, an apartment, a good grade, or a speeding ticket, it is especially damaging.

A recent case on the TV program *The People's Court* involved the owner of an apartment house who contracted a realtor to provide potential renters. The realtor was asked to "screen the applicants," so she did, ensuring that they had good jobs, good credit histories, and references from previous landlords. But when she brought the first applicant around to view the apartment, she discovered that the owner meant something else entirely. He said: "That applicant is Black! You were supposed to screen applicants!" The realtor quit (and was sued for breach of contract). One wonders how many other realtors do not quit, how often unwritten and unspoken agreements allow discrimination to continue.

Institutional Discrimination. Screening out Black applicants for an apartment or house is illegal in the United States. I may be free to behave in a hostile or impolite fashion toward anyone I choose, but I may not deny members of certain minority groups equal access to housing, jobs, public services, and selected social rewards. Nevertheless, unequal access continues to be common.

Institutional discrimination is the most subtle and pervasive type of discrimination, deeply embedded in such institutions as the educational system, the business world, health care, criminal justice, and the mass media. These social institutions promote discriminatory practices and traditions that have such a long history they just "seem to make sense," and minority groups become the victims of systematic oppression, even when only a few people, or none at all, are deliberately trying to discriminate. If unchecked, institutional discrimination undermines the very idea of a society based on individual achievement, merit, and hard work. Democracies must institute laws that prevent it and provide remedies when it happens.

The Fair Housing Act of 1968 banned discrimination in housing, but institutional discrimination persists. African Americans and Latinos are turned down for home loans twice as often as Whites with the same qualifications. The HUD Housing Discrimination Study of 2000 found that adverse treatment against

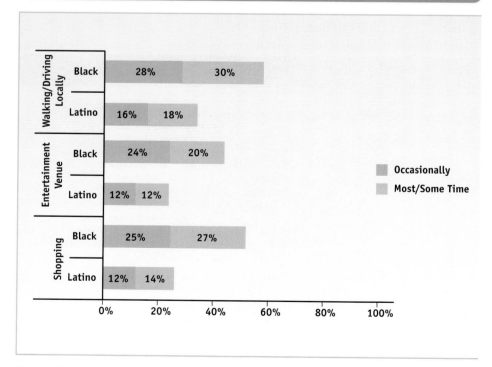

Figure 8.6 Subtle Discrimination: Feeling Out of Place in Various Public Venues

(*Source:* Center for Survey Research, Stony Brook University, "Black and Latino Experiences with Discrimination on Long Island," November 2008. Reproduced with permission of ERASE Racism.)

One way to find out whether our society has made racial progress is to track racial attitudes over time. In the 1920s, sociologist Emory Bogardus devised a *social distance scale* to measure the extent to which we use racial and ethnic categories in the choices we make about our social life (Bogardus, 1925, 1933). He asked a national sample of college students, aged 18 to 35 (about 10 percent of his respondents were Black), a set of questions designed to measure their distance from other groups. These included whether you would make personal friends with them, accept them as neighbors on your street, work in the same office, and date or marry someone from that group. Bogardus predicted that the social distance among groups would decline.

Every 10 years, these questions have been asked of a national sample, and the students ranked their preferences among 30 different groups—mostly Europeans, but also Black Americans, Canadians, Japanese Americans, and various Asian groups. There was some fluctuation over this half-century of surveys. Blacks, for example, moved up from the bottom to the

Changing Racial Attitudes

middle of the group. But generally the rankings listed White Americans, Canadians, Northern and Western Europeans in the top third, South and Central and Eastern Europeans in the middle third, and racial minorities in the bottom third. (Italians were the only Southern European group to make the top 10 eventually.) Americans were surprisingly consistent.

In 2001, sociologists Vincent Parillo and Christopher Donoghue updated these categories and administered the survey again to a large national sample of college students. It was administered in the six weeks following September 11. Italians had jumped to second place, even ahead of Canadians and the British, and Blacks had cracked the top 10. The last two categories now were filled by Muslims and Arabs (Parillo, 2006; Parillo and Donoghue, 2005).

Black applicants occurred in 22 percent of cases and against Hispanic applicants in 26 percent of cases: They were less likely to be told that a unit was available, were less likely to be offered a unit for inspection, and were quoted higher rents. The discrimination rate varied from city to city, from 14 percent in Chicago to 30 percent in Atlanta for Black renters, and from 15 percent in Denver to 32 percent in Chicago for Hispanic renters.

Segregation and Integration. For many years in the United States, physical separation between the White majority and the minority groups (especially African Americans), or **segregation,** was law. Discrimination means unequal treatment, and in the 1896 *Plessy vs. Ferguson* decision, the Supreme Court ruled that "separate but equal" accommodations for Blacks and Whites were not discriminatory. In fact, they were necessary to cater to the different needs of the races and ensure racial harmony. There were separate neighborhoods, separate businesses, separate sections on buses and in restaurants, separate schools and colleges, even separate washrooms and drinking fountains. In mainstream (that is, White) movies, Blacks

appeared only as servants and entertainers, but in their own "separate but equal" movies, they played rugged action heroes, mystery sleuths, romantic leads, every imaginable role.

Usually, however, the "separate" meant "inferior." Black schools received only a fraction of the resources of White schools. The Black section of the bus was at the back. The Black section of the restaurant was in the kitchen.

In the case of the system of apartheid, that inferiority was institutionalized and legal. **Apartheid** means "separation" (think: apartness), and it was a system that mandated segregation of different racial groups. In South Africa, apartheid was a political system institutionalized by the White minority in 1948, and all social life was determined by whether you were one of four races: White, Black, "coloured" (mixed race), or Indian (South Asian). There were separate schools, restaurants, hospitals, churches, drinking fountains—and even separate buses and bus stops. Apartheid remained in effect until 1990, when Nelson Mandela, the leader of the African National Congress, was freed from prison and soon elected president of South Africa.

In 1954, the Supreme Court heard the *Brown vs. the Board of Education* case and reversed its decision, concluding that "separate but equal" was never equal. So segregation was replaced by legal **integration,** physical intermingling of the races, which presumably would lead to cultural intermingling and racial equality. Fifty years later, integration has not been entirely achieved. We have integrated washrooms and drinking fountains in the United States, but most people, especially poor Blacks and rich Whites, continue to live in same-race neighborhoods and attend same-race schools. Segregation continues to separate poor people of color from education and job opportunities and isolate them from successful role models, helping to create a permanent minority underclass (Massey and Denton, 1993).

Affirmative Action or "Reverse Discrimination"? In 1965, President Lyndon Johnson asked employers to "take affirmative action to ensure that applicants are employed, and that employees are treated . . . without regard to their race, color, creed, or national origin." He established the Equal Opportunity Commission, which administers many **affirmative action** programs to ensure that minorities get fair treatment in employment applications.

Affirmative action programs are controversial. Opponents complain that minority applicants are "stealing jobs" from more qualified White applicants, a sort of "reverse discrimination." Recently I appeared on a television talk show opposite three "angry White males" who felt they had been the victims of workplace discrimination. The show's title, no doubt created to entice a large potential audience, was "A Black Woman Stole My Job." In my comments to these men, I invited them to consider what the word "my" meant in that title. Why did they believe the job was "theirs" to begin with? Why did they feel entitled to it? When a Black female applicant was hired instead, was she really stealing it from them? Why wasn't the title of the show "A Black Woman Got *the* Job" or "A Black Woman Got *a* Job"?

One might even say that White males have been the beneficiaries of a 2,000-year "affirmative action" policy that favored them. In an article in *The Nation* a few years ago, the eminent historian Eric Foner ruminated on his own college experience as a beneficiary of that version of affirmative action:

> Thirty-two years ago, I graduated from Columbia College [the undergraduate college at Columbia University]. My class of 700 was all-male and virtually all white. Most of us were young men of ability; yet had we been forced to compete for admission with women and racial minorities, fewer than half of us would have been at Columbia. None of us, to my knowledge, suffered debilitating self-doubt because we were the beneficiaries of affirmative action—that is, favored treatment on the basis of our race and gender. . . . [In fact], I have yet to meet a white male in whom favoritism (getting a job, for example, through relatives or an old boys' network, or because of racial discrimination by a union or an employer) fostered doubt about his own abilities. . . .

"Despite our rhetoric," Foner concludes, "equal opportunity has never been the American way. For nearly all our history, affirmative action has been a prerogative of white men" (Foner, 1995).

In 1978, the Supreme Court heard the case of Allan Bakke, a white premed student who was twice denied admission to the University of California–Davis Medical School, even though his test scores were superior to many Black students who were admitted. A 5–4 split decision acknowledged that race was a legitimate determining factor in medical school admission but held that strict racial quotas were unconstitutional. That is, admissions departments can take race into account as a factor in admission but cannot reserve a set number of places for any particular group.

Today, around 2 percent of the 91,000 cases of job discrimination pending before the Equal Employment Opportunity Commission are for reverse discrimination, and state affirmative action measures have been abolished in California, Washington, and Florida (for college admissions only). In 2003, the Supreme Court ruled in a 6–3 decision that the University of Michigan's affirmative action policy in undergraduate admissions, which awarded 20 extra points to Black, Hispanic, and Native American applicants, was unconstitutional (though it was allowed to remain in place in the Law School).

Sometimes affirmative action programs can lead to **tokenism,** in which a single member of a minority group is present in the office, workshop, or the classroom. When you are a *token,* you occupy a curious position. You are simultaneously invisible and hypervisible. You are a representative of your race, ethnicity, gender, or sexual identity—not a person. Nobody sees you, everybody sees your characteristics, and they are using those characteristics to form new stereotypes of your group. Your individual quirks and shortcomings will become stereotypes of the entire group. This is a huge responsibility. You have to be on your best behavior and be very careful to not do anything that might support a stereotype. This can lead to social paralysis: You are afraid to speak or act because everyone is watching and making conclusions about your group.

Hate Groups. People join hate groups to promote discrimination against ethnic and other minorities, usually because they feel that the main society is not doing a very good job of it. The Know-Nothing Party was formed in 1849 to promote anti-Catholic and anti-immigrant legislation. The Ku Klux Klan (KKK), formed shortly after the end of slavery in 1863, tried to prevent newly freed blacks from acquiring social equality with both political legislation and the more immediate tactics of violence and intimidation. When open discrimination is commonplace in the main society, these groups can acquire a great deal of political power. The Know-Nothings managed to dominate several state legislatures, including Massachusetts, and promoted the sitting president, Millard Fillmore, in the 1852 presidential election (he lost, but not due to an anti-immigrant agenda). At its height in the 1920s, the second Ku Klux Klan had over 4,000,000 members and was praised by many public figures, including President Warren Harding.

When open discrimination is frowned upon in the main society, it becomes more difficult for hate groups to get laws passed or sponsor successful political candidates. Former KKK Grand Wizard David Duke rose highest, when he captured 55 percent of the White vote in the 1989 Louisiana gubernatorial election, although he had to explain that his KKK membership was a "youthful mistake." Hate groups today usually do not hope to legislate discriminatory policies. Instead, they want to make their presence known,

Supreme Court Justice Clarence Thomas has repeatedly suggested that as the only African-American on the court he is not a token, opposing affirmative action because he believes it taints minority achievements like his own as unearned.

win supporters, and promote individual acts of discrimination, especially violence.

In the twenty-first century, many hate groups have moved beyond marching in strange costumes or starting fistfights on talk shows to using up-to-date tools of mass media and marketing: attractive, professionally produced books, music, Web pages, and social networking sites that hide their racist beliefs under a veneer of respectability. In public presentations, they never use racist slurs. They say that they are interested in science, Christianity, or patriotism rather than racism. The number of hate groups in the United States has risen by over 50 percent since 2000, so today there are over 900 groups active across the United States (Southern Poverty Law Center, 2009). Yet there are perhaps only 50,000 hard-core members of hate groups and no more than 500,000 "fellow travelers," people who read the literature, browse the websites, and agree with racist ideologies (Potok, 2006). A more subtle threat of hate groups is to draw attention away from everyday forms of prejudice and discrimination. After listening to the outrageous statements of a hate group, or seeing their ultraviolent behavior, people may believe that their own prejudice is harmless and

Race and class often intersect, as these mostly white male workers see the chief threat to their job security not from corporate policies of outsourcing and downsizing, but from immigrant laborers.

inconsequential. After all, they do not believe that non-White people are children of Satan, and they would never dream of bombing a Black church, so what does it matter if they feel uncomfortable in a Black neighborhood?

Although membership in organized hate groups is relatively low, there is an alarming increase in violent crimes in which the victim was chosen because of his or her membership in some minority group (Figure 8.5 on page 229). In 2005, the FBI documented 7,163 hate crimes. The most (2,630) were against Blacks, and 828 were against Whites. The second highest group, however, was anti-Jewish (848). There are more anti-Semitic crimes than against all other religious groups combined. The 128 anti-Islamic crimes, however, are by far the fastest growing type of bias crime (U.S. Department of Justice, 2005c).

This increase in hate crimes is not just an American problem. Significant increases in immigrant populations in European countries, coupled with fears of terrorism and the economic downturn, have provoked many into targeting immigrants. Across Europe, national governments are alarmed at the dramatic increases in hate crimes against Muslims.

Theories of Prejudice and Discrimination

Social scientists and philosophers have wondered about prejudice for centuries. Why does prejudice exist? Why are we prejudiced against some groups and not others? Why do we believe certain stereotypes and not others? And most importantly, what can we do about it?

The **primordial theory** suggests that a conflict exists between in-groups and out-groups, but doesn't explain how some groups come to be classified as out-groups. Is there any evidence that we have an "innate preference for people like us"? Often we prefer people who are not at all like us. In fact, many times, "opposites attract." These "innate" theories disregard the political, social, and economic processes behind individual prejudices. People can and do become racist through deliberate choice and socialization, not through any innate preferences.

According to *frustration-aggression theory*, people are goal directed, and when they can't

	Black	Latino
Missed out on housing because of a real estate agent	34%	15%
Missed out on housing because of a White landlord/home owner	31%	12%
Experienced some form of housing discrimination	*39%*	*21%*
Stopped by the police because of race/ethnicity	42%	19%
Verbally/physically harassed by neighbor	16%	16%
Experienced at least one of 4 forms of discrimination	*60%*	*40%*

Table 8.1
Experience with Institutional Discrimination

(*Source:* Center for Survey Research, Stony Brook University, "Black and Latino Experiences with Discrimination on Long Island," November 2008. Reproduced with permission of ERASE Racism.)

reach their goals, they become angry and frustrated. If they cannot find the source of their frustration, or if the source is too powerful to challenge, they will direct their aggression toward a **scapegoat,** a weak, convenient, and socially approved target. Considerable evidence shows racial and ethnic hostility increases during periods of economic instability (Blackwell, 1982). Sometimes people may become convinced that the scapegoat is actually the cause of their frustration—for instance, that they are unemployed because illegal immigrants have stolen their job—but often they are just lashing out at someone convenient. This theory does not explain why some groups become scapegoats and others do not or why we are prejudiced against groups who are not immediately visible.

Most sociologists see prejudice as a tool used by the elites, people at the top of the social hierarchy, to "divide and conquer" those at the bottom, making them easier to control and manipulate (Pettigrew, 1998). Racial and ethnic stereotypes are used to legitimate systemic inequality. For instance, if Blacks are really lazy, we can explain why there are so few working in high-power corporate jobs without having to deal with institutional discrimination. This theory is supported by research suggesting that prejudice decreases when racism is not institutionally supported (Pettigrew, 1998), but it ignores the role of race in the lives of those at the bottom of the hierarchy.

Sociologist Robert Blauner (1972) proposed that African Americans in the United States didn't resemble a classical minority group (like Jews in Europe or like the Irish or Italians in the United States). Instead, he used the model of the European imperialist conquest of Africa or Latin America as a metaphor to propose that Blacks represented an **internal colony.** Unlike other minority groups, Blacks did not come to the United States voluntarily; they were sub-

ject to specific laws that constrained their activity and movement and subject to economic and even sexual subordination (the rape of slave women, for example).

In the United States and worldwide, members of minority groups are often prejudiced against other minority groups, and they can harbor their own stereotypes about the elites (Kinloch, 1999; Phinney, Gerguson, and Tate, 1997; Tsukashima, 1983). For example, Puerto Rican shopkeepers who own small neighborhood grocery stores (called bodegas) are deeply suspicious that the Asian greengrocers have been supported by the city's wealthy to drive the Puerto Ricans out of business. Cross-cultural historical studies show that racial and ethnic minorities often promote prejudice against other minorities to try to increase their own wealth, power, and privilege (see, for example, Dreier, Mollenkopf, and Swanstrom, 2005).

Intersectionality. Race overlaps with other social categories, like ethnicity, gender, and sexuality. Stereotypes about stigmatized groups in all of these categories are remarkably similar: The group in question is considered illogical (childlike), overly emotional, primitive, potentially violent, and sexually promiscuous. Consequently, these stereotypes and prejudices often combine, and the effects of racism are compounded by the effects of classism, sexism, heterosexism, and the other "isms."

Indeed, sociologists understand that one cannot easily tease apart these different, yet entangled, strands. As a result, sociologists today discuss *intersectionality*—the ways in which our experience as members of different groups intersect with one another. Sometimes these experiences reinforce each other; sometimes they contradict each other. But to the sociologist, the key fact is that they are inseparable. One does not stop being African American when one is working class, female, or lesbian. All these experiences taken together compose what sociologist Patricia Hill Collins (1990) calls a **matrix of domination**—an interlocking system of control in which each type of inequality reinforces the others so that the impact of one cannot be fully understood without also considering the others (Figure 8.7).

Often, this intersectionality offers a painful reminder of marginality, and the ways in which even the oppressed groups can still hold prejudices. I have a friend who is a Black lesbian. She commented that whenever she is around other Black people, she is keenly aware that she is lesbian "and I don't fit in." But, she said, when she is around other lesbians, she remains keenly aware that she is Black "and I don't fit in there either." Often, the intersections of different categories of identity leave us feeling marginal—even when we are in a group of "our own."

Can Prejudice Be Overcome?

As we've seen, prejudice is a set of ideas, assumptions that we have about other groups. Is there any way to reduce prejudice? Some social scientists in the 1950s believed that prejudice could be changed by exposure to members of minority groups (Allport, 1954). We might believe that Italians are passionate, Blacks are lazy, or Jews are greedy because we haven't met enough members of these groups who don't fit the stereotypes. A few handshakes, therefore, will end the prejudice.

During the 1960s and 1970s, a huge amount of time and money was invested in busing students from segregated schools, not only to equalize instruction but to introduce Black and White students to each other. It didn't work: Contact alone does not diminish prejudice. People who have never met even one member of another particular group may not be prejudiced, while people who are surrounded by members of the minority group may still be prejudiced. In *Searching for Aboriginal Languages* (1984), linguist John Dixon finds that many of the White residents of Queensland, Australia, are prejudiced against the aboriginals and believe they are more sexually promiscuous. Dixon found that aboriginals actually select romantic partners on the basis of a very complex system of clans, kinship roles, and informal alliances dating back hundreds of years. The White residents saw aboriginals every day, talked to them, and worked with them but were completely oblivious to anything except "jumping into bed."

Social psychologist Mark Snyder (1987) found that even awareness of prejudice and desire to change were insufficient. You can realize that prejudice is wrong, and you can try to stop, but you might still believe stereotypes: They are beyond the reach of reason and goodwill. You will tend to notice and remember the ways in which a person from a minority group seems to fit a stereotype, whether you want to or not.

One of the problems in combating prejudice is that it is not merely a matter of individual perceptions. Gordon Allport (1954) called prejudice "a self-fulfilling prophecy." We see what we expect to see and don't see what we don't expect to see. Thus, what we see "fulfills" our expectations, and the stereotypes are confirmed. In a classic illustration of this, Gordon Allport reports the following conversation with an anti-Semite:

> Mr. X: The trouble with the Jews is that they only take care of their own group.
>
> Mr. Y: But the record of the Community Chest campaign shows that they give more generously, in proportion to their numbers, to the general charities of the community, than do non-Jews.

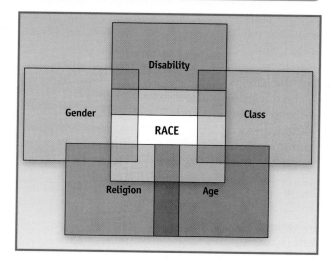

Figure 8.7 Matrix of Domination

President Barack Obama is biracial; the son of a black Kenyan father and a white American mother—that is, truly "African-American." Here, the young Obama sits between his maternal grandparents, who played a significant role in his life.

Mr. X: That shows they are always trying to buy favor and intrude into Christian affairs. They think of nothing but money; that is why there are so many Jewish bankers.

Mr. Y: But a recent study shows that the percentage of Jews in the banking business is negligible, far smaller than the percentage of non-Jews.

Mr. X: That's just it; they don't go in for respectable business; they are only in the movie business or run night clubs. (Allport, 1954, pp. 13–14)

The same expectation effect can happen on the job, among friends, in families, and among strangers—even within the group that has been negatively stereotyped. We tend to modify our beliefs and behaviors to correspond to a social role, even if that role is a negative stereotype. In 1997, John Ogbu, an anthropologist at the University of California, Berkeley, wondered why middle-class African American students in affluent Shaker Heights, Ohio, got lower grades than their White classmates (an average of C instead of B). Usually such disparities are explained by economic and social inequalities, but in this case, both groups of students were attending well-funded middle-class schools. He concluded that the Black students were afraid of being labeled as "acting White" if they studied too hard or got good grades (see Ogbu and Davis, 2003). Sociologist Pedro Noguera (2004) found that young Black men are so disconnected from school that they are the only group for whom there is no positive correlation between self-esteem and academic achievement.

More recent research in inner-city schools suggests an even more compelling picture. It turns out that Black *girls* who do well in school are indeed accused of "acting White," but Black boys who do well are accused of "acting like girls" (A. Ferguson, 2001; Fordham, 1999). Collins's "matrix of domination" suggests a correlation between gender and racial oppression: For these boys, being seen as a girl is even worse than being seen as White.

The Bradley Effect

The phenomenon of White people saying the right thing publicly but still acting in discriminatory ways privately has a name. It's called "the Bradley Effect," named after former Los Angeles mayor Tom Bradley. Leading handily in every preelection poll, Bradley lost the 1982 California governor's race because many Whites had told pollsters they would vote for Bradley, a Black man, and actually voted for his opponent in the privacy of the voting booth. After dire predictions, though, the Bradley Effect did not materialize at all during the 2008 presidential election.

Did You Know?

However, there is hope. People can and do decrease their prejudice. Mere contact is not enough, but when people of different groups must work together toward a common goal (Miller, Brewer, and Edwards, 1985), most measures of prejudice decrease. Other important factors are strong role models that contradict the stereotypes and a decrease in institutional forms of discrimination that make inequality seem normal and natural.

Unfortunately, some evidence suggests that many people are just learning what answers look best on surveys, regardless of how they really feel or react. Discrimination, especially of the backhanded "have a nice day" sort, seems to be on the rise. In a 1997 Gallup poll, 79 percent of Whites believed that Blacks and Whites were always treated equally, but only 49 per-

cent of Blacks agreed. Thirty percent of Black respondents said that they had encountered discrimination during the past month, while shopping, at work, while dining out, while using public transportation, or with the police. The percentage increased to 70 percent for young Black men, who were especially likely to experience discrimination while shopping (45 percent) and in interactions with the police (35 percent). A 1995 survey of the racial climate at Indiana State University (Terre Haute, Indiana) found that 64 percent of Black students had heard racial jokes or seen racial graffiti, 55 percent felt they had been left out of social activities, 48 percent had been insulted intellectually, and 47 percent had been called names or racial slurs. Most surprisingly, 40 percent had been insulted in class by a teacher.

Ethnic Groups in the United States

Every group has some distinctive norms, values, beliefs, practices, outlooks, and cultural artifacts, but when they emerge historically and tend to set the group apart from other groups, physically and culturally, they can

be called an ethnicity. In some ways, ethnicity is like race in that you belong to it whether you want to or not. If you have a Pakistani ethnicity, you will never acquire a Swedish ethnicity, even if you become a citizen of Sweden, learn to speak fluent Swedish, join the Swedish Lutheran Church, write 12 books on Swedish culture, and claim to love lutefisk. But in other ways,

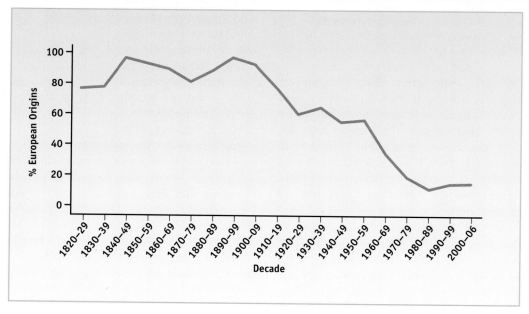

Figure 8.8 Percentage of Legal Immigrants Reporting European Origins, 1820–2006

(*Source:* Department of Homeland Security, *Yearbook of Immigration Statistics 2006.* Available at: www.dhs.gov/ximgtn/statistics/publications/yearbool.shtm.)

ethnicity and race are different. Because ethnicity is not based on biological difference (or the myth of biological difference), it can change from generation to generation, as culture becomes more or less significant. People "decide" just how "ethnic" they want to be. Immigrant groups find their ethnicities fading away, as children and grandchildren grow in the new country with fewer and fewer ties to home.

Ethnic groups share a common ancestry, history, or culture. They share similar geographic origins, language, cultural traditions, religion, and general values. When asked, "What ethnicity are you?" people whose families have lived in the United States for more than a few generations usually cannot answer. If they are White, they assume that their ancestors came from "somewhere in Europe," but English, French, Swiss, Prussian, Belgian, and Dutch immigrants intermingled so freely that they simply forgot about the homeland and its customs.

The United States is called a "nation of immigrants." Ever since the founding of the East Coast colonies by immigrants who had been thrown out of England for being too religious and "puritanical," different ethnic groups have not only "enriched" American life but make that life possible in the first place. President John F. Kennedy characterized the country's greatness as based on this fact, that America is "a society of immigrants, each of whom had begun life anew, on an equal footing." This was, he continued, the "secret" of America: "a nation of people with the fresh memory of old traditions who dared to explore new frontiers."

What are the origins of this nation of ethnic immigrants?

People from Europe

In the most recent census, 75 percent of the U.S. population was identified as White, most of European ancestry. The largest ethnic groups were German (23.3 percent), Irish (15.6 percent), Italian (4.9 percent), French (4.1 percent), and Polish (3.8 percent). We may now call them "European Americans" as a matter of convenience, but really we are saying "White people," referring to race rather than ethnicity. The differences today among many of these groups are

far smaller than they once were. The White European population will experience only a 7 percent increase during the next 50 years, increasing from 195.7 million in 2000 to 210.3 million in 2050.

People from North America

Native Americans (once called "Indians") were the original inhabitants of North America, present from at least 40,000 BCE. When the first Europeans and Africans arrived, there were between 2,000,000 and 10,000,000 people living north of the Rio Grande, divided into around 800 linguistic and cultural groups. Some were the nomadic hunter-gatherers of Hollywood-movie myth, but many were settled and agrarian, living in villages as large and prosperous as any villages among the European settlers. Still, the early European settlers usually approached the Native Americans through stereotypes: They were "noble savages," living without sin in a sort of Garden of Eden; or they were "wild savages," uncivilized and bestial. They were systematically deprived of their land and herded onto reservations, if not hunted and killed outright. William Henry Harrison and Andrew Jackson were both elected to the presidency primarily on their prestige as "Indian fighters." Political slogans and illustrations of the day showed them as noble, heroic White men "saving" America from the savage Indian threat. This threat was

Table 8.2
Selected Colleges and Universities That Changed Their Mascots

College	Former Mascot	Current Mascot	Date Changed
Dartmouth College, NH	Indians	Big Green	1969
Marquette University, WI	Warriors	Golden Eagles	1994
Northeastern State University, OK	Redmen	Riverhawks	2007
Seattle University, WA	Chieftains	Redhawks	1999
Shippensburg University, PA	Red Raiders	Raiders	2006
Simpson College, IA	Redmen	Storm	1992
Southeast Missouri State University	Indians	Redhawks	2004
Southern Nazarene University, OK	Redskins	Crimson Storm	1998
Southern Oregon University	Red Raiders	Raiders	1980
St. Bonaventure University, NY	Brown Indians	Bonnies	1979
Stanford University, CA	Indians	Cardinal	1972
Syracuse University, NY	Orangemen	Orange	1978
University of Massachusetts, Amherst	Redmen	Minutemen	1972
West Georgia University	Braves	Wolves	2006

contrived as the excuse to appropriate Native American land and natural resources and especially to clear a path for the transcontinental railroad. The stereotype of the Native American as uncivilized is still intact today, though it has changed from "violent" to "intuitive." Now movies have Native American sages teaching the White characters about listening to their hearts and staying close to nature.

Native Americans have long been used as mascots for sports teams. Did you know that half of all high school, college, and professional teams that used Native American mascots in 1960 have changed their mascots? Over 100 colleges and 1,000 schools use such mascots. Despite claims that these mascots are signs of "respect" for the tenacity and ferocity of the Native American tribes—tribes on whose appro-

priated land the colleges and universities may actually have been built—most Native Americans feel such mascots are insulting and perpetuate racial stereotypes (Table 8.2). "We simply chose an Indian as the emblem," explained one eighth grader when asked why his school had a Native American mascot. "We could have just as easily chosen any uncivilized animal."

In the most recent census, only about 1.5 percent of the population identified as Native American (alone or in combination with other races), but many more people have some Native American ancestry (most tribes require one-quarter ancestry to declare an official tribal affiliation). About half live in rural areas, mostly on reservations, and the rest are concentrated in big cities, especially Los Angeles, New York, Seattle, Chicago,

The NCAA started a policy in fall 2008 which prohibited collegiate teams from using Native American mascots. The former University of Illinois mascot was mistaken for an actual Native American Chief and even asked to perform weddings.

and Houston. The largest Native American nation, the Navajo or Dine of Arizona and New Mexico, has 269,000 members and many distinctive cultural institutions, including its own newspaper, radio station, and college. Its language is thriving. But most of the other Native American cultures are slowly dying out. Before the Europeans arrived, California was home to some 300 languages, more than the whole of Europe. Today 50 remain, though they are spoken by only a few people, almost all of them elderly.

The history of contact between European immigrants and Native Americans left many tribes destroyed, decimated, or displaced onto "reservations" (which were ironically conceived as places to "protect" the Native Americans from further harm by Whites who were stealing their land). As a result, today, Native Americans are worse off than other minorities in many measures of institutional discrimination:

- A 65 percent high school graduation rate and 9 percent college attendance rate, far below the national average
- A poverty rate of 32.2 percent, higher than any other ethnic group
- The highest rate of suicide in the 18- to 24-year-old age group
- A lower percentage of "current drinkers" than Whites and Hispanics, yet a higher rate of alcoholism
- A lower life expectancy than the nation as a whole (Ho, 2009; Housing Assistance Council, 2008)

Reservation life has grown mean and difficult, and funds are scarce for needed services. Many Native American cultures have taken advantage of tax and legal opportunities to open casinos (because reservations are not legally restricted from gambling) as a way to raise money since federal and state funds have all but dried up. This presents Native tribes with a cynical "choice": Either open a casino and feed the nation's gambling addiction or fail to provide needed services for their people.

Nonetheless, many Native Americans continue to embrace their cultural heritage. *Pan-Indianism* today emphasizes common elements that run through Native American cultures, creating an identity that goes beyond the individual nations.

People from Latin America

In the most recent census, 12.5 percent of the U.S. population declared that they were Hispanic or Latino/Latina, with ancestry in Latin America (the Caribbean, Mexico, and Central and South America). Since then, they have accounted for half of all U.S. population growth (Pew Hispanic Center, 2009). Latinos are now the largest ethnic minority group in the United States, and they are growing almost three times faster than the population as a whole (2.9 percent per year versus 1 percent per year in the general population), due both to immigration and higher birth rates (Figure 8.9). By 2050, the Hispanic population will nearly triple, from 35.6 million to 102.6 million.

Because these regions were originally settled by Native Americans, Europeans, Africans, and Asians, Hispanics may be of any race. Most speak Spanish at home, but they may speak Portuguese, French, Creole, Japanese, Italian, or an Indian language. Most are Roman Catholic, but they can be Protestant (usually Pentecostal), Jewish, Muslim, or followers of an Afro-Caribbean religion like Santería. Some do not approve

Pass the Salsa

Salsa has replaced ketchup as the most popular condiment. And in 2007, for the first time in American history, Hispanic names made the top 10 list of last names in America. Garcia (#8) and Rodriguez (#9) were both ahead of Wilson (#10) (Goldenberg, 2007).

Did You Know?

We are a nation of immigrants. President John F. Kennedy said this was the secret "secret" of America: "a nation of people with the fresh memory of old traditions who dared to explore new frontiers." Latinos represent the nation's largest ethnic minority (Spanish Harlem, New York City).

of dozens of distinct cultures being lumped together into people from a continent, so they prefer to be called Mexican Americans (or Chicanos), Cuban Americans, and so on.

Latinos in the United States come from various countries of origin:

- *From Mexico: 34.3 million*. This is the most established of the Hispanic subgroups: Just 36 percent are foreign born, and many have had ancestors in California, Arizona, or Texas since those states were part of Mexico.

- *From Central America: 2.3 million, mainly from El Salvador, Guatemala, Honduras, and Nicaragua*. These people live mostly in California, Texas, Florida, and New York. They tend to be foreign born (71 percent),

and 34 percent immigrated within the past decade. About 22 percent fall beneath the poverty line.

- *From South America: 1.7 million, mainly from Colombia, Ecuador, and Peru*. They tend to be foreign born (74 percent), and 33 percent immigrated within the past year. Many are well educated and belong to the middle class. About 35 percent of the foreign born have college degrees.

- *From Cuba: 1.2 million*. Of this group, 68 percent are foreign born, but most arrived more than a decade ago. Most have settled in Florida. They tend to be more affluent than other Hispanic subgroups. About a third of the foreign-born adults have some college education.

Figure 8.9 U.S. Hispanic Population by County

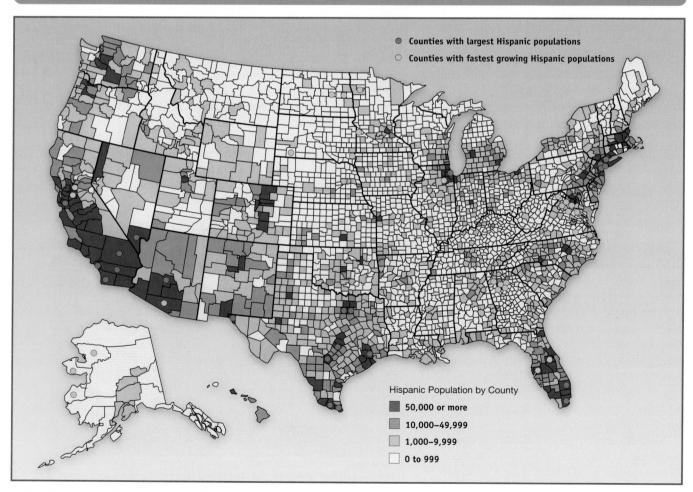

- *From the Dominican Republic: 912,000.* Over half live in New York. They are among the most impoverished of the Hispanic subgroups; 36 percent fall below the poverty line.
- *From Puerto Rico: about 3.5 million (not counting the 3.8 million in Puerto Rico itself).* About a third live in New York. They are among the most impoverished of the Hispanic subgroups: More than 30 percent are below the poverty line (Passel and Suro, 2005; U.S. Census Bureau, 2008).

Hispanic Americans are not only the fastest growing minority group in the United States: They also have the fastest growing affluence. Their disposable income may top $1 trillion by 2010 (Humphreys, 2006), and their earnings growth has not yet reached its peak (Moreno, 2008). Marketing executives have noticed. Hispanic people appear regularly on television commercials as purveyors of "traditional American values." Ten years ago, when Mexican American actor Mario Lopez starred in the teen sitcom *Saved by the Bell,* his character had to be made Anglo: Executives feared that no one would watch a show "with a Mexican in it."

Today, Hispanic actors are still often assigned to play gangsters, thugs, and servants, or else asked to play Anglo, but some, such as Penelope Cruz, America Ferrera, Benicia Del Toro, Antonio Banderas, and Jennifer Lopez, have "gone mainstream": They not only refuse to hide their ethnicity, they celebrate it. In South Florida, cable TV offers three all-Spanish channels, but they are not marketing only to the Hispanic community. The most popular *telenovelas* (prime-time soap operas) come with English-language subtitles so Anglos can watch too.

People from Sub-Saharan Africa

In the most recent census, 12.5 percent of the U.S. population was identified as Black or African American, with ancestry in sub-Saharan Africa. The two terms are often used interchangeably, but technically *Black* is a race that includes Andaman Islanders, Australian aboriginals, and other people from outside sub-Saharan Africa and does not apply to the White, Asian, and Khoisan

residents of Zimbabwe or Zaire. African American is an ethnicity, referring to the descendants of Black Africans who came to North America as slaves between 1500 and 1820 and who after slavery were subject to "Jim Crow" laws that kept Blacks and Whites separate and unequal. They therefore do share a history and cultural traditions. African Americans are the only group to immigrate to the United States against their will, as they were forcibly abducted to serve as slaves in the South and in the Caribbean.

To reinforce that common cultural tradition, some have celebrated June 19, called "Juneteenth," the day that word of the Emancipation Proclamation reached the slaves of the South; others have invented new holidays, like Kwanzaa. Some have fashioned a distinctive dialect of English, called "Ebonics," with some terms and grammatical structures borrowed from West African languages. The creation of new, and distinctly African American, names is also an invented way to "preserve" traditions. (Historically, slaves were named by their masters and likely to bear Anglo names like Sally and Bill; the power to name your child a more African-sounding name, like, say, Shaniqua or Kadeem, illustrates the power to control the fate of that child.)

Thus, in the process, they transformed race into ethnicity in its own right. (These invented traditions are controversial in the African American community itself because they replace more Christian holidays like Christmas.) Contemporary immigrants from Nigeria or South Africa may be Black, White, or Asian, but they would not be African American.

The African American population is expected to experience modest growth by 2050, growing from 40.2 million to 61.4 million.

At the turn of the last century, the great African American sociologist W. E. B. DuBois said that "the problem of the twentieth century is the problem of the color line." There are many racial and ethnic minority groups

The Origin of Hip

The words *hip-hop, hippie,* and *hip* all come from the African American *hep,* "cool" or "up-to-date," which ultimately derives from the Yoruba *hipikat,* "one who is aware, finely tuned to his or her environment." Other words and phrases derived from West African languages include *guy* (gay, "people"), *dig* (dega, "understand"), *jamboree* ("gathering"), *bug* ("bother"), *bogus* (boku, "fraud"), and *kick the bucket* (*kikatavoo,* "die").

Did You Know?

in the United States, and African Americans are not even the largest, yet they have always been the "standard" minority. Studies of prejudice and discrimination often concentrate on White and Black, ignoring everyone else, and indeed most of the racist legislation in the United States has been directed primarily if not exclusively against African Americans. The Civil Rights movement of the 1960s did not need to be more specific: Everyone realized that it was about the civil rights of African Americans.

Today, African Americans have achieved some measure of political and economic success. There is a sizeable Black middle class, with educational background and earnings comparable to those of middle-class Whites. Overall, however, African Americans lag behind White non-Hispanic Americans in high school graduation rate by 15 percentage points (Mishel and Joydeep, 2006) and college graduation rate by 20 percentage points (*Journal of Blacks in Higher Education*, 2007a). Black men's median earnings are 75 percent of what White men earn (women are roughly equal) (*State of Black America*, 2008). Twenty-five percent of Black people and 8 percent of white people are below poverty level (U.S. Census Bureau, 2008). Young Black men are nine times more likely to be murdered than are White men, and Black women three times as likely as White women (*National Urban League*, 2008). In recent years, there has been much debate about paying "reparations" to the descendants of former slaves because they worked for no payment and had their lives torn apart through slavery. (Jews have received reparations from the German and Swiss governments that profited from seizing their assets during World War II, and Black South Africans have received reparations for what was lost during apartheid.) Opponents claim that it would be too costly and would result in profiteering by minorities.

People from East and South Asia

About 4.6 percent of the U.S. population traces its ancestry to East, Southeast, or South Asia. These groups include China (22 percent), the Philippines (15 percent), India

Athletes like 2007 All-Star Game MVP Ichiro Suzuki defy stereotypes of Asians as weaklings and submissive nerds.

(15 percent), Korea (10 percent), Vietnam (10 percent), and Japan (9 percent). Harsh quotas limited immigration before the 1960s, so most are recent immigrants. They differ tremendously in language, religion, and culture, and often they have long-standing ethnic and national conflicts back home (Korea versus Japan, China versus Vietnam, and so on) that make the umbrella term *Asian American* problematic.

Even within a nationality, there are many ethnic differences. People from China may speak Mandarin, Cantonese, or any of a dozen other varieties of Chinese or a hundred local languages. People from India may be Hindu, Muslim, Christian, Buddhist, Sikh, Jain, or atheist. People from Mindanao, the largest and most industrialized island of the Philippines, may look down on people from other islands as uncouth and uncivilized. So even *Chinese American, Indian American,* and *Filipino/a* become a problem. The Asian American population is expected to triple by 2050, rising from 10.7 million to 33.4 million, primarily due to immigration (U.S. Census Bureau, 2008).

Asian Americans are often depicted as "the model minority." Many measures of discrimination are significant only for Blacks and Hispanics (like school achievement, college enrollments, prison populations); Asian Americans score the same as

Whites or surpass them. They have the highest college graduation rate of any ethnic group. Though Asian Americans are just less than 5 percent of the total population, they comprise 15 percent of all U.S. physicians and surgeons, 15 percent of all computer and mathematical occupations, 10 percent of all engineers, and 16 percent of the student body at Ivy League colleges (Kim, 2006). They are less likely to become victims of racially motivated hate crimes than any ethnic group except Whites.

Even the stereotypes of Asian Americans are somewhat different. Prejudiced beliefs about Blacks and Hispanics mark them as barbaric, unpredictable, violent, and sexually dangerous. *The Bell Curve* and other works claimed that African Americans were genetically inferior to Whites, had a lower native intelligence—that is, the arguments were about "nature" and no amount of "nurture" could compensate for their natural inferiority (Hernnstein and Murray, 1996). Prejudiced ideas about Asian Americans mark them as weak, passive, and asexual. In the mass media, they commonly appear not as thugs and drug dealers but as mystical sages and science nerds—stereotypes that are equally unfair but not nearly as threatening (Hamamoto, 1994). The success of Asian Americans, though, is attributed to their incredible work ethic, discipline, and parental influence—that is, as the result of "nurture." Few would be so consistent as to posit that Asian Americans were genetically superior to other groups. Of course, all of these are broad and false stereotypes. The point is that racist arguments are inconsistent; people refer to whichever one suits their purposes.

Scholars wondering about the "success" of the Asian American population have come up with several explanations. First, most Asian immigrants belonged to the middle class in their home country, so they find it easier to enter the middle class in the United States. They are more likely to be fluent in English. Because there are relatively few of them, they are unlikely to live in segregated neighborhoods and much more likely to marry someone of another racial/ethnic group (Asian American Cultural Center, 2005; Wong, 1986). Finally, if prejudice boils down to light versus dark, they may profit by being relatively light skinned.

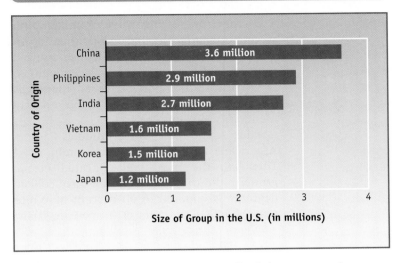

Figure 8.10 Major Asian American Groups

(*Source:* 2006 American Community Survey, <http://factfinder.census.gov>.)

People from the Middle East

The U.S. Census does not give them a separate category, but about 2 million people in the United States trace their ancestry to the Middle East or North Africa. About 1,500,000 are recent immigrants who have arrived since 1970. About one-third of these are Iranian, one-third Turkish, and the other one-third are Arabs, Israelis, Cypriots, and others. There have been two broad migrations of Middle Easterners to the United States:

- Between 1880 and 1920, refugees came here from the failing Ottoman Empire, especially Lebanon, Cyprus, Syria, and Armenia. They were mostly working class and poor, about 75 percent Christian and the rest Muslim or Jewish. They settled primarily in the industrial Northeast and Midwest.

- After 1970, many middle-class Israelis, Arabs, and Iranians immigrated to America. Of those, 73 percent were Muslim. They settled primarily in large cities, especially Los

The Mother Mosque

The first building in the United States designed for exclusive use as a mosque was constructed in Cedar Rapids, Iowa, in 1934. It was sold in 1971, becoming a youth center and a church, and then abandoned. In 1990, the Islamic Council of Iowa acquired and restored the building, and the "Mother Mosque" is now listed on the National Register of Historic Places as an "essential piece of American religious history."

Did You Know?

Angeles, New York, Chicago, Houston, and Washington, D.C.

Members of the first wave of immigration were assimilationist; like most other immigrants of the period, they hid or minimized their Middle Eastern ancestry and sought to fit in. During the past 50 years, there has been an increase in efforts to retain separate identity as Muslims.

Like Asian Americans, Middle Eastern Americans tend to be a "model minority." They are the most well-educated ethnic group in the United States: Half have college degrees, as opposed to 30 percent of White non–Middle Easterners. The median salary of Middle Eastern men is slightly higher than the national mean. However, nearly 20 percent live below the poverty level (U.S. Census Bureau, 2008).

Stereotypes about Middle Easterners tend to be more extreme, and more commonly believed, than stereotypes about other minority groups. Many Americans unaware of the political, cultural, and religious differences in the Middle East tend to believe that all Middle Easterners are Arabs, Muslims, or even Bedouins, who live in tents and ride camels. The men are stereotyped as wide-eyed terrorists; the women as subservient chattel. Even the hero of Disney's *Aladdin* (1993), who was an Arab but evidently not "as Arab" as everyone else, complains of the barbarity of his country: "They'll cut off your nose to spite your face, but hey, it's home." The conventional movie villain was once German, then Russian, then "Euro-terrorist"; now he is a Middle Eastern Arab.

Prejudice and discrimination against Middle Easterners, Arabs, and Muslims increased significantly after the 9/11 terrorist attacks. In 2003, the Pew Forum on Religion and Public Life found 38 percent of respondents would not vote for a well-qualified Muslim for president (a higher percentage than for any minority except gays), and half believed that half or more of all Muslims are anti-American (Pew Forum on Religion and Public Life, 2003). The FBI documented an increase of 1,600 percent in hate crimes against Arabs in 2001, jumping from 28 reported crimes in 2000 to 481 in 2001. Today, the number of anti-Islamic bias crimes is down to 156 incidents, a figure still second only to anti-Jewish crimes, which tower atop the list at 1,027 reported crimes (U.S. Department of Justice, 2007). In most countries of the European Union, intolerance has also increased significantly, first following September 11 and then spiking in different countries in the aftermath of incidents in each. Eighty percent of Muslims in the United Kingdom said they had experienced discrimination in 2001, a jump from 45 percent in 2000 and 35 percent in 1999; hostility increased in Spain and Germany after the Madrid train bombing and in the Netherlands after the murder of filmmaker Theo van Gogh, both in 2004 (International Helsinki Federation for Human Rights, 2006).

Ethnic groups compose niche markets that develop their own lifestyles and patterns of consumption. Young Muslim women can embrace the traditional and the modern at the same time.

Ethnicity: Identity and Conflict

Ethnicity is fluid; sometimes ethnic identification is stronger than at other times. For some groups for whom discrimination has largely disappeared, such as the Irish and the Italians, ethnic identity has become mostly a choice (Gans, 1962; Waters, 1990). Ethnicity becomes "situational"—to be asserted in times and situations when it will increase their prestige and downplayed or ignored when it may decrease their prestige. Or it becomes symbolic ethnicity, something to participate in on special occasions, like St. Patrick's Day or Passover, but ignored the rest of the time. Just as old ethnicities can fade away, new ethnicities can emerge. Members of the Yoruba, Ibo, Fulani, and other West African ethnic groups transported to the United States during the slavery era were forcibly stripped of their distinctive cultures, until only a few customs remained, but they banded together to form a new ethnic group, African American.

Ethnic Conflict

When several different ethnic groups are present in a single nation, they often compete for power and resources. Because there are around 5,000 ethnic groups in the world trying to share 190 nations, ethnic conflict is common, ranging from discrimination to violence and sometimes even civil war. Since 1945, 15 million people have died in conflicts involving ethnicity to some degree (Doyle, 1998).

At its most brutal, ethnic conflict can result in **genocide,** the planned, systematic destruction of a racial, political, or cultural group. The most infamous modern example of genocide is the Nazi massacre of 6 million Jews, Gypsies, gays, and other "undesirables" during World War II, but there have been a number of others. Between 1915 and 1923 the Turkish elite of the Ottoman Empire killed over 1 million ethnic Armenians. In the 1990s, the dominant Hutu ethnic group killed hundreds of thousands of minority Tutsi in Rwanda and Burundi; and a new euphemism for genocide, "ethnic cleansing," arose when majority Serbs killed hundreds of thousands of minority Muslims in Bosnia. War in Kosovo in 1999 was prompted by the charges that Serbian forces were engaging in "ethnic cleansing" of the Kosovar Albanians.

Why do ethnic minorities live in relative harmony in some countries while in others they are at each other's throats? There are no easy answers, but one factor appears to be heterogeneity. If there are many ethnic groups in the country, it is less likely that any one will dominate and the others feel left out. However, if there are only two or three, it is easy for them to characterize each other as demonic. Another factor is the rights and privileges given to minorities. In countries where ethnic minorities are accepted as ordinary parts of the political structure, they are less likely to compete for resources, real or imagined, and ethnic conflict is less common (Gurr, 2000; van Amersfoort, 1982).

Immigration ≠ Increased Crime

Increased immigration does not lead to an increase in crime. (See Figure 8.11.) Research by sociologist Robert Sampson found that Mexican American immigrants in Chicago were 45 percent less likely to commit violence than third-generation Americans. Immigrants, he found, are "less violent than people born in America, particularly when they live in neighborhoods with high numbers of other immigrants." Instead of moving from the multicultural city to the more homogeneous suburbs to avoid crime, we should move to an immigrant neighborhood. They're safer (Sampson, 2006)!

Did You Know?

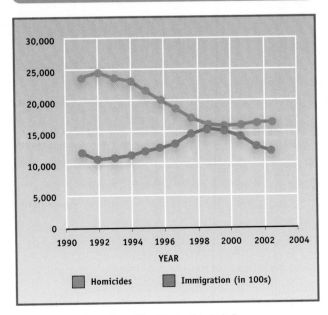

Figure 8.11 U.S. Immigration Flows and Homicide Trends

(*Source:* From "Open Doors Don't Invite Criminals," by Robert J. Sampson, *New York Times*, March 11, 2006.)

Melting Pot (Assimilation) and Multiculturalism (Pluralism)

My grade school social studies textbook—that same one with the pictures illustrating the three races—glowingly described America as a *melting pot.* The United States was praised for its acceptance of difference, lack of prejudice, and our ability to melt down all cultural differences into a single, savory American soup.

Sociologically, this process seems unlikely because the dominant groups are rarely willing to let their characteristics melt away into the pot. Instead, the minority groups were subject to **assimilation,** nearly abandoning their cultural traditions altogether and embracing the dominant culture. Only a few of their traditions entered the pot, mostly food (like pizza) and slang terms (like *pal* for friend, from the Romany word for "brother"); most traits and traditions were left behind. It was Italian Americans in the process of assimilating, not Italy, that gave us pizza—it was unknown in Palermo until a Pizza Hut franchise opened there. Besides, only White Europeans were invited to melt down. Asians, Native Americans, and Blacks weren't even given the option.

Some immigrant groups felt that assimilation was not desirable. They didn't want to lose

U.S. / Them

Who's Foreign Born?

The United States proudly calls itself "a nation of immigrants." What percent of the population in the following countries is foreign born—and what percent of those immigrants are citizens of their new country?

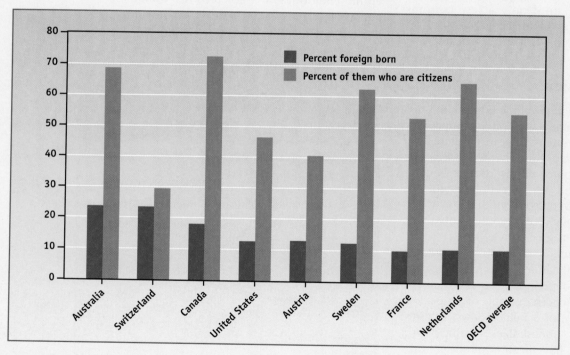

(*Source:* "Immigrant population," in OECD Factbook 2009: *Economic, Environmental and Social Statistics.* Copyright © OECD, 2009. Reproduced by permission.)

1. Only a few countries have higher percentages of foreign-born people than the United States, but the percent of that group who are citizens of their new country varies dramatically. What might explain the differences between Australia and Switzerland, for example?

2. Why is the percentage of foreign-born people higher than the average in the United States and the percent who are citizens lower than average?

What do **you** think?

The Melting Pot

Often referred to as a melting pot society, the United States boasts a rich variety of ethnic customs and traditions. As a society, we are trying to find a balance between assimilation and division. So, what do you think?

Some people say that it is better for a country if different racial and ethnic groups maintain their distinct customs and traditions. Others say that it is better if these groups adapt and blend into the larger society. Which of these views comes closer to your own?

○ It is better for society if groups maintain their distinct customs and traditions.

○ It is better for society if groups adapt and blend into the larger culture.

What does **America** think?

(These are based on actual survey data from the General Social Survey, 2004.)

The responses to this question were split almost in half. Slightly more than 50 percent of respondents thought it was better if groups adapted and blended into the larger society. White respondents (55.4 percent) were more likely to think that than were Black respondents (52.8 percent), and those who identified as other race were least likely to feel groups should assimilate (45.7 percent).

Thinking Critically about Survey Data

1. Why do you think there were only very small differences in responses by racial classification?

2. In many areas of the world, the question of assimilation and group difference leads to civil war and even genocide. Why do you think that does not happen in the contemporary United States?

References: See Davis et al., page 511.

---

their distinctive customs, social norms, language, and religion. Why couldn't they continue to speak their native language, read newspapers from home, eat the same food they ate at home, and still be Americans? Maybe in the nineteenth century, when the journey from the homeland to the United States took months and there was little chance of ever returning, assimilation made sense, but now the homeland was only a short plane flight away, and friends and relatives back home as close as a telephone call or email message.

During the 1980s and 1990s, many minority groups proposed pluralism as an alternative to the melting pot. **Pluralism** maintains that a stable society need not contain just one ethnic, cultural, or religious group. The different groups can treat each other with mutual respect instead of competing and trying to dominate each other. Thus,

minority cultures can maintain their own distinctiveness and still participate in the greater society without discrimination.

Multiculturalism. At its most stable, pluralism becomes multiculturalism, in which cultural groups exist not only side by side but equally. Real multiculturalism seems to be rare—one language, religion, or culture will usually dominate, either by numbers or by prestige, and people will be drawn to it, even in the absence of institutional discrimination. India has 22 official languages, but official

The Immigrant Press

The number of foreign-language newspapers in the United States increased every year from 1885 (when there were 822) until 1913 (when there were 1,323). There were daily newspapers in Swedish, Yiddish, Polish, German, Russian, Chinese, Italian, French, Chinese, Albanian, Greek, Hungarian, Croatian, Welsh, and many others. The immigrant press was a force for diversity as well as for cultural assimilation, as most papers promoted citizenship, instructed readers about American institutions, and encouraged consumerism through paid advertising (Kaestle et al., 1993; University of Chicago Library, 2007).

Did You Know?

communication in the national arena must be conducted in Hindi or English, and for everyday communication people tend to prefer English.

Advocates of multiculturalism like to point out the case of Switzerland, where four linguistic and cultural groups enjoy complete equality under the law. But are they really equal in everyday life? Nearly two-thirds (65 percent) of the population speaks German, 18 percent French, 10 percent Italian, and 0.8 percent Romansch (descended from Latin). Street signs are usually in the local language and German. In Parliament, speeches may be given in any of the national languages, but most politicians choose German, even if they speak something else at home. All schoolchildren must learn a second national language, but schools usually offer only German and French, so learning Italian or Romansch is not an option. People outside the German-speaking cantons often pretend that they do not understand German at all, as a way of resisting what they feel is linguistic imperialism by the "dominant" linguistic group. Clearly, the other languages do not enjoy the same prestige.

Bilingualism. The American assimilation model meant that English was preferred by society at large to the home language. The dominant culture expected that immigrants would enroll in English classes the moment they arrived; and, even if children were not punished for using their parents' birth language, they might grow up thinking that it was old-fashioned and outdated, a relic of their parents' generation. Today, however, many immigrants continue to speak their "native" language. Spanish is especially popular.

The United States is increasingly multicultural—and our institutions show it. Many American cities now have street signs in several languages, depending on the ethnic composition of the neighborhood. (This picture was taken in Chinatown, in New York City.)

The Hispanic preference for speaking Spanish has led to some controversy that speakers of Bengali, Muong, and Byelorussian do not generate. In the United States, 29 million people use Spanish as their everyday language, more than any non-Spanish nation in the world, yet 23 states have laws declaring English their official language and permitting only English in official documents.

Race and Ethnicity in the Twenty-First Century

Like class or gender, race and ethnicity are vital elements of our identity and also the basis for discrimination and inequality. Every one of us constructs our identity, at least in part, through race and ethnicity. It is one of the most important foundations of identity, an anchor that ties us to family, tradition, and culture. And yet virtually every one of us also wants to be treated as an individual, by our talents and achievements alone. We love it when race and ethnicity give us a sense of belonging and community; we hate it when our race and ethnicity are used against us, to deny us opportunities.

Maybe it is simply that we each want to be the ones who decide when race matters and when it doesn't: It should matter when we need to feel the connections among our roots, and it shouldn't matter when we want to be seen as individual trees.

But just as race and ethnicity seem to tie us to one common ancestry, a place of blood and birth, those categories are shifting dramatically in the contemporary world. These processes expose the *sociology* of race and ethnicity: The experiences of fixed and essential characteristics are the invention of different groups as they come into contact with each other. (After all, virtually every culture that had no contact with other people did not have an understanding of race; they simply called themselves "human beings.") Race, as an idea, requires interaction with others—that is, it requires not biology but society and culture.

And the changes in racial and ethnic identities are liable to be dramatic and lasting. In 2050, White Europeans will constitute 50 percent of the U.S. population (which will be 420 million), Latinos 24 percent, African Americans 15 percent, and Asian Americans 8 percent. We will be a multiracial nation, but will we be a multicultural one? In 1998, then-President Bill Clinton heralded a rich and multicultural future:

> Today, largely because of immigration, there is no majority race in Hawaii or Houston or New York City. Within five years, there will be no majority race in our largest state, California. In a little more than 50 years, there will be no majority race in the United States. No other nation in history has gone through demographic change of this magnitude in so short a time. [These immigrants] are energizing our culture and broadening our vision of the world. They are renewing our most basic values and reminding us all of what it truly means to be American.

Do you agree? After all, as we have seen, an increase in numbers does not necessarily bring equality. Will White privilege still be intact? Will "White" still be invisible, the unmarked category? In a well-known essay, sociologist Norman Glazer (1998) states, "We are all multiculturalists now." Will we start acting like it?

Chapter Review

1. The Sociology of Race and Ethnicity

Race and **ethnicity** are systems for categorizing people. Sociologists recognize that they are important for identity, are often the basis for inequality, and aren't set in stone—rather, definitions vary over time and by place, as they are social constructions rather than biological facts. Although there is no "pure" race, interracial relationships were stigmatized historically. Multiraciality is increasingly common, and many prominent personalities are bi- or multiracial, but race and ethnicity remain important for identity. A **minority group** member is part of an **in-group** with others of the same minority, compared with the **out-group,** the socially dominant **majority group.** Historically, race has been socially constructed in terms of "we" and "they."

race Social category, still poorly defined, that depends on an assumption of biological distinction to rate and organize social groups. (p. 220)

ethnicity Social category that depends on an assumption of inherent cultural differences to rate and organize social groups. (p. 220)

minority group A group one is born into, which has a distinguishable identity and whose members have less power and access to resources than other groups in society because of that group membership. (p. 223)

in-group A group with which you identify and that you feel positively toward, producing a "we" feeling. (p. 224)

out-group One to which you do not belong and toward which you feel either neutral or hostile; the "they" who are perceived as different from and of lower stature than ourselves. (p. 224)

majority group A group whose members experience privilege and access to power because of their group membership. With regard to race, lighter-colored skin usually means membership in the majority group. (p. 224)

2. Prejudice, Discrimination, and Racism

Prejudice, racism, and **discrimination** are often based on a **stereotype. Overt racism** includes discrimination, and is more obvious than **subtle racism,** which may be unconscious thoughts based on stereotypes. **Institutional discrimination** is particularly damaging, being pervasive, systematic, sometimes without willful intent. **Segregation** refers to racial separation; like **apartheid,** it perpetuates and sanctions discrimination and inequality. In the United States, **integration** occurred when segregation's inequalities were acknowledged by the Supreme Court, although in reality segregation and inequality continue to some degree. **Affirmative action** was intended to end discriminatory hiring practices, but because of underrepresentation of minorities in schools and work settings, it can result in **tokenism. Primordial theory** is one theory of prejudice; another is frustration-aggression theory, which sees minorities as a **scapegoats** for aggression.

A conflict orientation emphasizes the utility of racism and prejudice in maintaining subjugation of the underclass by legitimating structural inequality. Theories often don't address why a particular minority is subject to discrimination or stereotyping. It has been proposed that U.S. Blacks are an **internal colony.** Having multiple minority identities results in an interlocking intersection of control called a **matrix of domination.** Prejudice and discrimination may be abating, but people still feel the effects of racism.

prejudice A set of beliefs and attitudes that cause us to negatively prejudge people based on their social location. (p. 226)

racism A particularly powerful form of prejudice that includes not only a belief in general stereotypes but also a belief that one race (usually White) is inherently superior to the others. Racism is a prejudice that is systematically applied to members of a group. (p. 226)

discrimination A set of actions based on prejudice and stereotypes. (p. 226)

stereotype Generalization about a group that is oversimplified and exaggerated and that fails to acknowledge individual differences in the group. (p. 226)

overt racism Systematic prejudice applied to members of a group in clear, manifest ways, such as speech, discrimination, or a refusal to associate with members of that group. (p. 228)

subtle racism Systematic prejudice applied to members of a group in quiet or even unconscious ways; a simple set of mental categories that one may possess about a group based on stereotypes. (p. 228)

institutional discrimination The most subtle and pervasive type of discrimination, it is deeply embedded in such institutions as the educational system, the business world, health care, criminal justice, and the mass media. These social institutions promote discriminatory practices and traditions that have such a long history they just "seem to make sense," and minority groups become the victims of systematic oppression, even when only a few people, or none at all, are deliberately trying to discriminate. (p. 230)

segregation The practice of physically separating races by law and custom in institutions and communities. (p. 231)

apartheid A race-based caste system that mandated segregation of different racial groups. In South Africa it was a political system institutionalized by the White minority in 1948 and remained in effect until 1990. (p. 231)

integration The physical intermingling of the races organized as a concerted legal and social effort to bring equal access and racial equality through racial mixing in institutions and communities. (p. 232)

affirmative action Programs and policies developed to ensure that qualified minority group members are not discriminated against in the workplace, school admission, and the like. Affirmative action policies generally apply to race, ethnicity, and gender, among other categories. (p. 232)

tokenism When a single member of a minority group is present in an office, workplace, or classroom and is seen as a representative of that minority group rather than as an individual. (p. 233)

primordial theory A general theory that the origins of conflict may be found in our ties to blood and kinship groups—race, ethnicity, nation, tribe. (p. 234)

scapegoat A convenient, weak, and socially approved target for economic or social loss or insecurity. (p. 235)

internal colony Internal colonialism is a theory of race relations that argues that the position of African Americans in the United States is analogous to the position of colonies to the imperialist powers at the turn of the 20th century. An internal colony is the name for the subjugated group. (p. 235)

matrix of domination An interlocking system of control in which each type of inequality reinforces the others, so that the impact of one cannot be fully understood without also considering the others. (p. 236)

3. Ethnic Groups in the United States

U.S. citizens have origins in many countries and cultures. Ethnicity changes from generation to generation. The further removed generationally people are from their origins, the fewer the ties to their original culture and to people sharing those traditions. This is how people lose identification with an **ethnic group.** In a few generations, U.S. citizens with European origins, the largest percentage of Americans, have typically lost identification with their culture of origin. There are few Native American people left in the United States. This group suffers stereotyping and deprivation, with few resources, as a result of "protection" on reservations as their lands were diminished. Although few original tribal cultures remain, their ethnic identity is a source of pride. People with Latin American origins have great diversity due to the numerous countries and languages of origin. Together they are the largest ethnicity in the United States, with the greatest growing affluence and population. People of sub-Saharan African origin, called African Americans, share a unique heritage, having been brought here against their will, abducted and transported as slaves, and later subjected to "Jim Crow" laws. Asian Americans and Middle Eastern Americans often come from middle-class backgrounds originally and are often well off and highly educated compared to other U.S. ethnic groups. Both groups suffer from stereotyping, and the latter, most recently, are victims of increased hostility and discrimination.

ethnic group A group that is set apart from other groups by language and cultural traditions. Ethnic groups share a common ancestry, history, or culture. (p. 239)

4. Ethnicity: Identity and Conflict

Ethnic conflict arises from ethnic diversity in a nation, coupled with differential power and resources. Conflict includes discrimination, violence, civil war, and, at its most extreme, **genocide.** The more diversity, the less likely that any one ethnicity will be demonized. Conflict is also less likely when ethnic groups are part of a nation's political structure. Instead of conflict, **assimilation** may occur in a "melting pot," as in the United States, although this results in loss of ethnic identity for minority ethnicities, with dominance of the majority. An alternative is **pluralism,** which preserves and respects diversity, resulting in true multiculturalism.

genocide The planned, systematic destruction of a racial, political, or ethnic group. (p. 247)

assimilation Occurs when two groups come into contact and the minority group abandons its traditional culture to embrace the dominant culture. (p. 248)

pluralism Maintains that different groups in a stable society can treat each other with mutual respect and that minority cultures can maintain their own distinctiveness and still participate in the greater society without discrimination. (p. 249)

5. Race and Ethnicity in the Twenty-First Century

Race and ethnicity, as sources of identity, can give us feelings of pride and belonging but can also be the source of stereotype, prejudice, and discrimination. America is increasingly a multiracial nation.

Self-Test: Check Your Understanding

1. Which of the following is an action or behavior, rather than a belief or an attitude?
   a. Racism
   b. Prejudice
   c. Stereotype
   d. Discrimination

2. One of your classmates states that members of certain ethnic minorities are bound to get better grades on the exam because they are smarter. Your classmate's statements are examples of:
   a. racism.
   b. prejudice.
   c. a stereotype.
   d. discrimination.

3. According to sociologists, race:
   a. is a biological fact.
   b. is a social construct.
   c. depends on country of origin.
   d. follows from culture.

4. Which of the following is not true of minority groups?
   a. Members are always fewer in number than the majority.
   b. The group has less social power than the majority.
   c. Group members have less access to resources than the majority.
   d. All of the above are true of minority groups.

5. Sociologists working from a conflict perspective view racism in terms of:
   a. the justification that it provides for perpetuating inequality.
   b. an in-group and out-group identity process.
   c. the opportunity to vent aggressions and hostilities.
   d. the cost to society through loss of productive workers.

6. In the United States, the fastest-growing ethnic group is comprised of people originating in:
   a. sub-Saharan Africa.
   b. Asia.
   c. Latin America.
   d. the Middle East.

7. "Ethnic cleansing" is another name for:
   a. civil war.
   b. genocide.
   c. prejudice.
   d. discrimination.

8. A pluralistic society is one in which:
   a. everyone comes together in a "melting pot" and ethnic minorities assimilate.
   b. the majority is the standard for what is considered normal and minorities suffer.
   c. there are no minority groups because everyone is similar with a shared ethnicity.
   d. minority groups preserve their distinctive identities and have political participation.

Self-Test Answers: 1. d, 2. c, 3. b, 4. a, 5. a, 6. c, 7. b, 8. d

Integrate and Explore: Points to Consider

1. Is ethnic conflict inevitable? What are the conditions that make ethnic conflict more, and less, likely? Are prejudice and discrimination inevitable? Under what circumstances are prejudice and discrimination reduced? How do sociologists view power and conflict in relation to racism and discrimination?

2. How is a multicultural society different from a "melting pot" society? Will globalization increase pluralism or result in assimilation?

succeed with mysoclab PEARSON

Self-scoring practice tests, flashcards for learning key terms, streaming audio of the entire text, and multimedia, including:

Watch—*1963 March on Washington/Martin Luther King's "I Have a Dream" Speech*

Watch—*Synagogue Doubles As Mosque*

Explore—Interactive Map: *U.S. Census Data on Race and Origin*

Map—Social Explorer: *The Melting Pot Theory*

MySocLibrary—Cornel West: *Race Matters*

9

Sex and Gender

Barbie turned 50 in 2009. First introduced by Mattel in 1959, Barbie quickly became an international icon of femininity. Today, with over 1 billion sold (two dolls every second) in 150 countries, Barbie's shelf life encompasses both the challenges and the changes in our understanding of gender.

Barbie dolls were given a voice—literally— in 1992. Among Teen Talk Barbie's phrases were "Will we ever have enough clothes?" "I love shopping!" and "Math class is tough!" These sentiments suggested a distinctly female world of looking attractive and steering clear of science and math, where public life takes place in shopping malls.

The idea that men and women are fundamentally different pervades many cultures—including

ours—today. We have romantic "chick flicks" for women and violent action-adventure movies and video games for men. Intuitive, care-taking professions like early childhood education and nursing are seen as "women's jobs," while men are thought to be suited for analytical fields like engineering and computers. Women are believed to be best at cooperating and helping, while men are made for competitive environments and leadership, from sports, to corporate management, to public office.

"Men are from Mars, women are from Venus," that's how John Gray's international best-seller put it in 1992—the very same year Barbie began to speak. It has since been the title of a movie, a television show, a Broadway show, and a board game. It expresses what many people have come to believe is a basic and simple truth about gender: Men and women "think, feel, perceive, react, respond, love, need and appreciate differently" (Gray, 1992, p. 5)—so differently that we might as well be from different planets.

Yet, despite these differences, you are probably attending a coeducational school, where you sit in the same classes, live in the same dorms, eat in the same cafeteria, listen to the same lectures, read the same texts, take the same tests, and are graded (you hope) by the same criteria as members of the opposite sex. At home, we live in the same houses, prepare and eat the same meals, use the same bathrooms, and often watch the same television programs as our opposite-sex family members or spouses. We live in a world of *both* gender difference *and* gender similarity.

Gender is one of the fundamental ways in which we develop an identity. Every society in the world classifies people by whether they are male or female, and a host of social roles and relationships are prescribed as a result. Virtually every society assumes that, in some basic ways, women and men are different.

And gender is one of the fundamental ways in which societies organize themselves. In virtually every society, women and men are not equal. Gender inequality is a nearly universal phenomenon: To be a man or a woman means not only difference but also hierarchy.

"We live in a world of both gender difference and gender similarity. Women and men do often appear to be rather different creatures, and yet we are also so fundamentally similar in so many ways that we can work together, learn together and even live together."

Why does virtually every society differentiate people on the basis of biological sex? And why is virtually every known society also based on gender inequality, on the dominance of men over women? These are the two questions that animate the sociological study of gender.

To many observers, the answer is simple: Men dominate women because men and women are so different. Biological differences between women and men lead inevitably to different political, social, and economic outcomes. Men and women are unequal because nature made them different.

But sociologists take a different view. Sociologists believe that if gender inequality were simply the product of gender difference, then gender inequality would look pretty much the same everywhere. And, as we will see, gender inequality varies enormously from one culture to another. Plus, if gender difference itself were simply a reflection of natural differences, then these differences, too, would be universal. As we will see, they are far from universal.

We live in a world of *both* gender difference *and* gender similarity. Women and men do often appear to be rather different creatures, and yet we are also so fundamentally similar in so many ways that we are able to work together, learn together, and even live together. Even Barbie. After all, she's not only been an elementary school teacher, aerobics instructor, nurse, flight attendant, and McDonald's cashier, but also a surgeon, U.S. Army officer, fire fighter, police officer, pilot, business executive, and three-time presidential candidate!

Sex and Gender: Nature *and* Nurture

Sociologists begin by distinguishing sex and gender. When we refer to **sex** we refer to the biology of maleness and femaleness—our chromosomal, chemical, anatomical organization.

Gender refers to the meaning that societies give to the fact of biological difference. What is the significance of biological difference? Does it mean that you must—or must not—perform certain tasks, think certain thoughts, or do certain things? Sex is male and female; gender is the cultural meaning of masculinity and femininity.

Biological sex varies little—males everywhere have a Y chromosome, for example—but gender varies enormously. Specifically, gender varies in four crucial ways:

1. *Gender varies from culture to culture.* What it means to be a man or a woman in one culture may be quite different from that in another.
2. *Definitions of gender change over time.* What it may mean to be a man or a woman in the United States today is different from what it meant in 1776.
3. *Definitions of gender vary within a society.* Within any one society it may mean different things to be a man or a woman depending on race, religion, region, age, sexuality, class, and other social categories (see Kimmel, 2003).
4. *Gender varies over the life course.* What it means to be a man or a woman at age 20 is probably quite different from what it will mean to you at age 40 or at age 70.

Each of the social and behavioral sciences contributes to the study of gender. Anthropologists can help illuminate the cross-cultural differences, while historians can focus our attention on the differences over time. Developmental psychologists explore how definitions of masculinity and femininity vary over the course of one's life. And it has been sociology's contribution to examine the ways in which our different experiences, based on other bases of identity—class, race, and the like—affect our definitions of gender.

Gender identity refers to our understanding of ourselves as male or female, what we think it means to be male or female. Sociologists are aware that other identities, like class or race, dramatically affect gender identity. Sociologists who observe the *intersection* of

16th ASEAN Regional Forum

Increased gender equality has meant that many women are now entering positions formerly reserved for men. But they still have to maintain a balance between competent professional and feminine. Here, Secretary of State Hillary Clinton wears a suit, like the men—but distinctly feminine.

these identities speak, then, of gender identities as plural: *masculinities* and *femininities*. In fact, the differences *among* men and *among* women are often greater than the differences that we imagine *between* women and men. So, for example, although there are small differences between girls and boys in math and language abilities, we all know plenty of boys who are adept at languages and can barely learn the times tables and plenty of girls who whiz through math class but can't conjugate a Spanish verb.

The other major aspect of gender is inequality. **Gender inequality** has two dimensions: the domination of men over women and the domination of some men over other men (by virtue of class inequality or race inequality, for example) and some women over other women. Making the category of identity plural doesn't mean that all masculinities or femininities are considered equal.

All known societies are characterized by some amount of gender inequality, in which men dominate women (see Coult, 1965). This is called *male domination,* or patriarchy. **Patriarchy** literally means "the rule of the fathers," and while fathers don't rule in every case, men do hold power over women.

And most societies also grant more power and resources to some men and some women. One definition of masculinity or femininity comes to dominate and becomes the standard against which everyone comes

to be measured and to measure themselves. This is where race and class and the other bases of identity and inequality come in.

In 1963, the sociologist Erving Goffman described masculinity in the United States this way:

> In an important sense, there is only one complete unblushing male in America: a young, married, white, urban, northern, heterosexual, Protestant, father, of college education, fully employed, of good complexion, weight and height, and a recent record in sports. (p. 128)

In the next sentence, Goffman described what it feels like to *not* have all those characteristics. "Any male who fails to qualify in any one of these ways is likely to view himself—during moments at least—as unworthy, incomplete, and inferior." Because it is certain that all males will, at some point, fail to measure up to all those criteria, what Goffman is saying is that *all* males will, at some point, feel "unworthy, incomplete, and inferior."

Why do men and women in every country seem to be so different from each other? And why do we everywhere observe gender inequality?

This balance between gender identity and professional identity is equally true for minority men. Can you be corporate and still be styling? It's a difficult balance.

The Biology of Sex and Gender

Most everyday explanations of gender identity and gender inequality begin—and often end —with biology. The observed biological differences between women and men are thought to lead naturally, and inevitably, to the inequality we observe. Because we're different, the argument goes, we shouldn't try to be similar. And if these differences are natural, gender inequality is inevitable; changes in male–female relations contradict nature's plan and are therefore best avoided. (This is, of course, the "nature" side of the debate; we will also discuss the "nurture" side.)

Biological arguments rest on three types of evidence: evolutionary adaptation, different brain structures and chemistry, and hormonal differences. Sociologists must be aware of these sorts of arguments because sociological perspectives on sex and gender often run counter to them.

Evolutionary Imperatives. According to evolutionists, the differences we observe between women and men are the results of thousands of years of evolutionary adaptation (Daly and Wilson, 1999; Dawkins, 1978). Males and females developed different "reproductive strategies" to ensure that they reproduce successfully and that they are able to pass on their genetic material to the next generation. This is called the **evolutionary imperative.**

Biologically, the male's part in reproduction ends at ejaculation. He produces millions and millions of sperm cells, and his goal is to inseminate as many females as possible, increasing his chances that his offspring will survive. Evolutionary biologists argue that men are "naturally" promiscuous and extremely reluctant to commit to a relationship. The female's part in reproduction really begins at conception. She must invest a significant amount of energy to ensure that her offspring is born and survives a very long infancy. For this reason, females are considered "naturally" monogamous; they seek a committed relationship with one male to help them protect the dependent offspring. Thus, men are more aggressive, want more casual sex, and avoid commitment; females are nurturing, passive, and desire commitment (Symons, 1985).

To sociologists, these evolutionary arguments are unpersuasive. They work backward, by observing some difference in sexual behavior among contemporary people and then reasoning back to its supposed evolutionary origin. Proponents of such evolutionary imperatives use selective data and ignore other "natural" behaviors like altruism and cooperation. One could take the same evidence, in fact, and construct an equally plausible evolutionary explanation for exactly the opposite results. In fact, that's exactly what primatologist Sarah Blaffer Hrdy did (see the "Sociology and Our World" box).

Brain and Hormone Research. There are also some differences between male and female brains, and surely the **sex hormones**—any of the various hormones, such as testosterone or estrogen, that affect the development or growth of the male and female reproductive organs—result in very different gendered behaviors for women and men. Or do they?

Actually, scientists disagree about what those differences mean. Once it was thought that because males' brains were bigger than females', males were smarter. But it turned out that brain size was simply a reflection of body size and did not matter. However, recent studies of the brain do suggest some differences in which side of the brain dominates and the level of connection or separation between the two halves of the brain.

The right hemisphere is associated with visual and spatial ability; the left hemisphere controls language and reading. Males are thought to be more right brained, females more left brained; and the separation between the two sides is more pronounced in males than in females. Researchers at Indiana University's medical school measured brain activity of women and men while they listened to a subject read a John Grisham novel (see Holtz, 2000). The men showed much more activity on the left side of their brains; the women showed activity on both sides. But what this means is far from clear. One could say that such brain structure means that men are better able to compartmentalize, or it could mean that women use the entire brain.

Falling outside of your culture's standard definitions of masculinity or femininity can be uncomfortable at best. Often the consequences are severe and can affect your relationships, job opportunities, and quality of life.

Perhaps the sex hormones that trigger sex development provide the causes of sex differences. Sex differentiation, the process by which males and females diverge biologically, is most pronounced at two points:

1. During fetal development, when **primary sex characteristics**—those characteristics that are anatomically present at birth, like the sex organs themselves—develop in the embryo.
2. At puberty, when sex hormones trigger the development of **secondary sex characteristics,** such as breast development in girls, the lowering of boys' voices, and boys' development of facial hair.

Much hormone research concerns the effect of testosterone on behavior because males have much higher levels than females, and its effects seem far more noticeable. Everyone "knows," for example, that testosterone "causes" aggression. Increases in testosterone levels are associated with increases in aggression. But it is also true that aggressive behavior leads to an increase in production of testosterone. So biology causes behavior, and behavior (which may be culturally induced) causes biological changes. For example, one study matched two males in athletic contests. The one whose testosterone level was higher usually won. But then they put two males with equal testosterone levels in the competition: The winner's testosterone level went up after winning, and the loser's went down. Testosterone levels are thus responsive to changes in our social circumstances as well, so it is difficult to say that biology caused those changes (see Kemper, 1990; Sapolsky, 1997).

Biology is not necessarily destiny. Biology gives us the raw material from which we develop our identities. That raw material is shaped, molded, and given meaning within the culture in which we find ourselves. As in the example of testosterone studies, it makes far more sense to understand the *interaction* of biology and culture—to explore *both* nature *and* nurture—than to pretend that something as complicated as personal identity and social arrangements between women and men can be reduced to either nature *or* nurture.

Cross-Cultural Variations of Sex and Gender

One way in which social scientists have demonstrated that gender behavior cannot all be biologically determined is to observe the

Monogamous Masculinity, Promiscuous Femininity

Evolutionary psychologists argue that the size and number of reproductive cells lead inevitably to different levels of parental "investment" in children. (Males produce millions of tiny sperm; females produce only a few dozen comparatively huge eggs.) Sarah Blaffer Hrdy (1981) adds a few more biological facts to the mix. Unlike other mammals, she notes, human females conceal estrus; that is, they are potentially sexually receptive throughout their entire menstrual cycle, unlike other female mammals that go "into heat" when ovulating and who are otherwise utterly uninterested in sex. What is the evolutionary reason for this? Hrdy asks. (*Hint:* The female knows that the baby is hers, but the male can never be exactly sure.)

Could it be, she asks, that females might want to mate with as many males as possible, to ensure that all of them will provide food and protection to the helpless and dependent infant, thereby increasing its chances of survival? (Remember that infant mortality in those preindustrial cultures of origin was extraordinarily high.) Could it be that females have a natural propensity toward promiscuity to ensure the offspring's survival and that males have a natural propensity toward monogamy, lest they run themselves ragged to provide food and protection to babies who may—or may not—be theirs? Wouldn't it be more likely for males to devise a system that ensured women's faithfulness—monogamy—and institutionalize it in marriage and then develop a cultural plan that would keep women in the home (because they might be ovulating and thus get pregnant)? And because it often takes a couple more than one "try" to get pregnant, wouldn't regular couplings with one partner be a more successful strategy for a male than a one-night stand?

Of course, no one would suggest that this interpretation is any more "true" than the evolutionary psychologists'. But what Hrdy revealed is that one can use the same—or even better—biological evidence and construct the exact opposite explanation. If that's possible, it means that we should be *extremely* cautious in accepting evolutionary arguments.

remarkable differences in women and men among different cultures. Cultural definitions of masculinity and femininity vary significantly; thus, sex differences are "not something deeply biological." This quote is from Margaret Mead, perhaps the most famous anthropologist to study these cultural differences.

In her landmark book *Sex and Temperament in Three Primitive Societies* ([1935] 2001), Mead described three South Seas cultures that had remarkably different ideas about what it meant to be a man or a woman. In two cultures, women and men were seen as very similar: among the Arapesh, both men and women were what we might label "feminine"—kind, gentle, and emotionally

"Biology Is Destiny"

In the nineteenth century, opponents of women's equality used biological arguments to prevent women from going to work and to college, from voting, or even from serving on juries. Women were said to be too weak, irrational, or emotional, or too fragile and delicate.

Some tried to use statistical data to prove that women were not biologically capable of a college education.

According to Edward C. Clarke, Harvard's first professor of education, the demands of a college education would be too taxing for women, and if women went to college their brains would grow bigger and heavier, but their wombs would shrink.

His evidence? It turned out that college-educated women had fewer children than non–college-educated women. And 42 percent of women admitted to mental hospitals were college educated, compared with only 16 percent of men. (In the Middle Ages, the cause of insanity for women was believed to be a detached uterus that then floated through the body poisoning it; the word *hysteria* means "wandering womb"; thus, "hysterectomies.") Could it be that college education was actually driving women crazy—and causing them to stop having babies?

As we've seen earlier, in Chapter 4, one can draw no causal inferences from even such a strange correlation. Today, we would be more likely to attribute the decrease in family size to women's expanding opportunities, not to their shrinking wombs.

---

warm, "trustful" involved parents, while among the Mundugamor, both men and women were what we might call "masculine"—"violent, competitive, aggressively sexual, jealous." The Tchambuli might sound more familiar to us. They believed that women and men were very different. One sex was more "charming, coquettish and graceful" and spent their days gossiping and shopping; they wore their hair long and loved dressing up with feathers and shell necklaces. They were the men. The women were dominant, energetic economic providers. They wore their hair short, wore no adornments, and were efficient and business-like. They ran economic and political life.

So, which one was "biological"? Well, if you were to have asked them, they would all say that their way was the "natural" one. All cultures, Mead argued, develop cultural explanations that claim that their way is the natural way to do things. But all arrangements are equally culturally based.

The Value of Cross-Cultural Research. Cross-cultural research explores both universality of gender difference and gender inequality and also the remarkable variety in our cultural prescriptions of masculinity and femininity and the proper relations between them. It shows that the question is not biology or culture—nature or nurture—but both. Our biological sex is one factor, the raw material of gender identity. But it is shaped, molded, and given meaning only within a culture. How much inequality does a culture have? How different do they think men and women are? Is there any room for change? If gender identity and inequality can vary so much, it can also be changed.

Contemporary anthropologists still observe two cultural universals, a gendered division of labor and gender inequality. Why does every known society organize itself so that men are assigned to do some tasks and not others, while women are assigned to do some tasks and not others? And why would they then rank the tasks that men do as more

Cultural variations in gender differences and inequalities imply that our differences stem not only from biology but also from cultural forces that shape our identities. In some societies, males take on roles and identities that are often traditionally associated with females, and vice versa. Male beauty contest among the Wodaabe in Niger.

valuable and distribute resources and rewards disproportionately to men?

Sociologists used to believe that a gendered division of labor was *functional*—that as societies became more complex, dividing work from family life made more sense, and because females had and nursed the babies, they should remain at home and do all the house-based tasks while the males went off to hunt or fish.

It turned out that prehistoric societies were far more cooperative than we earlier thought. Archeologists suggest that whole villages—men, women, and older children—would all participate in hunting (see Zihlman, 1989). And everyone would tend the hearths, prepare meals, and raise children. And even if it could be shown that such a division of labor was once an efficient way to organize social life, the entry of women into every area of public life has certainly made it an anachronism.

Cross-cultural researchers offer several theories to explain the universality of gender inequality. In the mid-nineteenth century, German philosopher Frederich Engels, the collaborator of Karl Marx, observed that the three foundations of modern society—private property, the modern nation-state, and the nuclear family—all seem to have emerged at the same time. He claimed that private property both caused male domination and helped shape all modern political institutions.

Originally, Engels wrote, all families were large communal arrangements, with group marriages and gender equality. But the idea of private property brought with it several problems. How do you know what property is yours? How do you make sure your children can inherit it? How do you ensure an orderly transfer of property if you want to sell it or give it away?

The solution to these questions was the modern *nuclear family*, with a father at the head, establishing which children were his, and modern law that guaranteed the orderly transfer of property. These laws required enforcement, which led to the formation of nation-states and police. In this way, the creation of private property brought with it the modern family and the modern state.

Some contemporary anthropologists have studied why gender inequality seems so universal. Karen Sacks (1974), for example, examined what happens when a market economy is introduced in a traditional culture. She found that the more people got involved in producing for a market, instead of for themselves, the more gender unequal the culture became.

Marvin Harris (1977) argued that warfare and the preparations for war are the main causes of male domination because warfare demands that there be a core group of highly valued fathers and sons to carry out its military tasks. Males come to control the society and develop patriarchal religion—monotheism—to justify their domination.

What determines women's status?

- *Size and strength*. The more a society needs and values physical strength and highly developed motor skills, the greater the level of gender inequality (see Kimmel, 2003). Larger family size also leads to a perception of greater gender difference.

  This is because if the family is small, as in a nuclear family, males and females will cross over and perform each other's tasks because there is no one else to do them (Bacon, Barry, and Child, 1957).

- *Women's economic activity*. Women's economic activity is perhaps the chief predictor of gender equality (Sanday, 1981). The more property a woman produces or controls—especially after she gets married—the higher her status.

- *Child care*. When the females are entirely responsible for child care, their status tends to be lower. Sociologist Scott Coltrane (1996) found that the closer the relationship between father and son, the higher the status of women is likely to be because men's participation in domestic life indicates that the sexes are seen as more similar.

Blurring the Boundaries of Gender. Another major contribution of cross-cultural research has been to challenge the simple dichotomy of two biological sexes (male and female) and two gender identities (masculinity and femininity). Some biologists have pointed out that even the simple dichotomy of male and female sex is a convenience that fails to consider all

The berdache is a great example of how cultures blur gender roles—in some cultures a person of one sex will adopt the social role of the opposite sex. Most berdaches are males who take on the female gender identity.

the various possible experiences in between, as for example about intersexed people. Anthropologists take on the gender "binary" in the same way, suggesting that there may be far more genders out there than we know. Both sex and gender may be continual and not discrete categories.

Some societies recognize more than two genders—sometimes three or four. The Navaho appear to have three genders—one for masculine men, one for feminine women, and one called the *nadle* for those whose sex is ambiguous at birth. One can be born or choose to be a nadle; they perform tasks for both women and men and dress appropriately, depending on the tasks they are performing. And they can marry either men or women.

Numerous cultures have a clearly defined gender role for the *berdache*. A berdache is a member of one biological sex who takes the social role of the other sex, usually a biological male who dresses and acts as a woman. In most cases, they are not treated as freaks or deviants but are revered as special and enjoy high social and economic status; many even become shamans or religious figures (Williams, 1986). There are fewer female berdaches, although one Native American culture permits parents to decide that, if they feel they have produced too many daughters, they may therefore raise one as a son.

Becoming Gendered: Learning Gender Identity

How do we become gendered? How do little biological males and females grow up to be adult men and women? In a sense, our entire society is organized to make sure that happens, that males and females become gendered men and women. From large-scale institutions like family, religion, and schools, to everyday interactions like the kinds of toys we play with and the television programs we watch—we are constantly inundated with messages about appropriate gender behavior.

In a critique of biological research on gender differences, Harvard biologist Ruth Hubbard writes:

> If a society puts half its children into short skirts and warns them not to move in ways that reveal their panties, while putting the other half into jeans and overalls and encouraging them to climb trees, play ball, and participate in other vigorous outdoor games; if later, during adolescence, the children who have been wearing trousers are urged to "eat like growing boys" while the children in skirts are warned to watch their weight and not get fat; if the half in jeans runs around in sneakers and boots, while the half in skirts totters about on spike heels, then these two groups will be biologically as well as socially different. (1990, p. 69)

And what if the half in jeans and sneakers, eating heartily, were female, she seems to want us to ask, and the ones in frilly dresses and high heels and on constant diets were males? Would there be complete gender chaos, or would we simply come to believe that boys and girls were naturally like that?

Gender Socialization

Gender socialization is the process by which males and females are taught the appropriate behaviors, attitudes, and traits for their biolog-

"Sex brought us together, but gender drove us apart."

ical sex. Gender socialization begins at birth and continues throughout our lives. Before you know anything else about a baby, you know its sex. "It's a boy!" or "It's a girl!" is the way we announce the newborn's arrival. Even at the moment of birth, researchers have found, boys and girls are treated differently: A girl is held closer, spoken to in a softer voice about how pretty she is; a boy is held at arm's length, and people speak louder about how strong he looks.

From infancy onward, people interact with children based at least as much on cultural expectations about gender as on the child itself. In one experiment, adults were told that the baby was either a boy or girl, and the adults consistently gave gender-stereotyped toys to the child—dolls and hammers—regardless of the child's reaction to them. However, the babies were assigned at random, and the boys were often dressed in pink and the girls in blue. In another experiment, adults were shown a videotape of a 9-month-old infant's reaction to a jack-in-the-box, a doll, a teddy bear, and a buzzer. Half the adults were told it was a boy; half were told it was a girl. When asked about the child's emotional responses, the adults interpreted the exact same reaction as fear if they thought the baby was a girl and anger if they thought it was a boy (Condry and Condry, 1976).

All through childhood boys and girls are dressed differently, taught to play with different toys, and read different books; they even watch different cartoon shows on TV. As children, girls are rewarded more for physical attractiveness, boys for physical activity. Although boys and girls play together as toddlers, they are increasingly separated during childhood and develop separate play cultures.

This often means that boys play on one side of the playground and girls play on the other. In a study of children's play, sociologist Barrie Thorne (1993) found that girls who attempt to cross over to the boys' side are labeled "tomboys," and they may have a much easier time being accepted by the boys than a boy who crosses over to the girls' side. He is likely to be labeled a "sissy" and will be shunned by both boys and girls.

In this way, boys and girls not only learn gender difference, but they learn gender inequality: The consequences are different if girls move "up" in the hierarchy or if boys try to move "down." This is the double message of gender socialization: You learn difference and inequality at the same time. "If I were a

Did You Know?

Pink for Boys and Blue for Girls

Little boys and girls were not always dressed differently. In fact, it used to be the opposite of what it is now. Before the late nineteenth century, boys and girls were dressed identically. When children began to wear color-coded clothing, the rule was pink for boys and blue for girls. Pink was declared to be "a more decided and stronger color" and thus more suitable for boys, while blue was "more delicate and dainty." A debate in the 1910s and 1920s began to reverse that trend, and blue became the boy color and pink the girl color. And today we dress little girls more like little boys—in overalls, T-shirts, and sneakers (Paoletti, 1987, 1989, 1997).

Sociology and Our World

The M–F Test

In 1936, social psychologist Lewis Terman, the creator of the IQ test, turned his attention to gender. Terman sensed that parents were anxious about their children, and, with his student, Catherine Cox Miles, Terman tried to identify all the various traits, attitudes, behaviors, and preferences that could codify masculinity and femininity. Gender identity became the successful adoption of this bundle of traits and attitudes in their famous study, *Sex and Personality* (1936).

They believed that masculinity and femininity were end points on a continuum and that all children could be placed along that continuum, from M to F. The "job" of families, schools, and other agents of socialization was to make sure that boys ended up on the M side and girls ended up on the F side. The M–F test was perhaps the single most widely used means to determine successful acquisition of gender identity and was still being used up until the 1960s.

After you took the test, the researchers could place you on the continuum from M to F. At parent–teacher conferences, parents could be counseled on how to help their "feminine" son or "masculine" daughter move back to the gender-appropriate side. Terman and Miles were especially concerned that boys who scored high on the F side would turn out to be homosexual: "If they showed undue feminine tendencies special care should be exercised to give them opportunity to develop masculine characteristics" (Terman and Miles, 1936).

girl," one third grader said, "everybody would be better than me, because boys are better than girls."

Socialization is pervasive. If the traits and behaviors we observe among women and men were so "natural" and biologically based, why would we need such constant supervision to make sure we do them right? And why would we punish those who don't do them right so harshly?

After all the differential socialization boys and girls receive, what, then, are the real psychological differences between women and men? When social psychologists Eleanor Maccoby and Carol Jacklin (1987) surveyed more than 1,600 empirical studies, they found "a surprising degree of similarity" between the sexes and in how they are raised, especially in the first few years of life. They found only four areas with significant and consistent gender differences:

1. Girls have somewhat higher verbal ability.
2. Boys have somewhat better visual and spatial ability.
3. Boys do somewhat better on mathematical tests.
4. Boys were significantly more aggressive than girls.

A recent review of all available research on gender differences found little or no difference on virtually every other characteristic or behavior (Hyde, 2005).

The Social Construction of Gender

Sociologists speak of gender as socially constructed. The **social construction of gender** means that we construct our gender identities all through our lives, using the cultural materials we find around us. Our gender identities are both voluntary—we choose to become who we are—and coerced—we are pressured, forced, and often physically threatened to conform to certain rules. We don't make up the rules we have to play by, but we do bend them and shape them to make them feel like they're ours.

Gender Roles and Gender Relations. Consider our lives to be a dramatic play, says the sociologist Erving Goffman (1974). We need props and lots of rehearsing to get it right; then we try it out on the public stage, and the audience lets us know if we are doing it well—or not. Think of how many times

you've rehearsed a line, using different inflections or emphases, before you actually said it. In large part, then, gender identity is a performance. We use our bodies, language, and actions all to communicate to others that we are acting our part effectively.

Some psychologists use the term "sex roles" or **gender roles** to define the bundle of traits, attitudes, and behaviors that is associated with biological males and females. Roles are blueprints that prescribe what you should do, think, want, and look like, so that you can successfully become a man or a woman.

Sociologists have suggested that the role model ignores several important dimensions of gender identity and gender inequality. For one thing, it seems to assume that the two gender roles are independent and equal: "his" and "hers." But sociologists point out that masculinity and femininity are not independent; we know what it means to be a man or a woman by reference to the other. Nor are they equal: Masculinity—and especially the traits associated with it—is more highly valued than femininity (Stacey and Thorne, 1985).

Nor does the term *role* adequately capture gender in its complexity. It makes as much sense to speak of "sex roles" as it does to speak of "race roles" or "class roles"—which is to say, not very much sense at all. So sociologists usually speak of gender *relations* to emphasize how the definitions of masculinity and femininity are developed in relation to each other.

Gendered Institutions. Sociologists see another dimension to gender: an institutional level. Gender is not a "possession," something that you "get" through socialization and "have" for the rest of your life. It is a dynamic in all of our interactions. And it's part of the institutions we inhabit and the organizations we create. The positions we occupy—such as, for example, soldier or nurse—demand that we act in a certain way, and these ways of acting are also gendered. Soldiers are supposed to be stoic and aggressive, no matter whether that soldier is male or female; nurses are supposed to act caring and nurturing, regardless of whether that nurse is male or female. (As a result, male nurses and female soldiers have to constantly prove that they are masculine or feminine, respectively; see Williams, 1992.)

Women have entered virtually every field formerly reserved for men only. Globally, this can result in cultural confusion, as this Spanish soldier encounters a more gender-segregated society in Iraq.

engineering professorships might be due to biology (Summers, 2005).

But consider the question sociologically. Most professors—no matter what their field, even sociology!—complete their formal professional training by their mid- to late 20s, after which they typically become assistant professors. The next seven years, until they earn tenure, is often the most intense work time of their lives, when they have to devote 12 to 16 hours a day to work. By the time they "arrive," they are often in their mid-30s, and only then do they finally have time for a social life, to get married and have children.

Obviously, this arrangement works better for men, who may have wives who do the housework and child care, than it does for women, who might want to spend time developing a romantic relationship and having and raising children. It is therefore not surprising that there are more male than female full professors. Nor is it surprising that so many of those women who pursue their careers do not have children. The surprise is often that *any* mothers can balance both family and career as well as they do.

Observing how institutional arrangements are gendered often helps explain whether more men or women occupy those positions. In 2005, Lawrence Summers, then president of Harvard University, caused a big stir by suggesting that the reason that there were so few women at the top ranks of science and

Gender is a foundation of our identity, and it is also woven into the fabric of social structures. It is one of the ways in which social activities are organized. Like race, age, class, and sexuality, both aspects of gender—individual and institutional—are bases of gender inequality.

Gender Inequality on a Global and Local Scale

Discrimination against women is a global problem. Just about every country in the world treats its women less well than it treats its men (Kimmel, Lang, and Grieg, 2000). In developing countries, problems appear more fundamental and pervasive. Significant gender gaps are found in everything from literacy to education to employment to income to health in the developing world, and these

gaps are larger in nonindustrialized countries. Women are disproportionately represented among the world's poor. They are often denied access to critical resources, such as credit, land, and inheritance. Their labor is far less rewarded. Their health care and nutritional needs are underserved. They have far less access to education and support services. Their participation in decision making at home and in the community can be minimal but is routinely lower than men's (U.N. Development Program [UNDP], 2006). As a result, gender inequality can be said to hurt women somewhat more in poorer nations than it does in wealthier ones.

While the "feminization of poverty" indicates the disproportionate concentration of poverty among women, women around the world have also begun to lead political demonstrations and social movements. In the protests over the most recent elections in Iran (shown at left), thousands of women led the demonstrations against the current regime's political crackdown.

However, this is not to say that gender discrimination in industrial countries is an insignificant problem. When the World Economic Forum measured the global gender gap in 2008, publishing an international ranking of countries based on measures like women's economic opportunity and participation, political empowerment, educational attainment, and health and well-being, many wealthy countries ranked quite poorly in overall scores. Of 58 countries studied, Japan ranked 97 and Italy 67. The United States ranked only 27, well behind Norway (1), Sweden (3), New Zealand (5), the United Kingdom (13), France (15), and others (World Economic Forum, 2008).

Even U.S. women who are well off by world standards are badly harmed by discrimination based on sex—and so are their families. The U.S. **gender wage gap**—the gap between the median wages for women and for men—costs American families $200 billion every year (Murphy and Graff, 2005). If working women earned the same as men for the same jobs, U.S. poverty rates would be cut in half.

Nearly two-thirds of all hungry adults in America are women; globally, 7 out of 10 of the world's hungry are women and girls (U.N. World Food Program, 2009). More women around the world are working than ever before, but women face a higher unemployment rate than men, receive lower wages, and number 60 percent of the world's 550 million working poor—those who do not earn enough to lift themselves and their families above the poverty line of $1 a day (International Labour Organization, 2008). Taken together, trends like these have come to be known as the **feminization of poverty**—a term that refers to the disproportionate concentration of poverty among women, especially among female-headed households. Coined in the 1970s, by sociologist Diana Pearce, the feminization of poverty is a worldwide phenomenon that also afflicts U.S. women (Pearce, 1978).

In the United States, women of color are even more burdened by gender inequality because it is usually compounded by racial inequality. In all the indicators above, the racial gap is wide. Like White women, women of color also perform what sociologists call the "second shift," the housework and child care that need to be done after the regular work shift is over. But minority women also tend to hold the lowest-paying, least-rewarding jobs, often without health care benefits or sick days (Marchevsky and Theoharis, 2006; Women's Institute for a Secure Retirement [WISER], 2008). Recent immigrants may face an additional layer of discrimination, as cultural expectations derived of paternalistic cultures further compound the burdens of gender-based poverty and racism (U.N. Development Program, 2006).

Moreover, the global economy means the economic condition of both women and men in the United States is linked to that of people in other parts of the world. Driven by

U.S.-based multinational corporations, all workers have become part of an international division of labor. (See Chapter 12.) Corporations scanning the globe for the least expensive labor available frequently discover the cheapest workers are women or children. As a result, the global division of labor is taking on a gender dimension. Women workers, usually from the poorest countries in the world, provide the lowest-wage labor to manufacture products sold in wealthier industrial countries (Oxfam International, 2004; U.N. Development Program, 2006).

Globalization has also changed the dynamics of global gender inequality. Just as globalization tends to unite us in increasingly tight networks through the Internet and global cultural production, it also separates us. Globalization has dramatically affected geographic mobility as both women and men from poor countries must migrate to find work in more advanced and industrial countries. This global geographic mobility is extremely sex segregated: Men and women move separately. Men often live in migrant labor camps, or dozens pile into small flats, each saving to send money back home and eventually bring the family to live with them in the new country. Women, too, may live in all-female rooms while they clean houses or work in factories to make enough to send back home (Hondagneau-Sotelo, 2001).

Some women and girls are kidnapped or otherwise lured into a new expanding global

U.S. / Them

The Global Gender Gap

Each year, the World Economic Forum, a European-based nonpartisan policy institute, ranks 130 countries on their level of gender inequality. The WEF uses four criteria: level of economic participation, educational attainment, health, and political empowerment.

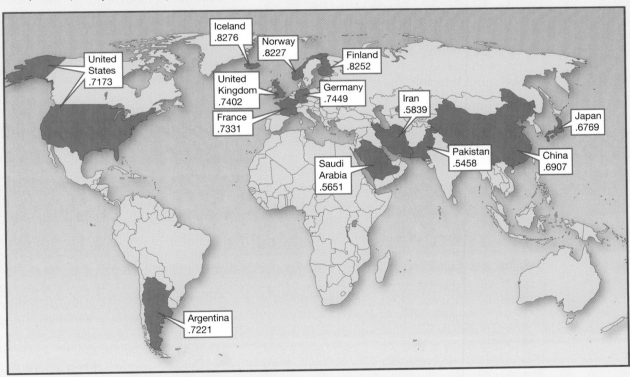

Iceland .8276
Norway .8227
Finland .8252
United States .7173
United Kingdom .7402
Germany .7449
Iran .5839
Japan .6769
France .7331
Pakistan .5458
China .6907
Saudi Arabia .5651
Argentina .7221

(*Source:* World Economic Forum, Global Gender Gap Report 2008, The Global Gender Gap Index 2008 Ratings. Reproduced by permission.)

1. Why do you think the top-ranked countries are all in Scandinavia? And why do you think the countries ranked lowest are in the Middle East and South Asia?

2. If you were a policy maker, how would you mix cultural ideology and social policy to reduce the gender gap?

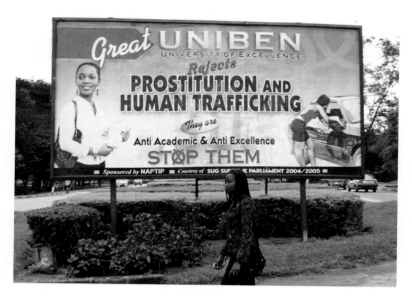

This billboard in Nigeria indicates a growing awareness of the problems and issues surrounding the profitable global sex trade.

sex trade, in which brothels are stocked with terrified young girls who borrowed from the traffickers enough money to pay their transportation, believing they were going to work in factories. They are forced into prostitution to repay these debts, and their families are often threatened should they try to escape (International Labour Organization, 2005). Global sex trafficking and global sex "tourism" are among the ugliest elements of globalization and ones that the advanced nations are increasingly policing.

Although gender inequality is a worldwide phenomenon, its expressions can and do vary from country to country and from region to region within countries. In some countries, like Saudi Arabia, women may not own or drive cars, but in other Muslim countries, like Pakistan and the Philippines, women have been heads of state.

Gender Inequality in the United States

In the United States, gender inequality can be seen in every arena of social life—from the workplace to school to families, to even the most intimate and personal aspects of our lives, like to those whom we choose to love.

The Gendered World of Work

The work we do is "gendered." We have definite ideas of what sorts of occupations are appropriate for women and which are appropriate for men. These ideas have persisted despite the fact that the workforce has changed dramatically in the past century. The percentage of women working has risen from around 20 percent in 1900 to more than 60 percent today. And this percentage holds for women who have children—even if they have children under 6 years old. It's also true for all races, and for every single occupation, from low-paid clerical and sales jobs to all the major professions. Today, women represent a majority of clerical and support workers and also half or more of students in medical school and law school (American Bar Association, 2008; Association of American Medical Colleges, 2008; Bureau of Labor Statistics, 2008).

Yet traditional ideologies persist about women and work. Women who are successful are often thought to be "less than" real women, while men who are successful are seen as "real men." Such ideology translates into practices: Women are paid less, promoted less, excluded from some positions, and assigned to specific jobs deemed more appropriate for them.

Gender discrimination in the workplace was once far more direct and obvious: Women were simply prohibited from entering certain fields. Until the late 1960s, classified advertising was divided into "Help wanted—Male" and "Help wanted—Female." Women were discouraged from "taking slots away from men" if they applied for jobs, or they might be asked in a job interview whether they planned to marry and have children (because that would mean they would leave the job). Can you imagine a male applicant being asked questions like that? In the summer of 1968, the EEOC ruled 3–2 that it violated the Civil Rights Act for employers to separate male and female "help wanted" ads in newspapers, except where sex was a bona fide occupational qualification.

Sex Segregation in the Workplace. The chief way that gender inequality is sustained in the workforce is through sex segregation. Sex segregation "refers to women's and men's concentration in different occupations, industries, jobs, and levels in workplace hierarchies" (Reskin, 1996, p. 94). Because different occupations are seen as more "appropriate" for one gender or the other, then the fact that one job is paid more than another is seen as resulting from the job, not the gender that does it.

How many of you have worked as a babysitter when you were a teenager? If your experience is like that of my students, most of the women have, many of the men have not. And the women were paid between $5.00 and $10.00 an hour, about $20 to $50 a day. Now, how many of you have also shoveled snow or mowed lawns? Most of the men have done this, but few of the women have. Snow shovelers and lawn mowers are paid somewhere around $25 a house and make up to $100 to $150 a day. Why?

Many of you are saying that shoveling snow and mowing lawns is "harder." And by that you mean requiring more physical exertion. But in our society, we usually pay those who use their brawn far *lower* wages than we pay those who use their brains—think of the difference between an accountant and a professional lawn mower. And besides, the skills needed for babysitting—social, mental, nurturing, caring, and feeding—are generally considered much more valuable than the ability to lift and move piles of snow. And most people would agree that the consequences of bad babysitting are potentially far worse than

Professions like teaching are often marked by a level of gender imbalance—female teachers outnumber male teachers. Sex segregation is pervasive and sustains inequality; it's no coincidence that teachers earn relatively low salaries.

those of bad lawn mowing! When grown-ups do these tasks—as lawn mower and baby nurse—their wages are roughly equivalent to each other. What determines the difference is simple: Girls babysit, and boys mow lawns. That is how sex segregation hides the fact that gender discrimination is occurring.

Sex segregation is so pervasive that economists speak about a **dual labor market** based on gender. The idea of a dual labor market is that work and workers are divided into different sectors—primary or secondary, formal or informal, and, in this case, male or female (Table 9.1). Men and women rarely compete

Table 9.1
The Most Male- and Female-Dominated Occupations

Male-Dominated Occupations	Percent Women
Construction managers	8.2%
Engineering managers	6.3%
Railroad conductors and yardmasters	4.7%
Crane and tower operators	3.7%
Aircraft mechanics and service technicians	1.7%
Power-line installers and repairers	1.4%
Carpenters	1.5%
Electricians	1.0%

Female-Dominated Occupations	Percent Women
Dental hygienists	97.7%
Preschool and kindergarten teachers	97.6%
Child care workers	95.6%
Secretaries and administrative assistants	96.1%
Word processors and typists	92.2%
Registered nurses	91.7%
Payroll clerks, bookkeeping and auditing clerks	90.8%*
Maids and housekeepers	90.1

*Average of three categories within 0.6% of each other.

(*Source:* Bureau of Labor Statistics, 2008.)

Lilly Ledbetter's Fight for Equal Pay

It wasn't until January 2009 that legal remedies were available for women who were the victims of wage discrimination. Lilly Ledbetter, a production supervisor at a Goodyear Tire plant in Alabama had been paid less than her male counterparts for decades, but she didn't find out about it until right before her retirement in 1998. She filed an equal pay lawsuit under the Civil Rights Act of 1964, but the courts refused it because the 180-day statute of limitations had long expired. Congress dramatically expanded the time under which a woman can file such a claim because wage discrimination is often not visible when salaries are not public. The Lilly Ledbetter Fair Pay Act was the first congressional act that President Obama signed into law.

Did You Know?

Pay Inequity Awareness Day

Every year in early April, the president of the United States declares "National Pay Inequity Awareness Day." Why in early April? Because the average woman in a full-time job would need to work for a full year and then more than three additional months all the way until April of the next year to catch up to what the average man earned the year before.

Did You Know?

against each other for the same job at the same rank in the same organization. Rather, women compete with other women, and men compete with other men, for jobs that are already coded as appropriate for one and not the other. And while we might think that different sexes are "naturally" predisposed toward certain jobs and not others, that is not the same everywhere. While most dentists in the United States are male, in Europe most dentists are female. In New York City, only 25 women are firefighters, out of a force of 11,500, while in Minneapolis, 23 *percent* of firefighters are women, as is the fire chief. The issue is less about the intrinsic properties of the position that determine its wages and prestige and more about which sex performs it. So widespread is this thinking that in occupations from journalism, to medicine, to teaching, to law, to pharmacy, sociologists have noted a phenomenon dubbed **feminization of the professions,** in which salaries drop as female participation increases (Menkel-Meadow, 1987; Wylie, 2000).

The Wage Gap. No matter where you look, women earn less than men. In a 2007 U.S. Census Bureau report, the median annual income for men working full time was $40,333; for women it was $30,887, or 77 percent of men's income (DeNavas-Walt, Proctor, and Lee, 2006; WISER, 2008). (The gap narrowed very slightly the next year, with women earning 77.8 percent of what men earn, according

to the Institute for Women's Policy Research, 2008.) That means, on average, a woman brings home about roughly $190 less per week than a man. Women of color fare considerably worse, with Latinas earning barely more than one-half the median income of White men (Figure 9.1). The lifetime impact of the pay gap is enormous for any woman, but particularly for a woman of color. A Black woman will earn approximately $471,000 less than the average White man over a 35-year career. A Latina will earn $654,00 less (Arons, 2008; Wiser, 2007).

For college graduates, the gap is similar: According to the *Economic Policy Institute*, recent female graduates made an average of $18.17 per hour, compared to the $21.09 per hour on average paid to recent male college graduates. One year out of college, the average woman is earning about 80 percent of her male colleagues' wages; ten years out of college, she is earning only 69 percent (American Association of University Women [AAUW], 2007).

And the gap continues to grow as women move up the professional ladder. At the management level, for every dollar earned by a White male manager, a White female manager earns just 59 cents; a Black woman manager gets only 57 cents, and a Latina manager an even smaller 48 cents (Becker, 2002). And women of all racial and ethnic backgrounds pay an enormous price for taking any time out of the full-time workforce (Crittenden, 2001; Rose and Hartmann, 2004).

The wage gap has been remarkably consistent. In biblical times, male workers were valued at 50 pieces of silver, female workers at 30, or 40 percent less (Rhode, 1997). In the United States since the Civil War, women's wages have ranged between 50 percent and 66 percent of men's. In recent years, the wage gap has been closing, but women's wages still average about 75 percent of men's. It turns out that this is not because women's wages have been rising so much, but rather because men's wages have been falling, and falling faster than women's (Bernhardt, Morris, and Handcock, 1995).

Glass Ceilings and the Glass Escalator. Gender inequality also extends to promotions. Women often hit a "glass ceiling," a barrier beyond which they cannot go, despite the fact that they can see others above them. The glass ceiling refers to "those artificial barriers . . . that prevent qualified individuals from advancing upward within their organization into management level positions" (Martin, 1991, p. 1). For example, women hold less than 14 percent of all corporate board seats. The median salary for the 100 male CEOs of the largest U.S. companies is about twice the median salary of women CEOs, and the median male bonus is about three times that of women (Dobrzynski, 2008).

One reason the glass ceiling persists is because of negative stereotypes about ambitious women. In a famous Supreme Court case (*Hopkins vs. Price Waterhouse*, 1989), a woman was not promoted to partner of a prestigious accounting firm, even though she had outperformed all the male candidates who were promoted. Her supervisors said she wasn't ladylike enough and advised her "to walk more femininely, talk more femininely, dress more femininely, wear makeup, have her hair styled and wear jewelry." The Court ordered that she be compensated and made partner.

The "glass ceiling" is different for men when they enter traditionally female-dominated occupations. As we note in the chapter on the economy and work, sociologist Christine Williams found that male librarians, nursery school teachers, and nurses do not hit a glass ceiling but rather ride a "glass escalator" to the top—in part as a way to preserve masculinity. Male nurses and librarians are promoted to administrative positions much more rapidly than their female colleagues (Williams, 1992, 1995).

Sexual Harassment at Work. Sexual harassment is also a form of gender discrimination in the workplace. **Sexual harassment** creates an unequal work environment by singling out women for different treatment. There are two types of sexual harassment. The first type is called *quid pro quo harassment,* and it occurs when a supervisor uses his (or her) position to try to elicit sexual activity from a subordinate by threatening to fire, or promising to promote, or even just repeatedly pressuring a subordinate for a date or for sex. The second type is called *hostile environment,* and it occurs when a person feels threatened or unsafe because of the constant teasing or threatening by other workers. This type of harassment is far more common but more difficult to prove. It seems to happen most often when male workers resent the "invasion" of women into a formerly all-male work environment.

Although most cases of sexual harassment happen between male supervisors and female employees, courts also recognize that women can harass men. The key is that someone uses his or her superior occupational rank to coerce someone else. In 1999, the Supreme Court also recognized that men can sexually harass another man, even if all the men are heterosexual.

Currently, in the United States, the Equal Employment Opportunity Commission (EEOC) receives about 5,000 sexual harassment claims a year (U.S. Equal Opportunity Commission, 2005).

Balancing Work and Family. Women also face discrimination if they try to balance work and family life. If employees who get pregnant, bear children, and take care of them are less likely to get promoted, then women who want to balance work and family will face painful choices. And men may experience such discrimination, too. Men who say they want a better balance between work and family, or want to take parental leave, are often scoffed at by their colleagues and supervisors as not sufficiently committed to their careers; they may be put on an informal "daddy track" and passed over for promotion or high-profile accounts (Kimmel, 1993; Jarrell, 2007).

Figure 9.1 Overall Wage Gap

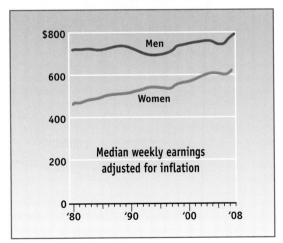

(*Source:* Hannah Fairfield, "Metrics: Why Is Her Paycheck Smaller?" *New York Times,* March 11, 2009, p. 4.)

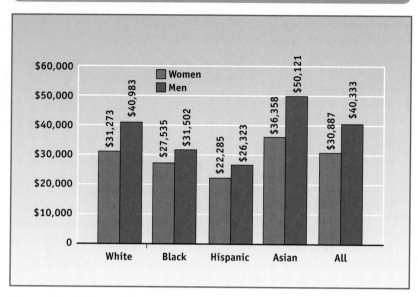

Figure 9.2 The Wage Gap: Median Annual Earnings by Race and Sex (Full-Time)

(*Source:* "Minority Women's Income," A report by WISER, Women's Institute for a Secure Retirement, 2008.)

Though nearly all of us, women and men, work for a living outside the home, women also do the great majority of work *inside* the home. Sociologist Arlie Hochschild (1989) calls this the **second shift**—the housework and child care that also need to be done after a regular working shift is over. Housework and child care are largely women's responsi-

bilities. Seeing housework and child care as "women's work" illustrates gender inequality, the "gender politics of housework"; women do not have a biological predisposition to do laundry or wash dishes.

Men's share of housework increased somewhat during the twentieth century, largely in response to the increasing numbers of women working outside the home. In the 1920s, 10 percent of working-class women said their husbands spent "no time" doing housework; by the late 1990s, only 2 percent said so (Pleck and Masciadrelli, 2003; Pleck, 1997). Between the 1960s and today, men's contribution to housework increased from about 15 percent to about 30 percent of the total (Fisher et al., 2006). Still, international study of men's share of housework found that U.S. men spend no more time on housework today than they did in 1985 and do only four more hours of housework per week than they did in 1965 (Institute for Social Research, 2002). Another international study of 20 industrialized countries found that over the past 40 years, men's proportional contribution to family work, including housework, shopping, and child care—where the most dramatic increases in men's contributions have been found—grew from about one-fifth to about one-third (Bianchi, Robinson, and Milkie, 2005; Coltrane, 2004; Fisher et al., 2006; Sullivan, 2006). Today, despite a gradual convergence

"First of all, Harrington, let me tell you how much we all admire your determination not to choose between job and family."

(*Source:* © Lee Lorenz/CondeNast/www.cartoonbank.com. Reprinted by permission.)

Women and Politics

The gender distribution in U.S. politics is still very unequal, with local and state governments tending to have more female representatives than the national government. So, what do you think?

1. Most men are better suited emotionally for politics than are most women.

○ Agree   ○ Disagree

2. If your party nominated a woman for president, would you vote for her if she was qualified for the job?

○ Yes   ○ No   ○ Wouldn't vote

What does **America** think?

(These are actual survey data from the General Social Survey, 2004.)

1. In 1972, slightly more than half of respondents said they disagreed with this statement. There was virtually no gender difference in responses. In 2004, more than three-quarters of respondents disagreed, with females being slightly more likely to disagree than were males.

2. In 1974, 80 percent of all respondents said they would vote for a qualified female presidential candidate. In 1998, the latest date for which statistics are available, that number had risen to above 90 percent. In both years, there was very little gender difference.

Thinking Critically about Survey Data

1. Why do you think there was virtually no gender difference in responses? Were you expecting that finding? Why or why not?

2. More respondents said they would vote for a female president than said that women were as emotionally suited for politics as men are. What do you think explains that difference?

References: See Davis et al., page 511.

in the amount of time both women and men spend in paid work and family work, U.S. women spend 60 percent more time on chores than men do—an average of 27 hours a week. International comparisons of seven countries—the United States, Sweden, Russia, Japan, Hungary, Finland, Canada—revealed that Swedish men do the most housework (24 hours per week) while Japanese men clock the least time (four hours weekly). Swedish women spend 33 hours a week on housework, and Japanese women spend 29 hours. However, men and women in every nation surveyed reported that routine housework was the least enjoyable use of their time (Fisher et al., 2006; Hook, 2006).

The impact of gender inequality in the family on women's equality in the workplace is significant. If women are responsible for housework and child care, they are pulled away from their workplace commitments, have less networking time, and may be perceived as having less ability to relocate, all important factors in career advancement (Allen et al., 2002). They may also be less rested and more stressed, which can affect their ability to get raises and promotions (Blair-Loy, 2003; Hochschild, 1989).

Gender Inequality in School

Remember Barbie's first words in 1992. "Math class is tough!" Her hundreds of millions of owners were learning all about gender—and gender inequality.

From the earliest ages, our educations teach us far more than the ABCs. We learn all about what it means to be a man or a woman. This is part of what sociologists refer to as the *hidden curriculum*—all the "other" lessons we're learning in school. In nursery schools and kindergarten classes, we often find the heavy blocks, trucks, and airplanes in one corner and the miniature tea sets in another. Subjects are often as gender coded as the outfits toddlers wear. From elementary school through higher education, male students receive more active instruction than do females (Sadker and Sadker, 1994). Teachers call on boys more often, spend more time with them, and encourage them more. Many teachers expect girls to hate science and math and love reading, and they expect boys to feel exactly the opposite. This led researchers to describe a "chilly classroom climate" for girls, a climate that holds girls back from achieving as much as they are capable (see AAUW, 2007). In response, some pundits have asked, "What about the boys?" This question suggests that all the initiatives developed to help girls in science and math, in sports, and in acceptable classroom behavior actually hurt boys. It's not girls but the ideology of masculinity that often prevents boys from succeeding in school. Educational reforms are hardly a winner-takes-all game: What's good for girls is usually good for boys, too.

Close observation by ethnographers in classrooms can reveal the ways in which boys and girls approach their educations differently. Listen to how one Australian boy described his feelings about English and math class:

> I find English hard. It's because there are no set rules for reading texts . . . English isn't like math where you have rules on how to do things and where there are right and wrong answers. In English you have to write down how to feel and that's what I don't like.

A girl in the same class felt completely different about it:

> I feel motivated to study English because . . . you have freedom in English—unlike subjects such as math or science—and your view isn't necessarily wrong. There is no definite right or wrong answer and you have freedom to say what you feel is right without being rejected as a wrong answer. (Martino, 1997)

Such differences are often magnified by differences of race and class. Middle-class White boys can often get away with being disruptive in class, while working class and minority boys might be punished. Sociologists John Ogbu and Signithia Fordham found that urban Black students used race and gender to disengage from academic success. When Black girls did well in school they were accused of "acting White." Black boys, by contrast, were accused of "acting like girls" (Fordham, 1994; Noguera, 2008; and Ogbu, 2003). Education is often hailed as the major way to get ahead in our lives. Gender inequality in education makes that promise more difficult for everyone to achieve.

Gender equality in education is often uncomfortable. One teacher decided to treat boys and girls exactly equally; and, to make sure she called on boys and girls equally, she always referred to the class roster, on which she marked who had spoken. "After two days the boys blew up," she told a journalist. "They started complaining and saying that I was calling on the girls more than them." Eventually, they got used to it. "Equality was hard to get used to," the teacher concluded, and the boys "perceived it as a big loss" (Orenstein, 1994, p. 27).

They were uncomfortable, but they got used to it. Today, state and local governments work to eliminate gender inequality in schools because discrimination, stereotypes, and harassment hurt both girls *and* boys. Gender inequality in education actually ends up producing the differences we think are so natural.

Gender Inequality in Everyday Life

Gender difference and gender inequality also have a profound impact on our everyday lives, in our relationships, friendships, marriages, and family life. During the eighteenth or nineteenth century, only men were thought capable of the emotional depths and constancy that true intimacy demanded. These days, though, intimate life is seen largely as the province of women. Women are seen as the relationship experts, capable of the emotional expression and vulnerability that today define intimacy.

How did this change? Sociologists believe that the answer has far less to do with men being from Mars and women from Venus and far more to do with our history. The Industrial Revolution drove a wedge between home and work, emotional life and rational life. For the first time, most men had to leave their homes for work that was competitive and challenging; success in that dog-eat-dog world required that they turn off their emotions and become competitors. Women's sphere remained the emotional refuge of home and hearth. Men learned to separate love and work, while women's work *was* love. Women are "expected, allowed and required to reveal certain emotions, and men are expected or required to deny or suppress them" (Tavris, 1999, fn. 43).

As a result, women have come to be seen as the experts on love and friendship. (Men became the experts on sex, which we discuss in Chapter 10.) Sociological research on friendship finds that women talk more with their friends, share their feelings more, and actually have more friends. Seventy-five percent of women could identify a best friend; only 33 percent of men could do so (Rubin, 1986). Men tend not to sustain friendships over time but rather pick up new ones in new situations. As sociologists and psychologists understand intimacy to be based on verbal and nonverbal sharing of feelings, mutual disclosure, vulnerability, and dependency, then men's friendships are "emotionally impoverished."

Yet other elements of masculinity—such as reliability and consistency, practical advice, and physical activity—also provide a solid foundation for friendship. Few sociologists would suggest that women have a monopoly on those qualities that make good friends.

Women are also seen as the love experts, so much so that sociologist Francesca Cancian speaks of "the feminization of love" (1987). That is because our society so positively values talking and expressing our feelings, but we also downplay "practical help, shared physical activities, spending time together, and sex," which men are more comfortable with. Of course, close loving relationships require a good deal of both emotional sharing and practical activity. The separation of spheres leaves both women and men unfulfilled. "Who is more loving," Cancian asks rhetorically, "a couple who confide most of their experiences to each other but rarely cooperate or give each other practical help, or a couple who help each other through many crises and cooperate in running a household but rarely discuss their personal experiences?"

Race also complicates the gender of friendship. For example, impassivity and inexpressiveness for men may be an adaptive

Did You
Know?

A Fine Bromance

"Bromance" movies, like *I Love You, Man* and *The Hangover,* are one of Hollywood's hottest genres. The difference between "his" friendships, or lack of them, and "her" friendships, and their deep intimacy, is the subtext of many films, like *Knocked Up* and *Superbad,* as well as the *Sex and the City* television series and film.

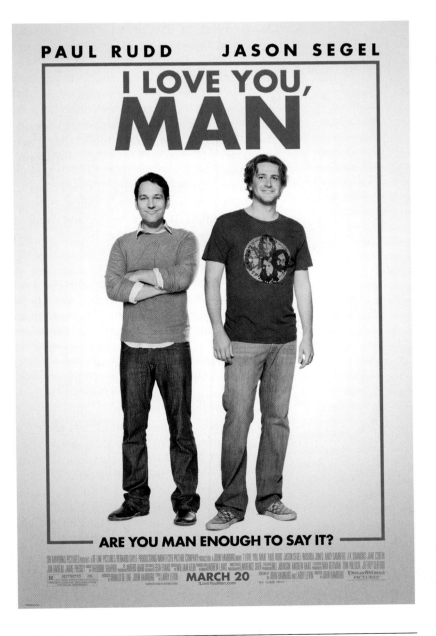

strategy to "disguise painful emotions such as shame and sadness influenced by frustrations encountered with mainstream society." On the other hand, Black men exhibit significant emotional expressiveness, often designed to release anger and resentment towards the existing social structure. (Thus the expressive styles of Black men, which Whites come to assume are part of Black culture, are in fact adaptive strategies to deal with the outrage and injustice of racism and economic inequality.) Class also shapes Black men's emotional experiences. Working-class Black male friendships are often self-disclosing and close, in part due to a shared political ideology. Yet upwardly mobile Black men have fewer friends, and those they have are less intimate, than their working-class counterparts, in part because they have accepted traditional definitions of masculinity (Harris, 1992; Franklin, 1992).

While research suggests that, at younger ages, cross-race friendships are more common, by fifth grade, they are less common and less stable than same-race friendships. Both Blacks and Whites rate their cross-race friendships as "less intimate" than their "same-race" friendships (Aboud, Mendleson, and Purdy, 2003; Clark, 1985). In college, cross-race friendships become more common if one's roommate is of a different race, but classroom integration has little effect (Stearns, Buchmann, and Bonneau, 2009).

Racial stereotypes both encourage and inhibit cross-race friendships. For both White boys and girls, Blacks may be seen as rebellious, and less obedient, and therefore associating with them might increase a White person's status as tough, rebellious, or independent. Stereotypes of Black masculinity hold that Black boys are "more masculine" than White boys, while stereotypes of Black femininity hold that they are "less feminine" than White girls. Interviews with college-aged White males found many placing a high premium on "scoring a Black dude" as a friend to enhance a guy's status with his other friends (Kimmel, 2008).

Similarly, racial stereotypes often inform cross-race romantic involvement.

Friendship and love are fragile because they are not secured by any social institu-

tions; in other words, there are no formal rules for friendship or love, just an emotional bond. Marriage, by contrast, is a formal contract, a set of mutual and equal obligations.

Marriage is a deeply gendered institution. Consider how we think of it. A woman devises some clever scheme to "trap" a man into marriage. When she succeeds, her friends throw her a shower to celebrate her triumph. The groom's friends throw a raucous party, often with strippers or prostitutes, to mark his "last night of freedom."

According to this model, marriage is something she wants and he resists—as long as he can. She wins, he loses. Yet the sociological research suggests something quite different. In the 1970s, sociologist Jessie Bernard (1972) identified two types of marriage—"his" and "hers." And, she argued, "his is better than hers." Marriage benefits men more than it does women. Married men are happier and healthier than either single men or married women. They live longer, earn more money, and have more sex than single men; they have lower levels of stress and initiate divorce less often than married women (Gove, 1972; Gove, Hughes, and Style, 1983). They also remarry more readily and easily.

Why would this traditional definition of marriage benefit men more than women? Because it is based not only on gender differences between women and men but also on gender inequality. In the gender division of labor, she works at home, and he doesn't; outside the home, he works, and so does she (although perhaps not for as many hours). And she provides all the emotional, social, and sexual services he needs to be happy and healthy. "Marriage is pretty good for the goose much of the time," writes a science reporter surveying the field, "but golden for the gander practically all of the time" (Angier, 1999).

Of course marriage is also good for women. Married people live longer and healthier lives, have more and better sex, save more money, and are less depressed than unmarried people (Centers for Disease Control, 2006b). But as long as there is gender inequality in our marriages, it's a better deal for men.

The Politics of Gender

Because sociologists study the links between identity and inequality—whether based on race, class, sexuality, age, or gender—sociologists also study the various movements that have been organized to challenge that inequality and enhance the possibilities of those identities. Gender politics includes those who are uncomfortable with the limitations placed on them by gender roles as well as more concerted social movements that would redress more structural and institutional forms of inequality.

Opposition to Gender Roles

Many men and women have found the traditional roles that were prescribed for them to be too confining, preventing them from achieving the sorts of lives they wanted. Both women and men have bumped up against restrictive stereotypes or arbitrary rules that excluded them. Historically, women's efforts to enter the labor force, seek an education, vote, serve on a jury, or join a union served as the foundation for contemporary women's efforts to reduce discrimination, end sexual harassment or domestic violence, or enable them to balance work and family life. Women soon understood that they could not do these things alone, and their opposition to gender roles became political: They opposed gender inequality.

Many men, however, continue to find traditional definitions of masculinity restrictive. Beginning in the 1970s, they sought "liberation" from parts of that role—as "success object" or "emotionless rock." "Men's liberation" never really took off as a social movement, but many thousands of men have become involved with groups that promise a more fulfilling definition of masculinity. Unfortunately, this is often to be achieved by returning to traditional, anachronistic, ideas of femininity as well. For example, the evangelical Christian group Promise Keepers embraces a traditional nineteenth-century vision of masculinity as responsible father and provider—as long as their wives also return to a traditional nineteenth-century definition of femininity, staying home and taking care of the children.

The Women's Movement(s)

Change requires political movements, not only individual choices. The modern women's movement was born to remove obstacles to women's full participation in modern life. In the nineteenth century, the "first wave" of the women's movement was concerned with women's *entry* into the public sphere.

Gender inequality remains a significant social problem—whether in representation in politics or in corporations, or in art museums. Some feminist organizations use humor to make their point.

Campaigns to allow women to vote (suffrage), to go to college, to serve on juries, to go to law school or medical school, or to join a profession or a union all had largely succeeded by the middle of the twentieth century. The motto of the National Woman Suffrage Association was, "Women, their rights and nothing less! Men, their rights and nothing more!"

In the 1960s and 1970s, a "second wave" of the women's movement appeared, determined to continue the struggle to eliminate obstacles to women's advancement but also equally determined to investigate the ways that gender inequality is also part of personal life, which includes their relationships with men. Second-wave feminists also focused on men's violence against women, rape, the denigration of women in the media, and women's sexuality and lesbian rights, as well as wage disparities and the glass ceiling. Their motto was, "The personal is political."

Today, a "third wave" of the women's movement has emerged among younger women. While third-wave feminists share the outrage at institutional discrimination and interpersonal violence, they also have a more playful relationship with mass media and consumerism. While they support the rights of lesbians, many third wavers are also energetically heterosexual and insist on the ability to be friends and lovers with men. They are also decidedly more multicultural and seek to explore and challenge the "intersections" of gender inequality with other forms of inequality, such as class, race, ethnicity, and sexuality. They are equally concerned with racial inequalities or sexual inequalities and see the ways in which these other differences construct our experiences of gender. Third-wave feminists also feel more empowered than their foremothers; they often feel there is no need for feminism because they can now do anything they want. Their motto could be, "Girls rule!"

There are also men who support gender equality. These "profeminist" men believe not only that gender equality is a good thing for women but that it would also transform masculinity in ways that would be positive for men, enabling them to be more involved fathers, better friends, more emotionally responsive partners and husbands—fuller human beings.

Gloria Steinem became one of the most enduring symbols of the U.S. women's movement after she infiltrated the Playboy Club to write an expose article about the life of a bunny. In 1972, she was one of the founders of Ms. Magazine.

Feminism

The political position of many young women today, however, is "I'm not a feminist, but . . . ." Most young women subscribe to virtually all the tenets of feminism—equal pay for equal work, right to control their bodies and sexuality—but they believe that they are already equal to men and therefore don't need a political movement to liberate them and that the term *feminist* carries too many negative connotations.

Feminism is the belief that women should have equal political, social, sexual, economic, and intellectual rights to men. It insists on women's equality in all arenas—in the public sphere, in interpersonal relations, at home and at work, in the bedroom and the boardroom. As a political theory, feminism rests on two foundations: one an empirical observation and the other a moral stand. The empirical observation is that women and men are not equal; that is, that gender inequality still defines our society. The moral stand is that this inequality is wrong and should change. A feminist once said that "Feminism is the radical idea that women are people" (Kramarae and Treichler, 1997). One can, of course, be a feminist and like men, want to look attractive, and shave one's underarms and wear mascara. Or not. Feminism is about women's choices and the ability to choose to do what they want to do with no greater obstacles than the limits of their abilities.

There are several major strands of feminism. Each emphasizes a different aspect of gender inequality and prescribes a different political formula for equality.

Liberal Feminism. **Liberal feminism** follows classical liberal political theory and focuses on the individual woman's rights and opportunities (Kraditor, 1981). Liberal feminists want to remove structural obstacles (institutional forms of discrimination in the public arena) that stand in the way of individual women's entry and mobility in their occupation or profession or the political arena. Liberal feminists have been at the forefront of campaigns for equal wages and comparable worth, as well as reproductive choice. The Equal Rights Amendment, which did not pass as a constitutional amendment in the 1970s, is an example of a liberal feminist political agenda. The amendment states simply that: "Equality of rights under the law shall not be denied or abridged by the United States or by any State on account of sex."

Liberal feminists have identified and sought to remove many of the remaining legal, economic, and political barriers to women's equal opportunity. Critics, however, claim that the focus on removing barriers to individual rights ignores the root causes of gender inequality, that liberal feminists tend to be largely White and middle class, and that their focus on career mobility reflects their class and race background (Dworkin, 1985, 2002; hooks, 1981, 1989).

Radical Feminism. **Radical feminism** states that women are not discriminated against just economically and politically; they are also oppressed and subordinated by men directly, personally, and most often through sexual relations (Brownmiller, 1976; Dworkin, 1985). Radical feminists often believe that patriarchy is the original form of domination and that all other forms of inequality derive from it. To radical feminists, it is through sex that men appropriate women's bodies.

Radical feminists have been active in campaigns to end prostitution, pornography, rape, and violence against women. Many argue that it is through "trafficking" in women's bodies—selling their bodies as prostitutes or making images of that trafficking in pornography—that gender inequality is reproduced (MacKinnon, 1987). Pornography provides a rare window into the male psyche: This is how men see women, they argue. "Pornography is the theory, rape is the practice," is a slogan coined by radical feminist writer Robin Morgan (1976). Radical feminists have also been successful in bringing issues of domestic violence and rape to international attention. They have created a growing worldwide concern for the new and revived sex slave marketplace.

However, radical feminism relies too much on unconvincing blanket statements about all men and all women, without taking into account differences among men and among women. Thus, it's often "essentialist," claiming that the single dividing line in society is between men and women. That is, of all feminists, it may be radical feminists who believe that men are from Mars and women from Venus. Their claims about universal sisterhood have not been convincing to Black feminists who feel that when radical feminists say "women," they really mean "White women" (see hooks, 1981).

Multicultural Feminism. Does liberal feminism or radical feminism apply equally to all women? Do Black women or Latino women or older women or rural women have the same sets of issues and problems as middle-class suburban White women? These divisions among women are often dismissed by liberal feminists who want women to be seen as individuals and by radical feminists who believe that all women face the same oppression *as women*.

Multicultural feminism argues that the experience as people of color cannot be extracted from the experience as women and treated separately. "Where does the 'Black' start and the 'woman' end?" asked one of my students. Multicultural feminists emphasize the historical context of racial and class-based inequalities. For example, sociologist Patricia Hill Collins (1998) shows how the treatment of slaves in the antebellum South (before the Civil War) was also part of a differential treatment of African women and African men. Slavery was not only racial inequality; it was also gender inequality, woven into it and inextricable from it.

Bell hooks (1989) argues that the focus on the family, the workplace, or sexuality as the sites of gender inequality does not track perfectly for Black women. For Black women, the family and sexuality may have been sources of power and pride, not oppression, and the workplace may not be an arena of expressing your highest aspirations.

The impact of multicultural feminism has been enormous. Today, most sociologists are following the lead of third-wave feminists and exploring the "intersections" of gender, race, class, age, ethnic, and sexual dimensions of inequality. Each of these forms of inequality shapes and modifies the others.

Gender Inequality in the Twenty-First Century

There is little doubt that around the world gender inequality is gradually being reduced. The International Conference on Women sponsored by the United Nations in 1985 proclaimed a universal declaration of women's rights as human rights, including the right to reproductive control and a strong condemnation of female genital mutilation.

Living in times of great historical transformation, we often forget just how recent are the changes we today take for granted. There are still women who remember when women could not vote, drive a car, serve on a jury, become doctors or lawyers, serve in the military, become firefighters or police officers, join a union, or go to certain colleges. All these changes happened in the twentieth century. They've "come a long way, baby," as the advertisement for a ladies' cigarette used to say.

At the same time, today, there is significant backlash against gender equality (see Faludi, 1991). Some people believe that women's rights are simply morally wrong, that gender equality violates some theological or eternal truth, or that it would violate our biological natures. Many men have resorted to theological or biological arguments to try to force women to return to their traditional positions of housewives and mothers (Dobson, 2004).

The struggle for gender equality has a long history, filled with stunning successes and anguishing setbacks. But for women (and their male allies) who believe in gender equality, there is no going back.

Chapter Review

1. Sex and Gender: Nature *and* Nurture

Every society has inequality based on **sex. Gender** is fundamental to human identity, differentiated everywhere on Earth. While sex has little variation, gender varies widely—cultural meanings of masculinity and femininity vary within a society, across cultures, over time, and even across the life course of a single individual. Gender provides a primary identity, **gender identity,** but it is also the basis for **gender inequality,** as all societies exhibit some degree of **patriarchy.** Sexual differentiation, an evolutionary adaptation, ensures propagation and continuation of our species—the **evolutionary imperative.** Physical differences between the sexes arise from **sex hormones** during development and growth, resulting in **primary sex characteristics** and **secondary sex characteristics,** but sociologists focus on gender, the social understanding and meaning given to sexual differentiation, and question why there is so much variation in gender inequality. Explanations for gender inequality include functional explanations by task, relations to the means of production, warfare, family size, and child care. Cross-cultural research demonstrates so much variation in what it means to be a man or a woman that we know gender is not biologically determined. Even the number of gender identities, assumed to be biological, varies cross-culturally.

sex A biological distinction; the chromosomal, chemical, and anatomical organization of males and females. (p. 256)

gender A socially constructed definition based on sex category, based on the meanings that societies attach to the fact of sex differences. (p. 256)

gender identity Our understanding of ourselves as male or female and what it means to be male or female, perhaps the most fundamental way in which we develop an identity. (p. 256)

gender inequality Gender inequality has two dimensions: the domination of men over women, and the domination of some men over other men and some women over other women. (p. 257)

patriarchy Literally, "the rule of the fathers"; a name given to the social order in which men hold power over women. (p. 257)

evolutionary imperative The term used to imply that the chief goal of all living creatures is to reproduce themselves. (p. 258)

sex hormones Testosterone and estrogen, the hormones that trigger development of secondary sex characteristics, such as breast development in girls and the development of facial hair in boys. (p. 258)

primary sex characteristics Those anatomical sex characteristics that are present at birth, like the sex organs themselves, which develop in the embryo. (p. 259)

secondary sex characteristics Those sex characteristics, such as breast development in girls and the lowering of voices and development of facial hair in boys, that occur at puberty. (p. 259)

2. Becoming Gendered: Learning Gender Identity

Sex, a product of nature, is realized at the moment of conception, but **gender socialization** begins as soon as the developing fetus is identified as a boy or a girl and continues throughout our lives in the **social construction of gender.** The meaning attached to a child's sex is apparent in the different ways that boy and girl babies are treated—how they are talked to, how they are dressed, the toys they are given, and even the traits or behaviors that are focused on. Differential treatment and differing expectations for behavior continue throughout our lives, as we learn and fulfill the expectations society holds for what it means to be male or female—how to act like a member of our gender, fulfilling **gender roles** that are even institutionalized.

gender socialization Process by which males and females are taught the appropriate behaviors, attitudes, and traits for their biological sex. It begins at birth and continues throughout their lives. (p. 262)

social construction of gender The sociological idea that gender is something we construct all through our lives, using the cultural materials we find around us. Our gender identities are simultaneously voluntary, based on choices, and coerced by social pressures, sometimes including physical threats, to conform to certain rules. (p. 264)

gender roles Psychology-based term to define the bundle of traits, attitudes, and behaviors that are associated with biological males and females. Roles are blueprints that prescribe what you should do, think, want, and look like, so that you can successfully become a man or a woman. (p. 264)

3. Gender Inequality on a Global and Local Scale

Across the globe, women are overrepresented among the world's poor, experiencing higher rates of unemployment, lower wages, and greater hardship on a number of indicators, including hunger, and access to health care. Even here in the United States there is a **gender wage gap.** The **feminization of poverty** is more extreme in developing countries, but in industrial nations, too, women (and more so women of color) experience greater hardship than men, in the workplace, with lower-paying and lower-status jobs, and in the home, where working women bear the additional burden of housework and child care.

gender wage gap The significant and remarkably consistent gap between earnings of men and women. The gap

between White men and women of color is larger than between White men and White women. (p. 266)

feminization of poverty This term describes a worldwide phenomenon that also afflicts U.S. women, that of women's overrepresentation among the world's poor and tendency to be in the worse economic straits than men in any given nation or population. (p. 266)

4. Gender Inequality in the United States

Although most women work, and over half of those training for a profession are women, traditional ideologies about gender roles persist, with detrimental effects for women in the labor force. In the **dual-labor market,** work that is seen as "women's work" is less well paid. **Feminization of the professions** results in lower wages even for professional women. Women in traditionally men's professions bump up against a glass ceiling in advancement, while men in traditionally women's professions rise rapidly. **Sexual harassment** is illegal but still happens. Women face hardships that men do not while trying to balance work and family, including discrimination in the workplace and the additional burden of the **second shift.** Our experiences in the workplace are preceeded by the inequality we experience in school, where gender socialization occurs through differential treatment and expectations for behavior. This socialization that occurs in school for both males and females is part of the "hidden curriculum." Not just in school and in the workplace, but in all aspects of life, there is gendered division of labor, with inequality permeating even love and friendship relationships.

dual labor market A theory of economic inequality in the labor market between the "primary" sector, characterized by high wage, high benefits jobs and the "secondary" market, characterized by low wage, few benefits, and seasonal or marginal employment. A "gendered" dual labor market indicates that the level of sex segregation in the labor force is high. (p. 269)

feminization of the professions The phenomenon in which salaries drop as female participation increases, revealing that it is less the intrinsic properties of the position that determine its wages and prestige and more which sex does it. (p. 270)

sexual harassment A form of gender discrimination in the workplace that singles out women for differential treatment. There are two types: "quid pro quo," which occurs when a supervisor uses his (or her) position to elicit sexual activity from a subordinate; and the more common "hostile environment," which occurs when a person feels threatened or unsafe because of constant teasing or threatening by other workers. (p. 271)

second shift The term coined by sociologist Arlie Hochschild to describe how working women typically must work both outside the home for wages and inside the home doing domestic management and child care. (p. 272)

5. The Politics of Gender

Men and women seek opportunities outside of traditionally restrictive gender roles. Successive waves of the women's movement have moved women into the public sphere in the nineteenth century, toward political and personal equality in the 1960s and 1970s, and today, toward greater personal freedom and equality across gender, race, class, ethnicity, and sexuality. Many today don't identify themselves as feminists, although they hold to the tenets of equality of **feminism,** because they believe that men and women are already equal and have no need of a political movement. Different forms of feminism exist, each focusing on particular issues of inequality, including **liberal feminism, radical feminism,** and **multicultural feminism.**

feminism A system of beliefs and actions that rests on two principles: Gender inequality defines our society; and such inequality is wrong and must change. (p. 278)

liberal feminism One of the three main branches of feminism today; focuses on the individual woman's rights and opportunities. (p. 279)

radical feminism One of the three main branches of feminism today; moves beyond discrimination economically

and politically to argue that women are oppressed and subordinated by men directly, personally, and most often through sexual relations. (p. 279)

multicultural feminism One of the three main branches of feminism today; argues that the experience of being a woman of color cannot be extracted from the experience of being a woman. Multicultural feminists emphasize the historical context of racial and class-based inequalities. (p. 279)

6. Gender Inequality in the Twenty-First Century

Gains have been made toward greater gender equality but only quite recently, in the grand scheme of things. Even today, in the twenty-first century, there is still a long way to go until the goal of global human rights, including gender equality, is reached. There are still those who oppose equality.

Self-Test: Check Your Understanding

1. _____ refers to the biological distinction of being male or female, while _____ refers to the meanings that societies attach to these biological differences.
   a. Gender; sex
   b. Feminism; oppression
   c. Sex; gender
   d. Physiology; sociology

2. As revealed by cross-cultural research, how many gender roles are found in each society?
   a. Only one
   b. Always two
   c. At least three
   d. It varies by society.

3. How prevalent are division of labor by gender and gender inequality today?
   a. Both are universal.
   b. Developing countries have division of labor by gender, while industrial societies have gender inequality.
   c. Developing countries have gender inequality, while industrial societies have division of labor by gender.
   d. Although both were prevalent in prehistoric societies, neither exist in society today.

4. How are infants of differing sexes treated?
   a. Infants of different sexes are treated identically by adults.
   b. They are treated the same by women but differently by men.
   c. They are treated the same by men but differently by women.
   d. Adults treat infants of different sexes differently.

5. According to the text, for which trait has a significant gender difference been found?
   a. Intelligence
   b. Violence
   c. Extroversion
   d. No significant differences have been found.

6. The second shift Arlie Hochschild wrote about refers to:
   a. the overtime a woman would have to work to earn as much as a man does for the same job.
   b. the fact that women get the less desirable shifts in the workplace due to their lower status.
   c. the extra hours working women work, compared with men, as they do the housework, too.
   d. the next shift in awareness, when women are not only legally recognized as equal but actually treated as such.

7. Which of the following is the result of the "hidden curriculum," according to the text?
   a. Men learn they are expected to like math and science.
   b. Women learn to talk more in class, to fulfill the expectation that women are chattier.
   c. Men learn that reading comes naturally to them, while women have to struggle with it.
   d. Men and women get the message that they are valued equally and have equal potential.

8. Identify which of the following is not one of the principles of feminism identified in the text.
   a. The moral position that inequality is wrong and should change
   b. The empirical observation that men and women are not equal in our society
   c. The fact that men and women have different abilities, and so have different contributions that they can make, but that both are equally valuable to society
   d. All of these are principles of feminism that were identified in the text.

Self-Test Answers: 1. c, 2. d, 3. a, 4. d, 5. b, 6. c, 7. a , 8. c

Integrate and Explore: Points to Consider

1. There is inequality across genders, but there is also stability and social cohesion in maintaining the status quo. How does this fact make it difficult for change, such as increased equality, to take place within a society? How might this fact contribute to conflict between societies as diverse cultures, with differing gender roles, interact globally?

2. What are some of the challenges that women in particular face, as a result of globalization? Are there additional challenges for women of color? Which challenges are best understood at a macrolevel and which at a microlevel?

succeed with mysoclab

Self-scoring practice tests, flashcards for learning key terms, streaming audio of the entire text, and multimedia, including:

Watch—Michael Kimmel, *How Gender Became Visible to Sociologists*

Watch—Michael Kimmel, *How Gender Bias Operates in Everyday Life*

Map—Social Explorer: *Gender Stratification in Wealth, Power and Privilege*

MySocLibrary—Judith Lorber, *Night to His Day: The Social Construction of Gender*

MySocLibrary—Gloria Steinem, *If Men Could Menstruate*

The "Sociological Body": Age, Health, and Sexuality

The untimely death of Michael Jackson in 2009 left the music world saddened by the loss of a great talent. But Jackson's physical transformation over the course of his career was deeply disturbing to many people. Each stage of his career seemed to be accompanied by a correspondingly new physical persona.

We think of our bodies as a possession, something uniquely and distinctly ours. "It's *my* body," says transgender theorist Susan Stryker, "I live here. I don't rent. And that means I can do with it whatever I want." As a result, we also consider our bodies to

be a "project"—something we can "work" on, a canvas of our own creation.

On the other hand, we think our bodies are biological entities, subject to natural processes such as aging, health, maturation, and decay. We experience ourselves to be driven by "urges," or needs that seem to come from inside the body but outside our control. Sometimes we even think parts of our bodies have a mind of their own.

Sex, for example, is among our most intimate and private experiences. We rarely discuss our sexual experiences honestly with family and friends. We may think of our desires as irrational, out-of-control impulses, some too shameful to even utter. Yet sex is also pretty much everywhere we look. References to sex and the sexual body are sprinkled liberally through our daily conversations. Sex is everywhere—online, in books and magazines, on TV, and in movies and music. And these images reflect cultural notions of what is sexy to people while they also help shape our personal experiences and expressions of sexual desire as well.

And when it comes to sexual identities, we think of them as fixed and permanent—something we are, not something we become. At the same time, though, we debate about whether or not homosexuals can teach our children without trying to recruit them and offer "conversion" therapies to help gays become heterosexual.

"We think of our bodies as a possession, something uniquely and distinctly ours, a "project" or a canvas of our own creation. But to the sociologist, there are few entities more social than the body—from the definitions of what constitutes health or beauty to the social controls that tell us what is "normal" or permissible and what is not."

So which is it—public or private? Sexuality biologically fixed or malleable and changing? To the sociologist, the answer to these questions is rarely one or the other. It's both. Sex is both private and public. It is a central part of our identity, and it evolves and changes over the course of our lives. What we desire, what we do, and what we think about what we do are all social.

To a sociologist, there are few entities that are more social than the body: from the definitions of what constitutes health or beauty, to the techniques and rationales we will use to achieve them; from our ideas of what we want to do with our bodies—aesthetically, medically, sexually—to the social controls that tells us what is "normal" or permissible and what is not.

The Social Body

At first glance, finding someone attractive might feel purely instinctive: You experience an immediate "gut reaction" of interest, without even thinking about it. But if desire were instinctive, the standards of physical attractiveness would be the same across human cultures; and, with a few exceptions (big eyes, a symmetrical face), they are not. They change dramatically from culture to culture.

Cultural Standards of Beauty

What we think of as beautiful is less a matter of individual perception and more about ever-shifting cultural standards. Standards of beauty vary enormously from culture to culture and, within the United States, among different racial and ethnic groups, ages, and even classes. In general, standards of women's beauty vary depending on economic trends and the status of women: When the economy goes up, women's standards become increasingly "feminine," exaggerating biological differences to suggest that male breadwinners can afford to have their wives stay at home. When women's status rises, men tend to become more interested in their own upper-body muscles, and beards and mustaches increase.

In the United States, women's beauty is placed at such a high premium and the standards of beauty are so narrow that many women feel trapped by what feminist writer Naomi Wolf (1991) called the "beauty myth"—a nearly unreachable cultural ideal of feminine beauty that "uses images of female beauty as a political weapon against women's advance-ment." By this standard, women are trapped in an endless cycle of cosmetics, beauty aids, diets, and exercise fanaticism (Wolf, 1991, pp. 10, 184; see also Rodin, Silberstein, and Striegel-Moore, 1985; Striegel-Moore, Silberstein, and Rodin, 1986). The body shape and weight that are considered ideal also vary enormously. And it appears that standards are becoming harder and harder to achieve.

Feeding and Starving the Female Body. In 1954, Miss America was 5' 8" and weighed 132 pounds. Today, the average Miss America contestant still stands 5' 8", but now she weighs just 117 pounds. In 1975, the average female fashion model weighed about 8 percent less than the average American woman; by 1990 that disparity had grown to 23 percent. And though the average American woman today is 5' 4" tall and weighs 140 pounds, the average model is 5' 11" and weighs 117 pounds. No wonder 42 percent of girls in first through third grades say they want to be thinner, and 81 percent of 10-year-olds are afraid of being fat. Almost half of 9- to 11-year-olds are on diets; by college the percentage has nearly doubled (Gimlin, 2002; Robbins, 2008).

Young women are particularly concerned with their weight. Research on adolescents suggests that a large majority consciously trade off health concerns in their efforts to lose weight. As a result, increasing numbers of young women are diagnosed with either anorexia nervosa or bulimia every year. **Anorexia nervosa** involves chronic and dangerous starvation dieting and obsessive exercise; **bulimia** typically involves "binging and purging" (eating large quantities and then either vomiting or taking enemas to excrete them). These are serious problems,

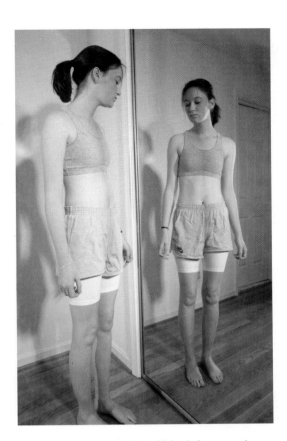

Most girls are preoccupied with body image and their weight—at least most middle-class White girls are (body image varies by class and race). At one end of the continuum are fad diets and efforts to stay fit and in shape. At the other end lie dangerous, and potentially lethal, eating disorders, such as anorexia.

often requiring hospitalization, which can, if untreated, threaten a girl's life. To a sociologist they represent only the farthest reaches of a continuum of preoccupation with the body that begins with such "normal" behaviors as compulsive exercise or dieting.

While rates of anorexia and bulimia are higher in the United States than in any other country—close to 4 percent of girls in the United States experience one or the other, more than ten times the rate for European countries—rates among American girls vary by race or class (Efron, 2005; Fitzgibbon and Stolley, 2000; U.S. Department of Health and Human Services, 2006).

Pumping up the Male Body. While men have long been concerned about appearing strong, the emphasis on big muscles seems to increase as an obsession during periods when men are least likely to actually have to use their muscles in their work (Gagnon,

1971; Glassner, 1988). Today, successful men's magazines like *Men's Health* encourage men to see their bodies as women have been taught to see theirs— as ongoing works-in-progress. In part, this coincides with general concerns about health and fitness, and in part it is about looking young in a society that does not value aging. But more than that, it also seems to be about gender.

Many men experience what some researchers have labeled **muscle dysmorphia,** a belief that one is too small, insufficiently muscular. Harvard psychiatrist Harrison Pope and his colleagues call it the **Adonis complex** —the belief that men must look like Greek gods, with perfect chins, thick hair, rippling muscles, and washboard abdominals (Pope, Phillips, and Olivardia, 2000).

The standards for men, like those for women, are becoming increasingly impossible to achieve. If the 1974 GI Joe action figure had been 5' 10" tall, he would have had, proportionally, a 31-inch waist, a 44-inch chest, and 12-inch biceps—strong and muscular but at least within the realm of the possible. If the 2002 GI Joe is still 5' 10" tall, his waist has shrunk to 28 inches, his chest has expanded to 50 inches, and his biceps are now 22 inches—nearly the size of his waist. Such proportions would make one a circus freak, not a role model (Pope et al., 2000).

The Obesity Problem. In the United States, we're getting fatter. In 1990, 11.3 percent of Americans were obese; by 2006, it was 32 percent (obesity is measured as having a body mass index [BMI] of over 30 [Centers for Disease Control (CDC), 2007]). About one out of three Americans under age 19, and about two-thirds of all adults, qualify as overweight or obese (Hellmich, 2006). About 5 percent of Americans are "morbidly obese," which is so fat that they qualify for radical surgery (Crister, 2003). If current trends continue, by 2030, most American adults—a projected 86 percent—will be overweight or obese (Liang, Cabellero, and Kumanyika, 2009).

Did You Know?

Figure 10.1 Global Obesity Forecast

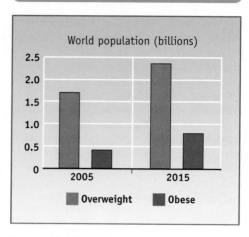

World population (billions)

2.5
2.0
1.5
1.0
0.5
0

2005   2015

■ Overweight ■ Obese

(*Source:* World Health Organization, 2005.)

Globally, obesity is a growing health problem, the mirror image of hunger and starvation (see Figure 10.1). The World Health Organization predicts there will be 2.3 billion over-weight adults in the world by 2015 and claims that there are already as many overnourished people as undernourished on Earth (BBC, 2008; Crister, 2003; Newman, 2004). Despite their connection, we think of starvation and obesity very differently. We have pity for the hungry and do-nate significantly to chari-ties that minister to hun-ger. We have contempt for the obese and believe it is their fault that they are fat.

While wealthy countries worry about obe-sity, poor countries worry about malnutrition and starvation. Developing countries, particu-larly those that are realizing economic gains due to globalization, are in between, seeing waistlines expand with economic develop-ment that includes urbanization, less exer-cise, and high-fat foods that are cheap and readily available.

Yet within the developed countries, the rich are significantly thinner than the poor. The wealthier you are, the more likely you are to eat well and exercise regularly; poorer people eat more convenience foods with high fats and suffer more weight-related illnesses, like diabetes.

Embodying Identity

Virtually all of us spend some time and energy in some forms of bodily transformation: We wear clothing we think makes us look good, or jewelry, or other adornments. But until recently, only a few "deviant" groups like motorcycle gangs, criminals, or transvestites practiced permanent bodily transformation—from piercing to tattoos, cosmetic surgery, and even the rare case of sex-change operations.

Today, body piercing involves far more than the earlobes and can include the tongue, eye-brows, navel, nose, lips, nipples, and even the genitals. Increasing numbers of young people are also getting tattoos. Given their vaguely "naughty" character in American society, tat-toos and piercing denote a slight sexualized un-dertone—if only because they indicate that the bearer is aware of his or her body as an instrument of pleasure and object of desire.

Tattoos: Inking Identity. Tattoos have long been a way to decorate the body among people in North and South America, Meso-america, Europe, Japan, China, Africa, and elsewhere. Their decline in Europe occurred with the spread of Christianity (Sanders, 1989). Today, however, tattoos have become quite common. Nearly one-third of Ameri-cans ages 25 through 29 have tattoos, as do 12 percent of those 40 through 49. Tattoos are more common in the West than other regions of the country, twice as common among Whites and Latinos as among African Americans, and more common among gay, lesbian, and bisexual Americans than among many other groups (Harris Poll, 2008). Overall, about 24 percent of all Americans between 18 and 50 have at least one tattoo, more than double the prevalence in 1985—

Obesity has become a global problem, not restricted to industrialized consumer societies. And imported im-ages of the beautiful body, as in the poster looking over this Chinese teenager's shoulder, also become the standard against which everyone is measured.

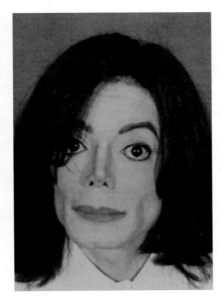

Beginning in the mid-1980s, Michael Jackson's appearance began changing dramatically. His nose narrowed, his skin lightened. In a 1993 televised interview with Oprah Winfrey, Jackson dismissed suggestions that he bleached his skin, declaring publicly that he suffered from the skin condition vitiligo, and used thick makeup to cover the resulting blotches. After Jackson's death, his friend and health guru Dr. Deepak Chopra told The Daily Beast that the singer's "compulsion with plastic surgery was an expression of self-mutilation . . . He was so ashamed of his body image, he had no self-esteem." "It was only on stage, when performing," Chopra said, "that he became someone comfortable in his own skin."

making tattoos slightly more common in the United States than DVD players (Rian, 2008).

Tattoos are seen as a way people can design and project a desired self-image (Atkinson, 2003). In cultures becoming increasingly image oriented, tattooing is conscious identity work. Tattoo design and placement are often sexually charged; over a third of tattoo wearers say it makes them feel more rebellious, and almost a third of say it makes them sexier. (On the other hand, almost 40 percent of nontattoo wearers think it makes other people less sexy.) While this mystique may attract people to tattoos, the motivation for middle-class people to "get inked" today has a lot to do with social groups. Tattoos are increasingly seen to symbolize traits valued by peers, including environmental awareness, athletic ability, artistic talent, and academic achievement (Harris Poll, 2008; Irwin, 2001). Of course, gangs and other marginalized groups continue to use tattoos as specific markers of identity.

Cosmetic Surgery. One of the fastest growing methods of bodily transformation is cosmetic surgery. According to the American Society of Plastic Surgeons, the total number of cosmetic procedures increased from 413,208 in 1992 to 11.8 million in 2007, and will top 55 million by 2015 (American Society of Plastic Surgeons, 2008). Reality television shows like *Extreme Makeover* make cosmetic surgery increasingly normal; one recent survey found these shows influenced about 80 percent of cosmetic surgery patients (Singer, 2007).

Though women continue to be the primary consumers of such cosmetic surgery, male patients have gone from 54,845 in 1992 to 1.1 million in 2007 and now comprise more than 10 percent of all surgical procedures. Teenagers are also having more plastic surgery, especially rhinoplasty (nose jobs), now the second most common cosmetic surgery in the United States after breast augmentation (American Society of Plastic Surgeons, 2006).

Once the preserve of wealthy Whites, cosmetic surgery has become increasingly common among non-Whites and the middle class. The number of people of color seeking cosmetic surgery tops 1 million a year, quadruple what it was ten years ago (American Society of Plastic Surgeons, 2008). And it is not just the United States that is witnessing accelerated growth in cosmetic procedures. Europe accounts for more than one-third of all cosmetic procedures performed worldwide, second only to the Americas.

> **Tattoo Barbie**
>
> The 50th anniversary edition of Barbie is "Totally Stylin' Tattoos Barbie." Her tattoos are removable.

Did You Know?

Age: Identity and Inequality

People often undertake cosmetic surgery to stay "young looking," to keep from getting old. But what does *old* mean, anyway? Sociologists believe that age is less a biological condition than a social construction. Depending on the norms of their society, 15-year-olds may play with toy soldiers or fight in real wars, 20-year-olds may receive a weekly paycheck or a weekly allowance, 40-year-olds may be changing the diapers of their children or grandchildren, and 60-year-olds may be doddering and decrepit or in the robust prime of life. It is not the passing of years but the social environment that determines the characteristics of age.

Age remains one of our major social identities; we assess ourselves and each other—positively and negatively—based on age as frequently as on class, race, ethnicity, gender, and sexuality. These judgments result in social stratification, for distributing rewards and punishments, and for allocating status and power.

To the sociologist, age is a basis for identity and a cause of inequality. As an identity, sociologists differentiate between your **chronological age**—a person's age determined by the actual date of birth—and **functional age**—a set of observable characteristics and attributes that are used to categorize people into different age cohorts. An **age cohort** is a group of people who are born within a specific time period and therefore assumed to share both chronological and functional characteristics.

Traditionally, the sociological study of aging was called **gerontology,** which is defined in the *American Heritage Dictionary* as the "scientific study of the biological, psychological, and sociological phenomena associated with old age and aging." However, sociologists now understand that such a study, while essential, tells only half the story. While age is a facet of identity at all moments through the life cycle, most of the inequality based on age occurs at the upper *and lower* ends of the life span—that is, among the young and the elderly. In high-income countries like the United States, older people often wield a great deal of political power, but

Many cultures celebrate rituals that mark the end of one life stage and the beginning of another. An example of such a ritual is this quinceañera (a young woman's celebration of her fifteenth birthday) in Salina, Kansas.

they still must battle negative stereotypes and limited social services. Children, teenagers, and young adults often lack any power, prestige, and resources, but they are seen as filled with potential, and we strive to look like them. And while we tout compassion for our elders and commitment to our kids, our social and economic policies often shortchange or harm both of these vulnerable groups. Today, the study of age and aging in sociology requires that we study both identity and inequality among both the young and the old—as well as everyone in between.

The Stages of Life

All societies—whether tribal, agrarian, or industrial—have always divided the **life span** into stages, seasons, or age groups. Each stage is expected to have its own **age norms**—distinctive cultural values, pursuits, and pastimes that are culturally prescribed for each age cohort. Life stages create predictable social groupings, allowing us to know in advance what to expect from strangers and new acquaintances and how to respond to them.

From ancient times through the early modern period of the seventeenth century, the rough division into childhood, adulthood, and old age was sufficient. Beginning about 1800, advances in sanitation, nutrition, and medical knowledge pushed up the average life expectancy in the United States and Western Europe. (**Life expectancy** is the average number of years that people born in a certain year could expect to live.) At the same time, the Industrial Revolution required that most children would grow up to work in factories and offices rather than on farms. They had to go to school to learn to read, write, and do basic arithmetic, and many of them stayed in school well into their teens. They weren't children anymore, but they weren't adults, either.

New stages of life were coined to accommodate the changes. The term *adult* entered the English language around 1656. **Adolescence** gained its current meaning, a life stage between childhood and adulthood, in the late nineteenth century. The adjective *teenage* appeared during the 1920s, and the noun *teenager* in 1941. The stages advanced as well: Adulthood started near the end of the teens, and elderly meant over 60, then over 65.

Today, increasing affluence, better nutrition, and more sophisticated medical expertise have increased the average life expectancy (in rich countries). Now, we often become adults at 25 or 30, and "elderly" means well over 70. With such a longer life expectancy, we need more life stages than "childhood," "adolescence," "adulthood," and "old age." We now divide adulthood and old age into new stages, roughly ten years apart:

- 25–35: young adulthood
- 35–45: "young" middle age
- 45–55: middle age
- 55–65: "old" middle age
- 65–75: "young" old age
- 75–85: "old" old age
- 85 and over: "oldest" old age

Of course, the boundaries of these life stages are subject to lots of variation and change.

In most societies, the transitions between life stages are occasions of great importance, marked by important milestones, ceremonies, and rituals. Many nonindustrial societies require grueling rites of passage, such as weeks in a sweat lodge or embarking on some "spirit quest" in the wilderness. Today many transitional stages are marked by bar or bat mitzvahs, religious confirmations, high school and college graduations, and coming-out parties. Middle-class milestones—like getting a driver's license, being allowed to drink alcohol, or getting a first apartment—are also marked by many people.

Adolescence. Before the eighteenth century, people were certainly aware of the physiological transformation that children undergo as they become adults, and they even called it "adolescence." But, as with childhood, they did not recognize it as a distinct sociological stage. Through the eighteenth century, teenagers were also considered "miniature adults." Then they were considered "big kids," just as innocent and carefree. In fact, through the early twentieth century, they were expected to have the same pastimes and interests as younger children. But as labor became more specialized, children required more specialized training, not only in the 3 Rs (readin', writin', and 'rithmetic) but in Latin, algebra, bookkeeping, and world history: They had to go to high school. Between 1880 and 1940, the high school graduation rate increased from 2 percent to 50 percent and the college graduation rate from under 2 percent to 9 percent. Faced with postponing adulthood from the early teens to the late teens or even later, adolescence became a new life stage between childhood and adulthood, with its own norms, values, pastimes, and pursuits.

Young Adulthood. Young adulthood is a transitional stage from adolescence, marking the beginning of our lives as fully functioning members of society. Sociologists have identified five milestones that define adulthood: (1) establishing a household separate from our parents; (2) getting a full-time job so we are no longer financially dependent; (3) getting married; (4) completing our education; and (5) having children. Major structural changes in the economy, as well as media images that encourage us to stay young longer, have pushed the age at which we complete these from about 22 to close to 30 (see Arnett, 2004; Kimmel, 2008).

In 1950, close to half of all women in the United States were married for the first time by age 20 (and men a few years later). By 1975, the median age (when half were married) was 21, and today it's risen to about 27 (27.4 for men, 25.6 for women), although these numbers vary by race, ethnicity, class, and region (Census Bureau, 2008a). We're starting families later, too. In 1970, the average age for women at the birth of their first child was 21.4 in the United States (men weren't asked). Today, it is about 25, although it, too, differs by race and ethnicity: African American and Hispanic women tend to be younger than White women when they have a first child, and Asian women tend to be slightly older (CDC, 2009). One of the reasons for the delay for all women is greater gender equality. Since 1970, the percentage of women graduating from college has nearly doubled, and the number in the labor force has gone up from 40 percent to almost 60 percent (Population Reference Bureau, 2008).

Putting off all adult responsibilities may be a response to increased longevity: If I'm going to live 20 years longer than my grandparents did, then maybe I have 20 more years to "grow up." But it is also a response to the fluid nature of contemporary adulthood. The milestones that once spelled the entrance to adulthood, definitively and finally, now occur throughout life, so it is little wonder that people feel like adolescents at age 30, 40, 50, or even as old as 60.

Middle Age. Because they're starting young adulthood later, people are also starting middle age later, in their 50s instead of their 40s, but eventually they are bound to notice some physiological changes. Some of these changes are class and race related. Difficult manual labor obviously ages one more rapidly than working in an office, and painting houses will age you more quickly than painting on a canvas.

If there is a developmental task of middle age, then it is this: acceptance. One must accept one's life as it is and "put away childish things"—like the dreams that you will drive a Ferrari, be a multimillionaire, or get to say "you're fired" on national television. Many adults have a difficult time achieving that acceptance; indeed, the constant emphasis on youth and glamour makes it increasingly difficult.

In earlier generations, parents hoped that they would live long enough to see their chil-

What do **you** think?

Teen Sex

Rites of passage have cultural and personal significance; one of these rites of passage is becoming sexually active. So, what do you think?

For those in their early teens, 14–16 years old, sex before marriage is:

○ always wrong.

○ almost always wrong.

○ sometimes wrong.

○ not wrong at all.

What does **America** think?

(These are actual survey data from the General Social Survey, 2004.)

For those in their early teens, 14 to 16 years old, sex before marriage is always wrong, according to 70 percent of all respondents in 2004. Women were more likely than men to report thinking it was always wrong. Another 17 percent of respondents thought it was almost always wrong. Ten percent thought it was sometimes wrong, and almost 4 percent thought it was not wrong at all. Middle-class respondents seemed to be more conservative in their views on teen sex, while upper-class respondents seemed to be the most liberal.

Thinking Critically about Survey Data

1. Why do you think women are more conservative in their views toward teen sex than men?

2. How do you explain the social class differences in responses about attitudes toward teen sex?

References: See Davis et al., page 511.

dren marry. Today they often live to see their grandchildren and great-grandchildren marry (or establish domestic partnerships). But the increase in longevity and the delay in child-bearing means that many middle-aged adults find themselves in the **sandwich generation,** caring for dependent children and aging parents at the same time. The sandwich generation is often stressed, worried, strapped, and squeezed (*General Social Survey,* 2006).

Old Age. A hundred years ago, half of the population of the United States was under 23 years old, and only 4 percent was 65 or older. But the number of older Americans has increased dramatically: In 2010, they numbered 40 million, or about 13 percent of the population (Federal Interagency Forum on Aging Related Statistics, 2008). Jerry Gerber and his coauthors (1990) argue that in the next few decades, the dramatic growth in the proportion of people over age 65 will produce an "age-quake" with similar radical social transformations. By 2050, the elderly will number 86.7 million, more than the entire U.S. population in 1900. They will comprise more than 20 percent of the population of the United States and about 20 percent of the population of the world (Federal Interagency Forum on Aging Related Statistics, 2008). The fastest-growing segment will be people 85 and older. By 2050, there will be 19 million of them (5 percent of the total population).

Three factors have led to the increase in the percentage of the population that is elderly and the gradual "graying of America." First, the birth rate has been declining for more than a century. The fact that women have been working outside the home meant that they were unable to raise a large number of children, and advances in birth control technology served to limit unexpected pregnancies. As a result, the U.S. birth-rate is at its lowest level since national data have been available and is 153rd in the world (Central Intelligence Agency, 2006).

Second, while the birthrate has been going down, life expectancy has been going up. In the United States, it shot up over 20 years during the first half of the century, from 47.3 in 1900 to 68.2 in 1950. During the last half of the century, it increased almost 10 more years, to 78.1, hitting record highs for White men (76 years) and Black men (70 years), as well as White women (81 years) and Black

"*This is our son, Eddy. He's just graduated from school and is entering a void this fall.*"

women (76.9 years) (CDC, 2008b). And the United States actually lags behind most of the wealthy nations, including Canada, France, Germany, New Zealand, Spain, the United Kingdom, and Japan (82.7 years) (Central Intelligence Agency, 2008). A third factor is the historical anomaly of the "baby boom"—the surge of births after World War II—who are now beginning to hit retirement age.

Some of the life expectancy increases are quite dramatic, but they also vary significantly by global economic status and by race, gender, and class within countries. Life expectancy for the United States as a whole has been increasing, as it has in the other wealthy countries of the OECD (the Organization for Economic Cooperation and Development, the organization of the world's 30 most developed nations) (OECD, 2009). But within that, affluent people have experienced greater gains, widening the gap in life expectancy between rich and poor in America and elsewhere (Pear, 2008) (see Figure 10.2).

Turn 65 and Move to Florida

The old joke that when you turn 65 you are required to move to Florida is close to the truth. In 2008, more than 17 percent of Florida's population was over 65, the highest percentage in the United States (California had the highest raw number of elderly persons). By 2030, six states are expected to have elderly populations of 25 percent or more: Florida, Maine, Montana, New Mexico, North Dakota, and Wyoming (*Newsweek*, 2009a; U.S. Census Bureau, 2008c).

Did You Know?

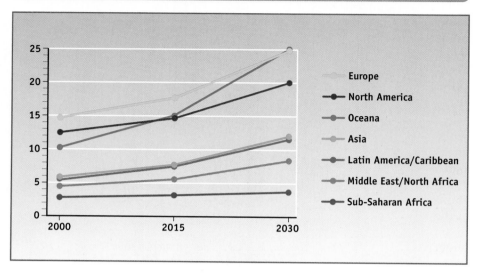

Figure 10.2 Percent of Population 65 Years or Older by Region: 2000, 2015, and 2030

Legend:
- Europe
- North America
- Oceana
- Asia
- Latin America/Caribbean
- Middle East/North Africa
- Sub-Saharan Africa

(*Source:* U.S. Census Bureau, International Data Base, 2004.)

In poor countries, life expectancy did not rise significantly during the twentieth century. In fact, while life expectancy has increased globally by almost 20 years in the past half century, in Botswana, Swaziland, Zimbabwe, and other parts of sub-Saharan Africa, life expectancy for men and women has actually been reduced by 20 years. A man in Zimbabwe can now expect to live to 38 years of age (World Health Organization, 2008). It's not that people are dying of age-related illnesses like heart disease and cancer at the age of 37 or 39, but rather that malnutrition and disease, especially HIV, keep most people in these countries from living to see middle age. Things are getting higher and lower, better and worse at the same time.

There are three life stages among the elderly. The "young old," ages 65 to 75, are likely to enjoy relative good health and financial security. They tend to live independently, often with a spouse or partner. The "old old," ages 75 to 85, suffer many more health and financial problems. They are more likely to be dependent. The "oldest old," ages 85 and higher, suffer the most health and financial problems (Belsky, 1990). However, these experiences vary enormously by class. For the lower classes, aging is often a crisis, in some cases a catastrophe. Working-class and poor people have the greatest number of health problems and the lowest rates of insurance, the least savings and retirement benefits, and the greatest financial needs.

Age and Inequality

Many societies place great value on the wisdom and authority that elders provide (Etzioni, 2005); *old* is a term of respect in Japanese, bestowed on people who are not elderly at all. But in the West, and especially in the United States, *old* means feeble, fragile, worn out, and outdated.

Physician Robert Butler, the first head of the National Institute on Aging, coined the term **ageism** in 1969 to refer to differential treatment based on age (usually affecting the elderly rather than the young). But it's equally true that dramatic inequalities exist at the younger end of the age spectrum as well. Young people are virtually powerless. As children and adolescents, they cannot vote, and they have few activist groups—their political participation occurs almost entirely under the supervision of their parents. Their unemployment rate is nearly double that of middle-aged people. They are just as vulnerable as elders, but they have no voice. As young adults, they have more opportunities for political action, but they still cannot match the economic vitality and political clout of the older generations. In the United States today, more people under age 18 are minorities—34 percent of Hispanics and 30 percent of African Americans are under 18, as compared with 24 percent of the total population—and nearly half of children under five are minorities (U.S. Census Bureau, 2009b). This dimension may compound the inequalities that accompany youth.

The Elderly and Poverty. In 1959, 33 percent of elderly men and 38 percent of elderly women in the United States were living below the poverty level. Today, seniors as a whole are more affluent than ever before, in wealth (accumulated net worth) if not in annual income. Elderly households headed by those 65 through 74 have a median net worth of $190,100, and although older White households and older married households have substantially higher net worth than elderly Blacks or singles, all older Americans still compare favorably to those under 35—who have a much smaller median net worth of $12,287 (U.S. Census Bureau, 2008c). Of

Why Women Live Longer Than Men

Because women live longer than men, the elderly are more likely to be female. In the United States, the ratio of women to men is 11.4 to 10 at age 65 through 69, but rises to 21 to 10 by age 85 and over (U.S. Administration on Aging, 2008).

But why do women live longer? Physicians have speculated that women have stronger constitutions and more immunity to disease. They are less likely to fall victim to heart disease because testosterone increases the level of "bad" cholesterol (low-density lipoprotein) while estrogen increases the level of "good" cholesterol (high-density lipoprotein). British researcher David Goldspink (2005) found that men's hearts weaken much more rapidly as they age: Between the ages of 18 and 70, their hearts lose one-fourth of their power, but healthy 70-year-old women have hearts nearly as strong as 20-year-olds (but don't worry, guys, regular cardiovascular exercise can slow or stop the decline).

Because the gap is decreasing, one cannot attribute this difference to biology alone. What sociological reasons might account for women living longer? Between the ages of 18 and 24, men are four to five times more likely to die than women, mostly from accidents: During this period of late adolescence and early adulthood, men often prove their masculinity through reckless and risky behavior, while women do not. At every age, men spend more time in the public sphere, where they are more likely to get into accidents, commit violent crimes, be victimized by crime, and be exposed to illnesses and hazardous material. Meanwhile, women spend more time at home. So, as gender inequality lessens and more women work outside the home, we would predict that the gap will decrease.

The problem is that the gap is decreasing everywhere, in both gender-polarized and gender-egalitarian countries: 5.80 years in Norway and 5.70 years in Sri Lanka, 7.95 years in France and 4.31 years in Mongolia. In fact, it seems to be shrinking more rapidly in gender-polarized countries: 2.51 years in Ethiopia, 1.81 years in Pakistan. And in seven countries, including Bangladesh, Malawi, Namibia, and Afghanistan, men are living longer than women.

Sociologists explain this by pointing out that rich and poor countries are diverging far more than women and men are in those countries. In poor countries, both women and men are increasingly susceptible to poor nutrition or health care, HIV, or violence and war. In wealthy countries, better health care and nutrition mean that both women and men are living longer. By 2040, European and American women will live to be about 100, and men will live to be 99 (Woods, 2005).

---

elderly people, more than 81 percent owned their own home in 2005, as opposed to 69 percent of all householders (Statistical Abstract of the United States, 2007).

Still, many elderly people lack the savings, investments, or pensions to be self-supporting after retirement, and the economic crisis that hit at the end of 2007 has magnified this problem. Most rich countries provide extensive benefits to their elderly populations, but the United States does not. Consequently, the poverty rate for senior citizens in the United States is about 10 percent, which is lower than the national average, but also much higher than it is in other rich nations (see Figure 10.3). The old are both richer and poorer than they ever have been.

In old age, inequalities based on race and gender are magnified. While they are age 18 to 64, African Americans and Hispanics are twice as likely to fall beneath the poverty threshold as their White non-Hispanic counterparts, but in the over-65 age group, they are *three* times as likely. Elderly women of all

Age inequalities are often compounded by inequalities of class, race, and gender.

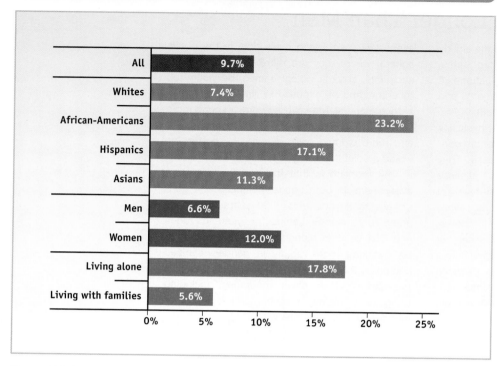

Figure 10.3 Poverty Rates among the Elderly (Age 65 and Older)

- All — 9.7%
- Whites — 7.4%
- African-Americans — 23.2%
- Hispanics — 17.1%
- Asians — 11.3%
- Men — 6.6%
- Women — 12.0%
- Living alone — 17.8%
- Living with families — 5.6%

(0% 5% 10% 15% 20% 25%)

(*Source:* U.S. Administration on Aging, 2008.)

hoods, unemployed, or working in low-income jobs that don't participate in the program will receive the lowest stipends, even though they need the money the most. In old age, the rich get richer, and the poor get poorer.

Youth and Poverty. Poverty is unequally distributed towards the young as well as the old. In 2007 the poverty rate for children under 18 in the United States was 18 percent—higher than in any other age group and almost 3 percent higher than it had been in 2000. (By comparison, the poverty rate for adults aged 18 to 64 was 10.9 percent and for senior citizens aged 65 and over, 9.7 percent) (National Center for Children in Poverty, 2008). Forty-three percent of children (more than 10 million) live in low-income families, defined as income below twice the federal poverty level. The poverty rate for children also varies by race and ethnicity, as shown in Figure 10.4.

Many countries around the world offer "family allowances" for children under 18, reasoning that they are unable to work and therefore require support. In France, family allowances cover the cost of childbirth, maternity and paternity leaves, and day care or babysitting services and provide a small monthly stipend for each child. In the United States, parents are expected to provide full financial support for their children. Federal programs like ADC (Aid to Dependent Children) and WIC (Women, Infants and Children) are available for low-income single parents, but the support is far from adequate.

Making young people's lives increasingly vulnerable are inequalities in health care. In the United States, nearly 12 percent of children and adolescents under 18 have no health insurance (Allegretto, 2006). The percentages are much higher for African Americans (14 percent), Hispanics (20 percent), and people living in poverty (20 percent). Young adults fare little better. More than 13 million Americans age 19–29 lack health insurance, up by 2.3 million since

races are more likely to be poor than elderly men—11.5 percent live at or below the poverty line, as compared with 6.6 percent of senior men—and they are three times more likely when they reach the "oldest old" life stage of 85 and up. When disenfranchised gender and racial categories are combined, the income inequality becomes more pronounced: 21 percent of elderly African Americans and 17 percent of elderly Hispanics are poor. Asian Americans are less dependent on Social Security than other aging Americans, but the poverty rate among elderly Asians is still 12 percent, which is higher than White Americans (Cawthorne, 2008a). The **Social Security** program, begun in 1940, improved the financial situation of the elderly. However, people who were poor during their adult-

Children in the Workforce

More than 246 million children aged 5 to 17 are in the workforce, about 16%. These children are contributing to family finances, often providing a major source of income. Sub-Saharan Africa has by far the highest percentage of children under 15 in the workforce (22 percent), followed by Asia (15.3 percent). Their jobs differ considerably from the teen workers in the United States: 70 percent are in agriculture, 8 percent in manufacturing, 8 percent in retail trade, and only 7 percent in service industries, including domestic work and child care. Forced and bonded labor occupies 5.7 million children and adolescents. A little over 1 million have been trafficked or transported to other regions or countries, and the rest work close to home (International Labour Organisation, 2006).

Did You Know?

2000. While young adults are only 17 percent of the under-65 population, they are nearly 30 percent of the nonelderly uninsured (Commonwealth Fund, 2009).

The Meaning of Age. The status of elders may rise as baby boomers start hitting retirement age, and because boomers grew up at the start of the information revolution, they will have the computer expertise that previous cohorts of the elderly lacked. They vote at a higher rate than the general population. They also own a greater share of the wealth, which means they wield a great deal of economic and political power.

But more than that, young people and old people are constantly changing the meaning of age in our society. In the future we will certainly live longer lives, and children will delay assuming full adult responsibilities for longer and longer periods—that is, we will be both old and young for a longer amount of time. It remains to be seen whether living longer will enable all of us to also live better or whether the rich will live longer and hap-

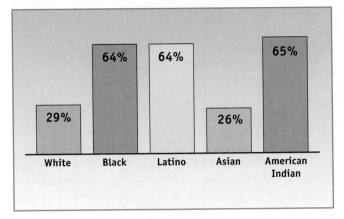

Figure 10.4 Young Children in Low-Income Families in the United States, by Race

(*Source:* © National Center for Children in Poverty [nccp.org], National Demographic Profiles used by permission of nccp.)

pier lives and the poor will live shorter, unhappy lives. What seems less controversial is that age will be an increasingly important element of our identities and a key axis of inequality.

The Body in Sickness and in Health

The health of our bodies is among the most profoundly social experiences we have. For one thing, not everyone gets sick with the same illnesses in the same ways. Health and illness are not randomly distributed around the world, in the United States, or even in our own individual community. Health and illness vary enormously by social factors including race, gender, and class, as well as age.

Age and Health

Our health changes as we age. Not only does our general health decline, but our susceptibility to various illnesses shifts. For example, men aged 25 to 44 are twice as likely to die of HIV or unintentional injuries than they are to die of heart disease or cancer. By age 45 through 64, though, these two leading causes of death for young men barely scratch the surface, and heart disease and cancer are about 20 times more likely to be the cause of death.

Projections indicate that life expectancy will continue to increase, particularly in the

rich world. As our population gradually ages, the divisions between the "young old" and the "old old" will sharpen, and people will come to expect to live into their 80s and 90s as a matter of course. The burden of health care will fall disproportionately on the younger members of society throughout the developed world (OECD, 2009).

Race, Class, and Health

In the United States and throughout the world, the wealthier you are, the healthier you are. People in more developed countries live longer and healthier lives; and, in every country, the wealthy live longer and healthier lives. Of course, wealthy people are not immune to illness simply because they are wealthy. But they have better nutrition, better access to better quality health care, and better standards of living—and these all lead to healthier lives.

Just as being wealthy is a good predictor of being healthy, so too is being poor a good predictor of being ill. Lower-class people work in more dangerous and hazardous jobs with fewer health insurance benefits and often live in neighborhoods or in housing that endangers health (peeling lead-based paint,

Globally, health varies with wealth: the poorer the country the poorer its citizens' health. According to the United Nations, 60 percent of all children living in Haiti, like these seen here, are malnourished. In the developing world, the major cause of death is infectious diseases, many of which are transmitted by unclean water.

Americans have lower life expectancy than others, and die at higher rates than other Americans from tuberculosis (600 percent higher), diabetes (189 percent higher), and injuries (152 percent higher). But Latinos, too, die of several leading causes of death at far higher rates than do Whites, including liver disease, diabetes, and HIV. Racism itself is harmful to health: The stress brought about by discrimination and inequality may contribute to the higher rates of stress-related diseases, hypertension, and mental illness (Brown, 2003; Harvard Project on American Indian Economic Development, 2006; Jackson and Stewart, 2003; Waitzkin, 1986).

While new scientific research suggests some medicines may be more or less effective depending on the patient's race, poverty is a far better explanation for health disparities (Degroat, 2006). As health care costs and the number of Americans living in poverty or in the ranks of the working poor all increase, health and health care disparity depend on inability to pay—for screening and preventive care, treatment and follow-up, as well as safe and healthy living conditions. Thus, those who need health care the most actually have the least access and the poorest care. Those at the bottom end of the socioeconomic ladder are also less likely to have health insurance, and, if they do, their insurance is more likely to place strict constraints on spending. Most have no insurance at all. America is paying a huge price in terms of health inequalities for its growing class inequalities.

The Global Distribution of Health and Illness

Globally, the problem of health and inequality is enormous. The wealthier the country, the healthier its population. In the poorest countries, high rates of poverty also means there are high rates of infectious diseases, malnutrition, and starvation. In Haiti, for example, a newborn baby has only a 50–50 change of surviving to age 5.

The cause of death for most people in the developed world is chronic diseases—such as heart attacks, cancers, and others. Over one-half of all deaths in the developing world are the result of infectious diseases or complications during pregnancy and childbirth to either the mother or the baby. But even some wealthy countries do not manage to safeguard health for their citizens or take care of the ill

exposed and leaky pipes that attract disease-bearing rodents or insects, unsanitary water and food supplies, for example). Stated most simply, inequality kills.

In the United States, men with less than 12 years of education (a broad measure of class position) are more than twice as likely to die of chronic ailments such as heart disease and almost twice as likely to die of communicable diseases than those with 13 or more years of education. Women with family income under $10,000 per year are three times more likely to die of heart disease and nearly three times as likely to die of diabetes than those with incomes above $25,000. White men earning less than $10,000 a year are 1.5 times more likely to die prematurely as those earning $34,000 or more (Isaacs, 2004).

Poor urban Blacks and Native Americans have the worst health of any ethnic group in the United States. One-third of all poor Black 16-year-old girls in urban areas will not reach their 65th birthdays. High rates of heart disease, cancer, and cirrhosis of the liver make African American men in Harlem less likely to reach age 65 than men in Bangladesh (Epstein, 2003). Native

A Common Cause of Death

Globally, leading causes of death vary from what we experience in the United States. Common diarrhea is the sixth leading cause of mortality throughout the world, killing roughly 1.8 million people each year. Tuberculosis, largely a treatable disease in the United States, is the seventh leading cause of death around the world (World Health Organization, 2008). Living conditions, clean water, access to medicine and medical care, and other sociological factors affect these rankings.

Did You Know?

or fragile in their populations. Despite the fact that the U.S. health care system is among the world's most advanced, the United States does not rank particularly high on many of the most basic health indicators. We rank 45th in life expectancy and 29th in infant mortality; in both cases, those rankings have been falling, particularly as compared with the developed world (CDC, 2008a; CIA, 2008).

In fact, when comparing wealthy countries, there is considerable variation in the levels of health achieved. To look at the amount of money spent on health care, one would think the United States is the healthiest country in the industrialized world. Today, U.S. health expenditures equal $6,714 per person per year while Japan spends just $2,474 (in U.S. dollars). France spends $3,499 (OECD, 2008). Yet life expectancy in Japan is the highest in the 10 most industrialized countries of the world and life expectancy in the United States is lowest of all these countries. France, which spends just over half what the United States does, boasts a life expectancy three years longer than ours (CIA, 2008; OECD, 2009). Canada spends $3,165 per capita, yet the average Canadian's life expectancy is nearly three years longer than the average American's. Moreover, on many measures of health care quality, the United States ranks at the bottom when compared with other developed countries, including Canada, Britain, and Australia.

HIV/AIDS. AIDS (acquired immune deficiency syndrome) is a disease of the immune system caused by HIV (human immunodeficiency virus), which attacks the white blood cells and thus makes the body vulnerable to infections that seize the "opportunity" of a compromised immune system. The disease can take up to several years to become manifest, and thus many people are HIV-positive (they have been infected) but remain asymptomatic and can transmit the disease to others.

HIV is both a sexually transmitted disease, like other STDs such as syphilis, gonorrhea, and HPV (human pappalomavirus), and also able to be transmitted with exchange of other body fluids, like blood. Widespread misunderstanding of the disease, and the stigma attached to it, leads to its uneven spread across different groups.

When HIV/AIDS was first diagnosed in 1981, it was so localized among urban gay men that in the United States it was called GRID (gay-related immune deficiency). Today, Black people are especially vulnerable to HIV, either because of unprotected same-sex behavior among males (which also makes women vulnerable) or higher rates of sharing IV drug paraphernalia. Blacks make up 12 percent of the U.S. population but account for half of all new reported HIV infections (see Figure 10.5). Initially, AIDS was also a "gendered" disease, with men accounting for nearly 9 of every 10 cases in the industrial West. Even as late as 2003, 85 percent of all HIV cases were male, but in the developing world today HIV/AIDS affects women and men in equal numbers.

Globally, AIDS is "the greatest health crisis in human history." As of 2008, 33 million people were infected with HIV worldwide. There were 2.7 million new infections and two million deaths in 2008 (UNAIDS, 2008). Initially, HIV/AIDS was a disease of the industrial countries, but it has gradually spread to the developing world. Today, the epicenter of the disease is sub-Saharan Africa. There, a 15-year-old boy or girl faces a 50–50 chance that he or she will contract HIV/AIDS.

One reason for the dramatic shift from the developed to the developing world has to do with global poverty. Medical breakthroughs since the 1990s transformed the disease from an almost universal likelihood of death to a chronic disease that can be managed with a combination of drug therapies. These drug therapies were enormously costly to develop and are enormously costly to purchase. Only those who are wealthy

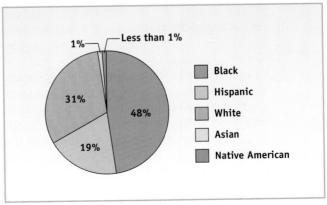

Figure 10.5 Percentage of AIDS Cases by Race/Ethnicity in the United States

(*Source:* Centers for Disease Control and Prevention, 2008.)

The Body in Sickness and in Health

enough or who have excellent health care coverage can afford the "AIDS drug cocktail"—which can cost more than $3,000 a month (*The Medical News*, 2008). In poorer countries, virtually no one can afford these drugs, and the governments do not have enough money to pay for them. Today, global philanthropic efforts to provide new drugs to low- and middle-income countries may be slowing the death rate (UNAIDS, 2008).

In addition, campaigns to raise public awareness of HIV risks in the developed world have led to dramatic changes in behavior. Young people today are urged to practice "safe sex,"—which means that during sexual activity, one should not exchange any bodily fluids (a condom prevents the exchange of fluids)—and IV drug users are cautioned to avoid sharing needles and to clean their needles with bleach solution to kill any potential infectants. The gay community's active mobilization around the AIDS epidemic led to a dramatic transformation of gay male sexual practices and to the development of institutions that promoted safe sex.

In the developing world, however, the transmission of the disease is different, and often cultural and religious beliefs have made campaigns to reduce risk difficult. Some people in Africa believe that HIV is a Western "import" and infects only gay men. Some men in southern African have begun to seek out young girls who are virgins as sex partners, on the assumption that they could not possibly be infected with the disease. As a result, many young girls are becoming infected because the men were HIV positive and did not know.

Health as an Institution

A crucial sociological aspect of health and illness is the set of institutions that are concerned with health care. From medical professionals (and their respective professional organizations) to hospitals, medical insurance companies, and pharmaceutical companies, health care is big business. Spending on health care in the United States in 2008 was $2.4 trillion and is projected to reach $3.1 trillion by 2012—roughly four times the total military and defense spending (Keehan, 2008; Sharp, 2009). (See Figure 10.6.)

As a percentage of the U.S. federal spending, however, health care runs a distant second to the military budget because our government provides comparatively little of our health care coverage, especially when compared with other industrialized countries (Friends Committee on National Legislation, 2008). The United States has both the most advanced health care delivery system in the world and one of the most expensive and inequitable among industrial nations. The United States is the only industrialized nation that does not guarantee coverage for essential medical services; and rations care by income, race, and health; and allows for-profit insurance companies to exclude people who need care.

Americans pay 17 percent of health care costs directly; private health insurance covers 38 percent, and direct public spending pays for about 45 percent of all health care costs. Increasing costs of drugs, medical technology, and the profit-oriented insurance industry guarantee that these percentages will continue to shift against individual health care consumers. The number of Americans without health coverage is increasing. Almost 50 million (16 percent) Americans lack any health coverage at all, including more than 32 percent of Hispanics, nearly 20 percent of Blacks, nearly 17 percent of Asian Americans, and over 14 percent of Whites (U.S. Census Bureau, 2008d).

But even those figures probably underestimate the real numbers. A 2009 study found that 86.7 million—one out of every three Americans—was uninsured at some point during 2007–2008, almost two-thirds of them for nine months or more. While African Americans and Latinos were much more likely to be uninsured, half (49.8 percent) were White. Eighty percent were in working families. And, nearly half—49.5 percent—were young people 19 to 24 years old (Families USA, 2009).

Many of the problems in the American health care system derive from its scale and size. Health care is a massive enterprise, involving every American, every single government—state, local, federal—and a host of corporations and professions (doctors, hospitals, medical technology, drugs, insurance). With no coherent national health care policy, the American system is a patchwork of competing interests and conflicting views.

This system is also the product of competing values. As we saw earlier, in Chapter 1,

Americans hold two different types of values, and these often collide. On the one hand, we believe that "all men are created equal" and that "human life is sacred." These values would push us toward supporting policies that would make basic health care a basic human right, not a privilege of the rich or the employed. On the other hand, we believe hard work should be rewarded, individual initiative and entrepreneurship should be unimpeded, and government should neither control profits nor tax Americans to pay for the welfare of those most needy. These values would lead us to "rationing" health care to those who can best afford it.

We hold both sets of values but tend to weigh them differently. In the abstract, we probably prefer to keep spending and taxation low, but our values change if we or a loved one is suddenly in urgent need of medical care. Then we want "the best" treatment options available, regardless of the cost.

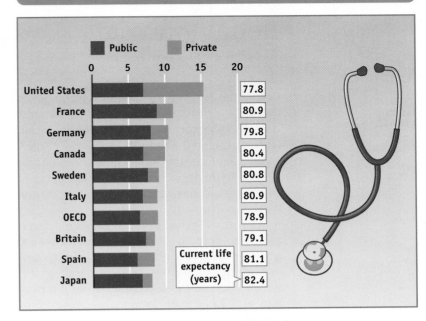

Figure 10.6 Health Spending as Percentage of GDP

(*Sources:* "Society at a Glance," OECD, 2009; United Nations.)

Health Care Reform

In the United States, efforts to reform the health care system have been shaped by the powerful lobbying efforts by the health insurances companies, the pharmaceutical companies, and the professional associations of doctors. These efforts have expanded the privatization of health care, resulting in slightly greater health care options for some and in significantly greater disparities in health care between the haves and the have-nots. With the passage of the Health Care Reform Act of 2003, individual choices expanded a little bit, but at the expense of decreased health care for America's poor.

In the absence of federal action, states have begun to take the lead on comprehensive health care reform. A number of states have reform laws pending in their legislatures, and numerous others have established commissions to develop recommendations for how to expand coverage. As of July, 2009, three states—Massachusetts, Vermont, and Maine—had enacted universal coverage legislation and 14 states had announced comprehensive reform proposals (Kaiser Commission on Medicaid and the Uninsured, 2009). While questions remain about the long-term financing for such policies, definitions of affordability, and about whether employers will respond by reducing their levels of coverage, they are advancing the debate about how to address the problem of the nation's uninsured.

The Obama administration launched a comprehensive health care reform drive in 2009. It recognizes that the number of uninsured Americans will continue to rise (to a projected 61 million Americans by 2020, not including the underinsured or part-year insured), as will health care spending, which is projected to double between 2009 and 2020 (The Commonwealth Fund, 2009). It also acknowledges that nearly one-third of all health care spending in the United States consists of profits and waste. As our population ages, the demands on the health care system are increasing at a faster rate than ever before (*The Economist*, 2009a; Commonwealth Fund, 2009). As a result, health care has become one of the most urgent political, economic—and sociological—issues in America. As the famous journalist Walter Cronkite once remarked, "Our healthcare system is neither healthy, nor caring, nor a system."

Many Insured Go Bankrupt

Three-fourths of all people who are driven to bankruptcy by health care costs actually had health insurance (*New York Times*, 2009b).

Did You Know?

Studying Sexuality: Behaviors and Identities

One of the ways we experience our bodies as distinctly private and personal is sexually. And yet few experiences are also more social. Once considered simply a biological "urge," social scientists now understand sexuality to be among the most important components of identity—and one of the most hotly debated bases for inequality.

As you will recall from the gender chapter, scientists draw a distinction between **sex,** referring to one's physiology (typically, but not always, male or female), and *gender,* which refers to the social and cultural meanings associated with being male, female, or something else. Sex is biological, standard across the human species, but gender is a social construction that differs from culture to culture and across time.

When discussing sexuality, we usually try distinguishing desire (physical attraction), behavior (sex), and identity (sexuality). When we discuss "sex" in the context of sexuality, we are not referring to one's biological sex but rather sexual behavior, or "sexual conduct"—the things people do from which they derive sexual meanings. Think of sex as whatever people do to experience sexual pleasure.

The term **sexuality** also refers to the identities we construct that are often based on our sexual conduct. Our identities may derive from the biological sex of the person whom we desire or with whom we have sex; that is, we may consider ourselves heterosexual, homosexual, bisexual.

Because sexual desire, sexual behavior, and sexual identity are so social, they are subject to values about their "correctness" and norms governing their enactment and even their expression. Some behaviors and identities are pronounced proper and others immoral or unnatural. There is therefore significant inequality based on sexual identity and sexual behavior. Sexual behavior is, in this sense, no different from all the other behaviors in our lives. We learn it from the people and institutions and ideas around us and assemble it into a coherent narrative that comes to be our sexuality.

Every culture develops a **sexual script,** a set of ideas and practices that answer the basic questions about sex: With whom do we have sex? What do we do? How often? Why? These scripts form the basic social blueprint for our sexual behaviors and identities (Gagnon and Simon, 1967). Over the course of childhood and adolescence, even through adulthood, your understanding of your culture's sexual scripts begins to cohere into a preference. This is your **sexual socialization.**

There are four ways in which sexuality can be seen as socially constructed:

1. Sexuality varies enormously from one culture to the next.
2. Sexuality varies within any one culture over time.
3. Sexuality varies among different groups in society. Race, ethnicity, age, and religion—as well as gender—all construct your sexualities.
4. Sexual behavior changes over the course of your life. What you might find erotic as a teenager may not be a preview of your eventual sexual tendencies; sexual tastes develop, mature, and change over time.

"I used to hate my body. Now, instead, I hate the forces that conspire to make me hate my body."

© William Haefeli/CondeNast Publications/www.cartoonbank.com. Reprinted by permission.

The Interplay of Biology and Society

Where does sexuality come from? We know that orientation is pretty stable by about the age of 5 (maybe earlier—we just can't interview newborns very effectively) and unchangeable—you like whom you like throughout your life, regardless of how much society approves or disapproves. But were you born with a sexual orientation, or did it evolve during those five years? Because heterosexual identity has so much social prestige, there's been little research on how people "become" heterosexual. Research, instead, typically is directed to explain the experiences of the "other." But we can take the research on gay people and expand it to include other orientations.

Many scientists claim that sexual orientation is the result of biology: chromosomes, brain chemistry, differences in our pubertal hormones. Some researchers have claimed they've discovered the "gay gene" or the "gay brain," but these studies are based on small samples with very large margins for error. Cross-cultural studies seem to indicate that about 5 percent of every human male population and 3 percent of every human female population is going to have exclusive same-sex interests, regardless of how much their culture praises or condemns same-sex activity. (And same-sex behavior is extremely common in the animal kingdom, which dispels evolutionary arguments.)

Sociologists generally believe that sexual orientation is both biologically based and socially constructed. One probably has an innate, biologically based interest in a certain sex, but the way that interest is understood, the ways we learn to act on it, to feel about it, and to express it are all learned in society.

Desires and Behaviors

Sexual behavior is any behavior that brings sexual pleasure or release (typically, but not always, involving sex organs). But again, behavior differs widely from culture to culture. Some practices, like oral–genital and genital–genital contact, occur everywhere, but others are extremely rare.

Even within the same society, different groups have vastly different incidences of specific sexual activities. In the United States, S&M, or sadomasochism (deriving sexual pleasure from inflicting or receiving pain), is

Most scientists now agree that sexual identity is the result of the interaction of biological, cultural, and social influences. But one thing is clear: In industrialized countries, there is increased acceptance of all sexual identities. The founding charter of the European Union prohibits discrimination based on sexual identity.

much more popular among Whites and Asian Americans than among African Americans.

Like sexual desire, sexual behavior is monitored and policed by social institutions, which are constantly giving us explicit messages about what is desirable and what is bad, wrong, and "deviant." If you dislike someone or something, you are likely to use an all-purpose insult accusing him, her, or it of engaging in a certain "deviant" sexual behavior, and the hand gesture that you might use while driving to indicate your displeasure at a bad driver was originally an invitation to engage in another sort of "deviant" sexual behavior.

In the contemporary United States, genital–genital contact is often presented as the most natural, normal, and fulfilling sexual behavior; other behaviors are often considered "not really sex" at all. Sexual behavior refers not only to what you do sexually but with whom you do it, how, how often, when, where, and so on. Sexual customs display a dizzying array that, taken together, imply that sexual behavior is anything but organized around reproduction alone. Where, when, how, and with whom we have sex vary enormously within cultures as well as from one culture to another.

For example, Ernestine Friedel, an anthropologist, observed dramatic differences in sexual customs between two neighboring tribes in New Guinea (1975). One, a highland tribe, believes that heterosexual intercourse

Everyone knows "sex sells"—and it is used to sell every-thing. Sex has never been as private as we imagine it was, but it is more public now than ever.

makes men weaker and that women threaten men with their powerful sexuality. Many men who would otherwise be interested in women prefer to remain celibate rather than risk the contact. As a result, population remains relatively low, which this culture needs because they have no new land or resources to bring under cultivation.

Not far away, however, is a very different culture. Here, people enjoy sex and sex play. Men who have sex with women worry about whether their partners are sexually satisfied, and they get along relatively well. They have higher birth rates, which is manageable because they live in a relatively abundant and uncultivated region, where they can use all the hands they can get to farm their fields and defend themselves.

American sexual behavior looks something like this: Take the typical American couple, Mr. and Mrs. Statistical Average. They're White, middle-aged, heterosexual, and married. They have sex once or twice a week, at night, in their bedroom, alone, with the lights off, in the "missionary position"—the woman on her back, facing the man who lies on top of her. The encounter—from the "do you want to?" to kissing, foreplay, and intercourse (always in that order) and finally to "Goodnight, sweetheart"—lasts about 15 minutes.

Now consider other cultures: Some cultures never have sex outside. Others believe that having sex indoors would contaminate the food supply because they live in one large room. Some cultures have sex two or three times a night, others perhaps once a month—or less. Some cultures practice almost no fore-play at all but go directly to intercourse; others prescribe several hours of touching and caress-ing, in which intercourse is a necessary but sad end to the proceedings.

While for us, kissing is a virtually universal initiation of sexual contact—"first base," as it is often known—other cultures find it disgusting because of the possibility of exchanging saliva. "Putting your lips together?" say the Siriono of the Brazilian Amazon. "But that's where you put food!"

Among heterosexuals in our culture, men are supposed to be the sexual initiators, and women are supposed to be sexually resistant. How different are the Trobriand Islanders, where women are seen as sexually insatiable and take the initiative in heterosexual rela-tions? Or a culture in Brazil where the women commit adultery, not men, but they justify it by saying that it was "only sex?" The men in that culture secretly give the women anaphro-disiacs to reduce their sexual ardor. These are but a few examples. When questioned about them, people in these cultures give the same answers we would. "It's normal," they'll say. Sexual norms can take many forms, but none is more "natural" than any other.

Sexual behavior can occur between people of the same gender or different genders, alone or in groups. It can be motivated by love or lust, money or reproduction, anger, passion, stress, or boredom. For example, some cul-tures forbid same-sex behavior and endorse only sexual activity between men and women. Some cultures develop elaborate rituals to credit the behaviors the culture endorses and to discredit those of which it disapproves.

Same-sex activity is treated differently from culture to culture. In 1948, anthropologist Clyde Kluckohn surveyed North American Indian tribes and found same-sex behavior ac-cepted in 120 of them and forbidden in 54 (this is not to say that it did not occur; it was simply considered bad or wrong). In the West, same-sex marriage has become legal only re-cently, but some traditional cultures (Lango in East Africa, Koniag in Alaska, and Tanala in Madagascar) have permitted it for thousands of years.

Sexual Identities

Norms about sexual behavior govern not only our sexual conduct but also how we develop a sexual identity. Our sexual identities cohere around a preference—for a type of person or a specific behavior. These preferences are more flexible than we typically think.

Take, for example, sadomasochism, or S&M. While this preference for specific behaviors is often understood as "deviant" sexual behavior, most Americans have experienced erotic stimulation of some kind from either inflicting or receiving pain (biting, scratching, slapping). Some percentage will find that they like that experience so much that they want to do it again, and a smaller percentage will actually incorporate it into their sexual script, as a preference. An even smaller percentage will find that they *really* like it, enough to make it a requirement of sexual conduct, and a tiny fraction will find that they can be aroused only through this behavior.

In that way, sexual behavior is rarely an either/or proposition—either you like it or you don't. Most people experience it a little bit, but they don't make it the defining feature of their sexual identity.

Heterosexuality and Homosexuality. Typically, we understand **sexual identity** (or, sometimes, orientation) to refer to an identity that is organized by the gender of the person (or persons) to whom we are sexually attracted. If you are attracted to members of the opposite sex, you are presumed to be heterosexual; if you are attracted to members of your own sex, you are presumed to be gay or lesbian. If you are attracted to both, you are bisexual. For all these orientations, the organizing principle is how your gender contrasts with or complements the gender of your potential partners.

Worldwide, the most common sexual identity is **heterosexuality,** sexual behavior between people of different genders. *Hetero* comes from the Greek word meaning "different." In most cultures, heterosexuality is considered "normal," which means that it is seen as occurring naturally. In most cultures, heterosexuality is also "normative," meaning that those who do not conform to it are often seen as deviant and subject to sanction. Although it is seen as normal, heterosexuality is learned within culture.

Although our sexual behavior may have very little to do with the institution of marriage, we typically understand heterosexual behavior only in relation to marriage. As a result, surveys often list only three types of heterosexual behavior: "premarital" (which takes place before marriage); "marital" (sex within the confines of a marriage); and "extramarital" (sex outside the confines of marriage). Even if a college student, for example, doesn't even think about marriage when deciding whether or not to have heterosexual relations, it will be understood as fitting into one of those three categories. (To be more accurate, we use the term *nonmarital* instead of *premarital* elsewhere in this book.)

The term **homosexuality** refers to sexual desires or behaviors with members of one's own gender. This comes from the Greek word *homo*, which means "same." As we have seen, homosexuality has been documented in most cultures, but sometimes it is praised, and sometimes it is condemned or even presumed not to exist.

Whether you are gay or lesbian, heterosexual, or bisexual, sounds straightforward: Gay men and lesbians are attracted to members of the same sex, heterosexuals to the opposite sex, and bisexuals to both. But again, sexual orientation turns out to be far more complex. Many people who identify as heterosexual engage in same-sex practices, and many who identify as gay engage in heterosexual practices. Their identity is derived from the people and institutions around them and assembled into a coherent narrative and experiences that don't fit are left out: The lesbian who has sex with men may explain it as "trying to fit in" rather than evidence she is "really" bisexual,

Sexuality is about both behaviors and identities, but they are often difficult to separate. The current "don't ask/don't tell" policy on gays in the military discriminates only against the behavior—you can be gay as long as you don't tell anyone or do anything about it.

The Heterosexual Questionnaire

In the 1980s, a young writer named Michael Rochlin composed a questionnaire to illustrate the impact of homophobia on the way heterosexuals understand sexuality. Among the questions:

1. What do you think caused your heterosexuality?
2. When and how did you first decide you were a heterosexual?
3. Is it possible your heterosexuality is just a phase you may grow out of?
4. Is it possible your heterosexuality stems from a neurotic fear of others of the same sex?
5. To whom have you disclosed your heterosexual tendencies? How did they react?
6. Why do you heterosexuals feel compelled to seduce others into your lifestyle?
7. Why do you insist on flaunting your heterosexuality? Can't you just be what you are and keep it quiet?
8. A disproportionate majority of child molesters are heterosexuals. Do you consider it safe to expose your children to heterosexual teachers?
9. With all the societal support marriage receives, the divorce rate is spiraling. Why are there so few stable relationships among heterosexuals?

and the heterosexual man who enjoys same-sex activity may explain it as "fooling around," irrelevant to his heterosexual identity.

Oddly, most cultures around the world have gotten along fine without any sexual identities at all. There were desires and behaviors, but the very idea that one's desire or behavior was part of the foundation of one's identity dates to the middle of the nineteenth century, when the terms *heterosexual* and *homosexual* were first used as nouns (describing identity) rather than as adjectives (describing behaviors).

That distinction between behaviors and identities is crucial in some cultural prohibitions. In some cases, it is the identity that is the problem, not the behaviors: You can do pretty much what you want; just don't make it the basis of your identity. In other cases it is the behaviors that are troubling, not the identity. The Roman Catholic Church's official position on homosexuality—love the sinner, hate the sin—is an example of the latter.

Can sexual orientation change? Though some gay men and lesbians have sought various treatments to help them "convert" to het-

erosexuality, such techniques almost always fail (see Duberman, 1991). One can surely stop the behaviors, but the orientation most often remains intact. Recent religious "conversion therapies" replace psychiatric models with theological ones but produce similar results (Wolkomir, 2005).

Bisexuality. We're so used to the gay/straight dichotomy that we often believe that you have to be one or the other: Gay/straight sounds as natural and normal as young/old, rich/poor, Black/White. But what about **bisexuality**—a sexual identity organized around attraction to both women and men?

First, bisexuality in not indiscriminate. You're attracted to men in some circumstances and women in others. You fall in love with men, but feel a sexual attraction only to women, or vice versa. Or you've had sex only with women, but you wouldn't say no if Brad Pitt called. The variety of experiences differs considerably.

Second, few understand you. Tell a date that you are bisexual, and you may get weird looks, a lecherous request to "watch" sometime, or outright rejection. Your straight friends believe that you are really straight but "confused" or "experimenting" or going through a phase. Your gay friends believe that you're really gay but too frightened to admit it.

Third, in spite of the jokes and the invisibility, you may also have a great deal of pride. Bisexuals often argue that they are more spiritual, or more psychologically developed, than gay or straight people, because they look at a person's character and personality rather than at trivial details like gender. They may be exaggerating a bit: Most bisexuals are just as attracted to certain physical types, and not as attracted to others, as gay and straight people. They just include some men and women in the category of "people to whom I'm attracted."

Identifying as a bisexual requires a coming-out process, a realization that both your same-sex and opposite-sex relations "count." Few organizations exist specifically for bisexuals, and scholars have not paid them much attention. Within the past decade, however, things have been changing. But bisexuals still have a long way to go before the average person stops assuming automatically that a new acquaintance must be gay or straight (Burleson, 2005; Fox, 2004; Rust, 1995, 1999; Storr, 1999; Tucker, 1995; Weinberg, Williams, and Pryor, 1994).

Figure 10.7 LGTBI Rights in the World

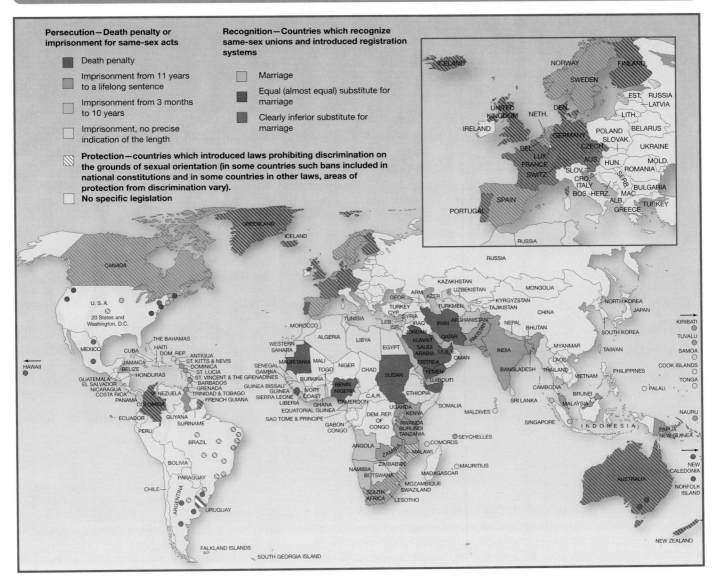

(*Source:* International Lesbian and Gay Association, http://www.ilga.org/map/LGBTI_rights.jpg. Reproduced with permission.)

Identities as Behaviors. There are other sexual identities based more on sexual behaviors than the gender of your partner. For example, some people may experience erotic attraction to specific body parts (partialism) or to objects that represent sexual behaviors (fetishism). Or they may become sexually aroused by the presence of real or imagined violence and power dynamics (sadomasochism) or find that they can be aroused only when having sex in public (exhibitionism) or when they observe others having sex (voyeurism). While many of these behaviors are present in routine sexual experiences—the fear of getting caught, wearing sexy clothing, biting and pinching— only a small percentage of the population make them the only activities in their sexual repertoire.

Asexuality. Everybody has a sexual orientation, right? Regardless of whether you are currently sexual, everybody is attracted to men, women, or both. Not necessarily. Some people state they have no sexual desire for anyone. They aren't gay/lesbian or heterosexual; they're **asexual.** Some estimates suggest that about four percent of men and women self-identify as asexual (Poston and

Baumle, 2006), while other studies have found that about one percent of people report experiencing no sexual desire at all (Bogaert, 2004).

Friends, family, and the medical establishment are quick to diagnose them as confused, conflicted, suffering from a hormone deficiency, or traumatized by child abuse. But asexuals counter that their sexuality is not a problem that needs to be cured: It is a perfectly valid sexual orientation. Asexuals have their own organizations, websites, slogans, coming-out stories, and lots of merchandise to buy (Harris, 2006).

American Sexual Behavior and Identities

You might not personally be a fan of any specific sexual behavior, but how do you feel about people who are? During the past 30 years, the General Social Survey has asked a number of questions about attitudes toward various sexual behaviors, and while disapproval of interracial and same-sex relationships has declined considerably, most attitudes have remained fairly stable. For instance, today about 95 percent of respondents state that sex between teenagers is "always wrong" or "almost always wrong," a percentage that has barely budged since 1972.

But such consistency in attitudes may be deceiving. For one thing, there is often a wide gap between those moral positions we take with regard to other people's behaviors and those we take with regard to our own behaviors. Also, attitudes may describe a position without telling us much about how someone actually applies that moral position in his or her everyday life. Take, for example, attitudes about homosexuality. In the 1970s, 75 percent of Americans believed that same-sex behavior was "always wrong" or "almost always wrong." If these respondents happened to discover that a co-worker or relative was gay, they might have been horrified, cutting all contact with the person. Their negative attitude could predict negative behavior.

Today, 50 percent of Americans believe that same-sex behavior is "always wrong" or "almost always wrong," but they are likely to be polite and tolerant to gay co-workers or relatives and even make gay friends. In other words, their negative attitude does not necessarily predict negative behavior.

Women's sexuality has changed enormously in the past decades. Once, a woman who was actively sexual with multiple partners would have been universally despised; in Sex and the City it's just one of several different sexual options for women.

The Gender of Sexuality

How do Americans construct their sexual identities? The single most important organizing principle of sexuality is gender. Men and women are raised to have very different attitudes toward sexual desire, behavior, and identity. One might say that there are "his" and "her" sexuality.

For many years, it was assumed that only men experienced sexual desire at all; women were interested in romance and companionship but not sex. Women who flirted with

For decades, sex researchers have noticed a strange thing: Men and women reported different numbers of partners. A recent survey found that men reported a median number of seven sexual partners over the course of their lives, while the median number of partners for women was four. How can this be? After all, it's a mathematical impossibility for men to average almost twice the number of partners that women average (if they are exclusively heterosexual, anyway).

Perhaps one reason is what we might call the "stud versus slut" effect: Men might overestimate their numbers to appear more like a stud; women might underestimate their numbers to appear less like a slut. So men might exaggerate, and women might minimize. For example, while about 10 percent of Americans have sex outside their marriage in any given year, the percentages vary significantly depending on how the questions are asked. In face-to-face interviews, about 1 percent of women say they have been unfaithful; on anonymous computer surveys, about 6 percent of women say they have. It might also be that men are picking partners from outside the surveyed population—for example, going to prostitutes, or having sex in other countries when they travel—in numbers far greater than women.

There's also the problem of retrospective analysis: People's memories don't tell you what actually happened but reveal more about what they believe or want to have happened—or what they believe should have happened. That is, asking people about the past tells you more, sometimes, about the present.

How Many Sex Partners Do People Have?

All of these may contribute to the disparity. But it turns out that this difference shows up only among some groups and only when they are asked some types of questions. For the 90 percent of Americans who have had 20 or fewer lifetime partners, the male–female ratio is close to 1—that is, they report the same number of partners. And if you ask men and women how many different partners they had in the past year, the ratio again is close to 1.

The entire discrepancy is a result of measurement error among the remaining 10 percent—that is, those who have had more than 20 partners over their lifetime. Four-fifths of these people tend to report their numbers in round numbers (25, 50, 100, and so on), and men tend to round up and women tend to round down. When you have had that many partners, most people just don't keep an exact tally.

It may simply be that these forces—normative expectations for studs and sluts, a "prostitute effect," or gendered memory for only those with the most partners—are in operation only for some groups and only when they are asked certain questions (Morris, 1993; Parker-Pope, 2008).

men were not expressing sexual desire but trying to "snare" men into marrying them or buying them something.

Although today many people agree that women have some degree of sexual desire, they consider it inappropriate to express openly. Men are expected to express how "horny" they are; women are not. Men who have a lot of sex are seen as "studs," and their status rises among their peers. Women who have a lot of sex are seen as "sluts," and their status falls. "Women need a reason to have sex," commented comedian Billy Crystal. "Men just need a place."

Whether gay or heterosexual, sexual behaviors, desires, and identities are organized more by the gender of the actor than by the genders of those toward whom he or she might be erotically inclined. That is to say, on all available measures, gay and straight men are far more similar to each other than either is to gay or straight women. Men are socialized to express a "masculine" sexuality, and women are socialized to express a "feminine" sexuality, regardless of their sexual orientation.

In our culture, the sexual double standard encourages men to pursue sex as an end in itself, to seek a lot of sex with many different partners, outside of romantic or emotional commitment. And women are taught to consider sex with one partner and only in the context of an emotional relationship. For example, there is a significant gender gap in attitudes about fidelity in a relationship (see Pew Research Center, 2006). As a result we see the highest rates of sexual activity among gay men (masculine sexuality times two), and the lowest rates among lesbians (feminine sexuality times two). Gay men have an average of over 30 partners during their lifetime, while lesbians have fewer than three. Gay men have the lowest rates of long-term committed relationships, straight men the next, then straight women, and finally, lesbians have the highest rates. Thus, it appears that men—gay or straight—place

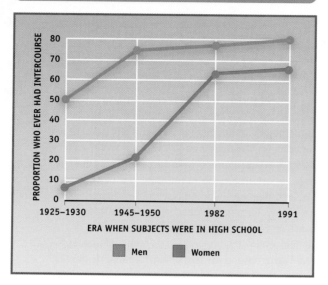

Figure 10.8 Trends in Heterosexual Experience among Teens

(*Source:* "Trends in Heterosexual Experience among Teens," from *The Gender of Sexuality: Sexual Possibilities*, by Pepper Schwartz, 1998. Used by permission of Rowman & Littlefield Publishing Group.)

sexuality at the center of their lives, and that women—gay or straight—are more interested in affection and caring in the context of a long-term love relationship.

In recent years, there has been increased convergence in women's and men's sexual attitudes and behaviors. Women's sexuality is becoming increasingly similar to men's; in fact we might even speak of a "masculinization" of sex. The **masculinization of sex** includes sexual intercourse starting earlier (Figure 10.8), the pursuit of pleasure for its own sake, the increased attention to orgasm, increased numbers of sexual partners, the interest in sexual experimentation, and the separation of sexual behavior from love. These are partly the result of the technological transformation of sexuality (from birth control to the Internet) and partly the result of the sexual revolution's promise of greater sexual freedom with fewer emotional and physical consequences (see Parker-Pope, 2008; Pew Research Center, 2006; Rubin, 1990; Schwartz and Rutter, 1998).

Convergence on Campus: Hooking Up. One place where one can observe the political ramifications of the gender convergence in sexual behavior is on campus, where a culture of "hooking up" has virtually erased the older pattern of "rating-dating-mating" observed by sociologist Willard Waller way back in 1937 (Waller, 1937).

Hooking up is a deliberately vague blanket term; one set of researchers defines it as "a sexual encounter which may nor may not include sexual intercourse, usually occurring on only one occasion between two people who are strangers or brief acquaintances" (Lambert, 2003, p. 129). While that seems to cover most cases, it fails to include those heterosexuals who hook up more than once or twice, or "sex buddies" (acquaintances who meet regularly for sex but rarely if ever associate otherwise), or "friends with benefits" (friends who do not care to become romantic partners but may include sex among the activities they enjoy together).

On many campuses, the sexual marketplace—gay and straight—is organized around groups of same-sex friends who go out together to meet appropriate sexual partners in a casual setting like a bar or a party. Party scenes feature hooking up as the standard mode of sexual interaction. For heterosexual students, hooking up covers a multitude of behaviors, including kissing and nongenital touching (34 percent), manual stimulation of the genitals (19 percent), oral sex (22 percent), and intercourse (23 percent). Almost all hooking up involves more alcohol than sex: Men averaged 4.7 drinks on their most recent hookup, women 2.9 drinks (England, Shafer, and Fogerty, 2008; Kimmel, 2008).

Convergence on Campus: Just Saying No. If hooking-up culture is the dominant campus sexual culture, then "abstinence pledgers" may represent a counterculture. Abstinence campaigns encourage young people to take a "virginity pledge" and refrain from heterosexual intercourse until marriage (the campaigns assume that gay and lesbian students do not exist).

At first glance, such campaigns appear to be successful. One study found that the total percentage of high school students who say they've had heterosexual sex had dropped from more than 50 percent in 1991 to slightly more than 45 percent ten years later. Teen pregnancy and abortion rates have decreased somewhat, and proponents point to the success of abstinence-based sex education and elaborate publicity campaigns in a 10 percent drop in teen sexual activity.

Abstinence campaigns do appear to have *some* effect, but they do not offset the other messages teenagers hear. Sociologist Peter

Chapter 10 The "Sociological Body": Age, Health, and Sexuality

Bearman and Hannah Bruckner (2001) analyzed data from over 90,000 students and found that taking a virginity pledge does lead an average heterosexual teenager to delay his or her first sexual experience—by about 18 months. And the pledges were effective only for students up to age 17. By the time they are 20 years old, over 90 percent of both boys and girls are sexually active.

The pledges were not effective at all if a significant proportion of students at the school was taking them. That is, taking the pledge seems to be a way of creating a "deviant" subculture, or a counterculture, what Bearman and Bruckner called an "identity movement"—add "virgins" to the Goths, jocks, nerds, preppies, and rappers. When pledgers did have heterosexual intercourse, they were *far less likely* to use contraception.

Sex education is controversial in the United States—but not in other industrialized countries. The evidence is clear that the more young people know about sex, the lower the rates of teen pregnancies, STIs, and abortions.

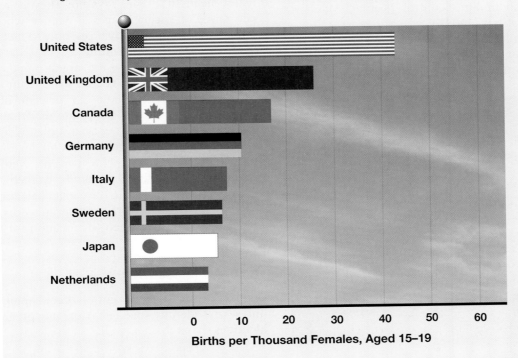

U.S. / Them

Birth Rate to Teen Mothers

The United States has the highest birth rate to teen mothers, aged 15 to 19, in the developed world. The birth rate to young females in the United States is more than double the rate of the next highest country, the United Kingdom, and more than eight times that of Japan.

- United States
- United Kingdom
- Canada
- Germany
- Italy
- Sweden
- Japan
- Netherlands

0   10   20   30   40   50   60

Births per Thousand Females, Aged 15–19

(*Source:* United Nations, *World Fertility Patterns 2007*, 2008.)

1. What factors might predict the rates of unwanted pregnancies?

2. Or, what might you infer culturally, if there were not "unwanted" pregnancies after all?

Another survey of 527 never-married heterosexual students at a large Midwestern university found that 16 percent had taken virginity pledges but that 61 percent of them had broken their pledge before graduating from college (Lipsitz, Bishop, and Robinson, 2003).

Since abstinence-based programs are often used instead of actual sex education, few people really know exactly what "counts" in keeping your pledge. In one recent survey of 1,100 college freshmen, 61 percent believed they were still abstinent if they had participated in mutual masturbation; 37 percent if they had had oral sex; and 24 percent if they had had anal sex. On the other hand, 24 percent believed that kissing broke their abstinence pledge (Bearman and Bruckner, 2001; Lipsitz et al., 2003). As a result, one recent study found abstinence-only programs had no impact on teen sexual activity or rates of unprotected sex (Trenholm et al., 2008). A secondary analysis of data gathered from over 1,700 heterosexual teenagers nationwide found that those who received abstinence-only education (24 percent of the students) were 50 percent more likely to report a pregnancy than those who received comprehensive sex education, which includes information about birth control (Kohler, Manhart, and Lafferty, 2008).

While abstinence-only sex education has little or no effect on reducing rates of abortion, unwanted pregnancy, or sexually transmitted diseases, comprehensive sex education lowers rates on all three measures (Alan Guttmacher Institute, 2001; Dailard, 2001; Darroch, Landry, and Singh, 2000; Kaiser Family Foundation, 2000; Kirby, 2001; Kohler et al., 2008; Landry, Laeser, and Richards, 1999). Globally, those countries with the most comprehensive sex education have far lower rates of unwanted pregnancies and sexually transmitted infections (Alan Guttmacher Institute, 2001; Sullivan/Anderson, 2009; United Nations, 2005).

Rape and Sexual Assault

Although women's and men's sexualities are becoming more similar, there remain some important differences. One of the most important is in the area of nonconsensual sexual activity, a form of sexual assault. On many college campuses, more than half of all sexual assaults take the form of "date rape," in which a woman is assaulted while on a date with a man. Some studies have estimated the rates to be significantly higher. Some men may take advantage of a woman while she is intoxicated and unable to resist, or they may simply be unaware that she "really means it" if she says no: They have been raised on media images of women who violently resist a man's advances, only to melt into his arms at the last minute.

While women comprise the largest proportion of victims of sexual assault, male victims are not uncommon: About 23 percent of women and 4 percent of men state that they have been forced to have sex against their will. Male perpetrators are more common in assaults against women (21.6 percent were assaulted by men, and 0.3 percent by women), but in assaults against men, the gender balance is about equal (1.9 percent were assaulted by men, 1.3 percent by women) (Laumann et al., 1996; Koss et al., 1994).

Diverse Sexualities

Gender may be the most central force shaping our sexual identity and behavior, but other identities shape them as well.

On America's college campuses, more than half of all sexual assaults take the form of "date rape," in which a woman is assaulted while on a date with a man. Getting a woman so drunk that she cannot consent—or say no—to sex is a prelude to assault, not lovemaking.

Race. For example, Blacks hold more liberal sexual values than Whites and have slightly more sex partners, but they also masturbate less frequently, have less oral sex, have less anal sex, and are slightly less likely to have same-sex contacts than Whites. Hispanics are also more sexually liberal in their attitudes than Whites, and they masturbate more often than both Whites and Blacks. Yet they also have less oral sex and have fewer sex partners, either same sex or opposite sex, than do Whites or Blacks (Centers for Disease Control, 2005; Laumann and Michael, 2000). Of all the large ethnic groups in the United States, Asian Americans are the least sexually liberal, masturbate least often, and have the fewest sex partners of either same or opposite sex (Laumann and Michaels, 2000).

Age. Age affects our sexuality, both directly and indirectly. After a certain age, younger people tend to have more sex than older ones, although there are variations by race and ethnicity (Centers for Disease Control, 2005). The aging body responds differently to sexual stimuli, and our sexual interests shift over time. And as we age we are more likely to be married or partnered—with children. And few things diminish sexual activity more than having children. Couples—gay and straight—with children report far less sexual activity than couples without children. There

is less time, less freedom, and less privacy—and greater fatigue.

Culture. It turns out that politics also affects sex. The more equal women and men are, the more satisfied women and men are with their sex lives. In a recent survey of 29 countries, sociologists found that people in countries with higher levels of gender equality—Spain, Canada, Belgium, and Austria—reported being much happier with their sex lives than those in countries with lower levels of gender equality, like Japan. The reason has to do with women's pleasure: "Male-centered cultures where sexual behavior is more oriented toward procreation tend to discount the importance of sexual pleasure for women," said sociologist Ed Laumann (Laumann and Michael, 2000).

Within each country, the greater the level of equality between women and men, the happier women and men are with their sex lives. It turns out that those married couples who report the highest rates of marital satisfaction—and the highest rates of sexual activity in the first place—are those in which men do the highest amounts of housework and child care (Laumann and Michael, 2000).

Sexual Inequality

Our sexual identities and sexual behaviors are the bases for significant social inequality. Although heterosexuals and homosexuals both express their sexuality through gender, there are some important differences between them. Only heterosexuality is credited as a "legitimate" sexual behavior, officially sanctioned.

Sexual desire, behavior, and identity are policed by social institutions through two distinct practices. **Homophobia** is an attitude, a socially approved dislike of gay men and lesbians, the presumption that they are inferior to straight people. **Heterosexism** is the institutionally based inequality that may derive from homophobia. As a set of practices rather than an ideology, heterosexism may be more pervasive.

Gay men and lesbians encounter heterosexism constantly. Sometimes it is in specific norms and laws that reflect these institutional practices.

Gay men and lesbians are criminals in the 13 states with antisodomy laws, and same-

sex couples are permitted to marry in only six states as of June 2009 (although they may marry in Canada and in most European countries). Most religious bodies in the United States do not permit them to become members. They can be fired from most jobs and evicted from most apartments with no legal recourse. (In Europe all members of the European Union subscribe to laws that prevent any discrimination against gays and lesbians.) Every year there are thousands of hate crimes directed against them, not to mention harassment, jokes, defamation (e.g., using "gay" as an all-purpose term for anything bad), and physical and sexual abuse. Studies of homophobia in both the United States and abroad have estimated that millions of lesbian, gay, and bisexual students are the frequent targets of homophobic harassment in school, at times by the teachers and staff, yet schools and governments don't deal effectively with the problem (Bochenek and Brown, 2001; Westall, 2009).

The systematic devaluation of same-sex desire and behavior, the stigma attached to

Figure 10.9 Acceptance of Homosexuality by Society: Survey Results

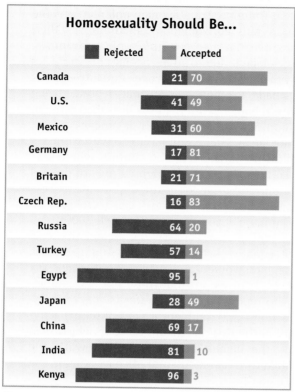

Homosexuality Should Be...

	Rejected	Accepted
Canada	21	70
U.S.	41	49
Mexico	31	60
Germany	17	81
Britain	21	71
Czech Rep.	16	83
Russia	64	20
Turkey	57	14
Egypt	95	1
Japan	28	49
China	69	17
India	81	10
Kenya	96	3

(*Source*: National Pew Global Attitudes Survey, Pew Global Attitudes Project, a project of the Pew Research Center, pewglobal.org, October 4, 2007. Reproduced by permission.)

asked why his raps almost always included derogatory references to "faggots." In response, he said:

> The lowest degrading thing you can say to a man . . . is to call him a faggot and try to take away his manhood. Call him a sissy, call him a punk. "Faggot" to me doesn't necessarily mean gay people. "Faggot" to me just means taking away your manhood. (cited in Kim, 2001, p. 5)

Because they mistakenly assume that all gay men are feminine and lesbians masculine, heterosexuals also demonstrate that they are "not gay" by exaggerating gender-stereotyped behavior. In this way, homophobia reinforces the gender of sex, keeping men acting hypermasculine and women acting ultrafeminine.

Sexual Minority Communities

In response to sexual inequality, people with minority sexual orientations often band together, both to find suitable partners and to escape the hostility of the mainstream society. If there are enough of them and they manage to find each other, they can form their own subcultures, with their own gathering places, social hierarchies, norms, values, and group cohesion. Sometimes they can even work to change social disapproval. Gay men and lesbians have probably been the most successful at creating social change. Thirty years ago, the mass media commonly carried articles about crazy "homosexuals." How could anybody engage in such behavior? Today it is just as likely to carry articles about crazy homophobes. How could anyone be so prejudiced? This is a big change in a short time. What happened?

Why was the gay rights movement so successful? One answer may be the connections with nongay people: The movement arose simultaneously with the youth counterculture of the late 1960s, when millions of college-aged people were protesting all sorts of injustices, from the Vietnam War to racial inequality. The gay rights activists were mostly college aged, members of that same counterculture. One of their early slogans was "We are your children." Political and social leaders were faced, for the first time, with gay men and lesbians who looked and acted like other young people, who could indeed be their children.

In fact, the gay rights movement may have been too successful to remain a counterculture or a subculture; it is now part of the mainstream culture. Many strictly gay social

being gay, becomes a crucial element in one's identity (Plummer, 1992). Homophobia constricts gay and lesbian experience because gays are painfully aware that they are not seen as equal—only because of the gender of their partner (see Figure 10.9). But we are often less aware of the power of homophobia to structure the experiences and identities of heterosexuals. Heterosexuals, especially men, spend a significant amount of time and energy making sure that no one gets the "wrong" idea about them. For men, the stakes are enormously high: Being "accused" of being gay, even for a moment, implies that they are less than fully masculine.

In an interview in 2001, Eminem was

Gay-Friendly Churches

The vocal antigay statements of some Christian denominations sometimes make us think that all organized religion is antigay. But in fact religious bodies were instrumental in the gay liberation movement of the 1970s, and today a number of Christian churches permit gay members and clergy, including the Episcopal Church, the United Church of Christ, the Disciples of Christ, the Lutheran Church (ELCA), the Presbyterian Church in America, and the American Baptists. In all, about 30 percent of Protestants in the United States belong to gay-friendly denominations.

Did You Know?

The modern gay and lesbian movement is about more than removing discrimination against homosexuals. It is also about the right to live openly as parents, workers, and neighbors.

institutions are struggling to survive. Gay bookstores are going out of business because gay-themed books are available at every bookstore. Why join a gay church, when gay people are welcomed in the church down the street? It is not that antigay prejudice and discrimination no longer exist but that they can now be fought more effectively within mainstream social institutions. It may often be the case that the more successful a social movement is, the less it is felt to be needed.

Sexuality as Politics

Sex has always been political—that is, people have always been arguing about what we *should* be able to do—and with whom, how, under what circumstances. It has often been the task of religion to regulate sexual activity, and it is increasingly the task of the state to do so. For example, laws regarding the age of consent, extramarital sex, the relationship of sex and commerce (regulating prostitution), reproductive rights, all involve the state in intimate decision making. Historically, the state sought to regulate sexual behavior to ensure clear lines of inheritance (barring children born out of wedlock from inheriting property) and to cement the connection between church and state.

Contemporary sexual politics involve political, scientific, and religious issues. Often these collide, as when scientific breakthroughs enable a wider range of sexual choices free of reproductive complications (such as the morning-after pill); often they coincide, as when the state seeks to protect children from predatory pedophiles.

Sex Tourism: The Globalization of Sex

For centuries, wealthy men have sought sexual adventures with "exotic" strangers in foreign countries. In some respects, **sex tourism** represents the globalization of prostitution. Like other global industries, well-organized groups direct the flow of the "consumer" (wealthy men) to the "commodities" (poor men and women). Like prostitution, there is far less "choice" on the part of the locals and far more coercion than typically meets the eye. According to the U.S. State Department, as many as 4 million people each year are lured by traffickers to destinations all over the world with promises of high-paying legitimate employment, only to end up as prostitutes and "rent boys."

Sex tourism uses the Internet to advertise its wares. For example, www.exotictours.com promises that on their tours "you will be with girls who want to make you happy and will honestly consider a marriage offer." Part of a recent Chinese itinerary promised that on your first night "girls will fight to get into the taxi with you. After picking out your night's entertainment, it's back to the hotel."

Current concern within the European community about sex trafficking, however, reveals a less erotic side of these transactions. In some Eastern European countries and new nations of the former Soviet Union, as well as Africa, young girls and boys are abducted or lured to European cities to serve as virtual sex slaves, paying off debts incurred in transporting them to their new homes. Globally, about 1.2 million women are sold or bartered as sex slaves every year; over half of them are from East Asia and South Asia (Kara, 2009). In the United States, the CIA estimates that 50,000 young women and girls are smuggled into the country every year.

Some countries, such as Thailand, have become destinations of choice for sex tourists (mostly middle-aged men from Germany and the United States) and have well-developed sex tourism industries. This industry was begun in the 1960s, when Thailand contracted with the U.S. military to provide "rest and recreation" services for troops stationed in Vietnam (Nagel, 2003). Proprietors take advantage of high unemployment and traditional attitudes about women to ensure a steady "supply" and use the exoticism of the "Orient" and traditional stereotypes about docile and compliant Asian women to ensure a steady "demand" from their heterosexual customers.

Sex tourism thus expresses the unequal relationships between countries who "sell" sex and countries who can "buy" it, as well as the inequalities between men and women, both globally and locally. Sociologist Joane Nagel notes how the geography of sex trafficking expresses its inequality: Men, women, and children from Latin America, Asia, Eastern Europe, and Africa are moved to the United States, from Nepal to India, from Burma to Thailand, from India and Pakistan to the Middle East (Nagel, 2003).

Global trafficking in women and men is big business. More than $1 billion per year is spent by sex tourists worldwide. Southeast Asia is a major market, as traffickers take advantage of local economic conditions to lure girls to the city. Sometimes, they just kidnap them.

The "Sociological Body" in the Twenty-First Century

Sexuality and age are foundations of identity, just like race or class or gender. And they are bases for inequality—the unequal distribution of rewards and punishments, of resources and recognition.

Attitudes about sexual differences or stereotypes about aging may change more slowly than social movements might hope, but they change faster than the policies our countries derive to keep things the same. Gay men and lesbians still face enormous discrimination, but most industrial societies are far less homophobic than they were just a decade ago. For example, membership in the European Union requires adherence to policies that prohibit all discrimination against people based on sexual orientation. Organizations such as the AARP have pressed for more social recognition and equality for older people. And young people are organizing in new ways to gain visibility and clout in a range of social arenas.

Changing attitudes will eventually lead to changed policies. In some cases, it may simply be a function of age. While 75 percent of people over 60 oppose legalizing gay marriage, 75 percent of people under 30 support legalizing it. Globally, people are becoming both more tolerant of sexual diversity and less tolerant, as the world often divides along lines of the acceptance of difference as a basis for citizenship.

In recent years, the intersection of age, health, and sexuality has become particularly important. One of the most significant changes in our experience of aging and living longer has been the transformation of our sexual lives. Just as young people enter puberty earlier than ever, so, too, are people remaining sexually active longer than ever, expanding the age of sexual activity from about 20 years often to expectations of triple that number and beyond. The old and the young continue to push the boundaries, aided oftentimes by cultural changes and technological advances that show no signs of slowing as the twenty-first century unfolds.

Chapter Review

1. The Social Body

Our bodies are subject to natural processes, but our understandings of our bodies are social constructs, varying by time and place, and we transform them accordingly. Beauty, for example, is a social construct, and ideals of beauty vary by culture, and even economic climate. The beauty standard in the United States is unnaturally thin or muscular but highly valued. **Anorexia nervosa** and **bulimia** rates among young women here are the highest worldwide, and men suffer from **muscle dysmorphia** and the **Adonis complex,** while our population is increasingly obese. Globally more people are overweight, although there are still nations combating malnutrition. As nations gain wealth, they gain weight, but the richest people are the healthiest as a result of diet and exercise, while the poor suffer ill health. Tattooing today exemplifies the body as a projection of our identity and a work in progress, subject to transformation. Plastic surgery is also increasingly common, and even **transgenderism** is more common than previously.

anorexia nervosa A potentially fatal syndrome characterized by chronic and dangerous starvation dieting and obsessive exercise. (p. 286)

bulimia A potentially fatal syndrome characterized by food "binging and purging" (eating large quantities and then either vomiting or taking laxatives or enemas to eliminate it). (p. 286)

muscle dysmorphia A belief that one is insufficiently muscular. (p. 287)

Adonis complex Term coined by psychiatrist Harrison Pope and his colleagues for the belief that men must look like Greek gods, with perfect chins, thick hair, rippling muscles, and washboard abdominal muscles. (p. 287)

2. Age: Identity and Inequality

Sociologists understand age as a social construct important for identity and also the basis for inequality. **Chronological age** is less important than **functional age,** shared by members of your **age cohort. Gerontology** focuses on aging, but the very young also suffer as a result of reduced social power and status; inequality is prevalent at both ends of the **life span.** Each stage of the **life span** has particular **age norms.** Our **life expectancy** is greater than any time previously, and norms have changed, too. **Adolescence** is longer than it has ever been historically, as a result of economic changes, better medical care, and longer life, resulting in stress for the **sandwich generation** that deferred childbearing, leaving them with a double burden of care—their own children as well as aging parents. Our nation's population, like many, is aging, but poverty and disease keep life spans short in some nations. **Ageism** frequently targets the elderly, although they have more power than the very young. The very young are without benefits and political power and suffer more from poverty than any other age group. Many elderly are relatively well off in the United States, helped by **Social Security,** but U.S. seniors still fare

worse than those in other developed nations. As we've seen in the United States, the rich do very well, but everyone else does poorly.

chronological age A person's age as determined by the actual date of his or her birth. (p. 290)

functional age A set of observable characteristics and attributes that are used to categorize people into different age cohorts. (p. 290)

age cohort A group of people who are born within a specific time period and therefore assumed to share both chronological and functional characteristics, as well as life experiences. (p. 290)

gerontology Scientific study of the biological, psychological, and sociological phenomena associated with old age and aging. (p. 290)

life span The average or the maximum amount of time an organism or object can be expected to live or last. (p. 290)

age norms Distinctive cultural values, pursuits, and pastimes that are culturally prescribed for each age cohort. (p. 290)

life expectancy The average number of years a person can expect to live; varies greatly by country and region. (p. 290)

adolescence Term coined by psychologist G. Stanley Hall (1904) to name the years coinciding with puberty as a distinct—and perilous—life stage. (p. 291)

sandwich generation Popular term for middle-aged adults who are caring for both their young children and their aging parents. (p. 293)

ageism Term coined by physician Robert Butler to refer to differential treatment based on age—usually the elderly rather than the young. (p. 294)

Social Security The U.S. government program wherein citizens contribute a small portion of their earnings while working and then collect a cash supplement after retirement. The program has been credited with preventing tens of millions of elderly from living in poverty and hunger. (p. 296)

3. The Body in Sickness and in Health

Illness and health are unequally distributed, varying by social factors like age, wealth, race, and class, which predict health or illness. Life expectancy also varies dramatically by social location. In wealthier nations chronic diseases are the main cause of death, but in poor nations infectious disease, diarrhea, and death in childbirth are preventable correlates of poverty. America's ranking on indicators of health, including infant mortality, are at the bottom of industrialized countries. Differences in the experience of HIV in industrialized nations compared with sub-Saharan Africa exemplify differences between rich and poor nations. Compared with other developed nations, the United States spends significantly less on health care and is the only such nation that does not provide health care for everyone. Because great wealth or insurance is needed due to the high cost of medical care here, a huge and growing number do without, and the population is progressively unhealthy. The burden of ill health is growing as our population ages, so health care reform is a current issue on the U.S. policy agenda.

4. Studying Sexuality: Behaviors and Identities

We consider **sex** to be biological, and sexuality to be personal and private, but sociologists also see **sexuality** as a social construction, an important component of identity, and the arena where social negotiation, control, and inequality play out in the **sexual script** we learn and in **sexual socialization. Sexual behavior** varies widely, but there is social control at all levels about what is considered normal and what is deviant, which varies widely by culture. We usually think about **sexual identity** in terms of **heterosexuality, homosexuality,** or **bisexuality,** but behavior not uncommonly diverges from this limited range of identities. We may have other preferences, either consistently or depending on circumstance, or we may be **asexual.**

sex A biological distinction; the chromosomal, chemical, and anatomical organization of males and females. (p. 302)

sexuality Identity we construct that is often based on our sexual conduct and often intersects with other sources of identity, such as race, class, ethnicity, age, or gender. (p. 302)

sexual script Set of ideas and practices that answer basic questions about sexual identity and practices: With whom do we have sex? What do we do? How often? Why? (p. 302)

sexual socialization The process by which your sexual scripts begin to cohere into a preference and sexual identity. (p. 302)

sexual behavior Any behavior that brings sexual pleasure or release (typically, but not always, involving sex organs). (p. 303)

sexual identity Refers to an identity that is organized by the gender of the person (or persons) to whom you are sexually attracted. Also called *sexual orientation.* (p. 305)

heterosexuality The most common sexual orientation worldwide, it is sexual attraction between people of different genders. (p. 305)

homosexuality Sexual desire toward members of one's own gender. (p. 305)

bisexuality Feeling attracted to sexual partners of both sexes. (p. 306)

asexual Having no sexual desire for anyone. (p. 307)

5. American Sexual Behavior and Identities

Our expectations for gendered behavior are so powerful that, regardless of our choice of sexual partners, men act more like other men and women more like other women regarding sexual behavior and preferences. Gay, straight, or otherwise, we usually conform to the sexual double standard, although this is changing as there is an increasing **masculinization of sex** for women. **Hooking up** is common on campuses. Teens are taking abstinence pledges, but education is more effective at preventing negative consequences of sexual behavior. The United States has the highest rate of teen birth in the developed world, and women are most often the victims of nonconsensual sex and assault, including date rape. Men are sometimes victimized, too, but the assailant is almost always male. The greater the equality between men and women, the happier everyone is with their sex lives.

masculinization of sex The pursuit of sexual pleasure for its own sake, increased attention to orgasm, increased numbers of sexual partners, interest in sexual experimentation, and separation of sexual behavior from love. That is partly the result of the technological transformation of sexuality (from birth control to the Internet) and partly the result of the sexual revolution's promise of greater sexual freedom with fewer emotional and physical consequences. (p. 310)

hooking up A sexual encounter that may or may not include sexual intercourse, usually occurring on only one occasion between two people who are strangers or brief acquaintances. (p. 310)

6. Sexual Inequality

Not only gender, but race, age, and culture exert an influence on sexuality. **Homophobia** is a pervasive ideology justifying the **heterosexism** that affects people directly. Like other minority groups, people who share a culture and suffer prejudice or discrimination on the basis of sexuality join together. Sexuality as an organizing principle for social movement has been so successful as to now be unnecessary, as evidenced by gay rights. Religion historically regulated sexual behavior, but as the state took over the role of regulation, churches were important in the organization of social movements. **Sex tourism** captures the inequality and exploitation that exists between those with wealth and power and those they exploit—industrialized developed nations in the West who use these services and the less-developed countries who provide them, as well as the inequality between men with power and the women and children who are the powerless and exploited victims.

homophobia A socially approved dislike of gay men and lesbians. (p. 313)

heterosexism Institutionally based inequalities that may derive from homophobia. (p. 313)

sex tourism Effectively the globalization of prostitution, a well-organized business whereby the flow of "consumers" (wealthy men) is directed to the "commodities" (poor men, women, and children). Like prostitution, there is far less "choice" on the part of the locals and far more coercion than typically meets the eye. The tourists seem to be men and women who are being friendly and flirtatious, but the locals are usually victims of kidnapping and violence. (p. 315)

7. The "Sociological Body" in the Twenty-First Century

Sexual lives are lengthening, as we enter puberty sooner and enjoy vitality into later years. Age, health, and sexuality intersect. Policy is slow to change, but society is catching up with people's sexual behaviors. As attitudes change, policies will follow. There is increasing tolerance in many parts of the globe, but differences are still sources of exclusion in others.

Self-Test: Check Your Understanding

1. Which of the following is not one of the causes for the increase in the percentage of elderly in the American population identified in the text?
   a. Decline in birth rate
   b. Increased life expectancy
   c. The large cohort of baby boomers reaching retirement age
   d. All of the above are factors identified in the text, resulting in an increase in the percentage of elderly in America.

2. Who lives longer, men or women?
   a. Men
   b. Women
   c. Men live longer in developing countries, but women live longer in industrialized countries.
   d. Women live longer in developing countries, but men live longer in industrialized countries.

3. Where does the United States rank in life expectancy compared with other nations worldwide?
   a. Number 1, with the longest life expectancy
   b. In the top ten
   c. In the top 20
   d. 45th, and dropping

4. Sociologists recognize that initial sexual preference probably stems from
   a. socialization and social control.
   b. early learning of gender roles.
   c. innate biological preferences.
   d. social control.

5. Cross-cultural studies reveal that the rates of preference for exclusively same-sex partners
   a. are similar across cultures.
   b. vary widely across cultures.
   c. are similar for men across cultures but vary widely for women.
   d. are impossible to assess, because of how unacceptable this practice is believed to be.

6. Which of the following is the most effective in reducing negative consequences of sexual behavior, including rates of abortion, unwanted pregnancy, and sexually transmitted diseases, according to the text?
   a. Abstinence-based education
   b. Comprehensive sex education
   c. Government-subsidized free birth control
   d. All of the above have been shown to be equally effective, according to the text.

7. The majority of slaves in captivity today come from
   a. sub-Saharan Africa.
   b. Asian countries.
   c. South American countries.
   d. Thailand.

8. The trend in homophobia is
   a. decreasing in both Europe and America.
   b. increasing in both Europe and America.
   c. decreasing in Europe; increasing in America.
   d. increasing in Europe; decreasing in America.

Self-Test Answers: 1. d, 2. b, 3. d, 4. c, 5. a, 6. b, 7. b, 8. b

Integrate and Explore: Points to Consider

1. Why are some sexual behaviors considered deviant in some cultures and normal in others? What challenges with regard to sexual behavior might be expected with increased globalization, since sexual scripts vary by cultures? Do you expect multiculturalism to result in greater or decreased tolerance for diverse sexual behaviors and identities?

2. What does it mean to say that age is a social construct? Do all nations experience each age the same, or are there differences? How much do life expectancies differ? How has the social experience of age changed as a result of industrialization and development?

succeed with PEARSON mysoclab

Self-scoring practice tests, flashcards for learning key terms, streaming audio of the entire text, and multimedia, including:

Watch—*Sexual Violence Billboards*
Watch—Mindy Stombler, *What is "Social" About Sex?*
Explore—*Gen X-ers and Boomers*
MySocLibrary—Greg Critser, *Let Them Eat Fat*

11

The Family

Almost daily, we hear some political pundit predict the end of the family. The crisis of the family is so severe that in 2000, the U.S. Congress passed a Family Protection Act, as if the family were an endangered species, like the spotted owl. Divorce and remarriage have never been more common. Millions of children are growing up with single parents or in blended households. Millions of young adults are putting off marriage until their 30s, or cohabiting instead of getting married, or opting to stay single. People are selecting household arrangements today that would mystify our ancestors. Even the staid U.S. Census Bureau has given in and added the category "cohabiting partners" to the old list of single, married, widowed, or divorced.

On the other hand, the family has never been more popular. Suddenly, everyone seems to want one: single people, gay men and lesbians, even the elderly and widowed. Prime-time sitcoms have made a staple of both lovably dysfunctional nuclear families (like *The George Lopez Show*) and fractured divorced families *(Two and a Half Men, The New Adventures of Old Christine, Gary Unmarried)* where ex-spouses try to navigate a postnuclear world. And the wedding industry generates sales of about $50 billion every single year.

The family is in crisis. The family has never been more popular.

The gay marriage debate is a good example of both sides of the argument. Opponents say it would wreak "a potentially fatal blow to the traditional family," leading "inexorably to polygamy and other alternatives to one man/one woman unions" (Dobson, 2004). At the same time, gay couples across the country have been eager to pledge their love and commitment by getting married. And millions of supporters believe matrimony should not be limited to only some couples but open to everyone who wants to enter into it. How much more popular can the idea of marriage get?

The great novelist Thomas Wolfe said "You can't go home again." A few years

"Is the family in crisis—or has it never been more popular, or more supported? We believe both—in part, sociologists understand, because both are true."

The great novelist Thomas Wolfe said "You can't go home again." A few years earlier, the poet Robert Frost wrote that "Home is the place where, when you have to go there, they have to take you in." We believe both statements—in part, sociologists understand, because both are true. The family has never been more popular in part *because* it is in crisis— and all the cultural media, from TV to movies to pop songs, are trying to reassert

its predominance in an increasingly individualized and global world. And the family is in crisis in part *because* of those institutional forces, like the global marketplace and its ideology of individualism, which constitute the dominant ideology around the world.

One thing is certain: The family is hardly a separate realm from the rest of society. It is a political football, tossed around by both liberals and conservatives, who appeal to it abstractly and develop policies that shape and mold it concretely. It is the foundation of the economy. And it is the basic building block of society. Always has been. Probably always will be.

What is the family? Where did it come from? Is it still necessary? How do sociologists understand the forces that hold it together and the forces that pull it apart?

The Family Tree

Unlike most animals, human beings are born helpless. For the first few years of their lives, they require round-the-clock care; and, for the first decade, they require nearly constant supervision, or they won't survive to adulthood. But even after they learn basic survival skills, humans are still not qualified to make their own way in the world—an adult has to provide for all of their needs for 10 or 15 years or more. You are born into a group—and your survival depends on it. This group is, of course, the family.

The Family Unit

The family is both hard and easy to define. In the most common sense, it is defined as "a group of people related by blood or marriage; relatives." But that's not all. The family is also a collection of cross-generational descendants. It's a term that comprises all members of any category that are related to one another, as in a family of numbers. In biology, it's a subdivision of a class of plants or animals.

The core element of all these definitions is the fact of relatedness—the members are logically or legally related to each other. And that is why the idea of the family has become such a political hot potato. Relatedness is everything. Excluding some people from establishing that relationship prevents them from being in a family.

Among humans, we can accept the initial definition above. Yet even that "group of people related by blood or marriage" comes in an enormously varied number of types, from the father-mother-kids model that we see on evening sitcoms to longhouses where everyone lives together. However, individual families are usually differentiated from others with a separate dwelling, their own house, apartment, cabin, or tent. Even when the entire tribe lives together in a single longhouse, each family gets its own cooking fire and personal space to differentiate it from the other families and signify that they belong together.

Chances are that you will occupy at least two different family units during your lifetime. While you are a child, you belong to a **family of origin**—the family you are born into—with your biological parents or others who are responsible for your upbringing. When you grow up, if you marry or cohabit with a romantic partner, you now also belong to a **family of procreation,** which is the family you choose to belong to in order to reproduce. Often we consider any adults you are living with as a family of procreation, even if none of them is actually doing any procreating. In modern societies, it is customary to change residences to signify that you have moved to a new family unit, but most premodern societies didn't differentiate: Either new wives moved in with their husbands' family, or new husbands moved in with their wives' family, or everyone kept right on living together (Fox, 1984; Stone, 2000).

Families usually have some rationale, real or imaginary, for being together. They, and everyone else in the community, assume that they "belong" together because of a common biological ancestry, legal marriage or adoption, some other bond of kinship, or the connection to others by blood, marriage, or adoption. Sometimes they can't prove biological ancestry, but they still insist on a common ancestor in the distant past, whether human, god, or animal. When all else fails, they create symbolic kinship, blood brothers, aunties, and "friends of the family."

Families as Kinship Systems

Every human society has divided the adults into cooperative groups who take charge of the care and feeding of the children. This is the origin of the **family,** defined as "the basic unit in society traditionally consisting of two parents rearing their children" but also "any of various social units differing from but regarded as equivalent to the traditional family"—such as single parents with children, spouses without children, and several generations living together. Families also refer to those related to you through blood or marriage, extended back through generations.

Families provide us with a sense of history, both as individuals and as members of a particular culture. Families themselves are part of **kinship systems,** cultural forms that locate individuals in the culture by reference to their families. Kinship systems are groupings that include all your relatives, mapped as a network from closest (mother, father, siblings) to a little more distant (cousins, aunts, uncles) to increasingly distant (your great-uncle twice removed). Your kinship system can be imagined as a "family tree." Tracing your family tree is especially popular these days because it provides a sense of history.

Family trees can be organized in several ways to ground you in that history, depending on how you trace your descent, where you live, and whom you marry. These different ways of constructing a family tree give you a different cognitive map of the world and your place in it. Your line of descent can be:

- **Matrilineal:** through your mother's side of the family

- **Patrilineal:** through your father's side of the family

- **Bilateral:** through both your parents' sides, equally

In many cases, your surname (last name) provides a minihistory of your ancestry. In some languages, it is literally in your name, like Johnson or Stevenson in English, Jonasdottir in Icelandic, Petrov in Russian. These names suggest different ways of tracing your family tree and lineage.

Families are not simply an expression of love between people who want to have children. They are fundamental cultural institutions that have as much to do with economics, politics, and sex as they do with raising children. As the fundamental unit of society, the social functions of the family and the regulation of sexuality have always been of interest to sociologists.

For one thing, families ensure the regular transfer of property and establish lines of succession. For another, families restrict the number of people you can have sex with. In prehistoric times, a mighty hunter might spend three weeks tracking down and killing a single mastodon. He didn't want to go through all of that time and expense to feed a child that his next-door neighbor had produced. But how could he be sure that his next-door neighbor *wasn't* the father of the children his best girlfriend had given birth to? To solve this problem, almost every society has established a type of marriage—a relationship that regulates sexual activity to ensure **legitimacy,** that is, to ensure that men know what children they have produced (women have an obvious way to know). Families then bear the economic and emotional burden of raising only the children that belong to them (Malinowski, [1927] 1974).

No society allows its members to marry or have sex with anyone they might take an interest in, but the specifics of who can marry whom vary from place to place and over time. The most common arrangement is **monogamy,** marriage between two people. Most monogamous societies allow men and women to marry each other because it usually takes one of each to make a baby, but

Multiple Wives

The family form mentioned most often in the Bible is polygyny (multiple female partners). In fact, all of the patriarchs—Abraham, Isaac, Jacob, and Joseph—had numerous wives and concubines (sexual partners to whom they were not married). Solomon was reputed to have had 1,000 wives, products of his many political alliances.

Did You Know?

Families are kinship systems that anchor our identities in shared history and culture.

same-sex monogamy is surprisingly common. Historian John Boswell found evidence of same-sex marriages existing alongside male-female marriages even in early Christian Europe (1995).

Many societies have instituted some form of **polygamy,** or marriage between three or more people, although most of those allow monogamy as well. The most common form of polygamy is **polygyny,** one man with two or more women, because a man can have children with several women at the same time. Among the Yoruba of northern Nigeria, women can have only one husband, but *they* can have as many wives as they want, so they practice a type of same-sex polygyny: One woman marries two or more women (Roscoe, 2001). **Polyandry,** one woman marrying two or more men, is rare, but it has been documented in Tibet and a few other places where men are absent for several months of the year.

Only a few societies practice **group marriage,** two or more men marrying two or more women, with children born to anyone in the union "belonging" to all of the partners equally. Group marriages appeared from time to time in the 1960s counterculture, but they rarely lasted long (Hollenbach, 2004).

Marriage does more than ensure that the proper people are responsible for the upbringing of the child; it ensures that when the child grows up, he or she will know who is off limits as a marriage partner. Almost every human society enforces **exogamy:** Marriage to (or sex with) members of your family unit is forbidden. This is the incest taboo, which Sigmund Freud argued was the one single cultural universal. (Without it, lines of succession and inheritance of property would be impossible!)

Of course, who counts as family varies from culture to culture and over time. Mom, Dad, brother, sister, son, or daughter are always off limits, except in a few cases of ritual marriage (the ancient Egyptian pharaohs married their sisters). But uncles and nieces commonly married each other through the nineteenth century, and first cousins are still allowed to marry in most countries in Europe and 26 of the U.S. states. In the Hebrew Bible, God struck Onan dead because he refused to have sex with his widowed sister-in-law and thereby produce an heir for his brother. But nowadays an affair with one's sister-in-law would be thought of as creepy at best.

The Historical Development of the Family

When our son was 5 years old, we were wandering through the ethnological exhibits at the Museum of Natural History. There were lifelike dioramas of other cultures—Eskimo, Polynesian, Amazonian—and also displays that portrayed the evolution of modern society through the Neolithic, Paleolithic, and Pleistocene ages. In each case, the diorama had exactly the same form: In the front, a single male, poised as a hunter or fisherman. Behind him, by a fire toward the back of the tableau, sat a single woman, cooking or preparing food, surrounded by several small children.

It wasn't until we passed into the hall of the animals, however, that anything seemed amiss. The dioramas kept to form: A single male—lion, gorilla, whatever—standing proudly in front, a single female and offspring lounging in the back waiting for him to bring home fresh meat.

"Look, Dad," Zachary said. "They have families just like we do."

I started to simply say "uh huh," the way parents do, half listening to their children. But something made me stop short. "Uh, actually, they don't," I said. "Most of these animals actually live in larger groupings, extended families and cooperative bands. And lionesses do most of the hunting (and caring for the young) while the males lounge about lazily most of the day."

Nor was every family throughout human history a nuclear family, a residential arrangement of only two generations, the parents and their children. Indeed, the nuclear family emerged only recently, within the past few thousand years. For most of human existence, our family forms have been quite varied and significantly larger, including several generations and all the siblings all living together.

Until my son pointed it out, though, I had never noticed that these exhibits in the museum were not historically accurate reflections of human (or animal) history but normative efforts to make the contemporary nuclear family appear to have been eternal and universal, to read it back into history and across species—in a sense, to rewrite history so that the family didn't have a history but instead to pretend it had always been the way it is.

Nothing could be further from the truth. Families have developed and changed enormously over the course of human history.

Families evolved to socialize children, transmit property, ensure legitimacy, and regulate sexuality. They also evolved as economic units. Because children went to work alongside the adults, they contributed to the economic prosperity of the family; in fact, the family became a unit of economic production. Property and other possessions were passed down from the adults of the family to the children. Occupation, religion, language, social standing, and wealth were all dependent on kinship ties.

In all agrarian societies, including Europe and the United States as late as the nineteenth century, the household has been the basic economic unit. Production—and consumption—occurred within the household. Everyone participated in growing and eating the crops, and the excess might be taken to market for trade.

There was no distinction between family and society: Family life *was* social life. Families performed a whole range of functions later performed by social institutions. The family was not only a site of economic production and consumption. It was:

- *A school.* Any reading and writing you learned was at your parents' knee.

- *A church.* The head of the household led the family prayers; you might see the inside of a "real" church or temple once or twice a year.

- *A hospital.* Family members knew as much as there was to know about setting broken bones and healing diseases.

- *A day care center.* There were no businesses to take care of children, so someone in the family had to do it.

- *A police station.* There were no police to call when someone wronged you, so you called on your family to take care of the situation.

- *A retirement home.* If you had no family to take care of you in your old age, you would end up in debtor's prison or begging on the streets.

Obviously, all these functions cannot be met by the nuclear family model. The most common model in the premodern era was the **extended family,** in which two or three generations lived under the same roof or at least in the same compound. No one left the household except to marry into another family, until the group got too big for the space available and had to split up. And even then, they would build a new house nearby, until eventually everyone in the village was related to everyone else.

The Origins of the Nuclear Family

Just as families are no longer concerned exclusively with socializing children, marriage developed far more functions than simple sexual regulation, ensuring that parents and children know who each other is. Marriage could also validate a gentleman's claim to nobility and establish that a boy had become a man. It could form a social tie between two families or bring peace to warring tribes. In the Middle Ages, European monarchs often required their children to marry the child of a monarch next door, on the theory that you are unlikely to go to war with the country that your son or daughter has married into (it didn't work—by the seventeenth century, all of the European monarchs were second or third cousins, and they were always invading each other).

Marriage has also come to represent a distinctive emotional bond between two people. In fact, the idea that people should select their own marriage partner is actually a very recent phenomenon. For thousands of years, parents selected partners to fulfill their own economic and political needs or those of the broader kinship group. Arranged marriages are still the norm in a number of countries. People still fall in love—romantic love is practically universal across human societies—but not necessarily with the people they intended to marry. The tradition of courtly love, praised

Romantic love is virtually universal, found in all cultures. This Hindu couple in South Asia participates in their marriage ceremony.

by the troubadours of medieval France, was actually about adultery, falling in love with someone else's spouse (De Rougemont, 1983).

Only about 200 years ago did men and women in Western countries begin to look at marriage as an individual affair, to be decided by the people involved rather than parents, church, and state.

Like the **companionate marriage,** in which individuals choose their marriage partners based on emotional ties and love, the nuclear family is a relatively recent phenomenon. It emerged in Europe and the United States in the late eighteenth century. Its emergence depended on certain factors, such as the ability of a single breadwinner to earn enough in the marketplace to support the family and sufficient hygiene and health so that most babies would survive with only one adult taking care of them.

Historians like Carl Degler (1980) trace the new nuclear family, as it emerged in the White middle class between 1776 and 1830, and Christopher Lasch (1975) suggests the theory of "progressive nucleation" to explain how it gradually superseded the extended family and became the norm. During the nineteenth century, industrialization and modernization meant that social and economic needs could no longer be met by kin. It became customary for children to move far from their parents to go to school or look for work. With no parents around, they had to be responsible for their own spouse selection; and, when they married, they would have to find their own home. Eventually adult children were expected to start their own households away from their parents, even if they were staying in the same town. When they had children of their own, they were solely responsible for the child rearing; the grandparents had only small and informal roles to play.

The change was not always beneficial: In every generation, husbands and wives had to reinvent child-rearing techniques, starting over from scratch, with many possibilities for mistakes. As Margaret Mead stated (1978), "Nobody has ever before asked the nuclear family to live all by itself in a box the way we do. With no relatives, no support, we've put it in an impossible situation."

The nuclear family is also a more highly "gendered" family—roles and activities are allocated increasingly along gender lines. On the one hand, because the nuclear family was by definition much smaller than the extended family, the wife experienced greater autonomy. On the other hand, in her idealized role, she was increasingly restricted to the home, with her primary role envisioned as child care and household maintenance. She became a "housewife."

Because the home was seen as the "women's sphere," middle-class women's activities outside the home began to shrink. The husband became the "breadwinner," the only one in the family who was supposed to go to work and provide economic support for the household. (Of course, families of lesser means could not always survive on the salary of a single earner, so wives often continued to work outside the home.)

As the attention of the household, and especially the mother, became increasingly centered on children, they were seen as needing more than food, clothing, education, and maybe a spanking now and then. They were no longer seen as "little savages," barbarians who needed civilizing, or corrupt sinners who would go to Hell unless they were baptized immediately. Instead, they were "little angels," pure and innocent, born "trailing clouds of glory" as they descended from heaven. Therefore they had to be kept innocent of the more graphic aspects of life, like sex and death, and they needed love, nurturing, and constant care and attention. The number of children per family declined, both because they would no longer be providing economic support for the family and because each child now required a greater investment of time and emotional energy.

In modern societies, children don't often work alongside their parents, and the family has become a unit of consumption rather than production; its economic security is tied to the workplace and the national economy. Instead, the major functions of the family are to provide lifelong psychological support and emotional security. The family has been so closely associated with love and belonging that friends and even groups of co-workers express their emotional intimacy by saying they are "a family."

Although the contemporary stereotype of the American family is a nuclear family, consisting of mother, father, and their 2.2 children, in reality, American families are quite varied. Only about a third of American families conform to this pattern. And not all family roles are assigned by gender—as this Chicano family illustrates at dinnertime.

Family and Ethnicity

The contemporary American nuclear family—the breadwinning husband, his homemaker wife, and their 2.2 children, who live in a detached single-family house in a suburb we call Anytown, USA—developed historically. But even today, it is only one of several family forms. Families vary not only from culture to culture but also within our society—by race and ethnicity. As each racial and ethnic group has a different history, their family units developed in different ways, in response to different conditions. For example, how can we understand the modern African American family outside the deliberate policies of slavery whereby families were broken up and husbands, wives, and children deliberately sold to different slave owners, so as to dilute the power of family as a tie of loyalty to something other than the master?

Sociologists are interested in the diversity of family forms by race and ethnicity. Some of these differences are now so well documented that to enumerate them sounds almost like a stereotype. And, to be sure, each ethnic group exhibits wide variation in their families. Some of these differences may be as much a result of class as they are of specific ethnic culture. For example, working-class families—regardless of the family's ethnic background—are less stable than middle-class families and more likely to be "matrifocal." As a result, sociologists are also interested in the process by which one family form became the standard against which all other family forms were measured—and found wanting. Although these family adaptations are seen largely among ethnic minorities, they are also seen among the White working class, which suggests that they are less "ethnic" adaptations to a White family norm and more "class" adaptations to a middle- and upper-class family norm. As each ethnic group develops a stable middle class, their families come to resemble the companionate-marriage nuclear family of the White middle class. It may be the case not that the nuclear family is inevitable, but that it is *expensive*—and that without significant governmental support, it does not flourish.

The European American Family

This family form that became the dominant model was itself the product of a variety of social factors that are unlikely to return. Based initially on the Anglo-Irish family of the seventeenth century, the European American family has also taken on characteristics from each of the large immigrant groups, especially those that arrived in the late nineteenth century. Many of these immigrant families were Catholic and did not use birth control, so their families tended to be larger than those of the Protestant immigrants, who did practice birth control.

Native Americans are often torn between the social norms of their traditional culture and those of the dominant society. This grandparent shows his grandson how to mend fishing nets.

But the contemporary family is also the result of deliberate social policies beginning in the first decades of the twentieth century. These policies held up a specific model as normal and natural and then endeavored to fulfill that vision by prohibitions on women's entry into the workplace or pushing them out once they found their way there, ideologies of motherhood and birth control to limit family size, a "eugenics" movement that demanded that all new immigrants conform to a specific standard of marriage and family, and a new educational and child-rearing ideology that specified how parents should raise their children. American families have always been subject to deliberate policies to encourage certain types of families and discourage others, a process that continues today.

The end of World War II saw the largest infusion of government funding toward the promotion of this new nuclear family—the interstate highway system that promoted flight to the suburban tract homes, the massive spending on public schools in those suburbs, and policy initiatives coupled with ideologies that pushed women out of manufacturing work and back into the home, while their veteran husbands were reabsorbed into the labor force or went to college on the GI Bill.

The family form that finally emerged in the 1950s—idealized in classic situation comedies of the 1950s and early 1960s like *Father Knows Best* and *Leave It to Beaver* on that newly emergent and culturally unifying medium, television—was far less a naturally emergent evolutionary adaptation and far more the anomalous result of deliberate social planning.

The Native American Family

Prior to the arrival of the Europeans, most Native Americans lived in small villages where extended families dominated; you could trace a blood relationship with almost everyone you knew, and most social interaction—from food distribution to village government—depended on kinship ties and obligations. Strangers were considered enemies unless they could be somehow included in the kinship network (Wilkinson, 1999). One of the primary means of creating kinship alliances was exogamy, the requirement that people marry outside of their clan. Marriages created allies, which were useful in any disputes with other clans in the tribe.

Native American families are, themselves, quite diverse. Most marriages are monogamous, but some tribes permitted polygyny, and a few permitted men to sleep with other women when their wives were pregnant or lactating. Many tribes, such as the Zuni and Hopi in the Southwest and the Iroquois in the Northeast, were matrilineal. Hopi children were raised by their mothers and uncles (and, to an extent, their fathers). Girls continued to live with their mothers throughout their lives. When they married, they brought their husbands home with them. When boys entered puberty, they moved into the men's ceremonial house. Eventually most of them married women of other clans and moved in with their wife's family.

The father had limited authority in the family: He was considered a guest in his wife's home, and her brothers or cousins made all of the major economic and child-rearing decisions. Children went to their uncle, not their father, for approval of their life choices.

Still, children—especially boys—learned a lot from their fathers. Although uncles had the greatest authority over their life decisions, their biological fathers taught them their occupational skills, hunting, herding animals, or growing crops.

Native American family and kinship systems were developed to provide for people's fundamental needs, such as producing enough food and defending against outsiders. Although kin often shared strong emotional bonds, families did not develop primarily out of people's desire for love, intimacy, and personal fulfillment but out of the desire to survive.

Native Americans are often torn between the social norms of their traditional culture and those of the dominant society (Garrett, 1999; Yellowbird and Snipp, 1994). One-third marry outside their ethnicity, and the extended family model of the tribal society is common only on the reservations. In the cities, most Native Americans live in nuclear families (Sandefur and Sakamoto, 1988).

As with other minority groups, social problems such as poverty put significant strains on both extended and nuclear families (Harjo, 1999; Strong, 2004).

The African American Family

Before slavery was abolished, most slaves in the United States and elsewhere were prohibited from legal marriages. It was common practice to separate husbands and wives, and children and parents, on arrival and to make sure they were sold to different plantations, which, slave owners reasoned, would keep them more obedient and less likely to maintain any attachments other than to the plantation. As a result, slaves created their own permanent marital bonds, developing strong kinship ties similar to those in the extended family models of West Africa. Mutual aid and emotional support remained centered in kinship long after slavery (Strong, 2004).

Since the early 1970s, economic changes have resulted in a massive loss of blue-collar jobs (disproportionately held by minorities), and as a result the nuclear family model has become even less common. African Americans have lower marriage rates and higher divorce rates than other ethnic groups (Clarkwest, 2006) and a greater percentage of single mothers. Over half of African American families consist of only one parent, usually the mother.

The completely self-sufficient nuclear family model is difficult enough with two parents, but only one parent trying to provide full-time emotional and financial support is often severely overextended. As a survival mechanism, many African American communities have adopted the convention of "fictive kinship"—that is, stretching the boundaries of kinship to include nonblood relations, friends, neighbors, and co-workers, who are obligated to help out in hard times and whom one is obligated to help out in turn (Stack, 1974).

Fictive kinship can also extend to women who have children with the same man. Far from considering each other competition or "home wreckers," they often consider each other kin, with the same bonds of obligation and emotional support due to sisters or sisters-in-law. When a woman has children with several different men, each of whom has children with several different women, the bonds of fictive kinship can extend across a community.

The Asian American Family

Asian Americans trace their ancestry to many different cultural groups in more than 20 languages, so they brought many different family systems to the United States with them. The more recent the immigration, the more closely their family system reflects that of their original culture. But even third- and fourth-generation families, who are demographically almost identical to White middle-class nuclear families (same percentage of married couples, two-parent families, and male heads of household), show some differences in orientation and family style.

Suzuki (1985) studied Chinese American and Japanese American families and found that the roles and responsibilities of various family members are based on the Confucian principles that have informed Chinese society for 2,000 years. They are more collectively based than Euro-American families, emphasizing the family as a unit rather than a group of individuals. Grown-up Euro-American children may reject their parents' wishes, saying "I have to live my own life," but Chinese and Japanese American children are more concerned about not bringing shame or dishonor to the family.

Euro-American families tend to be democratic, with every member having a voice in such decisions as what to have for dinner or where to go on vacation. In contrast, Chinese and Japanese American families are more hierarchical. Parents and older siblings exert authority over children and younger siblings and require respect and obedience from them. The only exceptions are made for gender—in some situations, boys may have authority over their mothers and older sisters.

The Hispanic Family

Like Asian Americans, Hispanic Americans trace their ancestry to many different cultures with different languages, religions, and different family systems: Cuban families are very different from Puerto Rican families, which are very different from Chicano families, and so on (Baca Zinn, 2005; Carrasquillo, 1994). Also like Asian Americans, the more recently Hispanic Americans have arrived in the

United States, the more closely their family system resembles that of their original culture.

Demographically, Hispanic families fall somewhat between Euro-American and African American families. Most are nuclear families, but they do have characteristics of extended families, with grandparents, aunts, uncles, and more distant relatives living close together, visiting each other frequently, and bearing some of the responsibilities for child rearing and emotional support.

They tend to be hierarchical by age and gender, like Asian American families, but here, too, Hispanic families exhibit significant variation. Chicano and Puerto Rican families are more egalitarian than Dominican and Cuban families; and those from South America are somewhat more likely to be middle class, smaller, and more egalitarian than those from the Caribbean.

Gender equality also increases with length of residence in the United States. The longer the family has been in the United States, the more egalitarian it will tend to be. The families of second- and third-generation immigrants tend to be more egalitarian than families of older generations (Chilman, 1999; Wilkinson, 1999). This is probably the result of social mobility rather than ethnicity—the longer the residence in the United States, the more likely is the family to belong to the middle class.

Forming Families

Sociologists study the variations in the family form and also the processes by which we form families. To most of us, it probably seems pretty straightforward: After a few years of dating, you become increasingly serious with one special someone, you fall in love, you gradually realize that this one is "it," and you decide to marry. Historically, this has been a process known as courtship, the intensification and institutionalization of an intimate relationship from meeting to mating to marrying. And it is so common, so casually assumed, we often have no idea just how unusual and recent this process is.

Courtship and Dating

In the famous musical *Fiddler on the Roof,* a drama that centers on the breakdown of a traditional Jewish family in a small Russian village in the late nineteenth century, as each of the three daughters chooses to marry an increasingly troublesome man, the girls' parents reminisce about their courtship. "The first time I met you was on our wedding day," Golde tells her husband, Tevye. That was not uncommon. So he asks if she loves him. "Do I what?!?" she answers.

Courtship was largely unknown in ancient society. Marriages were arranged, and children often were betrothed (promised, engaged) as toddlers. But even in the days when marriages

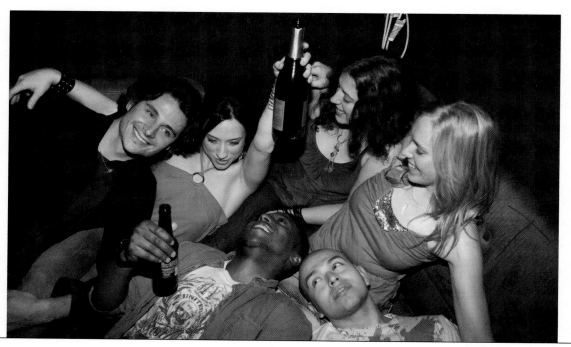

Dating and courtship in college has been partly replaced with a "hook up" culture, in which groups of friends socialize and then individuals may pair off later. Hooking up usually entails few, if any, expectations of an actual relationship.

were arranged by parents, children often had a voice in the selection process, and they found ways to meet and evaluate potential partners so they could make their preferences known. By the turn of the twentieth century, they were classmates at coed high schools, and they formed romantic bonds with people that their parents didn't even know.

The custom of dating, engaging in recreational activities in pairs rather than groups and with the goal of establishing or strengthening a romantic commitment, did not arise until the 1920s. Children of working-class immigrants in major American cities were trying to distance themselves from the old-fashioned supervised visits that their parents insisted on, and fortunately they enjoyed both a great deal of personal freedom and a wide range of brand-new entertainment venues (Bailey, 1989).

By the 1930s, the custom had spread to the middle class. College-aged men and women participated in a process called "rating and dating," whereby they were rated on their desirability as a date and would ask or accept dates only with people of similar ratings. Dating was based on physical attractiveness, social desirability, and other qualities—not family name and position. Most importantly, dating was supervised and scrutinized by one's peer group, not one's parents (Nock, 2003; Waller, 1937).

College and high school became the time of unparalleled freedom for American youth and were increasingly taken up by dating and courtship. Campus wits joked that girls were attending college just to get their "Mrs." degree. By the 1950s, parents were eagerly awaiting their son or daughter's first date as a sign of their entry into adulthood. There were many stages: casual dating, going steady (dating only one person), being pinned (wearing a class ring or pin as a sign of commitment), and finally becoming engaged. Boys and girls were supposed to begin dating early in high school and date many people over the period of years, perhaps going steady several times, until they found "the one" to marry. But not for too many years: "Still dating" in the late 20s was considered sad and slightly unwholesome. In the 1970s, the increased incidence of divorce sent many people in their middle years into the world of dating again, until there was little stigma about dating at the age of 30, 40, or 50.

Today it seems that everyone is dating. Kindergarteners go on "play dates," married couples go on dates, and the recently widowed or divorced are encouraged to date

Dating in Japan

In 1955, parents arranged 63 percent of all marriages in Japan. In 1998, the percentage had dropped to 7 percent (Retherford, Ogawa, and Matsukura, 2001). Yet, relative to the United States, Japan has not developed a strong dating culture. You're not expected to bring a date to every recreational activity, and if you're not dating anyone at the moment, your friends don't feel sorry for you and try to fix you up. The expectation that dating leads to marriage is also absent. Japanese television and other mass media don't glorify marriage and ridicule or pity single people, as American television often does (Orenstein, 2001).

Outside of high school and college, there are few places where single men and women meet and interact. Forty-five percent of heterosexual women over the age of 16 say that they have no male friends at all. However, practically all of the heterosexual women with one or more male friends have engaged in premarital sex (probably with the male friends) (Retherford et al., 2001).

With no societal push to marriage and premarital sex available, it is no wonder that they don't feel pressured into getting married right away, or at all. In 2001, schoolgirls around the world were asked whether they agreed with the statement that "everyone should be married." Three-quarters of American schoolgirls agreed. But 88 percent of Japanese schoolgirls disagreed (Coontz, 2005).

again almost immediately. Internet dating sites are among the Web's most popular, and your potential dates are neatly categorized by age, gender, race, and sexual orientation. And yet it also seems that no one is dating. On campuses, the preferred mode of social and sexual interaction is "hooking up," which is so loose and indiscriminate that its connection to dating and mating has been lost.

Marriage—and Its Alternatives

Marriage is the most common foundation for family formation in the world. The marriage of two people—a woman and a man—is universal in developed countries, although there are significant variations among different cultures.

Marriage is not identical to a nuclear family, although the two tend to go together. One can imagine, for example, marriage as a relationship between two people who are, themselves, embedded in an extended family or a communal child-rearing arrangement (such as the kibbutz). Sociologically, its universality suggests that marriage forms a stable, long-lasting, and secure foundation for the family's functions—child socialization, property transfer, legitimacy, sexual regulation—to be securely served.

Men Favor Marriage

American men are more eager to marry than American women. From 1970 to the late 1990s, men's attitudes toward marriage became more favorable, while women's became less so. By the end of the century, more men than women said that marriage was their ideal lifestyle (Coontz, 2005).

Marriage is also a legal arrangement, conferring various social, economic, and political benefits on the married couple. This is because the state regards marriage—that is, stable families—as so important that it is willing to provide economic and social incentives to married couples. As a result, people who have been legally excluded from marrying—the mentally ill, gays and lesbians—have sought to obtain that right as well.

Marriage is certainly not the only living arrangement for people in society (see Figure 11.5 on page 339). In America over the past century, the number of adults living alone increased by more than 20 percent, single parents and children by more than 10 percent, unmarried partners by well over 60 percent, and unmarried partners with their children by nearly 90 percent. In several developing countries, marriage is also occurring later and bringing with it numerous positive social outcomes. In industrialized countries like the United States, the implications of the shift toward later marriage and less marriage are a source of extensive sociological research and social debate.

Multigenerational households (adults of more than one generation sharing domestic space) increased by 38 percent between 1990 and 2000, until today they comprise about 3 percent of all households. In about two-thirds, the grandparents are in charge of the family, sharing their home with their grown children and grandchildren (or only their grandchildren), while in about one-third, the grown children are in charge of the family, sharing their home with both their parents and their children (Figure 11.1).

Marriage varies widely by race, ethnicity, education, and income. Nearly two-thirds (63 percent) of White women over 18 who make more than $100,000 a year are married, while only 25 percent of Black women over 18 who earn less than $20,000 per year are married (Center for Changing Families, 2007). Marriage, itself, has changed. It no longer signifies adulthood or conveys the responsibilities and commitment that it once did. In a society where pop stars marry and divorce within a day but couples who have been together for 30 years are forbidden from marrying, it is, in some people's eyes, discredited and corrupt. People are putting off marriage, cohabiting, or opting for singlehood. On the other hand, marriage has become more desirable than ever before, bringing together couples from varying backgrounds and repeat performers and inspiring many who've been excluded to fight for the right to marry. Some of these changes are temporary, like delayed marriage and, in most cases, cohabitation (which usually leads to marriage). Others, like singlehood, have become more permanent and less transitory.

Delayed Marriage. Early marriage—usually arranged by parents—is still the rule in sub-Saharan Africa and South and Central Asia. Approximately one-third of girls living in the developing world (excluding China) will be married before they are 18; one of out seven before their 15th birthday (Population Council, 2009). In Southern Asia, 48 percent of young women—nearly 10 million—are married before the age of 18. In Africa, it's 42 percent; in Latin America and the Caribbean, 29 percent. More than half of all girls under 18 are married

---

Figure 11.1 Trends in Coupling

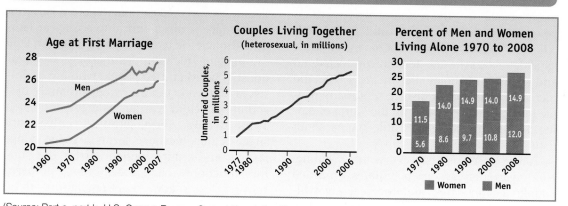

(*Source:* Part a, part b, U.S. Census Bureau, Current Population Survey; part c, www.catalyst.org, 2009.)

in some countries, including Afghanistan, Bangladesh, Yemen, India, and the Palestinian Territories. In Ethiopia and some areas of West Africa, some girls are married as early as age 7 (International Planned Parenthood Federation, 2006). However, the prevalence is decreasing significantly around the world. Since 1970, the median age of first marriage has risen substantially worldwide—for men from 25.4 years to 27.2 and for women from 21.5 to 23.2 (U.N. Population Fund [UNFPA], 2005).

In the United States, young people are experiencing longer periods of independent living while working or attending school before marriage. A 25-year-old American man today is far more likely to be single and childless than he would have been 50 years ago—or even 25 years ago. Among 25-year-old women, the fastest-growing demographic status is single, working, childless, head of household (Fussell and Furstenberg, 2006). The United States still has one of the industrial world's *lowest* age for first marriage. Differences among Black, White, and foreign-born populations in education and labor market opportunities have narrowed since the 1960s, creating more similarities in the lives of people of color and their White peers. However, significant educational and economic inequalities, in addition to cultural differences, mean that different groups will continue to vary in the ages of first marriage.

Staying Single. Not long ago, people who were "still not married" by their late 20s were considered deviant. Men were considered "big babies," who "refused to grow up" and "settle down." Women were "old maids," thought to be too unattractive or socially inept to attract a husband.

But singlehood has become commonplace, if not exactly respectable. Just over half of all Americans aged 25 (50.3 percent) and over are not married or cohabiting (U.S. Census Bureau, 2009a). This represents a historic milestone: Over half of all households in the United States do not have a married couple living there. More than 60 percent of all unmarried Americans have never been married. Although the percentage of single people is rising for all Americans, those rates vary considerably by gender, race, and ethnicity. Between 1970 and 2000, the proportion of White adults who had never married rose from 16 percent to 20 percent, 19 percent to 28 percent among Hispanics, and 21 percent to 39 percent among African Americans (U.S. Census Bureau, 2008).

While the age of marriage is increasing worldwide, child marriages are still common in many countries. This Kurdish couple appears to be about 10.

In Europe, the proportion of women who have never married ranges from 7 percent in Bulgaria to 36 percent in Iceland. The proportion of men is substantially higher.

Women are more likely to be single than men. In fact, the majority of American women (53 percent) is living without a spouse (U.S. Census Bureau, 2009a). Single women are better educated, have higher levels of employment and income, and have better mental health than single men (Catalyst, 2009; Fowlkes, 1994; Marks 1996).

Cohabiting. The term **cohabitation** refers to unmarried people in a romantic relationship living in the same residence. A few decades ago, when nonmarital sex was illegal in most states, cohabitation was virtually impossible—landlords wouldn't rent to people unless they were related by blood or marriage. Hotel managers could lose their license if they rented rooms to unrelated people. Today, cohabitation has become commonplace, largely lacking in social disapproval (Jayson, 2008). Nearly half of people 25 to 40 years of age in the United States have cohabited (Pew Research Center, 2007; Teachman, 2003); today, 10 percent of all opposite-sex couples living together are unmarried (U.S. Census Bureau, 2008a).

Globally, cohabitation is common in liberal countries—in Sweden, it is four times as prevalent as in the United States. That is largely because those countries provide universal health care and education to everyone, so you don't need to get married to be covered by your spouse's health plan or to ensure your children can go to university. However, it is rare in more

Figure 11.2 Living Together

Country	1995	2000s
Canada	13.9%	18.4%
Denmark	24.7%	24.4%
France	13.6%	17.2%
Germany	8.2%	11.2%
Italy	3.1%	3.8%
Netherlands	13.1%	13.3%
Sweden	23%	28.4%
United Kingdom	10.1%	15.4%
USA	5.1%	7.6%

Unmarried cohabitors as percent of all couples

(*Source:* The National Marriage Project at the University of Virginia, 2008. Reprinted with permission.)

conservative countries and remains illegal in some countries.

Is cohabitation a stage of courtship, somewhere between dating and marriage, sort of the equivalent of "going steady" among high school students? Many scholars and cohabiters have thought so—in the 1980s, it was even called "trial marriage." Women cohabiters were found to be more likely to desire marriage than men (Blumstein and Schwartz, 1983), but about 25 percent did not expect to marry the man they were currently living with (Fowlkes, 1994; Seltzer, 2001). Today, with more extensive information about cohabitants and more sophisticated research methods, many researchers are working to understand the many reasons couples cohabit before marriage, with some seeing cohabitation as a family form in its own right.

For some cohabiters, their living situation has nothing to do with marriage. More than one million elderly Americans cohabit, for example—for a significant financial reason. While the government strongly encourages marriage among the young and middle-aged with tax cuts and other benefits, elderly men and women receiving Social Security cannot marry without losing a significant percentage of their combined individual incomes (Brown, Lee, and Bulanda, 2006; Chevan, 1996).

Race and social class have an impact on who will cohabit and who will marry. Despite the popular assumption that opposite-sex cohabitation is a lifestyle of the rich and famous or of radical social rule breakers, it is actually more common among young, working-class, and poor people with less education and financial

wherewithal (Bumpass and Lu, 2000; Casper and Bianchi, 2002; Raley and Sweeney, 2007). Nearly one-third of opposite-sex cohabitators are both under 30 (versus 7 percent of married couples); and 22 percent earn less than $25,000 per year (versus 12 percent of married partners). One in ten adult Hispanic women currently cohabit, and 9 percent of White women, but only 6 percent of African American women (Figure 11.2).

Gay and lesbian cohabiters tend to diverge from many of these patterns, in several respects coming much closer to the demographics of straight married couples. While only 13 percent of opposite-sex cohabitants are middle-aged (45–64), for example, 28 percent of gay and lesbian cohabitants fall in this age range—as do 32 percent of straight married couples. About the same percentage of gay cohabitants and straight married couples are paying a mortgage on a home they own (59 percent for gay male couples and marrieds, 58 percent for lesbian couples), as compared with 35 percent for opposite-sex cohabitants. Gay and lesbian cohabitants tend to be better educated—25 percent of gay male couples and 26 percent of lesbian couples both hold college degrees versus just 10 percent of opposite-sex cohabitors—and more affluent: Thirty percent of gay male couples and 26 percent of lesbian couples earn over $100,000 per year, as compared with just 11 percent of opposite-sex partners living together (Elliott and Dye, 2005).

But opposite-sex cohabitants are more similar to straight married couples when it comes to raising kids. Forty-four percent of opposite-sex cohabitants have children under 18 in the household, as do 47 percent of straight married couples; only 38 percent of lesbian couples and 27 percent of gay men living together do (Elliot and Dye, 2005). In total, there are about 2.2 million children living with two unmarried parents in the United States: Forty-seven percent are White; 30 percent are Hispanic; and 15 percent are Black (U.S. Census Bureau, 2008a).

A lot of research has been conducted on the emotional stability of cohabiting couples. Some research finds that cohabiting women are more prone to depression than married women, especially if there are children involved. Maybe they are more prone to stress because they know that their unions can dissolve more easily than marriages; if they dissolve, there will be no legal means of distributing household resources equitably, and no spousal support after the "divorce." Other research has focused on the effects of cohabitation on marital stability. Twenty-five years ago, researchers found that cohabitation before marriage increased the risk of divorce (Teachman, 2003). Today, researchers find the odds of divorce among women who married their only cohabiting partner are significantly lower than among women who never cohabited before marriage—but they are twice as high for those who cohabit with a romantic partner more than once. The risk seems to be a higher risk of divorce if one cohabits many times or does not cohabit at all (Lichter and Qian, 2008; Teachman, 2003).

Explanations of Nonmarital Choices. Sociologists offer numerous explanations for the increases in delayed marriage, singlehood, and cohabitation. First, these changes are partially explained by new practices, such as courtship and dating. After all, arranged marriages usually take place when the children are younger. But courtship and dating are linked to the worldwide increase in the status of women. While it's true that arranged marriages affected both boys and girls, increased individual choice of marriage partners enables more women to seek educational and economic advancement and rests on increasing choices for women.

Second, these changes tend to be associated with higher levels of education—for both males and females.

Almost half of people 25 to 40 in the United States have cohabited, and 60 percent of all marriages formed in the 1990s began with cohabitation.

Third, these changes are partially explained by changing sexual behaviors and attitudes, especially increased acceptance of "premarital sex." For a long time, sexual activity before marriage was referred to as "premarital" because it was assumed that the couple involved would be in a serious, committed relationship and intend to marry. However, some people engage in sexual relations during a casual dating relationship, when marriage has not yet

Figure 11.3 Married Couple and Unmarried Partner Households

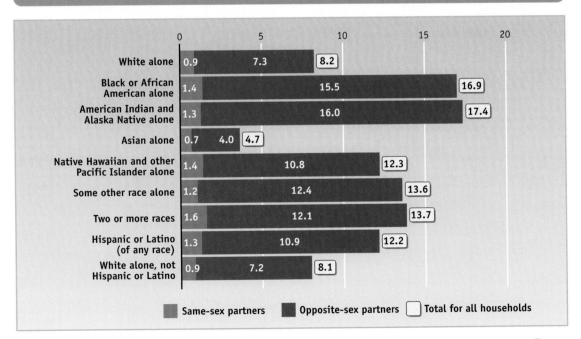

	Same-sex partners	Opposite-sex partners	Total for all households
White alone	0.9	7.3	8.2
Black or African American alone	1.4	15.5	16.9
American Indian and Alaska Native alone	1.3	16.0	17.4
Asian alone	0.7	4.0	4.7
Native Hawaiian and other Pacific Islander alone	1.4	10.8	12.3
Some other race alone	1.2	12.4	13.6
Two or more races	1.6	12.1	13.7
Hispanic or Latino (of any race)	1.3	10.9	12.2
White alone, not Hispanic or Latino	0.9	7.2	8.1

(*Source: Vital Statistics of the United States: Births, Life Expectancy, Deaths, and Selected Health Data,* 2nd ed., Helmut F. Wendel and Christopher S. Wendel, eds. U.S. Databook Series, Bernan Press, 2006.)

Figure 11.4 Acceptance of Interracial Dating

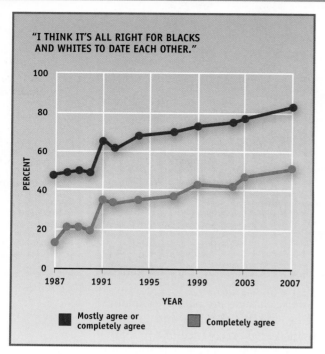

"I THINK IT'S ALL RIGHT FOR BLACKS AND WHITES TO DATE EACH OTHER."

Mostly agree or completely agree

Completely agree

(*Source:* From "Trends in Political Values and Core Attitudes: 1987–2007; Political Landscape More Favorable to Democrats," released March 22, 2007. Reprinted by permission of Pew Research Center for the People and the Press.)

become a topic of discussion. Some view sex as an appropriate conclusion to a first date. Still others "hook up" and don't even go as far as dating. Others never intend to marry, or they lack the right to marry, but they still have sex, sometimes in committed relationships, sometimes not. Therefore, a more precise term might be **nonmarital sex**—sex that is not related to marriage.

In wealthy countries, especially in northern Europe, nonmarital sex has become increasingly acceptable, even during the teen years. These countries provide sex education and health care services aimed at equipping young people to avoid negative consequences of sex by encouraging contraceptive use. In the United States, public attitudes toward nonmarital sex have changed significantly over the past 20 years. In a national survey in the early 1970s, 37 percent of respondents said that nonmarital sex is always wrong. By 1990 this number had fallen to 20 percent (Michael et al., 1994). Today, nearly twice that proportion of adults 18 through 64 say nonmarital births are not or only sometimes wrong (Pew Research Center, 2007). However, attitudes differ by race and ethnicity, (as well as by age). Nearly half (48 percent) of Blacks say premarital sex is al-

ways or almost always wrong, as compared to 38 percent of Whites and 28 percent of Hispanics (Pew Research Center, 2007). Nearly two-thirds of Whites say unmarried couples having children is bad for society, whereas 58 percent of Blacks and 45 percent of Hispanics do (Pew Research Center, 2007). American social and political institutions reflect this complex picture and have changed slowly. As a result, rates of teen pregnancy and sexually transmitted diseases are much lower in Europe than in the United States, although their rates of sexual activity are no higher (Alan Guttmacher Institute, 2008; *Washington Post*, 2006).

Biracial Marriage

Through most of the history of the United States, marriage or sexual relations between men and women of different races were illegal. Not until the Supreme Court's *Loving vs. State of Virginia* decision of 1967 were men and women of different races permitted to marry in all U.S. states.

Social barriers still place dating, courtship, and marriage within clear racial categories. However, interracial marriage is evolving from virtually nonexistent to merely atypical. Today, 5 percent of the population of the United States claims ancestry in two or more races, and 22 percent of Americans have a relative in a mixed-race marriage (Pew Research Center, 2007). Blacks are twice as likely as Whites to have an immediate family member in an interracial marriage, while Hispanics fall in the middle of those two groups. The most common interracial couple in the United States is a White husband married to an Asian wife (14 percent of all interracial couples).

Euro-Americans are least likely to intermarry: Only 3.5 percent of White, non-Hispanic individuals are married to someone of another race. And non-Hispanic Whites, along with people over 65, are less accepting of interracial dating than are African Americans, Hispanics, and younger people of all races (Pew Research Center, 2007; Figure 11.4).

For Black–White couples, the most common pattern (73 percent) is a White woman and an African American man. Among cohabiting couples, there is even a sharper gap: Five times as many Black men live with White women as White men with Black women. Oddly, in the mass media, Black man–White woman couples are almost nonexistent. Instead, we are far more likely to see a White man and a Black woman, like Rose and her husband on *Lost*.

For Asian–White couples, the most common pattern (over 75 percent) is White men and Asian women. The difference is less severe in cohabitation: Twice as many White men are living with Asian women as Asian men living with White women. Asian–Black pairings are rare, but they are even more unbalanced than interracial pairings involving Whites. Black husband–Asian wife patterns outnumber Asian husband–Black wife by 6 to 1.

There is little imbalance among Hispanics. Just under 18 percent of married Hispanic women have non-Hispanic husbands, and just over 15 percent of married Hispanic men have non-Hispanic wives.

Despite the increasing frequency of biracial marriage, many couples still face disapproval—sometimes even from the members of their own families.

Same-Sex Marriage

Same-sex couples have been cohabiting for hundreds of years, although sometimes societal pressures forced them to pretend that they were not couples at all. In the seventeenth and eighteenth centuries, for example, middle-class men often "hired" their working-class partners as valets or servants, so they could live together without question. Sometimes they pretended to be brothers or cousins. In the eighteenth and nineteenth centuries, it was so common for women to spend their lives together that there was a special name for their bonds, "Boston marriages."

To some, gay marriage is an indication that the family is falling apart; to others, that it has never been stronger and more desirable. A very "traditional" church wedding—in a gay and lesbian church.

Recent sociological research allows us to paint a portrait of the typical lesbian or gay couple, at least the ones who are open (all following data are from Ambert, 2005; Bianchi and Casper, 2000; and Black et al., 2000):

They're urban. More than half of lesbian or gay male couples live in just 20 U.S. cities, including "gay meccas" like Los Angeles; San Francisco; Washington, D.C.; New York; and Atlanta.

They're well educated. They tend to have higher educational attainments than men and women in heterosexual marriages.

They are less likely to have children. Nearly half of married couples versus 38 percent of lesbian couples and 27 percent of gay male couples are living with children of their own. Many are the products of previous heterosexual marriages, although artificial insemination and adoption are increasingly common.

They tend to be more egalitarian. They are more likely to share decision making and allot housework more equally than married couples and have less conflict as a result (Allen and Demo, 1995; Carrington, 2002).

And they are not permitted to marry in most of the United States. As of 2009, 29 states had a constitutional amendment restricting marriage to one man and one women, 13 states had a law (not affecting their constitution) restricting marriage to a man and a woman, and the United States is debating a federal constitutional amendment to ban gay marriage (McKinley, 2009). Nineteen states have constitutional amendments that bar gay or lesbian couples from hospital visitation, inheritance, and more than 1,000 other rights that heterosexual couples enjoy (Human Rights Campaign, 2007). As of mid-2009, five states provided the equivalent of state-level spousal rights to gay couples and three states plus Washington, D.C., provided some state-wide spousal rights.

However, reserving marriage and domestic partnerships to men and women applies only in the United States. As of this writing, same-sex couples can marry or enter into civil partnerships with the same rights as heterosexual couples in most European countries and can enter into civil partnerships with most of the same rights as heterosexual couples in nine others, including Brazil, France, Israel, South Africa, and Switzerland.

Parenting

Just as children have never been so important in our cultural values, parents have never been considered so important in the lives of their children. More people have wanted to become parents than ever before, including some who would rarely have considered parenting just 20 or 30 years ago: teenagers, 50-year-olds, gay and lesbian couples, infertile heterosexual couples. Ironically, even though parents are thought to be so utterly decisive in the outcomes of their children's lives, we also seem to believe that it's all hereditary, and socialization plays a very minor role in how our children turn out. Of course, to a sociologist, both sides are true: Parental socialization of children is enormously important, and parents also overvalue their role. The questions, as you've learned in this book, are not whether or not parents are important or biology trumps socialization, but in which arenas and under what circumstances does parental influence make a decisive difference, and does it do this in all groups, around the world?

And while it's true that children have never been so valued and desired, it's equally true that they have never been so undervalued and neglected. Children around the world are facing poor health care, compromised education, and the lack of basic services. In the United States, families get virtually no financial assistance to raise their children, although they receive a lot of advice about having them.

The core relationship of the family has always been between parents and children. Yet today that bond has been both loosened by other forces pulling families apart (like technology and overscheduling) and tightened by ideas that only parents know what is best for their children. It may be the case that the less time parents spend with their children, the more we insist that they spend time together.

Gender and Parenting

Although the majority of women are now working outside the home, numerous studies have confirmed that domestic work remains women's work (Gerstel and Gross, 1995). Most people agree with the statement that housework should be shared equally between both partners, and more men in male–female households are sharing some of the housework and child care, especially when the woman's earnings are essential to family stability (Perry-Jenkins and Crouter, 1990). But still, the women in male–female households do about two-thirds of the housework (Bianchi et al., 2000; Sullivan and Coltrane, 2008). That includes child care: Mothers spend much more time than fathers interacting with their children. They do twice as much of the "custodial" care, the feeding and cleaning of the children (Sullivan and Coltrane, 2008). A survey of American secondary students revealed that 75 percent of girls but only 14 percent of boys who planned to have children thought that they would stop working for awhile, and 28 percent of girls but 73 percent of boys expected their partner to stop working or cut down on work hours (Bagamery, 2004).

Over 5 million women are stay-at-home mothers, staying out of the workforce to care for their children (under the age of 15). However, there are only about 140,000 stay-at-home fathers (U.S. Census Bureau, 2008a). On the other hand, American fathers are more active and involved parents than ever before. Today's new fathers (those between 20 and 35 years old) do far more

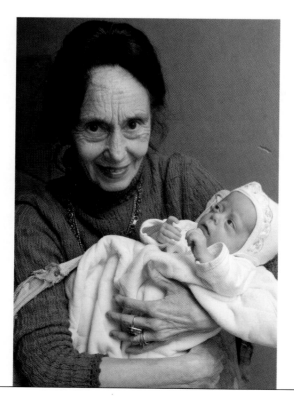

Nurture helps nature: Fertility treatments and in-vitro fertilization has also changed who can become a parent. Here, Professor Adriana Illiecu, 66, the world's oldest mother holds her daughter, Eliza, born in 2005. Eliza was conceived by IVF with donor sperm and eggs. So, although Adriana gave birth to Eliza, she has no genetic relationship to her.

Figure 11.5 Changing Household Composition, 1995 and 2010

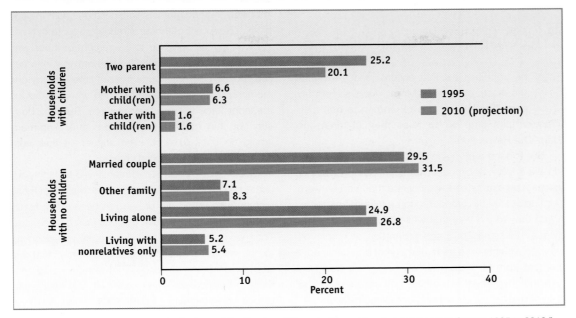

(*Source:* Jennifer Cheeseman Day, "Projections of the Number of Households and Families in the United States: 1995 to 2010." U.S. Bureau of the Census, *Current Population Reports*, Series P-25-1129. Washington, DC: U.S. Government Printing Office, April 1996, p. 11.)

child care than their own fathers did and are willing to decline job opportunities if they include too much travel or overtime (Pleck and Masciadrelli, 2004).

Single-Parent Families

During the first half of the twentieth century, the primary cause of single-parent families was parental death. By the end of the century, most parents were living—but many were living elsewhere. Currently more than 26 percent of children are being raised in single-parent families, the vast majority of them in single-mother households (U.S. Census Bureau, 2008a). Single-parent families have become more common in all demographic groups, but the greatest increases have been among less-educated women and among African American families (Sidel, 2006; U.S. Census Bureau, 2008a). Sometimes the parents are cohabiting, but most often one parent lives elsewhere and does not contribute to the day-to-day emotional and economic support of the child. Sometimes the other parent is not in the picture at all.

Most single parents are not so by choice. The pregnancy may have been an unexpected surprise that prompted the father to leave, or the relationship ended, leaving one parent with custody. Young, unprepared mothers predominate: Nearly 90 percent of teenage mothers are unmarried, but only 12 percent of mothers aged 30 to 44 are unmarried (Childstats.gov, 2009). Teen moms have the highest poverty rate of any demographic group in the United States, and those who do marry are much more likely to get divorced: Fifty percent of women who marry before age 18 are divorced within ten years, as compared with only 20 percent of those who marry at 25 or older (Dubner, 2008). At the same time, an increasing number of women are choosing single motherhood, either through fertility clinics and sperm banks or through adoption. White college-educated women led this trend, many of whom are in professional and managerial jobs (Bock, 2000; DeParle, 1993; Hertz, 2006; Mattes, 1994).

Single mothers predominate both because it is easier for a father to become absent during the pregnancy and because mothers are typically granted custody in court cases. Although mothers predominate, the gender disparity varies from country to country. Among the countries for which data are available, Belgium has the smallest proportion of women who are the single parent ("only" 75 percent—that is, 25 percent of

The Opt-Out Revolution

The popular view that children require round-the-clock care from Mom, not Dad or day care, has led millions of women to quit their jobs or take time off to raise their children—an "Opt-Out Revolution."

But is such a revolution really taking place? How do we know? Sociologist Kathleen Gerson and her colleagues examined the evidence that women were "opting out" of the workforce to be full-time mothers. What they found was that while it was true that between 1998 and 2002, the proportion of employed women with children under the age of one declined 4 percent from 59 percent to 55 percent, it was also true that 72 percent of mothers with children over the age of one are either working or looking for work.

One would expect that highly educated women with high-paying jobs would be the most likely to opt out, because they can afford to, but in fact they are less likely. Among mothers with children under the age of six, 75 percent of those with postgraduate degrees are working, as opposed to 65 percent of those with high school diplomas only. It turns out that one can see "opting out" only if one freezes time—at any one moment, there are, indeed, women who are leaving the labor force to raise their children. But they don't stay out; they go back to work soon after. And many would go back to work even sooner—if their husbands did a little more child care.

Sociologist Pamela Stone interviewed 54 highly educated successful White women, and found that those women who opted out did so not because of family commitments but because of *workplace* experiences. Their workplaces were so inflexible, so unwelcoming to the effort to balance work and family, that the women left. Stone concludes that women would continue to balance work and family—if only their workplaces would let them (Gerson, 2003; Stone, 2007).

single parents are the fathers) with Norway, Sweden, and Finland close behind. Estonia has the largest (95 percent). Those countries in which women's status is higher would tend to have lower percentages of women who are single parents.

Single mothers do not necessarily raise their children single-handedly. They are often interdependent with friends, family, and other members of their social networks, sharing support and care-work (DePaolo and Trimberger, 2008; Hertz, 2006; Hertz and Ferguson, 1998; Trimberger, 2005).

Grandparenting

Your kids grow up and go off to college, and your parenting is done. When they have kids of their own, you are not involved except for birthday cards and occasional visits at Thanksgiving. For good or bad, that's the nuclear family model. For good or bad, it is increasingly inaccurate. The number of grandparents raising their grandchildren has grown from 957,000 in 1970 to more than 1.5 million today. The number of multigenerational families living in grandparents' homes with at least one parent present has grown even more, from 2.4 million in 1970 to 4.3 million today (U.S. Census Bureau, 2009a).

The first group, grandparents raising their grandchildren alone, tends to be African American, living in urban centers, and poor.

Twenty-seven percent of children being raised by grandparents (and 63 percent being raised by grandmothers alone) are living in poverty. They tend to be working full time: Seventy-two percent of grandfathers and 56 percent of grandmothers, as opposed to 33 percent and 24 percent, respectively, who aren't raising their grandchildren.

What happened to the parents? Often the father has abandoned the child, and the mother is incompetent, in prison, or on drugs. Courts are much more likely to grant custody of a child to a blood relative than to a legal stranger. Grandparents can even legally adopt their grandchildren, in effect becoming their parents.

Adoptive Parents

When Angelina Jolie and Madonna each adopted babies from orphanages in Africa, they were ridiculed for trying to save the world one baby at a time. These Hollywood celebrities were not an elite vanguard but latecomers to a well-worn trend in the industrial world. In the United States alone there are 1.7 million adopted children—over 2 percent of all children (U.S. Census Bureau, 2008a; Jones, 2008).

Historically, adoption was considered an option to resolve an unwanted pregnancy—that is, it was about the biological mother. For centuries, all over Europe, foundling hospitals (hospitals that received unwanted newborn babies) enabled mothers to anonymously leave babies at a back door or on the steps, and nuns would find willing families to raise the children as their own. Today, however, the interest has shifted to the adoptive families, as more and more people who want to have children use various services to adopt babies. Adoption has shifted from being about "helping a girl in trouble" to "enabling a loving family to have a child."

There are many different types of adoptions, including:

- *Foster care adoption:* Adoption of children in state care for whom reunification with their birth parents is not feasible for safety or other reasons.

- *Private adoption:* Adoption either through an agency or independent networks.

- *Intercountry adoption (ICA):* Adoption of children from other countries by U.S. citizens. The top three countries for international adoption in 2006 were China (6,500 adoptions), Guatemala (4,135), and Russia (3,706) (U.S. State Department, 2007).

- *Transracial adoption:* Adoption of a child of a different race from the adopting parents; this involves about 10 to 15 percent of all domestic adoptions and the vast majority of ICAs.

Motivations for adoption vary. The couple may be incapable of conceiving a child themselves; they may be infertile or gay. Some single women adopt, while others use assisted reproductive technologies to become pregnant. In some cases, fertile couples adopt because they choose to adopt.

Adoption seems to have largely beneficial effects for all concerned (birth parents, adoptive parents, and adoptees). However, a sizeable minority of birth parents characterize their adoption experiences as traumatic, and many birth parents and adoptees spend significant time trying to locate each other and experience some reunions or closure in their relationships.

The number of adoptions by nonrelatives has declined sharply since 1970. The availability of birth control and legal abortion has meant that fewer women are having unwanted children, and adoption is still stigmatized in the United States; it is seen, as one sociologist put it, as "not quite as good as having your own" (Fisher, 2003).

Not Parenting

Childlessness is becoming increasingly common. In 1976, about 10 percent of women aged 40 to 44 (near the end of their childbearing years) had never conceived a child. According to the U.S. Census Bureau, that percentage has grown to 20 percent (U.S. Census Bureau, 2008). Today one in five women in America is remaining childless throughout her life, twice the proportion of just a generation ago (U.S. Census Bureau, 2007).

Education is an important predictor of childlessness: The more education a woman

Intercountry adoption (ICA) is often also transracial adoption. Pop star Madonna adopted her daughter, Mercy, from Malawi.

Attitudes toward Abortion

A central function of the institution of the family is to produce new members of society. Hence, family planning is a key element of the institution. Whether, and when, to have children is a personal or family decision, yet this decision is informed by societal norms and laws. Let's look at how you and other Americans view abortion and at how attitudes toward abortion have changed or not over time. So, what do you think?

Do you think it should be possible for a pregnant woman to obtain a legal abortion if:

1. The woman's own health is seriously endangered by the pregnancy?

○ Yes   ○ No

2. She is married and does not want any more children?

○ Yes   ○ No

3. The family has a low income and cannot afford any more children?

○ Yes   ○ No

4. She became pregnant as a result of rape?

○ Yes   ○ No

What does **America** think?

(These are the Actual Survey Data from General Social Survey. Reproduced by permission.)

1. In 2004, 86 percent of respondents said, "yes" and 14 percent said "no." These results are almost identical to 1972 responses. The percentage of respondents saying "yes" peaked in 1991 at 91.5 percent.

2. In 2004, 41.8 percent of respondents said "yes" and 58.2 percent said "no." The percentage of people saying "yes" peaked in 1994 at 48 percent, but otherwise, the data were almost identical to 1972, and attitudes have remained pretty steady since then.

3. The responses from 2004 showed 41 percent of respondents saying "yes" and 59 percent saying "no." The response for those saying "yes" was rather lower than 1972 and again peaked in 1994.

4. In 2004, 76.2 percent of respondents said "yes" and 23.8 percent said "no." The response for those saying "yes," was lower than it was in 1972 and peaked in 1991.

References: See Davis et al., page 511.

No Kids Required

A majority of Americans do not believe that children are "very important" for a successful marriage. In a survey in 2007, only 41 percent agreed, down 24 percent from 1990. The biggest increase in what is very important? Sharing household chores, up 15 percent (Pew Research Center, 2007).

Did You Know?

has, the more likely she is to bear no children. The proportion of childless women with graduate or professional degrees is about one in four; for those with a high school diploma, it's less than one in six (U.S. Census Bureau, 2007). The longer women put off children, the more likely they are to opt out of having children altogether, perhaps because they become accustomed to a child-free lifestyle. The U.S. trend toward later childbearing and the growing propor-tion of childless women are in tune with patterns across developed countries (Pilkington, 2008).

Race is also significant: White women are the most likely to be childless, at 23 percent; Hispanic women are the least likely to remain childless, at only 14 percent. (The number of children a Hispanic woman has, however, decreases sharply depending on how many generations her family has lived in the United States.) Sixteen percent of Black women and 18 percent of Asian American women are childless (U.S. Census Bureau, 2007). However, people have many reasons for remaining "child-free by choice," from concern about overpopulation to a desire to concentrate on their career to just not liking children or feeling they were not important to a happy marriage. In one study, women said they enjoyed the freedom and sponta-neity in their lives, while some others gave financial considerations, worries about stress, relationships too fragile to withstand children, being housebound, and diminished career opportunities. Men usually cite more practical considerations, including commitment to career and concern about the financial burden (Arnoldi, 2007; Gerson, 1985; Lunneborg, 1999; Scott, 2009).

Family Transitions

Through most of European and American history, marriage was a lifelong commitment, period. Divorce and remarriage were impossible. Though couples could live separately and find legal loopholes to avoid inheritance laws, they could never marry anyone else. In the sixteenth century, the English King Henry VIII had to behead two wives, divorce two others, found a new church (the Anglican Church), and close all the monasteries in England to get out of marriages he didn't like. Today, it's a little bit easier.

Divorce is the legal dissolution of a marriage. Grounds for divorce may vary from "no-fault" divorces, in which one party files for divorce, to those divorces that require some "fault" on the part of one spouse or the other (adultery, alienation of affection, or some other reason). Divorces are decrees that dissolve a marriage; they do not dissolve the family. Parents must still work out custody arrangements of children, alimony payments, child support. Just because they are no longer husband and wife does not mean they are no longer Mommy and Daddy.

In the United States, the divorce rate rose steadily from the 1890s through the 1970s (with a dip in the Depression and a spike after World War II). During the past 25 years, it has fallen significantly, along with marriage rates overall. The annual national divorce rate is at its lowest since 1970, while marriage is down 30 percent and the number of unmarried couples living together is up tenfold since 1960 ("The State of Divorce," 2007).

These trends are led by the middle class. At the lower end of the scale, however, the picture is reversed, leading some sociologists to describe a "divorce divide" based on class and race (Martin, 2006; see Figure 11.6).

Whatever these different sociological dimensions, some commentators broadly blame divorce for nearly every social ill, from prostitution (where else are divorced men to turn?) to serial murder (evidently watching their parents break up has kids reaching for the nearest pickax). More moderate voices worry that quick and easy divorce undermines the institution of the family, forcing the divorced adults to start courting again when they should be engaged in child rearing and teaching children that dysfunction is the norm.

Sociologists understand that both statements are, at least, partially true. Some people believe that the easy availability of divorce weakens our belief in the institution of marriage. On the other hand, sociologists often counter that divorce makes families stronger by allowing an escape from damaging environments and enabling both parents and children to adapt to new types of relationships.

Who usually wants the divorce? On the average, men become more content with their marriages over time, while women become less content; the wife is usually the one who wants out. A study of divorces that occurred after age 40 found that wives initiated two-thirds of them (Coontz, 2005).

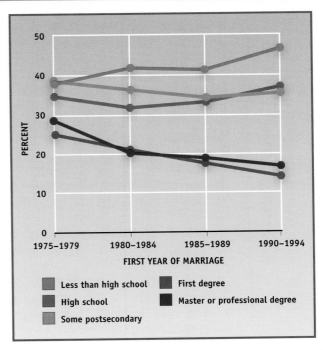

Figure 11.6 More Education, Less Divorce

Less than high school
High school
Some postsecondary
First degree
Master or professional degree

(*Source:* Adapted from "Trends in Marital Dissolution by Women's Education in the United States," by Steven P. Martin, *Demographic Research*, December 13, 2006, Vol. 15, #20, pp. 537–560, © 2006 Steven P. Martin. Reprinted by permission.)

Instant Divorce

Does religion "cause" divorce? It's a silly question, right? It's true, though, that aside from Nevada, the state that is the home of the "instant divorce," the states that have the highest divorce rates are those in the Bible Belt. The average divorce rate in the United States is 4.2 for every thousand people. The states with the highest rates were Nevada, Tennessee, Arkansas, Alabama, Oklahoma, New Hampshire, Wyoming, Idaho, Kentucky, and Arizona. Those states with the lowest rates were in the northeast: Connecticut, Massachusetts, New Jersey, New York, and Maryland.

How would a sociologist explain this? First, divorce varies with income: Lower-income people have significantly higher divorce rates than wealthier people. (This makes sense: Higher income shields you from greater money problems, and lower rates of money worries means lower marital conflict.) The states with the highest divorce rates also have the lowest household incomes.

Does religion play a role? Yes, to a degree. The states with the lowest divorce rates have the highest percentages of Catholics and Jews and the lowest percentages of evangelical Protestants. Jews have very low divorce rates, and Catholics have a lower rate than Protestants because they are, technically, prohibited from getting a divorce.

It's also true that the likelihood of divorce increases as the age of marriage decreases: The younger you are, the more likely is divorce. And those states have lower ages of marriage—in part because they also are states that mandate abstinence-only sex education, which means they have the highest rates of teen pregnancy and therefore so-called "shotgun" marriages (Bryner, 2009).

Overall, if you want to get divorced, you can increase your chances significantly by living in a Southern state, being poor, evangelical, taking an abstinence pledge, and getting married young.

After Divorce

Married couples opt for divorce for all sorts of reasons, and the divorce itself can be easy or hard, so it is understandable that research on the impact of divorce on the husband and wife is mixed. Some studies find that people are happier after their divorce than before (Wilson and Oswald, 2005). Others find psychological scars that never heal unless the divorcees remarry (Johnson and Wu, 2002). Still others find that individual attitudes make the difference in well-being after a divorce (Amato and Sobolewski, 2001; Wood, Goesling, and Avellar, 2007).

"His" and "Her" Divorces. In the 1960s, sociologist Jessie Bernard found that "there are two marriages, his and hers—and his is better than hers." The same is true for divorce. There are differences between men's and women's divorce, and, in general, his is better than hers. In a large majority of divorces, women's standards of living decline, while men's go up. Those men who are used to being the primary breadwinner may suddenly find that they are supporting one (plus a small amount for child support) on a salary that used to support the whole family. Those women who are more accustomed to being in charge of the house-

hold, with a secondary, part-time, or even no job, may suddenly find that their income must stretch from being a helpful supplement to supplying most of the family's necessities.

It is crucial to remember that the breadwinning husband with an income-supplementing a stay-at-home wife has rarely been an option for many minority families. Black women, for example, have a longer history of workforce participation than women of other races (Page and Stevens, 2005). Divorce plays an even bigger economic role for Black households than for Whites in the United States, partly because of this difference. While family income for Whites falls about 30 percent during the first 2 years of divorce, it falls by 53 percent for Blacks (Page and Stevens, 2005). Three or more years after divorce, White households recoup about one-third of the lost income, but the income of Black families barely improves. This may have to do with the fact that when divorce occurs, the probability of Black mothers working does not change, while recently divorced White women have an 18 percent greater probability of working (Page and Stevens, 2005).

Children of Divorce. After a divorce, children of all races and ethnicities are still more likely to live with the mother, while the father visits

United States Is World Leader in Divorce

The United States has the highest divorce rate in the world.

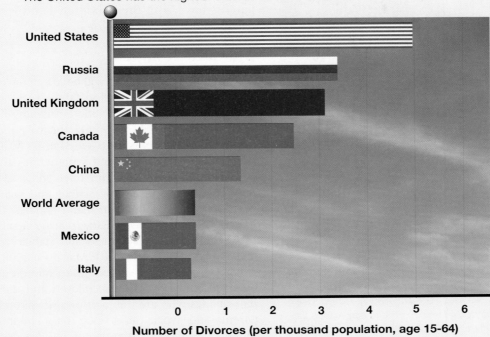

Number of Divorces (per thousand population, age 15-64)

1. Why does the divorce rate vary so much? What holds families together, and what pulls them apart?

2. Does "reform" mean making divorce harder to obtain or strengthening marriage? Or is it "both/and"?

Source: www.nationmaster.com, accessed May 8, 2009. Reprinted by permission.

on specified days or weeks. Not only do the children have to handle this new living situation, but many will soon move to a new home, enroll in a new school, and face the stress and depression of a mother who has suddenly entered or reentered the workforce as the primary breadwinner. And that's when the divorce is amicable. At times there is open hostility between the mother and father, with each telling the children how horrible the other is or even trying to acquire full custody, with many potential negative outcomes (Coontz, 1988).

Psychologist Judith Wallerstein (2000) studied 131 children of 60 couples from affluent Marin County, California, who divorced in 1971. She followed these children through adolescence and into adulthood, when many married and became parents of their own. She found a sleeper effect: Years later, their parents' divorce is affecting the children's relationships. They fear that their relationships will fail, fear betrayal, and, most significantly, fear any change at all. Divorce, she argued, was bad for children—both immediately and later in their lives. Couples, politicians argued, should, indeed, stay together, "for the sake of the children."

However, Wallerstein's findings have been quite controversial—and, in fact, have been disconfirmed by most sociological studies. After all, Wallerstein studied only children who came to see her as a therapist—that is, she based her findings on those children who were already having difficulties *before their parents divorced.* And she studied children only in wealthy ultraliberal Marin County, California. She attributed their subsequent problems in relationships to their parents' divorce, when it is just as plausible that it was the conflict between the parents that led to both the divorce *and* the children's problems. Staying together might have been the worst imaginable outcome.

Sociological research consistently finds that children are resilient and adapt successfully to their parents' divorces. Mavis Hetherington (2002), for example, studied more than 2,500 children from 1,400 families over a period of 30 years and found that

> ### Divorce in the 1950s
>
> Aside from a huge spike in divorce immediately after World War II, divorce rates in the 1950s were higher than in any previous decade except the Depression. Almost one in three marriages formed in the 1950s eventually ended in divorce (Coontz, 2005).

Did You Know?

Divorce is rarely a "pleasant" experience, but its impact varies significantly by race, gender, and class. Women's standard of living declines more sharply than men's (which may even rise). Poor and minority women's standards of living decline even more, and they recoup that lost income more slowly than White women do—if at all.

the fear of a devastating effect of divorce on children is exaggerated, with 75 to 80 percent of children coping reasonably well. Other scholars agree that, although parental divorce increases the risk of psychological distress and relationship problems in adulthood, the risks are not great (Amato, 2003; see also Ahrons, 2004).

Perhaps the outcome of divorce depends less on whether one gets a divorce and more on how civilly the parents behave toward each other and how much ongoing investment they maintain in their children's lives. That is to say, what's better for children is explained less well by whether the parents are married or divorced and better by the quality of the relationships the parents have with their children—and with each other.

Blended Families

At least half of all children will have a divorced and remarried parent before they turn 18 (Ahrons, 2004). They face different issues, depending on how old they are, the role that their biological parents have, whether it's Mom or Dad who remarries, and whether it's the custodial parent. Usually they must adjust to a new residence and a new school and share space with new siblings. In many families, finances become a divisive issue, placing significant strains on the closeness and stability of blended families (Korn, 2001; Martinez, 2005). Several studies have found that children in blended families—both stepchildren and their half-siblings who are the joint product of both parents—do worse in school than children raised in traditional two-parent families (see Ginther, 2004). Boys tend to have a more difficult time coping with half- or stepsiblings than girls do (Tillman, 2008).

While the dynamics of blended families tend to be similar across class and race, the likelihood of blending families tends to be far more common among the middle classes, where parents have sufficient resources to support these suddenly larger families. Lower-class families may be "blended" in all but name: They may cohabit with other people's children but not formalize it by marrying.

Violence in Families

The famous French sociologist Alexis de Tocqueville spoke of the family as a "haven in a heartless world," but for some the family is a violent nightmare. In many families, the person who promised to love and honor you is the most likely to physically assault you; the one who promised to "forsake all others" is also the most likely to rape you; and the one who is supposed to protect you from harm is the one most likely to cause that harm.

Intimate Partner Violence

Intimate partner violence (IPV) represents violence, lethal or nonlethal, experienced by a spouse, ex-spouse, or cohabiting partner; boyfriend or girlfriend; or ex-boyfriend or exgirlfriend. It is commonly called "domestic violence," but because some does not occur in the home, IPV is the preferred term. IPV is the single major cause of injury to women in the United

States. Women experience nearly 5 million intimate partner–related physical assaults each year, according to the Centers for Disease Control (CDC, 2006). IPV represents more than 21 percent of all nonfatal violent assaults on females aged 12 and over and 30 percent of all homicides against women and girls (U.S. Department of Health and Human Services, 2008).

IPV is more common among the poor—women in households with annual incomes below $7,500 have the highest rates of IPV—and the young: Women aged 20 through 24 have the highest rates, followed by women aged 25 through 34. Young women are also more likely to suffer dating assaults: One in 11 American adolescents reports being a victim of dating violence, with one in five high school girls reporting being physically or sexually abused by a dating partner (CDC, 2006). Dating violence is most prevalent among Black adolescents (14 percent), followed by 9 percent for Hispanics and 7 percent for Whites (CDC, 2006).

Globally, the problem of family violence is widespread. A study released in 2006 by the World Health Organization found that rates of IPV ranged from a low of 15 percent of women in Japan to a high of 71 percent of women in rural Ethiopia. (Rates in the European Union and United States were between 20 and 25 percent.) In six of the 15 sites of study, at least 50 percent of the women had been subjected to moderate or severe violence in the home at some point.

Perhaps more telling, the majority of the 25,000 women interviewed in the study said that it was the first time they had ever spoken of the abuse to anyone (García-Moreno et al., 2006).

In the United States, IPV knows no class, racial, or ethnic bounds. Yet there are some differences by race and ethnicity, as well as class and age. Native American women experience the highest rate of intimate partner violence, followed by Black women; Asian women are least likely to be victims of IPV (U.S. Department of Health and Human Services, 2008) (see Figure 11.7).

Black females experienced domestic violence at a rate 35 percent higher than that of White females, and Black males experienced domestic violence at a rate about 62 percent higher than that of White males (Rennison and Welchans, 2000).

Among Latinos the evidence is contradictory: One study found significantly less violence in Latino families than in Anglo families, while another found a slightly higher rate. Rates were directly related to two factors, the strains of immigrant status and the variations in ideologies of male dominance (Klevens, 2007).

In many cases, however, these racial and ethnic differences disappear when social class is taken into account. Sociologist Noel Cazenave examined the same National Family Violence Survey and found that Blacks had *lower* rates of wife abuse than Whites in three of four income categories—the two highest

Figure 11.7 Intimate Partner Violence among Females by Race/Ethnicity and Age

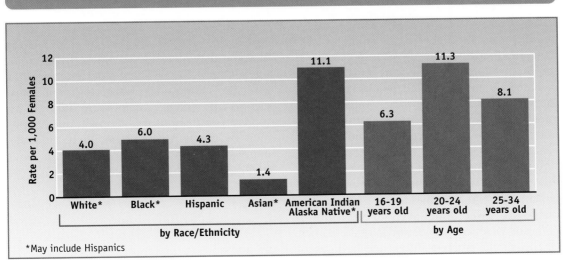

(*Source:* U.S. Department of Health and Human Services, Health Resources and Services Administration, Maternal and Child Health Bureau. *Women's Health 2008.* Rockville, MD: U.S. Department of Health and Human Services, 2008.)

How do we know what we know?

Gender Symmetry in IPV

Despite dramatic gender differences, there are some researchers and political pundits who claim that there is "gender symmetry" in domestic violence—that rates of domestic violence are roughly equal by gender (see, for example, Brott, 1994). One reason this symmetry is underreported is because men who are victims of domestic violence are so ashamed they are unlikely to come forward—a psychological problem that one researcher calls "the battered husband syndrome" (Steinmetz, 1978).

But a close look at the data suggests why these findings are so discordant with the official studies by the Department of Justice and the FBI. Those studies that find gender symmetry rely on the "conflict tactics scale" (CTS) developed by family violence researcher and sociologist Murray Straus and his colleagues over 30 years. The CTS asked couples if they had ever, during the course of their relationship, hit their partner. An equal number of women and men answered "yes." The number changed dramatically, though, when they were asked who initiated the violence (was it offensive or defensive?), how severe it was (did she push him before or after he'd broken her jaw?), and how often the violence occurred. When these three questions were posed, the results shifted back: The amount, frequency, severity, and consistency of violence against women are far greater than anything done by women to men.

There were several other problems with the CTS as a measure (see Kimmel, 2002). These problems included:

1. *Whom did they ask?* Studies that found comparable rates of domestic violence asked only one partner about the incident. But studies in which both partners were interviewed separately found large discrepancies between reports from women and from men.
2. *What was the time frame?* Studies that found symmetry asked about incidents that occurred in a single year, thus equating a single slap with a reign of domestic terror that may have lasted decades.
3. *Was the couple together?* Studies that found gender symmetry excluded couples that were separated or divorced, although violence against women increases dramatically after separation.
4. *What was the reason for the violence?* Studies that find symmetry do not distinguish between offensive and defensive violence, equating a vicious assault with a woman hitting her husband to get him to stop hitting the children.
5. *Was "sex" involved?* Studies that find symmetry omit marital rape and sexual aggression; because a significant amount of IPV occurs when one partner doesn't want to have sex, this would dramatically change the data.

Of course, women can be—and are—violent toward their husbands and partners. Criminologists Martin Schwartz and Walter DeKeseredy estimate that women commit as much as 3 to 4 percent of all spousal violence (Schwartz and DeKeseredy, 2008). But research such as this requires that we look more deeply at the questions asked. Sometimes, the answers are contained in the questions.

and the lowest. Higher rates among Blacks were reported only by those respondents in the $6,000 to $11,999 income range (which included 40 percent of all Blacks surveyed). Income and residence (urban) were also the variables that explained virtually all the ethnic differences between Latinos and Anglos (Cazenave and Strauss, 1979; Leeder, 2006).

Gay men and lesbians can engage in IPV as well. A recent informal survey of gay victims of violence in six major cities found that gay men and lesbians were more likely to be victims of domestic violence than of antigay hate crimes.

The single greatest difference in rates of IPV is by gender. According to the Bureau of Justice Statistics, 75–85 percent of all victims of domestic violence are women (CDC, 2006; see Kimmel, 2002). The gender imbalance of intimate violence is staggering. Of those victims of violence who were injured by spouses or ex-spouses, women outnumber men by about nine to one. Eight times as many women were injured by their boyfriends as men injured by girlfriends.

Family Violence between Generations

In addition to violence between domestic partners, there is also a significant amount of intergenerational and intragenerational violence in families. Intergenerational violence refers to violence between generations, such as parents to children and children to parents. Intragenerational violence refers to violence within the same generation—that is, sibling violence.

Sibling Violence. Sibling violence goes beyond routine sibling rivalry. Earlier reports found that as many as 80 percent of American children had engaged in an act of physical violence toward a sibling (Straus and Gelles, 1990). In a recent sociological study, David Finkelhor and his colleagues (2006) found that 35 percent of all children had been attacked by a sibling in the previous year. Of these, more than a third were serious attacks.

The consequences of sibling violence can be severe. Children who were repeatedly attacked were twice as likely to show symptoms of trauma, anxiety, and depression, including sleeplessness, crying spells, thoughts of suicide, and fear of the dark (Butler, 2006). Finkelhor and his colleagues found that attacks did not differ by class or race or even by gender, although boys were slightly more likely to be victims than girls. They occurred most frequently on siblings aged 6 to 12 and gradually tapered off as the child entered adolescence.

Sometimes, children use violence against their parents. About 18 percent of children used violence against their parents in the past year—about half of which was considered "nontrivial," serious enough to cause pain or injury (Agnew and Huguley, 1989; Cornell and Gelles, 1982; Straus, Gelles, and Steinmetz, 1980). Rates of child-to-parent violence decrease as the child ages; it is more often younger children who hit their parents. Injuries to parents are rare, but they do happen. If the parent reacts to a child's violence with violence, the child has learned a lesson that could last a lifetime.

Elder Abuse. A significant amount of family violence occurs towards the elderly. The term *elder abuse* was coined in 1988 by a Congressional Committee investigating the problem. Elder abuse consists of physical, sexual, psychological, and financial abuse and neglect. It is estimated that about 3.5 percent of the nation's 39 million Americans over age 65 have experienced one or more of these forms of elder abuse (National Center on Elder Abuse, 2006).

About one-fifth of elder abuse involves neglect by caregivers; 15 percent consists of emotional, psychological, or verbal abuse, and another 15 percent involves financial abuse. Only 1 percent involves sexual exploitation. Two-thirds of victims of elder abuse are female, and just over half of the abusers are female as well. This seems to be the result of different life-expectancy rates for women and men; because women outlive men, they are more likely to be victimized. And women are more likely to be the caretakers of the elderly as well.

Because the elderly often have smaller support systems and fewer resources, the impact of the abuse is magnified. Like young children, they are more vulnerable and dependent, and sometimes a single incident is enough to trigger a downward spiral to serious illness, depression, or despair (Burgess and Hanrahan, 2006).

Child Abuse. The rates of parental violence against children are significantly more serious. In recent years, American society has also been vitally concerned about the problem of child abuse (violence against children) and child sexual abuse (the sexual exploitation of children).

According to the Department of Health and Human Services, rates of victimization and the number of victims have been decreasing in the first decade of the twenty-first century. An estimated 872,000 children were determined to be victims of child abuse or neglect for 2004 (the last year for which there are data). More than 60 percent of child victims were neglected by their parents or other caregivers. The United States has rates that are significantly higher than rates in other English-speaking countries such as Australia, Canada, and Great Britain, partly, but not entirely, due to the higher rates of child poverty in the

Elder Abuse at Home

Although we often fear that placing the elderly in retirement homes and elder-care facilities increases their risk of elder abuse, the majority of cases occur in their homes and by their families. In the most recent survey of more than 565,000 cases of reported elder abuse, only 16 percent of perpetrators were strangers. One-third was adult children; 22 percent were other family members, and 11 percent were spouses or intimate partners (National Center for Victims of Crime, 2009).

Did You Know?

United States (poverty is a significant risk factor).

Rates of child abuse and child sexual abuse vary significantly by class but less by race or ethnicity. According to some research (Daly and Wilson, 1981), living with a stepparent significantly increases the risk of both abuse and sexual abuse. Yet other research, using the conflict tactics scale, found little difference—in generally very high rates overall. In one study, 63 percent of children who lived with both genetic parents, 47 percent of those who lived with a stepparent, and 60 percent of those who lived with a foster parent were subject to violence, and about 10 percent were subjected to severe violence in all three categories (Gelles and Harrop, 1991).

Globally, the problem of child abuse and neglect is equally serious—and includes forms of abuse that are not found in the economic North. In 2006, the United Nations commissioned the first global investigation into child abuse. They found that between 80 and 98 percent of children suffer physical punishment in their homes, with a third or more experiencing severe physical punishment resulting from the use of implements.

Despite these global differences, it is equally true that Americans are far more accepting of violence against children than they may realize. Over half of all American parents (55 percent) believe that corporal punishment, including spanking, is acceptable; and one-third of parents have used corporal punishment against their adolescents (Straus, 2005). These numbers are significantly less than the 94 percent who supported the use of corporal punishment in 1968 and the two-thirds who used it with adolescents in 1975 (Straus, 2005). But it is still the case that nearly all parents—94 percent—used corporal punishment with toddlers, and they did so, on average, three times a week.

Corporal punishment—typically, "paddling," which is hitting with a hard, wooden paddle measuring a foot and a half long—is also quite prevalent in U.S. schools. It is legal in 21 states, and the U.S. Department of Education reported that more than 223,000 students nationwide received corporal punishment at least once during the 2006–2007 academic year (Human Rights Watch, 2008).

Corporal punishment disproportionately affects African American students and, in some areas, Native American students. In the 2006–2007 school year, African American students made up 17.1 percent of the nationwide student population but 35.6 percent of those paddled. In the same year, in the 13 states with the highest rates of paddling, 1.4 times as many African American students were paddled as might be expected given their percentage of the student population. Although girls of all races were paddled less than boys, African American girls were nonetheless physically punished at more than twice the rate of their White counterparts in those 13 states during this period. Special education students—students with mental or physical disabilities—also receive corporal punishment at disproportionate rates (HRW, 2008).

There is actually little empirical evidence that spanking serves any developmental purpose, but there is a wealth of evidence that spanking is developmentally harmful. The American Academy of Pediatrics recommends that parents avoid spanking (2007). In fact, 94 percent of all studies of the effects of corporal punishment on children showed a relationship between such forms of punishment and aggression, delinquency in childhood, crime and antisocial behavior as an adult, low levels of empathy or conscience, poor parent–child relations, and mental health problems such as depression (Gershoff, 2002; HRW, 2008).

Family violence is often difficult to remedy through policy initiatives. Globally, fewer than 10 percent of all countries even have laws against certain forms of child abuse, let alone programs to offer aid and support to victims and to prosecute perpetrators (*Rights of the Child,* 2006). In the United States, policymakers have long taken the approach that what happens "behind closed doors" is a private matter, not a social problem that can be remedied through public policy. Rates of all forms of family violence are dramatically underreported; fear of retaliation, shame, and a general cultural acceptance of violence all greatly reduce the likelihood of reporting. And the continuum of violence, from spanking a child to murdering a spouse, is part of a culture that does not universally condemn violence but sees some instances of violence as legitimate and even appropriate and sees perpetrators as entitled to use violence.

The Family in the Twenty-First Century: "The Same as It Ever Was"

In the first line of his novel *Anna Karenina*, the great Russian novelist Leo Tolstoy wrote, "Happy families are all alike; every unhappy family is unhappy in its own way." How unsociological! Families, happy or unhappy, are as varied as snowflakes when viewed close up and as similar around the world as all the sand in the desert.

Families are as old as the human species. We've always had them; indeed we couldn't live without them. And families have always been changing, adapting to new political, social, economic, and environmental situations. Some expectations of family may be timeless, yet families have always been different, and new relationships, arrangements, and patterns are emerging all over the world today, just as they always have been. As the musician David Byrne sang in the 1980s, the family is "the same as it ever was."

Yes, it's probably true that family is still the place where, when we go there, they have to take us in. But even if we can go home again, it's never the same.

Chapter Review

1. The Family Tree

The family is changing as social structures change, which is alarming and yet causes nostalgia, even as alternatives develop; but it has changed before. Unlike premodern families, we move from our **family of origin** to a separate residence with our **family of procreation. Family** is more than a nuclear family, including **kinship systems** traced by **matrilineal descent, patrilineal descent,** and **bilateral descent.** Families serve many social functions, including care of the children and economic transfer by establishing **legitimacy,** as well as regulation of sexual activity and procreation through variations besides **monogamy,** including **polygamy, polygyny, polyandry,** and even **group marriage. Exogamy** is the one constant. The nuclear family is a recent phenomenon. The **extended family** was the norm before the modern era. Before **companionate marriage,** spouses were selected by parents to solidify family position. The role of marriage and of spouses and children within the marriage changed in the modern era, moving from a practical unit of economic production to an isolated nuclear unit organized around emotional connection.

family of origin A child's biological parents or others who are responsible for his or her upbringing. (p. 322)

family of procreation The family one creates through marriage or cohabitation with a romantic partner. Today, we consider any adults you are living with as a family of procreation, even if none of them is actually doing any procreating. (p. 322)

family The basic unit in society, it traditionally consists of two parents rearing their children but may also be any of various social units differing from but regarded as equivalent to the traditional family, such as single parents with children, spouses without children, and several generations living together. (p. 323)

kinship systems Social systems that locate individuals by reference to their families, that is, by common biological ancestry, legal marriage, or adoption. (p. 323)

matrilineal descent Tracing one's ancestry through the mother, her mother, and so on. (p. 323)

patrilineal descent Tracing one's ancestry through the father, his father, and so on. (p. 323)

bilateral descent Tracing one's ancestry through both parents, rather than only the mother (*see matrilineal*) or only the father (*see patrilineal*). (p. 323)

legitimacy Social arrangements that ensure men know what children they have produced (women usually know). Families then bear the economic and emotional burden of raising only the children that belong to them. (p. 323)

monogamy The most common arrangement; marriage between two people. Most monogamous societies allow men and women to marry each other because it takes one of each to make a baby, but same-sex monogamy is surprisingly common. (p. 323)

polygamy Marriage between three or more people. (*See* polyandry and polygyny.) (p. 324)

polygyny The most common form of polygamy, a marriage between one man and two or more women. (p. 324)

polyandry Rare form of polygamy in which one woman marries two or more men. (p. 324)

group marriage Rare marriage arrangement in which two or more men marry two or more women, with children born to anyone in the union "belonging" to all of the partners equally. (p. 324)

exogamy The insistence that marriage to (or sex with) members of your family unit is forbidden. This is the incest taboo, which Sigmund Freud argued was the one single cultural universal. (p. 324)

extended family The most common model in the premodern era, the family model in which two or three generations lived under the same roof or at least in the same compound: grandparents, parents, unmarried uncles and aunts, married uncles and aunts, sisters, brothers, cousins, and all of their children. (p. 325)

companionate marriage The (comparatively recent) idea that people should select their own marriage partner based on compatibility and mutual attraction. (p. 326)

2. Family and Ethnicity

Family structures varying by ethnicity, culture, and class are often adaptations resulting from historical circumstance. The American nuclear family changed from ethnic origins to small isolated nuclear families as a result of social planning. Native American families differed by tribe but were typically extended families, with kinship obligations important for survival. Many were matrilineal. When African American families in America were separated by slave owners, slaves created kinship networks. Most African American families are female-headed single-parent households, with "fictive kinships" as supportive ties of obligation and assistance. Asian American families are often collectivist, hierarchical rather than democratic, and based on traditional Confucian principles of familial obligation and honor, obedience, and respect. Hispanic families vary greatly, depending on country of origin. Length of residence increases egalitarianism, with upward social mobility. Like all ethnic variations, the further from the original culture, the more families resemble other American families.

3. Forming Families

Historically, families selected mates for children who had little say in the matter. Courtship is a recent development. Children of immigrants raised in coed high schools distanced themselves from tradition by dating. Peers became important in rating and dating, and courtship became ritualized, with specific steps leading to marriage. Today hookups often replace dating in college. In less developed parts of the world, arranged marriages persist, and girls are married off at early ages; but, in the developed world, we are increasingly marrying late, as there are alternatives to marriage, including being paired in **cohabitation,** and greater acceptability of **nonmarital sex,** with more people remaining single. Although marriage is decreasing, for many, family structures are changing in other ways. **Multigenerational households** are on the rise, with grandparents increasingly present to raise children. Biracial couples are more common; and, in many parts of the world, and increasingly in America, same-sex unions are legal.

cohabitation Once called "shacking up" or "living in sin," now more often called just "living together," the sociological term for people who are in a romantic relationship but not married living in the same residence. (p. 333)

nonmarital sex Sexual relations outside marriage. (p. 336)

multigenerational households Adults of more than one generation sharing a domestic space. (p. 332)

4. Parenting

Women do the majority of child care as well as the housework, but men are increasingly involved as parents. Often both parents work. More than a quarter of all children are raised in single-parent homes, most female headed, with the majority unmarried teen mothers; but some older well-educated women are choosing to become single parents. Two percent of American children are adopted, many from overseas. An increasing number of women, particularly well-educated older women, are opting out of childbirth.

5. Family Transitions

Like most things, divorce rates vary. Jews and Catholics are less likely to divorce, as are the wealthy, who experience less stress and marital discord due to their wealth. Those who marry very young are more likely to divorce. Women and children typically become poorer with divorce; minorities suffer a greater long-term cost. The transitions resulting from divorce can be difficult, as can adjusting to the blended families that often result; but children are resilient, and most adjust relatively well.

6. Violence in Families

Intimate partner violence (IPV) is the leading cause of injury to women and is more common among young poor women, often including dating violence. Although women are by far the most common victims, men, particularly gay men, suffer, as well. Violence also occurs between and across generations in families. Sibling violence, which occurs most between ages of 6 and 12, has severe consequences and does not vary by gender, race, or class. Elder abuse occurs most often in the home, by family members. Child abuse is epidemic globally, and often legal, and even in the United States it is tacitly accepted.

intimate partner violence (IPV) Violence, lethal or nonlethal, experienced by a spouse, ex-spouse, or cohabiting partner; boyfriend or girlfriend; or ex-boyfriend or ex-girlfriend. It is commonly called "domestic violence," but because some does not occur in the home, IPV is the preferred term. (p. 346)

7. The Family in the Twenty-First Century: "The Same as It Ever Was"

Families vary across time and place, and the one constant seems to be that families change. Though we worry about the family vanishing, or changing, and hold in our mind an image of what a family is, or should be, the fact is that families do continue, but in new, emerging forms, just as they always have.

Self-Test: Check Your Understanding

1. According to the text, historically, families served as which of the following?
   a. Production units
   b. Consumption units
   c. Emotional support
   d. All of the above are historical functions of the family.
2. Historically the most common family arrangement has been the
   a. fictive kinship.
   b. nuclear family.
   c. extended family.
   d. group marriage.
3. The term for the requirement that people marry outside their own family is
   a. polyandry.
   b. exogamy.
   c. legitimacy.
   d. polygamy.
4. Mutual ties of obligation and support among non–blood relations that develop in poor communities are referred to as:
   a. honorary aunties.
   b. blood brothers.

   c. godparents.
   d. fictive kinship.
5. Which of the following is not declining in incidence?
   a. Marriage
   b. Childbirth
   c. Single-parent households
   d. All of these are in decline.
6. Globally, attitudes toward same-sex marriage are
   a. largely unknown, due to taboos.
   b. becoming more restrictive.
   c. becoming more accepting.
   d. remaining unchanged.
7. The nuclear family emerged as a result of
   a. industrialization.
   b. birth control.
   c. Social Security.
   d. immigration.
8. In modern society, the role of the family is
   a. production.
   b. consumption.
   c. emotional support.
   d. procreation.

Self-Test Answers: 1. b, 2. c, 3. b, 4. d, 5. c, 6 .c, 7. a, 8. c

Integrate and Explore: Points to Consider

1. Compare the functions or roles family has served historically with the roles or functions family serves today. In which places are these historical functions still served primarily by family? What factors relate to changes in the family? How do families today meet the needs once met by the family in other eras?
2. How does the number of children, number of parents in the household, or likelihood of marriage vary by race, ethnicity, religion, or social class? Are there any trends or changes in family structure occurring across these social categories?

succeed with mysoclab PEARSON

Self-scoring practice tests, flashcards for learning key terms, streaming audio of the entire text, and multimedia, including:

Watch—*Marriage in India*
Explore—*Census Marriage Data*
Map—Social Explorer: *The Increase of Single Women with Children*
MySocLibrary—Stephanie Coontz, *The Way We Weren't: The Myth and Reality of the "Traditional Family"*
MySocLibrary—Lisa E. Phillips, *Love American Style*

Economy and Work

Americans spend an average of 1,804 hours per year working. That's 200 hours more than in France or Sweden, over 300 more than in Germany, but 550 hours less than Korea (OECD, 2007a). An American who works full-time from age 18 to age 65, with three weeks off for vacations and holidays each year, will spend about 91,000 hours doing things that are more likely to be boring, degrading, and physically exhausting than they are fun, interesting, and exciting. Why do we do it? It depends on whom you ask.

Ask a janitor or a sales clerk, and you are likely to hear: *for the money*. No one gets a free ride: Food, clothing, and shelter all come with price tags. Work is, well, *work*, not play. Unless you win the lottery, you just have to find some way to get through each day. Maybe you can think about your real life after hours, with family, friends, and leisure.

Ask a photojournalist or a trial lawyer, and you are likely to hear: *for the satisfaction*. A job is a "calling," the fulfillment of talent, skill, training, and ambition, not something you *do* but something you *are*. Even when the work day is supposedly over, you are constantly getting new ideas or thinking about problems. There is no "after hours." This *is* your life.

Clearly, our motivations for working are not either/or, but both. For most of us, it's a combination of the two. The janitor and the sales clerk probably find some degree of worth, meaning, and satisfaction in their jobs in addition to paychecks, and the photojournalist and the trial lawyer would be far less likely to consider their jobs a "calling" if they weren't paid.

A job provides both identity and financial support. Both sales clerks and lawyers are engaged in various markets, where people buy, sell, and trade what they have—resources, things, their abilities to work, and their skills—to others. The economy is the arena in which they do that. Given that we spend so much of our lives in that arena, sociologists understand the economy as one of the primary institutions of social life. And, just like the family, you'd think that such an important institution would be stable, secure, and relatively equal. Yet as just about everyone

in the world could tell you, the economy is unstable. Our jobs often feel insecure, our prosperity is precarious, and our sense of continuity between generations as tenuous as ever in history. And it's all connected: When we hear that the stock market in Asia goes down a few points, everyone on Wall Street braces for a bad day. Little ripples in Singapore or Spain send shock waves back to San Francisco and New York. And vice versa. The global economy has never been more connected—but neither has our place in it ever felt more local and fragmented.

> "A job provides both identity and financial support . . . Yet our jobs feel insecure, our prosperity precarious. The sociological analysis of the economy explores both sides."

The Economy and Society
Theories of the Economy
The Changing Economy
Economic Systems

The American Economy in Global Perspective
The Impact of Industrialization: Displacement and Consolidation
Corporations

Work, Identity, and Inequality
How We Work
Types of Jobs
Alternatives to Wage Labor
Unemployment

Diversity in the Workplace
Racial Diversity
Gender Diversity
Sexual Diversity

Work and Economy in the Twenty-First Century

355

The Economy and Society

We all need material resources to survive, like food, clothing, and shelter. But an adequate quality of life requires more, like transportation, communication, education, medical care, and entertainment. A vast array of goods and services is available to meet these needs: cars, cell phones, college classes, day care, diapers, DVD players, magazine subscriptions, microwave ovens, postage stamps, and psychiatric appointments. One person or household could never produce everything, so we must organize collectively to produce and distribute resources. The result is an economy.

Theories of the Economy

An **economy** is a set of institutions and relationships that manages natural resources, manufactured goods, and professional services. These resources, goods, and services are called **capital**. The major economic theories of the world diverge on the question of whether the people serve the economy or the economy serves the people. British empiricists like John Locke ([1689] 1988) and Thomas Hobbes ([1658] 1966) believed that no economy could ensure that everyone has adequate resources. Therefore people must compete with each other. We are motivated by rational self-interest, a desire to meet our own material needs even though we see others going without. Economies form when individuals band together to protect their common resources or to make their competition more congenial and predictable. If asked why they work, they will answer, like the janitor and sales clerk: *for the money*.

Adam Smith ([1776] 2000), the greatest theorist of capitalism, argued that social life involves much more than individuals striving for social gain: People cooperate as often as they compete. There are many Good Samaritans, many altruistic acts, many collective struggles over fairness and justice. If you ask them why they work, they will answer, like the photojournalist and the trial lawyer: *for the satisfaction*.

Karl Marx (Marx and Engels, [1848] 1998) believed that both answers were true—and therein lay the problem. Marx believed that an economic system based on private property divided people into two unequal and competing classes: The upper class worked because they achieved satisfaction by owning all the goods and services and controlling politics and social life. The working class worked because they had to—because they were, in effect, slaves to the upper classes. Eventually, he believed, if the workers controlled and owned everything, everyone would work for the pleasure of it.

By contrast, Émile Durkheim ([1893] 1997) argued that, in modern societies, we are all interdependent: Every person must depend on hundreds or thousands of others for goods and services. Thus, economies are not an isolating, divisive force at all, but a unifying force. They foster strong social ties and create social cohesion, or *organic solidarity*.

There is some truth to all these theories. Every economic system requires some degree of competition and some degree of cooperation. An economy is essential to the common good, but it also serves to emphasize or exacerbate the gap between rich and poor, middle class and working class, having a house and having an apartment, driving a car and taking the bus. It produces both identity and inequality.

The Changing Economy

The first human societies, tens of thousands of years ago, were nomadic hunter-gatherer groups of 20 to 40 people. They had few rules about the production and distribution of capital. Sometimes a particularly talented or interested person might specialize in a task, like making pottery or spears, but otherwise everyone worked together to provide food, shelter, and clothing, and there were few other material resources available (nomads can't own a lot) (Panter-Brick, Layton, and Rowley-Conwy, 2001). Then came the Agricultural Revolution.

The Agricultural Economy. Around 10,000 years ago, people living along the great rivers in Mesopotamia, Egypt, and China learned how to plow the land and grow regular, predictable crops of rice, wheat, or corn. No longer nomadic, they could acquire more goods. And because agriculture is far more productive (more food produced per hour of work) than hunting and gathering, not everyone had to be involved in providing food, shelter, and clothing for the group. Farmers could use their surplus crops to pay professional potters, builders, or priests. A division of labor began.

Sometimes a village might have a surplus of pottery makers and start exchanging its pottery with a village downstream, which had a surplus of spear makers. **Markets,** regular exchanges of goods and services, began, and with them the economy became a social institution. The agricultural economy, with its characteristics of permanent settlements, job specialization, and intergroup trade, lasted for thousands of years, through the great empires of Greece, Rome, China, and Mesoamerica (Cameron and Neal, 2002; Cipolla, 1994; North and Thomas, 1976).

The Industrial Economy. Before 1765, all work was done by human or animal muscle, except for an occasional windmill or waterwheel. Then James Watt marketed the first reliable, high-functioning steam engine, and the era of the machine began. Within a century, hundreds of new machines powered by steam or electricity appeared, including lithographs, telegraphs, steam locomotives, sewing machines, slot machines, lawn mowers, and refrigerators. By 1900, there were typewriters, phonographs, electric stoves, and automobiles. The **Industrial Revolution** ushered in a new economy, based on factory production: the **industrial economy.** This economy differed from agricultural economies in five ways (Hobsbawm, 2000; Oshima, 1986; Stearns, 2001):

1. *Power.* Machines were powerful: They could do 100 times the work of human or animal muscles.

2. *Centralization.* Manufacturing required bulky, expensive machines unfeasible for home use, so most jobs moved away from family farms to centralized offices and factories. For the first time, people had leave home in the morning and *go to work,* juggling two distinct worlds.

3. *Specialization.* Instead of a toy maker hammering, sewing, and painting every toy from start to finish, perhaps taking two entire days to complete one doll, it would be more efficient for one person to do nothing but affix arms. Where 20 start-to-finish toy makers could produce 10 dolls in a day, 20 specialized toy makers could produce 600.

Industrialization ushered in large-scale factories, assembly-line production, and more routinized labor, and thus transformed the experience of work itself. Assembly line at a generator factory of the Ford Motor Company.

4. *Wage labor.* Instead of being paid for the end result of their labor, workers got a regular paycheck in exchange for performing a specific task. Usually they never saw the end result. They received the same pay, no matter how successful their product was, while the handful of people who owned the factories kept all the profits.

> **A Car for $360**
>
> In 1910, Ford's Model T automobile sold for $780, a fairly high price at the time. Using an assembly line and the specialization of division of labor, Ford increased productivity tenfold, and the price dropped to $360 per car. It was mass production that made automobiles accessible to the majority of Americans.

5. *Separation of work and home.* The family farm was both home and workplace. But the coming of the industrial factory meant that home and work were separate, with enormous consequences for both realms.

Did You Know?

The Modern Consumer Economy. As more efficient machines and assembly lines made manufacturing increasingly simple, the emphasis of industrial economies shifted from **production** (how to get more goods out there) to **consumption** (how to decide from among the goods available). Advanced economies focus more on what we buy than on what we make. Advertising became an essential part of business. Products received brand names, trademarks, slogans, and spokespeople. General stores were replaced by department stores like Harrod's in London and Wanamaker's in the United States. In 1904, Macy's, on Herald Square in New York City, was advertised as "the largest store on Earth," with nine stories, 33 elevators, four escalators, and a system of pneumatic tubes. "Window shopping," looking through shop windows for items that one would like to possess, became a common pastime (Lancaster, 1995).

In 1899, Thorstein Veblen coined the term **conspicuous consumption** to mark the shift to this consumer economy in which prestige was based on accumulating as many possessions as possible and showing them off. Veblen argued that the real symbols of wealth were those that made it look as though you didn't have to work: Fashions like long fingernails, high heels, and tight skirts for women were a sign that they were pampered and didn't need to work; and wealthy men were shown sailing, skiing, and otherwise experiencing the leisure that only true wealth can bring.

With industrialization came the decline of agriculture as a livelihood. In 1700, before the Industrial Revolution, 60 percent of all workers in the United States were involved in the three Fs (farming, fishing, and forestry). As late as 1900, it was 30 percent. Today, the three Fs occupy less than 1 percent of the American workforce. Of course, there is little need for more workers. In 1880, a typical farmer could grow enough food to sustain five people (about the size of the typical farm family). Today's high-tech agribusiness specialists can feed about 80 people apiece.

The Post-industrial Economy. Industrial economies flourished for over 200 years (Mathias and Pollard, 1989). Industrialized—or "developed"—nations remain the world's economic leaders. Perhaps the simplest way to determine how rich or poor a country is would be to compare the percentage of its labor force involved in agriculture to the percentage in industry. In Switzerland, it's 5 percent agriculture, 26 percent industry. In Bangladesh, it's 63 percent agriculture, 11 percent industry.

Worldwide, jobs are shifting to the services sector, although unevenly, with developed economies seeing far greater increases in employment in services and declines in agriculture (see Figure 12.1). More than 42 percent of the world's workers are employed in the services sector, with more than 70 percent of those in developed economies, including the United States and the nations of the European Union. Nearly 35 percent work in agriculture (less than 4 percent in developed economies) and 22 percent in industry (about one-fourth of them in developed economies) (International Labour Organization [ILO], 2008). Ten years ago, 41 percent of worldwide employees worked in agriculture, and only 37.5 percent worked in services (ILO, 2008). Three social changes characterize "postindustrial" economies: knowledge work, rootlessness, and globalization (Bell, 1976; Kumar, 1995; Vallas, 1999).

Knowledge Work. Postindustrial economies shift from production of goods to production of ideas. In 1940, during the peak of the industrial economy, roughly half of all U.S. workers were working in factories. Today, with automation, outsourcing, and the decline of production, that number is about 7 percent. Blue-collar jobs (production of various types) now comprise about a quarter of the American workforce, while about one-third are white-collar (management and the professions) and more than 40 percent are pink-collar (predominantly female) service and office/clerical jobs (Bureau of Labor Statistics, 2008b). This shift has affected more than work—it has had an impact on attitudes, lifestyles, and worldviews.

Often postindustrial economies are called knowledge economies. A **knowledge economy** is less oriented around the actual production of a commodity and more concerned with the idea of the commodity, its marketing, its distribution, and its relationship to different groups of consumers. For example, a toy company may require very few people to attach doll arms on the assembly line, but it requires many people to conduct market research, direct TV commercials, design tie-in websites, negotiate with government and parental groups, and acquire global distribution rights. Postindustrial workers work not in factories, but in R&D (research and development), finance, investment, advertising, education, and training. They manipulate words and numbers rather than tools. Ideas, information, and knowledge have become the new forms of capital (Adler, 2001; Powell and Snellman, 2004).

Because knowledge-based workers now design, develop, market, sell, and service, they need classes in public speaking, technical writing, global business management, and Java programming. That is, they need to go to college—at least. The proportion of American workers doing jobs that call for complex skills has grown three times as fast as employment in general, and other economies are moving in the same direction, raising global demand for educated workers (*The Economist*, 2006e). But the United States is losing ground compared to other countries' high school graduation rates: The high school graduation rate in the United States is below both the OECD (Organization for Economic Cooperation and Development, the organization of the world's 30 most developed nations) average and the EU19 (the 19 member states of the European Union) average—well below graduation rates in countries including Greece, Korea, Ireland, the Czech Republic, Hungary, and Slovenia (The College Board, 2009).

In the **postindustrial economy,** some countries and some groups of people race down the "information superhighway" while others do not even have a paved road, let alone a superhighway. What happens to people with limited education in a postindustrial economy? Fifty years ago, they would have become blue-collar workers. Assembly-line work did not require a lot of education, and it paid nearly as much as white-collar jobs. But now, instead of finding assembly-line work, they are stuck in low-paying service jobs. They cannot afford houses in the same neighborhoods as the white-collar workers. Often, they cannot afford houses at all. The gap between "comfortable" and "barely getting by" shrank during the industrial economy, but now it is growing again (Krugman, 2002).

Globalization. In addition to knowledge economies, postindustrial economies are often called *global economies* (Hirst, 1997). They have produced a global division of labor, interconnecting workers but also dividing them along socioeconomic lines. As we saw in Chapter 1, globalization is a process of interaction and integration among the people, companies, and governments of different nations, a process driven by international trade

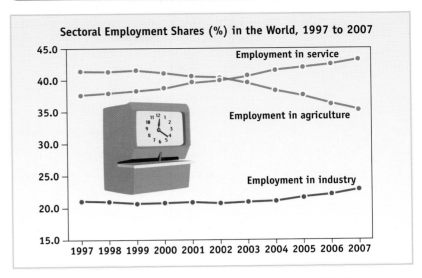

Figure 12.1 Global Changes in Employment by Sector of the Economy, 1997–2007

(*Source:* International Labor Organization, *Global Employment Trends*, 2007b.)

and investment and aided by information technology. Different societies experience this differently, but there is no doubt that globalization effects the environment, culture, political systems, and economic development and prosperity everywhere.

Global production refers to the fact that corporations derive raw materials from all over the world and use manufacturing and assembly plants in many different countries, using international labor forces. **Global distribution** ensures that these products are marketed and distributed all over the world as well. The products we buy are likely made of materials from several countries, assembled in another country, packaged and distributed from yet another, with advertising campaigns and marketing schemes drawn from yet another.

During the Industrial Revolution, the raw materials may have been drawn from other countries, but the entire manufacturing and marketing processes were located in the industrial country. Now, however, the process is fragmented, and each economic function may be located in another country, or several countries. This has also led to **outsourcing,** the contracting out to another company of work that had once been done internally by your company. Initially, technology and IT were outsourced to cheaper call centers in developing nations like India and China. Then, production line jobs began to move overseas where labor

Table 12.1
Occupations Most
Vulnerable to
Offshoring

Rank	Occupation	Annual Mean Wage	Number Employed
1	Computer programmers	$72,010	394,710
2	Data entry keyers	26,350	286,540
3	Electrical and electronics drafters	51,710	32,350
4	Mechanical drafters	46,690	74,260
5	Computer and information scientists, research	100,640	28,720
6	Actuaries	95,420	18,030
7	Mathematicians	90,930	3,160
8	Statisticians	72,150	20,270
9	Mathematical science occupations (all other)	61,100	6,930
10	Film and video editors	61,180	17,410

(*Source:* Alan S. Blinder, "How Many U.S. Jobs Might Be Offshorable?" *CEPS Working Paper 142* [March 2007]: and Bureau of Labor Statistics, *National Occupational Employment and Wage Estimates,* May 2007, www.bls.gov/oes/current/oes_nat.htm, accessed May 28, 2008.)

was cheaper and factories could be built without bowing to environmental regulations. Now even white-collar jobs like sales and service have also been outsourced (see Table 12.1).

Although research, development, production, and distribution occur in many different countries, the "knowledge labor" tends to occur in wealthier countries while unskilled and semiskilled factory work takes place in poorer countries. Even on the global level, the gap between rich and poor is increasing as globalization reinforces or even increases the stark inequalities of income and wealth around the world (Figure 12.2).

Globalization links owners and managers into an interlocking system of a managerial elite; often managers from Sri Lanka and Belgium will have more in common with each other (consumption patterns, tastes in art and music, and so on) than either will with the working class in his or her own country. However, while the elite at the top become more integrated and cohesive, the working classes will remain fractured and distant from each other, asserting local, regional, and cultural differences as a way to resist integration. In this way, also, the globalizing rich become richer and the globalized poor become poorer.

Rootlessness. Industrial economies move workers from home to factories, and postindustrial economies move them out into the wide, wide world. The production of ideas does not require all of the workers to be in the same building or even on the same continent. A decade ago, they could phone in their ideas and fax their presentations; now they can transmit entire volumes by IM, e-mail,

Internet, and other digital media. And when you call for technical support, you may be speaking to someone on another continent.

"Rush-hour traffic" is quickly becoming a meaningless term because many people don't have to be in some physical location called "work" every day between 9 a.m. and 5 p.m. They are on the road constantly, en route between home, office, meetings, and the airport. Service workers *are* stuck in some physical location, but their day might begin at 11 a.m., 4 p.m., or midnight, or they could work a "split shift," with four hours in the morning and four in the evening. So the streets are always crowded.

Even time becomes meaningless to the postindustrial worker. Clients and co-workers live in every part of the globe, so there is no "quitting time": Work can happen any time of the day or night. As a result, the 200-year-old distinction between home and work, livelihood and leisure, is fading away.

Economic Systems

All societies must deal with three fundamental economic issues: (1) production, (2) distribution, and (3) consumption. An **economic system** is a mechanism that deals with the production, distribution, and consumption of goods and services in a particular society.

Capitalism. **Capitalism** is a profit-oriented system based on the private or corporate ownership of the means of production and distribution. It arose in the Netherlands and Britain during the seventeenth century, when private investors began to fund the wealth-

Figure 12.2 World Wealth Levels, 2000

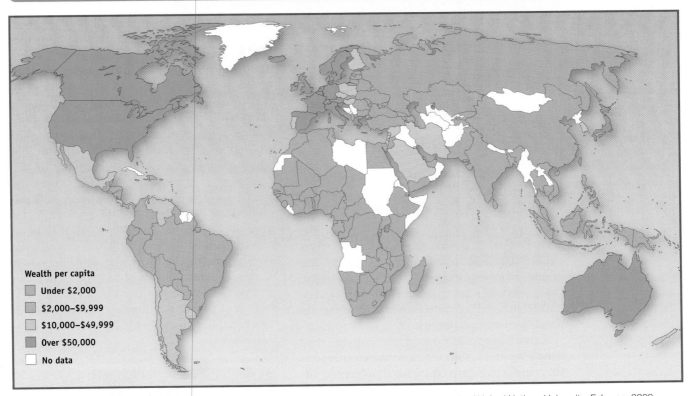

Wealth per capita
- Under $2,000
- $2,000–$9,999
- $10,000–$49,999
- Over $50,000
- No data

(*Source:* From *World Distributing Household Wealth*, World Institute for Development Economic Research of United Nations University, February 2008. Reprinted with permission.)

accumulating journeys of traders, explorers, and eventually colonists. Individual companies competed with each other for customers and profits with no government interference.

Classical capitalism has three components:

- *Private ownership* of the means of production (natural resources and production machinery).

- *An open market,* with no government interference. Kings and queens (and later prime ministers and presidents) should *"laissez-faire,"* or keep their hands off.

- *Profit* (receiving more than the goods cost to produce) as a valuable goal of human enterprise.

Each of these varies enormously, even among capitalist countries. In the United States, most people believe that the *political system* of democracy would be impossible without the *economic system* of capitalism. But capitalism has also turned out to be compatible with other political forms. Fascist Italy and the Communist former Soviet Union acted as capitalist nations in the global marketplace. The state just kept most of the profits.

Actually, democracy and capitalism often contradict each other. Capitalism, after all, frees individuals to pursue their own private interests in the marketplace; it promotes unconstrained liberty. Democracy, on the other hand, constrains individual liberty in the name of the common good. For instance, in capitalism, it makes sense for a factory to toss its toxic waste into the nearest river: The money saved on proper waste disposal can go into the stockholders' pockets, maximizing profits. But in democracy, concern for the common good (unpolluted rivers) requires the factory to dispose of its toxic waste properly, limiting its individual liberty and reducing its profits (see Figure 12.3).

As a result of the tension, capitalism in democratic countries has developed in different ways, in an attempt to balance individual liberty and the common good or, as the issue is sometimes framed, freedom and responsibility.

Laissez-Faire Capitalism. The original form of capitalism, theorized by Adam Smith, "laissez-faire" means "to leave alone" in French; under this system, governments would leave the marketplace alone to organize the economy,

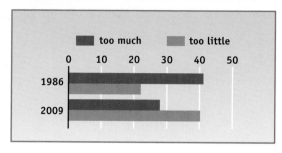

Figure 12.3 Percentage of Americans Saying That Federal Government Regulates Business

(*Source:* CBS News Poll, Wednesday, October 1, 2008.)

without government interference. Markets should be able to compete freely to sell goods, acquire raw materials, and hire labor. No government interference is necessary: The "invisible hand" of supply and demand creates a self-regulating economy.

Laissez-faire dominated in Europe and North America through the nineteenth century, but it has proved ineffective in preventing economic crises. (The current recession was caused largely by the absence of regulation—government "interference"—in financial markets.) Thus, the relationship between the government and economy can no longer be a question of whether or not the government should be involved in economic life: Today the questions are how much should the government be involved? In what sectors? In what ways?

State Capitalism. State capitalism requires that the government use a heavy hand in regulating and constraining the marketplace. Companies may still be privately owned, but they must also meet government-set standards of product quality, worker compensation, and truth in advertising. In turn, the government provides some economic security to companies to avoid catastrophic losses and controls foreign imports to help local companies compete in world markets. This system is still common in the rapidly developing countries of the Pacific Rim, such as Japan, South Korea, and Singapore.

Welfare Capitalism. Most contemporary capitalist countries also include extensive social welfare programs, and the government regulates some of the most essential services, such as transportation, health care, and the mass

media (Barr, 2004; Esping-Anderson, 1990; Stephens and Huber, 2001). This is called welfare capitalism.

The U.S. economy incorporates elements of all three forms of capitalism. Many companies seek to operate with as little government regulation as possible and set up corporate headquarters so they do not have to pay taxes in the United States (laissez-faire). Companies like Wal-Mart resist the unionization of their workers and undermine minimum wage regulations. Other industries, like the airlines and automobile manufacturers, agree to fare regulation or automotive emission controls in return for a more stable economic environment (state capitalism) and the promise that if they go bankrupt, as A.I.G. and General Motors did in 2008 and 2009, the government will bail them out. And the massive public sector—federal, state, and local bureaucracies and political systems—work as a kind of welfare capitalism, attempting to ensure that everyone obtains at least a minimum standard of living.

The relationship between corporations and government is complex and depends on the industry. Some companies are less regulated than others. In Europe, all utilities are government controlled, but the trend in the United States is toward privatization. Some public utilities are either heavily regulated or are actually part of a partnership between government and private interests.

Socialism. Although capitalism became the dominant economic system in the West by the end of the eighteenth century, it was not without its detractors. Utopians argued that it would be more equitable to cooperate instead of compete, so that everyone could share the goods and services. In the nineteenth century, many socialist communes were founded in the United States, where all property was commonly owned and all decisions made as a body. However, no one tried it on a national level.

Later, Karl Marx argued that the pursuit of rational self-interest was inhumane and oppressive. The *bourgeoisie* (owners) kept all the profits for themselves, while the *proletariat* (workers) had no choice but to work for them at wages barely enough to ensure survival. Marx hypothesized that the huge economic gap between the groups would cause increasing hostility and resentment and would eventually result in violent revolution.

Marx proposed to adapt socialism to national governments by ensuring that workers rather than owners controlled the means of production and that everyone would be treated fairly. Strong government controls would be put into place to ensure equitable distribution of resources. Thus, socialism is the exact opposite of laissez-faire capitalism, offering:

- *Collective (public sector) ownership.* Private property is limited, especially property used to generate income. Goods and services are available equally to all, regardless of individual wealth.
- *Collective goals.* Capitalism celebrates profit as the entrepreneurial spirit, but socialism condemns profit as greed. Individuals should concentrate on the common good.
- *Central planning.* Socialism operates through a "command economy." The government controls all production and distribution.

On the national level, many countries, both rich and poor, have socialist economies, but they allow for a degree of entrepreneurship, some profit, and differences in individual wealth, resulting in a "democratic socialism" that looks and feels much like welfare capitalism (Lichtheim, 1982; Rose and Ross, 1994). In Sweden, for instance, about 12 percent of economic production is "nationalized" (state controlled), and the rest is in private hands. High taxation, aimed especially at the rich, funds a wide range of social welfare programs for everyone, including universal health and child

"Can't we put in something about rich white guys don't have to pay taxes?"

© Michael Shaw/Condé Nast Publications/www.cartoonbank.com. Reprinted by permission.

care. Scholars differ on whether this economy should be classified as socialist or capitalist.

Communism. Many people confuse the two economic systems, but communism is *not* socialism. Marx believed that socialism was a necessary transition from the oppression of capitalism to the ideal economic system of communism. **Communism** is an economic system based on collective ownership of the means of production and is administered collectively, without a political apparatus to ensure equal distribution. It's utopian, and Marx believed that communism could be achieved only after many years of socialism.

Socialism requires strong government intervention; but, in a communist state, government is abolished. Socialism retains a difference between high-status and low-status work, so the janitor receives a lower salary than the physician, but in the communist paradise, the principle of distribution will become "from each according to his or her ability, to each according to his or her need." Thus, the janitor and the physician will receive the same stipend for personal expenses. Neither will lack anything, so both will be happy and content. Social inequalities will disappear, along with crime, hunger, and political strife.

What do **you** think?

The Rich and Taxes

Some think the rich should pay more taxes than they do, while others maintain that the rich contribute to society in other ways, such as providing jobs and revenue for middle- and working-class Americans. So, what do you think?

Do you think that people with high incomes should pay a larger share of their income in taxes than those with low incomes, the same share, or a smaller share?

○ Much larger share   ○ Larger   ○ Same share

○ Smaller share   ○ Much lower share

What does **America** think?

(These are actual survey data from the General Social Survey, 2002.)

In the 2002 General Social Survey, 23 percent of respondents said the rich should pay a much larger share of their income in taxes. Almost 44 percent said the rich should pay a larger share. Thirty-one percent thought the current share paid was adequate. When broken down by race, there was a significant difference between Black and White respondents, with Black respondents being much more likely (32 percent) to think that the rich should pay a much larger share of their income in taxes.

1. Why do you think the survey responses broke down by race the way they did?

2. How do you think responses might differ if they were broken down by social class? Go to the website and check for yourself. How did your prediction compare to the data?

References: See Davis et al., page 511.

Strangely, communist ideas did not take hold in industrialized, capitalist countries where the gap between owners and workers was most evident, but in agricultural countries, usually after revolutions or civil wars, such as in Russia (1917), China (1949), Vietnam (1954), Cuba (1959), and Yemen (1969). These countries usually called themselves socialist rather than communist because the government had not yet "withered away."

But as time passed, the government never withered away. Bureaucracy and regulation actually expanded, until the governments were stronger and more centralized than in capitalist countries. And social and class divisions remained strong (Muravchik, 2002; Pipes, 2001). What happened?

Sociologists explain that social stratification isn't simply a matter of economics. It involves power and status as well as wealth, so eliminating income disparities will not result in paradise. In fact, the communist governments created a new class of political elite. In the Soviet Union, about 10 percent of the population in 1984 belonged to the Communist Party. Called the *nomenklatura*, they got to shop in the best stores, send their children to the best schools, vacation at exclusive resorts, and travel abroad (Taylor, 1987; Voslensky, 1984).

The worker's paradise that Marx envisioned never happened and probably never could. After half a century of trying, most of the communist governments of the world have shifted to some form of capitalism. Today there are only five communist countries left (China, Cuba, Laos, North Korea, and Vietnam), and all except North Korea are busily decentralizing government controls and encouraging entrepreneurship (Hall, 1994; Oh and Hassig, 2000; Schopflin, 1993).

The American Economy in Global Perspective

What is the American "economic system"? How did the American economy develop?

The Impact of Industrialization: Displacement and Consolidation

The United States was formed at the start of the Industrial Revolution, as the agricultural economy was gradually superseded by the new industrial economy and new institutions were developing to match industrial complexity (Atack, 1994). By 1860, 16 percent of the U.S. population lived in urban areas, and a third of the nation's income came from manufacturing. But most industries were located in the Northeast, while the South remained rural and agricultural. The gap between North and South is reminiscent of the gap between rich, industrialized countries and poor, agricultural countries today.

The Civil War (1861–1865) was, in the economic sense, a clash between the two economic systems, and the Northern victory and the abolition of slavery sealed the industrial future of the United States. Industry surged ahead. Industrialization has also meant the gradual displacement of small shopkeepers and artisanal craft workers. Colonial America was a nation of small businessmen—whether farmers in the countryside or shopkeepers in the towns. Industrialization means consolidation, as big supersized stores undercut small shops and agribusinesses gobble up small farms.

Today, the opening of a Wal-Mart, the world's largest employer, usually means the closing of several dozen small shops nearby. Pushed down from the lower middle class into the working class, or impoverished, these small shopkeepers and farmers lose more than their stores; they lose their sense of independence and economic autonomy.

Consolidation. This impulse toward consolidation began in earnest in the late nineteenth century, often referred to as the Gilded Age, when a handful of so-called robber barons—Rockefeller, Ford, Carnegie, Vanderbilt, Gould, and Morgan—exercised almost total control over the American economy (Chernow, 1990,

1998; Schmitz and Kirby, 1995). At one point Rockefeller controlled 90 percent of the oil reserves in America, and Carnegie controlled 25 percent of the steel (Conte and Karr, 2001). Despite some government regulation in the early twentieth century, the economy grew almost unchecked until the catastrophic crash of 1929, and after the 1932 election President Franklin Roosevelt launched "the New Deal," which ushered in significant government regulation of the economy. Many of the most important laws and institutions that we take for granted in contemporary America started with the New Deal (Gilbert and Howe, 1991; Quadagno, 1984), including:

- Minimum wage, providing a floor below which wages cannot go

- Social Security, which provides pensions to the elderly and disabled based on payments they made when part of the workforce

- Regulation of the stock market by the government (the Securities and Exchange Commission, or SEC)

- Insurance of bank deposits by the government (the Federal Deposit Insurance Corporation, or FDIC)

If this sounds like recent history, it's because it is! The Reagan Revolution of the 1980s led the government out of the economy again (Reagan declared that government was "the problem, not the solution") until, unchecked during the Bush years, new Robber Barons emerged (especially in the financial sector) and the economy again collapsed. In this new era of regulation and reform, populist cries to cap executive salaries, regulate banks, and support homeowners indicate a return to Roosevelt's policies.

Corporations

Industrial and postindustrial economies would be impossible without corporations. The **corporation** is a business that is treated legally as an individual. It can make contracts, incur debts, sue, and be sued, but its obligations and liabilities are legally distinct from those of the owners: If you sue a corporation and are awarded $1,000,000 in damages, none of the money comes from the personal bank account of the CEO. Incorporating (that is, creating a corporation) thus separates individual investors from the profits or losses of their business and gives them the freedom to take more risks than they would otherwise.

Corporate capitalism has developed in four stages: family, managerial, institutional corporations, and multinational (Micklethwait and Woodridge, 2003).

Family Corporations. Even in agricultural economies, farmers, merchants, and artisans usually passed their tools and workshops on to their children, and in the early days of capitalism, entrepreneurs followed their lead by sharing their investments, customers, production, and profits with relatives. By the nineteenth century, entrepreneurs were putting their relatives into most of the managerial positions in their companies. John D. Rockefeller (1839–1937) got his start in the oil business in partnership with two nonrelatives, but eventually he bought them out and handed the reins of Standard Oil over to his son and grandsons. When they distributed stock only to family members as well, they could create huge entrepreneurial dynasties but still keep it all in the family.

Managerial Corporations. As companies grew, there were not enough qualified family members available to fill all of the necessary positions, or children and grandchildren didn't want to participate in the family business, so entrepreneurs began to hire outside managers. Eventually outsiders displaced family members in almost all managerial positions. The owners sold shares in the company's assets (stocks) to strangers who sought to share also in the company's profits, and the company became an entity separate from the family, just as work separated from home early in the Industrial Revolution.

Through most of the twentieth century, the corporate world was the domain of a new relationship, different from family and friends. Coworkers came together not because of kinship ties nor because they liked each other (they may or they may not) but solely in the interest of personal and corporate profit. Corporations developed their own culture, distinct from social worlds of family and friends, with their own procedures and practices, stated and unstated norms, values, goals, and vocabulary.

Managerial corporations were larger, more versatile, and stronger than family-run businesses, and more stable as well—as anyone who has ever tried to work with a family member can tell you. On the other hand, the larger and more impersonal forces of the corporation spelled the end of the workplace as an extension of family life.

Institutional Corporations. During the last half of the twentieth century, corporations began to hold shares in *other* corporations. The same people would serve on boards of directors of several companies at once, until many corporations were interconnected through a small network of power players. Their decision-making practices changed because they were concerned not only with their own company but with all of the companies in which they had a stake. Competition changed to cooperation in the pursuit of profits. The result was a maze of major, minor, and subsidiary corporations, connected not through legal documents but through boardroom small talk, golf games, and handshakes.

The networks of corporations began acting less like businesses and more like enterprise webs—central cores that link an array of business interests and continuously contract with similar webs all over the world (Chandler and Mazlish, 2005).

Multinational Corporations. Some corporations remain centered in the United States, with overseas offices and production plants clearly dependent parts of the central operation. But most, especially the largest, operate globally; they are called transnational or **multinational corporations** because they are no longer clearly located anywhere. Instead of a "home office," they operate through a network of offices all over the world. Even employees who are officially assigned to an office in one location may live in a dozen cities, or even a dozen countries, working together through e-mail, Web conferencing, and cell phones. Multinational corporations are the corporate form for the new global capitalist economy.

The products of multinational corporations do not really "come from" anywhere, in spite of the "Made in America" or "Made in China" labels. A toy may be designed by engineers living in Belgium, Switzerland, and South Africa through teleconferencing at an office in Brazil, while the parts are outsourced to a manufacturer based in Japan but with the factories located in India and Thailand; assembly occurs in a factory in Mexico, and the marketing campaigns are devised in the United States. The toy is sold in 128 countries, and the television commercials appear in 32 languages. Where is it made? Notice that my hypothetical toy is not assembled in factories in Germany, France, or Japan, and the engineers are not from Mexico or Thailand. "Outsourcing" and

Gone are the days when a group of local artisans created children's toys—or anything else. Even the simple "Made in Japan" label of the 1960s is obsolete. Today, toys designed in the United States are likely to be assembled in China from parts produced in Thailand and India.

"offshoring" are not random: They are based on economic division between First World and Third World. Every episode of *The Simpsons*, for example, is written and storyboarded in the United States, then outsourced to Korea for the tedious work of animation.

To sociologists, like Bonacich and Appelbaum (2000), the multinational corporation illustrates how modern corporations are both national and international, global and local, at the same time. They studied the global production of clothing sold in America. They found that two-thirds of it was "outsourced," produced in peripheral countries, where factory workers could be paid a small percentage of U.S. wages (in China, workers were thrilled to get $40 per month). They note a **race to the bottom:** Manufacturers and retailers like Wal-Mart and Kmart will go wherever on Earth they need to, to maximize profits by paying the lowest possible wages.

It used to be said that "what's good for General Motors is good for America." It meant that the success of companies led to prosperity for people in their home countries. But today, that old adage is ringing false. (It is not even clear, at this writing in spring 2009, that General Motors will still exist by the time you are reading this book!)

Globalization has "decoupled" the old win-win relationship between corporate and national interests. Corporate interests in making profits may no longer benefit the entire society. In fact, those profits may actually hurt most people. In the past, fatter profits led companies to hire more workers and offer higher wages. This is no longer true. In today's global economy, multinational companies are not really attached to a home country any more, so they don't put their profits back into it in the form of more hiring or better benefits. Increased profits are just as likely to result in cutbacks and layoffs as they are to increase hiring. They are not "sharing the wealth," so to speak—at least not at home.

The world's 40 biggest multinationals now employ 55 percent of their workforces in foreign countries and earn 59 percent of their revenues abroad (*The Economist*, 2006). In Europe, the trend is quite pronounced. Only 43 percent of all jobs at companies in France's CAC 40 (France's stock market index) are actually based in France. In Germany, just over half (53 percent) of employees of companies listed in its DAX 30 are based in Germany. But this is also happening more and more in the United States. Already, more than one-third of General Motors's employees don't work in America (*The Economist*, 2006).

Because the big multinational corporations are maximizing profits abroad, they are not spending in home countries on jobs and wages. What's more, the threat of further outsourcing continues to keep wages down at home. Even in countries with very strong unions, such as France or Germany, workers have been pressed to accept pay and benefit cuts—if they want to keep jobs at all (Gross, 2006).

What are companies doing with the profit gains? Some are investing in foreign operations—because that's increasingly where their markets are and profits are coming from. For now, in the United States, a bigger slice of the increase in national income has gone to corporate profits than in any economic recovery since 1945 (*The Economist*, 2006).

Work, Identity, and Inequality

Since the beginning of human society, our working lives have occupied the majority of our waking hours. From sunup to sundown, people in nonindustrial cultures have hunted and gathered, planted and sown, fished and farmed to provide for their society's members. This is still true today for most of the world's population. In contemporary industrial societies, it was only in the early twentieth century that we cut the working day to eight hours. And political movements in Europe are suggesting cutting the work week from 40 to 35 hours and the work day to seven or even six hours a day. In that sense, we work fewer hours today than ever before.

At the same time, we constantly hear how we are working longer and harder than ever before. Top-level managers in corporations and young lawyers in large firms often log 100-hour work weeks. Countless CEOs boast about virtually living in their offices. Americans are working harder and longer than residents of all but six other countries.

Sociologists understand that both these phenomena are true: The organization of our economies makes it possible for us to work fewer hours and also often makes it necessary for us to work longer hours.

How We Work

In the early days of mass production, the assembly line basically imagined workers as machines. People were simply trained to do a task with scientific precision and then asked to do it repeatedly. No one really cared whether the workers felt challenged, bored, intimidated, or humiliated. As industrialization progressed, management scientists began to research how

we respond to the workplace, to co-workers, to bosses, and to labor itself. Happier workers, who felt less bored and more valued, it turned out, were more productive—and that spelled higher profits.

The Hawthorne Effect. The earliest experimental study of work productivity was conducted between 1927 and 1932 at the Western Electric Hawthorne factory in Chicago. Researcher Elton Mayo chose six female assembly-line workers and assigned an observer to watch them, ask for their input, and listen to their complaints. Then he made a variety of environmental changes, including breaks of various lengths, different quitting times, different quotas, a day off, and a free lunch. To his surprise, almost every change increased productivity. And when he changed things back to the default, productivity increased again (Mayo, 1933)!

Mayo concluded that the changes themselves weren't responsible for the increase in productivity. It was that the workers had some input. The workers chosen for the experiment had no boss telling them the "proper" procedure. They were allowed to work in their own way; in fact, the observer displayed a keen interest in their individual work styles. They were treated as intelligent, creative individuals rather than as mindless machines.

The "Hawthorne Effect" or the "Somebody Upstairs Cares Syndrome" soon became a standard in management textbooks: People work better and faster when they feel valued. Except for one small problem: It wasn't exactly true. Economist Steve Levitt, coauthor with Steven Dubner of the best-selling book *Freakonomics* (2005), looked at Mayo's original data and found something interesting: The lighting was changed on a Sunday, so that the change would take effect on Monday when workers returned to work. But Levitt found

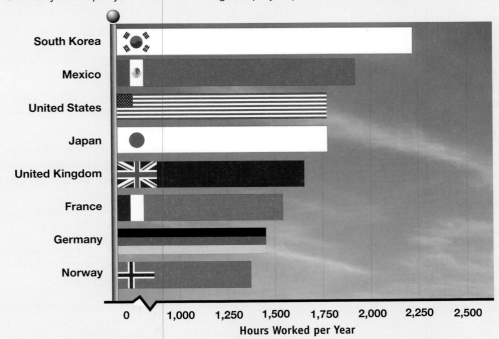

U.S. / Them

How Much Do We Work?

Americans work long and hard—but not as long as some countries, and lots longer than others. How many hours per year does the average employed person work in these selected countries?

Hours Worked per Year

(*Source:* OECD Factbook 2009: Economic, Environmental and Social Statistics. Copyright © OECD, 2009. Reproduced by permission.)

1. What sorts of factors influence how long we work?

2. What would we do with the 444 extra hours that Norwegians have every year? That's 18.5 full 24-hour days, or 55.5 working (eight-hour) days—more two full working months!

---

that productivity *always* went up on Mondays, whether there was a change of lighting or not (*The Economist*, 2009).

Theory X and Theory Y. In 1960 Douglas McGregor published *The Human Side of Enterprise*, about two theories of work (McGregor, [1960] 2005). Theory X assumes that people naturally dislike work, so they will slack off unless they are coerced and threatened. On the assembly line, a line supervisor must be watching them at all times. In white-collar jobs, they must fill out time sheets, goals statements, and allocation lists.

Theory Y is based on the assumption that people naturally like work, so they will do it if they feel they are a valued part of a team (as in the Hawthorne Effect). The job of the supervisor is to create team spirit, solve problems, and offer advice, not monitor productivity. On the assembly line, there should be suggestion

boxes and team meetings. White-collar workers might go on retreats where they fall backwards into each other's arms to learn trust.

McGregor argued that both theories are valid and can increase productivity, depending on the task and the maturity and responsibility of the workers. The biggest mistake of management is to implement Theory X all the time and never consider the possibility of Theory Y.

Manufacturing Consent. Sociologist Michael Burawoy (1980) wondered why so many people work so hard, making only their managers rich. It's not a desire for promotion because people work just as hard at dead-end jobs. It's not fear of being fired. Why don't they slack off or rebel against the oppressive system? Why do they care? To find out, he took a blue-collar job at "Allied Corporation" and carefully observed both management and workers. He found that management engaged in three strategies designed to **manufacture consent,** by which workers came to embrace a system that also exploited them. Manufacturing consent is the production of values and emotions (in addition to the actual things they produce) that bind workers to their company:

- *Piece-rate pay system.* The workers competed with each other to produce the highest quotas. Though the "prizes" were only minor pay raises, workers devoted a lot of time to "making out," strategizing new ways to increase their production. Even Burawoy found himself working harder.

- *Internal labor market.* Increasing job mobility within the company gave the workers the illusion that their dead-end jobs had potential.

- *Collective bargaining.* Unions gave workers the illusion that they, as individual workers, held power.

The ideas in *Manufacturing Consent* have been applied to many jobs, white collar as well as blue collar. For instance, in academia, promotion and tenure are based to a great extent on publications, but often tenure committees look only at the number of publications, not the quality. So professors find their own way of "making out." They publish a lot of short articles that do not involve extensive research rather than working on a big, meaningful project.

Types of Jobs

There are several different types of jobs, often categorized by the color of the collar you are thought to wear. Of course, these color codings are not always followed, but the job categories remain relatively stable.

White-Collar Jobs. White-collar work is knowledge-based work, with the day spent manipulating symbols: talking, speaking, reading, writing, and calculating. Most white-collar jobs require considerable education, usually a bachelor's degree and often today a master's degree. In 1900, only about 16 percent of American workers had white-collar jobs, but today the figure is about half (Bureau of Labor Statistics, 2008). "Professionals" are among the elite of the white-collar jobs. This category includes doctors, lawyers, and teachers as well as scientists, engineers, librarians, architects, artists, journalists, and entertainers. Professions can generally be distinguished from other jobs by four characteristics:

1. *Theoretical knowledge.* You must have not only technical training in a skill but also a theoretical understanding of a field. Architecture became a profession only when it became less about constructing buildings and more about understanding the dynamics of inhabited space.

2. *Self-regulating practices.* Other jobs have procedures, but professions observe a code of ethics.

3. *Authority over clients.* Based on their extensive training, professionals are qualified to advise their clients and expect them to obey directions. You expect that your doctor knows more than you do about your rash.

4. *Community orientation.* Rather than merely seeking personal income, the professional has a duty to the community.

Alongside the professionals are the white-collar workers in business. Perhaps, as President Calvin Coolidge said, "the business of America is business." Business administration remains the most popular college major, comprising nearly a quarter of all bachelor's degrees awarded in 2005 (U.S. Department of Education, 2006a). Yet less than 15 percent of American workers are actually employed in management, business, and financial occupations. Of these, 45 percent are women; the vast majority are White, about 8 percent are Black, 6 percent Hispanic, and 4 percent Asian (Bureau of Labor Statistics, 2008). Sales is usually considered white collar because it is knowledge work, persuading people to buy things, but sometimes it is categorized with service jobs because of its low salary and low prestige. Seventeen percent of American workers are in sales, about equally divided between men and women. Most are White, with 10 percent Hispanic, 9 percent Black, and 4 percent Asian (Bureau of Labor Statistics, 2008). Because white-collar jobs offer the highest salaries and the most opportunity for advancement, many sociologists, including C. Wright Mills (1959), have argued that white-collar workers are more in agreement with capitalism than blue- or pink-collar workers. However, contemporary scholars note that, in the postindustrial economy, most white-collar jobs are becoming more regimented and bureaucratic, and white-collar workers are experiencing a decay in autonomy, creativity, and advancement potential similar to that of the blue-collar workers as they shift downward to service (Fraser, 2001).

Blue-Collar Jobs. The term *blue collar* was first coined in 1951 for jobs involved with production rather than knowledge, because factory workers traditionally wore blue jumpsuits. In 1900, 60 percent of American workers were blue collar. Today that proportion is less than a quarter (Blinder, 2006). There are several types of blue-collar jobs—like natural resource and construction, factory work, and skilled crafts work.

Natural resource and construction work includes farming, fishing, and forestry, plus the construction trades (electricians, bricklayers, plumbers), and also auto and airplane repair, heating, air conditioning, and refrigeration. About 10 percent of American workers are involved. Of these, 96 percent are men, and only 4 percent are women. Sixty-six percent are White, 25 percent Hispanic, 7 percent Black, and 2 percent Asian (Bureau of Labor Statistics, 2008c). About 12 percent of American workers have jobs in production, which includes not only traditional factory jobs but driving buses, trucks, taxis, and cars, and running trains, and piloting airplanes. Like natural resources and construction, these jobs are heavily male oriented (78 percent men, 22 percent women). Of production workers, 61 percent are White, 20 percent Hispanic, 14.5 percent Black, and 4 percent Asian (Bureau of Labor Statistics, 2008c).

Pink-Collar Jobs. The term *pink collar* was coined by Louise Kay Howe in 1977, in her book *Pink Collar Workers: Inside the World of Woman's Work*. Howe found that jobs in offices, restaurants, and stores—such as secretary, waitstaff, or sales clerk—were often held by women. Today these jobs are still stigmatized as "women's work," and therefore most are low paying and low prestige. Some highly

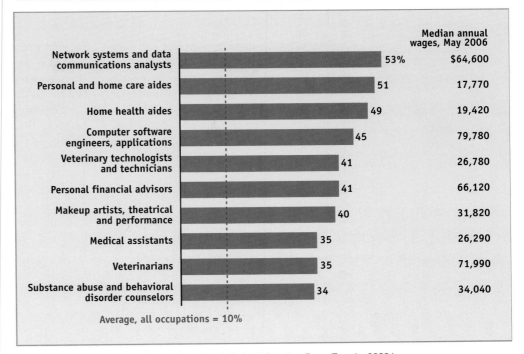

Figure 12.4 Top Ten Fastest-Growing Occupations, 2006–2016

		Median annual wages, May 2006
Network systems and data communications analysts	53%	$64,600
Personal and home care aides	51	17,770
Home health aides	49	19,420
Computer software engineers, applications	45	79,780
Veterinary technologists and technicians	41	26,780
Personal financial advisors	41	66,120
Makeup artists, theatrical and performance	40	31,820
Medical assistants	35	26,290
Veterinarians	35	71,990
Substance abuse and behavioral disorder counselors	34	34,040

Average, all occupations = 10%

(*Source:* Bureau of Labor Statistics, Population Bulletin: U.S. Labor Force Trends, 2008.)

experienced and lucky pink-collar workers can work their way up to the salary of a white-collar job, but most barely make a living wage, like the factory workers of the nineteenth century.

Many of the most dominant pink-collar jobs are in clerical and sales work. These are jobs in office production: typists, file clerks, data entry clerks, receptionists, secretaries, administrative assistants, and office managers, plus cashiers, insurance agents, and real estate agents. In 1900, clerical and office work occupied only 7.5 percent of the U.S. working population. Today this number is 25 percent, though the percentage is declining as more and more white-collar workers are asked to do their own administrative tasks. These jobs are heavily female oriented (more than two-thirds are women) (U.S. Department of Labor, 2008). Seventy-eight percent of pink-collar workers are White, 13.5 percent Black, 12 percent Hispanic, and 4 percent Asian (Bureau of Labor Statistics, 2008.

Service Work. This category includes food preparation and service, personal services (hair stylists, launderers, child care workers), and maintenance workers (janitors, garbage collectors), plus police officers and

Labor Unions

A hallmark of blue-collar employment has been the labor union. In the early days of industrialized economies, owners spent as little as they could on workers. The work day lasted 12 hours or more, often under horrible conditions, with no days off, no benefits, and poverty-level wages. Workers had no rights and no political influence, so if they were injured on the job or if they complained, they were fired.

Soon workers discovered that if they banded together in **labor unions** modeled on the medieval guilds, they could redress the balance of power through collective bargaining, appealing to owners as a group. Only a few labor unions appeared during the eighteenth and nineteenth centuries, and because they were local or limited to a single occupation, they were not successful at creating large-scale change. Then the American Federation of Labor (AFL) was founded to coordinate the activities of many different occupational unions, so that, for instance, steelworkers could assist railroad conductors. Later the AFL merged with the Committee for Industrial Organization and became the extremely influential AFL-CIO.

During the first decades of the twentieth century, organized labor used work slowdowns, work stoppages, and strikes to fight for many of the benefits that we take for granted today: the 40-hour work week, overtime pay, a minimum wage, unemployment insurance, workers' compensation for on-the-job injuries, child labor laws, and worker safety and health codes. All of these were opposed by the companies and granted only grudgingly after the government intervened (Fernie and Metcalf, 2005; Hannan and Freeman, 1987; Lichtenstein, 2002).

Union membership increased rapidly during the 1930s and 1940s, until by 1950 more than a third of all nonfarm workers in the United States belonged to unions. Membership declined after 1970, sometimes sharply, both because blue-collar employment was declining and because federal regulations to protect workers made a great deal of union negotiation obsolete. In 2006, only 12 percent of American nonfarm workers belonged to unions. But beginning in 2006, the weak economy for the majority of Americans fostered an uptick in union membership that increased in 2007 and 2008 (*The State of Our Unions*, 2008).

Globally, unionization varies tremendously, from 2 percent (Gabon) to 70 percent (Iceland). Overall, rich countries tend to be more heavily unionized, at 30 percent or more. But union membership is in decline almost everywhere (International Labour Organization, 2008).

firefighters. Of American workers, 17 percent have service jobs; of these, 57 percent are women, and 43 percent men; 59 percent are White, 20 percent Hispanic, 16 percent Black, and nearly 4 percent Asian (U.S. Department of Labor, 2008). Service work is also age oriented: It includes the oldest and the youngest workers, like the retirees who greet you at Wal-Mart and the local teenagers who are flipping your burgers at a fast food restaurant.

Service jobs include many of the lowest paid, least prestigious occupations, and the ones with fewest—if any—health and retirement benefits. Many service jobs sit at the minimum wage.

Green-Collar Jobs. As the global economy continues to change, a new type of job has begun to emerge. "Green-collar" jobs are in those industries that are involved with new and renewable energy. Today green-collar workers are installing solar panels, retrofitting buildings to make them more efficient, constructing transit lines, refining waste oil into biodiesel, erecting wind farms, repairing hybrid cars, and building green rooftops. In 2006 renewable energy and energy efficiency technologies generated 8.5 million new jobs, nearly $970 billion in revenue, and more than $100 billion in industry profits. In December 2007, then-President Bush signed the Green Jobs Act, authorizing $125 million to train workers for green-collar jobs. It targeted especially those who were most likely to be displaced by globalization: veterans, displaced workers, at-risk youth, and families in extreme poverty. Green-collar jobs refute the notion that environmental health comes at the expense of economic expansion. Growth and conversation need not be opposites (www.greenforall.org/resources/green-collar-jobs-overview/green-collar-jobs-overview).

Wages: High, Minimum, and "Living" Wages. The *minimum wage* in the United States is $7.25 per hour. (That's the federal mandate; some states may have higher rates.) That's about $58 a day. Maybe that could sustain a teenager living at home, with only entertainment expenses to worry about, but a person living alone, without parental support, could never acquire adequate food, clothing, and shelter for that amount (and don't even think about supporting children!). Yet today some two million adults (aged 16 and over) earn minimum wage or less (Bureau of Labor Statistics, 2008) including 9 percent of service workers and 8 percent of office workers. Nearly 40 percent of minimum wage workers are working full-time.

Nearly one in seven workers (especially Black, Hispanic, and women workers) spend at least half of the their work lives stuck at or near minimum wage (Carrington and Fallick, 2001). These workers, plus the 25 million more who earn a dollar or two an hour above the minimum wage, are called the working poor.

The real value of the minimum wage (that is, its equivalent in the contemporary workplace) rose through the 1960s to a high of $7.18 (in 1968). It fell steadily during the Reagan and Bush presidencies, to a low point of $4.80 (in 1989). President Clinton raised it to $5.89, but it fell again under George W. Bush. All the while, worker productivity, corporate profits, and CEO pay have all surged.

An obvious solution would be to raise the minimum wage—to at least $8.00 per hour, the minimum necessary for a single full-time worker to acquire adequate food, clothing, shelter, and transportation (but not health insurance, which most low-income jobs don't offer anyway). Opponents argue that raising the minimum wage will hurt businesses, thereby fueling inflation, increasing unemployment, and ultimately harming low-skill workers. But several studies reveal that the costs to businesses, even small businesses, would be minimal. Retail businesses with fewer than 20 employees would stand to lose 1.0 percent of their current net receipts. Large social service agencies (with 500 or more employees) would lose the most, 10.1 percent of net receipts. But they would save on recruitment, training, and retention costs; reduce turnover and absenteeism; and improve quality of work, all positively affecting profits (Sklar, Mykyta, and Wefald, 2001).

Americans seem to prefer capping the salaries of top-level executives during the current crisis, rather than raising the minimum wage. Perhaps we don't believe that a rising tide lifts all boats but rather that a waning tide ought to sink more yachts.

More than 130 municipalities around the country have legislated "living wage" ordinances since 1994, including big cities such

Table 12.2
Who Earns Minimum Wage?

	Percent Distribution Total	At Minimum Wage	Below Minimum Wage
By Age:			
Men and women, age 16–24 years	50.4	56.3	49.5
Men, 16–24 years	17.3	20.3	16.8
Women, 16–24 years	33.2	36.0	32.7
By Race/Ethnicity and Sex:			
White men and women	80.1	75.2	80.8
White men	25.2	22.7	25.5
White women	55.0	52.8	55.3
Black men and women	13.8	17.1	13.4
Black men	5.5	5.9	5.4
Black women	8.4	11.2	7.9
Asian men and women	3.1	3.8	3.0
Asian men	1.2	1.0	1.2
Asian women	1.9	2.8	1.8
Hispanic men and women	14.6	13.6	14.7
Hispanic men	5.9	5.2	6.0
Hispanic women	8.6	8.0	8.7

(*Source:* Bureau of Labor Statistics, 2008.)

The Poor Work Harder Than the Rich

One of the most enduring myths in Western culture is the myth that people are poor because they don't work hard enough. Consistently, sociologists have debunked this myth by surveys of hours worked, comparisons that show the minimum wage doesn't even come close to helping people live above the poverty line, and other methods. Recently, though, sociologists and journalists have gone deeper into the working lives of working people and found something somewhat startling: Poor people work much harder than rich people.

Sociologist Katherine Newman (1999) sent teams of her graduate students into minimum-wage jobs, like flipping burgers in a fast food restaurant she called "Burger Barn." The researchers were surprised to see just how honest and hard-working the workers were, but what's more, they noted how workers had to scramble frantically to try and put a few dollars aside for the future because they had neither health benefits nor retirement plans. The workers were proud to work, in fact, preferring to make it on their own than rely on public assistance.

And journalist Barbara Ehrenreich (2001) went even further: She took six months and worked in a variety of entry-level jobs that define low-wage service work in the global economy. She worked as a cleaning woman in Maine, as a waitress in Key West, and as an "associate" in a Wal-Mart in Minneapolis. (Documentarian Morgan Spurlock later did the same thing, but for a much shorter stint, making *30 Days at Minimum Wage* [2005], the first of a reality series of programs about month-long excursions into unfamiliar social milieu that ran for three seasons in the English-speaking world, plus Latin America, Norway, and Sweden, until 2009.) At Wal-Mart, Ehrenreich had to stay late (and off the books) to clean up and arrive early (off the books) to set up. Working two jobs, she could not afford rent on an apartment and ended up, as did the other women she worked with, living out of a car or in a run-down weekly rate motel, eating soup out of cans she heated on a hot plate (studies have found that even basic groceries are more expensive in poor neighborhoods [Talukdar, 2007]). Ehrenreich had to wear an adult diaper because she was not permitted to take bathroom breaks during her shift. She often relied on the kindness of strangers, as her co-workers were always offering to share what little they had. Only the working poor, she sadly concluded, actually believe in the Protestant work ethic—that if you work hard enough, you can make it in America. The middle class has long since abandoned such illusions.

"Most civilized nations," Ehrenreich concludes, "compensate for the inadequacy of wages by providing relatively generous public services such as health insurance, free or subsidized child care, subsidized housing and effective public transportation." What, she wonders at the end of the book, does that say about us?

as New York, Chicago, Boston, Detroit, Cleveland, Los Angeles, and Miami. The highest of the minimum "living wages" are $11.00 per hour with health insurance (Santa Cruz, CA) and $12.25 per hour without health insurance (Santa Monica, CA). Some foreign cities, such as Toronto, Canada, have long had fair wage standards in place; in 2007, London, England, began a major living wage campaign (Jackson, 2007).

Alternatives to Wage Labor

Working for wages is not the only way that people work. In fact, much of our labor is not for wages at all. Economists have identified several "alternatives" to the wage-labor system.

Working off the Books. Many people depend on informal, under-the-table, off-the-books work for a substantial part of their income. The informal economy—also called the "underground economy" and the "gray market"—includes several types of activities. Although some people are uncomfortable thinking of crimes as drug dealing, prostitution, shoplifting, gambling, car theft, and burglary as part of the underground economy, studies of arrests have found that most perpetrators think of themselves as "taking care of business." They "go to work" as deliberately as someone with an office job. They follow rules, procedures, protocols, and a code of ethics; they take occupational risks (such as being injured or going to prison).

"Informal" does not mean "unorganized." Nationally and globally, billions of dollars of goods, services, and money change hands through complex networks of crime families, gangs, corrupt officials, smugglers, and money-laundering specialists (Portes, Castells, and Benton, 1989).

Illegal immigration fosters another type of underground economy. Illegal immigrants are particularly vulnerable to unscrupulous entrepreneurs who offer sweatshop working conditions at well below minimum wage. Although some manage to find white-collar jobs or are self-employed, the majority of illegal immigrants take service jobs, including house cleaning, gardening, and food preparation. In fact, illegal immigrants' share of low-wage jobs has grown in recent years, to 17 percent in 2008 (Pew Hispanic Center, 2009). The median household income of illegal immigrant families is less than $36,000 per year, considerably less than the $50,000 of legal residents (Pew Hispanic Center, 2009).

Most often, however, neither the work nor the worker is illegal; the underground economy comes into play only because the money is undeclared and therefore untaxed. A waiter receives an average of $30 in tips every night, but at income tax time, he reports only his official salary, not the extra $7,500. A collector buys a vase at a garage sale for $5 and sells it on eBay for $100, pocketing the money but forgetting about it at tax time. People fix cars, do laundry, mow lawns, babysit informally for friends and neighbors, adding perhaps $60 to their pocketbooks this week and $80 next week, resulting in an extra $4,000 at the end of the year that the IRS doesn't know about.

The size of the informal economy varies among countries and regions. In many developing countries, the informal economy amounts to more than 50 percent of the gross domestic product. In India, 83 percent of workers are informal; in sub-Saharan Africa, about 76 percent are (Barta, 2009). In the high-income countries of the OECD, it is about 15 percent (OECD, 2008a). Estimates of undocumented income alone, excluding crime and the work of illegal aliens, calculate it at 10 to 15 percent of the regular economy in the United States. That's more than $1 trillion per year and $100 billion in lost taxes (*The Economist*, 2006b).

All socioeconomic classes participate in the informal economy, but the $95 profit that the collector made on the eBay vase is a negligible contribution to a middle-class income (and the IRS is unlikely to be terribly concerned about it). But money earned off the books and under the table may easily double a $7.25 per hour

The informal economy includes work most often paid in cash or services with no benefits and often includes workers in restaurants and bars, housecleaners, and child care workers.

minimum wage income. The working poor are likely to depend on the informal economy for their everyday survival; in many developing countries, the informal economy is the only safety net people have (Barta, 2009; ILO, 2007c; Newman, 1999).

Unpaid Work. For most of human history, all work was unpaid. People provided their own food, clothing, housing, and entertainment. For jobs that were too big for one person or household, favors could be called in from friends and family. Sometimes people bartered something they had for something they needed. With the advent of capitalism, most of the goods and services that families or groups used to provide for themselves, from clothing to entertainment to police protection, increasingly became someone's job and required pay.

But we still do a tremendous amount of unpaid work. The best example is taking care of our own household, doing the dusting, vacuuming, dishwashing, food preparation, and so on. It is denigrated as "women's work," assumed to be the domain of full-time "housewives," even though husbands, unmarried partners, relatives, and friends all sometimes stay home to take care of the household,

Did You Know?

while someone else "goes to work" to provide the financial support. Before capitalism, there was no division between work and home: Everything took place at or near home. But as the division between home and work grew, and men began to work in the public arena for wages, they began to perceive themselves as "breadwinners," solely responsible for the economic vitality of the household, for "putting food on the table."

The idea that unpaid household labor had nothing to do with "real" economy was set in stone as early as the 1920s. Domestic labor lost the status of "work" and became a part of the heterosexual marital bond. Presumably women found household maintenance similar to wrapping a present—a joyful "labor of love," technically work, but worth it to please their husbands.

Self-Employment. Entrepreneurship has always been the hallmark of the American dream. In some socioeconomic classes, parents send their children off to sell seeds or magazine subscriptions to their neighbors nearly as soon as they can walk, to put them on the road to self-made fame and fortune. Even today, in the age of corporate dominance, 6.6 percent of nonagricultural workers in the United States—about 10.4 million working-age Americans—are self-employed (U.S. Census Bureau, 2009a). Their jobs range from blue-collar carpet and floor installing to white-collar management analysis and professional photography. More men than women are self-employed, and Whites are considerably more likely than African Americans or Hispanics to work for themselves (Bureau of Labor Statistics, 2008c). (These differences are due to differences in education, access to credit, and family resources; see Dunn and Holtz-Eakin, 2000; Fairlie and Woodruff, 2005; and Lofstrom, 2002.)

Often self-employed people start small businesses and become employers of their own: More than 19 million Americans work for companies employing fewer than 20 employees, and another 18.4 work for companies with more than 20 but fewer than 100 employees. These small businesses are a continued source of energy for the American economy, typically producing about three-fourths of all new jobs created in any given year. They tend to hire more older workers and part-timers, so they tend to be points of entry into the economy for new groups.

During the past decade or so, women have been leading the way in small businesses (perhaps due to their frustration with corporate culture). The estimated growth rate in the number of women-owned firms was nearly twice the growth rate of male-owned firms, and their employment and revenues grew faster than male-owned firms. Today about 40 percent of all privately held businesses in the United States are women owned. They employ over 13 million people and generate nearly $2 trillion in annual sales (Center for Women's Business Research, 2008). The trend has been even more pronounced for women of color (Figure 12.5). Between 2002 and 2008, these firms grew faster than all privately held firms in the United States, employing more than 1.2 million people and generating more than $165 billion in sales (Center for Women's Business Research, 2008).

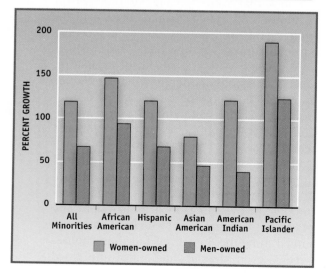

Figure 12.5 Women-of-Color Entrepreneurs

(*Source:* From *Center for Women's Business Research,* 2008. Reprinted with permission.)

Part-Time Work. About 25 percent of the American workforce is employed part-time (fewer than 35 hours per week) (Bureau of

Labor Statistics, 2008c). The percentage has remained fairly stable for the past 40 years. Women are more than twice as likely as men to work part-time (Economic Policy Institute, 2007; OECD, 2006). Globally, part-time workers are becoming increasingly common, ranging from 6 percent of the workforce in Greece to 36 percent in the Netherlands. However, women remain the primary part-time workers: They account for 73 percent of part-time employment in wealthy nations (OECD, 2007b).

Many people work part-time by choice because they want to attend to other commitments (part-time jobs have been traditional for high school and college students for years). However, over a quarter want full-time work but are prevented by the lack of suitable jobs; transportation or child care problems; or by employers who keep them just below the 35-hour-per-week limit to avoid paying full-time salaries and benefits. A surge in part-time employment began as a result of the weak economy: The number of Americans who saw their full-time jobs cut to part-time doubled in 2008, to 3.7 million—the largest figure since the U.S. government began tracking such data more than a half century ago (Goodman, 2008; Stern, 2009). In the industrialized world, more than 60 percent of people working at or below minimum wage are part-time (Bureau of Labor Statistics, 2008). Often, to make ends meet, they must take a part-time job in addition to a full-time job, or two or three part-time jobs.

Contingent and "On-Call" Work. Many employers have discovered the economic benefit of replacing permanent employees with employees hired to do a specific project or for a specific time period, or to be "on call," working only when their services are needed. According to the U.S. Department of Labor, about 4 percent of the American workforce are contingent, nearly 2 percent work "on call," and 1.5 percent are contract workers or "temps" (Bureau of Labor Statistics, 2005a; Novak, 2009). The ranks of temporary works have been swelling since the mid-1990s, both in the United States and globally. More than twice as many temps are employed in the United States as in any other country, but they are on the rise elsewhere, including emerging markets such as Brazil, South Africa, and Mexico (Coe, Johns, and Ward, 2008; Stern, 2009).

Globalization has shifted much industrial production to the developing world, and many manufacturing plants in the United States and Europe have closed.

Because there is no presumption of permanent employment, employers of contingent workers in the United States need not offer retirement pensions; cost-of-living raises; paid holidays, vacations, or sick leave; or health insurance (55 percent of traditional employees receive health insurance from their employees, but only 30 percent of on-call workers, 20 percent of contingency workers, and 10 percent of temporary workers do). They need not find more work for employees who have finished their duties early or pay overtime if their duties take longer than expected. They can lay off employees at any time without investing in expensive severance packages.

The characteristics of these workers vary widely. Independent contractors tend to be middle aged, White, and male, while temporary workers tend to be young, ethnic minority, and female. A large percentage of independent contractors, on-call workers, and contingency workers have white-collar jobs in management, the professions, or sales, but temporary workers are overrepresented in low-skill, low-paying jobs. Of independent contractors, more than 80 percent state that they prefer their arrangements, while well over 40 percent of temporary workers would prefer permanent jobs (Bureau of Labor Statistics, 2005a).

Unemployment

Even when the economy is functioning as smoothly as possible, there are always some people out of work, looking for work, or un-

During the Great Depression, millions of male breadwinners suddenly needed free coffee and doughnuts themselves, as the nation's unemployment rate hit 25 percent in 1934. In today's Great Recession, the unemployment rate has topped 10 percent.

able to work. Some people work only during some times of the year and not others; others are in between jobs, looking for a new position; others cannot find work in their field or are somehow disqualified from some jobs.

Social scientists typically distinguish among three different types of unemployment; the first two tend to be more temporary than the last:

1. *Seasonal unemployment* refers to the changes in demand for workers based on climate or seasonal criteria. For example, demand for agricultural labor drops dramatically after the harvest, and demand for workers in the tourist industry peaks only during "high season" for tourists.
2. *Cyclical unemployment* is a response to normal business cycles of expansion and contraction. During periods of economic expansion, demand for labor increases, and the unemployment rate goes down. But during recessions and economic downturns, demand for labor goes down, people are laid off or downsized, and unemployment rates increase.
3. *Structural unemployment* refers to more permanent conditions of the economy.

In some cases, it may be caused by a mismatch—say, between the skills needed by employers and the skills possessed by workers or between the geographic locations of employment and the location of potential workers. Structural unemployment can benefit corporations, who can hold labor costs down in a "buyer's market." In the 1980s and 1990s, more than 10 million American workers lost their jobs due to structural shifts in the economy, including the transformation of the auto and steel industries, the rise of high-technology jobs, and the offshore movement of many jobs.

Countries measure unemployment by counting people who are actively looking for jobs. The unemployment rate takes that number as a percentage of all employable workers (that means that the unemployment rate is lower than the actual number of people who do not have jobs, as some people simply give up and don't look for jobs. Part-time workers are also not included in the unemployment rate). In 2007, the unemployment rate in the United States was 4.4 percent. However, by

The Sociology of the Current Recession

"In Epidemic of Layoffs, No One Is Immune," read one headline about the dramatic increase in unemployment during the current recession. But it turns out that some are more immune than others. While the nightly news focuses on laid-off Wall Street brokers, the national reality looks quite different. The most vulnerable employees are, it turns out, the most "vulnerable" to unemployment. The current unemployment rate for those workers over 25 who have a college degree is 4.3 percent—half the national rate. For college-educated and White workers, the rate is 2.3 percent. But the unemployment rate for African Americans over 16 years old was 13.3 percent, and it was 11.4 percent for Hispanics. Without a high-school diploma? That number is 13.3 percent. And far more males than females are unemployed. In part, this is because manu-

facturing has declined more rapidly than sales and service jobs. But it also indicates the sociological observation that periods of economic crises reveal the lines of inequality already in place. Recovery can either remedy or reproduce these inequalities (Karabell, 2009).

Even if the rich are not getting richer, the poor are getting *much* poorer. People in developing countries are harder hit by the current downturn than those in wealthier countries. The continuing high cost of food and the dramatic drop in demand for raw materials have dramatically affected many in the developing world. Nearly three of four Mexicans say food prices have affected them "a great deal" (compared with one-third of U.S. residents and one-fourth of Canadians). More than nine of ten Kenyans say they are greatly affected (BBC World Service, 2009).

July 2009 it had more than doubled, to 9.5 percent. (And the "broad" unemployment rate, including part-timers and those not looking for work was 16.1 percent (Leonhardt, 2009). Since the recession began in December 2007, 6.5 million American jobs have been lost. These are both cyclical and structural; many of these lost jobs will not return when the economy turns around (Boushey, 2009).

Globally, while more people are working than ever before, so, too, are more people unemployed than ever before. Globally, the International Labor Organization (ILO) estimates that as much as 7.1 percent of the global workforce is unemployed, or an estimated 200 to 250 million people worldwide by the end of 2009, an all-time high (ILO, 2009a).

The Middle East and North Africa have the highest unemployment rate in the world (over 12 percent), while the unemployment rate in Latin

America and the Caribbean is about 8 percent. Almost half of the unemployed are the world's young people aged 15 to 24, who are more than three times as likely as adults to be out of work (ILO, 2008).

FIGURE 12.6 Unemployment Rates Total and Youth, World and Regions

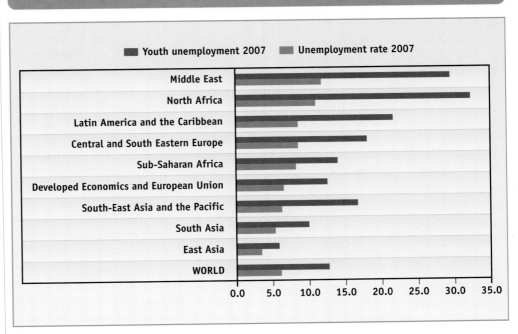

(*Source:* International Labor Organization, *Global Employment Trends,* January 2008.)

Diversity in the Workplace

Domestic comedy movies from the 1950s often begin at a suburban train station, where a crowd of White middle-class men, all dressed in identical gray suits, prepare for their work day in the big city. And, in fact, the middle-class work world in 1950 was nearly that homogeneous. In 1950, White men occupied over 90 percent of white-collar jobs in the United States. Today they occupy less than 50 percent of managerial, and about 40 percent of both sales professional jobs (Bureau of Labor Statistics, 2008c). Women and ethnic minorities are catching up.

During the next 50 years, the number of Hispanics and Asian Americans in the United States will triple, while the White non-Hispanic population will increase a mere 7 percent. The United States will be a "majority minority" country, with more than half the population belonging to ethnic minority groups (Friedman, 2006; U.S. Census Bureau, 2004b). The upward trends in minority population predict a corresponding increase in racial diversity in the workforce (Table 12.3). Coupled with increases in women's workforce participation, this means that White men may soon become a minority in the workplace.

Racial Diversity

Higher representation does not mean equality in the workplace. The salaries of people of color consistently lag behind those of White men. For every dollar that White men earn, Black and Hispanic men earn 65 cents, Black women 58 cents, and Hispanic women 48 cents. Two problems are becoming increasingly common in the racially diverse workforce—tokenism and the glass ceiling (see Figure 12.7).

When only a few members of a minority group occupy a job, they often believe (and are treated as if) they were hired as **tokens,** as representatives of their group rather than individuals. They are hypervisible: Everything they say or do is taken as what group members *always* say or do. If they get angry, for instance, their co-workers will conclude that everyone in the group gets angry easily. Their failures will be taken as evidence that the group as a whole is incompetent. Under constant pressure to reflect well on their group, tokens must be on guard at all times. They must consistently outperform their co-workers just to be perceived as equal (Moss-Kanter, 1977; Yoder, 1991).

Think about a time when you were the only member of some group in a larger group. You could have been the only woman or man, White person or person of color, straight or gay or bisexual, old or young, Christian, Muslim, or Jew—whatever set you apart. Let's say you were the only Latino. At some point, someone turns to you, innocently enough, and asks, "Well, how do Latinos feel about this?" At that moment, you become invisible as an individual, but you are hypervisible only as a member of the group. Of course, the only sensible answer is, "How should I know? I'm just an individual. I can only answer for myself. But I bet there are sociologists who have surveyed Latinos, and we can find out what most of them think about the question."

Gender Diversity

In 1900, less than 20 percent of American women (aged 15 and over) worked outside the home. Today over half do, and the percentage is increasing worldwide.

Surprisingly, women's employment is highest in poor countries, where everyone who can work does: The proportion is 82.8

Table 12.3
Increasing Racial Diversity in the U.S. Labor Force

	1995	2005	2020
White, non-Hispanic	76%	73%	68%
Hispanic	9%	11%	14%
African American	11%	11%	11%
Asian American	4%	5%	6%

(*Source: Workforce 2020: Work and Workers in the 21st Century,* by Richard Judy and Carol D'Amico, 1997. Reprinted with permission of the Hudson Institute.)

Figure 12.7 Unemployment Rates by Race/Ethnicity and Education, 2007

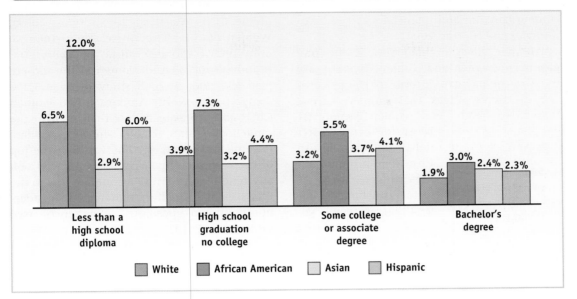

(*Source:* Bureau of Labor Statistics, 2008.)

percent of women in Mozambique, 80.4 percent in Cambodia, and 74.7 percent in Kenya of women working outside the home. In wealthy OECD countries, where women in male–female households have the option of staying home, workforce participation of women (aged 20 to 64) ranges from 76 percent (Denmark) to 71 percent (United States) to 60 percent (Japan). However, for college-educated women, the percentages are much higher: 89 percent in Denmark, 82 percent in the United States, and 63 percent in Japan.

The increase in the number of women in the workforce during the past 50 years has been called the "quiet revolution" because its consequences have been gradual but wide-sweeping—a transformation of consumer patterns, workplace policies, dating and relationships, parenting, household maintenance, and self-concepts for both men and women. But that transformation is incomplete. Men and women are still not equal, either in the workplace or at home.

As we saw in Chapter 9, inequality in the workplace has several distinctive characteristics, whether by gender or any other factor. Sex segregation concentrates women and men in different jobs and then explains those differences in terms of individual preferences (women and men simply want different jobs) rather than in terms of structural opportunities and barriers. About half the world's workers are in sex-segregated occupations (see Figure 12.8). In the United States, men comprise 98 percent of construction workers and 97 percent of airline pilots, for instance, while women comprise 76 percent of cashiers and 75 percent of clerical workers. While the overall sex segregation declined significantly in the 1970s, there is evidence of a recent

Figure 12.8 U.S. Women in Business

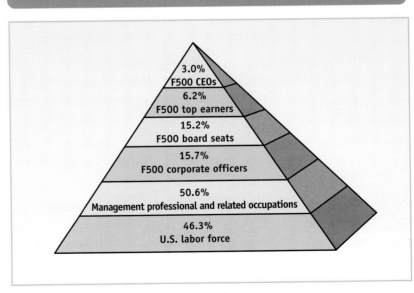

(*Source:* Catalyst Research; February 2, 2009, reproduced by permission.)

slowdown and resegregation of jobs within broad occupations (Charles and Grusky, 2004; Padavic and Reskin, [1994] 2002), including banking and financial services (Skuratowicz and Hunter, 2004).

Another effect of inequality is the **pay gap** between men and women. Typically, we think of the pay gap in terms of the percentage of men's wages that women earn—that is, we read about women earning 81 cents for every man's dollar. Yet we could also turn that around and say that men earn $1.23 for every woman's dollar—that is, men get a bonus, a "masculinity dividend" just for being men (Connell, 1995). In 2008, the median weekly earnings for full-time workers were $822 for men and $652 for women. The gap is noticeable across all racial divisions, although it is smaller for Blacks and Hispanics than for Whites and Asians (Table 12.4). The gap varies considerably by geographic location and by age—it is much smaller among young workers (25 to 34) than middle-aged and older ones (Bureau of Labor Statistics, 2006).

The gender wage gap is a global phenomenon. In most economies around the world, women still earn 90 percent or less of what their male co-workers earn (ILO, 2007). Even in typically "female professions" worldwide—jobs such as teaching and nursing—wage inequality persists for women (International Labour Organisation, 2009).

A third dynamic of gender inequality is the "glass ceiling." While women have been making small gains consistently for half a century, White men still control nearly all of the top jobs in corporate America. Women comprise more than half of all managers and professionals but less than 16 percent of the Fortune 500 corporate officers, only about 6 percent of the top earners, and only 3 percent of the CEOs (Catalyst, 2008; Jones, 2009). Women of color fare worse: They comprise only one corporate officer of every 100 (Catalyst, 2003). And women at the top are paid less, too. A 2008 study of over 3,200 companies in North America found women CEOs earn 15 percent less than men in the same jobs (Jones, 2009). The Glass Ceiling Commission observes: "The world at the top of the corporate hierarchy does not yet look anything like America." (Compare this to the "glass escalator" effect that men in gender-nontraditional positions experience [see Williams, 1995].)

In the EU, women hold only a tiny sliver of CEO positions but are significantly better represented on corporate boards (Catalyst, 2009).

Work–Family Dynamics. Our family lives also reinforce workplace gender inequality. Beginning in 2002, for the first time, the majority (51 percent) of married male–female couples in America were dual income (perhaps not surprisingly because the middle-class lifestyle that used to be feasible on one income now takes two). As women break into the ranks of the top earners, salary differences sometimes upset the traditional designation of the male partner as the "breadwinner": Twenty-six percent of all women in dual-wage households earn more than their husbands (Bureau of Labor Statistics, 2009). Among all married couples where the wife works (but not necessarily the husband), 33 percent of the wives earned more (Bureau of Labor Statistics, 2009).

However, household maintenance is still widely assumed to be a woman's job. A Western woman spends an average of 10 hours per week on household maintenance and a man about five hours. Sociologists have found that living arrangements don't change the average much: Two women living together will still spend about the same amount of time, as will two men. When men and women marry, the woman will perform 50 percent more housework than the man, even if they are both working full-time outside the home (Couprie, 2007). Once children arrive, the gap actually grows. American mothers do three times as much housework as men, spending 17 hours a week on average, while fathers spend just six (Seward et al., 2006).

Table 12.4
The "Masculinity Dividend": Median Weekly Pay Gap between Men and Women, 2009

	Men	Women
White	$855	$666
Black	$595	$559
Hispanic	$577	$510
Asian	$951	$773

(*Source:* Bureau of Labor Statistics, 2009.)

While new laws and regulations try to reduce the amount of workplace discrimination based on gender or sexuality, old stereotypes persist, keeping economic gender or sexual equality elusive. One way to see these dynamics is to observe what happens when people—not their workplaces—change. In a fascinating study, sociologist Kristen Schilt and economist Matthew Wiswall examined earnings records of recent male-to-female and female-to-male transgender people. Because they are really still the same people, their experiences may reveal something about gender dynamics in the workplace.

Schilt and Wiswall found that average earnings for female-to-male employees increased slightly

Workplace Discrimination

following their sexual reassignment surgery, but the wages of male-to-female transgender people fell by nearly one-third! Becoming a woman led several MTFs to lose authority and prestige as well as wages—along with increased harassment and often termination. On the other hand, becoming a man brought a slight increase in respect and authority (Schilt and Wiswall, 2008).

The United States ranks number eight among wealthy nations in the percentage of mothers in the labor force, with more than 60 percent of all mothers and more than 53 percent of mothers with children under 1 year old in the workforce (Cohany and Sock, 2007). In other nations, the percentage ranges from 76 percent (Sweden) to 32 percent (Czech Republic). Sixty-four percent of American working mothers are White, and 36 percent are women of color (OECD, 2006).

For many years, working mothers have been struggling to make corporate culture see children not as "problems" or distractions but as part of "business as usual." As parents, they want more flexibility in their hours and in their career paths, more options, updated criteria for success. Recently some men have joined them, reframing the issue from "women's right to work" to "parenting and the workplace."

Employers could benefit significantly from accommodating working parents of either sex. The skills one learns from parenting, including communication, emotional availability, multitasking, efficient organization, and patience, are valuable in the twenty-first-century workplace (Crittenden, 2005). Levine (1997) found that "working fathers," or fathers heavily invested in their children's daily lives, perform better and are more comfortable in a diverse workplace than the traditional "breadwinners."

Sexual Diversity

The workplace originated in a heterosexual division of labor: the male husband/father/ breadwinner and the female wife/mother/ domestic worker. Early decisions about wages and benefits assumed a single breadwinner for the entire family—and assumed that he was not only male but heterosexual. Many companies continue to assume that all of their employees, stockholders, and customers are heterosexual. There are no federal regulations barring discrimination on the basis of sexual orientation, so employers can refuse to hire gay men and lesbians or fire them at any time. As a result, most gay or lesbian employees must pretend that they are heterosexual, but even those who are out tend to bump up against what they call a "lavender ceiling."

Corporate culture is built around the assumption of heterosexuality, with conversations and jokes from the boardroom down to the loading dock focused on husbands and wives, other-sex boyfriends and girlfriends, and the attractiveness of various movie stars. Employees who refuse to participate are perceived as cool, distant, and snobbish, not "team players." Employees who mention same-sex partners, interests, and experiences are perceived as "problems." As a result, they are passed over at promotion time. In spite of the stereotype that all gay men are sophisticated interior designers living in Manhattan high-rise apartments, for example, gay and lesbian salaries lag far behind those of heterosexual workers (Raeburn, 2004).

Some changes have occurred recently, Over half of all Fortune 500 companies offer benefits for same-sex partners, and 410 include sexual orientation in their nondiscrimination policies. Not one of the Fortune 500 CEOs is openly gay or lesbian (Human Rights Campaign, 2006).

Work and Economy in the Twenty-First Century

The workplace as we know it today was created by the needs of an industrial economy. But now we are moving into a postindustrial, knowledge-based economy. The stereotypic office workplace, 9 to 5 workday, and single-field career are all becoming obsolete. What sorts of new arrangements will arise to take their place?

In the future, only a small percentage of workers will do a single job throughout their lives, changing only to move up to positions of greater authority (such as teachers becoming principals). Instead, they will develop a portfolio of skills and credentials that they will use to move horizontally, between jobs in many different career fields. Sometimes they will even occupy different jobs simultaneously.

The increased flexibility means that workers will have more control over their work and more creativity. However, they will have no job security because employers will be able to hire and fire them at will. And productivity will suffer because training and recruitment will be never ending: Workers will devote more time and energy to learning new skills and finding work than actually *doing* work.

In the future, we'll be more mobile. At present, such mobility is an option only for white-collar workers; the blue and pink collars are left behind. Also, it is unclear what benefits the white-collar employees will receive as mobility becomes more common. Greater flexibility, perhaps? More creativity? Greater autonomy? They will be working and playing at the same moment, answering personal and professional e-mails, watching movies while checking figures, surfing the Web while videoconferencing. Does this blurred boundary between work and leisure increase the quality of either? Or does it eat into private lives, cause higher stress, and create an army of slaves to e-mail?

And what will be the shape of the new economy as the world emerges from the current recession? Will the gap between rich and poor countries close significantly, or will it continue to widen? The global boom of the 1990s and early 2000s benefited the wealthy and the superwealthy and actually left those below the top 10 percent in worse economic shape than they had been in the 1980s. In a lighter moment, former President George W. Bush addressed his constituency as "the haves and the have-mores." But what about the swelling ranks of the "have-nots"? Will they have had enough and rebel, or will they find relatively comfortable places at the economic table?

In the future, will we be working more and enjoying it less, or working less and enjoying it more? Will the economy be the engine of spectacular wealth or grinding poverty? To the sociologist, the answer is both. It will depend on whom you talk to, where they live, and what they do for a living.

Chapter Review

1. The Economy and Society

Economy is vital to society, managing and distributing **capital.** Whether we view people as self-interested rationalists in competition, as did Locke and Hobbes, or idealist and cooperative, as Adam Smith did, or some split between the two, as did Marx, we are, as Durkheim observed, interdependent, relying on one another for goods and services that we cannot provide on our own. Economies unify us through connections, even as they are sources of identity that divide us through inequality. Economies began with agriculture, resulting in stability and surplus, leading to exchange in a **market.** The **Industrial Revolution** led to dramatic changes to society in an **industrial economy,** where work became **wage labor** for specialized jobs outside the home in centralized locations with powered machinery. With increasing efficiency, economic emphasis moved from **production** to **consumption,** and ultimately consumerism and **conspicuous consumption.** Our **postindustrial economy** is a **knowledge economy,** as the nature of work has changed, with **global production, global distribution,** and **outsourcing.** Less developed countries do the less skilled work, while developed nations join the managerial elite for whom work is no longer dictated by time or place. Each society has an **economic system,** which may include **capitalism,** which is dominant in the West and compatible with many political systems, such as **socialism, communism,** or some variation.

economy A set of institutions and relationships that manage capital. (p. 356)

capital Natural resources, manufactured goods, and professional services. (p. 356)

market Regular exchange of goods and services within an economy. (p. 357)

Industrial Revolution Transformation of the economy due to a large-scale shift from home-based craft work by individuals to machine-based mass production in factories. (p. 357)

industrial economy Economy based on factory production and technologies. (p. 357)

wage labor The arrangement by which workers get a regular paycheck in exchange for performing a specific task, rather than being paid for the end product of their labor. (p. 357)

production The creation of value or wealth by producing goods and services. (p. 357)

consumption The purchase and use of goods and services. (p. 357)

conspicuous consumption Thorstein Veblen's term to describe a new form of prestige based on accumulating and displaying possessions. (p. 358)

knowledge economy One defining element of the postindustrial economy in which ideas, information, and knowledge have become new forms of capital. (p. 358)

postindustrial economy Economy that shifts from the production of goods to the production of ideas. (p. 359)

global production A term that describes how, in a global economy, goods are manufactured from raw materials and produced in factories all over the world in complex production chains. (p. 359)

global distribution A term that describes how the products we buy are likely made of materials from several countries, assembled in another country, packaged and distributed from yet another, with advertising campaigns and marketing schemes drawn from yet another. (p. 359)

outsourcing Also called "offshoring," refers to the practice of hiring out any phase(s) of product development to lower-wage countries or groups. (p. 359)

economic system A mechanism that deals with the production, distribution, and consumption of goods and services in a particular society. (p. 360)

capitalism An economic system in which free individuals pursue their own private interests in the marketplace. In laissez-faire capitalism, markets freely compete without government intervention. State capitalism requires that the government use a heavy hand in regulating and constraining the marketplace, and welfare capitalism creates a market-based economy for most goods and services, yet also has social welfare programs and government ownership of essential services. (p. 360)

socialism Economic system in which people are meant to cooperate rather than compete, share goods and services, own property collectively, and make decisions as a collective body. (p. xxx)

communism Envisioned as the ideal economic system by Karl Marx, communism would produce and distribute resources "from each according to his or her ability, to each according to his or her need," erasing social inequalities along with crime, hunger, and political strife. (p. 363)

2. The American Economy in Global Perspective

America was born with the Industrial Revolution, and manufacturing flourished in the North, while the South remained agriculturally based. In the resulting Civil War, the modern model triumphed. Differences between these two economic systems can be seen not only by comparing nations globally but also by looking at the North and South in America today. The advent and subsequent growth of the **corporation** and the 1929 crash led to legislation to provide for citizens, eerily similar to the recent crash and bailouts today, which also followed laissez-faire growth, and again resulted in legislation to protect and prevent excess and profiteering by robber barons. Corporate entities also grew in scale and complexity, from family holdings, expanded to business with hired management, to institutional networks, and finally, **multinational corporations,** which engage in a **race to the bottom** to maximize profit by minimizing cost. Multinational corporations do not share interests with any one nation; they serve only themselves.

corporation A business that is treated legally as an individual. It can make contracts, incur debts, sue, and be sued, but its obligations and liabilities are legally distinct from those of its owners. (p. 365)

multinational corporation Also called a "transnational corporation," a giant company that is not clearly located in any one country but operates through a network of offices all over the world. (p. 366)

race to the bottom Bonacich and Appelbaum's term for outsourcing jobs to wherever manufacturers and retailers can pay the lowest possible wages so as to maximize profits. (p. 367)

3. Work, Identity, and Inequality

Traditionally people worked as long as there was daylight. In the modern age, that workday has shortened, but Americans work longer hours than other developed nations. Research and theories abound addressing why we work and what makes us work harder, including the Hawthorne Effect, Theory X and Theory Y, and **manufactured consent,** which considers how workers are bound to the company through values and emotion and strive to maximize productivity. White-collar workers do knowledge work, and higher education is required; professions are the most prestigious knowledge jobs. Blue-collar production jobs are male-dominated, while pink-collar jobs, including clerical positions, are female dominated, with less pay and prestige. Blue-collar workers can benefit from collective bargaining through a **labor union.** Service jobs are at the bottom of the pay scale. Minimum wages are not enough to live on, and the working poor suffer great hardship. Some places have mandated a higher "living wage" instead. The working poor often rely on working off the books in the underground or informal economy, including criminal activity and immigrant labor, or any untaxed jobs. Unpaid work includes household labor, which historically is not recognized, as it was assumed that men supported their wives, who worked for love. Self-employment is a cherished goal for Americans; while business ownership is rising for women, most part-time workers are women. Part-time workers include temps, as well as unemployed seasonal workers and workers experiencing cyclical unemployment. Unemployment is a growing globally.

manufactured consent Michael Burawoy's term for the strategies by which companies get workers to embrace a system that also exploits them. (p. 370)
labor union A group of workers who act collectively address common issues and interests. (p. 372)

4. Diversity in the Workplace

The U.S. white-collar workforce used to be homogeneously middle-class White males. Women and minorities are catching up in representation but lag behind in wages and can be treated as **tokens.** Gender inequality includes occupational segregation by gender, as well as the **pay gap** in the workplace and inequality in domestic unpaid labor, with women earning less and working more. There is also discrimination in the workplace by sexual orientation.

token Representative of a traditionally disenfranchised group whose hypervisibility results in constant pressure to reflect well on his or her group and to outperform co-workers just to be perceived as equal. (p. 380)
pay gap The consistent, worldwide difference between what men are paid and what women are paid for the same labor. (p. 382)

5. Work and Economy in the Twenty-First Century

As we move into the postindustrial knowledge-based economy, we can expect even less job security, less career stability, increased mobility, and overall more change. Not everyone is suffering equally in the current recession, and it is certain that our economic futures depend on our particular social location.

Self-Test: Check Your Understanding

1. Economies are born of rational self-interest, according to
   a. Locke and Hobbes.
   b. Adam Smith.
   c. Karl Marx.
   d. Emile Durheim.
2. Collective goals and central planning are hallmarks of which political system?
   a. Capitalism
   b. Socialism
   c. Communism
   d. Collective goals and central planning are hallmarks of all of the above political systems.
3. Identify the correct historical progression of the corporation in America, from earliest to most recent.
   a. Managerial, family, institutional, multinational
   b. Institutional, managerial, multinational, family
   c. Managerial, multinational, family, institutional
   d. Family, managerial, institutional, multinational
4. The original founding tenet of capitalism was "laissez-faire," which translates as
   a. "to leave alone."
   b. "the body politic."
   c. "free profit."
   d. "fair laziness."
5. According to the text, the underlying conflict in the American Civil War was
   a. the issue of slavery as either a fundamental right, or an abomination.
   b. Fighting for freedom to make a profit and own property under capitalism.

   c. a clash between a traditional agricultural economy and a modern industrial one.
   d. a fight for territory and expansion of an ideology of exploitation and submission.
6. Theoretical knowledge, self-regulating practices, and community orientation are hallmarks of
   a. white-collar jobs.
   b. blue-collar jobs.
   c. pink-collar jobs.
   d. professions.
7. Research in which sociologists and journalists joined the working poor revealed that
   a. most people working low-paying jobs are poor because they have poor work ethics and are lazy.
   b. most of the money the poor earn is spent on things like lottery tickets, alcohol, and eating out at fast food restaurants.
   c. the poor have strong work ethics but don't make enough to survive; still, they would rather work than take a handout.
   d. America provides few social services so as to encourage workplace participation because the poor would rather receive subsidies or welfare benefits than work.
8. In which of the following is the greatest percentage of working women found?
   a. In Western developed countries
   b. In the poorest countries
   c. In the wealthiest countries
   d. In European developed countries

Self-Test Answers: 1. a, 2. b, 3. d, 4. a, 5. d, 6. d, 7. c, 8. c

Integrate and Explore: Points to Consider

1. What was the basis for the economy prior to industrialization, and what was a typical workday like? Since industrialization, does everyone globally share the same work experience? How has global consumption and production led to decreasing or increasing inequality worldwide?

2. As many nations move toward knowledge-based economies, is inequality in the workplace lessening, increasing, or staying the same? In the recent recession, were all groups equally likely to lose their jobs, or were some groups hit harder than others? Why?

succeed with mysoclab PEARSON

Self-scoring practice tests, flashcards for learning key terms, streaming audio of the entire text, and multimedia, including:

Explore—*Debt Addiction*
Explore—*Auto Industry Layoffs*
Explore—*Latino Laborers*
Map—Social Explorer: *Different Industries and Income Extremes*
MySocLibrary—Robert Perrucci and Earl Wysong, *The Global Economy and the Privileged Class*

13

Politics and Media

The election of President Barack Obama in 2008 was a historic event for many reasons. Not only was he the first African American elected to the American presidency, but his campaign seemed to contradict the old American adage: "You can't fight City Hall." His answer? "Yes we can."

He was also the first to harness the political power and fundraising capacity of the Internet. Small donations poured in through websites and Internet campaigns that eventually dwarfed the finances of the Republican candidate, John McCain—and the Republicans are supposed to be the party of "big money"!

The campaign and Obama's election highlighted the issues when sociologists look at politics and the media. In some ways, we have more political power than ever before. The media give us constant access to political discussion and protest. Local groups constantly organize to change things. Yet we also have less power than ever. Every week, it seems, a new scandal reveals how the big money behind big corporations seems to dictate public policy. Labor strikes no longer work. Worldwide protests against wars and invasions have little impact on policy makers.

We're more politically aware than ever. Round-the-clock news stations broadcast every detail of major and minor political disputes. C-Span lets us glimpse every moment of every session of Congress. Twitter and other social media tools help activists communicate with each other and report on their progress quickly and constantly. Telephone and Internet polls chart changes in public opinion minute by minute. Yet we're also less politically engaged than ever. Party membership is down. Voting rates are low compared to other industrialized nations— even in elections full of hot-button issues.

We're more politically polarized than ever before. The divisions between Democrat and Republican have never been greater. No journalist half a century ago would have thought to divide the country into red and blue states. Yet we're also less politically coherent than ever before. Legislation that passes one year is rescinded the next.

"We are both more informed and more apathetic, more empowered and more disenfranchised, and the world is both more and less democratic than ever. Understanding these dynamics is sociology's unique contribution to the study of the media and of politics."

Few voters pull the lever for a straight party line any longer. Liberals vote for conservative candidates, conserv-atives vote for liberal candidates, and many people just give up on labels and vote for a mixed bag of Republicans, Democrats, independents, and Greens.

WO

Finally, in some ways, the world is more democratic than ever before. People everywhere celebrate democracy as an ideal, and virtually every nation claims, in its constitution or in its official name, to be a democracy—including the People's Republic of China, the Islamic Republic of Iran, and the Democratic People's Republic of Korea. Yet many of these countries are authoritarian regimes, ruled by political or theocratic elites rather than the "consent of the governed." And many democracies are also corrupt or run like individual fiefdoms, so the world sometimes seems less democratic than ever before.

Which is it? More or less power? More or less informed? More or less politically aligned? More or less democratic?

To the sociologist, the answer to these questions isn't one or the other. It's both. The processes and dynamics of how we can be both more *and* less informed, powerful, or democratic are sociology's unique contributions to the study of media and of politics.

Politics: Power and Authority

Politics is the art and science of government. Politics is about **power,** the ability to make people do what you want them to do— whether they want to do it or not. And it is about **government**—the organization and administration of the actions of the inhabitants of communities, societies, and states. And politics is about **authority**—power that is perceived as legitimate by both power holders and those who are subjected to it. If politics is working well, it is through government that power is transformed into authority.

Sociologists have always wondered about power: how we get it, how we use it, why some of us have so much of it and some of us have so little (Faulks, 2000; Lukes, 1986; Orum, 2000). Back in the nineteenth century, Marx saw power as purely a characteristic of social class. The owners of the means of production had complete control over the workers' tasks, schedules, and salaries. The workers had no power at all. They had no control over their wages or working conditions and could vote only for candidates who were handpicked by the factory owners.

Class, Status, and Power

No society has ever been built around pure coercion. A few have come close—the slave society of the antebellum South, for example, or Romania under Nicolai Ceausescu—but they are always vastly inefficient because they must expend almost all of their resources on keeping people in line and punishing dissidents. And even there, the leaders must supplement coercion with other techniques, like persuasion and indoctrination.

That's why Max Weber (1978) argued that power is not a simple matter of absolutes: Few of us have total power over others, so force won't work. And few of us have no power at all, so we rarely have to resort to trickery. Most often, people do what we want them to do willingly, not because they are being coerced or tricked. Drivers who obey the speed limits are probably not worried about being fined—after all, hundreds of cars are zooming past them at 90 mph without punishment. Instead, they have decided that they want to obey the speed limit, because they're good citizens, and that's what good citizens do.

In most societies, cultures, subcultures, families, and other groups, coercion remains a last resort, while by far the most common means of exercising power is authority. Authority is power that is perceived as legitimate, by both the holder of power and those subject to it. People must believe that the leader is entitled to make commands and that they should obey.

Types of Authority

Weber argued that leaders exercise three types of authority: traditional authority, charismatic authority, and legal-rational authority.

Traditional authority is a type of power that draws its legitimacy from tradition. We do things this way because we have always done them this way. In many premodern societies, people obeyed social norms for hundreds, sometimes thousands, of years. Their leaders spoke with the voice of ancient traditions, issuing commands that had been issued a thousand times before. They derived their authority from who they were: the descendants of kings and queens, or perhaps the descendants of the gods, not from their educational background, work experience, or personality traits.

Traditional authority is very stable, and people can expect to obey the same commands that their ancestors did. Its remnants still exist today in many social institutions, including religion, government, and the family, where we obey some rules because we have always done so. But even in ancient times, large-scale political, economic, and social changes sometimes occurred, such as invasion, war, or natural disaster, and new generations faced situations and challenges unknown to their ancestors, thus putting a great strain on traditional authority. That's when a second form, charismatic authority, would emerge.

Charismatic authority is a type of power in which people obey because of the personal characteristics of the leader. Charismatic leaders are so personally compelling that people follow them even when they have no traditional claims to authority. Indeed, they often ask their followers to break with tradition. We read in the New Testament that Jesus frequently said "it is written, but I say unto you...," contrasting traditional authority (Jewish law) with charismatic authority (his teachings).

Charismatic leaders are often religious prophets, but even when they are not, their followers can be as passionate and devout as religious believers. Some presidents, like Franklin D. Roosevelt and John F. Kennedy, developed a popularity that cannot be explained by their performance in office alone. Many other political leaders of the past and present depend, to some degree, on charisma in addition to other types of authority.

Charisma is morally neutral—as a personal quality, it can be found at all points in an ethical spectrum: Hitler, Gandhi, Osama bin Laden, and Nelson Mandela all possessed personal qualities that elicited obedience from their followers.

But pure charisma is also unstable because it is located in the personality of an individual, not a set of traditions or laws. And because they defy other forms of authority, charismatic leaders rarely live long—they are exiled (like the Dalai Lama in 1959), assassinated (Gandhi, Kennedy), or imprisoned (Mandela). When they are gone, their followers are faced with a crisis. How do you maintain the emotional high that you felt when the leader was with you?

Weber argued that after the leader's departure, a small group of disciples will create a set of rules and regulations by which one can continue being a follower. Thus, charismatic authority is replaced by the rules, regulations, and rituals of legal-rational authority.

In the third form of authority, **legal-rational authority,** leaders are to be obeyed, not primarily as representatives of tradition or because of their personal qualities, but because they are voicing a set of rationally derived laws. They must act impartially, even sacrificing their own opinions and attitudes in obedience to the laws of the land.

Legal-rational authority has become the most common form of authority in contemporary societies. In fact, many argue that modern government would be impossible without it. Governments operate under a set of regulations flexible enough to withstand changing social situations. Traditional authority is unable to handle much change without breaking down. And no leader, however charismatic, would today be able to sway tens of millions of people of diverse socioeconomic classes, races, religions, and life situations, on the basis of his or her personality alone.

Political Systems

Political systems determine how group leaders exercise their authority. Virtually all political systems fall into one of two categories, authoritarian or democratic.

Authoritarian Systems

In an **authoritarian political system,** power is vested in a single person or small group. That person holds power sometimes through heredity, sometimes through force or terror.

Although dictators rule by violence, they often have significant popular support. Adolf Hitler arriving at a rally in Nuremberg in 1936.

Did You Know?

Legitimate Dictators?

The three most ruthless dictators of the twentieth century acquired their power legitimately. King Victor Emmanuel of Italy appointed Mussolini prime minister in 1922. That same year, in the Soviet Union, Joseph Stalin was elected president of the Communist Party. German president Paul von Hindenburg appointed Adolph Hitler as chancellor in 1933. As soon as they came to power, though, they took over the press, dismantled parliament, outlawed political opposition, exiled or executed their enemies, and generally ignored whatever democratic ideals that gave them power in the first place.

Monarchy. One of the first political systems was the rule by a single individual, or **monarchy** (*mono* means "one," and *archy* means "rule").

The rule of an individual was legitimized by traditional authority. The rulers of ancient Egypt, China, Japan, and Peru all claimed that their families descended from the gods. Medieval monarchs derived their power from divine right: They were not literally descended from God, but their power was based on God's will. By the time of the Renaissance, most of the kings and queens of Europe were "absolute monarchs": Their word was law, even when their word contradicted the law of the land. It might be illegal for the average person to commit murder, but the king or queen could call for the execution of anyone, for any reason or for no reason (so it made sense to stay on his or her good side).

Gradually a more egalitarian climate began to prevail. We can find traces of "rule of the people" as early as the English Magna Carta (1215), which established government as a relationship between monarchy and the people. During a relatively short period, the English Civil War and revolutions in France, America, and Haiti either deposed hereditary rulers or made them answerable to parliaments of elected officials (Birn, 1992; Wedgwood, 1990; Winks and Kaiser, 2003). Other kingdoms became "constitutional monarchies" peacefully, adopting constitutions and electing parliaments with the full support of the kings or queens. A constitutional monarchy may still have a hereditary ruler, but he or she functions as a symbol of the country and a goodwill ambassador, while elected officials make the everyday political decisions based on the principles embedded in a constitution.

Today only a few absolute monarchies remain, such as in Kuwait, Saudi Arabia, and Swaziland, but even those countries often legislate a system of checks to keep the rulers from overstating their power.

Totalitarianism and Dictatorship. In **totalitarianism,** political authority is extended over all other aspects of social life—including culture, the arts, and social relations. Any political system may become totalitarian when no organized opposition is permitted and political information is censored. Secret police and paid informers closely monitor the people to ensure that they remain loyal to a rigidly defined ideology. Propaganda, misinformation, and terror are used to ensure obedience (Arendt, [1958] 1973).

Other than the brutal attempts to control the thoughts and behaviors of their citizens, modern totalitarian governments have little in common. They can start out as democracies (Nazi Germany), constitutional monarchies (Italy under Mussolini), or socialist states (the Soviet Union under Stalin). They span economic systems, although free-enterprise capitalism is uncommon because it is difficult to control. They tend to be more common in rich nations than in poor nations because they are expensive to maintain (North Korea expends 25 percent of its resources on the military). Or they can be **dictatorships,** in which one person, with no hereditary claim, can come to power, by military takeover or by being elected or appointed.

Democratic Systems

The great British statesman Winston Churchill once commented that democracy is the worst form of government—except for all the others. Democracy is messy and noisy, and order is difficult because, in its basic idea, democracy gives a political voice to everyone.

Democracy (from *demos,* or people) puts legislative decision making into the hands of the people rather than a single individual or a noble class. The concept originated in ancient Greek city-states like Athens and Sparta, in which all questions were put to a vote in an assembly, and every adult male citizen had voting rights. City officials were selected by lottery (Hansen, 1999).

Pure democracy, or **participatory democracy,** with every person getting one vote and the majority ruling, can work only in very small, homogeneous units, like classrooms, families, communes, clubs, churches, and small towns. If many people participate, it becomes impossible to gather them all together for decision making. If the population becomes heterogeneous, simple majority rule obliterates the needs of minorities.

The idea of democracy vanished when ancient Greece became part of the Roman Empire (510–23 BCE). It reappeared during the Enlightenment (1650–1800), when philosophers began to argue that all human beings have natural rights, including the right to select their own political leaders. Because nation-states were too big for participatory democracy, they developed the theory of **representative democracy,** in which citizens elect representatives to make the decisions for them. Representative democracy requires an educated citizenry and a free press. High-speed communication and transportation are also helpful; during the nineteenth century, it took weeks to calculate the popular votes in presidential elections and months before everyone in the country was informed of the results. However, there are often several steps between the people and the decisions, such as an electoral college, to minimize chaos while things get counted.

In 1900, there were only a few democracies in the world, and none with **universal suffrage** (voting for all adults, both men and women). Today 70 percent of the world's nations are democracies, more than twice the percentage just 20 years ago,

and another 14 percent are constitutional monarchies, all with universal suffrage (see Figure 13.1). The remaining 16 percent of the world's nations are a mixture of colonies, territories, absolute monarchies, communist states, Islamic republics or other forms of theocracy (rule by a religious group), military juntas, and dictatorships, plus one ecclesiastical state (Vatican City) and two states with no central government (Somalia, which is in chaos after 20 years of civil war; and Iraq, which is under American occupation as of this writing).

But even these countries are experiencing strong pressure toward democratization from both home and abroad. Globalized mass media constantly put rich people on display as examples of "ordinary" citizens of the United States, Japan, or Western Europe, thereby associating democracy with wealth, privilege, and power. International humanitarian agencies often associate democracy with freedom and condemn autocracies as necessarily oppressive. The only way to resist the pressure is to strictly censor outside media, thereby transforming the state into a totalitarian regime.

Problems of Political Systems

Democracies are messier than authoritarian systems; populations in open societies are more difficult to control. But both authoritarian and democratic systems are prone to the same types of problems.

Figure 13.1 Number of Democracies Worldwide, 1989–2008

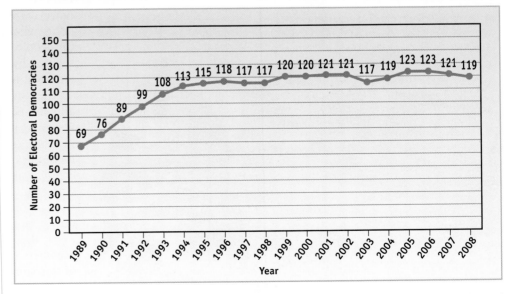

(*Source:* www.freedomhouse.org, Freedom House, Freedom in the World 2009: Global Data. Reprinted by permission.)

Corruption. An international agency called Transparency International (www.transparency.org) ranks nations on a scale of 0 (not corrupt) to 10 (highly corrupt) on the basis of three variables:

1. Outside interests donate large sums of money to elected officials.
2. New members of parliament or Congress obey special interest groups rather than the views of the people they are supposed to represent.
3. Officials misuse government funds or the power of their office for personal gain.

Corruption seems to have little to do with whether the country is democratic or authoritarian. For instance, Papua New Guinea, which rated a 10 on democratic institutions, ranked a 7.9 in corruption; and Kuwait, which rated a –7 on democratic institutions, ranked 4.7 in corruption. Instead, corruption seems to be characteristic of poor nations, where there are few economic opportunities, so people use their political influence to make money or exercise illicit power.

Bureaucracy. As we saw in Chapter 3, bureaucracies develop in all complex societies. Politically, Max Weber argued that bureaucracies were antagonistic to democracy. In a democracy, after all, one is elected to a fixed term (and with contemporary "term limits," these are increasingly short terms). This means that elected officials do not become "entrenched" but are constantly subordinate to the will of the people. By contrast, **bu-**

The appeal of democracy as a political ideal has become nearly universal. The first national election in Iraq in 2005.

reaucracies are staffed by people who are appointed, often for a "life tenure," which means that they are accountable to no one but the bureaucracy itself. Bureaucracies therefore almost always suffer from "bureaucratic entrenchment" (Weber, 1978). In the United States, most people who operate the government are never elected by anyone and not directly accountable to the people, and there are many possibilities of mismanagement, inefficiency, and conflict of interest (Etzioni-Halevy, 1983). The administrative staffs of organizations often wield enormous influence over policies, as do lobbyists and other interested groups.

Class, Race, Gender, and Power. The rich have far more political clout than the poor. Every U.S. president elected in the past 100 years has been wealthy when elected, and most were born into wealth. Today millions of dollars are necessary to successfully finance the campaigns of presidents, governors, senators, and even local officials like mayors: Grassroots door knocking and envelope stuffing can never compete with high-tech prime-time TV commercials and glossy full-page magazine ads. In recent years, several enormously wealthy men, like Michael Bloomberg, current mayor of New York City, have spent hundreds of millions of their own dollars to run for public office—and win.

Corporations and special interest groups spend millions, sometimes billions, of dollars on lobbying and **political action committees (PACs),** often leaving the average citizen's concerns far behind. As a result, the average citizen often feels that neither party is doing what is needed, that no one is listening to "people like me." Minorities feel particularly slighted by their parties and by the party system (Kittilson and Tate, 2004).

The interconnections between the wealthy and the powerful have been a major area of research interest to sociologists. Beginning in 1969, G. William Domhoff began to document these connections between corporate executives and elected officials. What he found was that formal mechanisms for influence, such as lobbying organizations or PACS, show only a moral public side of influence. In many cases, the private side is far more important. Members of the corporate elite are graduates of the same elite prep schools and Ivy League colleges as the legislators and political officials they seek to influence. They all send their chil-

Political campaigns have become so costly that often only the wealthiest can mount one. Billionaire Michael Bloomberg spent tens of millions of his own money to run for mayor of New York City in 2002 and again in 2009.

dren to the same schools and are even members of the same social organizations or fraternities. Thus, their influence is exerted informally: A corporate CEO calls up his "old school chum" who happens to be a senator, and after chatting about their families, mentions his interest in a particular bill. Domhoff even found that the top level corporate CEOs and political power brokers go away together each year on a retreat to a camp in northern California, where they spend the weekend partying (Domhoff, 1967, 1974).

The representation of women and minorities in elected offices is small. Of 535 seats in Congress, 91 are women—just 17 percent. Twenty-one of them are women of color: 12 black, 7 Latina, and 2 Asian-American (Center for American Women in Politics, 2009). Only 15 percent (81 members) are minorities: 43 African-American (42 in the House, 1 in the Senate); 30 Latinos (27 in the House, 3 in the Senate) and 8 Asian Americans and Pacific Islanders (6 House, 2

Senate). The 111th Congress that began in January 2009 saw the first openly gay candidate to be elected as a freshman; he joined three others, all of whom came out once they were already serving as members. Most minorities occupy seats in the lower House of Representatives, not the Senate; in fact, African American men are overrepresented in the House (Kittilson and Tate, 2004). On the state and local levels, the situation is similarly unequal. For instance, the average representation of women in state legislatures nationwide is less than 25 percent, and has increased less than 4 percent in the past 15 years (National Conference of State Legislatures, 2009).

The commonsense explanation for the underrepresentation of minorities in high government positions is simple: discrimination. Either minorities lack the financial resources to successfully run for office or else voter prejudice keeps them from being elected. Prejudices about the "qualifications" of various minorities to adequately represent the majority often induce people to vote for "majority" candidates.

This, though, raises another question: If the minorities cannot adequately represent the majority, how can the majority claim to adequately represent the minorities? If democracy is defined as the rule of the majority, what happens to those who are not in the majority? Will there be, as some sociologists predicted, a "tyranny of the majority," in which power becomes a zero-sum game and the winners get it and the losers don't, or will there be protections of the minorities to ensure they are not trampled politically? (Of course, middle-aged wealthy White men, who dominate all elective offices, are the statistical *minority* of all voters. By a landslide.)

Discrimination does not, however, explain what happens in countries with multiple electoral systems, combining "winner take all" (the U.S. practice) with proportional representation (or PR). In a **proportional representation** system, each party would receive a proportion of the legislative seats and thus would be more likely to govern "from the center" and build coalitions. This would tend to increase minority representation because coalitions of minority groups can form a majority. Countries that use proportional representation elect many times more women to their legislatures than winner-take-all systems (Rule and Hill, 1996).

Women in Parliament

The percentage of women in national legislatures varies enormously around the world. The highest rates tend to be among the most developed European nations, but not necessarily. Some developing countries, like Rwanda and South Africa, have fairly new constitutions, which require higher percentages of women.

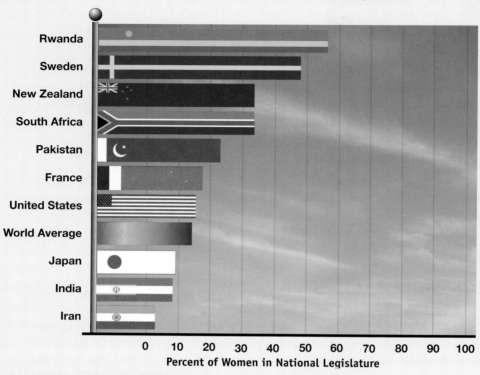

Rwanda
Sweden
New Zealand
South Africa
Pakistan
France
United States
World Average
Japan
India
Iran

0   10   20   30   40   50   60   70   80   90   100
Percent of Women in National Legislature

Source: Inter-Parliamentary Union, in *The Economist*, April 4, 2009.)

1. What might explain the differences in the number of women in elected office?

2. What sorts of policies might a country adopt in order to increase women's representation—assuming that increasing women's representation is a positive goal? Ought it to be a goal?

The Political System of the United States

In the American political system, citizens are protected as individuals from the exercise of arbitrary control by the government, but individual citizens have little impact on changing the system. Individuals must band together at every level—local, state, and national—to hope to sway policies. And even then, it is only through one's elected representatives that change can be accomplished. The system is so large and complex that organized bureaucratic political parties dominate the political landscape.

Political parties are groups that band together to petition for political changes and to support candidates to elected office. Most of the world's democracies have many parties: Germany has six, Japan seven, France 19, Italy 30, and Argentina 49. Usually, however, only two or at most three dominate in parliament or Congress. British elected officials traditionally belong to either the Labour Party or the Conservative Party; there are many other parties, but the most successful, the Liberal

Democrats, occupy only 9.6 percent of the seats in parliament.

With only two major political parties, the United States is something of an anomaly among democratic nations. Sociologists generally attribute the fact that most other countries have many more political parties to America's winner-take-all electoral system. With legislative representation based on proportional voting, as in Europe, for example, smaller parties can gain seats, have influence, and even be included in coalition governments. In the United States, it doesn't make sense to spend money and launch major campaigns if you are a third (or fourth, and so on) party because if you don't win, you get nothing, no matter how many votes you received. Republicans and Democrats tend to have different platforms (opinions about social and economic concerns) and different ideas about the role of government in the first place. According to conventional thinking, the Republicans run "against" government, claiming that government's job should be to get out of the way of individuals and off the back of the average taxpayer. Democrats, by contrast, believe that only with active government intervention can social problems like poverty or discrimination be solved. It is the proper role of government to provide roads, bridges, and other infrastructure, as well as services such as welfare, health insurance, and minimum wages to those who cannot fend for themselves.

Both sides point to the other side's failures as evidence that their own strategy is better. Republicans argue that overspending on welfare has made poor people lazy and dependent, unable and unwilling to help themselves, victims, as President Bush said, of the "soft bigotry of low expectations." Democrats point to the devastating human toll of Hurricane Katrina, for a recent example, which was made infinitely worse because of Republican policies of cutting funding to reinforce the levees surrounding New Orleans, while they offered massive tax cuts to the wealthy.

To a sociologist, however, this question—whether the government should intervene in personal life or not—is a good example of how framing the issue as "either/or" misses the most important issues. It's always both—and both parties believe that the government should both intervene in private life and stay out of it. It is rather *where* they want to stay out of your life and *where* they want to intervene that is the question.

American Political Parties: The Politics of Race, Class, and Gender

What makes people affiliate with—that is, join, support, or vote for—Republicans, Democrats, or a third party? Surprisingly, it's not often the issues, and rarely the "great divide" of government intervention versus hands off. The answer is that people are socialized into party affiliation. They vote to express their group identity. If you were to tell me your educational background, class, race, and gender, I would probably be able to predict who you are going to vote for with considerable accuracy (Burdick and Broadbeck, 1977; Popkin, 1994). Party affiliation tends to follow from:

You'd Better Vote

Twenty-seven of the world's democracies make voting compulsory. Usually nonvoters face no penalty, or they can get off with just an explanation and a fine (the equivalent of $2.50 in Switzerland, $25 to $250 in Austria, $400 in Cyprus). In Chile, Egypt, and Fiji, they can go to prison.

Did You Know?

1. *Class.* Poor, working-class, lower-middle-class, and blue-collar trade unionists tend to be Democrats, while wealthy, upper-middle-class, white-collar individuals tend to be Republicans. In 2008, Republican John McCain beat the Democrat Barack Obama among households earning between $100,000 and $200,000 a year, although he lost by 6 percentage points among highest-earning households over $200,000 per year.

2. *Education.* Generally, the higher educational levels go Democratic, and the lower Republican. However, in 2008, Barack Obama beat John McCain at every education level, and most decisively among those no high school (63 percent to 35 percent) and those with post-graduate degrees (58 percent to 40 percent).

3. *Race.* Since the 1930s, most racial and ethnic minorities have been Democratic. Before 2008, the percentage had been declining as more minorities became more affluent and professional. But Barack Obama received a majority of minority votes in 2008, including 67 percent of Latinos, 95 percent of African Americans, and 62 percent of Asian Americans (Limonic, 2008). Whites were the only group that voted for McCain over Obama (55 percent to 43 percent) (see Figure 13.2).

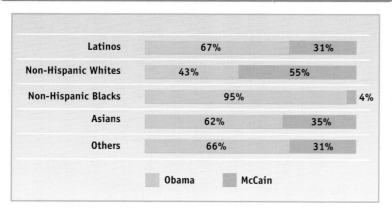

Latinos	67%	31%
Non-Hispanic Whites	43%	55%
Non-Hispanic Blacks	95%	4%
Asians	62%	35%
Others	66%	31%

Obama   McCain

(*Source:* Center for Latin American, Caribbean & Latino Studies, Laura Limonic, "Latinos and the 2008 Presidential Elections: A Visual Data Base," December 2008, p. 4. http://web.gc.cuny.edu/lastudies. Reproduced by permission.)

4. *Gender.* Women are more likely than men to vote Democratic, but again the percentages have been declining (54 percent in 2000, 51 percent in 2004). The decrease has occurred primarily among White women. In 2008, women voted for Obama over McCain 56 percent to 43 percent, but women of color overwhelmingly supported Obama: The Democrat won 96 percent of Black women and 68 percent of Latinas. (Only White women preferred McCain, by a margin of 53 to 46 percent.)

5. *Age.* When they vote, younger people tend to lean Democratic. In 2008, only voters over 65 preferred McCain, by 53 to 45 percent. Among the youngest voters, 18 through 29, Barack Obama got 95 percent of Black votes, 76 percent of Latinos, and 54 percent of Whites.

Interest Groups

Parties are not the only organized groups that influence political decisions. Individuals, organizations, and industries often form **interest groups** (also known as *special interest groups, pressure groups,* and *lobbies*) to promote their interests among state and national legislators and often to influence public opinion. *Protective groups* represent only one trade, industry, minority, or subculture: Labor unions are represented by the AFL-CIO, African Americans by the NAACP, women by NOW, and conservative Christians by Focus on the Family. *Promotional groups,* however, claim to represent the interests of the entire society: Greenpeace tries to preserve the planet's ecology, and Common Cause promotes accountability in elected officials (Grossman and Helpman, 2001; Miller, 1983).

Increasingly, interest groups do not try to represent an entire political agenda. Instead, they fight for or against a single issue, like gun control. As the number of "hot-button" issues has become more visible in the media, the number of interest groups has increased, especially now that the Internet provides an easy, risk-free place for mobilization: Potential members need only push a button indicating that they support the cause and key in their credit card number to make a donation.

Interest groups are very visible in Washington. Lobbying organizations and political action committees often have a staff of full-time professional lobbyists who influence politicians for a living. In fact, many people believe that interest groups have too much power and can buy votes in any election by pumping money into their campaign—or the campaigns of their opponents. As a result of widespread public suspicion, interest groups are also subject to restriction. They must be registered, and they must submit detailed reports of their activities.

Interest groups organize to lobby around specific issues. These Greenpeace polar bears are protesting against global warming.

Straw Polls

Polling is nearly as old as the United States. In the 1820s, newspapers began to do straw polls to test the mood of the electorate. The term comes from an old trick used by farmers, who would throw a few pieces of straw into the air to see which way the wind was blowing. The "straw poll" was designed to tell which way the political wind was blowing.

Did You Know?

Political Change

Political life is not merely a matter of orthodox social institutions: political parties, voting, and elections. History shows us that some groups find their objectives or ideals cannot be achieved with this framework—or are actively blocked by it. They need to develop "unorthodox" political action. Some types of efforts for political change, social movements and revolutions, are internal; others, like war and terrorism, are attempted from outside the society.

Social Movements

When people seek to effect change, they may engage in political revolutions, but more commonly they start **social movements—** collective attempts to further a common interest or secure a common goal through action outside the sphere of established institutions. They may try to influence public opinion with advertising campaigns or by convincing a celebrity to act as their spokesperson. They may try to get legislators' attention through marches, sit-ins, media "zaps" (invasions of televised media events),

Internet protests, boycotts, or work stoppages. Or they may try more colorful (and illegal) methods of getting their points across, like animal-rights activists who splash blood on actors wearing fur coats (McAdam, 1996; Meyer, Whittier, and Robnett, 2002; Morris and Mueller, 1992; Tarrow, 1998).

Today there are thousands of social movements, dedicated to supporting every imaginable political agenda. Many social movements are international and rely heavily on use of information technology to link local campaigners to global issues. They are as evident a feature of the contemporary world as the formal, bureaucratic political system they often oppose.

Revolutions

Revolution, the attempt to overthrow the existing political order and replace it with a completely new one, is the most dramatic and unorthodox form of political change. Many social movements have a revolutionary agenda, hoping or planning for the end of the current political regime. Some condone violence as a revolutionary tactic; many terrorists are hoping to start a revolution.

Successful revolutions lead to the creation of new political systems (in France, Russia, Cuba, and China), or brand new countries (Haiti, Mexico, and the United States). Unsuccessful revolutions often go down in the history books as terrorist attacks (Defronzo, 1996; Foran, 1997).

Earlier sociologists believed that revolutions had either economic or psychological causes. Marx believed that revolutions were the inevitable outcome of the clash between two social classes. As capitalism proceeded, the rich would get richer and the poor would get poorer, and eventually the poor would become so poor that they had nothing else to lose, and they would revolt. This is called the **immiseration thesis**—you get more and more miserable until you lash out.

Talcott Parsons (1966) and other functionalists maintained that revolutions were not political at all and had little to do with economic deprivation. They were irrational responses by large numbers of people who were not sufficiently connected to social life to see the benefits of existing conditions and thus could be worked into a frenzy by outside agitators.

This theory is clearly wrong. Revolutions are almost never caused by mass delirium but by people who want a change in leadership. A number of sociologists showed that revolutions were just a type of social movement, rationally planned, with mobilization strategies, grievances, and

specific goals in mind (see, for example, Gamson, 1975; Paige, 1975; Tilly, 1978; Zald and McCarthy, 1987). But Marx was also wrong—especially about which groups will revolt. It is not people with nothing left to lose, but people who are invested in the social system and have something at stake. Don't expect a revolt from the homeless and unemployed but from the lower middle classes in the cities and the middle-rung peasants in the countryside. Political scientist Ted Robert Gurr (1971) coined the term **relative deprivation** to describe how misery is socially experienced by constantly comparing yourself to others. You are not down and out: You are worse off than you used to be (downward mobility), or not as well off as you think you should be (rising expectations), or, perhaps, not as well off as those you see around you.

Sociologists typically distinguish among different types of revolutionary events, along a continuum from the least dramatic change to the most. A **coup d'état** simply replaces one political leader with another but often doesn't bring with it any change in the daily life of the citizens. (Some coups do bring about change, especially when the new leader is especially charismatic, as in Argentina under Perón.)

A **political revolution** changes the political groups that run the society, but they still draw their strength from the same social groups that supported the old regime. For example, the English Revolution between 1640 and 1688

The immediate aftermath of Iran's disputed election in June, 2009, witnessed two new developments in social movements in that country. First, women led the street protests for the opposition candidate Mirhossein Mousavi, and second, governmental repression was so significant that activists used Twitter and YouTube to broadcast their activities to the rest of the world.

reversed the relationship between the king and aristocracy on the one hand and the elected parliament on the other, but it didn't change the fact that only property owners were allowed to vote.

Finally, a **social revolution** changes, as Barrington Moore (1966) put it, the "social basis of political power"—that is, it changes the social groups or classes that political power rests on. Thus, for example, the French Revolution of 1789 and the Chinese Revolution of 1949 swept away the entire social foundations of the old regime—hereditary nobility, kings and emperors, and a clergy that supported them—and replaced them with a completely new group, the middle and working classes in the French case and the peasantry in the Chinese case.

War and Terrorism

War. In Hebrew and Arabic, the standard word for *hello* and *goodbye* is *shalom* or *salaam*, meaning "peace." War was so common in the ancient world that the wish for peace became a clichéd phrase, like the English *goodbye* (an abbreviated version of the more formal "God be with you"). By some estimates, there were nearly 200 wars in the twentieth century, but they are increasingly hard to pin down. The old image of war, in which two relatively evenly matched groups of soldiers from opposing states try to capture each other's territory, has become increasingly meaningless in the days of long-range missiles, smart bombs, and ecoterrorism. However, war still occurs as a standard, perhaps inevitable characteristic of political life: In his classic *On War* ([1832] 1984), Carl von Clausewitz wrote, "War is not an independent phenomenon, but the continuation of politics by different means."

The frequency of war suggests that it is an inevitable problem of human societies, but extensive research has found no natural cause and no circumstances under which human beings will inevitably wage war. In fact, governments worldwide expend considerable time and energy to mobilize their people for warfare (Brown, 1998; Stoessinger, 2004). They offer special privileges to those who enlist in military service, glorify warfare as "freedom fighting," schedule parades and exhibitions of military power, and portray enemies or potential enemies as monsters out to destroy us. The United States spends more money on its military than the next 46 highest spending countries combined; in 2008, it spent $711 billion. China

A perceived threat is often a justification for war— whether it turns out to be true or not. In February 2003, at the United Nations, the U.S government presented its case for the invasion of Iraq by showing maps of chemical and biological weapons storehouses. After the invasion, no such weapons were ever found.

spent "only" $122 billion; Russia $70 billion; France, Britain, and Germany combined $147 billion (Center for Arms Control and Non-Proliferation, 2008). If we look at expenditures per capita, we find that Israel leads with over $2,300 per person, but the United States is number two in the world at $2,000.

Sociologist Quincy Wright (1967) identified five factors that serve as root causes of most wars:

1. *Perceived threats.* Societies mobilize in response to threats to their people, territory, or culture. If the threats are not real, they can always be manufactured, such as the claim that Saddam Hussein possessed weapons of mass destruction, which was the pretext for the war in Iraq in 2002.
2. *Political objectives.* War is often a political strategy. Societies go to war to end foreign domination, enhance their political stature in the global arena, and increase their wealth and power.

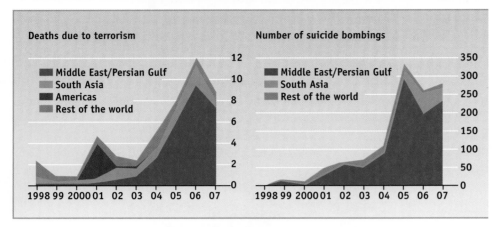

Figure 13.3 Reign of Terror

(*Source:* Used by permission of START: A Center of Excellence of the U.S. Department of Homeland Security, University of Maryland.)

3. *"Wag the dog" rationale.* When internal problems create widespread unrest at home, a government may wage war to divert public attention and unify the country behind a common, external enemy.

4. *Moral objectives.* Leaders often infuse military campaigns with moral urgency, rallying people around visions of, say, "freedom" rather than admitting they fight to increase their wealth or power. They claim that wars are not acts of invasion but heroic efforts to "protect our way of life." The enemy is declared "immoral," and morality and religion are mobilized for the cause.

5. *Absence of alternatives.* Sometimes, indeed, there is no choice. When your country is invaded by another, it is hard to see how to avoid war.

Terrorism. **Terrorism** means using acts of violence and destruction against military or civilian targets (or threatening to use them) as a political strategy. For instance, an individual or group interested in acquiring independence for the Basque people of northern Spain might engage in terrorism in the hope that the Spanish government will acquiesce to their demands for autonomy. Frequently, however, terrorism has no specific political goal. Instead, it is used to publicize the terrorist's political agenda or simply to cause as much damage to the enemy as possible. Interviews with terrorists who bomb abortion clinics reveal that they do not believe that their actions will cause the Supreme Court to reverse the *Roe v. Wade* decision; they simply want to kill abortion doctors. Similarly, when al-Qaeda orchestrated the 9/11 attacks, they did not expect Americans to embrace their extremist form of Islam en masse; they simply wanted to hurt Americans (Hoffman, 1998; Juergensmeyer, 2003).

Terrorism can be used *by* the regime in power to ensure continued obedience and to blot out all dissent. For example, Stalin in the Soviet Union, Pol Pot in Cambodia, Saddam Hussein in Iraq, and the apartheid regime in South Africa all used terrorist violence to maintain control. Because totalitarian states can survive only through fear and intimidation, many make terrorism lawful, a legitimate tool of government.

But usually we think of terrorism as the actions *against* the existing regime. Usually terrorists have little or no political authority, so they use terror to promote or publicize their viewpoints, just as nonviolent groups might use marches and protests.

While terrorism is not new, recent technological advances have made weapons easier to acquire or produce and communication among terrorist groups easier, so that terrorism is increasingly common. According to the U.S. National Counterterrorism Center, in 2008 there were 11,800 terrorist attacks worldwide, resulting in 54,000 deaths. The Near East had the largest number of reported attacks—40 percent of the total—while South Asia saw the greatest number of fatalities (National Counterterrorism Center, 2009).

Democratic societies reject terrorism in principle, but they are especially vulnerable to terrorists because they afford extensive civil liberties to their people and have less extensive police networks (as compared with totalitarian regimes). This allows far more freedom of expression, freedom of movement, and freedom to purchase terrorist weaponry. The London subway attacks of July 2005 and airport attacks in Glasgow, Scotland, of 2007 were possible only because people are free to move about the city at will; in a totalitarian state they would be subject to frequent searches and identification checks, and they would not be allowed in many areas unless they could prove that they had legitimate business. And the absence of checking and monitoring duty means that democratic countries have smaller police forces to respond to emergencies.

Terrorism is always a matter of definition. It depends on who is doing the defining: One person's terrorist might be another's "freedom fighter." Had the colonies lost the Revolutionary War, the patriots would have gone down in history books as a group of terrorists. The same group can be labeled terrorist or not, depending on who their foes are: In the 1980s, when they were resisting the Soviet Union, the Taliban groups in Afghanistan were portrayed in the media as "freedom fighters," but in 2001, when they were resisting the United States, they were portrayed as terrorists.

Everyday Politics

Most political activity does not occur in political caucuses and voting booths, through large-scale social movements, or even through the violence of war, terrorism, and revolution. Politics happens in everyday situations that have nothing to do with candidates.

Being Political. In 1969, Carol Hanisch wrote an article for the book *Feminist Revolution* ([1969] 1979) titled "The Personal Is Political," arguing that even the most intimate, personal actions make a political statement: "Personal problems are political problems," she concluded. Or, to put it another way, every problem is a political problem. For example, you are making a political statement when:

- Someone makes a racist, sexist, or homophobic comment, and you agree, disagree, or stay silent.

- You make a friend who belongs to a different race, gender, or sexual orientation, or who doesn't.

- A company exploits the workers in its foreign factories, but you buy its products anyway, or refuse to buy its products, or don't know about it.

- You seek out a "green" product, or don't, or don't notice whether it is environmentally friendly.

Sociology and Our World

A Tale of Two Terrorists

In 1992, an American GI returning from the Gulf War wrote a letter to the editor of a small, upstate New York newspaper complaining that the legacy of the American middle class had been stolen by an indifferent government. Instead of the American dream, he wrote, most people are struggling just to buy next week's groceries. That letter writer was Timothy McVeigh from Lockport, New York. Three years later, he blew up the Murrah Federal Building in Oklahoma City in what is now the second-worst act of terrorism ever committed on American soil.

McVeigh's background and list of complaints were echoed, ironically, by Mohammed Atta, the mastermind of the September 11 attack and the pilot of the first plane to hit the World Trade Center. Looking at these two men through a sociological lens sheds light on both the method and the madness of the tragedies they wrought.

McVeigh emerged from a small legion of White supremacists, mostly younger, lower-middle-class men, educated through high school. They are the sons of skilled industrial workers, of shopkeepers and farmers. But global economic shifts have left them little of their fathers' legacies. They

face a spiral of downward mobility and economic uncertainty. They complain they are squeezed between the omnivorous jaws of global capitalism and a federal bureaucracy that is, at best, indifferent to their plight.

Most of the terrorists of September 11 came from the same class and recited the same complaints. Virtually all were under 25, educated, lower middle class, and downwardly mobile. Many were engineering students for whom job opportunities had dwindled dramatically. And central to their political ideology was the recovery of manhood from the emasculating politics of globalization.

The terrors of emasculation experienced by lower-middle-class men all over the world will no doubt continue, as they struggle to make a place for themselves in shrinking economies and inevitably shifting cultures. Globalization feels to them like a game of musical chairs in which, when the music stops, all the seats are handed to others by nursemaid governments. Someone has to take the blame, to be held responsible for their failures. As terrorists, they didn't just get mad. They got even.

In short, you are "being political" all the time.

Everyday politics is not a replacement for organized political groups. In fact, the two complement each other. Small, seemingly inconsequential everyday acts have a cumulative impact, creating grassroots support for the legislative changes for which political groups lobby. These acts also express political identity, enhance solidarity, and promote social change (Scott, 1987).

Frequently, groups with little formal power still attempt to resist what they perceive as illegitimate or dictatorial authority, using symbolic and cultural expressions. For example, historian Kenneth Stampp found that instead of being docile and helpless, American slaves were constantly rebelling in numerous small symbolic ways: breaking tools, stealing from their owners, and working really slowly (Stampp, 1956). When Estonia was under Soviet occupation in the 1980s, citizens would pretend they spoke only Estonian or put signs on hotels in Russian that said "No Vacancy" (Suny, 1985). In France and Spain, schools in Brittany, Catalonia, or the Basque country often teach subjects in the local language rather than French or Spanish, to preserve local traditions.

Politics and Media: Interdependence. "Everyday politics" often relies on the media to make its points. Hands-on events depend on media coverage to enhance their impact on policy and public opinion; consumer actions need media coverage to spread the word about tactics, reasons, and goals. Sociologist Todd Gitlin (1980) coined the term "staged politics" to describe the conscious use of the mass media to create political events out of everyday actions.

Politics and the media have a long history of interdependence stretching back to the dawn of America itself, when colonial newspapers were used to publicize revolutionary ideas and drum up public support for military action. Today, political actors and media organizations engage in increasingly sophisticated relationships. Office-holders, organizations, and political candidates time and tailor their statements to news broadcasts, while media organizations sponsor polls and hire countless commentators, developing streams of content out of political sentiment and events. Today, many question the impact of the media in politics. Do the media shape or reflect the political scene? Do they create or reflect the public opinion on which political decision making is based?

This debate about the power of the media echoes across many social questions of the day. Think how many times we have heard variations of it: Does pornography lead men to commit rape? Does gangsta rap, or video games, or violent movies, or violent heavy metal music lead to increased violence in our society? Do the media incite social problems like violence or racism or sexism, or do they merely reflect how prevalent they already are in our society?

The sociologist does not choose between these two positions. It's both: The media both reflect the society in which they were created and also affect our behaviors and attitudes. If they didn't reflect our society, then they wouldn't make any sense. And if they didn't have some effect on our attitudes or behavior, then they wouldn't "work"—which means that the entire advertising industry would be out of business. Instead of asking whether media shape or reflect our society, the sociologist asks: How and in what ways do the media shape and reflect our lives?

What Are the Mass Media?

Media (the plural of *medium*) are the ways that we communicate with each other. If I am talking, I am using the medium of speech. I could also sing, gesture, and make smoke signals. In the Canary Islands, people used to communicate through the medium of whistling. Right now I am writing, or more precisely typing, using alphabetic symbols instead of sounds.

Technological innovations like the printing press, the radio, the television, and the personal computer have created **mass media,** ways to communicate with vast numbers of people at the same time, usually over a great distance. Mass media have developed in countless directions: There are books, newspapers, magazines, motion pictures, records and tapes, CDs and DVDs, radio and television programs, comic strips and comic books, and a whole range of new digital media. New forms of mass media are constantly being developed, and old forms are constantly falling into disuse.

Sometimes the new forms of mass media can revive or regenerate the old. Teenagers used to keep their diaries hidden in their rooms, with little locks to deter nosy siblings. Today they are likely to publish them on the Internet as blogs.

Sociologists are interested in the access to media by different groups with different resources and also in the effects of media—how they affect our behaviors and attitudes, how they bring us together or drive us apart, how they shape the very rhythm of our days.

Types of Mass Media

There are many types of mass media. All have experienced enormous growth since the nineteenth century, and today media animate—and some would say dominate—our everyday lives.

Print Media. The printing press, which appeared in China in the eighth century and Europe in the fifteenth, changed the way we record and transmit information (Eisenstein, 1993). The new technology allowed media to be produced more quickly, more cheaply, and in larger numbers. Reading shifted from a privilege of upper-class males to a much wider population, and the literacy rate in Europe jumped from less than 1 percent to between 10 and 15 percent.

In the first decades of the twentieth century, reading became a mass middle-class activity (Radway, 1999). People read cheap paperbacks, newspapers, and magazines.

The newspaper and the magazine were originally vehicles for general interest. Today, the nearly 20,000 magazines published in the United States are increasingly specialized publications, of interest to only a selected audience (Magazine Publishers of America, 2008).

Consuming media can link people around the world into networks and even movements. We may feel we have more in common with Madonna fans in Russia—who might buy this matroyshka (a traditional Russian wooden doll)—than we do with Beyoncé fans in the next town.

Both newspapers and magazines have experienced challenges by the Internet for audiences and, especially, for revenue. Newspapers are faring worse. The number of daily newspapers in the United States has shrunk significantly over the past century, and both numbers of papers and circulations have declined considerably over the past two decades: Between 1990 and 2007, U.S. daily newspaper circulation dropped by more than ten million (Isaacson, 2009). Newspaper ad revenues have been declining steadily since 2000 and sharply since 2006. Some papers are in bankruptcy; others have lost three-quarters of their value (Project for Excellence in Journalism, 2009). One of the few bright spots is Hispanic newspapers, where total circulation grew between 2005 and 2008. The number of Hispanic weekly newspapers in the United States increased to over 400 in 2008 (Project for Excellence in Journalism, 2009).

But the ethnic as well as the mainstream press is rapidly moving to the online format to stay afloat financially and reach fast-growing audiences there. Most newspapers are now available online (worldwide, more than 5,000) because that's where the readers are: Unique newspaper audiences surged from about 40 million a month to nearly

While mass general-interest magazines have declined, there are thousands of special-interest magazines—for every imaginable hobby. These magazines unite small communities, but "buttonhole" them into separate and definable niches.

70 million between 2004 and 2008 alone. In 2008, the percentage of people who get most of their national and international news on the Internet surpassed those who get it by reading the paper (Pew Center for People and the Press, 2009). Newspaper publishers are struggling to capture the revenue these growing audiences represent since advertising is down even online, and newspaper content on the Web has historically been free.

As for magazines, 85 percent of Americans over 18 read them, and the average number of issues they read per month has actually increased since 2003 (Magazine Publishers of America, 2008). Unique visitors to many magazine websites have grown steadily between 2006 and 2008, including visitors to several newsmagazine sites (Project for Excellence in Journalism, 2009). Revenues from digital operations at magazines are a small but fast-growing part of their business.

Sociology and Our World

Do Women's Magazines Oppress Women or Liberate Them?

In 1963, Betty Friedan published *The Feminine Mystique,* a blockbuster bestseller that many say launched the modern women's movement. Friedan argued that women's magazines are the main way that culture brainwashes women into believing that their highest value is in fulfilling their femininity, that true happiness can only come from catching a man, marrying him, and becoming a homemaker and mother.

Some 40 years later, the discussion continues, but now some best-selling authors are blaming women's magazines for leading women astray—in the opposite direction. These critics now say women's magazines brainwash women into wanting careers and independence, leading them away from the homes and families that represent their true pursuit of happiness (Crittenden, 1999; Shalit, 1999).

Which is it? Are women's magazines instruments of women's oppression by keeping women in the home—or by forcing them to seek fulfillment outside of the home? Are they guidebooks to fulfillment by encouraging women to marry and be mothers—or to build careers, businesses, and individual success in the world?

To the sociologist, the answer is not one or the other—it's both. From the very beginning, American women's magazines have presented readers with competing messages and have asked them to select which ideas to accept and which to resist and to resolve conflicting messages in their own ways (Aronson, 2002).

That diversity of perspectives remains true today. Women's magazines remain highly profitable and popular; four women's titles—*Good Housekeeping, Family Circle, Women's Day,* and *Ladies' Home Journal*—rank among the top ten best-selling magazines in the nation. The major magazines also have international editions published in dozens of countries around the world. And modern versions still carry at least some of the competing messages that readers have long expected and enjoyed. See for yourself: Look at any popular women's magazine—*Glamour, O, Jane, Latina, Cosmopolitan*—or check out even the great-grandmothers like *Good Housekeeping* or *Ladies' Home Journal.* See if you notice competing perspectives among the articles, the ads, and the editorials.

Globally, one can discern the difference between rich and poor nations by their newspaper circulation. Japanese and Norwegians are the most avid newspaper readers in the world, with 631 and 601 issues sold per 1,000 people, more than one per household. It's 98 in Germany, 241 in the United States, and 139 in Poland. But look at the poor countries: 51 issues per 1,000 people in South Africa, 11 in Kenya. Ethiopia is the lowest, at 0.3 (World Association of Newspapers, 2008). (See Figure 13.4.) Obviously the newspapers in these countries are not suffering greatly from Internet competition: Most people are too poor to afford newspapers and unable to read them anyway (Ethiopia has a 36 percent literacy rate).

Radio, Movies, and Television. Before 1880, if you wanted music, you had to make it yourself or hire someone. That all changed when Thomas Edison recorded his voice. Within a few decades, the gramophone (a machine that enabled you to listen to recorded music) was a staple of American life. And, at the same time, entrepreneurs sought to harness the power of transmitting sound via invisible "radio waves" and make them profitable. Movies were born with a 12-minute clip of *The Great Train Robbery* in 1903—and the media world changed forever.

By the mid-1930s, over half of the U.S. population went to the movies—every week. And this would include, typically, two full-length features, newsreels, serial dramas, cartoon shorts—and commercials. And television, introduced in the late 1940s, was geared to commercial sponsorship of shows. With variety shows and commercial spots every few minutes, the connection between selling products and consuming media was indelibly tightened. (European television and radio are state sponsored and, until the 1980s, had no commercials at all.)

The irony of American television is that, between 1955 and 1985, television was arguably the most popular form of mass media in the United States. Virtually everyone was watching—and everyone was watching the same channels. There were only three national networks: NBC, ABC, and CBS. Whole generations were defined by their preferred television programs: *I Love Lucy* in 1955, *Bonanza* in 1965, *All in the Family* in 1975.

Today, the average American home has more television sets than people—2.5 people versus 2.86 TVs (Nielsen, 2009). But television is so fragmented that even the top-rated shows draw only a small percentage of viewers. Only 18 percent of all households with TVs tune in to *American Idol,* the top-rated show of 2008, compared to 74 percent who watched *I Love Lucy,* the top-rated show in the 1950s (Poniewozik, 2009; Hof, 2006). Today's viewers can choose from among hundreds of channels, and the traditional networks lose numbers every year in favor of specialized niche channels.

In theory, television is as democratic a medium as you can find: Everyone who has a TV can watch whatever he or she chooses. But television also plays to a collection of "niche" markets. Thus, while we may witness an increase in the percentage of Black characters in prime time, or even an increase

The American Idol finale for 2009, at which openly gay pop sensation Adam Lambert was a close second place, drew over 28 million viewers—when it aired live. But it's also been viewed by far more people on DVRs, websites such as YouTube and Hulu, and other media that give us more access to television, whenever we want it.

Confidence in the Press

In an age of globalization and media conglomerates, many sources of news are controlled by a small number of large corporations and powerful individuals, but the rise of the Internet as a means of conveying information has changed the media landscape. So, what do you think?

As far as the people running the press are concerned, would you say you have a great deal of confidence, only some confidence, or hardly any confidence at all in them?

○ A great deal   ○ Only some   ○ Hardly any

What does **America** think?

(These are actual survey data from the General Social Survey, 2004. Reproduced by permission.)

The GSS survey results for 2004 indicate that almost 44 percent of the population have hardly any confidence in the press. Almost half of respondents had only some confidence in the press. Those in the upper class were most likely to reporting having a great deal of confidence in the press and at the same time were also the group most likely to report having very little confidence in the press. The percentage of respondents report confidence in the press has steadily declined since 1972 for all social class categories.

1. Take a good look at the social class differences in responses. They are complex. How do you explain them?

   Go to this website to look further at the data. You can run your own statistics and crosstabs here:

References: See Davis et al., page 511.

Video Games

More than 300 million people worldwide play video games. The global video game market totaled $50 billion in 2008, outselling box office receipts for movies, books, CDs, and DVDs by a landslide. (Movies, in second place, made $28 billion globally.) Over 225 million computer games—about two games *per household*—are sold every year in the United States.

Did You Know?

in Black-themed shows, this may not lead to significant racial progress. Why? Because the "cross-over" goes only one way. In 2004, Jane Brown and Carol Pardun examined the top 10 television shows watched by White and Black teenagers. They found that almost the same percentage of White and Black teens watched the top 10 "White" shows, such as *The Simpsons* and *Boy Meets World*. But very few White teens watched any of the "Black" shows, such as *The Parkers* or *Moesha*. On TV, as in other arenas of social life, the "marginalized" know more about the "center" than the center knows about the marginalized.

Each new form of media brings the world closer together—satellite TV and radio broad-

cast shows around the world. And yet media also can fragment us into niches and exacerbate the gap between rich and poor (those

Many new media forms are marketed to, and enjoyed by, different groups. There are "his" and "her" video and computer games, but, as a genre, it's mostly "his."

who have media access and those who do not). Globally, television is similar to the newspaper, saturating rich countries, rare in poor countries. In the United States, there are 740 television sets per 1,000 people; there are fewer than half that in Portugal (313) or Turkey (300), but that's more than enough to immerse the population in the latest game shows and reality series. Among poorer countries though—with 58 TVs per 1,000 people in India, 16 in Somalia, and four in Haiti, for example—there is no unifying national television culture (CIA, 2008).

The Internet. There was a home computer on the market as far back as 1975: the Altair 8800, which came unassembled, with a price of $5,000 (in today's dollars, that would be $18,000). Personal computers were a business tool, not a mass medium. But with the development of the World Wide Web in the 1980s, the computer had transformed the world yet again. With development of the Internet, online usage grew 3,000 percent per year: There were 10,000 network hosts in 1987 and 1,000,000 in 1992. By 2008, every country in the world, with a very few exceptions (Monserrat, the Isle of Man, Palau), was online (Abbate, 2000; Campbell-Kelly, 2004; *World Internet Statistics,* 2008).

The Internet has not only transformed mass media but is a new form of mass media in its own right. A website is its own medium, like nothing that has ever come before, with text, graphics, and sounds combined in a way that no previous medium could do. Information is scattered across hundreds of sites in dozens of countries; and because there is little or no regulation of Internet content, it often becomes difficult to distinguish fact from opinion and opinion from diatribe.

The Internet has been accused of facilitating increased isolation—all those millions of teenagers who spend the time they should be doing their homework in chat rooms, playing online poker, blowing up the galaxy on online games, or downloading songs and pornography. But at the same time, it's also a new form of community, a virtual town square, where you offer intimate details about yourself and your romantic (and sexual) desires, meet your friends on Friendster or Facebook, and interact with like-minded members of your virtual network. As former President George W. Bush noted, "With the Internet, you can communicate instantly with someone halfway across

Personal computers, now nearly universal in the industrialized world, are the centerpiece of our interface with media—they store information, give access to the Web, and store music, video, movies, TV, and old love letters. The first general-purpose computer, called the Electronic Numerical Integrator and Computer (ENIAC), was built by the U.S. Army in the 1940s. It weighed 30 tons, was eight feet high, three feet deep, and 100 feet long, and contained over 18,000 vacuum tubes that were cooled by 80 air blowers. And it mainly stored information.

the world and isolate yourself from your family and neighbors." It's not either/or—it's both (Bumiller, 2006).

In the United States, Internet use is common but varies socially. Men and women use the Internet at roughly similar rates, but they use it for different things. Men use it more quickly and tend to surf more widely, while women tend to use the Internet to build community; women use e-mail more often and spend longer at each website they visit (Schrank, 2009). Only about half of all Americans with an income between $25,000 and $35,000 are online, while 93 percent of those whose income is over $100,000 are online. While two-thirds of White households are on-line, fewer than half of Black (45 percent) and Hispanic (43 percent)

Preponderance of Pornography

More than one-fourth of all Internet sites are "adult" themed. In the United States, gross sales of all pornographic media are well over $12 billion a year for the whole industry—more than the NFL, the NBA, and Major League Baseball combined, or, in media terms, with revenues greater than ABC, NBC, and CBS combined (Edelman, 2009). And while pornography use is generally associated with more "liberal" and secular values, pornography use is greater in states with conservative ideologies about sex, in those with fundamentalist perspectives about God, and in 8 out of 10 states that voted Republican in 2008 (the two blue states were Florida and Hawaii).

Did You Know?

households and more than three-fourths of Asian American households (76 percent) are online. (See the National Telecommunications Information Administration, 2007.)

Blogs. The Internet has also produced a new form of journalism: the **blog.** Short for "Weblog," a blog is essentially an online personal journal or diary where an author can air his or her opinions directly to audiences. Some call it "personal journalism." Others call it "citizen journalism." Some say it doesn't qualify as journalism at all. Blogs, you might say, put the "me" back in "media."

Blogs have become amazingly popular: There are about 112.8 million of them—and this doesn't include the 73 million blogs in China (Helmond, 2008)! Half of all bloggers worldwide are 18 to 34 years old (Technorati, 2008), but many are also written by professors, journalists, scientists, and other adults of various professions. Seventy percent have college degrees; 44 percent are parents (Technorati, 2008).

There is controversy about both the definition and the growing power of blogs. Are blogs the first form of journalism to truly harness the democratic potential of the World Wide Web? Are they the way ordinary citizens can speak up, voicing their views without having to get past media company gatekeepers, editors, or advertisers? Blogs became so influential in both fundraising and opinion making in recent presidential campaigns that it is considered a strategic essential for political candidates to have a "blog-meister" on staff. On the other hand, traditional news journalism, whether print, broadcast, or online, must meet established standards of fairness and accuracy. Bloggers are under no obligation to be scrupulous and diligent in their research, news gathering, and reporting. They never need admit when their reports are fraudulent, unfair, or wrong. In fact, quite the contrary—and to some that's the whole point. Plus, the blogosphere is becoming increasingly commercialized; one-third of bloggers have been approached by companies to be "brand advocates" in their posts (Technorati, 2008).

Saturation and Convergence: The Sociology of Media

We live in an age saturated by the media. The average American home today has 3 television sets, 1.8 VCRs, 3.1 radios, 2.6 tape players, 2.1 CD players, 1.4 video game players, and at least one computer. American kids between 8 and 18 spend seven hours a day interacting with some form of electronic media—which may explain why 40 percent of 8- to 13-year-olds said they did not read any part of a book on the previous day, a figure that shoots up to 70 percent of kids 14 to 18.

TV is omnipresent: The average American household tuned in to TV for 8 hours and 18 minutes per day from September 2007 through September 2008, a record high since the days Nielsen began measuring television viewing in the 1950s (Nielsen, 2008). About 60 percent of families with children have the TV on during dinner, and more than 40 per-

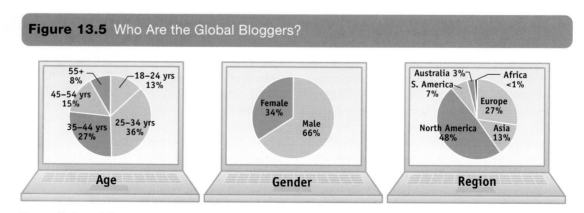

Figure 13.5 Who Are the Global Bloggers?

Age — 55+ 8%, 18–24 yrs 13%, 45–54 yrs 15%, 35–44 yrs 27%, 25–34 yrs 36%

Gender — Female 34%, Male 66%

Region — Australia 3%, S. America 7%, Africa <1%, Europe 27%, North America 48%, Asia 13%

(*Source:* Technorati, State of the Blogosphere, 2008, http://technorati.com/blogging/state-of-the-blogosphere/who-are-the-bloggers.)

cent are "constant television households"—that is, they have a TV on virtually all day, whether or not anyone is actually watching it.

Not long ago, the various types of mass media used to be vastly different, using distinct forms of technology. Now they are all digital. Even if a real book appears at the end of the production process, it is still written, edited, and produced in the form of word processing documents, spreadsheets, jpegs, mpgs, and wav files, and stored as computer files. The gap between forms of mass media is shrinking constantly. We can already gain access to the Internet from our television sets, watch TV on our computers, and play video games on either. The difference is just a matter of social context: We tend to watch TV in a group, and the computer is a solitary device.

Scholars have only just begun to speculate on the sociological implications of media convergence, but one effect is certain. Older people have always complained that the preferred mass media of their youth were far superior to the mass media today. Reading books was far superior to listening to the radio: You were active, engaged, and you had to use your imagination. Then: Listening to the radio was far superior to watching television, for the same reasons: active, engaged, used imagination. Then: Watching television was far superior to playing video games: active, engaged, used imagination. When every mass medium appears on flickering computer screens, there will be no nostalgic "active, engaged, imaginative" medium to look back on.

Both the cognitive demands that new media require from their viewers and their effects seem actually to be *more* engaging than those of previous generations. Surely, computer games require more manual dexterity and eye–hand coordination, as well as the ability to hold several different plotlines in your head simultaneously, while a TV show or radio show—not to mention sitting quietly and reading a book—required less physical connection. The "good old days" of media may not have demanded any more from the consumer and did not leave you as dizzy from so many choices.

Media Production and Consumption

For years, there seemed to be a strict division between media production and media consumption. A group of writers, editors, directors, actors, artists, and supporting personnel, all working for corporate executives in high-rise offices, produces and distributes the books, magazines, and television programs. The books, magazines, and television programs appear in their respective mass media, and we consume them. We have little input; a million irate letters failed to save *Star Trek* from cancellation in 1967.

This boundary is being increasingly blurred. Audiences increasingly run the show. Viewers of *American Idol,* for example, determine through their voting how the show turns out.

These days, media producers are all consumers themselves. The people who write, act in, and direct television programs go home every night and watch television themselves. Consumers are not just sitting idly by, consuming media as if they were popcorn; they create their own fan fiction, blogs, chat rooms, message boards. They twitter, and their "tweets" become news, become advertising, become culture. Consumers are also producers, using the same technologies to write books and magazines and produce movies.

However, the distinction between mass media production and consumption is still useful, particularly as we try to figure out exactly what happens as a message goes from my brain into words, sounds, and pictures (is "encoded"), is transmitted over a long distance through a mass medium, and then gets into your brain (is "decoded"). It's not at all like talking to you or showing you pictures face-to-face. To paraphrase Marshall McLuhan, the medium changes the message. Actually, the medium changes everything.

The Power of Twitter

The microblogging platform Twitter evolved by its users. And as Twitter's capabilities have multiplied, so have its uses. In 2009 alone, Twitter was used to track references to fever and possible "swine" flu cases and to organize an anticommunist uprising in Moldova. Twitter has become so widely used among activists that the governments of Iran and China attempted to block access to it to censor news—in Iran about protests following its presidential election and in China about the 20th anniversary of the Tiananmen Square massacre (Grossman, 2009).

Did You Know?

"Culture Industries" and Multicultural Voices

Sociologists of media are often interested in **culture industries**—the mass production of cultural products that are offered for consumption. Instead of crafting an individual work of creative genius, movie studios and radio stations are like assembly lines, producing cultural products as if they were loaves of bread. They may recycle the same images and themes because they have been successful in the past. If you've seen one cowboy movie (or one episode of *CSI*), you've seen them all. Every sitcom covers the same territory, with the same jokes. As a result, some sociologists have argued, con-sumers become passive and uncritical. We are said to absorb the simplistic, repetitive images with no questions asked, never having their preconceptions, stereotypes, and ideologies challenged (Horkheimer and Adorno, [1944] 1972; Steinert, 2003).

The concept of culture industries is helpful in explaining why so many mass media promote old-fashioned, even oppressive, ideologies. In a free-market economy, the producers must make the product appealing to as many potential consumers as possible. Therefore they select the themes and situations that are familiar and unthreatening. Sociologist Todd Gitlin coined the phrase "the logic of safety" to describe the continuing tendency of media producers to repackage time-tested themes and formulas to minimize programming risks and maximize profits (Gitlin, 2000). In so doing, the mass media also reinforce and may actually promote acceptance of inequalities.

But media production and media consumption are more complex than the culture industries idea proposes. Producers cannot churn out exactly the same old images audiences have seen before; some originality, some tweak, something novel is needed to attract an audience. Some mass media producers do have artistic visions in their own right, and sometimes they do challenge preconceptions, stereotypes, and ideologies.

What's more, media consumers are not the passive zombies culture industries fear. Rather, audiences are active; we participate in the process of making meaning out of media. Mass media can be more democratic, spreading ownership and consumption of media to more and more people and enabling previously voiceless minorities access to connection and visibility. For example, Black Entertainment Television (BET) and Black-owned record companies, Hispanic broadcasters such as Telemundo and Uni-vision, digital media companies, and magazines have identified and sustained a new media market and also, in the pro-cess, helped to create that market. Ethnic media markets have grown robustly in the United States in the twenty-first century (see Figure 13.6). Telemundo now out-performs its English-language counterparts in prime-time programming and news ratings in major U.S. markets. Viewership at BET has surged in recent years, reaching 87 million house-holds in 2008 (Project for Excellence in

Global media means diverse media outlets. Developed in 1966 as an alternative to western journalism's reporting on the Arabic world, Al Jazeera (the name means "the peninsula" as in the Arab peninsula) broadcasts on TV, the Internet in both English and Arabic, and claims a total of over 150 million viewers. At the same time, it offers Arabian Islam as the distinctly Muslim identity, which often clashes with practices in Indonesia, the world's largest Muslim nation.

Journalism, 2009). Overall, at least one-quarter of the adult population is either a primary or secondary consumer of ethnic media today (Project for Excellence in Journalism, 2006). Cyberspace further facilitates media democratization. After a racial incident at a school in Louisiana in 2006 had been all but ignored by the mainstream media, a group of Black blog-gers organized a collective to break the story. Since then, the number of Black blogs in the "Afrosphere" has increased by over 90 percent.

But media can also, simultaneously, be less democratic, as those at the top can concentrate increasing amounts of media power. **Media consolidation** refers to the increased control of an increasing variety of media by a smaller and smaller number of companies. A small number of companies control virtually all the media in the United States today, and huge conglomerates own or hold large stakes in a variety of media.

This consolidation raises fears about what gets produced and also about the quality and reliability of media products, particularly news. When a small group of people controls how information circulates, the spectrum of available ideas, opinions, and images seems likely to narrow. Moreover, big media companies will prefer programming and voices that conform to their own financial interests, and they are in a position to block most smaller, independent companies from rising to offer alternatives.

The Importance of Advertising

Advertising is a form of mass media and also a kind of media text. Advertising can appear as phrases, pictures, songs, cartoons, or short films ("commercials"), but its purpose is always the same: to convincing prospective consumers that they want or need a product—soap, soda, sports cars—but also services (like monster.com for job seekers) and other media ("Must-See TV"). Occasionally advertisements merely discuss the qualities of the product. But usually ads try to associate the product with a desirable quality or activity (Fox, 1997; Marchand, 1986; Samuel, 2002). The flavor of a soda is not nearly as important as the surge in popularity you experience with just one sip. Who cares about the nutritional content or taste of the cereal purveyed by the wise, wholesome general store proprietor?

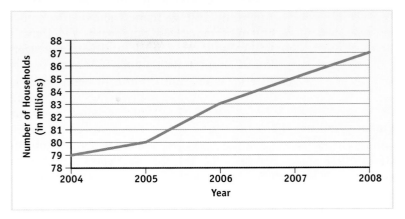

Figure 13.6 BET Viewership

(*Source:* The Pew Research Center's Project for Excellence in Journalism. The State of the News Media, stateofthemedia.org, July 16, 2009. Copyright © 2009 The Project for Excellence in Journalism. Reproduced by permission.)

Advertising is an engine of media production; most media depend on advertising to survive and profit. Because most of these mass media forms themselves are free (like TV or online newspapers) or cheap (like print newspapers or magazines), ads pay for most of the cost of production as well as the profits. As a rule, the more the medium depends on advertising for its revenue, the more it will shy away from challenging preconceptions and stereotypes (Pipher, 2000; Williamson, 1994). I have never seen an interracial couple on any television commercial, though they are increas-ingly common in real life (see Chapter 12, Family).

We consume many more ads than anything else, dozens every day, hundreds every week. They are everywhere. And ads present by far the most pervasive stereotypes of any form of mass media: Almost every commercial shows affluent nuclear families in huge suburban houses, with Dad reading the newspaper and Mom in the kitchen. Dad does not mop the floor, and whenever he cooks dinner, he botches the job and takes the kids out to a fast food restaurant. How does a steady diet of such images affect our ideas about how life works or how it should work?

Bilingual Newspapers

There have always been newspapers in other languages to serve America's diverse population. But since native-born Hispanics now outnumber Hispanic immigrants in the United States, a new bilingual audience has emerged. There are now over 200 bilingual (Spanish *and* English) newspapers in the United States, double the number from 2000—and with a combined circulation of 5.6 million (Project for Excellence in Journalism, 2009).

Did You Know?

Celebrities

Actors and singers are among the most common mass media products today. Many Americans cannot name their own senators and representatives, but nearly all of them know who Chris Rock is; they may even know about how in 2008 he accused former President Bill Clinton of being unwilling to even say the name of his wife's rival for the Democratic presidential nomination on *The Tonight Show*. Celebrity news often makes the front page of newspapers in the United States and Europe, particularly in Britain. Why? Celebrity stories sell papers—and magazines and products.

Mass media created celebrity. There were professional performers before, of course. But even the most diligent theatergoer might see the same actor only twice in a given year. With the advent of radio, listeners could hear their favorite comedians or singers every week. With movies, you could *see* your favorite performers almost as often. Celebrity magazines grew up around the American film industry, developing the thirst for details on the smallest doings of stars. Television is even more intimate than movies: You can see your favorite performers every week, in your own living room. These people are not simply performers; they are *celebrities*, famous not necessarily because of their talent or accomplishments but because they appear so often in mass media texts that audiences feel that they know them personally (Dyer, 1987; Gamson, 1994). And, in some ways, you do: In talk shows, magazine interviews, and fan articles, you learned every detail of their everyday lives, sometimes more intimately than your real friends. Of course, celebrities are not your friends; the intimacy is one-sided. They are neither friends nor strangers; Richard Schickel (1985) calls them "intimate strangers."

Today, celebrity itself has become the product—rather than a device for marketing films or music. Now there are "faux celebrities" everywhere—from the winners (and runners-up) of reality shows like *Survivor, The Bachelor, American Idol,* and others, to Anna Nicole Smith, to Jack and Kelly Osbourne, to Paris Hilton. Recently, Nadya Suleman, a young single mom in Los Angeles, delivered octuplets (after already having six other children), in what many believed to be a reality-based "audition" for future celebrity status. Celebrities and their agents even collaborate with photographers to stage shots that appear to be intrusions into their private lives in exchange for more control over their image and a share of the profits when those photographs are sold.

And sell they do. The two biggest U.S. celebrity gossip magazines, *People* and *US Weekly*, each sold more copies in 2008—amidst the economic recession—than they did in 2001 (*The Economist*, 2009a). And celebrity purveyors are continually expanding into new platforms and products. There are multiple celebrity news aggregator sites online, and *People* sustains an empire that includes a fashion portal, a Spanish-language magazine, a pet website, a country issue, and an iPhone application whose website receives 13 million unique visitors per month (*The Economist*, 2009a).

Did You Know?

Famous for Being Famous

A Hungarian-born socialite named Zsa Zsa Gabor (1917–) was probably the first celebrity created purely by media exposure. She was technically an actress, with a string of bad movies to her credit. But she didn't become one of the most recognizable people in the world because of her movies. She appeared on talk shows to talk about her marriages, her diamonds, her appearances at posh functions, her jet-set lifestyle. She became "famous for being famous."

The mass media crave celebrities—they sell papers and magazines, and we watch them on TV. The media also create a cult of celebrity, drawing us to certain people sometimes for no other reason than the fact that they are featured and photographed.

Consuming Media, Creating Identity

Whatever the producers may intend, consumers use media texts for their own ends. Through our consumption of media, we actively create our identities. In fact, it is largely *through* our media consumption that we know who we are and where we fit in society. Consumers have five broad goals in consumption:

1. *Surveillance, to find out what the world is like.* This is the main reason that we consume news and information programs, nonfiction books, magazines, and newspapers. However, we also acquire information from fiction. The best-selling novel *The Da Vinci Code* is both a mystery and a guided tour of modern Paris and the art of its famous museum, the Louvre.

2. *Decision making.* I may watch a YouTube clip before deciding to download a song or read a review of a club or restaurant before deciding to go there.

3. *Aesthetics.* Media objects are works of art because they create a particular vision of reality. I can appreciate the theme, style, and technique of *SpongeBob SquarePants* as easily as (maybe even more easily than) *Macbeth*.

4. *Diversion.* If we're being entertained, the reasoning goes, we are not engaged in big, important, useful work. We are diverted from improving ourselves, thinking about our problems, saving the world. However, diversion performs an important function. It's like a short vacation. By stepping outside of everyday reality for a moment, we are refreshed and may be better prepared to think about that big, important, useful work.

5. *Identity.* Consuming mass media texts allows us to create and maintain a group identity. If you belong to the upper class, chances are you will not listen to country-western music (or will keep the CDs hidden when company comes around), because your class identity requires that you like classical music instead.

There is no single, definitive meaning in media texts. Media texts may emphasize or "prefer" certain hegemonic meanings over others (Hall, 1993), but ultimately meaning is in the mind of the beholder. Readers and viewers interpret what they see in different

Media also create interpretive communities, groups that cohere around similar media tastes and create a subculture. At Comic-Con International, a group of Bat-people pose as some Ghostbusters look on.

ways; they notice, follow, value, and understand things in different ways and so "create" the meaning of a media text for themselves. No single meaning is "correct": There are always multiple possibilities.

One reason is that we never consume media texts in a vacuum: We consume the media text within an **interpretive community** (Fish, 1980; Lewis, 1992). Interpretive communities are groups that guide interpretation and convey the preferred meanings of mass media texts. Families, friends, classmates, chat groups, and Facebook friends are all interpretive communities. In subtle ways, they offer rewards for "correct" meanings and punishments for "incorrect" meanings. Sometimes the rewards and punishments are formal, like a grade in school. Usually, however, they are informal, approval or ridicule—just try to defend a "chick flick" if you are a guy, enjoy folk music if you are Black, or say the typical summer blockbuster is a mess of mindless explosions among teen or twenty-something friends!

Interpretive communities also produce fans. A **fan** is someone who finds significant personal meaning through allegiance to a larger social group: a sports team, for example. In the media, fandom refers to a heightened awareness of and allegiance toward a specific text—a story, a series, a performer—so that the fan gains satisfaction by belonging to an interpretive community.

Fandom is a public affiliation, not just a private love. It is a public proclamation of identity, a choice that your allegiance to some media product reveals a core element of yourself. It was important for fans of Harry Potter to buy the latest installment in the series the second it went on sale—in part to display publicly to other fans (or themselves) the strength of their allegiance. Rap and hip-hop fans may express their affiliation through clothing, jewelry, verbal affectations, social interactions. "Deadheads" will bedeck themselves in tie-dyed shirts (preferably with skulls on them) and, if they are male, wear their hair long. The hard-core *Star Trek* fan might write fan fiction (sometimes complete novels), start websites, organize conventions, use the hand gesture and expression "live long, and prosper," even walk around with Mr. Spock's pointed ears.

Fandom is a good example of the ways the media both create and reflect audience desires. Movie studios, television producers, and record producers offer websites and merchandise schemes to entice and sustain existing fans. These and other devices reflect the fandom of those who already like a particular star or show. But they also set the standard for "true" fandom: Suddenly you can't be a "real" fan unless you subscribe to these magazines, wear these clothes, and purchase these products. The media both meet "demand" (offering services) and create the very demand they then service.

Globalization of the Media

A few years ago, I was visiting Morocco, and I stayed in a fourteenth-century Moorish castle converted into a hotel. My room was furnished with ornate tile work, panels inlaid with lapis lazuli, fringed pillows. It was like moving into another world. I turned on the TV. What were they watching in this ancient, mysterious country? *Beavis & Butthead*.

American movies were being shown around the world as early as the 1920s, but the immersion has increased dramatically during the last 20 years. *The Simpsons* is broadcast in Central and South America, Europe, South Africa, Israel, Turkey, Japan, South Asia, and Australia . . . Almost every country in the world—even those that lack running water—has its own version of *American Idol*.

The mass media have become truly global in nature. CNN broadcasts via 23 satellites to more than 212 countries and territories in all corners of the globe. Major sporting events are seen by hundreds of millions of people worldwide. The 2008 Beijing Olympics was watched by 4.7 billion people—70 percent of the population of the world (Nielsen, 2008). The Internet is growing more global every day, allowing tens of millions of users from all over the world to come online to seek and share information, post opinions and creative work, and shop for items previously available only to those who physically traveled to other countries.

In the 1960s, the path-breaking media scholar Marshall McLuhan predicted that the rise of global electronic media would bring the world closer together. He coined the term **global village** to describe an environment in which people everywhere could make their voices heard to one another, thus compelling "commitment and participation" and making human beings "irrevocably involved with, and responsible for, each other" (McLuhan and Fiore, 1967, p. 24). Four decades later, is that what globalization means?

What Is Media Globalization?

Media globalization has two main concerns. First, there is the technological innovation that allows us to communicate instantaneously over vast distances. In many countries today, there is no need to be physically close by to work together; images, sounds, the thoughts of almost anyone, from anywhere, can potentially be available to billions of people. Technology is giving increasing numbers of people the power to produce culture. And technology is making it as easy to communicate with someone on another continent as it is with someone down the hall.

But media globalization also concerns the cultural products that are available around the world. In that area, sociologists are finding that McLuhan's vision of a global village is far from today's reality. Commercial interests, rather than humanitarian ideals of education, understanding, or equality, are driving media globalization. Large media conglomerates from a few wealthy industrialized nations are dominating global markets. In fact, both media production and consumption are strongly oriented toward the wealthier members of the world's population. As a result, the global media often function to highlight and help reproduce global inequality (Croteau and Hoynes, 2003).

Cultural Imperialism

The media products of the West, especially of the United States, are so dominant in global markets that some sociologists call it **cultural imperialism.** Imperialism is economic control of one country by another. Cultural imperialism, then, is cultural control of one country by another. One culture's art, music, television, and film are defined and controlled by another. And from Latin America to Asia to the Middle East, the West, but particularly the United States, is decried for its pervasive cultural dominance around the world.

Cultural imperialism is not simply the cultural domination of poor countries by rich ones, however. In Europe, for example, American movies make up anywhere from 54 to 92 percent of movies shown in theaters, while European films make up only 3 percent (Croteau and Hoynes, 2003). Of all movies shown on European television, over 50 percent are made in America (De Bens, Kelly, and Bakke, 1992). The overwhelming majority of music in the global marketplace is sung in English—usually by Americans. In Japan, songs sung in English make up 50 percent of radio playlists. In Germany, it's 80 percent (Barnet and Cavanaugh, 1994; Croteau and Hoynes, 2003).

Of the top-grossing films of all time at the global box office, all of the top ten are American films (Figure 13.7). Indeed, of the top 100, all are American. (The highest box office rank achieved by a film produced outside the United States is the UK's *Slumdog Millionaire,* at number 133) (IMDb, 2009).

The issue is not jealousy of American lifestyles or dislike of global media products like MTV, Hollywood films, English-language pop music, and American soap operas. The cultural imperialism thesis holds that this kind of Western media dominance, driven by the relentless desire for profits, will shape all the cultures of the world and ensure their Westernization. Playing everywhere and blocking out opportunities for local productions, this media dominance will substitute American values like individualism and consumerism for the local values of countries where media products are sold. Eventually, cultural distinctiveness will be eroded, threatening national and cultural identity. Other nations will be so thoroughly indoctrinated with U.S. cultural, political, and economic images and ideals that they will forget who they are.

U.S. cultural products are having an immense impact around the world, but sociologists are finding that for a number of reasons the cultural imperialism thesis offers only a partial picture. For now anyway, U.S. products are dominating some media and markets, while other media continue to be locally produced. Plus, different audiences still interpret foreign fare differently, and there are apparent limits to the appeal of Western—particularly U.S.—culture in other countries. Finally, different countries have created local variations of American or Western programs, giving imported formats a local resonance. Media globalization has induced successful "fusions" in film, television, and, perhaps especially, music, which circulate and sell well in originating countries and beyond. Many locally produced fusions have been so popular that they have allowed local producers to successfully compete with much larger media conglomerates.

Overall, then, it's not a question of domination or resistance, global or local, but both.

Lost in Translation?

The Middle Eastern Broadcasting Company in Dubai currently broadcasts a dubbed version of *The Simpsons* called *Al Shamsoon* to most of the countries in the Persian Gulf. In the Arabic version, Homer becomes Omar, and Bart is Badr. Some scenes have to be cut to avoid offending conservative Muslim censors: no girls in bikinis, no bacon for breakfast, and no alcohol. Homer cannot be shown drinking or talking about beer, and his after-work hangout, Moe's Tavern, no longer exists.

Did You Know?

Figure 13.7 Top Ten Grossing Films of All Time at the International (non–U.S.) Box Office

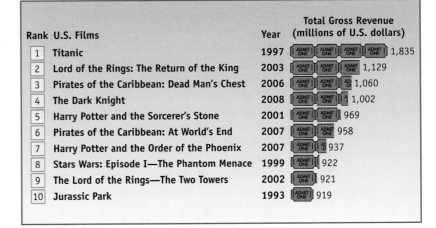

Rank	U.S. Films	Year	Total Gross Revenue (millions of U.S. dollars)
1	Titanic	1997	1,835
2	Lord of the Rings: The Return of the King	2003	1,129
3	Pirates of the Caribbean: Dead Man's Chest	2006	1,060
4	The Dark Knight	2008	1,002
5	Harry Potter and the Sorcerer's Stone	2001	969
6	Pirates of the Caribbean: At World's End	2007	958
7	Harry Potter and the Order of the Phoenix	2007	937
8	Stars Wars: Episode I—The Phantom Menace	1999	922
9	The Lord of the Rings—The Two Towers	2002	921
10	Jurassic Park	1993	919

(*Source:* From Internet Movie Database, www.IMDb.com.)

New Media, New Voices

For example, developments such as satellite TV and the Internet have allowed local groups to develop a voice that they never had before, no matter how strictly local governments may control media access. Before around 1990, the West heard a single, monolithic Arab "opinion" on everything from Israel to Islam, even though there were 18 predominantly Arab countries stretching from Morocco to Iraq, with people from all ethnic groups, social classes, religions, and political persuasions. Minority opinions were censored. Now they are talking, and through approved channels. And their voices are diverse. Among Morocco's 15 online newspapers and news websites are the progressive feminist *Femmes du Maroc* (published in French) and the socialist *Libération*. Saudi Arabia forbids its citizens from publishing or having access to any information that disagrees with official policy, but there are hundreds of clandestine groups, including over 500 on Yahoo.com.

Al Jazeera, an independent television network based in Qatar (on the Persian Gulf), is one of the most popular media sites in the world, with several specialized channels devoted to sports, music, and children's programs and over 50 million regular viewers (it launched Al Jazeera International, an English-language channel available in the United States via satellite, in late 2006). Its main claim to infamy is its dedication to presenting alternatives to official policies of the Arab world. Several Arab countries have claimed that the network is too pro-Israel or pro-U.S. On the other hand, after the 9/11 attacks, when Al Jazeera broadcast statements from Osama bin Laden, many Westerners claimed that it was merely a front for terrorists. Journalists from the network have had their credentials revoked in both Arab and Western countries, and when an English-language version of its website premiered in 2003, hackers immediately rerouted visitors to a picture of an American flag (Lynch, 2005; Rugh, 2004).

Today's media are helping other cultures to preserve and help "alternative" voices to be heard. After Al Jazeera launched in 1996, it spawned dozens of pan-Arab satellite TV competitors that together have loosened the information stranglehold of authoritarian governments across the Middle East (McHugh, 2006). In the United Kingdom, Sianel Pedwar Cymru, the Welsh fourth channel, is helping to support Welsh language and culture. In Mexico, the Zapatista movement was able to bypass established media to communicate with the world via the Internet. Broadcasting among the Bedouin tribes of the Sahara has helped revive a sense of collective identity (Abu-Lughod, 1989; Williams, 2003).

Politics and Media in the Twenty-First Century

The Greek philosopher Aristotle once wrote that "man is by nature a political animal." We are also political animals "by nurture"—because social life requires it. Politics remains a contentious arena, in which people organize together, formally and informally, to fight for their positions and influence the policies that, in turn, influence their lives. It is an arena in which the divisions among people—by class, race, gender, and age—are most evident, and the arena in which the power of some groups over other groups is declared to be legitimate because "the governed" have consented to it.

Both the lines of division and the terms of consensus among "the governed" are increasingly shaped by the mass media. In today's complex political environment, in which few of us have direct access to leaders and policymakers, the media provide most of our political information and also serve as a site of political mobilization. The mass media shape our political experience as well as reflect our political will.

Politics remains the arena in which we believe we can develop and maintain democracy, in which we all feel somewhat connected to each other because we are able to participate in the political process. It is rarely a question of whether politics unites us or divides us—indeed, politics both unites and divides. The questions remain, as always—united toward what goals, inspired by what vision, and divided by what factors?

And do the media shape or reflect these persistent questions? Yes. They do both. And they will do so increasingly as the new century unfolds.

Chapter Review

1. Politics: Power and Authority

Today we are both more politically involved and less, and globally we are moving toward greater democracy, while there are still numerous authoritarian strongholds. These contradictions are understood by sociologists who study **politics** and are interested in **power** and **government.** Weber identified three types of **authority** used by leaders: **traditional authority, charismatic authority,** and **legal-rational authority.**

politics The art and science of government. (p. 390)

power The ability to extract compliance despite resistance or the ability to get others to do what you want them to do, regardless of their own desires. (p. 390)

government The organization and administration of the actions of the inhabitants of communities, societies, and states. (p. 390)

authority Power that is perceived as legitimate, by both the holder of power and those subject to it. For a leader to exercise power, the people must believe he or she is entitled to make commands and that they should obey; indeed, that they want to obey. (p. 390)

traditional authority Dominant in premodern societies, including ancient Egypt, China, and Mesoamerica, the form of authority that people obeyed because they believed their society had always done things that way; derives from who the leaders are: the descendants of kings and queens, or perhaps the descendants of the gods, not from their educational background, work experience, or personality traits. (p. 390)

charismatic authority Authority derived from the personal appeal of a specific leader. (p. 391)

legal-rational authority Form of authority where leaders are to be obeyed not primarily as representatives of tradition or because of their personal qualities but because they are voicing a set of rationally derived laws. They must act impartially, even sacrificing their own opinions and attitudes in obedience to the laws of the land. (p. 391)

2. Political Systems

The two main kinds of political systems are **authoritarian political systems,** including **monarchy** and **totalitarianism;** and **democracy,** which includes **participatory democracy** and **representative democracy. Universal suffrage** is increasing. Problems associated with political systems include corruption, bureaucratic entrenchment, and under representation of minorities and the undue influence of money and power. A solution to the latter problem is **proportional representation.**

authoritarian political system When power is vested in a single person or small group. Sometimes that person holds power through heredity, sometimes through force or terror. (p. 391)

bureaucracy An efficient hierarchical formal organization with clear rules and regulations and division of labor (see discussion in Chapter 3). (p. 394)

dictatorship A type of totalitarian political system in which power is held by one person, who may or may not have a hereditary claim on power, usually with military support. (p. 392)

monarchy One of the first political systems; rule by a single individual (*mono* means "one," and *archy* means "rule"), typically hereditary. (p. 392)

totalitarianism A political system in which no organized opposition is permitted and political information is censored. (p. 393)

democracy Derived from the Greek word *demos* (people); puts legislative decision making into the hands of the people rather than a single individual or a noble class. (p. 393)

participatory democracy Also called "pure democracy," a political system in which every person gets one vote and the majority rules. (p. 393)

representative democracy System in which citizens elect representatives to make the decisions for them; requires an educated citizenry and a free press. (p. 393)

universal suffrage Granting of the vote to any and all citizens who meet specified, universal criteria, such as legal citizenship and a minimum age. (p. 393)

PAC (political action committee) A type of partisan political organization that is not subject to the same regulations as political parties, that attempt to influence elections and mobilize public opinion. (p. 394)

proportional representation In contrast to the winner-take-all system used in the United States, proportional representation gives each party a proportion of the legislative seats based on the number of votes its candidates garner. (p. 395)

3. The Political System of the United States

In the American political system, as in most democratic societies with elected representatives, an individual cannot effectively change the system, so we become members of a **political party.** Unlike other countries, there are mainly only two parties in America, with third parties having little influence. Party affiliation is typically based on class, education, race, gender, and age. An **interest group** is another group that is influential in the political process.

political party Group that bands together to petition for political chances or to support candidates for elected office. (p. 396)

interest group Also called special interest group, pressure group, and lobby, such a group promotes its interests among state and national legislators and often influences public opinion. There are two kinds: Protective groups represent only one trade, industry, minority, or subculture; promotional groups seek to represent the interests of the entire society. (p. 398)

4. Political Change

Political change can occur through means other than political parties and interest groups. A **social movement** is one way that people organize collectively; a **revolution** is more extreme, seeking to replace the existing order. Marx supposed class inequality would drive the underclass to revolution through the **immiseration thesis,** but the fact that people experience **relative deprivation** suggests otherwise. Other changes include **coup d'état,** a change in the head of state; **political**

revolution, when another political group supplants the previous ruling group; and, more fundamental to society as well as more dramatic, **social revolution.** War seems to be an inevitable part of political systems, and although it isn't predictable when a war will occur, a number of root causes have been identified underlying wars. Many different kinds of groups engage in acts of **terrorism,** for different reasons, with increasing frequency made possible by ease of access to technology. Those in power, or those opposed, may commit terrorist acts. Although politically motivated, they are often intended to cause damage or harm. Even our everyday actions, choices, or lack of action can be viewed as political. Media coverage can reflect our actions and choices, as well as form and inform them.

social movement Collective attempt to further a common interest or secure a common goal through action outside the sphere of established institutions. (p. 399)

revolution The attempt to overthrow the existing political and social order of a society and replace it with a new one. (p. 399)

immiseration thesis Marx's theory that, as capitalism proceeded, the rich would get richer and the poor would get poorer, and that eventually the poor would become so poor that they had nothing else to lose and would revolt. (p. 400)

relative deprivation Describes how misery is socially experienced by constantly comparing yourself to others. You are not down and out: You are worse off than you used to be (downward mobility), not as well off as you think you should be (rising expectations), or, perhaps, not as well off as those you see around you. (p. 400)

coup d'état The violent replacing of one political leader with another; often doesn't bring with it any change in the daily life of the citizens. (p. 400)

political revolution Changes the political groups that run the society, but they still draw their strength from the same social groups that supported the old regime. (p. 400)

social revolution Revolution that changes the social groups or classes that political power rests on. (p. 400)

terrorism Using acts of violence and destruction (or threatening to use them) as a political strategy. (p. 402)

5. What Are the Mass Media?

We use **media** to communicate; the term **mass media** refers to larger-scale communication. Different forms have emerged in our history, dependent on technology, and we have become increasingly influenced by them, as they transform society. Printing processes led to more books, which led to increased literacy; while today, newspapers are failing with the dominance of the Internet. Media draw the world closer, in a global community, while simultaneously fragmenting us into niche markets with great proliferation of choice. The Internet is perhaps the most democratizing medium of all, as every country has access to some degree; yet over one-quarter of all websites are devoted to pornography. Journalism has changed with the advent of the **blog.** Television and video games take up a tremendous amount of our day, particularly for younger people, as books and newspapers are read less frequently.

media The plural of *medium*, they are the ways that we communicate with each other. (p. 404)

mass media Ways to communicate with vast numbers of people at the same time, usually over a great distance. Mass media have developed in countless directions: books, newspapers, magazines, motion pictures, records and tapes, CDs and DVDs, radio and television programs, comic strips and comic books, and a whole range of new digital media. (p. 405)

blog Short for "weblog"; online opinion site. (p. 410)

6. Media Production and Consumption

Although individual voices proliferate in the media today, thanks to Twitter and blogs, there are still **culture industries** producing products for mass consumption, such as television shows and movies, and the power is increasingly concentrated in fewer and fewer corporations with **media consolidation,** which means that dominant voices and viewpoints are increasingly heard to the exclusion of minority or alternative choices. Advertising fuels media, and the more important the ad revenue is to the medium, the more it will tend to support stereotypical ideals. These advertising images predominate, and in turn they shape our lives. Celebrity is now a popular, lucrative, and marketable product. We use or consume media for many of our own purposes: to learn about the world, to gather information for making decisions, for an aesthetic or diverting experience, and to create and maintain an identity. Media may have a message, but we are free to take our own interpretations, which occur in **interpretive communities** that support and enforce particular understandings informally. As **fans,** we can create identity and find belonging.

culture industries The idea that American media productions are industrial products like any other product, a mode of production that empties them of original or complex content and soon renders their audiences passive and uncritical. (p. 412)

media consolidation The ongoing trends in media ownership in which only a handful of very large companies own and control the vast majority of media around the world. (p. 413)

interpretive communities Groups that share certain assumptions and interpretations of any cultural form (a text, for example). This sociological argument means that texts do not have meaning outside of the set of cultural assumptions groups of people bring to them. (p. 415)

fan Someone who finds significant personal meaning through a heightened awareness of and allegiance toward a specific media text—a story, a series, a performer. Fandom is a public affiliation, a public proclamation that your allegiance to some media product reveals a core element of your identity. (p. 415)

7. Globalization of the Media

Mass media are available globally, and much of them are the same. The dream of a **global village,** where everyone would have a voice, instead has resulted in what some claim is **cultural imperialism,** as the same voices dominate globally in both rich and poor nations—it is overwhelmingly American, with little diversity, ethnic or local variety, or minority voice, all of which leads to increasing Westernization. Recently, cable television has made local alternatives increasingly available.

global village Marshall McLuhan's term for his vision of the way global electronic media would unite the world through mutual interaction and involvement. (p. 416)

cultural imperialism The deliberate imposition of one country's culture on another country. (p. 417)

8. Politics and Media in the Twenty-First Century

Our social nature requires us to be political creatures, as we organize together and strive to have an impact on the policies that affect our lives. We can observe the divisions in who governs and who is governed in class, race, gender, and age, although we believe that we can have an influence on those policies that shape our lives. Increasingly, mass media reflect and shape our political will, but few of us, except those in power, have direct access to the media, even though we believe we can have an impact on policy through participation in politics. This is likely to continue, as we move further into the new century.

Self-Test: Check Your Understanding

1. Which classic figure discussed the historical progression and types of authority found in society?
   a. Durkheim   c. Marx
   b. Weber   d. Goffman
2. Charismatic authority is found
   a. in authoritarian political systems.
   b. in democratic political systems.
   c. in religious movements.
   d. Charismatic authority may be found in any of the above.
3. In which of the following is corruption more often found, according to the text?
   a. Authoritarian governments
   b. Democratic governments
   c. Richer nations
   d. Poorer nations
4. Which of the following is not one of the characteristics associated with party affiliation discussed in the text?
   a. Education   c. Age
   b. Religion   d. Class
5. In which type of nation are acts of terrorism more likely to occur?
   a. In totalitarian regimes, where people are likely to strike out against harsh rulers
   b. In poor nations, where there are great numbers of "have nots"
   c. In democratic nations, where there is unchecked freedom
   d. Terrorism is equally likely to occur in all of the above.
6. A small nation experienced a change in leadership when the nation's leader was arrested by the military police and replaced by a general in the military. The buses and trains continued to run, schools remained open, and there was no change in business or industry. This is an example of
   a. a coup d'état.
   b. political revolution.
   c. social revolution.
   d. terrorism.
7. Worldwide consumption of _____ is on the decline, while consumption of _____ is on the rise.
   a. television; newspapers
   b. books; newspapers
   c. newspapers; television
   d. television; magazines
8. Media productions that rely on advertising tend to be
   a. edgier and more avant garde.
   b. more likely to portray and reinforce stereotypes.
   c. more likely to have realistic portrayals of their audience.
   d. more likely to present alternative voices to meet niche markets.

Self-Test Answers: 1. b , 2. d, 3. d, 4. b, 5. c, 6. a, 7. c, 8. b

Integrate and Explore: Points to Consider

1. Which media do you regularly consume? How difficult is it for you to find a product of media that you have recently consumed with origins in another nation, culture, or ethnicity? If you have traveled to another country, how prevalent are locally produced media, in comparison with media originating in America? Has the ideal of the global village been realized?
2. Do we choose what we consume by our tastes, or are our tastes informed by what we consume? Which factors have been identified as influencing political views or party membership? Is politics influenced by the media? How influential are the media in politics if one corporation owns a movie studio, a cable news station, and newspapers in major cities and presents, in films, broadcasts, editorials, and stories, one view of political affairs? Is this a realistic scenario?

succeed with mysoclab

Self-scoring practice tests, flashcards for learning key terms, streaming audio of the entire text, and multimedia, including:

Watch—Amy Aronson, *Students Live in a Mediated World*
MySocLibrary—Benjamin R. Barber, *Jihad vs. McWorld*
MySocLibrary—Gregory Mantsios, *Media Magic: Making Class Invisible*
MySocLibrary—C. Wright Mills, *The Power Elite*

Education, Religion, and Science

In October, 2004, the Dover, Pennsylvania, Board of Education added a statement to the school district's biology curriculum that required that "Students . . . be made aware of the gaps/problems in Darwin's theory" and that they also be exposed to "other theories of evolution, including . . . intelligent design," as an alternative "explanation of the origin of life."

The district's science teachers refused to read that statement to their ninth-graders, citing a state education code that says that teachers may not present information they believe to be false. (A school administrator read the statement.) Eleven parents of current students sued the school district for violating the U.S. Constitution, which separates church and state, arguing that "intelligent design" is really "religion in disguise."

In December 2005, the U.S. District Court in Pennsylvania agreed with the parents, that teaching intelligent design violates the Constitution because the theory "cannot uncouple itself from its creationist, and thus religious, antecedents."

This event was but a small skirmish in the centuries-old struggle between religion and science. In the sixteenth century, the Church forced Galileo to recant his "theory" that Earth revolved around the sun because the Church held that Earth was the center of the universe. And education is often the arena in which these battles are fought.

Education, as an institution, is not only how we teach our children about their world; it is also a summary of what we know about that world in the first place. In that sense, science and religion may be thought to have competing views about the world and the methods by which we are to understand it.

To the sociologist though, religion and science have much in common, as well as significant differences. All three—education, religion, and science—are crucial social institutions, arenas that explain and inform social life. Both educational and religious institutions are among the primary institutions in a person's socialization,

> "Education, religion, and science are crucial social institutions, arenas that explain and inform social life. They are among the primary institutions in a person's socialization, grounding us in a moral view of the world and providing a set of tools with which we interact with that world."

grounding us in a moral view of the world and providing a set of tools with which we interact with that world.

Education in Social Context

Every day in the United States, 74.1 million people gather in auditoriums, classrooms, and laboratories, in the open air and in online chat rooms, to learn things from 4.6 million teachers, teaching assistants, lab assistants, instructors, and professors (*Digest of Educational Statistics,* 2009). They can learn an endless variety of subjects: Babylonian cuneiform and nuclear physics, short-story writing and motorcycle repair, conversational Portuguese and managerial accounting, symphony conducting and cartoon animation, existential philosophy and the gender politics of modern Japan.

Most people spend a quarter of their lives (or even more) becoming *educated*. If you live to be 70, you will devote 19 percent of your life to preschool, elementary school, and high school, and another 6 percent to college (assuming you graduate in four years). A Ph.D. might easily take another eight years. You would then finish your education at age 30, with 43 percent of your life over.

Education doesn't end at high school, college, or graduate school. Many people return to school after they received their degree, for additional degrees, courses, and certificates. Some want to learn a new skill or develop a new interest. And many others depend on education for their livelihood: They become teachers, administrators, and service personnel; they write and publish textbooks; they build residence halls and manufacture three-ring binders; they open restaurants and clothing shops in college towns to draw student business. In the United States, we spend $550 billion a year on elementary and secondary schools and another $200 billion on colleges and universities (U.S. Department of Education, 2009).

Why do we do it? How does it work? How does it both enable and restrict our own mobility? Sociologists define **education** as a social institution through which society provides its members with important knowledge—basic facts, job skills, and cultural norms and values. It provides socialization, cultural innovation, and social integration. It is accomplished largely through schooling, formal instruction under the direction of a specially trained teacher (Ballantine, 2001).

Like most social institutions, education has both manifest (clearly apparent) and latent (potential or hidden) functions. The manifest function is the subject matter: reading and writing in grade school, sociology and managerial accounting in college. Latent functions are by-products of the educational process, the norms, values, and goals that accrue because we are immersed in a specific social milieu. Education teaches both a subject and a **hidden curriculum:** individualism and competition, conformity to mainstream norms, obedience to authority, passive consumption of ideas, and acceptance of social inequality (Gilborn, 1992).

In addition to teaching a subject matter and various sorts of hidden norms and values, education establishes relationships and social networks, locating people within social classes. Randall Collins (1979) notes that the United States is a **credential society:** You need diplomas, degrees, and certificates to qualify for jobs; you can open a medical practice only if you have an MD degree, regardless of how smart you are; and you have to pass the state bar exam to practice law, regardless of how much law you know. Diplomas, degrees, certificates, examination scores, college majors, and the college you graduate from say "who you are" as much as family background. They tell employers what manners, attitudes, and even skin colors the applicants are likely to have. They provide gatekeeping functions that restrict important

In addition to the formal curriculum in class, students also participate in a "hidden curriculum" in which they learn social lessons about hierarchy, peer pressure, and how to act around the opposite sex.

and lucrative jobs to a small segment of the population.

History

For most of human history, there were no schools. Your parents taught necessary skills, or they hired you a tutor. Sometimes people with special skills opened academies, where you could pay tuition to study philosophy, music, or art. But there was no formal, structured system of education.

In many cultures, schools developed out of a need to train religious leaders. In ancient Babylonia, priests-in-training went to school so they could learn to read sacred texts and write the necessary rituals. In India, *gurukuls*, connected to temples and monasteries, offered instruction in Hindu scriptures, theology, astrology, and other religious topics (Ghosh, 2001). In China, citizens who wanted to become civil servants on any level had to pass a series of "imperial examinations." Examinations were theoretically open to anyone, but only the wealthy could afford to spend the years of preparation necessary for even the lowest exam (Chaffee, 1985; Gernet, 1982).

European schools also developed to teach priests and other religious workers necessary subjects, like Latin, theology, and philosophy. We still call the highest academic degree a PhD, or doctor of philosophy. When the Protestant Reformation began to teach that all believers, not just priests, should be able to read and interpret the Bible, many churches began to offer all children instruction in reading and writing. By the sixteenth century, formal schooling for children was available in many European countries, though only the wealthy had enough money and free time to participate (Bowen, 1976; Boyd and King, 1978). The United States was among the first countries in the world to set a goal of education for all of its citizens, under the theory that an educated citizenry was necessary for a democratic society to function. Yet the founding fathers disagreed about its purpose. Some believed that education would enable citizens to use reason to protect their freedom and to challenge government policies; others thought education should teach citizens to accept the social order, to be, as Daniel Webster argued, "citizens educated to be humble, devout, and submissive to legitimate authority" (Urban and Wagoner, 2003, p. 79). This tension in the purpose of education between free-thinking rebels and docile obedient participants persists, in some form, to the present day.

Educational opportunity and retention are organized by class and race. Lower-income and minority students are far more likely to drop out than middle-class and White students. The highest dropout rate is among lower-income Hispanic girls.

A free public education movement began in 1848, and soon there were free, tax-funded elementary schools in every state, with about half of young people (ages 5 to 19) attending (Urban and Wagoner, 2003). They often attended for only a few years or for only a few months of the year, squeezed in between their duties at home, and instruction was very basic—"reading, writing, and arithmetic." By 1918, every state had passed a mandatory education law, requiring that children attend school until they reached the age of 16 or completed the eighth grade, and a variety of new subjects were available, including higher levels of mathematics, science, social studies, foreign languages, art and music, and "practical subjects" like bookkeeping and typing. By the mid-1960s, a majority of American adults were high school graduates. Today about seven out of ten have high school diplomas.

Why did the educational curriculum expand so much? As industry expanded in the mid-nineteenth century, occupations became more differentiated, and work skills could no longer be passed down from parents to children. There was a great need for specialized education in the skills necessary for the modern workforce, especially English composition, mathematics, and the sciences. Abstract learning in subjects such as history and Latin did not provide immediate work skills, but they did signify that the student had the cultural background necessary to move into the middle class (Willis et al., 1994). They were not only the key to advancement; they were the key to impressing people.

On the college level, the United States ranks among the best-educated countries in the world, with the highest graduation rate for adults over 35 (one in four adults now has a bachelor's degree) and boasts the majority of the world's best universities (*The Economist*, 2008). But among younger Americans aged 25 through 34, the United States has slipped to tenth in the percentage who hold an associate degree or higher (National Center for Public Policy and Higher Education, 2008). And on the high school level, our graduation rate has been declining for the past three decades, with racial and ethnic minorities graduating at lower rates than Whites. The United States also has more dropouts and underpreparedness than any other industrialized country, and we are falling behind in math, science, and problem-solving skills (Organization for Economic Cooperation and Development, 2006).

Some groups have consistently enjoyed more educational success than others. Women received less elementary and secondary education than men through the nineteenth century and were all but excluded from higher education until the early twentieth century. The vast majority of high school dropouts come from low-income families, and the vast majority of college students come from high-income families.

Research confirms the funneling effect of the educational system. The high school graduation rate is significantly lower among minorities: The on-time graduation rate is 77.5 percent nationally, but for African Americans it is 69 percent, and for Hispanics it is 72 percent (National Center for Public Policy and Higher Education, 2008) (see Figure 14.1). Black and Hispanic boys graduate at even lower rates than do girls from the same groups; and for those who do graduate, only 65 percent of Blacks and 58 percent of Hispanics go on to enroll in college the next fall, as compared with 73 percent of Whites. Financial barriers play a large part in these differences: More than 90 percent of high school students from families in the highest income group enroll in college, while only 78 percent of middle-income students do. For the lowest income group, it is 52 percent.

From there, the funnel continues to narrow. Fewer minorities are able to complete a four-year college degree within six years.

Figure 14.1 U.S. High School Graduation Rate

Graduation Rate
Class of 2005

- 90–100%
- 80–90%
- 70–80%
- 60–70%
- 50–60%
- Less than 50%

DC

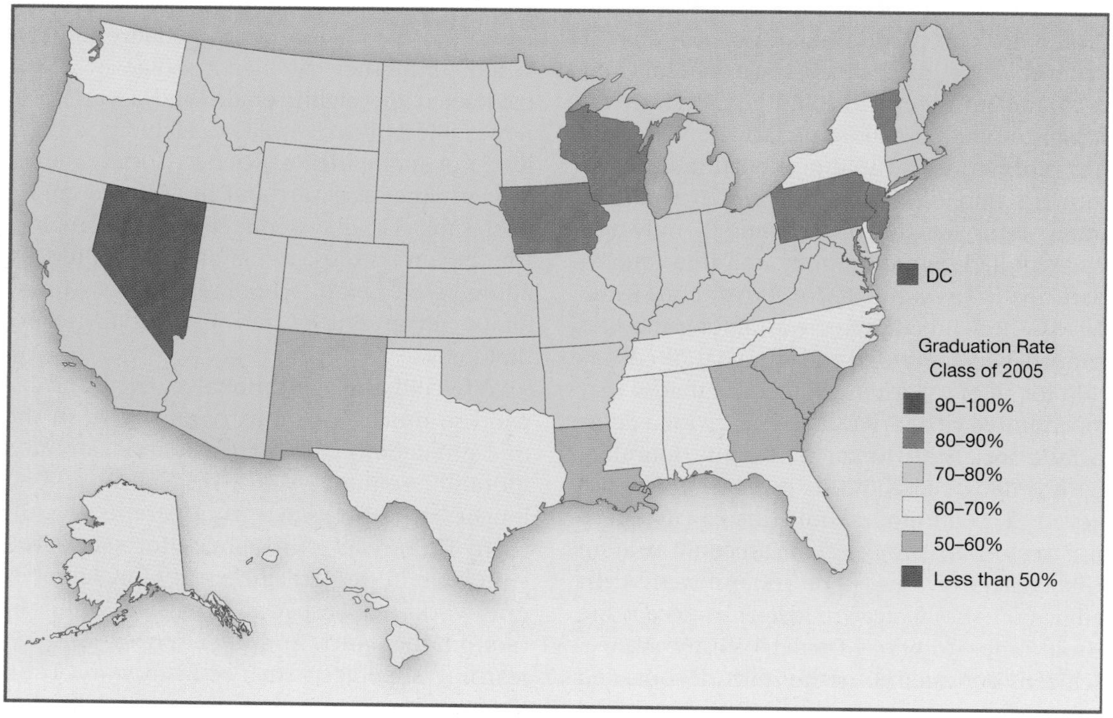

(*Source:* EducationWeek, "Diplomas Count, 2008," www.edweek.org.)

Chapter 14 Education, Religion, and Science

While 73 percent of White students graduate with a bachelor's degree within that time, only 59 percent of Blacks and 47 percent of Hispanics do (National Center for Public Policy and Higher Education, 2008). Americans with only a high school diploma have seen wage declines since the early 1970s, and those with only some college have seen virtually no wage growth since that time. Then when it comes to the advanced degrees that enable workers to garner increasingly higher wages in today's global knowledge economy, only 25 percent of Blacks and 17 percent of Hispanics 25 and over have attained any postsecondary degree, as compared to 38 percent of Whites and 56 percent of Asian Americans (Goldin and Katz, 2007).

The Hispanic dropout rate is particularly troubling because that group is a top driver to future workforce growth. Twenty-two percent of Hispanics aged 16 to 24 are high school dropouts, as compared with about 11 percent of Blacks and 6 percent of Whites (National Center for Education Statistics, 2008). There are many causes for this disparity: low incomes, a language barrier, and low-quality schooling that discourages participation.

Globalization

Around the world, too, education is closely tied to economic success. In low- and middle-income nations like India, Uganda, and Malawi, boys and girls may spend several years in school, but their learning is limited to the practical knowledge they need to farm or perform other traditional tasks. They don't have time for much else. A child in a high-performing country such as Norway, by contrast, can expect 17 years of education, double that of a child in Bangladesh and four times as much as a child in Niger (UNESCO, 2004).

Yet progress has been made in the past decade. With the major exception of Africa, most children around the world now receive some primary education, and the chance of a child continuing from primary school into the secondary grades is more than 80 percent in most countries. Beyond that, however, enrollment percentages drop dramatically in most regions of the world. In China, Malaysia, and Mexico, for example, the 90 percent of students who are enrolled at the lower secondary level drops to under 50 percent in the upper grades (The World Bank, 2009; UNESCO, 2004).

Gender also determines educational opportunity. One in three children worldwide lives in a country that does not ensure equal access to education for boys and girls. And in all countries without gender parity, it is girls who are disadvantaged. Gender disparity is even more widespread at the secondary level; in fact, the magnitude of inequity increases by educational level. Ironically, while disadvantages for girls in secondary education are common in low-income countries, girls tend to outnumber boys in high-income countries, including the United States (The World Bank, 2009).

As a result, the literacy rate is extremely low in poor countries. Among the Arab states, 19.8 percent of men and 41.1 percent of women were not literate as of 2006. Globally, 40 percent of Africans, 30 percent of Asians, and 15 percent of Latin Americans are illiterate (UNESCO, 2006). When most citizens cannot read and write at ordinary levels, they cannot compete in the global marketplace, and their nations remain impoverished. What's more, where women are better educated, children fare better in health, growth, and survival. Educated mothers are more likely to get prenatal care, to ensure children are immunized, and to provide a healthy diet, among other factors. One study of 65 countries found that doubling the proportion of girls educated at the secondary level would result in a drop of more than 50 percent in the infant mortality rate (State of the World's Mothers, 2008).

Some developing countries have made enormous strides in education. China now boasts very high enrollments in primary grades and almost 96 percent literacy. And yet enrollment drops considerably after ninth grade, especially in poorer regions, and there are large gender gaps.

A number of developing nations have begun intensive efforts to improve education, from grade school through university and professional schools. India has the world's youngest population, with 500 million people aged 18 and younger. If they could be educated, they would prove a formidable economic force. Government spending on education has grown rapidly. As a result, approximately 90 percent of all Indian children are enrolled in school. The literacy rate is up to 65 percent—from 53 percent in 1995. The number of Indians attending colleges and universities almost doubled in the 1990s. However, there is wide variation in literacy rates by location—wealthy districts have 98 percent literacy while poorer, rural ones have 48 percent—and especially by sex: The best districts have female literacy rates of 98 per-

cent, while the worst have 34 percent (Indicus Analytics, 2008). And India still has a high dropout rate—75 percent of Indian students drop out after eighth grade, and 78 percent of girls and 48 percent of boys fail to graduate from high school (ASER, 2008; NSSO, 2008).

In the 1980s, China also planned for universal education for grades 1 through 9 by 2000. As a result, there was an immense expansion of the educational system. Enrollment is high—at least through grade nine—so the literacy rate is 90 percent nationally, and 96 percent among young adults (age 12 to 40) (UNDP, 2008; *The Economist*, 2005). There has also been a massive university expansion, especially at the doctoral level; China is catching up to the United States particularly in doctorates awarded in science and engineering (National Science Foundation, 2008; *The Economist*, 2005).

U.S. / Them

Top Ten Countries Performance by 15-Year-Olds in Math and Reading

Once the world leader in education, the United States spends more per child on education than any other country. Yet the United States has slipped in recent years and is not even in the top 10 in global reading and math performance.

Top Ten Countries in Math Performance	Top Ten Countries in Reading Performance
1. Finland	1. Finland
2. South Korea	2. South Korea
3. Netherlands	3. Canada
4. Switzerland	4. Australia
5. Canada	5. New Zealand
6. Japan	6. Ireland
7. New Zealand	7. Sweden
8. Belgium	8. Netherlands
9. Australia	9. Belgium
10. Denmark	10. Norway
-- --	-- --
25. United States	25. United States

(*Source:* Organization for Economic Cooperation and Development and U.S. Department of Education.)

1. What might be some of the reasons that students in Finland do so well?

2. What sorts of policies might the United States implement to improve its standing? Does the low U.S. ranking indicate inferior performance, poor preparation, or less ability to take national standardized tests?

The Sociology of Education

Is there a set of information that everyone should know, or is it all a matter of personal preference? Is the person who can discuss Shakespeare's *The Tempest* but has never seen an episode of *Star Trek* really better educated than the person who can argue the merits of Kirk versus Picard but looks for the remote when Shakespeare's play is performed on PBS? More qualified for a white-collar job? Better able to select a candidate on Election Day?

E. D. Hirsch Jr. thinks so. A University of Virginia professor of humanities, Hirsch caused some controversy with his *Cultural Literacy: What Every American Needs to Know* (1988). He argued that the modern school curriculum, with its emphasis on diversity, is depriving children of the background that they need to be effective American citizens. They learn trivia, rather than a sound core curriculum.

So what do Americans need to know? Hirsch compiled a 600-plus-page *Dictionary of Cultural Literacy* (Hirsch, Kett, and Trefil, 2003). He doesn't reveal much about his criteria for inclusion: He selected items that are not too broad or too narrow, that appear frequently in national periodicals, and that have found "a place in our collective memory." It sounds like an outline of the "hidden curriculum," a reproduction of elite knowledge, and indeed there is little about minorities, very little about non-Western cultures. *Star Trek* is mentioned, as well as Batman and the *Peanuts* comic strip. However, most of the entries have to do with "high culture," elite knowledge. For example, here are some things that every "educated person" should know:

- "The Ballad of Reading Gaol," a poem by Oscar Wilde
- Absurdist playwright Samuel Beckett
- François Rabelais, who wrote the sixteenth-century masterpiece *Gargantua and Pantagruel*
- Thomas Aquinas, whose *Summa Theologica* is a classic of medieval theology
- Novelist Sir Walter Scott
- William Gladstone, prime minister of England during the Victorian era

OK, tell the truth: How many did you know? How many did your *instructor* know? Why are these more important to know than, let's say, the lyrics to a Bob Dylan song or who Lord Voldemort is?

And what about **scientific literacy,** which is, according to the National Academy of Sciences, the "knowledge and understanding of the scientific concepts and processes required for personal decision making, participation in civic and cultural affairs, and economic productivity." Scientific literacy has doubled over the past two decades, but, still, only about 28 percent of Americans are scientifically savvy and alert, according to Jon D. Miller, director of the Center for Biomedical Communications at Northwestern University Medical School (Miller, 2007). Low scientific literacy undermines our ability to take part in the democratic process today. One can't be an effective citizen without it, given that we are facing such issues as stem cell research, infectious diseases, nuclear power, and global warming.

Education and Inequality

If education doesn't make you smarter, at least it makes you richer. The higher your level of education, the higher your income will likely be.

The same holds true in other countries. While men at all levels of education earn more than equally educated women, and Whites earn more than racial and ethnic minorities, the relative earnings of all people of greater education are higher than those with lesser educational attainment (OECD, 2006).

But is this because educated people get paid more or because people who are already in the upper classes have enough resources to make sure their children go further in their education and because upper-class people value education more and therefore push their children? Most of us believe that education is a ticket to social mobility. And it's partly

The Shortest School Year

Americans like to talk about our intense work ethic as compared with people in other countries, especially Europeans. But school children are a national exception to the rule. Americans have one of the shortest school years anywhere—180 days versus 195 for OECD countries (Organization for Economic Cooperation and Development, the organization of the world's 30 most developed nations) and more than 200 for East Asian countries—and one of the shortest school days, too: the six-and-a-half-hour American school day equals 32 hours per week, far fewer than in countries like Belgium (44) or Sweden (60). And American children do only about one hour's worth of homework per day, an amount that shocks the Japanese and Chinese (*The Economist*, 2009).

Did You Know?

Figure 14.2 Mean Income by Years of Education and Gender, 2006

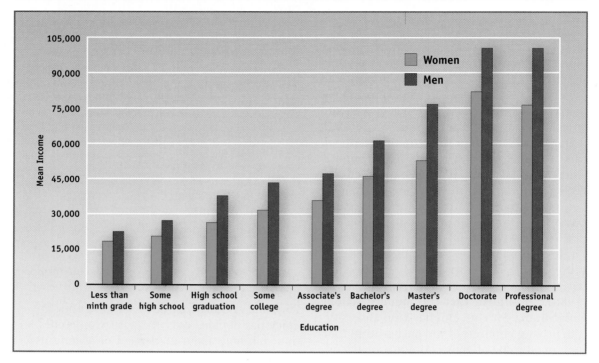

(*Source:* U.S. Department of Commerce, Bureau of the Census, Current Population Reports, Series P-60, "Money Income of Households, Families, and Persons in the United States," "Income, Poverty, and Valuation of Noncash Benefits," various years; and Series P-60, "Money Income in the United States," various years. From *Digest of Education Statistics 2005.*)

true. Over the course of American history, different groups of immigrants—for example, Jews, Koreans, and Cubans—have successfully used educational advancement as a vehicle for social mobility for the entire ethnic group. But education is also one of the primary vehicles by which society reinforces social inequalities based on race, ethnicity, class, and gender. As long as we believe that education is a strict meritocracy—the best get ahead—we believe that different educational outcomes (some groups do better than others) are based on characteristics of those individuals or those groups: They try harder and do more homework, or their culture rewards educational achievement more than other groups.

There is also a different dynamic, a "hidden" curriculum, through which education not only creates social inequalities but makes them seem natural, normal, and inevitable (Bowles, 1976; Lynch, 1989; Margolis, 2001). Of course, some teachers and administrators deliberately introduce stereotypes, marginalization, and exclusion into their lesson plans. But the problem goes much deeper than that. Educators need not *try* to reproduce social inequalities. They are

reproduced in textbooks, in test questions, and in classroom discussions.

The most important lessons of the hidden curriculum actually take place outside the classroom, on the playground, in the cafeteria, in the many informal interactions that take place during every school day, from kindergarten through college. Students learn which of their peers are "supposed" to dominate and which are "supposed" to be bullied, beaten, laughed at, or ignored. They learn about gender hierarchies (call a boy a "girl" to humiliate him, or "gay" to humiliate him even more). They learn about racial hierarchies. They learn about social status. The lessons they learn will influence their future decisions, whether they are in the boardroom or the courtroom, whether they are applying for a job or doing the hiring, regardless of how often the formal curriculum includes units on diversity.

The types of schools and the uneven distribution of resources for schools result in often dramatic differences in student achievement. One in nine American schoolchildren attends a private school, which most of us believe are superior to public schools. The evidence is far from clear, although parents, children, and even public school teachers all believe that private schools offer a better education.

Wealthy versus Poor School Districts. Parents say they switch to private schools—or want to—because of the crumbling buildings, overcrowded classrooms, bare-bones curriculum, and poor instruction in many public schools today. Unfortunately, those parents most able to afford private schools probably live in districts where the public schools are actually pretty good. Because education is funded largely by local property taxes, wealthier neighborhoods and communities have more money to spend on schools than poorer ones. Public schools in wealthy neighborhoods can afford state-of-the-art labs and libraries, small classes, and highly paid teachers. It is the poor neighborhoods that have the crumbling buildings, overcrowded classrooms, and overworked, underpaid teachers. The pattern holds up in every city and every state, reproducing the same class privileges that we find in the public/private school divide (Oakes, 1990).

Racial Segregation. The Supreme Court's *Brown v. Board of Education* decision (1954) outlawed the practice of **segregation**—requiring White and non-White students living in the same district to attend separate schools. In 1954, nearly 100 percent of Black students were attending intensely segregated (predominantly minority) schools. Busing programs began to decrease segregation in favor of **integration,** in which the school's ethnic distribution is more balanced.

Integration in U.S. classrooms peaked in 1988, then began to reverse when the 1991 Supreme Court ruling allowed the return of neighborhood schools. In 1998, more than 70 percent of Black students attended intensely segregated schools. The most dramatic (and largely ignored) trend affects Hispanic Americans. In 1968, a little more than 20 percent of Hispanic students were enrolled in intensely segregated schools. In 1998, more than a third were. Hispanics face serious levels of segregation by race and also poverty, with particularly large increases in segregation in the West, the first area in the nation to have predominantly minority public school enrollment (Orfield, 2004).

Segregation is strongly associated with poverty for all groups: Nearly 90 percent of intensely segregated Black and Latino schools have student bodies with concentrated poverty (Orfield, 2004). Concentrated poverty means students with worse health care, lower nutrition, less-educated parents, more frequent moves, weaker preschool skills, and often limited English skills. They have two strikes against them in their quest for educational excellence already, and then they must contend with outdated textbooks, inadequate facilities, overcrowded classrooms, and, often, inexperienced, uncredentialed teachers.

Gender Inequality. Education not only reproduces racial inequality, it reproduces gender stereotypes. In the hidden curriculum, teachers, administrators, and peers require us to conform to narrow definitions of what it means to be a "boy" or a "girl," and they punish deviance, subtly or not. However, education also allows us to move beyond stereotyping: The classroom is perhaps the only place where a boy can be praised for being quiet and studious and a girl can be praised for knowing the answer.

In their book, *Failing at Fairness* (1994), David and Myra Sadker documented some of the subtle ways teachers reinforce both gender difference and gender inequality. They named it the "chilly classroom climate" for girls, describing that class materials used often reflect stereotyped differences between women and men, boys and girls. Because of such disparities, there has been an effort to increase the number of active girls in schoolbooks and also in children's media.

Grades reflect both students' achievement and teachers' expectations. In one study, girls and Asian Americans received better grades than other students—even when their test scores were the same. The researchers concluded that this was because they conformed to teachers' perceptions of how good students behave.

The Racial Achievement Gap

I n *No Excuses: Closing the Racial Gap in Learning* (2003), Abigail and Stephan Thernstrom argue that African American educational underachievement stems from a variety of factors:

- Low birth weight, which can impair intellectual development
- High number of single-parent families led by young mothers unprepared to give children good educational guidance
- Inadequate funding
- Difficulty recruiting good teachers to work in schools attended primarily by Blacks

By contrast, Ronald Ferguson (2001) studied middle- and upper-middle-class students in Ann Arbor, Michigan, a wealthy, well-educated community, the site of the University of Michigan. Students in the city's three high schools had an average SAT score in 2004 of 1,165, over 100 points higher than the national average. In 2003, they had 44 National Merit finalists. Eighty-five percent of high school seniors go on to four-year colleges and universities. Quite an elite bunch!

Even in middle-class college-bound high schools, African American students typically had a C average, White students a B. African Americans typically scored 100 points below White students on the SAT. Why?

Some of the reasons Ferguson found were environmental: Even in the same community and the same schools, the African American students were less affluent: Twenty-one percent were upper middle class or upper class, compared to 73 percent of the White students. But there was more. The parents of African American students lacked access to the networks White parents had to trade information about the best teachers, classes, and strategies for success. They felt less entitled, less able to be demanding and advocate for their children.

Teachers often misread signals from the Black students. In high-stress, high-achievement schools, students who are trying hard and not doing well perceive themselves as failures. It's better to act as though you are simply uninterested in doing well than to acknowledge that you are struggling. Teachers see laziness and indifference, lower their expectations, and give students less support—which Ferguson found matters a great deal to minority students. They then try harder to pretend that they are uninterested, resulting in a self-fulfilling prophecy.

There have also been dramatic changes outside the classroom. Title IX legislation forbids discrimination against girls and women in all aspects of school life. As a result, many elementary and secondary schools have increased funding for girls' sports, allowing more girls the opportunity to participate. And, contrary to some expectations, girls have shown they love sports.

Still, one of the chief lessons taught in school is what it means to be a man or a woman. Gender conformity—adhering to normative expectations about masculinity or femininity—is carefully scrutinized. We get messages everywhere we look—in the content of the texts we read, the rules we are all supposed to follow, and the behaviors of teachers and administrators as role models. But it is most significantly taught by peers, who act as a sort of "gender police," enforcing the rules. Often we learn it by a sort of negative reinforcement: Step out of line, even the tiniest bit, and your friends and other students will let you know, clearly and unequivocally, that you have transgressed. Do it again, and they may begin to doubt you as a potential friend. Do it consistently, and you will be marginalized as a weirdo, a deviant, or, most importantly, as "gay."

Every American teenager knows that the most constant put-down in our high schools and middle schools these days is "that's so gay." Ordinarily this gay-baiting—calling people or something they do "gay" as a way of ridiculing them or putting them down—has little to do with sexual orientation: Calling someone's shirt or hairstyle or musical preference "gay" doesn't typically mean that you suspect he might actually be homosexual. It means that you don't think he is acting sufficiently masculine. "Dude, you're a fag," is the way one kid put it (Pascoe, 2005). The constant teasing and bullying that occur in middle schools and high schools have become national problems (Jovenen, Graham, and Schuster, 2003; Olweus, 1993). Bullying is not one single thing but a continuum stretching from hurtful language through shoving and hitting to criminal assault and school shootings. Harmful teasing and bullying happen to more than one million schoolchildren, both boys and girls, a year. The evidence of bullying's ubiquity alone is quite convincing. In one study of middle and high schools students in Midwestern towns, 88 percent reported having observed bullying, and 77 percent reported being a victim of bullying at some point during their school years. In another, 70 percent had been sexually harassed by their peers; 40 percent had experienced physical dating violence, 66 percent had been victimized by emotional abuse in a dating relationship, and 54 percent had been bullied. Many middle and high school students are afraid to go to school; they fear locker rooms, hallways, bathrooms, lunchrooms, and playgrounds, and some even fear their classrooms.

Educational Reform and Public Policy

The Department of Education oversees the nation's public schools. How can schools be more responsive to the people they are intended to serve? What sorts of policies can government and communities develop? Several of these policies are controversial.

Bilingual Education. Up to the 1960s, public education in the United States was always conducted in English (except for classes designed to teach foreign languages). In 1968, Congress passed the Bilingual Education Act, asserting that these children were being denied equal access to education and that school districts should "take affirmative steps to rectify the language deficiency." These steps included courses in ESL (English as a second language) and often classroom instruction in the student's native language on the primary level.

Some critics argue that the programs are costly and inefficient; that there simply aren't enough qualified teachers fluent in Navajo, Somali, and Thai to go around; and that students tend to do poorly in tests of both English and their native language. But often the question boils down to melting pot versus multiculturalism. Should everyone be learning English as quickly as possible, or is there room for Navajo, Somali, and Thai in our schools and in our society?

But researchers have concluded that bilingual education helps students to learn English. When students have only conversational English, they tend to fall behind their peers whose first language is English. A long-awaited, federally commissioned report was supposed to summarize existing data to determine whether bilingual education helps students who speak other languages to read English, but its release was cancelled by the government. It is known that the researchers involved conclude that it helps ("Tongue-Tied on Bilingual Education," 2005).

Privatization. One of the most popular types of school reform during the last few decades has been privatization, allowing some degree of private control over public education. There are two types of privatization, vouchers and charter schools.

The **voucher system** uses taxpayer funds to pay for students' tuition at private schools. It was first proposed by economist Milton Friedman in 1955, based on the idea of the free market: If there is competition for a product or service, quality will increase. However, it is controversial. Is the marketplace the best model on which to organize education, or should schools provide a service that should be shielded from the marketplace? A school district in Wisconsin instituted the first voucher program in 1990, and 15 years later only two more states (Ohio and Florida) and the District of Columbia

Bullying has become an increasingly important problem in schools. More than 1 million school children a year are bullied. More than just a problem of individual bullies and victims, sociologists point to bullying as a social experience that can compromise educational goals. Challenging bullying must involve changing school culture.

Random School Shootings

On April 16, 2007, Seung Hui Cho, a 23-year-old student at Virginia Tech, murdered two students in a dorm, waited about an hour, and then calmly walked to an academic building, chained the entrance, and started shooting methodically. In the end, he killed 30 students and faculty before shooting himself—the deadliest shooting by an individual in our nation's history. While obviously mentally ill, he had managed never to be ill "enough" to attract serious attention. In the time between the shootings, he recorded a video in which he fumed about all the taunting, teasing, and being ignored he had endured and how this final conflagration would even the score. In February, 2008, a 27-year-old former student at Northern Illinois University, Stephen Kazmierczak, opened fire on a crowded lecture hall at Northern Illinois University, killing four students before turning the gun on himself.

And then there was Columbine High School in Littleton, Colorado. The very word *Columbine* has become a symbol; kids today often talk about someone "pulling a Columbine." The connection between being socially marginalized, picked on, and bullied every day propelled Eric Harris and Dylan Klebold deeper into their video-game-inspired fantasies of a vengeful bloodbath. On April 20, 1999, Harris and Klebold brought a variety of weapons to their high school and proceeded to walk through the school, shooting whomever they could find. Twenty-three students and faculty were injured, and 15 died, including one teacher and the perpetrators.

What all these boys—virtually all school shooters have been boys—have in common is a self-

justifying narrative of victimization. All claimed to have been bullied, taunted, teased—maliciously, routinely, and with absolute impunity. Their actions came from a sense of "aggrieved entitlement"—they had been wronged and sought revenge. One boy, Luke Woodham, who killed two classmates in 1997, said, "I am not insane. I am angry. I killed because people like me are mistreated every day. I am malicious because I am miserable." Another boy, Michael Carneal, told psychiatrists weighing his sanity that "people respect me now" (Blank, 1998).

Several recent works emphasize the serious psychiatric disorders of these rampage shooters. While it's true that they did have serious psychological problems, a sociological perspective also considers the patterns of these shootings and the similarities among the perpetrators. What's more, we don't profile only the shooters, but also the schools: Did the schools have any characteristics in common?

Students understand these common characteristics, even if some observers do not. In a national survey of teenagers' attitudes, nearly nine of ten teenagers (86 percent) said that they believed that the school shootings were motivated by a desire "to get back at those who have hurt them" and that "other kids picking on them, making fun of them, or bullying them" were the immediate causes. Other potential causes, such as violence on television, movies, computer games or videos, mental problems, and access to guns, were significantly lower on the adolescents' ratings (Gaughan, Cerio, and Myers, 2001).

---

have followed suit, with a total of only about 36,000 students. Voters have defeated proposed voucher programs in many states, including California, Michigan, Texas, South Carolina, and Indiana.

Charter schools are publicly funded elementary or secondary schools that set forth in their founding document (charter) goals they intend to meet in terms of student achievement. In return, these schools are privately administered and exempt from certain laws regarding education. They encompass a wide range of curricula and style, from

no-nonsense, "back-to-basics" reading, writing, and mathematics to technology-rich science and math schools to intimate academies modeled on the more elite private schools. The first charter school was authorized in Minnesota in 1991, and they have been proliferating ever since. Now there are 4,600 charter schools educating about 1.4 million of the nation's 50 million public school students (Center for Education Reform, 2008; Dillon, 2009).

Do charter schools make a difference? A recent survey looked at schools in 16 states found that 17 percent of charter schools provided a better education than traditional public schools in the same states. But 37 percent of charter schools offered a worse education than traditional public schools in those states (Center for Research on Educational Outcomes [CREDO], 2009).

Homeschooling. About 3 percent of students ages 5 through 17—1.5 million—are being homeschooled in the United States, an increase of 400,000 since 2003 (National Center for Education Statistics [NECS], 2009).

They are homeschooled in all grades, from kindergarten through twelfth grade.

Why do parents homeschool their children? Eight-five percent of parents cited concern about the environment of traditional schools. Almost as many (72 percent) said that they wanted to provide the religious or moral instruction missing in traditional schools. Only 20 percent said they wanted a nontraditional approach to their child's education (NCES, 2009).

Thus, homeschooling is a phenomenon largely of the political far left and the far right. Liberals might complain about classroom conduct, watered-down academics, and the lack of attention to individual learning styles; conservatives and religious homeschoolers complain about having a required multicultural curriculum, with no school prayer and the teaching of evolution.

No Child Left Behind. In January 2002, then-President George W. Bush signed Public Law 107–110, the Elementary and Secondary School Act, better known as "No Child Left Behind" (NCLB). The 670-page law outlines a top-down approach to school performance, with a number of sweeping, even revolutionary, provisions:

- Students in elementary school (grades 3 through 8) must take annual tests to ensure that they have met minimal standards of competency in reading and math.
- Students in schools that are falling behind can transfer to better schools on the government's tab.
- Every child should learn to read and write English by the end of the third grade.

The cost of enforcing this law is immense: The Department of Education budget increased from $14 billion to $22.4 billion to handle it. And the goals, though broadly defined, have become difficult to enforce. Teachers complain that they must spend an excessive amount of class time preparing students for the reading and math tests, while ignoring other essential subjects like history and science. They complain that the program doesn't target the students who need the most help and even forces them to dumb down accountability measures that were already in place.

School districts complain that the law tends to reproduce the same inequalities that it is intended to combat. It treats every school district alike, ignoring special challenges faced by districts with many impoverished or non-English-speaking students or students with learning disabilities. Education critic Alfie Kohn argues that the main effect of NCLB has been "to sentence poor children to an endless regimen of test-preparation drills" (Kohn, 2007). Although reading and math scores have improved slightly, the policy remains controversial.

Higher Education

In 1949, there were 2.4 million college students in the United States. Fifty years later, there were 16 million. The population of the country had doubled during that period, but the proportion of the population going to college increased by 800 percent. About one in four Americans now has a college degree. And it is not merely a matter of intellectual interest: Today people need bachelor's degrees, and sometimes master's degrees, to get jobs that would have required a high school diploma or less 50 years ago. What happened?

In 1949, college degrees were simply unnecessary. A high school diploma qualified you for almost every job, and if you needed additional training, you could apply directly to a law or medical school. The wealthy went to college to "become educated," learn the social skills, and build the social networks necessary for an upper-class life (Altbach, 1998; Lucas, 1996; Rudolph, 1990).

After World War II, GI loans brought many of the returning soldiers to college for the first

---

A Bachelor's Degree

A typical four-year college degree is a "Bachelor's" degree in Arts or Science. Why? In the original vulgar Latin (Latin spoken by the common people), *baccalaris* meant a poor unmarried "farmhand" and *baccalaureus* meant "advanced student" (from *bacca laureus*, the laurel branch used to honor degree holders). Both words entered the English language in the late fourteenth century, but because they sounded almost the same, they both became *bachelor*.

Did You Know?

Figure 14.3 Undergraduate Enrollment: Total Undergraduate Enrollment in Degree-Granting Two- and Four-Year Postsecondary Institutions with Projections, by Sex: Fall 1970 through 2017

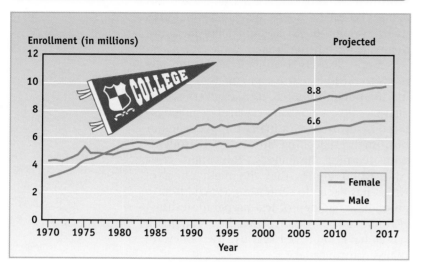

(*Source:* National Center for Education Statistics, and W. Hussar Projections of Education Statistics to 2017.)

time. Most were the first in their families to attend college, and they weren't quite sure what to expect. Some studied "liberal arts" such as English, history, and philosophy, but most wanted courses directly related to the jobs they would get afterward. Colleges filled

the need with job-oriented majors and courses. Employers, faced with a glut of applicants more qualified than usual, began to require more advanced degrees for entry-level jobs: Why hire someone with just a high school diploma for the typist job, when there were a dozen applicants with college degrees? Majors and career paths became more specialized: Why hire someone with an English degree for the advertising job, when there were a dozen applicants who majored in advertising? Today most students still major in one of the liberal arts, but job-oriented majors are very popular.

Higher Education and Inequality. High school graduation is only the rim of the funnel of educational privilege. Of those minorities and lower- and working-class persons who graduate from high school, few go on to college. Of those who do attend college, few graduate from college. And so on. By the time they turn 26, 59 percent of people from affluent families but just 7 percent of people from low-income households have a bachelor's degree (Education Trust, 2006).

The class barrier to higher education is actually increasing. The proportion of students from upper-income families attending the most elite colleges declined dramatically after World War II, but it is growing again. Only 3

Sociology and Our World

The Chosen

Sociologist Jerome Karabel graduated from Harvard University and now teaches at the University of California at Berkeley (and served on the admissions committee), so he may be the ideal person to write *The Chosen: The Hidden History of Admission and Exclusion at Harvard, Yale, and Princeton* (2005). He examined a century of admissions decisions at these three Ivy League schools to determine who gets in—and how.

Prior to the 1920s, all applicants who met high academic standards were accepted. The administration of these schools became concerned about the increasing numbers of well-qualified Jewish applicants (20 percent of the Harvard freshman class of 1918): How could they maintain a Protestant majority if they admitted everyone with a rash of A's? Instead, they established admissions committees and limited the "super bright" to about

10 percent of available spots. For the rest, grades were less important than "character": manliness, congeniality, leadership potential, and other qualities that they believed lacking in Jewish men.

Other universities followed the example of the Big Three; and, for the rest of the century, admissions committees from the top to the bottom tier of universities regularly rejected applicants whom they believed belonged to an "undesirable" race, ethnic background, religion, or socioeconomic status. "Character" was further delineated by looking at applicants' extracurricular activities and soliciting letters of recommendation. That system is still in place today. Though no admissions committee would dare ask about an applicant's race or religion today, they still weed out applicants with the wrong "character," and that rarely means the children of wealthy alumni.

percent come from the bottom quartile of the income, and only 10 percent come from the bottom half.

But it is not just elite colleges. Across the spectrum, colleges are drawing more members from upper-income households and fewer from average or below-average income households. Because the income gap between the college educated and the noncollege educated was 66 percent in 1997 (up from 31 percent in 1979) (*The Economist,* 2005), it seems that the universities are reproducing social advantage instead of serving as an engine of mobility.

The poorer students are priced out of the market for higher education by soaring tuition increases (which means that financial aid is extending farther up the income ladder than it used to). (See Figure 14.4.) We might think, "Oh, there are always scholarships for the smart ones," but being smart is not a replacement for having money. Seventy-eight percent of the top achievers from low-income families go to college. But 77 percent of the *bottom* achievers from high-income families also manage to get in ("Dreams Only Money Can Buy," 2003).

The Transformation of Higher Education. The "traditional" college experience celebrated in the Hollywood film—a leafy residential campus, ivy climbing on grand nineteenth-century buildings at a private four-year liberal arts college—has never captured the majority of students' experience in higher education. Those small, private, liberal arts colleges account for only about 10 percent of all higher-education students. "State" and "Tech" are far more common than Yale and Harvard. Over half of all students attend colleges that charge less than $9,000 a year in tuition—that is, are publicly funded (College Board, 2009) (see www.collegeboard.com/student/pay/add-it-up/4494.html).

Community Colleges. About one-third of all students attend two-year or community colleges (College Board, 2009). Unlike the traditional four-year liberal arts curriculum, the community college attracts a far more diverse student body, especially in terms of class and age. By offering classes at night, on weekends, during the summer, and online, the community college has proved quite responsive to the new 24/7 global economy and serves the needs of an increasingly diverse student population—older people and even retirees, veterans, people who have jobs, people with families—making the community college classroom a heterogeneous and diverse learning environment. The overwhelming majority of community college students are first-generation students (meaning that their parents did not go to college), making them truly an expression of the American belief that everyone deserves a chance.

On the other hand, community colleges also reproduce the very inequalities they attempt to address. They have no endowments and minuscule resources, pay their faculty far less than four-year schools and work them harder, and have far more part-time faculty who receive no benefits. While 46 percent of U.S. undergraduates go to community colleges, two-year schools receive less than one-tenth of the money that four-year

Figure 14.4 Soaring College Tuitions

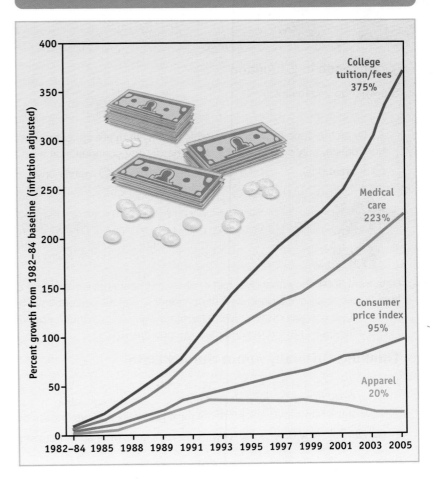

(*Source:* www.edweek.org.)

schools get from the federal government (Fitzpatrick/Austin, 2009). In that sense, too, they are a case study in the sociology of education: both challenging and reproducing inequalities at the very same time.

Privatization of Higher Education. One of the dominant recent educational trends, in primary and secondary education as well as in higher education, has been the spread of the marketplace. For centuries, colleges and universities were a sort of refuge from the market, a place where the pursuit of dollars didn't interfere with the pursuit of knowledge. Not anymore. Traditional universities are not-for-profit organizations. However, an increasing number of proprietary or **for-profit universities** have arisen in recent years. They have some advantages over traditional universities: The cost is comparatively low, the university rather than the

professors owns the curriculum, and students can graduate relatively quickly. They omit or severely curtail the traditional social activities of a college; their facilities are usually very limited; and their degrees lack the prestige of a degree from a traditional university. However, many students today are far more interested in developing practical, job-related skills than a "total college experience," and they have found proprietary schools a viable alternative. Each school has developed its own practical market niche:

- Strayer concentrates on telecommunications and business administration.
- Cardean University offers online business education, including MBAs.
- Concord Law School, owned by Kaplan (in turn owned by the *Washington Post*) has one of largest law school enrollments in the United States.

What do **you** think?

Confidence in Education

So, what do you think?

> As far as the people running the education system are concerned, would you say you have a great deal of confidence, only some confidence, or hardly any confidence at all in them?
>
> ○ A great deal   ○ Only some   ○ Hardly any

What does **America** think?

(*Source:* General Social Survey, 2004. Reproduced by permission.)

Data from 2004 show that over half of all respondents have only some confidence in the educational system. Slightly more than 30 percent have a great deal of confidence, and 13 percent have hardly any. Differences by race were significant and interesting. Black respondents were far more likely than White respondents to have confidence in the education system. These differences have remained steady since the 1970s.

Thinking Critically about Survey Data

1. The differences in survey response by race were striking. Why do you think that Black respondents were dramatically more likely to have a great deal of confidence in the education system than were White respondents, particularly in view of the fact that Black students have generally and historically been underserved by the educational system?

2. Conversely, why do you think White respondents were so pessimistic about the educational system?

References: See Davis et al., page 511.

Students develop a subculture that their professors (and their parents!) often find foreign and even a bit disconcerting. According to this stereotype, student life revolves around drinking, partying, playing video games and online poker, watching pornography on the Internet, sports, and sleeping. At many colleges, it appears that academic life—studying, homework, reading in the library, doing research—is almost an incidental afterthought, the least important part of a student's day. Occasionally, a professor goes "underground" and lives in a dorm or fraternity or sorority house for a semester and writes an exposé of campus life, designed to shock adults into paying attention to student culture (see Moffatt, 1989; Nathan, 2005).

In the late 1980s, anthropologist Michael Moffatt moved into the dorms at Rutgers and wrote a scathing exposé of campus life (Moffatt, 1989)—a world of indiscriminate drunken sex, copious drinking, no studying but lots of sleeping, and a lack of serious intellectual engagement. College, he wrote, is really about the pursuit of "fun."

Moffatt's description seemed a bit over the top to Northern Arizona University anthropologist Cathy Small. She wanted to understand why students didn't come to her office hours, didn't seem to do the readings for her classes, and fell asleep and ate during class time. In the fall of 2002, she enrolled in her own university and spent a year in the dorms as an incoming first-year student. She told virtually no one that she was a professor. And she published the results under a pseudonym to try to conceal her identity, but journalists figured it out within a week of the book's publication (Nathan, 2005).

The Ethnography of Campus Life

Small found students to be amazingly busy: Most work at part-time jobs for at least 15 hours a week, juggle five courses, and try to join campus activities to pad their college résumés to gain a competitive advantage in the job market. Sure, they drink and sleep, hook up, and party down. And they expect their colleges to both "educate and entertain" them.

Small found that the biggest differences between campus life today and when she was a student in the 1970s were the virtual lack of any free time in the lives of her students, the absence of a sense of campus "community," and the absence of any impact by faculty on the lives of students. Students also never discussed intellectual, political, or philosophical issues outside of class and rarely, if ever, discussed anything that happened in class with their friends.

Recent surveys support Small's observations, consistently finding that students are working harder and longer today than they ever did. Students study harder, and nearly half have paid jobs outside of school. Students also have far less sex and drink far less than observers—and students themselves—imagine (Perkins, 2003). As with most sociology, it isn't the case that students are complete party-going, alcohol-sodden, sex-addicted sports fans or serious academic nerds who live to study. They're both—although preferably not at the same time.

The University of Phoenix, the largest for-profit university in the United States, is also the largest university in the United States, period. It has 345,300 students on 239 campuses and various satellite campuses around the world, including some in China and India, and enrollment is growing at 25 percent per year.

Phoenix is the brainchild of John Sperling, a Cambridge University–educated economist turned entrepreneur. While teaching at a state university, he noticed that the curriculum was designed for "traditional" 18- to 22-year-old students and ignored adult learners. But, in the new economy, people 10 or 20 years past high school often decide that they

need college, and those with degrees often return to update their skills or retool their résumés. Sperling decided to found a new university catering to working adults, with convenient class schedules, many centers in conveniently located areas instead of one giant central campus (beginning in the 1990s, entire degrees could be taken online), and an emphasis on practical subjects that will help them build careers.

Nontraditional students now account for 95 percent of the Phoenix student body. They are over 25 years old, hoping to enhance their job possibilities rather than broaden their intellectual interests, and not particularly interested in immersing themselves in

College is no longer the sole domain of traditional-age students. Adult learners over 23 years old now make up about 10 percent of all college students—and more than 90 percent at some for-profit schools.

the traditional college environment. In some ways, the University of Phoenix has proved more successful than traditional colleges in meeting the needs of nontraditional students.

However, as institutions for higher learning, for-profits strip the university of its other functions. There are no science labs, and no faculty members do research; nor are professors protected by tenure or any forms of academic freedom. Faculty members are paid only to teach, and they are paid hourly wages that don't approach the salaries of professors at most colleges and universities. In a sense, these private universities separate the different dimensions of higher education and concentrate on some while ignoring others.

Religion and Science

As an institution, education is governed by standards, methods, and logic derived from the natural and social sciences, and types of inquiry drawn from the humanities. The stated goals of education are to enable the student to engage more fully with the social, natural, and cultural worlds. However, as we have pointed out, education also reproduces—and even legitimizes—some of the inequalities we have observed in society.

For centuries, the norms of science have governed our educational institutions. Injecting of nonscientific standards—religious conformity or political ideologies—has been resisted as an intrusion on the sanctity of the classroom. So, you might think that, as more and more people are educated, more and more people would embrace scientific or secular ideas, and fewer people would declare themselves religious.

That's certainly what some sociologists thought. For decades, sociologists predicted a gradual **secularization** of American life: As education became more pervasive, the bright clear light of scientific inquiry would triumph over the dark haze of religion.

They were wrong. Throughout the developing world, there is a religious resurgence. The collapse of communism in Russia led to sharp rises in religion. It's only in the Western European countries that religion has declined sharply. And, of course, one of the most significant sociological facts about the United States is

that increased reliance on science and technology has not come at the expense of adherence to religious ideals. Indeed, both religion and science have grown dramatically.

Again: It's not "either/or," religion *or* science. It's religion *and* science.

Comparing Religion and Science

Sociologists view science and religion as similar institutions. Both are organized and coherent systems of thought that are organized into social institutions. Both make claims to "truth." Both make claims to govern our conduct: Science governs our conduct toward the natural world, regulating how we are able to understand it, and religion orients people toward social interaction in this world as an expression of its beliefs in the next world. Both have professionals who devote many years to study and training to acquire the credentials necessary to speak as experts.

However, there are also many differences between the two institutions. **Religion** is a set of beliefs about the origins and meaning of life, usually based on the existence a supernatural power. It is primarily concerned with the big questions of existence, such as: What is the meaning of life? Where did I come from? Where am I going? The emphasis of science is more methodological. **Science** is the accumulated systematic knowledge of the physical or material world, which is obtained through experimentation and observation. Religion deals with big questions of existence; science deals with smaller questions of classification or processes. Scientific journals are full of articles about the cell walls of mollusks and the effect of a certain quantity of electricity on a strontium compound. Only a few branches of science consider ultimate questions of existence, and even then they don't focus on the individual. They ask, "Where did the universe come from?"

Religion acquires its ideas through **revelation:** God, spirits, prophets, or sacred books give us the answers to the questions of existence. On the other hand, science acquires its knowledge through **empirical verification:** Information is developed, demonstrated, and double-checked using an experimental method. Science bases its claims on what has been shown this way, rather than asking you to believe something on faith. Occasionally, religion may seek to offer proof of the truth of its claims—through miracles, for example—but even these may be a matter of faith. Scientific types believe it when they see it; religious types are more likely to see it when they believe it.

Science is interested in only the physical world. It concedes that a spiritual world may exist, but it is undetectable to scientific research. No systematic experiments have demonstrated its existence, or the existence of spiritual beings like ghosts or spiritual powers like ESP. The parapsychologists who study such matters have had mixed, unreliable results.

Religion and science both change over time. There are new interpretations of the revealed message, new emphases, or even new revelations. Scientific discoveries that are accepted as empirically demonstrated one day may be replaced by new discoveries, also empirically verified. Neither religion nor science changes overnight. Neither has a smooth, uncontroversial change from one set of beliefs to another. Instead, they advance by dramatic breaks with accepted wisdom. In religion, these breaks generally come when a new prophet or charismatic leader draws people away from established institutions. In science, these breaks come from scientists who challenge accepted assumptions and begin to draw followers into newer empirical areas of scientific exploration.

Classical Sociological Theories of Religion

Religion is a **cultural universal**—that is, it exists in every single culture. No human society has yet been discovered that lacks an organized, coherent system of beliefs about a spiritual world. However, religions vary tre-mendously. Some have no gods, some have many, and some have only one. Some believe in a heaven or a hell, some in reincarnation, some in both, and some do not believe in an afterlife at all. Sociologists are less interested in debating the truth of religious doctrine than in the function of religion. Why do all societies have one? What does it do for the society?

Durkheim and Social Cohesion. For Emile Durkheim, religion served to integrate society, to create a sense of unity out of an enormously diverse collection of individuals. Religion provides a sort of social glue that holds society together, binding us into a common destiny and common values.

But how? Durkheim went back to the origins of society. He surmised that primitive cultures were so overcome by the mystery and power of nature—lightning striking a tree, for instance—that they would come together as a group. These events were seen as **sacred**—holy moments that evoked that sense of unity. Cultures then try to re-create these moments in **rituals**—solemn reenactments of the sacred events. Rituals would remind individuals that they are part of a whole that is greater than its parts. Durkheim's emphasis on what holds a society together is important to sociologists who study modern societies, where the greater complexity and diversity pose many challenges to social unity. Sociologist Robert Bellah (1967) suggested that modern, secular societies develop a **civil religion** in which secular rituals—such as reciting the Pledge of Allegiance, singing the national anthem at professional sports events, lighting fireworks on the Fourth of July—create the intense emotional bonds among people that used to be accomplished by religion.

Marx and Social Control. Karl Marx believed that religion kept social change from happening by preventing people from revolting against the miserable conditions of their lives. In feudal society, Marx argued, religion served as a sort of ideological "blinder" to the reality of exploitation. Because the lords of the manor owned everything, including the rights to the labor of the serfs, anyone could tell that there was brutal inequality. So how could the lords stay in power? How come the serfs didn't revolt?

Marx argued that religion provided a justification for inequality. For example, the belief in the "Great Chain of Being," in which all creatures, from insects to kings, were arranged on a single hierarchical arrangement ordained by God, obviously justified the dominion of those at the top over those at the bottom. Marx called religion "the opiate of the masses," a drug that made people numb to the painful reality of inequality.

Weber and Social Change. Max Weber, in contrast, argued that religion could be a catalyst to change. Weber's earliest work wondered why capitalism developed in Western Europe in the way that it did. After all, he noted, capitalist economic activity (profit-maximizing buying and selling) had certainly existed as the dominant economic form of life in other times and places—notably in ancient China, ancient India, and among the ancient Jews. But none of these societies sustained capitalist activity. Only western Europe, in the fifteenth and sixteenth centuries, broke out of feudalism, its established social order, by developing instead a type of capitalism that was self-sustaining. Why?

Weber reasoned that it might have had something to do with the impact of religious ideas on economic activity. In the other three cases, religious ideas interfered with economic life, restrained trade, and made it more difficult for capitalism to become a self-sustaining system. He noticed that Protestant countries (Britain, Holland, Germany, the United States) had advanced earlier and further than Catholic countries such as Italy, Portugal, Spain, and France.

Perhaps the Protestant Reformation had freed individuals from constraints and enabled each individual to develop his or her relationship to God directly, without priests or churches as intermediaries. While Catholicism offered certainty—believers were certain they were going to heaven if they fulfilled the sacraments—Protestantism offered only insecurity; one could never know God's plan. This insecurity led Protestants, especially Calvinists, to begin to work exceptionally hard in this life to reduce the insecurity about where they might be going when they die (because that could not be known). Thus, Weber argued, individuals began to work harder and longer, to approach economic life rationally, through careful calculation of costs and benefits, and to resist the temptation to enjoy the fruits of their labor—which led to rapid and dramatic accumulation of capital for investment. And this accumulation eventually enabled capitalism in the West to become self-sustaining.

Weber was pessimistic about the future of this economic activity. Without the original ethical and religious foundation, Weber predicted, we would become trapped in an "iron cage" of routine, senseless economic acquisition. The very activities that we believed would give meaning to our lives would turn out to eventually leave us empty.

All three of these classical theorists shared several sociological insights. First, although we may experience our religious beliefs as individuals, religion is a profoundly social phenomenon. And they all believed that **religiosity,** the extent of one's religious belief, typically measured by attendance at religious observances or maintaining religious practices, would decline in modern societies. None would have predicted that religion would be as important to Americans as it is today.

Religious Groups

There are many forms of religious organizations. Some are small scale, with immediate and very personal contact; others are larger institutions with administrative bureaucracies that rival those of complex countries. These differ not only in size and scale but also in their relationship to other social institutions, the level of training for specific roles within the religion, and the levels of administration (Table 14.1).

Table 14.1
Types of Religious Organizations

	Cult	Sect	Denomination	Ecclesia
Size	Small	Small	Large	Universal
Wealth	Poor	Poor	Wealthy	Extensive
Beliefs	Strict	Strict	Diversity tolerated	Diversity tolerated
Practices	Variable	Informal	Formal	Formal
Clergy	Untrained	Some training	Extensive training	Extensive training
Membership	Emotional commitment	Accepting doctrine	Birth/decision to join	By belonging to a society

Chapter 14 Education, Religion, and Science

Cults. The simplest form of religious organization, a **cult,** forms around a specific person or idea drawn from an established religion. It is often formed by splitting off from the main branch of the religion. Cults are distinguished by the measure of loyalty they extract from members. Typically small, they are also composed of deeply fervent believers. Members of cults leave behind their membership in older religious institutions and often live on the margins of society. Thus they typically run afoul of local and national governments. And that may mean violent repression, such as the 1993 raid on the Branch Davidian compound outside Waco, Texas. And some cults can develop murderous messianic tendencies as well. In 1995, a cult called Aum Shinrikyo (Supreme Truth) released sarin gas on the Tokyo subway during the morning rush hour, killing 12 people and injuring thousands of others.

Does globalization increase or decrease the number of cults? Both. On the one hand, the Internet facilitates recruitment and enables cult members to remain connected despite large distances. On the other hand, cults often require intense interpersonal interaction.

Sects. A **sect** is a small subculture within an established religious institution. Like cults, they break from traditional practices, but unlike cults they remain within the larger institution. For example, the Jehovah's Witnesses are usually classified as a Christian sect. Sects typically arise when some members of an established religious institution believe that the institution is drifting from its true mission, becoming sidetracked by extraneous, more "worldly" pursuits.

Many sects are short lived. This is generally the case either because the group initially arises in response to specific institutional practices, which may then be incorporated into the established institution, or because it arises to follow a **charismatic leader,** who inspires the initial break with established institutions, but who then leaves (by exile, execution or natural causes). Others sects become "established sects" and develop their own formal institutional arrangements within a larger institutional framework (see Yinger, 1970). In Christianity, the Latter-Day Saints or the Amish are established sects.

Denominations. A **denomination** is a large-scale, extremely organized religious body. It has an established hierarchy, methods for cre-

Sects are smaller subcultures within denominations. The compound of the Fundamentalist Church of Jesus Christ of Latter Day Saints, a Mormon splinter group, was raided in April 2008, and 416 children were removed from the polygamous sect's West Texas ranch by officials. The children were placed in temporary custody of the state, but later returned to their families.

dentialing administrators, and much more social respect than either a cult or a sect. Members of cults and sects are often subject to prejudice and discrimination in the mainstream society, but members of denominations are usually considered "normal." The various Pentecostal churches were considered cults or sects as long as their members were mostly poor, urban, and African American; but once they began to gain White middle-class converts, they quickly became denominations.

In the United States, the overwhelming majority of the population belongs to one of the denominations of Christianity. The largest is the Roman Catholic Church (23 percent). Nearly 70 percent of all Americans claim membership in a Protestant denomination (chiefly Methodist, Baptist, Presbyterian, or Lutheran). There are 5.9 million Jews in the United States, 3 million Muslims, 2 million Buddhists, and 1 million Hindus.

Ecclesiae. There is one more formal religious organization, the **ecclesiae,** or religion so pervasive that the boundary between state and church is nonexistent. In such societies, the clerical elite often serve as political leaders or at least formal advisors to political

The International Society of Krishna Consciousness (or Hare Krishnas) is considered a cult in the United States. In India, however, it is an established Hindu sect.

leaders. Everyone in the society belongs to that faith by birth, not individual decision, and those who do not belong to the faith cannot become citizens. Until the French Revolution, the clergy in France was one of the two pillars on which the monarchy rested (the other was the nobility). Today, the Muslim clerics in Saudi Arabia and the Shi'ite mullahs in Iran are nearly identical with political leadership. Such merging of politics and religion is not inevitable. Some societies with established state churches remain remarkably free of clerical influence in political matters. In Sweden, for instance, the Lutheran Church has official status, but it exerts virtually no influence on political decision making.

Religion: Globally and Locally

Sociologists are not only fascinated by religion as a cultural universal; they are also interested in the remarkable diversity of religious belief and practice. In most places, local, traditional religions have given way to **world religions,** religions with a long history, well-established traditions, and the flexibility to adapt to many different cultures.

Western Religions

Three of the world's major religions, Judaism, Christianity, and Islam (plus a few smaller ones) are called "Western religions" because, while they originated in the Middle East, their adherents are largely among Western nations. They all trace their spiritual ancestry to the same event: About 2000 BCE, a nomadic tribe living in ancient Mesopotamia recognized that their god, Yahweh, was not specific to their tribe, but was the god of all the world. (In the Bible, it is Abraham who is the first ethical monotheist, a believer in only one God who is concerned that you act morally in this world. Thus, Western religions may also be called "Abrahamic" in that they all trace their origins to him.) They eventually founded Judaism (after Judea, where they settled), and they tried to follow God's law as revealed in the Torah, his sacred book. Christianity arose 2,000 years later out of a protest against the "corruption" of Judaism, and Islam 600 years

after that as a protest to the "corruption" of both, so all three religions share many beliefs and practices. Because Christianity and Islam emerged from these critiques of previous religions, they share several characteristics:

- They are exclusive: They believe they have the one true faith.
- They are evangelistic: They want you to choose their faith.
- There is only one god (although sometimes there are intermediaries, like saints and angels).
- There is usually a heaven and a hell, where we will experience eternal joy or torment.
- There is a sacred book, usually revealed by God, which followers are expected to read and obey.
- Believers are expected to attend regular worship services, held on the holiest day of the week.
- A messiah is coming to save us. (For Christians, he has already come, but he's coming back; the Shi'ite is the only Muslim denomination that believes this.)

Judaism and Christianity spread west, through Europe, while Islam spread east and south, throughout the Arabian peninsula and into India and Central Asia. Today, of course, all three religions have adherents worldwide.

Judaism believes that the covenant between God and Abraham around 2000 BCE became the foundation of Jewish law, as recorded in the Pentateuch (first five books of the Bible). Judaism flourished in the ancient world; it is estimated that 10 percent of the population of the Roman Empire was Jewish. Today there are about 15 million Jews in the world (0.2 percent of the world's population), divided into three branches: Orthodox, who follow traditional Jewish law very strictly; Reformed, who attempt to modernize dress, dietary laws, and worship practices (for instance, synagogue services are conducted in the usual language of the country, not in Hebrew); and Conservative, who rebelled against the overmodernization of the Reformed branch.

Christianity was founded 2,000 years ago by the disciples of Jesus, who declared him to be the son of God. Christians revere the Jewish Bible (which they call the Old Testament), as well as the New Testament, a collection of writings recounting the life of Jesus and the history of early Christianity. Today, Christianity is the world's largest single religion, with 2.1 billion adherents (about one-third of all the world's people), although it is divided into so many different denominations with widely varying beliefs and practices that it is often treated as a group of religions. There are three main branches, Roman Catholicism, Eastern Orthodoxy, and Protestantism, as well as many sects.

Islam was founded about 1,400 years ago when God grew displeased with the corruption of the teachings of his earlier prophets and gave his last prophet, Mohammed, a new sacred text, the Koran. Islam means "Submission to God," and Muslim, "one who has submitted to God." Islam is more communal than Christianity, especially its Protestant variety, and is often seen as requiring the fusion of religion and government. There are two main branches, Shi'ite and Sunni, which differ in a number of beliefs and practices; for instance, Shi'ite Muslims revere holy men, or imams. Today about 20 percent of the world's population is Muslim. Like Christianity, the numbers have increased dramatically, from 529 million to 1.3 billion (Figure 14.5).

All three of these religions are divided into various denominations and sects, based on

The World's Fastest-Growing Religion

What is the fastest growing religion in the world? The Church of Jesus Christ of Latter-Day Saints (LDS), also known as Mormons. Combining conservative family values (and downplaying its history of beliefs in polygamy and racism) and aggressive missionary activity, the Mormons now number over 13.5 million. If present trends continue, there will be 265 million members worldwide by 2080. (They are also the second-fastest-growing church in the United States [Reuters, 2009].)

Did You Know?

Figure 14.5 World Religions

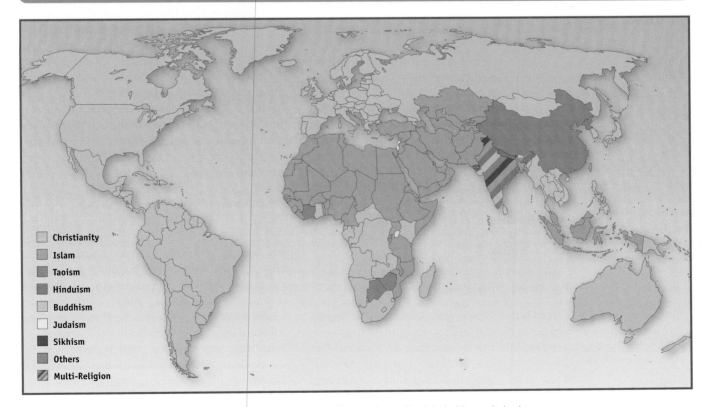

Christianity
Islam
Taoism
Hinduism
Buddhism
Judaism
Sikhism
Others
Multi-Religion

(*Source:* "World Religions," from Maps of the World website, www.mapsoftheworld.com. Reprinted with permission.)

Figure 14.6 World Religions by Percentage of Adherents

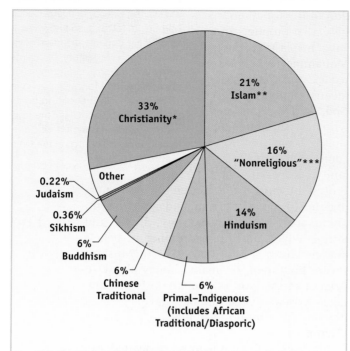

- 33% Christianity*
- 21% Islam**
- 16% "Nonreligious"***
- 14% Hinduism
- Other
- 0.22% Judaism
- 0.36% Sikhism
- 6% Buddhism
- 6% Chinese Traditional
- 6% Primal–Indigenous (includes African Traditional/Diasporic)

* Christianity includes Catholic, Protestant, Eastern Orthodox, Pentecostal, Anglican, Moniphysite, African Initiated Churches, Latter-Day Saints, Evangelical, Seventh-Day Adventist, Jehovah's Witnesses, Quakers, Assembly of God, nominal, etc.

** Islam includes Shi'ite, Sunni, etc.

*** "Nonreligious" includes agnostic, atheist, secular humanist, people answering "none" or no religious preference. Half of this group is "theistic" but nonreligious.

(*Source:* From Adherents.com. Reprinted with permission.)

interpretations of their religious texts. Some interpret these texts liberally and thus enable religious belief to casually coexist with modern life. Others are more demanding. At the extreme ends of all these religions are fundamentalist groups, which claim to be the purest and truest followers of their religion. **Fundamentalism** tries to return to the basic precepts, the "true word of God," and live exactly according to his precepts.

Eastern Religions

Three other major religions of the world, Hinduism, Buddhism, and Confucianism (plus some minor ones), are called "Eastern" because they arose in Asia, although, like the Western religions, they have adherents around the world. They have many beliefs and practices in common, some of which might baffle

people raised in a Western religion. They are not doctrinally exclusive: It may be possible to practice Buddhism, Hinduism, Confucianism, Taoism, and any other religion you want, all at the same time. There are many gods (although often religious scholars interpret them as emanations of a single god). There is no heaven or hell, just an endless series of reincarnations until you achieve enlightenment (except in Confucianism). There is no specific sacred book, although sometimes there are vast libraries of sacred texts to be revered. And there are no regular worship services. Temples are used for special rituals.

Hinduism developed from many indigenous religions in India around 1500 BCE. Hinduism is based largely on oral tradition, passed on from one generation to the next by storytellers. There are also many sacred texts, notably the Vedas and the Upanishads. There are many gods, but most people, most of the time, revere one of the main three, Brahman (who creates life), Vishnu (who preserves or maintains life), and Shiva (who destroys or renews life). Some of the avatars or incarnations of Vishnu are also popular, especially Krishna (portrayed as a blue-skinned youth) and Ganesha (portrayed as an elephant-headed man). Enlightenment is available only after countless incarnations, so most Hindus do not hope for it to happen in this lifetime; instead, they try to behave in a moral fashion to ensure a favorable reincarnation. Today there are nearly one billion Hindus (14 percent of all religious adherents), mostly in South Asia and in Indian communities around the world.

Just as Protestantism developed as a reaction to the "corruption" of Catholicism, **Buddhism** developed as a reaction to the "corruption" of Hinduism. (And, like Protestantism, there are many varieties of Buddhism.) It was originally founded by Siddhartha Gautama (560–580 BCE), later called the Buddha, or "The Enlightened One." While Hinduism taught that enlightenment could come only after countless lifetimes of reincarnation, the Buddha taught that enlightenment was possible in this lifetime, through the "Tenfold Path" of physical and spiritual discipline. Today there are two main branches of Buddhism, Hinayana ("The Small Cart"), which is common primarily in Southeast Asia and Tibet; and Mahayana ("The Large Cart"). There are 376 million Buddhist (6 percent of all adherents), mostly in East Asia.

The philosopher K'ung Fu Tzu or Confucius (551–479 BCE) lived in China about the same

446   **Chapter 14** Education, Religion, and Science

Buying Muslim

Conventional wisdom holds that as societies become more consumerist, they become less devout. Yet across the globe, both governments and companies are discovering that consumerism can be consistent with a Muslim lifestyle. In fact, a wide range of new products and services that comply with Islamic principles may help the world's 1.6 billion Muslims to more readily practice their religion in the modern world.

It began with food. Buying Muslim used to mean avoiding alcohol and pork and buying your meat from a halal butcher, who slaughtered it in accordance with Islamic law. Today, multinational food corporations are offering a range of Muslim-friendly mainstream selections. Dominos offers halal pepperoni from Malaysia on their pizzas. Food giants like Nestle and McDonalds control an estimated 90 percent of the $630 billion halal foods market worldwide (Power, 2009).

Governments, too, are getting involved. Several countries in the Middle East and Asia are investing in customized systems to ensure that halal standards are maintained in food storage. And because food production is increasingly globalized, chicken farmers in Brazil (who raise most of Saudi Arabia's chicken), lamb exporters in New Zealand, and food shippers in the Netherlands are all getting into the act (Millstone and Lang, 2008). Frozen halal foods are becoming more popular as more Muslim women are going to college and working outside the home (Esposito and Mogahed, 2008; Power, 2009).

A growing number of Muslims, especially the young, are also "buying Muslim" as part of a "conscientious consumerism": their clothing brands, cosmetics, even the apps for their mobile phones. One popular free download provides verses from the Koran; another helps users find the direction to Mecca (Micheletti, 2003; Micheletti and Stolle, 2006; Stolle and Houghe, 2005).

---

time as the Buddha in India. The faith he founded, **Confucianism,** remained the official religion of China until the People's Republic officially became atheist in 1949; it also had a strong impact on other Asian countries, especially Japan and Korea. Confucianism does not have much to say about gods or the afterlife. Instead, it establishes a strict social hierarchy. Confucianism sees Heaven and Earth as linked realms that are constantly in touch with each other. People in Heaven are the ancestors of those on Earth. It is hard to determine the number of adherents because officially no religions are practiced in mainland China, but it is safe to say that every aspect of Chinese culture owes a debt to Confucianism.

Eastern religions tend to be somewhat more tolerant of other religions than Western religions. Without the privileged access to revealed truth—by which conversion of nonbelievers is a mission of love—there is not as much need for coerced conversion or the bloody religious wars that have appeared for millennia in the West.

Religion in the United States

Around the time the United States was founded, Thomas Jefferson confidently predicted that people would eventually think of

the Bible as a book of myths, like Greek mythology. Yet faith in the literal truth of the Bible remains strong, and the United States remains one of the world's most churchgoing societies (see Figure 14.7). Why have rates of religious belief and participation declined in every European country but not in the United States?

Buddhist priests practice meditation and a strict physical and spiritual discipline to reach enlightenment. These Thai priests pray before their tea ceremony.

Figure 14.7 How Americans Describe Their Religious Identity

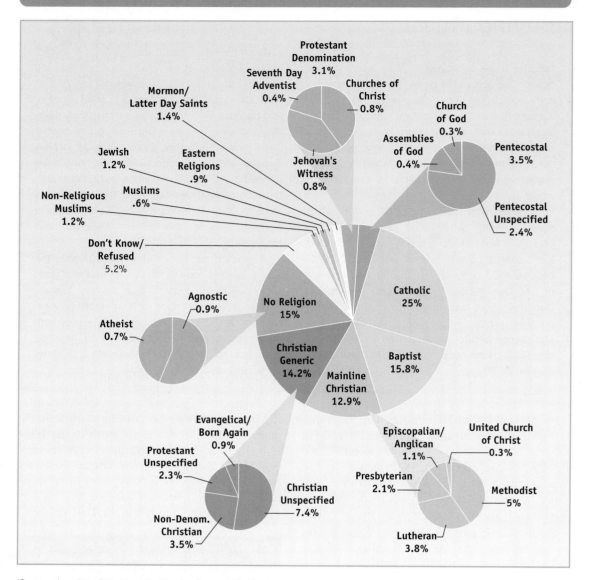

Protestant Denomination 3.1%
Seventh Day Adventist 0.4%
Churches of Christ 0.8%
Mormon/ Latter Day Saints 1.4%
Church of God 0.3%
Assemblies of God 0.4%
Pentecostal 3.5%
Jewish 1.2%
Eastern Religions .9%
Jehovah's Witness 0.8%
Pentecostal Unspecified 2.4%
Non-Religious Muslims 1.2%
Muslims .6%
Don't Know/ Refused 5.2%
Agnostic 0.9%
No Religion 15%
Catholic 25%
Atheist 0.7%
Christian Generic 14.2%
Baptist 15.8%
Mainline Christian 12.9%
Evangelical/ Born Again 0.9%
Episcopalian/ Anglican 1.1%
United Church of Christ 0.3%
Protestant Unspecified 2.3%
Presbyterian 2.1%
Methodist 5%
Christian Unspecified 7.4%
Non-Denom. Christian 3.5%
Lutheran 3.8%

(*Source:* American Religious Identification Survey [ARIS], 2008.)

One factor might be that the United States has been, since its inception, more than simply a nation of immigrants; it's actually a nation of religious immigrants. Since the Pilgrims were kicked out of England, the United States has always been a haven for those who were constrained from practicing their religion elsewhere—European Jews, Chinese Christians, Russian Orthodox believers, and so on. As some nations become increasingly secular, those who are religious may seek a haven in the United States. As a result, increased religiosity and increased secularism coexist.

Another factor is that the United States has been swept by several waves of increased religious passion. There were two Great Awakenings, one in the 1720s and one in the 1820s, which witnessed a democratization of religion. Some consider the current levels of religiosity an indication of a **Third Great Awakening,** a sort of religious democratization that makes the sacred available to more Americans with less effort.

Still a third factor has been the way that American religious institutions have grown as providers of social support and cultural interaction. In Europe, churches are often tourist attractions, but locals rarely set foot inside. During my first trip to London, I thought it might be a good idea to attend a service in Westminster Abbey. But services are held in the Abbey only on Sundays; every other day they're held in a tiny basement chapel—with about 30 people in attendance. Even the great cathedrals of Europe, like Notre Dame in Paris, or St. Peter's in Rome, or the Cathedral of Seville, have sparse attendance at mass—and then the congregation is composed largely of tourists.

American churches, by contrast, are almost always full. Churches are often the social and cultural center of the town. Every night there are groups that meet there, from Alcoholics Anonymous to Bible study to social gatherings for divorced parents. Religious institutions not only run parochial schools, but many organize preschool and day-care facilities (these are provided by the government in European countries). Churches sponsor soccer leagues and wilderness retreats, picnics and bingo nights. They have become the social—as well

Church attendance in all industrialized countries except the United States is at or near all-time lows. Even in Italy, home of the Pope, church attendance is significantly less than it has been in several centuries. At this evening mass in St. Peter's Basilica in Rome, many of the people are actually tourists.

as the spiritual—hub of American communities, especially important as other civic supports have declined.

Finally, it may be that the assumptions that one had to choose between religious and secular life were invalid. Americans hold religious beliefs in ways that can fit readily into an otherwise secular life. (For Americans, it is not a question of religion versus business, but religion *and*.) American religious beliefs are modified so that we can be both sacred and secular. Christian bookstores are open on Sundays; children come to church dressed in their soccer uniforms (Gibbs, 2004).

Religious Experience and Identity

Even though many of us claim to be highly religious, our knowledge of the dominant U.S. religions is rather limited. Over half of Americans (58 percent) cannot name even five of the Ten Commandments, and just under half know that Genesis is the first book of the Bible. And 12 percent of Americans believe that Joan of Arc was Noah's wife (she was really an early-fifteenth-century war heroine and political martyr) (McKibben, 2005). It may be that the dramatic rise of evangelical Christianity in the United States—nearly 40 percent of Americans identify themselves as "born-again" Christian or evangelical—has less to do with its doctrinal rigidity and more to do with how well it sits with other "American" values. In America, God is intimately involved in the minutest details of your everyday life. (Forget that old idea of a distant, abstract, and judgmental God; in the American version, God is close enough to be your best friend.) "While more Americans than ever consider themselves born again, the lord to whom they turn rarely gets angry and frequently strengthens self-esteem," according to sociologist Alan Wolfe (2003, p. 3).

Like our consumer economy, some evangelical religious organizations have "supersized," so that today, many Americans worship in megachurches such as Chicago's Willow Creek Community Church (17,000 weekly

The Secular "Muslim" Nation

The world's largest "Muslim nation" isn't a "Muslim nation" at all. Indonesia is the world's largest "Muslim" nation; the overwhelming majority of its nearly 200 million people are Muslim. (There are also 24 million Christians and Hindus and over 300 other ethnic groups.) But the country is a secular nation and has a tradition of religious tolerance and *pancasila*, a secular nationalist ideology. Apparently, there is nothing inherent in the religion that demands control of the government.

Did You Know?

Evangelical megachurches have "supersized" religion in the United States. At Willow Creek Community Church, in South Barrington, IL (outside Chicago), about 17,000 attend weekly services.

Muscular Christianity

The historical association of religiosity and femininity has troubled some theologians. At the turn of the last century, a movement called Muscular Christianity proclaimed Jesus a he-man, a religious Rambo, not the kind, sweet image of many mainstream churches. Jesus was no "dough-faced lick-spittle proposition," quipped Billy Sunday, a professional baseball player turned evangelist, "but the greatest scrapper that ever lived." Today, similar groups make masculine appeals. Seattle minister Mark Driscoll shouts down the "hippie, queer Christ" of mainstream churches, and JBC Men promote Jesus as action hero (JBC stands for "Jesus–Beer–Chips") (Worthen, 2009).

Did You Know?

attendance) or Bellevue Baptist Church outside Memphis (10,000 attendees). If these mainstream pop-culture renditions of Protestantism seem either too remote or too commercial, other smaller churches offer a relaxed experience in "house churches" where ministers are likely to wear blue jeans and speak to congregants informally (see Leland, 2004). All are relatively "seeker friendly," offering spiritual redemption and psychological therapy in the same package. With congregations numbering in the tens of thousands on any given Sunday, American megachurches are less somber religious affairs and more like a mixture of arena rock concerts and old-time tent preaching.

Variations in Religious Experience. Religions don't vary only by denomination; we vary in our degree of religious affiliation and in the intensity of our beliefs. Different groups express different levels of religiosity.

For example, age matters: The older you are, the more religious you are likely to be. And where you live matters: The rural are more religious than the suburban, and the suburban are more religious than the urban (the major exception to this is urban Blacks, who have high rates of religiosity, as we will discuss below).

And sex matters: Although they have long been excluded from leadership positions in several major religions, women remain more religious than men. Women attend religious services more frequently and report higher levels of religiosity (intense religious feelings) than do men (Pew Center, 2009). But why would women be more likely to adhere to a spiritual discipline that portrays them as second-class citizens? Many researchers point to more psychological explanations: Women are socialized to be more "dependent" and thus would "lean" on religion. But it turns out that men who are not in the labor force exhibit equally high levels of religiosity as women who are not in the labor force, and women's level of religiosity declines significantly when they enter the paid labor force (deVaus and McAllister, 1987).

Most Western religions also condemn homosexuality as contrary to divine law. Though actual references to homosexuality in the Bible are few, those who condemn homosexuality point to a passage in Leviticus (18:22) that reads, "And with a man you shall not lie with as a man lies with a woman; it is an abomination." Despite this, several religious denominations have begun to include gay men and lesbians, including some Protestant denominations, conservative and reform Judaism, and most non-Western religions. The consecration of an openly gay priest as an Episcopal bishop in 2005 split the American Episcopal Church from other national synods.

Both denominational affiliation and rates of religiosity also vary by race and ethnicity as well. In the United States, more than 92 percent of Blacks and Hispanics practice some religious denomination, while only about 88 percent of Whites do. Of those, more than 67 percent of Hispanics are Catholic, while only 22.4 percent of Whites and a mere 4.25 percent of Blacks are. Almost 83 percent of Blacks are Protestant, as compared with 57 percent of Whites and 19.6 percent of Hispanics (Pew Forum on Religion and Public Life, 2007). When it comes to religious observance, 84 percent of U.S. Blacks say religion is very important in everyday life, while only 68 percent of Hispanics and 39 percent of Whites feel the same way (Figure 14.8).

Overall, Americans are highly fluid in our religious affiliation—we change affiliation early and often. About half of all American adults have changed religions at least once in their lifetime, and many of those do so more than once (Pew Forum on Religion and Public Life, 2009). The group that has grown the most is those Americans who have left their religion to become unaffiliated, and they have done so for a range of reasons. More than 70 percent of former Catholics and former Protestants say they drifted away from their religions. Two-thirds of former Catholics and half of former Protestants say they stopped believing in its teachings. Large numbers also left their religions because they see religious people as judgmental, hypocritical, or insincere; because they see many religions, not just one, as offering some truth; or because they feel religious organizations focus too much on rules, on money, or on power, and not enough on spirituality and truth. A smaller proportion, about one-third of unaffiliated Americans, left their religion because they believe science had proved religion a superstition (Pew Forum on Religion and Public Life, 2009).

Most churches in the United States are populated by Whites or Blacks; rarely do they worship together. As Dr. Martin Luther King Jr. once put it, "The most segregated hour of Christian America is 11 o'clock on Sunday morning." Just as the White church has been, for centuries, an important social institution, so too has the Black church evolved as one of the central institutions of the African American community.

Actually, to speak of a singular "Black church" in America is a bit misleading; the "Black church" is really the vast array of Black churches, usually Protestant, that have developed over the course of U.S. history. The massive importation of African slaves in the seventeenth and eighteenth centuries was coupled with efforts to crush their traditional African-based religions (which were seen as a threat to their enslaved status) and to convert them to Christianity. Often slaves were required to attend church with their White masters but relegated to the balconies.

Gradually, however, slaves began to appropriate parts of the service, identifying with the biblical stories of the Jews, who were slaves in Egypt, and their liberation in the book of Exodus. After the Civil War, they established their own churches, which quickly became the cultural and social centers of the

newly arrived free Blacks to the northern cities and in the small southern towns where the descendents of former slaves settled.

Sociologist E. Franklin Frazier (1974) studied the Black church in America and especially noted how it answered secular as well as sacred needs for its community. He was impressed with the way that these churches became a training ground for activist ministers who began the Civil Rights movement—Jesse Jackson, Al Sharpton, Martin Luther King Jr. himself—and were consistently inspired by biblical stories of nonviolent resistance.

Today the Black church remains influential, both as a source of religious inspiration and for political mobilization (Battle, 2006; Billingsley, 1999). Ministers like Jesse Jackson mounted serious campaigns for the presidency; ministers are often powerful orators who inspire and mobilize. The Black church's contribution to American society has been enormous, including being the origins of soul and gospel music (Sam Cooke and Aretha Franklin got their start in gospel groups).

Religion on Campus. It is on college campuses that science and religion most often clashed. Many of the nation's first colleges and universities, such as Harvard and Yale, were originally designed for the training of ministers, but they soon expanded into other fields; and, even at church-related colleges today, only a small percentage of students major in religion. Public

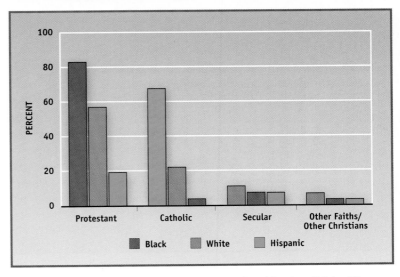

Figure 14.8 Denominational Distribution by Race/Ethnicity

(*Source:* "Changing Faiths: Latinos and the Transformation of American Religion," Pew Forum on Religion & Public Life and Pew Hispanic Center, projects of the Pew Research Center, pewforum.org, April 4, 2007. Reproduced by permission.)

The Black church often integrated elements of traditional and long-suppressed African religion into its services, including singing and dancing, and especially call-and-response-styles of preaching and praying. These women are members of the Temple of Deliverance Church of God and Christ in Memphis.

universities are often so careful to maintain the separation of church and state that some have no departments of religious studies or even any courses devoted to any religion.

The higher your level of educational attainment, the less devout you will be in practicing your religion. That means that professors, who usually have PhDs, tend to number among the nation's unfaithful. But their students are often quite religious. Most come to school already religious. Religious belief and practice have never been stronger on college campuses. More students are enrolling in reli-

gion courses and majoring in religion; more are living in dormitories or houses where spirituality and faith are parts of daily life; and groups are springing up where students can discuss religious ideas as a means of understanding the world in addition to (or instead of) science (Finder, 2007).

While church attendance among college students is lower than that of the nation as a whole (in part because services are held on Sunday morning, not an attractive time slot after a Saturday night of partying), the first national survey on the spiritual lives of college students (2004) found that more than two-thirds of college freshman pray, and almost 80 percent believe in God (Higher Education Research Institute, 2004). Church-affiliated colleges have seen faster enrollment increases than secular colleges, with evangelical Christian schools showing gains of 24 percent between 1980 and 1998 (as compared to less than 5 percent growth elsewhere) (Reisberg, 1999). Enrollment increases have been particularly strong among Black students; the number of Christian colleges that are now at least 10 percent Black has tripled in the past decade, with some schools showing enrollment increases of more than 40 percent (Journal of Blacks in Higher Education, 2008).

Religiosity varies by race and gender. A 2005 survey of more than 112,000 college students at 236 colleges and universities found that African Americans are far more engaged with religion and spirituality than other groups, while women were slightly more religious than men; however, these differences were not as great as in the general population. Latino and Asian American college students were the least religious, and Asian Americans scored highest on measures of religious skepticism. For the most part, religion on campus is likely to support diversity and respect for all religious beliefs; this religious pluralism coincides with religious vitality. Many on campus are religious, but comparatively few try to impose their views on others (Cherry, DeBerg, and Porterfield, 2003).

Religion as Politics. Religion has always been "political"—indeed, manifesting the vision of one's religious beliefs in the political arena is often an essential part of the religion. The great religious leaders, like Moses, Jesus, and Muhammad, found out firsthand that existing authorities find new religious beliefs threatening to their political control.

"I don't belong to an organized religion. My religious beliefs are way too disorganized."

In the twentieth century, religion has been embroiled in political debates on all sides of the political spectrum. In the former Soviet Union or in China today, just professing religion could be threatening to social control by the Communist party, providing an alternative authority structure. In twentieth-century Latin America, **liberation theology** within the Catholic Church was a source of popular mobilization against ruthless political dictators. Liberation theology focuses on Jesus not only as savior but as the savior of the poor and oppressed and emphasizes the Christian mission of bringing justice to the poor.

Most commonly, religious mobilization has aimed to move society to the political right, to restore a conservative agenda of a "Christian America" or an "Islamic Republic." In contemporary America, the mobilization of the Christian right has had an enormous effect on everyday life, from the sorts of books one can read in classrooms and libraries, to whom one can fall in love with. A few Muslim countries have instituted shari'a, or the Islamic law outlined in the Koran, which, when strictly interpreted, includes such penalties as cutting off the hand for robbery and death by stoning for adultery.

The secular side also exerts an influence. While we often hear about religious institutions being intolerant of political diversity, it is also common for secular politics to be intolerant of religious diversity. In the United States, Jehovah's Witnesses have been fined or jailed for refusing to salute the flag. In 2003, French President Jacques Chirac banned the wearing of any religious symbols in French public schools—including Catholic crucifixes, Jewish yarmulkes, Muslim cha-

New Age Religions

In addition to organized Western and Eastern religions, Americans enjoy a variety of New Age beliefs and practices. **New Age** is an umbrella term for many different groups and individual practices, so it is very often called simply "spirituality." New Age believers are often very open minded and pluralistic. Few groups demand strict obedience to a set of rules. Some people use New Age practices as a sort of individualized flavoring on traditional religious beliefs; still others meld several strands into a truly individualized spirituality. It would not be unusual for a New Ager to practice Buddhist meditation, read his or her horoscope, channel a spirit guardian, practice yoga, and receive a Shiatsu massage. In that sense, New Age spirituality is often syncretic—able to reconcile a variety of different religious beliefs.

New Age beliefs have benefited from increased globalization because followers can now travel the world in search of meaningful rituals. Indeed, travel companies have developed that cater especially to the spiritual nomads, who travel the world seeking meaning (Gooch, 2002). The rapid development and number of these groups also suggests that we are, in essence, a spiritual nation—with a spirituality that covers vast areas of our mental landscape and welcomes multiple beliefs but does not go very deep.

dors, and Sikh turbans (Sciolino, 2004). Although the constitutional principle of the separation of church and state was meant to protect liberty and ensure democracy in the United States, it also enabled religion and science to develop and expand separately. In recent years, however, the boundaries between the two have become increasingly blurry, and several political debates currently strain their happy coexistence, such as evolution versus creationism, school prayer, and embryonic stem cell research.

Science in Sociological Perspective

While we usually think of religious teachings as eternal, timeless truths, at least to the believer, we think of science as a gradual, progressive accumulation of information. We think that scientists all follow the same rigorous scientific method and perform their research objectively, without worrying about any political or moral implications. We think

that scientific breakthroughs are the result of individual genius, a greater-than-the-rest scientist who applies existing research and generates a revolutionary application or theoretical revelation.

Sociologists, however, see science quite differently. As we saw above, to the sociologist, religion and science share many characteristics, organizationally and ideologically. Sociologists observe the interactions among scientists, ranging from the way they interact within a scientific laboratory to the ways they form and sustain scientific communities, groups of scientists working on similar or related problems in a number of different settings. Other socio-logists take a more institutional approach, focusing on the role of the scientist and scientific institutions within a society.

Just as there are many different religions, there are many different types of science in the world. Scientists usually practice only one and know little about the others:

- Biological sciences study living organisms, including microorganisms (microbiology), animals (zoology), plants (botany), physiology, and biochemistry. Medicine and agriculture are applied branches of biological science.

- The physical sciences study nonliving processes, including the basic physical laws of existence (physics), organic and inorganic matter (chemistry), Earth sciences (geology, meteorology, and oceanography), and the stars and planets (astronomy). The various types of engineering are applied branches of physical science.

- Mathematics provides the quantitative foundation of all other sciences. Most research is purely theoretical, but there is an applied branch, computer science.

- Social sciences concern human beings, their mental processes (psychology), culture (anthropology), social structures (sociology), history, economics, and political science. There are several applied branches, including social work and criminal justice.

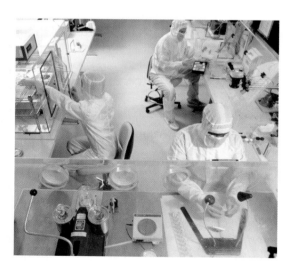

Private corporations inject enormous amounts of money into research for new drugs, but they are guided by the marketplace—not human needs or the interests of the scientific community—and seek to control access to their discoveries in order to increase profits.

Like all social institutions, science has norms that govern interactions among scientists and relationships between scientists and the rest of society and between scientific institutions and other social institutions. These norms are understood to govern these relationships and set the standards for scientific research.

The most important norm of science is **objectivity,** in which judgments are based on empirical verification, not on personal feelings or opinions. Scientists must check their personal lives at the laboratory door, and differences in class, race, and nationality should make no difference in procedure or results. Anyone using the scientific method should be able to arrive at the same conclusions—regardless of his or her personal characteristics.

But how often have you heard the results of research dismissed because of exactly those characteristics? Can we trust social scientific research done by people who do not have the experience they are studying? Would a White person simply be too biased to arrive at any reliable conclusions about Black people? Or would a Black or White person be too biased to reliably research his or her own group?

A second norm of science is that scientific knowledge should be open to everyone. Research results should be public knowledge; data should be shared with colleagues. Technological advances in applied science can be patented, but the pure research, the science behind the technology, is available to all. Einstein never tried to patent his theory of relativity, nor could he.

The most common method of providing this access is through publication in scholarly journals. Although there is no law that requires publication, scientists feel obliged by the norm of common ownership to publish their studies and to make their data available to anyone who wishes to replicate their studies. For example, the data sets of the General Social Survey are available at cost from NORC (the National Opinion Research Center), so that all social scientists can benefit from their use.

However, this norm of common ownership is constantly being threatened or undermined. As public money for basic research has shrunk in recent years, two "interested" parties have filled the funding gap: the military and private industry. Much scientific research about nuclear fission or on chemical or biological weapons is not published in scholarly journals at all, to avoid giving terrorists and other enemies access to it. Much research on the effects of drugs is funded by the drug companies, and you can be pretty sure they have certain results they would like to see!

These two interests came to a boil in 2001, as two teams raced to complete the mapping of the human genome. One team was funded by a private company, and the other was part of a government laboratory. Many believed that if the private company "won" the race, they would "own" the map of the human genome and could establish patents on human genetic sequences. (Eventually the two groups compromised and shared the publication of the map of the human genome.)

Another important scientific norm is **disinterestedness.** Scientific research should not be conducted for personal goals, such as fame or glory, and certainly not for money, but for the pursuit of scientific truth. Unfortunately, this norm is constantly undermined. The new partnerships between universities and private corporations push scientists away from performing basic research and more toward applied research. Second, the enormous amount of money that is possible if one has a financial interest in discoveries that can be big business—drugs, energy, weapons, for example—also lures science away from the disinterested pursuit of truth.

Scientific Networks

Popular images of scientific work often depict the mad scientist, his hair wild and unkempt, his eyes glazed over in demented genius, working all day and all night alone in his laboratory. All of a sudden, he has his revelation, his "Eureka!" moment, and he makes a new discovery. Such a view is unrealistic. Science is work, and like most forms of work, it is a collaborative effort, requiring the interaction of many different people with different roles, tasks, and social locations.

Sociologists are interested in "the network of communication and social relationships between scientists working in given fields or in all fields" (Ben-David, 1984, p. 3). Scientists develop rules of conduct, and those who do not accept these rules are excluded from scientific networks. Established scientists control research by acting as gatekeepers: They edit and review articles for scientific journals and decide who receives research grants. If you

don't do science by their rules, you don't get to do science.

In that sense, science is no different from any other workplace—and most religious and educational institutions as well. Those at the top of the hierarchy are the gatekeepers, making sure that scientific research conforms to what *they* think is worthy. In other words, scientific communities are like religious elites: They decide what the doctrine says, how you are to think about it, and what you can and cannot know.

These sociological dynamics explain the continued lack of women, for example, at the highest reaches of science and engineering professorships, as well as the abundance of Asian men, but not Latino or African American men, in those positions. And those groups are consistently paid less than White males. In one study, even after accounting for seniority, experience, and age, female scientists earned 23 percent less than their male counterparts (*The Economist*, 2006c). This is not the result of individual malevolence; indeed, many university departments claim to be eager to hire women

Scientific organizations work like any other social organization, with entrenched gatekeepers and bureaucratic processes. As a result, they reflect the same sociological characteristics of other organizations—a hierarchy dominated by white men. In 2004, Massachusetts Institute of Technology became the first major scientific university to inaugurate a female president, Sue Hockfield, a noted neuroscientist.

	Female (%)	Male (%)	White (%)	Asian (%)	Black (%)	Hispanic (%)
All science and engineering	27	73	75	14	4.3	4.3
Biological/ life scientist	43.3	56.5	76	14	3.7	4.2
Computer and information scientist	27.6	72.4	71	18.2	5	3.9
Mathematical scientist	60	40	76.5	11.6	7.4	3
Physical sciences	28.5	71.5	79	12.2	2.7	4
Engineers	11	89	77	12.5	3.3	5

Table 14.2 Working Scientists: Employment in Science and Engineering by Gender and Race

(*Source:* Adapted from National Science Foundation, 2006.)

and minorities. But the work they believe qualifies as breakthrough science and the unexamined prejudices they may harbor often conspire to form barriers that are difficult to overcome. Changing the gender and racial composition of the scientific community will take more than simply adding a few women or minorities; it will require changing the structure of the enterprise itself (see Table 14.2).

Scientific Breakthroughs

Scientific breakthroughs happen much the same ways that religions change. In a path-breaking study of the history of science, Thomas Kuhn (1962), a theoretical physicist, proposed that science changes in a similar way. Instead of scientific progress being gradual and linear, it is erratic and often unpredictable. Long periods of dull routine science are punctuated by dramatic breakthroughs.

Kuhn observed that, at any one time, there is a prevailing paradigm, or model, and scientists work within the paradigm. This is what Kuhn calls "normal" science. Normal science follows social customs: Older, more established scientists train younger ones to work within the existing fields of knowledge. These younger scientists extend the reach of the paradigm, but they seldom dare to challenge the paradigm itself. If they do, they often find they don't get published, receive research grants, or get tenure.

Yet sometimes, scientists doing normal science find results they cannot explain by existing theories. Initially, the scientific establishment discredits these "anomalies" (findings that differ from the norm) and gives the cold shoulder to the scientists. But eventually, these anomalies are too numerous and too significant to ignore. And then the old paradigm is replaced by a new one, one that can explain the older research and the new findings as well. In this way, long periods of normal science are punctuated by these scientific breakthroughs.

The Role of the Scientist in Society

Until the sixteenth century, individual members of the Church or nobility financed scientific research. This form of private support for science (as well as the arts) is called patronage, and it enabled many influential scientists to conduct their research in the absence of government or university jobs. Gradually, in the seventeenth and eighteenth centuries, European scientists were increasingly supported by the government, through subsidies and grants. Groups of scientists joined together into colleges and universities, under government sponsorship, to pursue their increasingly complex and expensive research. By the twentieth century, most scientific breakthroughs were made by professors, working in state-funded laboratories on university campuses.

Take, for example, the history of the Nobel Prize. During the nineteenth century, European scientists were heavily supported by the government. But two world wars, with a depression between, all but eliminated the money for government support in Europe. At the same time, the development of graduate training in the sciences and the space race with the Soviet Union after World War II propelled the United States into scientific leadership in the world. As a result, the number of European scientists who have won a Nobel Prize in the sciences has fallen, while the number of Americans has grown dramatically (www.Nobelprize .org). (We should point out, however, that many of the American Nobel laureates have been immigrants, who received their training in Europe and came to the United States to escape Nazi or Communist regimes.)

Today, scientific research around the world is supported both by governments, through grants for research, and by private companies, which employ scientists to develop new products—everything from new types of paint to robots that can land on the moon, from flavoring for soda to genetically modified crops that grow faster, stronger, or more plentifully even in adverse climates.

Typically, private enterprise and government fund different aspects of research. The government funds basic science—that is, scientific research that has no immediate application other than the furtherance of knowledge. Private companies are interested in developing new products, and they fund research that has possibilities for commercial application. In addition, large-scale scientific research requires so much money in start-up costs that global scientific cooperation has become the norm, as different groups, operating in different countries, often specialize in some smaller piece of the larger puzzle.

Recently, however, foundations, states, and university consortiums have stepped into many high-profile areas where neither government nor private companies have been willing to go. For example, since its inception in 2000, the Bill and Melinda Gates Foundation has given $8.5 billion toward global health, pursuing the prevention and treatment for diseases afflicting poor countries of low priority to for-profit drug companies (Hitt, 2008).

Education, Religion, and Science in the Twenty-First Century

As a society, we are becoming increasingly scientific. Human beings are curious about the world and always want to understand it better; science gives them that opportunity. On an almost daily basis, scientists change how we understand the world—from the furthest reaches of the universe to the tiniest subatomic particles.

We are also becoming increasingly religious. Human beings are also spiritual beings, and religion helps us navigate our way through the spiritual world. Some religious institutions may decline in membership, but others are growing dramatically, and new ones are constantly arising.

Our belief in the value of education is based half on science (getting an education will get me a better job and more money, which is empirically true), and half on faith (the optimistic idea that a better job with more money will lead to a happier life). Chances are you share this faith. That's why you are here, enrolled in a college, in this class, reading this book. The belief in the value of education is one of the pillars of America's civil religion. And then there is the "science of religion" and the "religion of science." Some scientists are attempting to explain religion scientifically, proposing that there is a "God gene," or that human beings, unlike other species, are either biologically programmed or evolutionarily adapted to believe in the supernatural (see, for example, Dennett, 2006, and Harris, 2004). Evolutionary biologist Richard Dawkins (2007) argues that morality results largely from genetic instincts evolved because humans benefit from cooperation and that religion itself is a by-product of mental abilities evolved for other reasons. Children, he argues, are "wired" to believe what their parents tell them because so much of what parents impart is useful or essential information. But this programming is vulnerable to error, becoming an avenue for useless information that gets passed along for no other reason than tradition.

At the same time, some evangelical ministers use scientific skepticism (one can never be absolutely certain that scientific discoveries are the truth) to question biological facts like evolution or geological facts like the age of Earth. A 2006 *Time* magazine poll found that nearly two-thirds (64 percent) of Americans say they would continue to believe what their religion teaches—even if scientists proved it to be wrong (Masci, 2007).

Some scholars predict a long period of tension between religion and science, followed by the triumph of one over the other. However, it seems just as likely that religion and science will coexist, as the growth of both religious ideas and scientific progress in the United States seems to suggest. Politically, there is always a danger that either religious fanatics or antireligious totalitarians will seize control of a country, as in Iran or Afghanistan as well as the former Soviet Union and China. But even there, it seems impossible to eradicate religion or science. In Iran today, science is undergoing a dramatic increase, just as, under Soviet rule, many continued to practice their religions. Science and religion may even "need" each other: As Albert Einstein once commented, "Science without religion is lame, and religion without science is blind" (cited in Lazare, 2007, p. 26). It seems that the human quest to know and understand one's world, and one's place in it, is as basic and unquenchable as human life itself.

Chapter Review

1. Education in Social Context

Science and religion are both institutions socializing us to a worldview. Education, religion, and science provide tools for understanding the world around us. We typically spend over a quarter of our lives getting an **education.** The educational system serves manifest and latent functions, providing content in subjects and a socializing environment advancing values, goals, and norms. This **hidden curriculum** includes obedience to authority, conformity, individualism, and competition. In a **credential society,** gatekeepers rely on this for associates of educational attainment, including social class, attitudes, and race. Historically the wealthy hired tutors for their children. Early schools provided religious instruction. In sixteenth-century Europe, the wealthy sent their children to schools, but America pioneered mandatory free education for all, vital for democracy. The curriculum expanded as jobs changed. Unequal access to education exists in America, with women and minorities faring the worst and the wealthy attaining the most. Globally, educational attainment has increased. Except in Africa, most children receive primary and often some secondary education, but wealthier nations do better. Poor nations have higher rates of illiteracy, particularly among women. Female literacy increases a society's well-being, reducing infant mortality. Countries working to improve education, like China, see greater economic success.

education A social institution through which society provides its members with important knowledge—basic facts, job skills, and cultural norms and values. It provides socialization, cultural innovation, and social integration. It is accomplished largely through schooling, formal instruction under the direction of a specially trained teacher. (p. 424)

hidden curriculum Means of socialization through which education not only creates social inequalities but makes them seem natural, normal, and inevitable. (p. 424)

credential society A society based more on the credentialing aspects of education than any substantive knowledge. (p. 424)

2. The Sociology of Education

What constitutes a good education—high culture or **scientific literacy?** Which better prepares citizens? Education equals greater earning for everyone, but because minorities have less access to education, the hidden curriculum supports and justifies inequality. Historically and today, **segregation** is associated with poverty, while **integration** improves education and opportunity, as schools improve. Education may allow us to break free of stereotypes, but minorities and girls often face perpetuation of inequality, and boys too find gender stereotypes enforced, through the powerful informal socialization occurring in schools. Debatable public policies regarding education include bilingual education, particularly for Spanish-speaking children, the **voucher system** to increase market competition to improve schools, and **charter schools,** although research suggests they usually lower educational quality. Parents often home-school for religious or moral reasons. "No Child Left Behind" assessed schools and led to a slight increase in test scores, but many believe it is detrimental for students and schools. Higher education is required for many jobs today. Class inequality is increasing, as education predicts income, but the upper class dominates higher education, perpetuating inequality. For the rest, there are community colleges and technical colleges, or a **for-profit university,** providing job skills and credentials without the whole college experience.

scientific literacy According to the National Academy of Sciences, it is the "knowledge and understanding of the scientific concepts and processes required for personal decision making, participation in civic and cultural affairs, and economic productivity." (p. 429)

segregation The practice of physically separating Whites from other races by law and custom in institutions and communities. (p. 431)

integration The physical intermingling of the races organized as a concerted legal and social effort to bring equal access and racial equality through racial mixing in institutions and communities. (p. 431)

voucher system First proposed in 1955, a free-market approach to school reform in which taxpayer funds are used to pay for students' tuition at private school, ostensibly upping competition and increasing quality in public schools. (p. 433)

charter schools Privatization-oriented school reform initiative in which schools are financed through taxpayer funds but administered privately. (p. 434)

for-profit university An institution of higher learning that is proprietary and is characterized by lower tuition costs and a faster path to degrees for students. Facilities are usually limited, and faculty is not tenured. (p. 438)

3. Religion and Science

Religiosity is on the rise, in spite of **secularization** in higher education. **Religion** and **science,** as social institutions, have many similarities but also many differences; for example, in knowledge acquisition—**revelation** versus **empirical verification.** Religion is a **cultural universal,** so sociologists question why it exists and the function it serves. Durkheim found that the **sacred** created unity in a social group. Bellah noted that modern secular societies have civic rituals that fulfill a similar function. Marx thought that religion justified inequality and blinded people to exploitation, while Weber's analysis showed that religion caused social change, as capitalism emerged from the protestant beliefs. Overall, sociologists predicted a decline in **religiosity,** but the opposite occurred. Religious organizations have many forms, including **cults, sects** (often headed by a **charismatic leader**), **denominations,** and **ecclesiae.**

secularization The process of moving away from religion and toward the worldly. (p. 440)

religion The set of beliefs about the origins and meaning of life, usually based on the existence of a supernatural power. (p. 440)

science The accumulated systematic knowledge of the physical or material world, obtained through experimentation and observation. (p. 440)

revelation A religious way of learning answers to fundamental questions of existence; God, spirits, prophets, or sacred books reveal what we need to know. (p. 441)

empirical verification The scientific way of learning answers to questions, in which knowledge is developed, demonstrated, and double-checked through experiments. (p. 441)

cultural universal Rituals, customs, and symbols that are evident in all societies. (p. 441)

sacred A place, time, object, or person in which the worlds of the spiritual and the worldly come together. (p. 441)

ritual Enactment by which members of a culture engage in a routine behavior to express their sense of belonging to the culture. (p. 441)

civil religion Secular rituals in a modern, secular society that create intense emotional bonds among people that used to be accomplished by religion like singing the national anthem at sporting events or lighting fireworks on Fourth of July. (p. 441)

religiosity The extent of one's religious belief, typically measured by attendance at religious observances or maintaining religious practices. (p. 442)

cult The simplest form of religious organization, characterized typically by fervent believers and a single idea or leader. (p. 443)

sect A small subculture within an established religious institution. (p. 443)

charismatic leader A person whose extraordinary personal qualities touch people enough to break with tradition and follow him or her. (p. 443)

denomination A large-scale, extremely organized religious body with established hierarchy and methods for credentialing administrators. (p. 443)

ecclesiae Religious institutions so pervasive that the boundary between church and state is nonexistent and in which the clerical elite also serves the political elite. (p. 443)

4. Religion: Globally and Locally

Local traditional religions are usually replaced by **world religions,** including the Western monotheistic religions: **Judaism, Christianity,** and **Islam,** with the most extreme or literal versions practicing **fundamentalism.** Eastern religions emerged from Asia; these world religions include **Hinduism, Buddhism,** and **Confucianism.** While Europe today is becoming less religious, America is becoming more so, perhaps because we are a nation founded by religious pilgrims, on the principle of religious freedom, or because our churches serve as community centers. Whatever the reason, we seem to be in the middle of a **Third Great Awakening.** We differ in religiosity and affiliation by gender, race, and ethnicity. Blacks and Whites typically attend different churches. Many Americans have **New Age** spiritual practices. Religion and politics often go hand in hand; for example, **liberation theology** mobilizes social justice, and the religious right and Islamic fundamentalists have faith-based political agendas.

world religions Those religions with long histories, well established traditions, and the flexibility to adapt to many different cultures. (p. 444)

Judaism The first monotheistic religion; believes the covenant between God and Abraham took place around 2000 B.C.E. and became the foundation of Jewish law. Today there are about 15 million Jews worldwide. (p. 444)

Christianity The world's largest religion today, it was founded 2,000 years ago by the disciples of Jesus, who declared him to the be the son of God. (p. 445)

Islam Founded about 1,400 years ago when God was displeased with the corruptions of earlier prophets and gave his last prophet, Mohammed, a new sacred text, the Koran. It requires the fusion of religion and government and two main branches—Shi'ite and Sunni. (p. 445)

fundamentalism The extreme end of many religions, fundamentalism tries to return to the basic precepts, the "true word of God," and live exactly according to his precepts. (p. 446)

Hinduism Developed in India around 1500 BCE, it believes in many gods, but most of the time people revere one of the main three Brahmin (creator of life); Vishnu (preserver of life); Shiva (destroyer or renewer of life). Today there are 900 million Hindus, mostly in South Asia and in Indian communities worldwide. (p. 446)

Buddhism Founded by Siddhartha Gantana, later called Buddha, it teaches that enlightenment is possible in this lifetime, through the Tenfold Path. There are two main branches—Hinayana and Mahayana. Today there are 376 million Buddhists, mostly in East Asia. (p. 446)

Confucianism Ethical and philosophical system developed from the teachings of the Chinese sage Confucius that focuses primarily on secular ethics and the cultivation of the civilized individual to create a civilized and peaceful society. (p. 447)

Third Great Awakening What some term a current religious revival in the United States that further demonstrates spirituality, making a relationship with the sacred attainable to even greater numbers of Americans, with even less effort or religious discipline. (p. 448)

New Age An umbrella term for many groups that practice and develop a distinct spirituality. New Age groups draw on organized religions and even traditions like astrology and a belief in life in outer space. (p. 453)

liberation theology A movement within the Catholic Church in Latin America that was a source of popular mobilization for social change. Liberation theology stressed the nobility of the poor and promoted a religious response to hunger, disease, and poverty. (p. 453)

5. Science in Sociological Perspective

Science is an institution, like religion, that is studied by sociologists. Both religion and science have practitioners who adhere to norms, and both have ways of knowing. **Objectivity** and **disinterestedness** are two of the norms guiding science. Science is the work of people in social networks, with gatekeepers among the scientific elite who decide who makes it in and which research gets funded and published. Science was historically funded by patronage, then by governments, and now even private individuals and foundations are funding scientific research.

objectivity The scientific norm that stipulates scientific knowledge must be based on objective criteria, not political agendas or personal preferences. (p. 454)

disinterestedness The scientific norm that stipulates scientific research should not be pursued for personal goals, but in the pursuit of scientific truth. (p. 455)

6. Education, Religion, and Science in the Twenty-First Century

We are becoming both increasingly scientific, and simultaneously increasingly religious. Even in repressive regimes, both religion and science ultimately prevail, as humans have a need to know, and understand their world, be it through religion, or science, or both!

Self-Test: Check Your Understanding

1. Which of the following is not common to both science and religion?
   a. It is an institution.
   b. It promotes a worldview.
   c. It is a way of knowing.
   d. All of these are common to both science and religion.

2. All of the following are Western world religions, except
   a. Islam.
   b. Judaism.
   c. Buddhism.
   d. Christianity.

3. Which of the following is a characteristic of Western, rather than Eastern, world religions?
   a. Church attendance on the holiest day of the week is expected.
   b. There is no one holy or divine book.
   c. There are many gods.
   d. You may practice more than one doctrine.

4. Singing the national anthem at a ball game is an example of a unifying ritual in contemporary secular society, according to:
   a. Durkheim.
   b. Bellah.
   c. Weber.
   d. Kuhn.

5. Religion is the opiate of the masses, according to:
   a. Martin Luther.
   b. Durkheim.
   c. Goffman.
   d. Marx.

6. Mennonites are Christian Anabaptists who base their way of life on the views of Menno Simons, a religious figure who lived in the 1500s. Their dress and way of life set them apart from mainstream society, so they are sometimes victims of discrimination and prejudice. Based on the discussion in the text, Mennonites can be identified as an example of a(n):
   a. cult.
   b. sect.
   c. denomination.
   d. ecclesiae.

7. Of the following, which group has the greatest religiosity?
   a. Women
   b. Men
   c. Young adults
   d. All of the above are equally religious.

8. Science differs from religion in that:
   a. it is an institution.
   b. it has norms for behavior.
   c. results should be replicable by anyone.
   d. it has a particular worldview and way of knowing.

Self-Test Answers: 1. d, 2. c, 3. a, 4. b, 5. d, 6. b, 7. a, 8. c

Integrate and Explore: Points to Consider

1. What characteristics are shared by both religion and science? In what ways are science and religion different? Globally, what changes are taking place with regard to religion? What changes are taking place with regard to education globally? What impact are these changes having for individual nations?

2. How does education enhance equality? How does education perpetuate inequality? Which groups stand the most to gain from equal access to education, and which stand to lose?

succeed with PEARSON mysoclab

Self-scoring practice tests, flashcards for learning key terms, streaming audio of the entire text, and multimedia, including:

Watch—*Synagogue Doubles as a Mosque*

Watch—*Bible Verse Ban in High School*

Explore—*Failing Schools Across the Country*

MySocLibrary—Peggy Orenstein, *Learning Silence: Scenes from the Class Struggle*

Sociology of Environments: The Natural, Physical, and Human Worlds

On August 23, 2005, the summer's twelfth tropical depression formed over the Bahamas. Soon it was upgraded to a Category 1 hurricane named Katrina. In a busy hurricane season, most of the world didn't pay much attention as it made landfall in Florida, caused little damage, weakened into a tropical storm, and blew off into the Gulf of Mexico. But then the warm water strengthened it into a Category 5, with winds of 175 miles per hour, the most intense hurricane to ever hit the gulf. On August 28, New Orleans Mayor Ray Nagle ordered a mandatory evacuation of the entire city. By the morning of August 29, only 20 percent of the 1.3 million residents remained, mostly those too poor or sick to move. Shortly after landfall, a storm surge breached the levees in several places. Four-fifths of the entire city was under water.

So far this doesn't sound very much like the introduction to a chapter in a sociology textbook. Read on.

During the subsequent days and weeks, news reports described a city in chaos, with snipers, rapes and murders, people dying of hunger and exposure, bodies lying unattended in the streets. (Later it turned out that many of the reports were exaggerated or even made up.) National Guard and federal troops were mobilized, but were they in New Orleans to distribute food and water or to keep looters away from the pricey boutiques on Canal Street? Why did they take so long to arrive? Most of the survivors were poor and African American. And the spin of the news reports—African Americans "looting" but White people "search-

"We think of people and the natural and built environments in which they live as separate, even conflicted, realms. Sociologists are interested in the dynamic relationships among the human, the physical, and the urban environments."

ing for food"—suggested that the disaster was bringing long-hidden prejudices to light.

We think of human beings, the cities they live in, and the physical world of tropical depressions as separate realms, sometimes even conflicted ones. As the events leading up to and following Hurricane Katrina

demonstrate, they are related, even interdependent. The hurricane, the flooding of New Orleans, and the aftermath are parts of the same story. "Natural disasters" may have human causes as well as human consequences. All three environments—the human, the urban, and the natural—constrain and construct human action, help create and sometimes help destroy each other. Sociologists are vitally interested in the dynamic relationships among the human, the physical, and the urban environments. The connections among the natural world, social life, and the ways that technology shapes and transforms both arenas are at the heart of sociological investigation.

The Human Environment

Humans are a social species. We want—and need—to be around other people most of the time. People who go off by themselves on purpose are often considered strange, socially inept, or even psychologically disturbed.

A major part of our environment is the mass of other people around us, simply doing what people do: being born and growing up, moving into town and leaving town, getting sick and getting well, living and dying. **Demography** is the scientific study of human populations and one of the oldest and most popular branches of sociology. Demography is used to understand health, longevity, and even political representation, as the census is the basis for allocation of congressional seats. Demographers are primarily concerned with the statistics of birth, death, and migration (Yaukey and Anderton, 2001).

Being Born and Dying

Demographers use two birth measurements: **fertility** (the number of children that a woman has) and **fecundity** (the maximum number of children that she could possibly have). Women are physically capable of having a child every nine months, so in the years between menarche (the onset of menstruation) and menopause (the end of menstruation) they could give birth over 20 times (their fecundity). However, in the United States, women have an average of 2.08 children each (their fertility) (Hamilton, Martin, and Ventura, 2006). (Men are not counted because they could produce thousands of children if they found enough partners. King Sobhuza II of Swaziland [1899–1982] fathered 210 children with his 70 wives.)

Demographers measure fertility with the number of live births in the country per year. They measure fecundity with the **fertility rate,** the number of children who would be born to each woman if she lived through her childbearing years with the average fertility of her age group. Poor countries often have a fertility rate of four or more (it's 6.84 in Somalia), while in rich countries, the fertility rate often drops to less than two (1.61 in Canada) (CIA World Factbook, 2009). Very high fertility rates spell trouble: Children do not contribute to the economy until they are older, but they must be fed, clothed, educated, and given health care, thus putting a severe strain on already impoverished families. Women with so many children may still participate in the labor force, relying on older children or other kin to look after younger children, but it still strains the family economy. As the children grow into adulthood, there will not be enough jobs to accommodate them, resulting in widespread unemployment. On the other hand, more children mean more potential support for aging and infirm parents.

However, very low fertility rates are also a problem, suggesting that the population is aging faster than it can be replenished with new births (see Figure 15.1). Fewer people participate in the workforce as they grow old or retire, but at the same time they continue to require housing, food, transportation, and health care, again putting a strain on the economy. The low number of births means that in about 20 years there will not be enough adult workers to fill critical jobs in business and technology, putting the country at an economic disadvantage. On the other hand, lower birth rates mean that adults have far more geographic and occupational mobility.

Of course, everyone dies sooner or later, but the **mortality rate,** or the number of deaths per year for every thousand people, can tell demographers a great deal about the relative health of the country. In the United States, the mortality rate is 8.25; every year, a little over eight people in every thousand die. Most wealthy nations range between eight and twelve.

Strangely, poor nations can have either higher or lower mortality rates. A low mortality rate, as in Guatemala (6.81) or Tonga (5.35), does not necessarily mean that the people there enjoy a high **life expectancy** (the average number of years a person can expect to live). In fact, in Guatemala, it's rather low, 64.31 for men and 66.21 for women. It usually means that the fertility rate is so high that the proportion of older people in the population goes down. In the United States, about 12 percent of the population is 65 or older. It's 3.3 percent in Guatemala and 4.2 percent in Tonga (CIA World Factbook, 2009).

A higher mortality rate, as in Afghanistan (20.99) or Zambia (20.23), usually signifies that, due to famine, war, or disease, many people do not live to see old age. AIDS is causing a significant decline in population growth in many low-income countries.

Demographers are especially interested in the **infant mortality rate,** the number of deaths per year in each thousand infants up to one year old. As you might expect, the infant mortality rate is extremely low in wealthy countries (4.31 in France), and extremely high in poor countries, especially in sub-Saharan Africa: It's 70.49 in Nigeria and 192.5 in Angola (that is, one out of five babies born dies during his or her first year of life). Because infants are more vulnerable to disease and malnutrition than adults or older children, the infant mortality rate correlates with the effectiveness of the country's health care, the level of nutrition, and innumerable other quality of life factors. The infant mortality rate serves as a proxy for the overall health of the country and can guide policy makers in their allocation of funds for hospitals, medical care, and pregnancy counseling.

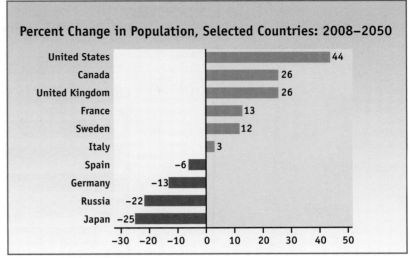

Figure 15.1 The Birth Dearth

Percent Change in Population, Selected Countries: 2008–2050

- United States: 44
- Canada: 26
- United Kingdom: 26
- France: 13
- Sweden: 12
- Italy: 3
- Spain: −6
- Germany: −13
- Russia: −22
- Japan: −25

(*Source:* Population Reference Bureau, 2008. Copyright © 2008 Population Reference Bureau. Reproduced by permission.)

Moving In, Moving Out

In addition to people being born and dying, demographers are interested in their physical movements, as they leave one territory (*emigrating*) and take up permanent residence in another (*immigrating*). People emigrate and immigrate either voluntarily or involuntarily. Most wealthy countries have sizeable populations of voluntary immigrants. In 2004, the United States gained 946,100 foreign nationals. Within the OECD (the Organization for Economic Cooperation and Development, the organization of the world's 30 most developed nations), the United Kingdom was next (with 302,800), followed by Canada, Germany, and France (OECD, 2007a).

Over 67 million people living today emigrated from their home territory involuntarily. Some 16 million are refugees; 26 million were displaced by political strife and war; and another 25 million were displaced by natural disasters. Pakistan hosts the most refugees (more than two million), followed by Syria, Iran, Germany, and Jordan (see Figure 15.2). As of 2008, the leading countries of origin were Afghanistan, whose 3.1 million refugees accounted for 27 percent of the global refugee population, followed by Iraq (2.3 million), Sudan (523,000), and Somalia (457,000) (UNHCR, 2008).

Voluntary migrants usually have two sets of motives for their move, called *push factors*

Life Expectancy

Life expectancy has increased dramatically among industrial countries, though it has actually decreased in some developing countries.

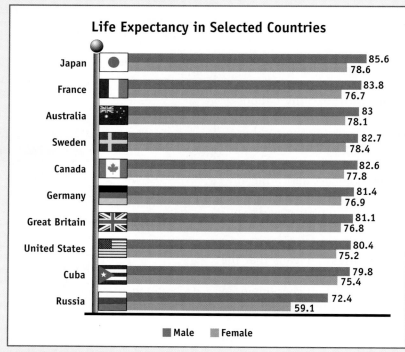

Life Expectancy in Selected Countries

Country	Female	Male
Japan	85.6	78.6
France	83.8	76.7
Australia	83	78.1
Sweden	82.7	78.4
Canada	82.6	77.8
Germany	81.4	76.9
Great Britain	81.1	76.8
United States	80.4	75.2
Cuba	79.8	75.4
Russia	72.4	59.1

■ Male   ■ Female

(*Source:* CIA, The World Factbook, 2008.)

1. What factors do you think contribute to these differences?
2. What sorts of government policies might be implements to increase life expectancy?

Refugee Next Door

Most refugees do not traverse the entire world in search of a safe haven. Most go to a neighboring country and thus stay within their region. The countries that received the most refugees in 2007 were Pakistan (over 2 million), Syria (1.5 million), and Iran (964,000). The United States received 281,000 (UNHCR, 2008).

Did You Know?

(reasons they want to leave their home territory in the first place) and *pull factors* (reasons they want to settle in this particular territory). The most common push factors are a sluggish economy, political and cultural oppression, and civil unrest—not enough to force them to leave, but enough to make their lives at home miserable. A slight downturn in one country's economic fortunes often leads to a rise in immigration in others. The most common pull factors are the opposite: a good economy, political and cultural tolerance, and civil stability. Because rich countries offer superior jobs and education and a great degree of political and cultural tolerance,

they tend to receive the most voluntary migrants.

Another extremely important pull factor is having someone you know in the territory you intend to immigrate to. People don't like to start out afresh in areas where they know no one and where possibly no one speaks their language or understands their culture, so when they have a choice, they often move to where family and friends are already located. Many relocate to follow a romantic partner.

There have been four major flows of immigration in modern history (Pagden, 2001):

1. Between 1500 and 1800, as Europe began to establish colonial empires around the world, millions of English, French, Spanish, and Portuguese citizens emigrated to the sparsely settled regions of North and South America, South Africa,

and Oceania. Some were forced to leave as punishment for a crime, but most chose to leave voluntarily, drawn by the promise of wealth or political freedom in the colonies.

2. At about the same time, Europeans transported over 11,000,000 East and West Africans to their New World colonies in North and South America and the Caribbean to work as slaves. Eventually they came to form a substantial part of the population of the United States, the Caribbean, and many regions of South America, especially Brazil. Because they maintained so much cultural continuity with their African homeland, they are now sometimes called "The African Diaspora" (Gomez, 2004; Thornton, 1998).

3. Beginning in about 1800, East Asians began to emigrate from China and to a lesser extent other countries, with motives similar to those of the Europeans who settled the New World (Takaki, 1998). They immigrated to major cities in the United States, Latin America, Africa, and the Middle East. Today Brazil has the largest population of Japanese ancestry (1.5 million) outside of Japan. In the newly independent United States, this was an era of rapid westward migration of European settlers, and the often-violent displacement of indigenous peoples.

4. Between about 1880 and 1920, millions of Southern and Eastern Europeans emigrated as they faced increasing political and economic strife as their countries modernized. High school textbooks in the United States tend to portray only immigrants arriving at Ellis Island, but they also settled in Canada, South Africa, Australia, New Zealand, and Latin America. By 1914, 30 percent of the population of Argentina was foreign born and speaking Italian, Russian, Polish, Czech, English, Yiddish, and German. In some districts, the proportion was as high as 50 percent (Shumway, 1993).

Studying Immigration

The **immigration rate** is the number of people entering a territory each year for every thousand of the population. The **emigration rate** is the opposite, the number of people leaving per thousand. However, few territories are so terrible that they cannot attract at least a

Many refugees cluster in places where their ethnic group has gained a foothold. There are 18,000 Hmong, political refugees from Laos, in the United States, almost all in a few cities in Minnesota, Wisconsin, and California. Here, Hmong third graders join a class in St. Paul, Minnesota.

few immigrants, or so wonderful that no one ever decides to emigrate (although some authoritarian states forbid their citizens from emigrating). Therefore demographers study the changing population by examining the **net migration rate,** the difference between the immigration and emigration rates in a given year.

Because rich countries offer the greatest educational and job opportunities and the most freedom from oppression, more people want to

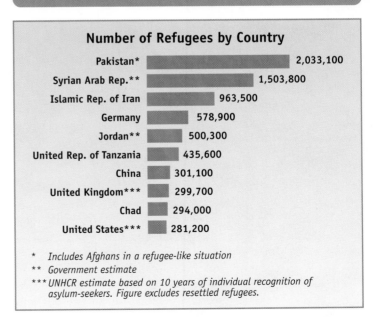

Figure 15.2 Major Refugee Hosting Countries

Number of Refugees by Country

Country	Refugees
Pakistan*	2,033,100
Syrian Arab Rep.**	1,503,800
Islamic Rep. of Iran	963,500
Germany	578,900
Jordan**	500,300
United Rep. of Tanzania	435,600
China	301,100
United Kingdom***	299,700
Chad	294,000
United States***	281,200

*   *Includes Afghans in a refugee-like situation*
** *Government estimate*
*** *UNHCR estimate based on 10 years of individual recognition of asylum-seekers. Figure excludes resettled refugees.*

(*Source:* UNHCR, 2007 Global Trends: Refugees, Asylum-Seekers, Returnees, Internally Displaced and Stateless Persons, Copyright © UNHCR, June 2008. Reproduced by permission.)

Did You Know?

move to them than to leave, so they tend to have positive net migration rates (5.9 in Canada, 3.31 in the United States, 2.18 in Germany). A negative net migration rate means that more people are emigrating than immigrating, suggesting that the country is too poor to offer many jobs or else is undergoing a political crisis (Iran, −2.64; Mexico, −4.57). The lowest net migration rate in the world is in Micronesia, where 21 more people per thousand leave than arrive every year. With one-fifth of the population unemployed, palm trees and ocean breezes haven't been sufficient incentive to stick around (CIA, 2006).

Internal migration means moving from one region to another within a territory. The average American moves 11 times during his or her life—more for young, middle-class professionals. Most of these migrations occur within the same city or to adjacent cities, as people seek bigger and better residences while staying "close to home."

Young college-educated people are more likely to move and to move longer distances. Married or single, they have fewer long-term responsibilities to tie them to a place, no kids to take out of school or houses to put up on the market. Also, people looking for jobs that require a college degree often conduct a national job search instead of a local search. By income group, the affluent are the most likely to move (Pew Research Center, 2008). Although most Americans have moved at least once in their lifetime, a significant portion—nearly 40 percent—have never left the place they were born. Overall, U.S. internal migration has been drifting downward for decades; less than 12 percent of Americans moved between 2007 and 2008, the smallest share since the government began tracking such numbers in the 1940s (Pew Research Center, 2008). (See Figure 15.3.)

Internal and international migrations are regulated by similar push and pull factors: People want jobs and freedom. Two million African Americans moved from the rural South to the urban North between 1900 and 1940, to escape stagnating rural economies and oppressive Jim Crow laws. Another five million moved north between 1940 and 1970 (Lemann, 1992). Since World War II, there has been an ongoing migration of young gay men and lesbians from small towns to big cities, to escape from the homophobia and heterosexism back home (Weston, 1995). This simultaneous push (discrimination) and pull (attraction of a community) created and sustain the now well-established gay areas in San Francisco, New York, Miami, Atlanta, and other major cities (see Levine, 1979).

Today most internal migration flows from the cities of the Northeast and the Midwest, where economies are stagnating—the so-called Rust Belt, from the reliance on heavy industry and especially the homes of the steel and auto industries—toward places with high economic prospects, the Sun Belt of the New South and the Southwest.

An influx of new immigrants, either internal or international, can provide new talent for the community, but it also puts a strain on the local infrastructure, as utility companies, school districts, real estate, and retailers try to

The United States has always proclaimed itself "a nation of immigrants," and immigrants' rights have always been hotly debated. Here, Corina Payan demonstrates with thousands of other Mexican-Americans for immigrants' rights in Denver. "We're here to make a better life . . . ," she said. "They treat us like criminals and we're not."

Figure 15.3 Interstate Migration in the United States

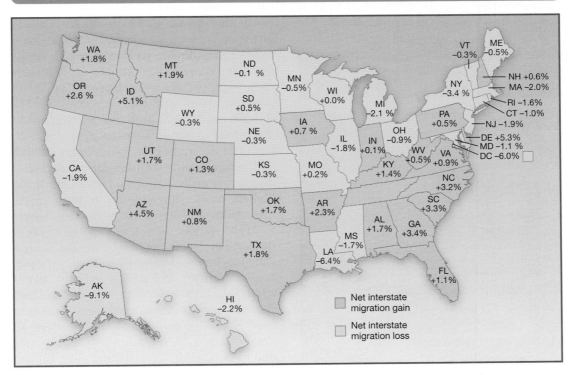

(*Source:* "Net Interstate Migration, by State, 2007" a Social & Demographic Trends report, Pew Research Center, pewsocialtrends.org, December 17, 2008. Reproduced by permission.)

deal with the influx. Meanwhile, the territories losing population experience a loss of talent, failed businesses, deserted downtowns, and a "sinking ship" feeling. Today, global migration is a politically volatile issue. Millions of immigrants from less-developed countries pour into industrial countries in North America, Europe, and Australia. As the global economy slows down, they are vulnerable targets for political opposition and economic protectionism, especially if they have entered the country illegally.

Population Composition

Comparing births and deaths, emigration and immigration, can give demographers only a partial understanding about what's going on in a country or region. They also want to know the **population composition**—that is, the comparative numbers of men and women and various age groups.

The male:female ratio is never 50:50. Due to physiological differences in X and Y chromosomes, 106 boys tend to be born for every 100 girls. A significantly lower birth ratio sug-

gests that environmental pollution is having an impact on the human body at the chromosomal level (Davis, Gottlieb, and Stampnitzky, 1998). A significantly higher ratio, especially in countries where boys are strongly preferred over girls—for instance, China (109), South Korea (110), and Guam (114)—suggests to demographers that women are more likely to choose abortions if they find that they are carrying girls.

After birth, the ratio of men to women decreases in every age group because men are more likely to die in accidents, warfare, and of certain diseases. If the ratio is too high or not high enough, demographers conclude that the country is especially unpleasant or unattractive for men or women. During the middle years of life (ages 15 to 64), the highest disproportion of men to women occurs in countries that draw a substantial

Educated Immigrants

Although we often see recent immigrants doing menial work, most immigrants to industrial countries are actually better educated and more highly qualified workers than those in the host country. Immigrants to Spain, Sweden, Italy, and Denmark are twice as likely as locals to be overqualified, and immigrants to Greece are three times as likely to be overqualified (*The Economist*, 2008).

Did You Know?

number of male foreign workers (there are 2.28 men for every woman in Qatar). Countries that lose many men to foreign employment tend to have a disproportionate number of women (there are 0.92 men for every woman in Puerto Rico).

The distribution of people of different age groups can best be represented by a graph called a **population pyramid,** which shows five- or ten-year age groups as different-sized bars, or "blocks" (Figure 15.4). Many poor countries, like Mexico, have "expansive pyramids" that look like real pyramids. They have a broad base to signify a high fertility rate, and every "block" gets smaller as the age group shrinks due to accident, disease, or other mortality factors, until the highest block (the elderly) is very small. Rich countries often have "constrictive pyramids." The base is not very broad because the fertility rate is not very high, but there's a big block of middle-aged and older people. Some countries, like Italy, even look somewhat top heavy because the middle and apex of the pyramid are bigger than the base; there are many more people over 30 than children. A few countries have "stationary pyramids," which look like pillars. Because few people in each age group die of accident or disease, every block is about the same size, beginning to shrink only a little beginning with the 60-year-olds. Demographers predict that while the United States is slightly constrictive now, it will be more stationary by 2030 (Young, 1998). In the United States, the higher fertility rates of immigrants help account for a less-constrictive pyramid than in some other wealthy countries (*The Economist*, 2005a; Population Reference Bureau, 2008).

Population pyramids can also be divided by gender, with men on one side and women on the other. If one of the blocks is larger on one end than the other, it means that one sex outnumbers the other in that age group. In the United States, women begin outnumbering men around the age of 70, but in India, they begin outnumbering men around the age of 40.

Demographers use population blocks to determine current and future social service needs of the society. In the United States, the baby boomer block has been a bulge in the pyramid, working its way upward since the 1950s, allowing demographers to predict a need for more child-oriented facilities, then more colleges and universities, and now more facilities for elderly people.

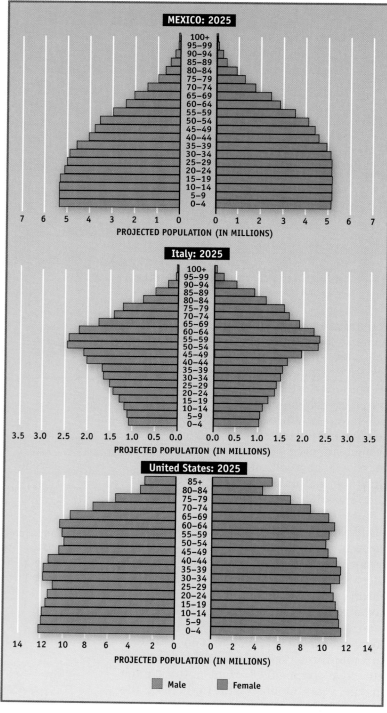

Figure 15.4 Population Pyramids: Comparing Mexico, Italy, and the United States, 2025

(*Source:* U.S. Census Bureau, International Data Base.)

Bare Branches

What happens when men are told constantly that they are worthless, a disgrace to their ancestors, and a failure to their country, unless they produce sons? And then modern medical techniques allow them to determine the sex of their children early in the pregnancy, early enough for an abortion? And strict birth control policies allow only one child per couple, unless it's not a son—then they can keep trying?

A lot of sons get born, and not very many daughters.

And, 20 years later, there's a new generation of young men who have been told constantly that they are worthless unless *they* produce sons. Except now there are fewer women around for them to produce the sons with.

In China they are called "bare branches," these men who do not produce sons, mostly due not to physiological malfunction or lack of heterosexual interest but to the lack of female partners. (The phrase refers to the bare branch on the family tree.) And their numbers are increasing. Nationwide, 2 million more boys than girls are being born every year. By 2020, that will mean 40 million more young adult men than women (Lim, 2004), a population the size of Spain. The Chinese government fears widespread rape, prostitution, and other sex crimes, but unless it can change 2,500 years of Confucian teachings and give these men a purpose in life besides having sons, the psychological consequences may outweigh the sociological.

Theories of Global Population Growth

Cities and countries grow or shrink for a variety of reasons: **natural population increase** (the number of births every year subtracted by the number of deaths), immigration and emigration, and changing boundary lines when territories are annexed or lost. But the world as a whole grows for only one reason, natural increase, and it is growing fast, at a rate of 1.3 percent per year. As of this writing, there are 6.5 billion people living on Earth, but by the time this book is published, it will probably be 6.75 billion. If you are 20 years old today, you can expect to see the world's population reach 8 billion before your fortieth birthday and 9 billion long before you retire (Cohen, 1995).

How did we get so many people? And what are we going to do with them?

For thousands of years, children meant prosperity. They started working alongside their parents as soon as they could walk, thus adding to the family's economic productivity. Women were pregnant as often as they could be. With a high infant mortality rate and virtually no effective medical care, only about half of the babies born survived to age 14

(Kriedte, 1983), so it was prudent to have as many children as possible to ensure that a few would survive to maturity.

In modern societies, most children survive to adulthood, so it is imprudent to give birth to more than you expect to raise. And far from meaning endless prosperity, they are an economic burden. For the first 20 years or so of their lives, parents provide their room, board, braces, medicine, school supplies, books, toys, and probably an allowance, while at least in the middle classes the children contribute little or nothing to the family budget (they may have a part-time job, but it's usually for their own spending money).

Fewer children, therefore, make more economic sense than lots of children. But tell that to men and women in cultures where a household with ten children is infinitely more prestigious than a household with just one. Even if they grudgingly admit that it might be a good idea to limit the number of their children, they may be unaware of birth control techniques, or they are unable to acquire the proper devices.

Even where industrialized countries find children an economic liability, in the absence of social safety nets like Social Security and elderly care facilities, people may want large families to ensure care in their old age. High fertility may be encouraged for religious or political reasons. Also, if women's opportunities are limited, childbearing, especially at an early age, is one of the few roles open to them.

Low infant mortality plus the prestige of large families meant that beginning about 1750, the world's population started to inch upward. Then the inch became a foot. Not only the population itself, but the rate of increase started to climb. It was this climb that sparked the growth of demography as a field of sociological study.

In 1900, the world's population was about 1.7 billion. During the twentieth century, it quadrupled to over 6 billion, due to plummeting infant and maternal mortality rates (the result of improved health care for both pregnant women and their infants and of better neonatal nutrition) and dramatically increased longevity. Although the peak slowed a bit after 1970, due to a declining fertility rate in rich countries and the world pandemic of HIV/AIDS, we are still gaining 77 million people each year, or the equivalent of the entire population of the United States every four years (Figure 15.5).

Ninety-six percent of the population growth is taking place in poor countries. Somalia, one of the poorest countries in the world, adds 3.38 percent to its population every year. This means that the people having the most children are precisely the ones least economically capable of providing for them. Many rich countries, on the other hand, have a stable population, and some are in decline. Demographers consider a population growth rate of 0.4 percent or so stable; but, in 40 of the 42 countries in Europe, the growth rate is lower than that, and in some it is actually shrinking. The birth rate and immigration rate are too low to replace those who die and emigrate.

Booms and Bombs

Thomas Robert Malthus (1766–1834), an English economist and clergyman, was one of the first to suggest that population growth might spin out of control and lead to disaster ([1798], 1999). Though the population of England was only about 6 million at the time, **Malthusian theory** held it would increase by geometric progression, doubling in each generation—a man and a woman would have four children, and those four would have eight, and those eight sixteen, and so on. However, because farm land has a limited fertility, even with new technology, food production can only increase by arithmetic progression—20 tons becomes 40, then 60, then 80, and so on. Eventually—and quite rapidly—there would be more people than food, leading to starvation on a global level.

While in principle his theory made sense, Malthus failed to foresee several cultural trends. First, the birth rate in England began to drop around 1850 as children were increasingly seen as an economic liability and people began to use birth control. Also, Malthus underestimated human ingenuity—irrigation, fertilizers, pesticides, and selective breeding have greatly increased farm productivity. So the population did not increase quite as fast as he thought, and there has been no global starvation. Yet. In rich countries, the problem is often quite the opposite—we consume far more than we need to survive.

Karl Marx was highly critical of Malthus's basic assumption that population growth would be a source of hardship for the masses. He argued that unequal distribution of resources was a far more significant factor. To Marx, the problem was that the rich get richer and the poor get babies. The political question was not how to reduce the number of babies but how to get the poor some of those riches.

Figure 15.5 World Population (in Billions): 1950 to 2050

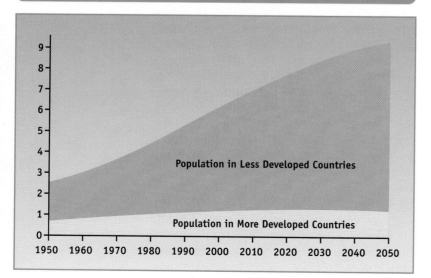

(*Source:* Population Reference Bureau, 2008. Copyright © 2008 Population Reference Bureau. Reproduced by permission.)

But Marx has been criticized for failing to take uneven population growth into account as a contributing factor in global inequality. For example, India is the second most populous country in the world, with a little over a billion people in 2005. Its population increases by 18 million per year, with an expected 50 percent increase by 2050. It currently faces a severe water shortage. This is not a resource that can be redistributed.

In 1968, Paul Ehrlich published *The Population Bomb,* which put a modern take on Malthus. He argued that even a moderate 1.3 percent population increase would soon spin out of control. Before the year 3000, he predicted, Earth's population would grow to 60 million billion, or 100 people for each square yard of the world, including the oceans and mountaintops. Of course, we would run out of food and usable water long before that. Ehrlich predicted that the first mass starvations would begin in the 1990s. He turned out to be slightly off as well. Millions of people are malnourished across the world, but not nearly as many as he predicted. Erlich later argued that an increased population combined with an alarming depletion of natural resources can only lead to chaos. His solution was a global effort to achieve **zero population growth**—where the number of births does not exceed the number of deaths. This would involve not only global stability in population but a decrease in poor countries and a redistribution of resources to those countries.

Frank Notestein (1945) argued that population growth is tied to technological development. **Demographic transition theory** holds that the population and technology spur each other's development. This transition has three stages:

1. *Initial stage.* The society has both a high birth rate and a high death rate, so the population size remains stable or else grows very slowly. Preindustrial societies were all at this stage.
2. *Transitional growth stage.* Industrialization leads to a better food supply, better medical care, and better sanitation, all resulting in a decrease in mortality at all age levels. However, the sociological prestige of large families has not decreased, so the birth rate remains high, and the population explodes. This is what Malthus observed, and it precipitated his theory of exponential growth.

Migration and fertility rates also affect the age demographics of a society. Russia loses 0.37 percent of its population every year, becoming older and grayer.

3. *Incipient decline stage.* Social forces and cultural beliefs catch up with technology. Both the birth and death rates are low, so population growth returns to minimal levels. Zero population growth is rare, but many industrialized countries like Germany are coming close.

This theory has been criticized for two reasons. First, it always works in the same direction, from high fertility/high mortality to high fertility/low mortality as technology increases, and then to low fertility/low mortality as social norms catch up. However, there have been many instances in history where the mortality rate moved from low to high, such as the periods immediately after the fall of the Roman Empire and the Mayan Empire. In contemporary sub-Saharan Africa, the high rate of HIV infection is offsetting the birth rate and causing countries to move backward, from stage two to stage one (high fertility/high mortality).

Second, it is not technology that causes a decrease in the mortality rate—but rather the *sociology,* the changes in personal and public health practices. Several major medical discoveries in the eighteenth and nineteenth centuries led to little change in the mortality rate. But when the public accepted the germ theory of disease, and therefore they began to sterilize implements, pasteurize their milk, immunize their children, wash their hands, and bathe regularly—then the mortality rate declined.

Life Expectancy

Y ou can go online or to an encyclopedia and find the life expectancy for men and women and different ethnic and occupational groups in every country in the world. But how do we know that a baby born today is likely to live to be 61, or 66, or 78, or 100? It's not easy.

First we have to find the crude death rate, the percentage of people of each age who were alive last year but are dead this year. For instance, if last year's records indicated that there were 1,000,000 people of age 30, and this year there are 900,000 people of age 31, then 30-year-olds have a 90 percent chance of seeing their thirty-first birthday, and their crude death rate is 10 percent. From this we can construct

a life table, a list of the probabilities that persons of age X will live to see age $X + 1$, $X + 2$, and so on. To find the life expectancy of the population, we take the mean of all the probabilities for a person of age 0 (a newborn baby).

Notice that the measure of life expectancy cannot predict the future. If the life expectancy in the country is 75, that doesn't mean that newborn babies will live for 75 more years, or that people who are 30 now have 45 years left to live. It is really a measure of how long people are living at this moment in time.

Life Expectancies at Birth by Race and Sex, 1904 and 2004 (in years)

Subgroup	1904	2004
White males	46.6	75.7
White females	49.5	80.8
Black males	29.1	69.8
Black females	32.7	76.5

(*Sources:* Joel Best, *Stat-Spotting,* University of California Press, 2008.)

Policies to Combat Population Growth

A number of organizations and nations have come together to try to decrease the population explosion. In the United States, Population Connection promotes the replacement level of only two children per family. The organization's website contains updates and policy briefs about different pressing environmental issues and has branches on many college campuses.

Several countries have started protocols intended to decrease overpopulation. In China, a family planning law was mandated in 1980. Although known worldwide as a "one child per couple" law, it is actually calculated by neighborhoods rather than couples: Each neighborhood is told the maximum number of births it can have per year. If

a couple wants to have a child, they must apply for a "pregnancy permit." They may be permitted to have more than one, if the neighborhood has not met its quota, and if there are extenuating circumstances (such as if they work on a farm, if their first child was a girl, if their first child is disabled, and so on); or they may not be permitted to have a child at all. Illegal pregnancy means losing privileges, paying fines, and even losing their jobs. Globally, some commentators worried about compromising personal freedom, and others worried about women accidentally getting pregnant and then being forced to have an abortion. However, the measures have been successful in controlling population. China has reduced its growth rate to 1.1 percent per year, half that of other poor nations.

The Urban Environment

In the U.S. farming town of Dekalb, Illinois, only 65 miles from downtown Chicago, live people who have never ventured to the city. Not to go to a Cubs game or the Art Institute, not to shop at Macy's. When questioned, they

seem surprised—who in their right mind would want to go into Chicago? It's crowded, dirty, ugly, expensive, and dangerous. Meanwhile, in the high-rise condos of Chicago's Gold Coast live people who have never ventured more than five miles west of the Loop. When they are questioned, they also seem surprised—where else is there to go? They're surrounded by nonstop excitement, cultural diversity, artistic innovation, and economic promise. Beyond Chicago there is nothing but small towns stuck in the 1930s, populated by narrow-minded bigots.

We think of cities as the capitals of civilization—culturally alive, commercially dynamic, exciting. We also think of cities as the centers and incubators of many of our most central social problems—crime, poverty, racial and ethnic antagonism. But it's not one or the other—it's both. The two sets of social issues are linked and interacting. To a great extent, one cannot exist without the other.

The City: Ancient to Modern

When people depend on farming for sustenance and don't have cars, they must live within walking distance of their farmland. Throughout most of human history, and in many undeveloped countries today, they have lived in villages scattered across the farmlands, with a population of only a few hundred, so small that everyone knows everyone else and is probably related through blood and marriage. Between 8000 and 5000 BCE, technological innovations in agriculture began to produce food surpluses, so some people could take on nonfarming jobs, mostly as priests and artisans. They could live in larger settlements—but not too much larger because 99 percent of the population had to be within walking distance of the fields or cattle. Many archaeologists name Çatalhöyük, in modern-day Turkey, as the first city. In 7000 BCE, it was home to 10,000 people—a tiny village today, but then by far the most populous settlement in the world (Mumford, 1968; Yoffee, 2005).

Most ancient cities grew up along major rivers, where enough food could be produced to feed a large nonfarming population. It still took up to 75 farmers to feed one nonfarmer, so these cities had to be small by modern standards. Most had no more than 10,000 residents. At the end of the first century BCE, a few cities in China and India reached a population of 300,000, and Rome was probably unique throughout the ancient world for its population of nearly one million.

The number of "large" cities stayed about the same throughout the Middle Ages and the Renaissance. For all of their fame as centers of Western civilization, European cities were surprisingly small. Of the ten most populous cities in the world in 1500, four were in China,

Cities, both ancient and modern, are often situated near major waterways—for trade, hygiene, and agriculture. This 1853 painting depicts the ninth-century Assyrian palaces of Ashurnasirpal II.

three in the Middle East, and two in India. Only one was in Europe: Paris, reaching number eight with a population of 185,000 (about the size of Dayton, Ohio, today). Beijing, China, number one, had a population of 672,000 (about the size of Memphis, Ten-nessee, today) (Chandler, 1987).

When the Industrial Revolution began around 1750, agricultural productivity increased exponentially, farming jobs began to diminish (a trend that continues today), and manufacturing took precedence. Factories needed hundreds of workers all in the same place, so thousands of people left the farms to move to the city (another trend that continues today). England and Western Europe became urbanized first and then the United States.

The Founders conceived of the United States as a nation of "gentlemen farmers," living on rural estates with their families and servants, with only a few towns scattered about. In 1790, only 5.1 percent of the population was urban. New York, the biggest city, had a population of 33,000. Philadelphia had 28,500 people, and Boston 18,000 (U.S. Census Bureau, 1998). These were small towns even by eighteenth-century standards; compare them to Paris, which had a population of 525,000 in 1790.

The former colonial empires in Africa, Asia, and Latin America urbanized more slowly. By 1900, nine of the ten most populous cities in the world were located in Europe or the United States; the most populous, London, had a population of 6.4 million. Today we can tell rich from poor countries

Urban demographers measure population density, which considers both the number of people and the area of the city itself. Some new expanding cities, like Mumbai, India, are extremely crowded, as people stream to the city from the countryside.

by the percentage of the population that lives in urban areas rather than rural areas: 97 percent in Belgium, 90 percent in the United Kingdom, 79 percent in Japan, as opposed to 31 percent in Mali, 25 percent in Vietnam, and 16 percent in Ethiopia (United Nations, 2006).

Ironically, where urbanization is high, people moving from rural areas have their choice of many cities, but where urbanization is low, there are fewer choices. Thus, poor countries with a high rural population are more likely to have megacities (cities with populations of 5,000,000 or more). Only six of the world's 40 megacities are in the United States or Western Europe, but over half are in poor countries.

Estimates of the population of the city itself are often misleading because suburbs and adjacent cities can double or triple the urbanized population, and in some regions the cities have blurred together into gigantic megacities. For instance, Chicago has an "official" population of about 2.9 million, but the PMSA (Primary Metropolitan Statistical Area), including all of the outlying suburbs and cities, brings it up to 8.6 million. Thus sociologists more often use "urban agglomerations"—a central city and neighboring communities linked to it, for example, by continuous built-up areas or commuters.

The number of people in a city is not always a good measure of what it feels like to live there. Does it feel crowded? Are the houses crammed together, or are there wide spaces between them? Is every inch of land built up,

or are there open areas, such as parks, lawns, and public squares? Are the streets narrow and clogged with cars? A better measure of how crowded a city feels is **population density,** the number of people per square mile or kilometer. Generally, older cities will have a larger population density, because they were constructed before the automobile allowed cities to spread out. Older neighborhoods will be denser than newer neighborhoods.

The most densely populated cities in the world are constricted; that is, there is no place for them to expand outward. Malé, capital of the Maldive Islands, is the most densely populated city on Earth, with 48,007 people per square kilometer (the total population of 81,000 is crammed onto a small atoll in the Indian Ocean). By contrast, New York has a population density of 10,292 (except on the island of Manhattan, which goes up to 25,849).

The more recently the city was founded, the lower the population density: Oklahoma City, founded in 1889, has a population density of 836 per square kilometer. Though cities with low population densities don't seem crowded, they have a downside. Everything is scattered, so it takes time and gas to get anywhere.

The Countryside

The U.S. Census Bureau used to define *urban* as living in an incorporated area with a population of 2,500 or more. However, so many people live in unincorporated areas adjacent to big cities or small towns that have been engulfed by big cities that many demographers suggest a change from a simple dichotomy of city and countryside to a rural–urban continuum, nine levels from #1 (county in a metropolitan area with one million people or more) to #9 (counties not adjacent to a major metropolitan area and with no city over 2,500). By that figure, 93.9 percent of the U.S. population was rural in 1800, 60.4 in 1900, and only 19 percent in 2000 (Northeast-Midwest Institute, 2002).

Globalization increasingly impoverishes the countryside, both by concentrating agricultural enterprises into larger and larger agribusinesses and by locating engines of industrial development in or near urban areas. Poverty and hunger are the ironic consequences of farm foreclosures and economic concentration in urban areas. Rural areas have higher rates of poverty than do urban areas, and rural Americans are more likely than city dwellers to use food stamps—despite the relative proximity to farms (National Rural Health Association, 2006). Rural areas in the United States also have increasingly higher suicide rates than cities—with all their urban alienation (National Association for Rural Mental Health, 2007).

Yet the scale and speed of migration from the countryside to cities have slowed in rich countries like the United States and in the European Union compared with poor and developing ones, especially in Asia and Africa. The United Nations reports that today's global urban population of 3.2 billion will rise to nearly 5 billion by 2030, when three out of five people worldwide will live in cities (U.N., 2005a). This surge of migrants will generally come into urban environments whose minimal infrastructure, squalid slums, and air and water pollution already make them fundamentally difficult and dangerous places to live and work.

Suburbs

Before the twentieth century, members of the upper classes always had at least two houses, one in the city and the other in the country, for weekend and summer visits (one of the most popular magazines for the upper class is entitled *Town and Country*). Everyone else had to live a mile or two at most from where they worked. Once Henry Ford's mass production made automobiles affordable, people could live much farther from work. What's more, the rapid migration of large numbers of Blacks from the rural South to northern cities in the decades after the Civil War led to racial fears of crime and violence. The White middle classes began moving out of the cities altogether, into outlying areas called **suburbs,** where their houses were separate from the others, with front and back yards, just like upper-class estates, instead of the cramped apartments and townhouses of the cities. The expression "a man's home is his castle" arose during this period (Jackson, 1987). The first mass-produced suburb, Levittown, opened in an unincorporated area on Long Island in 1951. By the time it was finished in 1958, there were 17,311 houses, plus shopping areas, churches, and recreation centers.

Suburbia has also received its share of detractors. Folksinger Malvina Reynolds complained that the suburbs were made of "Little Boxes," that were "all made out of ticky-tacky, and they all look just the same," not only the houses but the people: identical families, White, middle-class, heterosexual, husband, wife, 2.5 kids. Many comedies of the 1950s begin with long lines of cars driven by identically dressed wives, who drop identically dressed husbands off at the train station for their identical commutes into the city. Suburbs were criticized as deadening, soul destroying, isolated. They created a generation of robots—of "men in gray flannel suits" and "Stepford wives." But people still moved there in huge numbers.

Why? Safety, or assumed safety—because cities were increasingly seen as crime infested, poor, and populated by more "dangerous" minorities. Comfort—one could have a larger home, with all the new technological amenities, like televisions and barbecue pits. Ease of life—including the ability to have a car. Suburbs promised "the good life," and Americans followed the call.

Federal policies and programs after World War II propelled the suburbanization of America. The GI Bill, federal mortgage programs, the creation of the interstate highway system, and massive infusions of public funds for commuter railroads and local schools provided the opportunity to move to the

Large cities around the world usually offer a variety of public transportation options to enable people to move about more easily and with less traffic—even in a snowstorm. But "mass transit" is typically used by the working class and minorities. Some middle class people take public transportation from the suburbs; their trains and buses are often sleek and modern. The upper class is driven—by taxi or limo.

The post-World War II era witnessed the greatest migration of black Americans from the south to northern cities—and the great migration of whites from those cities to newly developed sub-urbs. William Levitt saw suburbanization as political, as well as residential. "No man who owns his own home . . . can be a Communist," he said.

the 1960s, suburbs grew at four times the rate of cities.

Jobs and amenities went with them. Downtown stores closed one by one as gigantic suburban shopping malls opened. Downtown movie palaces (with one movie playing) closed as gigantic multiplexes opened next to the shopping malls (12 or more movies playing on peanut-sized screens). Downtown businesses relocated to "business parks" in the suburbs. Because the middle classes and the poor rarely saw each other anymore, they often had enormous misconceptions about each other.

Once suburban areas had their own jobs and amenities, they were no longer simply "bedroom communities," empty during the day as the workers trekked into the city for their jobs, but cities in their own right, called "edge cities," with their own economic focus (often high tech). Sometimes they are called "beltway cities," because they are clustered around the interstate highways that loop around major cities. You might live in the edge city of Grand Prairie, Texas, and work in Fort Worth, 22 miles away, though you are actually

suburbs. The desire for a better life, and home ownership, combined with "White flight" (the movement of White middle-class residents from city to suburbs) provided the motive. By

Sociology and Our World

Celebration, Florida

Celebration, Florida, is a "created suburb," laid out by the Disney Corporation in a rural area a short commute from Orlando and opened in 1996. Disney "imagineered" a small town right out of its own nostalgia movies. According to its website, Celebration is a "place where memories of a lifetime are made, it's more than a home; it's a community rich with old-fashioned appeal and an eye on the future" and "people are connecting in ways that build vibrant, caring, and enduring traditions."

Such vibrant, caring, and enduring traditions come with a hefty price tag (bungalows start at $443,000 and cottages at $524,000), and there are more regulations than in a convent or military barracks. Every new resident must abide by a "Declaration of Covenants" that dictates everything from how long cars may be parked on the street to the number of occupants per bedroom (two). Residents are seen as "representatives" of the Disney vision of America, performers just as

much as the costumed Mickeys and Goofys who roam Disney World.

Much of Celebration seems geared more toward tourists than to its residents. The Market Street shopping area contains six upscale restaurants and 14 shops selling jewelry, dolls, and gifts—but there is no grocery store, drug-store, or gas station. The list of activities and civic organizations includes a nondenominational community church, a Rotary Club, Little League, the D.A.R. (Daughters of the American Revolution), and a chapter of the Republican Party (but not the Democratic Party).

Some 8,000 people believe that it is worth being on constant display to live in a clean, well-maintained, safe community. And they are not alone. Disney may be the most famous example, but some 40 million Americans are now living in privately owned communities that regulate how long you can park in the street and with whom you can share your bedroom (Ross, 1999).

Figure 15.6 U.S. Cities and Prosperity

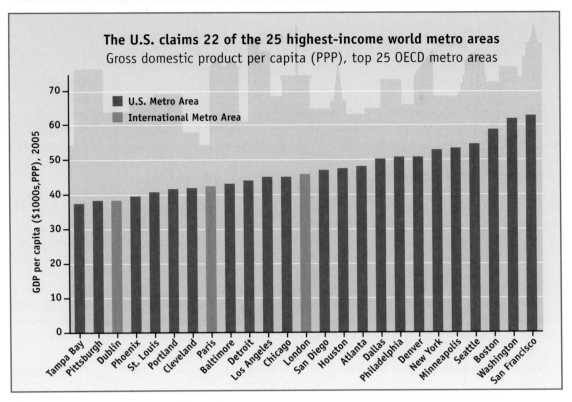

The U.S. claims 22 of the 25 highest-income world metro areas
Gross domestic product per capita (PPP), top 25 OECD metro areas

Legend:
■ U.S. Metro Area
■ International Metro Area

Y-axis: GDP per capita ($1000s, PPP), 2005

X-axis: Tampa Bay, Pittsburgh, Dublin, Phoenix, St. Louis, Portland, Cleveland, Paris, Baltimore, Detroit, Los Angeles, Chicago, London, San Diego, Houston, Atlanta, Dallas, Philadelphia, Denver, New York, Minneapolis, Seattle, Boston, Washington, San Francisco

(*Source:* Based on Figure 1.9. Ranking of OECD metro-regions by income in OECD (2006), *Competitive Cities in the Global Economy.* Copyright © OECD. Reproduced by permission.)

in a suburb of Dallas, 13 miles away. But it hardly matters because you depend on the nearby edge cities of Irving and Arlington to shop. Downtown is just for jury duty.

Revitalizing Downtown

During the 1980s and 1990s, many cities fought back, trying to revitalize their downtowns with hip shops, restaurants, and entertainment venues that would attract suburbanites looking for an evening of fun. Some especially hip young professionals even moved back in search of diversity and excitement, buying cheap houses and renovating them. Sometimes they took over whole downtown neighborhoods, raising the property values so much that poor and even middle-class people could no longer afford to live there (a process called **gentrification**). More commonly, cities annexed the suburbs, and any outlying areas that might become suburbs, so they could charge property tax.

Suburbs and edge cities are increasingly difficult to distinguish from inner cities. They have their own problems with traffic, crime, congestion, and pollution. Edge cities often have greater ethnic diversity than inner cities, in spite of "White flight" (Palen, 1995).

As suburbs expanded outward, it was inevitable that they would meet the suburbs of adjacent cities, until they all combined into one gigantic city, a **megalopolis.** These expanded metropolitan areas contain about two-thirds of the U.S. population and 68 percent of its jobs and generate about 75 percent of the gross domestic product (Brookings Institution, 2007). Megalopolises span hundreds of miles. You can drive from Nashua, New Hampshire (north of Boston), to Fairfax, Virginia (south of Washington, D.C.), through ten states and a bewildering number of city and county jurisdictions, without ever hitting unincorporated territory. Megalopolises face enormous structural problems. Their sheer size compounds the problems of air and water pollution, traffic congestion, crime, and joblessness. Civic improvement projects are often stalled by red tape, as different jurisdictions argue over whose responsibility they are.

Sociological Theories of the City

Many early sociologists were fascinated and appalled by life in cities. Ferdinand Töennies (1855–1936) theorized that families, villages, and perhaps neighborhoods in cities formed through *gemeinschaft,* or "commonality" (1957). They shared common norms, values, and beliefs. They had an instinctive trust; they worked together because they cared for each other. Instead, cities and states formed through *gesellschaft,* or "business company." They had differing, sometimes contradictory, norms, values, and beliefs. They had an instinctive mistrust. They worked together toward a definite, deliberate goal, not because they cared for each other but because everyone was acting to his or her own self-advantage.

Most sociologists today translate *gemeinschaft* and *gesellschaft* as "community" and "society," as two underlying motives for cementing bonds between people. Moving to the city undermines kinship and neighborhood, the traditional sources of social control and social solidarity. The personal freedom that the city provides comes at the cost of alienation.

The concepts of *gemeinschaft* and *gesellschaft* have been used most frequently to compare small towns and villages, where presumably everyone is one big happy family, with big cities, where presumably interpersonal connections are based on manipulation and fear. However, they can also be used to compare the "big happy family" of inner cities with the "isolation" of the suburbs.

Shortly after Töennies, Emile Durkheim theorized that village life was so much nicer because there was little division of labor. Almost everyone did the same work; they shared norms and values. Durkheim called this **mechanical solidarity,** a connection based on similarity. In the cities, by contrast, everyone was different: They worked at different jobs, they had different norms and values, they disagreed on what was right and wrong. What held them together was what he called **organic solidarity**—connections based on interdependence. Organic solidarity was more stable (if not as "nice") than mechanical solidarity because this interde-pendence meant that each individual was necessary to the functioning of the whole.

After working with the villagers of the Yucatan, anthropologist Robert Redfield (1941) decided that the division was not a matter of settlement size or division of labor but between rural (or "folk") and urban social networks. Folk societies are certainly characterized by homogeneity and a low division of labor; but, more importantly, the social networks are based on family. Family is everything. There are no friends or acquaintances. People who are not related to you by blood or marriage are by default enemies, unless you create sorts of fictional kinship ties in clans (presumed descent from a common ancestor) or in the common tradition of "blood brothers."

In urban societies, family is less important. Geographic mobility is greater, as is the emphasis on "chosen" communities—worplaces, neighborhoods—over kinship. You might call

Sociologists from Durkheim to Simmel to Jane Jacobs argued that, although frequently criticized as alienating and impersonal, urban neighborhoods are teeming with life and foster the development of cohesive communities.

your mother on her birthday and see the entire family over the Christmas holidays. "Secondary relationships"—friendships, work relationships—are more significant. In villages, kinship ties ensured that the person walking toward you would not rob or murder you. In cities, there was no such guarantee. There had to be rules of courtesy, and there had to be laws. The origins of the rituals such as shaking hands (to show you had no weapons) began in these new environments of strangers. Urban societies are more diverse, heterogeneous, and in constant flux.

In "The Metropolis and Mental Life" ([1902], 1971), the great German sociologist Georg Simmel worried about the overstimulation of the city environment. You are surrounded by so many sights and sounds, so many other humans, that you can't pay attention to everything. So, you pay attention to nothing. You develop a "blasé attitude." It is not that you are cold and unfeeling; it's that you have only enough brain cells to concentrate on your immediate concerns. If someone falls to the sidewalk in front of you, you might pass him or her by, assuming that someone in authority will provide the necessary assistance; anyway, it's none of your business.

On the other hand, in *The Death and Life of Great American Cities* (1961), urban analyst Jane Jacobs found that busy streets were not a source of overstimulation at all. Life happened on the street: Children played there; neighbors sat on stoops to gossip with each other; there was a sense of solidarity and belonging. In contrast, in the suburbs no one knew anyone else, and the streets were deserted except for people hurrying from their cars into their houses. Even deviance is under control in the city. Although many strangers are coming and going all the time, they are under constant scrutiny by people in the houses, who are making sure that nothing bad happens. But in the suburbs, no one is peering through windows, and deviance can go undetected.

Human Ecology

Looking at the spatial patterns of the city, sociologists noted that they share many characteristics in common with biological ecosystems. Both are based on the cooperative efforts of many specialized groups to distribute resources, eliminate waste, and maintain life. Even groups that seem scary and destructive serve a function: Predators are necessary to eat the herbivores and keep their population down, or else there would be so many of them that they would destroy the entire forest. In the same way, criminal activity demonstrates to the law-abiding population the limits on their behavior and creates a sense of "normalcy." Both human and biological systems are also extremely interdependent. A tiny problem with the smallest element can have catastrophic consequences for the whole. Just as the extinction of a "minor" species can destroy an entire ecosystem, the destruction of the roads leading into a city can lead to starvation and chaos in just a few days.

Human ecology arose as a discipline of the social sciences that looks at the interrelations of human beings within a shared social environment—the physical size and shape of the city, its social and economic dynamics, and its relationship to other cities and the natural world.

Urbanization. One of the most influential early studies of human ecology was Louis Wirth's "Urbanism as a Way of Life" (1938), drawing Durkheim and Töennies together to suggest that the move from villages to cities is not merely a change of residence but a change in the way people think and feel. He argued that people lose their kinship ties when they move from villages to cities; and, in the city, the size of the population, density, and social diversity make new social ties impossible to find. Therefore, they do not interact with people on more than a superficial level, resulting in loneliness and a feeling of rootlessness. Being around so many people leads to sensory overload, but now it makes city dwellers feel stressed and bad tempered—this is why when you walk down the street in a village, passersby will say "hello" to you, but in a city they pretend that you don't even exist.

The Urban Village. Herbert Gans (1962, 1968) disagreed with these human ecologists. He found that social networks are around the same size in both the city and the small town. You do not try to make friends with the one million people around you. You find community in a series of smaller worlds, people who share your tastes, interests, and socioeconomic background, just as you would in a village. Even slums, which to outsiders seem so threatening and merciless, can provide a strong sense of belonging to people.

Young people in America have always migrated to urban centers to start their careers and meet their future partners. Friends become the new family—as in the hit sit-com "How I Met Your Mother."

Gans (1968) found five types of people in the city:

- Cosmopolites—artists and intellectuals.
- Young, single professionals—people who would later be called Yuppies (young urban professionals, a term coined in the 1980s).
- Ethnic villagers—immigrants.
- The deprived—poor, often ethnic minorities.
- The trapped—poor elderly people.

Concentric Zones. Sociologists Robert Park, Ernest Burgess, and Robert McKenzie ([1925], 1967) studied how human ecology affected the use of urban space in the city. Inequalities of race and class (later sociologists added gender and sexual orientation) affected the distribution of resources. They believed that cities develop according to "concentric zones" of activity. These look much like the different zones in an archery target. Zone 1, the center of the city, is the political and cultural heart of the city, site of the most important businesses and government facilities and retail trade.

Zone 2 is an area of manufacturing and wholesale trade, providing the goods to sell in zone 1. It is also a zone of "social disorganization." Because no one has a sense of responsibility for the community, deviant activities such as crime, prostitution, and drunkenness, which would be swiftly dealt with in other zones, are allowed to flourish.

As people become upwardly mobile, they move away from the city core into zone 3 (working-class residential) and then into zone 4 (middle-class and upper-class residential). Or, if they are downwardly mobile, they move into

a zone closer to the city core. Zone 5 is a commuter zone.

The concentric zone theory may have characterized Chicago, at least for a period before middle-class flight to the suburbs.

Global Urbanization

For many years, urbanization was considered a sign of development, a sure sign that the nation was becoming richer and more prosperous. Recent trends suggest a more complicated picture (Figure 15.7). In 2000, 75 percent of the population of Latin America lived in urban areas, about the same as in the industrialized United States. Nearly half lived in cities with over one million inhabitants, and there were seven cities with more than 5 million: Mexico City, São Paulo, Buenos Aires, Rio de Janeiro, Bogotá, Lima, and Santiago. But the vast numbers of individuals moving to the city did not find sudden wealth.

Nearly half of the population of Latin America (43.4 percent) live in poverty, many in urban areas. More than one-third of urban dwellers live in slums. These vast neighborhoods in these cities lack adequate sanitation, housing, utilities, and police protection.

The gap between rich and poor is more noticeable in these urban centers than anywhere else in the world. In Rio de Janeiro, neighborhoods catering to tourists have a homicide rate of about 4 per 100,000. But in the favelas, slums only a few blocks away, the homicide rate can be as high as 150 per 100,000, among the highest in the world (Vanderschueren, 1996).

Figure 15.7 Urban Population of the World

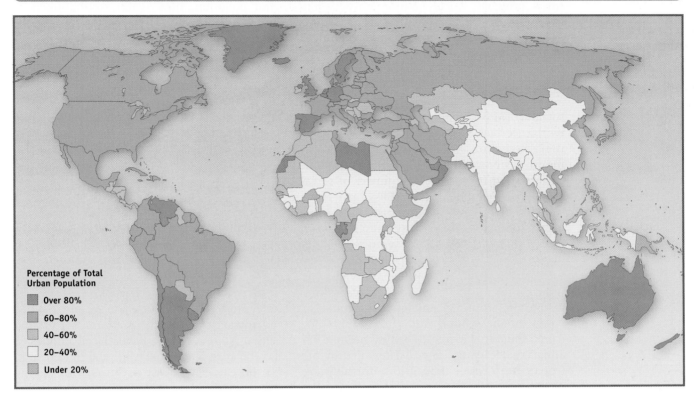

Percentage of Total Urban Population
- Over 80%
- 60–80%
- 40–60%
- 20–40%
- Under 20%

(*Source:* From Maps of the World website, www.mapsoftheworld.com. Reprinted with permission.)

Many cities around the world have global rather than local ties (Chase-Dunn, 1985). They are command centers not only of their own countries but also of the global economy. They are intimately involved in innovation and creation, producing not manufactured goods but information. They are more interdependent on each other than on the countries where they happen to be located. And they share a common culture of consumption. In New York, London, Tokyo, and, to a lesser extent, the second tier of global cities—Jakarta, Milan, Singapore, Rio de Janeiro—businessmen and -women armed with high-tech communication devices hold meetings in board rooms, read the *Financial Times* in English, and relax with American mass culture.

In 1991, Saskia Sassen introduced the term *global city*. She noted that New York, London, and Tokyo are actually located in three different countries on three different continents, with two languages in common use, so one might expect significant cultural differences. However, they have so many multinational ties that their exact location is meaningless. There are 2,500 foreign banks and financial companies in New York, employing one-quarter of all of the city's financial employees. National boundaries make little sense when the horizon of expectation for a city resident is the entire world.

The Natural Environment

Sociologists understand that the natural environment—the physical world, or more precisely, animals, plants, and the material substances that make up the physical world—is also organized into **ecosystems,** which are interdependent systems of organisms and their environment. Even if you have lived in Los Angeles your whole life and have never seen an open space other than a vacant lot, you are still participating in biological and geological ecosystems. You still breathe the air of the natural world. You drink its water, eat its food, and depend on its natural resources as raw materials for your manufactured products. Local natural disasters like fires and floods can disrupt your life as quickly as human warfare, and there are global environmental changes, slow-moving disasters, that threaten to disrupt all human life on the planet.

Early sociologists often theorized that the social world was a subcategory of the natural world. Herbert Spencer (1820–1903) argued that biological, social, psychological, and moral systems are all interrelated (2002). Others tried to analyze the impact of social life on the natural world. Ellsworth Huntington argued that Northern Europeans were so "advanced" because they lived in a tough climate, with harsh winters and the need to grow crops ([1915], 2001). Because they had to struggle to survive, they became industrious and hardworking. Meanwhile, people in tropical climates never had to worry about winter, and they could pick fruit right off the trees, so they became fat and lazy. He was wrong; sustenance in the tropics is no easier than in the north. There were "primitive" hunter-gatherers in the cold climates and advanced technological civilizations in the tropics.

After the first few decades of sociological thought, however, social sciences tended to ignore the environment, leaving it to the biologists, the geologists, and maybe the geographers. Sociology was about people, they figured, so why bother to worry about air and water pollution? Supplies were limitless, and even if they weren't limitless on Earth, we would soon be moving into space to mine the asteroid belt.

Then, during the 1970s, people began to envision Earth not as an infinite space, but as a small, fragile community, "Spaceship Earth" (Schnaiberg, 1980). Keep digging up iron and pumping out oil, and eventually there won't be any left. And, if we weren't going to be moving out to other planets, we had to make sure Earth stayed amenable for human life. The two most public environmental concerns of the 1970s were conservation, avoiding the depletion of natural resources, and pollution, avoiding "fouling our nest" (Schnaiberg, 1980).

At the same time, some sociologists began to criticize the discipline for being too "anthropocentric," or focused on human beings

(Catton and Dunlap, 1978). They began to look at the social production of conservation and pollution, how issues were framed as problems, how public perceptions and public policy could change, and the success or failure of environmental movements (Buttel, 1987). They looked into the role of technology in causing and potentially solving environmental problems (Bell, 2004; Hannigan, 1995; King, 2005). Finally, they looked at the problems themselves, what impact they were having on social relations, and how they might change social life in the future.

Energy and Other Resources

In 1900, even if your house was wired for electricity, you couldn't do much with it besides turn on electric lights. In 1930, you might have an electric telephone and radio; in 1960, an electric refrigerator, oven, and television set. In 2008, you would have a microwave oven, two or three television sets, a stereo system, several cell phones, a DVD player, a personal computer or two, and, in the garage, at least two cars. Our energy needs have skyrocketed. Sociologists want to know: What are the social implications of dependence on oil and the search for sustainable energy sources, like solar and hydroelectric? What sorts of political arrangements and business environments promote reliance of which types of energy (Rosa, Machlis, and Keating, 1988; Smil, 2005)?

The United States is by far the world's largest energy consumer, but not when consumption is calculated on a per capita basis (total amount of energy consumed divided by the population). In 2008, the United States consumed nearly 350 million BTU (British thermal units) of energy per capita; those countries with higher per capita rates tended to be either very cold (Norway), oil-producing nations (Kuwait, Norway, Qatar, United Arab Emirates), or small, underpopulated remote countries with very small and very wealthy populations where any essential service requires lots of energy to transport and provide (Netherlands Antilles, U.S. Virgin Islands, Gibraltar).

Only about 15 percent of energy consumed in the United States comes from renewable sources like nuclear, hydroelectric, geothermal, solar, or wind generators. The other 85 percent of our energy comes

Table 15.1

Environmental
Performance Index

Rank	Country	Score		Rank	Country	Score
1	Switzerland	95.5		14	United Kindgom	86.3
2	Sweden	93.1		15	Slovenia	86.3
3	Norway	93.1		16	Lithunia	86.2
4	Finland	91.4		17	Slovakia	86.0
5	Costa Rica	90.5		18	Portugal	85.8
6	Austria	89.4		19	Estonia	85.2
7	New Zealand	88.9		20	Croatia	84.6
8	Latvia	88.8		21	Japan	84.5
9	Columbia	88.3		22	Ecuador	84.4
10	France	87.8		23	Hungary	84.2
11	Iceland	87.6		24	Italy	84.2
12	Canada	86.6		25	Denmark	84.0
13	Germany	86.3		~39	United States	81.0

Prepared by the World Economic Forum, the Environmental Performance Index (EPI) evaluates the performance of 149 countries worldwide in areas including air pollution, sanitation, water resources and climate change. In 2008, the United States placed at the bottom of the Group of 8 industrialized countries, and 39th in the rankings overall.

Source: 2008 Environmental Performance Index.

from nonrenewable resources, especially oil and natural gas, by-products of millions of years of fossilization that stayed in the ground, undisturbed, until very recently. This is similar to global rates of consumption; worldwide, only 13.1 percent of the energy supply is from renewable sources like tide, solar, wind, and geothermal (*The Economist,* 2007).

Americans are 5 percent of the world's people, yet the United States consumes at least 25 percent of every type of energy and generates five times the world average of carbon dioxide (CO_2) emissions (Center for Environment and Population, 2008). Americans use about 20 million barrels of oil per day, far more than any other country in the world. Most wealthy countries use less than 2 million. At current levels of consumption, presuming no dependence on foreign oil, we have enough for 20 years (Roberts, 2005). And Americans use 64.4 billion cf (cubic feet) of natural gas per day, again far more than any other country in the world, twice as much as number two (Russia, with 38.8 billion cf). At current levels of consumption, we have enough for 34 years.

In addition, the United States produces 2.638 tetrawatt-hours of nuclear energy per million population per year, about the same as Bulgaria produces with six nuclear reactors. Sweden has 11 nuclear reactors and produces 7.288 tetrawatt-hours of nuclear energy per million population per year. Because we have invested so little in nuclear power in the past decades, our plants are old and inefficient, and there has been little effort to remain

Many of the new electronic gadgets that populate middle-class American homes consume greater and greater amounts of energy.

Chernobyl

The explosion of the nuclear power reactor at Chernobyl was the worst nuclear power plant accident in history. The radioactive fallout was 400 times greater than in Hiroshima after the atom bomb in 1945. Nuclear rain fell as far away as Ireland. Over 350,000 people were resettled as a result of the radioactivity.

competitive. This small investment is partly the result of political opposition to nuclear power, especially following the disasters at Three Mile Island, Pennsylvania, in 1979 and Chenobyl in what was then the Soviet Union (now in Ukraine) in 1986.

Vanishing Resources

Globally, forests are being depleted at the rate of one acre per second, depriving the world of a gigantic natural storage capacity for harmful carbon dioxide. Forests are unique in their capability to convert CO_2 during photosynthesis into carbon compounds that are then stored in wood, vegetation, and soil humus, a process called "carbon sequestration." Through this natural process, the world's forests store about one trillion tons of carbon—about one-and-a-half times the total amount found in the atmosphere. Deforestation, the clearing of these forests for crops and development, accounts for about 25 percent of all human-made emissions of carbon dioxide in the atmosphere—roughly the same amount as is produced by the United States, the world's largest polluter. Deforestation is often accomplished by burning, contributing to as much as 10 percent of the greenhouse effect (Bonnicksen, 2000). And, of course, the products that the forests might provide are also gone forever. The depletion of tropical rain forests is particularly disturbing because they cover only 7 percent of Earth's surface but account for up to 80 percent of the world's plant species, most of which have not been tested for medicinal effect.

Deforestation also results in the loss of topsoil because the cleared land is quick to erode. Covering huge stretches of land with concrete buildings and roads also increases erosion because there is nowhere for rainwater to go but onto undeveloped land. An estimated 26 billion tons of topsoil is being lost per year, transforming arable land into desert. The process of desertification can be seen in many parts of the world, especially sub-Saharan Africa.

Desertification, combined with the increased water use necessary for an increased population, means that the world is quickly losing groundwater—water tables are falling

in large swaths of many countries around the world, including the Great Plains and Southwest of the United States, most states in India, the entire northern half of China, and throughout the north of Mexico (Brown, 2005).

A final natural resource that we are quickly depleting is animal and plant species. We don't know exactly how many species there are—new ones are being discovered every day. But we do know that species are becoming extinct at a rate 1,000 times greater than before technological civilization, at a rate of 100 per day, usually as their natural environment is destroyed and they cannot adapt to their new surroundings. Worldwide, 25 percent of the world's mammals are threatened with extinction—a result of both habitat and hunting (International Union for Conservation of Nature, 2008). In the United States, the Fish and Wildlife Service lists 1,120 endangered animals, including such "common" animals as the brown bear, fox, otter, prairie dog, and red squirrel, as well as 748 endangered plants. Only a few hundred species have a specific economic or aesthetic value to humans, but we won't know which ones do and which do not if they disappear before we can test them. More important, however, is the contribution every species, even the most seemingly insignificant, makes to the delicate interbalance of an ecosystem. When an insect species goes extinct, the plant that it pollinated will die out soon, and then all of the animals that subsisted on that plant.

Environmental Threats

The natural environment is not only natural—it is "social" in that there is a constant interaction between the natural and the built environments, between people and the places where they live (and don't live), between nature and culture. The environment is today threatened by several human-created problems.

Pollution. There are three major sources of water pollution: domestic waste, industrial waste, and agricultural runoff. Indoor plumbing in urban areas means a huge amount of human waste, which is usually treated with toxic chemicals and then dumped into the nearest river. Many industrial processes require huge amounts of water, which is then dumped, along with more toxic chemicals. The petroleum industry is particularly prob-

Figure 15.8 Fossil Fuel Usage per Capita (World's 20 Largest Countries)

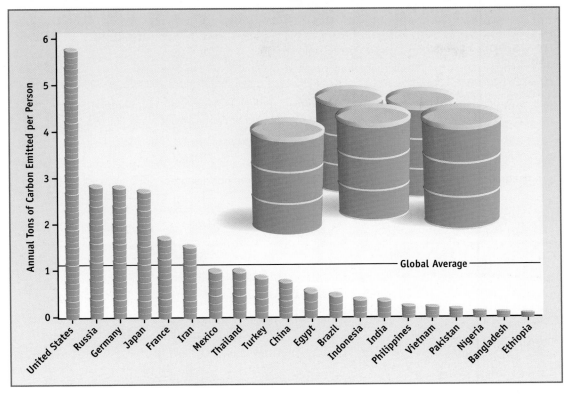

(*Source:* www.globalwarmingart.com.)

lematic; every year billions of gallons of oil are routinely deposited into the ocean during tank cleaning and other operations. Agricultural runoff includes not only topsoil but toxic pesticides and fertilizers. When it all ends up in the water supply, it can cause a huge number of unspecified health problems in humans.

Air pollution is concentrated in urban areas, the result of carbon monoxide, sulfur dioxide, and nitrogen oxide from cars, heaters, and industrial processes. These gases have a profound impact on the lungs and circulatory system; breathing the air in downtown Tokyo is the equivalent of smoking a pack of cigarettes every day. The gases have similar negative effects on every animal trying to breathe the same air, and when toxic gases combine with water molecules in the air, they can return to Earth as acid rain; enter lakes, rivers, and oceans through groundwater runoff; and destroy the ecosystems. Or they can rise up to the ozone layer, a band of oxygen isotopes 10 to 30 miles above Earth's surface, and bond with them, thus eliminating their effectiveness in shielding Earth from ultraviolet radiation. These invisible rays cause skin cancer, cataracts, and damage to the immune system and contribute to an increased production of carbon dioxide, which contributes to global warming.

Garbage. The 2008 State of Garbage in the U.S. report estimated that we produced 413 million tons of municipal solid waste, or MSW (household waste and waste from civic maintenance, like mowing parks and sweeping streets), an increase of 25 million tons since 2006. Seven percent was incinerated, just under 29 percent was recycled or composted, and 64.5 percent went into garbage dumps (Ljupka et al., 2008).

Many other countries are not as good at recycling. In poor countries, it typically doesn't happen at all: One hundred percent of waste

Warning to Future Civilizations

Some nuclear waste products will remain radioactive for 24,000 years—long after our civilization is forgotten. When the U.S. Department of Energy applied for permission to build a depository at Yucca Mountain, Nevada, they worried what would happen when future civilizations discovered what we had left behind. How to warn them? They decided on markers using six languages and a variety of symbols. In case everything is unknown to our descendants, they made the markers look unpleasant and foreboding, to give people an instinctive feeling of dread.

Did You Know?

Environmental Threats and Science

A great deal of controversy surrounds the topic of environmental threats. So, what do you think?

Many of the claims about environmental threats are greatly exaggerated.

○ Strongly agree

○ Agree

○ Neither agree nor disagree

○ Disagree

○ Strongly disagree

Modern science will solve our environmental - problems with little change to our way of life.

○ Strongly agree

○ Agree

○ Neither agree nor disagree

○ Disagree

○ Strongly disagree

What does **America** think?

(These are actual survey data from the General Social Survey, 2000.)

Less than 30 percent of respondents agreed or strongly agreed with this statement, and almost 43 percent disagreed or strongly disagreed. Those in the middle and upper classes were most likely to disagree, while those in the lower class were most likely to agree. Age and race differences were not significant.

Almost 50 percent of respondents disagreed or strongly disagreed with this statement, while only 22 percent agreed or strongly agreed. Those in the upper class were most likely to disagree.

Critical Thinking | Discussion Question

1. Why do you think there are social class differences in the survey responses?

References: See Davis et al., page 511.

goes into landfills. While rich countries have improved recycling rates over the last decade—46 percent of municipal waste is recycled in Germany, 39 percent in Belgium, 37 percent in Sweden, 34 percent in the United Kingdom (DEFRA, 2008; Eurostate, 2009)—landfills remain the predominant treatment for municipal waste throughout the OECD (OECD Key Environmental Indicators, 2009). Over 90 percent of municipal waste was landfilled in numerous Eastern European countries, including Latvia, Poland, and the Czech Republic (European Environment Agency, 2009).

Landfills pose two major problems. First, most of the garbage isn't biodegradable. Petroleum-based products, plastics, and styrofoam stay there forever, which means that the landfills fill up. A third of American landfills are already full, and by 2020, four-fifths of them will be full. There will be no place to put the garbage anymore.

When the garbage is biodegradable, it degrades into toxic chemicals, which seep into the groundwater and increase water pollution or into the air to increase air pollution. Degrading waste also increases the world's heat level, contributing to global climate change.

A particularly problematic kind of waste comes as a by-product of nuclear energy. Nuclear reactors produce waste that will be radio-active for thousands of years.

Climate Change. Since the nineteenth century, the global temperature has increased by about 0.6 degrees Celsius (1.08 degrees Fahrenheit), primarily because carbon dioxide, aerosols, and other gases released by human technology are prohibiting heat from escaping, resulting in a greenhouse effect. Many regions are already seeing an environmental impact: In Alaska and Canada, permafrost is thawing; 90 percent of the world's glaciers are in retreat. Because most of the world's major cities are on or near the ocean, a rise in the sea level due to melting glaciers and ice sheets could be catastrophic, like Hurricane Katrina with 200 million refugees. Other possible effects include a proliferation of hurricanes and extreme weather events, droughts and desertification, shortages of fresh water, and the extinction of species as their ecosystems are destroyed. Sociologists attempt to calculate the social ramifications of such climate shifts—where people will move, how they will survive—or even *if* they will survive (Figure 15.9).

The Sociology of Disaster

A disaster is a sudden environmental change that results in a major loss of life and property. It can be human orchestrated, such as a terrorist attack, or it can originate in nature, such as an earthquake or flood. Or it can be both. Bio-terrorism would involve unleashing a deadly disease like anthrax and causing a "natural" epidemic. A flu pandemic would involve the natural adaptability of the influenza virus, promoted by human factors like public health conditions, social mores and practices, and travel. The only operative term is "sudden," so that it comes on people with little or no warning.

For many years, sociologists were not much interested in disasters. They were interested in the social upheaval of wars and migration more than in fires and floods. One of the earliest sociological studies of a disaster was Kai T. Erikson's *Everything in Its Path* (1978), about the human response to a dam that burst and flooded Buffalo Creek in Logan County, West Virginia. One might expect survivors to experience long-term psychological trauma after losing many of their loved ones and everything they owned, but Erikson probed more deeply to investigate how they lost their individual and communal identity: The "furniture of self" had vanished.

In 1995, a week-long heat wave in Chicago was responsible for over 700 deaths. This was not a sudden catastrophe, so why were so many people unprepared? Eric Klineberg (2003) investigated the social conditions that led to and compounded the disaster. He found the obvious, that many poor and elderly people—and most of them Black women—had no air conditioning. Some were not aware of the neighborhood "cooling systems" or were afraid to go to them. Others did not realize that they were in danger; the news media downplayed the disaster, treating it as little more than a human-interest story.

The Asian tsunami of December 2004 that killed over 200,000 people may be too recent for a significant number of sociological studies, but they are certainly forthcoming, as is the study of the aftermaths of Hurricanes Katrina and Rita, as well as theorizing about the meaning of disaster in a sociology that has been too frequently concerned with societies as orderly and cohesive.

Garbage is among the most immediate environmental concerns, especially in countries with high levels of consumption. The United States dumps more than half of its garbage in landfills, but soon those landfills will be "land-full."

Figure 15.9 World Temperature Increases

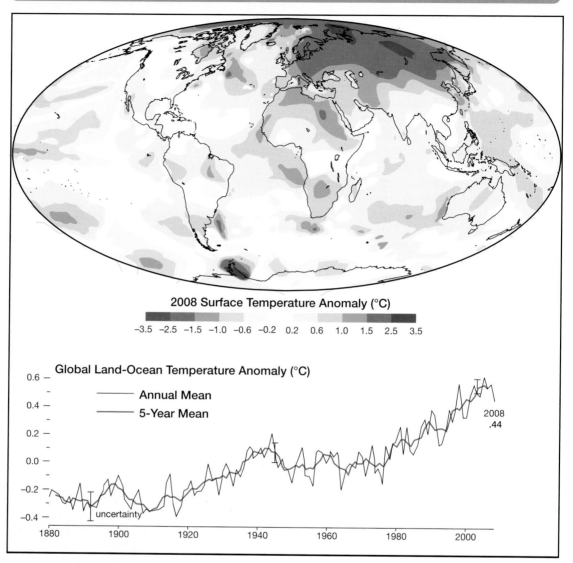

(*Source:* NASA, Earth Observatory 10th Anniversary, April 29, 2009.)

Environments in the Twenty-First Century

What do we do now? Do we sit alone in our room, waiting for the next hurricane, earthquake, tornado, nuclear accident, or biological pandemic, or a more gradual catastrophe caused by global warming, air pollution, desertification, or overpopulation? Do we play video games, eat nachos, and await the Apocalypse?

If Katrina and its aftermath have taught us anything, it is that we should be prepared. With foresight and planning, we can avoid some catastrophes altogether and lessen the impact of others. And one of the most important tools we have is a recognition of how the physical, urban, and human worlds interconnect. Nature is nurture—that is, the natural world does not exist except in relationship to the social and built worlds. City and countryside create each other; people are part of the ecosystem and also its greatest threat. Ignoring the interconnection nearly always leads to disaster. Recognizing and working with it may lead to a future.

Chapter Review

1. The Human Environment

Sociologists study not only our social environment but the interplay of the social and physical environment, too, because the human, the urban, and the natural are interdependent. **Demography** considers data on birth and death. Demographers look at **fertility, fecundity,** and **fertility rate** to understand a country. A low birth rate, as found in wealthy nations, means a country can't replace adults to care for the aging, although mobility increases, while poor nations have high birth rates, so there aren't enough resources for the children, or jobs for adults, although more children provide for aging parents. **Mortality rate** and **life expectancy** give insight into a nation's health. **Infant mortality rate** correlates with many quality of life factors and indicates how effective health policies are. Demographers look at population changes, including **immigration rate, emigration rate, net migration rate,** and **internal migration** and consider the push and pull factors behind these population changes. Economic opportunity and freedom in a region or nation is a pull, while oppression, discrimination, and lack of opportunity exert a push. The **population composition** and **population pyramid** are revealing. The former varies as a result of preferential selection for boy babies, environmental toxins, immigrant laborers, or wars; the latter by fertility and mortality.

demography The scientific study of human populations; one of the oldest and most popular branches of sociology. Demographers are primarily concerned with the statistics of birth, death, and migration. (p. 464)

fertility The number of children a woman bears. (p. 464)

fecundity The maximum number of children a woman could have during her childbearing years. (p. 464)

fertility rate The number of children who would be born to each woman if she lived through her childbearing years with the average fertility of her age group. (p. 464)

mortality rate The number of deaths per year for every thousand people. (p. 465)

life expectancy The average number of years a person can expect to live; varies greatly by country and region. (p. 465)

infant mortality rate The number of deaths per year in each thousand infants (up to one year old). (p. 465)

immigration rate The number of people entering a territory each year for every thousand of the population. (p. 467)

emigration rate Outflow of people from one society to another. (p. 467)

net migration rate The difference between immigration and emigration rates in a given year. (p. 467)

internal migration Moving from one region to another within a territory. (p. 468)

population composition The comparative numbers of men and women and various age groups in an area, region, or country. (p. 469)

population pyramid Type of graph that shows five- or ten-year age groups as different-sized bars, or "blocks." (p. 470)

2. Theories of Global Population Growth

In spite of other factors, with **natural population increase** the world's population is growing. In traditional society, children contribute to wealth, but few survive to adulthood, so birthrates are high; but, in modern society, children are expensive but also likely to survive. The population began to grow when prestigious large families combined with low mortality, but today almost all population growth is in poor nations. Changes in childbearing and agricultural production allowed us to avoid the disaster foretold by **Malthusian theory.** For Marx, the unequal distribution of resources was the main problem. One solution proposed to impending disaster due to overpopulation was **zero population growth.** **Demographic transition theory** implicates technology as a partner in population growth, through three stages of technological development and population changes, although this has been criticized for ignoring instances where the patterns differ and the theory doesn't fit and, when it does, overlooking the influence of social changes. Policies to reduce overpopulation include China's successful one child policy.

natural population increase Simple calculation of the number of deaths every year subtracted from the number of births. p. 471)

Malthusian theory Developed by the English economist and clergyman Thomas Robert Malthus (1766–1834), the theory held that population would increase by geometric progression, doubling in each generation—while the food supply would only increase arithmetically, leading to mass starvation, environmental disaster, and eventual human extinction. (p. 472)

zero population growth Paul Erlich's (1968) modern solution to Malthus's concerns, it entails a global effort to ensure that the number of births does not exceed the number of deaths, providing global population stability, a decrease in poor countries, and a redistribution of resources to those countries. (p. 473)

demographic transition theory Frank Notestein's (1945) theory that the population and technology spur each other's development. (p. 473)

3. The Urban Environment

Human settlements for most of our history were small villages amidst farmland; people could walk to their nearby fields. Surplus allowed larger villages, but ancient cities were quite small by modern standards and few in number. They were typically located on rivers to provide food for the bigger populations. Urbanization began in Europe with industrialization, as workers moved to work in factories. America began with few small cities and large farms but exceeded other parts of the world in the move to urbanization, due to industrialization. Urbanization correlates with wealth worldwide, with wealthier cities being more urban and having more large cities, while the poorest nations have rural populations and few, but very large, cities. Newer cities have lower **population density.**

Globalization has taken a toll on the countryside, and in many poor nations, cities are swelling as people move from the countryside into cities. The **suburb** developed in America with the automobile and with government policies enabling the middle class to live the "American Dream" outside cities swelling with immigrants, while commuting to work. **Gentrification** drew the middle class back into cities. About two-thirds of Americans now live in a **megalopolis.**

population density The number of people per square mile or kilometer. (p. 476)

suburb A residential community outside of a city but always existing in relationship to the city. (p. 477)

gentrification The process by which poorer urban neighborhoods are "upgraded" through renovation and development, often pushing out long-time residents of lesser means who can no longer afford to live there. (p. 479)

megalopolis A term coined by Jean Gottmann in 1961 to describe the integration of large cities and sprawling suburbs into a single organic urbanized unit, such as "Bo Wash," the Boston to Washington, D.C., corridor that includes New York and Philadelphia as well as the suburbs. (p. 479)

4. Sociological Theories of the City

Sociologists often prefer villages to cities. Töennies emphasized the connection and trust people had living together in villages, in *gemeinschaft*, or "commonality," while people in cities and suburbs organized by *gesellschaft* or "business company," and were isolated, mistrustful, self-interested, and without connection. Durkheim found villages had **mechanical solidarity,** while cities had **organic solidarity.** Anthropologists found the nature of the social network, kin or nonkin, is responsible for the observed differences, rather than size of community or work. Cities may lead us to withdraw and isolate ourselves from the barrage of stimulation or to participate in the vibrant social life around us. **Human ecology** studies these phenomena. Gans found social networks were the same size, whether urban or rural; city dwellers just found smaller groups for belonging. He identified five types of city dwellers. Others looked at the concentric zones of activity in cities, typified by Chicago, and how these zones related to social class, among other factors, and how people moved when upwardly or downwardly mobile. The global picture is complex. In some large cities in Latin America, people are poorer, not wealthier, and the gap between rich and poor is great. "Global cities" have so many multinational ties that their physical location is relatively meaningless.

mechanical solidarity Durkheim's term for a traditional society where life is uniform and people are similar. They share a common culture and sense of morality that bonds them. (p. 480)

organic solidarity Emile Durkheim's term for a modern society where people are interdependent because of the division of labor; they disagree on what is right and wrong but share solidarity because the division of labor makes them dependent on each other. (p. 480)

human ecology A social science discipline that looks at the relations among people in their shared environments. (p. 481)

5. The Natural Environment

We are part of an **ecosystem.** Spencer conceptualized interrelated subsystems, including the biological, psychological, social, and moral. Huntington saw climate and human behavior as related; he wrongly assumed life was easier in the tropics, with readily available food, and harder in the north, resulting in northern industriousness, ignoring the facts of hunter-gatherers in the north and advanced technology in the south. The 1970s brought renewed interest in the ecosystem and environmental concerns, including conservation and pollution. Energy is particularly important now. Sociologists consider how business and political relationships relate to energy policy and use. America's energy consumption, and contribution to global CO_2, is huge, although colder and isolated countries use more energy per capita. In America, as in the rest of the world, a small percentage of energy is from renewable sources. Another environmental concern is deforestation. Forests are vital for carbon sequestration. Deforestation removes potential pharmaceutical species; burning increases greenhouse gas; arable land becomes desert when topsoil is washed away; and more water is then needed, further depleting the water table. Other human-created ecological problems include air pollution, resulting in health problems, garbage storage, and even climate change. Sociologists are studying sudden disasters—how they disrupt our lives and why we aren't prepared or don't recognize them when they are occurring.

ecosystem An interdependent system in which the animals, plants, and the material substances that make up the physical world live. (p. 483)

6. Environments in the Twenty-First Century

We are a part of nature. We have a social world, and we modify our environment, but we are also part of the natural world, all of which have an impact on one another. We can best prepare for disaster by recognizing how human, physical, and urban worlds are interconnected. By doing this we can best prepare, and perhaps even prevent, forthcoming disasters. By understanding, we can create better futures.

Self-Test: Check Your Understanding

1. Which of the following is commonly used as an indicator of a nation's health policies, and general quality of life overall?
   a. Population composition
   b. Infant mortality rate
   c. Net migration rate
   d. Mortality rate

2. Who is notable for a theory of disaster resulting from geometric population growth and arithmetic growth of food sources, resulting in starvation and extinction?
   a. Thomas Malthus
   b. Karl Marx
   c. Herbert Gans
   d. Emile Durkheim

3. *Gemeinschaft* is found in:
   a. cities.
   b. suburbs.
   c. villages.
   d. All of the above have *gemeinschaft*.

4. Gans's "urban village" refers to:
   a. suburbs.
   b. rural town centers.
   c. global cities.
   d. social groups and neighbors.

5. According to Durkheim, villages have _____ while cities have _____.
   a. mechanical solidarity; organic solidarity
   b. *gemeinschaft; gesellschaft*
   c. organic solidarity; mechanical solidarity
   d. *gesellschaft; gemeinschaft*

6. The return of the middle class and professionals to urban centers is referred to as:
   a. "White flight."
   b. gentrification.
   c. urban villages.
   d. urbanization.

7. All of the following are types of city dwellers identified by Gans, except:
   a. ethnic villagers.
   b. cosmopolites.
   c. the trapped.
   d. dinks—dual income, no kids.

8. All of the following were identified in the text as important benefits of forests, except:
   a. carbon sequestration.
   b. habitat for diverse species.
   c. increased CO_2 emissions.
   d. prevention of erosion.

Self-Test Answers: 1. b, 2. a, 3. c, 4. d, 5. a, 6. b, 7. d, 8. c

Integrate and Explore: Points to Consider

1. How have people fared, generally, with the transition from rural to urban life? Does this hold for all cities? Has cultural diversity increased, or decreased, with the advent of global cities?

2. How is our social world affected by the natural world? How is the natural world affected by our social world? Do you think it is more useful to focus on technological solutions to ecological problems, or to human solutions? Is it possible to have one without the other?

succeed with mysoclab PEARSON

Self-scoring practice tests, flashcards for learning key terms, streaming audio of the entire text, and multimedia, including:

Watch—*World Population Report*
Watch—*World Climate Change*
Explore—*Toxic Town*
Explore—*Endangered Wheat*
MySocLibrary—Lester R. Brown, Gary Gardner, and Brian Halweil, *Sixteen Impacts of Population Growth*

Glossary

absolute poverty A global problem that afflicts half the world's population, the term for people who are so poor they do not have the ability to sustain their lives and lack the most basic necessities like food and shelter.

achieved status Status or social position based on one's accomplishments or activities.

adolescence Term coined by psychologist G. Stanley Hall (1904) to name the years coinciding with puberty as a distinct—and perilous—life stage.

Adonis complex Term coined by psychiatrist Harrison Pope and his colleagues for the belief that men must look like Greek gods, with perfect chins, thick hair, rippling muscles, and washboard abdominal muscles.

affirmative action Programs and policies developed to ensure that qualified minority group members are not discriminated against in the workplace, school admission, and the like. Affirmative action policies generally apply to race, ethnicity, and gender, among other categories.

age cohort A group of people who are born within a specific time period and therefore assumed to share both chronological and functional characteristics, as well as life experiences.

age norms Distinctive cultural values, pursuits, and pastimes that are culturally prescribed for each age cohort.

ageism Term coined by physician Robert Butler to refer to differential treatment based on age—usually the elderly rather than the young.

agents of socialization The people, groups, or institutions that teach people how to be functioning members of their society.

anomie A term developed by Emile Durkheim to describe a state of disorientation and confusion that results from too little social regulation, in which institutional constraints fail to provide a coherent foundation for action.

anorexia nervosa A potentially fatal syndrome characterized by chronic and dangerous starvation dieting and obsessive exercise.

anticipatory socialization The process of learning and adopting the beliefs, values, and behaviors of groups that one anticipates joining in the future.

apartheid A race-based caste system that mandated segregation of different racial groups. In South Africa it was a political system institutionalized by the White minority in 1948 and remained in effect until 1990.

ascribed status Status that is assigned to a person and over which he or she has no control.

asexual Having no sexual desire for anyone.

assimilation Occurs when two groups come into contact and the minority group abandons its traditional culture to embrace the dominant culture.

authoritarian political system When power is vested in a single person or small group. Sometimes that person holds power through heredity, sometimes through force or terror.

authority Power that is perceived as legitimate, by both the holder of power and those subject to it. For a leader to exercise power, the people must believe he or she is entitled to make commands and that they should obey; indeed, that they want to obey.

bilateral descent Tracing one's ancestry through both parents, rather than only the mother (*see* matrilineal) or only the father (*see* patrilineal).

bisexuality Feeling attracted to sexual partners of both sexes.

blog Short for "weblog"; online opinion site.

bourgeoisie Popularized by Karl Marx, term for the upper-class capitalists who owned the means of production. In Marx's time, they owned factories instead of farms. Today the term is also used to refer to upper-class managers who wield a lot of power.

broken windows theory Philip Zimbardo's proposition that minor acts of deviance can spiral into severe crime and social decay. Atmosphere and context are keys to whether deviance occurs or spirals.

Buddhism Founded by Siddhartha Gantana, later called Buddha, it teaches that enlightenment is possible in this lifetime, through the Tenfold Path. There are two main branches–Hinayana and Mahayana. Today there are 376 million Buddhists, mostly in East Asia.

bulimia A potentially fatal syndrome characterized by food "binging and purging" (eating large quantities and then either vomiting or taking laxatives or enemas to eliminate it).

bureaucracy Originally derived from the French word *bureau,* or office, a formal organization characterized by a division of labor, a hierarchy of authority, formal rules governing behavior, a logic of rationality, and an impersonality of criteria.

bureaucratic personality Robert Merton's term to describe those people who become more committed to following the correct procedures than they are to getting the job done.

canon   The officially recognized set of foundational sociologists.

capital   Natural resources, manufactured goods, and professional services.

capitalism   An economic system in which free individuals pursue their own private interests in the marketplace. In laissez-faire capitalism, markets freely compete without government intervention. State capitalism requires that the government use a heavy hand in regulating and constraining the marketplace, and welfare capitalism creates a market-based economy for most goods and services, yet also has social welfare programs and government ownership of essential services.

caste system   A fixed and permanent stratification system to which one is assigned at birth.

causality   The term used when one variable causes another to change.

charismatic authority   Authority derived from the personal appeal of a specific leader.

charismatic leader   A person whose extraordinary personal qualities touch people enough to break with tradition and follow him or her.

charter schools   Privatization-oriented school reform initiative in which schools are financed through taxpayer funds but administered privately.

christianity   The world's largest religion today, it was founded 2,000 years ago by the disciples of Jesus, who declared him to the be the son of God.

chronological age   A person's age as determined by the actual date of his or her birth.

class system   System of stratification in which people are ranked according to their economic position.

class   A group of people sharing the same social position in society. Class is based on income, power, and prestige.

cluster sample   A sampling technique used when "natural" groupings are evident in the population. The total population is divided into these groups (or clusters), and a sample of the groups is selected. Then the required information is collected from the elements within each selected group.

coercive organization   One in which membership is not voluntary, with elaborate formal rules and sanctions.

cohabitation   Once called "shacking up" or "living in sin," now more often called just "living together," the sociological term for people who are in a romantic relationship but not married living in the same residence.

colonialism   A political-economic system under which powerful countries establish, for their own profit, rule over weaker peoples or countries and exploit them for natural resources and cheap labor.

communism   Envisioned as the ideal economic system by Karl Marx, communism would produce and distribute resources "from each according to his or her ability, to each according to his or her need," erasing social inequalities along with crime, hunger, and political strife.

companionate marriage   The (comparatively recent) idea that people should select their own marriage partner based on compatibility and mutual attraction.

conflict theory   Theoretical approach that stresses the competition for scarce resources and unequal distribution of those resources based on social status (such as class, race, gender).

confounding variables   The things that might get in the way of an accurate measurement of the impact of one variable on another.

Confucianism   Ethical and philosophical system developed from the teachings of the Chinese sage Confucius that focuses primarily on secular ethics and the cultivation of the civilized individual to create a civilized and peaceful society.

conspicuous consumption   Thorstein Veblen's term to describe a new form of prestige based on accumulating and displaying possessions.

consumer crime   Crime in which the perpetrator uses a fake or stolen credit card to buy things for him- or herself or for resale. Such purchases cost both retailers and, increasingly, "e-tailers" over $1 billion per year, or nearly five cents for every dollar spent online.

consumption   The purchase and use of goods and services.

content analysis   Research method in which one analyzes artifacts (books, movies, TV programs, magazine articles, and so on) instead of people.

control group   In an experiment, the comparison group that will not experience the manipulation of the independent variable (the experimental group). Having a control group enables sociologists to compare the outcomes of the experiment to determine if the changes in the independent variable had any effects on the dependent variable.

control theory   Travis Hirschi's theory that people perform a cost-benefit analysis about becoming deviant, determining how much punishment is worth the degree of satisfaction or prestige the deviance will confer.

corporation   A business that is treated legally as an individual. It can make contracts, incur debts, sue, and be sued, but its obligations and liabilities are legally distinct from those of its owners.

correlation   The term for the fact of some relationship between two phenomena.

counterculture   Subculture that identifies itself through its difference and opposition to the dominant culture.

coup d'état   The violent replacing of one political leader with another; often doesn't bring with it any change in the daily life of the citizens.

credential society   A society based more on the credentialing aspects of education than any substantive knowledge.

crime   A deviant act that lawmakers consider bad enough to warrant formal laws and sanctions.

crowd An aggregate of individuals who happen to be together but experience themselves as essentially independent.

cult The simplest form of religious organization, characterized typically by fervent believers and a single idea or leader.

cultural capital French sociologist Pierre Bourdieu's term for the cultural articles—ideas, artistic expressions, forms of music or literature—that function as resources that people in the dominant class can use to justify their dominance.

cultural diffusion The spreading of new ideas through a society, independent of population movement.

cultural diversity Describes the vast differences between the cultures of the world as well as the differences in belief and behavior that exist within cultures.

cultural imperialism The deliberate imposition of one country's culture on another country.

cultural relativism A position that all cultures are equally valid in the experience of their own members.

cultural universal Rituals, customs, and symbols that are evident in all societies.

culture industries The idea that American media productions are industrial products like any other product, a mode of production that empties them of original or complex content and soon renders their audiences passive and uncritical.

culture lag The relatively gradual process by which non-material elements of culture catch up with changes in material culture and technology.

culture of poverty Oscar Lewis's theory that poverty is not a result of individual inadequacies but larger social and cultural factors. Poor children are socialized into believing that they have nothing to strive for, that there is no point in working to improve their conditions. As adults, they are resigned to a life of poverty, and they socialize their children the same way. Therefore poverty is transmitted from one generation to another.

culture shock A feeling of disorientation when the cultural markers that we rely on to help us know where we are and how to act have suddenly changed.

culture Both the material basis for social life and the sets of values and ideals that we understand to define morality, good and evil, appropriate and inappropriate.

cybercrime The growing array of crimes committed via the Internet and World Wide Web, such as Internet fraud and identity theft.

data The plural of datum. Data are systematically collected and systematically organized bits of information.

deductive reasoning Reasoning that logically proceeds from one demonstrable fact to the next. It often moves from the general to the more specific.

democracy Derived from the Greek word *demos* (people); puts legislative decision making into the hands of the people rather than a single individual or a noble class.

demographic transition theory Frank Notestein's (1945) theory that the population and technology spur each other's development.

demography The scientific study of human populations; one of the oldest and most popular branches of sociology. Demographers are primarily concerned with the statistics of birth, death, and migration.

denomination A large-scale, extremely organized religious body with established hierarchy and methods for credentialing administrators.

dependency theory Theory of poverty that focuses on the unequal relationship between wealthy countries and poor countries, arguing that poverty is caused by policies and practices by the rich that block economic growth of poor countries and exploit workers.

dependent variable The variable whose change depends on the introduction of the independent variable.

detached observation A perspective that constrains the researcher from becoming in any way involved in the event he or she is observing. This reduces the amount that the researchers' observations will change the dynamic that they are watching.

deviance Breaking or refusing to follow a social rule. The rule can be societywide or specific to a particular group or situation.

dictatorship A type of totalitarian political system in which power is held by one person, who may or may not have a hereditary claim on power, usually with military support.

differential association Edwin H. Sutherland's theory suggesting that deviance occurs when an individual receives more prestige and less punishment by violating norms than by following them.

discrimination A set of actions based on prejudice and stereotypes.

disinterestedness The scientific norm that stipulates scientific research should not be pursued for personal goals, but in the pursuit of scientific truth.

dramaturgy Erving Goffman's conception of social life as being like a stage play wherein we all work hard to convincingly play ourselves as "characters," such as grandchild, buddy, student, employee, or other roles.

dual labor market A theory of economic inequality in the labor market between the "primary" sector, characterized by high wage, high benefits jobs and the "secondary" market, characterized by low wage, few benefits, and seasonal or marginal employment. A "gendered" dual labor market indicates that the level of sex segregation in the labor force is high.

dyad A group of two people, the smallest configuration defined by sociologists as a group.

ecclesiae Religious institutions so pervasive that the boundary between church and state is nonexistent and in which the clerical elite also serves the political elite.

economic system A mechanism that deals with the production, distribution, and consumption of goods and services in a particular society.

economy A set of institutions and relationships that manage capital.

ecosystem   An interdependent system in which the animals, plants, and the material substances that make up the physical world live.

education   A social institution through which society provides its members with important knowledge—basic facts, job skills, and cultural norms and values. It provides socialization, cultural innovation, and social integration. It is accomplished largely through schooling, formal instruction under the direction of a specially trained teacher.

ego   Freud's term for the balancing force between the id and the superego; it channels impulses into socially acceptable forms.

emigration rate   Outflow of people from one society to another.

empirical verification   The scentific way of learning answers to questions, in which knowledge is developed, demonstrated, and double-checked through experiments.

ethnic group   A group that is set apart from other groups by language and cultural traditions. Ethnic groups share a common ancestry, history, or culture.

ethnicity   Social category that depends on an assumption of inherent cultural differences to rate and organize social groups.

ethnocentrism   The use of one's own culture as the reference point by which to evaluate other cultures; it often depends on or leads to the belief that one's own culture is superior to others.

ethnography   A type of field method in which the researcher inserts him- or herself into the daily world of the people he or she is trying to study to understand the events from the point of view of the actors themselves.

ethnomethodology   The study of the social knowledge, codes, and conventions that underlie everyday interactions and allow people to make sense of what others say and do.

evolutionary imperative   The term used to imply that the chief goal of all living creatures is to reproduce themselves.

exogamy   The insistence that marriage to (or sex with) members of your family unit is forbidden. This is the incest taboo, which Sigmund Freud argued was the one single cultural universal.

experiment   A testing process that is performed under controlled conditions to examine the validity of a hypothesis.

experimental group   In an experiment, the group that will have the change introduced to see what happens. (*See* control group.)

extended family   The most common model in the pre-modern era, the family model in which two or three generations lived under the same roof or at least in the same compound: grandparents, parents, unmarried uncles and aunts, married uncles and aunts, sisters, brothers, cousins, and all of their children.

extraneous variables   Variables that influence the outcome of an experiment but are not the variables that are actually of interest.

face work   In dramaturgical theory, the possible performance of ourselves, because when we make a mistake or do something wrong, we feel embarrassed, or "lose face."

fad   Short-lived, highly popular, and widespread behavior, style, or mode of thought.

family of origin   A child's biological parents or others who are responsible for his or her upbringing.

family of procreation   The family one creates through marriage or cohabitation with a romantic partner. Today, we consider any adults living together as a family of procreation, even if none of them is actually doing any procreating.

family   The basic unit in society, it traditionally consists of two parents rearing their children but may also be any of various social units differing from but regarded as equivalent to the traditional family, such as single parents with children, spouses without children, and several generations living together.

fan   Someone who finds significant personal meaning through a heightened awareness of and allegiance toward a specific media text—a story, a series, a performer. Fandom is a public affiliation, a public proclamation that your allegiance to some media product reveals a core element of your identity.

fashion   A behavior, style, or idea that is more permanent and often begins as a fad.

fecundity   The maximum number of children a woman could have during her childbearing years.

feminism   A system of beliefs and actions that rests on two principles: gender inequality defines our society; and such inequality is wrong and must change.

feminization of poverty   A worldwide phenomenon that also afflicts U.S. women, this term describes women's over-representation among the world's poor and tendency to be in worse economic straits than men in any given nation or population.

feminization of the professions   The phenomenon in which salaries drop as female participation increases, revealing that it is less the intrinsic properties of the position that determine its wages and prestige and more which sex occupies it.

fertility rate   The number of children who would be born to each woman if she lived through her childbearing years with the average fertility of her age group.

fertility   The number of children a woman bears.

feudalism   A fixed and permanent social structure based on mutual obligation, in which peasants worked the estates belonging to a small group of feudal lords, who fed and protected them. A peasant's only avenue to social advancement was to enter a convent or monastery.

folkway   One of the relatively weak and informal norms that are the result of patterns of action. Many of the behaviors we call "manners" are folkways.

for-profit university   An institution of higher learning that is proprietary and is characterized by lower tuition costs and a faster path to degrees for students. Facilities are usually limited, and faculty is not tenured.

functional age   A set of observable characteristics and attributes that are used to categorize people into different age cohorts.

functionalism (or structural-functionalism) Sociological theory that stressed the interconnectedness of social institutions forming stable and orderly social systems.

gender identity   Our understanding of ourselves as male or female and what it means to be male or female, perhaps the most fundamental way in which we develop an identity.

gender inequality   Gender inequality has two dimensions: the domination of men over women, and the domination of some men over other men and some women over other women.

gender roles   Psychology-based term to define the bundle of traits, attitudes, and behaviors that are associated with biological males and females. Roles are blueprints that prescribe what you should do, think, want, and look like, so that you can successfully become a man or a woman.

gender socialization   Process by which males and females are taught the appropriate behaviors, attitudes, and traits for their biological sex. It begins at birth and continues throughout their lives.

gender wage gap   The significant and remarkably consistent gap between earnings of men and women. The gap between White men and women of color is larger than between White men and White women.

gender   A socially constructed definition based on sex category, based on the meanings that societies attach to the fact of sex differences.

generalizability   Also called external validity or applicability; the extent to which the results of a study can be generalized to the general population.

generalized other   The organized rules, judgments, and attitudes of an entire group. If you try to imagine what is expected of you, you are taking on the perspective of the generalized other.

genocide   The planned, systematic destruction of a racial, political, or ethnic group.

gentrification   The process by which poorer urban neighborhoods are "upgraded" through renovation and development, often pushing out long-time residents of lesser means who can no longer afford to live there.

gerontology   Scientific study of the biological, psychological, and sociological phenomena associated with old age and aging.

global commodity chain   Worldwide network of labor and production processes, consisting of all pivotal production activities that form a tightly interlocked "chain" from raw materials to finished product to retail outlet to consumer. The most profitable activities in the commodity chain (engineering, design, advertising) are likely to be done in core countries, while the least profitable activities (mining or growing the raw materials, factory production) are likely to be done in peripheral countries.

global distribution   Describes how the products we buy are likely made of materials from several countries, assembled in another country, packaged and distributed from yet another, with advertising campaigns and marketing schemes drawn from yet another.

global inequality   Systematic differences in wealth and power among countries, often involving exploitation of the less powerful by the more powerful countries.

global production   A term that describes how, in a global economy, goods are manufactured from raw materials and produced in factories all over the world in complex production chains.

global village   Marshall McLuhan's term for his vision of the way global electronic media would unite the world through mutual interaction and involvement.

globalization   A set of processes leading to the development of patterns of economic, cultural, and social relationships that transcend geographical boundaries; a widening, deepening, and speeding up of worldwide interconnectedness in all aspects of contemporary life.

government   The organization and administration of the actions of the inhabitants of communities, societies, and states.

group cohesion   The degree to which individual members of a group identify with each other and with the group as a whole.

group marriage   Rare marriage arrangement in which two or more men marry two or more women, with children born to anyone in the union "belonging" to all of the partners equally.

group   Collection of individuals who are aware that they share something in common and who interact with one another on the basis of their interrelated roles and statuses.

groupthink   Irving Janis's term for social process in which members of a group attempt to conform their opinions to what they believe to be the consensus of the group, even if, as individuals, they may consider that opinion wrong or unwise.

hardcore members   The small number of group members, the "inner circle," who wield a great deal of power to make policy decisions.

hate crime   A criminal act committed by an offender motivated by bias against race, ethnicity, religion, sexual orientation, or disability status.

heterosexism   Institutionally based inequalities that may derive from homophobia.

heterosexuality   The most common sexual orientation worldwide, it is sexual attraction between people of different sexes.

hidden curriculum   Means of socialization through which education not only creates social inequalities but makes them seem natural, normal, and inevitable.

Hinduism   Developed in India around 1500 BCE., it believes in many gods, but most of the time people revere one of the three main Brahmin (creator of life); Vishnu (preserver of life); or Shiva (destroyer or renewer of life). Today there are 900 million Hindus, mostly in South Asia and in Indian communities worldwide.

homophobia   A socially approved dislike of gay men and lesbians.

homosexuality   Sexual desire toward members of one's own gender.

hooking up   A sexual encounter that may or may not include sexual intercourse, usually occurring on only one occasion between two people who are strangers or brief acquaintances.

human ecology   A social science discipline that looks at the relations among people in their shared environments.

hypothesis   A testable explanation for an event or phenomenon that assumes a relationship between two or more variables.

id   Sigmund Freud's label for that part of the human personality that is pure impulse, without worrying about social rules, consequences, morality, or other people's reactions.

immigration rate   The number of people entering a territory each year for every thousand of the population.

immiseration thesis   Marx's theory that, as capitalism proceeded, the rich would get richer and the poor would get poorer, and that eventually the poor would become so poor that they had nothing else to lose and would revolt.

impression management   Erving Goffman's term for our attempts to control how others perceive us by changing our behavior to correspond to an ideal of what they will find most appealing.

independent variable   In an experimental study, the agent of change, the ingredient that is added to set things in motion.

inductive reasoning   Research in which one reasons to a conclusion about all or many members of a class based on examination of only a few members of that class. Loosely, it is reasoning from the specific to the general.

industrial economy   Economy based on factory production and technologies.

Industrial Revolution   Transformation of the economy due to a large-scale shift from home-based craft work by individuals to machine-based mass production in factories.

infant mortality rate   The number of deaths per year in each thousand infants (up to one year old).

in-group heterogeneity   The social tendency to be keenly aware of the subtle differences among the individual members of your group.

in-group   A group with which you identify and that you feel positively toward, producing a "we" feeling.

institutional discrimination   The most subtle and pervasive type of discrimination, it is deeply embedded in such institutions as the educational system, the business world, health care, criminal justice, and the mass media. These social institutions promote discriminatory practices and traditions that have such a long history they just "seem to make sense," and minority groups become the victims of systematic oppression, even when only a few people, or none at all, are deliberately trying to discriminate.

integration   The physical intermingling of the races organized as a concerted legal and social effort to bring equal access and racial equality through racial mixing in institutions and communities.

interest group   Also called special interest group, pressure group, and lobby, such a group promotes its interests among state and national legislators and often influences public opinion. There are two kinds: Protective groups represent only one trade, industry, minority, or subculture; promotional groups seek to represent the interests of the entire society.

intergenerational mobility   Change in social class position, upward or downward, that takes place between generations. Your chances of getting ahead or falling behind the social class position of your parents is largely influenced by family income; those at the top tend to stay at the top or move even higher; those at the bottom tend to stay at the bottom or move even lower.

internal colony   Internal colonialism is a theory of race relations that argues that the position of African Americans in the United States is analogous to the position of colonies to the imperialist powers at the turn of the twentieth century. An internal colony is the name for the subjugated group.

internal migration   Moving from one region to another within a territory.

interpretive communities   Groups that share certain assumptions and interpretations of any cultural form (a text, for example). This sociological argument means that texts do not have meaning outside of the set of cultural assumptions groups of people bring to them.

intervening variable   A variable that helps explain a perceived relationship between an independent variable and a dependent variable. For example, in Pavlov's experiment on bell-ringing (independent) and dogs salivating (dependent), an intervening variable might have been the relative intelligence of the dogs themselves.

interview   Research method in which a researcher asks a small group of people open-ended questions.

intimate partner violence (IPV)   Violence, lethal or nonlethal, experienced by a spouse, ex-spouse, or cohabiting partner; boyfriend or girlfriend; or ex-boyfriend or ex-girlfriend. It is commonly called "domestic violence," but because some does not occur in the home, IPV is the preferred term.

intragenerational mobility   Change in social class position between members of the same generation, such as between sons and daughters or between Blacks and Whites of the same age group.

Islam   Founded about 1,400 years ago when God was displeased with the corruptions of earlier prophets and gave his last prophet, Mohammed, a new sacred test, the Koran. It requires the fusion of religion and government and two main branches–Shi'ite and Sunni.

Judaism   The first monotheistic religion; believes the covenant between God and Abraham took place around 2000 BCE. and became the foundation of Jewish law. Today there are about 15 million Jews worldwide.

kinship systems Social systems that locate individuals by reference to their families, that is, by common biological ancestry, legal marriage, or adoption.

knowledge economy One defining element of the postindustrial economy in which ideas, information, and knowledge have become new forms of capital.

labeling theory Howard Becker's term stresses the relativity of deviance, naming the mechanism by which the same act is considered deviant in some groups but not in others. Labels are used to categorize and contain people.

labor union A group of workers who act collectively to address common issues and interests.

language An organized set of symbols by which we are able to think and communicate with others; the chief vehicle by which human beings create a sense of self.

latent function Any function of an institution or process that is unintended, such as education keeps the streets safer, since young people are inside.

law A norm that has been organized and written down. Breaking this norm involves the disapproval not only of immediate community members but also of the agents of the state, who are charged with punishing such norm-breaking behavior.

leader All groups have leaders, people in charge, whether they were elected, appointed, or just informally took control.

legal-rational authority Form of authority where leaders are to be obeyed not primarily as representatives of tradition or because of their personal qualities but because they are voicing a set of rationally derived laws. They must act impartially, even sacrificing their own opinions and attitudes in obedience to the laws of the land.

legitimacy Social arrangements that ensure men know what children they have produced (women usually know). Families then bear the economic and emotional burden of raising only the children that belong to them.

liberal feminism One of the three main branches of feminism today; focuses on the individual woman's rights and opportunities.

liberation theology A movement within the Catholic Church in Latin America that was a source of popular mobilization for social change. Liberation theology stressed the nobility of the poor and promoted a religious response to hunger, disease, and poverty.

life chances A person's abilities to have access to material goods (food and shelter) and social resources (health care, education) that together control the quality of life.

life expectancy The average number of years a person can expect to live; varies greatly by country and region.

life span The average or the maximum amount of time an organism or object can be expected to live or last.

Likert scale The most common form of survey coding; arranges possible responses from lowest to highest.

literature review Reading and summary of other research on or closely related to the topic of a study.

looking-glass self Cooley's term for the process of how identity is formed through social interaction. We imagine how we appear to others and thus develop our sense of self based on the others' reactions, imagined or otherwise.

macrolevel analysis Analysis of the large-scale patterns or social structures of society, such as economies or political systems.

majority group A group whose members experience privilege and access to power because of their group membership. With regard to race, lighter-colored skin usually means membership in the majority group.

Malthusian theory Developed by the English economist and clergyman Thomas Robert Malthus (1766–1834), the theory held that population would increase by geometric progression, doubling in each generation—while the food supply would only increase arithmetically, leading to mass starvation, environmental disaster, and eventual human extinction.

manifest functions The intended consequences of an action or event.

manufactured consent Michael Burawoy's term for the strategies by which companies get workers to embrace a system that also exploits them.

market Regular exchange of goods and services within an economy.

masculinization of sex The pursuit of sexual pleasure for its own sake, increased attention to orgasm, increased numbers of sexual partners, interest in sexual experimentation, and separation of sexual behavior from love. That is partly the result of the technological transformation of sexuality (from birth control to the Internet) and partly the result of the sexual revolution's promise of greater sexual freedom with fewer emotional and physical consequences.

mass media Ways to communicate with vast numbers of people at the same time, usually over a great distance. Mass media have developed in countless directions: books, newspapers, magazines, motion pictures, records and tapes, CDs and DVDs, radio and television programs, comic strips and comic books, and a whole range of new digital media.

master status An ascribed or achieved status presumed so important that it overshadows all of the others, dominating our lives and controlling our position in society.

material culture The things people make and the things they use to make them—the tools they use, the physical environment they inhabit (forests, beaches, mountains, fertile farmlands, or harsh desert).

matrilineal descent Tracing one's ancestry through the mother, her mother, and so on.

matrix of domination An interlocking system of control in which each type of inequality reinforces the others, so that the impact of one cannot be fully understood without also considering the others.

McDonaldization The homogenizing spread of consumerism around the globe.

mechanical solidarity Durkheim's term for a traditional society where life is uniform and people are similar. They share a common culture and sense of morality that bonds them.

media consolidation The ongoing trends in media ownership in which only a handful of very large companies own and control the vast majority of media around the world.

media The plural of *medium,* they are the ways that we communicate with each other.

megalopolis A term coined by Jean Gottmann in 1961 to describe the integration of large cities and sprawling suburbs into a single organic urbanized unit, such as "Bo Wash," the Boston to Washington, D.C., corridor that includes New York and Philadelphia as well as the suburbs.

meritocracy Social system in which the greater the functional importance of the job, the more rewards it brings in salary, perks, power, and prestige.

microlevel analysis Analysis of small-scale social patterns, such as individual interactions or small-group dynamics.

minority group A group one is born into, which has a distinguishable identity and whose members have less power and access to resources than other groups in society because of that group membership.

modernism In sociology, a belief in progress that challenged tradition, religion, and aristocracies as remnants of the past and saw industry, democracy, and science as the wave of the future.

modernization theory W. W. Rostow's theory focusing on the conditions necessary for a low-income country to develop economically. Arguing that a nation's poverty is largely due to the cultural failings of its people, Rostrow believed poor countries could develop economically only if they give up their "backward" way of life and adopt modern Western economic institutions, technologies, and cultural values that emphasize savings and productive investment.

monarchy One of the first political systems; rule by a single individual (*mono* means "one," and *archy* means "rule"), typically hereditary.

monogamy The most common arrangement; marriage between two people. Most monogamous societies allow men and women to marry each other because it takes one of each to make a baby, but same-sex monogamy is surprisingly common.

mores Informally enforced norms based on strong moral values, which are viewed as essential to the proper functioning of a group.

mortality rate The number of deaths per year for every thousand people.

multicultural feminism One of the three main branches of feminism today; argues that the experience of being a woman of color cannot be extracted from the experience of being a woman. Multicultural feminists emphasize the historical context of racial and class-based inequalities.

multiculturalism The doctrine that several different cultures (rather than one national culture) can coexist peacefully and equitably in a single country.

multigenerational households Adults of more than one generation sharing a domestic space.

multinational corporations Large, international companies, also called transnational corporations, that manage production and/or deliver services in more than one country at once. Multinational corporations have a powerful influence in the local economies of the countries in which they operate, and in the global economy.

muscle dysmorphia A belief that one is insufficiently muscular.

natural population increase Simple calculation of the number of deaths every year subtracted from the number of births.

net migration rate The difference between immigration and emigration rates in a given year.

network Often conceived as a web of social relationships, a type of group that is both looser and denser than a formal group but connects people to each other, and, through those connections, with other people.

New Age An umbrella term for many groups that practice and develop a distinct spirituality. New Age groups draw on organized religions and even traditions like astrology and a belief in life in outer space.

nonmarital sex Sexual relations outside marriage.

nonmaterial culture Often just called "culture," the ideas and beliefs that people develop about their lives and their world.

norm One of the rules a culture develops that defines how people should act and the consequences of failure to act in the specified ways.

normative organization Voluntary organization wherein members serve because they believe in the goals of the organization.

objectivity The scientific norm that stipulates scientific knowledge must be based on objective criteria, not political agendas or personal preferences.

occupational crime The use of one's professional position to illegally secure something of value for oneself or for the corporation.

occupational prestige The degree of status accorded to an occupation.

opportunity theory Cloward and Ohlin's 1960 theory of crime, which holds that those who have many opportunities—and good ones at that—will be more likely to commit crimes than those with few good opportunities.

organic solidarity Emile Durkheim's term for a modern society where people are interdependent because of the division of labor; they disagree on what is right and wrong but share solidarity because the division of labor makes them dependent on each other.

organization A formal group of people with one or more shared goals.

organizational crime Illegal actions committed in accordance with the operative goals of an organization, such as antitrust violations, false advertising, or price fixing.

out-group homogeneity The social tendency to believe that all members of an out-group are exactly the same.

out-group   One to which you do not belong and toward which you feel either neutral or hostile; the "they" who are perceived as different from and of lower stature than ourselves.

outsourcing   Also called "offshoring," refers to the practice of hiring out any phase(s) of product development to lower-wage countries or groups.

overt racism   Systematic prejudice applied to members of a group in clear, manifest ways, such as speech, discrimination, or a refusal to associate with members of that group.

PAC (political action committee)   A type of partisan political organization that is not subject to the same regulations as political parties, and attempt to influence elections and mobilize public opinion.

paradigm   An example, pattern, or model, especially an outstandingly clear or typical example or archetype.

participant observation   Sociological research method in which one observes people in their natural habitat.

participatory democracy   Also called "pure democracy," a political system in which every person gets one vote and the majority rules.

patriarchy   Literally, "the rule of the fathers"; a name given to the social order in which men hold power over women.

patrilineal descent   Tracing one's ancestry through the father, his father, and so on.

pay gap   The consistent, worldwide difference between what men are paid and what women are paid for the same labor.

peer group   Our group of friends and wider group of acquaintances who have an enormous socializing influence, especially during middle and late childhood.

pluralism   Maintains that different groups in a stable society can treat each other with mutual respect and that minority cultures can maintain their own distinctiveness and still participate in the greater society without discrimination.

political party   Group that bands together to petition for political chances or to support candidates for elected office.

political revolution   Changes the political groups that run the society, but they still draw their strength from the same social groups that supported the old regime.

politics   The art and science of government.

polyandry   Rare form of polygamy in which one woman marries two or more men.

polygyny   The most common form of polygamy, a marriage between one man and two or more women. (*See* polyandry and polygyny.)

popular culture   The culture of the masses, the middle and working classes, that includes a wide variety of popular music, nonhighbrow forms of literature, any forms of spectator sports, and other popular forms of entertainment, like television, movies, and video games.

population composition   The comparative numbers of men and women and various age groups in an area, region, or country.

population density   The number of people per square mile or kilometer.

population pyramid   Type of graph that shows five- or ten-year age groups as different-sized bars, or "blocks."

postindustrial economy   Economy that shifts from the production of goods to the production of ideas.

postmodernism   A late-twentieth-century worldview that emphasizes the existence of different worldviews and concepts of reality, rather than one "correct" or "true" one. Postmodernism emphasizes that a particular reality is a social construction by a particular group, community, or class.

poverty line   Estimated minimum income required to pay for food, shelter, and clothing. Anyone falling below this income is categorized as poor.

power   The ability to extract compliance despite resistance or the ability to get others to do what you want them to do, regardless of their own desires.

predictability   The degree to which a correct prediction of a research outcome can be made.

prejudice   A set of beliefs and attitudes that cause us to negatively prejudge people based on their social location.

prestige   The amount of honor, respect, or deference accorded to social roles or statuses.

primary deviance   Any minor, usually unnoticed, act of deviance committed irregularly that does not have an impact on one's self-identity or on how one is labeled by others.

primary group   One such as friends and family, which comes together for expressive reasons, providing emotional support, love, companionship, and security.

primary sex characteristics   Those anatomical sex characteristics that are present at birth, like the sex organs themselves, which develop in the embryo.

primary socialization   A culture's most basic values, which are passed on to children beginning in earliest infancy.

primordial theory   A general theory that the origins of conflict may be found in our ties to blood and kinship groups—race, ethnicity, nation, tribe.

production   The creation of value or wealth by producing goods and services.

proletariat   Popularized by Karl Marx, the term for the lower classes who were forced to become wage laborers or go hungry. Today, the term is often used to refer to the working class.

property crime   A crime committed involving property, such as burglary, car theft, or arson, where there is no force or threat of force against a person.

proportional representation   In contrast to the winner-take-all system used in the United States, proportional representation gives each party a proportion of the legislative seats based on the number of votes its candidates garner.

purposive sample   Sample in which respondents are not selected randomly and are not representative of the larger population but are selected precisely because they possess certain characteristics that are of interest to the researcher.

qualitative methods   Inductive and inferential means to drawing sociological understanding, usually about less tangible aspects of social life, such as the actual felt experience of social interaction.

quantitative methods   Numerical means to drawing sociological conclusions using powerful statistical tools to help understand patterns in which the behaviors, attitudes, or traits under study can be translated into numerical values.

race to the bottom   Bonacich and Appelbaum's term for outsourcing jobs to wherever manufacturers and retailers can pay the lowest possible wages so as to maximize profits.

race   Social category, still poorly defined, that depends on an assumption of biological distinction to rate and organize social groups.

racism   A particularly powerful form of prejudice that includes not only a belief in general stereotypes but also a belief that one race (usually White) is inherently superior to the others. Racism is a prejudice that is systematically applied to members of a group.

radical feminism   One of the three main branches of feminism today; moves beyond discrimination economically and politically to argue that women are oppressed and subordinated by men directly, personally, and most often through sexual relations.

random sample   A sample chosen by an abstract and arbitrary method, such as tossing a piece of paper with each person's name on it into a hat. In this way, each person has an equal chance of being selected.

reference group   A group toward which one is so strongly committed, or one that commands so much prestige, that we orient our actions around what we perceive that group's perceptions would be.

relative deprivation   Describes how misery is socially experienced by constantly comparing yourself to others. You are not down and out: You are worse off than you used to be (downward mobility), not as well off as you think you should be (rising expectations), or, perhaps, not as well off as those you see around you.

relative poverty   A measure of the extent to which a household's financial resources fall below an average income threshold for that economy.

religion   The set of beliefs about the origins and meaning of life, usually based on the existence of a supernatural power.

religiosity   The extent of one's religious belief, typically measured by attendance at religious observances or maintaining religious practices.

representative democracy   System in which citizens elect representatives to make the decisions for them; requires an educated citizenry and a free press.

resocialization   Learning a new set of beliefs, behaviors, and values that depart from those held in the past.

revelation   A religious way of learning answers to fundamental questions of existence; God, spirits, prophets, or sacred books reveal what we need to know.

revolution   The attempt to overthrow the existing political and social order of a society and replace it with a new one.

ritual   Enactment by which members of a culture engage in a routine behavior to express their sense of belonging to the culture.

role conflict   What happens when we try to play different roles with extremely different or contradictory rules at the same time.

role exit   The process we go through to adjust when leaving a role that is central to our identity.

role performance   The particular emphasis or interpretation each of us gives a social role.

role strain   The experience of difficulty in performing a role.

role   Behavior expected of people who have a particular status.

sacred   A place, time, object, or person in which the worlds of the spiritual and the worldly come together.

sample   A limited group of research subjects whose responses are statistically developed into a general theme or trend that can be applied to the larger whole.

sandwich generation   Popular term for middle-aged adults who are caring for both their young children and their aging parents.

Sapir-Whorf hypothesis   A theory that language shapes our reality because it gives us a way to talk about the categories of life that we experience.

scapegoat   A convenient, weak, and socially approved target for economic or social loss or insecurity.

science   The accumulated systematic knowledge of the physical or material world, obtained through experimentation and observation.

scientific literacy   According to the National Academy of Sciences, it is the "knowledge and understanding of the scientific concepts and processes required for personal decision making, participation in civic and cultural affairs, and economic productivity."

second shift   The term coined by sociologist Arlie Hochschild to describe how working women typically must work both outside the home for wages and inside the home doing domestic management and child care.

secondary analysis   Analysis conducted on data previously collected by others for other reasons.

secondary deviance   The moment when someone acquires a deviant identity, occurring when he or she repeatedly breaks a norm and people start making a big deal of it, so the rule breaking can no longer be attributed to a momentary lapse in judgment or be justifiable under the circumstances but is an indication of a permanent personality trait.

secondary group   Co-workers, club members, or another group that comes together for instrumental reasons, such as wanting to work together to meet common goals. Secondary groups make less of an emotional claim on one's identity than do primary groups.

secondary sex characteristics Those sex characteristics, such as breast development in girls and the lowering of voices and development of facial hair in boys, that occur at puberty.

secondary socialization Occurring throughout the life span, it is the adjustments we make to adapt to new situations.

sect A small subculture within an established religious institution.

secularization The process of moving away from religion and toward the worldly.

segregation The practice of physically separating races by law and custom in institutions and communities.

segregation The practice of physically separating Whites from other races by law and custom in institutions and communities.

sex hormones Testosterone and estrogen, the hormones that trigger development of secondary sex characteristics, such as breast development in girls and the development of facial hair in boys.

sex tourism Effectively the globalization of prostitution, a well-organized business whereby the flow of "consumers" (wealthy men) is directed to the "commodities" (poor men, women, and children). Like prostitution, there is far less "choice" on the part of the locals and far more coercion than typically meets the eye. The tourists seem to be men and women who are being friendly and flirtatious, but the locals are usually victims of kidnapping and violence.

sex A biological distinction; the chromosomal, chemical, and anatomical organization of males and females.

sexual behavior Any behavior that brings sexual pleasure or release (typically, but not always, involving sex organs).

sexual harassment A form of gender discrimination in the workplace that singles out women for differential treatment. There are two types: "quid pro quo," which occurs when a supervisor uses his (or her) position to elicit sexual activity from a subordinate; and the more common "hostile environment," which occurs when a person feels threatened or unsafe because of constant teasing or threatening by other workers.

sexual identity Refers to an identity that is organized by the gender of the person (or persons) to whom you are sexually attracted. Also called *sexual orientation*.

sexual script Set of ideas and practices that answer basic questions about sexual identity and practices: With whom do we have sex? What do we do? How often? Why?

sexual socialization The process by which your sexual scripts begin to cohere into a preference and sexual identity.

sexuality Identity we construct that is often based on our sexual conduct and often intersects with other sources of identity, such as race, class, ethnicity, age, or gender.

social construction of gender The sociological idea that gender is something we construct all through our lives, using the cultural materials we find around us. Our gender identi-

ties are simultaneously voluntary, based on choices, and coerced by social pressures, sometimes including physical threats, to conform to certain rules.

social control theory As Walter Reckless theorized, people don't commit crimes even if they could probably get away with them due to social controls. There are outer controls—family, friends, teachers, social institutions, and authority figures (like the police)—who influence (cajole, threaten, browbeat) us into obeying social rules; and inner controls—internalized socialization, consciousness, religious principles, ideas of right and wrong, and one's self-conception as a "good person."

social Darwinism A model of social change that saw each succeeding society as developing through evolution and the "survival of the fittest."

social institution A formal organized system of roles, norms and values that are the major foundations of social life (i.e., the family, education)

social interaction The dynamic process by which two (dyad), three (triad) or more individuals relate to one another.

social mobility The movement from one class to another, it can occur in two forms: intergenerational—that is, your parents are working-class, but you became lower, or your parents are middle-class, but you became upper-class; and intragenerational—that is, you move from working to lower, or from middle to upper, all within your lifetime.

social movement Collective attempt to further a common interest or secure a common goal through action outside the sphere of established institutions.

social revolution Revolution that changes the social groups or classes that political power rests on.

Social Security The U.S. government program wherein citizens contribute a small portion of their earnings while working and then collect a cash supplement after retirement. The program has been credited with preventing tens of millions of elderly from living in poverty and hunger.

social stratification Taken from the geological term for layers of rock, or "strata," the ranking of people into defined layers. Social stratification exists in all societies and is based on things like wealth, race, and gender.

social structure A complex framework composed of both patterned social interactions and institutions that together organize social life and provide the context for individual action.

socialism Economic system in which people are meant to cooperate rather than compete, share goods and services, own property collectively, and make decisions as a collective body.

socialization The process by which we become aware of ourselves as part of a group, learn to communicate with others, and learn how to behave as expected.

society An organized collection of individuals and institutions, bounded by space in a coherent territory, subject to the same political authority, and organized through a shared set of cultural expectations and values.

socioeconomic status (SES) Your social connections, your taste in art, your ascribed and attained statuses, and more. Because there are so many components, sociologists today tend to prefer the concept of socioeconomic status to that of social class, to emphasize that people are ranked through the intermingling of many factors, economic, social, political, cultural, and community.

sociological imagination The ability to see the connection between our individual identities and the social contexts (family, friends, and institutions) in which we find ourselves.

sociology The study of human behavior in society.

status One's socially defined position in a group; it is often characterized by certain expectations and rights.

stereotype Generalization about a group that is oversimplified, selective, exaggerated and usually pejorative, which fails to acknowledge the individual differences in the group.

stigma An attribute that changes you "from a whole and usual person to a tainted and discounted one," as sociologist Erving Goffman (1963) defined it. A stigma discredits a person's claim to be normal.

strain theory Robert K. Merton's concept that excessive deviance is a by-product of inequality within societies that promote certain norms and versions of social reality yet provide unequal means of meeting or attaining them. Individuals respond to this strain either by conforming or by changing the goals or means of obtaining goals accepted by society.

stratified sample Sample in which research subjects are divided into proportions equal to the proportions found in the population at large.

structural functionalism A sociological paradigm that contends that all social life consists of several distinct, integrated levels that enable the world—and individuals who are within it—to find stability, order, and meaning.

structural mobility a general upward trend of the entire society. Structural mobility means that the entire society got wealthier, as occurred in post–World War II America.

subculture Group within a society that creates its own norms and values distinct from the mainstream and usually its own separate social institutions as well.

subjectivity The complex of individual perceptions, motivations, ideas, and emotions that give each of us a point of view.

subordinate Individual or group that possesses little or comparatively less social power.

subtle racism Systematic prejudice applied to members of a group in quiet or even unconscious ways; a simple set of mental categories that one may possess about a group based on stereotypes.

suburb A residential community outside of a city but always existing in relationship to the city.

superego Freud's term for the internalized norms, values, and "rules" of our social group that are learned from family, friends, and social institutions.

superordinate Individual or group that possesses social power.

survey Research method in which one asks a sample of people closed-ended questions and tabulates the results.

symbol Anything—an idea, a marking, a thing—that carries additional meanings beyond itself to others who share in the culture. Symbols come to mean what they do only in a culture; they would have no meaning to someone outside.

symbolic interactionism Sociological perspective that examines how individuals and groups interact, focusing on the creation of personal identity through interaction with others. Of particular interest is the relationship between individual action and group pressures.

systematic sample A type of sample that starts at a random position on a list and selects every nth unit (skip interval) of a population until the desired sample size is reached.

taboo The strongest form of norms, a taboo is a prohibition viewed as essential to the well-being of humanity.

terrorism Using acts of violence and destruction (or threatening to use them) as a political strategy.

tertiary deviance Occurs when members of a group formerly labeled deviant attempt to redefine their acts, attributes, or identities as normal—even virtuous.

Third Great Awakening What some term a current religious revival in the United States that further demonstrates spirituality, making a relationship with the sacred attainable to even greater numbers of Americans, with even less effort or religious discipline.

token Representative of a traditionally disenfranchised group whose hypervisibility results in constant pressure to reflect well on the group and to outperform co-workers just to be perceived as equal.

tokenism When a single member of a minority group is present in an office, workplace, or classroom and is seen as a representative of that minority group rather than as an individual.

total institution An institution that completely circumscribes your everyday life, cutting you off from life before you entered and seeking to regulate every part of your behavior.

totalitarianism A political system in which no organized opposition is permitted and political information is censored.

traditional authority Dominant in premodern societies, including ancient Egypt, China, and Mesoamerica, the form of authority that people obeyed because they believed their society had always done things that way; derives from who the leaders are: the descendants of kings and queens, or perhaps the descendants of the gods, not from their educational background, work experience, or personality traits.

underclass About 4 percent of the U.S. population, this group has no income, no connection to the job market, little education, inadequate nutrition, and substandard housing or none at all. They have no possibility of social mobility and little chance of achieving the quality of life that most people would consider minimally acceptable.

universal suffrage Granting of the vote to any and all citizens who meet specified, universal criteria, such as legal citizenship and a minimum age.

utilitarian organization Organization, like the college we attend or the company we work for, whose members belong for a specific, instrumental purpose or tangible material reward.

value If norms tell us how to behave, values tell us why. Values constitute what a society thinks about itself and so are among the most basic lessons that a culture can transmit to its young.

verstehen Max Weber's term for "intersubjective understanding," or the ability to understand social behavior from the point of view of those the sociologist is observing.

violent crime A crime of violence or one in which violence is a defining feature. According to the FBI, violent crime consists of four offenses: murder and nonnegligent manslaughter, forcible rape, robbery, and aggravated assault.

voucher system First proposed in 1955, a free-market approach to school reform in which taxpayer funds are used to pay for students' tuition at private school, ostensibly upping competition and increasing quality in public schools.

wage labor The arrangement by which workers get a regular paycheck in exchange for performing a specific task, rather than being paid for the end product of their labor.

white-collar crime Edward Sutherland's term for the illegal actions of a corporation or people acting on its behalf, by using the authority of their position to commit crime.

world religions Those religions with long histories, well-established traditions, and the flexibility to adapt to many different cultures.

world system theory Immanuel Wallerstein's theory that the interconnectedness of the world system began in the 1500s, when Europeans began their economic and political domination of the rest of the world. Because capitalism depends on generating the maximum profits for the minimum of expenditures, the world system continues to benefit rich countries (which acquire the profits) and harm the rest of the world (by minimizing local expenditures and therefore perpetuating poverty).

zero population growth Paul Erlich's (1968) modern solution to Malthus's concerns, it entails a global effort to ensure that the number of births does not exceed the number of deaths, providing global population stability, a decrease in poor countries, and a redistribution of resources to those countries.

References

AARP. *Baby Boomers Envision Their Retirement.* Washington, DC: AARP, 2001.

Abbate, Janet. *Inventing the Internet.* Cambridge, MA: MIT Press, 2000.

Aboud, F., M. Mendelson, and K. Purdy. "Cross-Race Peer Relations and Friendship Quality." *International Journal of Behavioral Development,* 27 (2), March 2003.

Abu-Lughod, L. "Bedouins, Cassettes, and Technologies of Public Culture." *Middle East Report,* 159 (1989): 7–11.

Adger, Neil, Saleemul Huq, Katrina Brown, Declan Conway, and Mike Hulme. "Adaptation to Climate Change: Setting the Agenda for Development Policy and Research," working paper. Norwich, UK: University of East Anglia, Tyndell Centre for Climate Change Research, 2002.

Adler, Jerry. "The New Naysayers." *Newsweek,* September 11, 2006.

Adler, Paul S. "Market, Hierarchy, and Trust: The Knowledge Economy and the Future of Capitalism." *Organization Science,* March–April 2001: 214–234.

Agnew, Robert, and Sandra Huguley. "Adolescent Violence towards Parents." *Journal of Marriage and the Family,* 5 (1, 1989): 699–711.

Ahrons, Constance. *We're Still Family: What Grown Children Have to Say about Their Parents' Divorce.* New York: HarperCollins, 2004.

Aileinikoff, Thomas Alexander, and Douglas B. Klusmeyer. *Citizenship Today: Global Perspectives and Practices.* New York: Carnegie Endowment for International Peace, 2001.

Alan Guttmacher Institute. "Abortion Common among All Women, Even Those Thought to Oppose Abortion," 1996. Available online at: www.agi-usa.org/pubs/archives/prabort2.html

Alan Guttmacher Institute. *Teenage Sexual and Reproductive Behavior in Developed Countries: Can More Progress Be Made?* New York: Alan Guttmacher Institute, 2001.

Alan Guttmacher Institute. "Facts on Induced Abortion Worldwide." New York: Alan Guttmacher Institute, October 2008.

Allan, Emilie Andersen, and Darrell J. Steffensmeier. "Youth Underemployment and Property Crime: Differential Effects of Job Availability and Job Quality on Juvenile and Young Adult Arrest Rates." *American Sociological Review,* 54 (1989): 107–123.

Allegretto, Sylvia. *U.S. Government Does Relatively Little to Lessen Child Poverty Rates.* Washington, DC: Economic Policy Institute, 2006.

Allen, K. R., and D. H. Demo. "The Families of Lesbians and Gay Men: A New Frontier in Family Research." *Journal of Marriage and the Family,* 57 (1995): 111–127.

Allen, Tammy D., Lillian T. Eby, Shane S. Douthitt, and Carrie L. Noble. "Applicant Gender and Family Structure: Effects of Perceived Relocation Commitment and Spouse Resistance." *Sex Roles,* December 2002.

Allport, Gordon. *The Nature of Prejudice.* New York: Anchor, 1954.

Altbach, Philip. *American Higher Education in the Twentieth Century: Social, Political, and Economic Challenges.* Baltimore, MD: Johns Hopkins University Press, 1998.

Amato, Paul R. "The Consequences of Divorce for Adults and Children." *Journal of Marriage and Family,* 62 (4, 2000): 1269–1287.

Amato, Paul R. "Reconciling Divergent Perspectives: Judith Wallerstein, Quantitative Family Research, and Children of Divorce." *Family Relations,* 52 (4, 2003): 332–339.

Amato, Paul R., and Alan Booth. "The Legacy of Marital Discord: Consequences for Children's Marital Quality." *Journal of Personality and Social Psychology,* 81: 627–638.

Amato, Paul R., and Juliana M. Sobolewski. "The Effects of Divorce and Marital Discord on Adult Children's Psychological Well-Being." *American Sociological Review,* 66 (2001): 900–921.

Ambert, Anne-Marie. *Same-Sex Couples and Same-Sex-Parent Families: Relationships, Parenting and Issues of Marriage.* Ottawa, Ontario, Canada: The Vanier Institute of the Family, 2005.

American Academy of Pediatrics, "Discipline," 2007. Available at: www.aap.org/publiced/BR_Discipline.htm

American Association of University Women (AAUW). *Women's Educational Gains and the Gender Earnings Gap.* Washington, DC: AAUW, 2007.

American Bar Association. *Charting Our Progress: The Status of Women in the Profession Today.* Chicago: American Bar Association, Commission on Women in the Profession, 2006.

American Bar Association. "First Year and Total J.D. Enrollment by Gender," 2008. http://www.abanet.org/legaled/statistics/charts/stats-6.pdf

American Civil Liberties Union. *Lesbian, Gay, Bisexual, Transgender Project, 2007.* Available at: www.aclu.org/lgbt/index.html

American Diploma Project. *Ready or Not: Creating a High School Diploma That Counts.* 2004. Available at: www.achieve.org/node/552

American Psychiatric Association. "Mental Health of the Elderly." 2007. Available at: http://healthyminds.org/mentalhealthofelderly.cfm

American Religious Identification Survey (ARIS), 2008. http://www.americanreligioussurvey~aris.org/

American Society of Plastic Surgeons. *Cosmetic Surgery Procedures,* 2006. Available at: www.plasticsurgery.org

American Sociological Association. "Sociology Degrees Awarded by Race, Ethnicity and Degree Level" and "Sociology Degrees Awarded by Level of Degree and Gender," 2007. Both available at: www.asanet.org (profession trend data).

Amnesty International. *Facts and Figures,* 2005. Available at: www.therepert.amnesty.org/eng

Amnesty International. "Death Sentences and Executions in 2008," 2009. Available at: www.amnesty.org/en/library/info/ACT50/003/2009/en

Anderson, E. "The Code of the Streets." *Atlantic Monthly,* 273, May 1994, 81–94.

Anderson, Elijah. *Streetwise: Race, Class and Change in an Urban Community.* Chicago: University of Chicago Press, 1992.

Anderson, Elijah. *Code of the Street: Decency, Violence, and the Moral Life of the Inner City.* New York: W. W. Norton, 2000.

Anderson, Sarah, John Cavanaugh, Chuck Collins, and Eric Benjamin. *Executive Excess, 2006.* Washington, DC: Institute for Policy Studies, 2006.

Andrew, John W. *Lyndon Johnson and the Great Society.* New York: Ivan R. Dee, 1999.

Angier, Natalie. *Woman: An Intimate Geography.* Boston: Houghton-Mifflin, 1999.

Angle, John. "A Mathematical Sociologist's Tribute to Comte: Sociology as Science." *Footnotes,* February 2007.

Annual Status of Education Report (ASER). "National Highlights." Pratham, India, 2008.

Appelbaum, Richard P., and Jeffrey Henderson. *States and Development in the Asian Pacific Rim.* Newbury Park, CA: Sage, 1992.

Arendt, Hannah. *The Origins of Totalitarianism* (1958). New York: Harcourt, 1973.

Arnett, Jeffrey Jensen. *Emerging Adulthood: The Winding Road from the Late Teens through the Twenties.* New York: Oxford University Press, 2004.

Arnold, Chris. "A Marriage of Hearts and Minåds . . . and Fortunes, Too." National Public Radio, February 10, 2007. Available at: www.npr.org/templates/story/story.php?storyId=7322722

Arnoldi, Ben. "America Becomes a More 'Adult-Centered' Nation." *The Christian Science Monitor*, July 10, 2007.

Aron-Dine, Aviva, and Isaac Shapiro. *Share of National Income Going to Wages and Salaries at Record Low in 2006; Share of Income Going to Corporate Profits at Record High.* Washington, DC: Center for Budget and Policy Priorities, March 2007.

Arons, Jessica. *Lifetime Losses: The Career Wage Gap.* Washington, DC: Center for American Progress, 2008.

Aronson, Amy. *Taking Liberties: Early American Women's Magazines and Their Readers.* Westport, CT: Praeger Press, 2002.

Arsova, Ljupka, Rob van Haaren, Nora Goldstein, Scott M. Kaufman, and Nickolas J. Themelis. "The State of Garbage in America: A Joint Study of Biocycle and the Earth Engineering Center of Columbia University." *Biocycle,* 49 (12, December 2008): 22.

Asch, Solomon. "Opinions and Social Pressure." *Scientific American,* 193 (5, 1955): 31–35.

Association of American Medical Colleges. "U.S. Medical School Applicants and Students 1982–3 and 2007–2008," 2008. http://www.aamc.org/data/facts/charts1982to2007.pdf

Atack, Jeremy. "Tenants and Yeomen in the Nineteenth Century." In Morton Rothstein and Daniel Field, eds., *Quantitative Studies in Agrarian History,* 3–29. Ames: Iowa State University Press, 1994.

Atkinson, Michael. *Tattooed: The Sociogenesis of a Body Art.* Toronto, Ont.: University of Toronto Press, 2003.

Auyero, Javier. *Poor People's Politics: Peronist Survival Networks and the Legacy of Evita.* Durham, NC: Duke University Press, 2000.

Axtell, R. E. *Do's and Taboos around the World.* New York: John Wiley & Sons, 1985.

Ayres, Irving, and Peter Siegelman. "Race and Gender Discrimination in Bargaining for a New Car." *American Economic Review,* 85 (3, 1995): 304–321.

Aziz, Mir Adnan. *An Era of Disparity.* New York: Global Policy Forum, 2008.

Bachman, R., and L. E. Saltzman. "Violence against Women: A National Crime Victimization Survey Report" (NCJ No. 154348). Washington, DC: U.S. Department of Justice, 1994.

Backman, Clifford R. *The Worlds of Medieval Europe.* Oxford, UK: Oxford University Press, 2002.

Bacon, Margaret, Herbert Barry, and Iruin Child, "A Cross-Cultural Survey of Some Sex Differences in Socialization." *Journal of Abnormal Social Psychology,* 53, 1957.

Baden, John. "Perverse Consequences (P.C.) of the Nanny State." *Seattle Times,* January 17, 1996, 1.

Bagamery, Anne. "Hearing Tomorrow's Workers." *International Herald Tribune,* April 14, 2004.

Bailey, Beth L. *From Front Porch to Back Seat: Courtship in Twentieth Century America.* Balti-more, MD: Johns Hopkins University Press, 1989.

Baldus, D. C., and G. Woodworth. "Race Discrimination and the Death Penalty: An Empirical and Legal Overview," in J. Acker, R. M. Bohm, and C. S. Lanier, eds., *America's Experiment with Capital Punishment,* pp. 385–416. Durham, NC: Carolina Academic Press, 1998.

Ballantine, Jeanne H. *The Sociology of Education: A Systematic Analysis.* Upper Saddle River, NJ: Prentice-Hall, 2001.

Barber, Benjamin. *Jihad vs. McWorld: How Globalization and Tribalism Are Reshaping the World.* New York: Crown, 1996.

Barnet, Richard J., and John Cavanagh. *Global Dreams: Imperial Corporations and the New World Order.* New York: Simon & Schuster, 1994.

Barr, Nicolas. *The Economics of the Welfare State.* New York: Oxford University Press, 2004.

Barta, Patrick. "The Rise of the Underground." *The Wall Street Journal,* March 14, 2009.

Bassuk, Shari S., Lisa F. Berkman, and Benjamin C. Amick II. "Socioeconomic Status and Mortality among the Elderly: Findings from Four U.S. Communities." *American Journal of Epidemiology,* 155 (6, 2002): 520–533.

Battle, Michael. *The Black Church in America: African American Christian Spirituality.* London: Blackwell, 2006.

BBC News, "Obesity: In Statistics," January 2, 2008. Available at: http://news.bbc.co.uk/2/hi/health/7151813.stm

BBC World Service. "Economic System Needs 'Major Changes': Global Poll." June 2009.

Bearman, Peter S., and Hannah Bruckner. "Promising the Future: Virginity Pledges and First Intercourse." *American Journal of Sociology,* 106 (4, 2001): 859–912.

Becker, Elizabeth. "Study Finds a Growing Gap between Managerial Salaries for Men and Women." *The New York Times,* January 24, 2002, p. 18.

Becker, Howard. *Art Worlds.* Berkeley: University of California Press, 1984.

Becker, Howard S. *Outside: Studies in the Sociology of Deviance.* New York: The Free Press, 1966.

Becker, Lee, Wilson Lowrey, Dane Claussen, and William Anderson. "Why Does the Beat Go On?" *Newspaper Research Journal,* Fall 2000: 1–11.

Bell, Daniel. *The Coming of Post-Industrial Society: A Venture in Social Forecasting.* New York: Basic Books, 1976.

Bell, Michael Mayerfield. *An Invitation to Environmental Sociology.* Thousand Oaks, CA: Pine Forge Press, 2004.

Bellah, Robert N. "Civil Religion in America." *Journal of the American Academy of Arts and Sciences,* 96 (1) (Winter, 1967): 1–21.

Bellah, Robert N., Richard Madsen, William M. Sullivan, Ann Swidler, and Steven M. Tipton. *Habits of the Heart.* New York: Harper & Row, 1986.

Belo, Roberto. *Blogs Take on the Mainstream,* December 31, 2004. Available at: http://news.bbc.co.uk/1/hi/technology/4086337.stm

Belsky, J. K. *The Psychology of Aging: Theory, Research and Intervention.* Pacific Grove, CA: Brooks/Cole, 1990.

Ben-David, Joseph. *The Scientist's Role in Society: A Comparative Study.* Chicago: University of Chicago Press, 1984.

Benjamin, C. I. Ravid. "From Geographical Realia to Historiographical Symbol: The Odyssey of the Word 'Ghetto.'" In *Essential Papers on Jewish Culture in Renaissance and Baroque Italy.* New York: Schocken, 1992.

Berger, Johannes. "The Capitalist Road to Communism: Groundwork and Practicability." *Theory and Society,* 15 (5, 1986): 689–694.

Berger, Peter L., and Thomas Luckmann. *The Social Construction of Reality: A Treatise in the Sociology of Knowledge.* New York: Anchor Books, 1966.

Berkowitz, Dan. "Refining the Gatekeeper Metaphor for Local Television News." *Journal of Broadcasting & Electronic Media,* Winter 1990: 55–68.

Bernard, Jessie. *The Future of Marriage.* New York: World, 1972.

Berner, Robert, and Adrienne Carter. "Swiping Back at Credit-Card Fraud." *Business Week,* July 11, 2005, 72.

Bernhardt, Annette, Martina Morris, and Mark S. Handcock. "Women's Gains or Men's Losses? A Closer Look at the Shrinking Gender Gap in Earnings." *American Journal of Sociology,* 101 (1995): 302–328.

Bianchi, S. M. "Maternal Employment and Time with Children: Dramatic Change or Surprising Continuity?" *Demography,* 37 (2000): 401–414.

Bianchi, S. M., and L. M. Casper. "American Families." *Population Bulletin* 55 (4, 2000): 1–43.

Bianchi, S. M., M. A. Milkie, L. C. Sayer, and J. P. Robinson. "Is Anyone Doing the Housework? Trends in the Gender Division of Household Labor." *Social Forces,* 79 (2000): 191–228.

Bianchi, Suzanne M., John P. Robinson, and Melissa A. Milkie. *Changing Rhythms of American Family Life.* New York: Russell Sage Foundation Publications, 2006.

Bieber, Irving, Toby Bieber, Cornelia Wilbur, and Alfred Rifkin. *Homosexuality: A Psychoanalytic Perspective.* New York: Basic Books, 1962.

Biernat, Monica, and Kathleen Fuegen. "Shifting Standards and the Evaluation of Competence: Complexity in Gender-Based Judgment and Decision Making." *Journal of Social Issues,* 57 (4), 2001, 707–724.

Billingsley, Andrew. *Mighty Like a River: The Black Church and Social Reform.* New York: Oxford, 1999.

Birdsong, David, ed. *Second Language Acquisition and the Critical Period Hypothesis.* Mahwah, NJ: Lawrence Erlbaum, 1999.

Birn, Raymond. *Crisis, Absolutism, Revolution: Europe, 1648–1789.* New York: Harcourt, 1992.

Black, D., Gary Gates, Seth Sanders, and Lowell Taylor. "Demographics of the Gay and Lesbian Population in the United States: Evidence from Available Systematic Data Sources." *Demography,* 37 (2000): 139–154.

Blackwell, J. E. "Persistence and Change in Inter-Group Relations: The Crisis upon U." *Social Problems,* 29 (1982): 325–346.

Blair-Loy, Mary. *Competing Devotions: Career and Family among Women Executives.* Cambridge, MA: Harvard University Press, 2003.

Blank, J. "The Kid No One Noticed." *U.S. News and World Report,* December 1998, 27.

Blau, Judith R., and Peter M. Blau. "The Cost of Inequality: Metropolitan Structure and Violent Crime." *American Sociological Review,* 47 (1, February 1982): 114–129.

Blau, Peter. *Exchange and Power in Social Life.* New York: Wiley, 1964.

Blau, Peter M., and Otis Duncan. *American Occupational Structure.* New York: John Wiley & Sons, 1967.

Blauner, Robert. *Racial Oppression in America.* New York: HarperCollins College Division, 1972.

Blinder, Alan. "Offshoring: The Next Industrial Revolution?" *Foreign Affairs* 85, 2 (2006), 113–128.

Blumstein, A., and A. J. Beck. "Population Growth in U.S. Prisons, 1980–1996," in M. Tonry and J. Petersilia, eds. *Prisons: Crime and Justice 26.* Chicago: University of Chicago Press, 1999.

Blumstein, Philip, and Pepper Schwartz. *American Couples.* New York: William Morrow, 1983.

Bochenek, M., and A. W. Brown. *Hatred in the Hallways: Violence and Discrimination against Lesbian, Gay, Bisexual, and Transgender Students in U.S. Schools.* New York: Human Rights Watch, 2001. Available at: www .hrw.org/reports/2001/uslgbt/toc.htm

Bock, Jane. "Doing the Right Thing? Single Mothers by Choice and the Struggle for Legitimacy." *Gender & Society,* 14 (1, 2000): 62–86.

Bogaert, A. F. "Asexuality: Its Prevalence and Associated Factors in a National Probability Sample." *Journal of Sex Research,* 41 (2004): 279–287.

Bogardus, Emery S. "Social Distance and Its Origins." *Sociology and Social Research,* 9 (1925): 216–225.

Bogardus, Emery S. "A Social Distance Scale." *Sociology and Social Research,* 22 (1933): 265–271.

Bonacich, Edna, and Richard P. Appelbaum. *Behind the Label: Inequality in the Los Angeles Garment Industry.* Berkeley: University of California Press, 2000.

Bonnicksen, Thomas. "Forests Can Give Us Breathing Room on Kyoto Rules." *Houston Chronicle,* November 15, 2000.

Booth, Alan, and Paul R. Amato. "Parental Predivorce Relations and Offspring Postdivorce Well-Being." *Journal of Marriage and the Family,* 63 (2001): 197–212.

Boswell, John. *Same-Sex Unions in Premodern Europe.* New York: Vintage, 1995.

Bouffard, J. A. "The Influence of Sexual Arousal on Rational Decision Making in Sexual Aggression." *Journal of Criminal Justice,* 30 (2, 2002): 121–134.

"Bound for Success." *Foreign Policy,* May–June, 2006, 26–27.

Bourdieu, Pierre. *Distinction: A Social Critique of the Judgment of Taste.* Cambridge, MA: Harvard University Press, 1984.

Bourgois, Phillippe. *In Search of Respect: Selling Crack in El Barrio.* New York: Cambridge University Press, 1995.

Boushey, Heather. "Recession Still Plagues Workers." Washington, DC: Center for American Progress, July 2, 2009.

Bowen, *James. A History of Western Education: Civilization of Europe, Sixth to Sixteenth Century.* New York: Palgrave Macmillan, 1976.

Bowles, Samuel. *Schooling in Capitalist America: Educational Reform and the Contradictions of Economic Life.* New York: Basic Books, 1976.

Boyd, Elizabeth A., Richard A. Berk, and Karl A. Hamner. "Motivated by Hatred or Prejudice: Categorization of Hate-Motivated Crimes in Two Police Divisions." *Law and Society Review,* 30 (4, 1996): 819–850.

Boyd, W., and E. King. *History of Western Education.* Lanham, MD: Littlefield Adams, 1978.

Boykoff, Maxwell T., and Jules M. Boykoff. "Balance as Bias: Global Warming and the U.S. Prestige Press." *Global Environmental Change,* 14 (2004): 125–136.

Brewer, Marilynn, and N. Miller. Beyond the Contact Hypothesis: Theoretical Perspectives on Desegregation. In N. Miller and M. Brewer, eds., *Groups in Contact: The Psychology of Desegregation.* New York: Academic Press, 1984.

Brodkin, Karen. *How Jews Became White Folks and What That Says about Race in America.* New Brunswick, NJ: Rutgers University Press, 1998.

Brohman, John. "Postwar Development in the Asian NICs: Does the Neoliberal Model Fit Reality?" *Economic Geography,* 72 (2, 1996): 107–130.

The Brookings Institution. *MetroNation: How U.S. Metro Areas Fuel American Prosperity.* Washington, DC, 2007.

Brooks, David. "Sex and the Cities." *New York Times,* May 1, 2004.

Brooks, David. "Nonconformity Is Skin Deep." *New York Times,* August 27, 2006.

Brott, Armin. "The Battered Statistic Syndrome." *Washington Post,* July 31, 1994.

Brown, Lester R. *Outgrowing the Earth: The Food Security Challenge in an Age of Falling Water Tables and Rising Temperatures.* New York: Norton, 2005.

Brown, Michael E., ed. *Theories of War and Peace.* Cambridge, MA: MIT Press, 1998.

Brown, Susan L., Gary R. Lee, and Jennifer Roebuck Bulanda. "Cohabitation among Older Adults: A National Portrait." *The Journals of Gerontology Series B: Psychological Sciences and Social Sciences,* 61 (2006): S71–S79.

Brown, Tony N. "Critical Race Theory Speaks to the Sociology of Mental Health: Mental Health Problems Produced by Racial Stratification." *Journal of Health and Social Behavior,* 44 (September 2003): 292–301.

Brownmiller, Susan. *Against Our Will.* New York: Simon and Schuster, 1976.

Bruns, Axel. *Gatewatching: Collaborative: Collaborative Online News Production.* New York: Peter Lang, 2005.

Bryner, Jeanna. "Teen Birth Rates Higher in Highly Religious States." MSNBC.com, September 16, 2009. Available at: www .msnbc.msn.com/id/32884806

Buchanan, Pat. *The Death of the West: How Dying Populations and Immigrant Invasions Imperil Our Country and Civilization.* New York: Thomas Dunne Books, 2002.

Bumiller, Elisabeth. "Bush Urges Graduates to Use Science to Protect Human Dignity." *New York Times,* May 7, 2006, 34.

Bumpass, Larry, and H. Lu. "Trends in Cohabitation and Implications for Children's Family Contexts in the United States." *Population Studies,* 54 (2000): 29–41.

Burawoy, Michael. *Manufacturing Consent.* Chicago: University of Chicago Press, 1980.

Burdick, Eugene, and Arthur J. Brodbeck. *American Voting Behavior.* Westport, CT: Geenwood Press, 1977.

Bureau of Labor Statistics. *Annual Averages of Occupations.* Washington, DC: Department of Labor, 2004a.

Bureau of Labor Statistics. *Small Business Research Summary.* Washington, DC: U.S. Department of Labor, 2004b.

Bureau of Labor Statistics. "Contingent and Alternative Employment Arrangements, February 2005." Washington, DC: U.S. Department of Labor, 2005a.

Bureau of Labor Statistics. "Wives Who Earn More Than Their Husbands, 1987–2003," Table 25, *Annual Economic Supplement.* Washington, DC: U.S. Department of Labor, 2005b. Available at: www.bls.gov/ cps/wlf-table25-2005.pdf

Bureau of Labor Statistics. *Employed Persons by Industry, Sex, Race, and Occupation.* Washington, DC: U.S. Department of Labor, 2006. Available at: www.bls.gov/cps/cpsaat17 .pdf

Bureau of Labor Statistics. "Employed Persons by Detailed Occupation, Sex, Race, and Hispanic or Latino Ethnicity," Household Data Annual Averages. Washington, DC: U.S. Department of Labor, 2008a.

Bureau of Labor Statistics. "Employed Persons by Occupation, Sex and Age," Washington, DC: U.S. Department of Labor, 2008b.

Bureau of Labor Statistics. "Labor Force Statistics from the Current Population Survey: Characteristics of Minimum Wage Workers," 2008c. Available at: www.bls .gov/cps.minwage2008tbls.htm

Bureau of Labor Statistics. *Population Bulletin,* U.S. Department of Labor, 63 (2), 2008d.

Bureau of Labor Statistics. "TED: The Editor's Desk: Wives Earning More Than Their Husbands, 1987–2006." Washington, DC: U.S. Department of Labor, January 9, 2009.

Burgess, A., and N. Hanrahan. "Identifying Forensic Markers in Elderly Sexual Abuse." Washington, DC: National Institute of Justice, 2006.

Burleson, William E. *Bi America: Myths, Truths and Struggles of an Invisible Community.* London: Harrington Park Press, 2005.

Burroughs, Edgar Rice. *Tarzan of the Apes.* New York: A. L. Burt, 1914.

Butler, Katy. "Beyond Rivalry: A Hidden World of Sibling Violence." *New York Times,* February 28, 2006.

Buttel, Frederick H. "New Directions in Environmental Sociology." *Annual Review of Sociology,* 13 (1987): 465–488.

Bryant, Jennings, and Dolf Zilman, eds. *Media Effects: Advances in Theory and Research.* Hillsdale, NJ: Lawrence Erlbaum, 1994.

Califano, J. A. "A Punishment-Only Prison Policy." *America* (February, 1998): 3–4.

Cameron, Rondo, and Larry Neal. *A Concise Economic History of the World.* New York: Oxford University Press, 2002.

Campbell-Kelly, Martin. *From Airline Reservations to Sonic the Hedgehog: A History of the Software Industry.* Cambridge, MA: MIT Press, 2004.

Cancian, Francesca. *The Feminization of Love.* New York: Cambridge University Press, 1987.

Candland, D. K. *Feral Children and Clever Animals: Reflections on Human Nature.* New York: Oxford University Press, 1993.

Cannon, Angie. "DWB: Driving While Black." *U.S. News and World Report,* March 15, 1999, 72.

Cardoso, Fernando, and Ernesto Faletto. *Dependency and Development in Latin America.* Berkeley: University of California Press, 1978.

Carrasquillo, Hector. "The Puerto Rican Family." In Ronald L. Taylor, ed., *Minority Families in the United States: A Multicultural Perspective,* pp. 82–94. Englewood Cliffs, NJ: Prentice Hall, 1994.

Carrington, Christopher. *No Place Like Home: Relationships and Family Life among Lesbians and Gay Men.* Chicago: University of Chicago Press, 2002.

Carrington, William J., and Bruce C. Fallick. "Do Some Workers Have Minimum Wage Careers?" *Monthly Labor Review* (May 2001): 18, 25.

Carter, Susan B., ed. *Historical Statistics of the United States.* New York: Cambridge University Press, 2006.

Caruso, Eugene M., Dobromir A. Rahnev, and Mahzarin R. Banaji. "Using Conjoint Analysis to Detect Discrimination: Revealing Covert Preferences in Overt Choices." *Social Cognition* 27 (1) (February 2009): 128–137.

Casper, Lynne M., and Suzanne M. Bianchi. *Continuity and Change in the American Family.* Thousand Oaks, CA: Sage Publications, 2002.

Castles, Stephen, and Alistair Davidson. *Citizenship and Migration: Globalization and the Politics of Migration.* New York: Routledge, 2000.

Catalyst. *Women of Color in Corporate Management: Three Years Later.* New York: Catalyst, 2003. Available at: www.catalystwomen.org

Catalyst. "Quick Takes: Single People." New York: Catalyst, 2009.

Catton, William Jr., and Riley E. Dunlap. "Environmental Sociology: A New Paradigm." *The American Sociologist,* 13 (1978): 41–49.

Cawthorne, Alexandra, "Elderly Poverty: The Challenge before Us." Washington, DC: Center for American Progress, 2008a.

Cawthorne, Alexandra. *Straight Facts on Women in Poverty.* Washington, DC: Center for American Progress, 2008b. Available at: www.americanprogress.org/issues/2008/10/women_poverty.html

Cazenave, N., and M. Straus. "Race, Class, Network Embeddedness and Family Violence: A Search for Potent Support Systems." *Journal of Comparative Family Studies,* 10, 3 (1979): 282–300.

CBS News. "U.S. Education: Less Bang for the Buck." September 16, 2003. Available at: www.cbsnews.com/stories/2003/08/20/national

CBS News. "Rich/Poor Income Gap Widening To Chasm." May 3, 2008. Available at: www.cbsnews.com/stories/2008/05/03/earlyshow/living/money/main4068795.shtml

Center for Arms Control and Non-Proliferation. "U.S. Military Spending vs. The World," February 22, 2008. Washington, DC.

Center for Changing Families. Online briefing, July 2, 2007.

Center for Educational Reform. "Charter Schools by State." 2007. Available at: www.edreform.com/upload/ncsw-numbers.pdf

Center for Research on Educational Outcomes (CREDO). "Multiple Choice: Charter Performance in Sixteen States." Stanford, CA: CREDO, June 2009.

Center for Women in Politics. "Fact Sheet: Women in Elective Office, 2009," 2009. Washington, DC.

Center for Women's Business Research. *Women-Owned Businesses in the United States, 2006: A Fact Sheet.* Washington, DC: Center for Women's Business Research, 2007.

Center for Women's Business Research. Research & Knowledge, 2009. Available at: www.nfwbo.org/

Centers for Disease Control (CDC). "First Birth Rates by Age of Mother, According to Race and Hispanic Origin," 2002. Available at: www.cdc.gov/nchs/data/statab/t991x02.pdf

Centers for Disease Control (CDC). "Sexual Behavior and Selected Health Measures: Men and Women 15–44 Years of Age." Atlanta: Centers for Disease Control, 2005.

Centers for Disease Control (CDC). *Healthy People, 2010.* Atlanta: Centers for Disease Control, 2006.

Centers for Disease Control (CDC). *Overweight, 2007.* Available at: www.cdc.gov/nchs/fastats/overwt.htm

Centers for Disease Control (CDC). "Recent Trends in Infant Mortality." National Center for Health Statistics Data Brief No. 9. Atlanta: Centers for Disease Control, 2008a.

Centers for Disease Control (CDC). "U.S. Deaths Down Sharply." CDC Online Newsroom, June 11, 2008b. www.cdc.gov/media

Centers for Disease Control (CDC). "Births." *National Vital Statistics Reports.* Atlanta: Centers for Disease Control, Jan. 7, 2009.

Central Intelligence Agency (CIA). *The World Factbook, 2006.* Washington, DC: CIA, 2006. Available at www.cia.gov/library/publications/the-world-factbook

Central Intelligence Agency (CIA). *The World Factbook, 2008.* Washington, DC: CIA, 2008.

Central Intelligence Agency (CIA). *The World Factbook, 2009.* Washington, DC: CIA, 2009.

Chaffee, John. *The Thorny Gates of Learning in Sung China: A Social History of Examinations.* New York: Cambridge University Press, 1985.

Chambliss, William J. *Power, Politics and Crime.* Boulder, CO: Westview Press, 2000.

Chambliss, William J., and Marjorie Zatz, eds. *Making Law.* Bloomington: Indiana University Press, 1993.

Chandler, Alfred Jr., and Bruce Mazlish. *Multinational Corporations and the New Global History.* Cambridge, UK: Cambridge University Press, 2005.

Chandler, Tertius. *Four Thousand Years of Urban Growth: An Historical Census.* Lewiston, NY: Edwin Mellen Press, 1987.

Chang, Jeff. *Total Chaos: The Art and Aesthetics of Hip-Hop.* New York: Basic Civitas Books, 2007.

Charles, Maria, and David B. Grusky. *Occupational Ghettos: The Worldwide Segregation of Women and Men.* Stanford, CA: Stanford University Press, 2004.

Chase-Dunn, Christopher. "The System of World Cities." In M. Timberlake, ed., *Urbanization in the World Economy,* pp. 269–292. Beverly Hills, CA: Sage, 1985.

Chatzky, Jean Sherman. "The Big Squeeze." *Money,* October 1, 1999.

Chen, Shaohua, and Martin Ravalon. "How Have the World's Poorest Fared since the Early 1980s?" Paper prepared for the World Bank, 2006.

Chernow, Ron. *The House of Morgan: An American Banking Dynasty and the Rise of Modern Finance.* New York: Atlantic Monthly Press, 1990.

Chernow, Ron. *Titan: The Life of John D. Rockefeller Sr.* New York: Random House, 1998.

Cherry, Conrad, Betty A. DeBerg, and Amanda Porterfield. *Religion on Campus.* Chapel Hill: University of North Carolina Press, 2003.

Chevan, A. "As Cheaply as One: Cohabitation in the Older Population." *Journal of Marriage and the Family,* 58 (1996): 656–667.

Children's Defense Fund. "Child Poverty in America." Washington, DC: August, 2008.

Childstats.gov. "Births to Unmarried Women." *America's Children: Key National Indicators of Wellbeing.* Washington, DC 2009.

Chilman, Catherine Street. "Hispanic Families in the United States: Research Perspectives." In Harriet Pipes McAdoo, ed., *Family Ethnicity: Strengths in Diversity.* Newbury Park, CA: Sage, 1999.

Christakis, Dimitri A. "Early Television Exposure and Subsequent Attention Problems in Children." *Pediatrics,* April 2004.

Cipolla, Carlo M. *Before the Industrial Revolution.* New York: Norton, 1994.

Clark, David D. *Analysis of Return Rates of the Inmate College Program Participants.* Albany: State of New York Department of Correctional Services, 1991.

Clark, M. L. "Gender, Race and Friendship Research." Paper presented at the annual meeting of the American Educational Research Association, Chicago, April 1985.

Clark, Nancy, and William H. Worger. *South Africa: The Rise and Fall of Apartheid.* Nashville, TN: Longmans, 2004.

Clarkwest, Andrew. "African American Marital Disruption in the 20th Century: What Changed? What Did Not?" Working paper. Ann Arbor: Institute for Social Research, University of Michigan, 2006.

Clausewitz, Claus von. *On War* (1832). Michael Howard and Peter Paret, trans. Princeton, NJ: Princeton University Press, 1984.

Cloward, Richard A., and Lloyd E. Ohlin. *Delinquency and Opportunity: A Theory of Delinquent Gangs.* New York: The Free Press, 1960.

CNNMoney.com. "Gap between Rich, Poor Seen Growing." October 12, 2007.

Coder, J., L. Rainwater, and T. M. Smeeding. 2001. "Poverty Across States, Nations, and Continents." In K. Vleminckx and T. M. Smedding (eds.), *Child Well-Being, Child Poverty, and Child Policy in Modern Nations: What Do We Know?* Bristol, UK: Policy Press; Toronto, Canada: University of Toronto Press, pp. 33–74.

Coe, Neil M., Jennifer Johns, and Kevin Ward. "The Embedded Transnational: The Internationalisation Strategies of the Leading Transnational Temporary Staffing Agencies." *Working Paper 10, Geographies of Temporary Staffing Unit.* Manchester, UK: University of Manchester, May 2009.

Cohany, Sharon R., and Emy Sock. "Trends in Labor Force Participation of Married Mothers of Infants." *Monthly Labor Review Online*, 130 (2, February 2007). Available at: www.bls.gov/opub/mlr/2007/02/art2exc

Cohen, Albert R. *Delinquent Boys: The Culture of the Gang.* New York: The Free Press, 1955.

Cohen, Joel E. *How Many People Can the Earth Support?* New York: Norton, 1995.

Cohen, Patricia. "As Ethics Panels Expand Grip, No Research Field Is Off Limits." *New York Times*, February 28, 2007, 1, 15.

Cohn, D'Vera, and Richard Morin. *American Mobility: Movers, Stayers, Places and Reasons.* Philadelphia, PA: The Pew Research Center, 2008.

Cole, David. "When Race Is the Reason." *The Nation*, March 15, 1999, pp. 22–24.

Cole, T. B. "Rape at U.S. Colleges Often Fueled by Alcohol." *Journal of the American Medical Association*, 296 (August 2, 2006): 504–505.

Coleman, Kenneth, ed. *A History of Georgia.* Athens: University of Georgia Press, 1991.

Coley, Richard, and Paul E. Barton. *Locked Up and Locked Out: An Educational Perspective on the U.S. Prison Population.* Princeton, NJ: Educational Testing Service, 2006.

The College Board. "Facts for Education Advocates: International Comparisons." New York: The College Board, 2009a.

The College Board. *Trends in College Pricing 2008.* New York: The College Board, 2009b.

Collins, Patricia Hill. *Fighting Words: Black Women and the Search for Justice.* Minneapolis: University of Minnesota Press, 1998.

Collins, Randall. *The Credential Society: A Historical Sociology of Education and Stratification.* New York: Academic Press, 1979.

Coltrane, Scott. *Family Man: Fatherhood, Housework, and Gender Equity.* New York: Oxford University Press, 1996.

Coltrane, Scott. "Fathering: Paradoxes, Contradictions and Dilemmas." In Marilyn Coleman and Lawrence Ganong, eds., *Handbook of Contemporary Families: Considering the Past, Contemplating the Future*, pp. 224–243. Thousand Oaks, CA: Sage, 2004.

The Commonwealth Fund. "How Will Comprehensive Reform Improve Health Care for Americans?" Supplement to the *Columbia Journalism Review*, September/October, 2009.

Computer Security Institute and Federal Bureau of Investigation. *Computer Crime and Security Survey. 2005.* Available at: www.cpppe.umd.edu/Bookstore/Documents/2005CSISurvey.pdf

Comte, Auguste. *Essential Writings*, Gertrud Lenzer, ed. New York: Harper, 1975.

Condry, J., and S. Condry. "Sex Differences: A Study in the Eye of the Beholder." *Child Development*, 47, 1976.

Conley, Kevin. "The Players." *The New Yorker*, July 11, 2005.

Connell, R. W. *Masculinities.* Berkeley: University of California Press, 1995.

Consoli, John. "Nielsen: TV Viewing Grows." *Mediaweek*, September 21, 2006. Available at: www.mediaweek.com/mw/news/recent_display.jsp?vnu_content_id7=1003154980

Conte, Christopher, and Albert R. Karr. "An Outline of the U.S. Economy," Chapter 3. International Information Programs, U.S. Government, 2001. Available at: http://usinfo.state.gov/products/pubs/econ/

Cookson, Peter W. Jr., and Caroline Hodges Percell. *Preparing for Power: America's Elite Boarding Schools.* New York: Basic Books, 1985.

Cooley, Charles Horton. *Human Nature and the Social Order* (1902). New York: Transaction, 1983.

Cooley, Charles Horton, *On Self and Social Organization* (1909). Hans Joachim-Schubert, ed. Chicago: University of Chicago Press, 1990.

Coontz, Stephanie. *Social Origins of Private Life: A History of American Families, 1600–1900.* New York: Verso, 1988.

Coontz, Stephanie. *Marriage: A History.* New York: Viking, 2005.

Cooper, Frederick. *Colonialism in Question: Theory, Knowledge, History.* Berkeley: University of California Press, 2005.

Cornell, Claire, and Richard Gelles. "Adolescent to Parent Violence." *Urban and Social Change Review*, 15 (1982): 8–14.

The Corporate Library. *Corporate Library's Annual CEO Pay 2007.* Portland, ME: Corporate Library, December, 2007.

Coser, Lewis A. *The Functions of Social Conflict.* Glencoe, IL: The Free Press, 1956.

Costa, P. T., and R. R. McCrae. "Age Difference in Personality Structure: A Cluster Analytic Approach." *Journal of Gerontology*, 31 (1978): 564–570.

Costello, B. J., and P. R. Vowell, "Testing Control Theory and Differential Association: A Reanalysis of the Richmond Youth Project Data." *Criminology*, 37 (4, 1999): 815–842.

Coult, Allan. *Cross-Tabulations of Murdock's World Ethnographic Sample.* Columbia: University of Missouri Press, 1965.

Council for American Private Education. *Benefits of Private Education, 2005.* Available at: www.capenet.org/benefits4.html#fn11

Couprie, Helene. "Time Allocation within the Family: Welfare Implications of Life in a Couple." *Economic Journal*, January 2007: 1–12.

Craig, Kellina M., and Craig R. Waldo. "So, What's a Hate Crime Anyway? Young Adults' Perceptions of Hate Crimes, Victims and Perpetrators." *Law and Human Behavior*, 20 (2, April 1996): 113–129.

Crary, David. "Bible Belt Leads U.S. in Divorces." Associated Press, November 12, 1999. Available at: www.ncpa.org/pd/social/pd111999g.html

Crister, Greg. *Fat Land: How Americans Became the Fattest People in the World.* Boston: Houghton Mifflin, 2003.

Crittenden, Ann. *The Price of Motherhood: Why the Most Important Job in the World Is Still the Least Valued.* New York: Metropolitan Books, 2001.

Crittenden, Ann. *If You've Raised Kids, You Can Manage Anything.* New York: Gotham, 2005.

Crittenden, Danielle. *What Our Mothers Didn't Tell Us: Why Happiness Eludes the Modern Woman.* New York: Simon & Schuster, 1999.

Crompton, Rosemary. *Class and Stratification: An Introduction to Current Debates.* Cambridge, UK: Polity, 1993.

Cross, Harry, Genevieve Kenney, Jane Mell, and Wendy Zimmerman. *Employer Hiring Practices: Differential Treatment of Hispanic and Anglo Job Seekers.* Washington, DC: The Urban Institute Press, 1990.

Croteau, David, and William Hoynes. *Media/Society: Industries, Images, and Audiences.* Thousand Oaks, CA: Pine Forge Press, 2003.

Cumings, Bruce. *Korea's Place in the Sun.* New York: W. W. Norton, 1998.

Cummings, H. J. "Permanent Temps." *Chicago Tribune*, 2004 (June 8), 12.

Currie, Elliot. *Confronting Crime: An American Challenge.* New York: Pantheon, 1985.

Dahl, Gordon, and Enrico Moretti. *The Demand for Sons: Evidence from Divorce, Fertility, and Shotgun Marriage.* Washington, DC: National Bureau of Economic Research, Paper #10281, February 2004.

Dailard, C. "Sex Education: Politicians, Parents, Teachers and Teens." *The Guttmacher Report on Public Policy*, 4 (1, 2001): 9–12.

Daly, Kathleen. "Neither Conflict Nor Labeling Nor Paternalism Will Suffice: Intersections of Race, Ethnicity, Gender, and Family in Criminal Court Decisions." *Crime and Delinquency*, 35 (1989): 136–168.

Daly, Kathleen, and M. Chesney-Lind. "Feminism and Criminology." *Justice Quarterly*, 5 (1988): 497–538.

Daly, Martin, and Margaret Wilson. "Child Maltreatment from a Sociobiological Perspective." *New Directions for Child Development*, 11 (1981): 93–112.

Daly, Martin, and Margo Wilson. *The Truth about Cinderella: A Darwinian View of Parental Love.* New Haven, CT: Yale University Press, 1999.

Darroch, J. E., David Landry, and Susheela Singh. "Changing Emphases in Sexuality Education in U.S. Public Secondary Schools, 1988–1999." *Family Planning Perspectives*, 32 (5, 2000): 204–211, 265.

Davis, Devra Lee, Michelle B. Gottlieb, and Julie R. Stampnitzky. "Reduced Ratio of Male to Female Births in Several Industrial Countries: A Sentinel Health Indicator?" *Journal of the American Medical Association*, 279 (13, April 1998).

Davis, James A., Tom W. Smith, and Peter V. Marsden. General Social Surveys

1972–2006: [Cumulative file] [Computer file]. 2nd ICPSR version. Chicago, IL: National Opinion Research Center [producer], 2005. Storrs, CT: Roper Center for Public Opinion Research, University of Connecticut/Ann Arbor, MI: Inter-University Consortium for Political and Social Research/ Berkeley, CA: Computer-Assisted Survey Methods Program, University of California [distributors], 2006. http://sda.berkeley.edu/cgi-bin/hsda?harcsda+gsso4

Davis, Kingsley, and Wilbert E. Moore. "Some Principles of Stratification." *ASR* 10 (2, 1945): 242–249.

Dawkins, Richard. *The Selfish Gene.* New York: Oxford University Press, 1976.

Dawkins, Richard. *The God Delusion.* Boston: Houghton-Mifflin, 2007.

De Bens, Els, Mary Kelly, and Marit Bakke. "Television Content: Dallasification of Culture?" In Kareen Siune and Wolfgang Treutzschler, eds., *Dynamics of Media Politics: Broadcast and Electronic Media in Western Europe,* pp. 75–100. London: Sage Press, 1992.

De Rougemont, Denis. *Love in the Western World.* Princeton, NJ: Princeton University Press, 1983.

Dean, Cornelia. "Scientific Savvy? In U.S., Not Much." *New York Times,* August 30, 2005.

Death Penalty Information Center. *The Death Penalty in 2008: Year End Report.* Washington, DC: December 2008.

Defronzo, James. *Revolutions and Revolutionary Movements.* Boulder, CO: Westview Press, 1996.

Degler, Carl N. *At Odds: Women and the Family in America from the Revolution to the Present.* New York: Oxford University Press, 1980.

Deloitte. *Global Security Survey. 2004.* Available at: www.deloitte.com/dtt/cda/doc/content/dtt_financialservices_2005GlobalSecuritySurvey_2004-07-21.pdf

Deloitte. *Global Security Survey. 2005.* Available at: www.deloitte.com/dtt/cda/doc/content/dtt_financialservices_2005GlobalSecuritySurvey_2005

DeNavas-Walt, Carmen, Bernadette D. Proctor, and Cheryl Hill Lee. *Income, Poverty, and Health Insurance Coverage in the United States: 2005.* Washington, DC: U.S. Census Bureau, 2006.

DeNavas-Walt, Carmen, Bernadette D. Proctor, and Jessica C. Smith, "Income, Poverty, and Health Insurance Coverage in the United States: 2007." U.S. Census Bureau, Current Population Reports, P60-235. Washington, DC: U.S. Government Printing Office, 2008.

Dennett, Daniel C. *Breaking the Spell: Religion as a Natural Phenomenon.* New York: Viking, 2006.

DePaolo, Bella, and E. Kay Trimberger. "Single Women." *Sociologists for Women in Society Fact Sheet,* Winter 2008. Available at: www.socwomen.org/wint08_fs.pdf

DeParle, Jason. "Census Reports a Sharp Increase in Never-Married Mothers; Puncturing Stereotypes of Out-of-Wedlock Births." *New York Times,* July 14, 1993.

Department for Environment, Food and Rural Affairs. "Municipal Waste Management Statistics 2007/08." London: DEFRA, November 2008.

Deux, Kay, and Lawrence S. Wrightsman. *Social Psychology,* 5th ed. Pacific Grove, CA: Thomson/Brooks Cole, 1988.

deVaus, David, and Ian McAllister. "Gender Differences in Religion: A Test of the Structural Location Theory." *American Sociological Review* 52 (1987): 472–481.

Digest of Educational Statistics, Table 254, "Bachelor's Degrees Conferred by Degree-Granting Institutes, by Discipline and Division, Selected Years, 1970–71 through 2004–05." Washington, DC: National Center for Education Statistics, 2006.

Dillon, Sam. "Education Chief to Warn Advocates That Inferior Charter Schools Harm the Effort." *New York Times,* June 22, 2009: A10.

"Divorce Rate Drops Like a High Fly Ball." *Rocky Mountain News,* October 15, 2007.

Dixon, John. *Searching for Aboriginal Languages: Memoirs of a Field Worker.* Chicago: University of Chicago Press, 1984.

Dobrzynski, Judith H. "The Highest Paid Women in Corporate America." *Forbes,* September 10, 2008.

Dobson, James. *Marriage under Fire: Why We Must Win This Battle.* Colorado Springs, CO: Multnomah Publishers, 2004.

Domhoff, G. William. *Who Rules America?* Englewood-Cliffs, NJ: Prentice-Hall, 1967.

Domhoff, G. William. *The Bohemian Grove and Other Ruling Class Retreats.* New York: Harper and Row, 1974.

Domhoff, G. William. *Who Rules America? Power and Politics,* 4th ed. Boston: McGraw-Hill, 2002.

Donnerstein, Edward. *The Question of Pornography.* New York: Free Press, 1985.

"Dossier: Red-State Values." *American Prospect,* January 4, 2006.

Doyle, Roger. "Ethnic Groups in the World." *Scientific American,* September 1998, 30.

"Dreams Only Money Can Buy." *Business Week,* April 14, 2003, 66.

Dreier, Peter, John Mollenkopf, and Todd Swanstrom. *Place Matters: Metropolitics for the Twenty-First Century.* Lawrence: University Press of Kansas, 2005.

DuBois, W. E. B. *The Philadelphia Negro* (1899). Elijah Anderson and Isabel Eaton, eds. Philadelphia: University of Pennsylvania Press, 1996.

DuBois, W. E. B. *The Souls of Black Folk* (1903). Bartleby.com, 1999.

Duberman, Martin. *Cures.* New York: Dutton, 1991.

Dudenhefer, Paul. "Poverty in the Rural United States." *Focus,* 15 (1, 1993): 37–46.

Duneier, Mitchell. *Sidewalk.* New York: Farrar, Straus and Giroux, 1999.

Dunn, T., and D. Holtz-Eakin. "Financial Capital, Human Capital and the Transition to Self-Employment: Evidence from Intergenerational Links." *Journal of Labor Economics,* 18 (2000): 282–305.

Durkheim, Emile. *The Division of Labor in Society* (1893). New York: The Free Press, 1997.

Durkheim, Emile. *The Rules of the Sociological Method* (1895). New York: The Free Press, 1997.

Durkheim, Emile. *Suicide* (1897). New York: Penguin Classics, 2007.

Dworkin, Andrea. *Intercourse.* New York: The Free Press, 1985.

Dworkin, Andrea. *Heartbreak: The Political Memoir of a Feminist Militant.* New York: Basic Books, 2002.

Dye, Jane Lawler. *Fertility of American Women.* Washington, DC: Current Population Reports, U.S. Census Bureau, 2008.

Dyer, Richard. *Heavenly Bodies: Film Stars and Society.* New York: St. Martins, 1987.

Ebaugh, Helen Rose Fuchs. *Becoming an Ex: The Process of Role Exit.* Chicago, IL: University of Chicago Press, 1988.

Eberstadt, Nicholas. "Why Poverty Doesn't Rate." *The Washington Post,* September 3, 2006, B01.

Economic Mobility Project. *Economic Mobility: Is the American Dream Alive and Well?* Philadelphia: The Pew Charitable Trusts, 2006.

Economic Policy Institute. *The State of Working America.* Washington, DC: Economic Policy Institute, 2007.

Economic Policy Institute. *State of Working America, 2008/2009.* Available at: www.epi.org

The Economist. "As They Don't Like It: Europe's Demographic Disaster Is Self-Inflicted but Not Terminal." 2005a (October 20).

The Economist. "Going Global: Why Street Things Are Getting Nastier." 2005b (February 26): 29.

The Economist. "Mind the Gap." 2005c (June 11).

The Economist. "New Thinking about an Old Problem." 2005d (September 17): 36.

The Economist. "Secrets of Success." 2005e (September 8).

The Economist. "An Underclass Rebellion." 2005f (November 10), 40.

The Economist. "Why Women Live Longer Than Men." 2005g (January 13).

The Economist. "A World of Opportunity." 2005h (September 8).

The Economist. "Calculating Casualties." 2006a (October 12), 52.

The Economist. "Decoupled: Companies' and Countries' Prosperity." 2006b (February 23).

The Economist. "The Flicker of a Brighter Future." 2006c (September 7), 51.

The Economist. "Mind the Gap." 2006d (September 9), 76.

The Economist. "Nollywood Dreams." 2006e (July 27), 48.

The Economist. "The World Is Our Oyster." 2006f (October 5), 35–37.

The Economist. "The World Goes to Town." Special section on Global Urbanization. 2007 (May 5), 3–11.

The Economist. "How to Smite Smoot: Gains from Immigration Could Be Greater Than Those from More Trade." 2008a (March 27).

The Economist. "In Search of a New Economy." 2008b (November 6).

The Economist. "Light Work: Questioning the Hawthorne Effect." 2009a (June 4).

The Economist. "Rags to Riches: America's Thriving Gossip Magazines." 2009b (June 20), 68–69.

The Economist. "A Special Report on Ageing Populations." 2009c (June 27).

The Economist. "Special Report on the New Middle Classes." 2009d (February 14), 6.

The Economist, "The Underworked American." 2009e (June 13), 40.

Edelman, Benjamin. "Red Light States: Who Buys Adult Online Entertainment?" *Journal of Economic Perspectives,* 23, 1 (Winter, 2009): 209–220.

Education Trust. *"Funding Gaps."* 2006. Available at: www2.edtrust.org/EdTrust/Press+Room/Funding+Gap+2006.htm

Edwards, S. S. M. "Neither Bad nor Mad: The Female Violent Offender Reassessed." *Women's Studies International Forum,* 9 (1986): 79–87.

Efron, Sonni. *"Eating Disorders on the Increase in Asia,"* 2005. Available at: www.dimensionsmagazine.com/news/asia/html

Egley, Arlen Jr., and Christina E. O'Donnell. *Highlights of the 2007 National Youth Gang Survey.* Washington, DC, Office of Juvenile Justice and Delinquency Prevention, 2009.

Ehrenreich, Barbara. *Nickel and Dimed: On (Not) Getting by in America.* New York: Owl Books, 2001.

Ehrlich, Paul. *The Population Bomb.* New York: Ballantine Books, 1968.

Eisenstein, Elizabeth. *The Printing Revolution in Early Modern Europe.* New York: Cambridge University Press, 1993.

Ekman, P., and Wallace V. Friesen. "A New Pan Cultural Facial Expression of Emotion." *Motivation and Emotion,* 10 (2, 1986): 886–891.

Ekman, Paul, and Wallace V. Friesen. *Facial Action Coding System: A Technique for the Measurement of Facial Movement.* Palo Alto, CA: Consulting Psychologists Press, 1978.

Elder, Glenn, and Elizabeth Pavalko. "Work Careers in Men's Later Years: Transitions, Trajectories and Historical Change." *Journal of Gerontology,* 48 (4, 1993): S180–S191.

Elliot, Jane. *The Eye of the Storm.* DVD, 1970. ABC News, New York.

Elliott, Diana B., and Jane Lawler Dye. "Unmarried Partner Households in the United States." A paper presented at the Annual Meeting of the Population Association of America, Philadelphia, March 31–April 2, 2005.

England, Paula, Emily Fitsgibbons Shafer, and Alison C. K. Fogerty. "Hooking Up and Forming Romantic Relationships on Today's College Campus." In Michael Kimmel and Amy Aronson, eds., *The Gendered Society Reader,* pp. 531–547. New York: Oxford University Press, 2008.

Ericson, Richard V., and Keven D. Haggerty. *Policing the Risk Society.* Oxford, UK: Clarendon Press, 1997.

Erikson, Erik. *Identity and the Life Cycle: Selected Papers.* Chicago: University of Chicago Press, 1959.

Erikson, Kai T. *Everything in Its Path: Destruction of Community in the Buffalo Creek Flood.* New York: Simon & Schuster, 1978.

Esbensen, F. A., and L. T. Winfree Jr. "Race and Gender Differences between Gang and Non-Gang Youth: Results From a Multi-Site Survey." *Justice Quarterly,* 15 (1998): 505–525.

Escobar, Gabriel, and Anne Swardson. "From Language to Literature, a New Guiding Lite." *Washington Post,* September 5, 1995, 1, A 18.

Esping-Anderson, G. *The Three Worlds of Welfare Capitalism.* Princeton, NJ: Princeton University Press, 1990.

Esposito, John, and Dalia Mogahed. "What Do Muslim Women Want?" Gallup, March 20, 2008.

Etzioni, Amitai. *A Comparative Analysis of Complex Organization: On Power, Involvement, and Their Correlates.* Revised and enlarged ed. New York: Free Press, 1975.

Etzioni, Amitai. "Going Soft on Corporate Crime." *Washington Post,* April 1, 1990, C3.

Etzioni, Amitai. "What Society Owes Older Generations." *The American Scholar,* Spring 2005, pp. 32–40.

Etzioni-Halevy, Eva. *Bureaucracy and Democracy: A Political Dilemma.* London: Routledge and Kegan Paul, 1983.

European Environment Agency. *Diverting Waste from Landfill: Effectiveness of Waste-Management Policies in the European Union.* Copenhagen, Denmark, 2009.

Evans, Peter B., and James E. Rauch. "Bureaucratic and Growth: A Cross-National Analysis of the Effects of 'Weberian' State Structures on Economic Growth." *American Sociological Review,* 64 (5, 1999): 748–765.

Fairlie, Robert W., and Christopher Woodruff, "Mexican-American Entrepreneurship." Paper presented at the Tenth Annual Meeting of the Society of Labor Economists, San Francisco, June 2005.

Faludi, Susan. *Backlash: The Undeclared War against American Women.* New York: Crown, 1991.

Families USA. *Americans at Risk: One in Three Uninsured.* March 2009. New York.

Farber, Susan L. "Identical Twins Reared Apart." *Science,* 215 (February, 1982): 959–960.

Farkas, G. *Human Capital or Cultural Capital? Ethnicity and Poverty Groups in an Urban School District.* New York: Aldine, 1996.

Farkas, G., R. P. Grobe, D. Sheehan, and Y. Shuan. "Cultural Resources and School Success: Gender, Ethnicity, and Poverty Groups within an Urban School District." *American Sociological Review,* 55 (1990a): 127–142.

Farkas, G., D. Sheehan, and R. P. Grobe. "Coursework Mastery and School Success: Gender, Ethnicity, and Poverty Groups within an Urban School District." *American Educational Research Journal,* 27 (4, 1990b): 807–827.

Farrell, Elizabeth, and Eric Hoover. "Getting Schooled in Student Life." *Chronicle of Higher Education,* July 29, 2005, 36.

Fass, Sarah, and Nancy K. Cauthen. *Who Are America's Poor? The Official Story.* National Center for Children in Poverty, 2006. Available at: www.nccp.org/publications/pub_684.html

Faulks, Keith. *Political Sociology: A Critical Introduction.* New York: New York University Press, 2000.

Featherman, D., and R. Hauser. *Opportunity and Change.* New York: Academic Press, 1978.

Federal Election Commission. *PAC Activity Increases.* Washington, DC: Federal Election Commission, August 30, 2006.

Federal Interagency Forum on Aging Related Statistics. *Older Americans 2008: Key Indicators of Well-Being,* 2008. Washington, DC.

Federal Trade Commission. *Consumer Fraud and Identity Theft Complaint Data, January–December 2006.* Washington, DC: Federal Trade Commission.

Federal Trade Commission. *Consumer Sentinel Network Data Book.* Washington, DC: Federal Trade Commission, February 2009.

Ferguson, Ann Arnett. *Bad Boys: Public Schools in the Making of Black Masculinity.* Ann Arbor: University of Michigan Press, 2001.

Ferguson, Ronald. "Cultivating New Routines That Foster High Achievement for All Students: How Researchers and Practitioners Can Collaborate to Reduce the Minority Achievement Gap." *ERS Spectrum,* 19 (4, Fall 2001).

Fernie, Sue, and David Metcalf. *Trade Unions: Resurgence or Decline?* New York: Routledge, 2005.

Ferrell, Jeff, and Eugene Stewart-Huidobro. *Crimes of Style: Urban Graffiti and the Politics of Criminality.* Boston: Northeastern University Press, 1996.

Festinger, Leon. *When Prophesy Fails.* New York: Harper and Row, 1957.

Fields, Jason. "Living Arrangements of Children." *Current Population Reports.* Washington, DC: U.S. Census Bureau, April, 2000: 9.

Fields, Jason, and Lynne M. Casper. "America's Families and Living Arrangements: March 2000." *Current Population Reports,* 2001: 520–537.

FIFA.com. "2006 World Cup Broadcast Wider, Longer and Farther Than Ever Before." February 6, 2007. Available at: www.fifa.com/aboutfifa/marketingtv/news/newsid= 111247.html

Filoux, J. C. "Inequalities and Social Stratification in Durkheim's Sociology." In S. P. Turner, ed., *Emile Durkheim: Sociologist and Moralist.* London: Routledge, 1993.

Finder, Alan. "Matters of Faith Find a New Prominence on Campus." *New York Times,* May 2, 2007, A16.

Finkelhor, David, Heather Turner, and Richard Ormrod. "Kid Stuff: The Nature and Impact of Peer and Sibling Violence on Younger and Older Children." *Child Abuse and Neglect,* 20 (2006): 1401–1421.

Firebaugh, Glen. "Does Foreign Capital Harm Poor Nations? New Estimates Based on Dixon and Boswell's Measures of Capital Penetration." *American Journal of Sociology,* 102 (2, 1996): 563–575.

Firebaugh, Glen. "Empirics of World Income Inequality." *American Journal of Sociology,* 104 (6, 1999): 1597–1630.

Firebaugh, Glen, and Frank D. Beck. "Does Economic Growth Benefit the Masses? Growth, Dependence, and Welfare in the Third World." *American Sociological Review,* 59 (5, 1994): 631–653.

Firebaugh, Glen, and Dumitru Sandu. "Who Supports Marketization and Democratization in Post-Communist Romania?" *Sociological Forum,* 13 (3, 1998): 521–541.

Fischer, Claude S. *To Dwell among Friends: Personal Networks in Town and City.* Chicago: University of Chicago Press, 1982.

Fischer, Claude, Michael Hout, Martin Sanchez-Jankowski, Samuel R. Lucas, Ann Swidler, and Kim Voss. *Inequality by Design: Cracking the Bell Curve Myth.* Princeton, NJ: Princeton University Press, 1996.

Fish, Stanley. *Is There a Text in This Class? The Authority of Interpretive Communities.* Cambridge, MA: Harvard University Press, 1980.

Fisher, Allen. "Still 'Not Quite as Good as Having Your Own'? Toward a Sociology of Adoption." *Annual Review of Sociology,* 2003: 335–361.

Fisher, Kimberley, Muriel Egerton, Jonathan I. Gershuny, and John P. Robinson. "Gender Convergence in the American Heritage Time Use Study (AHTUS)." *Social Indicators Research,* 2006.

Fitzgibbon, Marian, and Melinda Stolley. "Dying to Be Thin—Minority Women: The Untold Story." *Nova,* 2000. Available at: www.pbs.org/wgbh/nova/thin/minorities .html

Fitzpatrick/Austin, Laura. "Can Community Colleges Save the U.S. Economy?" *Time,* July 10, 2009, 48–51.

Fleisher, M. S., and J. L. Krienert. "Life-Course Events, Social Networks, and the Emergence of Violence among Female Gang Members." *Journal of Community Psychology,* 32 (2004): 607–622.

Foner, Eric. "Hiring Quotas for White Males Only." *The Nation,* June 26, 1995, 924.

Foote, Christopher, and Christopher Goetz. "Testing Economic Hypotheses with State-Level Data: A Comment on Donohue and Levitt (2001)." *Federal Reserve Bank of Boston Working Paper,* November 2005.

Foran, John. *Theorizing Revolutions.* New York: Routledge, 1997.

Fordham, Signithia, "Peer-Proofing Competition among Black Adolescents: 'Acting White' Black American Style." In Christine E. Sleeter, ed., *Empowerment through Multicultural Education.* Albany: SUNY Press, 1991.

Fordham, Signithia. *Blacked Out.* Chicago: University of Chicago Press, 1996.

Foucault, Michel. *Power/Knowledge: Selected Interviews & Other Writings, 1972–1977.* Colin Gordon, ed. New York: Pantheon Books, 1980.

Foucault, Michel. *Discipline & Punish: The Birth of the Prison* (1975). New York: Vintage, 1995.

Fowlkes, M. R. "Single Worlds and Homosexual Lifestyles: Patterns of Sexuality and Intimacy." In A. S. Rossi, ed., *Sexuality across the Life Course,* pp. 151–184. Chicago: University of Chicago Press, 1994.

Fox, Robin. *Kinship and Marriage: An Anthropological Perspective.* New York: Cambridge University Press, 1984.

Fox, Ronald C., ed. *Current Research in Bisexuality.* London: Harrington Park Press, 2004.

Fox, Stephen R. *The Mirror Makers: A History of American Advertising and Its Creators.* Urbana: University of Illinois Press, 1997.

Franklin, Clyde. 'Hey Home'—'Yo, Bro': Friendship among Black Men." In Peter Nardi, ed., *Men's Friendships.* Newbury Park, CA: Sage Publications, 1992.

Fraser, Jill Andresky. *White Collar Sweatshop: The Deterioration of Work and Its Reward in Corporate America.* New York: W. W. Norton, 2001.

Frazier, Franklin E. *The Negro Church in America.* New York: Schocken Books, 1974.

Freedman, Vicki A., Linda G. Martin, and Robert F. Schoeni. "Recent Trends in Dis-ability and Functioning among Older Adults in the United States." *Journal of the American Medical Association,* 288 (24, 2002): 3137–3146.

Frey, William H. *Metro America in the New Century: Metropolitan and Central City Demographic Shifts since 2000.* Washington, DC: Brookings Institute, 2005.

Friedan, Betty. *The Feminine Mystique.* New York: Dell, 1963.

Friedel, Ernestine. *Women and Men: An Anthropologist's View.* New York: Holt, Rinehart, 1975.

Friedman, Michael J. "Minority Groups Now One-Third of U.S. Population," July 14, 2006. Available at: USInfo.state .gov

Friedman, Milton. "The Role of Government in Education." In Robert A. Solo, ed., *Economics and the Public Interest.* New Brunswick, NJ: Rutgers University Press, 1955.

Friedman, Thomas. *The Lexus and the Olive Tree: Understanding Globalization.* New York: Farrar Straus and Giroux, 2000.

Friedman, Thomas. *The World Is Flat: A Brief History of the Twenty-First Century.* New York: Farrar, Straus and Giroux, 2005.

Friends Committee on National Legislation. "Allocation of U.S. 2009 Taxes." July 2008. Washington, DC.

Fulghum, Robert. *All I Really Need to Know I Learned in Kindergarten.* New York: Villard Books, 1988.

Fuller, Margaret. *Woman in the Nineteenth Century* (1845). Donna Dickenson, ed. New York: Oxford University Press, 1994.

Fussell, Elizabeth, and Frank Furstenberg. "The Transition to Adulthood during the 20th Century: Race, Nativity and Gender." In Richard R. Settersten Jr., Frank F. Furstenberg, and Ruben G. Rumbaut, eds., *On the Frontier of Adulthood: Theory, Research and Public Policy.* Chicago: University of Chicago Press, 2006.

Gagnon, John. "Physical Strength, Once of Significance." *Impact of Science on Society,* 21 (1, 1971): 31–42.

Gagnon, John, and William Simon. *Sexual Conduct.* Chicago: Aldine, 1967.

Gamson, Joshua. *Claims to Fame: Celebrity in Contemporary America.* Berkeley: University of California Press, 1994.

Gamson, Joshua, and Pearl Latteir. "Do Media Monsters Devour Diversity?" *Contexts,* 3 (3, 2004): 26–32.

Gamson, William. *The Strategy of Social Protest.* New York: Dorsey Press, 1975.

Gans, Herbert. *The Urban Villagers.* New York: The Free Press, 1962.

Gans, Herbert. *People and Places.* New York: The Free Press, 1968.

Gans, Herbert J. *Deciding What's News: A Study of CBS Evening News, NBC Nightly News, Newsweek, and Time.* New York: Random House, 1979.

Garbarino, James. *Lost Boys: Why Our Sons Turn Violent and How We Can Save Them.* New York: Anchor Books, 1999.

García-Moreno, Claudia, Henrica A. F. M. Jansen, Mary Ellsberg, Lori Heise, and Charlotte Watts. *WHO Multi-Country Study on Women's Health and Domestic Violence against Women.* Geneva: World Health Organization, 2006.

Gardner, Howard. *Frames of Mind: The Theory of Multiple Intelligences.* New York: Basic Books, 1983.

Garfinkel, Harold. *Studies in Ethnomethodology.* Englewood Cliffs, NJ: Prentice Hall, 1967.

Garrett, M. T. "Understanding the 'Medicine' of Native American Traditional Values: An Integrative Review." *Counseling & Values,* 43 (2, 1999): 84–99.

Gates, Jeff. *Statistics on Policy and Inequality. Global Policy Forum,* 1999. Available at: www.glob-alpolicy.org/socecon/inequal/gates99.htm

Gaughan, E., J. Cerio, and R. Myers. *Lethal Violence in Schools: A National Survey Final Report.* Alfred, NY: Alfred University, 2001.

Gelles, Richard, and John Harrop. "The Rise of Abusive Violence among Children with Nongenetic Caretakers." *Family Relations,* 40 (1, January 1991): 78–83.

General Accounting Office. *Death Penalty Sentencing: Research Indicates Pattern of Racial Disparities.* Washington, DC: GAO, 1990.

General Social Survey. Chicago: National Opinion Research Center, University of Chicago, 2006.

Gerber, Jerry, Janet Wolff, Walter Klores, and Gene Brown. *Lifetrends: The Future of Baby Boomers and Other Aging Americans.* New York: Macmillan, 1990.

Gereffi, Gary, and Miguel Korzeniewicz, eds. *Commodity Chains and Global Capitalism.* Westport, CT: Praeger, 1993.

Gernet, Jacques. *History of Chinese Civilization,* J. R. Foster (trans.). Cambridge, UK: Cambridge University Press, 1982.

Gershoff, T. E. "Corporal Punishment by Parents and Associated Child Behaviors and Experiences: A Meta-Analytic and Theoretical Review." *Psychological Bulletin,* 128 (4, 2002): 539–579.

Gerson, K. (2003, December 21). "Working Moms Heading Home? Doesn't Seem Likely." *The Oakland Tribune,* Op-Ed, December 21, 2003.

Gerson, Kathleen. *Hard Choices: How Women Decide about Work, Career and Motherhood.* Berkeley: University of California Press, 1985.

Gerstel, Naomi, and Harriet Engel Gross, "Gender and Families in the United States: The Reality of Economic Dependence." In Jo Freedman, ed., *Women: A Feminist Perspective,* pp. 92–127. Mountain View, CA: Mayfield, 1995.

Ghosh, Suresh. *The History of Education in Ancient India.* New Delhi, India: Munshiram Manoharlal Publishers, 2001.

Gibbs, Nancy. "And on the Seventh Day We Rested?" *Time,* August 2, 2004, 90.

Gilbert, Jess, and Caroline Howe. "Beyond State vs. Society; Theories of the State and New Deal Agricultural Policies." *American Sociological Review,* 56 (1991): 204–220.

Gilborn, D. "Citizenship, 'Race,' and the Hidden Curriculum." *International Studies in the Sociology of Education,* 2 (1992): 57–73.

Gilligan, Carol. *In a Different Voice: Psychological Theory and Women's Development* (1982). Cambridge, MA: Harvard University Press, 1993.

Gilman, Charlotte Perkins. *Herland* (1915). Denise D. Knight, ed. New York: Penguin, 1999.

Gilman, Charlotte Perkins. *Women and Economics* (1898). Michael Kimmel and Amy

Aronson, eds. Berkeley: University of California Press, 1998.

Gilman, Charlotte Perkins, and Julia Bates Dock. *Charlotte Perkins Gilman's "The Yellow Wallpaper and the History of Its Publication and Reception: A Critical Edition and Documentary Casebook.* University Park: Pennsylvania State University Press, 1998.

Gimlin, Debra. *Body Work: Beauty and Self-Image in American Culture.* Berkeley: University of California Press, 2002.

Ginther, Donna K. "Family Structure and Children's Educational Outcomes: Blended Families, Stylized Facts, and Descriptive Regressions." *Demography,* 41 (4, November 2004): 671–696.

Gitlin, Todd. *The Whole World Is Watching: Mass Media and the Unmaking of the New Left.* Berkeley: University of California Press, 1980.

Gitlin, Todd. *Inside Prime Time.* Berkeley: University of California Press, 2000.

Gladwell, Malcolm. "The Cool Hunt." *The New Yorker,* March 17, 1997.

Glassner, Barry. *Bodies.* New York: Putnam, 1988.

Glazer, Nathan. *We're All Multicultural Now.* Cambridge: Harvard University Press, 1998.

Gleckman, Howard, and Rich Miller. "More Risk—More Reward." *BusinessWeek,* July 25, 2005, 37.

Glenn, David. "Supply Side Education." *The Chronicle Review,* July 25, 2008.

Goffman, Erving. *The Presentation of Self in Everyday Life.* New York: Anchor Books, 1959.

Goffman, Erving. *Asylums.* New York: Doubleday, 1961.

Goffman, Erving. *Stigma: Notes on the Management of a Spoiled Identity.* Englewood Cliffs, NJ: Prentice-Hall, 1963.

Goldenberg, Suzanne. "Hispanic Names Make Top 10 in America." *The Guardian,* November 20, 2007.

Goldin, Claudia, and Katz, Lawrence. "Long-Run Changes in the U.S. Wage Structure: Narrowing, Widening, Polarizing." Paper prepared for the Brookings Institution, Washington, DC, 2007. Available at: www.brookings.edu/es/commentary/journals/bpea_macro/forum/200709goldin_katz.pdf

Goldschneider, Francis K., and Linda J. Waite. *New Families, No Families? The Transformation of the American Home. A RAND Study.* Berkeley: University of California Press, 1991.

Goldspink, David. "Why Women Outlive Men." 2005. Available at: www.thenakedscientist.com/html/content/news/news/405

Gomez, Michael A. *Reversing Sail: A History of the African Diaspora.* New York: Cambridge University Press, 2004.

Gooch, Brad. "Spiritual Retreats: Om-ward Bound." *Travel & Leisure,* October 5, 2002.

Goode, Erich. "The Ethics of Deception in Social Research: A Case Study." *Qualitative Sociology,* 19 (1996a): 11–33.

Goode, Erich. "Gender and Courtship Entitlement: Responses to Personal Ads." *Sex Roles,* 34 (3–4, 1996b), 141–169.

Goode, Erich. "Sexual Involvement and Social Research in a Fat Civil Rights Organization." *Qualitative Sociology,* 25 (Winter 2002), 501–534.

Goode, Erich. *Deviant Behavior,* 7th ed. Englewood Cliffs, NJ: Prentice-Hall, 2004.

Goode, William J., "A Theory of Role Strain." *American Sociological Review,* 25 (1960): 483–496.

Goodman, Peter S. "The Hidden Toll on Employment: Cut to Part Time." *The New York Times,* July 31, 2008.

Gottfredson, G. D., and D. C. Gottfredson. *Gang Problems and Gang Programs in a National Sample of Schools.* Ellicott City, MD: Gottfredson Associates, 2001.

Gottfredson, Michael, and Travis Hirschi. *A General Theory of Crime.* Stanford, CA: Stanford University Press, 1990.

Gottfredson, Michael R., and Travis Hirschi. "National Crime Control Policies." *Society,* 32 (2, January–February 1995): 30–36.

Gould, S. J. "Ghosts of Bell Curves Past." *Natural History* (February 1995): 12–19.

Gove, Walter R. "The Relationship between Sex Roles, Marital Status and Mental Illness." *Social Forces,* 51 (1972).

Gove, Walter R., Hughes, M., and Style, C. B. "Does Marriage Have Positive Effects on the Individual?" *Journal of Health and Social Behavior,* 24 (1983): 122–131.

Granovetter, Mark. *Getting a Job: A Study of Contacts and Careers,* 2nd ed. Chicago: University of Chicago Press, 1995.

Granovetter, Mark. "The Strength of Weak Ties."*American Journal of Sociology,* 78 (6, May 1973): 1360–1380.

Granovetter, Mark. *Getting a Job: A Study of Contacts and Careers.* Cambridge, MA: Harvard University Press, 1974.

Gray, John. *Men Are from Mars, Women Are from Venus.* New York: HarperCollins, 1992.

"Green Collar Jobs Overview," 2009. Retrieved October 11, 2009, from: www.greenforall.org/resources/green-collar-jobs-overview/green-collar-jobs-overview

Greenblat, Cathy. "How Do You Know You're in Love?" Unpublished manuscript, Rutgers University, 1998.

Greene, Jay P., and Marcus Winters. *Public High School Graduation and College-Readiness Rates: 1991–2002.* New York: Manhattan Institute, 2005.

Greene, Judith, and Kevin Pranis. *Gang Wars.* Washington, DC: Justice Policy Institute, 2007.

Greenwald, A. G., and S. D. Farnham. "Using Implicit Association Test to Measure Self-Esteem and Self Concept." *Journal of Personality and Social Psychology,* 79 (2000): 1022–1038.

Greenwald, A. G., D. E. McGhee, and J. L. K. Greenwald. "Measuring Individual Differences in Implicit Cognition: The Implicit Association Test." *Journal of Personality and Social Psychology,* 74 (6, 1998): 1464–1480.

Greenwald, A. G., D. E. McGhee, and J. K. L. Schwartz. "Measuring Individual Differences in Implicit Cognition: The Implicit Association Test." *Journal of Personality and Social Psychology,* 74 (1998): 1464–1480.

Gregory, Deborah. "Heavy Judgment." *Essence,* August 14, 1994.

Griffin, Gary A., and Harry F. Harlow. "Effects of Three Months of Total Social Depriva-tion on Social Adjustment and Learning in the Rhesus Monkey." *Child Development,* 37 (3, September 1966): 533–547.

Grimm, Matthew. "Bout Your G-G-Generation—Generation Y." *American Demographics,* September 2003, 38–41.

Gross, Daniel, "Invest Globally, Stagnate Locally." *New York Times,* April 2, 2006: 2.

Grossman, Gene M., and Elhanan Helpman. *Special Interest Politics.* Cambridge, MA: MIT Press, 2001.

Grossman, Lev. "Iran's Protest: Twitter, the Medium of the Movement." Time.com, June 17, 2009.

Grover, Ronald. "The Pornographers vs. the Pirates." *BusinessWeek,* June 19, 2006, 68–69.

Grusky, David B., ed. *Social Stratification: Class, Race, and Gender in Sociological Perspective.* Boulder, CO: Westview Press, 2000.

Gupta, Dipankar. *Interrogating Caste: Understanding Hierarchy and Difference in Indian Society.* New York: Penguin Books, 2000.

Gurr, Ted Robert. *Why Men Rebel.* Princeton, NJ: Princeton University Press, 1971.

Gurr, Ted Robert. *Peoples versus States: Minorities at Risk in the New Century.* Washington, DC: U.S. Institute of Peace, 2000.

Guzzo, Karen Benjamin. "How Do Marriage Market Conditions Affect Entrance into Cohabitation vs. Marriage?" Unpublished paper, Dept. of Sociology, University of Pennsylvania, September 2003.

Hagan, John, and Patricia Parker. "White Collar Crime and Punishment: The Class Structure and Legal Sanctioning of Securities Violations." *American Sociological Review,* 50 (3, June 1985): 302–316.

Hagan, John, and Ruth D. Peterson. *Crime and Inequality.* Stanford, CA: Stanford University Press, 1995.

Hall, G. Stanley. *Adolescence: Its Psychology and Its Relations to Physiology, Anthropology, Sociology, Sex, Crime, Religion, and Education.* New York: D. Appleton and Company, 1904.

Hall, J. A. "After the Fall: An Analysis of Post-Communism." *British Journal of Sociology,* 45 (4, 1994): 14–23.

Hall, Stuart. "Encoding, Decoding." In Simon During, ed., *The Cultural Studies Reader,* pp. 90–103. New York: Routledge, 1993.

Hamamoto, Darrell Y. *Monitored Peril: Asian Americans and the Politics of TV Representation.* Minneapolis: University of Minnesota Press, 1994.

Hamilton, Brady E., Joyce A. Martin, and Stephanie J. Ventura. "Births: Preliminary Data for 2005." Atlanta: Centers for Disease Control, 2006.

Hampton, R. L. "Family Violence and Homicides in the Black Community: Are They Linked?" In *Violence in the Black Family: Correlates and Consequences.* Lexington, MA: Lexington Books, 1987.

Hampton, R. L., and Richard Gelles. "Violence towards Black Women in a Nationally Representative Sample of Black Families." *Journal of Comparative Family Studies,* 25 (1, 1994): 105–119.

Hanisch, Carol. "The Personal Is Political." *Feminist Revolution,* March 1969, 204–205.

Hannan, Michael T., and John Freeman. "The Ecology of Organizational Founding: American Labor Unions, 1836–1985."

American Journal of Sociology, 92 (1987): 910–943.

Hannigan, John. *Environmental Sociology: A Social Constructionist Perspective.* New York: Routledge, 1995.

Hansen, M. H. *The Athenian Democracy in the Age of Demosthenes.* Norman: University of Oklahoma Press, 1999.

Harcourt, Bernard E., and Jens Ludwig. "Broken Windows: New Evidence from New York City and a Five-City Social Experiment." *University of Chicago Law Review,* 73, 1 (2006): 271–320.

Harjo, Suzan Shown. "The American Indian Experience." In Harriette Pipes McAdoo, ed., *Family Ethnicity: Strength in Diversity.* Newbury Park, CA: Sage, 1999.

Harlow, Harry F., Robert O. Dodsworth, and Margaret K. Harlow. "Total Social Isolation in Monkeys." *Proceedings of the National Academy of Sciences of the United States of America,* 54 (1, July 1965): 90–97.

Harlow, Harry F., Margaret K. Harlow, Robert O. Dodsworth, and G. L. Arling. "Maternal Behavior of Rhesus Monkeys Deprived of Mothering and Peer Associations in Infancy." *Proceedings of the American Philosophical Society,* 110 (1, February 1966): 58–66.

Harlow, Harry F., and Stephen J. Suomi. "Social Recovery by Isolation-Reared Monkeys." *Proceedings of the National Academy of Sciences of the United States of America,* 68 (7, July 1971): 1534–1538.

Harris, Lynn. "Asexual and Proud!" Salon. com, May 26, 2006. Available at: www .Salon.com

Harris, Marvin. *Cannibals and Kings.* New York: Random House, 1977.

Harris, Sam. *The End of Faith: Religion, Terror and the Future of Reason.* New York: W. W. Norton, 2004.

Harris, Shanette, "Black Male Masculinity and Same Sex Friendships." *Western Journal of Black Studies,* 16 (2), 1992.

Harris Interactive. "The Prestige Paradox: High Pay Doesn't Equal High Prestige." Available at www.harrisinteractive. com: Harris Interactive, 2008a.

Harris Interactive. "Three in Ten Americans Say Having a Tattoo Makes Them Feel Sexier." Harris Poll #15: February 12, 2008b.

The Harris Poll, May 8, 2004. Available at: www.harrisinteractive . com/harris_poll/index.asp?PID=464.

Hartney, Christopher. *U.S. Rate of Incarceration: A Global Perspective.* Washington, DC: National Council on Crime and Delinquency, 2006.

Harvard Project on American Indian Economic Development, "Facts on American Indian Health Disparities," 2006.

Hayward, M. D., and W. R. Grady. "Work and Retirement among a Cohort of Older Men in the United States, 1963–1983." *Demography,* 27 (3, 1990): 337–356.

Healy, J. *Endangered Minds: Why Children Don't Think and What We Can Do about It.* New York: Simon & Schuster, 1990.

Heilbroner, Robert L. *The Nature and Logic of Capitalism.* New York: W. W. Norton, 1986.

Heimann, C. F. Larry. "Understanding the Challenger Disaster: Organizational Structure and the Design of Reliable Systems."

American Political Science Review, June 1993: 26–28.

Hellmich, Nanci. "33% of Kids Tip Scales Wrong Way." *USA Today,* April 5, 2006, A-1.

Helmond, Ann. "How Many Blogs Are There? Is There Someone Still Counting?" *The Blog Herald,* February 11, 2008.

Hemenway, David. Quoted in Wirzbicki, Alan, "Gun Control Efforts Weaken in the South." *The Boston Globe,* September 4, 2005. Available at: www.boston.com/ news/nation/article/2005/09/07/gun. control/

Henshaw, S. K., and K. Kost. "Abortion Patients in 1994–1995: Characteristics and Contraceptive Use." *Family Planning Perspectives,* 28 (4, July/August 1996). Available online at: www.agi-usa.org/pubs/ journals/2814096.html

Henshaw, S. K., and G. Martire. "Abortion and the Public Opinion Polls: Morality and Legality." *Family Planning Perspectives,* 14 (2, March/April 1982): 53–60.

Hernnstein, Richard, and Charles Murray. *The Bell Curve: Intelligence and Class Structure in American Life.* New York: The Free Press, 1996.

Herskovits, Melville. *The Anthropology of the American Negro.* New York: Columbia University Press, 1930.

Hertz, R., & Ferguson, F. I. "Only One Pair of Hands: Ways That Single Mothers Stretch Work and Family Resources." *Community, Work, & Family,* 1 (1998): 13–37.

Hertz, Rosanna. *Single by Chance, Mothers by Choice.* New York: Oxford University Press, 2006.

Hertz, Tom. "Trends in the Intergenerational Elasticity of Family Income in the United States." *Industrial Relations,* 46 (1, January 2007): 22–50.

Hetherington, Mavis. *For Better or for Worse: Divorce Reconsidered.* New York: W. W. Norton, 2002.

Higher Education Research Institute. "The Spiritual Life of College Students." Los Angeles: UCLA Higher Education Research Institute, 2005.

Hill, G., and S. Hill. *Blacks on Television.* Lanham, MD: Scarecrow Press, 1985.

Hirsch, E. D. *Cultural Literacy: What Every American Needs to Know.* New York: Vintage, 1988.

Hirsch, E. D., Joseph F. Kett, and James Trefil. *Dictionary of Cultural Literacy.* Boston: Houghton Mifflin, 2003.

Hirschi, Travis. *Causes of Delinquency.* Berkeley: University of California Press, 1969.

Hirst, Paul. "The Global Economy—Myth and Realities." *International Affairs,* 73 (1997): 409–425.

Hitt, Emma. "A Boost for Vaccine Research." *Science,* March 28, 2008.

Ho, Vanessa. "Native American Death Rates Soar as Most People Are Living Longer." *Seattle Post-Intelligencer,* March 12, 2009.

Hobbes, Thomas. *Leviathan* (1658). New York: Modern Library, 1966.

Hobsbawm, E. J. *The Age of Revolution, 1776–1848.* New York: Anchor, 1962.

Hobsbawm, Eric J. *The Age of Capital.* London, UK: Widenfeld and Nicholson, 2000.

Hochschild, Arlie. *The Second Shift.* New York: Viking Press, 1989.

Hof, Robert D. "Who Needs Blockbusters?" *BusinessWeek,* July 17, 2006, 88.

Hoffman, Bruce. *Inside Terrorism.* New York: Columbia University Press, 1998.

Hofmann, Wilhelm, Bertram Gawronski, Tobias Gschwendner, Huy Le, and Manfred Schmitt. "A Meta-Analysis of the Correlation between the Implicit Association Test and Explicit Self-Report Measures." *Personality and Social Psychology Bulletin,* 31 (10, October 2005): 1369–1385.

Hollenbach, Margaret. *Lost and Found: My Life in a Group Marriage Commune.* Albuquerque: University of New Mexico Press, 2004.

Holston, J. A. *Cities and Citizenship.* Chicago: University of Chicago Press, 1999.

Holtz, Robert Lee. "Women Use More of Brain when Listening, Study Says." *Los Angeles Times,* November 29, 2000.

Home Office (Great Britain). 2005. *Statistics on Race and the Criminal Justice System.* London: The Home Office. Available at: www .homeoffice.gov.uk/rds/pdfs05/s95race04 .pdf

Home Office (Great Britain). *Offending, Crime and Justice Survey.* London: Home Office, 2006.

Hondagneu-Sotelo, Pierrette. *Domestica: Immigrant Workers Cleaning and Caring in the Shadows of Affluence.* Berkeley: University of California Press, 2001.

Hook, Jennifer L. "Care in Context: Men's Unpaid Work in 20 Countries, 1965–2003." *American Sociological Review,* 71, 4 (2006): 639–660.

hooks, bell. *Ain't I a Woman? Black Women and Feminism.* Boston: South End Press, 1981.

hooks, bell. *Talking Back: Thinking Feminist, Thinking Black.* Boston: South End Press, 1989.

Hoover, Stewart, Lynn Schofield Clark, and Lee Rainie. "Faith Online." *Report of the Pew Center on the Internet and American Life, 2004.* Washington, DC: Pew Center.

Hopkins, Terence, and Immanuel Wallerstein. *The Age of Transition: Trajectory of the World System, 1945–2025.* London: Zed Books, 1996.

Horkheimer, Max, and Theodor W. Adorno. "The Culture Industry: Enlightenment as Mass Deception" (1944). In *Dialectic of Enlightenment.* John Cumming, trans. New York: Herder and Herder, 1972.

Housing Assistance Council. "Housing on Native American Lands," June 2008. Available at: www.ruralhome.org/manager/ uploads/NativeAmerInfoSheet.pdf

Hout, Michael. "Status, Autonomy and Training in Occupational Mobility." *American Journal of Sociology,* 89 (1984): 1379–1409.

Howe, Louise Kay. *Pink Collar Workers: Inside the World of Women's Work.* New York: Putnam, 1977.

Howell, J. C., A. Egley Jr., and D. K. Gleason. "Modern Day Youth Gangs." *Bulletin, Youth Gang Series.* Washington, DC: U.S. Department of Justice, Office of Juvenile Justice and Delinquency Prevention, 2002.

Howell, James C. "The Impact of Gangs on Communities." *National Youth Gang Center Bulletin,* August 2006. Available at: www .iir.com/nygc/publications/NYGCbulletin_ 0806.pdf

Howell, Signe, and Roy Willis, eds. *Societies at Peace*. New York: Routledge, 1983.

Hrdy, Sarah Blaffer. *The Woman That Never Evolved*. Cambridge, MA: Harvard University Press, 1981.

Hrdy, Sarah Blaffer. *Mother Nature: A History of Mothers, Infants, and Natural Selection*. New York: Pantheon, 1999.

Hsiang-Shul, Chen. *Chinatown No More: Taiwan Immigrants in Contemporary New York*. Ithaca, NY: Cornell University Press, 1992.

Hubbard, Ruth. "The Political Nature of Human Nature." In Deborah Rhode, ed., *Theoretical Perspectives on Sexual Difference*. New Haven, CT: Yale University Press, 1990.

Hughes, Everett C. "Dilemmas and Contradictions of Status." *American Journal of Sociology*, 50 (1945): 353–354.

Human Rights Campaign. *Domestic Partner Benefits Employer Trends and Benefits Equivalency for the GLBT Family*. Washington, DC: Human Rights Campaign, 2006.

Human Rights Campaign. "State Prohibitions on Marriage for Same-Sex Couples." Washington, DC: Human Rights Campaign, 2007. Available at: www.hrw.org

Human Rights Watch, 2007. "Facts about Child Soldiers." Available at: http://hrw .org/campaigns/crp/fact_sheet.html

Human Rights Watch. *A Violent Education: Corporal Punishment of Children in U.S. Public Schools*. Washington, DC: Human Rights Watch, 2008.

Humphreys, Jeffrey. "The Multicultural Economy 2006," *Georgia Business and Economic Conditions*, 66 (3, 2006).

Humphreys, Laud. *Tearoom Trade: Impersonal Sex in Public Places*. New York: Transaction, 1970.

Hunt, G., K. Joe-Laidler, and K. MacKenzie. "Moving into Motherhood: Gang Girls and Controlled Risk." *Youth & Society*, 36 (2005): 333–373.

Huntington, Ellsworth. *Civilization and Climate* (1915). Honolulu: University Press of the Pacific, 2001.

Hyde, Janet. "The Gender Similarities Hypothesis." *The American Psychologist*, 60 (6, 2005): 581–592.

Iceland, John, and Kurt Bauman, "Income Poverty and Material Hardship: How Strong Is the Association?" *Journal of Socio-Economics*, 36 (2007).

Indicus Analytics. "Key Indicators on Literacy in India," October 2008. Available at: www.indicus.net/media/index.php/idl/ 1235-key-indicators-on-literacy-in-india

"Inside the Mind of Gen Y." *American Demographics*, September 2001.

Institute for Social Research. *Husbands Are Doing More Housework while Wives Are Doing Less*. 2002. Available at: www.umich.edu/news/index.html?Releases/2002/Mar02/chr031202a

International Helsinki Federation for Human Rights. *Report: Human Rights in the OSCE Region*. Helsinki, Finland: International Helsinki Federation for Human Rights, 2006.

International Institute for Democracy and Electoral Assistance. "Compulsory Voting." 2007. Available at: www.idea.int/vt/ compulsory_voting.cfm

International Labour Organization (ILO), 2001. *Annual Report 2001–02*. Geneva, Switzerland: ILO.

International Labour Organization (ILO). "Every Child Counts: New Global Estimates on Child Labour." Geneva, Switzerland April 2002.

International Labour Organization (ILO), *Global Employment Trends for Women*, 2004. Geneva, Switzerland: International Labour Organisation, March 2004.

International Labour Organization (ILO). *Global Estimates on Child Labour, 2000–2004*. Geneva: International Labour Office, 2005. Available at: www.ilo.org/dyn/declaris/ DECLARATIONWEB.DOWNLOAD_ BLOB?Var_DocumentID=6233

International Labour Organization (ILO). *Facts on Child Labor, 2006*. Available at: www.ilo .org/wcmsp5/groups/public/—dgreports/ dcomm/documents/publication/ wcms_067558.pdf

International Labour Organization (ILO). *Annual Report 2005–06*. Geneva, Switzerland: ILO, 2007a.

International Labour Organization (ILO). *Global Employment Trends Brief*, January 2007. Geneva, Switzerland: ILO, 2007b.

International Labour Organization (ILO). *The Informal Economy*. Geneva: 298th ILO Governing Body Session, 2007c.

International Labour Organization (ILO). *Global Employment Trends*. Geneva: International Labour Office: 2008.

International Labour Organization (ILO). *Global Employment Trends*. Geneva: International Labour Office, January 2009a.

International Labour Organization (ILO). *Global Wage Report 2008/09*. Geneva: International Labour Office, 2009b.

International Lesbian and Gay Association. *World Legal Survey 2006*. Available at: www .ilga.info/Information/Legal_survey/ ilga_world_legal_survey%20introduction .htm

International Lesbian and Gay Association. May, 2009 Available at: http://www.ilga .org/statehomophobia/ILGA_map_2009_ A4.pdf

International Monetary Fund (IMF). *World Economic Outlook Database*. Washington, DC. October 2008.

International Obesity Task Force. *Global Obesity Map*. London: IOTF, 2007.

Internet Movie Database (IMDb). "All-Time Box Office: World-Wide, 2009." Available at www.imdb.com/boxofficealltimegross? region=world-wide

Ironmonger, Duncan. "Counting Outputs, Capital Inputs and Caring Labor: Estimating Gross Household Product." *Feminist Economics*, 2 (3, 1996): 37–64.

Irwin, Katherine. "Legitimating the First Tattoo: Moral Passage through Informal Interaction." *Symbolic Interaction*, 24 (2001): 49–73.

Isaacs, Julia. *Economic Mobility of Black and White Families*. Washington DC: The Brookings Institution, 2007.

Isaacs, Julia. "Economic Mobility of Families across Generations." In Haskins, Ron, Julia Haskins, and Isabel V. Sawhill, eds., *Getting Ahead on Losing Ground: Economic Mobility in America*. Washington, DC: Center on Children and Families, 2009.

Isaacson, Walter. *Einstein: His Life and Universe*. New York: Simon and Schuster, 2007.

Isaacson, Walter. "How to Save Your Newspaper." *Time*, February 16, 2009.

Ito, Mizuko, Heather Horst, Matteo Bittanti, Danah Boyd, Becky Herr-Stephenson, Patricia G. Lange, C. J. Pascoe, and Laura Robinson. *Living and Learning with New Media: Summary of the Findings of the Digital Youth Project*. Chicago: John D. and Catherine T. MacArthur Foundation, November, 2008.

Jackson, Andrew. "Fighting Poverty through Municipal Wage Ordinances." *Progressive Economics Forum*, July 18, 2007.

Jackson, Kenneth. *Crabgrass Frontier: The Suburbanization of America*. New York: Oxford University Press, 1987.

Jackson, Pamela Braboy, and Quincy Thomas Stewart. "A Research Agenda for the Black Middle Class: Work Stress, Survival Strategies and Mental Health." *Journal of Health and Social Behavior*, 44 (September 2003): 442–455.

Jacobs, Jane. *The Death and Life of Great American Cities*. New York: Vintage, 1961.

Jacobsohn, J., S. Dunn, and Williams College. *Diversity and Citizenship: Rediscovering American Nationhood*. Lanham, MD: Rowman & Littlefield, 1996.

Janis, Irving L. *Victims of Groupthink*. Boston: Houghton-Mifflin, 1972.

Jarrell, Anne. "The Daddy Track." *Boston Globe*, July 7, 2007.

Jayson, Sharon. "Living Together No Longer 'Playing House.'" *USA Today*, July 28, 2008.

Johnson, David R., and Jian Wu. "An Empirical Test of Crisis, Social Selection, and Role Explanations of the Relationship between Marital Disruption and Psychological Distress: A Pooled Time-Series Analysis of Four-Wave Panel Data." *Journal of Marriage and Family*, 64 (2002): 211–224.

Johnson, Steven. *Everything Bad Is Good for You*. New York: Riverhead Books, 2005.

Jones, Arthur. "Global Sex Trade Prospers." *National Catholic Reporter*, May 25, 2001.

Jones, Del. "Hooters to Pay $3.75 Million in Sex Suit." *USA Today*, October 1, 1997, 1A.

Jones, Del. "Women CEOs Gain Slowly on Corporate America." *USA Today*, January 2, 2009.

Jones, J. "Adoption Experiences of Women and Men and Demand for Children to Adopt by Women 18–44 Years of Age in the United States, 2002." *National Center for Health Statistics, Vital Health Statistics*, 23 (27, 2008).

Jonson, Steve. "How Twitter Will Change the Way We Live (in 140 Characters or Less)." *Time*, June 15, 2009.

Journal of Blacks in Higher Education. "Black Student College Graduation Rates Inch Higher but a Large Racial Gap Persists," 2007a. Available at: www.jbhe.com/ preview/winter07preview.html

Journal of Blacks in Higher Education. "Black Student College Graduation Rates Remain Low, but Modest Progress Begins to Show," 2007b. Available at: www.jbhe .com/features/50_blackstudent_gradrates .html

Journal of Blacks in Higher Education. "Black Enrollments at Christian Colleges Are on the Rise." August 7, 2008.

Juergensmeyer, Mark. *Terror in the Mind of God: The Global Rise of Religious Violence.* Berkeley: University of California Press, 2003.

Juvonen, Jaana, Sandra Graham, and Mark Schuster. "Bullying among Young Adolescents: The Strong, the Weak and the Troubled." *Pediatrics,* 112 (6, December 2003): 1231–1237.

Kaestle, Carl F., H. Damon-Moore, Katherine Tinsley, Lawrence C. Stedman, and William Vance Trollinger Jr. *Literacy in the United States: Readers and Reading Since 1880.* New Haven, CT: Yale University Press, 1993.

Kaiser Commission on Medicaid and the Uninsured. "States Moving Toward Comprehensive Healthcare Reform," July 10, 2009. Washington, DC.

Kaiser Family Foundation. *Sex Education in America: A View from Inside the Nation's Classrooms.* Menlo Park, CA: Henry J. Kaiser Family Foundation, 2000.

Kaiser Family Foundation. *Generation M: Media in the Lives of 8-to-18-Year-Olds.* Menlo Park, CA: Henry J. Kaiser Family Foundation, 2004a.

Kaiser Family Foundation. *Sex Education in America: General Public/Parents Survey,* January 2004b. Available at: www.kff.org/newsmedia/upload/Sex-Education-in-America-General-Public-Parents-Survey-Toplines.pdf

Kanter, James. "One in Four Mammals Facing Extinction." *New York Times,* October 6, 2008.

Kanter, Rosebeth M. *Men and Women of the Corporation.* New York: Basic Books, 1977.

Kara, Siddarth. *Sex Trafficking.* New York: Columbia University Press, 2009.

Karabel, Jerome. *The Chosen: The Hidden History of Admission and Exclusion at Harvard, Yale, and Princeton.* Boston: Houghton-Mifflin, 2005.

Karabell, Zachary. "We Are Not in This Together." *Newsweek,* April 20, 2009, 30–31.

Katz, Jack. *Seductions of Crime: Moral and Sensual Attractions in Doing Evil.* New York: Basic Books, 1988.

Katz, Lawrence, Steven Levitt, and Ellen Shustorovich. "Prison Conditions, Capital Punishment, and Deterrence." *American Law and Economics Review,* 2 (2, 2003): 318–343.

Katz, Michael. *The Undeserving Poor.* New York: Pantheon, 1990.

Keay, Douglas. "AIDS, Education, and the Year 2000: An Interview with Margaret Thatcher." *Woman's Own,* September 23, 1987, 14.

Keehan, S., et al. "Health Spending Projections through 2017." *Health Affairs* 27 (2008): W145–W155.

Kellerman, A. L., and J. A. Marcy. "Men, Women and Murder: Gender-Specific Differences in Rates of Fatal Violence and Victimization." *Journal of Trauma,* 33 (1, 1992).

Kempadoo, Kamala, Jyoti Saghera, and Bandana Pattanaik, eds. *Trafficking and Prostitution Reconsidered: New Perspectives on Migration, Sex Work, and Human Rights.* Boulder, CO: Paradigm Publishers, 2005.

Kemper, Theodore. *Testosterone and Social Structure.* New Brunswick, NJ: Rutgers University Press, 1990.

Kennedy, Randall. *Nigger: The Strange Career of a Troublesome Word.* New York: Pantheon, 2002.

Kerbo, Harold R. *Social Stratification and Inequality: Class Conflict in Historical and Comparative Perspective.* New York: McGraw-Hill, 1996.

Kim, Richard. "Eminem—Bad Rap?" *The Nation,* March 13, 2001, 4.

Kim, Won. "Asian Americans Are at the Head of the Class." *Diversity Inc,* July/August 2006, 40.

Kimmel, Michael. "What Do Men Want?" *Harvard Business Review,* April, 1993.

Kimmel, Michael. *Manhood in America: A Cultural History.* New York: The Free Press, 1996.

Kimmel, Michael. "'Gender Symmetry' in Domestic Violence: A Substantive and Methodological Research Review." *Violence against Women,* 8 (11, 2002): 1332–1363.

Kimmel, Michael. *The Gendered Society.* New York: Oxford University Press, 2003.

Kimmel, Michael. *Guyland: The Perilous World where Boys Become Men.* New York: HarperCollins, 2008.

Kimmel, Michael, James Lang, and Alan Grieg. *Men, Masculinities and Development.* New York: U.N. Development Program (UNDP), 2000.

King, Leslie. *Environmental Sociology: From Analysis to Action.* Lanham, MD: Rowan & Littlefield, 2005.

Kinloch, Graham C. *The Comparative Understanding of Intergroup Relations: A Worldwide Analysis.* Boulder, CO: Westview Press, 1999.

Kinsella, Kevin, and David R. Phillips. *Global Aging: The Challenge of Success.* Washington, DC: Population Reference Bureau, 2005.

Kirby, D. *Emerging Answers: Research Findings on Programs to Reduce Teen Pregnancy.* Washington, DC: Campaign to Prevent Teen Pregnancy, 2001.

Kirp, David. "After the Bell Curve." *The New York Times Magazine,* July 23, 2006, 15–16.

Kitsuse, John. "The New Conception of Deviance and Its Critics." In Walter A. Gove, ed., *The Labelling of Deviance: Evaluating a Perspective,* pp. 381–392. Thousand Oaks, CA: Sage Publications, 1980.

Kittilson, Miki C., and Katherine Tate. "Political Parties, Minorities and Elected Office: Comparing Opportunities for Inclusion in the U.S. and Britain." University of California, Irvine: Center for the Study of Democracy, Paper 04–06, 2004. Available at: http://repositories.cdlib.org/csd/04-06

Klevens, Joanne. "Overview of Intimate Partner Violence among Latinos." *Violence against Women,* 13 (2, 2007): 111–122.

Klineberg, Eric. *Heat Wave: A Social Autopsy of Disaster in Chicago.* Chicago: University of Chicago Press, 2003.

Kohlberg, Lawrence. *Stages of Moral Development as a Basis for Moral Education.* Cambridge, MA: Harvard University Center for Moral Education, 1971.

Kohlberg, Lawrence, and Carol Gilligan. "The Adolescent as Philosopher." *Daedalus,* 100 (1971): 1051–1086.

Kohler, P. K., L. E. Manhart, and W. E. Lafferty. "Abstinence-Only and Comprehensive Sex Education and the Initiation of Sexual Activity and Teen Pregnancy." *Journal of Adolescent Health,* 42 (4, April 2008): 344–351.

Kohn, Alfie. "NCLB: Too Destructive to Salvage." *USA Today,* May 31, 2007.

Kohn, Melvin. "Social Class and the Exercise of Parental Authority." *American Sociological Review,* 24 (June 1959a): 352–366.

Kohn, Melvin. "Social Class and Parental Values." *American Journal of Sociology,* 64 (January, 1959b): 337–351.

Kohn, Melvin. "Social Class and Parent-Child Relationships: An Interpretation." *American Journal of Sociology,* 68 (January 1963): 471–480.

Kohn, Melvin. *Class and Conformity.* Chicago, IL: University of Chicago Press, 1977.

Kohn, Melvin. "On the Transmission of Values in the Family: A Preliminary Formulation." In Alan C. Kerckhoff (ed.), *Research in Sociology of Education and Socialization: A Research Annual,* Vol. 4, pp. 3–12. Greenwich, CT: JAI Press, 1983.

Kohn, Melvin. "Social Structure and Personality: A Quintessentially Sociological Approach to Social Psychology." *Social Forces,* 68 (September 1989): 26–33.

Kohn, Melvin, with Leonard I. Pearlin. "Social Class, Occupation, and Parental Values: A Cross-National Study." *American Sociological Review,* 31 (August 1966): 466–479.

Kohn, Melvin, with Carrie Schoenbach. "Social Stratification, Parents' Values, and Children's Values." In Dagmara Krebs and Peter Schmidt (eds.), *New Directions in Attitude Measurement,* pp. 118–151. Berlin and New York: Walter de Gruyter, 1993.

Kohn, Melvin, with Kazimierz Slomczynski and Carrie Schoenbach. "Social Stratification and the Transmission of Values in the Family: A Cross-National Assessment." *Sociological Forum,* 1 (Winter 1986): 73–102.

Kolb, Robert W. *Encyclopedia of Business Ethics and Society.* Thousand Oaks, CA: Sage Publications, 2008.

Konig, Susan. "Courting High Net Worth Women." *On Wall Street,* February 2005.

Korn, Donald Jay. "Yours, Mine, OURS." *Black Enterprise,* October 2001.

Koss, Mary, L. A. Goodman, A. Browne, L. F. Fitzgerald, G. P. Keita, and N. F. Russo, *No Safe Haven: Male Violence against Women at Home, at Work, and in the Community.* Washington, DC: American Psychological Association, 1994.

Kozol, Jonathan. *Death at an Early Age: The Destruction of Hearts and Minds of Negro Children in the Boston Public Schools.* Boston: Houghton-Mifflin, 1967.

Kraditor, Aileen. *The Ideas of the Woman Suffrage Movement, 1890–1920.* New York: Norton, 1981.

Krakovsy, Marina. "Global Psyche: National Poker Face." *Psychology Today,* January 2009, 34.

Kramarae, Cheris, and Paula A. Treichler. *A Feminist Dictionary.* Urbana: University of Illinois Press, 1997.

Kraybill, D. B. *The Fiddle of Amish Culture* (rev. ed.). Baltimore, MD: The Johns Hopkins University Press, 2001.

Kriedte, Peter. *Peasants, Landlords, and Merchant Capitalists*. New York: Cambridge University Press, 1983.

Kristof, Nicholas. "Believe It, or Not." *New York Times*, August 15, 2003, 33.

Kristof, Nicholas. "Marriage: Mix and Match." *New York Times*, March 3, 2004, A23.

Krugman, Paul. "The End of Middle-Class America." *The New York Times Magazine*, October 20, 2002, 62–67, 76–78, 141.

Krugman, Paul. "Graduates versus Oligarchs." *New York Times*, February 22, 2006, A-31.

Kuhn, Thomas. *The Structure of Scientific Revolutions*. Chicago: University of Chicago Press, 1962.

Kumar, K. *From Post-Industrial to Post-Modern Society: New Theories of the Contemporary World*. Oxford, UK: Blackwell, 1995.

Kurki, Leena. "International Crime Survey: American Rates About Average." *Overcrowded Times*, 8 (5, 1997): 4–7.

Lambert, Tracy. "Pluralistic Ignorance and Hooking Up." *Journal of Sex Research*, 40 (2, May 2003): 129.

Lancaster, B. *The Department Store: A Social History*. London, UK: Leicester University Press, 1995.

Landry, D. J., L. Kaeser, and C. L. Richards, "Abstinence Promotion and the Provision of Information about Contraception in Public School District Sexuality Education Policies." *Family Planning Perspectives*, 31 (6, 1999): 280–286.

Lane, Harlan. *The Wild Boy of Aveyron*. Cambridge, MA: Harvard University Press, 1979.

Lareau, Anette. *Unequal Childhoods: Class, Race and Family Life*. Berkeley: University of California Press, 2003.

Lasch, Christopher. "The Family and History." *New York Review of Books*, 8 (November 13, 1975): 33–38.

Lauer, Robert H., and Jeanette C. Lauer. *Marriage and Family: The Quest for Intimacy*, 5th ed. New York: McGraw-Hill, 2003.

Laumann, Edward, John Gagnon, Robert Michael, and Stuart Michaels. *The Social Organization of Sexuality*. Chicago: University of Chicago Press, 1996.

Laumann, Edward, and Robert Michael, eds. *Sex, Love, and Health in America: Private Choices and Public Policies*. Chicago: University of Chicago Press, 2000.

Lazare, Daniel. "Among the Disbelievers." *The Nation*, May 28, 2007, 27–28.

Leach, Karoline. *In the Shadow of the Dreamchild: A New Understanding of Lewis Carroll*. New York: Peter Owen, 1999.

Lee, Felicia. "Survey of the Blogosphere Finds 12 Million Voices." *New York Times*, July 20, 2006.

Leeder, Elaine J. *The Family in Global Perspective: A Gendered Journey*. Thousand Oaks: Sage, 2003.

Leibovich, Mark, and Grant Barrett. "The Buzzwords of 2008." *New York Times*, December 28, 2008.

Leland, John. "Hip New Churches Sway to a Different Drummer." *New York Times*, February 18, 2004, A-1, 17.

Lemann, Nicholas. *The Promised Land: The Great Black Migration and How It Changed America*. New York: Vintage, 1992.

Lemert, Edwin. *Human Deviance, Social Problems and Social Control*. Englewood Cliffs, NJ: Prentice-Hall, 1972.

Lenski, Gerhard. *Power and Privilege: A Theory of Social Stratification*. Chapel Hill: University of North Carolina Press, 1984.

Leonhardt, David. "Money Doesn't Buy Happiness. Well, on Second Thought." *New York Times*, April 16, 2008, C1,C7.

Leonhardt, David. "In Recession, a Bleaker Path for Workers to Slog." *New York Times*, July 15, 2009, A-1, 3.

Levine, James A. *Working Fathers*. New York: Perseus Books, 1997.

Levine, L. W. *Highbrow/Lowbrow: The Emergence of Cultural Hierarchy in America*. Cambridge, MA: Harvard University Press, 1988.

Levine, Martin. "Gay Ghetto." *Journal of Homosexuality*, 4 (4, Summer 1979).

Levine, Susan. "Laughing through Their Years." *Washington Post*, May 29, 1999, C-1.

Levinson, Daniel J. *The Seasons of a Man's Life*. New York: Alfred Knopf, 1978.

Levitt, Steven, and Stephen Dubner. *Freakonomics*. New York: William Morrow, 2005.

Lewin, Tamar. "Boys Are No Match for Girls in Completing High School." *New York Times*, April 19, 2006, A12.

Lewis, Lisa A. *The Adoring Audience; Fan Culture and Popular Media*. New York: Routledge, 1992.

Lewis, Oscar. *Five Families: Mexican Case Studies in the Culture of Poverty*. San Francisco: HarperCollins, 1965.

Lexington. "Minding the Gap." *The Economist*, June 11, 2005, 32.

Liang, Lan, Benjamin Caballero, and Shiriki Kumanyika. "Will All Americans Become Overweight or Obese? Estimating the Progression and Cost of the U.S. Obesity Epidemic." *Obesity*, 16 (7, July 2008): 1583–1602.

Liazos, Alexander, "Nuts, Sluts, and Perverts: The Poverty of the Sociology of Deviance." *Social Problems*, 20 (1, Summer 1972): 103–120.

Lichtenstein, Nelson. *State of the Union: A Century of American Labor*. Princeton, NJ: Princeton University Press, 2002.

Lichter, Daniel T., and Zhenchao Qian. "Serial Cohabitation and the Marital Life Course." *Journal of Marriage and Family*, 70 (2008): 861-878.

Lichtheim, George. *Marxism*. New York: Columbia University Press, 1982.

Liebman, J. S., J. Fagan, and V. West. "A Broken System: Error Rates in Capital Cases, 1973–1995." Available online at: http://papers.ssrn.com/paperstaf?abstract_id=232712 (June 12, 2000).

Liebow, Elliot. *Tally's Corner*. Boston: Little, Brown, 1968.

Lifton, Robert Jay. *The Nazi Doctors: Medical Killing and the Psychology of Genocide*. New York: Basic Books, 1986.

Lim, Louisa. "China Fears Bachelor Future." *BBC News International Edition*, April 4, 2004.

Limber, S. P., P. Cunningham, V. Florx, J. Ivey, M. Nation, S. Chai, and G. Melton. "Bullying among School Children: Preliminary Findings from a School-Based Intervention Program." Paper presented at the Fifth International Family Violence Research Conference, Durham, NH, June, 1997.

Limonic, Laura. "Latinos and the 2008 Presidential Elections: A Visual Data Base." New York: Center for Latin American, Caribbean and Latino Studies, CUNY Graduate Center, 2008.

Lind, Michael. "Are We Still a Middle-Class Nation?" *Atlantic Monthly*, 293 (1, 2004), 120–129.

Lipsitz, Angela, Paul D. Bishop, and Christine Robinson. "Virginity Pledges: Who Takes Them and How Well Do They Work?" Presentation at the Annual Convention of the American Psychological Association, August 2003.

Liu, T. S., and T. A. Miller. "Economic Analysis of the Future Growth of Cosmetic Surgery Procedures." *Plastic and Reconstructive Surgery*, 121 (6) (2008): 404e.

Living and Learning with New Media: Summary of Findings from the Digital Youth Project, Chicago, IL: MacArthur Foundation, 2008.

Livingston, J. *Crime and Criminology*. Englewood Cliffs, NJ: Prentice-Hall, 1992.

Locke, John. *Two Treatises of Government* (1689), ed. Peter Laslett. New York: Cambridge University Press, 1988.

Loehlin, John C., and Robert C. Nichols. *Heredity, Environment, and Personality*. Austin: University of Texas Press, 1976.

Lofland, John. "Collective Behavior: The Elementary Forms." In *Collective Behavior and Social Movements*, Russell Curtis Jr. and Benigno Aguirre, eds. Boston: Allyn and Bacon, 1993.

Lofstrom, Magnus. "Labor Market Assimilation and the Self-Employment Decision of Immigrant Entrepreneurs." *Journal of Population Economics*, 15 (1, 2002): 83–114.

Lucas, Christopher J. *American Higher Education: A History*. New York: Palgrave Macmillan, 1996.

Lukes, Steven. *Power*. New York: New York University Press, 1986.

Lunneborg, Patricia. *The Chosen Lives of Child-Free Men*. Westport, CT: Bergin & Garvey, 1999.

Luxembourg Income Study. *Relative Poverty Rates for the Total Population, Children and the Elderly*. Luxembourg: 2007. Available at: www.lisproject.org/keyfigures/povertytable.htm

Lynch, Kathleen. *The Hidden Curriculum: Reproduction in Education, a Reappraisal*. London: Falmer Press, 1989.

Lynch, Marc. *Voices of the New Arab Public: Iraq, Al-Jazeera, and Middle East Politics Today*. New York: Columbia University Press, 2005.

Maccoby, Eleanor, and Carol Jacklin. *The Psychology of Sex Differences*. Stanford, CA: Stanford University Press, 1987.

MacKinnon, Catherine. *Feminism Unmodified: Discoveries in Life and Law*. Cambridge, MA: Harvard University Press, 1987.

Magazine Publishers of America. *The Magazine Handbook 2008–09*. New York: Magazine Publishers of America, 2008.

Males, Mike. *The Scapegoat Generation: America's War on Adolescents*. San Francisco: Common Courage Press, 1996.

Males, Mike. *Ten Myths about the Next Generation.* San Francisco: Common Courage Press, 1998.

Malinowski, Bronislaw. *Sex and Repression in Savage Society* (1927). New York, Plume, 1974.

Malthus, Thomas Robert. *An Essay on the Principle of Population* (1798). New York: Oxford University Press, 1999.

Manning, Anita. "Aging Gracefully Is the Biggest Concern." *USA Today*, October 23, 2005, A-7.

Marchand, Roland. *Advertising the American Dream: Making Way for Modernity.* Berkeley: University of California Press, 1986.

Marchevsky, Alejandra, and Jeanne Theoharis. *Not Working: Latina Immigrants, Low-Wage Jobs, and the Failure of Welfare Reform.* New York: NYU Press, 2006.

Marchioso, Kathleen. "From Sambo to Brute: The Social Construction of African-American Masculinity." *The Edwardsville Journal of Sociology*, 1 (2001). Available at: www.sieu.edu/sociology

Margolis, Eric, ed. *The Hidden Curriculum in Higher Education.* New York: Falmer Press, 2001.

Markham, Victoria D. *U.S. Population, Energy and Climate Change.* New Canaan, CT: Center for Environment and Population, 2008.

Marks, N. "Flying Solo at Midlife: Gender, Marital Status and Psychological Wellbeing." *Journal of Marriage and the Family*, 58 (1996): 917–932.

Marshall, John. *John Locke: Resistance, Religion and Responsibility.* Cambridge, UK: Cambridge University Press, 1994.

Martens, Jens. "A Compendium of Inequality: The Human Development Report 2005." Global Policy Forum, 2005.

Martin, Bradley. *Under the Loving Care of the Fatherly Leader: North Korea and the Kim Dynasty.* New York: St. Martins, 2004.

Martin, Joyce A., Brady E. Hamilton, Paul D. Sutton, Stephanie J. Ventura, Fay Menacker, and Sharon Kirmeyer. "Births: Final Data for 2004." Atlanta, GA: National Center for Health Statistics, Centers for Disease Control, 2006.

Martin, Lynn. *A Report on the Glass Ceiling Initiative.* Washington, DC: U.S. Department of Labor, 1991.

Martin, Steven. "Reassessing Delayed and Forgone Marriage in the United States." Working paper, Maryland Population Research Center, June 2004.

Martin, Steven. *Growing Evidence for a "Divorce Divide"? Education, Race, and Marital Dissolution Rates in the U.S. since the 1970s.* New York: Russell Sage Foundation, 2006.

Martinez, Michael. "Blended Families Face Difficult Financial Decisions." *AP Business Wire*, June 17, 2005.

Martino, Wayne. "Gendered Learning Experiences: Exploring the Costs of Hegemonic Masculinity for Girls and Boys in Schools." *Gender Equity: A Framework for Australian Schools.* Canberra: Publications and Communications, Department of Urban Services, ACT Government, 1997.

Marx, Karl. *Capital* (1867). David McLellan, ed. New York: Oxford University Press, 1998.

Marx, Karl. *The Eighteenth Brumaire of Louis Napoleon.* New York: Monthly Review Press, 1965.

Marx, Karl, and Friedrich Engels. *The Communist Manifesto: A Modern Edition* (1848). E. J. Hobsbawm, ed. New York: Verso, 1998.

Masci, David. "How the Public Resolves Conflicts between Faith and Science." *Pew Forum on Religion and Public Life*, August 27, 2007.

Massey, Douglas S., and Nancy A. Denton. *American Apartheid.* Cambridge, MA: Harvard University Press, 1993.

Mathias, Peter, and Sidney Pollard. *The Cambridge Economic History of Europe, Vol. 8: The Industrial Economies: The Development of Economic and Social Policies.* Cambridge, UK: Cambridge University Press, 1989.

Mattox, William. "Diamonds Are Forever." 1999. Available at: www2.nando.net/noframes/story/0,2107,31812-51154-381237-0,00.html

Mattes, Jane. *Single Mothers by Choice: A Guidebook for Single Women Who Are Considering or Have Chosen Motherhood.* New York: New York Times Books, 1994.

Matus, Ron. "Public Officials, Private Schools." *St. Petersburg Times*, April 6, 2005, 1A.

Mayo, Elton. *The Human Problems of an Industrial Civilization.* New York: Macmillan, 1933.

McAdam, Doug, ed. *Comparative Perspectives on Social Movements: Political Opportunities, Mobilizing Structures, and Cultural Framings.* Cambridge, UK: Cambridge University Press, 1996.

McAll, Christopher. *Class, Ethnicity, and Social Inequality.* Montreal, Quebec, Canada: McGill-Queen's University Press, 1990.

McCarthy, J. D., and M. N. Zald. 1987. "Resource Mobilization and Social Movements: A Partial Theory," in S. M. Buechler and F. K. Cylke, eds., *Social Movements: Perspectives and Issues*, pp. 149–172. Mountain View, CA: Mayfield Publishing Company.

McGregor, Douglas. *The Human Side of Enterprise* (1960). New York: McGraw-Hill, 2005.

McHugh, Kristin. "The Sky's the Limit: Arab Media Thriving Amid Controversy Both in United States and Middle East." The Stanley Foundation, 2006. Muscatine, Iowa

McKibben, Bill. "The Christian Paradox." *Harper's Magazine*, August, 2005.

McKinley, James C. Jr. "Texas Battle on Gay Marriage Looms." *New York Times*, Oct. 2, 2009.

McLanahan, S., and E. Kelly. "The Feminization of Poverty: Past and Future." MacArthur Foundation Working Paper series. Available at: www.onlin.wustl.edu/Macarthur/working%20papers/wp-mclanahan3.htm

McLaughlin, Margaret L., Kerry K. Osborne, and Christine B. Smith. "Standards of Conduct on Usenet." In Steven G. Jones, ed., *Cybersociety*, pp. 90–111. Thousand Oaks, CA: Sage, 1995.

McLuhan, Marshall, and Quentin Fiore. *The Medium Is the Message.* New York: Bantam, 1967.

McPherson, M., L. Smith-Lovin, and M. E. Brashears. "Social Isolation in America: Changes in Core Discussion Networks Over Two Decades." *American Sociological Review*, 71 (2006): 353–375.

Mead, George Herbert. *Mind, Self and Society.* Chicago: University of Chicago Press, 1967.

Mead, Margaret. *Sex and Temperament in Three Primitive Societies* (1935). New York: Harper Perennial, 2001.

Mead, Margaret. "Interview." *New Realities*, June 1978.

The Medical News. "AIDS Healthcare Foundation Criticizes Etravirine's Pricing," January 22, 2008. Available at: www.news-medical.net/news/2008/01/22/34571.aspx

Medical World News. "Abortion Clinic's Toughest Cases." March 9, 1987, 55–61.

Meissner, Christian A., John C. Brigham, and David A. Butz. "Memory for Own- and Other-Race Faces." *Applied Cognitive Psychology*, 19 (January 2005): 545–567.

Menkel-Meadow, Carrie. *The Comparative Sociology of Women Lawyers: The "Feminization" of the Legal Profession.* Menlo Park, CA: Institute for Social Research, 1987.

Merton, Robert K. "Social Structure and Anomie." *American Sociological Review*, 3 (October 1938): 672–682.

Merton, Robert K. *Social Theory and Social Structure* (1949). New York: The Free Press, 1968.

Merton, Robert K. "Discrimination and the American Creed" (1949). In *Sociological Ambivalence and Other Essays*, 189–216. New York: The Free Press, 1976.

Meyer, David S., Nancy Whittier, and Belinda Robnett, eds. *Social Movements: Identity, Culture, and the State.* Oxford, UK: Oxford University Press, 2002.

Meyer, J. W., and Brian Rowan. "Institutional Organizations: Formal Structure as Myth and Ceremony." *American Journal of Sociology*, 83 (1977): 340–363.

Michael, R. T., J. H. Gagnon, E. O. Laumann, and G. Kolata. *Sex in America: A Definitive Study.* Boston: Little, Brown, 1994.

Micheletti, Michele. *Political Virtue and Shopping. Individuals, Consumerism, and Collective Action.* New York: Palgrave, 2003.

Micheletti, Michele, and Dietlind Stolle. "The Market as an Arena for Transnational Politics." In *Youth Activism: A Web Forum Organized by the Social Science Research Council*, June 7, 2006. Available at: http://ya.ssrc.org/transnational/Micheletti_Stolle

Micklethwait, John, and Adrian Woodridge. *The Company: A Short History of a Revolutionary Idea.* New York: The Modern Library, 2003.

Milgram, Stanley. "Behavioral Study of Obedience." *Journal of Abnormal and Social Psychology*, 67 (1963): 371–378.

Milgram, Stanley. *Obedience to Authority; An Experimental View.* New York: Harper and Row, 1974.

Miller, Jon. "Science Literacy and Pseudo-Science." American Association for the Advancement of Science Symposium, February 27, 2007.

Miller, Lisa. "The Authenticity Test." *Newsweek*, November 19, 2007.

Miller, Matthew, and Tatiana Serafin, eds. "The 400 Richest Americans." *Forbes*, September 21, 2006.

Miller, N., M. B. Brewer, and K. Edwards. "Cooperative Interaction in Desegregated Settings: A Laboratory Analog." *Journal of Social Issues*, 41 (3, 1985): 63–75.

Miller, Stephen. *Special Interest Groups in American Politics*. Piscataway, NJ: Transaction Publishers, 1983.

Miller, Walter B. "Lower Class Culture as a Generating Milieu of Gang Delinquency." In Marvin E. Wolfgang, Leonard Savitz, and Norma Johnston, eds., *The Sociology of Crime and Delinquency*. New York: Wiley, 1970. Originally published in *Journal of Social Issues*, 14 (1958): 5–19.

Mills, C. Wright. *White Collar: The American Middle Classes*. New York: Oxford University Press, 1959.

Milner, Murray Jr. *Freaks, Geeks, and Cool Kids: American Teenagers, Schools and the Culture of Consumption*. New York: Routledge, 2006.

Mishel, Lawrence, Jared Bernstein, and Heidi Shierholz. *The State of Working America 2008/2009*. Ithaca, NY: ILR Press, an imprint of Cornell University Press, 2009.

Mishel, Lawrence, and Roy Joydeep. *Rethinking High School Graduation Rates and Trends*. Washington, DC: Economic Policy Institute, 2006.

Moffatt, Michael. *Coming of Age in New Jersey*. New Brunswick, NJ: Rutgers University Press, 1989.

Molotch, Harvey. *Where Stuff Comes From: How Toasters, Toilets, Cars, Computers and Many Other Things Come to Be as They Are*. New York: Routledge, 2003.

Montagu, Ashley. *Man's Most Dangerous Myth: The Fallacy of Race* (1942). Lanham, MD: Altamira Press, 2000.

Moore, Barrington. *Social Origins of Dictatorship and Democracy: Lord and Peasant in the Making of the Modern World*. Boston: Beacon Press, 1966.

Moore, J. W., and Hagedorn, J. M. "Female Gangs: A Focus on Research." *Bulletin, Youth Gang Series*. Washington, DC: U.S. Department of Justice, Office of Juvenile Justice and Delinquency Prevention, 2001.

Moore, Molly. "Micro-Credit Pioneer Wins Peace Prize." *Washington Post*, October 14, 2006, A1.

Moore, Solomon. "Executions and Death Sentences in United States Dropped in 2008, Report Finds." *New York Times*, December 11, 2008.

Moreno, Jenalia, "Study Finds Growing Latino Affluence—Young Hispanics." *Houston Chronicle*, May 23, 2008, 14.

Morgan, Robin. *Sisterhood Is Powerful*. New York: Random House, 1976.

Morris, Aldon D., and Carol McClurg Mueller, eds. *Frontiers in Social Movement Theory*. New Haven, CT: Yale University Press, 1992.

Morris, Martina. "Telling Tails Explain the Discrepancy in Sexual Partner Reports." *Nature*, 365 (6445, 1993): 437–440.

Morsch, James. "The Problem of Motive in Hate Crimes: The Argument against Prescriptions of Racial Motivation." *Journal of Criminal Law and Criminology*, 82 (3, Autumn 1991): 659–689.

Moss-Kanter, Rosabeth. *Men and Women of the Corporation*. New York: Basic Books, 1977.

Mowry, George. *The Era of Theodore Roosevelt and the Birth of Modern America*. New York: Harper, 1958.

Mullen, B., and Hu, L. "Perceptions of In-Group and Out-Group Variability: A Meta-Analytic Integration." *Basic and Applied Psychology*, 10 (1989): 291–301.

Mumford, Lewis. *The City in History: Its Origins, Its Transformations, and Its Prospects*. New York: Harvest Books, 1968.

Mumola, Christopher J., and Jennifer Karberg. *Drug Use and Dependence, State and Federal Prisoners, 2004*. Washington, DC: U.S. Department of Justice, October 2006 (NCJ213530).

Muravchik, Joshua. "Marxism." *Foreign Policy*, 133 (November–December. 2002), 36–38.

Murdock, George P. *Social Structure*. New York: Macmillan, 1949.

Murray, Bobbi. "Living Wage Comes of Age." *The Nation*, July 23/30, 2001.

Mustard, David B. "Racial, Ethnic, and Gender Disparities in Sentencing: Evidence from the U.S. Federal Courts." *Journal of Law and Economics*, 44 (2001): 285–314.

Nagel, Joane. *Race, Ethnicity and Sexuality: Intimate Intersections, Forbidden Frontiers*. New York: Oxford University Press, 2003.

Nansel, T. R., M. Overpeck, R. S. Pilla, W. J. Ruan, B. Simons Morton, and P. Scheidt. "Bullying Behaviors among U.S. Youth: Prevalence and Association with Psychosocial Adjustment." *Journal of the American Medical Association*, 285 (16, 2001): 2094–2100.

Nathan, Rebekah. *My Freshman Year*. Ithaca, NY: Cornell University Press, 2005.

National Alliance for Caregiving. *National Caregiving Report*. Washington, DC: Author, 2004. Available at: www.caregiving.org/data/04finalreport.pdf

National Association for Rural Mental Health. "Suicide Rates in Rural Areas," 2007. Available at: www.highplainsmentalhealth.com/news.asp?ID=73

National Center for Children in Poverty. "Demographics of Young, Poor Children." New York: Columbia University, Mailman School of Public Health, 2008.

National Center for Education Statistics (NECS). *1.1 Million Homeschooled Students in the United States in 2003*. 2004. Available at: http://nces.ed.gov/nhes/homeschool/

National Center for Education Statistics (NECS). *Program for International Student Assessment (PISA)*. 2003. Available at: http://nces.ed.gov/surveys/pisa/

National Center for Education Statistics (NECS). *The Condition of Education 2008*. Washington, DC: U.S. Department of Education, 2008.

National Center for Education Statistics (NECS). *Digest of Educational Statistics*. Washington, DC: U.S. Department of Education, 2009a.

National Center for Education Statistics (NECS). "Issue Brief, December 2008: 1.5 Million Homeschooled Students in the United States in 2007." Washington, DC: U.S. Department of Education, 2009b.

National Center for Heath Statistics. *Health, United States, 2007*. Atlanta, GA: Centers for Disease Control, 2007.

National Center for Public Policy and Higher Education. *Measuring UP*, 2008. San Jose, CA:

National Center for Victims of Crime. "Elder Abuse," 2009. Available at: www.ncvc.org/ncvc/main.aspx?dbName=DocumentViewer&DocumentID=32350

National Center for Women and Policing. *Equality Denied: The Status of Women in Policing, 2001*. Washington, DC: National Center for Women and Policing, April 2002.

National Center on Elder Abuse. "Abuse of Adults 60 Years of Age and Older." Prepared for the National Center on Elder Abuse, 2006. Washington, DC.

National Council of La Raza. *Lost Opportunities: The Realities of Latinos in the Criminal Justice System*. Washington, DC, 2004.

National Council of State Legislatures. "Women in State Legislatures: 2009 Legislative Session," 2009. Washington, DC.

National Council on Crime and Delinquency. *U.S. Rates of Incarceration: A Global Perspective*. Washington, DC: 2006.

National Counterterrorism Center. *Report on Terrorist Incidents, 2006*. Washington, DC: National Counterterrorism Center, April 30, 2007.

National Counterterrorism Center. *2008 Report on Terrorism*. Washington, DC: National Counterterrorism Center, April 30, 2009.

National Crime Victimization Survey. "Trends in Violent Victimizations, 1973–2005." Washington, DC: U.S. Department of Justice, 2005.

National Family Caregivers Association. *National Caregiving Statistics*, 2007. Available at: www.nfcacares.org/who_are_family_caregivers/care_giving_statstics.cfm#1

National Gang Intelligence Center (NGIC). *National Gang Threat Assessment 2009*, January 2009. Available at: www.usdoj.gov/ndic/pubs32/32146/index.htm

National Governors Association. "Benchmarking for Success," 2008. Available at: www.nga.org/files/pdf/0812benchmarking.pdf

National Poverty Center. "Poverty in the United States." Ann Arbor: University of Michigan, 2008. Available at: www.npc.umich.edu/poverty/

National Retail Federation. *National Retail Security Survey, 2007*. Washington, DC: National Retail Federation, 2007.

National Rural Health Association. "Farm Bill Reauthorization: Implications for the Health of Rural Communities." Issue paper, November 2006.

National Sample Survey Organization (NSSO). "India's Literacy Rate Increase Sluggish," February 1, 2008. Kolkata, India: NSSO.

National Science Foundation. "Global Trends in Higher Education in Science and Engineering." *Science and Engineering Indicators, 2008*. Available at: www.nsf.gov/statistics/seind08/c2/c2s5.htm#c2s54

National Telecommunications Information Administration. "Current Population Survey. Households Using the Internet in and Outside the Home, by Selected Characteristics: Total Urban, Rural, Princi-

pal City 2007." Available at: www.ntia
.doc.gov/reports/2008/Table_Household
Internet2007.pdf

National Urban League. *The State of Black America*. Washington, DC: National Urban League, 2008.

National White Collar Crime Center, 2009. "National Public Survey on White Collar Crime." Available at: www.nw3c.org/ research/national_public_survey.cfm

National Youth Gang Center. *National Youth Gang Survey Analysis, 2007*. Washington, DC: National Youth Gang Center, 2007.

Needleman, Sarah E. "Doing the Math to Find Good Jobs: Mathematicians Land Top Spot in New Ranking of Best and Worst Occupations in the U.S." *The Wall Street Journal*, January 6, 2009.

Neilsen, Francois, and Arthur S. Adelson. "The Kuznets Curve and the Great U-Turn: Income Inequality in U.S. Counties, 1970 to 1990." *American Journal of Sociology*, 62 (1, 1997): 12–26.

Neugarten, Bernice. *The Meanings of Age*. Chicago, IL: University of Chicago Press, 1996.

New York Times. February 19, 2009a. A14. Moore, Solomon. "Study Shows Sharp Rise in Latino Federal Convicts." *New York Times*, February 18, 2009.

New York Times. July 1, 2009b. A1. Abelson, Reed. "Insured, but Bankrupted by Health Crises." *New York Times*, June 30, 2009.

Newman, Cathy. "Why Are We So Fat?" *National Geographic*, August 2004.

Newman, Katherine. *No Shame in My Game: The Working Poor in the Inner City*. New York: Alfred A. Knopf, 1999.

Newsweek. "The Graying of America," January 26, 2009a: 74.

Newsweek. "Stirring the Pot." January 26, 2009b: 70.

Newton, Michael. *Savage Girls and Wild Boys: A History of Feral Children*. New York: Thomas Dunne Books, 2003.

Nielsen. "More Than Half the Homes in the U.S. Have Three or More TVs." Nielsenwire, June 20, 2009. New York.

Nielsen Media Research. "Americans Can't Get Enough of Their Screen Time." November 24, 2008. New York.

Nisbet, Robert A. *The Social Bond: An Introduction to the Study of Sociology*. New York: Alfred A. Knopf, 1970.

Nock, Steven. "The New Chronology of Union Formation: Strategies for Measuring Changing Pathways." Paper prepared for Office of the Assistant Secretary for Planning and Evaluation, HHS, November 2003. Health and Human Services. Yes: Washington, DC.

Noguera, Pedro. "The Trouble with Black Boys." Paper presented at Harvard University Graduate School of Education, May 2004.

Noguera, Pedro. *The Trouble with Black Boys*. New York: John Wiley and Sons, 2008.

Norris, Pippa. *Democratic Phoenix: Reinventing Political Activism*. Cambridge, UK: Cambridge University Press, 2002.

North, Douglas, and Robert Paul Thomas. *The Rise of the Western World: A New Economic History*. Cambridge, UK: Cambridge University Press, 1976.

Northeast-Midwest Institute. "Rural Population as a Percent of State Total, by State," 2002. Available at www.nemw.org/ poprural.htm

Norwich, John Julius. *A History of Venice*. New York: Vintage, 1989.

Notestein, Frank. "Population—The Long View," in P. W. Schultz, ed., *Food for the World*. Chicago: University of Chicago Press, 1945.

Novak, Candace. "Behind the Rise of Temp Work: A Q & A with Vicky Smith, Author of *The Good Temp*." *U.S. News & World Report*, April 29, 2009.

Nussbaum, Emily. "My So-Called Blog." *New York Times Magazine*, January 11, 2004, 32.

Oakes, Jeannie. *Keeping Track: How Schools Structure Inequality*. New Haven, CT: Yale University Press, 1985.

Oakes, Jeannie. *Multiplying Inequalities: The Effects of Race, Social Class, and Tracking on Opportunities to Learn Mathematics and Science*. Santa Monica, CA: RAND Corporation, 1990.

Oates, Stephen B. *Abraham Lincoln: The Man behind the Myths*. New York: Perennial, 1994.

Offer, Daniel, Marjorie Kaiz Offer, and Eric Ostrov. *Regular Guys*. New York: Plenum, 2004.

Ogbu, John. "Understanding the School Performance of Urban Blacks: Some Essential Background Knowledge." In H. J. Walhberg, O. Reyes, and R. P. Weissberg, eds., *Children and Youth: Interdisciplinary Perspectives*. Thousand Oaks, CA: Sage Press, 1997.

Ogbu, John. *Black American Students in an Affluent Suburb: A Study of Academic Disengagement*. New York: Taylor & Francis, 2003.

Ogbu, John, and A. Davis. *Black American Students in an Affluent Suburb: A Study in Academic Disengagement*. Mahwah, NJ: Lawrence Erlbaum Publishers, 2003.

Ogbu, John, and Signithia Fordham. "Black Students' School Success: Coping with the Burden of 'Acting White,'" *The Urban Review*, 18 (3, 1986): 176–206.

Ogburn, William F. *Social Change with Respect to Culture and Original Nature* (1922). New York: Dell, 1966.

Oh, Kongdan, and Ralph C. Hassig. *North Korea: Through the Looking Glass*. Washington, DC: The Brookings Institution Press, 2000.

O'Hare, William P., and Sarah Savage. *Child Poverty in Rural America*. New York: National Center for Children in Poverty, Columbia University, Summer 2006.

Olweus, Dan. *Bullying at School: What We Know and What We Can Do*. New York: Blackwell, 1993.

Orenstein, Peggy. *Schoolgirls*. New York: Doubleday, 1994.

Orenstein, Peggy. *Flux: Women on Sex, Work, Love, Kids, and Life in a Half-Changed World*. New York: Academic Press, 2001.

Orfield, Gary. *Brown at 50: King's Dream or the Plessy Nightmare*. Cambridge, MA: Harvard University Press, 2004.

Organization for Economic Cooperation and Development (OECD). *Education at a Glance: OECD Indicators 2006*. Paris: OECD, 2006.

Organization for Economic Cooperation and Development (OECD). *OECD Factbook 2007: Economic, Environmental, and Social Statistics*. Paris: OECD, 2007a.

Organization for Economic Cooperation and Development (OECD). *Women and Men in OECD Countries*. Paris: OECD, 2007b.

Organization for Economic Cooperation and Development (OECD). "Competition Policy and the Information Economy." Global Forum on Economic Competition, December 2008a.

Organization for Economic Cooperation and Development (OECD). *OECD Health Data 2008*. Paris: OECD, 2008b.

Organization for Economic Cooperation and Development (OECD). *Key Environmental Indicators 2008*. Paris: OECD, 2009a.

Organization for Economic Cooperation and Development (OECD). *OECD Factbook*. Paris: OECD, 2009b.

Organization for Economic Cooperation and Development (OECD). *Society at a Glance*. Paris: OECD, 2009c.

Orum, Anthony M. *An Introduction to Political Sociology*, 4th ed. Englewood Cliffs, NJ: Prentice-Hall, 2000.

Oshima, Harry T. "The Transition from an Agricultural to an Industrial Economy in East Asia." *Economic Development and Cultural Change*, 34 (4, July 1986): 783–809.

Overell, Stephen. "Cheating—We're All at It." *Financial Times*, June 27, 2003, 53.

Oxfam International. *Trading Away Our Rights: Women Working in Global Supply Chains*. London: Oxfam, 2004.

Padavic, Irene, and Barbara F. Reskin. *Women and Men at Work* (1994). Thousand Oaks, CA: Pine Forge Press, 2002.

Pagden, Anthony. *Peoples and Empires: A Short History of European Migration, Exploration, and Conquest, from Greece to the Present*. New York: Modern Library, 2001.

Page, Marianne, and Ann Huff Stevens. "Understanding Racial Differences in the Economic Costs of Growing Up in a Single-Parent Family." *Demography*, 42: 1 (February 2005): 75–90.

Paige, Jeffrey. *Agrarian Revolutions*. New York: The Free Press, 1975.

Palen, J. John. *The Suburbs*. New York: McGraw-Hill, 1995.

Panter-Brick, Catherine, Robert H. Layton, and Peter Rowley-Conway. *Hunter-Gatherers: An Interdisciplinary Perspective*. Cambridge, UK: Cambridge University Press, 2001.

Paoletti, J. O. "Clothing and Gender in American Children's Fashions, 1890–1920." *Signs*, 13 (Autumn 1987): 136–143.

Paoletti, J. O. "The Children's Department." *Men and Women: Dressing the Part*. Washington, DC: The Smithsonian Institution Press, 1989.

Paoletti, J. O. "'Pink or Blue? What Color for Your Baby?' The Gendering of Infants' and Toddlers' Clothing in America." *The Material Culture of Gender/The Gender of Material Culture*. Winterthur, DE: The Henry Francis du Pont Winterthur Museum, 1997.

Parillo, Vincent. "Diversity in America: Past, Present, and Future." Paper presented to the Eastern Sociological Society, February 24, 2006.

Parillo, Vincent, and Christopher Donoghue. "Updating the Bogardus Social Distance Studies: A New National Study." *The Social Science Journal*, 422 (2005): 257–271.

Park, Robert E., Ernest Burgess, and Robert McKenzie. *The City: Suggestions for Investigation of Human Behavior in the Urban Environment* (1925). Chicago: University of Chicago Press, 1967.

Parker-Pope, Tara. "Love, Sex and the Changing Landscape of Infidelity." *New York Times*, October 28, 2008.

Parsons, Talcott. *The Structure of Social Action*. New York: The Free Press, 1937.

Parsons, Talcott. *The Social System*. New York: The Free Press, 1951.

Parsons, Talcott. *Societies: Evolutionary and Comparative Perspectives*. Englewood Cliffs, NJ: Prentice-Hall, 1966.

Pascoe, P. J. "'Dude, You're a Fag.'" *Sexualities*, 8 (3, 2005): 329–346.

Passel, Jeffrey S., and Roberto Suro. "Rise, Peak, and Decline: Trends in U.S. Immigration 1992–2004." Pew Hispanic Center Reports on Immigration, September 2005. Philadelphia, PA.

Paternoster, Raymond, Robert Brame, and Sarah Bacon, eds. *The Death Penalty: America's Experience with Capital Punishment*. New York: Oxford University Press, 2007.

PBS/*Frontline*. "Merchants of Cool." Airdate February 27, 2001.

Pear, Robert. "Gap in Life Expectancy Widens for the Nation." *New York Times*, March 23, 2008: 44.

Pearce, Diana. "The Feminization of Poverty: Women, Work, and Welfare." *Urban and Social Change Review*, 11 (1978): 28–36.

Pennar, K., and C. Farrel, "Notes from the Underground Economy." *BusinessWeek*, February 15, 1993, 98–101.

Pennycock, Alastair. "Language, Localization, and the Real: Hip-Hop and the Global Spread of Authenticity." *Journal of Language, Identity & Education*, 6 (2, 2007): 101–115.

Perkins, H. Wesley, ed. *The Social Norms Approach to Preventing School and College Age Substance Abuse: A Handbook for Educators, Counselors, and Clinicians*. San Francisco: Jossey-Bass, 2003.

Perry-Jenkins, M., and A. C. Crouter. "Implications of Men's Provider Role Attitudes for Household Work and Marital Satisfaction." *Journal of Family Issues*, 11 (2, 1990): 136–156.

Peter, Laurence J., and Raymond Hull. *The Peter Principle: Why Things Always Go Wrong*. New York: William Morrow, 1969.

Peterson, D., J. Miller, and F. Esbensen. "The Impact of Sex Composition on Gangs and Gang Delinquency." *Criminology*, 39 (2, 2001): 411–439.

Pettigrew, Thomas F. "Intergroup Contact Theory." *Annual Review of Psychology*, 49 (1998): 65–85.

Pettit, Becky, and Bruce Western. "Mass Imprisonment and the Life Course: Race and Class Inequality in U.S. Incarceration." *American Sociological Review*, 69 (April 2004): 151–169.

Pew Center for the People and the Press. "Online Newspapers Modestly Boost Readership." Philadelphia: The Pew Charitable Trusts, July 30, 2006.

Pew Center on the States, Public Safety Performance Project. *One in 100: Behind Bars in America 2008*. Philadelphia, (published by The Pew Charitable Trusts); 2008.

Pew Economic Mobility Project. "Opinion Poll on Economic Mobility and the American Dream." 2009. Available at: www.economicmobility.org/poll2009

Pew Forum on Religion and Public Life. "Religion and Politics: Contention and Consensus," 2003. Available at: http//pewforum.org/publications/surveys/religion-politics.pdf

Pew Forum on Religion and Public Life. *Changing Faiths: Latinos and the Transformation of American Religion*. Philadelphia: The Pew Charitable Trusts, 2007a.

Pew Forum on Religion and Public Life, 2007b. "Hispanics Transforming Nation." Available at: http://pewforum.org/news/display.php?NewsID=13310

Pew Forum on Religion and Public Life. "Faith in Flux: Changes in Religious Affiliation in the U.S." Philadelphia: The Pew Charitable Trusts, April 2009.

Pew Global Attitudes Project. "Among Wealthy Nations . . . U.S. Stands Alone in Its Embrace of Religion." Pew Research Center, 2002. Available at: http://pewglobal.org/reports/display.php?ReportID=167

Pew Global Attitudes Project. *47-Nation Pew Gobal Attitudes Survey*, October 4, 2007a. Philadelphia: The Pew Charitable Trusts.

Pew Global Attitudes Project. "Global Unease with Major World Powers," Philadelphia: The Pew Charitable Trusts, June 27, 2007b.

Pew Hispanic Center. "The Wealth of Hispanic Households: 1996–2002." Philadelphia, The Pew Charitable Trusts, October 2005.

Pew Hispanic Center. "Statistical Portrait of Hispanics in the United States, 2007." Philadelphia: The Pew Charitable Trusts, March 5, 2009.

Pew Research Center. *A Barometer of Modern Morals: Sex, Drugs and the 1010*. Philadelphia: The Pew Charitable Trusts, 2006.

Pew Research Center on the People and the Press. "Acceptance of Interracial Dating." Available at: http://people-press.org/reports/pdf/312.pdf

Pew Research Center for People and the Press. *Trends in Political Values and Core Attitudes: 1987–2007*. Philadelphia: The Pew Charitable Trusts, 2007.

Philipp, Steven F. "Race and Gender Differences in Adolescent Peer Group Approval of Leisure Activities." *Journal of Leisure Research*, 30 (2, 1998): 214–232.

Phillips, Scott. "Racial Disparities in the Capital of Capital Punishment." *Houston Law Review*, 45 (October 2008): 441–464.

Phinney, Jean S., Debora L. Gerguson, and Jerry D. Tate. "Intergroup Attitudes among Ethnic Minority Adolescents: A Causal Model." *Child Development*, 68 (5, October 1997): 955–969.

Piaget, J. *The Child's Conception of the World*. London: Routledge and Kegan Paul, 1928.

Piaget, J. *The Moral Judgment of the Child*. London: Kegan Paul, Trench, Trubner and Co., 1932.

Piaget, J. *The Origins of Intelligence in Children*. London: Routledge and Kegan Paul, 1953.

Piaget, J. *The Child's Construction of Reality*. London: Routledge and Kegan Paul, 1955.

Pilkington, Ed. "One in Five U.S. Women Remain Childless in Life." *The Guardian*, August 20, 2008.

Pipes, Richard. *Communism*. London, UK: Weidenfeld and Nicolson, 2001.

Pipher, Mary. *Can't Buy My Love: How Advertising Changes the Way We Think and Feel*. New York: Free Press, 2000.

Pizzo, Stephen, and Paul Muolo. *Profiting from the Bank and Savings and Loan Crisis*. New York: HarperCollins, 1994.

Pleck, Joseph H. "Paternal Involvement: Levels, Sources, and Consequences." In M. E. Lamb, ed., *The Role of the Father in Child Development*, 3rd ed., 66–103. New York: John Wiley, 1997.

Pleck, Joseph H., and Masciadrelli, Brian. "Paternal Involvement in U.S. Residential Fathers: Levels, Sources, and Consequences." In M. E. Lamb, ed., *The Role of the Father in Child Development*, 4th ed., 222–271. New York: Wiley, 2004.

Plummer, Ken. "Speaking Its Name: Inventing a Lesbian and Gay Studies." In Ken Plummer, ed., *Modern Homosexualities*, 3–25. London: Routledge, 1992.

Pollak, Otto. *The Criminality of Women* (1950). Westport, CT: Greenwood, 1978.

Pollack, William. *Real Boys: Rescuing Our Sons from the Myths of Boyhood*. New York: Owl Books, 1999.

Pomer, Marshall. "Intergenerational Occupational Mobility in the United States: A Segmentation Perspective." *Work and Occupations*, 10 (1983): 497–501.

Poniewozik, James. "Here's to the Death of Broadcast." *Time*, March 26, 2009.

Pope, Harrison, Katharine Phillips, and Roberto Olivardia. *The Adonis Complex: The Secret Crisis of Male Body Obsession*. New York: The Free Press, 2000.

Popkin, Samuel L. *The Reasoning Voter: Communication and Persuasion in Presidential Campaigns*. Chicago: University of Chicago Press, 1994.

Population Council. "Transitions to Adulthood: Child Marriage/Married Adolescents." Retrieved May 2009 from: www.popcouncil.org/ta/mar.html

Population Reference Bureau. "U.S. Labor Force Trends." *Population Bulletin*, 63 (2, June 2008).

Portes, A., M. Castells, and L. A. Benton. *The Informal Economy: Studies in Advanced and Less Developed Countries*. Baltimore: Johns Hopkins University Press, 1989.

Poston, Dudley L., and Amanda K. Baumle. "Patterns of Asexuality in the United States." Paper presented at the Annual Meeting of the American Sociological Association, Montreal, Canada, August 11, 2006.

Potok, Mark. *The Year in Hate, 2005*. Montgomery, AL: Southern Poverty Law Center, 2006. Available at: www.splcenter.org/intel/intelreport/article.isp?aid=627

Powell, Walter W., and Kaisa Snellman. "The Knowledge Economy." *Annual Review of Sociology*, 30 (August 2004): 199–220.

Power, Carla. "Buying Muslim." *Time*, June 15, 2009.

PricewaterhouseCoopers. *Global Economic Crime Survey.* New York, 2007.

Project for Excellence in Journalism. *The State of the News Media 2006.* Washington, DC: Author, 2006.

Project for Excellence in Journalism. "Digital Trends." *State of the News Media.* Washington, DC: Project for Excellence in Journalism, 2009.

Pullum, Geoff. *The Great Eskimo Vocabulary Hoax and Other Irreverent Essays.* Chicago: University of Chicago Press, 1991.

Putnam, Robert. *Bowling Alone: The Collapse and Revival of American Community.* New York: Simon and Schuster, 2000.

Quadagno, Jill. "Welfare Capitalism and the Social Security Act of 1935." *American Sociological Review,* 49 (1984): 632–647.

Quattrone, G. A., "On the Perception of a Group's Variability." In S. Worchel and W. Austin, eds., *The Psychology of Intergroup Relations,* 2nd ed. Chicago: Nelson-Hall, 1986.

Quattrone, G. A., and E. E. Jones, "Perceptions of Variability within In-Groups and Out-Groups." *Journal of Personality and Social Psychology,* 1980.

Quinney, Richard. *Class, State, and Crime: On the Theory and Practice of Criminal Justice.* New York: David McKay, 1977.

Radcliffe Public Policy Center. *Life's Work: Generational Attitudes toward Work and Life Integration.* Cambridge, MA: Radcliffe Institute of Advanced Study and Harris Interactive, 2001.

Radcliffe-Brown, A. R. *Structure and Function in Primitive Society.* London: Cohen and West, 1952.

Radelet, M. L., and H. A. Bedau. *In Spite of Innocence: Erroneous Convictions in Capital Cases.* Boston: Northeastern University Press, 1992.

Radway, Janice. *A Feeling for Books: The Book-of-the-Month Club, Literary Taste, and Middle-Class Desire.* Chapel Hill: University of North Carolina Press, 1999.

Raeburn, Nicole C. *Changing Corporate America from the Inside Out: Lesbian and Gay Workplace Rights.* Minneapolis: University of Minnesota Press, 2004.

Raley, Kelly R., and Megan M. Sweeney. "What Explains Race and Ethnic Variation in Cohabitation, Marriage, Divorce, and Nonmarital Fertility?" Los Angeles: California Center for Population Research, September 2007.

Ranis, Gustav, and Syed Akhtar Mahmood. *The Political Economy of Development Policy Change.* Oxford, UK: Blackwell, 1991.

Rawlings, M. Keith, R. J. Graff, R. Calderon, S. Casey-Bailey, and M. Pasley. "Patient and Provider Differences in What They Perceive as Having 'Had Sex': Implications for HIV/AIDS Prevention." Poster 889, 42nd Annual Meeting of the Infectious Diseases of America. Boston, MA: September, 2004.

Reckless, Walter. *American Criminology: New Directions.* New York: Appleton-Century-Crofts, 1973.

Redfield, Robert. *Folk Cultures of the Yucatan.* Chicago: University of Chicago Press, 1941.

Rennison, M., and W. Welchans. *Intimate Partner Violence, NCJ 178247.* Washington, DC: U.S. Department of Justice, Office of Justice Programs, Bureau of Justice Statistics, May 2000. Revised July 14, 2000.

Reskin, Barbara. "Sex Segregation in the Workplace." In P. Dubeck and K. Borman, eds., *Women and Work: A Handbook.* New York: Garland, 1996.

Resnick, Stephan A., and Richard D. Wolff. *Knowledge and Class: A Marxian Critique of Political Economy.* Chicago: University of Chicago Press, 1987.

Rettberg, Jill Walker. *Blogging.* Cambridge, UK: Polity Press, 2008.

Retherford, Robert D., Noah-iro Ogawa, and Rikiya Matsukura. "Late Marriage and Less Marriage." *Population and Development Review,* 27 (1, 2001): 65–78.

Rhode, Deborah. *Speaking of Sex: The Denial of Gender Equality.* Cambridge, MA: Harvard University Press, 1997.

Rian, Shari. "Social Stigma Drives Some Women to Remove Tattoos." *The Los Angeles Times,* July 21, 2008. Available at: http://latimesblogs.latimes.com/booster_shots/2008/07/social-stigma-d.html

Rich, Carole. *Writing and Reporting News.* Belmont, CA: Thomson Publishing, 2006.

Rights of the Child, Notes by the Secretary General of the United Nations. New York: United Nations, August 29, 2006.

Rimmerman, Craig. *The New Citizenship: Unconventional Politics, Activism, and Service.* Boulder, CO: Westview Press, 2001.

Ritzer, George. *The McDonaldization of America.* Thousand Oaks, CA: Pine Forge Press, 1996.

Robbins, Sarah. "Is Your Body Normal?" *Glamour,* July, 2008, 98.

Roberts, D. F. "The Dynamics of Racial Intermixture in the America Negro—Some Anthropological Considerations." *American Journal of Human Genetics,* 7 (December 1975): 361–367.

Roberts, Paul. *The End of Oil: On the Edge of a Perilous New World.* New York: Mariner Books, 2005.

Rodin, Judith, Lisa Silberstein, and Ruth Striegel-Moore. "Women and Weight: A Normative Discontent." In T. B. Sonderegger, ed., *Psychology and Gender: The Nebraska Symposium on Motivation 1984.* Lincoln: University of Nebraska Press, 1985.

Roediger, David. *The Wages of Whiteness: Race and the Making of the American Working Class.* New York: Verso, 1991.

Roethlisberger, Fritz J., and William J. Dickson. *Management and the Worker.* Cambridge, MA: Harvard University Press, 1939.

Rogers, J. W., and M. D. Buffalo. "Fighting Back: Nine Modes of Adaptation to a Deviant Label." *Social Problems,* 22 (1974): 101–118.

Rosa, Eugene, A., Gary E. Machlis, and Kenneth M. Keating. "Energy and Society." *Annual Review of Sociology,* 14 (1988): 149–172.

Roscoe, Will, ed. *Boy-Wives and Female Husbands: Studies of African Homosexualities.* London: Palgrave Macmillan, 2001.

Rose, Brad, and George Ross. "Socialism's Past, New Social Democracy, and Socialism's Futures." *Social Science History,* 18 (3, Autumn 1994): 439–469.

Rose, Heather, and Glenn E. Martin. "Locking Down Civil Rights: Criminal Record-Based Discrimination." *Race/Ethnicity: Multidisciplinary Global Perspectives,* 2, 1 (Autumn, 2008): 13–19.

Rose, Stephen J., and Heidi I. Hartmann. *Still a Man's Labor Market: The Long-Term Earnings Gap.* Washington, DC: Institute for Women's Policy Research, 2004.

Rosenthal, Robert, and Lenore Jacobson. *Pygmalion in the Classroom: Teacher Expectations and Pupil's Intellectual Development* (1968). New York: Irvington, 1992.

Ross, Andrew. *The Celebration Chronicles: Life, Liberty, and the Pursuit of Property Value in Disney's New Town.* New York: Ballantine Books, 1999.

Rostow, W. W. *Process of Economic Growth.* New York: W. W. Norton, 1962.

Rousseau, Jean-Jacques. *The Social Contract.* (1754). New York: bnpublishing.com, 2007.

Rubin, Lillian. *Intimate Strangers: Men and Women Together.* New York: HarperCollins, 1983.

Rubin, Lillian. *Just Friends.* New York: Harper and Row, 1986.

Rubin, Lillian. *Erotic Wars: What Happened to the Sexual Revolution?* New York: Farrar, Straus & Giroux, 1990.

Rudolph, Frederick. *The American College and University: A History.* Athens: University of Georgia Press, 1990.

Rugg, W. D. "Experiments in Wording Questions." *Public Opinion Quarterly,* 5 (1941): 91–92.

Rugh, William A. *Arab Mass Media: Newspapers, Radio, and Television in Arab Politics.* Westport, CT: Praeger, 2004.

Rule, Wilma, and Steven Hill. "Ain't I a Voter? Voting Rights for Women." *Ms.,* September–October 1996.

Rust, Paula Rodriguez. *Bisexuality and the Challenge to Lesbian Politics.* New York: New York University Press, 1995.

Rust, Paula Rodriguez. *Bisexuality in the United States: A Social Science Reader.* New York: Columbia University Press, 1999.

Sabol, William J., and Heather C. West. *Prisoners in 2007.* Washington, DC: US Department of Justice Bureau of Justice Statistics, December 2008 (NCJ224280).

Sacks, Karen. "Engels Revisited: Women, Organization of Production, and Private Property." *Women, Culture, and Society.* Stanford, CA: Stanford University Press, 1974.

Sadker, Myra, and David Sadker. *Failing at Fairness: How Schools Shortchange Girls.* New York: McGraw Hill, 1994.

Saguy, Abigal C. "Sex, Inequality, and Ethnography: Response to Erich Goode." *Qualitative Sociology* 25:4 (2002): 549–556.

Qui, Chen, Steven Salterio, and Pamela Murphy. "Fraud in Canadian Nonprofit Organizations as Seen through the Eyes of Canadian Newspapers, 1998–2008." *Philanthropist,* 22, 1 (2009).

Sampson, Robert J. "Open Doors Don't Invite Criminals." *New York Times,* March 11, 2006, A15.

Samuel, Lawrence R. *Brought to You by Postwar Television Advertising and the American Dream.* Austin: University of Texas Press, 2002.

Sanchez-Jankowski, Martin. *Islands in the Street: Gangs and American Urban Society.*

Berkeley: University of California Press, 1991.

Sanday, Peggy Reeves. *Female Power and Male Dominance: On the Origins of Sexual Inequality.* New York: Cambridge University Press, 1981.

Sandefur, Gary D., and Arthur Sakamoto. "American Indian Household Structure and Income." *Demography,* 25 (1, 1988): 71–80.

Sanders, Clinton R. *Customizing the Body: The Art and Culture of Tattooing.* Philadelphia: Temple University Press, 1989.

Sanders, Stephanie, and June Machover Reinisch. "Would You Say You 'Had Sex' If . . .?" *JAMA,* 281 (January 20, 1999): 275–277.

Sapir, Edward. *Language.* New York: Harcourt, Brace and World, 1921.

Sapolsky, Robert. *The Trouble with Testosterone.* New York: Simon and Schuster, 1997.

Sasseen, Jane. "White-Collar Crime: Who Does Time?" *BusinessWeek,* February 6, 2006, 60.

Sassen, Saskia. *The Global City: New York, London, Tokyo.* Princeton, NJ: Princeton University Press, 1991.

Saunders, Peter. *Social Class and Stratification.* London: Routledge, 1990.

Save the Children. *State of the World's Mothers.* 2008.

Saxton, Alexander. *The Indispensable Enemy: Labor and the Anti-Chinese Movement in California.* Berkeley: University of California Press, 1971.

Saxton, Alexander. *The Rise and Fall of the White Republic: Class Politics and Mass Culture in Nineteenth-Century America.* New York: Verso, 1990.

Sayer, L. S. "Time Use, Gender, and Inequality: Differences in Men's and Women's Market, Nonmarket, and Leisure Time." Ph.D. Dissertation, University of Maryland, 2001.

Schachter, Jason. *Why People Move: Exploring the March 2000 Current Population Survey.* Washington, DC: U.S. Bureau of the Census, 2001. Available at: www.census.gov/prod/2001pubs/p23-204.pdf

Schaffner, Laurie. *Girls in Trouble with the Law.* New Brunswick, NJ: Rutgers University Press, 2006.

Scheper-Hughes, Nancy. *Death without Weeping: The Violence of Everyday Life in Brazil.* Berkeley: University of California Press, 1992.

Schickel, Richard. *Intimate Strangers: The Culture of Celebrity.* Garden City, NY: Doubleday, 1985.

Schilt, Kristen, and Matthew Wiswall. "Before and After: Gender Transitions, Human Capital and Workplace Experiences." *Berkeley Electronic Journal of Economic Analysis and Policy,* 8 (1), 2008.

Schlesinger, Arthur. "Biography of a Nation of Joiners." *American Historical Review,* 50 (1, October 1944): 1–25.

Schmitz, Christopher, and Maurice Kirby. *The Growth of Big Business in the United States and Western Europe, 1850–1939.* Cambridge, UK: Cambridge University Press, 1995.

Schnaiberg, Allan. *The Environment: From Surplus to Scarcity.* New York: Oxford University Press, 1980.

Schopflin, George. *Politics in Eastern Europe.* New York: Blackwell, 1993.

Schrank, Delphine. "The Online Male Takes a Licking and Keeps on Clicking." *Washington Post,* February 17, 2009, HE06.

Schwartz, Martin, and Walter DeKeseredy. "Interpersonal Violence against Women: The Role of Men." *Journal of Contemporary Criminal Justice,* 24 (May 2008): 78.

Schwartz, Pepper, and Virginia Rutter. *The Gender of Sexuality.* Thousand Oaks, CA: Pine Forge Press, 1998.

Schwendinger, Herman, and Julia R. Schwendinger. *Sociologists of the Chair: A Radical Analysis of the Formative Years of North American Sociology (1883–1922).* New York: Basic Books, 1974.

Scott, James. *Weapons of the Weak: Everyday Forms of Peasant Resistance.* New Haven, CT: Yale University Press, 1987.

Scott, Janny, and David Leonhardt. "Does Class Still Matter?" *New York Times Upfront,* 138 (6, 2005), 10–16.

Scott, Laura S. *Two Is Enough: A Couple's Guide to Living Childless by Choice.* Berkeley, CA: Seal Press, 2009.

Selden, Steven. *Inheriting Shame: The Story of Eugenics and Racism in America.* New York: Teachers College Press, 1999.

Seltzer, J. A. "Families Formed Outside of Marriage." In *Understanding Families in the New Millennium: A Decade in Review.* Lawrence, KS: NCRF and Alliance Communication Group, 2001.

Sennett, Richard, and Jonathan Cobb. *The Hidden Injuries of Class.* New York: Norton, 1993.

Settersten, Richard A., Frank F. Furstenberg, and Ruben Rumbaut. *On the Frontier of Adulthood: Theory, Research, and Public Policy.* Chicago: University of Chicago Press, 2005.

Seward, Rudy Ray, Dale E. Yeatts, Iftekhar Amin, and Amy Dewitt. "Employment Leave and Fathers' Involvement with Children: According to Mothers and Fathers." *Men and Masculinities,* 8 (2006): 405–427.

Shah, Anup. "Poverty Facts and Stats." *Global Issues* website, 2007. Available at: www.globalissues.org/TradeRelated/Facts.asp

Shalit, Wendy. *A Return to Modesty: Discovering the Lost Virtue.* New York: The Free Press, 1999.

Sharp, Travis. "Growth in U.S. Defense Spending Over the Past Decade." Center for Arms Control and Non-Proliferation, February 26, 2009. www.armscontrolcenter.org/policysecurityspending/articles/022609_fy10_topline_growth_decade/

Shattuck, R. *The Forbidden Experiment: The Story of the Wild Boy of Aveyron.* New York: Kodansha International, 1980.

Sheehy, Gail. *Passages.* New York: Bantam, 1976.

Shumway, Nicholas. *The Invention of Argentina.* Berkeley: University of California Press, 1993.

Sidel, Ruth. *Unsung Heroes: Single Mothers and the American Dream.* Berkeley: University of California Press, 2006.

Siegel, Larry J. *Criminology: Theories, Patterns, and Typologies.* Belmont, CA: Wadsworth, 2000.

Simmel, Georg. "The Metropolis and Mental Life" (1902). In Donald Levine, ed., *Georg Simmel on Individuality and Social Forms.* Chicago: University of Chicago Press, 1971.

Simmel, Georg. *Conflict and the Web of Group Affiliations* (1908). New York: Free Press, 1956.

Singer, Natasia. "Who Is the Real Face of Cosmetic Surgery?" *New York Times,* August 16, 2007, G1, 3.

Sklar, Holly, Laryssa Mykyta, and Susan Wefald. *Raise the Floor.* New York: Ms. Foundation for Women, 2001.

Skocpol, Theda. *States and Social Revolutions: A Comparative Analysis of France, Russia, and China.* Cambridge, UK: Cambridge University Press, 1979.

Skuratowicz, Eva, and Larry W. Hunter. "Where Do Women's Jobs Come From? Job Resegregation in an American Bank." *Work and Occupations,* 31 (1, 2004): 73–110.

Smeeding, T. M. 2006. "Poor People in Rich Nations: The United States in Comparative Perspective." *Journal of Economic Perspectives,* 20 (1): 69–90.

Smelser, Neil, ed. *Karl Marx on Society and Social Change.* Chicago: University of Chicago Press, 1975.

Smil, Vaclav. *Energy at the Crossroads: Global Perspectives and Uncertainties.* Cambridge, MA: MIT Press, 2005.

Smith, Adam. *The Wealth of Nations* (1776). Robert B. Reich (ed.). New York: Modern Library, 2000.

Smock, Pamela J. "Cohabitation in the United States: An Appraisal of Research Themes, Findings, and Implications." *Annual Review of Sociology,* 26 (2000): 1–20.

Snyder, Howard N., and Metissa Sickmund. *Juvenile Offenders and Victims.* Washington, DC: National Center for Juvenile Justice, U.S. Department of Justice, March 2006.

Snyder, Mark. *Public Appearances, Private Realities: The Psychology of Self-Monitoring.* New York: W. H. Freeman, 1987.

Snyder-Grenier, Ellen M. *Brooklyn: An Illustrated History.* Philadelphia: Temple University Press, 2004.

Sollors, Werner, ed. *Interracialism: Black–White Intermarriage in American History, Literature, and Law.* New York: Oxford University Press, 2000.

Solon, Gary. "Intergenerational Income Mobility in the United States." *American Economic Review,* 82 (3, 1992): 393–408.

Southern Poverty Law Center. "The Year in Hate." Spring, 2009. Montgomery, AL. www.splcenter.org/intel/intelreport/intrep.jsp

"Special Report: CEO Compensation." Forbes.com, May 5, 2007.

Spencer, Herbert. *Principles of Biology.* Honolulu: University Press of the Pacific, 2002.

Stacey, Judith, and Barrie Thorne. "The Missing Feminist Revolution in Sociology." *Social Problems,* 21 (1985): 301–316.

Stack, Carol. *All Our Kin.* New York: Harper and Row, 1974.

Stamm, K., F. Clark, and P. R. Eblacas. "Mass Communication and Public Understanding of Environmental Problems: The Case of Global Warming." *Public Understanding of Science,* 9 (2000): 219–237.

Stampp, Kenneth. *The Peculiar Institution: Slavery in the Antebellum South.* New York: Knopf, 1967.

"The State of Divorce: You May Be Surprised." *Time,* May 28, 2007.

The State of Our Unions in 2008: A Profile in Union Membership in Los Angeles, California, and the Nation. Los Angeles: UCLA, 2008.

Stearns, Elizabeth, Claudia Buchmann, and Kara Bonneau. "Interracial Friendships in the Transition to College: Do Birds of a Feather Flock Together Once They Leave the Nest?" *Sociology of Education,* 82 (2), April 2009.

Stearns, Peter. *Consumerism in World History.* New York: Routledge, 2001.

Steenbergen, B. V. *The Condition of Citizenship.* Thousand Oaks, CA: Sage, 1994.

Steinberg, Ted. *Acts of God: The Unnatural History of Natural Disaster in America.* New York: Oxford University Press, 2000.

Steinert, Heinz. *Culture Industry.* Cambridge, UK: Polity Press, 2003.

Steinmetz, Susan. "The Battered Husband Syndrome." *Victimology,* 2 (1977–1978): 499–509.

Stephens, John D., and Evelyne Huber. *Development and Crisis in the Welfare State: Parties and Policies in Global Markets.* Chicago: University of Chicago Press, 2001.

Stern, Linda. "The New American Job." *Newsweek,* January 28, 2009.

Stoessinger, John G. *Why Nations Go to War.* New York: Wadsworth, 2004.

Stolle, Dietlind, and Marc Hooghe. "Inaccurate, Exceptional, One-Sided or Irrelevant? The Debate about the Alleged Decline of Social Capital and Civic Engagement in Western Societies." *British Journal of Political Science,* 35 (1) (2005): 149–167.

Stone, Linda. *Kinship and Gender: An Introduction.* Boulder, CO: Westview Press, 2000.

Stone, Pamela. *Opting Out? Why Women Really Quit Careers and Head Home.* Berkeley: University of California Press, 2007.

Storr, Mel. *Bisexuality: A Critical Reader.* New York: Routledge, 1999.

Straus, Murray. "Children Should Never, Ever, Be Spanked No Matter What the Circumstances." In D. R. Loseke, R. J. Gelles, and M. M. Cavanaugh, eds., *Current Controversies about Family Violence,* 2nd ed. Thousand Oaks, CA: Sage Publications, 2005.

Straus, Murray, and Richard Gelles, eds. *Physical Violence in American Families.* New Brunswick, NJ: Transaction Publishers, 1990.

Straus, Murray, Richard Gelles, and Susan Steinmetz. *Behind Closed Doors: Violence in America's Families.* New York: Anchor, 1980.

Streigel-Moore, Ruth, Lisa Silberstein, and Judith Rodin. "Toward an Understanding of Risk Factors for Bulimia." *American Psychologist,* 41(1986): 246–263.

Steurer, Stephen J., and Linda G. Smith. *Education Reduces Crime: Three-State Recidivism Study.* Centerville, UT: Management and Training Corporation, 2003.

Strong, Bryan. The Marriage and Family Experience, 9th ed. Belmont, CA: Wadsworth, 2004.

Sullivan, Oriel. *Changing Gender Relations, Changing Families: Tracing the Pace of Change over Time.* New York: Rowman & Littlefield, 2006.

Sullivan, Oriel, and Scott Coltrane. "Men's changing contribution to housework and child care." Paper presented at the 11th Annual Conference of the Council on Contemporary Families, April 25–26, 2008, University of Illinois, Chicago.

Sullivan/Anderson, Amy. "How to End the War over Sex Ed." *Time,* March 30, 2009, 40–43.

Summers, Lawrence. "Remarks at NBER Conference on Diversifying the Science and Engineering Workforce." January 14, 2005. Available at: www.president.harvard.edu/speeches/2005/nber.html

Sumner, William Graham. *Folkways: A Study of the Sociological Importance of Usages, Manners, Customs, Mores, and Morals.* (1906). Mineola, NY: Dover Publications, 2002.

Suny, Ronald. "Some Notes on National Character, Religions and Way of Life of the Armenians." Paper presented at the Lelio Basso Foundation, Venice, Italy, 1985.

Sutherland, Edwin H. "White Collar Criminality." *American Sociological Review,* 5 (February 1940): 1–12.

Suttles, Gerald. *The Social Construction of Communities.* Chicago: University of Chicago Press, 1972.

Suzuki, Bob. "Asian-American Families." In James Henslin (ed.), *Marriage and Family in a Changing Society,* 104–119. New York: Free Press, 1985.

Swidler, Ann. "Culture in Action: Symbols and Strategies." *American Sociological Review,* 51 (2, April 1986): 273–286.

Symons, Donald. "Darwinism and Contemporary Marriage." In Kingsley Davis, ed., *Contemporary Marriage: Comparative Perspectives on a Changing Institution.* New York: Russell Sage Foundation, 1985.

Takaki, Ronald. *Strangers from a Different Shore.* Boston: Little, Brown, 1998.

Talukdar, Debabrata. "Cost of Being Poor: Retail Price and Consumer Price Search Differences across Inner-City and Suburban Neighborhoods." *Journal of Consumer Research,* 35, 3 (October 2008): 457–471.

Tarrow, Sidney. *Power in Movement: Social Movements and Contentious Politics.* Cambridge, UK: Cambridge University Press, 1998.

Tarumoto, Hideki. "Multiculturalism in Japan: Citizenship Policy for Immigrants." *International Journal on Multicultural Societies,* 5 (1, 2003): 88–103.

Tatum, Beverly Daniel. *Why Are All the Black Kids Sitting Together in the Cafeteria? A Psychologist Explains the Development of Racial Identity.* New York: HarperCollins, 1997.

Tavris, Carol. *The Mismeasure of Women.* New York: Peter Smith, 1999.

Taylor, Frederic Winslow. *Principles of Scientific Management* (1911). New York: Norton, 1967.

Taylor, Michael. *The Possibility of Cooperation.* New York: Cambridge University Press, 1987.

Teachman, J. "Premarital Sex, Premarital Cohabitation, and the Risk of Subsequent Marital Dissolution among Women." *Journal of Marriage and Family,* 65 (2003): 444–455.

Tebbel, John, and Mary Ellen Zuckerman. *The Magazine in America, 1741–1990.* New York: Oxford University Press, 2005.

Technorati. "Blog Posts by Language—Q4," 2006. Available at: http://korlieng.exteen.com/20070513/technorati-chart

Technorati. *State of the Blogosphere 2008,* 2008.

Terman, Lewis, and Catherine Cox Miles. *Sex and Personality* (1936). Westport, CT: Praeger Press, 2001.

Thernstrom, Abigail, and Stephan Thernstrom. *No Excuses: Closing the Racial Gap in Learning.* New York: Simon and Schuster, 2003.

Thomas, W. I., and D. S. Thomas. *The Child in America.* New York: Alfred A. Knopf, 1928.

Thompson, Michael, and Dan Kindlon. *Raising Cain: Protecting the Emotional Life of Boys.* New York: Ballantine Books, 2000.

Thornberry, T. P., M. D. Krohn, A. J. Lizotte, C. A. Smith, and K. Tobin. *Gangs and Delinquency in Developmental Perspective.* New York: Cambridge University Press, 2003.

Thorne, Barrie. *Gender Play: Boys and Girls in School.* New Brunswick, NJ: Rutgers University Press, 1993.

Thornton, John. *Africa and Africans in the Making of the Atlantic World, 1400–1800.* New York: Cambridge University Press, 1998.

Tierney, John. "What's So Funny? Well, Maybe Nothing." *New York Times,* March 13, 2007, F1, F6.

Tillman, Kathryn T. "Non-Traditional Siblings and the Academic Outcomes of Adolescents." *Social Science Research,* 37 (2008): 88–108.

Tilly, Charles. *From Mobilization to Revolution.* Reading, MA: Addison-Wesley, 1978.

Tilly, Chris. *Half a Job: Bad and Good Part-Time Jobs in a Changing Labor Market.* Philadelphia: Temple University Press, 1996.

Tocqueville, Alexis de. *Democracy in America* (1835). New York: Library of America, 2004.

Töennies, Ferdinand. *Community and Society: Gemeinschaft und Gesellschaft.* Charles P. Loomis, trans. New York: Harper and Row, 1957.

"Tongue-Tied on Bilingual Education." Editorial in *New York Times,* September 2, 2005.

Trenholm, C., B. Devaney, K. Fortson, M. Clark, L. Q. Bridgespan, and J. Wheeler. "Impacts of Abstinence Education on Teen Sexual Activity, Risk of Pregnancy, and Risk of Sexually Transmitted Diseases." *Journal of Policy Analysis Management,* 29 (2, Spring 2008): 255–276.

Trimberger, E. K. *The New Single Woman.* Boston: Beacon Press, 2005.

Tsukashima, Ronald Tadao, "Chronological, Cognitive, and Political Effects in the Study of Interminority Group Prejudice." *Phylon,* 44 (3, 1983): 217–231.

Tuchman, Gaye. *Making News: A Study in the Construction of Reality.* New York: Macmillan, 1978.

Tucker, Naomi. *Bisexual Politics: Theories, Queeries, and Visions.* Binghamton, NY: Haworth Press, 1995.

Turkheimer, Eric, Brian D'Onofrio, Hermine Maes, and Lindon Eaves. "Analysis and

Interpretation of Twin Studies Including Measures of the Shared Environment." *Child Development*, 76 (6, November/December 2005): 1217–1233.

Turkheimer, Eric, Andreana Haley, Mary Waldron, Brian D'Onofrio, and Irving Gottesman. "Socioeconomic Status Modified Hereditability of IQ in Young Children." *Psychological Science*, 14 (6, November 2003): 623–628.

Twenge, Jean M. *Generation Me: Why Today's Young Americans Are More Confident, Assertive, Entitled—And More Miserable Than Ever*. New York: Free Press, 2006.

Uchitelle, Louis. *The Disposable American: Layoffs and Their Consequences*. New York: Alfred Knopf, 2006.

Uggen, Christopher. "Ex-Offenders and the Conformist Alternatives: A Job-Quality Model of Work and Crime." *Social Problems*, 46 (1, February 1999): 127–151.

Uggen, Christopher and Jeff Manza. *Locked Out: Felon Disenfranchisement and American Democracy*. New York: Oxford University Press, 2006.

UNAIDS. *2008 Report on the Global AIDS Epidemic*, 2008.

UNESCO. *World Culture Report*. Paris: UNESCO, 2000.

UNESCO. *Human Rights of Migrants*. Paris: UNESCO, NGLS Roundup 89, March 2002.

UNESCO. *Global Education Digest 2004: Comparing Education Statistics across the Globe*. Montreal: UNESCO, 2004.

UNESCO Institute for Statistics. *Literacy Rates, Youth (15–24) and Adult (15), by Region and Gender. September 2006 Assessment*. Paris: UNESCO, 2006.

UNHCR. *2007 Global Trends: Refugees, Asylum-Seekers, Returnees, Internally Displaced and Stateless Persons*, 2008.

United Nations. *World Urbanization Prospects Report*, 2005a. Available at: www.economist.com/images/20070505/CSU158.gif

United Nations. *World Youth Report*. New York: United Nations, 2005b.

United Nations. *World Urbanization Prospects, 2005*. New York: United Nations. Department of Economic and Social Affairs, 2006. Available at: http://esa.un.org/unup/index.asp?panel=1

United Nations. *World Fertility Patterns 2007*. New York, 2008.

U.N. Development Program (UNDP). *Taking Gender Equality Seriously*. New York: UNDP, 2006.

U.N. Population Fund (UNFPA). "Child Marriage Fact Sheet," 2005. Available at: www.unfpa.org/swp/2005/presskit/factsheets/facts_child_marriage.htm

U.N. World Food Program. "Hunger Statstics," 2009. Available at: www.wfp.org/hunger/stats

U.S. Administration on Aging. *Profile of Older Americans: 2008*. Washington, DC: U.S. Government Printing Office, 2008.

U.S. Census Bureau. *Population of the 24 Urban Places: 1790*, June 1998. Available at: www.census.gov/population/documentation/twps0027/tab02.txt

U.S. Census Bureau. *Median Household Income*. Washington, DC: U.S. Government Printing Office, April 2001a.

U.S. Census Bureau. "The 65 Years and Over Population: 2000." Washington, DC: U.S.

Bureau of the Census, October 2001b. Available at: www.census.gov/prod/2001pubs/c2kbr01-10.pdf

U.S. Census Bureau, Census 2000 Brief. "The Two or More Races Population, 2000." November, 2001c. Available at: http://www.census.gov/prod/2001pubs/c2kbr01-6.pdf

U.S. Census Bureau. "Average Travel Time to Work of Workers 16 Years and Over Who Did Not Work at Home," 2002a. Available at: www.census.gov/acs/www/Products/Ranking/2002/R04T160.htm

U.S. Census Bureau. "Marital Status of Women at First Birth by Age," 2002b.

U.S. Census Bureau. "More Diversity, Slower Growth: Census Bureau Projects Tripling of Hispanic and Asian Populations in 50 Years; Non-Hispanic Whites May Drop to Half of Total Population." Washington, DC: U.S. Department of Commerce, March 18, 2004a.

U.S. Census Bureau. "2004 American Community Survey." Washington, DC: U.S. Department of Commerce, 2004b.

U.S. Census Bureau. "Income, Poverty and Health Insurance Coverage." 2004. Washington, DC: U.S. Department of Commerce, August 2005a.

U.S. Census Bureau. "Who's Minding the Kids? Child Care Arrangements." Winter 2002. *Current Population Reports*. Washington, DC: U.S. Department of Commerce, 2005b.

U.S. Census Bureau. "American Community Survey (2005 supplement to the 2000 Census)." Washington, DC: U.S. Department of Commerce, 2006a.

U.S. Census Bureau. "Father's Day, 2006." 2006b. Available at: www.census.gov/PressRelease/www/releases/archives/facts_for_features_special_editions/006794.html

U.S. Census Bureau, "Income Poverty and Health Insurance Coverage in the U.S.: 2005." *Current Population Reports*. Washington, DC: U.S. Department of Commerce, August 2006c.

U.S. Census Bureau. "Life Expectancy at Birth by Region, Country, and Sex: 2002, 2025, and 2050." 2006d. Available at: www.census.gov/ftp/pub/ipc/www/idbsum

U.S. Census Bureau. "Population Estimates by Sex and Age, July." 2006e. Available at: www.census.gov/popest/national/asrh/NC-EST2006/NC-EST2006-02.xls

U.S. Census Bureau. "Poverty: 2005 Highlights." Current Population Survey Annual Social and Economic Supplement. Washington, DC: U.S. Department of Commerce, 2006f.

U.S. Census Bureau. "Voting and Registration in the Election of 2004." Population report P20-556. Washington, DC: U.S. Department of Commerce, 2006g.

U.S. Census Bureau. *Statistical Abstract of the United States: 2007*. Washington, DC: U.S. Department of Commerce, 2007.

U.S. Census Bureau, *America's Families and Living Arrangements: 2008*. Washington, DC: U.S. Department of Commerce, 2008a.

U.S. Census Bureau, Current Population Survey, *2008 Annual Social and Economic Supplement*, September, 2008. http://www.census.gov/apsd/techdoc/cps/cpsmar08.pdf

U.S. Census Bureau. *Facts for Features: Older Americans Month, 2008*. Washington, DC: U.S. Department of Commerce, 2008c.

U.S. Census Bureau. "Income, Poverty and Health Insurance Coverage in the United States: 2007." *Current Population Survey*. Washington, DC: U.S. Department of Commerce, August 2008d.

U.S. Census Bureau. *Current Population Survey, March and Annual Social and Economic Supplements, 2008 and Earlier*. Washington, DC: U.S. Department of Commerce, January 2009a.

U.S. Census Bureau. *Statistical Abstract of the United States: 2009*. Washington, DC: U.S. Department of Commerce, 2009b.

U.S. Census Bureau. "U.S. Census Bureau Estimates Nearly Half of Children under 5 Are Minorities." Washington, DC: U.S. Department of Commerce, May 14, 2009c.

U.S. Census Bureau. "Percentage of Childless Women 40 to 44 Years Old Increases Since 1976, Census Bureau Reports." Available at: www.census.gov/PressRelease/www/releases/archives/fertility/001491.html

U.S. Census Bureau. "Population Highlights, 2000." Washington, DC: U.S. Department of Commerce.

U.S. Department of Commerce, Bureau of Economic Analysis. "Current Dollar and 'Real' Gross Domestic Product." Posted July 27, 2007. www.bea.gov/national/xls/gdplev.xls

U.S. Department of Education, National Center for Education Statistics, Projections of Education Statistics to 2013. NCES 2004–2013. Washington, DC: U.S. Department of Education, 2003.

U.S. Department of Education. *Digest of Educational Statistics 2006*. Washington, DC: Institute for Education Sciences, 2006a. Available at: http://nces.ed.gov/programs/digest/d06/

U.S. Department of Education, National Center for Educational Statistics (NCES). *Integrated Postsecondary Education Data System (IPEDS) Completions, 1966–2004*. Washington, DC: NCES, 2006b. Retrieved on November 8, 2006, from http://caspar.nsf.gov

U.S. Department of Education. "Fiscal Year Budget, 2007." Available at: www.ed.gov/about/overview/budget/budget07/summary/edlite-appendix3.html

U.S. Department of Health and Human Services. "Eating Disorders: A Midlife Crisis for Some Women." *Health Reports*, 2006. Available at: www.healthfinder.gov

U.S. Department of Health and Human Services. "Women's Health USA 2008." Washington, DC: U.S. Government Printing Office, 2008.

U.S. Department of Justice, "Report to the Deputy Attorney General on the Events at Waco, Texas, February 28 to April 19, 1993." October 8, 1993. Available at: http://www.usdoj.gov/05publications/waco/wacotocpg.htm

U.S. Department of Justice. *Acquaintance Rape of College Students, Problem-Oriented Guide for Police Series #17*, Washington, DC: U.S. Government Printing Office, 2003.

U.S. Department of Justice. "Crime in the United States." 2005a. Available at: www.fbi.gov/ucr/ojcius.

U.S. Department of Justice, Bureau of Justice Statistics. "Crime and Victims Statistics." 2005b. Available online at: http://www.ojp.usdoj.gov/bjs/cvict.htm

U.S. Department of Justice, Bureau of Justice Statistics, Federal Bureau of Investigation, 2005c. "Hate Crime Statistics." 2005c. Available at: www.fbi.gov/ucr/hc2005/index.html

U.S. Department of Justice, Bureau of Justice Statistics. 2005. "Violent Victimization of College Students, 1995–2002." Available at: www.ojp.usdoj.gor/bjs/pub/pdf/vvcs02.pdf

U.S. Department of Justice, Federal Bureau of Investigation, "Full Time Law Enforcement Employees." *Crime in the United States*. Washington, DC: U.S. Government Printing Office, 2007.

U.S. Department of Justice, Bureau of Justice Statistics. *Criminal Victimization 2007*. Available online at: www.ojp.usdoj.gov/bjs/cvictgen.htm#findings

U.S. Department of Justice, Federal Bureau of Investigation, *Crime in the United States 2007*. Washington, DC: U.S. Government Printing Office, June 2008a.

U.S. Department of Justice, Bureau of Justice Statistics, *Criminal Victimization in the United States*, Washington, DC: U.S. Government Printing Office, 2008b.

U.S. Department of Justice. *Girls Study Group: Understanding and Responding to Girls' Delinquency*. Washington, DC: U.S. Government Printing Office, May 2008c.

U.S. Department of Justice, Federal Bureau of Investigation, *Crime in the United States 2007*. Washington, DC: U.S. Government Printing Office, 2009.

U.S. Department of Labor, Bureau of Labor Statistics. "A Profile of the Working Poor, 2003." Report 983, March 2005.

U.S. Department of Labor, Women's Bureau. "Employment Status of Women and Men in 2008." Washington, DC: U.S. Government Printing Office, 2008.

U.S. Equal Opportunity Commission. "Occupational Employment in Private Industry by Race/Ethnic Group/Sex and by Industry, United States, 2005." Available at: www.eeoc.gov/stats/jobpat/2005/national.html

U.S. State Department. "Immigrant Visas Issued to Orphans Coming to the U.S." 2007. Available at: http://travel.state.gov/family/adoption/stats/stats_451.html

UC Atlas of Global Inequality. "Income Inequality," 2007. Available at: http://ucatlas.ucsc.edu/income.php

University of Chicago Library. "Guide to the Chicago Foreign Language Press Survey Records, 1861–1938." Chicago: University of Chicago Library, 2007.

Urban, Wayne J., and Jennings L. Wagoner. *American Education: A History*. New York: McGraw-Hill, 2003.

Vallas, Steven P. "Rethinking Post-Fordism: The Meaning of Workplace Flexibility." *Sociological Theory*, 17 (1999): 68–101.

Valliant, G. E. *Adaptations to Life*. Boston: Little, Brown, 1978.

van Amersfoort, Hans. *Immigration and the Formation of Minority Groups: The Dutch Experience, 1945–1975*. New York: Cambridge University Press, 1982.

Vanderschueren, Franz. *From Violence to Justice and Security in Cities*. New York: UN-Habitat, 1996. Available at: www.unhabitat.org/downloads/docs/1899_49562_franz_paper

Van Kesteren, J. N., P. Mayhew, and P. Nieuwbeerta. *Criminal Victimization in Seventeen Industrialized Countries: Key Findings from the 2000 International Crime Victims Survey*. The Hague: Ministry of Justice, WODC, 2000.

Van Vugt, William E. *Britain to America: Mid Nineteenth-Century Immigration to the U.S.* Urbana: University of Illinois Press, 1999.

Veblen, Thorstein. *The Theory of the Leisure Class*. (1899). Robert Lekachman, ed. New York: Penguin Classics, 1994.

Velkoff, V., and V. Lawson. *International Brief: Gender and Aging Caregiving*. Washington, DC: U.S. Department of Commerce, iB/98-3, December 1998.

Venkatesh, Sudhir. *Gang Leader for a Day*. New York: Penguin, 2008.

Verhaag, Bertram. *Blue Eyed* [videorecording/DVD]. Denkmal Filmproductions; a Claus Stigal & Bertram Verhaag production; written and directed by Bertram Verhaag. 1996.

Villarroel, Maria, Charles Turner, Elizabeth Eggleston, Alia Al-Tayyib, Susan Rogers, Anthony Roman, Philip Cooley, and Harper Gordek. "Same Gender Sex in the United States: Impact of T-ACASI on Prevalence Estimates." *Public Opinion Quarterly*, 70 (2, Summer 2006): 166–196.

Voci, A. "Perceived Group Variability and the Salience of Personal and Social Identity." In W. Stroebe and M. Hewstone, eds., *European Review of Social Psychology*, 11 (2000): 177– 221.

Voslensky, Michael. *The Soviet Ruling Class*. New York: Doubleday, 1984.

Wacquant, Loic. *Body and Soul: Notebooks of an Apprentice Boxer*. New York: Oxford University Press, 2003.

Wacquant, Loic. "The 'Scholarly Myths' of the New Law and Order Doxa." *The Socialist Register*, 2006: 93–115.

Waitzkin, Howard B. *The Second Sickness: Contradictions of Capitalist Health Care*. New York: The Free Press, 1986.

Walch, Timothy. *Immigrant America: European Ethnicity in the U.S.* New York: Garland, 1994.

Walker, J. J., Senger, F. Villaruel, and A. Arboleda. *Lost Opportunities: The Reality of Latinos in the U.S. Criminal Justice System*. National Council of La Raza. 2004. Available at: www.nclr.org/content/publication/detail/27567/

Waller, Willard. "The Rating and Dating Complex." *American Sociological Review*, 2 (1937), 727–734.

Wallerstein, Immanuel. "The Rise and Future Demise of the World Capitalist System: Concepts for Comparative Analysis." *Comparative Studies in Society and History*, 16 (4, 1974): 387–415.

Wallerstein, Immanuel. *The Capitalist World-Economy*. Cambridge, UK: Cambridge University Press, 1979.

Wallerstein, Immanuel. "The Development of the Concept of Development." *Sociological Theory*, 2 (1984): 102–116.

Wallerstein, Immanuel. *World-Systems Analysis: An Introduction*. Durham, NC: Duke University Press, 2004.

Wallerstein, Judith. *The Unexpected Legacy of Divorce: A 25-Year Landmark Study*. New York: Hyperion, 2000.

Ward, Lester Frank. *Pure Sociology: A Treatise on the Origin of Spontaneous Development of Society* (1883). New York: Augustus Kelley Publishers, 1970.

Warrick, J. "The Warming Planet; What Science Knows." *Washington Post*, November 11, 1997, A1.

Washington Post. "In Western Europe," May 16, 2006.

Wasow, Bernard. "Illegal Immigrants, Our Low-Income Taxpayers." *Mother Jones*, May 26, 2006.

Waters, Mary. *Ethnic Options: Choosing Ethnic Identities in America*. Berkeley: University of California Press, 1990.

Weber, Max. *The Protestant Ethic and the Spirit of Capitalism* (1904, 1905). New York: Routledge, 2004.

Weber, Max. *From Max Weber*. Trans. and ed. by H. H. Gerth and C. Wright Mills. New York: Oxford University Press, 1958.

Weber, Max. *Economy and Society* (2 volumes). Berkeley: University of California Press, 1978.

Wedgwood, C. V. *The Thirty Years' War*. New York: Routledge, 1990.

Weich, Ronald, and Carlos Angulo. *Justice on Trial: Racial Disparities in the American Criminal Justice System*. Washington, DC: Leadership Conference on Civil Rights, 2000.

Weinberg, Martin S., Colin J. Williams, and Douglas W. Pryor. *Dual Attraction: Understanding Bisexuality*. New York: Oxford University Press, 1994.

Weisman, Jonathan. "Georgia GOP Congressman Calls Obama 'Uppity.'" *The Washington Post*, September 4, 2008.

Weitzman, Lenore J. "The Economic Consequences of Divorce Are Still Unequal: Comment on Peterson." *American Sociological Review*, 61 (3, 1996): 537–539.

Wendel, Helmut F., and Christopher S. Wendel, eds. *Vital Statistics of the United States: Births, Life Expectancy, Deaths, and Selected Health Data*, 2nd ed. New York: U.S. Databook Series, Bernan Press, 2006.

Westall, Sylvia. "Homophobia Damaging Lives across Europe—EU Study." Reuters, March 31, 2009. Available at: www.reuters.com/article/latestCrisis/idUSLU292053

Weston, Kath. "Get Thee to a Big City: Sexual Imaginary and the Great Gay Migration." *GLQ*, 2 (3, 1995): 253–277.

Wethington, Elaine. "Multiple Roles, Social Integration, and Health." In K. Pillemer, P. Moen, E. Wethington, and N. Glasgow, eds., *Social Integration in the Second Half of Life*. Baltimore: Johns Hopkins University Press, 2000.

Whorf, Benjamin Lee. "Science and Linguistics." In John B. Carroll, ed., *Language, Thought and Reality*. Cambridge, MA: MIT Press, 1956.

Whyte, William Foote. *Street Corner Society: The Social Structure of an Italian Slum*, 4th ed.

(First edition published 1943). Chicago: University of Chicago Press, 1993.

Wilkinson, Doris. "Family Ethnicity in America." In Harriette Pipes McAdoo, ed., *Family Ethnicity: Strength in Diversity.* Newbury Park, CA: Sage, 1999.

Williams, Christine. "The Glass Escalator: Hidden Advantages for Men in the 'Female Professions.'" *Social Problems,* 39 (3, 1992).

Williams, Christine. *Still a Man's World: Men Who Do "Women's Work."* Berkeley: University of California Press, 1995.

Williams, Jessica. "Facts That Should Change the World: America Spends $10 Billion Each Year on Porn." *New Statesman,* June 7, 2004.

Williams, Kevin. *Understanding Media Theory.* New York: Oxford University Press, 2003.

Williams, Robin Jr. *American Society: A Sociological Interpretation,* 3rd ed. New York: Alfred Knopf, 1970.

Williams, Walter. *The Spirit and the Flesh.* Boston: Beacon, 1986.

Williamson, Judith. *Decoding Advertisements.* London: Marion Boyars Publishers, 1994.

Willis, George, William H. Schubert, Robert V. Bullough, Craig Kridel, and John T. Holton (eds.). *The American Curriculum: A Documentary History.* Westport, CT: Praeger, 1994.

Willis, P. *Learning to Labor.* New York: Columbia University Press, 1977.

Wilmoth, Janet M., Gordon F. DeJong, and Christine C. Himes, "Immigrant and Non-Immigrant Living Arrangements in Later Life." *International Journal of Sociology and Social Policy,* 17 (1997): 57–82.

Wilson, Chris M., and Andrew J. Oswald. "How Does Marriage Affect Physical and Psychological Health? A Survey of the Longitudinal Evidence." *The Warwick Economics Research Paper Series (TWERPS)* 728. Coventry, UK: University of Warwick Department of Economics, 2005.

Wilson, J. Q., and G. L. Kelling, "Broken Windows: The Police and Neighborhood Safety." *Atlantic Monthly,* March 1982, 29–38.

Wilson, James Q. *Thinking about Crime.* New York: Alfred Knopf, 1985.

Winerip, Michael. "The Adult Store Goes Mainstream." *New York Times,* 2009 (June 28), ST-1.

Winks, Robin W., and Thomas E. Kaiser. *Europe, 1648–1815: From the Old Regime to the Age of Revolution.* Oxford, UK: Oxford University Press, 2003.

Wirth, Louis. "Urbanism as a Way of Life: The City and Contemporary Civilization." *American Journal of Sociology,* 44 (1938): 1–24.

Wirzbicki, Alan. "Gun Control Efforts Weaken in the South." *Boston Globe,* September 4, 2005.

Wolf, Naomi. *The Beauty Myth.* New York: William Morrow, 1991.

Wolfe, Alan. *The Transformation of American Religion: How We Actually Live Our Faith.* New York: Free Press, 2003.

Wolkomir, Michelle. *The Sacred and Sexual Struggles of Gay and Ex-Gay Christian Men.* New Brunswick, NJ: Rutgers University Press, 2005.

Women's Institute for a Secure Retirement (WISER). "African American Women and Retirement Income," 2008a. Washington, DC.

Women's Institute for a Secure Retirement (WISER). "Minority Women and Retirement Income." May, 2008b. Washington, DC.

Wong, Morrison G. "Post-1965 Asian Immigrants: Where Do They Come From, Where Are They Now, and Where Are They Going?" *Annals of the American Academy of Political and Social Science,* 487 (September 1986): 150–168.

Wood, Robert G., Brian Goesling, and Sarah Avellar. "The Effects of Marriage on Health: A Synthesis of Recent Research Evidence." Washington, DC: Department of Health and Human Services, 2007. Available at: http://aspe.hhs.gov/hsp/07/marriageonhealth

Woods, Richard. "Women Take Lead as Lifespan Heads for the Happy 100s." *Sunday Times* (London), October 30, 2005, p. 14.

The Working Poor Families Project. *Working Poor Families: Still Working Hard, Still Falling Short: New Findings on the Challenges Confronting America's Working Families* (2008). Available at: www.workingpoorfamilies.org/pdfs/NatReport08.pdf

World Association of Newspapers. "World Press Trends: Newspapers Are a Growth Business," June 2, 2008. http://www.wan-press.org/article17377.html

World Bank. *Monitoring Environmental Progress.* Washington, DC: World Bank, 1995.

World Bank. *World Development Indicators 2006.* Available at: www.devdata.worldbank.org

World Bank. *World Development Indicators 2008.* Washington, DC: World Bank, 2008.

World Bank. *Global Monitoring Report 2008.* World Bank: 2009.

World Economic Forum. *Global Gender Gap Report.* Brussels: World Economic Forum, 2009.

World Health Organization (WHO). *World Health Report 2008.* Geneva: WHO, 2008.

World Internet Statistics. "World Internet Usage Statistics," 2008. Available at: www.internetworldstats.com/stats.htm

Molly Worthen. "Who Would Jesus Smack Down?" *The New York Times Magazine,* January 6, 2009.

Wright, Quincy. *A Study of War,* 2nd ed. Chicago: University of Chicago Press, 1967.

Wylie, Cathy. *Trends in the Feminization of the Teaching Profession in OECD Countries, 1980–1995.* Geneva: International Labour Organization, 2000.

Yaukey, David, and Douglas L. Anderton. *Demography: The Study of Human Population.* Long Grove, IL: Waveland Press, 2001.

Yellowbird, Michael, and C. Matthew Snipp. "American Indian Families." In Ronald Taylor, ed., *Minority Families in the United States: A Multicultural Perspective,* 179–201. Englewood Cliffs, NJ: Prentice-Hall, 1994.

Yinger, John. *Closed Doors, Opportunities Lost.* New York: Russell Sage Foundation, 1995.

Yinger, John. "Evidence on Discrimination in Consumer Markets." *Journal of Economic Perspectives* 12 (1998): 23–40.

Yoder, J. "Rethinking Tokenism: Looking beyond Numbers." *Gender and Society,* 5 (1991): 178–192.

Yoffee, Norman. *Myths of the Archaic State: Evolution of the Earliest Cities, States, and Civilizations.* Cambridge, UK: Cambridge University Press, 2005.

Young, T. Kue. *Population Health: Concept and Methods.* New York: Oxford University Press, 1998.

Zehr, S. C. "Public Representations of Scientific Uncertainty about Global Climate Change." *Public Understanding of Science,* 9 (2000): 85–103.

Zerubavel, Eviator. *The Seven Day Circle: The History and Meaning of the Week.* Chicago: University of Chicago Press, 1989.

Zeune, Gary D. "Are You Teaching Your Employees to Steal?" *Business Credit,* April 2001.

Zihlman, Adrienne. "Woman the Gatherer: The Role of Women in Early Hominid Evolution." In Sandra Morgen, ed., *Gender and Anthropology.* Washington, DC: American Anthropological Association, 1989.

Zimbardo, Philip G. "The Human Choice: Individuation, Reason, and Order versus Deindividuation, Impulse, and Chaos." Nebraska Symposium on Motivation, 17 (1969): 237–307.

Zimring, Franklin E., and Gordon Hawkins. *Crime Is Not the Problem: Lethal Violence in America.* New York: Oxford University Press, 1997.

Zuckerman, Phil. "Atheism: Contemporary Rates and Patterns." In Michael Martin, ed., *The Cambridge Companion to Atheism.* Cambridge, UK: Cambridge University Press, 2005.

Name Index

Subject Index

Population, sex ratio in China, 471
The Population Bomb (Ehrlich), 473
Population composition, 469–471
Population density, 476
Population growth, 471–474
 demographic transition theory of, 473
 Malthusian theory of, 472–473
 natural population increase and, 471–472
 policies to combat, 471, 474
Population pyramids, 470
Pornography
 blogs and, 410
 on Internet, 409
Postindustrial economy, 358–359
Postmodernism, 29
Poverty, 198–204
 absolute, 198
 among children, 200, 296
 culture of, 202–203
 among elders, 200–201, 294–296
 feminization of, 201–202, 266
 health and, 296–297
 among mothers, 200
 personal initiative and, 202
 reducing, 203–204
 relative, 198
 structures of inequality and, 203
 in United States, 200–201
Poverty line, 198–199
Power, 190–191
 bureaucracies and, 84–85
 conflict theories and, 23–24
 dependency theory and, 211–212
 deviance and, 161
 minority groups and, 223
 politics and, 390. *See also* Authority
 social, 67
Predictability, 110
Prejudice. *See also* Discrimination; Racism;
 Segregation
 definition of, 226
 against obese people, 287
 overcoming, 236–238
 stereotypes and, 78, 226–228
 theories of, 234–236
Premodernism, 29
Preoperational stage, 132
Pressure groups, 398
Prestige, 190
 occupational, 190
Primary deviance, 160
Primary groups, 73–74
Primary sex characteristics, 259
Primary socialization, 135
Primates, socialization of, 129–130
Primordial theory, 234
Print media, 405–407
Prisons, 174–177
 privatization of, 177
Private ownership, capitalism and, 361
Privatization
 of higher education, 438–440
 of schools, 433–435
Probability, 110
Problem definition, 112
Production
 global, 359, 367
 modern consumer economy and, 357
Professional ethics, 117–118
Profit, capitalism and, 361
Proletariat, 189, 363
Promotional groups, 398
Property crimes, 165
Proportional representation (PR), 395
Prostitution, world economy and, 213
Protected groups, research and, 118
Protection as goal of incarceration, 176
Protestant churches, 443
The Protestant Ethic and the Spirit of Capitalism
 (Weber), 16–17
Psychological stage theories of development,
 131–135
 problems with, 133–135
Pull factors, immigration and, 466

Purposive samples, 103
Push factors, emigration and, 465–466

Qualitative methods, 97–98
Quantitative data analysis, 104–108
 secondary, of existing data, 106–108
 surveys and, 104–106
Quantitative methods, 96–98

Race. *See also* Ethnicity; *specific groups*
 biraciality and multiraciality and, 222–223
 childlessness and, 342
 class and, 196–197
 crime and, 170, 171–172
 cross-race friendships and, 275–276
 culture versus, 221
 definition of, 220, 221–222
 discrimination and. *See* Discrimination
 divorce and, 344
 of gang members, 155, 156
 hate crime and, 167
 health and, 298
 intelligence and, 228
 language and, 43
 minority groups and majority groups and,
  223–226
 multiculturalism and, 28
 organizations and, 83
 peer approval and, 141
 political party affiliation and, 397
 politics and, 395
 prejudice and. *See* Prejudice
 racial diversity in workplace and, 380
 racism and, 226, 228–229
 religious experience and, 450, 451
 school segregation and, 431
 sexuality and, 312–313
 in twenty-first century, 250–251
Race to the bottom, 367
Racial segregation in schools, 431
Racism
 definition of, 226
 DuBois's views on, 20
Radical feminism, 279
Radio, 407
Random samples, 104
Rape, 312
Reasoning, deductive and inductive, 96
Rebellion in strain theory, 162–163
Recession, current, 379
Reference groups, 75
Refugees, 466, 467
Regulations in bureaucracies, 84
Rehabilitation as goal of incarceration, 176–177
Relative poverty, 198
Religion, 440–453
 as agent of socialization, 137–139
 on campus, 451–452
 civil, 441
 as cultural universal, 441
 definition of, 440
 divorce and, 344
 Durkheim's views on, 441
 Eastern, 446–447
 fastest-growing, 445
 hate crime and, 167
 Marx's views on, 441–442
 merging of politics with, 443–444
 multiculturalism and, 26, 28
 New Age, 453
 as politics, 452–453
 religious groups and, 440–444
 science compared with, 440–441
 in twenty-first century, 457
 in United States, 447–449
 variations in religious experience and, 450–451
 Weber's views on, 442
 Western, 444–446
 world, 444–453
Religiosity, 442
Religious experience and identity, 449–453
Religious groups, 440–444
Remarriage, blended families and, 346
Reporting research findings, 113

Representative democracy, 393
Research methods, 92–122
 appropriate comparisons and, 108–109
 basic steps in, 112–113
 basic types of, 98
 causality and, 110–111
 content analysis and, 108, 109
 controversy and, 114–119
 emergent, 119–121
 ethics and, 117–118
 importance of, 94–98
 institutional review boards and, 118–119
 interview studies and, 99, 103, 107–108, 109
 objectivity and, 115
 observational, 99–103
 overstating results and, 115–117
 predictability and probability and, 110
 qualitative versus quantitative data and, 96–98
 scientific method and, 95–96
 surveys, 104–106, 109
 variables and, 98–99
Resocialization, 135
Resources, 484–486
 vanishing, 486
Responsibility, diffusion of, 77
Retreatism in strain theory, 163
Retribution as goal of incarceration, 175
Revelation, 441
Revolutions, 399–401
 political, 400–401
 social, 401
Rigidity of bureaucracies, 85
Ritual(s), 43–44, 441
Ritualism
 in bureaucracies, 85
 in strain theory, 162
Robber barons, 365
Role(s), 70–71
 gender. *See* Gender roles
Role conflict, 70
Role exit, 70–71
Role expectations, 70–71
Role performance, 68, 70–71
Role strain, 70
Roman Catholic Church, 443
Rules in bureaucracies, 84

Sacred events, 441
Sadomasochism (S&M), 305
Same-sex marriage, 337
Samples, 104–105
 cluster, 105
 purposive, 103
 random, 104
 stratified, 105
 systematic, 104–105
Sapir-Whorf hypothesis, 42
School(s). *See also* Education
 charter, 434–435
 privatization of, 433–435
 racial segregation in, 431
School districts, wealthy versus poor, 431
School shootings, 434
Science, 453–458
 definition of, 440–441
 disinterestedness and, 455
 objectivity and, 454
 religion compared with, 440–441
 role of scientists in society and, 456–457
 scientific breakthroughs and, 456
 scientific networks and, 455–456
 social, 9, 454
 in twenty-first century, 457
Scientific literacy, 429
Scientific method, 95–96
Searching for Aboriginal Languages (Dixon), 236
Seasonal unemployment, 378
Secondary analysis, 106–108, 109
Secondary groups, 74
Secondary sex characteristics, 259
Secondary socialization, 135
Second shift, 272–273
Sects, 442, 443
Secularization, 440

Photo Credits